A BRIEF HISTORY OF WESTERN CIVILIZATION

D1263572

A BRIEF HISTORY OF WESTERN CIVILIZATION

THE UNFINISHED LEGACY

FIFTH EDITION

Mark Kishlansky
Harvard University

Patrick Geary
University of California, Los Angeles

Patricia O'Brien
University of California, Los Angeles

PEARSON
Longman

New York   San Francisco   Boston
London   Toronto   Sydney   Tokyo   Singapore   Madrid
Mexico City   Munich   Paris   Cape Town   Hong Kong   Montreal

Acquisitions Editor: Janet Lanphier
Development Editor: Marion B. Castellucci
Executive Marketing Manager: Sue Westmoreland
Media Editor: Melissa Edwards
Production Manager: Donna DeBenedictis
Project Coordination, Text Design, and Electronic Page Makeup: Elm Street Publishing Services, Inc.
Cover Design Manager: John Callahan
Cover Designer: Maria Ilardi
Cover Image: *An Elegant Couple from Madrid*, c. 1770 (oil on canvas) by Teipolo, Lorenzo Baldissera (1736–76). © Palacio Real de Madrid,
    Spain/The Bridgeman Art Library
Photo Researcher: Photosearch, Inc.
Senior Manufacturing Buyer: Alfred C. Dorsey
Printer and Binder: Quebecor World Dubuque
Cover Printer: Phoenix Color Corporation

For permission to use copyrighted material, grateful acknowledgment is made to the copyright holders on pp. C-1–C-2, which are hereby made part of this copyright page.

Library of Congress Cataloging-in-Publication Data

Kishlansky, Mark A.
   A brief history of western civilization: the unfinished legacy / Mark Kishlansky, Patrick Geary, Patricia
O'Brien.—5th ed.
     p. cm.
Includes bibliographical references and index.
ISBN 0-321-43104-9 (single-vol. ed.)—ISBN 0-321-44997-5 (v. 1)—ISBN 0-321-44996-7 (v. 2)
1. Civilization, Western—History. I. Geary, Patrick J., 1948– II. O'Brien, Patricia, 1945– III. Title.

CB245.K548 2007
909'.09821—dc22

                                                                    2006017847

Copyright © 2007 by Pearson Education, Inc.

All rights reserved. No part of this publication may be reproduced, stored in a retrieval system, or transmitted, in any form or by any means, electronic, mechanical, photocopying, recording, or otherwise, without the prior written permission of the publisher. Printed in the United States.

Please visit us at http://www.ablongman.com/kishlansky

ISBN 0-321-43104-9 (Complete Edition)
ISBN 0-321-44997-5 (Volume I)
ISBN 0-321-44996-7 (Volume II)

1 2 3 4 5 6 7 8 9 10—QWD—09 08 07 06

BRIEF CONTENTS

DETAILED CONTENTS

Note: Each chapter ends with Questions for Review, Key Terms, Discovering Western Civilization Online, and Suggestions for Further Reading.

MAPS AND GEOGRAPHICAL TOURS

CHRONOLOGIES, GENEALOGIES, AND FIGURES

DOCUMENTS

PREFACE

When we set out to write *Civilization in the West*, we tried to write, first of all, a book that students would *want* to read. Throughout many years of planning, writing, revising, rewriting, and numerous meetings together, this was our constant overriding concern. Would the text work across the variety of Western civilization courses, with the different levels and formats that make up this fundamental course? We also solicited the reactions of scores of reviewers to this single question: "Would students *want* to read these chapters?" Whenever we received a resounding "No!" we began again—not just rewriting, but rethinking how to present material that might be complex in argument or detail or that might simply seem too remote to engage the contemporary student. Though all three of us were putting in long hours in front of computers, we quickly learned that we were engaged in a teaching rather than a writing exercise. And though the work was demanding, it was not unrewarding. We enjoyed writing this book, and we wanted students to enjoy reading it. We have been gratified to learn that our book successfully accomplished our objectives. It stimulated student interest and motivated students to want to learn about European history. *Civilization in the West* was successful beyond our expectations.

The text was so well received, in fact, that we decided to publish this alternative, brief version: *A Brief History of Western Civilization: The Unfinished Legacy.* In an era of rapidly changing educational materials, alternative formats and models should be available. We believe that students and general readers alike will enjoy a conveniently sized book that offers them a coherent, well-told story. In this edition of the brief text, we have enlarged and added detail to many of the full-color maps so that they are easier to see and use. We have also added a new feature, "Map Discovery," that teaches students to think critically about maps, have included new essays to give students a feel for the cultural exchanges that have taken place between the West and the non-West entitled "The West and the Wider World," and have replaced several of the chapter-opening "Visual Record" narratives.

APPROACH

The approach used in *A Brief History of Western Civilization: The Unfinished Legacy,* Fifth Edition, upholds and confirms a number of decisions made early in the writing of *Civilization in the West.* First, this brief, alternative version is, like the full-length text, a mainstream text in which most of our energies have been focused on developing a solid, readable narrative of Western civilization that integrates coverage of women and minorities into the discussion. We highlight personalities while identifying trends. We spotlight social history, both in sections of chapters and in separate chapters, while maintaining a firm grip on political developments.

Neither *A Brief History of Western Civilization: The Unfinished Legacy* nor *Civilization in the West* is meant to be an encyclopedia of Western civilization. Information is not included in a chapter unless it fits within the themes of that chapter. In both the full-length and brief versions of this text, we are committed to integrating the history of ordinary men and women into our narrative. We believe that isolated sections placed at the end of chapters that deal with the experiences of women or minority groups in a particular era profoundly distort historical experience. We call this technique "cabooysing," and whenever we found ourselves segregating women or families or the masses, we stepped back and asked how we might recast our treatment of historical events to account for a diversity of actors. How did ordinary men, women, and children affect the course of world historical events? How did world historical events affect the fabric of daily life for men, women, and children from all walks of life? We also tried to rethink critical historical problems of civilization as gendered phenomena.

We take the same approach to the coverage of central and eastern Europe that we did to women and minorities. Even before the epochal events of the late 1980s and early 1990s

Chapter **14**

EUROPE AT WAR, 1555–1648

decisively shaped by this century of wholesale slaughter, during which dynastic and religious fervor finally ran its course. The survival of Protestantism, the disintegration of ~~the rise~~ *~~Holland~~*

Looking Ahead

As we will see in this chapter, warfare in the seventeenth century decisively reshaped power relations of families and

that returned this region to the forefront of international attention, we realized that many textbooks treated the Slavic world as marginal to the history of Western civilization. Therefore, we worked to integrate more of the history of eastern Europe into our text than is found in most others and to do so in a way that presented these regions, their cultures, and their institutions as integral rather than peripheral to Western civilization.

FEATURES

In *A Brief History of Western Civilization: The Unfinished Legacy,* we wanted to present features that would have the most immediate and positive impact on our readers and fulfill our goal of involving students in learning. Therefore, this edition features the following:

The Visual Record: Pictorial Chapter Openers

In these pictorial chapter openers, an illustration—a painting, a photograph, an artifact, or an edifice—appears at the beginning of each chapter, accompanied by text through which we explore the picture, guiding students across a canvas or helping them to see in an artifact or a piece of architecture details that are not immediately apparent. It is the direct combination of text and image that allows us to achieve this effect, to "unfold" both an illustration and a theme. All of the opening images have been chosen to illustrate a dominant theme within the chapter, and the dramatic and lingering impression they make helps to reinforce that theme. A section at the end of each essay called "Looking Ahead" provides a brief overview of chapter coverage and further strengthens the connection between the subject of the opener and the major topics and themes of the chapter.

Geographical Tours of Europe

Six times in the book, we pause in the narrative to take a tour of Europe. In these "Geographical Tours of Europe," sometimes we follow an emperor as he tours his realm; sometimes we examine the impact of a peace treaty; sometimes we follow the travels of a merchant. Whatever the thematic occasion, our intention is to guide the student around the changing contours of the geography of Western history. In order to do this effectively, we worked with our cartographer

---

362   Chapter 18   The Balance of Power in Eighteenth-Century Europe

GEOGRAPHICAL TOUR
A Grand Tour of Europe in 1714

In the eighteenth century, young noblemen from every European nation com~~~~ tour. Usually in comp palaces, castles, and c learn a little of the lan class who were engag who took the grand to witnessed the redrawi new balance of power The political geogr

Both agreements reflected the dynamics of change that had taken place over the previous century. The rise of France on the Continent and of Britain's colonial empire around the globe were facts that could no longer be ignored. The decline of Sweden and Poland and the emergence of Russia as a great power were the beginning of a long-term process that would

Expansion of Western Europe

Perhaps the most obvious transformation in the political geography of western Europe was the expansion of European power around the globe.

Colonies in the Americas. In the Atlantic, Spain remained the largest colonial power, controlling all of Mexico and Central America, the largest and most numerous of the Caribbean islands, North America from Colorado to California (as well as Florida), and most of South America (see **Map B**). The other major colonial power in the region was Portugal, which held the richly endowed colony of Brazil.

■ **Map B. The Americas.** Much of the American continents was still uncharted with most settlements in the coastal areas.

Mexico. France also claimed the territory of Louisiana, named for Louis XIV, which stretched from New Orleans to Montana. The British settlements ranged along the Atlantic seaboard from Maine to Georgia. Unlike the French, the British settled their territory and were interested in expansion only when their population, which was doubling every 25 years, outgrew its resources. By the early eighteenth century, the ports of Boston, New York, Philadelphia, and Charleston were thriving commercial centers.

Colonies in the Far East. Europeans managed their eastern colonial territories differently than they did those in the Atlantic. Initially, the Portuguese and the Dutch had been satisfied with establishing trading factories—coastal fortresses in Africa and Asia that could be used as warehouses and defended against attack. But in the seventeenth century, the European states began to take control of vital ports and lucrative islands (see **Map C**). Here, the Dutch were the acknowledged leaders, replacing the Portuguese, who had begun the process at the end of the sixteenth century. Holland held, by force or in conjunction with local leaders, all the Spice Islands in the Pacific. The Dutch also occupied both sides of the Malay Peninsula and nearly all the coastal areas of the islands in the Java Sea. Dutch control of Ceylon was strategically important for its Indian trade. Compared to the Dutch, all other European states had only a minor territorial presence in the

■ **Map C. India and the East Indies.** The famous Spice Islands were still controlled by the Dutch while the British gained footholds on both coasts of India.

A WOMAN REPORTER BEHIND THE LINES OF THE WAR IN CHECHNYA

Anne Nivat was the Moscow correspondent for the French daily newspaper Libération *in October 2000 when she interviewed the rebel president of Chechnya. Fluent in Russian and holding a doctorate in political science, Nivat traveled to southern Russia disguised as a Chechen woman to cover the war from the Chechen side. Her newspaper reports led to antiwar protests in Paris.*

Focus Questions
What indications does the Chechen rebel leader give that he sees guerrilla warfare within Chechnya as the best means of defeating Russia? What are his motives for opposition to the presence of Russian troops in Chechnya?

I finally find Maskhadov. He is wearing a military uniform with a pistol in his belt and appears to be in perfect health. Seated on a comfortable sofa in a "safe house," he seems relaxed and eager to share his thoughts on the situation in Chechnya. Outside, Russian armored vehicles pass through the autumn mist. Since he left Grozny the previous winter,

their army but to conserve our own forces. While they occupy our territory—that is, while they remain inactive—their forces grow weaker, while ours get stronger. Our men are everywhere. The Russians know it, and yet they never mount an offensive. Their army is demoralized." . . .

Maskhadov is silent for a moment. He lets out a deep sigh. The Chechens, he admits, are tired of this war. "I recognize that the situation is difficult for the civilian population, which has become the target of the Russian army. I also regret that thousands of my countrymen have had to leave for Ingushetia or elsewhere. But each time I send out my representatives, they come back with the same message: 'Continue the fight. We're with you.' We can't afford to lose face, and the population knows it as well as I do. One way or another, the Russians will be forced to come to the negotiating table. I...

---

476   **Chapter 23**   State Building and Social Change in Europe, 1850–1871

QUESTIONS FOR REVIEW

1. How did the process of creating nation-states in Germany and Italy differ?
2. What social and political circumstances explain the different reforms undertaken in France, Britain, and Russia?
3. How did industrialization change women's lives, and how did such changes depend on a woman's social class?
4. What were the connections between Darwin's ideas about nature and Marx's ideas about society?
5. What forces inspired the creation of the Paris Commune, and what did its fate suggest about the possibility of revolution in the late nineteenth century?

KEY TERMS

Eastern question, p. 464
natural selection, p. 474
Paris Commune, p. 475
Proclamation of the German Empire, p. 462
realism, p. 472
realpolitik, p. 466
Reichstag, p. 467
Risorgimento, p. 464
zemstvos, p. 470

DISCOVERING WESTERN CIVILIZATION ONLINE

You can obtain more information about state building and social change in Europe between 1850 and 1871 at the websites listed below. See also the Companion Website that accompanies this text, www.ablongman.com/kishlansky, which contains an online study guide and additional resources.

Building Nations: The Politics of Unification
The Crimean War (1853–1856)
www.hillsdale.edu/oldacademics/history/war/19Crim.htm
Electronic texts of officers' and soldiers' accounts of the battles of the Crimean War.

Changing Values and the Force of New Ideas
Florence Nightingale
www.kings.edu/womens_history/florence.html
Annotated bibliography of literature on Florence Nightingale.
The Eighteenth Brumaire of Louis Napoleon

The West and the Wider World
THE NUTMEG WARS

A seed about the size of an acorn connected Portugal, Holland, and England to a small string of islands in the Pacific Ocean to the eastern seaboard of North America. It created a series of trading wars among the European powers in the seventeenth century and resulted in a number of trade treaties with the leaders of the Banda Islands, in what is now Indonesia. East and West became linked as great European sailing ships made port at the juncture of the Indian and Pacific Oceans in search of the seeds of the tree *Myristica Fragrans*, which grew only on the Banda Islands and which had the singular virtue of producing two rare spices greatly prized by Europeans: mace and, especially, nutmeg.

Flimsy in appearance, the seeds of the *Myristica Fragrans* could be harvested with no greater effort than the shaking of its branches. The open waters of the seed pod yielded the delicate spice mace that was used in cookery and as a base for fragrances. The pod itself after husking, drying, and cracking yielded the nutmeg, a versatile spice (some think it is the distinctive ingredient in Coca Cola) that experienced a craze in the first decades of the seventeenth century. Its use as a flavor-

origins suggested mystical power. By the end of the century, when the Dutch entered the trade and annual imports grew toward 100 tons, nutmeg was widely believed to be an aphrodisiac, and since aphrodisiacs work on the mind rather than the body, what was believed was all that mattered. Demand

■ Engraving of the Banda Islands, based on a sixteenth-century map by Theodore de Bry.

rose and supply fell. By the beginning of the seventeenth century, when the English contested Dutch supremacy in global trade, the two nations were bringing back a staggering 200 to 250

Indeed, nutmeg was so valuable to Europeans in the seventeenth century that their quest to obtain it led three nations to dispatch their merchants on eighteen-month journeys from which most never returned. If they did not perish during the long sea voyage around the horn of Africa, along the Coromandel Coast of India, and past the great pepper island of Java, they were imperiled by barely submerged razor-sharp volcanic rocks that guarded the Banda Islands on which the trees flourished. Shifting trade winds also made the islands inaccessible six months a year. Only those with good guides or good luck laid anchor there. If the merchants survived the dangers of nature, then they faced those of man. Every European captain claimed his nation held exclusive trading rights to these miraculous seeds, and in the open waters of the Pacific Ocean might made right. More than one great sailing ship had its hull punctured by cannon balls, its mast burned by flaming arrows, its crew killed or scuttled by rival merchants.

Even to reach an island port in safety was no guarantee of success. The indigenous peoples were fierce, capable, and resolutely independent. As one Eng...

---

to develop small, detailed maps to complement the overview map that appears at the beginning of each tour section. We know that only the most motivated students will turn back several pages to locate on a map a place mentioned in the text. Using small maps allows us to integrate maps directly into the relevant text, thus relieving students of the sometimes frustrating experience of attempting to locate not only a specific place on a map but perhaps even the relevant map itself. We have also added labels to all the tour maps and have included in-text references to direct students to relevant maps at specific points in the tour.

Primary Source Documents

A Brief History of Western Civilization: The Unfinished Legacy contains selections from primary sources in order to stimulate students' interest in history by allowing them to hear the past speak in its own voice. The extracts relate directly to discussion within the chapter, thus providing students with a fuller understanding of a significant thinker or event. Each selection is accompanied by an explanatory headnote that identifies the author and work and provides the necessary historical context. "Focus Questions" following the headnote guide students' reading and spark critical thinking about the document.

Discovering Western Civilization Online

"Discovering Western Civilization Online" encourages students to explore the study of Western civilization beyond the confines of a textbook. These end-of-chapter website resources link students to enriching documents, images, and cultural sites. They have been updated for this fifth edition.

CHANGES IN THE NEW EDITION

In the fifth edition of *A Brief History of Western Civilization: The Unfinished Legacy,* we have made several changes to the book's content and coverage.

New! The West and the Wider World

To engage students with historical subjects we have included the new two-page "The West and the Wider World" feature that appears six times in the book. These new essays focus on instances of dynamic cultural encounters and exchanges between the West and the non-West at different points in history. The topics for this new feature were chosen to enhance the student's sense of connections among the events, phenomenon, politics, and products of the West and the wider world. At the end of each feature, we have included questions to spark class discussion and to reinforce such connections.

Revised and Improved Map Program

When teachers of Western civilization courses are surveyed, no single area of need is cited more often than that of geographical knowledge. Most students simply have no mental image of Europe, no familiarity with those geophysical features that are a fundamental part of the geopolitical realities of Western history. We realized that maps, carefully planned and skillfully executed, would be an important component of our text. In this edition, we have revised the entire map program, improving the look of the maps and increasing the sizes of many of them for easier readability. The great number of maps throughout the text, the specially designed "Geographical Tour of Europe" and "Map Discovery" features, and the ancillary programs of map transparencies and workbook exercises combine to provide the strongest possible program for teaching historical geography.

New! Visual Record Pictorial Essays

New "The Visual Record" pictorial essays were developed for the fifth edition as well. Chapter 9, "The High Middle Ages, 900–1300," opens with a pictorial essay on a Syrian castle and its influence on Edward I and his own castle in Wales; Chapter 12, "The European Empires," opens with an examination of a portrait of a king; Chapter 30, "The End of the Cold War and New Global Challenges, 1970 to the Present," begins with an examination of the 1989 fall of the Berlin Wall. We believe that each of these new pictorial essays will help students understand the dominant themes of their respective chapters.

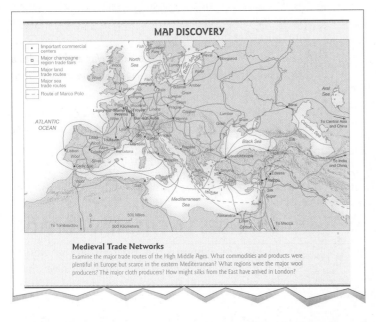

MAP DISCOVERY

Medieval Trade Networks

Examine the major trade routes of the High Middle Ages. What commodities and products were plentiful in Europe but scarce in the eastern Mediterranean? What regions were the major wool producers? The major cloth producers? How might silks from the East have arrived in London?

New! Map Discovery

To complement the standard map program and "Geographical Tours," we have tadded another map-based feature to this edition. "Map Discovery," which appears two to three times per chapter, offers specially designed maps with supporting caption information and questions designed to engage students in analyzing the map data and making larger connections to chapter discussions. We have found that focusing students' attention on the details of a map and asking them to consider why that information is important is an effective way to strengthen critical thinking skills, as well as to expand geographical knowledge.

New! Key Terms and Glossary

In each chapter, key terms are highlighted in boldface type to alert students to principal concepts and events discussed in the chapter. A page-referenced list of the key terms is included at the end of the chapter to help students review the main ideas and events covered in the chapter. A new glossary included at the end of the book provides definitions for the key terms.

Chapter Content Changes

Chapter 3, "Classical and Hellenistic Greece, 500–100 B.C.E.," includes additional material on Hellenistic medicine and includes a new feature on representing the Buddha. Chapter 5, "Imperial Rome, 146 B.C.E.–192 C.E.," includes a new discussion of the study of science and astronomy in the empire. Chapter 7, "The Classical Legacy in the East: Byzantium and Islam," includes expanded coverage of Islamic civilization, including additional material on Muslim scientists and philosophers, and a new essay on the secrets of silk production from China introduced into Byzantium. Chapter 9, "The High Middle Ages, 900–1300," includes a new section on the expansion of the Mongol Empire and its impact on the West. In Chapter 10, "The Later Middle Ages, 1300–1500," there is a new discussion of the impact of events outside Europe on the decline of Italian economic power. Chapter 11, "The Italian Renaissance," contains a new section on Renaissance science, particularly the biological and life sciences. Chapter 12, "The European Empires," includes an expanded discussion of the legacy of the Encounters and the origin of the African slave trade. Chapter 17, "Science and Commerce in Early Modern Europe," includes expanded coverage of the early slave trade and a new feature on European trade competition in the East and the resulting Nutmeg wars. In Chapter 18, "The Balance of Power in Eighteenth-Century Europe," a new feature essay explores the formation of the British Raj in India.

Parts of Chapter 20, "The French Revolution and the Napoleonic Era, 1789–1815," were reorganized and streamlined to present more succinctly the factors leading to the crisis of the Old Regime and the early stages of the revolution. The chapter now also includes a feature on guillotine justice in the revolution. Chapter 23, "State Building and Social Change in Europe, 1850–1914," includes a new section on the new technology and art of photography and an expanded discussion of the Civil War in the United States. In Chapter 24, "The Crisis of European Culture, 1871–1914," a new section explores the arts in the shaping of the new consciousness and a new feature essay examines the influence of African art on Western artists and the influence of the industrial West on African art. Parts of Chapter 26, "War and Revolution, 1914–1920," were reorganized to better present the Russian Revolution and its impact on the Great War, and the discussion of settling the peace was expanded. Chapters 29, "The Cold War and Postwar Economic Recovery: 1945–1970," and Chapter 30, "The End of the Cold War and New Global Challenges, 1970 to the Present," have been reorganized to highlight the significance of postwar economic and social transformations and geopolitical shifts and to better present the developments of the Cold War and its conclusion. Chapter 29 now begins with the origins of the Cold War and includes a new feature on the post–World War II rise in Japanese manufacturing. Chapter 30 has been updated and also includes expanded coverage of the European Union; analysis of ethnicity, nationalism, and terrorism in the early twenty-first century; and a new section on French laws on secularism.

There are many new features in our text and much that is out of the ordinary. We hope that there are many things in this book that teachers of Western civilization will find valuable. But we also hope that there are things here with which you will disagree, themes that you can develop better, arguments and ideas that will stimulate you. A textbook is only one part of a course, and it is always less important than a teacher. What we hope is that by having done our job successfully, we will have made the teacher's job easier and the student's job more enjoyable.

ACKNOWLEDGMENTS

We want to thank the many conscientious historians who gave generously of their time and knowledge to review our manuscript. We would like to thank the reviewers of the first four editions as well as those of the current edition. Their valuable critiques and suggestions have contributed greatly to the final product. We are grateful to the following:

Daniel F. Callahan, *University of Delaware*; Michael Clinton, *Gwynedd-Mercy College*; Bob Cole, *Utah State University*; Gary P. Cox, *Gordon College*; Peter L. de Rosa, *Bridgewater State College*; Frank Lee Earley, *Arapahoe Community College*; Steven Fanning, *University of Illinois at Chicago*; Patrick Foley, *Tarrant County College*; Charlotte M. Gradie, *Sacred Heart University*; Richard Grossman, *Northeastern Illinois University*; David Halamy, *Cypress College*; Gary J. Johnson, *University of Southern Maine*; Cynthia Jones, *University of Missouri at Kansas City*; John Kemp, *Truckee Meadows Community College*; Janilyn Kocher, *Richland Community College*; Lisa M. Lane, *MiraCosta College*; Oscar Lansen, *University of North Carolina at Charlotte*; Michael R. Lynn, *Agnes Scott College*; Mark S. Malaszczyk, *St. John's University*; John M. McCulloh, *Kansas State University*; David B. Mock, *Tallahassee Community College*; Don Mohr, Emeritus, *University of Alaska, Anchorage*; Martha G.

Newman, *University of Texas at Austin*; Lisa Pace-Hardy, *Jefferson Davis Community College*; Marlette Rebhorn, *Austin Community College*; Steven G. Reinhardt, *University of Texas at Arlington*; Kimberly Reiter, *Stetson University*; Robert Rockwell, *Mt. San Jacinto College*; Maryloy Ruud, *University of West Florida*; Jose M. Sanchez, *St. Louis University*; Erwin Sicher, *Southwestern Adventist College*; and Ruth Suyama, *Los Angeles Mission College*; David Tengwall, *Anne Arundel Community College*; Janet M. C. Walmsley, *George Mason University*; John E. Weakland, *Ball State University*. Rick Whisonant, *York Technical College*.

Our special thanks go to our colleagues at Marquette University for their longstanding support, valuable comments, and assistance on this edition's design: Lance Grahn, Lezlie Knox, Timothy G. McMahon, and Alan P. Singer.

We also acknowledge the assistance of the many reviewers of *Civilization in the West* whose comments have been invaluable in the development of *A Brief History of Western Civilization: The Unfinished Legacy*:

Joseph Aieta, III, *Lasell College*; Ken Albala, *University of the Pacific*; Patricia Ali, *Morris College*; Gerald D. Anderson, *North Dakota State University*; Jean K. Berger, *University of Wisconsin, Fox Valley*; Susan Carrafiello, *Wright State University*; Andrew Donson, *University of Massachusetts, Amherst*; Frederick Dotolo, *St. John Fisher College*; Janusz Duzinkiewicz, *Purdue University*; Brian Elsesser, *Saint Louis University*; Bryan Ganaway, *University of Illinois*; David Graf, *University of Miami*; Benjamin Hett, *Hunter College*; Mark M. Hull, *Saint Louis University*; Barbara Klemm, *Broward Community College*; Lawrence Langer, *University of Connecticut*; Elise Moentmann, *University of Portland*; Alisa Plant, *Tulane University*; Salvador Rivera, *State University of New York*; Thomas Robisheaux, *Duke University*; Ilicia Sprey, *Saint Joseph's College*; George S. Vascik, *Miami University, Hamilton*; Vance Youmans, *Spokane Falls Community College*; Achilles Aavraamides, *Iowa State University*; Meredith L. Adams, *Southwest Missouri State University*; Arthur H. Auten, *University of Hartford*; Suzanne Balch-Lindsay, *Eastern New Mexico University*; Sharon Bannister, *University of Findlay*; John W. Barker, *University of Wisconsin*; Patrick Bass, *Mount Union College*; William H. Beik, *Northern Illinois University*; Patrice Berger, *University of Nebraska*; Lenard R. Berlanstein, *University of Virginia*; Raymond Birn, *University of Oregon*; Donna Bohanan, *Auburn University*; Werner Braatz, *University of Wisconsin, Oshkosh*; Thomas A. Brady, Jr., *University of Oregon*; Anthony M. Brescia, *Nassau Community College*; Elaine G. Breslaw, *Morgan State University*; Ronald S. Brockway, *Regis University*; April Brooks, *South Dakota State University*; Daniel Patrick Brown, *Moorpark College*; Ronald A. Brown, *Charles County Community College*; Blaine T. Browne, *Broward Community College*; Kathleen S. Carter, *High Point University*; Robert Carver, *University of Missouri, Rolla*; Edward J. Champlin, *Princeton University*; Stephanie Evans Christelow, *Western Washington University*; Sister Dorita Clifford, BVM, *University of San Francisco*; Gary B. Cohen, *University of Oklahoma*; Jan M. Copes, *Cleveland State University*; John J. Contreni, *Purdue University*; Tim Crain, *University of Wisconsin, Stout*; Norman Delaney, *Del Mar College*; Samuel E. Dicks, *Emporia State University*; Frederick Dumin, *Washington State University*; Laird Easton, *California State University, Chico*; Dianne E. Farrell, *Moorhead State University*; Margot C. Finn, *Emory University*; Allan W. Fletcher, *Boise State University*; Luci Fortunato De Lisle, *Bridgewater State College*; Elizabeth L. Furdell, *University of North Florida*; Thomas W. Gallant, *University of Florida*; Frank Garosi, *California State University, Sacramento*; Lorne E. Glaim, *Pacific Union College*; Joseph J. Godson, *Hudson Valley Community College*; Sue Helder Goliber, *Mount St. Mary's College*; Manuel G. Gonzales, *Diablo Valley College*; Louis Haas, *Duquesne University*; Eric Haines, *Bellevue Community College*; Paul Halliday, *University of Virginia*; Margaretta S. Handke, *Mankato State University*; David A. Harnett, *University of San Francisco*; Paul B. Harvey, Jr., *Pennsylvania State University*; Neil Heyman, *San Diego State University*; Daniel W. Hollis, *Jacksonville State University*; Kenneth G. Holum, *University of Maryland*; Patricia Howe, *University of St. Thomas*; David Hudson, *California State University, Fresno*; Charles Ingrao, *Purdue University*; George F. Jewsbury, *Oklahoma State University*; Donald G. Jones, *University of Central*

Arkansas; William R. Jones, *University of New Hampshire;* Richard W. Kaeuper, *University of Rochester;* David Kaiser, *Carnegie-Mellon University;* Jeff Kaufmann, *Muscatine Community College;* Carolyn Kay, *Trent University;* William R. Keylor, *Boston University;* Joseph Kicklighter, *Auburn University;* Charles L. Killinger, III, *Valencia Community College;* Alan M. Kirshner, *Ohlone College;* Charlene Kiser, *Milligan College;* Alexandra Korros, *Xavier University;* Cynthia Kosso, *Northern Arizona University;* Lara Kriegel, *Florida International University;* Lisa M. Lane, *MiraCosta College;* David C. Large, *Montana State University;* Catherine Lawrence, *Messiah College;* Bryan LeBeau, *Creighton University;* Robert B. Luehrs, *Fort Hays State University;* Donna J. Maier, *University of Northern Iowa;* Margaret Malamud, *New Mexico State University;* Roberta T. Manning, *Boston College;* Lyle McAlister, *University of Florida;* Therese M. McBride, *College of the Holy Cross;* David K. McQuilkin, *Bridgewater College;* Victor V. Minasian, *College of Marin;* David B. Mock, *Tallahassee Community College;* Robert Moeller, *University of California, Irvine;* R. Scott Moore, *University of Dayton;* Ann E. Moyer, *University of Pennsylvania;* Pierce C. Mullen, *Montana State University;* John A. Nichols, *Slippery Rock University;* Thomas F. X. Noble, *University of Virginia;* J. Ronald Oakley, *Davidson County Community College;* Bruce K. O'Brien, *Mary Washington College;* Dennis H. O'Brien, *West Virginia University;* Maura O'Connor, *University of Cincinnati;* Richard A. Oehling, *Assumption College;* James H. Overfield, *University of Vermont;* Catherine Patterson, *University of Houston;* Sue Patrick, *University of Wisconsin, Barron County;* Peter C. Piccillo, *Rhode Island College;* Peter O'M. Pierson, *Santa Clara University;* Theophilus Prousis, *University of North Florida;* Marlette Rebhorn, *Austin Community College;* Jack B. Ridley, *University of Missouri, Rolla;* Constance M. Rousseau, *Providence College;* Thomas J. Runyan, *Cleveland State University;* John P. Ryan, *Kansas City Community College;* Geraldine Ryder, *Ocean County College;* Joanne Schneider, *Rhode Island College;* Steven Schroeder, *Indiana University of Pennsylvania;* Steven C. Seyer, *Lehigh County Community College;* Lixin Shao, *University of Minnesota, Duluth;* George H. Shriver, *Georgia Southern University;* Ellen J. Skinner, *Pace University;* Bonnie Smith, *University of Rochester;* Patrick Smith, *Broward Community College;* James Smither, *Grand Valley State University;* Sherill Spaar, *East Central University;* Charles R. Sullivan, *University of Dallas;* Peter N. Stearns, *Carnegie-Mellon University;* Saulius Suziedelis, *Millersville University;* Darryl B. Sycher, *Columbus State Community College;* Roger Tate, *Somerset Community College;* Janet A. Thompson, *Tallahassee Community College;* Anne-Marie Thornton, *Bilkent University;* Donna L. Van Raaphorst, *Cuyahoga Community College;* James Vanstone, *John Abbot College;* Steven Vincent, *North Carolina State University;* Richard A. Voeltz, *Cameron University;* Faith Wallis, *McGill University;* Sydney Watts, *University of Richmond;* Eric Weissman, *Golden West College;* Christine White, *Pennsylvania State University;* William Harry Zee, *Gloucester County College.*

Each author also received invaluable assistance and encouragement from many colleagues, friends, and family members over the years of research, reflection, writing, and revising that went into the making of this text:

Mark Kishlansky thanks Ann Adams, Robert Bartlett, Ray Birn, David Buisseret, Ted Cook, Frank Conaway, Constantine Fasolt, James Hankins, Katherine Haskins, Richard Hellie, Matthew Kishlansky, Donna Marder, Mary Beth Rose, Victor Stater, Jeanne Thiel, and the staffs of the Joseph Regenstein Library, the Newberry Library, and the Widener and Lamont Libraries at Harvard.

Patrick Geary wishes to thank Mary, Catherine, and Anne Geary for their patience, support, and encouragement. He also thanks Anne Picard, Dale Schofield, Hans Hummer, and Richard Mowrer for their able assistance throughout the project.

Patricia O'Brien thanks Christopher Reed for his loving support; Tristan Reed for his intellectual engagement; and Erin and Devin Reed for "keeping me in touch with the contemporary world."

MARK KISHLANSKY
PATRICK GEARY
PATRICIA O'BRIEN

SUPPLEMENTS

For Qualified College Adopters

- **Instructor's Resource Manual**   This thorough instructor's manual includes an introductory essay on teaching Western civilization and a bibliographic essay on the use of primary sources for class discussion and analytical thinking. Each chapter contains a chapter summary, key terms, list of important geographic locations, discussion questions, and an annotated list of films (not supplied by Longman).

- **Test Bank**   This supplement contains more than 1,200 multiple-choice, true/false, and essay questions. Multiple-choice and true/false questions are referenced by topic and text page number.

- **TestGen-EQ Computerized Testing System**   This flexible, easy-to-master computerized test bank on a dual-platform CD includes all of the items in the printed test bank and allows instructors to select specific questions, edit them, and add their own items to create exams.

- **Instructor Resource Center (IRC) (www.ablongman.com/irc)**   Through the Instructor Resource Center, instructors can log into premium online products, browse and download book-specific instructor resources, and receive immediate access and instructions to installing course management content.

- **Research Navigator and Research Navigator Guide**   Research Navigator is a comprehensive website offering EBSCO's ContentSelect Academic Journal & Abstract Database, the *New York Times* Search-by-Subject Archive, *Financial Times* Article Archive and Company Financials, and "Best of the Web" Link Library. The Research Navigator Guide provides your students with access to the website and includes reference material and hints about conducting online research.

- **Study Card for Western Civilization**   Colorful, affordable, and packed with useful information, Longman's Study Cards make studying easier, more efficient, and more enjoyable.

- **Text-Specific Transparency Set**   A set of full-color transparency map acetates drawn from *Civilization in the West*, Sixth Edition.

- **History Video Program**   A list of more than 100 videos from which qualified college adopters can choose. Restrictions apply.

- **History Digital Media Archive CD-ROM**   This CD-ROM contains electronic images and interactive and static maps, along with media elements such as video. It is fully customizable and ready for classroom presentation. All images and maps are available in PowerPoint™ as well.

- **Discovering Western Civilization Through Maps and Views**   Created by Gerald Danzer, University of Illinois at Chicago, and David Buisseret, this unique set of 140 full-color acetates contains an introduction to teaching history through maps and a detailed commentary on each transparency. The collection includes cartographic and pictorial maps, views and photos, urban plans, building diagrams, and works of art.

- **Interpretations of the Western World**   General Editor Mark Kishlansky has prepared a customizable database of secondary source readings. Selections are grouped topically so that instructors can assign readings that illustrate different points of view about a given historical debate.

For Students

- **Study Guide**   Available in two volumes, each chapter in the study guide includes a summary; a timeline activity; map and geography questions; key terms, people, and events; and identification, multiple-choice, and critical-thinking questions.

- **The Western Civilization Companion Website http://www.ablongman.com/westerncivilization**   Students can take advantage of this online course companion that includes practice tests, Web links, and flash cards that cover the scope of topics covered in a typical Western civilization class.

- **Mapping Western Civilization: Student Activities**   Created by Gerald Danzer, University of Illinois at Chicago, this map workbook features exercises designed to teach students to interpret and analyze cartographic materials such as historical documents.

- **Western Civilization Map Workbook**   These two volumes test and reinforce basic geography literacy while building critical-thinking skills.

- **Longman Atlas of Western Civilization**   This 52-page atlas features carefully selected historical maps that provide comprehensive coverage for the major historical periods.

- **A Short Guide to Writing About History,** Fifth Edition   Written by Richard Marius, late of Harvard University, and Melvin E. Page, Eastern Tennessee State University, this engaging and practical text helps students get beyond merely compiling dates and facts. Covering both brief essays and the documented resource paper, the text explores the writing and researching processes, identifies different modes of historical writing, including argument, and concludes with guidelines for improving style.

MyHistoryLab (www.myhistorylab.com)

MyHistoryLab provides students with an online package complete with the entire comprehensive electronic textbook and numerous study aids. With several hundred primary sources, many of which are assignable and link to a gradebook, pre- and post-tests that link to a gradebook and result in individualized study plans, videos and images, as well as map activities with gradable quizzes, the site offers students a unique, interactive experience that brings history to life. The comprehensive site also includes a History Bookshelf with fifty of the most commonly assigned books in history classes and a History Toolkit with tutorials and helpful links. Other features include gradable assignments and chapter review materials; a Test Bank; and Research Navigator.

Delivered in CourseCompass, Blackboard, or WebCT, as well as in a non-course-management version, MyHistoryLab is easy to use and flexible. MyHistoryLab is organized according to the table of contents of the comprehensive textbook. With the course-management version, instructors can create a further customized product by adding their own syllabus, content, and assignments, or they can use the materials as presented.

Longman Library of World Biography Series

Pocket-sized and brief, each biography in the Library of World Biography series relates the life of its subject to the broader themes and developments of the time. Series titles include: *Ahmad al-Mansur: Islamic Visionary* by Richard Smith (Ferrum College); *Alexander the Great: Legacy of a Conqueror* by Winthrop Lindsay Adams (University of Utah); *Benito Mussolini: The First Fascist* by Anthony L. Cardoza (Loyola University); *Fukuzawa Yûkichi: From Samurai to Capitalist* by Helen M. Hopper (University of Pittsburgh); *Ignatius of Loyola: Founder of the Jesuits* by John Patrick Donnelly (Marquette University); *Jacques Coeur: Entrepreneur and King's Bursar* by Kathryn L. Reyerson (University of Minnesota); *Katô Shidzue: A Japanese Feminist* by Helen M. Hopper (University of Pittsburgh); *Simón Bolívar: Liberation and Disappointment* by David Bushnell (University of Florida); *Vasco da Gama: Renaissance Crusader* by Glenn J. Ames (University of Toledo); and *Zheng He: China and the Oceans in the Early Ming, 1405–1433* by Edward Dreyer (University of Miami).

Penguin-Longman Partnership

The partnership between Penguin Books and Longman Publishers offers a discount on a wide range of titles when bundled with any Longman history survey textbook. Visit www.ablongman.com/penguin for more information.

MARK KISHLANSKY   Mark Kishlansky is Frank B. Baird, Jr., Professor of English and European History and has served as the Associate Dean of the Faculty at Harvard University. He was educated at the State University of New York at Stony Brook, where he first studied history, and at Brown University, where he received his Ph.D. in 1977. For 16 years, he taught at the University of Chicago and was a member of the staff that taught Western Civilization. Currently, he lectures on the History of Western Civilization at Harvard. Professor Kishlansky is a specialist on seventeenth-century English political history and has written, among other works, *A Monarchy Transformed, The Rise of the New Model Army,* and *Parliamentary Selection: Social and Political Choice in Early Modern England.* From 1984 to 1991, he was editor of the *Journal of British Studies* and is presently the general editor of *History Compass,* the first on-line history journal. He is also the general editor for Pearson Custom Publishing's source and interpretations databases, which provide custom book supplements for Western Civilization courses.

PATRICK GEARY   Holding a Ph.D. in Medieval Studies from Yale University, Patrick Geary has broad experience in interdisciplinary approaches to European history and civilization. He has served as the director of the Medieval Institute at the University of Notre Dame as well as director for the Center for Medieval and Renaissance Studies at the University of California, Los Angeles, where he is currently Distinguished Professor of History. He has also held positions at the University of Florida and Princeton University and has taught at the École des Hautes Études en Sciences Sociales in Paris, the Central European University in Budapest, and the University of Vienna. His many publications include *Readings in Medieval History; Before France and Germany: The Creation and Transformation of the Merovingian World; Phantoms of Remembrance: Memory and Oblivion at the End of the First Millennium; The Myth of Nations: The Medieval Origins of Europe;* and *Women at the Beginning: Origin Myths from the Amazons to the Virgin Mary.*

PATRICIA O'BRIEN   is a specialist in modern French cultural and social history and received her Ph.D. from Columbia University. She has held appointments at Yale University, the University of California, Irvine, the University of California, Riverside, the École des Hautes Études en Sciences Sociales in Paris, and the University of California, Los Angeles. Between 1995 and 1999, Professor O'Brien worked to foster collaborative interdisciplinary research in the humanities as director of the University of California Humanities Research Institute. Since 2004, she has served as Executive Dean of the College of Letters and Science at UCLA. Professor O'Brien has published widely on the history of French crime and punishment, cultural theory, urban history, and gender issues. Representative publications include *The Promise of Punishment: Prisons in Nineteenth-Century France;* "The Kleptomania Diagnosis: Bourgeois Women and Theft in Late Nineteenth-Century France" in *Expanding the Past: A Reader in Social History;* and "Michel Foucault's History of Culture" in *The New Cultural History,* edited by Lynn Hunt. Professor O'Brien's commitment to this textbook grew out of her own teaching experiences in large, introductory Western civilization courses. She has benefited from the contributions of her students and fellow instructors in her approach to the study of Western civilization in the modern period.

A BRIEF HISTORY OF
WESTERN CIVILIZATION

INTRODUCTION

THE IDEA OF WESTERN CIVILIZATION

The West is an idea. It is not visible from space. An astronaut viewing the blue-and-white terrestrial sphere can make out the forms of Africa, bounded by the Atlantic, the Indian Ocean, the Red Sea, and the Mediterranean. Australia, the Americas, and even Antarctica are distinct patches of blue-green in the darker waters that surround them. But nothing comparable separates Asia from Europe, East from West. Viewed from 100 miles up, the West itself is invisible. Although astronauts can see the great Eurasian landmass curving around the Northern Hemisphere, the Ural Mountains—the theoretical boundary between East and West—appear faint from space. Certainly they are less impressive than the towering Himalayas, the Alps, or even the Caucasus. People, not geology, determined that the Urals should be the arbitrary boundary between Europe and Asia.

Even this determination took centuries. Originally, Europe was a name that referred only to central Greece. Gradually, Greeks extended it to include the whole Greek mainland and then the landmass to the north. Later, Roman explorers and soldiers carried Europe north and west to its modern boundaries. Asia too grew with time. Initially, Asia was only that small portion of what is today Turkey inland from the Aegean Sea. Gradually, as Greek explorers came to know of lands farther east, north, and south, they expanded their understanding of Asia to include everything east of the Don River to the north and of the Red Sea to the south.

Western civilization is as much an idea as the West itself. Under the right conditions, astronauts can see the Great Wall of China snaking its way from the edge of the Himalayas to the Yellow Sea. No comparable physical legacy of the West is so massive that its details can be discerned from space. Nor are Western achievements rooted forever in one corner of the world. What we call Western civilization belongs to no particular place. Its location has changed since the origins of civilization, that is, the cultural and social traditions characteristic of the *civitas,* or city. "Western" cities appeared first outside the "West," in the Tigris and Euphrates river basins in present-day Iraq and Iran, a region that we today call the Middle East. These areas have never lost their urban traditions, but in time, other cities in North Africa, Greece, and Italy adapted and expanded this heritage.

Until the sixteenth century C.E., the western end of the Eurasian landmass was the crucible in which disparate cultural and intellectual traditions of the Near East, the Mediterranean, and northern and western Europe were smelted into a new and powerful alloy. Then "the West" expanded by establishing colonies overseas and by giving rise to the "settler societies" of the Americas, Australia and New Zealand, and South Africa.

Western technology for harnessing nature, Western forms of economic and political organization, Western styles of art and music are—for good or ill—dominant influences in world civilization. Japan is a leading power in the Western traditions of capitalist commerce and technology. China, the most populous country in the world, adheres to Marxist socialist principles—a European political tradition. Millions of people in Africa, Asia, and the Americas follow the religions of Islam and Christianity, both of which developed from Judaism in the cradle of Western civilization.

Many of today's most pressing problems are also part of the legacy of the Western tradition. The remnants of European colonialism have left deep hostilities throughout the world. The integration of developing nations into the world economy keeps much of humanity in a seemingly hopeless cycle of poverty as

the wealth of poor countries goes to pay interest on loans from Europe and America. Hatred of Western civilization is a central, ideological tenet that inspired terrorist attacks on symbols of American economic and military strength on September 11, 2001, and that fuels anti-Western terrorism around the world. The West itself faces a crisis. Impoverished citizens of former colonies flock to Europe and North America seeking a better life but often finding poverty, hostility, and racism instead. Finally, the advances of Western civilization endanger our very existence. Technology pollutes the world's air, water, and soil, and nuclear weapons threaten the destruction of all civilization. Yet these are the same advances that allow us to lengthen life expectancy, harness the forces of nature, and conquer disease. It is the same technology that allows us to view our world from outer space.

How did we get here? In this book we attempt to answer that question. The history of Western civilization is not simply the triumphal story of progress, the creation of a better world. Even in areas in which we can see development, such as technology, communications, and social complexity, change is not always for the better. However, it would be equally inaccurate to view Western civilization as a progressive decline from a mythical golden age of the human race. The roughly 300 generations since the origins of civilization have bequeathed a rich and contradictory legacy to the present. Inherited political and social institutions, cultural forms, and religious and philosophical traditions form the framework within which the future must be created. The past does not determine the future, but it is the raw material from which the future will be made. To use this legacy properly, we must first understand it, not because the past is the key to the future, but because understanding yesterday frees us to create tomorrow.

Chapter 1

THE FIRST CIVILIZATIONS

The Visual Record

ÖTZI'S LAST MEAL

The idea that we can visit with an ancestor from three hundred generations past seems incredible. And yet a discovery in the Italian Alps a decade ago has brought us face to face with Ötzi (so-named for the valley where he was found), an ordinary man who faced a cruel death more than five thousand years ago. Ötzi's perfectly preserved body, clothing, tools, and weapons allow us to know how people lived and died in Western Europe before it was Europe—before indeed it was the West.

Ötzi was small by modern European standards: he stood at just 5 feet 4 inches. Around 40 years old, he was already suffering from arthritis, and his several tattoos were likely a kind of therapy. He probably lived in a village below the mountain whose inhabitants survived by hunting, simple agriculture, and goat herding.

One spring day around 3000 B.C.E., Ötzi enjoyed what would be his last meal of meat, some vegetables, and flat bread made of einkorn wheat. He dressed warmly but simply in a leather breechcloth with a calfskin belt covered by a leather upper garment of goatskin sewn together with animal sinews. Below, he wore leather leggings and sturdy shoes made of bearskin soles and deerhide tops, lined with soft grasslike socks. On his head was a warm bearskin cap.

Ötzi carried an ax with a blade of almost pure copper and a flint knife in a fiber scabbard. He secured his leather backpack on a pack-frame made of a long hazel rod bent into a U-shape and reinforced with two narrow wooden slats. Among other things it held birch bark containers, one filled with materials to start a fire, which he could ignite with a flint he carried in his pouch. He also equipped himself with a multipurpose mat made from long stalks of Alpine grass and a simple first-aid kit consisting of inner bark from the birch tree—a substance with antibiotic and styptic properties.

For so small a man, Ötzi carried an imposing weapon: a yew-wood bow almost six feet long and a quiver of arrows. He must have been working on the weapon shortly before he died; the bow and most of the arrows were unfinished.

For ten years after the discovery of Ötzi's body, scholars and scientists studied his remains and speculated on why and how he died. Was he caught by a sudden storm or did he perhaps injure himself and die of exposure? And what was he doing so high in the

mountains—six hours from the valley where he had his last meal, without adequate food or water? Finally, another X-ray of his frozen corpse revealed a clue: the shadow of a stone point lodged in his back.

Apparently, Ötzi left the lower villages that fateful spring day frightened and in a great hurry. Alone at an altitude of over 10,000 feet, desperately trying to finish his bow and arrows, he was fleeing for his life, but his luck ran out. Ötzi was shot in the back with an arrow. It pierced his shoulder between his shoulder blade and ribs, paralyzing his arm and causing extensive bleeding. Exhausted, he lay down in a shallow cleft in the snowy rocks. In a matter of hours he was dead, and the snows of centuries quietly buried him.

What does Ötzi's life and death tell us about the story of Western civilization? Although during his lifetime radically new urban societies and cultures were appearing just east of the Mediterranean, Ötzi still belonged to the Stone Age. None of his clothing was woven, although such basic technology was common in western Asia. The only metal was his ax head of soft copper, not the much harder bronze favored in the eastern Mediterranean. And yet, something vital connected Ötzi's world and that distant cradle of civilization: his last meal. Einkorn wheat is not native to western Europe but originated in the region of the Tigris and Euphrates. From there, both the grain itself and the technology of its cultivation spread slowly, ultimately reaching Ötzi's Alpine village. Other components of civilization would follow: weaving, metal working, urbanization, writing, and ways to kill men and women like Ötzi with greater efficiency.

Looking Ahead

This first chapter begins before Ötzi with the origins of humankind and chronicles the great discoveries that led to the first urban-based civilizations of Mesopotamia and Egypt. It examines as well the seminomadic herding societies that lived on their margins and developed the first great monotheistic religious tradition. ➤

BEFORE CIVILIZATION

The human race was already ancient by the time that Ötzi died, and civilization first appeared around 3,500 years before the Common Era, the period following the traditional date of the birth of Jesus. (Such dates are abbreviated B.C. for "before Christ" or B.C.E. for "before the Common Era"; A.D., the abbreviation of the Latin for "in the year of the Lord," is used to refer to dates after the birth of Jesus. Today, scholars use simply C.E. to mean the Common Era. To indicate an approximate date for an event that cannot be dated precisely, the abbreviation *ca.*, or *circa*, "approximately," is used.) The first human-like creatures whose remains have been discovered date from as long as five million years ago. One of the best-known finds, nicknamed "Lucy" by the scientist who discovered her skeleton in 1974, stood only about four feet tall and lived on the edge of a lake in what is now Ethiopia. Lucy and her band did not have brains that were as well developed as those of modern humans. They did, however, use simple tools such as sticks, bone clubs, and chipped rocks. Although small and relatively weak compared with other animals, Lucy's species of creatures—neither fully ape nor human—survived for over four million years.

Varieties of the modern species of humans, *Homo sapiens* ("thinking human"), appeared well over 100,000 years ago and spread across the Eurasian landmass and Africa. The earliest *Homo sapiens* in Europe, the *Neanderthal,* differed little from us today. They were roughly the same size and had the same cranial capacity as we. They spread throughout much of Africa, Europe, and Asia during the last great ice age. To survive in the harsh tundra landscape, they developed a cultural system that enabled them to modify their environment. Customs such as the burial of their dead with food offerings indicate that Neanderthals may have developed a belief in an afterlife. Although a bit shorter and heavier than most people today, they were clearly our close cousins. Nevertheless, DNA studies suggest that Neanderthals are not directly related to modern humans. Their subspecies appears to have been a dead end.

No one knows why or how the Neanderthals were replaced by our subspecies, *Homo sapiens sapiens* ("thinking thinking human"), around 40,000 years ago. Whatever the reason and whatever the process—extinction, evolution, or extermination—this last arrival on the human scene was universally successful. All humans today—whether blond, blue-eyed Scandinavians, Australian aborigines, Africans, Japanese, or Amerindians—belong to this same subspecies. Differences in skin color, type of hair, and build are minor variations on the same theme. The identification of races, while selectively based on some of these physical variations, is, like civilization itself, a fact not of biology but of culture.

Early *Homo sapiens sapiens* lived in small kin groups of 20 or 30, following game and seeking shelter in tents, lean-tos, and caves. People of the **Paleolithic era** or Old Stone Age (ca. 600,000–10,000 B.C.E.) worked together for hunting and defense and apparently formed emotional bonds that were based on more than sex or economic necessity. The skeleton of a man found a few years ago in Iraq, for example, suggests that although he was born with only one arm and was crippled further by arthritis, the rest of his community supported him and he lived to adulthood. Clearly, his value to his society lay in something more than his ability to make a material contribution to its collective life.

The Dominance of Culture

During the upper or late Paleolithic era (ca. 35,000–10,000 B.C.E.), **culture,** meaning everything about humans that is not inherited biologically, was increasingly determinant in human life. Paleolithic people were not on an endless and all-consuming quest to provide for the necessities of life. They spent less time on such things than we do today. Therefore, they were able to find time to develop speech, religion, and artistic expression. Wall paintings, small clay and stone figurines of female figures (which may reflect concerns about fertility), and finely decorated stone and bone tools indicate not just artistic ability but also abstract and symbolic thought.

The end of the glacial era marked the beginning of the Mesolithic, or Middle Stone Age (ca. 10,000–8000 B.C.E.). This period occurred at different times in different places as the climate grew milder, vast expanses of glaciers melted, and sea levels rose. Mesolithic peoples began the gradual domestication of plants and animals and sometimes formed settled communities. They developed the bow and arrow and pottery, and they made use of small flints (microliths) and fishhooks.

Paintings: A Cultural Record.   An amazing continuous record of the civilizing of the West is found in the arid wastes of Africa's Sahara Desert. At the end of the last ice age, around 10,000 B.C.E., much of North Africa enjoyed a mild, damp climate and supported a diverse population of animals and humans. At Tassili-n-Ajjer in modern Algeria, succeeding generations of inhabitants left over 4,000 paintings on cliff and

CHRONOLOGY	
BEFORE CIVILIZATION	
ca. 100,000 B.C.E.	*Homo sapiens*
ca. 40,000 B.C.E.	*Homo sapiens sapiens*
ca. 35,000–10,000 B.C.E.	Late Paleolithic era (Old Stone Age)
ca. 8000–6500 B.C.E.	Neolithic era (New Stone Age)
ca. 3500 B.C.E.	Civilization begins

cave walls that date from about 6000 B.C.E. until the time of Jesus. Like a pictorial time line, these paintings show the gradual transformations of human culture.

The earliest cave paintings were produced by people who, like the inhabitants of Europe and the Near East, lived by hunting game and gathering edible plants, nuts, and fruit. Through this long period, humans perfected the making of stone tools; learned to work bone, antler, and ivory into weapons and utensils; and organized an increasingly complex society.

Sedentarization.   Sometime around 5000 B.C.E., the artists at Tassili-n-Ajjer began to include images of domesticated cattle and harnesslike equipment in their paintings. Such depictions give evidence of the arrival in North Africa of two of the most profound transformations in human history: sedentarization, that is, the adoption of a fixed dwelling place, and the agricultural revolution. These fundamental changes in human culture began independently around the world and continued for roughly 5,000 years. They appeared first around 10,000 B.C.E. in the Near East, then elsewhere in Asia around 8000 B.C.E. By 5000 B.C.E. the domestication of plants and animals was under way in Africa and what is today Mexico.

Around 10,000 B.C.E., many hunter-gatherers living along the coastal plains of what is today Syria and Israel and in the valleys and the hill country near the Zagros Mountains between modern Iran and Iraq began to develop specialized strategies that led, by accident, to a transformation in human culture. Rather than constantly traveling in search of food, people living near the Mediterranean coast stayed put and exploited the various seasonal sources of food, fish, wild grains, fruits, and game. In communities such as Jericho, people built

and rebuilt their mud brick and stone huts over generations rather than moving on as their ancestors had. Such a sedentary existence was easier on the very young and the very old, and consequently infant mortality dropped and life expectancy rose. In the Zagros region, sedentary communities focused on single, abundant sources of food at specific seasons, such as wild sheep and goats in the mountains during summer and pigs and cattle in the lower elevations in winter. These people also harvested the wild forms of wheat and barley that grew in upland valleys.

Social Organization, Agriculture, and Religion

No one really knows why settlement led to agriculture. As population growth put pressure on the local food supply, gathering activities demanded more formal coordination and organization and led to the development of political leadership. This leadership and the perception of safety in numbers may have prevented the traditional breaking away to form other similar communities in the next valley, as had happened when population growth pressured earlier groups. In any case, people no longer simply looked for favored species of plants and animals where they occurred naturally. Now they introduced these species into other locations and favored them at the expense of plant and animal species that were not deemed useful. Agriculture had begun.

Control of Nature.   The ability to domesticate goats, sheep, pigs, and cattle and to cultivate barley, wheat, and vegetables changed human communities from passive harvesters of nature

■ In this cave painting in northern Africa, animal magic evokes help from the spirit world in ensuring the prosperity of the cattle herd. A similar ceremony is still performed by members of the Fulani tribes in the Sahel, on the southern fringe of the Sahara.

to active partners with it. These peoples of the **Neolithic era,** or New Stone Age (ca. 8000–6500 B.C.E.), organized sizable villages. Jericho, which had been settled before the agricultural revolution, grew into a fortified town complete with ditch, stone walls, and towers and sheltered perhaps 2,000 inhabitants. Çatal Hüyük in southern Turkey may have been even larger.

The really revolutionary aspect of agriculture was not simply that it ensured settled communities a food supply. The true innovation was that agriculture was portable. For the first time, rather than looking for a place that provided them with the necessities of life, humans could carry with them what they needed to make a site inhabitable. This portability also meant the rapid spread of agriculture throughout the region.

Religion.   Agricultural societies brought changes in the form and organization of formal religious cults. Elaborate sanctuary rooms decorated with frescoes, bulls' horns, and sculptures of heads of bulls and bears indicate that structured religious rites were important to the inhabitants of Çatal Hüyük. At Jericho, human skulls covered with clay, presumably in an attempt to make them look as they had in life, suggest that these early settlers practiced ancestor worship. In these larger communities the bonds of kinship that had united small hunter-gatherer bands were being supplemented by religious organization, which helped to control and regulate social behavior. The nature of this religion is a matter of speculation. Images of a female deity, interpreted as a guardian of animals, suggest the religious importance of women and fertility.

Around 1500 B.C.E., a new theme was depicted on the cliff walls at Tassili-n-Ajjer: men herding horses and driving horse-drawn chariots. These drawings indicate that the use of horses and chariots, which had developed over 1,500 years before in Mesopotamia, had now reached the people of North Africa. Chariots symbolized a new, dynamic, and expansive phase in Western culture. Constructed of wood and bronze and used for transport and especially for aggressive warfare, they are symbolic of the culture of early river civilizations, the first civilizations in western Eurasia.

MESOPOTAMIA: BETWEEN THE TWO RIVERS

Need drove the inhabitants of Mesopotamia—a name that means "between the rivers"—to create a civilization; nature itself offered little for human comfort or prosperity. The upland regions of the north receive most of the rainfall, but the soil is thin and poor. In the south the soil is fertile, but rainfall is almost nonexistent. There the twin rivers provide life-giving water but also bring destructive floods that usually arrive at harvest time. Therefore, agriculture is impossible without irrigation. But irrigation systems, if not properly maintained, deposit harsh alkaline chemicals on the soil, gradually reducing its fertility. In addition, Mesopotamia's only natural resource is clay. It has no metals, no workable stone, no valuable minerals of use to ancient people. These

very obstacles pressed the people to cooperative, innovative, and organized measures for survival. Survival in the region required planning and the mobilization of labor, which was possible only through centralization.

Until around 3500 B.C.E., the inhabitants of the lower Tigris and Euphrates lived in scattered villages and small towns. Then the population of the region, which was known as Sumer, began to increase rapidly. Small settlements became increasingly common; then towns such as Eridu and Uruk in what is now Iraq began to grow rapidly. These towns developed in part because of the need to concentrate and organize population in order to carry on the extensive irrigation systems necessary to support Mesopotamian agriculture. These towns soon spread their control out to the surrounding cultivated areas, incorporating the smaller towns and villages of the region. They also fortified themselves against the hostile intentions of their neighbors.

Nomadic peoples inhabited the arid steppes of Mesopotamia, constantly trading with and occasionally threatening settled villages and towns. Their menace was as ever-present in Near Eastern history as drought and flood. But nomads were a minor threat compared with the dangers posed by settled neighbors. As population growth increased pressure on the region's food supply, cities supplemented their resources by raiding their more prosperous neighbors. Victims sought protection within the ramparts of the settlements that had grown up around religious centers. As a result, the populations of the towns rose along with their towering temples, largely at the expense of the countryside. Between about 3500 and 3000 B.C.E., the population of Uruk quadrupled, from 10,000 to 40,000. Other Mesopotamian cities, notably Umma, Eridu, Lagash, and Ur, developed along the same general lines as they concentrated water supplies within their districts with artificial canals and dikes. At the same time, the number of smaller towns and villages in the vicinity decreased rapidly. The city had become the dominant force in the organization of economy and society, and the growth of the Sumerian cities established a precedent that would continue throughout history.

The Ramparts of Uruk

Cities did more than simply concentrate population. Within the walls of the city, men and women developed new technologies and new social and political structures. They created cultural traditions such as writing and literature. The pride of the first city dwellers is captured in a passage from the *Epic of Gilgamesh,* the earliest known great heroic poem, which was composed sometime before 2000 B.C.E. In the poem, the hero Gilgamesh boasts of the mighty walls he had built to encircle his city, Uruk:

> Go up and walk on the ramparts of Uruk
> Inspect the base terrace, examine the brickwork:
> Is not its brickwork of burnt brick?
> Did not the Seven Sages lay its foundations?

MAP DISCOVERY

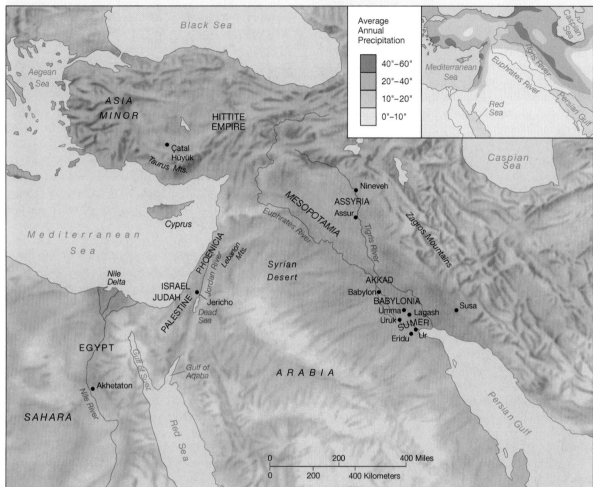

The Ancient World

Notice the locations of the earliest civilizations. What geographical similarities can you see between the Nile Valley and the valleys of the Tigris and Euphrates rivers that might have encouraged the appearance of complex civilizations? How dependent on rainfall were the agricultures that supported these civilizations? What problems do river valleys pose to settlement that civilization might solve?

Gilgamesh was justifiably proud of his city. In his day (ca. 2700 B.C.E.) these walls were marvels of military engineering; even now their ruins remain a tribute to his age. Archaeologists have uncovered the remains of the ramparts of Uruk, which stretched over five miles and were protected by some 900 semicircular towers. These massive protective walls enclosed about two square miles of houses, palaces, workshops, and temples. Uruk may with reason be called the first true city in the history of Western civilization.

Urban Life.   Within Uruk's walls the peculiar circumstances of urban life changed the traditional social structure of

Mesopotamia. In Neolithic times, social and economic differences within society had been minimal. Urban immigration increased the power, wealth, and status of two groups. In the first group were the religious authorities who were responsible for the temples. The second consisted of the emerging military and administrative elites, such as Gilgamesh, who were responsible for the construction and protection of the cities. These two groups probably encouraged much of the migration to the cities.

Whether they lived inside the city or on the farmland it controlled, Mesopotamians formed a highly stratified society that shared unequally in the benefits of civilization. Slaves, who did most of the unskilled labor within the city, were the primary victims of civilization. Most were prisoners of war, but some were people forced by debt to sell themselves or their children. Most of the remaining rural people were peasants who were little more than slaves. Better off were soldiers, merchants, and workers and artisans who served the temple or palace. At the next level were landowning free persons. Above all of these were the priests responsible for temple services and the rulers. Rulers included the *ensi,* or city ruler, and the *lugal,* or king, the earthly representative of the gods. Kings were powerful and feared.

Women's Status.

Urban life also redefined the role and status of women, who in the Neolithic period had enjoyed roughly the same roles and status as men. In cities, women tended to exercise private authority over children and servants within the household, while men controlled the household and dealt in the wider world. This change in roles resulted in part from the economic basis of the first civilization. Southern Mesopotamia has no sources of metal or stone. To acquire these precious commodities, trade networks were extended into Syria, the Arabian Peninsula, and even India. The primary commodities that Mesopotamians produced for trade were textiles, and these were produced largely by women captured in wars with neighboring city-states. Some historians suggest that the disproportionate numbers of low-status women in Mesopotamian cities affected the status of women in general. Although women could own property and even appear as heads of households, by roughly 1500 B.C.E. the pattern of patriarchal households predominated. Throughout Western history, while individual women might at times exercise great power, they did so largely in the private sphere.

Tools: Technology and Writing

Changes in society brought changes in technology. The need to feed, clothe, protect, and govern growing urban populations led to major technological and conceptual discoveries. Canals and systems of dikes partially harnessed water supplies. Farmers began to work their fields with improved plows and to haul their produce to town, first on sleds and ultimately on carts. These land-transport devices, along with sailing ships, made it possible not only to produce greater agricultural surplus but also to move this surplus to distant markets. Artisans used a refined potter's wheel to produce ceramic vessels of great beauty. Government officials and private individuals began to use cylinder seals, small stone cylinders engraved with a pattern, to mark ownership. Metalworkers fashioned gold and silver into valuable items of adornment and prestige. They also began to cast bronze, an alloy of copper and tin, which came into use for tools and weapons about 3000 B.C.E.

Pictograms.

Perhaps the greatest invention of early cities was writing. As early as 7000 B.C.E., small clay or stone tokens with distinctive shapes or markings were being used to keep track of animals, goods, and fruits in inventories and bartering. By 3500 B.C.E., government and temple administrators were using simplified drawings—today termed **pictograms**— that were derived from these tokens to assist them in keeping records of their transactions. Scribes used sharp reeds to impress the pictograms on clay tablets. Thousands of these tablets have survived in the ruins of Mesopotamian cities.

Cuneiform.

The first tablets were written in Sumerian, a language related to no other known tongue. Each pictogram represented a single sound, which corresponded to a single object or idea. In time, these pictograms developed into a true system of writing called **cuneiform** (from the Latin *cuneus,* "wedge") after the wedge shape of the characters. Finally, scribes took a radical step. Rather than simply using pictograms to indicate single objects, they began to use cuneiform characters to represent concepts. For example, the pictogram for "foot" could also mean "to stand." Ultimately, pictograms came to represent sounds divorced from any particular meaning.

The implications of the development of cuneiform writing were revolutionary. Since symbols were liberated from meaning, they could be used to record any language. Over the next thousand years, scribes used these same symbols to write not only in Sumerian but also in the other languages of Mesopotamia, such as Akkadian, Babylonian, and Persian. Writing soon allowed those who had mastered it to achieve greater centralization and control of government, to communicate over enormous distances, to preserve and transmit information, and to express religious and cultural beliefs. Writing reinforced memory, consolidating and expanding the achievements of the first civilization and transmitting them to the future. Writing was power, and for much of subsequent history a small minority of merchants and elites and the scribes in their employ wielded this power. In Mesopotamia, this power served to increase the strength of the king, the servant of the gods.

Gods and Mortals in Mesopotamia

Uruk had begun as a village like any other. Its rise to importance resulted from its significance as a religious site. A world of many cities, Mesopotamia was also a world of many gods, and Mesopotamian cities bore the imprint of the cult of their gods.

Mesopotamian Divinities.

The gods were like the people who worshipped them. They lived in a replica of human society, and each god had a particular responsibility. Every object and element from the sky to the brick or the plow had its own active god. The gods had the physical appearance and personalities of humans as well as human virtues and vices. Greater gods such as Nanna and Ufu were the protectors of Ur and Sippar. Others, such as Inanna, or Ishtar, the goddess of love, fertility, and wars, and her husband Dumuzi, were worshiped throughout Mesopotamia. Finally, at the top of the pantheon were the gods of the sky, the air, and the rivers.

■ The Standard of Ur, made of shells, lapis lazuli, and limestone, was found at Ur. In the top panel, known as *War*, soldiers and horse-drawn chariots return victorious from battle. In the lower panel *Peace*, the king celebrates the victory, captives are paraded before him, and the conquered people bring him tribute.

Temples and Rituals. Mesopotamians believed that the role of mortals was to serve the gods and to feed them through sacrifice. By around 2500 B.C.E., although military lords and kings had gained political power, the temples still controlled a major portion of economic resources. They owned vast estates where peasants cultivated crops and tended flocks to support the priests, scribes, artisans, laborers, farmers, teamsters, smiths, and weavers who operated these complex religious centers. A **ziggurat**, or tiered tower, dedicated to the god stood near many temples.

Although Mesopotamians looked to hundreds of personal divinities for assistance, they did not attempt to establish personal relationships with their great gods. However, since they assumed that the gods lived in a structured world that operated rationally, they believed that mortals could deal with the gods and enlist their aid by following the right rituals. Rites centered on the worship of idols. The most important care was feeding. At the temple of Uruk the gods were offered two meals a day, each consisting of two courses served in regal quantity and style.

Through the proper rituals a person could buy the god's protection and favor. Still, mortal life was harsh, and the gods offered little solace in coping with the great issues of human existence. This attitude is powerfully presented in the *Epic of Gilgamesh*, which, while not an accurate picture of Mesopotamian religion, does convey much of the values of this civilization. In this popular legend, Gilgamesh, king of Uruk, civilizes the wild man Enkidu, who was sent by the gods to temper the king's harshness. Gilgamesh and Enkidu become friends and undertake a series of adventures. However, even their great feats cannot overcome death. Enkidu displeases the gods and dies. Gilgamesh then sets out to find the magic plant of eternal life with which to return his friend from the somber underworld. On his journey he meets Ut-napishtim, the Mesopotamian Noah, who recounts the story of the Great Flood and tells Gilgamesh where to find the plant. Gilgamesh follows Ut-napishtim's advice and is successful but loses the plant on his journey home. The message is that only the gods are immortal, and the human afterlife is at best a shadowy and mournful existence.

Sargon and Mesopotamian Expansion

The temple was one center of the city; the palace was the other. As representative of the city's god, the king was the ruler and highest judge. He was responsible for the construction and maintenance of religious buildings and the complex system of canals that maintained the precarious balance between swamp and arid steppe. Finally, he commanded the army, defending his community against its neighbors and leading his forces against rival cities.

Competition and War.   The cultural and economic developments of early Mesopotamia occurred within the context of almost constant warfare. From around 3000 B.C.E. until 2300 B.C.E. the rulers of Ur, Lagash, Uruk, and Umma fought among themselves for control of Sumer, their name for the southern region of Mesopotamia. The population was a mixture of Sumerians and Semites, peoples who spoke Semitic languages related to modern Arabic or Hebrew, all jealously protective of their cities and gods and eager to extend their domination over their weaker neighbors.

The Akkadian Empire.   The extraordinary developments in this small corner of the Middle East might have remained isolated phenomena were it not for Sargon (ca. 2334–2279 B.C.E.), king of Akkad and the most important figure in Mesopotamian history. During his long reign of 55 years, Sargon built on the conquests and confederacies of the past to unite, transform, and expand Mesopotamian civilization. Born in obscurity, he was worshipped as a god after his death. In his youth he was the cupbearer to the king of Kish, another Sumerian city. Later, Sargon overthrew his master and conquered Uruk, Ur, Lagash, and Umma. This made him lord of Sumer. Such glory had satisfied his predecessors, but not Sargon. Instead, he extended his military operations east across the Tigris, west along the Euphrates, and north into modern Syria, thus creating the first great multiethnic empire state in the West.

The Akkadian state—so named by contemporary historians for Sargon's capital at Akkad—consisted of a vast and heterogeneous collection of city-states and territories. Sargon attempted to rule it by transforming the traditions of royal government. Rather than eradicating the traditions of conquered cities, he allowed them to maintain their own institutions but replaced many of their autonomous ruling aristocracies with his own functionaries. At the same time, however, he tried to win the loyalty of the ancient cities of Sumer by naming his daughter high priestess of the moon-god Nanna at Ur. He was thus the first in a long tradition of Near Eastern rulers who sought to unite his disparate conquests into a true state.

Sargon did more than just conquer cities. Although a Semite, he spread the achievements of Sumerian civilization throughout his vast state. Akkadian scribes used cuneiform to write the Semitic Akkadian language. So important did Sargon's successors deem his accomplishments that they ordered him to be worshiped as a god.

The Akkadian state proved as ephemeral as Sargon's accomplishments were lasting. All Mesopotamian states tended to undergo a cycle of rising rapidly under a gifted military commander and then beginning to crumble under the internal stresses of dynastic disputes and regional assertions of

autonomy. Thus weakened, they could then be conquered by other expanding states. First Ur, under its Sumerian king and first law codifier, Shulgi (2094–2047 B.C.E.), and then Amoritic Babylonia, under its great ruler, Hammurabi (1792–1750 B.C.E.), assumed dominance in the land between the rivers. From about 2000 B.C.E. on, the political and economic centers of Mesopotamia were in Babylonia and in Assyria, the region to the north at the foot of the Zagros Mountains.

Hammurabi and the Old Babylonian Empire

In the tradition of Sargon, Hammurabi expanded his state through arms and diplomacy. He expanded his power south as far as Uruk and north to Assyria. In the tradition of Shulgi, he promulgated an important body of law, known as the Code of Hammurabi. In the words of its prologue, this code sought:

> To cause justice to prevail in the country
> To destroy the wicked and the evil,
> That the strong may not oppress the weak.

Law and Society.   As the favored agent of the gods, the king had responsibility for regulating all aspects of Babylonian life, including dowries and contracts, agricultural prices and wages, and commerce and money lending. Hammurabi's code addresses professional behavior of physicians, veterinarians, architects, and boat builders. It offers a view of many aspects of Babylonian life, though always from the perspective of the royal law. The code lists offenses and prescribes penalties, which vary according to the social status of the victim and the perpetrator. Hammurabi's code thus creates a picture of a prosperous society composed of three legally defined social strata: a well-to-do elite, the mass of the population, and slaves. Each group had its own rights and obligations in proportion to its status. Even slaves enjoyed some legal rights and protection, could marry free persons, and might eventually obtain freedom.

Much of the code sought to protect women and children from arbitrary and unfair treatment. Husbands ruled their households but did not have unlimited authority over their wives. Women could initiate their own court cases, practice various trades, and even hold public positions. Upon marriage, husbands gave their fathers-in-law a payment in silver or in furnishings. The wife's father gave her a dowry over which she had full control. Some elite women personally controlled great wealth.

The Code of Hammurabi was less a royal attempt to restructure Babylonian society than an effort to reorganize, consolidate, and preserve previous laws in order to maintain the established social and economic order. What innovation it did show was in the extent of such punitive measures as death or mutilation. Penalties in earlier codes had been primarily compensation in silver or valuables.

Mathematics.   Law was not the only area in which the Old Babylonian kingdom began an important tradition. To handle the economics of business and government administration, Babylonians developed the most sophisticated mathematical

THE CODE OF HAMMURABI

The society revealed in the Code of Hammurabi was a complex world of landed aristocrats, merchants, and simple workers and shopkeepers. Its economy functioned on a complex system of credit relationships binding the various members of the society together, as seen in the following selections.

Focus Questions

What occupations were pursued in the Old Babylonian Empire? How did gender and social status affect legal penalties?

If a merchant lent grain at interest, he shall receive sixty *qu* of grain per *jur* as interest [equal 20 percent rate of interest]. If he lent money at interest, he shall receive one-sixth shekel six *se* (i.e., one-fifth shekel) per shekel of silver as interest.

If a seignior who incurred a debt does not have the money to pay it back, but has the grain, the merchant shall take grain for his money with its interest in accordance with the ratio fixed by the king.

If a seignior gave money to another seignior for a partnership, they shall divide equally in the presence of god the profit or loss which was incurred.

If a woman wine seller, instead of receiving grain for the price of a drink, has received money by the large weight and so has made the value of the drink less than the value of the grain, they shall prove it against that wine seller and throw her into the water.

If an obligation came due against a seignior and he sold the services of his wife, his son, or his daughter, or he has been bound over to service, they shall work in the house of their purchaser or obligee for three years, with their freedom reestablished in the fourth year.

If an obligation came due against a seignior and he has accordingly sold [the services of] his female slave who bore him children, the owner of the female slave may repay the money which the merchant paid out and thus redeem his female slave.

---

system known before the fifteenth century C.E. Babylonian mathematics was based on a numerical system from 1 to 60. (Today we still divide hours and minutes into 60 units.) Babylonian mathematicians devised multiplication tables and tables of reciprocals. They also devised tables of squares and square roots, cubes and cube roots, and other calculations needed for computing such important figures as compound interest. Although Babylonian mathematicians were not interested primarily in theoretical problems and were seldom given to abstraction, their technical proficiency indicates the advanced level of sophistication with which Hammurabi's contemporaries could tackle the problems of living in a complex society.

For all its achievements, Hammurabi's state was no more successful than those of his predecessors at defending itself against internal conflicts or external enemies. Despite his efforts, the traditional organization that he inherited from his Sumerian and Akkadian predecessors could not ensure orderly administration of a far-flung collection of cities. Hammurabi's son lost over half of his father's kingdom to internal revolts. Weakened by internal dissension, the kingdom fell to a new and potent force in Western history: the Hittites.

The Hittite Empire.   The Hittite state emerged in Anatolia in the shadow of Mesopotamian civilization. The Hittite court reflected Mesopotamian influence in its art and religion and in its adaptation and use of cuneiform script. Unlike the Sumerians, the Semitic nomads, the Akkadians, and the Babylonians, the Hittites were an Indo-European people. Their language was part of the linguistic family that includes most modern European languages as well as Persian, Greek, Latin, and Sanskrit. From their capital of Hattushash (modern Bogazköy in Turkey), they established a centralized state based on agriculture and trade in the metals mined from the ore-rich mountains of Anatolia and exported to Mesopotamia.

CHRONOLOGY
BETWEEN THE TWO RIVERS

ca. 3500 B.C.E.	Pictograms appear
ca. 3000–2316 B.C.E.	War for control of Sumer
ca. 2700 B.C.E.	Gilgamesh
ca. 2334–2279 B.C.E.	Sargon
1792–1750 B.C.E.	Hammurabi
ca. 1600 B.C.E.	Hittites destroy Old Babylonian state
ca. 1286 B.C.E.	Battle of Kadesh

The Hittites were among the earliest people to succeed in smelting iron.

Perfecting the light horse-drawn war chariot, the Hittites expanded into northern Mesopotamia and along the Syrian coast. They were able to destroy the Babylonian state around 1600 B.C.E. The Hittite Empire was the chief political and cultural force in western Asia from about 1400 to 1200 B.C.E. Its gradual expansion south along the coast was checked at the battle of Kadesh about 1286 B.C.E., when Hittite forces encountered the army of an even greater and more ancient power: the Egypt of Ramses II.

THE GIFT OF THE NILE

Like that of the Tigris and Euphrates valleys, the rich soil of the Nile Valley can support a dense population. There, however, the similarities end. Unlike the Mesopotamian floodplain, the Nile floodplain required little effort to make the land productive. Each year, the river flooded at exactly the right time to irrigate crops and to deposit a layer of rich, fertile silt. The Nile flows from south to north, emptying into the Mediterranean Sea. South of the last cataracts (rapids or falls), the fertile upriver region called Upper Egypt is about eight miles wide and is flanked by high desert plateaus. Downriver, in Lower Egypt near the Mediterranean, the Nile spreads across a lush marshy delta more than one hundred miles wide. Egypt knew only two environments: the fertile Nile Valley and the vast wastes of the Sahara Desert surrounding it. This inhospitable and largely uninhabitable region limited Egypt's contact with outside influences. Thus while trade, communication, and violent conquest characterized Mesopotamian civilization, Egypt knew self-sufficiency, an inward focus in culture and society, and stability. In its art, political structure, society, and religion, the Egyptian universe was static. Nothing was ever expected to change.

The earliest sedentary communities in the Nile Valley appeared on the western margin of the Nile Delta around 4000 B.C.E. In villages such as Merimda, which had a population of over 10,000, huts constructed of poles and adobe bricks huddled together near *wadis*, fertile riverbeds that were dry except during the rainy season. Farther south, in Upper Egypt, similar communities developed somewhat later but achieved an earlier political unity and a higher level of culture. By around 3200 B.C.E., Upper Egypt was in contact with Mesopotamia and had apparently borrowed something of that region's artistic and architectural traditions. During the same period, Upper Egypt developed a pictographic script.

These cultural achievements coincided with the political centralization of Upper Egypt under a series of kings. Probably around 3150 B.C.E., King Narmer or one of his predecessors in Upper Egypt expanded control over the fragmented south, uniting Upper and Lower Egypt and

establishing a capital at Memphis on the border between these two regions. For over 2,500 years, the Nile Valley, from the first cataract to the Mediterranean, enjoyed the most stable civilization the Western world has ever known.

■ Ancient Egypt. The thin strip of rich land bordering the Nile saw the development of an extraordinary civilization that endured for more than 2,000 years.

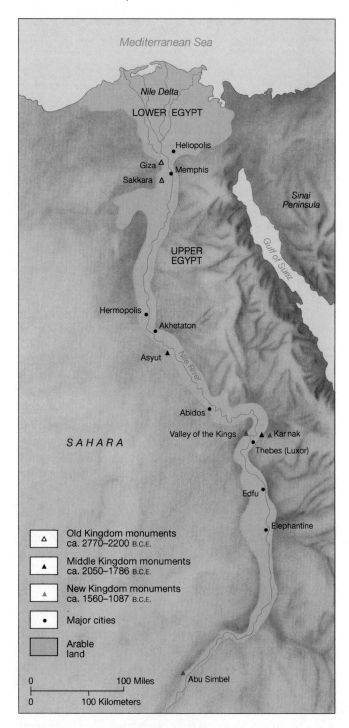

Tending the Cattle of God

Historians divide the vast sweep of Egyptian history into 31 dynasties, regrouped in turn into four periods of political centralization: pre- and early dynastic Egypt (ca. 3150–2770 B.C.E.), the Old Kingdom (ca. 2770–2200 B.C.E.), the Middle Kingdom (ca. 2050–1786 B.C.E.), and the New Kingdom (ca. 1560–1087 B.C.E.). The time gaps between kingdoms were periods of disruption and political confusion termed intermediate periods. While minor changes in social, political, and cultural life certainly occurred during these centuries, the changes were less significant than the astonishing stability and continuity of the civilization that developed along the banks of the Nile.

God Kings. Divine kingship was the cornerstone of Egyptian life. Initially, the king was the incarnation of Horus, a sky and falcon god. Later, the king was identified with the sun-god Ra (subsequently known as Amen-Re, the great god), as well as with Osiris, the god of the dead. As divine incarnation, the king was obliged above all to care for his people. It was he who ensured the annual flooding of the Nile, which brought water to the parched land. His commands preserved **maat,** the ideal state of the universe and society, a condition of harmony and justice. In the poetry of the Old Kingdom, the king was the divine herdsman; the people were the cattle of god:

Well tended are men, the cattle of god.
He made heaven and earth according to their desire
and repelled the demon of the waters . . .
He made for them rulers (even) in the egg,
a supporter to support the back of the disabled.

Unlike the rulers in Mesopotamia, the kings of the Old Kingdom were not warriors but divine administrators. Protected by the Sahara, Egypt had few external enemies and no standing army. A vast bureaucracy of literate court officials and provincial administrators assisted the god-king. They wielded wide authority as religious leaders, judicial officers, and, when necessary, military leaders. A host of subordinate overseers, scribes, metalworkers, stonemasons, artisans, and tax collectors rounded out the royal administration. At the local level, governors administered provinces called *nomes,* the basic units of Egyptian local government.

Gender and Bureaucracy. Women of ancient Egypt were more independent and involved in public life than those of Mesopotamia. Egyptian women owned property, conducted their own business, entered legal contracts, and brought lawsuits. They shared in the economic and professional life of the country at every level except one: women were apparently excluded from formal education. The professional bureaucracy was open only to those who could read and write. As a result, the primary route to public power was closed to women, and the bureaucratic machinery remained firmly in the hands of men.

The role of this bureaucracy was to administer estates, collect taxes, and channel revenues and labor toward vast public works projects, which focused on the king. The king lived in the royal city of Memphis in the splendor of a *Per-ao,* or "Great House," from which comes the word *pharaoh,* the Hebrew term for the Egyptian king.

The Pyramids. During the Old and Middle Kingdoms, great pyramid temple-tomb complexes more imposing than the Great House were built for the kings. Within the temples, priests and servants performed rituals to serve the dead kings just as they had served the kings when they were alive. Even death did not disrupt the continuity that was so vital to Egyptian civilization. The cults of dead kings reinforced the monarchy, since veneration of past rulers meant veneration of the reigning king's ancestors.

Building and equipping the pyramids focused and transformed Egypt's material and human resources. Artisans had to be trained, engineering and transportation problems had to be solved, quarrying and stoneworking techniques had to be perfected, and laborers had to be recruited. In the Old Kingdom, whose population has been estimated at perhaps 1.5 million, more than 70,000 workers at a time were employed in building these great temple-tombs. No smaller work force could have built such a massive structure as the Great Pyramid of Khufu (ca. 2600 B.C.E.), which stood 481 feet high and contained almost 6 million tons of stone. In comparison, the great Ziggurat of Ur, built around 2000 B.C.E., rose only some 120 feet above the Mesopotamian plain. The pyramids were constructed by peasants working when the Nile was in flood and they could not till the soil. Although actual construction was seasonal, the work was unending. No sooner was one complex completed than the next was begun.

Feeding the masses of laborers absorbed most of the country's agricultural surplus. Equipping the temples and pyramids provided a constant demand for the highest-quality luxury goods, since royal tombs and temples were furnished as luxuriously as palaces. Thus the construction and maintenance of these vast complexes focused the organization and production of Egypt's economy and government.

Democratization of the Afterlife

In the Old Kingdom, future life was available through the king. The graves of thousands of his attendants and servants surrounded his temple. All the wealth, labor, and expertise of the kingdom thus flowed into these temples, reinforcing the position of the king. Like the tip of a pyramid, the king was the summit, supported by all of society.

Decline of Royal Power. Gradually, however, the absolute power of the king declined. The increasing demands for consumption by the court and the cults forced agricultural expansion into areas where returns were poor, thus decreasing the flow of wealth. As bureaucrats increased their efforts to supply the voracious needs of living and dead kings and their attendants, they neglected the maintenance of the economic system that supplied these needs. The royal government was not protecting society; the "cattle of god" were not being well tended. Finally, tax-exempt religious foundations, established to ensure the perpetual cult of the dead, received donations of vast amounts of property, and their power came to rival the king's. This removed an ever greater amount of the country's wealth from the control of the king and his agents. Thus the wealth and power of the Egyptian kings declined at roughly the time that Sargon was expanding his Akkadian state in Mesopotamia. By around 2200 B.C.E., Egyptian royal authority collapsed entirely, leaving political and religious power in the hands of provincial governors.

The Middle Kingdom.   After almost 200 years of fragmentation, the governors of Thebes in Upper Egypt reestablished centralized royal traditions, but with a difference. Kings continued to build vast temples, but they did not resume the tremendous investments in pyramid complexes on the scale of the Old Kingdom. The bureaucracy was opened to all men, even sons of peasants, who could master the complex pictographic writing. Private temple-tombs proliferated and with them new pious foundations. These promised eternal care by which anyone with sufficient wealth could enjoy a comfortable afterlife.

The memory of the Old Kingdom's shortcomings introduced a new ethical perspective that was expressed in the literature written by the elite. For the first time, the elite voiced the concern that justice might not always be served and that the innocent might suffer at the hands of royal agents. In a popular tale from around 1900 B.C.E., Sinuhe, an official of Amenemhet I (d. 1962 B.C.E.), flees Egypt after the death of his king. He fears that through false reports of his actions he will incur the wrath of Amenemhet's son. Though he returns in his old age and is received honorably, the moral is clear: The state system at times failed in its responsibility to safeguard *maat*.

The Hyksos.   The greater access to power and privilege in the Middle Kingdom benefited foreigners as well as Egyptians. Assimilated Semites rose to important administrative positions. By around 1600 B.C.E., when the Hittite armies were destroying the state of Hammurabi's successors, large bands of Semites had settled in the eastern Delta, setting the stage for the first foreign conquest of Egypt. A series of kings referred to by Egyptian sources as "rulers of foreign lands," or Hyksos, overran the country and ruled the Nile Valley as far south as Memphis. These foreigners adopted the traditions of Egyptian kingship and continued the tradition of divine rule.

The Hyksos kings introduced their military technology and organization into Egypt. In particular, they brought with them the light horse-drawn war chariot. This mobile fighting platform—manned by warriors armed with bows, bronze swords of a type previously unknown in Egypt, and lances—transformed Egyptian military tactics. These innovations

remained even after the Hyksos were expelled by Ahmose I (1552–1527 B.C.E.), the Theban founder of the Eighteenth Dynasty, with whose reign the New Kingdom began.

The Egyptian Empire

Ahmose did not stop with the liberation of Egypt. He forged an empire. He and his successors used their newfound military might to extend the frontiers of Egypt south up the Nile beyond the fourth cataract and well into Nubia. To the east

■ This painted limestone head of Hatshepsut was originally from a statue. She is shown wearing the crown of Egypt and the stylized beard that symbolized royalty and was often seen on the statues and death masks of pharaohs.

they absorbed the caravan routes to the Red Sea, from which they were able to send ships to Punt (probably modern Somalia), the source of the myrrh and frankincense that were needed for funeral and religious rituals. Most important was the Egyptian expansion into Canaan. Here Egyptian chariots crushed their foes as kings pressed on as far as the Euphrates. Thutmose I (1506–1494 B.C.E.) proclaimed, "I have made the boundaries of Egypt as far as that which the sun encircles."

Thutmose's immediate successors were his children, Thutmose II (1494–1490 B.C.E.) and Hatshepsut (1490–1468 B.C.E.), who married her brother. After the death of Thutmose II, Hatshepsut ruled both as regent for her stepson Thutmose III (1490–1436 B.C.E.) and as co-ruler. She was by all accounts a capable ruler, preserving stability and even personally leading the army on several occasions to protect the empire.

In spite of the efforts of Hatshepsut and her successors, the Egyptian Empire was never as grand as its kings proclaimed. Many of the northern expeditions were raids rather than conquests. Still, the expanded political frontiers meant increased trade and unprecedented interaction with the rest of the ancient world. The cargo excavated from the wreck of a ship that sank off the coast of what is now Turkey around 1350 B.C.E. vividly portrays the breadth of international exchange in the New Kingdom. The lost ship carried a cargo of exotic merchandise from around the Mediterranean world. As private merchants were virtually unknown in the Egyptian empire, the voyage was likely a royal venture or perhaps carried gifts and tributes to the god-king.

Religious and Royal Consolidation Under Akhenaten

Religion was both the heart of royal power and its only limiting force. Although the king was the embodiment of the religious tradition he was also bound by that tradition as it was interpreted by an ancient and powerful system of priesthoods, pious foundations, and cults. The intimate relationship between royal absolutism and religious cult culminated in the reign of Amenhotep IV (1364–1347 B.C.E.), the most controversial and enigmatic ruler of the New Kingdom, who challenged the very basis of royal religious control. In a calculated break with over a thousand years of Egyptian religious custom, Amenhotep attempted to abolish the cult of Amen-Re along with all of the other traditional gods, their priesthoods, and their festivals. In their place he promoted a new divinity, the sun-disk god Aten. Amenhotep moved his capital from Thebes to a new temple city, Akhetaton, near modern Tel al-'Amarna, and changed his own name to Akhenaten ("It pleases Aten").

Akhenaten has been called the first monotheist, a reformer who sought to revitalize a religion that had decayed into superstition and magic. Yet his monotheism was not complete. The god Aten shared divine status with Akhenaten himself. Akhenaten attacked other cults, especially that of Amen-Re, to consolidate royal power and to replace the old priesthoods with his own family members and supporters.

A New Aesthetic.   In attempting to reestablish royal divinity, Akhenaten temporarily transformed the aesthetics of Egyptian court life. Traditional archaic language gave way to the everyday speech of the fourteenth century B.C.E. Wall paintings and statues showed people in the clothing that they actually wore rather than in stylized parade dress. This new naturalism rendered the king at once more human and more divine. It differentiated him from the long line of preceding kings, emphasizing his uniqueness and his royal power.

The strength of royal power was so great that during his reign, Akhenaten could command acceptance of his radical break with Egyptian tradition. However, his ambitious plan did not long survive his death. His innovations annoyed the Egyptian elite, while his abolition of established festivals alienated the masses. His son-in-law, Tutankhamen (1347–1337 B.C.E.), the son of Akhenaten's predecessor, was a child when he became king upon Akhenaten's death. Under the influence of his court advisers, probably inherited from his father's reign, he restored the ancient religious traditions and abandoned the new capital of Akhetaton for his father's palace at Thebes.

The Hittites.   Return to the old ways meant return to the old problems. Powerful pious foundations controlled fully 10 percent of the population. Dynastic continuity ended after Tutankhamen, and a new military dynasty seized the throne. These internal problems provided an opportunity for the growing Hittite state in Asia Minor to expand south at the expense of Egypt. Ramses II (1289–1224 B.C.E.) checked the Hittite expansion at the battle of Kadesh, but the battle was actually a draw. Eventually, Ramses and the Hittite king Hattusilis III signed a peace treaty whose terms included nonaggression and mutual defense. The agreement marked the failure of both states to unify the Fertile Crescent, the region stretching from the Persian Gulf northwest through Mesopotamia and down the Mediterranean coast to Egypt.

The mutual standoff at Kadesh did not long precede the disintegration of both Egypt and the Hittite state. Within a century, states large and small along the Mediterranean coast from Anatolia to the delta and from the Aegean Sea in the west to the Zagros Mountains in the east collapsed or were destroyed in what seems to have been a general crisis of the civilized world. The various raiders, sometimes erroneously called the "Sea Peoples," who struck Egypt, Syria, the Hittite state, and elsewhere, were not the primary cause of the crisis. It was rather internal political, economic, and social strains within both Egypt and the Hittite state that provided the opportunity for various groups—including Anatolians, Greeks, Israelites, and others—to raid the ancient centers of civilization. In the ensuing confusion, the small Semitic kingdoms of Syria and Canaan developed a precarious independence in the shadow of the great powers.

CHRONOLOGY
THE GIFT OF THE NILE

ca. 3150–2770 B.C.E.	Predynastic and early dynastic Egypt
ca. 2770–2200 B.C.E.	Old Kingdom
ca. 2600 B.C.E.	Pyramid of Khufu
ca. 2050–1786 B.C.E.	Middle Kingdom
ca. 1560–1087 B.C.E.	New Kingdom
1552–1527 B.C.E.	Ahmose I
1506–1494 B.C.E.	Thutmose I
1494–1490 B.C.E.	Thutmose II
1490–1468 B.C.E.	Hatshepsut
1364–1347 B.C.E.	Amenhotep IV (Akhenaten)
1347–1337 B.C.E.	Tutankhamen
1289–1224 B.C.E.	Ramses II

BETWEEN TWO WORLDS

City-based civilization was an endangered species throughout antiquity. Just beyond the well-tilled fields of Mesopotamia and the fertile delta of the Nile lay the world of the Semitic tribes of seminomadic shepherds and traders. Of course, not all Semites were nonurban. Many had formed part of the heterogeneous population of the Sumerian world. Sargon's Semitic Akkadians and Hammurabi's Amorites created great Mesopotamian nation-states, adopting the ancient Sumerian cultural traditions. Along the coast of Canaan, other Semitic groups established towns and joined in the trade between Egypt and the north. But the majority of Semitic peoples continued to live a life that was radically different from that of the people of the floodplain civilizations. From these, one small group, the Hebrews, emerged to establish a religious and cultural tradition that was unique in antiquity.

The Hebrew Alternative

Sometime after 2000 B.C.E., small Semitic bands under the leadership of patriarchal chieftains spread into what is today Syria, Lebanon, Israel, and Palestine. These bands crisscrossed the Fertile Crescent, searching for pasture for their flocks. Occasionally, they participated in the trade uniting Mesopotamia and the towns of the Mediterranean coast. For the most part, however, they pitched their tents on the outskirts of towns only briefly, moving on when their sheep and goats had exhausted the supply of pasturage. Semitic Aramaeans and Chaldeans brought with them not only their flocks and families, but Mesopotamian culture as well.

Mesopotamian Origins. Hebrew history records such Mesopotamian traditions as the story of the flood (Genesis 6–10), legal traditions strongly reminiscent of those of Hammurabi, and the worship of the gods on high places. Stories such as that of the Tower of Babel (Genesis 11) and the garden of Eden (Genesis 2–4) likewise have a Mesopotamian flavor, but with a difference. For these wandering shepherds, urban culture was a curse. In the Hebrew Bible (the Christian Old Testament) the first city was built by Cain, the first murderer. The Tower of Babel, probably a ziggurat, was a symbol not of human achievement but of human pride.

At least some of these wandering Aramaeans, among them the biblical patriarch Abraham, rejected the gods of Mesopotamia. Religion among these nomadic groups focused on the specific divinity of the clan. In the case of Abraham, this was the god El. Abraham and his successors were not monotheists. They did not deny the existence of other gods. They simply believed that they had a personal pact with their own god.

In its social organization and cultural traditions, Abraham's clan was no different from its neighbors. These independent clans were ruled by a senior male (hence the Greek term *patriarch*—"rule by the father"). Women, whether wives, concubines, or slaves, were treated as distinctly inferior, virtually as property.

Egypt and Exodus. Some of Abraham's descendants must have joined the steady migration from Canaan into Egypt that took place during the Middle Kingdom and the Hyksos period. Although they were initially well treated, after the expulsion of the Hyksos in the sixteenth century B.C.E., many of the Semitic settlers in Egypt were reduced to slavery. Around the thirteenth century B.C.E., a small band of Semitic slaves numbering fewer than 1,000 left Egypt for Sinai and Canaan under the leadership of Moses. The memory of this departure, known as the Exodus, became the formative experience of the descendants of those who had taken part and those who later joined them. Moses, a Semite who carried an Egyptian name and who, according to tradition, had been raised in the royal court, was the founder of the Israelite people.

During the years that they spent wandering in the desert and then slowly conquering Canaan, the Israelites forged a new identity and a new faith. From the Midianites of the Sinai Peninsula, they adopted the god Yahweh as their own. Although composed of various Semitic and even Egyptian groups, the Israelites adopted the oral traditions of the clan of Abraham and identified his god, El, with Yahweh. They interpreted their extraordinary escape from Egypt as evidence of a covenant with this god, a treaty similar to those concluded between the Hittite

■ A relief on a basalt obelisk (ca. 830 B.C.E.) depicts Jehu, a king of Israel, making obeisance to the Assyrian monarch Shalmaneser III. This is the oldest identified portrait of an Israelite.

kings and their dependents. Yahweh was to be the Israelites' exclusive god; they were to make no alliances with any others. They were to preserve peace among themselves, and they were obligated to serve Yahweh with arms. This covenant was embodied in the law of Moses, a series of terse absolute commands ("Thou shall not . . .") that were quite unlike the conditional laws of Hammurabi ("if . . . , then . . ."). Inspired by their new identity and their new religion, the Israelites swept into Canaan. Taking advantage of the vacuum of power left by the Hittite-Egyptian standoff following the battle of Kadesh, they destroyed or captured the cities of the region. In some cases, the local population welcomed the Israelites and their religion. In other places, the indigenous people were slaughtered down to the last man, woman, and child.

A King Like All the Nations

During its first centuries, Israel was a loosely organized confederation of tribes whose only focal point was the religious shrine at Shiloh. This shrine, in contrast with the temples of other ancient peoples, housed no idols, only a chest, known as the Ark of the Covenant, which contained the law of Moses and mementos of the Exodus. In times of danger, temporary leaders would lead united tribal armies. The power of these leaders, who were called judges in the Hebrew Bible, rested solely on their personal leadership qualities. This charisma indicated that the spirit of Yahweh was with the leader. Yahweh alone was the ruler of the people.

By the eleventh century B.C.E., this disorganized political tradition placed the Israelites at a disadvantage in fighting their neighbors. The Philistines, who dominated the Canaanite seacoast and had expanded inland, posed the greatest threat. By 1050 B.C.E., the Philistines had defeated the Israelites, captured the Ark of the Covenant, and occupied most of their territory. Many Israelites clamored for "a king like all the nations" to lead

them to victory. To consolidate their forces, the Israelite religious leaders reluctantly established a kingdom. Its first king was Saul, and its second was David.

David (ca. 1000–962 B.C.E.) and his son and successor, Solomon (ca. 961–922 B.C.E.), brought the kingdom of Israel to its peak of power, prestige, and territorial expansion. David defeated and expelled the Philistines, subdued Israel's other enemies, and created a united state that included all of Canaan from the desert to the sea. He established Jerusalem as the political and religious capital. Solomon went still further, building a magnificent temple complex to house the Ark of the Covenant and to serve as Israel's national shrine. David and Solomon restructured Israel from a tribal to a monarchical so-

■ The Kingdoms of Israel and Judah. From its greatest extent under Solomon, the Kingdom of Israel split into rival northern and southern kingdoms and then progressively lost ground against Assyria and Babylon.

ciety. The old tribal structure remained only as a religious tradition. Solomon centralized land divisions, raised taxes, and increased military service to strengthen the monarchy.

The cost of this transformation was high. The kingdom under David and especially under Solomon grew more tyrannical as it grew more powerful. Solomon behaved like any other king of his time. He contracted marriage alliances with neighboring princes and allowed his wives to practice their own cults. He demanded extraordinary taxes and services from his people to pay for his lavish building projects. When he was unable to pay his Phoenician creditors for supplies and workers, he deported Israelites to work as slaves in Phoenician mines.

Exile

Not surprisingly, the united kingdom did not survive Solomon's death. The northern region broke off to become the Kingdom of Israel with its capital in Shechem. The south, the Kingdom of Judah, continued the tradition of David from his capital of Jerusalem. These small, weak kingdoms did not long maintain their independence. Beginning in the ninth century B.C.E., a new Mesopotamian power, the Assyrians, began a campaign of conquest and unprecedented brutality throughout the Near East. The Hebrew kingdoms were among their many victims. In 722 B.C.E., the Assyrians destroyed the Kingdom of Israel and deported thousands of its people to upper Mesopotamia. In 586 B.C.E., the Kingdom of Judah was conquered by Assyria's destroyers, the New Babylonian empire under King Nebuchadnezzar II (604–562 B.C.E.). The temple of Solomon was destroyed, Jerusalem was burned, and Judah's elite were deported to Babylon.

The Babylonian captivity ended some 50 years later when the Persians, who had conquered Babylonia, allowed the people of Judah to return to their homeland. Those who returned did so with a new understanding of themselves and their covenant with Yahweh, who was now seen as not just one god among many but as the one universal God. This new understanding was central to the development of Judaism.

The fundamental figures in this transformation were Ezra and Nehemiah (fifth and fourth centuries B.C.E.), who were particularly concerned with keeping Judaism uncontaminated by other religious and cultural influences. They condemned those who had remained in Judaea and who had intermarried with foreigners during the exile. Only the exiles who had remained faithful to Yahweh and who had avoided foreign marriages could be the true interpreters of the **Torah,** or law. This ideal of separatism and national purity came to characterize the Jewish religion in the post-exilic period.

Among its leaders were the Pharisees, a group of zealous adherents to the Torah, who produced a body of oral law termed the **Mishnah,** or second law, by which the law of Moses was to be interpreted and safeguarded. In subsequent centuries this oral law, along with its interpretation, developed into the Talmud, which did not assume its final form until almost a thousand years after the Babylonian exile. Pharisees believed in resurrection and in spirits such as angels

and devils. They also believed that a messiah, or savior, would arise as a new David to reestablish Israel's political independence. Among the priestly elite, the hope for a Davidic messiah was seen as more universal: a priestly messiah would arise and bring about the kingdom of glory. Some Jews actively sought political liberation from the Persians and their successors. Others were more intent on preserving ritual and social purity until the coming of the messiah. Still others, such as the Essenes, withdrew into isolated communities to await the fulfillment of the prophecies.

NINEVEH AND BABYLON

The Assyrian state that destroyed Israel accomplished what no other power had ever achieved. It tied together the floodplain civilizations of Mesopotamia and Egypt. But the Assyrian state was not just larger than the nation-states that had preceded it; it differed in nature as well as in size. The nation-states of Akkadia, Babylonia, the Hittites, and even the Egyptian empire were essentially diverse collections of city-states. Each preserved its own institutions and cultural traditions while diverting its economic resources to the capital. The Assyrian empire was an integrated state in which conquered regions were reorganized and remade along the model of the central government. By the middle of the seventh century B.C.E., the Assyrian empire stretched from the headwaters of the Tigris and Euphrates rivers to the Persian Gulf, along the coast from Syria to beyond the Nile Delta, and up the Nile to Thebes.

The Assyrian Empire

The Assyrian plain north of Babylonia had long been the site of a small Mesopotamian state threatened by seminomads and great powers such as the Babylonians and later the Hittites. Its early history was similar to that of so many earlier Mesopotamian empires. Early expansion soon gave rise to internal revolt and external threats. However, revolt paved the way for the ascension of Tiglath-pileser III (746–727 B.C.E.), the greatest empire builder of Mesopotamia since Sargon. Tiglath-pileser and his successors transformed the structure of the Assyrian state and expanded its empire. In the sense that the Assyrians not only conquered but created an administrative system by which to rule, theirs was the first true empire, and as such, it served as a model for Persia, Macedonia, and Rome.

From his palace at Nineveh, Tiglath-pileser combined all of the traditional elements of Mesopotamian statecraft with a new religious ideology and social system to create the framework for a lasting multiethnic imperial system. The heart of Tiglath-pileser's program was the most modern army the world had ever seen. In place of traditional armies of peasants and slaves supplied by great aristocrats, he raised professional armies from the conquered lands of the empire and placed them under the command of Assyrian generals. The Assyrian army was also the first to make massive use of iron weapons, which were superior to the bronze swords and shields of their enemies. Assyrian forces were well balanced, including not only infantry, cavalry, and chariots, but also engineering units for constructing the siege equipment that was needed to capture towns. Warfare had become a science.

In addition to the professional army, Tiglath-pileser created the most developed military-religious ideology of any ancient people. Kings had long been agents of the gods, but Ashur, the god of the Assyrians, had but one command: Enlarge the empire! Thus warfare was the mission and duty of all, a sacred command paralleled through the centuries in the cries of "God wills it" of the Christian crusaders and "God is great" of Muslims.

Tiglath-pileser restructured his empire, both at home in Assyria and abroad, so that revolts of the sort that had nearly destroyed it would be less likely. Within Assyria he increased the number of administrative districts, thus decreasing the strength of each, which reduced the likelihood of successful rebellions launched by dissatisfied governors. Outside Assyria proper, the king liquidated traditional leaders whenever possible and appointed Assyrian governors or at least assigned loyal overseers to protect his interests. To shatter regional identities, which could lead to separatist movements, Tiglath-pileser deported and resettled conquered peoples on a massive scale. He transported the Hebrews to Babylon, sent 30,000 Syrians to the Zagros Mountains, and moved 18,000 Aramaeans from the Tigris to Syria.

Finally, in the tradition of his Assyrian predecessors, Tiglath-pileser and his successors maintained control of conquered peoples through a policy of unprecedented cruelty and brutality. One ruler, for example, boasted of once having flayed an enemy's chiefs and used their skins to cover a great pillar that he erected at their city gate and on which he impaled his victims.

The New Babylonian Empire

Ironically, while the imperial military and administrative system created by the Assyrians became in time the blueprint for future empires, its very ferocity led to its downfall. The hatred inspired by such brutality led to the destruction of the Assyrian empire at the hands of a coalition of its subjects. In what is today Iran, Indo-European tribes coalesced around the Median dynasty. Egypt shook off its Assyrian lords under the leadership of the pharaoh Psamtik I (664–610 B.C.E.). In Babylon, which had always proven difficult for the Assyrians to control, a new Aramaean dynasty began to oppose Assyrian rule. In 612 B.C.E., the Medes and Babylonians joined forces to attack and destroy Nineveh. Once more, the pattern begun by Sargon, of imperial expansion, consolidation, decay, and destruction, was repeated.

However, the lessons that the Assyrians taught the world were not forgotten by the Babylonians, who modeled their imperial system on that of their predecessors. Administration of the New Babylonian empire, which extended roughly over the length of the Tigris and extended west into Syria and Canaan, owed much to Assyrian tradition. The Code of Hammurabi once more formed the fundamental basis for justice. Babylonian kings restored and enriched temples to the Babylonian gods, and temple lands, administered by priests appointed by the king, played an important role in Babylonian economy and culture. Babylonian priests, using the mathematical methods developed during the Old Kingdom, made important advances in mathematical astronomy.

Under King Nebuchadnezzar II, the city of Babylon reached its zenith, covering some 500 acres and containing a population of over 100,000, more than twice the population of Uruk at its height. The city walls, later counted among the seven wonders of the world by the Greeks, were so wide that two chariots could ride abreast on them. Yet this magnificent fortification was never tested. In 539 B.C.E., a Persian army under King Cyrus II (ca. 585–ca. 529 B.C.E.), who had ousted the Median dynasty in 550 B.C.E., slipped into the city through the Euphrates riverbed at low water and took the city by surprise.

CONCLUSION

The legacy of the first 3,000 years of civilization is more than a tradition of imperial conquest, exploitation, and cruelty. It goes beyond a mere catalog of discoveries, inventions, and achievements, impressive as they are. The legacy includes the basic structure of Western civilization. The floodplain civilizations and their neighbors provided the first solutions to problems of social and political organization and complex government. They built what we now recognize to have been the first cities, city-states, nation-states, and finally multinational empires. They attacked the problems of uneven distribution of natural resources through irrigation, long-distance trade, and communication. Their religious traditions, from polytheism to monotheism, provided patterns for subsequent Western religious traditions. Mesopotamian astronomy and mathematics and Egyptian engineering and building were fundamental for future civilizations. The immediate successors of these civilizations, however, would be to the west of the great river valleys, in the mountainous peninsulas and scattered islands of southern Europe.

CHRONOLOGY
BETWEEN TWO WORLDS

ca. 1050 B.C.E.	Philistines defeat the Israelites
ca. 1000–961 B.C.E.	David, king of Israel
ca. 961–922 B.C.E.	Solomon, king of Israel
722 B.C.E.	Assyrians destroy kingdom of Israel
604–562 B.C.E.	Nebuchadnezzar II
586 B.C.E.	Nebuchadnezzar II conquers kingdom of Judah

QUESTIONS FOR REVIEW

1. What cultural developments allowed people to secure food, organize society, and overcome hostile environments before the rise of the first cities?
2. How did urbanization, the invention of writing, and political centralization first develop in the resource-poor area between the Tigris and Euphrates rivers?
3. How did the differing geographic conditions of Mesopotamia and Egypt shape the development of civilization in each?
4. What was the Hebrew people's covenant with Yahweh, and how did this help make a society quite different from the societies around it?
5. What political, religious, and military innovations made the Assyrian Empire more vast and powerful than any previously seen?

KEY TERMS

culture, *p. 6*

cuneiform, *p. 10*

maat, *p. 15*

Mishnah, *p. 20*

Neolithic era, *p. 8*

Paleolithic era, *p. 6*

pictograms, *p. 10*

Torah, *p. 20*

ziggurat, *p. 11*

DISCOVERING WESTERN CIVILIZATION ONLINE

You can obtain more information about the first civilizations at the websites listed below. See also the Companion Website that accompanies this text, www.ablongman.com/kishlansky, which contains an online study guide and additional resources.

General Websites

NM's Creative Impulse: References—Western Civilization

history.evansville.net/referenc.html#West

This section of Nancy B. Mautz's Creative Impulse: The Artist's View of World History and Western Civilization Website provides a directory of Western Civilization websites and pages for further exploration

Before Civilization

Origins of Humankind

www.pbs.org/wgbh/evolution/humans/humankind/

Educational information on prehistory of humanity.

Rock Art Links—Petroglyphs and Pictographs

www.electronics-ee.com/Art/Art_History/Rock_Art.htm

Online database of links to prehistoric rock art throughout the world.

Çatal Hüyük

catal.arch.cam.ac.uk/catal/catal.html

A site devoted to Çatal Hüyük, one of the earliest settlements to have developed into a sedentary agricultural community.

Prehistoric Cultures

www.d.umn.edu/cla/faculty/troufs/anth1602/

A course website at the University of Minnesota Duluth that links to materials on prehistoric cultures around the world.

Mesopotamia

ABZU: Guide to Resources for the Study of the Ancient Near East Available on the Internet

www.etana.org/abzu/

A major site for all aspects of Ancient Mesopotamia and Egypt maintained by the Oriental Institute of The University of Chicago.

Mesopotamia (Ur)

www.taisei.co.jp/cg_e/ancient_world/ur/aur.html

The city of Ur reproduced with computer graphics.

Egypt

NM's Creative Impulse: Egypt

history.evansville.net/egypt.html

Award-winning site for Egyptian history.

Survey of Ancient Egypt

www.cofc.edu/~piccione/hist270/index.html

Excellent class web page on Ancient Egypt.

Egyptian Kings

touregypt.net/kings.htm

A site that provides information on all of the pharaohs.

Giza Plateau Computer Model

www.oi.uchicago.edu/OI/DEPT/COMP/GIZ/MODEL/Giza_Model.html

A site devoted to Giza with a computer model of its pyramids and other monuments.

Israel

The Hebrews: A Learning Module
www.wsu.edu/~dee/HEBREWS/HEBREWS.HTM
An excellent course site devoted entirely to the ancient Hebrews.

The Israel Museum, Jerusalem: Archaeology
www.imj.org.il/eng/archaeology/
Site on early Israel archaeology.

Nineveh and Babylon

The Palace of Ashurnasirpal II
ccat.sas.upenn.edu/arth/asrnsrpl.html
A three-dimensional animated fly-through of the Palace of Ashurnasirpal II.

Babylon
www.geocities.com/Area51/Cavern/5178/main.html
A tour of Babylon in the year 580 B.C.E.

SUGGESTIONS FOR FURTHER READING

General Reading

Cambridge Ancient History, vol. 1 (Cambridge: Cambridge University Press, 1990). Contains essays on every aspect of ancient civilizations.

Barbara S. Lesko, ed. *Women's Earliest Records from Ancient Egypt and Western Asia: Proceedings of the Conference on Women in the Ancient Near East* (Atlanta: Scholars Press, 1989). Important collection of essays on all aspects of women in ancient societies.

Donald B. Redford, *Egypt, Canaan and Israel in Ancient Times* (Princeton: Princeton University Press, 1992). A synthesis of the interrelations among three great Near Eastern civilizations.

Before Civilization

Lewis R. Binford, *In Pursuit of the Past* (New York: Thames & Hudson, 1988). A general introduction to prehistoric archaeology by an expert, intended for a general audience.

Barry Cunliffe, *Prehistoric Europe: An Illustrated History* (Oxford: Oxford University Press, 1997). An engaging introduction to early Europe.

Brian M. Fagan, *People of the Earth: An Introduction to World Prehistory,* 7th ed. (New York: HarperCollins, 1992). Excellent introduction to the prehistory of Europe and Asia.

Mesopotamia: Between the Two Rivers

Jean Bottero, *Everyday Life in Ancient Mesopotamia* (Baltimore: Johns Hopkins University Press, 2001). Social history of Mespotamia by a leading expert.

Gwendolyn Leick, *The Babylonians, An Introduction* (New York: Routledge, 2003). General introduction to Babylonian history.

Susan Pollock, *Ancient Mesopotamia: The Eden that Never Was* (Cambridge: Cambridge University Press, 1999). An original introduction to the earliest phase of Mesopotamian history.

The Gift of the Nile

Cyril Aldred, *The Egyptians,* 3rd rev. ed. (New York: Thames & Hudson, 1998). Readable general history of ancient Egypt focusing on culture.

Erik Hornung, *History of Ancient Egypt: An Introduction* (Ithaca, NY: Cornell University Press, 1999). A brief survey of Egypt by a great European scholar.

Ian Shaw, ed. *The Oxford History of Ancient Egypt* (Oxford: Oxford University Press, 2000). Comprehensive collaborative survey of ancient Egypt.

Between Two Worlds

John Curtis, *Ancient Persia* (Cambridge, MA: Harvard University Press, 1990). Brief overview of ancient Iran.

Roland De Vaux, *Ancient Israel: Its Life and Institutions* (Grand Rapids, MI: Wm. B. Eerdmans Publishing Co., 1997). A classic account of religious and social life in ancient Israel.

Henry Jackson Flanders, Robert Wilson Crapps, and David Anthony Smith, *People of the Covenant: An Introduction to the Hebrew Bible,* 4th ed. (New York: Oxford University Press, 1996). A balanced introduction to Hebrew and Jewish history that draws on both Jewish and Christian scholarship.

A. T. Olmstead, *History of Assyria* (Chicago: University of Chicago Press, 1975). The fundamental survey of the Assyrian Empire.

For a list of additional titles related to this chapter's topics, please see www.ablongman.com/kishlansky.

Chapter 2

EARLY GREECE, 2500–500 B.C.E.

The Visual Record

HECUBA AND ACHILLES

The wrath of the great warrior Achilles is the subject of Homer's *Iliad,* the first and greatest epic poem of the Mediterranean West, written shortly after 750 B.C.E. Angered by a perceived slight to his honor, Achilles sulks in his tent while the other Achaeans, or Greeks, fight a desperate and losing battle against their enemies, the defenders of the city of Troy. Only after his friend Patroclus is slain by the Trojan Prince Hector does Achilles return to the battle to avenge his fallen comrade and propel the Achaeans to victory. Near the end of the epic, after he has slain Hector in hand-to-hand combat, Achilles ties his foe's body to the back of his chariot and drags it three times around Patroclus's tomb to appease his friend's spirit. The gods are horrified at this demeaning treatment of the body of one who had always been faithful in his sacrifices. Zeus, the chief god, sends his messenger Iris to Hector's mourning parents, his father, Priam, king of Troy, and his mother, Hecuba. Iris urges them to ransom their son's body from Achilles. Moved by the message, Priam goes to Achilles' tent to plead for Hector's body. Achilles, moved by pity and grief for his own father and for Patroclus, grants the old king his request, and Priam returns in sorrow to Troy bearing the body of his son for burial.

The first portions of this episode are brilliantly rendered on the side of the sixth century B.C.E. *hydria,* or water pitcher, shown here. At the center, Achilles leaps into his chariot. The naked body of Hector stretches below him, and the chariot rushes around the tumulus, or burial mound, of Achilles' friend, represented by the white hill to the right. Above it, the small winged spirit of Patroclus watches. But even as Achilles carries out his deed of vengeance, Iris, the winged messenger of Zeus, rushes to Hector's parents, who are shown under a columned portico, which represents Troy. Typically, the artist has taken some liberty with the story. It is not the grieving father the artist has chosen to feature but rather Hecuba, Hector's disconsolate mother. In a vivid manner, totally alien to previous artistic traditions, the Greek artist, like the Greek poet, has captured the essentials of human tragedy.

For all its violent action, the *Iliad* is concerned less with what people do than with how they face the great challenges of life and death. Hector had died well and, in so doing, won immortal fame from his enemies, the Greeks. Achilles eventually acted well and, in his encounter with Priam, faced the universal elements of human destiny: life, love, suffering, endurance, death. Such sentiments, expressed by Homer, became an enduring heritage of Greek civilization and, through it, the civilization of the West.

Looking Ahead

In this chapter, we will explore the first Greek-speaking societies in the Eastern Mediterranean, their collapse, and then the emergence of a new and powerful form of civilization created in the cities of Archaic Greece. ➤

GREECE IN THE BRONZE AGE TO 700 B.C.E.

Early in the *Iliad,* Homer pauses to list the captains and ships of the besieging forces. The roll call of heroes and their homelands is more than a literary device. It is the distant echo of a vanished world, the world of "the goodly citadel of Athens, wealthy Corinth, Knossos and Gortys of the great walls, and the established fortress of Mycenae." The poet lived in an age of illiterate warrior herdsmen, of impoverished, scattered, and sparsely populated villages. Still, in the depths of this "Dark Age," roughly from 1200 to 700 B.C.E., the distant memory of a time of rich palaces, teeming cities, and powerful kings lived on. Homer and his contemporaries could not know that these confused memories stemmed from the last great Bronze Age (ca. 3500–1200 B.C.E.) civilization of the Mediterranean. Still less could they have imagined that they were preparing the foundations of a far greater and lasting civilization, that of classical Greece.

Unlike the rich floodplains of Mesopotamia and Egypt, Greece is a stark world of mountains and sea. The rugged terrain of Greece, only 10 percent of which is flat, and the scores of islands that dot the Aegean and Ionian seas favor the development of small, self-contained agricultural societies. The Greek climate is uncertain, constantly threatening Greek farmers with failure. Rainfall varies enormously from year to year, and arid summers alternate with cool, wet winters. Wheat, barley, and beans were the staples of Greek life. Greek farmers struggled to produce the Mediterranean triad of grains, olives, and wine, which first began to dominate agriculture around 3000 B.C.E. Constant fluctuations in climate and weather from region to region helped to break down the geographical isolation by forcing insular communities to build contacts with a wider world in order to survive.

Islands of Peace

To Homer, the Greeks were all Achaeans, whether they came from the Greek mainland, the islands in the Aegean Sea, or the coast of Asia Minor. Since the late nineteenth century, archaeologists have discerned three fairly distinct late Bronze Age cultures—the Cycladic, the Minoan, and the Mycenaean—that flourished in the Mediterranean before the end of the twelfth century B.C.E.

The Cyclades.   The first culture appeared on the Cyclades, the rugged islands strewn across the bottom of the Aegean from the Greek mainland to the coast of Asia Minor. As early as 2500 B.C.E., artisans in small settlements on the islands of Naxos and Melos developed a high level of metallurgical and artistic skill. Cycladic society was not concentrated into towns, nor, apparently, was it particularly warlike. Many of the largest Cycladic settlements were unfortified. Cycladic religion, to judge from fragments of large clay statues of female figures found in a temple on the island of Ceos, focused on female deities, perhaps fertility goddesses.

This early Bronze Age society slowly faded, but not before influencing its neighbors, especially Crete, the large Mediterranean island to the south. There, beginning around 2500 B.C.E., a sophisticated centralized civilization developed that was termed Minoan after the legendary King Minos of Crete.

Minoan Crete.   Knowledge of **Minoan civilization** burst on the modern world suddenly in 1899. In that year, the English archaeologist Sir Arthur Evans made the first of a series of extraordinary archaeological discoveries at Knossos, the legendary palace of Minos. Crete's location between the civilizations of the Fertile Crescent, Egypt, and the barbarian worlds of the north and west made the island a natural point of exchange and amalgamation of cultures. Still, during the golden age of Crete, roughly between 2000 and 1550 B.C.E., the island developed its unique traditions.

Great palace complexes were constructed at Knossos, Phaistos, Hagia Triada, and elsewhere on the island. They appear as a maze of storerooms, workrooms, and living quarters clustered around a central square. Larger public rooms may have existed at an upper level, but all traces of them have disappeared. Palace bureaucrats, using a unique form of syllabic writing known as Linear A, controlled agricultural production and distribution as well as the work of skilled artisans in their surrounding areas.

Cretan Society and Religion.   Like other ancient civilizations, Minoan Crete was strongly stratified. The vast peasantry paid a heavy tribute in olive oil and other produce. Tribute or taxes flowed to local and regional palaces and

CHRONOLOGY	
GREECE IN THE BRONZE AGE	
ca. 2500 B.C.E.	Beginning of Minoan civilization in Crete
ca. 2000–1500 B.C.E.	Golden Age of Crete
ca. 1600 B.C.E.	Beginning of Mycenaean civilization in Greece
ca. 1450 B.C.E.	Cretan cities, except Knossos, destroyed
ca. 1375 B.C.E.	Knossos destroyed
ca. 1200–700 B.C.E.	Greek Dark Age
ca. 1200 B.C.E.	Mycenaean sites in Greece destroyed; Knossos destroyed again
ca. 1100–1000 B.C.E.	Writing disappears from Greece

MAP DISCOVERY

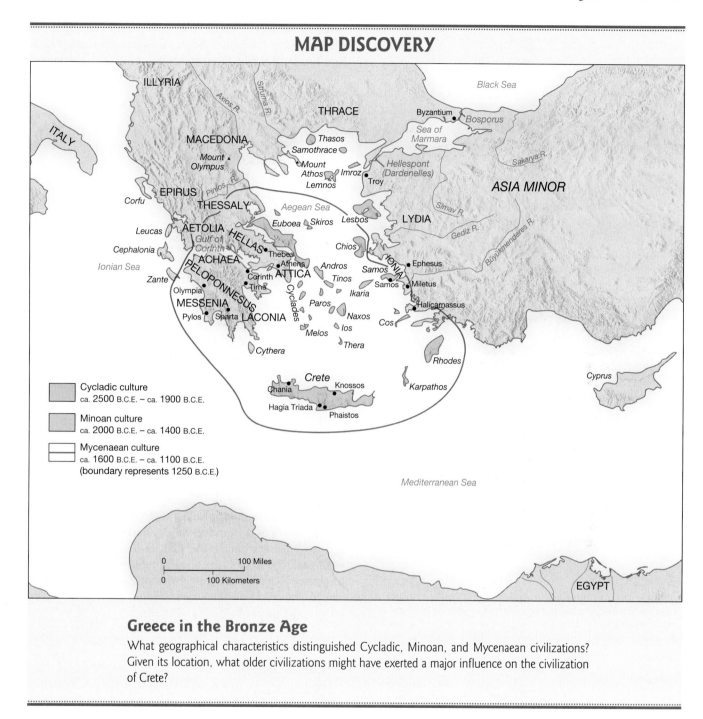

Greece in the Bronze Age

What geographical characteristics distinguished Cycladic, Minoan, and Mycenaean civilizations? Given its location, what older civilizations might have exerted a major influence on the civilization of Crete?

ultimately to Knossos, which stood at the pinnacle of a four-tiered network uniting the island. To some extent, the palace elites redistributed this wealth back down the system through their patterns of consumption.

Though the system may have been exploitive, it was not militaristic. None of the palaces or towns of Crete was fortified. Nor was the cult of the ruler particularly emphasized. Monumental architecture and sculpture designed to exalt the ruler and to overwhelm the commoner are entirely absent from Crete. A key to this unique social tone may be Cretan

religion and, with it, the unusually high status of women. Although male gods received veneration, Cretans particularly worshipped female deities. Chief among the female deities was the mother goddess, who was the source of good and evil. However, one must be careful not to paint too idyllic an image of Cretan religion. Children's bones found in excavations of the palace of Knossos show traces of butchering and the removal of slices of flesh.

Although Minoan society was not clearly matriarchal, it nevertheless differed considerably from the floodplain

■ Female divinity from Knossos, ca. 1600 B.C.E. Snakes, symbols of the underworld, are balanced by the bird of prey on the head of this divinity.

civilizations of the Near East and the societies that were developing on the mainland. At least until the fourteenth century B.C.E., both men and women seem to have played important roles in religious and public life and together built a structured society without the need for vast armies or warrior kings.

Around 1450 B.C.E., a wave of destruction engulfed all of the Cretan cities except Knossos, which was finally annihilated around 1375 B.C.E. The causes of this catastrophe continue to inspire historical debate. Some argue that a natural disaster such as an earthquake or the eruption of a powerful volcano on Thera was responsible for the destruction. More likely, given the martial traditions of the continent and their total absence on Crete, the destruction was the work of mainland Greeks taking control of Knossos and other Minoan cen-

ters. Around this same time, true warrior graves equipped with weapons and armor begin to appear on Crete and at Knossos for the first time. Following this violent conquest, only Knossos and Phaistos were rebuilt, presumably by Greek lords who had eliminated the other political centers on the island. Knossos was ravaged again around 1200 B.C.E.

Mainland of War

The contrast between the vulnerable islands and the violent Greek mainland was particularly marked. Around 1600 B.C.E., a new and powerful warrior civilization arose on the Peloponnesus at Mycenae. The only remains of the first phase of this civilization are 30 graves found at the bottom of deep shafts arranged in two circles. The swords, axes, and armor that fill the graves emphasize the warrior lives of their occupants. By 1500 B.C.E., mainland Greeks were using huge *tholoi*, or beehive-shaped tombs, for royal burials. Over 50 such tombs have been found on the Greek mainland, as have the remains of over 500 villages and great palaces at Mycenae, Tiryns, Athens, Thebes, Gla, and Pylos. This entire civilization, which encompassed not only the mainland but also parts of the coast of Asia Minor, is called **Mycenaean,** although there is no evidence that the city of Mycenae actually ruled all of Greece.

The Mycenaeans quickly adopted artisanal and architectural techniques from neighboring cultures, especially from the Hittites and from Crete, and incorporated these techniques into a distinctive tradition of their own. Unlike the open Cretan palaces and towns, Mycenaean palaces were strongly walled fortresses. From these palaces, Mycenaean kings and their staffs controlled the collection of taxes and tribute as well as the production of bronze and woolen cloth and governed maritime trade. Palace administrators adopted the Linear A script of Crete, transforming it to write their own language, a Greek dialect, in a writing known as **Linear B,** which appears to have been used almost exclusively for record keeping in palaces.

The Dark Age

Mycenaean domination did not last for long. Around 1200 B.C.E., many of the mainland and island fortresses and cities were sacked and totally destroyed. In some areas, such as Pylos, the population fell to roughly 10 percent of what it had been previously. Centralized government, literacy, urban life—civilization itself—disappeared from Greece for over 400 years. Why and how this happened are among the great mysteries of world history.

In later centuries, the Greeks believed that after the Trojan War, new peoples, especially the Dorians, had migrated into Greece, destroying Mycenae and most of the other Achaean cities. More recently, some historians have argued that catastrophic climatic changes, volcanic eruptions, or some other natural disaster wrecked the cities and brought famine and tremendous social unrest in its wake. Neither theory is accurate. No single invasion or natural disaster destroyed

Mycenaean Greece. It self-destructed. Its disintegration was part of the widespread crisis affecting the eastern Mediterranean in the twelfth century B.C.E. The pyramid of Mycenaean lordship, built by small military elites commanding maritime commercial networks, was always threatened with collapse. Overpopulation, the fragility of the agrarian base, the risks of overspecialization in cash crops such as grain in Messenia and sheep raising in Crete, and rivalry among states—all made Mycenaean culture vulnerable. The disintegration of the Hittite empire and the near-collapse of the Egyptian empire disrupted Mediterranean commerce, exacerbating hostilities among Greek states.

As internal warfare raged, the delicate structures of elite lordship disappeared in the mutual sackings and destructions of the palace fortresses. The Dark Age poet Hesiod (ca. 800 B.C.E.), although writing about his own time, probably got it about right:

> *Father will have no common bond with son*
> *Neither will guest with host, nor friend with friend*
> *The brother-love of past days will be gone . . .*
> *Men will destroy the towns of other men.*

With the collapse of the administrative and political system on which Mycenaean civilization was built, the tiny elite that had ruled it vanished as well. From roughly 1200 until 800 B.C.E., the Aegean world entered what is generally termed the Dark Age, a confused period about which little is known, during which Greece returned to a more primitive level of culture and society.

A New Material Culture.

In the wake of the Mycenaean collapse, bands of northerners moved slowly into the Peloponnesus while other Greeks migrated out from the mainland to the islands and the coast of Asia Minor. As these tribal groups merged with the indigenous populations, they gave certain regions distinctive dialectic and cultural characteristics. Thus, the Dorians settled in much of the Peloponnesus, Crete, and southwest Asia Minor. Ionians made Attica, Euboea, and the Aegean islands their home; a mixed group called Aeolians began to migrate to central and northwest Asia Minor. As a result, from the eleventh century B.C.E., both shores of the Aegean became part of a Greek-speaking world. Still later, Greeks established colonies in what is today southern Ukraine, Italy, North Africa, Spain, and France. Throughout its history, Greece was less a geographical than a cultural designation.

Everywhere in this world, between roughly 1100 and 1000 B.C.E., architecture and urban traditions declined, and writing disappeared along with the elites for whose exclusive benefit these achievements had served. The Greece of this Dark Age was much poorer, more rural, and more simply organized. It was also a society of ironworkers. Iron began to replace bronze as the most common metal for ornaments, tools, and weapons. At first this was a simple necessity. The collapse of long-distance trade deprived Greeks of access to tin and copper, the essential ingredients of bronze. Gradually, however,

■ A golden funeral mask (ca. 1500 B.C.E.) found in the royal tombs of Mycenae. The mask was once thought to be the likeness of Agamemnon, the king of Mycenae in the Homeric epics.

the quality of iron tools and weapons began to improve as smiths learned to work hot iron into a primitive steel.

What little is known of this period must be gleaned from archaeology and from Homer's two great epic poems that were written down around 750 B.C.E., near the end of the Dark Age. The archaeological record is bleak. Pictorial representation of humans and animals almost disappears. Luxury goods and most imports are gone from tombs. Pottery made at the beginning of the Dark Age shows little innovation, crudely imitating forms of Mycenaean production.

Gradually, beginning in the eleventh century B.C.E., things began to change a bit. New geometric forms of decoration began to appear on pottery. New types of iron pins, weapons, and decorations appeared that owed little or nothing to the Mycenaean tradition. Cultural changes accompanied these material changes. Around the middle of the eleventh century B.C.E., Greeks in some locations stopped burying their dead and began to practice cremation. Whatever the meaning of these changes, they signaled something new on the shores of the Aegean.

The Evidence of Homer.

The two epic poems—the *Iliad* and the *Odyssey*—hint at this something new. The *Iliad* is the older poem, dating probably to the second half of the eighth century B.C.E. The *Odyssey* dates from perhaps 50 years later. Traditionally ascribed to Homer, these epics were actually the work of oral bards or performers who composed as they chanted. Although the Homeric poems explicitly harken back to the Mycenaean age, much of the description of life, society, and culture actually reflects Dark Age conditions. Thus Homer's heroes were petty kings, chieftains, and nobles, whose positions rested on their wealth, measured in land and flocks, on personal prowess, on networks of kin and allies, and on military followings. The Homeric hero Odysseus is typical of these Dark Age chieftains. In the *Iliad* and the *Odyssey* he is king of Ithaca, a small island on the west coast of Greece. He retained command of his men only as long as he could lead them to victory in the raids against their neighbors. Odysseus describes his departure for home after the fall of Troy with pride:

> The wind that bore me from Ilios brought me . . . to Ismarus, whereupon I sacked their city and slew the people. And from the city we took their wives and much goods, and divided them among us, that none through me might go lacking his proper share.

When present, the king was judge, gift giver, lawgiver, and commander. Absent, no legal or governmental institutions preserved his authority. Instead, the nobility, lesser warriors who were constantly at odds with the king, sought to take his place. In the *Odyssey*, only their mutual rivalry saves Odysseus's wife, Penelope, from being forced to marry one of these haughty aristocrats who were eager to replace the king. Odysseus's son Telemachus summoned the assembly of the people to listen to his complaints against the noble suitors of his mother. Thus the people were not entirely excluded from public life; but this does not mean that they were particularly effective. The assembly listened to both sides and did nothing. Still, a time was coming when changes in society would give hitherto unimagined power to the silent farmers and herdsmen of the Dark Age.

From the Bronze Age civilizations, speakers of Greek had inherited distant memories of an original, highly organized urban civilization grafted onto the rural, aristocratic warrior society of the Dark Ages. Most important, this common dimly recollected past gave all Greek-speaking inhabitants of the Mediterranean world common myths, values, and identity.

ARCHAIC GREECE, 700–500 B.C.E.

Between roughly 800 and 500 B.C.E., extraordinary changes took place in the Greek world. The descendants of the farmers and herdsmen of Homer's Dark Age brought about a revolution in political organization, artistic traditions, intellectual values, and social structures. In a burst of creativity forged in conflict and competition, they invented politics, abstract thought, and the individual. Greeks of the Archaic Age (ca. 700–500 B.C.E.) set the agenda for the rest of Western history.

HECTOR AND ANDROMACHE

The Trojan hero Hector is almost as central to the Iliad *of Homer as is Achilles. Unlike the latter, Hector is a dutiful, reliable support to his city and to Andromache, who is not only his wife but his closest and dearest companion. The description of their last meeting is one of the great expressions of the heroic ethos and of the bonds of man and woman in that culture.*

Focus Questions
How would you describe the relationship between Hector and Andromache? What is the ideal future that Hector wishes for his son?

At last his own generous wife came running to meet him, Andromache, the daughter of high-hearted Eëation. . . . She came to him there, and beside her went an attendant carrying the boy in the fold of her bosom, a little child, only a baby, Hector's son, the admired, beautiful as a star shining. . . . Andromache, stood close beside him, letting her tears fall, and clung to his hand and called him by name and spoke to him: "Dearest, your own great strength will be your death, and you have no pity on your little son, nor on me, ill-starred, who soon must be your widow." . . .

Then tall Hector of the shining helm answered her: "All these things are in my mind also, lady; yet I would feel deep shame before the Trojans, and the Trojan women with trailing garments, if like a coward I were to shrink aside from fighting. . . . But it is not so much the pain to come of the Trojans that troubles me . . . as the thought of you, when some bronze-armored Achaian leads you off, taking away your day of liberty in tears; and in Argos you must work at the loom of another." . . .

Then taking up his dear son he tossed him about in his arms and kissed him, and lifted his voice in prayer to Zeus and the other immortals:

"Zeus, and you other immortals, grant that this boy, who is my son, may be as I am, pre-eminent among the Trojans, great in strength, as I am, and rule strongly over Ilion;

And someday let them say of him: 'He is better by far than his father,' as he comes from the fighting; and let him kill his enemy and bring home the blooded spoils, and delight the heart of his mother."

From the *Iliad* of Homer, Book VI.

MAP DISCOVERY

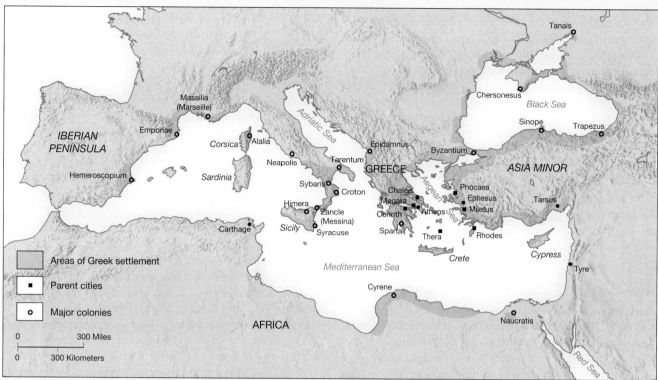

Greek Cities and Colonies of the Archaic Age

Where are the areas of Greek settlement and major colonies in the Archaic Age? What does the location of Greek settlements tell us about the relationship between Greek culture and geography? What regions of Europe and the Near East lacked Greek colonies? Why?

The first sign of radical change in Greece was a major increase in population in the eighth century B.C.E. In Attica, for example, between 780 and 720 B.C.E., the population increased perhaps sevenfold, possibly because of a shift from herding to agriculture. The consequences were enormous. First, population increase meant more villages and towns, greater communication among them, and thus the more rapid circulation of ideas and skills. Second, the rising population placed impossible demands on the agricultural system of much of Greece. Third, it led to greater division of labor and, with an increasingly diverse population, to fundamental changes in political systems. The old structure of loosely organized tribes and chieftains became inadequate to deal with the more complex nature of the new society.

The multiplicity of political and social forms developing in the Archaic Age set the framework within which the first flowering of Greek culture developed. Economic and political transformations laid the basis for intellectual advance by creating a broad class with the prosperity to enjoy sufficient leisure for thought and creative activity. Finally, maritime relations brought people and ideas from around the Greek world together, cross-fertilizing artists and intellectuals in a way never before seen in the West.

Ethnos and Polis

In general, two forms of political organization developed in response to the population explosion of the eighth century B.C.E. On the mainland and in much of the western Peloponnesus, people continued to live in large territorial units called *ethne* (sing. *ethnos*). In each **ethnos,** people lived in villages and small towns scattered across a wide region. Common customs and a common religion focusing on a central religious sanctuary united them. The ethnos was governed by an elite, or **oligarchy** (meaning "rule by the few"), made up of major landowners who met from time to time in one or another town within the region. This form of government, which had its roots in the Dark Ages, continued to exist throughout the classical period.

A much more innovative form of political organization, which developed on the shores of the Aegean and on the islands, was the **polis** (pl. *poleis*), or city-state. Initially, *polis* meant simply "citadel." Villages clustered around these fortifications, which were both protective structures and cult centers for specific deities. These high, fortified sites—*acropolis* means "high citadel"—were sacred to specific gods: in Athens and Sparta, to Athena; in Argos and Samos, to Hera; at Corinth and Thermon, to Apollo. In addition to protection, the polis offered a marketplace, or *agora,* where farmers and artisans could trade and conduct business. The rapid population growth of the eighth century B.C.E. led to the fusion of these villages and the formation of real towns. Each town was independent, each was ruled by a monarchy or an oligarchy, and each controlled the surrounding region, the inhabitants of which were on an equal footing with the townspeople. At times of political or military crisis, the rulers might summon an assembly of the free males of the community to the agora to participate in or to witness the decision-making process. In the following centuries these city-states became the center for that most dramatic Greek experiment in government: democracy.

Technology of Writing and Warfare

The general model of the polis may have been borrowed from the eastern Mediterranean Phoenicians, the merchant society that was responsible for much of the contact Greeks of the eighth century B.C.E. had with the surrounding world. The Phoenicians were certainly the source of an equally important innovation that appeared in Greece at the same time: the reintroduction of writing. Sometime in the eighth century B.C.E., Greeks adopted the Phoenician writing system. But unlike the abandoned Mycenaean script, the purpose of the new writing system was not primarily central administrative record keeping. From the start, this writing system was intended for private, personal use and was available to virtually anyone. The Greeks radically transformed the Phoenician system, making its Semitic characters stand for arbitrary sounds and adding vowel notation in order to record poetry. Soon this writing system was used to indicate ownership of objects, to record religious and secular vows, and even to entertain.

Within the polis, political power was not the monopoly of the aristocracy. The gradual expansion of the politically active population resulted largely from the demands of warfare. In the Dark Age, warfare had been dominated by heavily armed, mounted aristocrats who engaged their equals in single combat. In the Archaic Age, such individual combat between aristocratic warriors gave way to battles that were decided by the use of well-disciplined ranks of infantrymen called *phalange* (sing. **phalanx**). Although few Greeks could afford costly weapons, armor, and horses, between 25 and 40 percent of the landowners could provide the shields, lances, and bronze armor needed by the infantrymen, or **hoplites.**

The democratization of war led gradually to the democratization of political life. Those who brought victory in the phalanx were unwilling to accept total domination by the aristocracy in the agora. The rapid growth of the urban population, the increasing impoverishment of the rural peasantry, and the rise of a new class of wealthy merchant commoners were all challenges that traditional forms of government failed to meet. Everywhere, traditional aristocratic rule was being undermined, and cities searched for ways to resolve this social conflict. No one solution emerged, and one of the outstanding achievements of archaic Greece was the almost limitless variety of political forms elaborated in its city-states.

■ A Corinthian vase showing hoplites marching into battle.

Colonists and Tyrants

Colonization and tyranny were two intertwined results of the political and social turmoil of the seventh century B.C.E. Population growth, changes in economy, and opposition to aristocratic power led Greeks to seek change externally through emigration and internally through political restructuring.

Late in the eleventh century B.C.E., Greeks had begun to migrate to new homes on the islands and along the coast of Asia Minor, in search of commercial advantages or a better life. By the eighth century B.C.E., Greeks had pushed east as far as Al Mina in northern Syria and Tarsus in eastern Asia Minor.

Beginning around 750 B.C.E., a new form of colonization began in the western Mediterranean. The impetus for this expansion was not primarily trade, but rather the need to reduce population pressure at home. The first noteworthy colony, Cumae, near Naples, was founded by emigrants from Euboea. Soon other cities sent colonists to southern Italy and Sicily. Around 700 B.C.E., similar colonies appeared in the northeast in Thrace, on the shores of the Black Sea, and as far as the mouth of the Don River. The colonists were not always volunteers. At Thera, for example, young men were chosen by lot to colonize Cyrene. The penalty for refusing to participate was death and confiscation of property. Usually, colonists were only single males, the most volatile portion of the community. Colonies were thus a safety valve to release the pressures of population growth and political friction. Although colonies remained attached culturally to their mother cities, they were politically independent. The men who settled them were warriors as well as farmers or traders and carved out their new cities at the expense of the local population.

Colonization relieved some of the population pressure on Greek communities, but it did not solve the problem of political conflict. As opposition to entrenched aristocracies grew, first in Argos, then at Corinth, Sicyon, Elis, Mytilene, and elsewhere, new leaders opposed to aristocratic rule seized power. These rulers were known as **tyrants,** a term that originally meant the same as king. In the course of the later sixth century B.C.E., "tyrant" came to designate those who had achieved supreme power without benefit of official position. Often, this rise to power came through popularity with hoplite armies. However, the term tyrant did not carry the negative connotation associated with it today. Early tyrants were generally welcomed by their fellow citizens and played a crucial role in the destruction of aristocratic government and the creation of civic traditions.

Tyrants weakened the power of entrenched aristocratic groups, promoted the prosperity of their supporters by protecting farmers and encouraging trade, undertook public works projects, founded colonies, and entered into marriage alliances with rulers of other cities, which provided some external peace. Although they stood outside the traditional organs of government, tyrants were frequently content to govern through them, leaving magistracies and offices intact but ensuring that through elections these offices were filled with the tyrant's supporters. Thus at Corinth, Mytilene, Athens, and elsewhere, tyrants preserved and even strengthened constitutional structures as a hedge against the return to power of aristocratic factions.

The great weakness of tyrannies was that they depended for their success on the individual qualities of the ruler. Tyrants tended to pass their powers on to their sons, and as tyrannies became hereditary, cities came to resent incompetent or excessively cruel successors. As popular tyranny gave way to harsh and arbitrary rule, opposition brought on civil war and the deposition or abdication of the tyrant. Gradually, "tyranny" acquired the meaning it bears today, and new forms of government emerged. Still, in spite of the bitter memory Greek tyranny left in people's minds, in many cities tyrants had for a time solved the crisis of political order and had cleared the way for broader participation in public life than had ever before been known.

Gender and Power

Military, political, and cultural life in the city-states became more democratic, but this democratization did not extend to women. Greek attitudes toward gender roles and sexuality were rigid. Except in a few cities and in certain religious cults, women played no public role in the life of the community. They remained firmly under male control throughout their lives, passing from the authority of their fathers to that of their husbands. For the most part, friendship existed only between members of the same sex, and this friendship was often intensely sexual. Bisexuality was the norm in Greek society, although neither Greek homosexuality nor heterosexuality was the same as in modern society. Rather, they coexisted and formed parts of a sexuality of domination by those considered superior in age, rank, or sex over others. Mature men took young boys as their lovers, helped to educate them, and inspired them by word and deed to grow into ideal warriors and citizens. We know less about such practices among women, but teachers such as Sappho of Lesbos (ca. 610–ca. 580 B.C.E.), who was also a wife and mother, formed similar bonds with their pupils, even while preparing them for marriage.

Those women who were in public life were mostly slaves, frequently prostitutes. These ranged from impoverished streetwalkers to *hetairai,* educated, sophisticated courtesans who entertained men at *symposia* (sing. *symposion*), or male banquets, which were the centers of cultural and social life. Many female slaves were acquired by collecting and raising female infants who had been abandoned. Greek society did not condemn or even question abandonment of infants, prostitution, or sexual exploitation of women and slave boys. These practices formed part of the complex and varied social systems of the developing city-states.

Gods and Mortals

Greeks and their gods enjoyed an ambivalent, almost irreverent relationship. On the one hand, Greeks made regular offerings to the gods, pleaded with them for help, and gave them thanks for assistance. On the other, the gods were thoroughly human, sharing in an exaggerated manner not only human strengths and virtues but also weaknesses and vices.

Greeks offered sacrifices to the gods on altars, which were raised everywhere—in homes, in fields, in sacred groves. No group had the sort of monopoly on the cult of the gods that Mesopotamian and Egyptian priests enjoyed. Unlike the temples of other societies, Greek temples were houses of the gods, not centers of ritual. The so-called Doric temple, which housed a statue of the god, consisted of an oblong or rectangular room covered by a pitched roof and circled by columns. These temples reflected the wealth and patriotism of the city. They stood as monuments to the human community rather than to the divine.

On special occasions, festivals were celebrated at sanctuaries, honoring the gods of the city with processions, athletic contests, and feasts. Some of these celebrations drew participants from all of the Greek world. The two greatest pan-Hellenic (meaning "all Greek," from *Hellas,* the Greek word for Greece) sanctuaries were Olympia and Delphi. Because both were remote from centers of political power, they were insulated from interstate rivalry and provided neutral ground on which hostile neighbors could meet in peace.

Beginning in 776 B.C.E., every four years, wars and conflicts were temporarily suspended while athletes from the whole Greek world met at Olympia to participate in contests in honor of Zeus. The competitions were sometimes violent. Wrestling in particular could be deadly, since matches continued until one participant signaled that he had had enough. Many wrestlers chose death rather than defeat. Olympic victors were treated as national heroes.

Delphi, the site of the shrine of Apollo, god of music, archery, medicine, and prophecy, was the second pan-Hellenic cult center. Like Olympia, Delphi drew athletes from the whole Greek world to its athletic contests. However, Delphi's real fame lay in its oracle, or spokeswoman, for the god Apollo. From the eighth century B.C.E., before undertaking any important decision such as establishing a colony, beginning a war, or even contracting a marriage, individuals and representatives of distant cities traveled to Delphi to ask Apollo's advice or to seek purification from the guilt attached to shedding others' blood and reconciliation with their fellow citizens. For a stiff fee, visitors were allowed to address questions to the god through a female medium. She entered a trance state and uttered a reply, which lay priests at the shrine then put into verse form and transmitted to the petitioner. The ambiguity of the Delphic replies was legendary.

Though gods were petitioned, placated, and pampered, they were not privileged or protected. Unlike the awe-inspiring gods of the Mesopotamians and Egyptians, the traditional Greek gods, inherited from the Dark Age, were represented in ways that showed them as all too human, vicious, and frequently ridiculous. Zeus was infamous for his frequent rapes of boys and girls. His lust was matched only by the fury of his jealous wife, Hera. According to one story, a visitor to Athens asked why its citizens so often use the phrase "By Zeus!" The answer came back: "Because so many of us are." The Greek gods were immortal, superhuman in strength, and able to interfere in human affairs. But in all things they reflected the values and weaknesses of the Greek mortals, who could bargain with them, placate them, and even trick them.

Religious cults were not under the exclusive control of any priesthood or political group. Therefore there were no official versions of stories of gods and goddesses. This is evident both from Greek poetry, which often presents contradictory stories of the gods, and from pottery, which bears pictorial versions of myths that differ greatly from written ones. No one group or sacred site enjoyed a monopoly on access to the gods. Like literacy and government, the gods belonged to all.

Myth and Reason

The glue holding together the individual and frequently hostile Greek poleis and the ethne scattered throughout the Mediterranean was their common stock of myths. Stories of gods and heroes, told and retold, were fashioned into *mythoi* (myths, literally, "formulated speech"), which explained and described the world both as it was and as it should be. Myths were told about every city, shrine, river, mountain, and island. Myths explained the origins of cities, festivals, the world itself. What is the place of humans in the cosmos? They stand between beasts and gods because Prometheus tricked Zeus and gave men fire with which they cook their food and offer the bones and fat of sacrificial animals to the gods. Why is there evil and misfortune? Because in revenge for Prometheus's trickery, Zeus offered humans Pandora (the name means "all gifts"), the first woman, whose beauty hid her evil nature. By accepting this gift, humans brought evil and misfortune on themselves. Such stories were more than simply fanciful explanations of how things came to be. Myths sanctioned and supported the authority of social, political, and religious traditions and provided a means of reasoning about the world.

Art and the Individual

Archaic Greeks borrowed from everywhere and transformed all that they borrowed. Just as they adopted and adapted the Phoenician alphabet and Mesopotamian science, they took Near Eastern and Egyptian painting and sculpture and made them their own. During the Dark Age, the Mycenaean traditions of art had entirely disappeared. Pottery showed only geometric decorations; sculpture was unknown. Gradually, from the ninth century B.C.E., stylized human and animal figures, lions, griffins, and other strange beasts began to appear within the tightly composed geometric patterns. By the eighth century B.C.E., such exotic subjects had given way to the Greek passion for human images taken from their own myths and

CHRONOLOGY
ARCHAIC GREECE

ca. 780–720 B.C.E.	Population increase in Greece
776 B.C.E.	First Olympic Games held
ca. 750–700 B.C.E.	Greeks develop writing system based on Phoenician model; Greeks begin colonizing western Mediterranean
ca. 700–500 B.C.E.	Archaic Age of Greece
ca. 700 B.C.E.	First stone temples appear in Greece
ca. 650 B.C.E.	Cypselus breaks rule of Bacchiads in Corinth; rules city as tyrant
594 B.C.E.	Solon elected chief archon of Athens; institutes social and political reforms
586 B.C.E.	Death of Periander ends tyrants' rule in Corinth
499 B.C.E.	Ionian cities revolt

■ The Calf-Bearer was commissioned for the temple of Athena, which was destroyed by the Persians in 480 B.C.E. when they captured Athens and burned the Acropolis.

legends. The preferred technique was the so-called black figure style, which developed first at Corinth. Subjects were painted in black silhouette on red clay, and then details were cut with a sharp point so that the background could show through. As the popularity of these mythic and heroic scenes increased, so too did the artists' technical competence. Greek artists competed with one another to overcome technical problems of perspective and foreshortening. From the sixth century B.C.E., many of the finest examples were signed. Such masterpieces celebrated not only the heroes of the past but also the artist as individual and as the interpreter of culture no less original than the poet.

Greek sculpture underwent a similar dramatic development. The earliest and most common subject of archaic sculpture was the standing male nude, or **kouros** figure, which was in wide demand as a grave monument, dedication to a god, or even cult statue of male deity. In Egypt, seventh century B.C.E. Greeks had seen colossal statues and had learned to work stone. They brought these techniques home, improved on them by using iron tools (the Egyptians knew only bronze ones), and began to create their own human images. The rigidly formulaic position of the kouros—standing, arms by the sides, looking straight ahead, left foot extended—followed Egyptian tradition and left little room for originality. Thus sculptors sought to give their statues originality and individuality, not as representations of individuals, but as the creations of the individual sculptor. To this end, they experimented with increasingly natural molding of limbs and body and began signing their works. Thus, as in vase painting, Greek sculpture reflected the importance of the individual, not in its subject matter, but in its creator. The female counterparts of the kouros figures, called *korai*, followed similarly rigid traditions to which sculptors added female attributes.

The real challenges in sculpture came in the portrayal of narrative in decorations on monuments, primarily temples. Unlike kouroi, which were usually private commissions intended to adorn the tombs of aristocrats, these public buildings were constructed as expressions of civic pride and were accessible to everyone. Here the creativity and dynamism of Greek cities could be paralleled in stone. Figures such as the Calf-Bearer (ca. 590 B.C.E.) from the Athenian acropolis are daring in the complexity of composition and the delicacy of execution. (See photo on p. 35.) These are statues that tell stories. In the Calf-Bearer, a master farmer carries a calf to be sacrificed to Athena. The two gentle heads and the cross formed by the farmer's hands and the calf's legs are individual traits without precedent in ancient art. Although formally intended for religious purposes, these figures serve not only the gods and the aristocratic elite, but the whole community.

A TALE OF THREE CITIES

The political, social, and cultural transformations that occurred in the Archaic Age took different forms across the Greek world. No community or city-state was typical of Greece. The best way to understand the diversity of Archaic Greece is to examine three very different cities that by the end of the sixth century B.C.E. had become leading centers of Greek civilization. Corinth, Sparta, and Athens present something of the spectrum of political, cultural, and social models of the Hellenic world. Corinth, like many cities, developed into a commercial center in which the assembly of citizens was dominated by an oligarchy. Sparta developed into a state in which citizenship was radically egalitarian but restricted to a small military elite. In Athens, the Archaic Age saw the foundations of an equally radical democracy.

Wealthy Corinth

Corinth owed its prosperity to its privileged site, dominating both a rich coastal plain and the narrow isthmus connecting the Peloponnesus to the mainland. In the eighth century B.C.E., as Greeks turned their attention to the west, Corinthians led the way. Corinthian pottery appeared throughout western Greece and southern Italy. Corinthian trade led to colonization, and settlers from Corinth founded Syracuse and other cities in Sicily and Italy, which served as markets for Corinthian products. Even more important to Corinthian prosperity was its role in the transport of other cities' products from east to west. By carrying goods across the isthmus and loading them onto other ships, merchants could avoid the long, dangerous passage around the Peloponnesus.

Social Tensions.   The precise details of early Corinthian government are uncertain. Still, it appears that in Corinth, as in many other cities, a tyranny replaced a ruling clan, and in time this tyranny ended with an oligarchic government. Until the middle of the seventh century B.C.E., Corinth and its wealth were ruled in typical Dark Age fashion by an aristocratic clan known as the Bacchiads. Corinth began its rise under this aristocratic rule, and individual Bacchiads led colonizing expeditions to Italy and Sicily. However, the increasing pressures of population growth, rapidly expanding wealth, and dramatic changes in the economy produced social tensions that the traditional aristocratic rulers were unable to handle. As in cities throughout the Greek world, these tensions led to the creation of a new order.

The early history of Corinth is obscure, but apparently around 650 B.C.E. a revolution led by a dissident Bacchiad named Cypselus (ca. 657–627 B.C.E.) and supported by non-Bacchiad aristocrats and other Corinthians broke the Bacchiads' grip on the city. The revolution led to the establishment of Cypselus as tyrant. Cypselus and his son Periander (ca. 627–586 B.C.E.) seem to have been generally popular with most Corinthians.

Corinth Under Its Tyrants.   In Corinth, as in many other cities, the tyrants restructured taxes, relying primarily on customs duties, which were less of a burden on the peasantry. Around 600 B.C.E., Periander began construction of a causeway across the isthmus on which ships could be hauled from the Aegean to the western Mediterranean. This causeway eventually became a major source of Corinth's wealth. Periander attacked conspicuous consumption on the part of the aristocracy. He introduced laws against idleness and put thousands of Corinthians to work in extensive building programs. He erected temples and sent colonists to Italy. Under his leadership, the Corinthian fleet developed into the most powerful naval force in the Adriatic and Aegean Seas. Under its tyrants, Corinth led the Greek world in the production of black figure pottery, which spread throughout the Mediterranean.

The tyrants also laid the foundation for broader political participation. Cypselus divided the population into eight tribes, based not on traditional ethnic divisions, but on arbitrary groupings by region. All of Corinth was divided into three large regions. The population of each region was distributed among each of the eight tribes. This assignment prevented the emergence of political factions based on regional disputes. Ten representatives from each tribe formed a council of 80 men. Under the tyrants this council was largely advisory and provided a connection between the autocratic rulers and the citizens.

In Corinth, as elsewhere, the strength or weakness of tyranny rested on the abilities and personality of individual tyrants. Cypselus had been a beloved liberator. His son Periander, in spite of his accomplishments, was remembered for his cruelty and violence. Shortly after Periander's death in 586 B.C.E., a revolt killed his successor, and tyranny in Corinth ended.

Oligarchy.   The new government continued the tribal and council system established by Cypselus. From the sixth century B.C.E. until its conquest by Macedonia in 338 B.C.E., Corinth was ruled by an oligarchy. Although an assembly of the *demos,* or adult males, met occasionally, actual government was in the hands of eight deliberators, or *probouloi,* and nine other men from each tribe who together formed the council of eighty. The oligarchs who made up the council avoided the kind of exclusive and arbitrary tendencies that had destroyed both the Bacchiads and the tyrants. They were remarkably successful in maintaining popular support among the citizens and provided a reliable and effective government.

Thus Corinth flourished, a city that was more open to commerce and wealth than most, moderate in its political institutions and eager for stability. As one fourth century B.C.E. poet wrote:

> [There] lawfulness dwells, and her sister,
> Safe foundation of cities,
> Justice, and Peace, who was bred with her;
> They dispense wealth to men.

Martial Sparta

At the beginning of the eighth century B.C.E., the Peloponnesus around Sparta and Laconia faced circumstances similar to those of Corinth and other Greek communities. Population growth, increasing disparity between rich and poor, and an expanding economy created powerful tensions. However, while Corinthian society developed into a complex mix of aristocrats, merchants, artisans, and peasants ruled by an oligarchy, the Spartan solution was a rigid two-tiered social structure. By the end of the Archaic Age, a small, homogeneous class of warriors called *homoioi* ("those alike"), or equals, ruled a vast population of state serfs, or *helots.* The two classes lived in mutual fear and mistrust. Spartans controlled the helots through terror and ritual murder. The helots in turn were "an enemy constantly waiting for the disasters of the Spartans." Yet, throughout antiquity the Spartans were the Greeks who were most praised for their courage, simplicity of life, and service to the state.

Messenia.   War was the center of Spartan life, and war lay at the origin of the Spartans' extraordinary social and political organization. In the eighth century B.C.E., the Spartans conquered the fertile region of Messenia and compelled the vanquished Messenians to turn over one-half of their harvests. The spoils were not divided equally but went to increase the wealth of the aristocracy, thus creating resentment among the less privileged. Early in the seventh century B.C.E., the Spartans attempted a similar campaign to take the plain of Thyreatis from the city of Argos. This time they were not so fortunate; they were defeated, and resentment of the ordinary warriors toward their aristocratic leaders flared into open conflict. The Messenians seized on this time as a moment to revolt, and for a time, Sparta was forced to fight at home and abroad for its very existence. In many cities, such crises gave rise to tyrants. In Sparta, the crisis led to radical political and social reforms that transformed the polis into a unique military system.

Reforms of Lycurgus.   The Spartans attributed these reforms to the legendary lawgiver Lycurgus (seventh century B.C.E.). Whether or not Lycurgus ever existed and was responsible for all of the reforms, they saved the city and ended its internal tensions at the expense of abandoning the mainstream of Greek development. Traditionally, Greeks had placed personal honor above communal concerns. During the crisis of the second Messenian war, Spartans of all social ranks were urged to look not to individual interest but to **eunomia,** good order and obedience to the laws, which alone could unite Spartans and bring victory. United, the Spartans crushed the Messenians. In return for obedience, poor citizens received equality before the law and benefited from a land distribution that relieved their poverty. Conquered land, especially that in Messenia, was divided and distributed to Spartan warriors. However, the Spartan warriors were not expected to work the land themselves. Instead, the state reduced the defeated Messenians to the status of helots and assigned them to individual Spartans. While this system did not erase all economic inequalities among the Spartans (aristocrats continued to hold more land than others), it did decrease some of the disparity. It also provided a minimum source of wealth for all Spartan citizens and allowed them to devote themselves to full-time military service.

This land reform was coupled with a political reform that incorporated elements of monarchy, oligarchy, and democracy. The state was governed by two hereditary kings, probably representing different groups that had formed the Spartan polis earlier, and a council of elders, the *gerousia.* In peacetime, the authority of the two royal families was limited to familial and religious affairs. In war, they commanded the army and held the power of life and death.

In theory at least, the central institution of Spartan government was the gerousia, which was composed of 30 men at least 60 years of age and included the two kings. The gerousia directed all political activity, especially foreign affairs, and served as high court. Members were elected for life by the assembly, or *apella,* which was composed of all equals over the age of 30 and approved decisions of the gerousia. However, this approval, made by acclamation, could easily be manipulated, as could the course of debate within the gerousia itself. Wealth, cunning, and patronage were more important than its formal structures in the direction of the Spartan state.

Actual administration was in the hands of five magistrates, termed *ephors,* whose powers were extremely broad. They presided over joint sessions of the gerousia and apella. They held supreme authority over the kings during wartime, acted as judges for noncitizens, and controlled the *krypteia,* or secret police. The krypteia were a band of youths who practiced state terrorism as part of their rite of passage to the status of equal. On the orders of the ephors, the krypteia assassinated, intrigued, arrested powerful people, and terrorized helots. Service in this corps was considered a necessary part of a youth's education.

Social Control.   The key to the success of Sparta's political reform was an even more radical social reform that placed everyone under the direct supervision and service of the state from birth until death. Although admiring aristocratic visitors often exaggerated their accounts of Spartan life, the main outlines are clear enough. Eunomia was the sole guiding principle, and service to the state came before family, social class, and every other duty or occupation.

Spartan equals were made, not born. True, only a man born of free Spartan parents could hope to become an equal, but birth alone was no guarantee of admission to this select body, or even of the right to live. Public officials examined infants and decided whether they were sufficiently strong to be allowed to live or should be exposed on a hillside to die. From birth until age seven, a boy lived with his mother; he then entered the state education system, or *agoge,* living in barracks with his contemporaries and enduring 13 years of rigorous military training. At age 12, training with swords and spears became more intense, as did the rigors of the lifestyle. Boys were given only a single cloak to wear and slept on thin rush mats. They were encouraged to supplement their meager diet by stealing food, although if they were caught, they were severely whipped, not for the theft but for the failure. All of this they were expected to endure in silence.

Much of the actual education of the youths was entrusted to older, accomplished warriors, who selected boys as their homosexual lovers. Such relationships were the norm throughout Greece but were more important in Sparta. The lover served as tutor and role model, and in time the two became a fighting team. At age 20, Spartan youths were enrolled in the krypteia. Each was sent out into the countryside with nothing but a cloak and a knife, forbidden to return until he had killed a helot.

If a youth survived the rigors of his training until age 30, he could at last be incorporated into the rank of equals, provided that he could pass the last obstacle. He had to be able to furnish a sufficient amount of food from his own lands for the communal dining group to which he would be assigned. This food might come from inherited property or, if he had proved himself an outstanding warrior, from the state. Those who passed this final qualification became full members of the assembly, but they continued to live with the other warriors. Men could marry at age 20, but family life in the usual sense was nonexistent. A man could not live with his wife until age 30 because he was bound to the barracks.

Although their training was not as rigorous as that of males, Spartan women were given an education and allowed a sphere of activity unknown elsewhere in Greece. Girls, like boys, were trained in athletic competition and, like boys, competed naked in wrestling, footraces, and spear throwing. This training was based not on a belief in the equality of the sexes but simply on the desire to improve the physical stamina and childbearing abilities of Spartan women. Women were able to own land and to participate widely in business and agricultural affairs; since men were entirely involved in military pursuits, women were expected to look after economic and household affairs. When a foreign woman commented that Spartan women were the only women who could rule men, a Spartan woman replied, "With good reason, for we are the only women who bring forth men."

Few Lacedaemonians (as Spartans were also called) ever became equals. Not only were there far more helots than Spartans, but many inhabitants of the region, termed *perioikoi,* or peripherals, although they were free citizens of their local communities, were not allowed into the agoge. Others were unable to endure the harsh life, and still others lacked the property qualifications to supply their share of the communal meals. For all the trappings of egalitarianism, equality in Sparta was the privilege of a tiny minority.

The total dedication to military life was reinforced by a deliberate rejection of other activities. From the time of the second Messenian war, Sparta withdrew from the mainstream of Greek civilization. Equals could not engage in crafts, trade, or any other forms of economic activity. Because Sparta banned silver and gold coinage, it could not participate in the growing commercial network of the Greek world. Although a group of free citizens of subject towns could engage in such activities, the role of Sparta in the economic, architectural, and cultural life of Greece was negligible after the seventh century B.C.E. Militarily, Sparta cast a long shadow across the Peloponnesus and beyond, but the number of equals was always too small to allow Sparta both to create a vast empire and to maintain control over the helots at home. Instead, Sparta created a network of alliances and nonaggression pacts with oligarchic neighbors. In time, this network came to be known as the Peloponnesian League.

Democratic Athens

Athens did not enjoy the advantages of a strategic site such as that of Corinth, nor was it surrounded by rich plains like Sparta. However, the "goodly citadel of Athens" was one of the few Mycenaean cities to have escaped destruction at the start of the Dark Age. Gradually, Athens united the whole surrounding region of Attica into a single polis, by far the largest in the Greek world. Well into the seventh century B.C.E., Athens followed the general pattern of the polis seen in Corinth and Sparta. Like other Dark Age communities, Athens was ruled by aristocratic clans, particularly the Alcmaeonids. Only the members of these clans could participate in the *areopagus,* or council, which they entered after serving a year as one of the nine *archons,* or magistrates, elected yearly. Until the seventh century B.C.E., Athens escaped the social pressures brought on by population growth and economic prosperity that led to civil strife, colonialism, and tyranny elsewhere. This was due largely to its relative abundance of arable land and its commercial prosperity based on the export of grain.

Social Tensions. By the late seventh century B.C.E., however, Athens began to suffer from the same class conflict that had shaken other cities. Sometime around 630 B.C.E., an aristocrat named Cylon attempted to seize power as tyrant. His attempt failed, but when he was murdered by one of the Alcmaeonids, popular revulsion drove the Alcmaeonids from the city. A decade of strife ensued as aristocratic clans, wealthy merchants, and farmers fought for control of the city. Violence between groups and families threatened to tear the community apart.

Reforms of Solon.   In 621 B.C.E., the Athenians granted a judge, Draco, extraordinary powers to revise and systematize traditional laws concerning vengeance and homicide. His restructuring of procedures for limiting vengeance and preventing bloodshed were harsh enough to add the term "Draconian" to Western legal vocabulary. When asked why death was the most common penalty he imposed, Draco explained that minor offenses merited death and he knew of no more severe penalty for major ones. Still, these measures did nothing to solve the central problems of political control. Finally, in 594 B.C.E., an Athenian merchant who was respected by both aristocrats and commoners was elected chief archon and charged with reforming the city's government. Solon (ca. 630–ca. 560 B.C.E.) based his reform on the ideal of eunomia, as had the Spartans, but he followed a very different path to secure good order.

In Sparta, Lycurgus had begun with a radical redistribution of land. In Athens, Solon began with the less extreme measure of eliminating debt bondage. Athenians who had been forced into slavery or into sharecropping because of their debts were restored to freedom. A law forbade mortgaging free men and women as security for debts. Athenians might be poor, but they would be free. This free peasantry formed the basis of Athenian society throughout its history.

Solon also reorganized the rest of the social hierarchy and broke the aristocracy's exclusive control of the areopagus by dividing the society into four classes based on wealth rather than birth and opening the archonship to the top two classes. He further weakened the areopagus by establishing a council of 400 members drawn from all four classes, to which citizens could appeal decisions of the magistrates.

Solon's efforts to resolve Athens's social tensions did not entirely succeed. His laws were more humane than those of Draco, but Solon himself did not consider his new constitution perfect, only practical. Asked whether he had given the Athenians the best laws that he could give them, he answered, "The best that they could receive." Resistance from the still powerful aristocracy prompted some Athenians to urge Solon to assume the powers of a tyrant to force through his reforms. He refused, but after his death, Peisistratus (d. 527 B.C.E.), an aristocrat who was strongly supported by the peasants against his own class, hired a mercenary force to seize control of the city. After two abortive attempts, Peisistratus ruled as tyrant from 545 B.C.E. until his death.

Athenian Tyranny.   Peisistratus and later his son Hippias (d. 490 B.C.E.), who succeeded him until 510 B.C.E., ruled through Solon's constitution but took care to ensure that the archons who were elected each year were their agents. Thus they strengthened the constitution even while they further weakened the aristocracy.

Peisistratus and Hippias drew their support from the *demos,* or people at large, rather than from an aristocratic faction. They claimed divine justification for their rule and made a great show of devotion to the Athenian gods. Peisistratus promoted annual festivals and, in so doing, began the great tradition of Athenian literature. At the festival of Athena, professional reciters of *rhapsoidiai* (epic poetry) recited large portions of the *Iliad* and the *Odyssey.* During a festival in honor of Dionysus, actors performed the first tragedies and comedies. The tyrants also directed a series of popular nationalistic public works programs that beautified the city, increased national pride, and provided work for the poor. They rebuilt the temple of Athena on the acropolis, for which the statue of the Calf-Bearer was commissioned. These internal measures were accompanied by support for commerce and export, particularly of grain. Soon, Athens was challenging Corinth as the leading commercial power and was trading in grain as far away as the Black Sea.

Peisistratus was firm. His son Hippias was harsh. Still, even Hippias enjoyed the support of the majority of the citizens of both popular and aristocratic factions. Only after the assassination of his younger brother did Hippias become sufficiently oppressive to drive his opponents into exile. Some of these exiles obtained the assistance of Sparta and returned to overthrow Hippias in 510 B.C.E. Hippias's defeat ended the tyrants' rule in Athens and won for Sparta an undeserved reputation as the opponent of all tyranny.

Athenian Democracy.   Following the expulsion of Hippias, some aristocrats attempted to return to the "good old days" of aristocratic rule. However, Athenians had been accustomed to Solon's constitution for more than 80 years and were unwilling to give it up. Moreover, the tyrants had created a fierce sense of nationalistic pride among all ranks of

■ An Athenian silver coin called a *tetradrachm,* dating from the fifth century B.C.E. The owl is the symbol of the goddess Athena.

Athenians, and few were willing to turn over government to the hands of only a few. When the aristocrats made their bid to recover power, their primary opponent, Cleisthenes (ca. 570–ca. 507 B.C.E.), a descendant of the Alcmaeonids, made the demos his faction and pushed through a final constitutional reform that became the basis for Athenian **democracy.**

The essence of Cleisthenes' reform lay in his reorganization of the major political units by which members of the council were selected. Previously, each citizen had belonged to one of four tribes, which were further broken down into 12 brotherhoods, or *phratries,* which were administrative and religious units. In a manner similar to that of Cypselus in Corinth, Cleisthenes reshuffled these phratries into 30 territorial units comprising urban, inland, or coastal regions. These 30 units in turn were grouped into 10 tribes, each consisting of one unit from each of the urban, inland, and coastal regions. The tribes elected the members of the council, military commanders, jurors, and magistrates. As in Corinth, this reorganization destroyed the traditional kin-based social and political pattern and integrated people of differing social, economic, and regional backgrounds. Aristocrats, merchants, and poor farmers had to work together to find common ground for political action, both regionally and nationally. With this new integrated democracy and its strong sense of nationalism, Athens emerged from the Archaic Age as the leading city of the Hellenic world.

THE COMING OF PERSIA AND THE END OF THE ARCHAIC AGE

By the end of the sixth century B.C.E., the products of Greek experimentation were evident throughout the Mediterranean. Greek city-states had resolved the crises of class conflict. Greek merchants and artisans had found ways to flourish despite poor soil and uncertain climate. Greek philosophers, poets, and artists had begun to celebrate the human form and the human spirit. Still, these achievements were the product of small, independent, and relatively weak communities on the fringe of the civilized world.

In the second half of the sixth century B.C.E., all this changed. The Persian empire, under its dynamic king Cyrus II, began a process of conquest and expansion west into Asia Minor, absorbing the kingdom of Lydia and conquering Ionia on the coast of Asia Minor. The Persians placed tyrants loyal to Cyrus to rule over these Greek communities, and for a few decades these centers of Greek culture and thought accepted foreign control. In 499 B.C.E., the passion for democracy, which had swept much of mainland Greece, reached Ionia. Cities such as Miletus, Ephesus, Chios, and Samos revolted, expelled their Persian-appointed tyrants, established democracies, and sent ambassadors to the mainland to seek assistance. Eretria and Athens, two mainland cities with Ionian roots, responded, sending ships and men to aid the Ionian rebels. Athenian interests were more than simple solidarity with their Ionian cousins. Athens depended on grain from the Black Sea region and believed its direct interests to lie with the area. The success of the revolt was short lived. The puny Greek cities were dealing with the largest empire the West had yet known. By 500 B.C.E., the Persian Empire included Asia Minor, Mesopotamia, Palestine, and Egypt, uniting all peoples from the Caucasus to the Sudan.

The giant Persian Empire responded slowly, but with force,

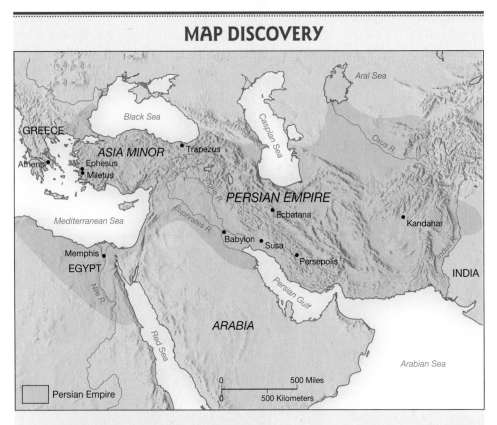

MAP DISCOVERY

The Persian Empire, ca. 500 B.C.E.

Examine the extent of the Persian Empire. Which ancient civilizations that you have studied so far were incorporated into the Persian Empire? What effects on cultural and economic exchange can you imagine to have resulted from this territorial conquest?

to the Greek revolt. King Darius I (522–486 B.C.E.) gathered a vast international force from throughout his empire and set about recapturing the rebellious cities. The war lasted five years and ended in a Persian victory. By 494 B.C.E., the Persians had retaken the cities of the coast and nearby islands. In the cities that were deemed most responsible for the revolt, the population was herded together, the boys were castrated and made into royal eunuchs, the girls were sent to Darius's court, the remainder of the population was sold into slavery, and the towns were burned to the ground. Once the rebels had been disposed of, Darius set out to punish their supporters on the mainland, Eretria and Athens. With the same meticulous planning and deliberate pace, the Persian king turned his vast armies toward the Greek mainland.

CONCLUSION

Civilization developed much later in the Mediterranean world than it had in the floodplains of the Near East. The earliest Bronze Age societies of Greece and the neighboring islands, while influenced by contact with the great civilizations of Mesopotamia and Egypt, developed distinctive societies and cultures that were tied closely to the sea around them. Still, they too were caught up in the general cataclysm of the twelfth century B.C.E. Out of the ruins emerged a society that was much less centralized, wealthy, or powerful but possessed an extraordinary dynamism.

The Archaic Age was an age of experimentation. Propelled by demographic and political pressures and inspired by the legends of vanished heroes, Greeks began in the eighth century B.C.E. to recast traditions and techniques acquired from their ancient neighbors into new forms. The multiplicity of independent communities, their relative isolation, and their differing traditions created a wide spectrum of political forms, social structures, and cultural values. Yet from Sicily to Asia Minor, Greeks felt themselves united by a common language, a common cultural heritage, and a common commitment to individual freedom within the community, whether that freedom was protected within a monarchy, a tyranny, an oligarchy, or a democracy. That commitment to freedom, fostered in the hoplite ranks, protected in the assembly, and increasingly expressed in poetry and sculpture, hung in the balance as Darius and the Persians marched westward.

QUESTIONS FOR REVIEW

1. What social and geographic factors shaped Greek culture in the age of the *Iliad* and the *Odyssey*?
2. What social forces spurred colonization, and what impact did colonization have on Archaic Greek civilization?
3. What do the gods, myths, and art of the Greek people reveal about their lives?
4. How did the Corinthian, Spartan, and Athenian cultures differ, and why did these city-states evolve in such different directions?

KEY TERMS

colonization, *p. 33*
democracy, *p. 40*
ethnos, *p. 31*
eunomia, *p. 37*
hoplites, *p. 32*

kouros, *p. 35*
Linear B, *p. 28*
Minoan civilization, *p. 26*
Mycenaean, *p. 28*
oligarchy, *p. 31*

phalanx, *p. 32*
polis, *p. 31*
tyrants, *p. 33*

DISCOVERING WESTERN CIVILIZATION ONLINE

You can obtain more information about early Greece at the Websites listed below. See also the Companion Website that accompanies this text, www.ablongman.com/kishlansky, which contains an online study guide and additional resources.

General Websites
The Perseus Digital Project
www.perseus.tufts.edu/
A digital library dedicated to all aspects of ancient Greek civilization.

Thomas R. Martin, An Overview of Classical Greek History
www.perseus.tufts.edu/cgi-bin/ptext?doc=1999.04.0009
This page of The Perseus Digital Project includes an extremely detailed outline of Greek history up to the death of Alexander, with wonderful links to other sources.

Greece in the Bronze Age

Palace of Knossos in Minoan Crete

www.dilos.com/region/crete/kn_01.html

A site devoted to the city of Knossos.

Bureaucrats and Barbarians

www.wsu.edu/~dee/MINOA/CONTENTS.HTM

A site devoted to Minoan and Mycenean civilizations.

Archaic Greece

The Ancient Greek World Index

www.museum.upenn.edu/Greek_World/Index.html

A comprehensive site dedicated to ancient Greece from the University of Pennsylvania Museum.

The British Museum Compass

www.thebritishmuseum.ac.uk/compass/

Search the British Museum Collection, which includes Greek antiquities.

Educated Women in Ancient Society

w3.arizona.edu/~ws/ws200/fall97/grp3/grp3.htm

A site devoted to elite women in Greece and their education.

Classical Myth: The Ancient Sources

web.uvic.ca/grs/bowman/myth/

A site devoted to classical mythology with iconography of Greek mythical figures.

A Tale of Three Cities

The Ancient City of Athens

www.Indiana.edu/~kglowack/athens/

A site dedicated to ancient Athens including architecture and sources.

Everything Spartan, Lakonian, and Messenian

www.geocities.com/Athens/Aegean/7849

A site dedicated to Sparta.

The Aegean Map of Greece

www.agn.gr/hellas/map.htm

A Greek government site with an interactive map of Greek locations including historical and modern information.

The Coming of Persia

Internet Ancient History Sourcebook: Persia

www.fordham.edu/halsall/ancient/asbook05.html

A site devoted to sources of ancient Persian history.

SUGGESTIONS FOR FURTHER READING

General Reading

S. B. Pomeroy, et. al. *Ancient Greece: A Political, Social, and Cultural History* (Oxford: Oxford University Press, 1998). An important introduction to Greek society and culture.

Greece in the Bronze Age to 800 B.C.E.

M. I. Finley, *Early Greece: The Bronze and Archaic Ages,* 2d ed. (New York: W. W. Norton, 1982). A very readable overview by a leading Greek historian.

Susan Langdon, ed. *New Light on a Dark Age: Exploring the Culture of Geometric Greece* (Columbia, MO: University of Missouri Press, 1997). Current essays on every aspect of society and culture in Dark Age Greece.

N. K. Sandars, *The Sea Peoples* (New York: Thames & Hudson, 1985). A survey of the controversy over the crisis of the twelfth century B.C.E.

William Taylour, *The Mycenaeans* (London: Thames & Hudson, 1990). General overview of Mycenaean civilization and daily life based on archaeology.

Archaic Greece, 800–500 B.C.E.

John Boardman, *The Greeks Overseas* (New York: Thames & Hudson, 1982). A description of varieties of Greek involvement abroad and their effects on Greece by a distinguished archaeologist.

———, *Greek Sculpture: Archaic Period* (New York: Thames & Hudson, 1985). A well-illustrated survey of early Greek sculpture.

Walter Burkert, *Structure and History in Greek Mythology and Ritual* (Berkeley: University of California Press, 1980). Burkert relates myth and religion to society and history.

Eva C. Keuls, *The Reign of the Phallus: Sexual Politics in Ancient Athens* (New York: Harper & Row, 1985). A controversial study of sexual politics.

Catherine Morgan, *Early Greek States beyond the Polis* (NewYork: Routledge, 2003). A reevaluation of the relationship between ethne and polis in the Archaic period.

S. B. Pomeroy, *Families in Classical and Hellenistic Greece: Representation and Realities* (Oxford: Oxford University Press, 1999). A history of the family in Greece by a leading feminist historian.

Anthony Snodgrass, *Archaic Greece: The Age of Experiment* (Totowa, NJ: Biblio Distribution Center, 1980). An excellent survey of the creative achievements of the Archaic period.

Christopher Tadgell, *Hellenic Classicism: The Ordering of Form in the Ancient Greek World.* (New York: Whitney Library of Design, 1998). A survey of Greek art and architecture to the construction of Athens' Acropolis.

A Tale of Three Cities

Paul Cartledge, *Sparta and Lakonia: A Regional History 1300–362 B.C.* 2nd ed. (New York: Routledge, Chapman & Hall, 2002). The best survey of Spartan history.

J. B. Salmon, *Wealthy Corinth: A History of the City to 338 B.C.* (New York: Oxford University Press, 1984). A comprehensive history of early Corinth.

David Whitehead, *The Demes of Attica (ca. 508–250 B.C.)* (Princeton, NJ: Princeton University Press, 1986). An excellent study of Athenian politics and society.

For a list of additional titles related to this chapter's topics, please see www.ablongman.com/kishlansky.

Chapter 3

CLASSICAL AND HELLENISTIC GREECE, 500–100 B.C.E.

The Visual Record

ALEXANDER AT ISSUS

The centuries of Greek glory opened and closed with war with Persia. The invasion of the Greek mainland by Darius I in 490 B.C.E. pitted the greatest empire the West had ever known against a few small, mutually suspicious states. His failure created among the Greeks a new belief in the superiority of the Greek world over the barbarian and of free men over Eastern despots. Darius III (336–330 B.C.E.) suffered a far more devastating defeat than his ancestor at the hands of Alexander the Great (336–323 B.C.E.) and a combined Greek army 157 years later. Darius I had lost his pride. Darius III lost his empire and, shortly afterward, his life.

Alexander had announced his expedition as a campaign to punish the Persians for their invasion of Greece over a century and a half earlier. Greeks rightly viewed Alexander's victory at Issus in 333 B.C.E. as the beginning of the end for the Persians, and it was long celebrated by Greek poets and artists. The most famous of these was Philoxenus of Eretria, whose paintings marked the high point of Greek pictorial art. His

masterpiece, like all other Greek paintings executed on wood, is long vanished. In the first century B.C.E., however, a wealthy Roman commissioned a mosaic copy of the painting for his villa at Pompeii in southern Italy. The mosaic, measuring some 16 feet by 8 feet and containing 1.5 million stones, each the size of a grain of rice, is itself a masterpiece. It is also a faithful copy of Philoxenus's painting, which a Roman critic had characterized as "surpassed by none."

In muted tones of red, brown, black, and yellow, Philoxenus captures this most dramatic moment of the battle. Alexander, with reckless disregard for his own safety, has

routed the Persians' left flank, cutting Darius's Greek mercenaries to pieces, scattering his Persian guard, and forcing Darius to flee for his life. The artist's use of bold foreshortening renders the rear of the horse in the center almost three dimensional as it runs in blind fury toward Darius's chariot. Although the entire scene is wildly chaotic, each man and each mount is portrayed as an individual, with his own expression of emotion and his own part to play in the violent action.

The young Alexander exudes the reckless courage and violence for which he was so famous. Yet he is not the center of the composition. That place of honor goes to Darius, whose kindly, tortured face looks back as his horses pull his chariot to safety. His hand stretches out in helpless sympathy toward the young Persian who has thrown himself between his king and Alexander, taking through his chest the spear that the Greek king had intended for the Persian ruler.

The artist has not depicted a simple juxtaposition of civilization against barbarity. Greeks fought on both sides at Issus, just as they had in the Persian wars of the fifth century B.C.E. Nor did Alexander's warriors despise their Persian enemies. Philoxenus's depictions of Darius and Alexander reflect the complexity of the situation. A similar degree of complexity characterized the entire panorama of classical Greek history.

Looking Ahead

The victories over the Persian forces of Darius and his successors brought an unprecedented period of political and cultural freedom and creativity, but also a deadly rivalry between Athens and Sparta, the leaders of the victorious Greeks. Only a generation after Athenian and Spartan troops had faced the Persians, they fought each other in a long and futile war. This left the Greek world exhausted and easy prey for the ambitious Macedonian dynasty, which nevertheless spread Greek culture through the Eastern Mediterranean and western Asia. ➤

WAR AND POLITICS IN THE FIFTH CENTURY B.C.E.

The vast Persian army moving west in 490 B.C.E. threatened the fruits of three centuries of Greek political, social, and cultural experimentation. The shared ideal of freedom within community and the common bond of language and culture seemed no basis on which to build an effective resistance to the great Persian Empire. Moreover, Darius I was not marching against the Greeks as such. Few Greek states other than Athens had supported the Ionians against their Persian conquerors. Many Greeks saw the Persians as potential allies or even rulers who were preferable to their more powerful Greek neighbors and to rivals within their own states. Separated by political traditions, intercity rivalries, and cultural differences, the Greeks did not feel any sense of national or ethnic unity. Particular interest, rather than patriotism or love of freedom, determined which cities opposed the Persian march. In the end, only Eretria, a badly divided Athens, and the small town of Plataea were prepared to refuse the Persian king's demand for gifts of earth and water, the traditional symbols of submission.

The Persian Wars

Initially, the Persian campaign followed the pattern established in Ionia. In the autumn of 490 B.C.E., Darius quickly destroyed the city of Eretria and carried off its population in captivity. The victorious Persian forces, numbering perhaps 20,000 infantrymen and mounted archers, then landed at the Bay of Marathon. Even with around 600 Plataeans, the total Athenian force was no more than half that of its enemies, but the Greeks were better armed and commanded the hills facing the Marathon plain on which the Persian troops had massed. The Athenians also benefited from the leadership of Miltiades (ca. 544–489 B.C.E.), an experienced soldier who had served Darius and who knew the Persian's strengths and weaknesses. For over a week, the two armies faced each other in a battle of nerves. Growing dissension in the Athenian ranks finally led the Greek generals to make a desperate and unexpected move. Abandoning the high ground, the Athenian hoplites rushed in disciplined phalanxes over almost a mile of open fields and then attacked the amazed Persian forces at a run. Although the Persians broke through the center of the Greek lines, the Athenians routed the Persian flanks and then turned in, enveloping the invaders in a deadly trap. In a few hours it was all over. Six thousand Persians lay dead, while fewer than 200 Athenians were buried in the heroes' grave that still marks the Marathon plain. The Persians retreated to their ships and sailed for the Bay of Phalerum near Athens, hoping to attack the city itself before its victorious troops could return. However, the Athenians, though exhausted from the battle, rushed the 23 miles home in under eight hours, beating the Persian fleet. When the Persians learned that they had lost the race, they turned their ships for Asia.

The almost miraculous victory at Marathon had three enormous consequences for Athens and for Greece in general.

First, it established the superiority of the hoplite phalanx as the finest infantry formation in the Mediterranean world. Second, Greeks expanded this belief in military superiority to a faith in the general superiority of Greeks over the "barbarians" (those who spoke other languages). Finally, by proving the value of the citizen army, the victory of the Athenians solidified and enhanced the democratic reforms of Cleisthenes.

Common citizens were determined that the victory won by the hoplite phalanx at Marathon should not be lost to an aristocratic faction at home. To guard against this danger, the Athenian assembly began to practice **ostracism,** a ten-year exile without loss of property, which was imposed on those who threatened to undermine the constitution of Cleisthenes. Each year, every Athenian citizen had the opportunity to write on a potsherd (in Greek, *ostrakon*) the name of the man he most wished to leave Attica. If at least 6,000 citizens voted, the state sent the individual receiving the most votes into temporary exile. No charges or accusations had to be made, much less proven. Anyone who had offended the Athenians or who, by his prominence, seemed a threat to democracy could be ostracized. At the same time, Athenians also began to select their chief officers not simply by direct election but by lot. This practice prevented any individual from rising to power by creating a powerful faction. Themistocles (ca. 528–426 B.C.E.), the son of a noble father and a non-Greek mother, took the lead in using the tools of ostracism and selection by lot to hold the aristocratic factions at bay.

Thermopylae and Salamis

Occupied by problems elsewhere in their vast empire and by the unexpected death of Darius I in 486 B.C.E., the Persians paid little attention to Greece for six years. After Darius's death, his son Xerxes (486–465 B.C.E.) began to amass foodstuffs, weapons, and armies for a land assault on his Greek enemies. Though some Greek states more or less willingly allied themselves with the Persians, the others met in Sparta in 481 B.C.E. to plan resistance. The allies agreed that the Spartans would take command of the combined land and sea forces.

Although larger than those mustered by Athens against Darius, the Greek forces were puny compared with Xerxes' infantry and 1,000 light and highly maneuverable Ionian and Phoenician ships. The Spartan commanders sought a strategic point at which the numerical superiority of the Persian forces would be neutralized. The choice fell on the narrow pass of Thermopylae and the adjacent Euboean strait. While a select force of hoplites held the pass, the Greek fleet, following a strategy devised by the Athenian leader Themistocles, harried the larger Persian one. Neither action produced a Greek victory, but none could have been expected.

At Thermopylae, the Greeks held firm for days against wave after wave of assaulting troops. Finally, Greek allies of the Persians showed them a narrow mountain track by which they were able to attack the Greek position from the rear. Seeing that all was lost, the Spartan king Leonidas (490–480 B.C.E.) sent most of his allies home. Then he and

■ The Persian Wars. Greeks fought on both sides in the Persian Wars, while many others remained neutral.

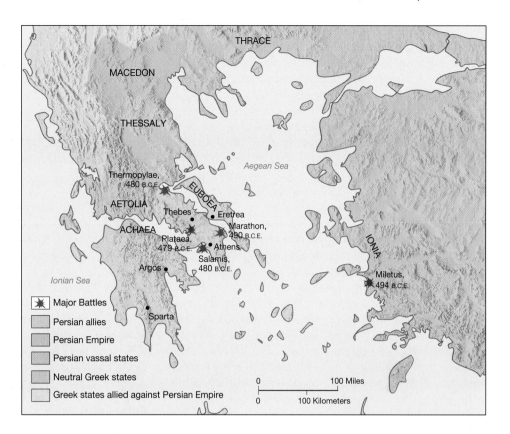

THRACE

MACEDON

THESSALY

Aegean Sea

Thermopylae, 480 B.C.E.

EUBOEA

AETOLIA

Thebes • • Eretrea

ACHAEA

Marathon, 490 B.C.E.

Plataea, 479 B.C.E.

• Athens

Salamis, 480 B.C.E.

Argos •

Ionian Sea

IONIA

Miletus, 494 B.C.E.

✸ Major Battles

Persian allies

Persian Empire

Persian vassal states

Neutral Greek states

Greek states allied against Persian Empire

Sparta •

0   100 Miles

0   100 Kilometers

his 300 Spartan equals faced certain death with a casual disdain characterized by the comment made by one Spartan equal. Told that when the Persians shot their arrows, they were so numerous that they hid the sun, the Spartan replied, "Good. If the Persians hide the sun, we shall have our battle in the shade."

While the Persian troops were blocked at Thermopylae, their fleet was being battered by fierce storms in the Euboean straits and harassed by the heavier Greek ships. Here, the Greeks learned that in close quarters they could stand up to Xerxes' Phoenician navy. This lesson proved vital a short time later. While the Persian army burned Athens and occupied Attica, Themistocles lured Xerxes' fleet into the narrow strait between Salamis and the mainland. There, the slower Greek vessels bottled up the larger and vastly more numerous enemy ships and cut them to pieces.

After Salamis, Xerxes lost his appetite for fighting Greeks. Without his fleet he could not supply a vast army far from home in hostile territory. Leaving a force to do what damage it could, he led the bulk of his army back to Persia. At Athenian urging, the Greek allies under Leonidas's kinsman Pausanias (d. ca. 470 B.C.E.) met the Persians at Plataea in 479 B.C.E. Once again, hoplite discipline and Greek determination overcame the enemy's numerical superiority. Athenian sea power and Spartan infantry had proven invincible. Soon the Athenians were taking the offensive, liberating the Ionian cities of Asia Minor and, in the process, laying the foundations of an Athenian empire that was every bit as threatening to their neighbors as that of Xerxes.

The Athenian Empire

Sparta, not Athens, should have emerged as the leader of the Greek world after 479 B.C.E. However, the constant threat of a helot revolt and the desire of the members of Sparta's Peloponnesian League to go their separate ways left Sparta too preoccupied with internal problems to fill the power vacuum left by the Persian defeat.

Athens, on the other hand, was only too ready to take the lead in bringing the war home to the Persians. With Sparta out of the picture, the Athenian fleet was the best hope of liberating the Aegean from Persians and pirates. Athenian propaganda emphasized the Persian menace and Ionian solidarity.

The Delian League. Athens accepted control in 478 B.C.E. of what historians have come to call the **Delian League,** after the island of Delos, a religious center that housed the league's treasury. Athens and some of the states with navies provided ships; others contributed annual payments to the league. Initially, the league pursued the war against the Persians, driving them back along the Aegean and the Black Seas. At the same time, Athens hurriedly rebuilt its defensive fortifications, a move that Sparta and other states correctly interpreted as directed more against them than against the Persians.

Athens's domination of the Delian League ensured its prosperity. Attica, with its fragile agriculture, depended on Black Sea wheat, and the league kept these regions under Athenian control. Since Athens received not only cash "contributions" from league members but also half of the spoils taken in battle, the state's public coffers were filled. The new riches made possible the reconstruction of the city, which had been burned by the Persians, into the most magnificent city of Greece.

The league was too vital to Athenian prosperity to stand and fall with the Persian threat. The drive against the Persian Empire began to falter after a league expedition to Egypt in 454 B.C.E. ended in total defeat. Discouraged by this and other setbacks, the Athenian Callias, acting for the league, apparently concluded a peace treaty with Persia in 449 B.C.E., making the alliance no longer necessary. For a brief moment it appeared that the Delian League might disband. But it was too late. The league had become an empire, and Athens's allies were its subjects.

Athenian Imperialism. The Athenian empire was an economic, judicial, religious, and political union that was held together by military might. Athens controlled the flow of grain through the Hellespont to the Aegean, ensuring its own supply and heavily taxing cargoes to other cities. Athens controlled the law courts of member cities and used them to repress anti-Athenian groups. Rich and poor Athenian citizens alike acquired territory throughout the empire. The rich took over vast estates confiscated from local opponents of Athenian dominance, while the poor replaced hostile populations in the colonies. Control over this empire depended on the Athenian fleet to enforce cooperation. Athenian garrisons were established in each city, and "democratic" puppet governments ruled according to the wishes of the garrison commanders. Revolt, resignation from the league, or refusal to pay the annual tribute resulted in brutal suppression. Persian tyranny had hardly been worse than Athenian imperialism.

Private and Public Life in Athens

During the second half of the fifth century B.C.E., Athens, enriched by tribute from its over 150 subject states, was a vital, crowded capital that drew merchants, artisans, and laborers from throughout the Greek world. At its height, the total population of Athens and surrounding Attica numbered perhaps 350,000, although probably fewer than 60,000 were citizens—adult males qualified to own land and participate in Athenian politics. Over one-quarter of the total population were slaves. Great landowners, unable to force ordinary freemen to work their estates, had turned to slave labor. Slaves were also vital in mining and other forms of craft and industrial work.

Greek slaves were not distinguished by race, ethnicity, or physical appearance. Anyone could become a slave. Prisoners of war, foreigners who failed to pay taxes, and victims of pirate raids could all end up on the auction blocks of the ancient world. Slaves were as much the property of their owners as land, houses, cattle, and sheep were. Many masters treated their slaves well, but they were under no obligation to do so, and beatings, sexual exploitation, tattooing, starvation, and shackling were all too common.

Metics. Roughly half of Athens's free population were foreigners—*metoikoi,* or **metics.** These were primarily Greek

citizens of the tributary states of the empire, but they might also be peoples from Africa or from Asia Minor, such as Lydians. The number of metics increased after the middle of the fifth century B.C.E.—both because of the flood of foreigners into the empire's capital and because Athenian citizenship was restricted to persons with two parents who were of citizen families. Metics could not own land in Attica, nor could they participate directly in politics. They were required to have a citizen protector and to pay a small annual tax. Otherwise, they were free to engage in every form of activity.

Women. More than half of those born into citizen families were entirely excluded from public life. These were the women who controlled and directed the vital sphere of the Athenian home, but who were considered citizens only for purposes of marriage, transfer of property, and procreation. From birth to death, every female citizen lived under the protection of a male guardian, either a close relative such as a father or brother, or a husband or son. Women spent almost their entire lives in the inner recesses of the home. Fathers arranged marriages, which were contracted to produce legitimate children and acquire wealth through dowries. A wife had no control over her dowry,

■ On this fifth-century B.C.E. Athenian vase women are depicted making preparations for a wedding.

which passed to her son. In the event of divorce or the death of her husband, the woman and her dowry returned to her father.

An honorable Athenian woman stayed at home and managed her husband's household. Only the poorest citizens sent their wives and daughters to work in the marketplace or the fields. For women, even the most casual contact with other men without permission was strictly forbidden, although men were expected to engage in various sorts of extramarital affairs. In the words of one Athenian male, "Hetairai we have for our pleasure, mistresses for the refreshment of our bodies, but wives to bear us legitimate children and to look after the house faithfully." The household, as Athenians never tired of repeating, was the foundation of all society.

Freedom in Community.   Male control over women may have resulted in part from fear. Women were identified with the forces of nature, which included both positive forces such as fertility and life and negative forces such as chaotic irrationality, which threatened civilization. These two poles were epitomized by the cult of Dionysus. He was the god of wine, lifeblood, and fertility, but he was also the deity whose female devotees, the *maenads,* were portrayed as worshipping him in a state of frenzied savagery that could include tearing children and animals limb from limb.

The male citizens of fifth-century B.C.E. Athens were free to an extent previously unknown in the world. But Athenian freedom was freedom *in* community, not freedom *from* community. The essence of their freedom lay in their participation in public life, especially self-government, which was their passion. This participation was always within a complex network of familial, social, and religious connections and obligations. Each person belonged to a number of groups: a deme, a tribe, a family, various religious associations, and occupational groups. Each of these communities placed different and even contradictory demands on its members. The impossibility of satisfying all of these demands, of responding to the special interests of each, forced citizens to make hard choices, to set priorities, and to balance conflicting obligations. This process of selection was the essence of Athenian freedom, a freedom that, unlike that of the modern world, was based not on individualism but on a multitude of collectivities. The sum of these overlapping groupings was Athenian society, in which friends and opponents alike were united.

Unity did not imply equality. Even in fifth-century B.C.E. Athens, not all Athenians were socially or economically equal. Most were farmers who looked to military service as a means of increasing their meager income. Others engaged in trade or industry, although metics, with their commercial contacts in their cities of origin, dominated much of these activities in Athens. However, the aristocracy was still strong, and most of the popular leaders of the century came from the ranks of old wealth and influence. Still, sovereignty lay not with these aristocrats but with the demos—the people.

In theory the adult male citizens of Athens were its sovereigns. Since the time of Solon, they had formed the **ekklesia,** or assembly. On particularly solemn occasions, as many as 6,000 citizens might convene in the *pnyx,* the meeting place of the assembly. They also made up the large juries, always composed of several hundred citizens, who decided legal cases less on law than on the political merits of the case and the quality of the orators who pleaded for each side. Such large bodies were too unwieldy to deal with the daily tasks of government. Therefore, control of these tasks fell to the council, or *boule,* composed of 500 members selected by lot by the tribes; the magistrates, who were also chosen by lot; and ten military commanders or generals, the only major officeholders who were elected rather than chosen at random.

Demagogues.   Paradoxically, the resolute determination of Athenian democrats to prevent individuals from acquiring too much power helped to create a series of extraconstitutional power brokers. Since most offices were filled by lot and turned over frequently, real political leadership came not from officeholders but from generals and from popular leaders. These so-called demagogues, while at times holding high office, exercised their power through their speaking skills, informal networks, and knowledge of how to get things done. Demagogues tended to be wealthy aristocrats who acquired this knowledge through their willingness to volunteer on committees or serve as unpaid government workers or in minor elected offices. Governing an empire demanded skill, energy, and experience, but Athenian democracy was formally run by amateurs. Small wonder that the city's public life was dominated by these popular leaders.

Pericles and Athens

For 30 years, one individual dominated Athenian public life: the general Pericles (ca. 495–429 B.C.E.), a great orator and successful military commander who led Athens during the decades of its greatest glory. Athens's system of radical democracy reached its zenith under his leadership, even while Athens's imperial program drew it into a long and fatal war against Sparta, the only state powerful enough to resist it.

Pericles was descended from the Alcmaeonids, a leading Athenian aristocratic family. Nevertheless, as one ancient author put it, he "took his side, not with the rich and the few, but with the many and the poor." Pericles acquired intimate knowledge of government through long service on various public works projects, projects that provided lucrative income to poorer citizens. He was also president of the commission responsible for constructing the great ivory and gold statue of Athena that stood in the Parthenon, the main temple in Athens. He served on the commission that built the Lyceum, or city exercise center, and the Parthenon itself. These enormous projects won him a great popular following while giving him an intimate knowledge of public finance and the details of Athenian government. He enhanced his position further through his great powers of persuasion.

Pericles never ruled Athens. As a general he could only carry out the orders of the ekklesia and the boule, and as a citizen he could only attempt to persuade his fellows. Still, he was largely responsible for the extension of Athenian democracy to all free citizens. Under his influence, Athens abolished the last property requirements for officeholding. He convinced the state to pay those who served on juries, thus making it possible for even the poorest citizens to participate in this important part of Athenian government. But he was also responsible for a restriction of citizenship to those whose mothers and fathers had both been Athenians. Such a law would have denied citizenship to many of the most illustrious Athenians of the sixth century B.C.E., including his own ancestors. The law also prevented citizens of Athens's subject states from developing a real stake in the fate of the empire.

Pericles believed that the Athenian empire had to be preserved at all costs. This policy ultimately drew Athens into deadly conflict with Sparta. The first clash between the two rival powers came around 460 B.C.E. at Megara, which lay between the Peloponnesus and Attica. The Athenians emerged victorious, checking Sparta and absorbing Megara, Aegina, and Boeotia. However, in 446 B.C.E., after the Athenian defeat in Egypt, Megara and Boeotia rebelled, and Sparta invaded the disputed region. Unable to face this new threat at home after the disastrous loss abroad, in 445 B.C.E. the Athenians, under the leadership of Pericles, concluded a peace treaty with Sparta whereby Athens abandoned all of its continental possessions. The treaty was meant to last for 30 years, but it held for only 14.

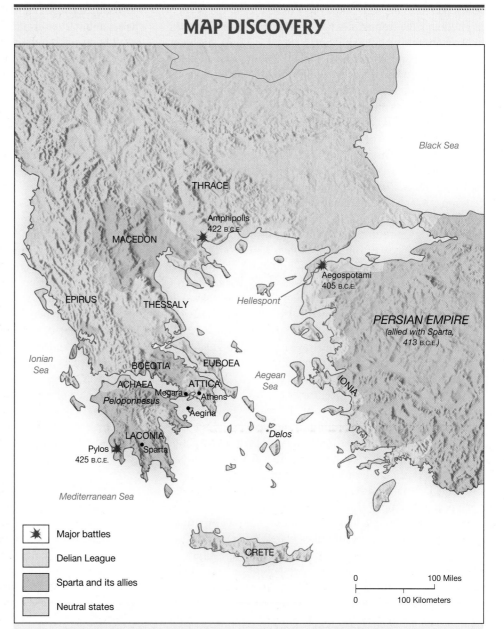

MAP DISCOVERY

The Delian League and the Peloponnesian War

When Athens turned the Delian League into its own empire, the resulting war pitted the Attica city-state against the combined forces of Sparta and Persia. Examine the extent of the Delian League, Sparta and its allies, and the neutral states. Why would Sparta and its allies feel threatened strategically and economically by the Delian League? Why was an alliance with Persia a vital part of Spartan strategy? What threats faced those states that remained neutral?

The two great powers were eager to preserve the peace, but the whole Greek world was a tinderbox ready to burst into flame. The spark came from an unexpected direction. In 435 B.C.E., Corinth and its colony Corcyra on the Adriatic Sea came to blows, and Corcyra sought the assistance of Athens. The Athenians agreed to a defensive alliance with Corcyra and assisted it in defeating its enemy. This assistance infuriated Corinth, an ally of Sparta, and in 432 B.C.E., the Corinthians convinced the Spartans that Athens's imperial ambitions were insatiable. The next year, Sparta invaded Attica, and the Peloponnesian War, which would destroy both great powers, had begun.

The Peloponnesian War

The Peloponnesian War was actually a series of wars and rebellions. Athens and Sparta waged two devastating ten-year wars, from 431 B.C.E. to 421 B.C.E. and then again from 414 B.C.E. to 404 B.C.E. At the same time, cities in each alliance took advantage of the wars to revolt against the great powers, eliciting terrible vengeance from both Athens and Sparta. Within many of the Greek city-states, oligarchs and democrats waged bloody civil wars for control of their governments. Moreover, between 415 and 413 B.C.E., Athens attempted to expand its empire in Sicily, an attempt that ended in disaster. Before it was over, the Peloponnesian War had become an international war, with Persia entering the fray on the side of Sparta. In the end, there were no real victors, only victims.

Initially, Sparta and Athens both hoped for quick victory. Sparta's strength was its army, and its strategy was to invade Attica, devastate the countryside, and force the Athenians into an open battle. Pericles urged Athens to a strategy of conserving its hoplite forces while exploiting its naval strength. Athens was a naval power and, with its empire and control of Black Sea grain, could hold out for years behind its fortifications, the great walls linking Athens to its port of Piraeus. At the same time, the Athenian fleet could launch raids along the coast of the Peloponnesus, thus bringing the war home to the Spartans. Pericles hoped in this way to outlast the Spartans.

The Archidamian War. The first phase of the war, called the Archidamian War after the Spartan king Archidamus (431–427 B.C.E.), was indecisive. Sparta pillaged Attica but could not breach the great wall or starve Athens. In 430 B.C.E., the Spartans received unexpected help in the form of plague, which ravaged Athens for five years. By the time it ended in 426 B.C.E., as much as one-third of the Athenian population had died, including Pericles. Still Athens held out, establishing bases encircling the Peloponnesus and urging Spartan helots and allies to revolt.

At Pylos in 425 B.C.E., the Athenian generals Cleon and Demosthenes captured a major force of Spartan equals. The Spartans offset this defeat by capturing the city of Amphipolis on the northern Aegean. The defeated Athenian commander, Thucydides (d. ca. 401 B.C.E.), was exiled for his failure and retired to Spartan territory to write his great history of the war. Exhausted by a decade of death and destruction, the two sides contracted peace in 421 B.C.E. Although Athens was victorious in that its empire was intact, the peace changed nothing, and tensions festered for five years.

THE TWO FACES OF ATHENIAN DEMOCRACY

Early in the Peloponnesian War, Thucydides summarized the virtues of Athenian democracy in the speech he ascribes to Pericles in honor of those who died in the first year of the war. By 416 B.C.E., the sixteenth year of the Peloponnesian War, Athenian imperialism no longer even paid lip service to the ideals of democracy or freedom. Thucydides illustrates this in his reconstructed debate between representatives of the Spartan colony of Melos, which had attempted to remain neutral, and representatives of the Athenians, who demanded their surrender and enslavement.

Focus Questions
What limits did the Athenians place on the ideal of democracy? How did the Athenians justify violence to maintain their empire?

Pericles' Funeral Oration
Our constitution is called a democracy because power is in the hands not of a minority but of the whole people. When it is a question of settling private disputes, everyone is equal before the law; when it is a question of putting one person before another in positions of public responsibility, what counts is not membership of a particular class, but the actual ability which the man possesses. No one, so long as he has it in him to be of service to the state, is kept in political obscurity because of poverty.

The Melian Debate
ATHENIANS: You know as well as we do that, when these matters are discussed by practical people, the standard of justice depends on the equality of power to compel and that in fact the strong do what they have the power to do and the weak accept what they have to accept.

MELIANS: And how could it be just as good for us to be the slaves as for you to be the masters?

ATHENIANS: You, by giving in, would save yourselves from disaster; we by not destroying you, would be able to profit from you.

MELIANS: So you would not agree to our being neutral, friends instead of enemies, but allies of neither side?

ATHENIANS: No, because it is not so much your hostility that injures us; it is rather the case that, if we were on friendly terms with you, our subjects would regard that as a sign of weakness in us, whereas your hatred is evidence of our power.

Ultimately the Melians rejected Athens's demands, and shortly after the Athenians captured the city, they executed all the men and sold the women and children as slaves.

From Thucydides, *History of the Peloponnesian War.*

Alcibiades and the Sicilian Expedition.   After the peace of 421 B.C.E., Pericles' kinsman Alcibiades (ca. 450–404 B.C.E.) came to dominate the demos. Well-spoken, handsome, and brave but also vain, dissolute, and ambitious, Alcibiades led the city into disaster. Although he was a demagogue who courted popular support, he despised the people and schemed to overthrow the democracy. In 415 B.C.E., he urged Athens to expand its empire westward by attacking Syracuse, the most prosperous Greek city of Sicily, which had largely escaped the devastation of the Archidamian War. The expedition went poorly, and Alcibiades, accused at home of having profaned one of the most important Athenian religious cults, was ordered home. Instead, he fled to Sparta, where he began to assist the Spartans against Athens. The Sicilian expedition ended in disaster. Athens lost over 200 ships and 50,000 men. At the same time, Sparta resumed the war, this time with naval support provided by Persia.

Suddenly, Athens was fighting for its life. Alcibiades soon abandoned Sparta for Persia and convinced the Athenians that if they would abandon their democracy for an oligarchy, Persia would withdraw its support of Sparta. In 411 B.C.E., the desperate Athenian assembly established a brutal, antidemocratic oligarchy, but when the war continued, Athens, amid bitter factionalism, reestablished its democracy. The Persian king renewed his support for Sparta, sending his son Cyrus (ca. 424–401 B.C.E.) to coordinate the war against Athens. Under the Spartan general Lysander (d. 395 B.C.E.), Sparta and its allies finally closed in on Athens. Lysander captured the Athenian fleet in the Hellespont, destroyed it, and severed Athens's vital grain supply. Within months, Athens was entirely cut off from the outside world and starving. In 404 B.C.E., Sparta accepted Athens's unconditional surrender. Athens's fortifications came down, its empire vanished, and its fleet, except for a mere twelve ships, dissolved.

The Peloponnesian War showed not only the limitations of Athenian democracy but the potential brutality of oligarchy as well. More ominously, it demonstrated the catastrophic effects of disunity and rivalry among Greek cities of the Mediterranean.

ATHENIAN CULTURE IN THE HELLENIC AGE

Most of what we today call Greek is actually Athenian. Throughout the Hellenic age (the fifth and early fourth centuries B.C.E., as distinct from the Hellenistic period of roughly the later fourth through second centuries B.C.E.), the turbulent issues of democracy and oligarchy, war and peace, hard choices and conflicting obligations found expression in Athenian culture even as the glory of the Athenian empire was manifested in art and architecture. The great dramatists Aeschylus, Sophocles, and Euripides were Athenian, as were the sculptor Phidias, the Parthenon architects Ictinus and Callicrates, and the philosophers Socrates and Plato. To Athens came writers, artists, and thinkers from throughout the Greek world.

The Examined Life

A primary characteristic of Athenian culture was its critical and rational nature. In heated discussions in the assembly and the agora, the courtroom and the private symposium, Athenians and foreigners drawn to the city no longer looked to the myths and religion of the past for guidance. Secure in their identity and protected by the openness of their radical democracy, they began to examine the past and present and to question the foundations of traditional values. From this climate of inquiry emerged the traditions of moral philosophy and its cousin, history.

The Ionian interest in natural philosophy, the explanation of the universe in rational terms, continued throughout the fifth century B.C.E. But philosophers began also to turn their attention to the human world, in particular to the powers and limitations of the individual's mind and the individual's relationship with society. By the end of his life, the philosopher Heraclitus had become intrigued with the examination of the rational faculties themselves rather than what one could know with them. In part, this meant a search for personal, inner understanding that would lead to proper action within society—in other words, to the search for ethics based in reason. In part, too, such an inquiry led to a study of how to formulate arguments and persuade others through logic.

The Sophists.   In the political world of fifth-century B.C.E. Athens, rhetoric, the art of persuasion, was particularly important because it was the key to political influence. Teachers called **sophists** ("wise people") traveled throughout Greece, offering to provide an advanced education for a fee. Although the sophistic tradition later gained a negative reputation, teachers such as Gorgias (ca. 485–ca. 380 B.C.E.) and Protagoras (ca. 490–421 B.C.E.) trained young men not only in the art of rhetoric but also in logic. By exercising their students' minds with logical puzzles and paradoxical statements, the sophists taught a generation of wealthy Greeks the powers and complexities of human reason.

Socrates.   The teacher Socrates (ca. 470–399 B.C.E.) was considered by many of his contemporaries as but one more sophist, but he himself reacted against what he saw as the amoral and superficial nature of sophistic education. He was interested in the search for moral self-enlightenment urged by Heraclitus. "Know thyself" was Socrates' plea. An unexamined life, he argued, was not worth living. Socrates refused any pay for his teaching, arguing that he had nothing to teach. He knew nothing, he said, and was superior to the sophists only because he recognized his ignorance while they professed wisdom. Socrates' method infuriated his contemporaries. He would approach individuals who had reputations for wisdom or skill and then, through a series of disarmingly simple questions, force them to defend their beliefs. The inevitable result was that in their own words the outstanding sophists, politicians, and poets of the day demonstrated the inadequacy of the foundations of their beliefs.

■ This bust of Socrates portrays him with the traditional beard of the philosopher. His features display the tradition that this man, whose thoughts were the most beautiful, was nevertheless of remarkably homely appearance.

Since Socrates refused to commit any of his teaching to writing, we know of him only from the conflicting reports of his former students and opponents. One thing is certain, however: While demanding that every aspect of life be investigated, Socrates never doubted the moral legitimacy of the

Athenian state. Condemned to death in 399 B.C.E. on the trumped-up charges of corrupting the morals of the Athenian youth and introducing strange gods, he declined the opportunity to escape into exile. Rather than reject Athens and its laws, he drank the fatal potion of hemlock given him by the executioner.

Understanding the Past

The philosophical interest in human choices and social constraints found echo in the historical writing of the age. In particular, two writers established the spectrum of how to understand the past.

Herodotus.   Herodotus (ca. 484–420 B.C.E.), the first historian, was one of the many foreigners who found in Athens the intellectual climate and audience he needed to write an account of the Persian wars of the preceding generation. His book of inquiries, or *historia,* into the origins and events of the conflict between Greeks and Persians is the first true history. Herodotus had traveled widely in the eastern Mediterranean, collecting local stories and visiting famous temples, palaces, and cities. In his study, he presents a great panorama of the civilized world at the end of the sixth century B.C.E. Herodotus did not hesitate to report myths, legends, and outrageous tales. His faith in the gods was strong, and he believed that the gods intervene in human affairs. Still, he was more than just a good storyteller. Often, after reporting conflicting accounts, he would conclude, "Both stories are told and the reader may take his choice between them." In other cases, after recounting a particularly far-fetched account heard from local informants, he would comment, "Personally, I think this story is nonsense."

As Herodotus explained in his introduction, his purpose in writing was first to preserve the memory of the past by recording the achievements of both Greeks and eastern non-Greeks and second to show how the two came into conflict. It was this concern to explain, to go beyond mere storytelling, that earned Herodotus the designation "father of history." Herodotus was less interested in the mythic dimensions of the conflict than in the human, and his primary concern was the action of individuals under the press of circumstances. Ultimately, the Persian wars became for Herodotus the conflict between freedom and despotism, and he described with passion how different Greek states chose between the two.

Thucydides.   The story of the Peloponnesian War was recorded by a different sort of historian, one who focused more narrowly on the Greek world and on political power. Thucydides had been an Athenian general and a major actor in the first part of the Peloponnesian War until his exile in 425 B.C.E. He began his account at the very outbreak of the conflict, thus writing a contemporary record of the war rather than a history of it. As Herodotus is called the father of history, Thucydides might be called the first social scientist.

For Thucydides, the central subject was human society in action. He viewed the Greek states as acting out of rational self-interest. His favorite device for showing the development of such policies was the political set speech in which two opposing leaders attempt to persuade their fellow citizens on the proper course of action. Although fictitious by modern standards, these speeches penetrate to the heart of the tough political choices facing the opposing forces. This hard-nosed approach to political decisions continues to serve as a model to historians and practitioners of power politics.

Still, morality is always just below the surface of Thucydides' narrative. Even as he unflinchingly chronicles the collapse of morality and social order in the face of political expediency, he recognizes that this process will destroy his beloved Athens. In his account of the second phase of the war, Athens acts with the full arrogance of a tyrant. Its overwhelming pride leads it to attack and destroy its weaker neighbors and ultimately to invade Sicily, with disastrous results. In the later, unfinished chapters (Thucydides died shortly after Athens's final defeat), the Peloponnesian War takes on the characteristics of a tragedy. Here Thucydides, the ultimate political historian, shows the deep influence of the dominant literary tradition of his day: Greek drama.

Athenian Drama

Since the time of its introduction by Peisistratus in the middle of the sixth century B.C.E., drama had become popular, not only in Athens but throughout the Greek world. Plays formed part of the annual feast of Dionysus and dealt with mythic subject matter largely taken from the *Iliad* and the *Odyssey*. Three types of plays honored the Dionysian festival. Tragedies dealt with great men who failed because of flaws in their natures. Comedies were more directly topical and political. They parodied real Athenians, often by name, and amused even while making serious points in defense of democracy. Somewhere between tragedies and comedies, satyr plays remained closest to the Dionysian cult. In them, lecherous drunken satyrs, mythical half-man, half-goat creatures, interact with gods and men as they roam in search of Dionysus.

Aeschylus.   Only a handful of the hundreds of Greek plays written in the fifth century B.C.E. survive. The first of the great Athenian tragedians whose plays we know is Aeschylus (525–456 B.C.E.), a veteran of Marathon and an eyewitness of the battle of Salamis. His one surviving trilogy, the *Oresteia*, traces the fate of the family of Agamemnon, the Greek commander at Troy. The three plays of the trilogy explore the chain of violent acts, vengeance, and conflicting obligations that ultimately must be settled by rational yet divinely sanctioned law.

Sophocles.   Aeschylus's younger contemporary Sophocles (496–406 B.C.E.), the most successful of the fifth century B.C.E. tragedians, sought in his mature plays to express human character. He shows how humans make decisions and carry them out, constrained by their pasts, their weaknesses, and their

vices, but free nonetheless. Sophocles' message is endurance, acceptance of human responsibility and, at the same time, of the ways of the gods, who overrule people's plans. The heroine of *Antigone,* for whom the play is named, is the sister of Polynices, exiled son of King Oedipus of Thebes. Polynices has died fighting his city, and Creon, its new ruler, commands under penalty of death that Polynices' body be left unburied. This would mean that his soul would never find rest, the ultimate punishment for a Greek. Antigone, with determination and courage equal to her love for her brother, buries Polynices and is entombed alive for her crime. Here the conflict between the state, which claims the total obedience of its people, and the claims of familial love and religious piety meet in tragic conflict. Creon, warned by a prophet that he is offending heaven, orders Antigone's release, but it is too late. Rather than wait for death, she has already hanged herself.

Euripides.   Compared with Aeschylus and Sophocles, Euripides (485–406 B.C.E.) was far more original and daring in his subject matter and treatment of human emotions. His female characters were often wronged and seldom accepted their lot. His plays abound in plot twists and unexpected, violent outbursts. Passion, not reason, rules Euripides' world. His characters are less reconciled to their fates and less ready to accept the traditional gods:

> *Does someone say that there are gods in heaven?*
> *There are not, there are not—unless one chooses*
> *To follow old tradition like a fool.*

Greek Comedy.   Neither passion nor reason but politics rules the world of Greek comedy. Rather than the timelessness of the human condition, Athenian comic playwrights focused their biting satire on the political and social issues of the moment. Particularly, the comic genius Aristophanes (ca. 450–ca. 388 B.C.E.) used wit, imagination, vulgarity, and great poetic sensitivity to attack everything that offended him in his city. In his plays, he mocks and ridicules statesmen, philosophers, rival playwrights, and even the gods. His comedies are full of outrageous turns of plot, talking animals, obscene jokes and puns, and mocking asides. Yet Aristophanes was a deeply patriotic Athenian, dedicated to the democratic system and to the cause of peace. In *Lysistrata*, written in 411 B.C.E., after Athens had renewed the war against Sparta, the women of Greece force their men to make peace by conspiring to refuse them sex as long as war continues. Through the sharp satire and absurd plots of his plays, Aristophanes communicates his sympathy for ordinary people, who must match wits with the charlatans and pompous frauds who attempt to dominate Athens's public life.

Art and the Human Image

The humanity in Greek drama found its parallel in art. In the late sixth century B.C.E., a reversal of the traditional black-figure technique had revolutionized vase painting. Artists had begun to outline scenes on unfired clay and then fill in the background with black or brown glaze. The interior details of the figures were also added in black. The results were a much more lifelike art, a lighter, more natural coloring, and the possibility of more perspective, depth, and molding.

Sculpture reflected the same development toward balance and realism contained within an ideal of human form. The finest bronzes and marbles of the fifth century B.C.E. show freestanding figures whose natural vigor and force, even when they are engaged in strenuous exertion, are balanced by the placidity of their faces and their lack of emotion. The tradition established by the Athenian sculptor Phidias (ca. 500–ca. 430 B.C.E.) sought a naturalism in the portrayal of the human figure, which remained ideal rather than individual.

The greatest sculptural program of the fifth century B.C.E. was that produced for the Athenian acropolis. The reconstruction of the acropolis, which had been destroyed by the Persians, was the culmination of Athenian art. The result was the greatest complex of buildings in the ancient world. One entered the acropolis complex through the monumental *propylaea,* or gateway, a T-shaped structure approached by a flight of steps. From the top of the steps, one could glimpse both Phidias's great bronze statue of Athena Promachos in the center of the acropolis and, to the right, the Parthenon. As visitors entered the acropolis itself, they passed on the right the small temple of Athena as Victory. Continuing on the Sacred Way, one saw on the left the delicate Erechtheum, which housed the oldest Athenian cults. On the right, visitors were overawed by the Parthenon, a monument as much to Athens as to Athena. Even today, the ruined temple seems a rectangular embodiment of order, proportion, and balance. Every surface, from the floor to the columns to the horizontal beams, curves slightly. The spacing of the columns varies, and each leans slightly inward. Those at the rear are larger than those at the front to compensate for the effect of viewing them from a greater distance. The optical illusion of flatness, regularity, and repetition in the Parthenon was the intended effect.

An illusion, too, was the sense of overwhelming Athenian superiority and grandeur the acropolis was intended to convey. By the time the Erechtheum was completed in 406 B.C.E., however, the Athenian empire was all but destroyed, the city's population was devastated, and its democracy was imperiled. Two years later, Athens surrendered unconditionally to Sparta.

The intellectual and artistic accomplishments of Athens were as enduring as its empire proved ephemeral. Writers and artists alike focused their creative energies on human existence, seeking a proper proportion, order, and meaning, a blend of the practical and ideal, which Athens's political leaders lacked.

FROM CITY-STATES TO MACEDONIAN EMPIRE, 404–323 B.C.E.

The Peloponnesian War touched every aspect of Greek life. The war brought changes to the social and political structures of Greece by creating an enduring bitterness between the elites and the populace and a distrust of both democracy and

traditional oligarchy. The mutual exhaustion of Athens and Sparta left a vacuum of power in the Aegean. Finally, the war raised fundamental questions about the nature of politics and society throughout the Greek world.

Politics After the Peloponnesian War

Over the decades-long struggle, the conduct of war and the nature of politics had changed, bringing new problems for victor and vanquished alike. Lightly armed professional mercenaries willing to fight for anyone who was able to pay gradually replaced hoplite citizen soldiers as the backbone of the fighting forces. As war became more professional and protracted, it also became more brutal. The rise of mercenary armies also meant trouble for democracies such as Athens as well as for Sparta with its class of equals.

Spartan Imperialism.   Victory left Sparta no more capable of assuming leadership in 404 B.C.E. than it had been in 478 B.C.E. Years of war had reduced the population of equals to fewer than 3,000. The Spartans proved to be extremely unpopular imperialists. As reward for Persian assistance, Sparta returned the Ionian cities to Persian control. Elsewhere, it established hated oligarchies to rule in a way favorable to Sparta's interests. In Athens, a brutal tyranny of 30 men took control in 404 B.C.E. With Spartan support, they executed 1,500 democratic leaders and forced 5,000 more into exile. The Thirty Tyrants evoked enormous hatred and opposition. Within a year the exiles recaptured the city, restored democracy, and killed or expelled the tyrants.

Similar opposition to Spartan rule emerged throughout the Greek world, shattering the fragile peace created by Athens's defeat. For over 70 years, the Greek world boiled in constant warfare. Mutual distrust, fear of any city that seemed about to establish a position of clear superiority, and the machinations of the Persian Empire to keep Greeks fighting each other produced a constantly shifting series of alliances.

Thebes.   Persia turned against its former ally when, in 401 B.C.E., Sparta supported an unsuccessful attempt by Cyrus to unseat his brother Artaxerxes II. Soon the unlikely and unstable alliance of Athens, Corinth, Argos, Thebes, and Euboea, financed by Persia, entered a series of vicious wars against Sparta. The first round ended in Spartan victory, due to the shifting role of Persia, whose primary interest was the continued disunity of the Greeks. By 377 B.C.E., however, Athens had reorganized its league and, with Thebes as an ally, was able to break Spartan sea power. The decline of Sparta left a power vacuum that was soon filled by Thebes. Athens, concerned by this new threat, shifted alliances, making peace with its old enemy. However, Spartan military fortunes had so declined that when Sparta attacked Thebes in 371 B.C.E., its armies were destroyed and Spartan power was broken. The next year, Thebes invaded the Peloponnesus and freed Messenia, the foundation of Sparta's economic prosperity. Sparta never recovered. Deprived of its economic base, its body of equals reduced to a mere 800, and its fleet gone, Sparta never regained its historic importance.

Theban hegemony was short-lived. Before long, the same process of greed, envy, and distrust that had devastated the other Greek powers destroyed Thebes. Athens's reconstituted league disintegrated as members opposed Athenian attempts once more to convert a free association of states into an empire. By the 330s B.C.E., all of the Greek states had proven themselves incapable of creating stable political units larger than their immediate polis.

Philosophy and the Polis

The failure of Greek political forms, oligarchy and democracy alike, profoundly affected Athenian philosophers. Plato (ca. 428–347 B.C.E.), an aristocratic student of Socrates, grew up during the Peloponnesian War and had witnessed the collapse of the empire, the brutality of the Thirty Tyrants, the execution of Socrates, and the revival of the democracy and its imperialistic ambitions. From these experiences he developed a hatred for Athenian democracy and a profound distrust of ordinary people's ability to tell right from wrong. Disgusted with public life, Plato left Attica for a time and traveled in Sicily and Italy, where he encountered different forms of government and different philosophical schools. Around 387 B.C.E., he returned to Athens and opened the Academy, a school to provide Athenian youth with what he considered to be knowledge of what was true and good for the individual and the state.

Platonic Forms.   To transmit his teachings, Plato chose the unlikely literary form of the dialogue, in the form of discussions between his teacher, Socrates, and a variety of students and opponents. While Plato shared with his mentor the conviction that human actions had to be grounded in self-knowledge, Plato's philosophy extended much further. His arguments about the inadequacy of all existing forms of government and the need to create a new form of government through the proper education of elite philosopher rulers were part of a complex understanding of the universe and the individual's place in it.

Plato argued that true knowledge is impossible as long as it focuses on the constantly changing, imperfect world of everyday experience. Human beings can have real knowledge only of that which is eternal, perfect, and beyond the experience of the senses, the realm of what Plato called the **Forms.** One would know these Forms from one's memories of a previous existence when one's spirits had direct contact with the universe of the Forms. Plato believed that when one judged individuals or actions to be true or good or beautiful, one did so not because those individuals or actions were truly virtuous, but because one recognized that they participated in some way in the Idea or Form of truth or goodness or beauty.

According to Plato, the evils of the world, in particular the vices and failures of government and society, result from ignorance of the truth. Most people live as though chained in a cave in which all they can see are the shadows cast by a fire on the walls. In their ignorance they mistake these flickering, imperfect images for reality. Their proper ruler must be a philosopher, one who is not deceived by the shadows. The philosopher's task is to break their chains and turn them toward the source of the light so that they can see the world as it really is.

Aristotelian Empiricism.   Plato's idealist view (in the sense of the Ideas or Forms) of knowledge dominated much of ancient philosophy. However, his greatest student, Aristotle (384–322 B.C.E.), rejected this view in favor of **empiricism,** a philosophy rooted in observation of the natural world. Aristotle came from a medical family of northern Greece, and although he was a student in Plato's Academy for almost 20 years, he never abandoned observation for speculation. Systematic investigation and explanation characterize Aristotle's vast work, and his interests ranged from biology to statecraft to the most abstract philosophy. In each field he employed essentially the same method. He observed as many individual examples of the topic as possible and from these specific observations extracted general theories. His theories, whether on the nature of matter, the species of animals, the workings of the human mind, ethics, or the proper form of the state, are distinguished by clarity of logical thinking, precision in the use of terminology, and respect for the world of experience.

In human affairs, Aristotle recommended moderation. Unlike Plato, he did not regard any particular form of government as ideal. Rather, he concluded that the type of government ultimately mattered less than the balance between narrow oligarchy and radical democracy. Consistent with his belief that "virtue lies in a mean," he advocated governments composed of citizens who were neither extremely wealthy nor extremely poor. Moderation was the key to stability and justice. Yet, during the very years that Aristotle was teaching, the vacuum created by the failure of the Greek city-states was being filled by the growing Macedonian monarchy that finally ended a century of Greek warfare and, with it, the independence of the Greek city-states.

The Rise of Macedon

The polis had never been the only form of the Greek state. Alongside the city-states of Athens, Corinth, Syracuse, and Sparta were more decentralized ethne ruled by traditional hereditary chieftains and monarchs. Macedonia, in the northeast of the mainland, was one such ethnos. Its kings, chosen by the army from within a royal family, ruled in cooperation with nobles and clan leaders. The Macedonian people spoke a Greek dialect, and Macedonian kings and elite identified with Greek culture and tradition. Macedonia had long served as a buffer between the barbarians to the north and the Greek mainland, and its tough farmers and pastoralists were geared to constant warfare. As Athens, Sparta, and Thebes fought each other to mutual exhaustion, Macedonia under King Philip II (359–336 B.C.E.) moved into the resulting power vacuum.

■ A Roman copy of a Greek statue of Aristotle. Many ancient Greek sculptures are known only through Roman copies.

After some early military successes against northern barbarians, Philip, a skillful politician and outstanding military strategist, turned his attention to the south and relentlessly swallowed up one Greek state after another. In 338 B.C.E., Philip achieved a final victory at Chaeronea and established a new league, the League of Corinth. However, unlike all those that had preceded it, this league was no confederation of sovereign states. It was an empire ruled by a king and supported by wealthy citizens whose cooperation Philip rewarded well. This new model of government, a monarchy drawing its support from a wealthy elite, became a fixture of the Mediterranean world for over 2,000 years.

Philip's success was based on his powerful military machine, which combined both Macedonian military tradition and the new mercenary forces that had emerged over the past century in Greece. The heart of his army was the infantry trained in the use of pikes some 14 feet long—4 feet longer than those of the Greek hoplites. Macedonian phalanxes moved forward in disciplined ranks, pushing back their foes, whose shorter lances could not reach the Macedonians. When the enemy was contained, the Macedonian cavalry charged from the flank and cut them to pieces.

No sooner had Philip subdued Greece than he announced a campaign against Persia. He intended to lead a combined Greek force in a war of revenge and conquest to punish the great empire for its invasion of Greece 150 years earlier and its subsequent involvement in the Greek world. Before he could begin, however, he was cut down by an assassin's knife, leaving his 20-year-old son, Alexander (336–323 B.C.E.), to lead the expedition. Within 13 years, Alexander had conquered the world.

The Empire of Alexander the Great

Alexander, envisioning himself a new Achilles, sought to imitate and surpass that legendary hero of the *Iliad*. Alexander's military genius, dedication to his troops, reckless disregard for his own safety, and ability to move both men and supplies across vast distances at great speed enabled him to lead the war machine that Philip had developed on an odyssey of conquest that stretched from Asia Minor to India. In 334 B.C.E., the first year of his campaign, Alexander captured the Greek cities of Asia Minor. Then he continued east. At Gordium, according to legend, he confronted an ancient puzzle, a complex knot tied to the chariot of the ancient king of that city. Whoever could loosen the knot, the legend said, would become master of Asia. Alexander solved that puzzle, as he did all of his others, with his sword. Two months later, he defeated the Persian king Darius III at Issus and then headed south toward the Mediterranean coast and Egypt. After his victories there, he turned again to the north and entered Mesopotamia. At Gaugamela in 331 B.C.E., he defeated Darius a second, decisive time. Shortly afterward, Darius was murdered by the remnants of his followers. Alexander captured the Persian capital of Persepolis with its vast treasure and became the undisputed ruler of the vast empire.

The conquest of Persia was not enough. Alexander pushed on, intending to conquer the whole world. His armies marched eastward, subduing the rebellious Asian provinces of Bactria and Sogdiana. He negotiated the Khyber Pass from what is now Afghanistan into the Punjab, crossed the Indus River, and defeated the local Indian king. Everywhere he went, he reorganized or founded cities, entrusting them to loyal Macedonians and other Greeks and settling them with veterans of his campaigns, and then pushed on toward the unknown. On the banks of the Hyphasis River in what is now Pakistan, his Macedonian warriors finally halted. Worn out by years of bloody conquest and exhausting travel, they refused to go further. "If there is one thing above all others a successful man should know," their spokesman told Alexander, "it is *when to stop*." Furious but impotent, Alexander led his troops back to Persepolis in 324 B.C.E. Although Alexander was keenly disappointed, no mortal had ever before accomplished such a feat of conquest.

Binding Together an Empire

Alexander is remembered as a greater conqueror than ruler, but his plans for his reign, had he lived to complete them, might have won him equal fame. Unlike his Macedonian followers, who were interested mainly in booty and power, he recognized that only by merging local and Greek peoples and traditions could he forge a lasting empire. Even while founding cities on the Greek model throughout his empire, he

carefully respected the local social and cultural traditions of the conquered peoples and encouraged his companions to marry the daughters of local elites. Whether his program of cultural and social amalgamation could have succeeded is a moot point. In 323 B.C.E., less than two years after his return from India, he died at Babylon at the age of 32.

The empire did not outlive the emperor. Vicious fighting soon broke out among his generals and his kin. Alexander's wife Roxane and son Alexander IV (323–317 B.C.E.) were killed, as were all other members of the royal family. The various units of the empire broke apart into separate kingdoms and autonomous cities in which each ruler attempted to continue the political and cultural tradition of Alexander in a smaller sphere. Alexander's empire became a shifting kaleidoscope of states, kingdoms, and cities, dominated by priest-kings, native princelings, and territorial rulers, all vying to enhance their positions while preserving a relative balance of power. By 275 B.C.E., three large kingdoms dominated Alexander's former domain. The most stable was Egypt, which Ptolemy I (323–285 B.C.E.), one of Alexander's closest

MAP DISCOVERY

The Empire of Alexander the Great

Compare the empire of Alexander with the map of the ancient world (p. 8). How do you account for the specific areas Alexander chose to conquer? Based on information presented in this chapter, what lasting effects remained in this region?

CHRONOLOGY
CLASSICAL GREECE

525–456 B.C.E.	Aeschylus
ca. 500–ca. 430 B.C.E.	Phidias
496–406 B.C.E.	Sophocles
490 B.C.E.	Battle of Marathon
485–406 B.C.E.	Euripides
ca. 484–ca. 420 B.C.E.	Herodotus
480 B.C.E.	Battles of Thermopylae and Salamis
478 B.C.E.	Athens assumes control of Delian League
ca. 470–399 B.C.E.	Socrates
ca. 460–430 B.C.E.	Pericles dominates Athens
ca. 450–ca. 388 B.C.E.	Aristophanes
431–421; 414–404 B.C.E.	Peloponnesian War
ca. 428–347 B.C.E.	Plato
384–322 B.C.E.	Aristotle
384–322 B.C.E.	Demosthenes
338 B.C.E.	Philip of Macedon defeats Athens
336–323 B.C.E.	Reign of Alexander the Great

THE HELLENISTIC WORLD

Although vastly different in geography, language, and custom, the Hellenistic kingdoms (so called to distinguish them from the Hellenic civilization of the fifth and early fourth centuries B.C.E.) shared two common traditions. First, great portions of the Hellenistic world, from Asia Minor to Bactria and south to Egypt, had been united at various times by the Assyrian and Persian empires. During these periods they had absorbed much of Mesopotamian civilization, in particular the administrative traditions begun by the Assyrian Tiglath-pileser. Therefore, the Hellenistic kings ruled kingdoms that were already accustomed to centralized government and could rely on the already existing machinery of tax collection and administration to control the countryside. For the most part, however, these kings had little interest in the native populations of their kingdoms beyond the amount of wealth that they could extract from them. Hellenistic monarchs remained Greek and lavished their attentions on the newly created Greek cities, which absorbed vast amounts of the kingdom's wealth.

These cities and their particular form of Greek culture were the second unifying factor in the Hellenistic world. In the tradition of Alexander himself, the Ptolemys, Seleucids, and Antigonids cultivated Greek urban culture and recruited Greeks for their most important positions of responsibility. Alexander had founded over 35 cities during his conquests. The Seleucids established almost twice as many throughout their vast domain, even replacing the ancient city of Babylon with their capital, Seleucia, on the Tigris. In Egypt, the Ptolemys replaced the ancient capital of Memphis with the new city of Alexandria. These cities became the centers of political control, economic consumption, and cultural diffusion throughout the Hellenistic world.

followers, acquired on Alexander's death and which he and his descendants ruled until Cleopatra VII (51–30 B.C.E.) was defeated by the Roman Octavian in 31 B.C.E. In the east, the Macedonian general Seleucus (246–226 B.C.E.) captured Babylon in 312 B.C.E., and he and his descendants ruled a vast kingdom reaching from what is today western Turkey to Afghanistan. However, whittled away over time by its neighbors, the Seleucid kingdom gradually shrank to a small region of northern Syria before it fell to Rome in 64 B.C.E. After 50 years of conflict, Antigonus Gonatas (276–239 B.C.E.), the grandson of another of Alexander's commanders, secured Macedon and Greece. His Antigonid successors ruled the kingdom until it fell to the Romans in 168 B.C.E.

Alexander's conquests brought Greek traditions of urban organization to a wide area, replacing indigenous ruling elites with Hellenized dynasties. But Alexander's successors never integrated this Greek culture and the more ancient indigenous cultures of their subjects. This failure proved fatal for the Hellenistic kingdoms. (See "The West and the Wider World: Representing the Buddha, pp. 60–61.)

Urban Life and Culture

The Hellenistic kingdoms lived in a perpetual state of warfare with one another. Kings needed Greek soldiers, merchants, and administrators and competed with their rivals in offering Greeks all the comforts of home. Hellenistic cities were Greek in physical organization, constitution, and language. They boasted an agora, or marketplace, temples to the Greek gods and goddesses, theaters, baths, and, most important, a *gymnasion*, or combination sports center and school for young men. Sophocles' tragedies played to enthusiastic audiences in an enormous Greek theater in what is today Ai Khanoum on the Oxus River in Afghanistan, and the rites of Dionysus were celebrated in third-century B.C.E. Egypt with processions of satyrs, maenads, free wine for all, and a golden phallus 180 feet long. These Greeks were drawn from throughout the Greek-speaking world, and in time a universal Greek dialect, *koine,* became the common language of culture and business.

For all their Greek culture, Hellenistic cities differed fundamentally from Greek cities and colonies of the past. Not only were they far larger than any earlier Greek cities, but their

The West and the Wider World

REPRESENTING THE BUDDHA: FROM APOLLO TO CHRISTIAN SAINT

East and West met long before the modern age. The cultures of eastern and western Eurasia have developed in close interdependency since antiquity, and beginning with the conquests of Alexander the Great, the mutual influences in religion, science, and art became ever more direct. However, they were far from one-sided. Consider the case of the Buddha, whose cult in the East was given a decisive direction by Hellenistic art, and whose cult, thinly disguised, later entered the mainstream of Western Christianity.

According to legend, Siddhartha Gottama, known as the Buddha (b. ca. 566 B.C.E.), had been the son of a powerful tribal leader in the foothills of the Himalayas. At his birth, a visionary predicted that he would become either a great king or a savior of humanity. To ensure his worldly career, his father surrounded him with wealth and luxury and sheltered him from all knowledge of poverty, suffering, and death. Nevertheless, Siddhartha encountered a poor man, a sick man, a beggar, and a corpse. Profoundly saddened, he abandoned his comfortable life for one of extreme self-deprivation and meditation that culminated in his enlightenment—the realization of how to break the endless cycle of sorrow and suffering. However, rather than escaping the cycle, he chose to remain in the world to share his insights, his "way," with the rest of humanity.

Siddhartha's followers were few until the third century B.C.E. when King Asoka of the Mauryan dynasty, who had unified India, adopted the way of the Buddha, renounced violence, and promoted Buddhism both within his empire and beyond by sending missionaries into the Mediterranean world. Though they followed the way of the Buddha, for centuries Buddhists opposed portraying Siddhartha in human form. This changed in the second century C.E. in the kingdom of Gandhara in modern Pakistan and Afghanistan, ruled by the Emperor Kanishka (ca. 129–160 C.E.). This area had once been part of the Alexandrian Empire and, as everywhere in the Empire, saw the arrival of Greek merchants, soldiers, artists, and colonists. Kanishka absorbed these Greek traditions into his kingdom and commissioned Greek sculptors to create tall statues of the Buddha for monasteries and other public places. But how to portray the Buddha? The artists, drawing on Mediterranean traditions of

■ The delicate facial features, elaborate hair, and flowing robe of this Gandharan Buddha, ca. 150 C.E., are derived from Hellenistic models of Apollo.

classical sculpture, chose to portray him as a young Apollo. One can see the similarities in the delicate, finely carved face and in the toga in which the Gandhara Buddha is dressed. This innovation was soon picked up by indigenous sculptors who combined Central Asian, Indian, and Hellenistic styles and elements into the first Buddhist representational art. Buddha had become a Greek god.

But Buddha's transformation was far from over. Sometime in the early Middle Ages, a legend emerged in Greek of Josaphat, the son of the Indian King Abenner who persecuted Christians. When a soothsayer predicted that Josaphat would himself convert, his father raised him in isolated luxury to keep all knowledge of the word from him. However, a Christian hermit, Barlaam, managed to reach the prince, inform him of sickness, old age, and death, and convert him to the Christian faith. At first his father tried to prevent his conversion, but eventually Abenner himself converted and abdicated his throne to live as a hermit. Later Josaphat, too, abdicated, adopted the life of a hermit with Barlaam, and spent the rest of his life in self-deprivation and meditation. After their deaths, Barlaam and Josaphat were revered in India as miracle workers. This thinly veiled version of the story of Buddha (even the name Josaphat is derived from the Persian Budasif or Bodhisattva) rapidly spread across the Christian world, with translations appearing in Greek, Syriac, Arabic, Ethiopic, Armenian, and Hebrew as well as in Latin and Western vernacular languages. Saints Barlaam and Josaphat were venerated in the Latin West on January 27. Only in the nineteenth century did Westerners realize that this Christian saint was the ancient Indian Bodhisattva who chose a life of meditation over riches and power.

Representation of powerful divinities and spiritual leaders was essential

■ A fifteenth-century manuscript illustration of the monk Barlaam, disguised as a merchant, speaking with the Indian prince Josaphat.

in both Eastern and Western religious devotion and, thanks to the rich cultural exchanges in the areas that are now Pakistan and Afghanistan, similar solutions emerged for the representation of these figures. Not long after the first portrayals of Buddha as Apollo, Christ would be depicted in the same way by artists and sculptors. Likewise, the values of renunciation, self-discipline, and a love of humanity were themes shared across Eurasia, perfectly exemplified by the Buddha, whether as

Christian saint or Indian guide to enlightenment.

QUESTIONS FOR DISCUSSION

Why might an Indian prince be attracted to the political and cultural tradition of Hellenism? What other kinds of exchanges and interactions took place between East and West during the Hellenistic period? How do these considerations change how we might imagine the division between East and West?

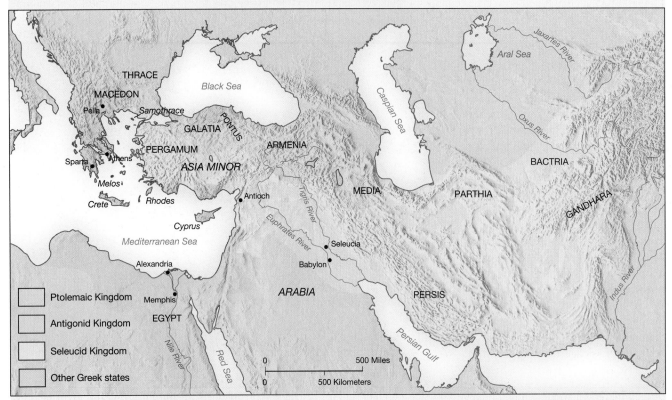

The Hellenistic Kingdoms

Consider the locations of the Hellenistic kingdoms carved out of Alexander's empire by his generals. From what you have read in previous chapters, which indigenous cultures do you think might have most influenced the Ptolemaic and Seleucid Kingdoms? Where would you expect to find Greek culture most important?

government and culture were different from those of other cities or colonies. Colonies had been largely independent poleis. The Hellenistic cities were never politically sovereign. The regional kings maintained firm control over the cities, even while working to attract Greeks from the mainland and the islands to them. This policy weakened the political significance of Greek life and culture. While these cities were in theory democracies, kings firmly controlled city government, and participation in the city councils and magistracies became the affair of the wealthy.

At the same time, Hellenistic cities were much less closed than were the traditional poleis of the Hellenic world. In the new cities of the east, Greeks from all over were welcomed as soldiers and administrators regardless of their city of origin. By the second century B.C.E., Greeks no longer identified themselves by their city of origin but as "Hellenes," that is, Greeks. Native elites could also become Greeks by adopting Greek language and culture.

Women in Public Life

The great social and geographical mobility that was possible in the new cities extended to women as well as men. No longer important simply as transmitters of citizenship, women began to assume a greater role in the family, in the economy, and in public life. Marriage contracts, particularly in Ptolemaic Egypt, emphasized the theoretical equality of husband and wife. In one such contract, the husband and wife were enjoined to take no concubines or male or female lovers. The penalty for the husband was loss of the wife's dowry; for the wife the punishment was divorce. Since women could control their own property, many engaged in business, and some became wealthy and influential.

The most powerful women in Hellenistic society were queens, especially in Egypt, where the Ptolemys adopted the Egyptian tradition of royal marriages between brothers and sisters. Arsinoë II (ca. 316–270 B.C.E.) ruled as an equal with her brother-husband Ptolemy II (286–246 B.C.E.). She inaugurated a tradition of powerful female monarchs that ended only with Cleopatra VII, the last independent ruler of Egypt, who successfully manipulated the Roman generals Julius Caesar (100–44 B.C.E.) and Mark Antony (81–30 B.C.E.) to maintain Egyptian autonomy.

Just as monarchs competed with one another in creating Greek cities, they vied in making their cities centers of Greek culture. Socially ambitious and newly wealthy citizens supported poets, philosophers, and artists and endowed gymnasia and libraries.

■ The *Nike,* or Winged Victory, is an outstanding example of Hellenistic sculpture. It was found in fragments on the island of Samothrace in the Aegean Sea in 1863. The head and arms were never discovered. The statue is now in the Louvre in Paris.

Alexandria

The most vibrant center of this rich complex of social change and culture was Alexandria in Egypt. Alexander the Great had founded it after having himself crowned pharaoh in the ancient capital of Memphis in 331 B.C.E. After Alexander's death, Ptolemy I made it not only his political and commercial center but the cultural center for Greek art, science, and scholarship for the whole world. In time, the library at Alexandria housed half a million book-rolls, including all of the great classics of Greek literature. Generations of poet-scholars edited and commented on the classics, in the process inventing literary criticism and preserving much of what is known about classical authors.

Hellenistic Literature

Hellenistic writers were not simply book collectors or critics. They also developed new forms of literature, including the romance, which often recounted imaginary adventures of Alexander the Great, and the pastoral poem, which the Sicilian Theocritus (ca. 310–250 B.C.E.) developed out of popular shepherd songs. Callimachus (ca. 305–ca. 240 B.C.E.) was the master of the short, witty epigram. Throughout antiquity, he was considered a model, more frequently quoted than any other poet but Homer. His influence on Roman poets, including Virgil and Ovid, was essential. Alexandria was able to attract the greatest scholars and poets of the Hellenistic world, but its greatest playwright, Menander (342–292 B.C.E.) refused to leave his native Athens for the rewards of Ptolemaic patronage. Menander's gift was for comedy, but it was a new type of comedy quite removed from the politically biting and often vulgar humor of Aristophanes. Menander wrote with great poetic skill and artistry some 100 wildly complicated, good-natured plays. More than any other ancient poet or playwright, he draws a sympathetic image of ordinary men and women.

Architecture and Art

Political rivalry also encouraged architectural and artistic rivalry, as kings competed for the most magnificent Hellenistic cities. Temples, porticoes, and public buildings grew in size and ornamentation, and Hellenistic architects and planners combined these buildings in harmonious urban ensembles, sometimes using natural hills and slopes to create elegant terraced vistas.

Freestanding statues and magnificent murals and mosaics adorned the public squares, temples, and private homes of Hellenistic cities. While artists continued the traditions of the Hellenic age, they displayed more freedom in portraying tension and restlessness as well as individuality in the human form. Sculptors demonstrated their skill in the portrayal of drapery that was tightly folded or fell naturally across the human form. The Nike (Victory) from Samothrace (ca. 200 B.C.E.) and the Aphrodite from Melos, known more commonly as the Venus de Milo (ca. 120 B.C.E.), are supreme examples of Hellenistic sculptural achievement.

Hellenistic Philosophy

Philosophy, too, flourished in the Hellenistic world, but in directions different from those initiated by Plato and Aristotle, who were both deeply committed to political involvement in the free polis. Instead, Cynics, Epicureans, and Stoics turned inward, advocating types of morality that were less directly tied to the state and society. These philosophies appealed to the rootless Greeks of the Hellenistic east, who were no longer tied by bonds of religion or patriotism to any community.

Cynics. The Cynic tradition was established by Antisthenes (ca. 445–ca. 365 B.C.E.), a pupil of Socrates, and Diogenes of Sinope (d. ca. 320 B.C.E.). The **Cynics** taught that excessive attachment to the things of this world was the source of evil and unhappiness. An individual achieves freedom by renouncing material things, society, and pleasures. The more one has, the more one is vulnerable to the whims of fortune. The Cynics' goal was to reduce their possessions, connections, and pleasures to the absolute minimum. "I would rather go mad than enjoy myself," Antisthenes said.

Epicureans. Like the Cynics, the **Epicureans** sought freedom, but from pain rather than from the conventions of ordinary life. Epicurus (341–270 B.C.E.) and his disciples have often been attacked for their emphasis on pleasure. "You need only possess perception and be made of flesh, and you will see that pleasure is good," Epicurus wrote. But this search for pleasure was not a call to sensual indulgence. Pleasure was to be pursued rationally, with awareness that today's pleasure could mean tomorrow's suffering. The real goal was to reduce desires to those that were simple and attainable. Therefore Epicureans urged retirement from politics, retreat from public competition, and concentration instead on friendship and private enjoyment. For Epicurus, reason properly applied illuminated how best to pursue pleasure. The traditional image of the Epicurean as an indulgent sensualist is a gross caricature. As Epicurus advised one follower, an Epicurean "revels in the pleasure of the body—on a diet of bread and water."

Stoics. The **Stoics** also followed nature, but rather than leading them to retire from public life, it led them to greater participation in it. Stoic virtue consisted in applying reason to one's life in such a way that one knowingly lived in conformity to nature. Worldly pleasures, like worldly pain, had no particular value. Both were to be accepted and endured. Stoics believed that just as the universe is a system in which stars and planets move according to fixed laws, so too was human society ordered and unified. As the founder of Stoicism, Zeno (ca. 335–ca. 263 B.C.E.), expressed it, "All men should regard themselves as members of one city and people, having one life and order." According to the Stoics, every person had a role in the divinely ordered universe, and all roles were of equal value. True happiness consisted in freely accepting one's role, whatever it was, while unhappiness and evil resulted from attempting to reject one's place in the divine plan.

Cynicism, Epicureanism, and Stoicism all emphasized the importance of reason and the proper understanding of nature. Hellenistic understanding of nature was one area in which Greek thinkers were influenced by the ancient Near Eastern traditions brought to them through the conquests of Alexander.

Mathematics and Science

Particularly for mathematics, astronomy, and engineering, the Hellenistic period was a golden age. Ptolemaic Egypt became the center of mathematical studies. Euclid (ca. 300 B.C.E.), whose *Elements* was the fundamental textbook of geometry until the twentieth century, worked there, as did his student Apollonius of Perga (ca. 262–ca. 190 B.C.E.), whose work on conic sections is one of the greatest monuments of geometry. Both Apollonius and his teacher were as influential for their method as for their conclusions. Their treatises follow rigorous logical proofs of mathematical theorems, which established the form of mathematical reasoning to the present day. Archimedes of Syracuse (ca. 287–212 B.C.E.) corresponded with the Egyptian mathematicians and made additional contributions to geometry, such as the calculation of the approximate value of pi, as well as to mechanics, arithmetic, and engineering. Archimedes was famous for his practical application of engineering, particularly to warfare, and legends quickly grew up about his marvelous machines with which he helped Syracuse defend itself against Rome.

Mathematical Astronomy. Many mathematicians, such as Archimedes and Apollonius, were also mathematical astronomers, and the application of their mathematical skills to the exact data collected by earlier Babylonian and Egyptian empirical astronomers greatly increased the understanding of the heavens and the earth. Archimedes devised a means of measuring the diameter of the sun, and Eratosthenes of Cyrene (ca. 276–194 B.C.E.) calculated the circumference of the earth to within 200 miles. Aristarchus of Samos (ca. 270 B.C.E.) theorized that the sun and fixed stars were motionless and that the earth moves around the sun. His theory was rejected by contemporaries. Hipparchus of Nicea (ca. 146–127 B.C.E.) placed the earth at the center of the universe. With slight adjustments made 300 years later by Ptolemy of Alexandria, Hipparchus's earth-centric theory remained predominant until the sixteenth century.

Medicine. Like astronomy, Hellenistic medicine combined theory and observation. In Alexandria, Herophilus of Chalcedon (ca. 270 B.C.E.) and Erasistratus of Ceos (ca. 260

B.C.E.) conducted important studies in human anatomy. The Ptolemaic kings provided them with condemned prisoners, whom they dissected alive; thus they were able to observe the functioning of the organs of the body. The terrible agonies inflicted on their experimental subjects were considered to be justified by the argument that there was no cruelty in causing pain to guilty men to seek remedies for the innocent. Through his studies, Herophilus recognized the brain as the center of the nervous system and was able to distinguish accurately between motor and sensory nerves. He also produced the first accurate descriptions of such organs as the eye, brain, liver, and salivary glands.

Cultural Resistance.   For all of their vitality, the Hellenistic cities remained parasites on the local societies. No real efforts were made to merge the two and to develop a new civilization. Some ambitious members of the indigenous elites tried to adopt the customs of the Greeks; others plotted insurrection. The clearest example of these conflicting tensions was that of the Jewish community. Early in the second century B.C.E., a powerful Jewish faction, which included the High Priest of Yahweh, supported Hellenization. With the assistance of the Seleucid king, this faction set up a gymnasion in Jerusalem where Jewish youths and even priests began to study Greek and participate in Greek culture. Some even underwent painful surgery to reverse the effects of circumcision so that they could pass for Greeks in naked athletic contests. This rejection of tradition infuriated a large portion of the Jewish population. When the Seleucids finally attempted to introduce pagan cults into the temple in 167 B.C.E., open rebellion broke out and continued intermittently until the Jews gained independence in 141 B.C.E.

This violent opposition was repeated elsewhere from time to time, especially in Egypt and Persia, where, as in Judaea, old traditions of religion and monarchy provided rallying points against the transplanted Greeks. In time, the Hellenistic kingdoms' inability to bridge the gap between Greek and indigenous populations proved fatal. In the east, the non-Greek kingdom of Parthia replaced the Seleucids in much of the old Persian Empire. In the west, continuing hostility between kingdoms and within kingdoms prepared the way for their progressive absorption by the new power to the west: Rome.

CONCLUSION

In the fifth century B.C.E., the rugged slopes, fertile plains, and arid islands of the Greek world gave rise to characteristic forms of social, political, and cultural organization that have reappeared in varying forms wherever Western civilization has taken root. In Athens, which emerged from the ruins of the Persian invasion as the most powerful and dynamic state in the Hellenic world, the give-and-take of a direct democracy challenged men to raise fundamental questions about the relationship between individual and society, freedom and absolutism, gods and mortals. At the same time, this society of free males excluded the majority of its inhabitants—women, foreigners, and slaves—from participation in government and fought a long and ultimately futile war to hold together an exploitive empire.

The interminable wars among Greek states ultimately left the Greek world open to conquest by a powerful semi-Greek monarchy that went on to spread Athenian culture throughout the known world. Freed from the particularism of individual city-states, Hellenistic culture became a universal tradition emphasizing the individual rather than the community of family, tribe, or religious association. Yet this universal Hellenistic cultural tradition remained a thin veneer, hardly assimilated by the masses of the ancient world. Its proponents, except for Alexander the Great, never sought a real synthesis of Greek and barbarian tradition. Such a synthesis would begin only with the coming of Rome.

QUESTIONS FOR REVIEW

1. Why did Athens become Greece's greatest power in the wake of the Persian wars?
2. What social concerns and cultural accomplishments were expressed in Greek philosophy, drama, and art?
3. What does the Peloponnesian War reveal about weaknesses and divisions in Greek culture?
4. What factors explain Alexander the Great's success in expanding his empire?
5. What changes did Greek culture experience as it was carried eastward with the creation of the Hellenistic kingdoms?

KEY TERMS

Cynics, *p. 64*

Delian League, *p. 47*

ekklesia, *p. 49*

empiricism, *p. 56*

Epicureans, *p. 64*

Forms, *p. 56*

metics, *p. 48*

ostracism, *p. 46*

sophists, *p. 52*

Stoics, *p. 64*

DISCOVERING WESTERN CIVILIZATION ONLINE

You can obtain more information about classical and Hellenistic Greece at the websites listed below. See also the Companion Website that accompanies this text: www.ablongman.com/kishlansky, which contains an online study guide and additional resources.

War and Politics in the Fifth Century B.C.E.

Articles on Ancient Persia
www.livius.org/persia.html
Links to articles on many aspects of ancient Persian history.

The Greeks: Crucible of Civilization
www.pbs.org/empires/thegreeks/
A Public Broadcasting System site devoted to ancient Greece.

The Ancient City of Athens
www.indiana.edu/~kglowack/athens/
An excellent site devoted to Athens.

The Peloponnesian War
www.multimania.com/sdelille/gdpa.html
A site developed by Sven Delille on the Peloponnesian War.

Diotima: Women and Gender in the Ancient World
www.stoa.org/diotima/
A site devoted to women and gender in antiquity.

The Ancient Greek World Index
www.museum.upenn.edu/Greek_World/
A University of Pennsylvania Museum online exhibit devoted to ancient Greek society.

Alexander the Great
history.boisestate.edu/westciv/alexander/
Dr. Ellis L. Knox's page devoted to Alexander the Great.

The Hellenistic World

A Brief History of Clocks: From Thales to Ptolemy
www.perseus.tufts.edu/GreekScience/Students/Jesse/CLOCK1A.html
A history of clocks in the Hellenistic world.

Archimedes
www.mcs.drexel.edu/~crorres/Archimedes/contents.html
A site devoted to Archimedes and Hellenistic science.

SUGGESTIONS FOR FURTHER READING

General Reading

Cambridge Ancient History, 2d ed., vols. 5 (1989) and 7 (1984). Contains essays on most aspects of Greek history.

Pierre Vidal-Naquet, *The Black Hunter: Forms of Thought and Forms of Society in the Greek World* (Baltimore: The Johns Hopkins University Press, 1998). A brilliant exploration of Greek society and politics approached through its margins, its contradictions, and its oppositions.

War and Politics in the Fifth Century B.C.E.

Sue Blundell, *Women in Ancient Greece* (Cambridge, MA: Harvard University Press, 1995). A good place to start for an understanding of women in classical Greece.

W. R. Connor, *The New Politicians of Fifth-Century Athens* (Indianapolis: Hackett, 1992). Reappraises the demagogues within the context of Athenian political life.

John Manuel Cook, *The Persian Empire* (New York: Schocken Books, 1983). The standard history of Persia from the perspective of history and archaeology.

Charles W. Fornara and Loren J. Samons II, *Athens from Cleisthenes to Pericles* (Berkeley: University of California Press, 1991). Detailed survey of the development of Athenian democracy and empire.

Yvon Garlan, *Slavery in Ancient Greece* (Ithaca, NY: Cornell University Press, 1988). A basic study of Greek slavery.

Lisa Kallet, *Money and the Corrosion of Power in Thucydides: The Sicilian Expedition and Its Aftermath* (Berkeley: University of California Press, 2002). A focused study of corruption in a crucial aspect of the Peloponnesian War.

Nigel M. Kennell, *The Gymnasium of Virtue: Education and Culture in Ancient Sparta* (Chapel Hill: University of North Carolina Press, 1995). An investigation of Spartan culture.

Helen King, *Hippocrates' Woman: Reading the Female Body in Ancient Greece* (New York: Routledge, 1998). A study of Greek medical theory concerning women and women's bodies.

P. J. Rhodes, *Ancient Democracy and Modern Ideology* (London: Duckworth Academic, 2003). An essay from a prominent Greek historian exploring the modern uses of Athenian democracy.

Athenian Culture in the Hellenic Age

J. Boardman, *Greek Art,* 3d ed. (New York: Thames & Hudson, 1985). A handbook introduction by period.

W. Burkert, *Greek Religion* (Cambridge, MA: Harvard University Press, 1985). General survey of the topic.

Simon Goldhill, *Reading Greek Tragedy* (New York: Cambridge University Press, 1986). A general introduction to Athenian tragedy.

G. E. R. Lloyd, *Aristotle: The Growth and Structure of His Thought* (New York: Cambridge University Press, 1968). A developmental approach to Aristotle.

C. J. Rowe, *Plato* (New York: St. Martin's, 1984). A good survey of the philosopher's thought.

From City-States to Macedonian Empire, 404–323 B.C.E.

A. B. Bosworth, *Conquest and Empire* (New York: Cambridge University Press, 1988). A scholarly but readable account of Alexander the Great.

J. R. Hamilton, *Alexander the Great* (Pittsburgh: University of Pittsburgh Press, 1973). Still the best biography of Alexander in English.

The Hellenistic World

J. Barnes et al., *Science and Speculation* (New York: Cambridge University Press, 1982). A collection of papers on Hellenistic science.

Peter Green, *Alexander to Actium: The Historical Evolution of the Hellenistic Age* (Berkeley: University of California Press, 1990). A broad examination of the Hellenistic period.

Peter Green, ed., *Hellenistic History and Culture* (Berkeley: University of California Press, 1993). A stimulating series of articles and debates on Hellenistic civilization.

For a list of additional titles related to this chapter's topics, please see www.ablongman.com/kishlansky.

Chapter 4

EARLY ROME AND THE ROMAN REPUBLIC, 800–146 B.C.E.

The Visual Record

ETERNAL ROME

Five miles from its mouth, the Tiber River snakes in a lazy S around the first highlands that rise from the marshes of central Italy. These weathered cliffs, separated by tributary streams, look down on the river valley that broadens to over a mile and a half wide, the first and only natural ford for many miles. Only three promontories—the Capitoline, Palatine, and Aventine—are separate hills. The others, the Quirinal, Viminal, Caelian, Oppian, and Esquiline, are actually spurs of the distant Apennines. Gradually, the pastoral villages that had been founded on these hills spread down to the valleys between them, united, and grew to a city whose name was synonymous with empire for over 2,000 years.

Rome wasn't built in a day. The earliest Roman villages were found on the Palatine, from whose heights the picture seen here was taken and which remained throughout Rome's history the favored residential area. The Capitoline with its steep cliffs, which begin at the extreme left of the photograph, served as an acropolis, the religious center of the community. Here were found not only temples but also the state archives and the city mint beside the temple of Juno the Admonisher, *Juno Moneta* (hence our word *money*). The Capitol, so the Romans thought, was indestructible and became a symbol of the eternal city. As Romans established colonies across Italy and throughout the Mediterranean, the colonies too had their hill temples, their so-called capitols.

The area in the center of the photograph between the Palatine and Capitoline was originally a low, marshy burial ground. In the seventh century B.C.E., Etruscan kings drained the marshes, making it possible to pave the area and turn it into a public meeting place, or forum. The Forum became the heart of the city. Through it ran the Sacred Way, the road that cuts diagonally from left to right in the photograph. At the south end, to the right of the photograph, was the marketplace, which bustled with shops and businesses. To the north, where the domed church of Saints Luca and Magartina now stands, was the Comitium, the meeting place of the citizens' assembly. Just below it still stands the Curia, the meeting place of the Roman Senate, which survives because it was converted into a Christian church in the seventh century C.E. Here, too, temples and monuments rose to meet religious and public needs.

As Rome grew from a simple city to an empire, the Forum reflected these changes. Simple Etruscan architecture gave way to the Greek style of building. Marble replaced brick and stucco. Near the Curia, the golden milestone marked the point from which all

distances were measured and to which all roads of the empire led. By the time of Julius Caesar and Augustus, Rome had replaced its Forum, just as it had replaced its republican constitution. Caesar had begun and Augustus completed new forums, known collectively as the Forum of the Caesars, which lay beyond the trees at the upper right of the picture. Their successor Trajan (98–117 C.E.) would build a still greater one just beyond it. Still, for centuries of Romans and for the Western societies that succeeded them, the narrow space encompassing the Capitoline, the Palatine, and the Forum was the center of the city and the world.

Looking Ahead

This chapter begins with a survey of the western Mediterranean and charts the gradual expansion of Roman power from but another Italian village at the site of this forum to the dominant power in the western Mediterranean. As its power expanded abroad, social and economic tensions grew at home, and from this tension arose a new culture, deeply indebted to Greek and Etruscan traditions but also deeply original in its political forms and social organization. ➤

THE WESTERN MEDITERRANEAN TO 509 B.C.E.

Civilization came late to the western Mediterranean, carried in the ships of Greeks and Phoenicians. While the great flood-plain civilizations of Mesopotamia and Egypt and the Greek communities of the eastern Mediterranean were developing sophisticated systems of urban life and political organization, western Europe and Africa knew only the scattered villages of simple farmers and pastoralists. These populations, such as the Ligurians of northern Italy, were the descendants of Neolithic peoples only remotely touched by the developments in the East. The West was rich in metals, however, and an indigenous Bronze Age culture developed slowly between 1500 and 1000 B.C.E., spreading widely north of the Alps and south into Italy and Spain. By the twelfth century B.C.E., workshops in northern Italy were producing bronze spearheads, swords, and axes both for local use and for export to Crete, Naxos, Corfu, and Mycenae. At the same time, southern Italians were importing bronze knives and ornaments from Greece. In addition to finished weapons and other objects, the Eastern cities sought in Italy and Spain unworked bronze, silver bullion, tin, and iron.

Sometime around the year 1000 B.C.E., a new, distinctive iron-using civilization first appeared in northern Italy. These **Villanovans,** so called for a major archaeological discovery of this civilization at Villanova near Bologna, differed from earlier Italian peoples in their use of iron, in the practice of cremating their dead and burying their ashes in large urns, and in the greater size and complexity of their settlements.

No one knows whether the Villanovans were new arrivals in Italy or simply the descendants of previous inhabitants. However, around this same time, small groups of people did begin to infiltrate Italy from the east and the north, occupying the mountainous terrain of the Apennines and pushing the indigenous society westward. These new arrivals shared no common organization or identity, but all spoke related Indo-European languages that we call *Italic,* including Latin. These newcomers were warriors. Like the Dark Age Greeks, they soon developed the art of making iron weapons, which gave them a decided advantage over the older inhabitants of the peninsula. By 800 B.C.E. they were in firm control of the mountainous region of central Italy and threatened the coastal societies of the west and south.

Carthage: The Merchants of Baal

Also around 800 B.C.E., Phoenicians arrived in the West from the regions of Tyre, Sidon, and Byblos. They established a series of bases along the route to and from Spain on the coast and on the islands of Corsica, Sicily, Ibiza, and Motya in the Mediterranean and at Utica and Carthage on the coast of North Africa. Carthage was initially no more than a small anchorage for ships. Gradually, however, Carthage established itself as the center of an expanding Phoenician presence in the western Mediterranean.

The city was perfectly situated to profit from both the land and the sea. Its excellent double harbor made it an ideal port. Here ships could lie at rest, protected from storms as well as from enemies by a narrow 70-foot entrance to the sea that could be closed with iron chains. The city was equally protected on land, situated on a narrow isthmus and surrounded by massive walls. As long as Carthage controlled the sea, its commercial center was secure from any enemies.

By the middle of the sixth century B.C.E., Carthage was the center of a real empire. But in contrast with the Athenian empire of the following century, Carthage was much more successful at integrating other cities and peoples into its mercenary military and thus sharing the burden of warfare. This multiethnic empire endured for three centuries, proving far more stable than any of those created by the Greeks.

Although superficially similar to many Greek cities, the Punic (from *Puni* or *Poeni,* the Roman name for the Carthaginians) state differed profoundly in the relationship between citizen and state. Ordinary citizens had little involvement and, apparently, little interest in government, and officials consistently came from among the wealthy and powerful merchant aristocracy. According to Aristotle, however, the aristocracy treated the rest of the population generously, sharing with it profits of its commercial and imperial wealth. Thus the class pressures that created the Greek tyrants never emerged in Carthage.

The Gods of Carthage.   The gods of Carthage were local variations of the Phoenician gods, especially Baal Hammon, the supreme god El of the Semitic world. Tanit, goddess of fertility, assumed an importance equal to that of Baal Hammon.

According to hostile Greek and Roman sources, all Carthaginian citizens were obligated to sacrifice their first-born sons. The sacrifice of children constituted the most important and, to their Greek and barbarian neighbors, the most repulsive aspect of Punic culture. The basic reliability of these reports was dramatically confirmed in 1922, when archaeologists excavated the first of several sites containing urns filled with the remains of hundreds of children. In areas excavated from later periods, these bones are mixed with the bones of sacrificed animals.

Stable, prosperous, and devout, Carthage was the master of the western Mediterranean. But its dominion was not undisputed. From the sixth century B.C.E., the Punic empire felt the pressure of ambitious Greek cities that were eager to gain a share of the West's riches.

The Western Greeks

The Greek arrival in the west was the result of a much more complex process than the trading policy of the Phoenicians. As we saw in Chapter 2, toward the end of the Dark Age, commerce, overpopulation, and civic tension sent Greek colonists out in all directions. In the eighth century B.C.E., Crete, Rhodes, Corinth, Argos, Chalcis, Eretria, and Naxos all established colonies in Sicily and southern Italy.

MAP DISCOVERY

Greek and Phoenician Colonies and Trade

Note the location of the major Phoenician and Greek colonies and the extent of the trade routes to and from these colonies. Where, if at all, did Greek and Phoenician colonies come into close proximity and competition? Did the two systems compete for the same trade goods?

In the seventh century B.C.E., Syracuse became the greatest city of Sicily and one of the most prosperous cities of the Greek world. Greek colonies spread slowly up the boot of Italy, known as Greater Greece, in pursuit of trade and arable land. By the last quarter of the seventh century B.C.E., the autonomous Greek colonies began to encroach on the Carthaginian empire's sphere of influence. Around 631 B.C.E., Greeks from Thera founded a colony at Cyrene in North Africa. The Greek city of Phocaea in Asia Minor established a colony at Marseille around 600 B.C.E.

Both commercial rivalry and open warfare characterized the relationship between Greeks and Phoenicians in the western Mediterranean. In the course of the sixth century B.C.E., Greeks in Sicily attempted to expel the Phoenicians from the island. In the fifth century B.C.E., Syracuse, under its tyrant Gelon (ca. 540–478 B.C.E.), threatened both Punic and Greek cities on the island. In an attempt to defend its colonies, in 480 B.C.E. Carthage launched an enormous force to support Gelon's Greek enemies. The attack took place, probably not

coincidentally, at the same moment that Xerxes invaded Greece. At the battle of Himera—fought, we are told, on the same day as the battle of Salamis—the Syracusans soundly defeated the Carthaginians.

Gelon's victory at Himera ushered in a period of prosperity and cultural achievement in Sicily. The tyrants of Syracuse, enriched with the spoils of victory, created a court whose magnificence, wealth, and generosity won admiration throughout the Greek world. This prosperity continued after the elimination of the tyranny in midcentury, and in 415 B.C.E., Syracuse was able to withstand Athens's attempt at conquest. (See Chapter 3, p. 52.)

A far more serious threat appeared in 410 B.C.E., when a new Carthaginian army arrived in Sicily seeking revenge. The Carthaginians rapidly captured and destroyed Himera, extending the boundaries of Punic Sicily. This invasion initiated a century of inconclusive conflict between Syracuse and Carthage.

Early on in their struggle with the Sicilian Greeks, the Carthaginians found allies in the third major civilization of the West. These were the Etruscans, who in the seventh century B.C.E. dominated the western part of central Italy, known as Etruria. The region today is Tuscany; its name derives from *Tusci,* the Roman term for this early people.

Italy's First Civilization

Etruscan civilization was the first great civilization to emerge in Italy. The **Etruscans** have long been regarded as a people whose origins, language, and customs are shrouded in mystery. However, in recent years, archaeologists have demonstrated that the Etruscans originated in western Italy with an indigenous cultural tradition that was apparently overwhelmed by the chaos of the twelfth-century B.C.E. crisis and the migration of Indo-Europeans from the north. This tradition shares much with Eastern civilizations, such as the importance of underworld gods, fertility cults, and the high status of women. And while the Etruscan language appears to be unrelated to any other language, bilingual inscriptions and careful analysis have enabled scholars to read many of the extant Etruscan texts.

Etruscan civilization coalesced slowly in Etruria over the course of the seventh century B.C.E. from diverse groups sharing a similar cultural and linguistic tradition. In the mid-sixth century B.C.E., in the face of Greek pressure from the south, 12 of these groups united in a religious and military confederation. Over the next 100 years, the confederation expanded north into the Po Valley and south to Campania. Cities, each initially ruled by a king, were the centers of Etruscan civilization, and everywhere the Etruscans spread, they either improved on existing towns or founded new ones. Towns in the north included Bologna, Parma, Modena, Ravenna, Milan, and Mantua; in the south were Nola, Nuceria, Pompeii, Sorrento, and Salerno. The Etruscan confederation remained loose and never developed into a centralized empire. Etruscan kings assumed power in conquered towns, but between the sixth and fifth centuries B.C.E., Etruscan kingship gave way to oligarchic governments, much as Greek monarchies had a bit earlier. In the place of kings, aristocratic assemblies selected magistrates, often paired together or combined into "colleges" to prevent individuals from seizing power. These republican institutions provided the foundation for later Roman republican government.

An Archaic Society.   The remnants of an ancient civilization, the Etruscans retained throughout their history social and cultural traditions that had long since vanished elsewhere in the Mediterranean. Society was divided sharply into two classes, lords and servants. The lords' wealth was based on the rich agricultural regions of Etruria where grain grew in abundance and on the equally rich deposits of copper and iron. The vast majority of the population were actual slaves, working the lands and mines of the aristocracy.

The aristocrats were aggressive and imaginative landowners. They developed hydraulic systems for draining marshes, produced a wine that was famous throughout the Mediterranean, and put their slaves to work in mines and in smelting. Still, they were largely absentee landlords, spending much of their time in the towns that characterized Etruscan civilization. These cities, with their massive walls, enclosed populations of as many as 20,000. Although little remains of their largely wooden houses and other buildings, their tombs were furnished with the wares of everyday life, including benches, beds, ornaments, utensils, and vessels and platters of Etruscan and Corinthian manufacture, providing a vivid image of how the Etruscans lived.

The most striking aspect of Etruscan life to Greek contemporaries and to later Romans was the elevated status of Etruscan women. As in the much earlier Minoan civilization, women played an active, public role in society. Unlike honorable Greek women, Etruscan women took part in banquets, attended and even occasionally presided over dances, concerts, and sporting events, and were active in political life. Greeks such as Aristotle regarded the public behavior of Etruscan women as lewd. When a king died, his successor had to be designated and consecrated by the Etruscan queen to establish his legitimacy. To later Romans, this practice was shocking.

Etruscan Dominance.   While the Etruscans were consolidating their hegemony in western Italy, they were at the same time establishing their maritime power. From the seventh to the fifth centuries B.C.E., Etruscans controlled the Italian coast of the Tyrrhenian Sea as well as Sardinia, from which their ships could reach the coast of what is today France and Spain. Attempts to extend farther south into Greek southern Italy and toward the Greek colonies on the modern French coast brought the Etruscans and the Greeks into inevitable conflict. Etruscan cities fought sporadic sea battles against Greek cities in the waters of Sicily as well as off the coasts of Corsica and Etruria.

Common hostility toward the Greeks as well as complementary economic interests soon brought the Etruscans into alliances with Carthage. Toward the end of the sixth century B.C.E., Etruscan cities including Rome signed a series of pacts with Carthage that created military alliances against the Phocaeans and Syracuse. Etruscan fleets were victorious over the Phocaeans, driving them from Corsica, but they were no match for Syracuse. In 474 B.C.E., shortly after the battle of Himera, the Syracusan fleet destroyed that of the Etruscans off Cumae.

Cumae marked the beginning of Etruscan decline. Through the fifth century B.C.E., Etruscan cities lost control of the sea to the Greeks. Around the same time, Celts from north of the Alps invaded and conquered the Po Valley. And to the south, Etruscans saw their inland territories progressively slipping into the hands of their former subjects, the Romans, who had begun to acquire the commercial, political, and military expertise that would drive their long rise to dominance.

■ On the Etruscan sarcophagus of Larthia Scianti, a matron reclines as at a banquet. Much of our knowledge of the first Italian civilization comes from the elaborate paintings and statuary found in Etruscan cemeteries.

FROM CITY TO EMPIRE, 509–146 B.C.E.

What manner of people were these Romans who, from obscure origins, came to rule an empire? Their own answer would have been simple: They were farmers and soldiers, simple people accustomed to simple, straightforward actions. Throughout their long history, Romans liked to refer to the clear-cut models provided by their semilegendary predecessors: Cincinnatus, the farmer, called away to the supreme office of dictator in time of danger, then returning to his plow; Horatius Cocles, the valiant warrior who held back an Etruscan army on the Tiber bridge until it could be demolished and then, despite his wounds, swam across the river to safety; Lucretia, the wife who chose death after dishonor. These were myths, but they were important myths to Romans, who preferred concrete models to abstract principles.

Later Romans liked to imagine the history of their city as one predestined by the gods for greatness. Some liked to trace the origins of Rome to Romulus and Remus, twin sons of the war god Mars and a Latin princess. According to legend, the children, after having been thrown into the Tiber River, were raised by a she-wolf. Other Romans, having absorbed the Homeric traditions of Greece, taught that the founder of Rome was Aeneas, son of the goddess of love, Aphrodite, and the Trojan Anchises, who had wandered west after the fall of Troy. All agreed that Rome had been ruled by kings, who underwent a steady decline in ability and morals until the last, Tarquin the Proud, was expelled by outraged Latins. These legends tell much about the attitudes and values of later Romans. They tell nothing about the actual origins of the city or its rise to greatness.

Latin Rome

Civilization in Italy meant Etruria to the north and Greater Greece to the south. In between lay Latium, a marshy region punctuated by hills on which a sparse population could find protection from disease and enemies. This population was an amalgam of aboriginal Ligurians and the more recently arrived Latins and Sabines, who lived a pastoral life in small, scattered villages.

The Alban Hills south of the Tiber were a center of Latin population. Sometime in the eighth century B.C.E., roughly 40 Latin villages formed a loose confederation, the Alban League, for military and religious purposes. Not long afterward, in the face of an expanding Etruscan confederation from the north and Sabine penetration from the east, the Albans established a village on the steep Palatine hill to the north. The Palatine was one of several hills overlooking a natural ford on the Tiber. This Alban village, called Roma Quadrata, was soon joined by other Latin and Sabine settlements on nearby hills. By the end of the eighth century B.C.E., seven Latin villages along the route from the Tiber to Alba had formed a league for mutual defense and shared religious cults.

Early Roman society was composed of households; clans, or *gentes;* and village councils, or *curiae* (sing. *curia*). The male head of each household, the **paterfamilias,** had the power of life and death over its members and was responsible for the proper worship of the spirits of the family's ancestors, on whom continued prosperity depended. Within some villages these families were grouped into gentes, which claimed descent from a semimythical ancestor.

Male members of village families formed councils, which were essentially religious organizations but also provided a forum for public discussion. These curiae tended to be dominated by gentes, but all males could participate, including those who belonged to the *plebians* or **plebs,** that is, families that were not organized into gentes. Later, the leaders of the gentes called themselves **patricians** ("descendants of fathers") and claimed superiority to the plebs, or common people.

Important plebeian and patrician families increased their power through a system of clientage, which remained a fundamental aspect of social and political organization throughout Roman history. Clients were free men who depended on the protection of a more powerful individual or family and who owed various services, including political support, in return for this protection.

Villages themselves grouped together for military and voting purposes into ethnic *tribus,* or tribes, each composed of a number of curiae. Each curia supplied a contingent of infantry, and each tribe cooperated to supply a unit of horsemen to the Roman army.

Assemblies of all members of the curiae expressed approval of major decisions, especially declaration of war and the selection of new kings, and thus played a real if limited political role. More powerful although less formal was the role of the Senate (assembly of elders), which was composed of heads of families. The Senate's power derived from the individual importance of its members and from its role in selecting a candidate for king, who was then presented to the assembly of the curiae for approval.

Kings served as religious leaders, the primary means of communication between gods and humans. Through the early Latin period, royal power remained fundamentally religious and limited by the Senate, curiae, gentes, and families.

The seven villages that made up primitive Rome developed independently of their Etruscan and Greek neighbors. Initially, Romans lived in thatched huts, tended their flocks on the hillsides, and maintained their separate village identities. By the seventh century B.C.E., they had begun fortifications and other structures indicating the beginnings of a dynamic civic life. This independent course of development changed in the middle of the seventh century B.C.E., when the Etruscans overwhelmed Latium and absorbed it into their civilization. Under its Etruscan kings, Rome first entered civilization.

Etruscan Rome

The Etruscans introduced in Latium, especially in Rome, their political, religious, and economic traditions. Etruscan city organization partially replaced Latin tribal structures. Etruscan kings and magistrates ruled Latin towns, increasing the power of traditional Latin kingship. The kings not only were religious leaders, but also led the army, served as judges, and held supreme political power. As Latium became an integral part of the Etruscan world, the Tiber became an important commercial route. For the first time, Rome began to enter the wider orbit of Mediterranean civilization. The town's population swelled with the arrival of merchants and artisans.

Urban Growth.   As Rome's importance grew, so did its size. Etruscan engineers drained the marshes into a great canal flowing to the Tiber, thus opening the lowlands between the hills to settlement. This in turn allowed them to create and pave the Forum. The Etruscans constructed a series of vast fortifications encircling the town. Under Etruscan influence, the fortified Capitoline hill, which served much like a Greek acropolis, became the cult center with the erection of the temple to Jupiter, the supreme god; Juno, his consort; and Minerva, an Etruscan goddess of craftwork who was similar to Athena. In its architecture, religion, commerce, and culture, Latin Rome was deeply indebted to its Etruscan conquerors.

As important as the physical and cultural changes brought by the Etruscans was their reorganization of the society. As in Greece, this restructuring was tied to changes in the military. The Etruscans had learned from the Greeks the importance of hoplite tactics, and King Servius Tullius (578–534 B.C.E.) introduced this system of warfare into Rome. This led to the abolition of the earlier curia-based military and political system in favor of one based only on property holding. Weakening the traditional Latin social units, the king divided Roman society into two groups: property owners and others. Landowners who were wealthy enough to provide armed military service were organized into five classes and ranked according to the quality of their arms and hence their wealth. Each class was further divided into military units called *centuries.* Members of these centuries constituted the centuriate assembly, which replaced the older curial assemblies for such vital decisions as the election of magistrates and the declaration of war.

The constitution and operation of this centuriate assembly ensured control by the most conservative forces within the society. Small centuries of wealthy well-armed cavalrymen and fully armed warriors outnumbered the more modestly equipped but more numerous centuries. Likewise, men over the age of 47, although in a minority, controlled over half the centuries in each class. Since votes were counted not by individuals but by centuries, this ensured within the assembly the domination of the rich over the poor, the older over the younger. The remainder of the society was the *infra classem* (literally "under class"), who owned no property and were thus excluded from military and political activity.

With this military and political reorganization came a reconstruction of the tribal system. Servius Tullius abolished the old tribal organization in favor of geographically organized tribes into which newcomers could easily be incorporated. Henceforth, while the family remained powerful, involvement in public life was based on property and geography. Latins, Sabines, Ligurians, and Etruscans could all be active citizens of the growing city.

Class Divisions.   While the old tribal units and curiae declined, divisions between the patricians and the plebeians grew more distinct. During the monarchy, the patricians came to compose an upper stratum of wealthy nobles. They forbade marriage outside their own circle, forming a closed, self-perpetuating group that monopolized the Senate, religious rites, and magisterial offices. Although partially protected by the kings, the plebeians, whether rich or poor, were pressed into a second-class status and denied access to political power.

In less than two centuries the Etruscans transformed Rome from a small collection of wood and reed villages into a prosperous, unified urban center that played an important role in the economic and political life of central Italy. They laid the foundations of a free citizenry, incorporating Greek models of military and social organization. The transformations brought about by the Etruscan kings became an enduring part of Rome. The Etruscans themselves did not. Just as the hoplite revolution in Greece saw the end of most Hellenic monarchies, around the traditionally reported date of 509 B.C.E. the Roman patricians expelled the last Etruscan king, Tarquin the Proud, and established a republic.

Rome and Italy

Just as in Rome, monarchy was giving way to oligarchic republics across Etruria in the sixth century B.C.E. Rome was hardly exceptional. However, the establishment of the Roman republic coincided roughly with the beginning of the Etruscan decline, allowing Rome to assert itself and to develop its Latin and Etruscan traditions in unique ways.

The Early Republic.   The patrician oligarchy had engineered the end of the monarchy, and patricians dominated the offices and institutions of the new republic at the expense of the plebs, who, in losing the king, lost their only defender. Governmental institutions of the early republic developed within this context of patrician supremacy.

Characteristic of republican institutions was that at every level, power was shared by two or more equals who were elected for fixed terms. This practice of shared power was intended to ensure that magistrates would consult with each other before making decisions and that no individual could achieve supreme power at any level. Replacing the king were the two *consuls,* each elected by the assembly for a one-year term. Initially, only the consuls held the **imperium,** the supreme power to command, to execute the law, and to impose the death penalty. Only in moments of grave crisis might a consul, with the approval of the Senate, name a single **dictator** with extraordinary absolute power for a very brief period, never more than six months. In time, other magistracies developed to perform specialized functions. *Praetors,* who in time also exercised the imperium, administered justice and defended the city in the absence of the consuls. *Quaestors* controlled finances. *Censors* assigned individuals their places in society, determined the amount of their taxes, filled vacancies in the Senate, and negotiated contracts for public construction projects. A variety of military commanders directed wars against neighboring cities and peoples under the imperium of the consuls. In all their actions these officeholders consulted with each other and with the Senate, which was composed of roughly 300 powerful former magistrates. The centuriate assembly functioned as the legislative organ of the state, but it continued to be dominated by the oldest and wealthiest members of society.

Patricians, Plebs, and Public Law.   During the early republic, wealthy patricians, aided by their clients, monopolized the Senate and the magistracies. Successful magistrates rose through a series of increasingly important offices, which came to be known as the *cursus honorum,* to the position of consul. Censors selected from among former magistrates in appointing new senators, thus ensuring that the Senate would be dominated by the patrician elite. Patricians also controlled the priesthoods, positions which they held for life. With political and religious power came economic power. The poorer plebs in particular found themselves sinking into debt to wealthy patricians, losing their property, and with it the basis for military service and political participation. In the courtroom, in the temple, in the assembly, and in the marketplace, plebeians found themselves subjected to the whims of an elite from which they were excluded.

The plebs began to organize in response to patrician control. On several occasions in the first half of the fifth century B.C.E., the whole plebeian order withdrew a short distance from the city, refusing to return or to serve in the military until conflicts with the patricians were resolved. In time, the plebs created their own assembly, the Council of the Plebs, which enacted laws that were binding on all plebeians. This council founded its own temples and elected magistrates called *tribunes,* whose persons were declared sacred to the gods. The tribunes protected the plebs from arbitrary patrician power. Anyone who harmed the tribunes, whether patrician or plebeian, could be killed by the plebs without trial. With their own assembly, magistracies, and religious cults, the plebeians were well on the way to creating a separate republic. This conflict between the plebeians and the patricians, known as the Struggle of Orders, threatened to tear Roman society apart just as pressure from hostile neighbors placed Rome on the defensive.

Political Expansion.   Roman preeminence in Latium had ended with the expulsion of the last king. The Etruscan town of Veii just north of the Tiber began periodic attacks against Rome. To the south, the Volscians had begun to expand northward into the Litis and Trerus valleys. This military pressure from the outside forced the patricians to seek a compromise with the plebeians. One of the first victories won by the plebs around 450 B.C.E. was the codification of basic Roman law, the Law of the Twelve Tables, which recognized the basic rights of all free citizens. The new law was posted publicly so that all could have access to it. Around the same time, the state began to absorb the plebeian political and religious organizations intact. Gradually, priesthoods, magistracies, and thus the Senate were opened to plebeians. The consulship was the last prize finally won by the plebs in 367 B.C.E. In 287 B.C.E., as the result of a final secession of the plebs, the decisions of the plebeian assembly became binding on all citizens, patrician and plebeian alike.

Bitter differences at home did not prevent patricians and plebs from presenting a united front against their enemies abroad. By the beginning of the fourth century B.C.E., the united patrician-plebeian state was expanding its rule both northward and southward. Roman legions, commanded by patricians but formed of the whole spectrum of property-owning Romans, reestablished Roman preeminence in Latium and then began a series of wars that brought most of Italy under Roman control. In 396 B.C.E., Roman forces captured and destroyed Veii and shortly afterward conquered the rest of southern Etruria. In the south, Roman and Latin forces turned back the Volscians. In 390 B.C.E., Rome suffered a temporary setback at the hands of the Gauls, or Celts, of northern Italy, who raided southward and sacked much of the city before being bought off with a large tribute payment. Even this event had a silver lining. The damage to Rome was short lived, but the Gauls had dealt a deathblow to the Etruscan cities of the north, clearing the way for later Roman conquest. By 295 B.C.E., Rome had secured its rule as far north as the Po Valley. In the south, Roman infantry and persistence proved the equal of professional Greek armies. Rome won a war of attrition against a series of Hellenistic commanders, the last of whom was the Greek king Pyrrhus of Epirus (319–272 B.C.E.). Pyrrhus, regarded as the greatest tactician of his day, won a number of victories that proved more costly to him than to his Roman opponents. In 275 B.C.E., after losing two-thirds of his troops in these "Pyrrhic victories," he withdrew to Sicily. By 265 B.C.E., Rome had absorbed the Hellenistic cities of the south.

Roman conquest benefited patrician and plebeian alike. While the patricians acquired wealth and power, the plebeians received a prize of equal value: land. After the capture of Veii, for example, the poor of Rome received shares of the conquered land. Since landowning was a prerequisite for military service, this distribution created still more peasant soldiers for further expeditions. Still, while the constant supply of new land did much to diffuse the tensions between orders, it did not actually resolve them. Into the late third century B.C.E., debt and landlessness remained major problems, creating tensions in Roman society. Probably not more than half of the citizen population owned land by 200 B.C.E.

Incorporating the Conquered.   The Roman manner of treating conquered populations, radically different from anything seen before, also contributed to Rome's success. In war, no one could match the Roman legions for ruthless, thorough destruction. Yet no conquerors had ever shown themselves so generous in victory. After Rome crushed the Latin revolt of 338 B.C.E., virtually all of the Latins were incorporated into the Roman citizenry. Later colonies founded outside of Latium were given the same status as Latin cities. Other, more distant conquered peoples were considered allies and were required to provide troops but no tribute to Rome. In time, they too might become citizens.

The implications of these measures were revolutionary. By extending citizenship to conquered neighbors and by offering the future possibility to allies, Rome tied their fate to its own. Rather than potentially subversive subjects, conquered populations became strong supporters. Thus, in contrast to the Hellenistic cities of the east, where Greeks jealously guarded their status from the indigenous population, Rome's colonies acted as magnets, drawing local populations into the Roman cultural and political orbit. Greeks were scandalized by the Roman tradition of giving citizenship even to freed slaves. By the end of the fourth century B.C.E., some of the sons of these freedmen were finding a place in the Senate. Finally, in all of its wars of conquest, Rome claimed a moral mandate. Romans went to great lengths to demonstrate that theirs were just wars, basing their claims on alleged acts of aggression by their enemies, on the appeal to Rome by its allies, and, increasingly, by presenting themselves as the preservers and defenders of Greek traditions of freedom. Both these political and propagandistic measures proved successful. Between 265 and 91 B.C.E. few serious revolts shook the peace and security of Italy south of the Po.

Benevolent treatment of the conquered spurred further conquest. Since subject cities and peoples did not pay tribute, the only way for Rome to benefit from its conquests or to exercise its authority was to demand and use troops. By 264 B.C.E., all of Italy was united under Roman hegemony. Roman expansion finally brought Rome into conflict with the great Mediterranean power of the west: Carthage.

Rome and the Mediterranean

Since its earliest days, Rome had allied itself with Carthage against the Greek cities of Italy. The zones of interest of the two cities had been quite separate. Carthage was a sea empire, whereas Rome was a land-based power without a navy. The Greeks, aspiring to power on land and sea, posed a threat to both Rome and Carthage. However, once Rome had conquered the Greek cities to the south, it became enmeshed in the affairs of neighboring Sicily, a region with well-established Carthaginian interests. There, in 265 B.C.E., a group of Italian mercenary pirates in Messina, threatened by Syracuse, requested Roman assistance. The Senate refused, but the plebeian assembly, eager for booty, exercised its newly won right to legislate for the republic and accepted. Shortly afterward, the Romans invaded Sicily, and Syracuse turned to its old enemy, Carthage, for assistance. The First Punic War had begun.

The First Punic War.   This war, which lasted from 265 to 241 B.C.E., was a costly, brutal, and drawn-out affair that Rome won by dint of persistence and methodical calculation rather than strategic brilliance. Rome invaded and concluded an alliance with Syracuse in 263 B.C.E. The war rapidly became a sea war. Rome had little previous naval experience but quickly learned the rules of the game and then rewrote them to its own advantage. Taking a wrecked Carthaginian ship as a model, Roman builders constructed twenty fast ships propelled by roughly 200 oarsmen to ram and sink opposing ships. Rome also built 100 larger ships with crews of 300,

MAP DISCOVERY

The Punic Wars

What accidents of geography and political expansion made war between Rome and Carthage almost inevitable? What advantages might Hannibal have seen in taking the route he did to attack Rome? What were the long-term effects of Hannibal's route for the inhabitants of the Iberian Peninsula and Gaul? What parts of Carthage's African Empire might have been most attractive to Roman conquerors?

manned by Roman allies. Unaccustomed to fighting at sea, Roman engineers turned sea battles into land battles by placing on their ships heavy gangplanks that could be dropped onto enemy ships. The gangplanks were equipped with a heavy iron spike to secure them to the enemy's deck. This allowed a contingent of legionnaires to march onto the enemy ship and fight as though on dry land.

With these innovations the Romans won impressive initial victories but still could not deliver a knockout blow in either Sicily or North Africa for over 20 years. Finally, in 241 B.C.E., Rome forced the Carthaginian commander, Hamilcar Barca

(ca. 270–229 B.C.E.), to surrender simply because the Romans could afford to build one more fleet than he. Carthage paid a huge indemnity and abandoned Sicily. Syracuse and Messina became allies of Rome. In a break with tradition, Rome obligated the rest of Sicily to pay a true tribute in the form of a tithe (one-tenth) of their crops. Shortly after that, Rome helped itself to Sardinia as well, from which it again demanded tribute, not simply troops. Rome had established an empire.

During the next two decades, Roman legions defeated the Ligurians on the northwest coast, the Celtic Gauls south of the Alps, and the Illyrians along the Adriatic coast. At the same time, Carthage fought a bitter battle against its own mercenary armies, which it had been unable to pay off after its defeat. Carthage then began the systematic creation of an empire in Spain. Trade between Carthage and Rome reached the highest level in history, but trade did not create friendship—only a wary peace. On both sides, powerful leaders saw the treaty of 241 B.C.E. as just a pause in a fight to the death. Hamilcar Barca had his nine-year-old son Hannibal swear to be Rome's eternal enemy. Fearful and greedy Romans insisted that Carthage had to be destroyed for the security of Rome. They were particularly disturbed by the growth of Carthage's Spanish empire, even though Hamilcar Barca assured the Senate that he was simply trying to raise funds to pay off Carthage's indemnity.

Securing Western Hegemony.   After the death of Hamilcar, Carthaginian successes in Spain, led by Hamilcar's son-in-law Hasdrubal (d. 221 B.C.E.) and his son Hannibal (247–183 B.C.E.), finally provoked Rome to war in 218 B.C.E. As soon as this Second Punic War had begun, Hannibal began an epic march north out of Spain, along the Mediterranean coast, and across the Alps. In spite of great hardships he was able to transport over 23,000 troops and approximately 18 war elephants into the plains of northern Italy.

Hannibal's brilliant generalship brought victory after victory to the Carthaginian forces. In the first engagement, on the Trebia River in the Po Valley, the Romans lost 20,000 men, two-thirds of their army. Carthaginian success encouraged the Gauls to join the fight against the Romans. Initially, Italian, Etruscan, and Greek allies remained loyal, but after Rome's catastrophic defeats at Lake Trasimene in Etruria in 217 B.C.E. and especially at Cannae in 216 B.C.E., a number of Italian colonies and allies, namely the cities of Capua and Syracuse, went over to the enemy. In the east, Philip V of Macedon (238–179 B.C.E.) made a treaty with Carthage in the hope of taking Illyria (today the coast of Croatia) from a defeated Rome.

As commanders chosen by the patrician-dominated Senate failed to stop the enemy, the Roman plebs became increasingly dissatisfied with the way the oligarchy was conducting the war. In 217 B.C.E., following the battle of Lake Trasimene, the Senate named the capable general Quintus Fabius Maximus (d. ca. 203 B.C.E.) dictator. He used delaying tactics successfully to slow the Carthaginians. The popular assembly, impatient for a decisive victory, elected a second dictator, thus effectively canceling the position of Quintus Fabius Maximus. The next year, popular pressure forced the election of Gaius Terentius Varro as consul. Varro quickly led the army to the greatest defeat in Roman history at Cannae. There, Hannibal surrounded and annihilated Varro's numerically superior army.

Three things, however, saved the Roman state. First, while some important allies and colonies defected, the majority held firm. Rome's traditions of sharing the fruits of victory with its allies, extending the rights of Roman citizenship, and protecting central and southern Italy against its enemies proved stronger than the appeals of Hannibal. Although he was victorious time and again, without local support Hannibal could not hold the terrain and cities he won. New allies such as Syracuse, which fell in 212 B.C.E., were forcibly

returned to the Roman camp. Fabius resumed his delaying tactics, and gradually Hannibal's victories slipped from his hands.

The second reason for Rome's survival was the tremendous social solidarity that all classes and factions of its population showed during these desperate years. In spite of the internal tensions between patricians and plebeians, their ultimate dedication to Rome never faltered. Much of this loyalty was due to the Roman system of strong family and patronage ties. Kinsmen and clients answered the call of their patriarchs and patrons to bounce back repeatedly from defeat. Roman farmer-soldiers stood firm.

The third reason for Rome's ultimate success was Publius Cornelius Scipio (236–184 B.C.E.), also known as Scipio the Elder, a commander who was able to force Hannibal from Italy. Scipio, who earned the title Africanus for his victory, accomplished this not by attacking Hannibal directly, but by taking the war home to the enemy, first in Spain and then in Africa. In 210 B.C.E., Scipio arrived in Spain and rapidly captured the city of Cartagena (New Carthage). Within four years he destroyed Punic power in Spain. Riding the crest of popular enthusiasm at home, he raised a new army and in 204

POLYBIUS DESCRIBES THE SACK OF NEW CARTHAGE

In the following selection, the Greek historian Polybius, who was a close friend of the adopted grandson of Scipio Africanus, describes the Roman capture of New Carthage (Carthago Nova) in Spain in 210 B.C.E. during the Second Punic War. Before a siege, Romans offered their enemies generous terms, but once the siege had begun, they offered none. The passage shows the combination of brutality and thoroughness with which the Romans liquidated those who defied them.

Focus Questions

Why did Scipio order his troops to kill everyone they found on entering the city? What incentives did Roman citizens have to fight in the Punic Wars?

Scipio, when he judged that a large enough number of troops had entered the town, let loose the majority of them against the inhabitants, according to the Roman custom; their orders were to exterminate every form of life they encountered, sparing none, but not to start pillaging until the word was given to do so. This practice is adopted to inspire terror, and so when cities are taken by the Romans you often see not only the corpses of human beings but dogs cut in half and the dismembered limbs of other animals, and on this occasion the carnage was especially frightful because of the large size of the population.

Scipio himself with about 1,000 men pressed on toward the citadel. Here [the Carthaginian commander] Margo at first put up some resistance, but as soon as he knew for certain that the city had been captured he sent a message to plead for his safety, and handed over the citadel. Once this had happened the signal was given to stop the slaughter and the troops then began to pillage the city. When darkness fell . . . Scipio . . . recalled the rest of his troops from the private houses of the city and ordered them through the military tribunes to collect all the spoils in the marketplace, each maniple bringing its own share. . . . Next day all the booty . . . was collected in the marketplace, where the military tribunes divided it among their respective legions, according to the Roman custom. . . . All those who have been detailed to collect the plunder then bring it back, each man to his own legion, and after it has been sold, the tribunes distribute the proceeds equally among all.

From Polybius, *The Rise of the Roman Empire.*

B.C.E. sailed for Africa. His victories there drew Hannibal home, where at Zama in 202 B.C.E. the Roman commander destroyed the Carthaginian army. Zama put an end to both the Second Punic War and Carthaginian political power. Saddled with a huge indemnity and forced to abandon all of its territories and colonies to Rome, Carthage was reduced to a small portion of the North African coast. It had become in effect a Roman subject.

The Final Destruction. Still, this humiliating defeat was not enough for Rome. While some Roman senators favored allowing Carthage to survive as a means of keeping the Roman plebs under senatorial control, others demanded destruction. Chief among them was the censor Marcus Porcius Cato, known as Cato the Elder (234–149 B.C.E.), who ended every speech with "Carthage must be destroyed." Ultimately, trumped-up reasons were found to renew the war in 149 B.C.E. In contrast to the desperate, hard-fought campaigns of the Second Punic War, the Third was an unevenly matched slaughter. In 146 B.C.E., Scipio Aemilianus (184–129 B.C.E.), or Scipio the Younger, the adopted grandson of Scipio the Elder, overwhelmed Carthage and sold its few survivors into slavery. As a symbolic act of final destruction, he then had the site razed, plowed, and cursed. Carthage's fertile hinterland became the property of wealthy Roman senators.

Expansion into the Hellenistic East. In the same year that Carthage was destroyed, Roman armies destroyed Corinth, a second great center of Mediterranean commerce. This victory marked the culmination of Roman imperialist expansion eastward into the Greek and Hellenistic world, which had begun with the conquest of Illyria. This expansion was not simply the result of Roman imperialist ambitions. The Hellenistic states, in their constant warring and bickering, had drawn Rome into their conflicts against their neighbors. Greek states asked the Roman Senate to arbitrate their disputes. Pergamum requested military assistance against Macedonia. Appealing to Rome's claims as "liberator," cities pressed the Senate to preserve their freedom in the face of aggressive expansion by their more powerful neighbors. In a series of intermittent, uncoordinated, and sporadic engagements, Rome did intervene, although its real focus was on its life-and-death struggle with Carthage.

Roman intentions may not have been conquest, but Roman intervention upset the balance of power in the Hellenistic world. The price of Roman arbitration, intervention, and protection was loss of independence. Gradually, the Roman shadow fell over the eastern Mediterranean.

The treaty that Philip V of Macedon concluded with Carthage during the Second Punic War provided an initial excuse for war, one that was seized on more eagerly by the plebeian assembly than by the Senate. Shortly after its victory at Zama, Rome provoked Philip to war and then easily defeated him in 197 B.C.E., proclaiming the freedom of the Greek cities and withdrawing from Greece. In 189 B.C.E., the Seleucid Antiochus III (223–187 B.C.E.) of Syria suffered the same fate, and Rome declared the Greek cities in Asia Minor that he had controlled free. The Greeks venerated the Roman commander, Titus Quinctius Flamininus (228–174 B.C.E.), as a god—the first Roman to be accorded this eastern honor.

In reality, the control of the freed cities lay in the hands of local oligarchs who were favorable to Rome. In 179 B.C.E., Philip's son Perseus (179–168 B.C.E.) attempted to stir up democratic opposition to Rome within the cities. This time, Rome responded more forcefully. The Macedonian kingdom was divided into four republics governed by their own senates and magistrates selected from among the local aristocrats. In Epirus, 70 cities were destroyed, and 150,000 people were sold into slavery. This harsh punishment prompted other Greek cities to react with panic even to the mere threat of Roman retribution. When the citizens of Rhodes heard that the Senate was contemplating declaring war on them, they quickly executed all of their anti-Roman fellows.

The final episode of Rome's expansionist drama unfolded during the Third Punic War. When Rome resumed its war with Carthage in 149 B.C.E., several Greek cities attempted once more to assert their autonomy from the hated oligarchies established by Rome. Retribution was swift. Roman legions crushed the rebel forces, and, as an example to all, Corinth was razed and its population was enslaved.

In the west, in northern Italy, Spain, and Africa, Roman conquest had been direct and complete. Tribal structures had been replaced by Roman provinces governed by former magistrates or proconsuls. In the east, Rome preferred to work through the existing political hierarchies. Still, Rome cultivated its image as

CHRONOLOGY	
THE ROMAN REPUBLIC	
509 B.C.E.	Expulsion of last Etruscan king; beginning of Roman Republic
ca. 450 B.C.E.	Law of the Twelve Tables
396 B.C.E.	Rome conquers southern Etruria
295 B.C.E.	Rome extends rule north to Po Valley
265–241 B.C.E.	First Punic War
264 B.C.E.	All of Italy under Roman control
218–202 B.C.E.	Second Punic War
149–146 B.C.E.	Third Punic War; Carthage is destroyed

protector of Greek liberties against the Macedonian and Seleucid monarchies and preferred indirect control to annexation. Its power was no less real for being indirect.

By 146 B.C.E., the Roman republic controlled the whole rim of the Mediterranean from Rhodes in the east across Greece, Dalmatia, Italy, southern Gaul, Spain, and North Africa. Even Syria and Egypt, although nominally independent, had to bow before Roman will. This subjugation had been graphically demonstrated in 168 B.C.E., when the Seleucid Antiochus IV (175–164 B.C.E.) invaded the kingdom of the Egyptian ruler Ptolemy VI (180–145 B.C.E.) and besieged Alexandria. The Ptolemys had long before made a treaty with Rome, and the Senate sent an envoy to Antiochus with written instructions to withdraw immediately from Egypt. The king replied that he would like to consult before making a decision. The Roman envoy immediately drew a circle around Antiochus, ordering him to give an answer before he stepped out of the ring. Such directness was unknown in the world of Hellenistic diplomacy. After a moment's hesitation, the deeply shocked Antiochus replied that he would do whatever the Romans demanded. Through perseverance and determination, Rome had risen from obscurity to become the greatest power the West had ever known. The republic had endured great adversity. It would not survive prosperity.

■ One of a series of Roman mosaics illustrating tasks appropriate to the months of the year. Here two laborers are using an olive press with a horizontal screw for the December olive pressing.

REPUBLICAN CIVILIZATION

Territorial conquest, the influx of unprecedented riches, and exposure to sophisticated Hellenistic civilization ultimately overwhelmed earlier Roman civilization. This civilization had been created by stubborn farmers and soldiers who valued authority, simplicity, and piety above all else. This unique culture was the source of strength that led Rome to greatness, but its limitations prevented the republic from resolving its internal social tensions and the external problems caused by the burden of empire.

Farmers and Soldiers

The ideal Roman farmer was not the great estate owner of the Greek world, but the smallholder, the dirt farmer of central Italy. Typical farm families, with holdings of perhaps as little as 10 acres, raised grain, beans, and hogs for their own consumption. In addition, they cultivated vineyards and olive groves for cash crops. But the most important crop of Roman farms was citizens. "From farmers come the bravest men and the sturdiest soldiers," wrote Cato the Elder. Nor was the ideal Roman soldier the gallant cavalryman but rather the solid foot soldier. Cavalry—composed of wealthy citizens who made up the elite **equestrian** order—and especially allies provided reconnaissance and protected Roman flanks. The main fighting force, however, was the infantry. Sometime in the early republic the Greek phalanx was transformed into the Roman legion, a flexible unit composed of 30 companies of 120 men each, armed with javelins and short swords.

Constant training, careful preparation, and painstaking execution characterized every aspect of Roman military expeditions. Wars were won as much by engineering feats as by feats of arms. Engineers constructed bridges, siege machines, and catapults. By the time of the late republic, Roman armies on the march could construct identical camps each night, quickly building a strong square fort 2,150 feet on a side. Within the camp, every unit had exactly the same location for its quarters, as did the commander and paymaster. The chain of command was rigidly maintained from the commander, a Roman consul, through military tribunes and centurions, two of whom commanded each company of 120 men.

These solid, methodical troops, the backbone of the republican armies that conquered the Mediterranean, were among the victims of that conquest. The pressures of constant international warfare were destroying the farmer-soldiers whom the traditionalists loved to praise. When the Roman sphere of interest had been confined to central Italy, farmers could do their planting in spring, serve in the army during the summer months, and return home to care for their farms in time for harvest. When Rome's wars became international expeditions lasting for years, many soldiers, unable to work their lands while doing military service, had to mortgage their farms in order to support their families. When they returned, they often found that during their prolonged absences they had lost their farms to wealthy aristocratic moneylenders. While aristocrats amassed vast landed estates worked by imported slaves, ordinary Romans and Italians lacked even a family farm capable of supporting themselves and their families. Without land they and their sons were excluded from further military service and sank into the growing mass of desperately poor, disfranchised citizens.

The Roman Family

In Roman tradition, the paterfamilias was the master of the family—which in theory included his wife, children, and slaves—over whom he exercised the power of life and death. This authority lasted as long as he lived. Only at his death did his sons, even if they were long grown and married, achieve legal and financial independence. The family was the basic unit of society, of the state.

Although not kept in seclusion as in Greece, Roman women theoretically never exercised independent power in this male-dominated world. Before marriage, a Roman girl was subject to the authority of her father. When she married, her father traditionally transferred legal guardianship to her husband, thus severing her bonds to paternal family. A husband could divorce his wife at will, returning her and her dowry to her father. However, wives did exercise real though informal authority within the family. Part of this authority came from their role in the moral education of their children and the direction of the household. Part also came from their control over their dowries. Widows might exercise even greater authority in the raising of their children.

Paternal authority over children was absolute. Not all children born into a marriage became members of the family. The Law of the Twelve Tables allowed defective children to be killed for the good of the family. Newborn infants were laid on the ground before the father, who decided whether the child should be raised. By picking up a son, he accepted the child into the family. Ordering that a daughter be nursed similarly signified acceptance. If there were too many mouths to feed or the child was simply unwanted, the father could command that the infant be killed or abandoned. Abandoned children might be adopted by childless couples.

Nor were all sons born into Roman families. Romans made use of adoption for many purposes. Families without heirs could adopt children. Powerful political and military figures might adopt promising young men as their political heirs. These adopted sons held the same legal rights as the father's natural offspring and thus were integral members of his family.

Slaves, too, were members of the family. On the one hand, slaves were property without personal rights. On the other, they might live and work alongside the free members of the family, worship the family gods, and enjoy the protection and endure the authority of the paterfamilias. In fact, the authority of the paterfamilias was roughly the same over slave and free members of the family. If he desired, he could sell the free members of the family into slavery.

The center of everyday life for the Roman family was the *domus,* the family house whose architectural style had developed from Etruscan traditions. Visitors entered through the front door into the *atrium,* a central courtyard containing a collecting pool into which rainwater for household use flowed from the roof through terra-cotta drains. In niches or on shelves stood wax or terra-cotta busts of ancestors and statues of the household gods. Around the atrium, openings gave on to workrooms, storerooms, bedrooms, offices, and small dining rooms.

Social Effects of Expansion

In the wake of imperial conquests, the Roman family and its environment began to change in ways that were disturbing to many of the oligarchy. Some women, perhaps in imitation of their more liberated Hellenistic sisters, began to take a more active role in public life. One example is Cornelia, a daughter of Scipio Africanus. After her husband's death in 154 B.C.E., she refused to remarry, devoting herself instead to raising her children, administering their inheritance, and directing their political careers.

Some married women, too, escaped the authority of their husbands. Fewer and fewer fathers transferred authority over their daughters to their husbands. Instead, daughters remained under their father's authority as long as he lived. This meant that on the father's death, they became independent persons, able to manage their own affairs without their husbands' consent or interference. Although some historians believe that sentimental bonds of affection may have increased between many husbands and wives and parents and children as legal bonds loosened, it also meant that the wife's relationship to her children was weakened. Roman mothers had never been legally related to their children. Wives and mothers were not fully part of their husbands' families. Their brother's families, not their own children, were their natural heirs. Just as adoption created political bonds, marriage to daughters sealed alliances between men. However, when these alliances fell apart or more advantageous ones presented themselves, fathers could force their daughters to divorce their husbands and to marry someone else. Divorce became increasingly common in the second century B.C.E. More and more, wives were temporary visitors in their husbands' homes.

Not every Roman family could afford its own domus, and in the aftermath of the imperial expansion, housing problems became acute for the poor. In Rome and other towns of Italy, shopkeepers lived in small houses attached to their shops or in rooms behind their workplaces. Peasants who were forced off their land and into cities found shelter in multistory apartment buildings, an increasingly common sight in the cities of the empire. In these cramped structures, families crowded into small, low rooms about ten feet square. In Roman towns throughout Italy, simple dwellings, luxurious mansions, shops, and apartment buildings existed side by side. The rich and the poor rubbed shoulders every day, producing a friction that threatened to burst into flame.

Roman Religion

Romans worshipped many gods, the more the better. Every aspect of daily life and work was the responsibility of individual powers, or *numina*. Every man had his *genius* or personal *numen,* just as every woman had her *juno.* Each family had its household powers, the *lares familiares,* whose proper worship was the responsibility of the paterfamilias. The *vesta* was the spirit of the hearth fire. The *lares* were the deities of farmland, the *domus,* and the guardians of roads and travelers. The *penates* guarded the family larder or storage cupboard. These family spirits exercised a binding power, a *religio,* on the Romans, and the pious Roman householder recognized these claims and undertook the *officia,* or duties, to which the spirits were entitled. These basic attitudes of religion, piety, and office lay at the heart of Roman reverence for order and authority. They extended to other traditional Roman and Latin gods such as Jupiter, the supreme god; Juno, his wife; Mars, the god of war; and the two-faced Janus, spirit of gates and new beginnings.

Outside the household, worship of the gods and the reading of the future in the entrails of sacrificed animals, the flight of birds, or changes in weather were the responsibilities of colleges of priests. Roman priests did not, as did those in the Near East, form a special caste but rather were important members of the elite who held priesthoods in addition to other public offices. Religion was less a matter of personal relationship with the gods than a public, civic activity that bound society together. State-supported cults with their colleges of priests, Etruscan- and Greek-style temples, and elaborate ceremonies were integral parts of the Roman state and society. The world of the gods reflected that of mortals. As the Roman mortal world expanded, so did the divine. Romans were quick to identify foreign gods with their own. Thus Zeus became Jupiter, Hera became Juno, and Aphrodite became Venus.

Still, the elasticity of Roman religion could stretch just so far. With the empire came not only the cults of Zeus, Apollo, and Aphrodite to Rome but that of Dionysus as well. Unlike the formal public cults of the other Greek deities, which were firmly in the control of authorities, that of Dionysus was largely outside state control. Women, in the tradition of the maenads, controlled much of the ecstatic and overtly sexual rituals associated with the god. Following the Second Punic War, the cult of Dionysus, known in Latin as Bacchus, spread rapidly in Italy. At its secret rites, or *Bacchanalia,* men and women were rumored to engage in every kind of sexual act.

In 186 B.C.E., the Senate decreed the cult of Bacchus a conspiracy and ordered an inquiry. The consul Spurius Postumius Albinus, acting on the false testimony of a former prostitute, began a brutal persecution. Rituals were banned, priests and adherents were arrested, and rewards were offered to informants, who provided lurid and fanciful accounts of what had taken place at the Bacchanalia. Hundreds of people were imprisoned, and greater numbers were executed. The Senate ordered all shrines to Bacchus destroyed and Bacchanalia banned throughout Italy. Perhaps more than any other episode, the suppression of the Bacchic cult showed the oligarchy's fear of the changes sweeping Roman civilization.

Republican Letters

As Rome absorbed foreign gods, it also absorbed foreign letters. From the Etruscans the Romans adopted and adapted the alphabet, the one in which most Western languages are written to this day. Early Latin inscriptions are largely funeral monuments and some public notices such as the Law of the Twelve Tables. The Roman high priest responsible for maintaining the calendar of annual feasts also prepared and updated annals, short accounts of important religious and secular events of each year. However, before the third century B.C.E., apart from extravagant funerary eulogies carefully preserved within families, Romans had no apparent interest in writing or literature as such. The birth of Latin letters began with Rome's exposure to Greek civilization.

Greek Historians of Rome. Early in the third century B.C.E., Greek authors had begun to pay attention to expanding Rome. The first serious Greek historian to focus on this new Western power was Timaeus (ca. 356–ca. 260 B.C.E.), who spent most of his productive life in Athens. There he wrote a history of Rome up to the Pyrrhic war, interviewing Roman and Greek witnesses to gain an understanding of this Italian city that had defeated a Hellenistic army. Polybius (ca. 200–ca. 118 B.C.E.), the greatest of the Greek historians to record Rome's rise to power, gathered his information firsthand. As one of a thousand eminent Greeks deported to Rome for political investigation, he became a close friend of Scipio Aemilianus and accompanied him on his Spanish and African campaigns. Polybius's history is both the culmination of the traditions of Greek historiography and its transformation, since it centers on the rise of a non-Greek power to rule "almost the whole inhabited world."

The Origins of Latin Literature. At the same time that Greeks began to take Rome seriously, Romans themselves became interested in Greece, in particular in the international Hellenistic culture of the eastern Mediterranean. The earliest Latin literary works were clearly adaptations if not translations of Hellenistic genres and texts. Already in 240 B.C.E., plays in the Greek tradition were said to have been performed in Rome. The earliest extant literary works, ironically for the sober image of the Roman farmer-soldier, are the plays of Plautus (ca. 254–184 B.C.E.) and Terence (186–159 B.C.E.), lightly adapted translations of Hellenistic comedies.

Scheming servants, mistaken identities, bedroom farces, young lovers, and lecherous elders make up the plots of the Roman plays. The authors of these comedies experimented with and transformed Greek literature. Plautus, in particular, while maintaining superficially the Greek settings of his plays, actually creates a world that is more Roman than Greek. References to Roman laws, magistrates, clients, and social situations abound, as do humorous derogatory comments on Greek mores. Terence, although remaining closer to Greek models, Romanized his material through the creation of an elegant, natural style. His plays rapidly became classics, influencing subsequent generations of Latin authors, who worked to create a literary language separate from but equal to Greek.

THE CRISIS OF ROMAN VIRTUE

Rome's rise to world power within less than a century profoundly affected every aspect of republican life. Magistrates operating far from senatorial control in conquered provinces exercised power and found opportunities for enrichment never before seen. Successful commanders, honored and even deified by Eastern cities, felt the temptation to ignore the strict requirements of senatorial accountability. During the time of a provincial command, it was said, one had to make three fortunes: the first to pay off the bribes it took to get the office, the second to pay off the jury that would investigate corruption after the command had expired, and a third to live on for the rest of one's life. Provincial commanders enriched themselves through extortion, collusion with dishonest government contractors and tax collectors, and wholesale bribe-taking. Ordinary citizens, aware of such abuses, felt increasingly threatened by the wealthy and powerful.

In the second century B.C.E., Romans found themselves in a dilemma as the old and the new exerted equal pressures. These tensions led to almost a century of bitter civil strife and ultimately to the disintegration of the republic. The complex interaction of these tensions can best be seen in the life of one man, Marcus Porcius Cato.

■ A memorial sculpture of Cato the Elder and his wife. Cato defended the ancient Roman traditions even as he himself was deeply influenced by the changes sweeping Rome.

Cato the Elder is often presented as the preserver of the old traditions, in contrast to Scipio Aemilianus, destroyer of Carthage and proponent of Hellenism in the Roman world. True, as censor, fighting against conspicuous consumption, and as self-conscious defender of the past, Cato cast himself in the mold of the traditional Roman. And Scipio, with his love of Hellenism and his political career defined more by personal achievement than traditional magistracies, represented a new type of Roman. But if the division between old and new, between Cato and Scipio, had been so clear-cut, the dilemma of republican Rome would not have been so great. As it was, Cato reflected in himself this contradictory clash of values. Like the two-faced god Janus, whom he invoked in all his undertakings, Cato was the stern censor, the guardian and proponent of traditional Roman virtue, as well as the new Roman of shrewd business acumen, influence, and power unimaginable to the simple farmers he professed to admire.

Cato was born in the Latin town of Tusculum in 234 B.C.E. and grew to maturity on a family estate in Sabine territory. He came of age just at the start of the Second Punic War and distinguished himself in campaigns against Hannibal in Italy and Syracuse in Sicily. In between campaigns he became even more famous for his eloquence in pleading legal cases. His talents and energy brought him to the attention of powerful members of the senatorial aristocracy, under whose patronage he came to Rome. There he began to rise through the offices of military tribune, quaestor, and ultimately consul and censor.

This first-generation senator became the spokesman for the traditional values of Rome, for severity and simplicity, for honesty and frugality in private and public life. Cato ridiculed Greek philosophy and education, and he glorified his own simple farm life, the care he took in the management of his estates and of his extended *familia*, and his working in his fields side by side with his slaves.

Actually, Cato, as much as anyone else, was deeply involved in the rapid changes brought about by the empire. He may have worked along with his slaves, but as soon as they grew old, he sold them to the state to avoid having to support them, something no conscientious paterfamilias would ever have done. Although he led the battle to prevent senators from participating in commerce, he was perhaps the first of that body to diversify his holdings and investments. He bought up land, hot baths, and mineral deposits. Although he avoided conspicuous consumption himself, as consul and censor he was responsible for many of the sumptuous building projects in Rome through which ordinary Romans first experienced the luxuries of the Hellenistic world. While scorning Greek culture, he worked bits of Greek authors even into his attacks on Greek civilization.

Cato was neither duplicitous nor hypocritical. He was simply typical. Many senators agreed with him that the old values were slipping away and, with them, the foundation of the republic. Many feared that personal ambition was undermining the power of the oligarchy. Yet these same people could not resist exploiting the changed circumstances for their own benefit.

CONCLUSION

Rome had come a long way since its origin as an outpost of the Alban League. At first overshadowed by its more civilized neighbors to the north and south, it had slowly and tenaciously achieved independence from and then domination over its more ancient neighbors. It absorbed or adapted ideas and institutions from the Etruscans, Greeks, and others with whom it came into contact. Rome's great success was largely due to Roman authoritarianism as well as to its genius for creative adaptation, flexibility, and thoroughness and its willingness to give those it conquered a stake in Roman victory. Until the middle of the second century B.C.E. this formula had served the republic well. After the final destruction of Carthage, however, an isolated and fearful oligarchy appeared unwilling or unable to broaden the base of those participating in the Roman achievement. The result was a century of conflict and civil war that destroyed the republican empire.

QUESTIONS FOR REVIEW

1. Why might the Greeks have been surprised by certain characteristics of Carthaginian and Etruscan society?
2. What social, political, and military practices made possible the expansion of Rome from a collection of villages into a power that ultimately destroyed Carthage in the Punic Wars?
3. How were family and household life organized in the domus of the Roman Republic?
4. Why were Romans like Cato the Elder concerned by the changes that accompanied the expansion of Roman international power?

KEY TERMS

dictator, *p. 75*

equestrians, *p. 80*

Etruscans, *p. 72*

imperium, *p. 75*

paterfamilias, *p. 73*

patricians, *p. 74*

plebs, *p. 73*

Villanovans, *p. 70*

DISCOVERING WESTERN CIVILIZATION ONLINE

You can obtain more information about early Rome at the websites listed below. See also the Companion Website that accompanies this text, www.ablongman.com/kishlansky, which contains an online study guide and additional resources.

General Websites

Ancient Rome
www.providence.edu/dwc/rome.htm
A course web page with links to every aspect of Roman history and civilization.

NM's Creative Impulse: Rome
history.evansville.net/rome.html
An excellent website dedicated to Roman history.

Places to Go: Carthage
www.tourismtunisia.com/togo/carthage/carthage.html
A brief introduction to Carthage designed for tourists but with historical information.

The Etruscan Civilization: Art and Archaeology Links
oncampus.richmond.edu/academics/classics/students/belanger/etruscolnks.html
A site dedicated to Etruscan civilization.

From City to Empire

Frank E. Smitha's World History: The Rise of Ancient Rome
fsmitha.com/h1/ch15.htm
An outline by Frank Smitha of early Roman history beginning with the legendary accounts of Rome's foundation.

The Forum Romanum: History and Religion
library.thinkquest.org/11402/homehis.html
A Thinkquest site on Roman history and religion including links to Roman archaeology.

Republican Civilization

Women's Life in Greece and Rome
www.stoa.org/diotima/anthology/wlgr/
A site devoted to women in Rome and Greece.

Republican Roman Government
www.utexas.edu/depts/classics/faculty/Riggsby/RepGov.html
A detailed explanation of the republican constitution of Rome.

SUGGESTIONS FOR FURTHER READING

Primary Sources

Many of the works of Polybius, Livy, Cato, Caesar, Cicero, and other Roman authors are available in English translation from Penguin Books. The first volume—*Roman Civilization, Selected Readings, Vol. I: The Republic* (1951), by Naphtali Lewis and Meyer Reinhold—contains a wide selection of documents with useful introductions. An excellent selection of Roman historical writing can be found in Ronald Mellor, *The Roman Historians* (New York: Routledge, 1999).

The Western Mediterranean to 509 B.C.E.

Graeme Barker and Tom Rasmussen, *The Etruscans* (Oxford: Blackwell Publishers, 2000). An introduction to Etruscan studies and history.

Serge Lancel, *Carthage: A History* (Oxford: Blackwell Publishers, 1997). A basic introduction.

From City to Empire, 509–146 B.C.E.

Nigel Bagnall, *The Punic Wars* (London: Hutchinson, 1990). Survey of the wars between Rome and Carthage.

Mary Beard and Michael Crawford, *Rome in the Late Republic* (Ithaca, NY: Cornell University Press, 1985). A short interpretive essay on the crisis of the late republic.

John Boardman, Jasper Griffin, and Oswyn Murray, *The Oxford History of the Roman World* (New York: Oxford University Press, 2001). A balanced collection of essays on all aspects of Roman history and civilization.

K. R. Bradley, *Slavery and Society at Rome* (New York: Cambridge University Press, 1994). The place of slavery in the Roman world.

P. A. Brunt, *Social Conflicts in the Roman Republic* (New York: Norton, 1971). Analyzes the continuing struggle between patricians and plebeians until the end of the republic.

Tim Cornell, *The Beginnings of Rome, 1000–264 B.C.* (New York: Routledge, 1995). A new look at the origins of Rome.

Michael Crawford, *The Roman Republic* (Cambridge, MA: Harvard University Press, 1978). A modern survey of the republican period, emphasizing political history.

Republican Civilization

Geza Alfoldy, *The Social History of Rome* (Berlin: Walter de Gruyter, 1988). A survey of Rome that emphasizes the relationship between social structure and politics.

Erich S. Gruen, *Culture and National Identity in Republican Rome* (Ithaca, NY: Cornell University Press, 1992). Important lectures by a major figure in the field.

Erich S. Gruen, *The Hellenistic World and the Coming of Rome,* 2 vols. (Berkeley: University of California Press, 1984). A detailed history of the Hellenistic world, presenting Rome's gradual and unintended rise to dominance in it.

Sarah B. Pomeroy, ed., *Women's History and Ancient History* (Chapel Hill: University of North Carolina Press, 1991). The place to begin for the history of women in antiquity.

The Crisis of Roman Virtue

Alan E. Astin, *Cato the Censor* (New York: Oxford University Press, 1978). An excellent biography of Cato that also analyzes his writings.

Pat Southern, *Pompey the Great* (Stroud, England: Tempus Publishing Ltd., 2002). The most recent biography of the triumvir.

For a list of additional titles related to this chapter's topics, please see www.ablongman.com/kishlansky.

Chapter 5

IMPERIAL ROME, 146 B.C.E.–192 C.E.

The Visual Record

THE ALTAR OF AUGUSTAN PEACE

In 27 B.C.E., Octavian, known to history as the Emperor Augustus, emerged as the absolute ruler of a Roman world tired of bloodshed. In 13 B.C.E., a grateful (and ingratiating) Senate decreed that Augustus be honored by the construction of an altar dedicated to the new goddess of peace, Pax, erected on the field long-sacred to her opposite, Mars, the god of war. Pax was one of Augustus's favorite divinities and the cornerstone of his political program. In return for abandoning all hopes of republican government, Augustus promised harmony, prosperity, and, above all, peace. More than any other surviving monument, the Altar of Augustan Peace, in its design and in the ideology of its elaborate carved friezes, embodies Augutus's vision of that peace.

The style of the Roman Pantheon, a 20-by-24-foot marble rectangle standing more than three feet tall and surrounded on three sides by a U-shaped counter, revived a form common hundreds of years earlier. Augustus, whose transformation of the Roman state and society was so radical that it has been rightly termed a revolution, was always careful to present the most daring innovations as restorations of ancient republican tradition.

To reach the altar, a visitor must climb a short flight of steps and enter through an enclosure wall erected of massive rectangular slabs of marble. The lower course of the external walls is decorated with delicate, intricately intertwined acanthus plants, a symbol of peaceful abundance that came to be intimately associated with Augustan art. The upper course contains exquisitely carved friezes representing the stories of the two mythical founders of Rome: Romulus, the abandoned child nursed by a she-wolf, and Aeneas, the legendary Trojan warrior who

wandered the Mediterranean in obedience to the gods until he arrived at the site of Rome. On the sides of the wall are images of processions. On the south, Augustus and his family prepare to celebrate the cult of the goddess of peace. On the north side magistrates and ordinary Roman citizens carry gifts, either to Augustus or to the Augustan Peace—it was really the same thing.

On the far side of the enclosure, the side most visible to passing Romans, the visitor encounters on the right the goddess Roma and on the left the goddess Pax herself. She sits upon a stone ledge amid lush flowers and plants. At her feet a sheep grazes and a cow reclines, the very image of prosperity and contentment. Pax holds two happy infants in her lap on whom she gazes with love.

Domesticity, abundance, fruitfulness, and the simplicity of an earlier time: This is the image of the Augustan Peace that the emperor and his advisors sought to create. This was to be the new reality of Rome restored, a vision so com-

pelling that subsequent generations referred to the empire of Augustus, the Roman Empire, simply as the *Pax Romana*. And yet, our translation of pax as peace unconsciously accepts Augustus's perspective: To thousands of victims of the empire, a better translation would be pacification. A Roman critic at the end of the first century put it: "They created a desert and called it peace."

Looking Ahead

This chapter explores the consequences of Roman imperial expansion throughout the Mediterranean, the long and violent crises that led to civil war and the end of the republic, and the new forms of government, society, and culture that were imperial Rome. ➤

THE PRICE OF EMPIRE, 146–121 B.C.E.

Roman victory defeated the republic. Roman conquest of the Mediterranean world and the establishment of the Roman Empire spelled the end of the republican system. Roman society could not withstand the tensions caused by the enrichment of the few, the impoverishment of the many, and the demands of the excluded populations of the empire to share in its benefits. Traditional Roman culture could not survive the attraction of Hellenistic civilization with its wealth, luxuries, and individualistic values. Finally, Roman government could not restrain the ambitions of its oligarchs or protect the interests of its ordinary citizens. The creation of a Mediterranean empire brought in its wake a century of revolutionary change before new and stable social, cultural, and political forms were achieved in the Roman world.

Winners and Losers

Rome had emerged victorious in the Punic and Macedonian wars, but the real winners were the members of the oligarchy, the **optimates** (the "best"), as they called themselves, whose wealth and power had grown beyond all imagining. These optimates included roughly 300 senators and magistrates, most of whom had inherited wealth, political connections, and long-established clientages. Since military command and government of the empire were entrusted to magistrates who were answerable only to the Senate of which they were members, the empire was essentially their private domain.

But new circumstances created new opportunities for many others. Italian merchants, slave traders, entrepreneurs, and bankers, many of lowly origin, poured into the cities of the East in the wake of the Roman legions. These newly enriched Romans constituted a second elite and formed themselves into a separate order, that of the *equites,* or equestrians, who were distinguished by their wealth and honorific military service on horseback but were connected with the old military elite. Since the Senate did not create a government bureaucracy to administer the empire, equestrian tax farmers became essential to provincial government. Companies of these *publicans,* or tax collectors, purchased the right to collect rents on public land, tribute, and customs duties from provincials. Whatever they collected beyond the amount contracted for by Roman officials was theirs to keep. Publicans regularly bribed governors and commanders to allow them to gouge the local populations with impunity and on occasion even obtained Roman troops to help them make their collections. Gradually, some of these "new men," their money "laundered" through investments in land, managed to achieve lower magistracies and even move into the senatorial order. Still, the upper reaches of office were closed to all but a tiny minority. By the end of the Punic Wars, only some 25 families could hope to produce consuls.

The losers in the wars included the vanquished who were sold into slavery by the tens of thousands; the provincials who bore the Roman yoke; the Italian allies who had done so much for the Romans; and even the citizen farmers, small shopkeepers, and free artisans of the republic. All four groups suffered

■ Roman slaves sifting grain. Roman victories in the Punic and Macedonian wars brought a huge influx of slaves from the conquered lands. Slaves were pressed into service on the estates and plantations of wealthy landowners.

from the effects of empire, and over the next century, all resorted to violence against the optimates.

Slave Revolts. The slaves revolted first. Thousands of them, captured in battle or taken after victory, flooded the Italian and Sicilian estates of the wealthy. Estimates vary, but in the first century B.C.E. the slave population of Italy was probably around two million, fully one-third of the total population. This vastly expanded slave world overwhelmed the traditional role of slaves within the Roman familia. Rural slaves on absentee estates enjoyed none of the protections afforded traditional Roman servants. Cato sold off his slaves when they reached old age; others simply worked them to death. Many slaves, born free citizens of Hellenistic states, found such treatment unbearable. Slaves rose up against their masters in Sicily in 135 B.C.E. and again a generation later and in southern Italy between 104 and 101 B.C.E. The most serious slave revolt occurred in Italy between 74 and 71 B.C.E. Gladiators—professional slave fighters trained for Roman amusement—revolted in Capua. Under the competent leadership of the Thracian gladiator Spartacus, over 100,000 slaves took up arms against Rome. Ultimately, eight legions, more troops than had met Hannibal at Zama, were needed to put down the revolt. All slave revolts succumbed to the superior strength and discipline of the Roman legions, and retribution was always terrible. After the defeat of Spartacus, crucified rebels lined the road from Rome to Naples.

Provincial Revolts. Revolts profoundly disturbed the Roman state, all the more because it was not just slaves who revolted. In many cases, poor free peasants and disgruntled provincials rose up against Rome. The most significant provincial revolt was that of Aristonicus, the illegitimate half-brother of Attalus III (ca. 138–133 B.C.E.) of Pergamum, a Roman client state. Attalus had left his kingdom to Rome at his death. In an attempt to assert his right to the kingdom, Aristonicus armed slaves and peasants and attacked the Roman garrisons. The hellenized cities of Asia Minor remained loyal to Rome, but this provincial uprising, the first of many over the centuries, lasted more than three years, from 133 to 130 B.C.E. In 88 B.C.E., the king of Pontus led a revolt against Romans in Asia Minor, a revolt that spread to Greece before it was quelled.

Revolts by slaves and provincials were disturbing enough. Revolts by Rome's Italian allies were much more serious. After the Second Punic War, these allies, on whose loyalty Rome had depended for survival, found themselves badly treated and exploited. Government officials used state power to undermine the position of the Italian elites. At the same time, Roman aristocrats used their economic power to drive the Italic peasants from their land, replacing them with slaves. Fregellae, south of Rome, revolted in 125 B.C.E. A broader and more serious revolt took place between 91 and 89 B.C.E. after the Senate blocked an attempt to extend citizenship to the al-lies. During this so-called Social War (from *socii*, the Latin word for allies), almost all the Italian allies rose against Rome. These revolts differed from those in the provinces in that the Italian elites as well as the masses aligned themselves against the Roman oligarchy. Even some ordinary Roman citizens joined the rebel forces against the powerful elite.

Optimates and Populares

The despair that could lead ordinary Roman citizens to armed rebellion grew from the social and economic consequences of conquests. While aristocrats amassed vast landed estates worked by cheap slaves, ordinary Romans often lacked even a family farm capable of supporting them and their families. Many found their way to Rome, where they swelled the ranks of the unemployed, crowded into shoddily constructed tenements, and lived off the public subsidies.

While many senators bemoaned the demise of the Roman farmer-soldier, few were willing to compromise their own privileged position to help. In the face of the oligarchy's unwillingness to deal with the problem, the tribune Tiberius Gracchus (ca. 163–133 B.C.E.) in 133 B.C.E. attempted to introduce a land-reform program that would return citizens to agriculture. Gracchus was the first of the **populares,** political leaders appealing to the masses. His motives were probably a mixture of compassion for the poor, concern over the falling numbers of citizens who had the minimum amount of land to qualify for military service, and personal ambition.

Tiberius Gracchus. During the previous century, great amounts of public land had illegally come into private hands. With the support of reform-minded aristocrats and commoners, Gracchus proposed a law that would limit the amount of public land an individual could hold to about 312 acres. He also proposed a commission to distribute to landless peasants the land recovered by the state as a result of the law. Because many senators who illegally held vast amounts of public land strongly opposed the measure, it faced certain failure in the Senate. Gracchus therefore took it to the plebeian assembly, where it was assured support from the rural poor. Moreover, he further influenced the assembly to depose one of the tribunes who threatened to veto it. The law passed, but Gracchus's maneuvering lost him many of his aristocratic supporters, who feared that a popular democracy led by a demagogue was replacing the senatorial oligarchy.

Also in 133 B.C.E., Gracchus introduced another bill that called for the royal treasury of the kingdom of Pergamum, bequeathed to Rome by Attalus III, to be used to help citizens receiving land to purchase livestock and equipment. These laws, which challenged the Senate's traditional control over finance and foreign affairs, angered the conservative elite; but as long as Gracchus held office, he was protected from any sort of attack by the traditional immunity accorded to tribunes. It was no secret, however, that the Senate planned to prosecute him as soon as his

THE REFORMS OF TIBERIUS GRACCHUS

In the following passage, the romanized Greek Appian of Alexandria (ca. 95–ca. 165 c.e.), drawing on earlier but now lost records, describes the positions of the two factions in the dispute over the land reform Tiberius Gracchus introduced in 133 B.C.E.

Focus Questions

How had wealthy Romans acquired vast amounts of public land? Why did the wealthy see Gracchus as so great a threat?

Tiberius Sempronius Gracchus, an illustrious man, eager for glory, a most powerful speaker, and for these reasons well known to all, delivered an eloquent discourse while serving as tribune, lamenting the fact that the Italians, a people so valiant in war and related in blood to the Romans, were declining little by little into pauperism and paucity of numbers without any hope of remedy. He inveighed against the multitude of slaves as useless in war and never faithful to their masters, and adduced the recent calamity brought upon the masters by their slaves in Sicily.... After speaking thus he again brought forward the law providing that nobody should hold more than 500 *iugera* of public domain. But he added a provision to the former law, that [two] sons of the occupiers might each hold one-half that amount and that the remainder should be divided among the poor by three elected commissioners, who should be changed annually.

This was extremely disturbing to the rich because, on account of the commissioners, they could no longer disregard the law as they had done before; nor could they buy from those receiving allotments, because Gracchus had provided against this by forbidding such sales. They collected together in groups, and made lamentation, and accused the poor of appropriating their fields of long standing, their vineyards, and their buildings. Some said they had paid the price of the land to their neighbors. Were they to lose the money with the land? Others said the graves of their ancestors were in the ground, which had been allotted to them in the division of their fathers' estates. Others said that their wives' dowries had been expended on these estates, or that the land had been given to their own daughters as dowry.... All kinds of wailing and expressions of indignation were heard at once. On the other side were heard the lamentations of the poor—that they were being reduced from competence to extreme poverty, and from that to childlessness, because they were unable to rear their offspring. They recounted the military services they had rendered, by which this very land had been acquired, and were angry that they should be robbed of their share of the common property.... Emboldened by numbers and exasperated against each other they kindled incessant disturbances, and waited eagerly for the voting of the new law, some intending to prevent its enactment by all means, and others to enact it at all costs.

one-year term expired. To escape this fate, he appealed to the assembly to reelect him for an unprecedented second consecutive term. To his opponents this appeal smacked of an attempt to make himself sole ruler, a democratic tyrant on the Greek model. A group of senators and their clients, led by one of Gracchus's own cousins, broke into the assembly meeting at which the election was to take place and murdered the tribune and 300 of his supporters.

Gaius Gracchus. The optimates in the Senate could eliminate Tiberius Gracchus, but they could not so easily eliminate the movement he had led. In 123 B.C.E., his younger brother, Gaius Sempronius Gracchus (153–121 B.C.E.), became tribune. During his two one-year terms he initiated an even broader and more radical reform program. Tiberius had been concerned only about poor citizens. Gaius attempted to broaden the citizenry and to shift the balance of power away from the Senate. Alarmed by the revolt at Fregellae, he attempted to extend citizenship to all Latins and to improve the status of Italian allies by extending to them the right to vote in the assembly. To check the power of senatorial magistrates in the provinces, he transferred to the equestrians the right to investigate provincial corruption. This move brought the wealthy equestrian order into politics as a counterbalance to the Senate. Gaius also improved the supply and distribution of grain in Rome and other Italian cities to benefit the urban poor. He reestablished his brother's land distribution project, extended participation to Latins and Italians, and encouraged colonization as a means to provide citizens with land. Finally, to protect himself and his party from the anticipated reaction of the Senate and to prepare to avenge his brother's death, he pushed through a law stipulating that only the people could condemn a citizen to death.

Gaius's program was extraordinary for several reasons. First, it was exactly that: a program, the first comprehensive attempt to deal with the problems facing Roman society. Second, it proposed a basic shift of power, drawing the equestrian order for the first time into the political arena opposite the Senate and making the assembly rather than the Senate the initiator of legislation. Finally, it offered a solution to the problem of the allies that, although rejected at the time, was finally adopted some 20 years later. In the short run, however, Gaius's program was a failure. In 121 B.C.E., he was not reelected for a third term and thus lost the immunity of the tribunate. Recalling his brother's fate, he armed his supporters. Once more the Senate acted, ordering the consul to take whatever measures he deemed necessary. Gaius and some 3,000 of his supporters died.

The deaths of Tiberius and Gaius Gracchus marked a new beginning in Roman politics. Not since the end of the monarchy had a political conflict been decided with personal violence. The whole episode provided a model for future attempts at reform. Reformers would look not to the Senate or the aristocracy but to the people, from whom they would draw their political power. The experience of the Gracchi also provided a model for repression of other reform programs: violence.

THE END OF THE REPUBLIC

With the Gracchi dead and the core of their reforms dismantled, the Senate appeared victorious against all challengers. At home the masses of ordinary Roman citizens and their political leadership were in disarray. The conquered lands of North Africa and the Near East filled the public coffers as well as the private accounts of Roman senators and publicans. In reality, Rome had solved neither the problem of internal conflict between rich and poor nor that of how to govern its enormous empire. The apparent calm ended when revolts in Africa and Italy exposed the fragility of the Senate's control and ushered in an ever increasing spiral of violence and civil war.

The Crisis of Government

In 112 B.C.E., the Senate declared war against Jugurtha (ca. 160–104 B.C.E.), a North African client state king, who, in his war against a rival, had killed some Roman merchants in the Numidian city of Cirta. The war dragged on for five years amid accusations of corruption, incompetence, and treason. Finally, in 107 B.C.E., the people elected as consul Gaius Marius (157–86 B.C.E.), a "new man" who had risen through the tribunate, and entrusted to him the conduct of the war. To raise an army, Marius ignored property qualifications and enlisted many impoverished Romans, arming them at public expense. Although recruiting of landless citizens had probably taken place before, no one had done it in such an overt and massive manner. Senators looked on Marius's measure with great suspicion, but the poor citizen recruits, who had despaired of benefiting from the land reforms proposed by the Gracchi, looked forward to receiving a grant of land at the end of their military service. Marius quickly defeated Jugurtha in 106 B.C.E.

In the following year, Celtic and Germanic barbarians crossed the Alps into Italy. Although technically disqualified

from further terms, Marius was elected consul five times between 104 and 100 B.C.E. to meet the threat. During this period he continued to recruit soldiers from among the poor and, on his own authority, extended citizenship to allies. To his impoverished soldiers, Marius promised land, but after his victory in 101 B.C.E., the Senate refused to give farms to veterans. As a result, Marius's armies naturally shifted their allegiance away from the Roman state and to their popular commander. Soon this pattern of loyalty became the norm. Politicians forged close bonds with the soldiers of their armies. Individual commanders, not the state or the Senate, ensured that their recruits received their pay, shared in the spoils of victory, and obtained land on their retirement. In turn, the soldiers became fanatically devoted to their commanders. Republican armies had become personal armies, potent tools in the hands of ambitious politicians.

The Civil Wars. The outbreak of the Social War in 91 B.C.E. marked the first use of these armies in civil war. Both Marius and the consul Lucius Cornelius Sulla (138–78 B.C.E.) raised armies to fight the Italians, who were pacified only after Roman citizenship was extended to all Italians in 89 B.C.E. The next year, Mithridates VI (120–63 B.C.E.), the king of Pontus, took advantage of the Roman preoccupation in Italy to invade the province of Asia. As soon as the Italian threat receded, Sulla, as the representative of the optimates, raised an army to fight Mithridates. Marius, as leader of the populares who favored reform, attempted to have Sulla relieved of command. Sulla marched on Rome, initiating a bloody civil war. In the course of this war, Rome was occupied three times, once by Marius and twice by Sulla. Each commander ordered mass executions of his opponents and confiscated their property, which he then distributed to his supporters.

Ultimately, Sulla emerged victorious and ruled as dictator from 82 to 79 B.C.E., using this time to shore up senatorial power. He doubled the size of the Senate to 600, filling the new positions with men drawn from the equites. He reduced the authority of tribunes and returned jury courts from the equites to the senators. To weaken the military power of magistrates, he abolished the practice of assigning military commands to praetors and consuls. Rather, they were to be held by proconsuls, or former magistrates, who would serve for one year as provincial governors.

In 79 B.C.E., his reforms in place, Sulla stepped down to allow a return to oligarchic republican rule. Although his changes bought a decade of peace, they did not solve the fundamental problems dividing optimates and populares. If anything, his rule had proved that the only real political option was a dictatorship by a powerful individual with his own army. During the last generation of the republic, idealists continued their hopeless struggle to prop up the dying republican system while more forward-thinking generals fought among themselves for absolute power.

Republican Crisis. Marcus Tullius Cicero (106–43 B.C.E.) reflected the strengths and weaknesses of the republican tradition in the first century B.C.E. Although cultivated, humane, and dedicated to the republican constitution, he was also ambitious, blind to the failings of the optimates, a poor judge of character, and out of touch with the political realities of his time. Like Cato in an earlier age, he was a "new man," the son of a wealthy equestrian who provided his children with the best possible education both in Rome and in Athens and Rhodes. In Greece, Cicero developed a lifelong attachment to Stoic philosophy and developed the oratory skills necessary for a young Roman destined for public life. After returning to Rome, Cicero quickly earned a reputation for his skills as a courtroom orator.

Cicero identified firmly with the elite, hoping that the republic could be saved through the harmonious cooperation of the equestrian and senatorial orders. Neither group was interested in following his program, but most considered him a safer figure than military strongmen like Sulla, who sought high office. In 63 B.C.E., Cicero was elected consul, the first "new man" to hold the office in over 30 years. The real threat to the existence of the republic was posed by the ambitions of powerful military commanders: Pompey (106–48 B.C.E.), Crassus (ca. 115–53 B.C.E.), and Julius Caesar (100–44 B.C.E.).

Pompey and Crassus, both protégés of Sulla, rose rapidly and unconstitutionally through a series of special proconsular commands by judicious use of fraud, violence, and corruption. Pompey first won public acclaim by commanding a victorious army in Africa and Spain. On his return to Rome in 70 B.C.E., he united with Crassus, who had won popularity for suppressing the Spartacus rebellion. Together, they worked to dismantle the Sullan constitution to the benefit of the populares. In return, Pompey received an extraordinary command over all of the coasts of the Mediterranean, in theory to suppress piracy but actually to give him control over all of the provinces of the empire. When, in 66 B.C.E., King Mithridates of Pontus again attacked Greece, Pompey assumed command of the provinces of Asia. His army not only destroyed Mithridates but continued on and conquered Armenia, Syria, and Palestine, acquiring an impressive retinue of client kings and increasing the income from the provinces by some 70 percent.

While Pompey was extending the frontiers of the empire to the Euphrates, Crassus, whose wealth was legendary—"no one should be called rich," he once observed, "who is not able to maintain an army on his income"—was consolidating his power. He allied himself with Julius Caesar, a young, well-connected orator from one of Rome's most ancient patrician families, who nevertheless promoted the cause of the populares. The Senate feared the ambitious and ruthless Crassus. It was to block the election of Crassus's candidate Catiline (Lucius Sergius Catilina, ca. 108–62 B.C.E.) to the consulate in 63 B.C.E. that the Senate elected Cicero instead. Catiline soon joined a conspiracy of Sullan veterans and populares, but Cicero quickly uncovered and suppressed the conspiracy and ordered Catiline's execution.

The First Triumvirate.   When Pompey returned from Asia in triumph in 62 B.C.E., he expected to find Italy convulsed

with the Catiline revolt and in need of a military savior in the tradition of Sulla. Instead, thanks to Cicero's quick action, all was in order. Although he never forgave Cicero for stealing his glory, Pompey disbanded his army and returned to private life, asking only that the Senate approve his organization of the territories he had conquered and grant land to his veterans. The Senate refused. In response, Pompey formed an uneasy alliance with Crassus and Caesar. This alliance was known as the **First Triumvirate,** from the Latin for "three men." Caesar was elected consul in 59 B.C.E. and the following year received command of the province of Cisalpine Gaul in northern Italy.

Pompey and Crassus may have thought that this command would remove the ambitious young man from the political spotlight. Instead, Caesar, who has been called, with only some exaggeration, "the sole creative genius ever produced by Rome," used his province as a staging ground for the conquest of a vast area of western Europe to the mouth of the Rhine. His brilliant military skills beyond the Alps and his dedication to his troops made Caesar immensely popular with his legions. His ability for self-promotion ensured that this popularity was matched at home, where the populares eagerly received news of his Gallic wars. In 53 B.C.E., Crassus died leading an army in Syria, leaving Pompey and the popular young Caesar to dispute supreme power. As word of Caesar's military successes increased his popularity at Rome, it also increased Pompey's suspicion of his younger associate. Finally, in 49 B.C.E., Pompey's supporters in the Senate relieved Caesar of his command and ordered him to return to Italy.

Return he did, but not as commanded. Rather than leave his army, as ordered, on the far side of the Rubicon River, which marked the boundary between his province of Cisalpine Gaul and Italy, Caesar marched on Rome at the head of his legions. This meant civil war, a vicious bloodletting that convulsed the whole Mediterranean world. In 48 B.C.E., Caesar defeated Pompey in northern Greece. Pompey was assassinated shortly afterward in Egypt. Still, the wars went on between Pompey's supporters and Caesar until 45 B.C.E., when, with all his enemies defeated, Caesar returned to Rome.

The Second Triumvirate.   In Rome, unlike Sulla, Caesar showed his opponents clemency as he sought to heal the wounds of war and to undertake an unprecedented series of reforms. He enlarged the Senate to 900 and widened its representation, appointing soldiers, freedmen, provincials, and above all wealthy men from the Italian towns. He increased the number of magistracies to broaden participation in government, founded colonies at Carthage and Corinth, and settled veterans in colonies elsewhere in Italy, Greece, Asia, Africa, Spain, and Gaul.

Still, Caesar made no pretense of returning Rome to republican government. In early 44 B.C.E., although serving that year as consul together with his general Mark Antony (ca. 81–30 B.C.E.), Caesar had himself declared perpetual dictator. This move was too much for some 60 die-hard republican senators. On 15 March, a group led by two enemies whom

MAP DISCOVERY

The Career of Julius Caesar

Examine the extent of the Roman Empire in ca. 49 B.C.E. and the movement of Julius Caesar's military campaigns. How vital was Gaul to the Roman Empire before Caesar's campaigns? Based on the locations of Caesar's campaigns during the Civil War, what can you assume about the center of power of his enemies? What geographical considerations might have led Pompey to seek an alliance with Egypt's Cleopatra?

Caesar had pardoned, Cassius Longinus and Marcus Junius Brutus, assassinated him as he entered the Senate chamber.

Cicero rejoiced when he heard of the assassination, clear evidence of his political naïveté. The republic was dead long before Caesar died, and the assassination simply returned Rome to civil war, a war that destroyed Cicero himself. Antony, Marcus Lepidus (d. 12 B.C.E.), another of Caesar's generals, and Caesar's grandnephew and adopted son Octavian (63 B.C.E.–14 C.E.), who took the name of his great uncle, soon formed the **Second Triumvirate** to destroy Caesar's enemies. After a bloody purge of senatorial and equestrian opponents, including Cicero, Antony and Octavian set out after Cassius and Brutus, who had fled into Macedonia. At Philippi in 42 B.C.E., Octavian and Antony defeated the armies of the two assassins (or, as they called themselves, liberators), who preferred suicide to capture.

After the defeat of the last republicans at Philippi, the members of the Second Triumvirate began to look suspi-

ciously at one another. Antony took command of the east, protecting the provinces of Asia Minor and the Levant from the Parthians and bleeding them dry in the process. Lepidus received Africa, and Octavian was left to deal with the problems of Italy and the west.

Initially, Octavian had cut a weak and unimposing figure. He was only 18 when he was named adopted son and heir in Caesar's will. He had no military or political experience and was frequently in poor health. Still, he had the magic of Caesar's name with which to inspire the army, he had a visceral instinct for politics and publicity, and he combined these with an absolute determination to succeed at all costs. Aided by more competent and experienced commanders, notably Marcus Agrippa (ca. 63–12 B.C.E.) and Gaius Maecenas (ca. 70–8 B.C.E.), he began to consolidate his power at the expense of his two colleagues. Lepidus attempted to gain a greater share in the empire but found that his troops would not fight against Octavian. He was forced out of his position and allowed to retire in obscurity, retaining only the honorific title of pontifex maximus.

Antony, to meet his ever-growing demand for cash, became dependent on the Ptolemaic ruler of Egypt, the clever and competent Cleopatra. For her part, Cleopatra manipulated Antony in order to maintain the integrity and independence of her kingdom. Octavian seized the opportunity to portray Antony as a traitor to Rome, a weakling controlled by an Oriental woman who planned to move the capital of the empire to Alexandria. Antony's supporters replied with propaganda of their own, pointing to Octavian's humble parentage and his lack of military ability. The final break came in 32 B.C.E. Antony, for all his military might, could not attack Italy as long as the despised Cleopatra was with him. Nor could he abandon her without losing her financial support. Instead, he tried to lure Octavian to a showdown in Greece. His plan misfired. Agrippa forced him into a naval battle off Actium in 31 B.C.E. in which Antony was soundly defeated. He and his Egyptian queen committed suicide, and Octavian ruled supreme in the Roman Empire.

A Life Worth Leading

Mere survival was a difficult and elusive goal through the last decades of the republic. Still, some members of the elite sought more. They tried to make sense of the turmoil around them and formulate a philosophy of life and a model of personal conduct. By now, the members of Rome's elite were in full command of Greek literature and philosophy, which they studied and adapted to their needs, creating a distinctive Latin cultural tradition. The most prominent figure in the late republic is Cicero, who combined his active life as lawyer and politician with an abiding devotion to Stoic philosophy. In the Stoics' belief in divine providence, morality, and duty to one's allotted role in the universe, Cicero found a rational basis for his deeply committed public life. In a series of written dialogues, Cicero presented Stoic values in a form that created a Latin philosophical language that was freed from slavish imitation of Greek. He also wrote a number of works of political philosophy, particularly *The Republic* and *The Laws,* in conscious imitation of Plato's concern for the proper order of society. For Cicero, humans and gods were bound together in a world governed not simply by might but by justice. The universe, while perhaps not fully intelligible, was nonetheless rational, and reason had to be the basis for society and its laws.

These same concerns for virtue are evident in the writings of the great historians of the late republic, Sallust (86–ca. 34 B.C.E.) and Livy (59 B.C.E.–17 C.E.). Sallust was a supporter of Julius Caesar, who had written his own stylistically powerful histories of the Gallic and Civil Wars. For Sallust, as well as for his younger contemporary, Livy, the chaos of civil war was the direct result of moral corruption and decline that followed the successes of the empire. For Sallust, the moral failing was largely that of the Senate and its members, who trampled the plebs in their quest for power and personal glory. Livy, who was much more conservative, condemned plebeian demagogues as well as power-hungry senators. Only those aristocratic conservatives who, like Cato, had stood for the ancient Roman traditions merited praise. In the second century B.C.E., the Greek historian Polybius had been fascinated with the rise of the Roman Republic to world supremacy. A century later the Roman historians were even more fascinated with its decline.

A different kind of morality dominated the work of Lucretius (ca. 100–55 B.C.E.), the greatest poet of the late republic. Just as Cicero had molded Stoicism into a Roman civic philosophy, Lucretius presented Epicurean materialist philosophy as a Roman alternative to the hunger for power, wealth, and glory. In his great poem *On the Nature of Things,* Lucretius presented the Epicurean's thoroughly physical understanding of the universe. He described its atomic composition, the evolution of humans from brutish beginnings to civilization, and the evil effects not only of greed and ambition but also of religion. All that exists is material reality, he believed. He also believed that religion, whether the state-supported cults of ancient Rome or the exotic cults introduced from the East, played on mortal fear of death, a fear that was irrational and groundless. "Death is nothing to us," Lucretius wrote. "It is only the natural fulfillment of life. A rational, proportional enjoyment of life is all that matters. Sorrow and anxiety come from but an ignorant emotionalism."

Emotion was precisely the goal of another poetic tradition of the late republic, that of the *neoteric* or new-style poets, especially Catullus (ca. 84–ca. 54 B.C.E.). Avoiding politics and moralistic philosophy, these poets created short, striking lyric poems that, although inspired by Hellenistic poetry, combine polished craftsmanship with a direct realism that is without precedent. Roughly two dozen of Catullus's poems are addressed to his lover:

> *My lady says that she wants to marry no one so much as me,*
> *Not even should Jupiter himself ask her.*
> *So says she. But what a woman says to her eager lover*
> *Should be written in the wind and rushing water.*

One of the most striking differences between such Latin poetry and its Greek antecedents is the reality and individuality of the persons and relationships expressed.

The same interest in the individual affected the way artists of the late republic borrowed from Greek art. Since Etruscan times, Romans had commemorated their ancestors in wax or wooden busts displayed in the atria of their homes. Hellenistic artists concentrated on the ideal, but Romans cherished the individual. The result was portraiture that caught the personality of the individual's face, even while portraying him or her as one of a type. Statues of the ideal nude, the armored warrior, or the citizen in his simple toga followed the proportions and conventions of Hellenistic sculpture. The heads, however, depict unique individuals who represent the last generation of the Roman Republic.

THE AUGUSTAN AGE AND THE *PAX ROMANA*

It took Octavian two years after his victory at Actium in 31 B.C.E. to eliminate remaining pockets of resistance and to work out a system to reconcile his rule with Roman constitutional traditions while not surrendering any of his power. That power rested on three factors: his immense wealth, which he used to secure support; his vast following among the surviving elites as well as among the populares; and his total command of the army. It also rested on the exhaustion of the Roman people, who were eager, after decades of civil strife, to return to peace and stability. Remembering the fate of Julius Caesar, however, Octavian had no intention of rekindling opposition by establishing an overt monarchy. Instead, in 27 B.C.E. he returned the republic from his own charge to the Senate and the people of Rome. In turn the Senate decreed him the title of Augustus, meaning "exalted."

This meant that Augustus, as Octavian was now called, continued to rule no less strongly than before, but he did so not through any autocratic office or title—he preferred to be called simply the "first citizen," or **princeps**—but by preserving the form of the traditional Roman magistracies. For four years he rested his authority on consecutive terms as consul, and after 23 B.C.E. he held a life position as tribune. The Senate granted him proconsular command of the provinces of Gaul, Spain, Syria, and Egypt, the major sources of imperial wealth and the locations of more than three-quarters of the Roman army. Later, the Senate declared his *imperium,* or command, of these "imperial" provinces superior to that of any governors of other provinces. Thus Augustus, through the power of the plebeian office of tribune, stood as the permanent protector of the Roman people. As simultaneously either consul or proconsul, he held the command of the army, the basis of the ancient patrician authority. He was the first and greatest emperor.

The Senate's formalities deceived no one. Augustus's power was absolute. However, by choosing not to exercise it in an absolutist manner, he forged a new constitutional system that worked well for himself and his successors. By the end of his reign, few living persons could remember the days of the republic, and fewer still mourned its passing. Under Augustus and his successors the empire enjoyed two centuries of stability and peace, the **Pax Romana,** or "Peace of Rome."

The Empire Renewed

Cicero had sought in vain a concord of the orders, a settlement of the social and political frictions of the empire through the voluntary efforts of a public-minded oligarchy. What could not happen voluntarily, Augustus imposed from above, reforming the Roman state, society, and culture.

The Senate.   Key to Augustus's program of renewal was the Senate, which he made, if not a partner, then a useful

CHRONOLOGY THE END OF THE REPUBLIC	
135–81 B.C.E.	Revolts against the republic
133–121 B.C.E.	Gracchi reform programs
107 B.C.E.	Gaius Marius elected consul
91–82 B.C.E.	Social War and Civil War (Marius vs. Sulla)
82–79 B.C.E.	Sulla rules as dictator
79–27 B.C.E.	Era of civil wars
63 B.C.E.	Cicero elected consul; First Triumvirate (Pompey, Crassus, Caesar)
59 B.C.E.	Caesar elected consul
45 B.C.E.	Caesar defeats Pompey's forces
44 B.C.E.	Caesar is assassinated; Second Triumvirate (Mark Antony, Lepidus, Octavian)
42 B.C.E.	Octavian and Mark Antony defeat Cassius and Brutus at Philippi
31 B.C.E.	Octavian defeats Mark Antony and Cleopatra at Actium
27 B.C.E.	Octavian is declared Augustus

subordinate in his reform. He gradually reduced the number of senators, which had grown to over 1,000, back down to 600. In the process, he eliminated the unfit and incompetent as well as the impoverished and those who failed to show the appropriate reverence toward the princeps. At the same time, he made membership hereditary, although he continued to appoint individuals of personal integrity, ability, and wealth to the body. Most conspicuous among the "new men" to enter the Senate under Augustus were the wealthy leaders of Italian cities and colonies. These small-town notables formed the core of Augustus's supporters and worked most closely with him to renew the Roman elite.

Augustus also shared with the Senate the governance of the empire, although again not on an equal footing. The Senate named governors to the peaceful provinces, while Augustus named commanders to the frontier imperial provinces where the bulk of the legions were stationed. Senators themselves served as provincial governors and military commanders. The Senate also functioned as a court of law in important cases. Still, the Senate remained a creature of the emperor, seldom asserting itself even when asked to do so by Augustus or his successors and competing within its own ranks to see who could be first to do the emperor's bidding.

The Equites.

Augustus undertook an even more fundamental reform of the equites, the wealthy businessmen, bankers, and tax collectors who had vied with the senatorial aristocracy since the reforms of Tiberius Gracchus. After Actium, many equites found themselves proscribed—sentenced to death or banishment—and had their property confiscated. Augustus began to rebuild their ranks by enrolling a new generation of successful merchants and speculators who became the foundation of his administration. Equestrians formed the backbone of the officer corps of the army, of the treasury, and of the greatly expanded imperial administration. The equestrian order was open at both ends. Freedmen and soldiers who acquired sufficient wealth moved into the order, and the most successful and accomplished equestrians were promoted into the Senate.

■ This idealized marble portrait statue of the emperor Augustus addressing his army was found in the villa of Livia, wife of Augustus, at Prima Porta in Rome. The carvings on his breastplate recall a diplomatic incident during his reign.

The Army.

The land crisis had provoked much of the unrest in the late republic, and after Actium, Augustus had to satisfy the needs of the loyal soldiers of his 60 legions. Drawing on his immense wealth, acquired largely from the estates of his proscripted enemies, he pensioned off 32 legions, sending them to colonies that he purchased for them throughout the empire. The remaining 28 legions became a permanent professional army stationed in imperial provinces. In time, the normal period of enlistment became fixed at 20 years, after which time Augustus provided the legionnaires with land and enough cash to settle in among the notables of their colonies. After 5 C.E., the state assumed the payment of this retirement bonus. Augustus established a small elite unit, the praetorian guard, in and around Rome as his personal military force. Initially, the praetorians protected the emperors; in later reigns, they would make them.

These measures created a permanent solution to the problem of the citizen-soldier of the later republic. Veteran colonies—all built as model Roman towns with their central forum, baths, temples, arenas, and theaters as well as their outlying villas and farms—helped to romanize the far provinces of the empire. These colonies, unlike the independent colonies of Greece in an earlier age, remained an integral part of the Roman state. Thus romanization and political integration went hand in hand, uniting through peaceful means an empire that had first been acquired by arms. Likewise, ambitious provincials, through service as auxiliaries and later as citizens, acquired a stake in the destiny of Rome.

Not every citizen, of course, could find prosperity in military service and a comfortable retirement. The problems of urban poverty in Rome continued to grow. By the time of Augustus, the capital city had reached a population of perhaps 600,000 people. A tiny minority relaxed in the comfortable homes built on the Palatine. Tens of thousands more crammed into wooden and brick tenements and jostled each other in the crowded, noisy streets. Employment was hard to find, since free men had difficulty competing against slaves. The emperors, their power as tribunes making them protectors of the poor, provided over 150,000 resident citizens with a basic dole of wheat brought from Egypt. The emperors also built aqueducts to provide water to the city. In addition, they constructed vast public recreation centers. These included both the sumptuous baths, which were combination bathing facilities, health clubs, and brothels, and arenas such as the Colosseum, where 50,000 spectators could watch gladiatorial displays, and the Circus Maximus, where a quarter of the city's population could gather at once to watch chariot races. Such mass gatherings replaced the plebeian assemblies of the republic as the occasions on which the populace could express its will. Few emperors were foolish enough to ignore the wishes that the crowd roared out in the Circus.

Divine Augustus.

Augustus's renewal of Rome rested on a religious reform. After the death of Lepidus in 12 B.C.E., Augustus assumed the office of pontifex maximus and used it to direct a reinvigoration of Roman religion. He restored numerous temples and revived ancient Roman cults. He established a series of public religious festivals, reformed priesthoods, and encouraged citizens to participate in the traditional cults of Rome. His goals in all these religious reforms were twofold. After decades of public authority controlled by violence and naked aggression, he was determined to restore the traditions of Roman piety, morality, sacred order, and faith in relationship between the gods and Roman destiny. An equally important goal was Augustus's promotion of his own cult. His adoptive father, Julius Caesar, had been deified after his death, and Augustus benefited from this association with a divine ancestor. His own genius, or guiding spirit, received special devotion in temples throughout the west dedicated to "Rome and Augustus." In the east, he was worshipped as a living god. In this manner, the emperor became identical with the state, and the state religion was closely akin to emperor worship. After his death, Augustus and virtually all of the emperors after him were worshipped as official deities in Rome itself.

Closely related to his fostering of traditional cults was Augustus's attempt to restore traditional Roman virtues, especially within the family. Like the reformers of the late republic, he believed that the declining power of the paterfamilias was at the root of much that was wrong with Rome. To reverse the trend and to restore the declining population of free Italians, Augustus encouraged marriage, procreation, and the firm control of husbands over wives. He imposed penalties for those who chose not to marry and bestowed rewards on those who produced large families. He enacted laws to prevent women from having extramarital affairs and even exiled his own daughter and granddaughter for promiscuity.

Poetry and Patronage. Augustus actively patronized those writers who shared his conservative religious and ethical values and who might be expected to glorify the princeps, and he used his power to censor and silence writers whom he considered immoral. Chief among the favored were the poets Virgil (70–19 B.C.E.) and Horace (65–8 B.C.E.). Through their poetry in praise of the emperor, these poets conferred immortality on Augustus.

Horace celebrated Augustus's victory at Actium, his reform of the empire, and reestablishment of the ancient cults that had brought Rome divine favor. In Horace's poems, Augustus is almost a god. His deeds are compared to those of the great heroes of Roman legend and judged superior. Interspersed with the poems praising Augustus are poems of great beauty praising the love of both boys and girls and the enjoyment of wine and music. To Horace, the glories of the new age inaugurated by Augustus with the secular games of 17 B.C.E. included not only the splendor of empire but also the enjoyment of privileged leisure.

Virgil began his poetic career with pastoral poems celebrating the joys of rural life and the bitterness of the loss of lands in the Civil Wars. Later, under the patronage of Maecenas and Augustus, Virgil turned directly to glorifying Augustus and the new age. The ultimate expression of this effort was the *Aeneid*, an epic that was consciously intended to serve for the Roman world the role of the Homeric poems in the Greek.

As he reworked the legend of Aeneas—a Trojan hero who escaped the destruction of the city, wandered throughout the Mediterranean, and ultimately came to Latium—Virgil presented a panoramic history of Rome and its destiny. Unlike the Homeric heroes, Achilles and Odysseus, who were driven by their own search for glory, Aeneas was driven by his piety, that is, his duty toward the gods and his devotion to his father. Aeneas had to follow his destiny, which was the destiny of Rome, to rule the world in harmony and justice. In the midst of his wanderings, Aeneas (like Odysseus before him) entered the underworld to speak with his dead father. There he saw a vision of Rome's greatness to come. He saw the great heroes of Rome, including Augustus, "son of a god," and he was told of the particular mission of Rome.

> Let others fashion in bronze more lifelike, breathing images
> Let others (as I believe they will) draw living faces from marble
> Others shall plead cases better and others will better
> Track the course of the heavens and announce the rising stars.
> Remember, Romans, your task is to rule the peoples
> This will be your art: to teach the habit of peace
> To spare the defeated and to subdue the haughty.

The finest of the poets who felt the heavy hand of Augustus's disfavor was Ovid (43 B.C.E.–17 C.E.), the great Latin poet of erotic love. In *Art of Love* and *Amores* he cheerfully preached the art of seduction and adultery. He delighted in poking irreverent fun at everything from the sanctity of Roman marriage to the serious business of warfare. In his great *Metamorphoses,* a series of artfully told myths, he parodied the heroic epic, mocking with grotesque humor the very material that Virgil used to create the *Aeneid.* By 8 C.E., Augustus had had enough. He exiled the witty poet to Tomis, a miserable frontier post on the Black Sea. There, Ovid spent the last nine years of his life, suffering from the harsh climate, the danger of nomadic attacks, and, most of all, the pain of exile from the center of the civilization he loved. Exactly what offense he committed is not clear. Perhaps for Augustus what was most intolerable was that, in spite of the emperor's efforts to foster an immortal poetic tradition glorifying the Roman virtues, Ovid was clearly appreciated by his contemporaries as the greatest poet of the age.

Augustus's Successors

Horace and Virgil may have made Augustus's fame immortal. His flesh was not. The problem of succession occupied him throughout much of his long reign and was never satisfactorily solved. Since the princeps was not a specific office, but a combination of offices and honors held together by military might and religious aura, formal dynastic succession was impossible. Instead, Augustus attempted to select a blood relative as successor, include him in his reign, and have him voted the various offices and dignities that constituted his own position.

Unfortunately, Augustus outlived all of his first choices. His nephew and adopted son Marcellus, to whom he married his only child Julia, died in 23 B.C.E. He then married Julia to his old associate Agrippa and began to groom him for the position, but Agrippa died in 12 B.C.E. Lucius and Gaius, the sons of Julia and Agrippa, also died young. Augustus's final choice, his stepson Tiberius (14–37 C.E.), proved to be a gloomy and unpopular successor but nevertheless was a competent ruler under whom the machinery of the empire functioned smoothly. The continued orderly functioning of the empire even under the subsequent members of Augustus's family—the mad Gaius, also known as Caligula (37–41), the bookish

but competent Claudius (41–54), and initially under Nero (54–68)—is a tribute to the soundness of Augustus's constitutional changes and the vested interest that the descendants of Augustus's military and aristocratic supporters had in them.

Nero was more than even they could bear, however. Profligate, vicious, and paranoid, Nero divided his time between murdering his relatives and associates—including his mother, his aunt, his wife, his tutors, and eventually his most capable generals—and squandering his vast wealth on mad attempts to gain recognition as a great poet, actor, singer, and athlete. (When he competed in games, other contestants wisely lost.) Finally, in 68 C.E., the exasperated commanders in

MAP DISCOVERY

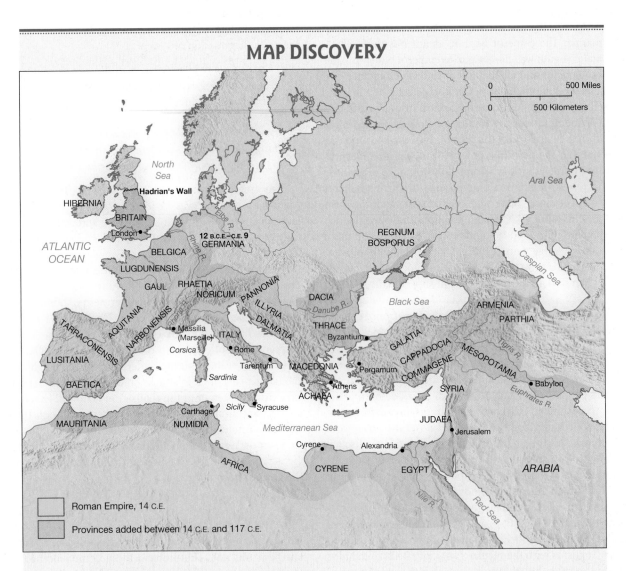

The Roman Empire, 14 and 117 C.E.

Examine the extent of the Roman Empire in 14 C.E. and in 117 C.E. What civilizations and empires that you have previously studied were incorporated into the Roman Empire by 14 C.E.? By 117 C.E.? Which regions had never before been part of ancient civilizations? What natural geographical features defined the boundaries of the empire in the west, north, south, and east?

Gaul, Spain, and Africa revolted. Once more, war swept the empire. Nero slit his own throat, and in the next year, the "Year of the Four Emperors," four men in quick succession won the office, only to lose their lives just as quickly. Finally, in 70 C.E., Vespasian (69–79 C.E.), the son of a "new man," who had risen through the ranks to the command in Egypt, secured the principate and restored order.

The first emperors had rounded off the frontiers of the empire, transforming the client states of Cappadocia, Thrace, Commagene, and Judaea in the east and Mauritania in North Africa into provinces. Claudius presided over the conquest of Britain in 43 C.E. These emperors introduced efficient means of governing and protecting the empire and tied together its inhabitants, roughly 50 million in the time of Augustus, in networks of mutual dependence and common interest. Augustus established peaceful relations with the Parthian empire, which permitted unhampered trade between China, India, and Rome. In the west, after a disastrous attempt to expand the empire to the Elbe ended in the loss of three legions in 9 C.E., the frontier was fixed at the Rhine. In the east, the northern border stopped at the Danube. The deserts of Africa, Nubia, and southern Arabia formed what many in the first century C.E. saw as the "natural" southern boundaries of the empire.

When Vespasian's troops fought their way into Rome in vicious hand-to-hand street fighting, the populace watched with idle fascination. The violence of 69 C.E., unlike that of the previous century, involved mostly professional legions and their commanders. The rest of the empire sat back to watch. In a few restive regions of the empire, some Gauls, the Batavians along the Rhine, and diehard Jewish rebels tried to use the momentary confusion to revolt, but by and large the empire remained stable. This stability was the greatest achievement of Augustus and his immediate successors.

The emperors of the Flavian dynasty, Vespasian and his sons and successors Titus (79–81) and Domitian (81–96), were stern and unpretentious provincials who restored the authority and dignity of their office, although they also did away with most of the trappings of republican legitimacy that Augustus and his immediate successors had used. They solidified the administrative system, returned the legions to their fairly permanent posts, and opened the highest reaches of power to provincial elites as never before. After the Flavian emperors, the Antonines (96–193)—especially Trajan (98–117), Hadrian (117–138), and Antoninus Pius (138–161)—ruled for what has been termed "the period in the history of the world during which the human race was most happy and prosperous."

Breaking the Peace.   Not all was peaceful in this period, however. Trajan initiated a new and final expansion of the imperial frontiers. Between 101 and 106 he conquered Dacia (modern Romania). He resumed war with the Parthians, conquering the provinces of Armenia and Mesopotamia by 116. During the second century the Palestinian Jews revolted in 115–117 and again in 132–135. The emperor Hadrian put down this second revolt and expelled the surviving Jews from Judaea. Along both the

CHRONOLOGY
THE ROMAN EMPIRE

Julio-Claudian Period, 27 B.C.E.–68 C.E.	Augustus (27 B.C.E.–14 C.E.)
	Tiberius (14–37 C.E.)
	Caligula (37–41)
	Claudius (41–54)
	Nero (54–68)
Year of the Four Emperors, 69 C.E.	
Flavian Period, 69–96	Vespasian (69–79)
	Titus (79–81)
	Domitian (81–96)
Antonine Period, 96–192	Trajan (98–117)
	Hadrian (117–138)
	Antoninus Pius (138–161)
	Marcus Aurelius (161–180)
	Commodus (180–192)

eastern and western frontiers, legions had to contend with sporadic border incidents. Within the borders, however, a system of Roman military camps, towns, and rural states constituted a remarkably heterogeneous and prosperous civilization.

Administering the Empire.   The imperial government of this vast empire was as oppressive as it was primitive. Taxes, rents, forced labor service, military levies and requisitions, and outright extortion weighed heavily on its subjects. To a considerable extent, the inhabitants of the empire continued to be governed by the indigenous elites whose cooperation Rome won by giving them broad autonomy. Thus, Hellenistic cities continued to manage their own affairs under the supervision of essentially amateur Roman governors. Local town councils in Gaul, Germany, and Spain supervised the collection of taxes, maintained public works projects, and kept the peace. In return for their participation in Roman rule, these elites received Roman citizenship, a prize that carried prestige, legal protection, and the promise of further advancement in the Roman world.

In those imperial provinces that were controlled directly by the emperor, the army was much more in evidence, and the professional legions were the ultimate argument of imperial tax collectors and imperial representatives, or *procurators*. Moreover, as the turmoil of the Year of the Four Emperors amply demonstrated, the military was the ultimate foundation of imperial rule itself. Still, soldiers were as much farmers as fighters.

Legions usually remained in the same location for years, and veterans' colonies sprang up around military camps.

Finally, much of the governing of the empire was done by the vast households of the Roman elite, particularly that of the princeps. Freedmen and slaves from the emperor's household often governed vast regions, oversaw imperial estates, and managed imperial factories and mines. The descendants of the old Roman nobility might look down their noses at imperial freedmen, but they obeyed their orders.

The empire worked because it rewarded those who worked with it and left alone those who paid their taxes and kept quiet. Local elites, auxiliary soldiers, and freedmen could aspire to rise to the highest ranks of the power elite. As provincials were drawn into the Roman system, they were also drawn into the world of Roman culture. Proper education in Latin and Greek, the ability to hold one's own in philosophical discussion, and the absorption of Roman ways, including styles of dress, recreation, and religious cults, all were essential for ambitious provincials. Thus, in the course of the first century C.E., the disparate portions of the empire competed, not to free themselves from the Roman yoke, but to become Roman themselves.

RELIGIONS FROM THE EAST

The same openness that permitted the spread of Latin letters and Roman baths to distant Gaul and the shores of the Black Sea provided paths of dissemination for other, distinctly un-Roman religious traditions. For many in the empire, the traditional rituals offered to the household gods and the state cults of Jupiter, Mars, and the other official deities were insufficient foci of religious devotion. Many educated members of the elite were actually vaguely monotheistic. Many others in the empire sought personal, emotional bonds with the divine world.

As noted in Chapter 4, in the second century B.C.E. the Roman world had been caught up in the emotional cult of Dionysus, an ecstatic, personal, and liberating religion entirely unlike the official Roman cults. Again in the first century C.E., so-called **mystery cults**—that is, religions promising immediate personal contact with a deity that would bring immortality—spread throughout the empire. Some were officially introduced into Rome as part of its open polytheism. These included the Anatolian Cybele or great mother-goddess cult, which was present in Rome from the late third century B.C.E. Devotees underwent a ritual in which they were bathed in the blood of a bull or a ram, thereby obtaining immortality. The cult of the Egyptian goddess Isis spread throughout the Hellenistic world and to Rome in the republican period. From Persia came the cult of Mithras, the ancient Indo-Iranian god of light and truth, who, as bringer of victory, found special favor with Roman soldiers and merchants eager for success in this life and immortality beyond the grave. Generally, Rome tolerated these alien cults as long as they could be assimilated into, or at least reconciled in some way with, the cult of the Roman gods and the genius of the emperor.

Jewish Resistance

With one religious group this assimilation was impossible. The Jews of Palestine had long refused any accommodation with the polytheistic cults of the Hellenistic kingdoms or with Rome. Roman conquerors and emperors, aware of the problems of their Hellenistic predecessors, went to considerable lengths to avoid antagonizing this small and unusual group of people. When Pompey seized Jerusalem in 63 B.C.E., he was careful not to interfere in Jewish religion and even left Judaea under the control of the Jewish high priest. Later, Judaea was made into a client kingdom under the puppet Herod. Jews were allowed to maintain their monotheistic cult and were excused from making sacrifices to the Roman gods.

Still, the Jewish community remained deeply divided about its relationship with the wider world and with Rome. At one end of the spectrum were the Sadducees, a party composed largely of members of priestly families, who enjoyed considerable influence with their foreign rulers. They were staunch defenders of the ancient Jewish law, or Torah, but not to the exclusion of other later religious and legal traditions. They were willing to work with Rome and even adopt some elements of Hellenism, as long as the services in the temple could continue.

At the other end of the spectrum were the Hasidim, those who rejected all compromise with Hellenistic culture and collaboration with foreign powers. Many expected the arrival of a messiah, a liberator who would destroy the Romans and reestablish the kingdom of David. One party within the Hasidim were the Pharisees, who practiced strict dietary rules and rituals to maintain the separation of Jews and Gentiles (literally, "the peoples," that is, all non-Jews). The Pharisees accepted the writings of the Hebrew prophets along with the Torah and abided by a still larger body of orally transmitted law, the "tradition of the elders." The most prominent figure in this movement was Hillel (ca. 30 B.C.E.–10 C.E.), a Jewish scholar from Babylon who came to Jerusalem as a teacher of the law. He began a tradition of legal and scriptural interpretation that, in an expanded version centuries later, became the Talmud. Hillel was also a moral teacher who taught peace and love, not revolt. "Whatever is hateful to you, do not to your fellow man: this is the whole Law; the rest is mere commentary," he taught.

For all their insistence on purity and separation from other peoples, the Pharisees did not advocate violent revolt against Rome. They preferred to await divine intervention. Another group of Hasidim, the Zealots, were less willing to wait. After 6 C.E., when Judaea, Samaria, and Idumaea were annexed and combined into the province of Judaea and administered by imperial procurators, the Zealots began to organize sporadic armed resistance to Roman rule. As ever, armed resistance was met with violent suppression. Throughout the first century

C.E., clashes between Roman troops and Zealot revolutionaries grew more frequent and more widespread.

The Origins of Christianity

The already complex landscape of the Jewish religious world became further complicated by the brief career of Joshua ben Joseph (ca. 6 B.C.E.–30 C.E.), known to history as Jesus of Nazareth and to his followers as Jesus the Messiah or the Christ. Jesus came from Galilee, an area known as a Zealot stronghold. However, while Jesus preached the imminent coming of the kingdom, he did so in an entirely nonpolitical manner. He was, like many popular religious leaders, a miracle worker. When people flocked around him to see his wonders, he preached a message of peace and love of God and neighbor. His teachings were entirely within the Jewish tradition and closely resembled those of Hillel. However, while many contemporary religious leaders announced the imminent coming of the Messiah, Jesus' closest followers, the apostles and disciples, began to think that he himself was the Messiah and expected him to restore the kingdom of Israel.

For roughly three years, Jesus preached in Judaea and Galilee, drawing large, excited crowds. Many of his followers pressed him to lead a revolt against Roman authority and reestablish the kingdom of David, even though he insisted that the kingdom he would establish was not of this world. Other Jews saw his claims as blasphemy and his assertion that he was the king of Jews, even if a heavenly one, as a threat to the status quo. Jesus became more and more a figure of controversy, a catalyst for violence. Ultimately, the Roman procurator, Pontius Pilate, decided that Jesus posed a threat to law and order. Pilate, like other Roman magistrates, had no interest in the internal religious affairs of the Jews. However, he was troubled by anyone who had the potential for causing political disturbances, no matter how unintentional. Pilate ordered Jesus scourged and put to death by crucifixion, a common Roman form of execution for slaves, pirates, thieves, and noncitizen troublemakers.

Spreading the Faith.   The cruel death of Jesus ended the popular agitation he had stirred up, but it did not deter his closest followers. They soon announced that three days after his death, he had risen and had appeared to them numerous times during the following few weeks. They took this resurrection as proof of his claims to be the Messiah and confirmation of his promise of eternal life to those who believed in him. Soon a small group of his followers, led by Peter (d. ca. 64 C.E.), formed another Jewish sect—preaching and praying daily in the temple. New members were initiated into this sect, which soon became known as Christianity—through baptism, a purification rite in which the initiate was submerged briefly in flowing water. They also shared a ritual meal in which bread and wine were distributed to members. Otherwise, they remained entirely within the Jewish religious and cultural tradition, and hellenized Jews and pagans who wanted to join the sect had to observe strict Jewish law and custom.

Christianity spread beyond its origin as a Jewish sect because of the work of one man, Paul of Tarsus (ca. 5–ca. 67 C.E.). Although Paul was an observant Jew, he was part of the wider cosmopolitan world of the empire and from birth enjoyed the privileges of Roman citizenship. He saw Christianity as a separate tradition, completing and perfecting Judaism but intended for the whole world.

Paul set out to spread his message, crisscrossing Asia Minor and Greece and even traveling to Rome. Wherever he went, Paul won converts and established churches, called *ecclesiae,* or assemblies. Everywhere Paul and the other disciples went, they worked wonders, cast out demons, cured illnesses, and preached. Paul's teachings, while firmly rooted in the Jewish historical tradition, were radically new. God had created the human race, he taught, in the image of God and destined it for eternal life. However, by the deliberate sin of the first humans, Adam and Eve, humans had lost eternal life and introduced evil and death into the world. Even then, God did not abandon his people but began, through the Jews, to prepare for their eventual redemption. That salvation was accomplished by Jesus, the son of God, through his faith, a free

■ A Roman tombstone inscribed with some of the earliest examples of Christian symbols. The anchor represents hope, while the fish recall Jesus' words, "I will make you fishers of men."

and unmerited gift of God to his elect. Through faith, the Christian ritual of baptism, and participation in the church, men and women could share in the salvation offered by God, Paul said.

How many conversions resulted from Paul's theological message and how many resulted from the miracles he and the other disciples worked will never be known, but another factor certainly played a part in the success of conversions. That was the courage Christians showed in the face of persecution.

Even Rome's elasticity and tolerance of new religions could be stretched only so far. The Christians' belief in the divinity of their founder was no problem. Their offer of salvation to those who participated in their mysteries was only normal. But their stubborn refusal to acknowledge the existence of the other gods and to participate in the cult of the genius of the emperor was intolerable. Christianity was an aggressive and successful cult, attracting followers throughout the empire. It was viewed not as religion, but as subversion. Beginning during Nero's reign, Roman officials sporadically rounded up Christians, destroyed their sacred scriptures, and executed those who refused to sacrifice to the imperial genius. But instead of decreasing the cult's appeal, persecution only aided it. For those who believed that death was birth into a new and better life, martyrdom was a reward, not a penalty. The strength of their convictions convinced others of the truth of their religion.

Christian Institutions. As the number of Christians increased in the face of persecution, the organization and teaching of this new faith began to evolve. A hierarchy developed within the various communities that Paul and the other apostles established. The leader of each community was the bishop, an office derived from the priestly leader of the Jewish synagogue, who was responsible for both charity and the Torah. Assisted by **presbyters** (priests), deacons, and deaconesses, bishops assumed growing responsibilities as expectations for the second coming receded. These responsibilities included presiding over the *eucharist,* or ritual meal, that was the center of Christian worship, as well as enforcing discipline and teaching.

Christian teaching focused on the Gospels, accounts of Jesus' life written toward the end of the first century; letters, or Epistles; and narratives and visionary writings by his early disciples and their immediate successors. In their preaching, bishops connected these texts to the tradition of Jewish Scriptures, explaining that the life of Jesus was the completion and fulfillment of the Jewish tradition. Over centuries, certain Gospels and Epistles and one book of revelation came to be regarded as authoritative and, together with the version of Jewish Scripture that was in use in Greek-speaking Jewish communities, constituted the Christian Bible. In the second and third centuries, the Christian message began to be challenged. Hellenistic moral philosophers and Roman

officials condemned Christianity as immoral and, because of its rejection of the cult of the emperor and the gods of Rome, atheistic. Neoplatonists found the teachings of Christianity philosophically naive. Even within the Christian community, different groups held different views. Monatists argued that Christians were obligated to fast and abstain from marriage until the second coming. Dualist **Gnostics** interpreted the Christian message as a secret wisdom, or *gnosis,* which, combined with baptism, freed men and women from their fates.

Bishops defended the faith and determined what was correct. By the end of the first century, episcopal (from the Greek word for bishop) authority was understood to derive from the bishops' status as successors of the apostles. Bishops of the churches that had been established directly by the apostles in Jerusalem, Antioch, Alexandria, and Rome—termed *patriarchates*—claimed special authority over other, less ancient communities. Gradually, the exalted position of the bishop and his assistants led to a distinction between the clergy and the laity, the rank and file of Christians. At the same time, women, who had played central roles in Jesus' ministry, were excluded from positions of authority within the clergy. In this process, the Christian community came to resemble closely the Roman patriarchal household, a resemblance that increased the appeal of the new sect to nonbelievers.

Although Christianity spread rapidly through the eastern Mediterranean in the first and second centuries, it remained a minor irritation in the eyes of the empire's rulers. Its fundamental role in the transformation of the Roman world would not become clear until the third and fourth centuries.

GEOGRAPHICAL TOUR
A Tour of the Empire

Each town in the sprawling empire, from York in the north of Britain to Dura Europus on the Euphrates, was a center of Roman culture, or *Romanitas,* in provinces that were still closely tied to local provincial traditions. Each boasted a forum where locals conducted business and government affairs. Each had an arena for gladiatorial games, baths, a racetrack, and a theater where Greek and Latin plays entertained the populace. Temples to the Capitoline Jupiter and to the deified emperors adorned the cities. Aqueducts brought fresh water from distant springs into the heart of the cities.

Connecting these towns was a network of well-maintained roads frequented by imperial administrators, merchants, the idle rich, and soldiers. Beginning in 120, the roads of the empire saw a most unusual traveler: the emperor Hadrian, who traveled them to conduct an extraordinary inspection of the length and breadth of his empire (see **Map A**). Hadrian, the adopted son and heir of Trajan, had received an excellent Greek education

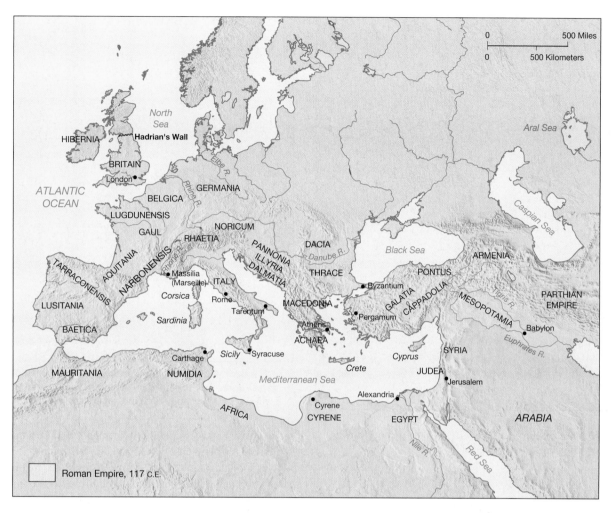

■ **Map A. The Roman Empire at the Time of Hadrian.** Hadrian's empire was a well-ordered world of provinces governed by a vast bureaucracy and held together by a common culture and the power of the imperial army.

and was an accomplished writer, poet, connoisseur, and critic. Still, he had spent most of his early career as a successful field commander and administrator in Dacia and the lower Danube. Years of military experience had made Hadrian very aware of the potential weaknesses of the vast Roman borders, and his primary interest was to inspect those military commands that were most critical for imperial stability.

The Western Provinces

Thus Hadrian set out westward, traveling first through the provinces of Gaul, prosperous and pacific regions long integrated into the Roman world (see **Map B**). Gaul was known for its good food, its pottery manufacture, and its comfortable, if culturally slightly backward, local elites. Much of Gaul's prosperity came from supplying the legions guarding the Rhine-Danube frontier, and it was across the Rhine toward Germany where the legions faced the barbarians of

"Free Germany," that Hadrian was headed. Legions stationed at Xanten, Cologne, and Trier (see **Map B**) were far removed from the Mediterranean world that formed the heart of the empire. The dark forests, cold winters, and crude life made Germany a hardship post. Hadrian threw himself into the harsh camp life of Germany in order to bolster discipline and combat readiness. He shared rough field rations, long marches, and simple conditions with his troops.

From Germany, Hadrian traveled down the Rhine through what is today Holland and then crossed over to Britain. Here, too, defense was utmost on his mind. Celts from the northern, unconquered portion of the island had been harassing the romanized society to the south. The emperor ordered the erection of a great wall over 50 miles long across Britain from coast to coast. South of the wall, Roman Britain was studded with hundreds of Roman villas, ranging from simple country farmhouses to vast mansions with more than 60 rooms. Over a hundred towns and villages were large enough to boast walls, ranging

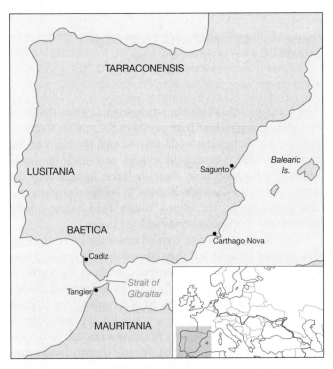

■ **Map B. The Provinces of Gaul.** Gaul was a vast agricultural region supplying legions posted along the Rhine River.

■ **Map C. Spain.** Roman Spain was a major source of gold, iron, and tin as well as a vital agricultural region.

■ **Map D. Asia.** Asia remained for Rome the center of Hellenistic civilization with its populous cities and vital trade routes.

from London with a population of roughly 30,000 to numerous settlements of between 2,000 and 10,000 inhabitants.

No sooner had he put things straight in Britain than Hadrian returned to Gaul, paused in Nîmes in the south (see **Map B**), and then headed south toward his native Spain (see **Map C**). By the second century C.E., Spain was even more thoroughly romanized than most of Gaul, having been an integral part of the empire since the Second Punic War. It was also far richer. Spanish mines yielded gold, iron, and tin, and Spanish estates produced grain and cattle. Since the reign of Vespasian, the residents of Spanish communities had been given some of the rights of Roman citizens, making them eligible for military service, a value even greater to the empire than Spain's mineral wealth. Problems with military service brought Hadrian to Spain. The populace was becoming increasingly resistant to conscription, a universal phenomenon, and Hadrian's presence strengthened the efforts of recruiters.

The Eastern Provinces

Hadrian soon set sail for the provinces of Asia (see **Map D**). There he was in the heart of the Hellenistic world, so central to the empire's prosperity. Its great cities were centers of manufacture, and its ports were the vital links in Mediterranean trade. As in Hellenistic times, these cities were the organizing principle of the region; local senates were largely self-governing, and rivalries among cities prevented the creation of any sort of provincial identities. In Asia, Hadrian worked with individual communities, showering honors and privileges on the most cooperative and founding new communities in the Anatolian hinterland. The last activity was particularly important because, for all of the civilized glory of urban Asia, the rural areas remained strongly tied to traditions that neither Greeks nor Romans had managed to weaken. The empire remained two worlds: one urban, hellenized, mercantile, and collaborationist; the other rural, traditional, exploited, and potentially separatist.

In 125, Hadrian left Asia for Greece (see **Map E**), where he participated in traditional religious cults. Greek culture continued to be vital for Rome, and by participating in the rituals of Achaea and Athens, the emperor placed himself in the traditions of the legendary Heracles and Philip of Macedon. Finally, in 127, Hadrian returned to Rome via Sicily, a prosperous amalgam of Greek and Latin cultures dominated by vast senatorial estates, or *latifundia*.

This restless emperor spent less than 12 months in Rome before setting out again, this time for Africa. There, as in Germany, his concern was the discipline and preparedness of the troops guarding the rich agricultural areas and thriving commercial centers of the coast from the marauding nomads on the edges of

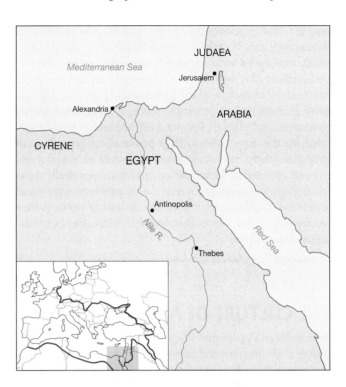

■ **Map F. Egypt.** Throughout the Roman period, Egypt was the breadbasket of the empire, supplying Rome and other cities with essential grain.

the desert. Shortly after that, he was again in Athens to dedicate public works projects he had undertaken as well as an altar to himself. From Greece he headed east, again crossing Asia and this time moving into Cappadocia and Syria (see **Map A**). His concerns here were again defense, but against a powerful civilized Parthian Empire, not barbarian tribes.

Moving southward, Hadrian stopped in Jerusalem, where he dedicated a shrine to Jupiter Capitolinus on the site of the destroyed Jewish temple before heading to Egypt for an inspection trip up the Nile (see **Map F**). Egypt remained the wealthiest Roman province and the most exploited. Since Augustus, Egypt had been governed directly by the imperial household, its agricultural wealth from the Nile Delta going to feed the Roman masses. At the same time, Alexandria continued to be one of the greatest cultural centers of the Roman world. This culture, however, was a fusion of Greek and Egyptian traditions, constantly threatening to form the basis for a nationalist opposition to Roman administrators and tax collectors. Hadrian sought to defuse this powder keg by disciplining administrators and by founding a new city, Antinopolis, which he hoped would create a center of loyalty to Rome.

Hadrian finally returned to the imperial residence on the Palatine in 131. He had spent over ten years on the road and had no doubt done much to strengthen and preserve the *Pax Romana*. Still, to the careful observer the weaknesses of the empire were as evident as its strengths. The frontiers were vast and constantly tested by a profusion of hostile tribes and

■ **Map E. Italy and Greece.** Italy, although economically dependent on the rest of the empire, was the vital center of the empire, while Greece was honored more for its glorious past than its actual importance.

peoples. Roman citizens from Italy, Gaul, and Spain were increasingly unwilling to serve in such far-flung regions. As a result, the legions were manned by progressively less romanized soldiers, and their battle readiness and discipline, poorly enforced by homesick officers, declined dangerously. In the more civilized eastern provinces, corrupt local elites, imperial governors, and officials siphoned off imperial revenues destined for the army to build their personal fortunes. Also, in spite of centuries of hellenization and Roman administration, city and countryside remained culturally and politically separated. Early in the second century, such problems were small clouds on the horizon, but in the following century they would grow into a storm that would threaten the very existence of the empire.

THE CULTURE OF ANTONINE ROME

True to Virgil's claim that Rome left it to others to "track the course of the heavens and announce the rising stars," Romans themselves took little interest in natural science. However, they supported Greek science pursued in the East, particularly in Alexandria, where centuries of Greek mathematics, astronomy, and geography came to fruition in the work of Claudius Ptolemaeus (ca. 85–ca.165 C.E.), usually known as Ptolemy.

■ This fifteenth-century Latin translation of Ptolemy's *Almagest* presents his model for the motion of the outer planets, Mars, Jupiter, and Saturn. The complicated cycles and epicycles are necessary to explain the motion of these planets while keeping the Earth at the center of the universe.

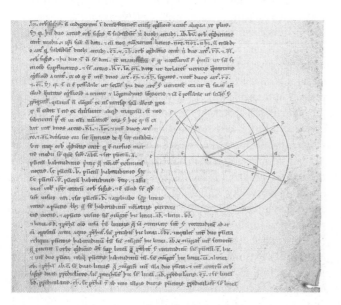

Ptolemy was a cartographer and geographer, but his greatest work was as a mathematician and astronomer.

Building on the work of Hipparchus, Ptolemy developed a complex model for the universe that could explain the apparent motion of the sun, moon, and planets. Because, as most ancient scientists, he believed the Earth to be the center of the universe, he sought a mathematically correct model to explain the apparent motions of the sun and the moon, which appear to move at varying speeds, and of the planets, which appear to move erratically when observed from Earth. His solution was first to posit a series of eccentric circles around the Earth. In order to explain the apparent variations in speed and direction, he posited a series of epicycles: that the planets move in uniform circular motion in a small circle while at the same time moving uniformly on the circumference of a larger circle. The result was a complex series of cycles and epicycles, but the mathematics work quite well. Ptolemy's theory remained the accepted model of the solar system for the next 1400 years.

Romans themselves, however, were more interested in how humans should lead their lives than in how the planets moved. Annius Florus, a poet friend of Hadrian, commenting on the emperor's exhausting journeys, wrote:

> *I do not want to be Caesar,*
> *To walk about among the Britons,*
> *To endure the Scythian hoar-frosts.*

To this, Hadrian replied:

> *I do not want to be Florus,*
> *To walk about among taverns,*
> *To lurk about among cook-shops.*

Like the other members of his dynasty, Hadrian enjoyed an easy familiarity with men of letters, and like other men of letters of the period, Florus was a provincial, an African drawn from the provincial world to the great capital. Another provincial, Rome's greatest historian, Cornelius Tacitus (ca. 56–ca. 120), recorded the history of the first century of the empire. Tacitus wrote to instruct and to edify his generation and did so in a style characterized by irony and a sharp sense of the differences between public propaganda and the realities of power politics. His picture of Germanic and British societies served as a warning to Rome against excessive self-confidence and laxity.

Tacitus's contemporaries, Plutarch (ca. 46–after 119) and Suetonius (ca. 69–after 122), were biographers rather than historians. Plutarch, who wrote in Greek, composed *Parallel Lives,* a series of character studies in which he compared an eminent Greek with an eminent Roman. Suetonius also wrote biographies, using anecdotes to portray character. Suetonius's biographies of the emperors fall short of the literary and philosophical qualities of Plutarch's character studies and far short of Tacitus's histories. Suetonius delighted in the rumors of private scandals that surrounded the emperors and used personal vice to explain public failings.

In the later second century, Romans in general preferred the study and writing of philosophy, particularly Stoicism, over history. The most influential Stoic philosopher of the century was Epictetus (ca. 55–135), a former slave who taught that people could be free by the control of their will and the cultivation of inner peace. Like the early Stoics, Epictetus taught the universal brotherhood of humankind and the identity of nature and divine providence. He urged his pupils to recognize that dependence on external things was the cause of unhappiness and therefore they should free themselves from reliance on material possessions, public esteem, and all other things prized by the worldly.

The philosophy of Epictetus found its most eager pupil in an emperor. Marcus Aurelius (161–180) reigned during a period when the stresses glimpsed by Hadrian were beginning to show in a much more alarming manner. Once more, the Parthians attacked the eastern frontier, while in Britain and Germany, barbarians struck across the borders. In 166, a confederation of barbarians known as the Marcomanni crossed the Danube and raided as far south as northern Italy. A plague, brought west by troops returning from the Parthian front, ravaged the whole empire. Like his predecessor Hadrian, Aurelius felt bound to endure the Scythian hoarfrosts rather than luxuriate in the taverns of Rome. He spent virtually the whole of his reign on the Danubian frontier, repelling the barbarians and shoring up the empire's defenses.

Throughout his reign, Aurelius found consolation in the Stoic philosophy of Epictetus. In his soldier's tent at night he composed his *Meditations,* a volume of philosophical musings. Like the slave, the emperor sought freedom from the burden of his office in his will and in the proper understanding of his role in the divine order. He called himself to introspection, to a constant awareness, under the glories and honors heaped upon him by his entourage, of his true human nature: "A poor soul burdened with a corpse."

Aurelius played his role well, dying in what is today Vienna, far from the pleasures of the capital. However, his Stoic philosophy did not serve the empire well. For all his emphasis on understanding, Aurelius badly misjudged his son Commodus (180–192), who succeeded him. Commodus, whose chief interest was in being a gladiator, saw himself as the incarnation of Heracles and appeared in public clad as a gladiator and as consul. As Commodus sank into insanity, Rome was once more convulsed by purges and proscriptions. Commodus's assassination in 192 did not end the violence. The *Pax Romana* was over.

CONCLUSION

The haphazard conquest of the Mediterranean world threw Roman republican government, traditional culture, and antagonistic social groups into chaos. The result was a century and a half of intermittent violence and civil war before a new political and social order headed by an absolute monarch established a new equilibrium. During the following two centuries, a deeply hellenized Roman civilization tied together the vast empire by incorporating the wealthy and powerful of the Western world into its fluid power structure while brutally crushing those who would not or could not conform. The binding force of the Roman Empire was great and would survive political crises in the third century as great as those that had brought down the republic 300 years before.

QUESTIONS FOR REVIEW

1. How were rifts in Roman society widened by Rome's expansion into an empire?
2. In what ways were the life and thought of Cicero indicative of an age characterized by civil conflict and the collapse of republican traditions?
3. How was religious reform an important part of Augustus's efforts to restore stability to Roman society?
4. What did the Flavian and Antonine emperors do to keep Rome's vast empire intact and in relative peace?
5. How did Paul of Tarsus transform the teachings of Jesus of Nazareth from an outgrowth of Judaism into a separate spiritual tradition?

KEY TERMS

First Triumvirate, *p. 92*

Gnostics, *p. 102*

mystery cults, *p. 100*

optimates, *p. 88*

Pax Romana, p. 95

populares, *p. 89*

presbyters, *p. 102*

princeps, *p. 95*

Second Triumvirate, *p. 93*

DISCOVERING WESTERN CIVILIZATION ONLINE

You can obtain more information about imperial Rome at the websites listed below. See also the Companion Website that accompanies this text, www.ablongman.com/kishlansky, which contains an online study guide and additional resources.

General Websites

Ancient/Classical History with N. S. Gill: The Gracchi
ancienthistory.about.com/od/gracchi/
An introduction to the Gracchi with links to other sites.

Pompeii Forum Project
www.iath.virginia.edu/pompeii/page-1.html
A great site devoted to the Roman city of Pompeii, which was destroyed by Mount Vesuvius in 79 C.E.

The End of the Republic

History & Literature of the Roman Revolution
johara.web.wesleyan.edu/CCIV274links.html
Dr. Jim O'Hara's web page devoted to the end of the Roman Republic.

The Cicero Home Page
www.utexas.edu/depts/classics/documents/Cic.html
A site dedicated to Cicero, including texts of his orations and a bibliography.

The Vergil Project
Vergil.classics.upenn.edu/
A site dedicated to providing resources and teaching materials on Virgil.

The Augustan Age and the *Pax Romana*

Augustus and the Foundation of the Empire
www.carthage.edu/outis/augustus.html
A web page devoted to the Emperor Augustus with links to archaeology and art of the Augustan age.

Virtual Tour of Rome
www.geocities.com/Athens/Forum/6946/virtual/virtual.html
A site that provides a virtual tour of the Roman Forum.

The Corinth Computer Project
corinth.sas.upenn.edu/corinth.html
A computer reconstruction of Roman Corinth.

The Dinur Center for Research in Jewish History: Second Temple and Talmudic Era
www.hum.huji.ac.il/dinur/Internetresources/historyresources/second_temple_and_talmudic_era.htm
A site at The Hebrew University of Jerusalem with links to many other sites concerning Judaism and early Christianity.

SUGGESTIONS FOR FURTHER READING

Primary Sources

Major selections of the works of Caesar, Cicero, Tacitus, Plutarch, Suetonius, and Marcus Aurelius are available in English translation from Penguin Books. The second volume by Naphtali Lewis and Meyer Reinhold, *Roman Civilization Selected Readings, Vol. II: The Empire* (1951), contains a wide selection of documents with useful introductions.

The Price of Empire

E. Badian, *Roman Imperialism in the Late Republic* (Ithaca, NY: Cornell University Press, 1968). A study of the contradictory forces leading to the development of the empire.

Mary Beard and Michael Crawford, *Rome in the Late Republic* (Ithaca, NY: Cornell University Press, 1985). An analysis of the political processes of the late republic as part of the development of Roman society, not simply the decay of the republic.

Henrik Mouritsen, *Plebs and Politics in the Late Roman Republic* (Cambridge: Cambridge University Press, 2001). A study of the political role of the masses in the last years of the republic.

The End of the Republic

Robert Gurval, *Actium and Augustus: the Politics and Emotions of Civil War* (Ann Arbor: University of Michigan Press, 1998). Important study of the end of the republic.

A. J. Langguth, *A Noise of War: Caesar, Pompey, Octavian, and the Struggle for Rome* (New York: Simon & Schuster, 1994). The era of the civil wars and the end of the republic.

D. Stockton, *Cicero: A Political Biography* (London: Oxford University Press, 1971). A biography of the great orator in the context of the end of the republic.

The Augustan Age and the *Pax Romana*

J. B. Campbell, *The Emperor and the Roman Army* (New York: Oxford University Press, 1984). Essential for understanding the military's role in the Roman Empire.

Albrecht Dihle, *Greek and Latin Literature of the Roman Empire: From Augustus to Justinian* (New York: Routledge, 1994). A survey of classical literature.

Catharine Edwards and Greg Woolf, ed., *Rome the Cosmopolis* (New York: Cambridge University Press, 2003). An innovative collection of essays examining the relationship between Rome and its empire.

Karl Galinsky, *Augustan Culture* (Princeton, NJ: Princeton University Press, 1998). An important study of the cultural world of Augustus.

Judith P. Hallett, *Fathers and Daughters in Roman Society and the Elite Family* (Princeton, NJ: Princeton University Press, 1984). A study of indirect power exercised by elite women in the Roman world as daughters, mothers, and sisters.

J. E. Lendon, *Empire of Honour: The Art of Government in the Roman World* (Oxford: Oxford University Press, 2001). A provocative study of Roman despotism and the support it enjoyed from the ruling classes of the provinces.

Fergus Millar, *The Emperor in the Roman World* (Ithaca, NY: Cornell University Press, 1992). A study of emperors, stressing their essential passivity by responding to initiatives from below.

D. A. West and A. J. Woodman, *Poetry and Politics in the Age of Augustus* (New York: Cambridge University Press, 1984). The cultural program of Augustus.

Religions from the East

Schuyler Brown, *The Origins of Christianity: A Historical Introduction of the New Testament,* rev. ed. (Oxford: Oxford University Press, 1993). A balanced and comprehensive introduction to early Christianity.

Ramsay MacMullen, *Paganism in the Roman Empire* (New Haven, CT: Yale University Press, 1981). A description of the varieties and levels of pagan religion in the Roman world.

Ekkehard W. Stegemann and Wolfgang Stegemann, *The Jesus Movement: A Social History of Its First Century* (Minneapolis: Fortress Press, 1999). A new survey of the first century of Christianity.

A Tour of the Empire

Jane F. Gardner, *Women in Roman Law and Society* (Bloomington: Indiana University Press, 1986). A study of the extent of freedom and power over property enjoyed by Roman women.

Peter Garnsey and Richard Saller, *The Roman Empire: Economy, Society, and Culture* (Berkeley: University of California Press, 1987). A topical study of imperial administration, economy, religion, and society, arguing the coercive and exploitative nature of Roman civilization in relation to the agricultural societies of the Mediterranean world.

Fergus Millar, *Rome, the Greek World, and the East: The Roman Republic and the Augustan Revolution* (Chapel Hill: University of North Carolina Press, 2000). A collection of essays by a leading historian surveying Rome's rise to empire.

For a list of additional titles related to this chapter's topics, please see www.ablongman.com/kishlansky.

Chapter 6

THE TRANSFORMATION OF THE CLASSICAL WORLD, 192–500

The Visual Record

A BRIDE'S TROUSSEAU

Venus, assisted by mythical sea creatures and *erotes,* or cupids, beautifies herself on the central panel of a magnificent silver chest that made up part of a fourth-century Roman bride's trousseau. On the top, the bride, Projecta, and her groom, Secundus, are depicted within a wreath held by two more cupids. The iconography and the execution of this sumptuous object—composed of solid silver with silver gilt and measuring almost two feet by one foot—testify to the high status of the bride and her deep attachment to the ancient classical traditions of Greco-Roman culture. Projecta and Secundus were Roman aristocrats, and their marriage was part of Roman rituals of class, wealth, and power as ancient as the goddess on the marriage chest.

Yet, within the thorough paganism of the symbolism and the lavish expense of the workmanship, the Latin inscription engraved on the rim across the front of the lid confronts the viewer with how utterly changed the Roman world had become. It reads, "Secundus and Projecta, live in Christ." In spite of the elaborate pagan symbolism of the casket, Secundus and Projecta were Christians, but they apparently saw nothing improper about commemorating their marriage in the age-old manner of their pagan ancestors. A bride could live in Christ and still be Venus.

Such was the world of late antiquity. By the time Projecta married Secundus, the once persecuted Christian sect was not only legal but well on its way to

becoming the established religion in the empire. Formerly a religion of hellenized Jews and freed slaves, it was attracting converts from among the highest classes of Roman society. And yet, aristocratic families, Christian as well as pagan, continued the ancient cultural traditions without a sense of betrayal or contradiction. Rome appeared as eternal and serene as Venus herself.

But the Projecta casket has more to tell us. It was found, along with over 60 other exquisite objects and 70 pounds of silver plate, on the Esquiline hill in Rome, where it had been hastily buried to hide it from some catastrophe. The probable catastrophe is not hard to guess: In 410, when Projecta would have been an elderly woman, the barbarian Visigoths sacked and pillaged Rome for three days, raping Roman women and looting them of such treasures as this marriage chest.

Yet these barbarians were themselves Christians, while the city of Rome had remained a pagan stronghold. Moreover, the Visigoths were an officially designated Roman army reacting to the failure of the state to provide them with

what they saw as their due. Such contrasts of paganism and Christianity, barbarity and Roman culture, were integral parts of a new Roman world, one that was characterized by radical transformations of Roman and barbarian culture that took place in the two centuries following the death of Marcus Aurelius in 180. Accelerating this process of change and transformation was the combination of events that are collectively referred to as the crisis of the third century.

Looking Ahead

This chapter follows the profound political and social transformations that turned both the Roman Empire and its barbarian neighbors into radically new societies with different political, religious, and social organizations. By the sixth century, the eastern half of the empire had become profoundly hellenized, while the western half had disintegrated into numerous Romano-barbarian kingdoms without losing its close identity with Rome. ➤

THE CRISIS OF THE THIRD CENTURY

From the reign of Septimius Severus (193–211) to the time of Diocletian (284–305), both internal and external challenges shook the Roman Empire. The empire survived, but its social, political, and economic structures were radically transformed.

Sheer size was a fundamental problem for the empire. Haphazard expansion in many regions—to the north and west, for instance—overextended the frontiers. The labor and resources needed to maintain this vast territory strained the economic system of the empire. Like a thread stretched to the breaking point, the thin line of border garrisons and forts was ready to snap.

The economic system itself was part of the reason for this strain on resources. For all of its commercial networks, the economy of the empire remained tied to agriculture. To the aristocrats of the ancient world, agriculture was the only honorable source of wealth. The goal of the successful merchant was to liquidate his commercial assets, buy estates, and rise into the leisured landholding elite. As a result, liquid capital for either investment or taxation was always scarce.

The lack of sophistication seen in commercial and industrial business practice characterized the financial system of the empire as well. Government had always been conducted on the cheap. The tax system of the empire had never been very efficient at tapping into the real wealth of the aristocracy. Each individual city made its own collective assessments. Individuals eager to win the gratitude of their local communities were expected to provide essential services from their own pockets. Even with the vast wealth of the empire at its disposal, the government never developed a system of public debt—that is, a policy of borrowing against future revenues. As a result, the only way to solve short-term cash-flow problems was to debase the coinage by using more copper and less silver. This practice became epidemic in the third century, when the price of a bushel of wheat rose over 200 percent.

The failure of the empire to develop a stable political base complicated its economic problems. In times of emergency, imperial control relied on the personal presence and command of the emperor. As the empire grew, it became impossible for this presence to be felt everywhere. Moreover, the empire never developed either a regular system of imperial succession or an adequate power base. Control of the army, which was the ultimate source of imperial power, was possible only as long as the emperor could lead his armies to victory.

Enrich the Army and Scorn the Rest

Through much of the late second and third centuries, emperors failed dismally to lead their armies to victory. The barely romanized provincials in the military bore the brunt of these attacks. When the emperors selected by the distant Roman Senate failed to win victory, frontline armies unhesitatingly raised their own commanders to the imperial office. These commanders set about restructuring the empire in favor of the army. They opened important administrative posts to soldiers, expanded the army's size, raised military pay, initiated expensive building programs in frontier settlements, and in general introduced authoritarian military discipline throughout society. To finance these costly measures, the new military government confiscated senatorial wealth, introduced new forms of taxation, and increasingly debased the coinage.

The Rise of the Military. With their first rise in real income, soldiers in the provinces could improve their standard of living while in service and buy their way into provincial elites on retirement. Free-spending soldiers and imperial extravagance helped the bleak settlements on the edges of military camps grow into prosperous cities with all the comforts of the older parts of the empire.

For the first time, capable soldiers could hope to rise to the highest levels of public power, regardless of their birth. One extraordinarily successful soldier was Publius Helvius Pertinax. Born the son of a freed slave in the north of Italy (Liguria) in 126, he abandoned a career as a schoolteacher to enter the military. By the time he was 50, his success as a military commander won for him the office of consul. He then held a series of military, civil, and proconsular positions in Syria, Britain, Italy, and Africa before returning to Rome. When the Emperor Commodus was murdered in 192, the palace guard proclaimed Pertinax emperor—the first emperor who had not come from the privileged senatorial class.

Economic Disaster. Soon, however, the military control of the empire turned into a nightmare even for the provinces and their armies. Exercising their newly discovered power, armies raised and then destroyed pretender after pretender, offering support to whichever imperial candidate promised them the greatest riches. Pertinax, the first of these soldier-emperors, was murdered by his soldiers less than three months after becoming emperor. The army's incessant demands for higher pay led emperors to lower the amount of silver in the coins with which the soldiers were paid. But the less the coins were worth, the more of them were necessary to purchase goods. And the more goods cost, the less valuable was the soldiers' salary. Such drastic inflation wrecked the economic stability of the empire and spurred the army on to greater and more impossible demands for raises. Emperors who could not meet the demands were killed by their troops. In fact, the army was much more effective at killing emperors than enemies. Between 235 and 284, 17 of the 20 more or less legitimate emperors were assassinated or killed in civil war.

External Threats. The crisis of the third century did not result only from economic and political instability within the empire. Rome's internal crises coincided with an increase of attacks from outside the empire. In Africa, Berber tribes harassed the frontiers. The Sassanid dynasty in Persia threatened Rome's eastern frontier. When the Emperor Valerian (253–260) attempted to prevent the Persian king of kings

■ This cameo was made to the order of Shapur I after the capture of Valerian during the great battle near Antioch in 260. The symbolic scene has Shapur seizing Valerian simply by grasping his hand.

Shapur I from seizing Roman Mesopotamia and Armenia, he was captured and held prisoner for the rest of his life.

The greatest danger to Rome came not from the south or east, but from the west. There, along the Rhine, various Germanic tribes known collectively as the Franks and the Alemanni began raiding expeditions into the empire. Along the lower Danube and in southern Ukraine, the Gothic confederation raided the Balkans and harassed Roman shipping on the Black Sea.

An Empire on the Defensive

The central administration of the empire simply could not deal effectively with the numerous barbarian attacks. Left on their own, regional provincial commanders at times even headed separatist movements. Provincial aristocrats who despaired of receiving any help from distant Rome often supported these pretenders. One such commander was Postumus, whom the armies of Spain, Britain, and Gaul proclaimed emperor. His nine-year separatist reign (ca. 258–268) was the longest and most stable of that of any emperor, legitimate or otherwise, throughout this whole troubled period.

Political and military instability had devastating effects on the lives of ordinary people. Citizenship had been extended to virtually all free inhabitants of the empire in 212, but that right was a formality given simply to enlarge the tax base, since only citizens paid inheritance taxes. Society became

sharply divided into the privileged **honestiores**—senators, municipal gentry, and the military—and the increasingly burdened **humiliores**—everyone else. The humiliores suffered the most from the tax increases because, unlike the honestiores, they could neither bribe their way out of them nor intimidate tax collectors with private armies. They were also frequent targets of extortion by the military and of violence perpetrated by bandits.

Slave and peasant bandits, rustlers, and even pirates played an ambivalent role in society. Often they terrorized the countryside, descending from the hills to attack villages or travelers. However, at times they also protected peasants from greedy tax collectors and military commanders. In Gaul and Spain, peasants and local leaders organized armed resistance movements, termed *Bacaudae,* to withstand the exorbitant demands of tax collectors. In the first centuries of the empire, bandits operated primarily in peripheral areas that had been recently and poorly subjugated to Roman rule. In the late second and third centuries they became an increasing problem in Italy itself.

The Barbarian Menace

Compounding the internal violence that threatened to destroy the Roman Empire were the external attacks of the Germanic barbarians. These attacks reflected changes within the Germanic world as profound as those within the empire.

Between the second and fifth centuries the Germanic world was transformed from a mosaic of small, decentralized, agricultural tribes into a number of powerful military tribal confederations capable of challenging Rome itself. We cannot understand the impact of the barbarians on the empire without understanding the social and political organization and the transformation of these people living beyond the frontier.

Germanic Society.   The Germanic peoples typically inhabited small villages organized into patriarchal households, which were integrated into clans, which in turn composed tribes. For the most part, clans governed themselves, and except in war, tribal leaders had little authority over their followers. In the second century, many tribes had kings, but they were religious rather than political leaders.

Germanic communities lived by farming, but cattle raising and especially warfare carried the highest social prestige. Men measured their status by the number of cattle they owned and by their martial ability. Women took care of agricultural chores and household duties. Like the number of cattle, the number of wives showed a man's social position. Polygyny was common among chiefs.

Warfare defined social groupings, and warriors dominated public life. Only within the clan was fighting inappropriate. But rival clans within the same tribe dealt with one another brutally. Conflict took the form of the feud, and each act of aggression was repaid in kind. If an individual within a clan had a grievance with an individual within another clan, all his kinsmen were obliged to assist him. Thus a single incident could result in a continuous escalation of acts of revenge.

Feuding and Peacemaking.   Clans in other tribes were fair game for raiding, looting, and conquering. Individuals, clans, and tribes built their wealth and reputations on warfare. The more successful a tribe was in warfare, the more clans it attracted and the greater its position became in the barbarian world.

The practice of feuding, especially within the tribe, had enormous costs. Families were decimated, and strong warriors who were needed to defend the tribe from outside attack faced constant danger from members of their own tribe. Tribal leaders attempted to reduce hostilities by establishing payments called **wergeld** in place of the blood vengeance demanded in reparation for crimes. Such wergeld, normally paid in cattle or slaves, was voluntary, since the right of vengeance was generally recognized, and the unity of the tribe remained precarious.

Tribes also attempted to reinforce unity through religious cults involving shared myths of common ancestry and rituals intended to underline group cohesion. When not fighting,

TACITUS ON THE GERMANS

At the end of the first century C.E., Tacitus wrote a brief account of the Germanic peoples living beyond the frontiers, in part to inform Romans about the neighboring people and in part to criticize the morals and practices of Roman society. In general, his information, although selective and filtered through Roman culture, appears quite accurate.

Focus Questions

What, according to Tacitus, are the various types of executive and legislative power among the Germanic peoples? Why was the feud so important in this society?

They pick their kings on the basis of noble birth, their generals on the basis of bravery. Nor do their kings have limitless or arbitrary power, and the generals win favor by the example they set if they are energetic, if they are distinguished, if they fight before the battle-line, rather than by the power they wield. But no one except the priests is allowed to inflict punishment with death, chains, or even flogging, and the priests act not, as it were, to penalize and at the command of the general, but, so to speak, at the order of the god, who they believe is at hand when they are waging war.... The nobles make decisions about lesser matters, all freemen about things of greater significance, with this proviso, nonetheless, that those subjects, of which ultimate judgment is in the hands of the mass of people, receive preliminary consideration among the nobles.... When the crowd thinks it opportune, they sit down fully armed. Silence is demanded by the priests, who then also have the right of compulsion. Soon the king or the chieftains are heard, in accordance with the age, nobility, glory in war, and eloquence of each, with the influence of persuasion being greater than the power to command. If a proposal has displeased them, they show their displeasure with a roar; but if it has won favor, they bang their *frameae* [spears] together; the most prestigious kind of approval is praise with arms.... There is an obligation to undertake the personal feuds as well as the friendships of one's father or blood-relative; but the feuds do not continue without possibility of settlement, for even murder is atoned for by a specific number of cattle and sheep and the entire family accepts the settlement, with advantage to the community, since feuds are the most dangerous when joined with freedom.

From Tacitus, *Germany.*

Germanic warriors spent much of their time drinking beer together at the table of their war leader. Communal beer drinking was a way of uniting potentially hostile neighbors. Not surprisingly, it could also lead to drunken brawls that reopened the very feuds drinking bouts were intended to end. These feuds could in turn lead to the hiving off of irreconcilable factions, which might in time form their own tribes.

Warrior Bands.   In contrast to the familial structure of barbarian society stood another warrior group that cut across kindred and even tribal units. This was the warrior band, called in Latin the *comitatus*. Some young warriors formed personal bonds with particularly able leaders and pledged them absolute loyalty. In return the leaders were obligated to lead their warriors to victory and to share with them the spoils of war. These warrior societies, far from being the basic units of a larger tribal military force, were organized for their own plunder and fighting. While they might be a valuable aid in intertribal warfare, they could also shatter the fragile peace by conducting raids on neighbors, thus bringing whole tribes into internal conflict. Successful warrior leaders might draw sufficient numbers of followers and conquer so many other groups that in time the band would become a new tribe.

Roman Influence in the Barbarian World

Intratribal and intertribal violence produced a rough equilibrium of power and wealth as long as small Germanic tribes lived in isolation. The presence of the Roman Empire, felt both directly and indirectly in the barbarian world, upset this equilibrium. Unintentionally, Rome itself helped to transform the Germanic tribes into the major threat to the imperial system.

The Lure of Roman Culture.   The direct presence of Roman merchants extended only about a 100 miles beyond the frontiers. However, the attraction of Roman luxury goods and the Romans' efforts to establish friendly Germanic buffer zones along the borders drew even distant tribes into the Roman imperial system. Across the barbarian world, tribal leaders and comitatus leaders sought the prestige that Roman goods brought them. Roman provincial commanders encouraged these leaders to enter into commercial arrangements with the Romans. In exchange for their cattle, which the Romans needed for their troops, the Germanic leaders received gold and grain. This outside source of wealth greatly increased economic disparity within Germanic society. In addition, some leaders made treaties with Rome, thus receiving the advantage of Roman support, which other tribal leaders lacked. In return for payments of gold and foodstuffs, chieftains of these "federated" tribes agreed to oppose tribes that were hostile to Rome and to prevent young hotheads of their own tribes from raiding across the frontier. Some chiefs supplied warriors for the Roman army. Others even led their comitatus into Roman service. By the late third century, the Roman army included Franks, Goths, and Saxons serving as

far away from their homes as Egypt. Such "imperial Germans" moved back and forth between the Roman and barbarian worlds, using each as a foundation for increased power in the other and obscuring the cultural and political differences between the two.

The West Germanic Revolution.   The effects of contact between barbarians and Romans reached far and wide throughout the empire and beyond the frontier. Along the Rhine and Danube the result was the so-called West Germanic Revolution. To survive in a time of constant warfare, tribes had to become armies. The armies needed a united and effective leadership. Among most of the western Germanic peoples, the tradition of the older tribal king was abandoned. A new kind of nonroyal chieftain emerged as the war leader of the people and as the representative of the war god Woden. In the later second and third centuries, the turmoil resulted in the formation of new tribes and tribal confederations: the Marcomanni, the Alemanni, and the Franks. By the end of the second century, this internal barbarian transformation spilled over into the empire in the form of the Marcomannian wars and the Saxon, Frankish, and Alemannic incursions into the western provinces.

The Gothic Confederation.   Around the same time, along the Oder and Vistula rivers to the north, a group later known as the Goths began their slow consolidation around a royal family. The Goths were unique in that their kings exercised more military authority than was usual for a Germanic tribe. These kings formed the nucleus of a constantly changing barbarian group. A Goth was not necessarily a biological descendant of the small second-century tribe living along the shore of the Baltic. Anyone who fought alongside the Gothic king was a Goth.

Between the second and fourth centuries, the bearers of this Gothic royal tradition began to filter to the south and east, ultimately transferring their model of barbarian organization to the area of present-day Kiev in southern Ukraine. This move was not so much a physical migration of thousands of people across Europe as the gradual confederation under Gothic leadership of various Germanic, Scythian, and other peoples living around the Black Sea. By the early third century, this Gothic confederation was strong enough to challenge Roman supremacy in the region. These first Gothic wars in the east were even more devastating than the later wars in the west.

THE EMPIRE RESTORED

By the last decades of the third century, the empire seemed in danger of crumbling under combined internal and external pressure. That it did not was largely due to the efforts of the soldier-emperor Aurelian (270–275), who was able to repulse the barbarians, restore the unity of the empire, and then set about stabilizing the internal imperial structure.

Diocletian, the God-Emperor

Diocletian (284–305), a Dalmatian soldier who had risen through the ranks to become emperor, completed the process of stabilization and reorganization of the imperial system begun by Aurelian. The result was a regime that in some ways increased imperial power and in other ways simply did away with the pretenses that had previously masked the emperor's true position.

No longer was the emperor *princeps,* or "first citizen." Now he was *dominus,* or "lord," the term of respect used by slaves in addressing their masters. He also assumed the title of *Iovius,* or Jupiter, thus claiming divine status, and demanded adoration as a living god. Diocletian recognized that the empire was too large and complex for one man to rule. To solve the problem, he divided the empire into eastern and western parts, each part to be ruled by both an augustus and a junior emperor, or caesar. Diocletian was augustus in the east, supported by his caesar, Galerian. In the west the rulers were the augustus Maximian and his caesar, Constantius.

The Tetrarchy. In theory, this **tetrarchy,** or rule by four, provided for regular succession. The caesars, who were married to daughters of the augusti, were to succeed them. Although from time to time subsequent emperors would rule alone, Diocletian's innovation proved successful and enduring. The empire was divided administratively into eastern and western parts until the death of Julius Nepos, the last legitimate emperor in the west, in 480.

In addition to this constitutional reform, Diocletian enacted or consolidated a series of measures to improve the functioning of the imperial administration. He reorganized and expanded the army, approximately doubled the number of provinces, separated their military and civil administration, and greatly increased the number of bureaucrats to administer them. He attempted to stem runaway inflation by increasing the amount of silver in coins and fixing maximum prices and wages throughout the empire. He restructured the imperial tax system, basing it on payments in goods and produce in order to distribute the burden more equitably among all citizens and to avoid problems of currency debasement.

A Militarized Society. The pillar of Diocletian's success was his victorious military machine. He was effective because, like the barbarian chieftains who had turned their tribes into armies, he militarized society and led this military society to victory. Like Diocletian himself, his soldiers were drawn from provincial marginal regions. They showed tremendous devotion to their god-emperor. By the time of Diocletian's reign, a career such as that of Pertinax had become the rule rather than the exception for emperors. For Diocletian and his soldiers, the periphery of the empire had become its center; the center was increasingly marginal to the program of the empire.

Fiscal Reform. Some aspects of Diocletian's program, such as the improvement of the civil administration and the military, were successful. Others, such as the reform of silver currency and wage and price controls, were dismal failures. One effect of the fiscal reforms was

MAP DISCOVERY

The Empire Under Diocletian

This map shows the extent of the empire in 305, at the end of Diocletian's reign. Compared with the map on page 103, what portions of the empire had been lost or abandoned during his reign? Why? What geographical challenges did the empire's size pose to the emperor? Note where Aurelius Gaius served. What were the troubles and disturbances that influenced his itinerary?

to bind **coloni,** or hereditary tenant farmers, to their lands, since they were forbidden to leave the villages where they were registered to pay their taxes. In this practice lay the origins of European serfdom. Another effect was the gradual destruction of the local city councils, since their members, the **decurions,** were held personally responsible for the payment of local assessments whether or not they could be collected from the other inhabitants. In time, this led to the dissolution of local civil government.

All of these measures were designed to marshal the entire population in the monumental task of preserving *Romanitas.* Central to this task was the proper reverential attitude toward the divine emperors who directed it. One group seemed stubbornly opposed to this heroic effort: the Christians. In 298, an incident occurred that seemed to confirm their subversive attitude. At a sacrifice in the presence of Diocletian, the Roman priests were unable to obtain the desired favorable omens; they attributed their failure to the presence of Christians, who were crossing themselves to ward off demons. Such blasphemous conduct—it might be compared, for instance, to desecrating the flag at a modern public assembly—led to the launching of the Great Persecution, which formally began in 303 and lasted sporadically until 313. It resulted in the death of hundreds of Christians who refused to sacrifice to the pagan gods.

Constantine, the Emperor of God

In 305, in the midst of the Great Persecution, Diocletian and his co-augustus Maximian took the extraordinary step of abdicating in favor of their caesars, Galerians and Constantius. This abdication was intended to provide for an orderly succession. Instead, the sons of Constantius and Maximian, Constantine (306–337) and Maxentius (306–312), drawing on the prejudice of the increasingly barbarian armies toward hereditary succession, set about wrecking the tetrarchy. In so doing, they plunged the empire once more into civil war as they fought over the western half of the empire.

Victory and Conversion.   Victory in the west came to Constantine in 312, when he defeated and killed Maxentius in a battle at the Milvian Bridge outside Rome. Constantine attributed his victory to a vision telling him to paint on the shields of his soldiers. For pagans, this symbol ☥ was the solar emblem of the cult of the Unconquered Sun. For Christians, it was the Chi-Rho, ☧, formed from the first two letters of the Greek word for Christ. The next year, in Milan, Constantine rescinded the persecution of Christians and granted Christian clergy the same privileges that pagan priests enjoyed. Constantine himself was not baptized until near death, a common practice in antiquity. However, during his reign, Christianity grew from a persecuted minority to the most favored cult in the empire.

Constantinople.   Almost as important as Constantine's conversion to Christianity was his decision to establish his capital in Byzantium, a city founded by Greek colonists on the narrow neck of water connecting the Black Sea to the Mediterranean. He transformed and enriched this small town, calling it the New Rome. Later it was known as Constantinople, the city of Constantine. For the next 11 centuries, Constantinople served as the heart of the Roman and then the Byzantine world. From his new city, Constantine began to transform the empire into a Christian state and Christianity into a Roman state religion.

The Triumph of Christianity

While paganism was being disestablished, Christianity was rapidly becoming the established religion. The effects of Constantine's conversion on the empire and on Christianity were enormous. Constantine made large financial contributions to Christian communities to repay them for their losses during persecutions. He erected rich churches on the model of Roman basilicas, or administrative buildings, and converted temples into Christian places of worship. He gave bishops the authority to act as magistrates within the Christian community. Once the particular subjects of persecution, bishops became favored courtiers. Constantine attempted to make himself the de facto head of the Church. He even presided at the Council of Nicaea in 325, at which the assembled bishops condemned the Arian teaching that Jesus as Son of God was not equal to God the Father. Constantine and his successors, with the brief exception of his nephew Julian (r. 361–363), sought to use the cult of the one God to strengthen their control over the empire.

Emperor and Church.   Although Constantine himself continued to maintain cordial relations with representatives of all cults and to use ambiguous language that would offend no one when talking about "the deity," his successors were less broad-minded. After Constantine's death in 337, they began restricting paganism. In 341, pagan sacrifice was banned, and by 355 the temples had been closed and the death penalty for sacrificing to pagan gods had been decreed, although not enforced.

Imperial control over Christianity was strong, but not total. One of the most powerful Christian successors to Constantine, Theodosius I (347–395), met his match in Ambrose (339–397), the bishop of Milan. In 390, the emperor, angered by riots in the Greek city of Thessalonica, ordered a general massacre of the population. Ambrose dared to excommunicate, or ban, the emperor from his church in Milan until Theodosius did public penance for that brutal act. Eventually, the emperor acquiesced, acknowledging that even he was subject to the rule of God as interpreted by the bishops. The incident was often cited later by church leaders to define the relationship between religious and secular authority.

Conversion.   Although imperial support was essential to the spread of Christianity in the fourth century, other factors encouraged conversion as well. Christian miracles, particularly

■ This mosaic found under St. Peter's Basilica in Rome is believed by many to be the earliest representation of Jesus, while others see it as Helios, the sun-god. The catacombs were underground passages near Rome used by the early Christians as cemeteries, for funeral and memorial services, and as places of refuge during times of persecution.

that of exorcism, or the casting out of demons, won many converts. The ancient world was believed to be filled with daimons, supernatural creatures whose power for good or ill no one doubted. Every village had its possessed persons—mad men and women, troubled youths, and hate-filled citizens. Wandering Christian preachers seemed more competent than others to deal with these tormentors, proving that their God was more powerful than the spirits and that their message was worthy of a hearing.

Over the course of the fourth century, the number of Christians rose from 5 to 30 million. Imperial support, miracles, and preaching could not, by themselves, account for this phenomenal growth. Physical coercion played a large part. The story was told that in one town, on imperial command, all of the local temples were destroyed and "a great number" of leading pagans who refused conversion were tortured to death. The remaining pagan population converted. Whether or not the story is true, it illustrates the essential role that naked force often played in the process of conversion. Conversion—by whatever method—also suited the emperors, who saw a unified cult as an essential means of bolstering their position.

IMPERIAL CHRISTIANITY

The religion to which Constantine converted had matured institutionally and intellectually since its origins as a reform movement within Judaism. By the late third century, Christian communities existed throughout the empire, each headed by a bishop who was considered divinely guided and answerable only to his flock and to God. These bishops replaced pagan philosophers as sources of wisdom and authority. In the west, the bishop of Rome, termed the pope, had acquired the position of first among equals, a position that was at times acknowledged by the eastern patriarchates as well, out of respect for the successor of Peter and Paul and bishop of the ancient capital. However, the Church as a whole was divided on fundamental questions of belief, and the growing importance of Christianity in the Roman Empire added to the gravity of these divisions. The two most contentious issues were, in the Greek-speaking regions of the empire, the nature of Christ, and in the Latin-speaking provinces, the extent to which individuals could earn their salvation through their own virtue.

Divinity, Humanity, and Salvation

Jesus, the savior or Christ, was at the heart of Christian belief, but individual Christian communities interpreted the nature of Christ differently as they attempted to reconcile their faith with the intellectual traditions of late antiquity. Christian Scriptures spoke of the Father, the Son, and the Spirit. Yahweh was generally accepted as the Father and Christ as the Son; the Spirit was understood to be the continuing presence of God sent by Jesus after his resurrection and ascension.

Christology. Generally, Christians saw God as a Trinity, at once one and three. But the relationship among the three was a source of endless debate, particularly for Greek-speaking Christians attempting to reconcile their faith with the Neoplatonic ideas of successive emanations from God to creation, which were incorporated into the Christian understanding of the Trinity. Was Christ just a man, chosen by God as a divine instrument, or was he God? If he was God, had he simply appeared to be human? These were not trivial or academic questions for Christians, since the possibility of salvation depended on their answers. Throughout the eastern half of the empire, ordinary people were ready to fight not only with words, but even with weapons to defend their positions.

Throughout the so-called **Christological controversies**—which began in the early third century and continued through the fifth—two extremes presented Christ as either entirely human or entirely God, with centrists attempting to hold a middle ground. At one extreme were the Monarchians, who emphasized the oneness of God by arguing that the three represented three activities although God possessed only one substance, and the Gnostics, who argued that Jesus had only appeared to be human but in reality was only divine. At the other extreme were the **Arians,** who explained that Jesus was a man and not divine.

MAP DISCOVERY

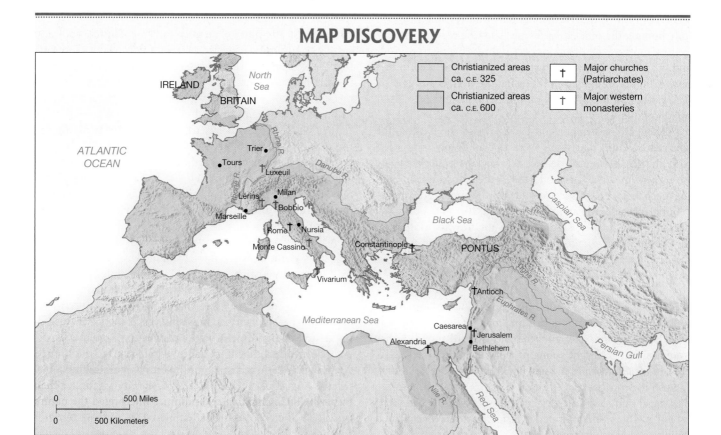

The Spread of Christianity

Examine the regions in which Christianity first became established. What is distinctive about the areas Christianized in the first three centuries of Christendom? What major differences can you detect between Christian centers in the eastern and western portions of the Roman Empire? To what extent did Christianity exist outside the empire by 600?

Origen of Alexandria. The first Christian intellectual to undertake a systematic exposition of the Trinity was the great Alexandrine theologian Origen (185–254). In all of his teachings, Origen moved Christian teaching from a literal to a symbolic understanding of Scripture and gave it a sound philosophical foundation by synthesizing the Neoplatonic tradition with Christianity. His trinitarian teachings insisted on the co-eternality of the Son with the Father, but, drawing as he did on Neoplatonic ideas of emanations, he seemed to subordinate the Son to the Father and to make the Spirit a creation of the Son. In the generations following Origen, the controversy continued, particularly between those who taught the equality of the persons of the Trinity and those who, like the Alexandrine theologian Arius (ca. 250–336), insisted that Jesus was not equal to God the Father but was a lesser divinity created by God. By the time of Constantine, the issue of whether or not Jesus was one with God threatened to destroy the unity of Christianity. To settle the controversy, the emper-

or commanded the bishops of the entire Church to assemble at Nicaea in 325. At the emperor's urging, the council condemned the teachings of Arius and adopted the term *homousion,* "of one being," to describe the equality of the Father and the Son.

The Council of Nicaea did not end the Christological controversy. For almost a century, Arians continued to win adherents to their denial of the divinity of Christ, even among the Christian emperors who succeeded Constantine. Before the Arian tradition finally died out within the empire, missionaries spread it to the barbarian Goths beyond the frontiers. Similarly, at the other extreme, Monophysites in Egypt and Syria argued that Christ had only one nature—the divine. A century after Nicaea, another council was held at Chalcedon in 451 to resolve the issue. Following the recommendation of the bishop of Rome, Pope Leo I (440–461), the bishops at Chalcedon agreed that in the one God there were three divine persons: the Father, the Son, and the Spirit. However, the second person of the Trinity, the Son, had two natures: one fully human, the other fully divine. The Chalcedon formulation established the orthodox, or "right-believing," position, and the full weight of the imperial machinery worked to impose it on all. In Egypt and Palestine the decree was greeted with outrage. Mobs of monks and laity rioted in the streets to oppose the "unclean synod of Chalcedon."

Although a western bishop had provided the formula for Chalcedon, Latin Christians were not as deeply concerned with the Christological debates as were the easterners. For westerners, the great question was less the nature of God than the mechanism of salvation and the role of humans in the salvational process. An attempt to answer this and other key doctrinal questions was provided by a man who, more than any other individual, would set the course of western Christianity and political philosophy for the next thousand years: Augustine of Hippo.

Augustine of Hippo.   Augustine (354–430) was born into a well-off North African family in the town of Tagaste and was quickly drawn into the good life and upward mobility that were available to bright young provincials in the fourth century. In his *Confessions*, the first psychological autobiography, Augustine describes how his skills in rhetoric took him to the provincial capital of Carthage and then on to Rome and finally Milan, the western imperial residence, where he gained fame as one of the foremost rhetoricians of the empire.

While in Milan, Augustine came into contact with kinds of people he had never encountered in Africa, particularly Neoplatonists and Christians. The most important of these was Ambrose, bishop of Milan. The encounter with a spiritual philosophy and a Christianity that was compatible with it profoundly changed the young professor. After a period of agonized searching, Augustine converted to the new religion. Abandoning his Italian life, he returned to the North African town of Hippo to found a monastery where he could devote himself to reading the Scriptures. However, his neighbors were determined to harness the intellectual talents of their brilliant native son. When their bishop died, they forcibly seized Augustine and made him their bishop.

Augustine spent the remainder of his life as bishop of this small provincial town, but his reputation as spokesperson for the Christian tradition spread throughout the empire. As a professor of rhetoric he had become an expert in debate, and much of his episcopal career was spent in refuting opponents within the Church as well as dealing with traditional pagans who blamed the problems of the empire on the new religion. Christians, they claimed, had abandoned the traditional gods and the traditional Roman virtues and justice that had made Rome great.

In responding to these attacks, Augustine elaborated a new Christian understanding of human society and the individual's relationship to God, which dominated Western thought for the next 15 centuries. His views were set forth in several works: *Confessions, On the Trinity,* and *City of God.* He rejected elitist attempts to identify the true Church with any earthly community. Likewise, he rejected the claim of pagans that the Roman tradition was the embodiment of true virtue. Instead, he argued that the true members of God's elect necessarily coexisted in the world with sinners. No earthly community, not even the empire or the visible Church, was the true "city of God." Earthly society participated in the true Church, the city of God, through the sacraments and did so quite apart from the individual worthiness of the recipients or even of the ministers of these rites. Belief that the presence of sinners within the Church blocked the plan of salvation or that responsibility for salvation lay with the individual was to deny the omnipotence of God.

According to Augustine, salvation was free, a gift not earned by virtuous lives but freely granted by God to the elect. In this way, Augustine argued for a distinction between the visible Christian empire and the Christian community. Earlier, the pharisaic Jew Paul had determined that Christianity would survive Judaism even as the latter was being destroyed by Rome. Now Augustine, the Roman rhetorician, determined that Christianity would survive the Roman Empire just as it was disintegrating into barbarian kingdoms. Even as Augustine lay dying in Hippo, the city was under siege by barbarian Vandals.

The Call of the Desert

At the same time that intellectuals like Augustine were attempting to explain Christian doctrine, less intellectual but equally determined men and women were searching for a different way of living Christ's message. This was the hermit, monk, or recluse, who taught less by his or her words than by his or her life, a life that was often so unusual that even the most ignorant and worldly citizen of the late empire could recognize in it the power of God. Beneath the apparent eccentricity, however, lay a fundamental principle: the radical rejection of society's values in favor of absolute dedication to God's.

Shortly after the death of Origen in 254, another Egyptian was undertaking a different path to enduring fame. Anthony (ca. 250–355), a well-to-do peasant, heard the same biblical text that later converted Augustine: "Go, sell all you have and give to the poor and follow me." Anthony was uneducated; it was said that he had been too shy as a boy to attend school. This straightforward peasant did exactly what the text commanded. He disposed of all his goods and left his village for the Egyptian desert. There, for the next 70 years, he sought to follow Christ in a life of constant self-mortification and prayer.

This dropout from civilization deeply touched his fellow Christians, many of whom were disturbed by the abrupt transformation of their religion from persecuted minority to privileged majority. By the time of his death this monk—the word comes from the Greek *monos*, "alone"—found himself the head of a large, loosely knit community of like-minded persons who looked to him as spiritual father, or abbot. Over the next few centuries, thousands rejected the worldliness of civilization and the easy life of the average Christian to lead a monastic life in the wildernesses of the empire.

Monastic Communities

Monasticism took two forms: communal organization and solitary life. Pachomius (ca. 290–346) and Basil the Great (ca. 329–379) in the east and Benedict of Nursia (ca. 480–547) in the west perfected the communal life. Faced with the impossibility of surviving in a harsh environment without cooperation, Egyptian monks banded together into small monastic towns. As many as 2,000 monks lived in these monasteries. They placed themselves under the control of the abbot, who served as spiritual guide and administrator of the community. These men and women sought spiritual perfection through physical self-mortification and through the subordination of their own wills to that of the abbot. Monks drank no wine, ate no meat, used no oil. They spent their days in prayer and work. Abbots organized their monks into houses according to their various crafts, and the surplus of their gardening, baking, basket making, and the like was sold in the villages and towns of Egypt. During the fourth century, this monastic tradition spread east to Bethlehem, Jerusalem, Caesarea, and Constantinople and west to Rome, Milan, Trier, Marseille, and Tours. In the following centuries, it reached beyond the borders of the empire when Egyptian-style monasticism was introduced into Ireland.

Intellectuals as well as peasants heard the call of monastic life. Chief among the intellectuals was Jerome (ca. 347–420), the greatest linguist of antiquity, who was so impressed by a visit to the monastic communities of the east that he became a priest and founded a monastery in Bethlehem. There, he translated the Bible into Latin. This Latin translation, known as the *Vulgate,* became the standard version of Christian Scripture in the west until the Reformation and, in Roman Catholic countries, until the twentieth century.

In the Greek-speaking world, the definitive form of the monastic community was provided by Basil the Great. Basil had visited the monasteries of Egypt, Palestine, and Syria before founding his own monastery at Pontus near his family estate at Annesi in present-day Turkey. Although he did not write a specific rule for the governance of his monastery, his collection of commentaries and spiritual advice to his followers outlined a form of monastic life in which a day of agriculture, craft work, and care for the sick and the poor was organized within an ordered progression of liturgical prayer. His emphasis on communal life rather than on heroic acts of individual asceticism provided the model for eastern monasticism from his day to the present.

Unlike Anthony of Egypt, Basil was a brilliant and well-educated intellectual who frequently left his monastery to throw himself into the ecclesiastical politics of the empire. By the end of his life, Basil had become bishop of Caesarea. Eastern monastic communities continued this active involvement in political and secular affairs. Monasteries provided the early religious training for most religious leaders. Monks and abbots often involved themselves wholeheartedly in the politics of the empire. Monks rioting in the streets of Constantinople over political issues were a familiar sight for over a thousand years.

In the west, Benedict of Nursia was as influential in structuring communal religious life as Basil was in the east. In time, Benedict became abbot of a small community of monks at Monte Cassino, between Rome and Naples. The rule that he drafted for the governance of his community, while drawn largely from earlier monastic rules circulating in Italy, became the definitive statement of western monasticism. Benedict's rule encouraged moderation and flexibility while emphasizing a life of poverty, chastity, and obedience to an elected abbot. Monks were required to perform some physical labor, and the monastery was intended to be a self-sufficient community. However, the real task of the monk was the continuous praise of God. This consisted of gathering at regular intervals through the day and night for communal prayer. Although Benedict lived and died in obscurity, within two and a half centuries his rule became the universal rule for western monasticism.

Western monasteries, too, provided their share of bishops, but unlike those in the east, western monks remained more isolated from population centers and from direct involvement in public affairs. However, western monasteries were not peripheral to western society and religion. Rather, these rustic communities were centers of religious and economic activity as well as education and learning in the largely rural west. They remained under the authority of the local bishops, who were usually drawn from the lay aristocracy of the empire in the west. Also, western monasteries depended on the political and economic support that they received from lay patrons.

Solitaries and Hermits

Although Anthony had begun as a hermit, he and most Egyptian monks eventually settled into communal lives. Elsewhere, particularly in the desert of Syria, the model of the monk remained the individual hermit. The Syrian desert, unlike that of Egypt, was particularly suitable for such an ascetic life. Here, the desert was milder, an individual could find food in wild roots and water in rain pools, and villages were never too far off. Moreover, the life of the wandering hermit was closely connected to traditional seminomadic lifestyles in the Fertile Crescent. But the Christian hermits who appeared across Syria in late antiquity were unlikely to be mistaken for the familiar Bedouin nomads. The Christian hermits were wild men and women who came down from the mountainsides and galvanized the attention of their contemporaries by their lifestyles. The most famous of the hermits, Simeon Stylites (ca. 390–459), spent 36 years perched at the top of a

■ A gold plaque from a sixth-century Syrian reliquary. The subject is Simeon Stylites on his pillar; the snake represents the vanquished devil. Clients could consult the holy man by climbing up the ladder on the left.

pillar 50 feet high. Two women, Marana and Cyra, lived 42 years chained in a small open-roofed enclosure.

Such people of God, rejecting civilized life in the most overt and radical ways, nevertheless met very real social and cultural needs of the population. Their lack of ties to human society made them the perfect arbitrators in the constant disputes that threatened to disrupt village life. They were individuals of power, whose proven ability to cast out demons and work miracles made them ideal community patrons at a time when traditional power brokers of the village were being lured away to imperial service or provincial cities. The greatest of these holy people, like Simeon Stylites, received as visitors not only local peasants but also emperors and empresses, who eagerly sought their advice.

Unlike the eastern monks, the Syrian hermits of the fourth and fifth centuries had few parallels in the west. Hermits did inhabit the caves and forests of Italy and Gaul, and pious women found solitude as recluses even in the center of Rome. But these westerners did not establish themselves either as independent sources of religious power or as political power brokers. Their monasticism remained a personal religious commitment. When one Roman woman was asked why she

remained shut up in her cell, she replied, "I am on a journey." When asked where she was going, she answered simply, "To God."

A PARTING OF THE WAYS

Those who remained in "the world" at the end of the fourth century could hardly take so serene a view of life. Christians and pagans might differ in their explanations for the ills that had befallen the empire, but none could deny their severity. The vulnerability of the Constantinian system became clear shortly after 376, when the Huns, a nomadic horse-riding people from central Asia, swept into the Black Sea region and threw the entire barbarian world once more into chaos. The Huns quickly destroyed the Gothic confederation and absorbed many of the peoples who had constituted the Goths. Others sought protection in the empire. The Visigoths, as they came to be known, were the largest of these groups, and their fate illustrated how precarious existence could be for all the inhabitants of the imperial frontier.

Driven from their lands and thus from their food supply, the Visigoths turned to the empire for assistance. But the Roman authorities treated them as brutally as had the Huns, forcing some to sell their children into slavery in return for morsels of dog flesh. In despair, the Visigoths rose up against the Romans, and against all odds, their desperate rebellion succeeded. They annihilated an imperial army at Adrianople in 378, and the emperor Valens himself was killed. His successor, Theodosius (379–395), was forced to allow the Visigoths to settle along the Danube and to be governed by their own leaders even though they lived within the boundaries of the empire.

Theodosius's treaty with the Visigoths set an ominous precedent. Never before had a barbarian people been allowed to settle as a political unit within the empire. Within a few years the Visigoths were again on the move, traveling across the Balkans into Italy under the command of their chieftain Alaric (ca. 370–410). In 410, they captured Rome and sacked it for three days, an event that sent shock waves throughout the entire empire. The symbolic effect of the Visigoths' victory far exceeded the amount of real damage, which was relatively light. Only after Alaric's death did the Visigoths leave Italy, ultimately settling in Spain and southern Gaul with the emperor's approval.

The Barbarization of the West

Rome did not fall. It was transformed. Romans participated in and even encouraged this transformation. Roman accommodation of the Visigoths set the pattern for subsequent settlement of barbarians in the western half of the empire. By this time, barbarians made up the bulk of the imperial army, and commanders were frequently themselves barbarians. However, these barbarian troops had been integrated into existing Roman military structures. Indeed, these so-called imperial Germans had often proved to be even more loyal to Rome than were the Roman provincial populations they were to protect. In the late fourth and fifth centuries, emperors accepted whole barbarian peoples as integral parts of the Roman army and settled them within the empire. Usually, the emperors diverted a percentage of tax revenues from the region's estates to support these "guests."

The Visigothic kingdom in southern Gaul and Spain was typical in this respect. Alaric's successor, Ataulf, was extremely eager to win the emperor's approval. He married Galla Placidia, the daughter of the Emperor Theodosius and the sister of Emperor Honorius, in a Roman ceremony in Narbonne in 414. Soon afterward, he established a government at Bordeaux directed by Gallo-Roman aristocrats. Although his opponents soon assassinated him, his successors concluded a treaty with Constantinople in which the Visigoths were recognized as a legitimate, established political presence within the empire. This so-called kingdom of Toulouse endured for almost a century. South of the Pyrenees, the Gothic kingdom of Toledo continued for almost 300 years.

The Visigoths were not the only powerful barbarian people to challenge the empire. The Vandals, who had entered the empire in 406, crossed over into Africa, the richest region of the western empire, and quickly conquered it. Avowed enemies of the empire, the Vandals used their base in North Africa to raid the European coastline and attack Roman shipping. In 455, they sacked Rome much more thoroughly than had the Goths 45 years earlier.

Another threat appeared in the 430s, when the Huns, formerly Roman allies, invaded the empire under their charismatic leader Attila (ca. 406–453). Although defeated in Gaul by a combined army of barbarians under the command of the Roman general Flavius Aetius in 451, they turned toward Italy and penetrated as far as Rome. There, they were stopped not by the rapidly disintegrating imperial forces but by the bishop of Rome, Pope Leo I, who met Attila before the city's gates. What transpired between the two is not known, but Attila's subsequent withdrawal from Italy vastly increased the prestige of the papacy. Now popes not only were successors of Saint Peter and bishops of the principal city of the west, but were replacing the emperor as protector of the city. The foundation of the political power of the papacy was established.

The confederation of the Huns collapsed after the death of Attila in 453, but imperial power did not revive in Italy. A series of incompetent emperors were pushed aside by barbarian generals who assumed power on the peninsula and sought recognition from Zeno, the emperor in the east. However, after the death in 480 of the last legitimate western emperor, Julius Nepos, Zeno conferred the title of patrician on the Ostrogothic king Theodoric. In 489, Theodoric invaded Italy with imperial blessing and established himself as ruler of Italy.

In Gaul, between the Seine and the Loire, the Roman general Flavius Aetius and, after his death, the general Syagrius continued to represent some imperial presence. But the armies that Aetius and Syagrius commanded consisted entirely of barbarians—particularly Visigoths and Franks—and they represented the interests of local aristocratic factions rather than those of Constantinople. So thoroughly barbarized had these last Roman commanders become in their military command and political control that the barbarians referred to Syagrius as "king of the Romans." Ultimately, in 486, Syagrius was defeated and replaced by the Frank Clovis, son of Syagrius's military commander Childeric, probably with the blessing of the emperor.

Britain met a similar fate. Abandoned by the Roman legions around 407, the Romano-Celtic population in this province concluded a treaty with bands of Saxons and Angles to protect Britain from other barbarian raiders. As had happened elsewhere in the empire, the barbarians came as federated troops and stayed as rulers. Gradually, during the fifth century, Germanic warrior groups conquered much of the island. The Anglo-Saxons pushed the native inhabitants to the west and the north. There, as the Cornish and the *Welsh* (in Anglo-Saxon, Welsh means simply "enemy"), they preserved the Christian religion but largely lost their other Roman traditions.

The New Barbarian Kingdoms

The establishment of barbarian kingdoms within the Roman world meant the end of the western empire as a political entity. However, the emperors in the east and west continued to pretend that all these barbarian peoples, with the exception of the Vandals, were Roman troops commanded by loyal Roman officers who happened to be of barbarian origin. The emperors gave the barbarian kings or war leaders official status within the empire as Roman generals or patricians and occasionally granted them portions of abandoned lands or existing estates. Local Roman elites considered these leaders rude and uncultured barbarians who nevertheless could be made to serve these elites' own interests more easily than better educated imperial bureaucrats.

As a result, the aristocracy of the west, the *maiores,* viewed the decay of the civil government without dismay. This decay was due largely to the poverty of the imperial treasury. In the fifth century, the entire public revenues of the west amounted to little more than the annual incomes of a few wealthy private aristocrats. Managing to escape both taxation and the jurisdiction of public officials, these individuals carved out for themselves vast estates, which they and their families controlled with private armies and which they governed as virtually autonomous lordships. Ordinary freemen, pressed by the remnants of imperial taxation and by barbarians, were forced into accepting the protection and hence control offered by aristocrats, who thereby came to control whole villages and districts.

The primary source of friction between barbarians and provincial elites was religion. Many Goths had converted to Christianity around the time that the Huns had destroyed the

MAP DISCOVERY

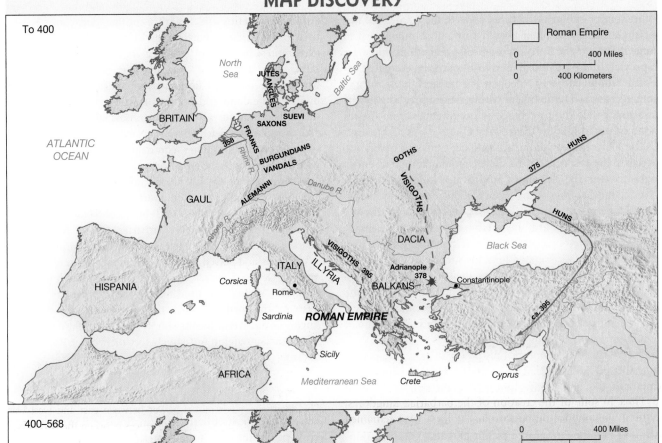

To 400

North Sea
JUTES
ANGLES
Baltic Sea
BRITAIN
SAXONS
SUEVI
ATLANTIC OCEAN
FRANKS
358
Rhine R.
BURGUNDIANS
VANDALS
GOTHS
HUNS
375
GAUL
ALEMANNI
Rhone R.
Danube R.
VISIGOTHS
HUNS
DACIA
Black Sea
VISIGOTHS 395
ITALY
ILLYRIA
Adrianople 378
Corsica
Rome
BALKANS
Constantinople
HISPANIA
ROMAN EMPIRE
ca. 395
Sardinia
Sicily
AFRICA
Mediterranean Sea
Crete
Cyprus

Roman Empire
0 400 Miles
0 400 Kilometers

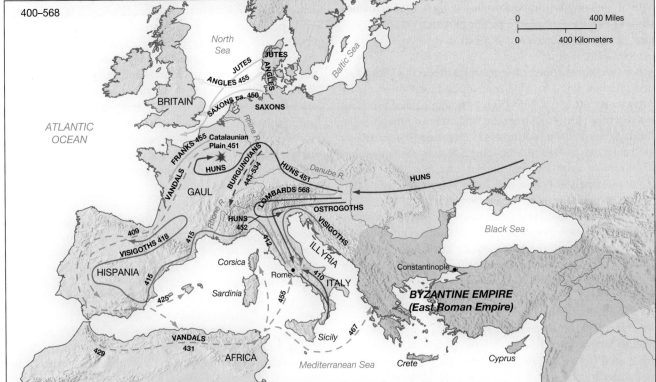

400–568

North Sea
JUTES
ANGLES
Baltic Sea
ANGLES 455
SAXONS ca. 450
SAXONS
BRITAIN
ATLANTIC OCEAN
Rhine R.
FRANKS 455
Catalaunian Plain 451
HUNS
BURGUNDIANS
443-534
HUNS 451
Danube R.
HUNS
VANDALS
GAUL
LOMBARDS 568
OSTROGOTHS
HUNS 452
VISIGOTHS
Black Sea
Rhone R.
412
ILLYRIA
409
VISIGOTHS 418
Corsica
Rome
410
ITALY
Constantinople
HISPANIA
415
425
Sardinia
455
BYZANTINE EMPIRE (East Roman Empire)
429
VANDALS 431
467
Sicily
AFRICA
Mediterranean Sea
Crete
Cyprus

0 400 Miles
0 400 Kilometers

Barbarian Migrations and Invasions

Study these maps of Barbarian migrations and invasions. Who were Rome's western neighbors in the fourth century? What effects did the Huns have on Barbarian migrations? From these maps, how might you explain the relative stability of the Eastern or Byzantine Empire in the sixth century compared with the Western?

Gothic confederation. However, they had chosen the Arian form of Christianity to appease the Arian emperors Constantius and Valens. But the Goths and most other barbarian peoples held to their Arian form of faith long after it had been abandoned in the empire. Therefore, wherever the barbarians settled, they were met with distrust and hostility from the orthodox clergy. In southern Gaul and Italy, this hostility created serious difficulties because during the fifth century bishops had assumed many of the traditional duties and powers held by provincial Roman administrators.

Although during the fifth century the western aristocracy had largely given up on the civil administration, these wealthy landowners increasingly identified with the episcopacy. In Gaul, bishops were regularly selected from members of the greatest Gallo-Roman senatorial families, establishing veritable episcopal dynasties. In Italy and Spain, too, bishops were drawn from the landed aristocracy. These bishops, most of whom were elected after long years of outstanding secular leadership, served as the primary protectors and administrators of their communities, filling the vacuum left by the erosion of other civil offices. They, more than either local civil officials or the Bacaudae, were successful in representing the community before imperial tax collectors or barbarian chieftains.

Thus, in spite of the creation of the barbarian kingdoms, cultural and political leadership at the local level remained firmly in the hands of the aristocracy. Aristocratic bishops, rather than hermits, monopolized the role of mediators of divine power just as their lay brothers, in cooperation with barbarian military leaders, monopolized the role of mediators of secular power.

Barbarian military leaders needed local ties by which to govern the large indigenous populations over whom they ruled. They found cooperation with these aristocrats to be both necessary and advantageous. Thus, while individual landowners might have suffered in the transition from Roman to barbarian rule, for the most part this transition took place with less disturbance of the local social or political scene than was once thought. During the fifth century, the imperial presence simply faded away as barbarian kings came to rule in the name of the emperor. After 480, the emperor resided exclusively in the east. The last western emperors disappeared without serious opposition either from western aristocrats or from their eastern colleagues.

The Hellenization of the East

The eastern half of the empire, in contrast to the west, managed to survive and even to prosper in the fifth and sixth centuries. In the east, beginning in 400, the trends toward militarization and barbarization of the administration were reversed, the strength of the imperial government was reaffirmed, and the vitality and integrity of the empire were restored.

Several reasons account for the contrast between east and west. First, the east had always been more urbanized and civilized than the west. It had an old tradition of civil control that antedated the Roman Empire itself. When the decay of Roman traditions allowed regionalism and tribalism to arise in the west, the same decay brought in the east a return to Hellenistic traditions. Second, the east had never developed the tradition of public poverty and private wealth that was characteristic of the west. In the east, tax revenues continued to support an administrative apparatus, which remained in the hands of civilians rather than barbarian military commanders. Moreover, the local aristocracies in the eastern provinces never achieved the wealth and independence of their western counterparts. Finally, Christian bishops, frequently divided over doctrinal issues, never managed to monopolize either sacred power, which was shared by itinerant holy men and monks, or secular power, which was wielded by imperial agents. Thus, under the firm direction of its emperors, especially Theodosius and later Zeno, the eastern empire not only survived but prepared for a new expansionist phase under the emperor Justinian.

CONCLUSION

The divergence in religious power between east and west was characteristic of the growing differences between the two halves of the Roman Empire at the close of late antiquity. The profound crises—military, social, and economic—that had shaken the empire and the barbarian world in the course of the third century left the west transformed. The new imperial system, based on an absolute ruler and an authoritarian Christianity, held the Roman world together for a few more centuries. Ultimately, however, the two halves of the old Mediterranean empire drifted in different directions as each formed a new civilization from Roman and indigenous traditions.

The east remained more firmly attached not only to Roman traditions of government but also to the much more ancient traditions of social complexity, urban life, and religious culture that stretched back to the dawn of civilization. The emperors continued to rule from Constantinople for another thousand years, but the extent of their authority gradually shrank to little more than the city itself. Furthermore, their empire was so profoundly hellenized in nature that it is properly called Byzantine (from the original name of Constantinople) rather than Roman.

The west experienced a transformation even more profound than that of the east. The triple heritage of late Roman political and military forms, barbarian society, and Christian culture coalesced into a new civilization that was perhaps less the direct heir of antiquity than was that of the east but was all the more dynamic for its distinctiveness. In culture, politics, and patterns of urban and rural life, the west and the east had gone separate ways, and their paths diverged ever more in the centuries ahead.

QUESTIONS FOR REVIEW

1. How did increasing contact between Roman civilization and the Germanic barbarians transform both?
2. How did Constantine's adoption of Christianity and the movement of his capital to Byzantium contribute to the decline of the western empire?
3. How did different views of the divinity of Christ and the means of salvation divide early Christians?
4. What was the attraction of monasticism, and why did it take so many different forms?
5. What were the differences in politics and culture in the eastern and western portions of the empire by the end of the fifth century C.E.?

KEY TERMS

Arians, *p. 118*

Christological controversies, *p. 118*

coloni *p. 117*

decurions, *p. 117*

honestiores, *p. 113*

humiliores, *p. 113*

monasticism, *p. 121*

tetrarchy, *p. 116*

wergeld, *p. 114*

DISCOVERING WESTERN CIVILIZATION ONLINE

You can obtain more information about the transforming Roman world at the websites listed below. See also the Companion Website that accompanies this text, www.ablongman.com/kishlansky, which contains an online study guide and additional resources.

General Websites

ORB Online Encyclopedia: Late Antiquity in the Mediterranean

www.nipissingu.ca/department/history/MUHLBERGER/ORB/LT-ATEST.HTM

A guide to late antiquity in the Mediterranean.

The Crisis of the Third Century

Worlds of Late Antiquity

ccat.sas.upenn.edu/jod/wola.html

A comprehensive site dedicated to late antiquity created by Professor James O'Donnell.

The Empire Restored

Diocletian's Palace

www.st.carnet.hr/split/diokl.html

A site devoted to Emperor Diocletian's palace in modern Split.

Imperial Christianity

Resources for Constantine the Great

shsu.edu/~eng_wpf/con-hist.html

Links connecting to sites concerning Constantine.

A Parting of the Ways

A Visual Tour Through Late Antiquity

www.nipissingu.ca/department/history/muhlberger/4505/show.htm

Images of people and places of late antiquity.

SUGGESTIONS FOR FURTHER READING

The Crisis of the Third Century

Peter Brown, *The World of Late Antiquity, A.D. 150–750* (New York: Harcourt Brace Jovanovich, 1971). A brilliant essay on the cultural transformation of the ancient world.

Averil Cameron, *The Later Roman Empire, A.D. 284–430* (Cambridge, MA: Harvard University Press, 1993). An important survey by an authority.

Hans-Werner Goetz, Jorg Jarnut and Walter Pohl, eds., *Regna and Gentes: The Relationship between Late Antique and Early Medieval Peoples and Kingdoms in the Transformation of the Roman World* (Leiden, The Netherlands: Brill, 2003). A series of essays on the transformation of the Classical world.

Malcolm Todd, *The Early Germans* (Oxford: Blackwell Publishers, 1992). A general introduction to pre-Roman Germanic society.

The Empire Restored

T. D. Barnes, *The New Empire of Diocletian and Constantine* (Cambridge, MA: Harvard University Press, 1982). A current examination of the transformations brought about under the two great emperors.

Ramsay MacMullen, *Paganism in the Roman Empire* (New Haven, CT: Yale University Press, 1981). A sensible introduction to the varieties of Roman religion in the imperial period.

Imperial Christianity

G. W. Bowersock, *Martyrdom and Rome* (New York: Cambridge University Press, 1995). A new look at Christian martyrdom in antiquity.

Peter Brown, *Authority and the Sacred: Aspects of the Christianisation of the Roman* (Cambridge: Cambridge University Press, 1995). A highly readable account of the emergence of Christianity in the Roman world by the leading historian of late antiquity.

W. H. C. Friend, *The Rise of Christianity* (London: Darton, Longman and Todd, 1984). A panoramic survey of Christianity from its origins to the seventh century.

Ramsay MacMullen, *Christianizing the Roman Empire (100–400)* (New Haven, CT: Yale University Press, 1984). A view of Christianity's spread from the perspective of Roman history.

A Parting of the Ways

Peter Brown, *The Rise of Western Christendom* (Cambridge, MA: Blackwell, 1996). A survey of late antiquity by a master scholar and stylist.

Patrick J. Geary, *The Myth of Nations: The Medieval Origins of Europe* (Princeton, NJ: Princeton University Press, 2001). An essay examining the relationship between modern nationalism and ethnic groups in late antiquity.

Judith Herrin, *The Formation of Christendom* (Princeton, NJ: Princeton University Press, 1987). A history of the transformed Mediterranean world, east and west, to 800 from the perspective of a noted Byzantinist.

Brian Ward-Perkins, *The Fall of Rome and the End of Civilization* (Oxford: Oxford University Press, 2005). An archaeologist's argument against seeing the end of Antiquity as a period of peaceful transition. An account of the decline in material culture at the end of Antiquity.

Herwig Wolfram, *The Roman Empire and Its Germanic Peoples* (Berkeley: University of California Press, 1997). Important general survey of the place of the barbarians in the Roman world.

For a list of additional titles related to this chapter's topics, please see www.ablongman.com/kishlansky.

Chapter 7

THE CLASSICAL LEGACY IN THE EAST: BYZANTIUM AND ISLAM

The Visual Record

FROM TEMPLE TO MOSQUE

First a temple dedicated to the Syriac god Hadad and then to the Roman Jupiter, later the Christian church of Saint John, and finally a mosque, the Great Mosque of Damascus in Syria bears testimony to the great civilizations that have followed one another in the Near East. Like the successive houses of worship, each civilization rose on the ruins of its predecessor, incorporating and transforming the rich legacy of the past into a new culture. Little of the pagan and Christian structures is visible, although the mosque owes much to both, as does the civilization it represents.

Nothing remains of the pre-Roman structure. In the first century C.E. the Romans rebuilt the temple to include an outer enclosure measuring 1,233 by 1,000 feet with four monumental gateways. In the interior was a porticoed court marked by four corner towers. Monumental portals, or gateways, in the east and west walls provided access to the inner court through triple doorways. In the center of the court stood a structure housing the statue of Jupiter.

Around the time of Constantine, the Roman temple was converted into a Christian church dedicated to Saint John the Baptist. Apparently, a portion of the interior porticoed court, which measured roughly 517 by 318 feet, was enclosed to provide a space for worshippers. Two of the four towers were raised to serve as bell towers.

For a time after Damascus fell to the Arabs in 635, Christians and Muslims shared the church. However, the Muslim population of the city grew rapidly, and by 705, Damascus was the capital of a vast, expanding Muslim empire, which would soon stretch from the Pyrenees to the Indus River. The caliph al-Walid (705–715) wanted a place of prayer befitting his capital's glory. He invited the Christian community to choose a site for another church. When they refused, he expelled them and hired Greek architects to adapt the structure to Muslim worship. They demolished the interior walls of the church, leaving only the ancient walls of a porticoed court and the tower at each of the four corners. These four Christian towers became the first minarets, towers from which Muslim religious leaders call the faithful to prayer five times each day. Al-Walid employed the finest artists available to cover the walls of the mosque with mosaics.

During the preliminary work, an underground chapel was said to have been found, containing a chest with a human head. On the chest was written, "This is the head of John, son of Zacharias." Al-Walid had the sacred relic placed under one of the pillars and a monument erected over it. To this day, the shrine survives in the mosque, a symbol of the continuity among Judaism, Christianity, and Islam.

This moment of artistic and religious cooperation was brief. Only a few years later, in 717, al-Walid's successor subjected Constantinople to the most fearful siege it would endure for 500 years. Still, the continuity of religious worship and the common taste for classical art show how deeply both the caliphate and the empire were bound together in the common heritage of late antiquity, of which both were the true heirs.

Looking Ahead

This chapter traces the fates of these two heirs of Mediterranean civilization, Byzantium and Islam, from the sixth to the fifteenth centuries. Inspired by central religious visions, they developed their common heritages into religious, artistic, and social forms that contrast with western Europe's path. ➤

THE BYZANTINES

At the end of the fifth century C.E., the eastern empire of Theodosius and Zeno had escaped the fate that its western counterpart had suffered at the hands of the Germanic peoples. Wealthier and more urbanized than the west, its population had also been accustomed to centralized government for more than a thousand years. Still, the long-term survival of the eastern empire seemed far from certain.

Little unified the empire of Constantinople. The population of the capital split into two rival political factions, whose violent conflicts often threatened the stability of the government. These rival groups, organized militarily and politically, controlled the Circus, or Hippodrome, where the games and chariot races that were the obsession of the city's population took place. These factions took their names, the Greens and the Blues, from their circus colors. When these two factions joined forces with the army, they were powerful enough to create or destroy emperors. Beyond Constantinople, the empire's population consisted of the more or less hellenized peoples of Asia Minor, Armenians, Slavs, Arabs, Syrians, Egyptian Copts, and others. Unlike western Europe, the east was still a world of cities, which were centers of commerce, industry, and Hellenistic culture. But the importance of these urban centers began to decline in favor of the rural peasant world,

which not only constituted the source of its great wealth but also fed the empire and provided generations of tough soldiers to protect it from its enemies.

Finally, the eastern empire was more divided than unified by its Christianity. Rivalry among the great cities of Antioch, Alexandria, Jerusalem, Rome, and Constantinople was expressed in the competition among their bishops, or patriarchs. The official "right teaching," or orthodox, faith of Constantinople and its patriarch was bitterly opposed by "deviant," or heterodox, bishops of other religious traditions, around which developed separatist ethnic political movements. By the time of Justinian (527–565), emperors were obsessed with maintaining absolute authority and imposing uniformity on their empire.

Justinian and the Creation of the Byzantine State

Strong-willed, restless, and ambitious, Justinian is remembered as "the emperor who never slept." Although his goals were essentially conservative, his attempts to return to the past and restore the territory, power, and prestige of the ancient Roman Empire created a new world. With the assistance of his dynamic wife Theodora, his great generals Belisarius and Narses, his brilliant jurist Tribonian, his scientists

■ A mosaic from the church of San Vitale in Ravenna. The emperor Justinian, along with secular and ecclesiastical officials, is shown bringing an offering to the church. The halo around his head signifies the sacred nature of the imperial office.

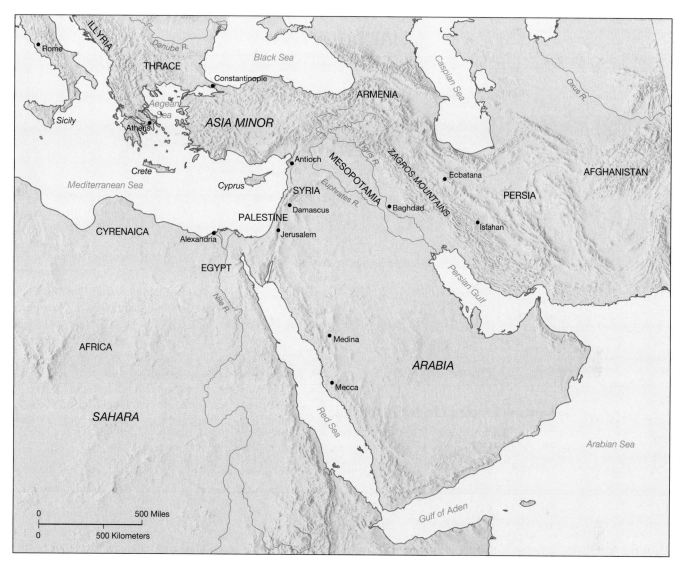

■ The Eastern Mediterranean. The Arabian Peninsula was peripheral to the Roman and Persian empires until the seventh century when the new Islamic faith suddenly emerged from Arabia to overwhelm its more ancient neighboring empires.

Anthemius of Tralles and Isidorus of Miletus, and his brutally efficient administrator and tax collector John of Cappadocia, he remade the empire.

Spurred on by Theodora, in 532 Justinian checked the power of the Circus factions by brutally suppressing a riot that left 30,000 dead in the capital city. Belisarius and Narses recaptured North Africa from the Vandals, Italy from the Ostrogoths, and part of Spain from the Visigoths, restoring for one last moment some of the geographical unity of the empire of Augustus and Constantine. Tribonian revised and organized the existing codes of Roman law into the *Justinian Code,* a great monument of western jurisprudence that remains today the foundation of most of Europe's legal systems. Anthemius and Isidorus combined their knowledge of mathematics, geometry, kinetics, and physics to build the Church of the Holy Wisdom (Hagia Sophia) in Constantinople, one of the largest and most innovative churches ever constructed.

This structure was as radical as it was simple. In essence, it is a huge rectangle, 230 by 250 feet, above which a vast dome 100 feet in diameter rises to a height of 180 feet and seems to float, suspended in air. Less well appreciated were the achievements of John of Cappadocia, who was able to squeeze the empire's population for the taxes to pay for these conquests, reforms, and building projects.

Ultimately, Justinian's spectacular achievements came at too high a price. He left his successors an empire that had been virtually bankrupted by the costs of his wars and his building projects, was bitterly divided by his attempts to settle religious controversies, and was poorly protected on its eastern border, where the Sassanid Empire was a constant threat. Most of Italy and Spain soon returned to barbarian control. In 602, the Sassanid emperor Chosroes II (d. 628) invaded the empire, capturing Egypt, Palestine, and Syria and threatening Constantinople itself. In a series of desperate campaigns, the

MAP DISCOVERY

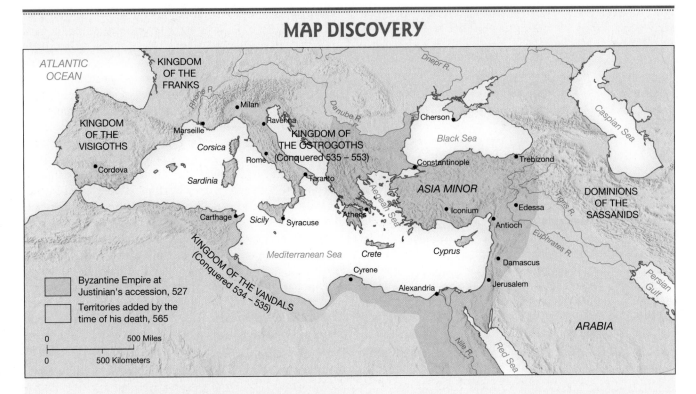

Byzantine Empire Under Justinian

Examine the boundaries of the Byzantine Empire under Justinian. Why would Justinian have been particularly eager to recover the areas that he reconquered? What problems were posed by the conquest of the Ostrogoths that were not present in the conquest of the Vandals?

---

emperor Heraclius (610–641) turned back the tide and crushed the Sassanids, but it was too late. A new power, Islam, had emerged in the deserts of Arabia. This new power was to challenge and ultimately absorb both the Sassanids and much of the eastern Roman Empire. As a result, the east became increasingly less Roman and more Greek—or, specifically, more *Byzantine*, a term derived from the original name of Constantinople, Byzantium.

For over 700 years, the Byzantine Empire played a major role in Western history. From the seventh through tenth centuries, when most of Europe was too weak and disorganized to defend itself against the expansion of Islam, the Byzantines stood as the bulwark of Christianity. When organized government had virtually disappeared in the west, the Byzantine Empire provided a model of a centralized bureaucratic state ruled according to principles of Roman law. When, beginning in the fourteenth century, western Europeans began once more to appreciate the heritage of Greek and Roman art and literature, they turned to Constantinople. There, the manuscripts of Greek writers such as Plato and Homer were available to contribute to a rebirth of classical culture in the west. The Slavic north, caught between the Latin Christians and the

Muslims, sought its cultural and religious orientation in the liturgical culture of Byzantine orthodoxy. Perhaps most important, when urban civilization had all but disappeared from the rest of Europe, Greeks and Latins could still look "to The City," *eis ten polin*, or, as the Turks pronounced it, Istanbul.

Emperors and Individuals

The classic age of Byzantine society, roughly from the eighth through the tenth centuries, has been described as "individualism without freedom." Individuals and small family groups stood as isolated units in a society characterized, until the mid-eleventh century, by the direct relationship between an all-powerful emperor and citizens of all ranks.

Governing Byzantium.   In part, this individualism resulted from the Byzantine form of government. The Byzantine state was, in theory and often in fact, an autocracy. Since the time of Diocletian, all members of society were subjects of the emperor, who alone was the source of law. How a person became emperor remained, as it had been in the Roman Empire, more a question of military power than of constitutional succession. Although in theory the emperor was elected by the Senate, army, and people of Constantinople, emperors generally selected their own successors and had them crowned in their own lifetimes.

As long as the empire remained a civilian autocracy, it was even possible for a woman to rule, either as regent for a minor son or as sovereign. Irene (780–802), widow of Leo IV (725–780), ruled first as regent for her son Constantine VI (780–797). However, when her son reached his majority, she had him blinded and deposed, and she ruled alone from 797 to 802, not merely as the *basilissa*, or wife of the emperor, but as the *basileus*—emperor. In the eleventh century, the empire was ruled at different times by two sisters, Zoe (1028–1034), daughter of one emperor and widow of another, and Theodora (1042–1056), who was dragged out of a church by an enthusiastic mob and proclaimed empress.

Male or female, emperors were above and beyond their subjects, often quite literally. In the tenth century, a mechanical throne was installed in the main audience room. The throne would suddenly lift the emperor high above the heads of astonished visitors. Like God the Father, with whom he was closely identified in imperial propaganda, the emperor was separated from the people by an unbridgeable gulf.

Thus the traditional corporate bodies of the Roman Empire wasted away or became window dressing for the imperial cult. The Senate gradually ceased to play any autonomous role, and its powers were officially abolished in the ninth century.

The Circus factions, which in the sixth century had the power to make or break emperors, met the same fate. From autonomous political groups, they too gradually became no more than participants in imperial ceremonies. By the tenth century, the Greens and the Blues were simply officially constituted groups whose role was to praise the emperor by mouthing traditional formulas on solemn occasions.

Bureaucracy and Army.   Although the emperor was the source of all authority, the actual administration of the empire was carried out by a vast bureaucracy composed of military and civilian officers. The empire was divided into roughly 25 provinces, or *themes*. The soldiers in each theme were also farmers, rather than full-time warriors. Each soldier received a small farm by which to support himself and his family. Soldiers held their farms as long as they served in the army. When a soldier retired or died, his farm and his military obligation passed to his eldest son. These farmer-soldiers were the backbone of both the imperial military and the economic system. They not only formed a regular, native, locally based army, but they also kept much of Byzantine agriculture in the hands of small free peasants rather than great aristocrats. The themes were governed by military commanders, or **strategoi,** who presided over both civilian and military bureaucrats.

In contrast to the military command of the themes, the central administration, which focused on the emperor and the imperial family, was wholly civil. The most important po-

sitions at court were occupied by eunuchs, castrated men who offered a number of advantages to imperial administration. Eunuchs often directed imperial finance, served as prime ministers, directed the vast bureaucracy, and even undertook military commands. Because they could not have descendants, there was no danger that they would attempt to turn their offices into hereditary positions or that they would plot and scheme on behalf of their children. Moreover, since the sacred nature of the emperor required physical perfection, eunuchs could not aspire to replace their masters on the throne. Finally, although at times their influence with the emperor made them immensely powerful, eunuchs were feared and despised by the general population. Therefore, they had little likelihood of building autonomous power bases outside of imperial favor. The extensive use of eunuchs was one of the keys to the survival of absolutist authority in the empire. Thus imperial authority was preserved at a time when both Islamic and Latin states were experiencing a progressive erosion of central power to the benefit of ambitious aristocratic families.

Families and Villages

A godlike emperor and a centralized bureaucracy left little room for the development of the hierarchies of private patronage, lordship, and group action that were characteristic of western Europe. In the Byzantine Empire, aristocrat and peasant were equal in their political powerlessness. Therefore, Byzantine society tended to be organized at the lowest level, that of the nuclear family. Daily life focused on the protective enclosure of the private home, which served as both shelter and workplace. Professional and craft associations continued to exist as they had in antiquity, but they were not autonomous professional groups intended to protect the interests of their members. Instead, they were fostered and controlled by imperial officials to regulate and tax urban industry.

Rural Life.   The countryside, which was the backbone of Byzantine prosperity into the eleventh century, was also a world with limited horizontal and vertical social bonds. Villages were the basic elements in the imperial system. The village court handled local affairs and tax assessments, but it in turn dealt directly with the imperial bureaucracy. Occasionally, villages might unite against imperial tax collectors, but villagers normally dealt with each other and with outside powers as wary individuals. Most peasants, whether they were landowners, peasant soldiers, or renters, survived on the labor of their own family and perhaps one or two slaves. Large cooperative undertakings, as in Islamic lands, and the use of communal equipment, as became the rule in the west, were unknown. Individual families worked their own fields, which were usually enclosed by protective stone or brick walls. Byzantine peasants would have agreed with the saying in the poem by New Englander Robert Frost: "Good fences make good neighbors."

Urban Life.   Like the villages, Byzantine towns were isolated in location and activities. The mountainous terrain of Greece and Asia Minor contributed to this isolation, cutting off ready overland communication among communities and forcing them to turn to the sea. In this respect, Constantinople was ideally situated to develop into the greatest commercial center of the west, at its height boasting a population of over one million. Because of Constantinople's strategic location on the Bosporus, that slim ribbon of water uniting the Black and Mediterranean Seas, all of the products of the empire and those of the Slavic, Latin, and Islamic worlds, as well as Oriental goods arriving overland from central Asia, had to pass through the city. Silks, spices, and precious metals were loaded onto ships at Trebizond and then transported south to Constantinople. Baltic amber, slaves, and furs from the Slavic world were carried down the Dnepr River to the Black Sea and then to the capital. There, all goods passing to the north or south had to be unloaded, assessed, and subjected to a flat import-export tariff of 10 percent.

The empire's cities were centers for the manufacture of luxury goods that were in demand throughout the Islamic and Christian worlds. Imperial workshops in Constantinople and closely regulated workshops in Corinth and Thebes produced fine silks, brocades, carpets, and other luxury products that were marketed throughout the Mediterranean, again subject to the state's customary 10 percent tax. (See "The West and the Wider World: Industrial Espionage in the Sixth Century," pp. 136–137.)

As vital as maritime commerce was to the empire, most Byzantines despised the sea. They feared it as a source of pirates, sudden storms, and hidden dangers. Moreover, particularly among the elite, commerce was considered demeaning. Never great mariners, Byzantines were largely content to allow others—first Syrians and Slavs and later Italians—to monopolize the empire's commerce.

A Foretaste of Heaven

The cultural cement that bound emperor and subjects together was **Orthodox Christianity.** The Islamic capture of Alexandria, Jerusalem, and Antioch had removed the centers of regional religious particularism from the empire. The barbarian domination of Italy had isolated Rome and reduced its influence. These two processes left Constantinople as the only remaining patriarchate in the empire and thus the undisputed center of Orthodox Christianity. However, like virtually every other aspect of Byzantine society and culture, the patriarch and the Orthodox faith he led were subordinated to the emperor.

In theory, patriarchs were elected; in reality, emperors appointed them. Patriarchs in turn controlled the various levels of the Church hierarchy, which included metropolitans, bishops, and the local clergy. This ecclesiastical structure reflected and reinforced the organization of the state bureaucracy. Local priests were drawn from the peasant society of which they were a part. They were expected to be married and to live

■ The Byzantine Empire in 814. By the ninth century, the empire had lost all its territories but Asia Minor, Greece, the boot of Italy, and the islands of Sardinia and Sicily.

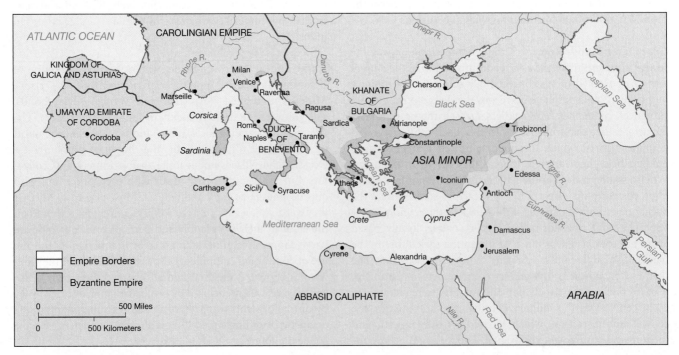

much like their neighbors. Bishops, metropolitans, and patriarchs were recruited from monasteries and were to be celibate. They were, so to speak, spiritual eunuchs who represented the emperor.

The essence of Orthodox religion was the liturgy, or ceremonies, of the Church, which provided, it was said, a foretaste of heaven. Adoration of God and veneration of the emperor went hand in hand as the cornerstone of imperial propaganda. Ecclesiastical and court processions ensured that order and stability reigned in this world as a reflection of the eternal order of the next.

Iconoclasm

The one aspect of religious life that was not entirely under imperial control was monasticism. Since the time of the desert fathers, monastic communities had been an essential part of Christianity. From the sixth century, numerous monastic communities were founded throughout the empire, and by the eleventh century there were at least 300 monasteries within the walls of Constantinople alone. Monasteries were often wealthy and powerful. Moreover, their religious appeal, often based on the possession of miracle-working religious images, or **icons,** posed an independent source of religious authority that was at odds with the imperial centralization of all aspects of Byzantine life. .

Beginning with Emperor Leo III, the Isaurian (717–741), the military emperors who had driven back Islam sought to curtail the independence of monastic culture and particularly the cult of icons that was an integral part of it. These emperors and their supporters, termed **iconoclasts** (literally, "breakers of images"), objected to the mediating role of sacred images in worship. Monasteries, with their miracle-working icons, became particular targets of imperial persecution. They were closed,

their estates were confiscated, and their monks were forced to marry. Imperial agents destroyed icons, statues, and illustrated manuscripts and painted over frescoes in churches. The defenders of icons—**iconodules,** or image venerators—were imprisoned, tortured, and even executed. Most bishops, the army, and much of the non-European population of the empire supported the iconoclast emperors, but monks, the lesser clergy, and the majority of the populace, particularly women, violently resisted the destruction of their beloved images.

For more than a century, the iconoclast dispute raged. Finally, in 843, the Empress Theodora (842–858), who ruled during the minority of her son, ended the persecution and restored image veneration. Monasteries reopened and regained much of their former wealth and prestige. Images were brought out of hiding or new ones were created, and they resumed their role in the eastern Christian church.

The iconoclastic struggle deeply affected Byzantium's relations with the west. Christians in western Europe, and particularly the popes of Rome, never accepted the iconoclast position. The popes considered the iconoclast emperors heretics and looked increasingly to the Frankish Carolingian family for support against them and the Lombards of Italy. In this manner, the Franks first entered Italian politics and began, with papal support, to establish themselves as a rival imperial power in the west, which culminated in the coronation of Charlemagne in 800.

Although Byzantium lost Italy and the city of Rome, the empire survived and even flourished. Between the sixth and ninth centuries, the reduced but still vital Roman Empire in the East developed a distinctive political and cultural tradition. The Byzantine system was based on imperial absolutism buttressed by a powerful religious tradition and an effective bureaucracy that dealt directly with individual subjects on behalf of the emperor.

■ In this manuscript illustration, an icon is being destroyed while priests try to persuade Leo V to abandon his iconoclast policies.

The West and the Wider World

INDUSTRIAL ESPIONAGE IN THE SIXTH CENTURY

The Emperor Justinian not only laid the political, institutional, and cultural foundations of Byzantium but, in a daring act of industrial espionage and smuggling, he also established what remained for centuries one of its most important export industries: silk manufacture. In the year 950, Bishop Liutprand of Cremona, emissary of the Emperor Otto I to the Byzantine court, was returning home from Constantinople after a humiliating encounter with Emperor Nicephorus when, as a final insult, his baggage was inspected and five valuable pieces of purple silk confiscated. The German emperor was deemed unworthy of the precious purple cloth. Liutprand fumed and complained but could do nothing. Silk, the most prized cloth in the world, was available only from Byzantium or the Far East. Its manufacture was a closely guarded secret and a state monopoly. But Justinian had stolen the secret in the sixth century, and his Byzantine successors had maintained their monopoly for four hundred years.

Silk is a miracle fabric: a single filament of silk is as strong as steel of the same thickness. It is also much less dense than cotton or wool and much more moisture absorbent, able to take in three times its own weight without appearing damp. It is durable, dyes beautifully, and resists mold and mildew. No wonder it has been a prized commodity for the past five thousand years. However, its production is extraordinary. Silk is produced from the cocoons of silkworm moths. The worms feed on mulberry leaves before spinning their cocoons in one continuous thread that can be as long as 1,000 feet. Before the worms can hatch into moths and destroy the cocoon, they are killed with hot air or steam, and the cocoon is softened and unraveled.

This laborious process was first discovered in China, the native habitat of the silkworm, and the Chinese monopolized its production for the first 3,000 years. Exports were strictly controlled. Only finished cloth could be exported, and no one was allowed to export eggs, cocoons, or silk worms under penalty of death. Only very gradually did this monopoly break down in Asia. Around 200 B.C.E.,

Chinese emigrants to Korea brought with them silkworms and mulberry plants and began Korean silk production. Japan and India acquired the secret technology around 300 C.E., but they were as careful as the Chinese to avoid further proliferation of the technique, especially farther west.

And the West was mad for silk. Already in antiquity caravan routes along what today is called the Silk Road reached from the western Chinese city of Xian across modern Afghanistan and into modern Iraq and Syria, ending in Damascus. Sea routes also connected Egypt and India through the Red Sea, providing an alternative route for silk to reach the Mediterranean world. Ancient Persians particularly admired the material and even unwove Chinese cloths so they could reuse the precious filaments to reweave them into clothing and textiles of their own. Alexander the Great was so impressed with the splendid silk robes worn by the vanquished Persian Emperor Darius III that he demanded vast amounts of the material from the conquered Persians as spoils of war. The

■ Eastern Han (25–220) tomb decoration showing silk weavers.

Romans first became aware of silk around 50 B.C.E., and the cloth became enormously popular (and enormously expensive). It was literally worth its weight in gold. Aristocratic women and particularly empresses amassed vast quantities of silk shawls and scarves. The conspicuous use of silk was a barometer of Roman morals: severe emperors such as Aurelian forbade his wife to own so much as a single silk shawl, while others like Caligula enjoyed wearing silk himself.

But where did silk come from? Although Aristotle was aware that the threads came from the cocoons of the silk worm, Romans had only a vague idea of its origins. Their best guess was that it grew on trees. And they certainly had no means of manufacturing it, being content with importing raw silk and then weaving and dying it according to their own taste. Thus Roman desire for silk was at the mercy of those who controlled the silk route from China and India: their enemies, the Persians.

All this changed around 530 when a group of monks from India appeared before the Emperor Justinian. These men, Nestorian Christians from a region of India that specialized in silk production, explained to the emperor that they could make it possible for the empire to free itself from its dependency on Persia to satisfy its appetite for silk. They revealed to him the origin of silk and the process of recovering it from cocoons. With his encouragement, they returned home and smuggled back to the Empire silk worm eggs and mulberry seeds, ac-

■ This Byzantine silk cloth, showing a hero or charioteer driving a quadringa (four-horse chariot) was found in Charlemagne's tomb—probably a gift from the Byzantine court to the Frankish emperor.

cording to legend, by hiding them in their hollow walking staffs. Soon, Byzantine silk production was under way, but the Byzantines, in the tradition of the Chinese and Indians before them, maintained silk manufacture as a strictly controlled state monopoly. Silk's beauty, its rarity, and its prestige were too great an economic and political asset to allow uncontrolled production. For centuries, until its monopoly was broken by Muslim silk production in Spain and eventually Italy, silks could be used not simply as commodities but as tools of politics to honor, or to shame, Byzantium's neighbors.

QUESTIONS FOR DISCUSSION

Why do you suppose that Western elites so desired Chinese and Indian silk? Was there a relationship between the expansion of Western religions such as Christianity and Islam into Asia and the end of the Asian silk monopoly?

THE RISE OF ISLAM

Arabs lived on the fringes of the Byzantine and Sassanid Empires. Trade routes had carried people from the Fertile Crescent and Egypt across northern Arabia for centuries. By the sixth century C.E., Arabic-speaking peoples from the Arabian Peninsula had spread through the Syrian Desert as far north as the Euphrates.

The northern borders of Arabia along the Red Sea had formed Roman provinces that even produced an emperor, Philip the Arab (244–249). Hira, to the south of the Euphrates, became a Sassanid puppet principality that, although largely Christian, often provided the Persians with auxiliaries. Within both the Byzantine and Sassanid Empires the distinction between Arab and non-Arab populations was blurred. Except for the Arabic language and a hazy idea of common Arabic kinship, nothing differentiated Arabs from their neighbors.

This was dramatically changed by an obscure merchant in the Arabian city of Mecca, who embarked on a career that would transform the world. Through faith, Muhammad (ca. 570–632) united the tribes of the Arabian Peninsula and propelled them on an unprecedented mission of conquest. Within a century of Muhammad's death, the world of Islam— a word that means "submission to the will of God"—included all of the ancient Near East and extended from the Syr Darya (formerly the Jaxartes) River in Asia south into the Indian subcontinent, west across the African coast to the Atlantic, north through Spain, and along the Mediterranean coast to the Rhone River. Just as their faith combined elements of traditional Arab worship with Christianity and Judaism, the Arabian conquerors and their subject populations created a vital civilization from a mix of Arabian, Roman, Hellenistic, and Sassanid traditions.

Arabia Before the Prophet

Southern Arabia, with relatively abundant rainfall and fertile soils, was an agricultural region long governed by monarchs. Here was the kingdom of Saba, the Sheba of the Bible, which had existed since the tenth century B.C.E. During the fifth century C.E., the kings of the Yemen had extended their influence north over the Bedouin tribes of central Arabia in order to control and protect the caravan trade between north and south. In the late sixth century, however, Ethiopian and then Persian conquerors destroyed the Arabian kingdom of the Yemen and absorbed it into their empires. The result was a power vacuum that left central Arabia and its trade routes across the deserts in confusion.

Bedouin Society.   The interior of the Arabian Peninsula was much less directly affected by the great empires to the north or the Arabian kingdoms to the south. Waterless steppes and seas of shifting sand dunes had long defeated Roman and Persian or Sassanid efforts to control the Arabic Bedouin.

These nomads roamed the peninsula in search of pasturage for their flocks. Theirs was a life of independence, simplicity, and danger.

Although they acknowledged membership in various tribes, the Bedouin's real allegiance was to much narrower circles of lineages and tenting groups. As in the Germanic tribes of Europe, kin relationships rather than formal governmental systems protected individuals through the obligation for vengeance and blood feud. In the words of a pre-Islamic poet, "Blood for blood—wiped out were the wounds, and those who had gained a start in the race profited not by their advantage." Tribal chieftains, called *sheikhs*, chosen from ruling families, had no coercive power, either to right wrongs or to limit feuds. They served only as arbitrators and executors of tribal consensus. The patriarch of each family held final say over his kin. He could ignore the sheikh and go his own way.

The individual was unimportant in Bedouin society. Private land ownership was unknown, and flocks and herds were often held in common by kindred. The pastoral economy of the Bedouin provided meat, cheese, and wool. Weapons, ornaments, women, and livestock could be acquired through exchange at the market towns around desert oases. More commonly, these goods and women were taken in raids against other tribes, caravans, and settlements or by exacting payments from weaker neighbors in return for protection. Raids, often launched in defense of family honor, were also the means of increasing prestige and glory in this warrior society. Prizes won in battle were lightly given away as signs of generosity and marks of social importance.

Some of the Arabs of the more settled south, as well as inhabitants of towns along caravan routes, were Christian or Jewish. As farmers or merchants, these groups were looked down upon by the nomadic Bedouin, most of whom remained pagan. Although they recognized some important gods and even a high god usually called Allah, Bedouin worshipped local tribal deities, who were often thought of as inhabiting a sacred stone or spring. Worship involved gifts and offerings and played only a small part in nomadic life. Far more important was commitment to the tribe, expressed through loyalty to the tribal cult and through unity of action against rival tribes.

Harams.   Rivalry and feuding among tribes could be set aside at a mutually accepted neutral site, which might grow up around a religious sanctuary. A sanctuary, or *haram*, which was often on the border between tribal areas, was founded by a holy man not unlike the Christian holy men of the Syrian Desert. The holy man declared the site and surrounding area neutral ground on which no violence could take place. Here, enemies could meet under truce to settle differences under the direction of the holy man or his descendants. Merchant communities sprang up within the safety of these sites, since the sanctuary gave them and their goods protection from their neighbors.

Mecca was just such a sanctuary, around whose sacred black rock, or Ka'bah, a holy man named Qusayy established himself and his tribe, the Quraysh, as its guardians sometime early in the sixth century. In the next century, under the patronage of the Quraysh, Mecca grew into an important commercial center. Through religious, diplomatic, and military means, Quraysh organized camel caravans, which could safely cross the desert from the Yemen in the south to Iran and Syria in the north. During the early seventh century, when increased hostilities between the Byzantine and Sassanid empires severed the direct trading links between the empires, the Quraysh network became the leading commercial organization in northern Arabia. Still, its effectiveness remained tied to the religious importance of Mecca and the Ka'bah. When Muhammad, a descendant of Qusayy, began to preach his monotheistic message, he was seen as a threat to the survival of his tribe and his city.

Muhammad, Prophet of God

More is known about Muhammad's life than about the lives of Moses, Jesus, Buddha, or any of the other great religious reformers of history. Still, Muhammad's adherents quickly wrapped his early years in a protective cloak of pious stories, making it difficult to discern truth from legend. A member of a lesser branch of the Quraysh, Muhammad was an orphan raised by relatives. At about age 20, he became the business manager for Khadijah, a wealthy widow whom he later married. This marriage gave him financial security among the middle ranks of Meccan merchants. In his thirties, he began to devote an increasing amount of time to meditation, retiring to the barren, arid mountains outside the city. There, in the month of Ramadan in the year 610, he reported a vision of a man who told him: "O Muhammad! Thou art the Messenger of God."

Preaching Islam.   Khadijah, to whom he confided his revelation in fear and confusion, became his first convert. Within a year he began preaching openly. His early teachings stressed the absolute unity of God, the evils of idolatry, and the threat of divine judgment. Further revelations to Muhammad were copied word for word in what came to be the Qur'an, or Koran. These messages offered Arabs a faith founded on a book. In their eyes, this faith was both within the tradition of the Christianity and Judaism of their neighbors and superior to them. The Qur'an was the final revelation and Muhammad the last and greatest prophet. To Muslims—the term means "true believers"—Muhammad is simply the Prophet.

Muslims believe that Allah's revelation emphasized, above all, his power and transcendence and that the duty of humans is worship. The prayers of Islam, in contrast with those of Christianity and Judaism, are essentially prayers of praise,

THE QUR'AN

The following passages from the Qur'an express the central importance of the revelation of Allah, compassion for Jews and Christians as sharers in the belief in the one God, and the condemnation of polytheistic idolaters.

Focus Questions
What are the characteristics of the righteous according to the Qur'an? How does the attitude of Islam differ toward Christians, Jews, and polytheists?

In the name of Allah, the compassionate, the Merciful. This Book is not to be doubted. It is a guide to the righteous, who have faith in the unseen and are steadfast in prayer; who bestow in charity a part of what We give them; who trust what has been revealed to you [Muhammad] and to others before you, and firmly believe in the life to come. These are rightly guided by their Lord; these shall surely triumph.

As for the unbelievers, whether you forewarn them or not, they will not have faith. Allah has set a seal upon their hearts and ears; their sight is dimmed and a grievous punishment awaits them. . . .

Men, serve your Lord, who has created you and those who have gone before you, so that you may guard yourselves against evil; who has made the earth a bed for you and the sky a dome, and has sent down water from heaven to bring forth fruits for your sustenance. Do not knowingly set up other gods besides Him. . . .

Believers, Jews, Christians, and Sabaeans [ancient rulers of Yemen believed to be monotheists]—whoever believes in Allah and the Last Day and does what is right—shall be rewarded by their Lord; they have nothing to fear or to regret. . . .

Yet there are some who worship idols, bestowing on them the adoration due to Allah (though the love of Allah is stronger in the faithful). But when they face their punishment the wrongdoers will know that might is His alone and that Allah is stern in retribution. When they face their punishment the leaders will disown their followers, and the bonds which now unite them will break asunder. Those who followed them will say: "Could we but live again, we would disown them as they have disowned us now."

Thus Allah will show them their own works. They shall sigh with remorse, but shall never come out of Hell.

From Qur'an, sura 2.

seldom prayers of petition. This reverential attitude places little premium on scriptural interpretation or theological speculation. Muslims regard the whole Qur'an as the exact and complete revelation of God, literally true and forming a unified whole, though revelations contained in it came at various times throughout the Prophet's life. It is the complete guide for secular and religious life, the fundamental law of conduct for Islamic society. The Prophet emphasized constantly that he was simply God's messenger and merited no special veneration or worship. For this reason, Muslims have always rejected the label *Muhammadan,* which nonbelievers often apply to them. Muslims are not followers of Muhammad but of the God of Abraham and Jesus, who chose to make the final and complete revelation of his power and his judgment through the Prophet.

Initially, such revelations of divine power and judgment neither greatly bothered nor influenced Mecca's merchant elite. Muhammad's earliest adherents, such as his cousin 'Ali ibn Abi (ca. 600–661), came from his own clan and from among the moderately successful members of the Meccan community—the "nearly haves" rather than the "have-nots," as one scholar put it. Elite clans such as the Umayya, who controlled the larger Quraysh tribe, saw little to attract them to the upstart. But soon Muhammad began to insist that those who did not accept Allah as the only God were damned, as were those who continued to venerate the sorts of idols on which Mecca's prosperity was founded. With this proclamation, toleration gave way to hostility. Muhammad and his followers were ostracized and even persecuted.

The Hijra.   Around 620, some residents of Medina, a smaller trading community populated by rival pagan, Jewish, and Islamic clans and racked by internal political dissension, approached the Prophet and invited him to govern the community in order to end the factional squabbles. Rejected at home, he answered their call. On 24 September 622, Muhammad and one supporter secretly made their way from Mecca to Medina. This short journey of less than 300 miles, known as the **Hijra,** was destined to change the world.

The Triumph of Islam

The Hijra marked the beginning of the Islamic dating system in the way that the birth of Jesus began the Christian dating system. The Hijra also marked the Prophet's shift from preaching to action. He organized his followers from Mecca and Medina into the **Umma,** a community that transcended the old bonds of tribe and clan. He set about turning Medina into a haram like Mecca, with himself as founding holy man and the Umma as his new family. But this was not to be a haram or indeed a family like any other. Muhammad was not merely a sheikh whose authority rested on consensus. He was God's messenger, and his authority was absolute. His goal was to extend this authority far beyond his adopted town of Medina to Mecca and ultimately to the whole Arab world.

First, he gained firm control of Medina at the expense of its Jewish clans. He had expected these monotheists to embrace his teachings. Instead, they rejected the unlettered Arab's attempt to transform Judaic and Christian traditions into an Arab faith. Rejection was their undoing. The Prophet expelled them in the name of political and religious unity. Those who were not expelled were executed.

Return to Mecca.   Muhammad then used this unified community to attack the Quraysh where they were most vulnerable—in their protection of camel caravans. Inability to destroy the upstarts or protect its trading network cost the Quraysh tribe much of its prestige. More and more members of Meccan families and local tribes converted to Islam. In 629, Muhammad and 10,000 warriors marched on Mecca and captured the city in a swift and largely bloodless campaign.

During the three years between Muhammad's triumphant return to Mecca and his death, Islam moved steadily toward becoming the major force in the Arabian Peninsula. The divine revelations increasingly took on legal and practical dimensions as Muhammad was forced to serve not just as Prophet, but as political leader of a major political and economic power. The Umma had become a sort of supertribe, open to all individuals who would accept Allah and his Prophet. The invitation was extended to women as well as to men.

Women in Early Islam.   Islam brought a transformation of the rights of women in Arabian society. This did not mean that they achieved equality with men any more than they did in any premodern civilization, east or west. Men continued to dominate Islamic society, in which military prowess and male honor were so valued. Women remained firmly subordinate to men, who could have up to four wives, could divorce them at will, and could keep women segregated from other men. In public matters, such as inheritance and in witnessing and giving testimony, women were valued at one-half of a man. When in public, Islamic women in many regions adopted the Syriac Christian practice of wearing a veil that covered all of the face but the eyes.

Islam did, however, forbid female infanticide, a common practice in pre-Islamic society. Brides, not their fathers or other male relatives, received the dowry from their husbands, thus making marriage more a partnership than a sale. All wives had to be treated equally. If a man was unable to do so, he had to limit himself to a single wife. Islamic women acquired inheritance and property rights and had protection against mistreatment in marriage. Although they remained second-class in status, at least women had a status, recognized and protected within the Umma.

An Arabian Faith.   The rapid spread of Islam within the Arab world can be explained by a number of religious and material factors. Men may have been attracted by the sensuous vision of the afterlife promised to believers. Paradise was presented as a world of refreshing streams and leafy bowers, where redeemed men would lie on divans, eat exotic foods served by handsome youths, and be entertained by beautiful virgins called houris, created especially for them by Allah. Probably more compelling than the description of heaven was the promise of the torments awaiting nonbelievers on the day of judgment: "For the wrongdoers we have prepared a fire which will encompass them like the walls of a pavilion. When they cry out for a drink they shall be showered with water as hot as melted brass, which will scald their faces. Evil shall be their drink, dismal their resting-place."

The concrete attractions of Islam in this world included both economic prosperity and the opportunity to continue a lifestyle of raiding and warfare in the name of Allah. Muhammad won over the leaders of the Quraysh by making Mecca the sacred city of Islam and by retaining the Ka'bah, cleansed of idols, as the center of Islamic pilgrimage.

Muhammad's message spread to other tribes through diplomatic and, occasionally, military means. The divisive nature of Bedouin society contributed to his success. Frequently, factions within other tribes turned to Muhammad for mediation and support against their rivals. In return for his assistance, petitioners accepted his religious message. Since the Qur'an commanded Muslims to destroy idol worship, conversion provided the occasion for holy wars (**jihads**) of conquest and profitable raids against their still-pagan neighbors. Converts showed their piety by sending part of their spoils as alms to Medina. The Qur'an permitted Christians and Jews living under the authority of Islamic communities to continue to practice their faith, but they were forced to pay a head tax that was shared among members of the Umma.

The Spread of Islam

Muhammad died in the summer of 632 after a short illness, leaving no successor and no directions concerning the leadership of the Umma. Immediately, his closest and most influential followers selected Abu Bakr (632–634), the fourth convert to Islam, to be **caliph,** or successor of the Prophet. Abu Bakr and, after his death two years later, the caliph 'Umar (634–644) faced formidable obstacles. Within the Umma, tensions between the early Medina followers of the Prophet and the Meccan elite were beginning to surface. A more critical problem was that the tribes that had accepted the Prophet's leadership believed that his death freed them from their treaty obligations. Now they attempted to go their own ways. Some sent emissaries to announce that, while they would remain Muslims, they would no longer pay alms. Others attempted to abandon Islam altogether.

To prevent the collapse of the Umma, Abu Bakr launched a war of reconversion. Purely by chance, this war developed into wars of conquest that reached far beyond the Arab world.

Commanded by Khalid ibn al-Walid (d. 642), the greatest early Islamic general, Muslim forces defeated tribe after tribe and brought them back into the Umma. But long-term survival demanded expansion. Since Muslims were forbidden to raid fellow believers and raids were an integral part of Bedouin life, the only way to keep recently converted Bedouin in line was to lead them on military expeditions against non-Muslims. Arab armies could move men and supplies quickly across the arid wastes, crush their enemies, and then retreat back into the desert, beyond the reach of Byzantine and Sassanid forces. Under Abu Bakr, Muslim expansion covered all of Arabia. Under 'Umar, Islam conquered Iran, Iraq, Syria, and Egypt.

The swift and total collapse of the Sassanid Empire and a major portion of the Byzantine Empire astounded contemporaries, not least the Muslims themselves. Their success seemed to be irrefutable proof that Muhammad's message was indeed from God. By 650, Islam stretched from Egypt to Asia Minor, from the Mediterranean to the Indus River.

Another factor that contributed to the Muslims' phenomenal success was the protracted fighting between the Byzantine and Sassanid Empires bs well as internal divisions within the Byzantine world. For over two decades (ca. 602–628) Egypt, Palestine, and Syria had been under Persian control. Although the Byzantine emperor Heraclius eventually reconquered them, these provinces had not yet recovered from the decades of warfare, and within them a whole generation had grown up with no experience of Byzantine government.

In addition, the reimposed Byzantine yoke was widely resented because of profound cultural differences between Greeks and the inhabitants of Syria, Iraq, and Egypt. Many looked on the Byzantines not as the liberators but as the enemy. Syria and Egypt had always been different from the rest of the Roman world. Although their great cities of Antioch and Alexandria had long been centers of Hellenistic learning and culture, the hinterlands of each enjoyed ancient cultural traditions that were totally alien to their urban neighbors. In Syria, this rural society was Aramaic and Arabic speaking. In Egypt, it was Coptic. With the steady decay of urban life and the rising demands on the rural economy, these local differences rose to greater prominence. Eventually, these peculiarities coalesced around traditions sustained by liturgies that were in the vernacular and sharply at odds with the Orthodox Christianity of Constantinople.

These profound cultural, ethnic, and social antagonisms were largely fought out in the sphere of doctrine, particularly over the nature of Jesus Christ. The form of Christianity that the emperors sought to impose, defined at the Council of Chalcedon in 451, insisted that Jesus was only one person but had two complete natures, one fully human, the other entirely divine. Such a distinction rested less on the language of the New Testament than on the Greek philosophical tradition. To the Syrian and Egyptian communities this position was heresy. "Anathema to the unclean Synod of Chalcedon!" wrote

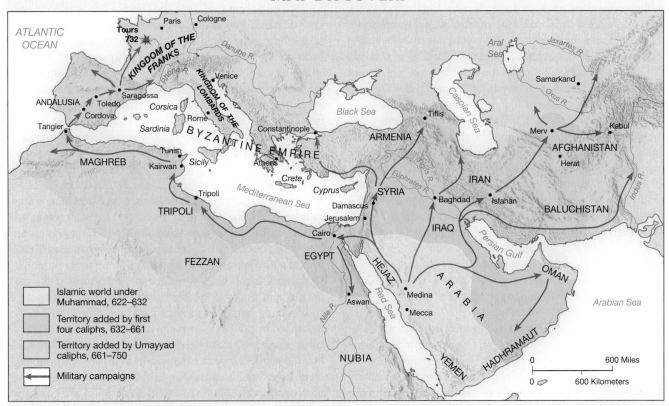

The Spread of Islam

Consider the geographical extent of the Islamic conquest. What trading and cultural networks were united by the spread of Islam? How did the geography of the Islamic world differ from those of its Roman and Sassanid predecessors? What may have prevented Islam's spread through Asia Minor and up the Iberian peninsula?

one Egyptian monk. Closer to the Jewish tradition of the transcendence of God, the Syriac and Egyptian Monophysite (meaning "one nature") Christians insisted that Christ had but a single nature and it was divine.

The two groups vented their intense hatred of each other in riots, murders, and vicious persecutions directed by zealous emperors. As a result, for many Christians of the Near East, the arrival of the Muslims, whose beliefs about the unity and transcendence of God were close to their own and who promised religious toleration and an end to persecution, was seen initially as a divine blessing.

Many Christians and Jews in Syria, Palestine, Egypt, and North Africa shared this view of the Muslim conquest as liberation rather than enslavement. Jews and Christians may have been second-class citizens in the Islamic world, but at least they had a defined place. Conquered populations were

allowed to practice their religion in peace. Their only obligation was to pay a head tax to their conquerors, a burden that was considerably less onerous than the money exacted by Byzantine tax collectors.

The Byzantines' defeat of the Sassanids indirectly facilitated the Muslims' conquest of Iraq. When the Bedouin realized that the Persians were too weakened to protect their empire against raiders, they intensified their attacks. Soon, recent converts to Islam, too late to profit from the conquests of Syria and Egypt, were spearheading the conquest. By 650, the great Sassanid Empire had disappeared, and the Byzantine Empire had lost Egypt, Syria, Mesopotamia, Palestine, portions of Asia Minor, and much of North Africa. During the reigns of Constantine IV (668–685) and Leo III (717–741), Constantinople itself faced besieging Muslim fleets. Each time, it survived only through the use of a secret weapon, so-called Greek fire, an explosive liquid that burst into flame when sprayed by siphons onto enemy ships. Although the city itself survived, the Muslim conquests reduced the once vast empire to little more than Greece, western Asia Minor, southern Italy, and the Balkans.

Authority and Government in Islam

Conquering the world for Islam proved easier than governing it. What had begun as a religious movement within Arabian society had created a vast multinational empire in which Arabs were a tiny minority. Nothing in the Qur'an, nothing in Arabian experience, provided a blueprint for empire. Thus, the Muslims' ability to consolidate their conquests is even more remarkable than the conquests themselves. Within the first decades following the Prophet's death, two models of governance emerged, models that continue to dominate Islamic politics to the present.

The Umma.   The first model was that of pre-Islamic tribal authority. The Umma could be considered a supertribe, governed by leaders whose authority came from their secular power as leaders of the superior military and economic elements within the community. This model appealed particularly to the Quraysh and local tribal leaders who had exercised authority before Muhammad. The second model was that of the authority exercised by the Prophet. In this model, the Umma was more than a supertribe, and its unity and purity had to be preserved by a religiously sanctioned rule exercised by a member of the Prophet's own family. This model was preferred by many of the more recent converts to Islam, especially the poor. Governance under each of the two models was attempted successively in the seventh and eighth centuries.

Regardless of their disagreements on the basis of political authority, both groups adopted the administrative systems of their conquered lands. Byzantine and Sassanid bureaucracy and government, only slightly adjusted, became the models for government in the Islamic world until the twentieth century. In Syria and Egypt, Byzantine officials and even churchmen were incorporated into the government, much as had happened in Europe following the Germanic conquests. For example, John of Damascus (ca. 676–ca. 754), a Christian theologian venerated as a saint, served as the caliph's chief councilor. His faithfulness to the Islamic government and opposition to Byzantine imperial iconoclasm earned him the title of "cursed favorer of Saracens [Muslims]" from the Byzantine emperor.

Likewise, the Muslims left intact the social structures and economic systems of the empires they conquered. Lands remained in the hands of their previous owners. Only state property or, in the Sassanid Empire, that of the Zoroastrian priesthood became common property of the Muslim community. The monastery of Saint Catherine on Mount Sinai, for example, founded by the emperor Justinian around 540, survived without serious harm and still shelters Orthodox monks today.

The Last Orthodox Caliphs.   The division of the spoils of conquest badly divided the Umma and precipitated the first crisis in the caliphate. Under 'Umar, two groups received most of the spoils of the conquests. First were the earliest followers of the Prophet, who received a disproportionate share of revenues. Second were the conquerors themselves, who were often recent converts from tribes on the fringes of Arabia. After 'Umar's death, his successor 'Uthman (d. 656), a member of the powerful Umayya clan of Mecca, attempted to consolidate control over Islam by Quraysh elite. He began to reduce the privileges of early converts in favor of the old Meccan elite. At the same time, he demanded that revenue from the provinces be sent to Medina. The result was rebellion, both within Arabia and in Egypt. 'Uthman's only firm support lay in distant Syria, ruled by members of his own clan. Abandoned at home and abroad, he was finally murdered as he sat reading the Qur'an in his home.

In spite of 'Uthman's unpopularity, his murder sent shock waves throughout the Umma. The fate of his successor, Muhammad's beloved son-in-law and nephew 'Ali (656–661), had an even more serious effect on the future of Islam. Although chosen as fourth caliph, 'Ali was immediately charged with complicity in 'Uthman's murder and was strongly opposed by the Umayyad commander of Syria. To protect himself, 'Ali moved the caliphate from Arabia to Iraq, but in 661, 'Ali was murdered by supporters of his Umayyad rivals. Still, the memory of the "last orthodox caliph" remained alive in the Islamic world, especially in Iraq and Iran. Centuries later, a tradition developed in Baghdad that legitimate leadership of Islam could come only from the house of 'Ali. Adherents to this belief developed into a political and religious sect known as Shi'ism. Although frequently persecuted as heretical by the majority of Muslims, **Shi'ites** remain a potent minority within the Islamic world today.

Umayyad and 'Abbasid Caliphates

The immediate effect of 'Ali's death, however, was the triumph of the old Quraysh and in particular the Umayyads, who established at Damascus in Syria a caliphate that lasted a century. The Umayyads made no attempt to base their rule on spiritual authority. Instead, they ruled as secular leaders, attempting to unite the Islamic empire through an appeal to Arab unity. Profits from this state went entirely to the Quraysh and members of Arabian tribes, who formed the backbone of the early Umayyad army, monopolized high administration, and acquired rich estates throughout the empire.

Umayyad Caliphate.   The Umayyads extended the Islamic Empire to its farthest reaches. In the north, armies from Syria marched into Anatolia and were stopped only in 677 by the Byzantine fleet before Constantinople itself. In the east, Umayyad armies pressed as far as the Syr Darya River on the edge of the Chinese Tang empire. In the south and southwest, the general Tariq ibn Ziyad (d. ca. 720) conquered the Mediterranean coast of Africa and in 711 crossed over the strait near the Rock of Gibraltar (the name comes from the Arabic *jabal Tariq,* "Tariq's mountain") and quickly conquered virtually the entire Iberian peninsula. Soon raiding parties had ventured as far north as the Loire Valley of what is today France. There they were halted by the Frankish commander Charles Martel in 732. Much of Spain, however, remained under Islamic control until 1492.

The Umayyad caliphate's external success in conquering failed to extend to its dealings with the internal tensions of the Umma. The Umayyads could not build a stable empire on the twin foundations of a tiny Arabian elite and a purely secular government taken over from their Byzantine predecessors. Arabs as well as Jews, Zoroastrians, and Christians converted in great numbers. Not all Muslim commanders looked favorably on such conversions. Far from practicing "conversion by the sword," as was often the case in Christian missionary activity, Muslim leaders at times discouraged the spread of Islam among the non-Arabs they had conquered. The reason was simple. Christians and Jews had to pay the head tax imposed on them. If they converted, they no longer paid the tax. In time, this growing population of non-Arab Muslims began to demand a share in the empire's wealth.

The 'Abbasid Revolution.

Not only were the numbers of Muslims increasing, so also was their fervor. Growing numbers of devout Muslims—Arabs and non-Arabs alike—were convinced that leadership had to be primarily spiritual and that this spiritual mandate was the exclusive right of the family of the Prophet. Ultimately, a coalition of dissatisfied Persian Muslims and Arabian religious reformers united under the black banners of the descendants of Muhammad's paternal uncle, 'Abbas (566–ca. 653). In 750, this group overthrew the Umayyads everywhere but in Spain and established a new caliphate in favor of the 'Abbasids.

With the fall of the Umayyad caliphate, Arabs lost control of Islam forever. The 'Abbasids attempted to govern the empire according to religious principles. These were found in the Qur'an and in the **sunnah,** or practices established by the Prophet and preserved first orally and then in the **hadith,** or traditions, which were somewhat comparable to the Christian Gospels. This new empire was to be a universal Muslim commonwealth in which Arabs had no privileged position. "Whoever speaks Arabic is an Arab," ran a popular saying. The 'Abbasids had risen to power as "the group of the saved," and they hoped to make the moral community of Islam the cornerstone of their government, with obedience to 'Abbasid authority an integral part of Islamic belief.

The institutional foundations of the new caliphate, however, like those of the Umayyads, remained firmly in the ancient empires they had conquered. The great caliph Mansur (754–775) moved the capital from Damascus to Baghdad, an acknowledgment of the crucial role of Iraqi and Iranian military and economic strength. The 'Abbasids constructed an autocratic imperial system on the model of their Persian predecessors. With firm control of the military, increasingly composed of slave armies known as mamluks, the 'Abbasids governed the Islamic empire at its zenith.

Division and Revolt.

Ultimately, however, the 'Abbasids were no more successful than the Umayyads in maintaining authority over the whole Muslim world. By the tenth century, local military commanders, termed **emirs,** took control of provincial governments in many areas while preserving the fiction that they were appointed by the 'Abbasid caliphs. The caliphs maintained the symbolic unity of Islam while the emirs went their separate ways. The majority of Muslims accepted this situation as a necessary compromise. In contrast to the Shi'ites, who continued to look for a leader from the family of 'Ali, the **Sunnis,** as they came to be known, remain to the present the majority group of Muslims. The Sunnis had no fixed theory of government or succession to the caliphate. Instead, they accepted the events of history in a practical manner, secure in the truth of the hadith: "My umma will never agree upon an error."

In the west, the 'Abbasids could not maintain even a facade of unity. The Shi'ites launched sporadic revolts and separatist movements. The most successful was that of 'Ubayd Allah the Fatimid (d. 934), who claimed to be the descendant of 'Ali and rightful leader of Islam. In 909, with the support of North African seminomadic Berbers, he declared himself caliph in defiance of the 'Abbasids at Baghdad. In 969, 'Ubayd's Fatimid successors conquered Egypt and established a new city, Cairo, as the capital of their rival caliphate. By the middle of the eleventh century, the Fatimid caliphate controlled all of North Africa, Sicily, Syria, and western Arabia. In Umayyad Spain, although the Muslim population remained firmly Sunni, the powerful emir 'Abd ar-Rahman III (891–961) in 929 also took the title of caliph, thus making his position religious as well as secular. Everywhere, the political and religious unity of Islam was being torn apart.

The Turks.

The arrival in all three caliphates of Muslim peoples who were not yet integrated into the civilization of the Mediterranean world accelerated this disintegration. From the east, Seljuk Turks, long used as slave troops, entered Iraq and in 1055 conquered Baghdad. Within a decade they had conquered Iran, Syria, and Palestine as well. Around the same time, Moroccan Berbers conquered much of North Africa and Spain, while Bedouin raided freely in what are today Libya and Tunisia. These invasions by Muslims from the fringes of the Islamic commonwealth had catastrophic effects on the Islamic world. The Turks, unaccustomed to commerce and to the administrative traditions of the caliphate, divided their empire among their war leaders, displacing traditional landowners and disrupting commerce. The North African

Berbers and Bedouin destroyed the agricultural and commercial systems that had survived successive Vandal, Byzantine, and Arabian invasions.

Islamic Civilization

The Islamic conquest of the seventh century brought peace to Iraq and Iran after generations of struggle and set the stage for a major agricultural recovery. In the tradition of their Persian predecessors, the caliphs organized vast irrigation systems, which made Mesopotamia the richest agricultural region west of China. Peasants and slaves raised dates and olives in addition to wheat, barley, and rice. Sophisticated hydraulics and scientific agriculture brought great regions of Mesopotamia and the Mediterranean coast into cultivation for the first time in centuries.

By uniting the Mediterranean world with Arabia and India, the 'Abbasid empire created the greatest trade network that had ever been seen. Muslim merchants met in bustling ports on the Persian Gulf and the Red Sea to trade silks, paper, spices, and horses from China for silver and cotton from India. Gold from the Sudan was exchanged for iron from Persia. Also offered were carpets from Armenia and Tabaristan, what is today Iran, and slaves from western Europe. Many of these luxury goods found their way to Baghdad, then known as the marketplace for the world.

The marketplace for ideas was as active as that for merchandise. Within a few generations, descendants of Bedouin established themselves in the great cities of the ancient Near East and absorbed the traditions of Persian, Roman, and Hellenistic civilization. However, unlike the Germanic peoples of western Europe, who quickly adopted the Latin language and Roman Christianity, the Muslims recast Persian and Hellenistic culture in an Arabic form. Even in Iran, where Farsi, or Persian, survived as the majority language, Arabic vocabulary and structure transformed the traditional language. While 'Abassid political unity was falling apart, this new civilization was reaching its first great synthesis.

Science and Faith. Islamic intellectuals synthesized and expanded Greek, Persian, and Indian traditions of astronomy and mathematics and sought to find the proper balance between science and faith. As early as the eighth century, caliphs collected Persian, Greek, and Syriac scientific and philosophical works and had them translated into Arabic. Because of the need to establish hours for prayer, Islamic scholars were particularly interested in practical aspects of astronomy and devices for determining time such as the astrolabe, which allows one to determine the time of day or night as well as to determine the exact time of sunrise and sunset and to solve various astronomical problems. Muslim scholars beginning with Ibrahim al-Fazari in ca. 771 perfected the astrolabe, and Islamic treatises and star tables, the most accurate ever devised, were disseminated both west across Europe and east as far as China.

Abu Ja'far Muhammad ibn Musa Al-Khwarizimi (790–850), known as the father of algebra, developed the solution to quadratic equations and wrote treatises that remained fundamental in the East and the West well into the Renaissance. Muslim intellectuals also introduced the so-called Arabic numerals from India and by the tenth century had perfected the use of decimal fractions. Later Muslim mathematicians such as Omar Khayyam (1048–1122) and Ghiyath al'Din Jamshid Mas'ud al'Kashi (1390–1450) investigated complex mathematical problems and developed mathematical concepts not surpassed until the nineteenth century.

Medicine was perhaps the area in which Muslims made the greatest contributions in both theory and practice. Charity is fundamental to Islam, and across the Islamic world hospitals

■ Muslim astronomers made many advances. They perfected the astrolabe, an instrument used to observe and calculate the positions of heavenly bodies.

were established where the sick could be cared for without cost. Al-Razi (864–930), an Iranian physician who became the head of the hospital in Baghdad, wrote a comprehensive medical encyclopedia that became a standard text, East and West. The Persian physician Ibn Sina (980–1037), known in the West as Avicenna, was perhaps the greatest of the classical Islamic physicians. He was the first to recognize the contagious nature of tuberculosis, the value of anesthetics, and the effectiveness of experimenting with new drugs on animals before administering them to humans. His *Encyclopedia* covered such topics as surgical removal of cancers, the importance of hygiene, and the uses of more than 700 specific drugs.

Islamic intellectuals also applied ancient learning to questions of Islamic faith. Legal scholars concerned with the authenticity of hadith used Greek rationalist methods to distinguish genuine from spurious traditions. Religious mystics called Sufis blended Neoplatonic and Muslim traditions to create new forms of religious devotion. Abu Hamid Al-Ghazali (1058–1128) combined his deep knowledge of Neoplatonism, law, mathematics, and science with his deep spiritual attachment to Islamic mysticism to produce powerful critiques of what he took to be the excesses of rational science.

Philosophy.   Although Islamic scientists were professional physicians, astronomers, or lawyers, most were also deeply concerned with abstract philosophical questions, particularly those raised by the works of Plato and Aristotle, which had been translated into Arabic. Many sought to reconcile Islam with that philosophical heritage in the same manner that Origen and Augustine had done for Christianity. Ya'qub al-Kindi (d. 873), the first Arab philosopher, noted that, "The truth . . . must be taken wherever it is to be found, whether it be in the past or among strange peoples." Ibn Sina, in addition to writing on science and medicine, attempted to synthesize Aristotelian thought into a Neoplatonic view of the universe. In the next century, the Cordoban philosopher Ibn Rushd (1126–1198), called Averroës in the West, went still further, teaching an authentic Aristotelian philosophy stripped of Neoplatonic mystical trappings. His commentaries on Aristotle were enormously influential even outside the Islamic world. For Christian philosophers of the thirteenth century, Averroës was known simply as "the Commentator."

The Islamic world also produced important Jewish scientists, physicians, and scholars, the most important of whom was Moses Maimonides (1135–1204). Born in Islamic Spain, he migrated to Morocco, Israel, and eventually Egypt where he became a successful physician. He wrote important texts in Arabic and Hebrew on Jewish law, but his most influential work was *The Guide to the Perplexed,* an Arabic treatise in which he attempts to reconcile Aristotelian and Neoplatonic philosophy to sacred Scripture. His rationalistic approach drew both criticism and praise from within the Jewish, Christian, and Islamic worlds and had a lasting effect on philosophers and thinkers in all three traditions.

Christian Invasion.   At the same time that Muslim thought and culture was at its most creative, Islam faced invasion from a new and unaccustomed quarter: Constantinople. In the tenth and early eleventh centuries, the Byzantines pressed the local rulers of northern Syria and Iraq in a series of raids, which reached as far as the border of Palestine. At the end of the eleventh century, western Europeans, encouraged and supported by the Byzantines, captured Jerusalem and established a Western-style kingdom in Palestine that survived for over a century. Once more, Constantinople was a power in the Mediterranean world.

THE BYZANTINE APOGEE AND DECLINE, 1000–1453

During the tenth and eleventh centuries, Byzantium dominated the Mediterranean world for the last time. Imperial armies under the Macedonian dynasty (867–1059) began to recover some lands that had been lost to Islam during the previous two centuries. Antioch was retaken in 969, and for over a century Byzantine armies operated in Syria and pushed to the border of Palestine. By the middle of the eleventh century, Armenia and Georgia, which had formed independent principalities, had been reintegrated into the empire. To the west, Sicily remained in Muslim hands, but southern Italy, which had been subject to Muslim raids and western barbarian occupation, was secured once more. Byzantine fleets recaptured Crete, cleared the Aegean of Muslim pirates, and reopened the vital commercial sea routes. To the north, missionaries spread not only the Christian religion but also Byzantine culture among the Slavic peoples beyond the frontiers of the empire. The most important missionaries were the brothers Cyril (ca. 827–869) and Methodius (ca. 827–885), who preached to the Khazars and the Moravians. They also invented the Cyrillic alphabet, which they used to translate the Bible and other Christian writings into Slavic. Their missionary activities laid the foundation for the conversion of Serbia, Bulgaria, and Russia. In 1018, Basil II (976–1025) destroyed the Bulgarian kingdom and brought peace to the Balkan Peninsula.

The conquests of the Macedonian dynasty laid the foundation for a short-lived economic prosperity and cultural renaissance. Conquered lands, particularly Anatolia, brought new agricultural wealth. Security of the sea fostered a resurgence of commerce, and customs duties enriched the imperial treasury. New wealth financed the flourishing of Byzantine art and literature. However, just as in the spheres of Byzantine liturgy and court ceremonial, the goal of Byzantine art was to reflect not the transient "reality" of their world but rather the permanent classical values inherited from the past. Thus, rarely in Byzantine art, literature, or religion was innovation appreciated or cultivated.

The language, style, and themes of classical Greek literature, philosophy, and history completely dominated Byzantine culture. Only in rare works such as the popular epic *Digenis Akrites* does something of the flavor of popular Byzantine life appear. The title of the work means roughly "the border defender born of two peoples," for the hero, Basil, was the son of a Muslim father and a Christian Greek mother. The epic consists of two parts, one describing the exploits of the father, a Muslim emir or general, and the other describing those of Digenis Akrites himself, fighting against both Muslims and bandits. The descriptions of his battles, his encounters with wild beasts and dragons, and his heroic death, as well as those of his intelligence, learning, and magnificent palace, are at once part of the Western epic tradition and a reflection of life on the edge of the empire. *Digenis Akrites* is unique for its close relation to popular oral traditions of Byzantine society.

The Disintegration of the Empire

In all domains, however, the successes of the Macedonian emperors set the stage for serious problems. Rapid military expansion and economic growth allowed new elites to establish themselves as autonomous powers and to position themselves between the imperial administration and the people. The constant demand for troops always exceeded the supply of traditional salaried soldiers. In the eleventh century, emperors began to grant imperial estates to great magnates in return for military service. These grants, termed *pronoia,* often included immunity from imperial taxation and the right to certain administrative activities traditionally carried out by the central government. The practice created in effect a largely independent, landed military aristocracy that stood between the peasantry and the imperial government. This policy weakened the centralized state and reduced its income from taxes.

Internal Conflict.   As generals became dissatisfied with the civilian central administration, they began to turn their armies against the emperors, launching over 30 revolts in as many years. To defend itself against both the Muslims without and the generals within, the central government, composed of intellectuals, eunuchs, and urban aristocrats, had to spend vast sums on mercenary armies. These armies, composed largely of Armenians, Germans, and Normans, soon began to plunder the empire they were hired to protect. Further danger came from other, independent Normans who, under their commander Robert Guiscard (ca. 1015–1085), conquered Byzantine Bari and southern Italy and then Muslim Sicily. Soon Guiscard was threatening the empire itself. The hostility between aristocracy and imperial administration largely destroyed the tradition of civilian government. "Do not wish to be a bureaucrat," one general advised his son. "It is not possible to be both a general and a comedian."

Under increasing pressure from local magnates on the one hand and desperate imperial tax collectors on the other, villages began to make deals with powerful patrons who would represent them in return for the surrender of their independence. Through the eleventh and twelfth centuries, the Byzantine peasantry passed from the condition of individualism without freedom to that of collectivism without freedom. Through the same process, landlords and patrons acquired the means to exercise a political role, which ended the state's monopoly on public power.

Commercial Threats.   At the same time that civil war and external pressure were destroying the provincial administration, Byzantine disdain for commerce was weakening the empire's ability to control its income from customs duties. Initially, the willingness to turn over commerce to Italians and others posed few problems. Those who were engaged in actual commerce were for the most part citizens of the empire and were in any case subject to the 10 percent tariffs. However, in the tenth and eleventh centuries, merchants of Amalfi, Bari, and then Venice came to dominate Byzantine commerce. Venetian merchant fleets could double as a powerful navy in times of need, and by the eleventh century the Venetians were the permanent military and commercial power in the Mediterranean. When Robert Guiscard and his Normans threatened the empire, the emperors had to turn to the Venetians for protection and were forced to cede them major economic privileges. The Venetians acquired the right to maintain important self-governing communities in major ports throughout the empire and were allowed to pay lower tariffs than the Byzantines paid.

In 1071, the year that Robert Guiscard captured the last Byzantine city in Italy, the empire suffered an even more disastrous defeat in the east. At Manzikert in Anatolia, the emperor Romanus IV (1067–1071) and his unreliable mercenary army fell to the Seljuk Turks, who captured Romanus. The defeat at Manzikert sealed the fate of the empire. Anatolia was lost, and the gradual erosion of the empire in both the west and the east had begun.

The Conquests of Constantinople and Baghdad

At the end of the eleventh century the Comnenian dynasty (1081–1185) briefly halted the political and economic chaos of the empire. Rather than fighting the tendency of the centralized state to devolve into a decentralized aristocratic one, Alexius I Comnenus (1081–1118) tied the aristocracy to his family, thus making it an instrument of imperial government. In the short run the process was successful. He expanded the use of pronoia to strengthen loyal aristocrats and granted them offices in the central administration that had been traditionally reserved for eunuchs. He stabilized Byzantine currency, which was the international exchange medium in the Islamic and Christian worlds

CHRONOLOGY
THE BYZANTINE EMPIRE AND THE RISE OF ISLAM

527–565	Reign of Justinian
610	Muhammad's vision
662	The Hijra, Muhammad's journey from Mecca to Medina
726–787	First phase of iconoclast dispute
732	Muslim advance halted by Franks
750	'Abbasids overthrow Umayyads; take control of Muslim world
802–843	Second phase of iconoclast dispute
843	Empress Theodora ends iconoclast persecution; restores image veneration
867–1059	Macedonian dynasty rules Byzantine Empire; begins recovering lands from Muslims
1054	Schism splits churches of Rome and Constantinople
1071	Robert Guiscard captures Sicily and southern Italy; Battle of Manzikert; Seljuk Turks defeat Byzantines
1099	First Crusade establishes Latin kingdom in Jerusalem
1221	Genghis Khan leads Mongol army into Persia
1453	Constantinople falls to Ottomans

Christianity had developed a number of rituals and beliefs that differed from Orthodox practice. This parting of the ways had already appeared during the iconoclastic controversies of the eighth and ninth centuries. In the eleventh, it was directed by an independent and self-assertive papacy in Rome, which claimed supreme authority throughout Christendom.

Disagreements between the patriarchs of Constantinople and the popes of Rome prevented cooperation between the two Christian worlds and led to further deterioration of relationships between Greeks and Latins. These disagreements came to a head in 1054, when the papal representative, or legate, Cardinal Humbert (ca. 1000–1061) met with the patriarch of Constantinople, Michael Cerularius (ca. 1000–1059), to negotiate ecclesiastical control over southern Italy and Sicily. Humbert was arrogant and demanding, Michael Cerularius haughty and uncompromising. Acting beyond his authority, Humbert excommunicated the patriarch and all his followers. The patriarch responded in kind, excommunicating Humbert and all connected with him. This formal excommunication was lifted in the 1960s, but the split between the churches of Rome and Constantinople continues to the present.

Excommunication was probably the least of the dangers the Byzantines faced from the West. The full fury of the often ignorant, greedy, and violent Western society reached the empire when, after the defeat at Manzikert, the emperor Alexius called on Western Christians for support against the Muslims. To his horror, adventurers of every sort, eager to conquer land and wealth in the name of the cross of Jesus, flooded the empire. In a penetrating and often cynical biography of her father, Alexius's daughter Anna (ca. 1093–1148) describes how, as quickly as possible, Alexius hurried these crusaders (from the Latin *cruciata*, "marked with a cross") on to Palestine before they could turn their violence against his empire. Even while recognizing that the crusaders were uncouth and barbarous, the Byzantines had to admit that the Latins were effective. Despite enormous hardships, the First Crusade was able to take advantage of division in the Muslim world to conquer Palestine and establish a Latin kingdom in Jerusalem in 1099.

The Sack of Constantinople. The crusaders' initial victories and the growth of Latin wealth and power created in Constantinople a temporary enthusiasm for western European styles and customs. The Byzantines soon realized, however, that the Latin kingdom posed a threat not only to Islam but to them as well. While crusaders threatened Byzantine territories, Venetian merchants imposed a stranglehold on Byzantine trade. When emperors granted other Italian towns concessions equal to those of the Venetians, they found that they had simply amplified their problems. Anti-Latin sentiment reached the boiling point in 1183. In the riots that broke out in that year, Italians and other westerners in Constantinople were murdered, and their goods were seized. Just 21 years later, in 1204, a wayward crusade, egged on by Venice, turned aside from its planned expedition

and had been dangerously devalued by his predecessors. Still, by the late twelfth century the empire was a vulnerable second-rate power caught between Latin Europe and Islam.

Initially, the Christian West was a more deadly threat than the Islamic East. In the eleventh century, after more than 500 years of economic and political weakness, western Europe was beginning to reach parity with Byzantium. Robert Guiscard and his Normans, who had conquered Sicily and southern Italy, were typical examples of the powerful militaristic aristocracy that was developing in the remains of the old western empire.

Dangers from the West. The military threat from the West was paralleled by a religious one. In the centuries that Rome had been largely cut off from Constantinople, Western to Palestine to capture a bigger prize: Constantinople. After pillaging the city for three days, the westerners established one of their own as emperor and installed a Venetian as patriarch.

The Byzantines did manage to hold onto a portion of their empire centering on Nicaea, and before long the Latins fell to bickering among themselves. In 1261, the ruler of Nicaea, Michael Palaeologus (ca. 1224–1282), recaptured Constantinople with the assistance of the Genoese and had himself crowned emperor in the Hagia Sophia. Still, the empire was fatally shattered, its disintegration into autonomous lordships complete. The restored empire consisted of little more than the district around Constantinople, Thessalonica, and the Peloponnesus. Bulgarians and Serbs had expanded far into the Greek mainland. Most of the rich Anatolian regions had been lost to the Turks, and commercial revenues were in the hands of the Genoese allies. The restored empire's survival for almost 200 years was due less to its own prerogative than to the internal problems of the Islamic world.

Eastern Conquests.   The caliphs of Baghdad, like the emperors of Constantinople, succumbed to invaders from the barbarous fringes of their empire. In 1221, the Mongol prince Temujin (ca. 1162–1227), better known to history as Genghis

■ The Ottoman Empire, ca. 1450. By the mid-fifteenth century the Ottoman Empire had absorbed virtually all of the Byzantine Empire.

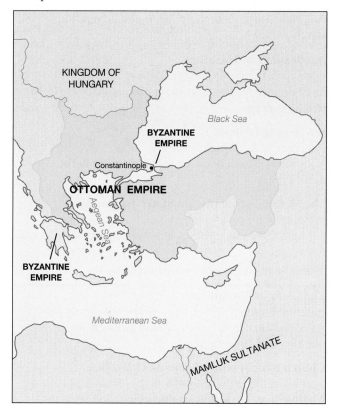

Khan ("Universal Ruler"), led his conquering army into Persia from central Asia. From there, a portion of the Mongols went north, invading Russia in 1237 and dividing it into small principalities ruled by Slavic princes under Mongol control. In 1258, a Mongol army captured Baghdad and executed the last 'Abbasid caliph, ending a 500-year tradition. The Mongol armies then moved westward, shattering the Seljuk principalities in Iraq, Anatolia, and Syria and turning back only before the fierce resistance of the Egyptian Mamluks.

From the ruins of the Seljuk kingdom arose a variety of small Turkish principalities, or emirates. After the collapse of the Mongol empire, one of these, the Ottoman, began to expand at the expense of both the weakened Byzantine Empire and the Mongol-Seljuk Empire. In the next centuries, the Ottomans expanded east, south, and west. Around 1350, they crossed into the Balkans as Byzantine allies but soon took over the region for themselves. By 1450, the Ottoman stranglehold on Constantinople was complete. The final scene of the conquest, long delayed but inevitable, occurred three years later.

For Greeks and for Italian intellectuals of the Renaissance, the conquest of Constantinople by the Ottomans was the end of an imperial tradition that reached back to Augustus. But Mehmed the Conqueror (1452–1481) could as easily be seen as its restorer. True, the city was plundered by the victorious army. But this was simply the way of war in the fifteenth century. The city, its palaces, and its religious edifices fared better under the Turks than they had under its previous, Christian conquerors. To mack the Orthodox Church, the Latins had placed a prostitute on the patriarch's throne in the Hagia Sophia. Mehmed, after purging the church of its Christian trappings, rededicated it to the worship of the one God. Once more, Constantinople, for centuries a capital without a country, was the center of a great Mediterranean empire.

CONCLUSION

Although often deadly enemies, the Byzantine and Islamic worlds were both genuine heirs of the great eastern empires of antiquity. The traditions of the Assyrian, Alexandrian, Persian, and Roman empires lived on in their cities, their bureaucracies, and their agricultural and commercial systems. Both also shared the monotheistic religious tradition that had emerged from Judaism. In their schools and libraries they preserved and transmitted the literary and scientific heritage of antiquity. Through Islam the legacy of the West reached East Asia. Through Byzantium the peoples of the Slavic world became heirs of the caesars. The inhabitants of western Europe long viewed the Byzantine and Islamic civilizations with hostility, incomprehension, and fear. Still, in the areas of culture, government, religion, and commerce, the West learned much from its eastern neighbors.

QUESTIONS FOR REVIEW

1. In what ways was Byzantine society characterized by individualism without freedom?
2. How and why did Muhammad both break from tribal and clan traditions and build upon them in creating Islam?
3. How did conflicts within Islam after Muhammad's death divide it spiritually but also contribute to Islam's expansion across Africa and Spain?

4. How did the rapid expansion of Byzantium under the Macedonian dynasty contribute to the empire's slow collapse?

KEY TERMS

caliph, *p. 141*

emirs, *p. 144*

hadith, *p. 144*

Hijra, *p. 140*

iconoclasts, *p. 135*

iconodules, *p. 135*

icons, *p. 135*

jihads, *p. 141*

Orthodox Christianity, *p. 134*

Shi'ites, *p. 143*

strategoi, *p. 133*

sunnah, *p. 144*

Sunnis, *p. 144*

Umma, *p. 140*

DISCOVERING WESTERN CIVILIZATION ONLINE

You can obtain more information about the classical legacy in the East at the websites listed below. See also the Companion Website that accompanies this text, www.ablongman.com/kishlansky, which contains an online study guide and additional resources.

The Byzantines

Byzantium: Byzantine Studies on the Internet
www.fordham.edu/halsall/Byzantium/
A major site with links to every aspect of Byzantine civilization maintained by Paul Halsall.

NM's Creative Impulse: Byzantium
history.evansville.net/byzantiu.html
An excellent guide to Byzantine studies on the web.

Medieval Sourcebook: The Institutes of Justinian, 535 C.E.
www.fordham.edu/halsall/basis/535institutes.html
www.fordham.edu/halsall/source/corpus1.html
Extensive selections from the *Institutes,* a digest of laws and legal opinions designed for law students. The *Institutes,* the *Codex Justinianus,* and the *Digest* were part of the *Corpus Iurus Civilis* (Body of Civil Law) issued under Justinian. This codification of Roman law stands as a great monument of Western jurisprudence.

The Rise of Islam

IslamiCity.com—Education
www.islamicity.com/education/islamiceducation
A site for Islamic history maintained by IslamiCity, dedicated to advancing Islamic information, fostering community, and educating people about Islam.

Internet Islamic History Sourcebook
www.fordham.edu/halsall/islam/islamsbook.html
Paul Halsall's site dedicated to sources on Islamic history and culture.

About Islam and Muslims
www.ummah.org.uk/what-is-islam/index.html
A site devoted to explaining Islam maintained by the UNN Islamic Society.

Welcome to Isfahan!
isfahan.apu.ac.uk/isfahan.html
A site devoted to eleventh-century Isfahan, capital of medieval Persia.

The Metropolitan Museum of Art: Islamic Art
metmuseum.org/collections/department.asp?dep=14
A guide to New York's Metropolitan Museum Islamic collection.

The Byzantine Apogee and Decline

The Glory of Byzantium
metmuseum.org/explore/Byzantium/byzhome.html
A site dedicated to Byzantine art and history at the Metropolitan Museum of Art.

Church History with a Focus on Orthodoxy
aggreen.net/church_history/c_histry.html
A site dedicated to Orthodox Christianity with links to Byzantine history and culture.

SUGGESTIONS FOR FURTHER READING

The Byzantines

Jonathan Harris, *Byzantium and the Crusades* (London and New York: Hambledon and London, 2003). A new treatment of relations between Byzantium and Western Europe.

Alexander P. Kazhdan, ed., *The Oxford Dictionary of Byzantium* (New York: Oxford University Press, 1991). Standard reference for Byzantine history and culture.

Alexander Kazhdan and Giles Constable, *People and Power in Byzantium* (Washington, DC: Dumbarton Oaks, 1982). An imaginative and controversial analysis of Byzantine culture by a Russian Byzantinist and a Western medievalist.

Cyril Mango, *Byzantium: The Empire of New Rome* (New York: Scribner's, 1980). An imaginative and provocative reevaluation of the Byzantine world.

John Moorhead, *Justinian* (New York: Macmillan, 1994). A readable biography of the great emperor.

Dimitri Obolensky, *Byzantium and the Slavs* (Crestwood, NY: St. Vladimir's Seminary Press, 1994). A survey of the Byzantine Empire's relations with eastern Europe.

Warren T. Treadgold, *A Concise History of Byzantium* (New York: St. Martin's Press, 2001). An up-to-date survey of Byzantine history.

The Rise of Islam

Aziz Al-Azmeh, *Arabic Thought and Islamic Societies* (London: Routledge, Chapman & Hall, 1986). A demanding but valuable introduction to Islamic intellectual history.

Albert Hourani, *A History of the Arab Peoples* (New York: Warner Books, 1992). A clear, thoughtful survey of Arab history for nonspecialists.

Robert G. Hoyland, *Arabia and the Arabs: From the Bronze Age to the Coming of Islam* (New York: Routledge, 2001). A comprehensive survey of the early history of Arabia.

Hugh Kennedy, *The Prophet and the Age of the Caliphates* (White Plains, NY: Longman, 1986). A valuable summary of the early political history of Islam.

Bernard Lewis, *Islam in History: Ideas, People, and Events in the Middle East* (Chicago: Open Court, 1993). Broad synthesis of Islam.

Bernard Lewis, *The Muslim Discovery of Europe* (New York: W. W. Norton, 1985). Views of the West by Muslim travelers.

Bernard Lewis, ed., *Islam and the Arab World* (New York: Knopf, 1976). An illustrated collection of essays on Islamic history and culture.

Fatima Mernissi, *Women and Islam: An Historical and Theological Enquiry* (Oxford: Basil Blackwell, 1991). Sympathetic study of women in Islam.

Roy P. Mottahedeh, *The Mantle of the Prophet: Religion and Politics in Iran* (New York: Simon and Schuster, 1985). An important introduction to the social values and structures of western Iran and southern Iraq in the tenth and eleventh centuries.

G. E. Von Grunebaum, *Classical Islam: A History, 600–1258* (Chicago: Aldine, 1970). A general introduction to early Islamic history.

The Byzantine Apogee and Decline, 1000–1453

Michael Angold, *The Byzantine Empire, 1025–1204* (White Plains, NY: Longman, 1997). A solid survey of the Byzantine Empire prior to the capture of Constantinople by the Latins.

P. M. Holt, *The Age of the Crusades: The Near East from the Eleventh Century to 1517* (White Plains, NY: Longman, 1986). An excellent survey of the political history of the Near East in the later Middle Ages.

For a list of additional titles related to this chapter's topics, please see www.ablongman.com/kishlansky.

Chapter 8

THE WEST IN THE EARLY MIDDLE AGES, 500–900

The Visual Record

THE CHAPEL AT THE WATERS

The Palatine Chapel in Aachen, now a small German city near the Belgian border, brings together a fascination with the traditions of the Roman past with the creativity of a new epoch. These two strands describe Europe during the early Middle Ages, generally the period between 500 and 900. Aachen was a favorite residence of the Frankish king Charles the Great, or Charlemagne (768–814), who often came there to enjoy its natural hot springs. In time, it came to be his primary residence, the capital of his vast kingdom, which stretched from central Italy to the mouth of the Rhine River. Around 792, Charlemagne commissioned an architect to design a palace complex, one that would rival the great Roman and Byzantine buildings of Italy and Constantinople.

Royal agents scoured Europe for Roman ruins from which columns, precious marble, and ornaments could be salvaged and reused. From these ancient stones, masons raised a complex of audience rooms, royal apartments, baths, and quarters for court officials. The whole ensemble was intentionally reminiscent of the Lateran Palace in Rome, which was the residence of the popes.

The central building of Charlemagne's palace complex was the chapel, a symmetrical octagon 300 feet on its principal axes, modeled on San Vitale in Ravenna. The choice of model was significant. Ravenna had been the former capital of Roman Italy and of Theodoric the Great, the Ostrogothic king whom Charlemagne greatly admired. But although modeled on Roman buildings, the Palatine Chapel was admirably suited to the glorification of Charlemagne.

The building was divided into three tiers. The first tier, on the ground floor, held the sanctuary, where priest and people met for worship. The topmost tier, supported by ancient Roman pillars, represented the heavens. Between the two was a gallery connected by a passage to the royal residence. On this gallery sat the king's throne. From his seat, Charlemagne could look down on the religious services being conducted below. Looking up to where he sat, worshippers were constantly reminded of the king's intermediary position between ordinary mortals and God. This architectural design boldly asserted that Charlemagne was more than a barbarian king. By 805, when the chapel was dedicated, he had made good this assertion. As a contemporary chronicler wrote while in Rome in the year 800:

On the most holy day of Christmas, when the king rose from prayer in front of the shrine of the blessed apostle Peter to take part in the Mass, Pope Leo placed a crown on his head and he was hailed by the whole Roman people. . . . He was now called Emperor and Augustus.

To Charlemagne and to his supporters, this coronation ceremony revived the Roman Empire in the west. Like his chapel in Aachen (long afterward known as Aix-la-Chapelle, the chapel at the waters), this empire was built on the remains of Roman traditions grafted onto a vigorous tradition of Germanic kinship and society. According to the Byzantines, who looked on Charlemagne and his imperial coronation with alarm, the western empire could not be revived because it had never really ended. According to them, the death of the last western emperor Julius Nepos in 480 had ended the division of the empire. Since then, the Byzantine emperors had pretended that they ruled both east and west. Charlemagne's claims, made through the ceremony in Rome and more subtly in the imperial architecture of his palace, represented to them not a revival of the empire but a threat to its existence.

Looking Ahead

This chapter will trace western Europe's progress toward Aachen, exploring the spectrum of barbarian successor states before concentrating on the unique blend of Roman, Christian, and Frankish institutions and culture that culminated in the Carolingian Empire, an empire whose legacy endured long after its unity dissolved into competing kingdoms and lordships. ➤

THE MAKING OF THE BARBARIAN KINGDOMS, 500–750

The existence of a united empire had long been but a dream. In the year 500, Emperor Anastasius I (491–518) could delude himself that he ruled the whole empire of Augustus, Diocletian, and Constantine, both east and west. Never mind that in the east, war against the Persians dragged on. Never mind that along the northern border of the empire the Bulgarians, a new multiethnic barbarian confederation, had begun to raid into the Balkans. Neither of these conflicts, Anastasius contended, threatened the stability of the empire. In the west, the governor who ruled Italy had sworn that he "rejoiced to live under Roman law, which we are prepared to defend by arms." The king of the once troublesome Vandals had concluded a marriage alliance with the Italian governor and seemed ready to accept Roman statecraft. Beyond the Alps, a Roman officer called a *patrician* ruled the regions of the upper Rhone, and a consul controlled Gaul. In Aquitaine and Spain, legitimate, recognized officers of the empire ruled both Romans and barbarians. What need was there to speak of the end of the empire in the West?

This imperial unity was more apparent than real. The Italian governor was the Ostrogothic king Theodoric the Great (493–526), whose Roman title meant less than his Ostrogothic army. The patrician was the Burgundian king Gondebaud (480–516). The Roman officer in Aquitaine and Spain was the Visigothic king Alaric II (485–507), and the Gallic consul was the Frankish king Clovis (482–511). Each of these rulers courted imperial titles and recognition, but none regarded Anastasius as his sovereign.

Italy: From Ostrogoths to Lombards

In the early sixth century, all of the Germanic peoples who were settled within the old Roman Empire acknowledged the Goths as the most successful of the "blond-haired peoples," as the Romans called the barbarians. The Ostrogoths had created an Italian kingdom in which Romans and barbarians lived side by side. The Visigoths ruled Spain and southern Gaul by combining traditions of Roman law and barbarian military might. Yet neither Gothic kingdom endured for more than two centuries.

The Ostrogothic Kingdom.
Theodoric the Ostrogoth was the most cultivated, capable, and sophisticated barbarian ruler. He was also the most powerful. Burgundians, Visigoths, and Alemanni looked to him for leadership and protection. Even Clovis, the ambitious Frankish king, usually bowed to his wishes. Theodoric had spent his teenage years as a pampered hostage in Constantinople. There, he had learned to understand and admire Roman ways. Later, after he had conquered Italy at the head of his Gothic army, he established a dual government, which respected both the remains of Roman civil administration and Gothic military organization.

■ A gold solidus coin bears a portrait of Theodoric. His left hand holds a globe on which stands a personification of victory. The inscription reads "King Theodoric," but the absence of a robe and diadem shows that he was not considered the equal of the emperor.

Religion as well as government divided Italy's population. The Ostrogoths were Arians; the majority of the Romans were orthodox Christians. Initially, Theodoric made no effort to interfere with the religion of his subjects, stating, "We cannot command the religion of our subjects, since no one can be forced to believe against his will." This religious toleration attracted into his government outstanding Roman intellectuals and statesmen. The Roman Boethius (480–524), while serving in Theodoric's government, was also trying to synthesize the philosophical traditions of Plato and Aristotle. Cassiodorus (ca. 490–ca. 585), a cultivated Roman senator, served as Theodoric's secretary and held important positions in his government before retiring to found monasteries, where he and his monks worked to preserve the literary and philosophical traditions of Rome. Following Theodoric's death in 526, internal conflict over the succession paved the way for a protracted and devastating invasion by the Byzantines, who destroyed not only the Ostrogothic kingdom but also much of what remained of Roman Italy.

Italy was simply too close to Constantinople and too important for the ambitious Emperor Justinian I (527–565) to ignore. Encouraged by his easy victory over the Vandals, he sent an army into Italy, where he anticipated an easy reconquest of the peninsula. Instead, he got almost 20 years of vicious warfare. Not only were the Goths more formidable foes than he had expected, but when Roman tax collectors arrived with the Roman armies, Justinian found that the Italian people did not greet their "liberators" with open arms. In addition, in the midst of the reconquest a new and terrible disease appeared throughout the Mediterranean world. The plague cut down as much as one-third of Europe's population in the next two centuries.

MAP DISCOVERY

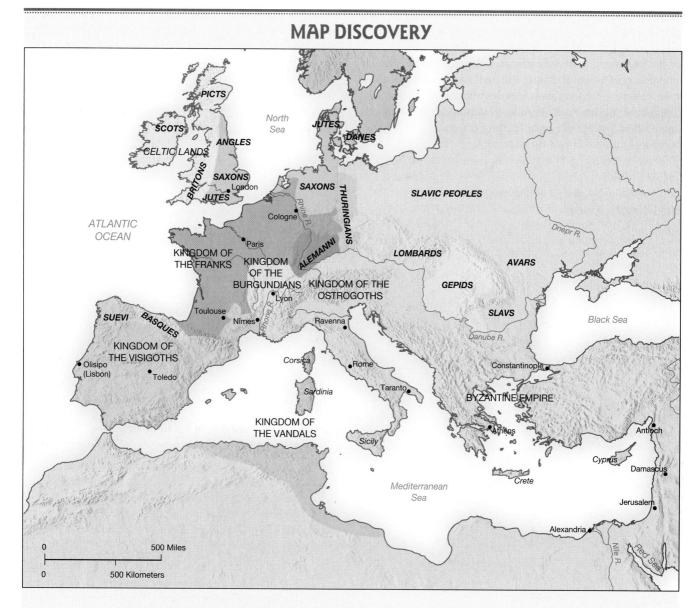

The Barbarian Kingdoms, ca. 526

Examine the locations of Barbarian Kingdoms in the sixth century. What strategic geographical advantages did the Ostrogothic kingdom hold that allowed Theodoric the Great to play a dominant role in the West? How did the relative isolation of the kingdom of the Franks aid its future development? Which Barbarian kingdoms were in a position to absorb the most Roman traditions? Which the least?

Lombard Conquest. The destruction of Italy by war and disease paved the way for its conquest by the Lombards. As allies in Justinian's army, some members of this Germanic tribe from along the Danube had learned of the riches of Italy firsthand. In 568, the whole Lombard people left the Carpathian basin to their neighbors, the Avars, and invaded the exhausted and war-torn Italian peninsula. By the end of

the sixth century, the Ostrogoths had disappeared, and the Byzantines retained only the heel and toe of the boot of Italy and a narrow strip stretching from Ravenna to Rome. The Byzantine presence in Rome was weak, and by default the popes, especially Gregory the Great (590–604), became the defenders and governors of the city. Gregory organized the resistance to the Lombards, fed the population during famines, and comforted them through the dark years of plague and warfare. A vigorous political as well as spiritual leader, he laid the foundations of the medieval papacy.

The Lombards largely eliminated the Roman tax system under which Italians had long suffered. In the sphere of religion, many of the Lombards initially were Arians, but in the early seventh century the Lombard kings and their followers accepted orthodox Christianity. This conversion paved the way for the unification of the society.

Visigothic Spain: Intolerance and Destruction

Rather than accepting a divided society as did the Ostrogoths or merging into an orthodox Roman culture as did the Lombards, the Visigoths of Gaul and Spain sought to unify the indigenous population of their kingdom through law and religion. Roman law deeply influenced Visigothic law codes and formed an enduring legal heritage to the West. Religious unity was a more difficult goal. The king's repeated attempts to force conversion to Arianism failed and created tension and mistrust. This mistrust proved fatal. In 507, Gallo-Roman aristocrats supported the Frankish king Clovis in his successful conquest of the Visigothic kingdom of Toulouse. Defeat drove the Visigoths deeper into Spain, where they gradually forged a unified kingdom based on Roman administrative tradition and Visigothic kingship.

The long-sought religious unity was finally achieved when King Recared (586–601) and the Gothic aristocracy embraced orthodox Christianity. This conversion further blurred the differences between Visigoths and Roman provincials in the kingdom. It also initiated an unprecedented use of the Church and its ideology to strengthen the monarchy. Visigothic kings modeled themselves after the Byzantine emperors, proclaimed themselves new Constantines, and used Church councils, held regularly at Toledo, as governing assemblies.

Still, the Visigoths continued to distrust anyone who was different, and their suspicion focused especially on the considerable Jewish population, which had lived in Spain since the *Diaspora,* or dispersion, in the first century of the Roman Empire. Almost immediately after Recared's conversion, he and his successors began to enact a series of anti-Jewish measures, culminating in 613 with the command that all Jews accept baptism or leave the kingdom. Although this mandate was never fully carried out, the virulence of the persecution of the Jews grew through the seventh century. At the same time, rivalry within the aristocracy weakened the kingdom and left it vulnerable to attack from without. In 711, Muslims from North Africa invaded and quickly conquered the Visigothic kingdom. While some remnants of the Visigoths held on in small kingdoms in the northwest, most of the population quickly came to terms with their new mas-

ters. Jews rejoiced in the religious toleration brought by Islam, and many members of the Christian elite converted to Islam and retained their positions of authority under the new regime.

The Anglo-Saxons: From Pagan Conquerors to Christian Missionaries

The motley collection of Saxons, Angles, Jutes, Frisians, Suebians, and others who came to Britain as federated troops and stayed on as rulers did not coalesce into a united kingdom until almost the eleventh century. Instead, these Germanic warriors carved out small kingdoms for themselves, enslaving the romanized Britons or driving them into Wales. Although independent, these little kingdoms (their number varied from five to as many as eleven at different times) maintained some sort of identity as a group. The king of the dominant kingdom enjoyed some deference from his fellow rulers. Other kings looked to him as first among equals and sought his advice and influence in their dealings with one another. Unlike the Goths, none of these peoples had previously been integrated into the Roman world. Rather than fusing Roman and Germanic traditions, they eradicated the former. Urban life disappeared and, with it, the Roman traditions of administration, taxation, and culture.

In their place developed a world whose central values were honor and glory, whose primary occupation was fighting, and whose economic system was based on plunder and the open-handed distribution of riches. In many ways, this Anglo-Saxon world resembled the heroic age of ancient Greece. This was a society dominated by petty kings and their aristocratic war leaders. These invaders were not, like the Goths, just a military elite. They also included free farmers who partly replaced and partly absorbed romanized British peasantry, introducing their language, agricultural techniques, social organization, and folkloric traditions to the southeastern part of the island. These ordinary settlers, much more than the kings and aristocrats, were responsible for the gradual transformation of Britain into England, the land of the Angles.

The Anglo-Saxons were pagans, and although Christianity survived, the relationship between conquered and conquerors did not provide a climate conducive to conversion. Christianity came instead from without. The conversion of England resulted from a two-part effort. The first originated in Ireland, the most western society of Europe and the one in which Celtic traditions had survived little changed for over 1,000 years. Ireland had never formed part of the Roman Empire and so had never developed the forms of urban life and centralized, hierarchical government or religion characteristic of Britain and the Continent. In the fifth century, merchants and missionaries introduced an eastern monastic form of Christianity to Ireland, which adapted easily to the rural tribal organization of Irish society. Although Irish

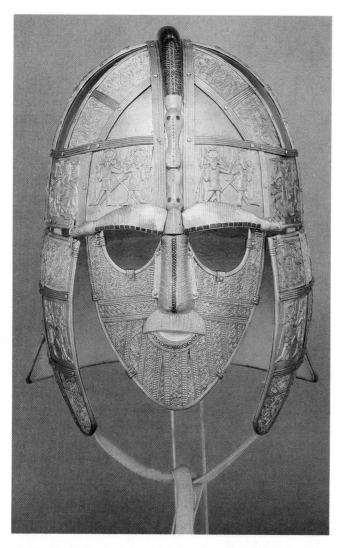

■ The elaborate helmet of a seventh-century Anglo-Saxon king, recovered from his ship burial at Sutton Hoo on the southeast coast of England, shows the wealth and culture of these rulers.

Christianity was entirely orthodox in its beliefs, the isolation of Ireland led to the development of numerous distinctive local practices. Thus, although Ireland had important bishops, the most influential churchmen were powerful abbots of strict ascetic monasteries, closely connected with tribal chieftains, who directed the religious life of their regions. Around 565, the Irish monk Columba (521–597) established a monastery on the island of Iona off the coast of Scotland. From there, wandering Irish monks began to convert northern Britain.

The second effort at Christianizing Britain began with Pope Gregory the Great. In 596, he sent the missionary Augustine (known as Augustine of Canterbury to distinguish him from the bishop of Hippo) to attempt to convert the English. Augustine laid the foundations for a hierarchical, bishop-centered church based on the Roman model. In time,

the pagan king Ethelbert and much of his southwest kingdom of Kent accepted Christianity, and the pope named Augustine archbishop of Canterbury.

As Irish missionaries spread south from Iona and Roman missionaries moved north from Canterbury, their efforts created in England two opposing forms of orthodox Christianity. One was Roman, episcopal, and hierarchical. The other was Celtic, monastic, and decentralized. The Roman and Celtic churches agreed on basic doctrines. However, each had its own calendar of religious feasts and its own rituals. King Oswy of Northumbria (d. 670) called an episcopal meeting, or **synod,** in 664 at Whitby to settle the issue. After hearing arguments from both sides, Oswy accepted the customs of the Roman Church, thus allying himself and ultimately all of Anglo-Saxon England with the centralized, hierarchical form of Christianity, which could be used to strengthen his monarchy.

During the century and a half following the Synod of Whitby, Anglo-Saxon Christian civilization blossomed. Contact with the Continent and especially with Rome increased. The monasteries of Monkwearmouth and Jarrow became centers of learning, culminating in the writings of Bede (673–735), the greatest scholar of his century. His history of the English church and people is the finest historical work of the early Middle Ages.

By the eighth century, England itself had begun to send Christian missionaries to the Continent to convert their still-pagan Germanic cousins. Until the late eighth and ninth centuries, when the Germanic Vikings began to attack Anglo-Saxon settlements, England furnished the Continent with many of its leading thinkers and scholars.

The Franks: An Enduring Legacy

In the fourth century, various small Germanic tribes along the Rhine coalesced into a loose confederation known as the Franks. A significant group of them, the Salians, made the mistake of attacking Roman garrisons and were totally defeated. The Romans resettled the Salians in a largely abandoned region of what is now Belgium and Holland. There, they formed a buffer to protect Roman colonists from other Germanic tribes and provided a ready supply of recruits for the Roman army. During the fourth and fifth centuries, these Salian Franks and their neighbors assumed an increasingly important role in the military defense of Gaul and began to spread out of their "reservation" into more settled parts of the province. Although many high-ranking Roman officers of the fourth century were Franks, most were neither conquerors nor members of the military elite. Rather, they were soldier-farmers who settled beside the local Roman peoples they protected.

In 486, Clovis, leader of the Salian Franks and commander of the barbarized Roman army, staged a successful coup (possibly with the approval of the Byzantine emperor), defeating and killing Syagrius, the last Roman commander in the West.

Although Clovis ruled the Franks as king, he worked closely with the existing Gallo-Roman aristocracy as he consolidated his control over various Frankish factions and over portions of Gaul and Germany that were held by other barbarian kingdoms. Clovis's early conversion to orthodox Christianity helped to ensure the effectiveness of this Gallo-Roman cooperation. Clovis converted, hoping that God would give him victory over his enemies and that his new faith would win the support of the Roman aristocracy in Gaul. The king's baptism convinced many of his subjects to convert as well and paved the way for the assimilation of Franks and Romans into a new society. This Frankish society became the model for European social and political organization for over 1,000 years.

The mix of Frankish warriors and Roman aristocrats spread rapidly across western Europe. Clovis and his successors absorbed the Visigothic kingdom of Toulouse, the Thuringians, and the kingdom of the Burgundians and expanded Frankish hegemony through modern Bavaria and south of the Alps into northern Italy. Unlike other barbarian kingdoms such as those of the Huns or Ostrogoths, which evaporated almost as soon as their great founders died, the Frankish synthesis was enduring. Although the dynasty established by Clovis, called the Merovingian after a legendary ancestor, lasted only until the mid-eighth century, the Frankish kingdom was the direct ancestor of both France and Germany.

After Clovis's death in 511, his kingdom was divided among his four sons. For the next 200 years, the heart of the Frankish kingdom, the region between the Rhine and Loire Rivers, was often divided into the kingdoms of Neustria, Burgundy, and Austrasia, each ruled by a Merovingian king. The outlying regions of Aquitaine and Provence to the south and Alemania, Thuringia, and Bavaria to the east were governed by Frankish dukes appointed by the kings. Still, the Frankish world was never as divided as Anglo-Saxon England. In the early eighth century, a unified Frankish kingdom reemerged as the dominant force in Europe.

LIVING IN THE NEW EUROPE

The substitution of Germanic kings for imperial officials made few obvious differences in the lives of most inhabitants of Italy, Gaul, and Spain. The vast majority of Europeans were poor farmers whose lives centered on their villages and fields. For them the seasons in the agricultural year, the burdens of rent and taxation, and the frequent poor harvests, food shortages, famines, and epidemics were more important than empires and kingdoms. Nevertheless, fundamental if imperceptible changes were transforming daily life at every level of society. The slaves and semifree peasants of Rome gradually began to form new kinds of social groups and to practice new forms of agriculture as they merged with the Germanic warrior-peasants. Elite Gallo-Roman landowners came to terms with their Frankish conquerors, and these two groups began to coalesce into a single unified aristocracy. In the same way that Germanic and Roman

society began to merge, Germanic and Roman traditions of governance united between the sixth and eighth centuries to create a powerful new kind of medieval kingdom.

Creating the European Peasantry

Three fundamental changes transformed rural society during the early Middle Ages. First, Roman slavery virtually disappeared. Second, the household emerged as the primary unit of social and economic organization. Third, Christianity spread throughout the rural world. Economics, not ethics, destroyed Roman slavery. In the kind of slavery that was typical of the Roman world, large gangs of slaves were housed in dormitories and directed in large-scale operations by overseers. This form of slavery demanded a highly organized form of estate management and could be quite costly, since slaves had to be fed and housed year-round. Since slaves did not always reproduce at a rate sufficient to replace themselves, the supply had to be replenished from elsewhere. However, as the empire ceased to expand, the supply of fresh captives dwindled. As cities shrank, many markets for agricultural produce disappeared, making market-oriented large-scale agriculture less profitable. Furthermore, the Germanic societies that settled in the West had no tradition of gang slavery.

As a result, from the sixth through the ninth centuries, owners abandoned the practice of keeping gangs of slaves in favor of the less complicated practice of establishing slave families on individual plots of land. The slaves and their descendants cultivated these plots, made annual payments to their owners, and also cultivated the undivided portions of the estate, the fruits of which went directly to the owner. Thus slaves became something akin to sharecroppers. Gradually, they began to intermarry with hereditary tenant farmers and others who, though nominally free, found themselves in an economic situation much like that of slaves. By the ninth century, the distinction between slaves who had acquired traditional rights to their farms, or **manses,** and free peasants who held and worked manses belonging to others was blurred. By the tenth and eleventh centuries, peasant farmers throughout much of Europe were subject to the private justice of their landlords, no matter whether their ancestors had been slave or free. Although not slaves in the classical sense, the peasantry had fused into a homogeneous unfree population.

Rural Households

The division of estates into separate peasant holdings contributed to the second fundamental transformation of European peasant society: the formation of the household. Neither the Roman tradition of slave agriculture nor the Germanic tradition of clan organization had encouraged the household as the basic unit of society. Now individual slaves and their spouses were placed on manses, which they and their children were expected to cultivate. The household had become the basic unit of Western economy.

The household was more than an economic unit, however. It was also the first level of government. The head of the household, whether slave or free, male or female—women, particularly widows, were often heads of households—exercised authority over its other members. This authority made the householder a link in the chain of the social order, which stretched from the peasant hovel to the royal court.

Peasant life centered on the house, the village, and the field. Peasant houses often consisted simply of two or three rooms in which dwelt both the human and animal members of the household. The rhythm of peasant life was tied to the agricultural cycle, which had changed little since antiquity. Although women and men worked together on the harvest, peasants normally divided labor into male and female tasks. Husbands and sons worked in the fields. Wives and daughters tended chickens, prepared the dark bread that was the staple of their diet, spun, and wove.

Peasant culture, like peasant society, experienced a fundamental transformation during the early Middle Ages: the peasantry became Christian. In antiquity, Christianity had been an urban phenomenon. The term for the rural population had been synonymous with "unbelievers." They were called pagans, that is, the inhabitants of the countryside, or *pagus*. The spread of Christianity throughout the rural world began in earnest in the sixth century, when bishops and monks began to replace the peasant's traditional agrarian cults with Christian feasts, rituals, and beliefs.

Christianity penetrated more deeply into rural society with the systematic establishment of parishes, or rural churches. By the ninth century, this parish system began to cover Europe. Bishops founded parish churches in the villages of large estates, and owners were obligated to set aside one-tenth of the produce of their estates for the maintenance of the parish church. The priests who staffed these churches came from the local peasantry and received a basic education in Latin and in Christian ritual from their predecessors and from their bishops. The continuing presence of priests in each village had a profound effect on the daily lives of Europe's peasants.

Creating the European Aristocracy

At the same time that a homogeneous peasantry was emerging from the blend of slaves and free farmers, a homogeneous aristocracy was evolving out of the mix of Germanic and Roman traditions. In Germanic society, the elite had owed its position to a combination of inherited status and wealth, perpetuated through military command. Families who produced great military commanders were thought to have a special war-luck granted by the gods. The war-luck bestowed on men and women of these families a near-sacred legitimacy. This legitimacy made the aristocrats largely independent of their kings. In times of war, kings might command, but otherwise, the extent to which they could be said to govern aristocrats was minimal.

The Roman aristocracy was also based on inheritance, but of land rather than leadership. During the third and fourth cen-

turies, Roman aristocrats' control of land extended over the people who worked that land. At the same time, great landowners were able to free themselves from provincial government. Like their Germanic counterparts, Roman aristocrats acquired a sacred legitimacy, but within the Christian tradition. They monopolized the office of bishop and became identified with the sacred and political traditions associated with the Church.

In Spain and Italy, the religious differences separating Arians and orthodox Christians impeded the fusion of the Germanic and Roman aristocracies. In Gaul, the conversion of Clovis and his people facilitated the rapid blending of the two worlds. North of the Loire River, where the bulk of the Franks had settled, Roman aristocrats soon became Franks. By the mid-sixth century, the descendants of Bishop Remigius of Reims, who had baptized Clovis, had Frankish names and considered themselves Franks. Still, the Roman aristocratic tradition of great landholders became an integral part of the identity of the Frankish elite.

In the late sixth century, this northern Frankish aristocracy found its own religious identity and legitimacy in the Irish monasticism introduced by Saint Columbanus (543–615) and other wandering monks. At home in Ireland, these monks had been accustomed to working not with kings but with leaders of clans. In Gaul, they worked closely with the Frankish aristocrats, who encouraged them to build monasteries on their estates. Eventually, these monasteries amassed huge landholdings and became major economic and political centers headed by aristocrats who abandoned secular life for the cloister.

South of the Loire River, conditions were decidedly different. Here, Irish monasticism was less important than episcopal office. The few Frankish and Gothic families who had settled in the south were rapidly absorbed into the Gallo-Roman aristocracy, which drew its prestige from control of local religious and secular power. Latin speech and Roman culture distinguished these "Romans," regardless of their ancestry.

Aristocratic Lifestyle

Aristocratic life was similar whether north or south of the Loire, in Anglo-Saxon England, Visigothic Spain, or Lombard Italy. Aristocratic family structures were loosely knit clans that traced descent from important ancestors through either the male or the female line. Clans jealously guarded their autonomy against rival clans and from royal authority.

Feasting and Fighting. The aristocratic lifestyle focused on feasting, hospitality, and the male activities of hunting and warfare. In southern Europe, great nobles lived in spacious villas, often surrounded by solid stone fortifications, an inheritance of Roman traditions. In the north, Frankish and Anglo-Saxon nobles lived in great wooden halls, richly decorated but lacking fortifications. During the fall and winter, aristocratic men spent much of their time hunting deer and wild boar in their forests. Hunting was not merely sport. Essentially, it was preparation for war, the activity of the summer months. In

FROM SLAVE TO QUEEN

Queen Balthild (d. ca. 680), an Anglo-Saxon woman captured and sold into slavery in Francia, became the wife of Clovis II, king of Neustria and Burgundy (639–657). Her career, including her regency for her son Clothar III and her eventual forced retirement to the monastery she had founded at Chelles, is typical of the complex role and reputation early medieval queens enjoyed. This laudatory account, which was probably written by a nun at Chelles, hints that Balthild had been forced into the convent by those opposed to her political role.

Focus Questions

What roles of a queen does this passage illustrate? What reforms did Balthild attempt to introduce in Frankish society?

Divine providence called her from across the seas. She, who came here as God's most precious and lofty pearl, was sold at a cheap price. Erchinoald, a Frankish magnate and most illustrious man, acquired her, and in his service the girl behaved most honorably. She gained such happy fame that, when the said lord Erchinoald's wife died, he hoped to unite himself to Balthild, that faultless virgin, in a matronal bed. But when she heard this, she fled and most swiftly took herself out of his sight. Thereafter it happened, with God's approval, that Balthild, the maid who escaped marriage with a lord, came to be espoused to Clovis, son of the former king Dagobert. Thus by virtue of her humility she was raised to a higher rank.

She acted as a mother to the princes, as a daughter to priests, and as a most pious nurse to children and adolescents. She distributed generous alms to everyone. She guarded the princes' honor by keeping their intimate counsels secret. In accordance with God's will, her husband King Clovis migrated from the body and left his sons with their mother. Immediately after him her son Clothar took up the kingdom of the Franks, maintaining peace in the realm. Then, to promote peace, by command of Lady Balthild with the advice of the other elders, the people of Austrasia accepted her son Childeric as their king and the Burgundians were united with the Franks. And we believe, under God's ordinance, that these three realms then held peace and concord among themselves because of Lady Balthild's great faith. She proclaimed that no payment could be exacted for receipt of a sacred rank. Moreover, she ordained that yet another evil custom should cease, namely that many people determined to kill their children rather than nurture them, for they feared to incur the public exactions which were heaped upon them by custom, which caused great damage to their affairs.

It was her holy intention to enter the monastery of religious women which she had built at Chelles. But the Franks delayed much for love of her and would not have permitted this to happen except that there was a commotion made by the wretched Bishop Sigobrand whose pride among the Franks earned him his mortal ruin. Indeed, they formed a plan to kill him against her will. Fearing that the lady would act heavily against them, and wish to avenge him, they suddenly relented and permitted her to enter the monastery.

From The Life of the Blessed Queen Balthild

March, as soon as the snows of winter had begun to melt and roads had become passable, aristocrats gathered their retainers, who had enjoyed their winter hospitality, and marched to war. The enemy varied. It might be rival families with whom feuds were nursed for generations. It might be raiding parties from a neighboring region. Or the warriors might join a royal expedition led by the king and directed against a rival kingdom. Whoever the enemy was, warfare brought the promise of booty and glory.

Women in Aristocratic Society. Within this aristocratic society, women played a wider and more active role than had been the case in either Roman or barbarian antiquity. In part, women's new role was due to the influence of Christianity, which recognized the distinct—though always inferior—rights of women, fought against the barbarian tradition of allowing chieftains numerous wives, and acknowledged women's right to lead a cloistered religious life. In addition, the combination of Germanic and Roman familial traditions permitted women to participate in court proceedings, to inherit and dispose of property, and, if widowed, to serve as tutors and guardians for their minor children. Finally, the long absence of men at the hunt, at the royal court, or on military expeditions left wives in charge of the domestic scene for months or years at a time. The religious life in particular opened to aristocratic women possibilities of autonomy and authority that had previously been unknown in the West. Saint Hilda of Whitby (614–680), an Anglo-Saxon princess, for example, established and ruled a religious community that included both women and men. It was in Hilda's community that the Synod of Whitby took place, and Hilda played an active role, advising the king and assembled bishops.

Governing Europe

The combination in the early Middle Ages of the extremes of centralized Roman power and fragmented barbarian organization produced a wide variety of governmental systems. At one end of the spectrum were the politically fragmented Celtic and Slavic societies. At the other end were the Frankish kingdoms, in which descendants of Clovis, drawing on the twin heritages of Roman institutions and Frankish tradition, attempted not simply to reign but to rule.

Kings and Aristocrats.   Rulers and aristocrats both needed and feared each other. Kings had emerged out of the Germanic aristocracy and could rule only in cooperation with aristocrats. Aristocrats were concerned primarily with maintaining and expanding their own spheres of control and independence. They perceived royal authority as a threat. Still, they needed kings. Strong kings brought victory against external foes and thus maintained the flow of booty to the aristocracy. Aristocrats in turn redistributed the spoils of war among their followers to preserve the bonds of warrior society. Thus, under capable kings, aristocrats were ready to cooperate, not as subjects but as partners.

As the successors of Germanic war leaders and late Roman generals, kings were primarily military commanders. During campaigns and at the annual **Marchfield,** when the free warriors assembled, the king was all-powerful. At those times he could cut down his enemies with impunity. At other times the king's role was strictly limited. His direct authority extended only over the members of his household and his personal warrior band.

Royal Justice.   The king's role in administering justice was similarly ambivalent. He was not the source of law, which was held to be simply the customs of the past, nor was he responsible for enforcing this customary law. Enforcement was the duty of individuals and families. Only if they wanted did they bring their grievances to the king or his agents for arbitration or judgment. However, even though they could not formally legislate, kings effectively molded law and legal procedure by collecting, selecting, clarifying, and publishing customary laws. Clovis presents a model for such legislative activity in the compilation of Salic law made during his reign. Visigothic and Anglo-Saxon kings of the seventh through tenth centuries did the same.

As heirs of Roman governmental tradition, kings sought to incorporate these traditions into their roles. By absorbing the remains of local administration and taxation, kings acquired nascent governmental systems. Through the use of written documents, Roman scribes expanded royal authority beyond the king's household and personal following. Tax collectors continued to fill royal coffers with duties collected in markets and ports.

Finally, by assuming the role of protector of the Church, kings acquired the support of educated and experienced ecclesiastical advisers and the right to intervene in disputes involving clergy and laity. Further, as defenders of the Church, kings could claim a responsibility for the preservation of peace and the administration of justice—two fundamental Christian (but also Roman) tasks.

Royal Administration.   Early medieval kings had no fixed capitals from which they governed. Instead, they were constantly on the move, supervising their kingdoms and consuming the produce of their estates. Since kings could not be everywhere at once, they were represented locally by aristocrats who enjoyed royal favor. In the Frankish world these favorites were called *counts,* and their districts were called *counties.* In England, royal representatives were termed *ealdormen,* and their regions were known as *shires.* Whether counts or ealdormen, these representatives were military commanders and judicial officers drawn from aristocratic families close to the king. Under competent and effective kings, partnership with these aristocratic families worked well. Under less competent rulers and during the reigns of minors, these families often managed to turn their districts into hereditary, almost autonomous regions. The sphere of royal authority thus shrank or expanded in large measure in response to the individual qualities of the king.

THE CAROLINGIAN ACHIEVEMENT

The Merovingian dynasty initiated by Clovis presided over the synthesis of Roman and Germanic society. It was left to the Carolingians who followed to forge a new Europe. In the seventh century, members of the new aristocracy were able to take advantage of royal minorities and dynastic rivalries to make themselves into virtual rulers of their small territories. By the end of the century, the kings had become little more than symbolic figures in the Frankish kingdoms. The real power was held by regional strongmen called *dukes.* The most successful of these aristocratic factions was that led by Charles Martel (ca. 688–741) and his heirs, known as the Carolingians.

Charles Martel.   This family had risen to prominence in the seventh century by controlling the office of mayor of the palace in Austrasia, the highest court official who advised the king as spokesman for the aristocracy. The Carolingians increased their influence by marrying their sons to daughters of other aristocratic families. In the late seventh century, they extended their control to include Neustria and Burgundy as well as Austrasia. By the second quarter of the eighth century, Charles Martel, while not king, was the acknowledged ruler of the Frankish kingdom.

Charles Martel was ruthless, ambitious, and successful. He crushed rivals in his own family, subdued competing dukes, and united the Frankish realm. He was successful in part because he molded the Frankish cavalry into the most effective military force of the time. His mounted, heavily armored warriors were extremely effective but very costly. He financed them with property confiscated from his enemies. In return for oaths of absolute fidelity, he gave his followers, or **vassals,** estates, which they held as long as they served him faithfully. With this new army he practiced a scorched-earth policy against his opponents that left vast areas of Provence and Aquitaine desolate for decades.

Charles Martel looked beyond military power to the control of religious and cultural institutions. He supported Anglo-Saxon missionaries such as Boniface (ca. 680–755), who were trying to introduce on the Continent the Roman form of Christianity they knew in England. This hierarchical style of Christianity served Carolingian interests in centralization, especially since Charles appointed his loyal supporters as bishops and abbots. Missionaries and Frankish armies worked hand in hand to consolidate Carolingian rule.

The ecclesiastical policy that proved most crucial to later Carolingians was Charles's support of the Roman papacy. Charles caught the attention of Pope Gregory III (731–741) in 732, after a battle near Tours in which Charles defeated a Muslim force that was attempting to continue the northward expansion of Islam. A few years later, when the pope needed protection from the Lombards to maintain his central Italian territories, he sought and obtained help from the Frankish leader.

Pippin III.   The alliance with the papacy solidified during the lifetime of Charles's son Pippin (ca. 714–768). Pippin inherited his father's power, but since he was not of the royal Merovingian family, he had no right to the title of king. No Frankish tradition provided a precedent by which a rival family might displace the Merovingians. Pippin turned instead to the pope, seeking legitimacy in religious authority. In a carefully orchestrated exchange between Pippin and Pope Zacharias (741–752), the latter declared that the individual who exercised the power of king ought also to have the title. Following this declaration the last Merovingian was deposed, and in 751 a representative of the pope anointed Pippin king of the Franks.

The alliance between the new dynasty and the papacy marked the first union of royal legitimacy and ecclesiastical sanction in European history. Frankish, Gothic, and Anglo-Saxon kings had been selected on secular criteria. Kings combined royal descent with military power. Now the office of king required the active participation of the Church. The new Frankish kingship led Europe into the first political, social, and cultural restructuring of the West since the end of the Roman Empire.

Charlemagne and the Renewal of the West

Pippin's son Charlemagne was the heir of the political, religious, and social revolutions begun by his grandfather and father. Charlemagne was a large man, over six feet tall, with piercing eyes, a robust physique, and a restless spirit. To his in-

■ This bronze equestrian statue of a king dates from the ninth century. The rider wears the typical Frankish attire of hose, tunic, and long riding cloak. The subject is often identified as Charlemagne or his grandson Charles the Bold.

timates, he was a generous lord constantly surrounded by friends. To his enemies, he was the man of iron—the grim and invincible warrior clad head to foot in steel, sweeping all before him. He was a conqueror, but he was also a religious reformer, a state builder, and a patron of the arts. As the leader of a powerful, united Frankish kingdom for over 40 years, Charlemagne changed the West more profoundly than anyone since Augustus.

Almost every spring, Charlemagne assembled his Frankish armies and led them against internal or external enemies. He subdued the Aquitainians and Bavarians, conquered the kingdom of the Lombards and assumed the title of king of the Lombards, crushed the Saxons, annexed the Spanish region of Catalonia, and destroyed the vast Pannonian kingdom of the Avars. In wars of aggression his armies were invincible. Not only were they better armed and mounted, but their ability to transport men and matériel great distances was unmatched.

MAP DISCOVERY

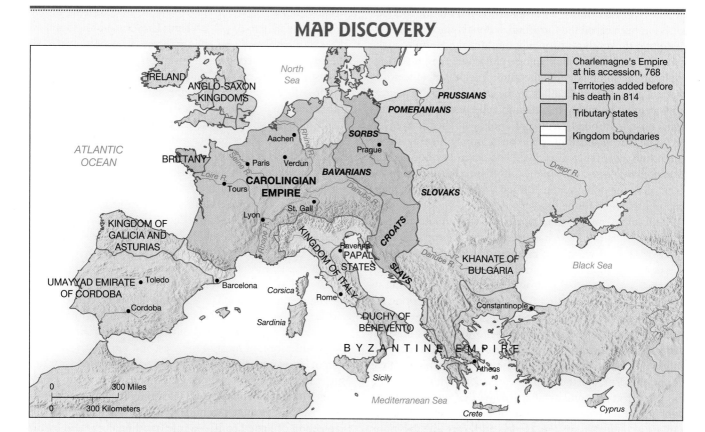

Charlemagne's Empire, 814

Compare the empire of Charlemagne with that of Hadrian (p. 103). How similar are they? How does Charlemagne's Frankish Empire compare geographically with the Byzantine Empire in 814 (p. 132)? What new Barbarian peoples now appear on the peripheries of the empire?

War booty fueled Charlemagne's renewal of European culture. As a Christian king, he considered it his duty to reform the spiritual life of his kingdom and to bring it into line with his concept of the divinely willed order. To achieve this goal, he needed a dedicated and educated clergy. Most of the native clergy were poorly educated and indifferent in their observance of the rules of religious life. Charlemagne set about creating a reformed, educated clergy.

The Carolingian Renaissance

Charlemagne recruited leading intellectuals from England, Spain, Ireland, and Italy to the royal court to lead a thorough educational program. The architect of his cultural reform, Alcuin of York (ca. 732–804), directed a school for young lay and ecclesiastical aristocrats in the king's palace and encouraged the king to finance a wide variety of educational programs. Charlemagne supported schools in great monasteries such as Fulda and St. Gall for the training of young clerics and laymen. These schools needed books. Charlemagne's educa-

tional reformers scoured Italy for fading copies of works by Virgil, Horace, and Tacitus with the same determination that his builders hunted antique marbles and columns for his chapel. Alcuin and others corrected and copied classical texts that had been corrupted by generations of haphazard transmission. The earliest extant manuscripts of virtually all classics of Roman antiquity date from the late eighth or early ninth century. Caroline **minuscule,** the new style of handwriting that was developed to preserve these texts, was so clear and readable that during the Renaissance, humanists adopted it as their standard script.

Ironically, Charlemagne, who fostered this blossoming of learning and who himself studied a number of subjects under the guidance of Alcuin, never mastered the art of writing. He could read, but according to Einhard, a contemporary biographer of Charlemagne, the emperor "used to keep writing-tablets and notebooks under the pillows on his bed, so that he could try his hand at forming letters during his leisure moments; but, although he tried very hard, he had begun too late in life and he made little progress."

The reformers of this era laid the necessary foundation for what has been called the **Carolingian Renaissance.** Their successors in the ninth century built on this foundation to make creative contributions in theology, philosophy, and historiography and to some extent in literature. The pursuit of learning was not a purely clerical affair. In the later ninth century, great aristocrats were highly literate and collected their own personal libraries. Count Everard of Friuli, who died in 866, left an estate that included over 50 books, among them works by Augustine, histories, saints' lives, and seven law books. Elite women participated fully in the Carolingian Renaissance. One example is the noblewoman Dhuoda, who composed a manual of instruction for her son.

Educational reform went hand in hand with reform of ecclesiastical institutions. Charlemagne and his son Louis the Pious (814–840) worked to establish the Benedictine rule as the norm for monastic life and to reform the parish clergy. The goal was a purified and organized clergy performing its essential role of celebrating Christian ritual and praying for the Frankish king. At the same time, the monasteries were to provide competent clerics to serve the royal administration at every level. These reforms were expensive. The fiscal reorganization of ecclesiastical institutions was as far-reaching as their cultural reform. For the first time, Frankish synods or councils made *tithing* mandatory, specifying that one-tenth of all agricultural harvests was to go to the maintenance of church buildings, support of the clergy, and care of the poor. Monasteries flourished.

Carolingian Government

Charlemagne recognized that conquest alone could not unify his enormous kingdom with its vast differences in languages, laws, customs, and peoples. The glue that held it together was loyalty to him and to the Roman Church. He appointed as counts throughout Europe members of the great Frankish families who had been loyal to his family for generations. Thus he created what might be termed an "imperial aristocracy" that was truly international in scope. In addition to supervising the royal estates in their counties, each spring these counts led the local military contingent, which included all the free men of the county. Counts also presided over local courts, which exercised jurisdiction over the free persons of the county. The king maintained his control over the counts by sending teams of emissaries, or **missi dominici,** composed of bishops and counts to examine the state of each county.

Charlemagne recognized that while his representatives might be drawn from Frankish families, he could not impose Frankish legal and cultural traditions on all his subjects. The only universal system that might unify the kingdom was Roman Christianity. Unity of religious practices, directed by the reformed and educated clergy, would provide spiritual unity. Furthermore, since the clergy could also participate in the administration of the kingdom, they could guarantee administrative unity as well. Carolingian monarchs did not intend the enriched and reformed Church to be independent of

royal authority; it was rather to be an integral part of the Carolingian system of government. However, at least some of the educated clerics and lay aristocrats who participated in the system formed a clear political ideology based on Augustinian concepts of Christian government. They attempted to educate Charlemagne and his successors to the duties of a king: maintaining peace and providing justice.

Carolingian government was no modern bureaucracy or state system. It was a mobile palace that included the royal household and ecclesiastical and secular aristocrats. The laymen and clerics who served the king were tied to him by personal oaths of loyalty rather than by any sense of dedication to a state or nation. Still, the attempts at governmental organization were far more sophisticated than anything that the West had seen for four centuries or would see again for another four. The system of counts and missi provided the most effective system of government before the thirteenth century and served as the model for subsequent medieval rulers.

The size of Charlemagne's empire approached that of the old Roman Empire in the West. Only Britain, southern Italy, and parts of Spain remained outside Frankish control. With the reunification of most of the West and the creative adaptation of Roman traditions of culture and government, it is not surprising that Charlemagne's advisers began to compare his empire to that of Constantine. This comparison was accentuated by Charlemagne's conquest of Lombard Italy and his protection of Pope Leo III—a role traditionally played by the Byzantine emperors. By the end of the eighth century, the throne in Constantinople was held by a woman. Irene (752–802) was powerful and capable, but Western male leaders considered her unfit by reason of her sex for such an office. All these factors finally converged in one of the most momentous events in Western political history: Charlemagne's imperial coronation on Christmas Day in the year 800.

Historians debate the precise meaning of this event, particularly since Charlemagne was said to have remarked afterward that he would never have entered St. Peter's Basilica in Rome had he known what was going to happen. Presumably, he meant that he wanted to be proclaimed emperor by his Frankish people rather than by the pope, since this is how he had his son Louis the Pious acclaimed emperor in 813. Nevertheless, the imperial coronation of 800 subsequently took on great significance. Louis attempted to make his imperial title the sole basis for his rule, and for the next thousand years, Germanic kings traveled to Rome to receive the imperial diadem and title from the pope. In so doing, they inadvertently strengthened papal claims to enthrone—and at times to dethrone—emperors.

Carolingian Art

The same creative adaptation of the classical heritage that gave birth to a new Western empire produced a new Western art. The artistic traditions of the barbarian world consisted almost entirely of the decoration of small, portable objects such as weapons, jewelry, and, after conversion, manuscripts.

Barbarian art was essentially nonrepresentational and consisted primarily of elaborate interlaced geometric forms of great sophistication.

For Charlemagne and his reformers, such abstract art was doubly inappropriate. Not only was it too distant from the Roman heritage that they were trying to emulate, but it could not be used for instruction or propaganda. Therefore, Charlemagne invited Italian and Byzantine artists and artisans to his kingdom to teach a form of representational art that would decorate as well as educate. However, these southern traditions were no more slavishly followed by northern artists than were Roman political traditions wholly taken over by Charlemagne's government. The synthesis of Mediterranean and northern artistic traditions produced a dynamic plastic style of representation in which figures seem intensely alive and active. These figures, which appear in manuscript illuminations, ivories, and bas-reliefs, are often arranged in narrative cycles that engage the mind as well as the eye.

GEOGRAPHICAL TOUR
Europe in the Ninth Century

The Carolingian Empire stretched from the Baltic Sea to the Adriatic and linked, through a network of commerce and exchange, the Germanic and Slavic worlds of the north, the Islamic world of Spain and the Near East, and the Mediterranean world of Byzantium (see **Map A**). Carolingian kings rebuilt roads, bridges, and ports to facilitate trade. Charlemagne also reformed Western currency, abandoning gold coinage in favor of the more easily obtainable silver.

Silver was the medium of exchange at the northern ports of Durstede near the mouth of the Rhine and Quentovic near modern Etaples, where Frankish merchants haggled with Anglo-Saxon and Danish traders over cloth, furs, and amber from the Baltic. Merchants along the Slavic frontier and down the Danube dealt primarily in human commodities. Great

■ **Map A. Europe in the Ninth Century.** In the course of the ninth century, individual kingdoms developed across Europe.

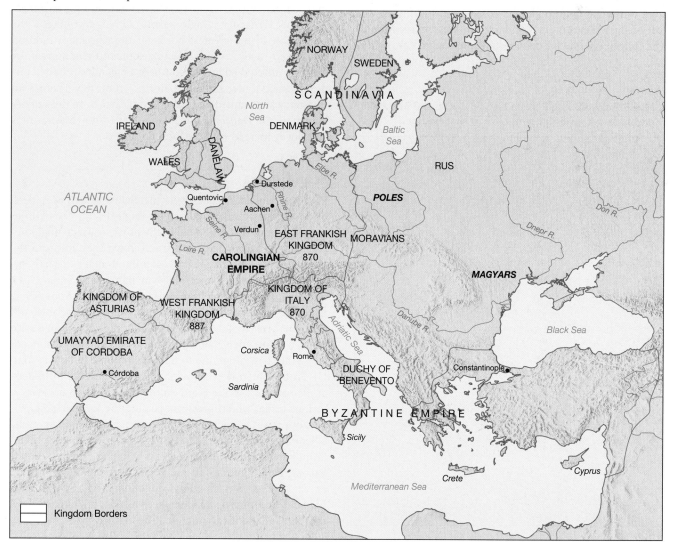

slave trains passed from these regions into the Rhine region. In Verdun, young boys were castrated at "eunuch factories" before being sent down the Rhone River to the cities of lower Provence, where they were sold to Muslim agents from Spain and North Africa. Jewish and Greek merchants supplied the Frankish church and aristocracy with luxury goods from Constantinople and the East. The travels of such a merchant in the early ninth century might begin with a short trip from Quentovic to the English coast and then continue clockwise around the Frankish world (see **Map A**).

England

A continental visitor in England (see **Map B**) would be well treated. In 796, Charlemagne had written to King Offa of Mercia (757–796), offering English merchants protection in his kingdom. Offa, the only king whom Charlemagne referred to as "brother," ruled a prosperous southeast England. Charlemagne's letter indicates that Mercia's prosperity owed much to trading, in which Anglo-Saxon woolens and silver were exchanged for wine, oil, and other products of the Continent.

Mercian supremacy did not long survive Offa. In the constant warfare among Anglo-Saxon kingdoms during the first half of the ninth century, Mercia fell to Wessex (see **Map B**). The cycle of rise and fall of little kingdoms might have contin-

■ **Map B. England.** Anglo-Saxon England was divided into a shifting number of small kingdoms ruled by rival dynasties.

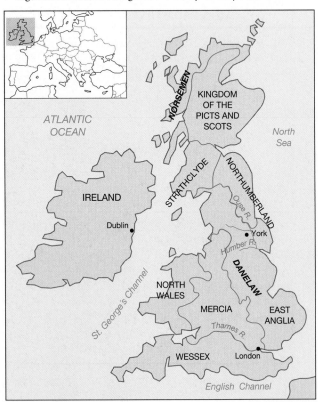

ued had the Vikings not come onto the scene. These Scandinavian raiders had been harassing the coast since 786. However, they did not pose a serious threat to England until 865, when a great Viking army interested not in raiding but in conquest landed north of the Humber River. All but one of the Anglo-Saxon kingdoms were destroyed.

The surviving king, Alfred of Wessex (870–899), reorganized his army, established a network of fortifications, created a navy, and thus temporarily halted the Viking conquest. Still, he realized that his military achievement could be consolidated only by the transformation of his political base. Few of Alfred's contemporaries saw him as the savior of England. He had first to win the loyalty of people in his own kingdom and then attract that of Anglo-Saxons outside it.

Alfred won support by reforming the legal and cultural foundations of his kingdom. His legal reforms aimed to reassure subjects of the various Anglo-Saxon kingdoms of equal treatment. At the same time, they emphasized the importance of oaths of loyalty and the gravity of treason. Finally, Alfred inaugurated a religious and cultural program to extend literacy and learning so that his people might better understand and follow God's word. Because, by this time, Latin was almost entirely unknown in England, Alfred and his reformers used the vernacular Anglo-Saxon. Alfred encouraged the translation of the greatest books of the Christian tradition into Anglo-Saxon, even translating some of them himself. By the time Alfred died in 899, southern England was united under Wessex leadership. The north, from the Thames to Chester, was occupied and colonized by Danes. In this region, known as the *Danelaw*, the Vikings settled down as farmers and slowly merged with the local population.

Scandinavia

Scandinavians in England were merchants as well as raiders. They sold furs, amber, and fish for English silver and cloth. A merchant who was interested in the northern trade might depart England from York and travel down the Ouse and the Humber to the North Sea (see **Map B**). To make this passage, he might sail with a Scandinavian merchant Viking in his longboat, that supreme expression of Viking culture. These magnificent ships, over 70 feet long, were fast, flexible, and easily maneuverable. A merchant's journey would begin with passage across the Channel, followed by a two-day sail north along the coast of Jutland to the mouth of the Eider (see **Map C**). From here, travelers could cross the peninsula to Hedeby at the head of the Slie Fjord on the Baltic. After a few days, a serious trader would press on, passing the Swedish archipelago, out past Oland and Gotland, through the narrow straits where Stockholm now stands, to Birka, the greatest port of Scandinavia. Here, Danes, Swedes, Franks, Frisians, Anglo-Saxons, Balts, Greeks, and Arabs met to trade furs, ivory, and amber for weapons, fine English cloth, silver, and gold. Like England, Scandinavia had long been an area of Frankish commercial and political interest. The Saxons had previously

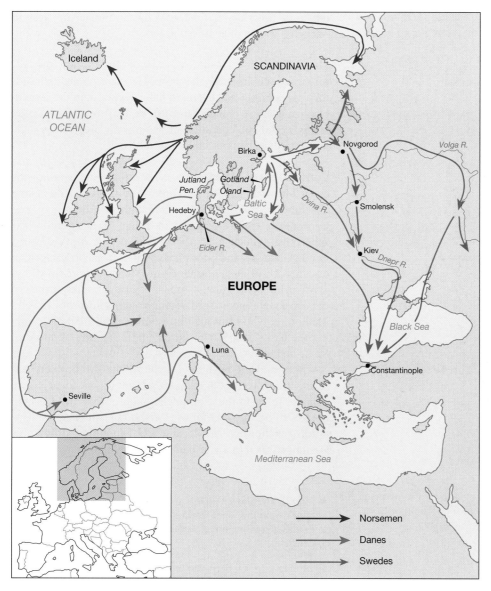

women could claim the right to divorce whenever they wished. In the ninth century, however, internal developments began to threaten the traditional independence of men and women alike, contributing to the Scandinavian expansion into the rest of Europe.

Royal Consolidation. Scandinavian kings were traditionally selected by groups of earls and exercised a position more as first among equals than as ruler. However, around the end of the eighth century, Scandinavian kings began to consolidate power at home and to look to the wealthy Anglo-Saxon and Frankish worlds as sources of booty and glory. Earls and royal pretenders, threatened or displaced by the kings, also began to go *viking*—that is, raiding—to replace abroad what they had lost at home.

Vikings. The directions in which Northmen went viking depended on the region of Scandinavia from which they came. Swedes looked eastward, trading with the Slavic world and Byzantium. Norwegians looked to Ireland and Scotland and later to Greenland, Iceland, and North America. The Danes tended to focus on England and the Frankish empire (see **Map C**).

Swedish merchant Vikings, known as the *Rus'*, traveled down

■ **Map C. Scandinavia.** Fleeing political consolidation at home, Scandinavian Vikings raided and settled into Russia and Ukraine, west to Iceland and the British Isles, down the Atlantic coast, and even into the Mediterranean.

formed a buffer between the Scandinavians and the Frankish world, but Charlemagne's conquests had brought the two societies into direct contact.

Norse Society. Scandinavian society resembled Germanic society of the first century. It was composed of three social classes. At the top were wealthy chiefs, or *jarlar* (earls), who had numerous servants, slaves, and free retainers. At the bottom were *thralls,* or bondsmen. In between were peasant freeholders, who formed the bulk of the population. Military ability and political cunning were equally prized in women and men. In this society, women enjoyed considerable freedom and authority that shocked observers from other cultures. An Arab merchant who visited Hedeby reported that

the Volga, Dvina, and Dnepr rivers as far as the Black and Caspian seas in search of furs and slaves (see **Map C**). There they met the trading routes of the Byzantine Empire and the caliphate of Baghdad. Rus'-fortified trading settlements at Novgorod, Smolensk, and Kiev (see **Map C**) became the nuclei of a Slavic-Scandinavian political unit to which the Rus' eventually gave their name: Russia.

Norwegians began their viking in Europe's western islands in the late eighth century. Ireland, until then undisturbed by either Roman or Germanic invaders, was the first victim. Other Norwegians raided south along the coast of the Frankish kingdom, Spain, and even into the Mediterranean, where they made forays into Provence, North Africa, and Italy (see **Map C**). The political consolidation in Norway under north to Scandinavia, east to Constantinople, or west to Aachen—was an open question.

Slavic Origins.   The development of Slavic society and culture was quite similar to that of the Germans. In the sixth century, Slavic tribes had begun to filter westward. In the seventh century, a Frank named Samo (d. ca. 660) organized a brief but powerful confederation of Slavs in the area between the Sudeten Mountains and the eastern Alps.

Conversion of the Slavs.   In the following century, the Great Moravian Empire developed out of Slavic tribes along the March River (see **Map D**). Both the Byzantine and Carolingian empires sought to bring Moravia into their spheres of influence. In the middle of the ninth century, Frankish, Italian, and Greek missionaries began to compete to organize a Christian church in this Slavic empire. In 852, a Slavic prince, particularly suspicious of the Franks, turned to the Greeks. He encouraged the missionary efforts of Cyril and Methodius, who translated liturgical texts into Slavonic, laying the basis for a Slavic church, and began the tradition of Slavic literacy.

The promising beginning made by the two brothers was short lived, as the Franks feared an independent Slavic church. In 864, the Carolingian king Louis the German (843–876) conquered Moravia. Methodius, who had been appointed archbishop of Moravia and Pannonia by the pope, was imprisoned in a German monastery. The Frankish hege-

■ An example of the animal style common in the Celtic-Germanic art of the early Middle Ages, this wooden animal head is the terminal of a post from a seventh-century Viking ship.

■ **Map D. The Slavic World.**   In the ninth century, new kingdoms appeared in the Slavic world under the influence of Vikings, Franks, Byzantine missionaries, Magyar raiders, and local chieftains.

Harold Finehair (860–933), which culminated in 872, led more Norwegians to go viking. Earls who objected to Harold's consolidation went abroad to maintain their freedom. Some settled in the Faroe Islands; others colonized Iceland.

The southernmost Scandinavians, the Danes, were most intimately familiar with the Frankish and Anglo-Saxon realms. Some of these Vikings, led by Danish kings, colonized whole areas such as Northumbria and the region at the mouth of the Seine. It was this latter region that later became Normandy—land of the Northmen.

The Slavic World

A merchant in Scandinavia might join an expedition of Swedish Rus' to cross the Baltic Sea and enter the Slavic world (see **Map D**) in search of ermine and slaves. The Carolingians' effects were felt, both in merchant activity and in the presence of imperialist armies and missionaries. The Slavic world of the ninth century was a rapidly changing amalgam of Germanic and Slavic peoples whose ultimate orientation—

mony lasted only a few decades. In 895, a new steppe people, the Magyars, or Hungarians, swept into Pannonia as had the Huns and Avars before them. These new invaders destroyed the Franks' puppet Moravian empire and split the Slavic world in two: the northern and southern Slavs. The Magyar kingdom (see **Map D**) proved to be a greater threat to the Franks than did the Slavs or Avars. Not only did the Magyars conquer Pannonia as far as the Enns River, but for 50 years they raided deep into the Carolingian empire.

Muslim Spain

The Slavic world was not only in contact with the Christian societies of Byzantium and the West. Muslim merchants used Arab gold to buy furs and slaves from Rus' traders at settlements along the Dnepr. A Spanish merchant might depart from Kiev and, to avoid the Magyars, travel down the Dnepr to the Black Sea, past Constantinople, and then across the length of the Mediterranean to Al-Andalus, as the Muslims called Spain (see **Map E**).

After the disintegration of the Umayyad caliphate (see Chapter 7, pp. 143–144), the last Umayyad, 'Abd ar-Rahman I (731–788), made his way to Spain, where in 756 he established an independent emirate. Under the centralized control of the Umayyad emirs, the economic and cultural life of urban Spain, which had stagnated under the Visigoths, experienced a renaissance as vital as that taking place across the Pyrenees in the Frankish empire.

The Umayyad Emirate.   To secure the emirate, 'Abd ar-Rahman and his successors had to overcome internal division and external aggression. The Spanish population included an elite minority of Arabs, recently arrived Syrians, North

African Berbers, converted Spaniards, Christian Spaniards, and Jews. In addition, Frankish aggression and Scandinavian Vikings continually harassed Al-Andalus.

In the short run, 'Abd ar-Rahman secured control by brute force. Relying on a professional army composed mainly of slaves, the emirs crushed revolts mounted by various Muslim factions. They strengthened a series of semiautonomous districts, or marches, commanded by military governors as buffers against the Frankish kingdom to the north. Finally, they established a line of guard posts along the coast to protect themselves against the Northmen. In the long run, the emirs sought stability in religion and law. They presented themselves as the champions and defenders of Islam and cultivated the study and application of Islamic law as a source of justice and social order.

The economic prosperity of Al-Andalus was based on an enlightened system of agriculture, which included the introduction of oranges, rice, sugarcane, and cotton from the eastern Mediterranean. Complementing agriculture was a renewed urban life bolstered by vigorous trade to the north, east, and south. In the ninth and tenth centuries, Spain was the most prosperous region of Europe and one of the wealthiest areas of the Muslim world.

In this climate of security and prosperity developed the most sophisticated and refined culture in the West. Arabic poetry and art developed in a manner exactly the opposite of that in the Carolingian world. Poetry, visual art, and architecture deemphasized physical forms and encouraged abstraction and meditation. Such abstract contemplative art did not develop in Western Christendom for centuries.

AFTER THE CAROLINGIANS: FROM EMPIRE TO LORDSHIPS

Alien, dynamic, and potentially threatening neighbors surrounded the Carolingian kingdom. To the west was Anglo-Saxon England; to the east were the Slavic and Byzantine worlds. Scandinavia lay to the north, and Al-Andalus threatened to the south. In the later ninth and tenth centuries, the Frankish kingdom collapsed, owing in part to the actions of these neighbors but primarily to the kingdom's own internal weaknesses.

Charlemagne, despite his imperial title, had remained dependent on his traditional power base, the Frankish aristocracy. For them, learned concepts of imperial renovation meant little. They wanted wealth and power. Under Charlemagne, the empire's prosperity and relative internal peace had resulted largely from continued successful expansion at the expense of neighbors. Its economy had been based on plunder and the redistribution of war booty among the aristocracy and wealthy churches. As wars of conquest under Charlemagne gave place to defensive actions against Magyars, Vikings, and Saracens, the supply of wealth dried up.

■ **Map E. Spain.**   Under the Umayyad emirs, Spain prospered as a center of agriculture, trade, and mixed Islamic, Jewish, and Christian cultures.

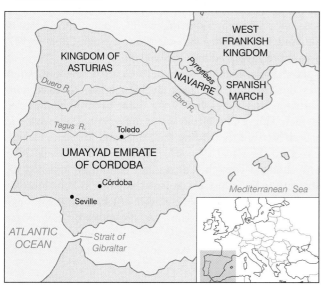

Aristocratic supporters were rewarded with estates within the empire and thus became enormously wealthy and powerful.

Disintegration of the Empire

Competition among Charlemagne's descendants as well as grants to the aristocracy weakened central authority. By fate rather than by design, Charlemagne had bequeathed a united empire to his son Louis the Pious (814–840). Charlemagne had intended to follow Frankish custom and divide his estate among all his sons, but only Louis survived him. Louis's three sons, in contrast, fought one another over their inheritance, and in 843 they divided the empire among them. The eldest son, Lothair (840–855), who inherited his father's imperial title, received an unwieldy middle portion that stretched from the Rhine south

MAP DISCOVERY

The Division of Charlemagne's Empire

Consider how Charlemagne's grandsons divided his empire. What major symbolic locations remained in the kingdom of Emperor Lothair? Do the kingdoms of Kings Charles and Louis appear more culturally and ethnically homogeneous than that of their brother? Into what states would their two kingdoms eventually develop?

through Italy. Louis the German (840–876) received the eastern portions of the empire. The youngest son, Charles the Bald (840–877), was allotted the western portions. In time, the western kingdom became France, and the eastern kingdom became the core of Germany. The middle kingdom, which included modern Holland, Belgium, Luxembourg, Lorraine (or Lotharingia, from "Lothair"), Switzerland, and northern Italy, remained a disputed region into the twentieth century.

The disintegration of the empire meant much more than its division among Charlemagne's heirs. In no region were his successors able to provide the degree of peace and public control that he had established. The Frankish armies, designed for wars of aggression, were too clumsy and slow to deal with the lightning raids of Northmen, Magyars, and Saracens. The constant need to please aristocratic supporters made it impossible for kings to prevent aristocrats from absorbing free peasants and churches into their economic and political spheres. Increasingly, these magnates were able to transform the offices of count and bishop into inherited familial positions. They also determined who would reign in their kingdoms and sought kings who posed no threat to themselves.

Most aristocrats saw this greater autonomy as their just due. Only dukes, counts, and other local lords could organize resistance to internal and external foes at the local level. They needed both economic means and political authority to provide protection and maintain peace. These resources could be acquired only at the expense of royal power. Therefore, during the late ninth and tenth centuries, much of Europe found its equilibrium at the local level as public powers, judicial courts, and military authority became the private possession of wealthy families.

Emergence of France and Germany

Ultimately, new royal families emerged from among these local leaders. The family of the counts of Paris, for example, gained enormous prestige from the fact that they had led the successful defense of the city against the Vikings from 885 to 886. For a time they alternated with Carolingians as kings of the West Franks. After the ascension of Hugh Capet in 987, they entirely replaced the Carolingians.

In a similar manner, the eastern German kingdom, which was divided into five great duchies, began to elect non-Carolingians as kings. In 919, the dukes of this region elected as their king Duke Henry of Saxony (919–936), who had proven his abilities fighting the Danes and Magyars. Henry's son, Otto the Great (936–973), proved to be a strong ruler who subdued the other dukes and definitively crushed the Magyars. In 962, Otto was crowned emperor by Pope John XII (955–964), thus reviving the empire of Charlemagne, though only in its eastern half. However, the dukes of this eastern kingdom chafed constantly at the strong control the Ottonians attempted to exercise at their expense. Although the empire Otto reestablished endured until 1806, he and his successors never matched the political or cultural achievements of the Carolingians.

By the tenth century, the early medieval kingdoms, based on inherited Roman notions of universal states and barbarian traditions of charismatic military leadership, had all ended in failure. After the demise of the Carolingian empire, the West began to find stability at a more local but also more permanent level. However, the local nature of Western society did not mean that the Roman and Carolingian traditions were forgotten. Carolingian religious reform, classical learning, and political ideology were preserved in the following centuries.

Cluny

Church reform took on a new life in 909 with the foundation of the monastery of Cluny in eastern France. Cluniac monks, drawn from the lesser aristocracy, were God's shock troops, fighting evil with their prayers with the same vigor that their secular cousins fought the enemy with their swords. Cluny, inspired by the monastic program of Louis the Pious and granted immunity from secular interference, became the center of an extraordinary expansion of Benedictine monasticism throughout the West.

The revival of classical learning that was begun in Carolingian schools, although hampered by the new wave of invasions that began in the latter ninth century, continued in centers such as St. Gall, Auxerre, and Corvey. During the late ninth and tenth centuries, Western Christian civilization spread to the north and east. By the year 1000, Scandinavia, Poland, Bohemia, and even Hungary had become Christian kingdoms with national churches whose bishops were approved by the pope. Among the aristocracy, just as all restraints on this warrior elite seemed to have been thrown off, a gradual process of transformation of their material and mental world began. Encouraged by Cluniac monasticism and by episcopal exhortations, nobles began to consider limiting their violence against one another and placing it instead in the service of Christendom.

CONCLUSION

Although the Magyar, Viking, and Saracen raids contributed to the disintegration of the Carolingian empire, their role was secondary. The internal dynamics of the Frankish world and its unresolved social and political tensions were the essential causes of the collapse of the Carolingian synthesis.

In the long run, however, the Carolingian synthesis left a powerful and enduring legacy. At the start of the Middle Ages in the West, a variety of Germanic kingdoms experimented with a whole spectrum of ways to reconcile the twin elements of barbarian and Roman tradition. The Ostrogoths attempted to preserve the two as separate entities and soon vanished. The Visigoths sought unification through coercion and found themselves isolated and weakened. In England, Germanic invaders sought to replace Roman traditions entirely. Only the Franks found a lasting means of amalgamating Roman and Germanic societies.

The key elements of this synthesis were orthodox Christianity, Roman administration, and Frankish military kingship. Between 500 and 800, these three elements coalesced into a vital new civilization. Although the political structure created by Charlemagne did not survive his grandsons, the Frankish model proved enduring in every other respect. The cultural renaissance laid the foundation of all subsequent European intellectual activities. The alliance between the Church and monarchy provided the formula for European kings for almost a thousand years. The administrative system with its central and local components provided the model for later medieval government in England and on the Continent. The idea of the Carolingian Empire, the symbol of European unity, has never entirely disappeared from the West.

QUESTIONS FOR REVIEW

1. What social and political forces encouraged division within the various Gothic, Anglo-Saxon, and Frankish kingdoms?
2. How did the household and the parish provide new units for organizing European society?
3. How did the aristocracy evolve out of Germanic and Roman traditions, and how was the aristocracy both a support and a threat to the kingdoms of the early Middle Ages?
4. What were Charlemagne's achievements?
5. Why did Charlemagne's empire not outlive him for long?

KEY TERMS

Carolingian Renaissance, *p. 164*

manses, *p. 158*

Marchfield, *p. 161*

minuscule, *p. 163*

missi dominici, *p. 164*

synod, *p. 157*

vassals, *p. 162*

DISCOVERING WESTERN CIVILIZATION ONLINE

You can obtain more information about the West in the early Middle Ages at the websites listed below. See also the Companion Website that accompanies this text, www.ablongman.com/kishlansky, which contains an online study guide and additional resources.

General Websites

The Labyrinth: Resources for Medieval Studies
www.georgetown.edu/labyrinth/labyrinth-home.html
Labyrinth is the central website for all medieval studies.

The Making of the Barbarian Kingdoms

Anglo-Saxon History: A Select Bibliography
www.wmich.edu/medieval/research/rawl/keynesbib/home.htm
A comprehensive bibliographical site on Anglo-Saxon civilization created and maintained by Simon Keynes.

Medieval Art at the Metropolitan Museum
metmuseum.org/collections/view50.asp?dep=17
A look at some of the Metropolitan Museum's collection of medieval art, including migration-period jewelry.

Living in the New Europe

Wharram Percy: The Lost Medieval Village
loki.stockton.edu/~ken/wharram/wharram.htm
A site devoted to exploring a lost medieval village from Roman times to the High Middle Ages.

The Carolingian Achievement

Carolingian Writing Centers
ccat.sas.upenn.edu/jod/map.html
A site with links to centers of Carolingian renaissance culture.

After the Carolingians

Viking Archaeology
bubl.ac.uk/link/v/vikingarchaeology.htm
A site devoted to Viking society and archaeology.

Kingship
ishi.lib.berkeley.edu/history155/slides/kingship/index.html
Interactive explorations of ninth- through eleventh-century images of kings.

SUGGESTIONS FOR FURTHER READING

The Making of the Barbarian Kingdoms, 500–750

James Campbell, ed., *The Anglo-Saxons* (Oxford: Phaidon, 1982). A collection of essays on Anglo-Saxon England by an outstanding group of archaeologists and historians.

Roger Collins, *Early Medieval Europe: 300–1000* (Basingstoke: Macmillan Education, 1991). A brief survey of the barbarian kingdoms in late antiquity and the early Middle Ages, with an emphasis on political history.

Rosamond McKitterick, ed. *The Early Middle Ages: Europe 400–1000* (New York: Oxford University Press, 2001). A collective introduction to early medieval history.

Walter Pohl, ed., with Helmut Reimitz, *Strategies of Distinction: The Construction of Ethnic Communities, 300–800* (Leiden, The Netherlands: Brill, 1998). An important collection devoted to early medieval ethnicity.

Ian Wood, *The Merovingian Kingdoms 450–751* (London: Longman, 1994). Excellent survey of early Frankish history with an emphasis on government.

Living in the New Europe

Lisa M. Bitel, *Land of Women: Tales of Sex and Gender from Early Ireland* (Ithaca: Cornell University Press, 1998). An intelligent and well-written look at women in early medieval Ireland.

Lisa M. Bitel, *Women in Early Medieval Europe, 400–1100* (Cambridge: Cambridge University Press, 2002). A valuable survey of women in the early Middle Ages.

Julia Bolton Holloway, Constance S. Wright, and Joan Bechtold, *Equally in God's Image: Women in the Middle Ages* (New York: P. Lang, 1990). Studies on medieval women from the end of antiquity to the Renaissance.

The Carolingian Achievement

Paul Fouracre, *The Age of Charles Martel* (New York: Longman, 2000). An exploration of the Frankish world in the early eighth century.

Rosamond McKitterick, *The Frankish Kingdoms Under the Carolingians, 751–987* (New York: Longman, 1983). A very detailed study of Carolingian history with an emphasis on intellectual developments.

Rosamond McKitterick, ed., *The New Cambridge Medieval History, c. 700–c. 900, vol. II* (Cambridge: Cambridge University Press, 1995). An excellent collective history of all aspects of Europe in the eighth and ninth centuries.

Janet L. Nelson, *The Frankish World, 750–900* (London: Hambledon Press, 1996). An excellent and balanced survey.

Pierre Riche, *The Carolingians: A Family Who Forged Europe* (Philadelphia: University of Pennsylvania Press, 1993). A general summary of Carolingian history by a leading French scholar.

Geographical Tour: Europe in the Ninth Century

Paul M. Barford, *The Early Slavs: Culture and Society in Early Medieval Eastern Europe* (Ithaca, NY: Cornell University Press, 2001). An introduction to eastern Europe in the early Middle Ages.

Roger Collins, *Early Medieval Spain: Unity in Diversity, 400–1000* (New York: St. Martin's Press, 1983). A balanced survey of Visigothic and Islamic Spain.

F. Donald Logan, *The Vikings in History* (New York: HarperCollins, 1991). General introduction to the Vikings.

Peter Sawyer, *The Age of the Vikings* (New York: St. Martin's Press, 1971). A good introduction to Scandinavian history.

After the Carolingians: From Empire to Lordships

Georges Duby, *The Early Growth of the European Economy: Warriors and Peasants from the Seventh to the Twelfth Century* (Ithaca, NY: Cornell University Press, 1974). An imaginative survey of the economic and social forces forming in Europe in the early Middle Ages.

Heinrich Fichtenau, *Living in the Tenth Century: Studies in Mentalities and Social Orders* (Chicago: University of Chicago Press, 1990). A brilliant evocation of the quest for order on the Continent following the dissolution of the Carolingian Empire.

Timothy Reuter, *Germany in the Early Middle Ages, 800–1056* (New York: Longman, 1991). A readable, original survey of early German history by a British scholar thoroughly knowledgeable about current German scholarship.

For a list of additional titles related to this chapter's topics, please see www.ablongman.com/kishlansky.

Chapter 9

THE HIGH MIDDLE AGES, 900–1300

The Visual Record

FROM THE SYRIAN DESERT TO THE WELSH MARSHES

On 16 August 1909, T. E. Lawrence, a young Oxford archaeology student, celebrated his twenty-first birthday by visiting the great Syrian castle of Krak des Chevaliers, which he described as "the best preserved and most wholly admirable castle in the world." Seven centuries earlier, another young Englishman, Prince Edward, was also inspired by the Krak des Chevaliers. His experience in the Syrian desert led him on a path toward the subjugation of the Welsh.

Krak is the most impressive of a series of castles standing guard over the Homs Gap, the vital route connecting the Mediterranean and the inland cities of Syria. Long a strategic site, in the eleventh century the Emir of Aleppo turned it over to a garrison of Kurds who gave it its Arab name: Husn Al Akrad, or castle of the Kurds. After it was captured by crusaders and turned over to the military order of the Knights of St. John Hospitallers, it became Krak des Chevaliers (castle of the knights). By the time Edward I arrived in Syria during the Ninth Crusade in 1271, the Knights had learned from their Arab and Kurdish enemies, adopting their military architecture and developing Krak further into the most extensive and advanced defensive structure in the world. The fortifications built by the Kurds became the inner fortification or keep, while a second, much more impressive series of walls ninety feet thick and protected by seven towers were raised on the cliffs which themselves rose almost 2,000 feet above the pass.

■ Krak des Chevaliers.

174

■ Beaumaris Castle.

Access to the castle was possible by a single road and gate protected by a drawbridge. Within the castle were built extensive accommodations, a meeting hall, chapel, the palace of the Grand Master of the Knights, and vast storage rooms that could hold sufficient supplies for sieges lasting years. Edward's crusade accomplished little, but he took home with him the knowledge of the most advanced castle architecture in the world. A few short years after assuming the crown in 1274, Edward found the perfect use of his newly acquired knowledge in Wales.

Edward represented a new kind of European ruler: a methodical warrior and ruthless foe who based his power not simply on military might but on bureaucracy and planning. During his long reign he transformed the royal court into an efficient government, able to extend royal justice at the expense of nobles' private courts, to regulate and control his agents throughout his kingdom, and to derive vast incomes from his subjects.

Much of this income went to conquer and subdue Wales. By 1284, the conquest was complete but his control of the hostile territory tenuous. To secure the region, he employed the master mason James of St. George to construct a series of 17 castles modeled on those he had seen in Syria. Perhaps the supreme achievement of St. George was Beaumaris Castle, an entirely new fortification erected at a new town, aptly named Newborough, to which the entire rebellious population of nearby Llanfaes was forced to move. Beaumaris consists of a powerful inner ring of walls and towers surrounded by a second, lower concentric wall itself surrounded by a moat. Entrance was through a massively fortified central gate with a drawbridge and further fortifications. Even though it was never entirely finished, prior to the age of gunpowder, Beaumaris was as impenetrable as Krak des Chevaliers. It was the ultimate in successful military construction, so obviously impregnable that it never saw serious action. With his massive castles and his massive taxes to fund them, Edward had achieved a concentration of power not seen in Europe for almost half a millennium.

Looking Ahead

This chapter analyzes the world of Edward, the peasants whose fields and villages were ultimately the source of the aristocracy's wealth, the knights and ladies who made up the courts, and the religious reform movements that introduced new values to Europe. It also visits the emerging cities of western and central Europe to understand the rebirth of commerce and trade and with it the urban society and culture it made possible. Finally, it traces the development of medieval monarchies, the new political powers created by men such as Edward I. ➤

THE COUNTRYSIDE

Between the years 1000 and 1300, Europe's population almost doubled, from approximately 38 million to 74 million. Various reasons have been proposed for this growth: less warfare and raiding, the decline of slavery, gradually improving agricultural techniques and equipment, and possibly a slowly improving climate.

During the tenth century, the great forests that had covered most of Europe began to be cut back as population spread out from the islands of cultivation. From around 1100, in the north of Germany and in what is today Holland, enterprising peasants began to drain marshes, a slow process of creating new land that would continue into the 1900s. This progress was not everywhere linear. In England, for example, forests actually gained on plow-land after the Norman Conquest of 1066. By the mid twelfth century, however, the acrid smoke from slash-and-burn clearing of the forest could be smelled all across Europe.

The Peasantry: Serfs and Freemen

The peasants who engaged in the opening of this internal frontier were the descendants of the slaves, unfree farmers, and petty free persons of the early Middle Ages. In the east along the frontier of the Germanic empire, in the Slavic world, in Scandinavia, in southern Gaul, in northern Italy, and in the reconquered portions of Christian Spain, they were free persons who owned land, entered into contracts with magnates, and remained responsible for their own fates. Across much of northwestern Europe, in particular in France in the eleventh century, the various gradations in status disappeared, and the peasantry formed a homogeneous social category loosely described as **serfs.** Although they were not slaves in a legal sense, their degraded status, their limited or nonexistent access to public courts of law, and their enormous dependency on their lords left them in a situation similar to that of the Carolingian slaves settled on individual farmsteads in the ninth century. Each year, peasants paid their lords certain fixed portions of their meager harvests. In addition, they had to work a certain number of days on the **demesne,** or reserve of the lord, the produce of which went directly to him for his use or sale. Finally, they were required to make ritual payments symbolizing their subordination.

Most peasants led lives of constant insecurity. They were poorly housed, clothed, and fed; subject to the constant scrutiny of their lords; and defenseless against natural or human-made disasters. Their homes were typically small one- or two-room shacks constructed of mud and wood and shared with their most valuable domestic animals. These huts usually had no windows and, until the sixteenth century, no chimneys. Smoke from the open hearth escaped through a hole in the roof.

Peasants' houses were clustered in villages on manors or large estates. In some parts of Europe, this was the result of their lord's desire to keep a close eye on his labor supply.

Beginning in the tenth century in central Italy and elsewhere, lords forced peasants to abandon isolated farmsteads and traditional villages and to move into small, fortified settlements. In these new villages, peasants were obligated to have disputes settled in the lord's court, to grind their grain in the lord's mill, and to bake their bread in the lord's oven—all primary sources of revenue for the lord. The same sort of monopoly applied to the Church. Villagers had to contribute a tenth of their revenues to the Church and to make donations in order to receive the sacraments. In some villages, these payments may have actually gone to the Church, but usually they too went to the lord.

Each morning men went out to their fields, which surrounded the village. In some villages, each peasant householder held thin strips of widely scattered land, while pasturage and woodland were exploited in common. Such an open-field system allotted all peasant households a portion of all the different sorts of land. In other villages, each household tended a unified parcel of land. Such closed fields generally corresponded with greater divergences in wealth within the village and encouraged more independence.

Agricultural Innovation.   Agricultural technology gradually changed the ways that peasants worked their land and the amount of food they could produce. Instead of a light plowshare that simply cut a furrow, a heavier plow with a moldboard—a curved iron plate attached above the plowshare to lift and turn the soil, depositing it to one side of the furrow—spread across Europe. It increased production in the heavy-soil areas north of the Alps and in bottom lands. The moldboard plow with wheels was often pulled by several pairs of oxen, which made it too expensive for the ordinary farmer working alone. The new plow thus promoted cooperative organization of the work of plowing and reliance on the open-field system of land tenure.

With the introduction of new technology for plowing came new systems of crop rotation. Traditionally, farmers divided their land into two parts, one planted, the other plowed (usually twice) but allowed to remain fallow. Around the eighth century, some peasants began to introduce a **three-field system:** one-third of the land was planted in autumn with wheat or rye, one-third remained fallow, and one-third was planted in spring with barley, rye, or a leguminous crop such as beans or peas that added nutrients to the soil. As this innovation became standard after the year 1000, the result was a greatly increased yield, a minimal increase in labor, and an improved diet.

While the men worked the fields, women took charge of the domestic tasks. These included carding wool, spinning, weaving, caring for the family's vegetable garden, bearing and raising children, and brewing the thick, souplike beer that was a primary source of carbohydrates in the peasant diet. During harvest, women worked in the fields alongside the men.

Beer, black bread, beans, cabbage, onions, and cheese made up the typical peasant diet. Meat was a rarity and usually came from pigs. Only in northern Europe, where the shortage of winter fodder necessitated culling herds each winter, did peasants occasionally enjoy beef. Inadequate agricultural methods and inefficient storage systems left the peasantry in constant threat of famine.

Negotiating Freedom.   The expansion of arable land offered new hope and opportunities to peasants. Population growth, as rapid as it was between the tenth and twelfth centuries, did not keep up with the increasing demand for laborers in newly settled areas of Europe. Lords were often willing to make special arrangements with groups of peasants to encourage them to bring new land under cultivation. From the beginning of the twelfth century, peasant villages acquired from their lord the privilege to deal with him and his representatives collectively rather than individually. Villages purchased the right to control petty courts and to limit fines imposed by the lord's representative. Peasants acquired protection from arbitrary demands for labor and extraordinary taxes.

These good times did not last forever. Gradually, during the late twelfth and thirteenth centuries, the labor market stagnated. Europe's population—particularly in France, England, Italy, and western Germany—began to reach a saturation point. As a result, lay and ecclesiastical lords found that they could profit more by hiring cheap laborers than by demanding customary services and payments from their serfs. They also found that their serfs were willing to pay for increasing privileges.

Peasants could purchase the right to marry without the lord's consent, to move to neighboring manors or nearby towns, and to inherit. They acquired personal freedom from their lord's jurisdiction, transformed their servile payments into payments of rent for their manses, purchased their own land, and commuted their labor services into annual or even one-time payments. In other words, they began to purchase their freedom. This free peasantry benefited the emerging states of western Europe, since kings and towns could extend their legal and fiscal jurisdictions over these persons and their lands at the expense of the nobility. Governments thus encouraged the extension of freedom and protected peasants from their former masters. By the fourteenth century, serfs were a rarity in many parts of western Europe.

This is not to say that these freed serfs and their descendants necessarily gained prosperity. Freedom often meant freedom from the protection that lords had provided. It meant the freedom to fail and even to starve. Some free peasants were able to participate in the emerging world of cash-crop farming and to tie into a growing trend toward agricultural specialization. Others, by the fourteenth century, roamed the countryside trying to survive, occasionally becoming the source of political and social turmoil.

Even as western serfs were acquiring a fragile freedom, the free peasants in much of eastern Europe and Spain were losing it. In much of the Slavic world, through the eleventh century, peasants lived in large, roughly territorial communes of free families. Gradually, however, princes, churches, and aristocrats began to build great landed estates. By the thirteenth century—under the influences of western and Byzantine models and of the Mongols, who dominated much of the Slavic world from 1240—lords began to acquire political and economic control over the peasantry. In Hungary during the twelfth century, free peasants and unfree servants merged to form a stratum of serfs subordinated to the emerging landed aristocracy and the lesser nobility composed of free warriors. A similar process took place in parts of Spain. In all of these regions the decline of the free peasantry accompanied the decline of public authority to the benefit of independent nobles. The aristocracy rose on the backs of the peasantry.

The Aristocracy: Warriors and Heiresses

Beginning in the late tenth century, writers of legal documents began to use an old term in a novel manner to designate certain powerful free persons who belonged neither to the old aristocracy nor to the peasantry. The term was *miles,* which in classical Latin meant "soldier." As it was used in the Middle Ages, we would translate it as "knight." The knightly function gradually came to entail a certain status and lifestyle.

The center of the knightly lifestyle was northern France. From there the ideals of knighthood, or **chivalry,** spread out across Europe, influencing aristocrats as far east as Byzantium. The essence of this lifestyle was fighting. Through warfare this aristocracy had maintained or acquired its freedom, and through warfare it justified its privileges. The origins of this small elite (probably nowhere more than 2 percent of the population) were diverse. Many of its members were descended from the old aristocracy of the Carolingian age. They traced descent through the male line. Inheritance was usually limited to the eldest sons, and daughters were given a dowry but did not share in inheritance. Younger sons had to find service with some great lord or live in the household of their older brothers. Even the eldest sons who became heads of households could not dispose of family property without consulting their kinsmen.

Such noble families, proud of their independence and ancestry, maintained their position through complex kin networks, mutual defense pacts with other nobles, and control of castles, from which they could dominate the surrounding countryside. By the twelfth century, nobles lived safely behind the castle walls, often even independent of the local counts, dukes, and kings. This lesser nobility absorbed control of such traditionally public powers as justice, peace, and taxation.

Aristocratic Education.   For the sons of such nobles, preparation for a life of warfare began early, often in the entourage of a maternal uncle or a powerful lord. Boys learned to ride, to handle heavy swords and shields, to manage a lance on horseback, and to swing an ax with deadly accuracy. They also learned lessons about honor, pride, and family tradition. The feats of ancestors or heroes, celebrated in such works as the *Song of Roland* and the legends of King Arthur, were sung by traveling minstrels at the banqueting table and provided models of knightly action. The culmination of this education for English and French nobles came in a ceremony of knighting. An adolescent of age 16 to 18 received a sword from an older, experienced warrior. No longer a "boy," he now became a "youth," ready to enter the world of fighting for which he had trained.

A youth was a noble who had been knighted but who had not married or acquired land either through inheritance or as a reward from a lord for service and thus had not yet established his own "house." He led the life of a warrior, joining in promising military expeditions and amusing himself with tournaments—mock battles that often proved as deadly as the real thing—in which one could win an opponent's horses and armor as well as renown. Drinking, gambling, and lechery were other common activities. This was an extraordinarily

■ A knight receives a token from a lady in this image from a manuscript from ca. 1300 that contains the works of more than 100 German courtly love poets. The ideals of chivalry and courtly love glorified women in literature and song, but in real life the subordinate status of women reflected the values of a martial society.

dangerous lifestyle, and many youths did not survive to the next stage in a knight's life, that of acquiring land, wife, honor, and his own following of youths.

The period between childhood and maturity was as dangerous for noblewomen as for men. Marriage was the primary form of alliance between noble houses, and the production of children was essential to the continued prosperity of the family. Therefore, the daughters of the nobility were generally brought up for marriage and procreation. They were usually married at around age 16 and then were expected to produce as many children as possible. Given the primitive knowledge of obstetrics and hygiene, bearing children was even more dangerous than bearing a lance. Many noblewomen died in childbirth, often literally exhausted by frequent successive births. Although occasionally practiced, contraception was condemned both by the Church and by husbands eager for offspring.

In this martial society, the official political and economic status of women declined considerably. Because they were considered unable to participate in warfare, in northern Europe women were also frequently excluded from inheritance, estate management, courts, and public deliberations. This at least was the theory, although we know that many individual women continued to control property, manage estates, and testify in court.

Still, the most powerful women were widows who had borne sons and who could play a major part in raising them. Such women were not uncommon. If a noblewoman was able to bear children successfully, she stood an excellent chance of surviving her husband, who was probably at least 15 years her senior and whose military pursuits placed him in constant danger. Such women, experienced in management by years of directing the households of their husbands, well connected by kinship, and experienced in court intrigue from years of attending assemblies in the company of their husbands and sons, could often hold their own with their male counterparts. Their support and alliances were actively sought by aristocrats, kings, and churches.

Land and Loyalty. The noble lifestyle required wealth, and wealth meant land. The nobility was essentially a society of heirs who had inherited not only land but also the serfs who worked their manors. Lesser nobles acquired additional property from great nobles and from ecclesiastical institutions in return for binding contracts of mutual assistance. This tradition was at least as old as the Carolingians, who granted their followers land in return for military service. In later centuries, counts and lesser lords continued this tradition, exchanging land for support. Individual knights became **vassals** of lay or ecclesiastical magnates, swearing fealty or loyalty to the lord and promising to defend and aid him. In return, the lord swore to protect his vassal and granted him a means of support by which the vassal could maintain himself while serving his lord. Usually, this grant, termed a **fief,** was a parcel of productive land and the serfs and privileges attached to it, which the vassal and his heirs could hold as long as they provided the designated service to the lord.

Individual lords often had considerable numbers of vassals, who might also be the vassals of other lay and secular lords. The networks formed vital social and political structures. In some unusual situations—as in England immediately after the Norman Conquest and in the Latin Kingdom of Jerusalem, founded in 1099—these structures of lords and vassals constituted systems of hierarchical government. Elsewhere, individuals often held fiefs from, and owed service to, more than one lord, and not all of the individuals in a given county or duchy owed their primary obligation to the count or duke. Likewise, often most of a noble's land was owned outright rather than held in fief, thus making the feudal bond less central to his status. As a result, these bonds—anachronistically called **feudalism** by French lawyers of the sixteenth and seventeenth centuries—constituted just one more element of a social system tied together by kinship, regional alliances, personal bonds of fealty, and the surviving elements of Carolingian administration inherited by counts and dukes. In much of Europe the society of the eleventh and twelfth centuries was one of intensely local autonomous powers in which public order and political authority were spread as widely as ever in European history.

The Church: Saints and Monks

The religious needs of the peasantry remained those that their pre-Christian ancestors had known: fertility of land, animals, and women; protection from the ravages of climate and the warrior elite; and supernatural cures for the ailments and disabilities of their harsh life. The cultural values of the nobility retained the essentials of the Germanic warrior ethos, including family honor, battle, and display of status. The rural Church of the high Middle Ages met the needs of both, although it subtly changed them in the process.

Most medieval people, whether peasants or lords, lived in a world of face-to-face encounters, a world in which abstract creeds counted for little. In this world, religion meant primarily action, and the essential religious actions were the liturgical celebrations performed by the clergy. Although many of the parish priests had received only rudimentary instruction from their predecessors and had minimal knowledge of Latin and theology, such intellectual shortcomings were not important. Ordinary lay people just wanted priests who would not extort them by selling the sacraments, would not seduce their wives and daughters, and would remain in the village to perform the rituals necessary to keep the supernatural powers well disposed toward the community.

The most important of these supernatural powers was not some distant divinity but the saints—local, personal, even idiosyncratic persons. During their lives, saintly men and women had shown that they enjoyed God's special favor. After their deaths they continued to be the link between the divine and earthly spheres. Through their bodies, preserved as relics

in the monasteries of Europe, they continued to live among mortals even while participating in the heavenly court. Thus they could be approached and won over through offerings, bribes, oaths, and rituals of supplication and submission. Praying and fasting, petitioners pilgrimaged to a saint's tomb, normally found in a monastery, and kept vigil there, beseeching the saint for protection. Some saints attracted national or even international pilgrimages. As the recipients of gifts to the saints, monastic communities became wealthy and powerful.

Monastic Culture.   In addition to orchestrating the cult of saints, monasteries also took responsibility for the cult of the ordinary dead. In particular, monastic communities commemorated and prayed for members of noble families who, through donations of land, had become especially associated with the monastic community. Association with such monasteries through gifts and exchanges of property, and particularly through burial in the monastic cemetery, provided the surest means of continuing noble families' honor and prestige into the next world. Across Europe, noble families founded monasteries on their own lands or invited famous abbots to reorganize existing monasteries.

Supported by both peasants and nobles, Benedictine monasteries reached their height in the eleventh and twelfth centuries. Within their walls developed a religious culture, the essence of which was the passionate pursuit of God. The goal was not simply salvation but perfection, and this required discipline of the body through a life of voluntary chastity and poverty and discipline of the spirit through obedience and learning. The Benedictine's life moved to the rhythm of the divine office, the ancient series of eight hours each day when the monks put aside work, study, or rest and assembled in the monastic church for the communal chanting of prayers, psalms, and hymns.

Monasteries were communities that specialized in prayer and therein found their social justification. They were also enormously rich and powerful. The monastery of Cluny, in saving souls through prayer, became the first international organization of monastic centers, with abbeys and dependent communities, called priories, throughout Europe. The abbots of Cluny were among the most powerful and influential people of the eleventh and twelfth centuries, considered to be the equals of kings, popes, and emperors. To remain in form for the strenuous liturgical commemoration of living and dead patrons, Cluniac monks largely abandoned the tradition of manual work, leaving such mundane activities to their thousands of serfs and lay agents.

Monastic Reform.   The Cluniac monks' comparative luxury and concentration on liturgy to the neglect of other spiritual activities led some monastic reformers to call for a return to simplicity, separation from the rest of society, and a deeper internal spirituality. Chief among these groups were the Cistercians, who, under the dynamic leadership of Bernard of Clairvaux (1090–1153), spread their rigorous ascetic form of monasticism from England to the Vienna woods. The Cistercians built monasteries in the wilderness and discouraged the kinds of close ties with secular society that the Cluniacs had established. Paradoxically, by establishing themselves in remote areas, organizing their estates in an efficient manner, and gaining a great reputation for asceticism, the Cistercians also became enormously wealthy and successful leaders in the economic changes taking place in the twelfth and thirteenth centuries.

The rural Church not only served the lay population but worked to transform it. Although monks and bishops were spiritual warriors, most abhorred bloodshed among Christians and sought to limit the violence of aristocratic life. This attitude combined altruistic and selfish motives, since Church property was often the focus of aristocratic greed. The decline of public power and the rise of aristocratic autonomy and violence were particularly marked in southern France. There, beginning in the tenth century, churchmen organized the Peace of God and the Truce of God, movements that attempted to protect peasants, merchants, and clerics from aris-

tocratic violence and to limit the times when warfare was allowed. During the eleventh century, the goals of warfare were shifted from attacks against other Christians to the defense of Christian society. This redirection produced the **Crusades,** religious wars of conquest authorized by popes and directed against Europe's non-Christian neighbors.

Crusaders: Soldiers of God

The Crusades left a complex and troubling legacy in world civilization. Between 1096 and 1272, waves of zealous and adventuresome European Christians set out to do battle with the Muslims. Eight main crusades were launched, each lasting from one to four years, except the Seventh Crusade (1248–1254), which dragged on longer. The First Crusade originated in 1095, when Pope Urban II (1088–1099), hoping to direct noble violence away from Christendom, urged Western knights to use their arms to free the Holy Land from Muslim occupation. In return, he promised to absolve them from all of the punishment due for their sins in this life or the

MAP DISCOVERY

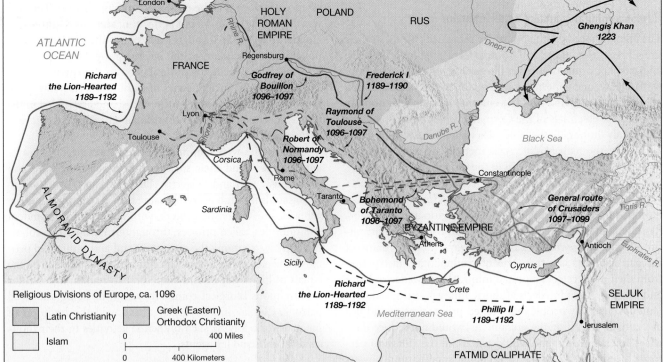

Religious Divisions of Europe, ca. 1096

- Latin Christianity
- Greek (Eastern) Orthodox Christianity
- Islam

0 — 400 Miles
0 — 400 Kilometers

The Crusades

Examine the religious divisions of Europe and the major crusade routes. What different geographical and political obstacles did crusaders face depending on whether they traveled by land or by water? How did the divisions of Christianity and Islam affect the course of the Crusades?

POPE URBAN II SUMMONS A CRUSADE

In 1095, Pope Urban II convened a Church council in Clermont, France. The primary focus of the council was to establish peace within the Christian community, but at the same time he launched his appeal for aid to the Byzantine Empire, thus launching what would be the First Crusade. We do not have his exact words, but this version of his sermon was preserved by Fulcher of Chartres, a cleric who participated in the crusade and who was present at the council.

Focus Questions

What effects does Urban hope the crusade will have within Christian society? What rewards does he promise those who participate?

Now that you, O sons of God, have consecrated yourselves to God to maintain peace among yourselves more vigorously and to uphold the laws of the Church faithfully, there is work to do. As most of you have been told, the Turks, a race of Persians, who have penetrated within the boundaries of the Byzantine Empire even to the Mediterranean to the Bosporus, in occupying more and more of the lands of the Christians, have overcome them, already victims of seven battles, and have killed and captured them, have overthrown churches, and have laid waste God's kingdom. Concerning this affair I, with suppliant prayer—not I, but the Lord—exhort you, heralds of Christ, to persuade all of whatever class, both knights and footmen, both rich and

poor, in numerous edicts, to strive to help expel that wicked race from our Christian lands before it is too late. I speak to those present, I send word to those not here, moreover, Christ commands it. Remission of sins will be granted for going thither, if they end a shackled life either on land or in crossing the sea, or in struggling against the heathen. I, being vested with that gift from God, grant this to those who go. Let those who are accustomed to wage private wars wastefully even against Believers, go forth against the Infidels in a battle worthy to be undertaken now and to be finished in victory. Now, let those, who until recently existed as plunderers, be soldiers of Christ; now let those who until recently existed as plunderers, against brothers and relations, rightly fight barbarians; now let those who recently were hired for a few pieces of silver, win their eternal reward.

Edward Peters, ed., *The First Crusade. The Chronicle of Fulcher of Chartres and Other Source Materials* (Philadelphia: University of Pennsylvania Press, 1971), pp. 30–31.

---

next. After terrible hardships, the crusaders succeeded in taking Jerusalem in 1099 and established a Latin Kingdom in Palestine. For over two centuries, bands of Western warriors went on armed pilgrimages to defend this precarious kingdom. The Second Crusade (1145–1149) ended in defeat and disaster at the hands of Seljuk Turks in Asia Minor. In 1187, the Muslim commander Saladin recaptured Jerusalem, causing Emperor Frederick Barbarossa and the kings of France and England, Philip II Augustus and Richard the Lion-Hearted, to embark on the Third Crusade (1187–1192). This crusade also failed, but Richard signed a peace treaty with Saladin. On his way home, the English king was captured and imprisoned in Austria until his mother, Eleanor, could raise the ransom to buy his freedom. Five subsequent crusades accomplished little.

The Idea of the Crusade

Although military failures, the Crusades appealed particularly to younger sons and knights who hoped to acquire in the East the status that constricting lineages denied them in the West. Other such holy wars were directed against the Muslims in Spain, the Slavs in eastern Europe, and even heretics and political opponents in France and Italy.

The Crusades were brutal and vicious, and the crusaders were often motivated as much by greed as by piety. Doubts about the spiritual significance of such wars contributed to their decline. So, too, did the rise of centralized monarchies, whose rulers usually viewed the Crusades as wasteful and futile. The age of the Crusades passed with the age of the independent warrior aristocracy.

In the eleventh and twelfth centuries, peasants, lords, and monks made up the great majority of Europe's population and lived together in mutual dependence, sharing involvement in the rhythm of the agrarian life. From the later part of the twelfth century, however, this rural world became increasingly aware of a different society: that of the growing cities and towns of Europe, whose citizens moved to the newer rhythms of commerce and manufacture.

MEDIEVAL TOWNS

To the traditional rural mind, towns seemed somehow immoral. Nobles disdained urban society for its lack of respect for aristocracy and its disinterest in their cult of violence. Still, as rude warriors were transformed into courtly nobles, these nobles were drawn to urban luxuries and became indebted to urban moneylenders to maintain their "gracious" lifestyles. For many peasants, towns were refuges from the hopelessness of their normal lives. "Town air makes one free," they believed, and many serfs fled the land to try their fortunes in the nearby towns.

Italian Cities

Urban life had never ceased in Italy, which had maintained its urban traditions and ties with the Mediterranean world since antiquity. Although urban populations had shrunk in late antiquity and they were dominated by their bishops, who exercised secular and ecclesiastical lordship, the towns of the Italian peninsula had continued to play commercial and political roles and to attract not only runaway serfs but even nobles, who maintained fortified towers within the town walls.

The coastal cities of Amalfi, Bari, Genoa, and especially Venice had continued to play important roles in commerce both with the Byzantines and with the new Muslim societies. For Venice, this role was facilitated by its official status as a part of the Byzantine Empire, which gave it access to Byzantine markets. With nothing of their own to trade but perhaps salt and, in Venice, glass, these cities acted as go-betweens for the transport of eastern spices, silks, and ivories, which they exchanged for Western iron, slaves, timber, grain, and oil. To protect their merchant ships, Italian coastal cities developed their own fleets, and by the eleventh century they were major military forces in the Mediterranean. Venice's fleet became the primary protector of the Byzantine Empire and was thereby able to win more favorable commercial rights than those enjoyed by Greek merchants.

Merchants and Capitalists.
As the merchants of the Italian towns penetrated the markets at the western end of the great overland spice routes connecting China, India, and central Asia with the Mediterranean, they established permanent merchant colonies in the East. When expedient, they did not hesitate to use military force to win concessions.

For the Italians, who had no scruples about trading with Muslims, the Crusades were primarily economic opportunities. Only the Italians had the ships and the expertise to transport the crusaders by sea, the only option that offered hope of success, and then to bring them supplies once they were in Palestine. Crusaders paid the Italian merchants handsomely for their assistance and also granted them economic and political rights in the Palestinian port cities such as Tyre and Acre. The culmination of this relationship between northern crusaders and Italians was the Fourth Crusade, which, short on funds, was sidetracked by the Venetians into capturing and sacking Constantinople, a blow from which the Byzantine Empire never recovered. Venice emerged as the undisputed Mediterranean power.

By the thirteenth century, Italian merchants had spread far beyond the Mediterranean. The great merchant banking houses of Venice, Florence, and Genoa had established offices around the Mediterranean and Black seas; south along the Atlantic coast of Morocco; east into Armenia and Persia; west to London, Bruges, and Ghent; and north to Scandinavia. Some individual merchants, the Venetian Marco Polo (1254–1324), for example, traded as far east as China and even entered the service of the Great Khan.

These international commercial operations required more sophisticated systems of commercial law and credit. Italian merchants responded by developing double-entry bookkeeping, limited-liability partnership, commercial insurance, and international letters of exchange. Complex commercial affairs also required a system of credit and interest-bearing loans, an idea that was abhorrent to traditional rural societies. Churchmen condemned borrowing and lending at credit, but bankers found ways of hiding interest payments in contracts, thus allowing lender and seller to participate in the growing world of credit-based transactions.

Underlying the expanding commercial developments was a basic change: a new mentality that considered commerce an honorable occupation. Since antiquity, aristocrats had considered only warfare and agriculture to be worthy pursuits. The strength of the Italian towns was that they were able to throw off the rural, aristocratic value system. The Italian passion for commerce spread from the seacoasts to the towns throughout Italy and from there to Marseille, Barcelona, and other cities in southern Europe. By the twelfth century, wealthy citizens, whether descended from successful merchants or from landed aristocrats, were indifferently termed magnates. The rest of the town's population were called *populars*. The difference between the two was essentially economic.

Communal Government.
In the eleventh and early twelfth centuries, many Italian towns bought off or expelled their traditional lords such as counts and bishops, thus allowing the magnates and populars of these cities to create their own governing institutions or communes. Within many towns the magnates formed their own corporation—the society of knights—to protect their privileged position. Families of nobles and magnates, whose cultural values were similar to those of the rural aristocracy, competed with each other for honor and power. Feuds fought out between noble families and their vassals in city streets were frequent events in Italian towns.

Opposing the magnates were popular corporations—the society of the people—which sought to rein in the violent and independent-minded nobles. Each of these popular organizations, dominated by the prominent leaders of craft and trade associations, had its own elected officers and its own military, headed by a "captain of the people," who might command as many as 1,000 troops against the magnates.

To tip the scales in their favor, differing parties frequently invited outside powers into local affairs. The greatest outside contenders for power in the Italian cities were the Germanic empire and the papacy. Most towns had an imperial faction (named Ghibelline after Waiblingen castle, which belonged to

MAP DISCOVERY

Medieval Trade Networks

Examine the major trade routes of the High Middle Ages. What commodities and products were plentiful in Europe but scarce in the eastern Mediterranean? What regions were the major wool producers? The major cloth producers? How might silks from the East have arrived in London?

the family of the emperor Frederick II), bitterly opposed by a papal faction (in time called Guelph after the Welf family, which opposed Frederick's family). Eventually, the Guelphs became the party of the wealthy who were eager to preserve the status quo, and the Ghibellines became the party of those out of power.

To maintain civic life in spite of these conflicts, cities established complex systems of government in which officers were selected by series of elections and lotteries designed to prevent any one faction from seizing control. Sovereignty lay with the *arengo,* or assembly, which included all adult male citizens. Except in very small communes this body was too large to function efficiently, so most communes selected a series of working councils. The great council might be as large as 400; an inner council had perhaps 24 to 40 members. Generally, executive authority was vested in consuls, whose numbers varied widely and who were chosen from various factions and classes. When these consuls proved unable to overcome the partisan politics of the factions, many towns turned to hiring

podestas, nonpolitical professional city managers from outside the community. These were normally magnates from other communes who had received legal educations and who served for relatively short periods. In Modena, for example, they served for six months. They were required to bring with them four judges, 24 cavalrymen, and sergeants and grooms to help maintain order. They could not have any relatives in Modena, could not leave town without permission of the great council, and could not eat or drink with local citizens lest they be drawn into factional conflicts.

Northern Towns

Merchant and manufacturing towns also developed along the Baltic and North Seas and the English Channel. Scandinavian fish and timber, Baltic grain, English wool, and Flemish cloth circulated by sea around Scandinavia, Lithuania, northern Germany, Flanders, and England, linking them in a common economic network.

The earliest of these interrelated communities were the cloth towns of Flanders, Brabant, and northern France. Chief among them were Ghent, Bruges, and Ypres and the wool-exporting towns of England, particularly London. In the eleventh century, Flanders, lacking the land for large-scale sheep grazing and facing a growing population, began to specialize in the production of high-quality cloth made from English wool. At the same time, England, which experienced an economic and population decline following the Norman Conquest, began to export the greater part of its wool to Flanders to be worked. The need for water to power looms and to wash the woolen cloth during production tended to concentrate this industry along waterways. By the late eleventh century, the production of wool cloth began to develop from a cottage occupation into Europe's first major industry. Now manufacture was concentrated in towns, and men replaced women at the looms. Furthermore, production was closely regulated and controlled by a small group of extremely wealthy merchant-drapiers (cloth makers).

Concentration of capital, specialization of labor, and increase of urban population created vibrant, exciting cities that were essentially composed of three social orders. At the top were wealthy patricians, the merchant-drapiers. Their agents traveled to England and purchased raw wool, which they then distributed to weavers and other master craftsmen. These craftsmen—often using equipment rented from the patricians—carded, dyed, spun, and wove the wool into cloth. Finally, the finished cloth was returned to the patricians, whose agents then marketed it throughout Europe. Through their control of raw materials, equipment, capital, and distribution the merchant-drapiers controlled the cloth trade and thus the economic and political life of the Flemish wool towns. Through their closed associations, or **guilds,** they controlled production and set standards, prices, and wages. They also controlled communal government by monopolizing urban councils.

At the bottom of urban society were the unskilled and semiskilled artisans, called "blue nails" because constant work with dye left their fingers permanently stained. These poorly paid workers led an existence that was more precarious than that of most peasants. In the early fourteenth century, the temporary interruption of grain shipments from northern

■ As towns grew, the numbers and types of jobs grew as well. In this fifteenth-century Flemish manuscript illumination, a master of the dyer's guild supervises as men of the guild dye cloth.

Germany to Ypres left thousands dead of starvation. Small wonder that from the thirteenth century on, blue nails were increasingly hostile to patricians. Sporadic rebellions and strikes spread across Flanders, Brabant, and northern France. Everywhere they were ruthlessly suppressed. The penalty for organizing a strike was death.

Between the patricians and the workers stood the masters, the skilled craftsmen who controlled the day-to-day production of cloth and lesser crafts. They organized into guilds to protect themselves from competition. The masters often leased their looms or other equipment from the merchant-drapiers and received from them raw materials and wages to be distributed to their workers.

The Fairs of Champagne

Tying together the northern and southern commercial worlds were the great fairs of Champagne. Six times during the year, the towns of Champagne—particularly Troyes and Provins—swelled with exotic crowds of merchants from Flanders, England, Scandinavia, Germany, Brabant, Spain, and Italy. Rich and poor people from the surrounding countryside also poured into the towns as merchants from north and south met to bargain and trade under the protection of the local counts.

Northern merchants offered cloth, which was known by the name of the town in which it was made. From Italy came merchants of great Italian trading companies to purchase northern cloth for resale throughout the Mediterranean. Southern merchants brought silks, sugar, salt, alum (a chemical that was essential in cloth manufacture), and, most important, spices to trade at the fairs. Medieval cooks gloried in the use of spices, of which they knew over 200. The liberal use of exotic spices may have served as a preservative, and spices probably hid the taste of half-rotten food. But the use of spices was primarily a part of the conspicuous consumption by which the rich displayed their wealth and status.

In addition to the trade in cloth and spices, leather from Spain, iron from Germany, copper and tin from Bohemia, salted or smoked fish and furs from Scandinavia, and local wines, cheeses, and foodstuffs also changed hands under the watchful eyes of fair officials, who supervised weights, measures, and currency exchanges. The fair staff also provided courts to settle disagreements among merchants. These great international exchanges connected the financial and marketing centers of the south with the manufacturing and trading communities of the north, tying the northern world to the south more effectively than had any system since the political institutions of the Roman Empire.

Scholasticism and Urban Intellectual Life

The urban world of the twelfth and thirteenth centuries created forms of religious and cultural expression particularly suited to it. The cathedral schools shifted away from monastic education to an education aimed more at participation in the affairs of the world. Young men were taught the essential urban skills of writing, computation, and law.

The Medieval University.   In the late eleventh and early twelfth centuries, the pace of urban intellectual life quickened. The combination of population growth, improved agricultural productivity, political stability, and educational interest culminated in what has been called the renaissance of the twelfth century. Bologna and Paris became the undisputed centers of the new educational movements. Bologna specialized in the study of law, while Paris became the leader in the study of liberal arts and theology. Students at Bologna organized a **universitas,** or guild of students, the first true university. The law students, many of them adults from wealthy backgrounds, controlled every aspect of the university from the selection of administrators to the exact length of professors' lectures. Professors and administrators were fined if they broke any of the regulations.

In the early twelfth century, students from across Europe flocked to Paris to study with the greatest and most original intellect of the century, Peter Abelard (1079–1142). Brilliant, supremely self-assured, and passionate, Abelard was in his early twenties when he arrived in Paris and quickly took the intellectual community by storm. He ridiculed the established teachers, bested them in open debate, and established his own school, which drew the best minds of his day. Abelard's intellectual method combined the tools of legal analysis perfected in Bologna with Aristotelian logic and laid the foundation of what has been called the **Scholastic method.** Logical reasoning, Abelard believed, could be applied to all problems, even those concerning the mysteries of faith.

So great was Abelard's reputation that an ambitious local cleric engaged him to give private instruction to his brilliant niece, Heloise. Soon Abelard and Heloise were having an affair. When Heloise became pregnant, the two were secretly married. Fearing to harm his clerical career, Abelard refused to make the marriage public, preferring to protect his career rather than Heloise's honor. Her outraged uncle hired thugs, who broke into Abelard's room and castrated him. After Abelard recovered from his mutilation, he and Heloise both entered monasteries, and Abelard spent years as the abbot of a small monastery in Brittany. In 1136, he returned to teach in Paris, where he quickly drew new attacks, this time led by Bernard of Clairvaux, who accused him of heresy. Abelard was convicted by a local council and forced to burn some of his own works. He sought protection from his persecutors in the monastery of Cluny, where he died in 1142.

Although Abelard met tragedy in his personal and professional life, the intellectual ferment that he had begun in Paris continued long after him. By 1200, education had become so important in the city that the universitas, or corporation of professors, was granted a charter by King Philip Augustus, who guaranteed its rights and immunities from the control of the city. Unlike that at Bologna, the University of Paris remained a corporation of masters rather than of students. It

■ This illustration from a fourteenth-century manuscript shows Henry of Germany delivering a lecture to university students in Bologna.

was organized like other guilds into masters; bachelors, who were similar to journeymen in other trades; and students, who were analogous to apprentices.

Students began their studies at around age 14 or 15 in the faculty of arts. After approximately six years, they received a bachelor of arts degree, which was a prerequisite to enter the higher faculties of theology, medicine, or law. After additional years of reading and commenting on specific texts under the supervision of a master, they received the title of master of arts, which gave them the license to teach anywhere within Christian Europe. During their years of study, students also enjoyed a spirited life that revolved around the taverns and brothels that filled the student district, or Latin Quarter. Drunken brawls were frequent, and relationships between students and townspeople were often strained because students enjoyed legal immunity from city laws.

The intellectual life of the universities through the thirteenth and fourteenth centuries was dominated by Aristotelian thought. The introduction of the works of Aristotle into the West between 1150 and 1250 created an intellectual crisis every bit as profound as that of the Newtonian revolution of the seventeenth century or the Einsteinian revolution of the twentieth. For centuries, Western thinkers had depended on the Christianized Neoplatonic philosophy of Origen and Augustine. Aristotle was known in the West only through his basic logical treatises, which in the twelfth century, thanks in large part to the work of Peter Abelard, had be-

come the foundation of intellectual work. Logic, or dialectic, was seen as the universal key to knowledge, and the university system was based on its rigorous application to traditional texts of law, philosophy, and Scripture.

The Aristotelian Challenge.   Beginning in the late twelfth century, Christian and Jewish scholars began translating Aristotle's treatises on natural philosophy, ethics, and metaphysics into Latin. Suddenly, Christian intellectuals who had already accepted the Aristotelian method were brought face to face with Aristotle's conclusions: a world without an active, conscious God, a world in which everything from the functioning of the mind to the nature of matter could be understood without reference to a divine creator. Further complicating matters, the texts arrived not from the original Greek, but normally through Latin translations of Arabic translations accompanied by learned commentaries by Muslim and Jewish scholars, especially by Averroës, the greatest Aristotelian philosopher of the twelfth century.

As the full impact of Aristotelian philosophy began to reach churchmen and scholars, reactions varied from condemnation to whole-hearted acceptance. To many, it appeared that there were two irreconcilable kinds of truth, one knowable through divine revelation and the other through human reason. Scholasticism attempted to bridge the gap by using reason to deepen one's understanding of that which is accepted on faith.

One Parisian scholar who refused to accept the dichotomy of faith and reason was Thomas Aquinas (1225–1274), a professor of theology and the most brilliant intellect of the High Middle Ages. Aquinas refused to accept the possibility that human reason, which was a gift from God, led necessarily to contradictions with divine revelation. His *Summa Against the Gentiles* (1259–1264) and his incomplete *Summa of Theology* (1266–1273) sought to defend the integrity of human reason and to reconcile it with divine revelation. Properly applied, the principles of Aristotelian philosophy could not lead to error, he argued. However, human reason unaided by revelation could not always lead to certain conclusions. Questions about such matters as the nature of God, creation, and the human soul could not be resolved by reason alone. In developing his thesis, Aquinas recast Christian doctrine and philosophy, replacing their Neoplatonic foundation with an Aristotelian base. Although not universally accepted in the thirteenth century, Aquinas's synthesis came to dominate Christian intellectual life for centuries.

Preaching and Poverty.   Aquinas was a member of a new religious order, the Dominicans, who along with the Franciscans appeared in response to the social and cultural needs of the new urbanized, monetized European culture. Benedictine monasticism was ideally suited to a rural, aristocratic world but had little place in the bustling cities of Italy, Flanders, and Germany. In these urban, commercial environments, Christians were more concerned with the problems of living in the world than escape from it. Lay persons and clerics alike were concerned with the growing wealth of ecclesiastical institutions, and across southern Europe especially, individual reformers attacked the wealthy lifestyles of monks and secular clergy as un-Christian.

Torn between their own involvement in a commercial world and an inherited Christian-Roman tradition that looked on commerce and capital as degrading, reformers called for a return to what they imagined to have been the life of the primitive Church, one that emphasized both individual and collective poverty. The poverty movement attracted great numbers of followers, many of whom also criticized clerical morality and questioned the value of sacraments and the priesthood. Although many reformers were condemned as heretics and were sporadically persecuted, the reform movement continued to grow and threatened to destroy the unity of Western Christendom.

The people who preserved the Church's unity aimed at reforming the Church from within. Francis of Assisi (1182–1226), the son of a prosperous Italian merchant, rejected his luxurious life in favor of one of radical poverty and service to others. He was a man of piety, simplicity, humility, and joy. As he wandered about, preaching repentance, he drew great numbers of followers from all ranks, especially from the urban communities of Italy. Convinced of the importance of obedience, Francis asked Pope Innocent III to approve the way of life he had chosen for himself and his followers. The

■ An altarpiece depicting Saint Francis of Assisi with six scenes from his life. His hands show the stigmata—symbolic marks that represent the wounds Christ received on the cross.

pope granted his wish, and the Order of Friars Minor, or Franciscans, grew by thousands, drawing members from as far away as England and Hungary.

Francis insisted that his followers observe strict poverty, both individually and collectively. The order could not own property, nor could its members even touch money. They were expected to beg for their food as they traveled from town to town, preaching, performing manual labor, and serving the poor. Francis did not approve of women followers leading such a life but insisted that they pursue radical poverty within cloistered convents that were often within the walls of towns.

In time, the expansion of the order and its involvement in preaching against heresy and in education brought about compromises with Francis's original ideals. The Franciscans needed churches in which to preach, books with which to study, and protection from local bishops. Most of the friars accepted these changes. These, the so-called conventuals, were bitterly opposed by the spirituals, or rigorists, who sought to maintain the radical poverty of their founder. In the fourteenth century, this conflict led to a major split in the order and ultimately to the condemnation of the spirituals as heretics.

The order of friars founded by Dominic (1170–1221) also adopted a rule of strict poverty, but their primary focus was on preaching. This order emphasized intellectual activity and higher education and spoke out against heresies. Thus the Dominicans too gravitated toward the cities of western Europe and especially toward its great universities. These new orders of preachers, highly educated, enthusiastic, and eloquent, began to formulate for the urban laity of Europe a new vision of Christian society, a society not only of peasants, lords, and monks, but also of merchants, artisans, and professionals. Their central organizations and their lack of ties to the rural aristocracies also made them the favorite religious orders of the increasingly powerful centralized monarchies.

THE INVENTION OF THE STATE

The disintegration of the Carolingian Empire in the tenth century left political power fragmented among a wide variety of political entities. In general, these were of two types. The first, the papacy and the empire, were elective traditional structures that claimed universal sovereignty over the Christian world, based on a sacred view of political power. The second, largely hereditary and less extravagant in their religious and political pretensions, were the limited kingdoms that arose within the old Carolingian world or on its borders.

The Universal States: Empire and Papacy

The Frankish world east of the Rhine River had been less affected than the kingdom of the West Franks by the onslaught of Vikings, Magyars, and Saracens. The eastern Frankish kingdom, a loose confederacy of five duchies—Saxony, Lorraine, Franconia, Swabia, and Bavaria—had preserved much of the Carolingian religious, cultural, and institutional traditions. In 919, Duke Henry I of Saxony (919–936) was elected king, and his son Otto I (936–973) laid the foundation for the revival of the empire. Otto inflicted a devastating defeat on the Magyars in 955, subdued the other dukes, and tightened his control over the kingdom. He accomplished this largely through the extensive use of bishops and abbots, whom he appointed as his agents and sources of loyal support. In 951, Otto invaded and conquered Lombardy. Eleven years later, he entered Rome, where he was crowned emperor by the pope.

The Medieval Empire. Otto, known to history as "the Great," had established the main outlines of German imperial policy for the next 300 years. This policy included conflict with the German aristocracy, reliance on bishops and abbots as imperial agents, and preoccupation with Italy. His successors, both in his own Saxon dynasty (919–1024) and in the succeeding dynasties, the Salians (1024–1125) and the Staufens (1138–1254), continued this tradition. Magnates elected the German kings, who were then consecrated as emperors by the pope. Royal fathers were generally able to

bring about the election of their sons, and in this manner they attempted to turn the kingship into a hereditary office. However, the royal families could not manage to produce male heirs in each generation, and so the magnates continued to exercise real power in royal elections.

The magnates' ability to expand their own power and autonomy at the expense of their Slavic neighbors to the east also contributed to the weakness of the German monarchy. In the 1150s, for example, Henry the Lion (ca. 1130–1195), duke of Bavaria and Saxony, carved out an autonomous principality in the Slavic areas between the Elbe and the Vistula, founding the major trading towns of Lübeck and Rostock. It was the goal of every great aristocratic family to extend its own independent lordship.

To counter such aristocratic power, emperors looked to the Church both for the development of the religious cult of the emperor as "the Anointed of the Lord" and as a source of military and political support. While the offices of count and duke had become hereditary within the great aristocracy, the offices of bishop and abbot remained public charges to which the emperor could appoint loyal supporters. Since these ecclesiastics had taken vows of celibacy, the emperor did not fear that they would attempt to pass their offices on to their children. Moreover, churchmen tended to be experienced, educated administrators who could assist the emperor in the administration of the empire. Like the Carolingians, the Saxon and Salian emperors needed a purified, reformed Church that was free of local aristocratic control to serve the interests of the emperor. This imperial church was the cornerstone of the empire.

The laymen on whom the emperor could rely, particularly from the eleventh century, were trusted household serfs whom the emperors used as their agents. Although unfree, these ministerials were entrusted with important military commands and given strategic castles throughout the empire. Despised by the freeborn nobility, they tended at first to be loyal supporters of the emperor. In the twelfth century, they adopted the chivalric ideals of their aristocratic neighbors and took advantage of conflicts between emperor and pope to acquire autonomy. As old noble families died out, ministerial families replaced them as a new hereditary aristocracy.

Otto the Great had entered Italy to secure his southern flank. His successors became embroiled in Italian affairs until, in the thirteenth century, they abandoned Germany altogether. As emperors, they had to be crowned by the pope. This was possible only if they controlled Rome. Moreover, the growing wealth of northern Italian towns was an important source of financial support if Lombardy could be controlled. As the emperors were drawn further into papal and Italian politics, frequently with disastrous results, Germany became merely a source of men and matériel with which to fight the Lombard towns and the pope. From the eleventh through the thirteenth centuries, emperors granted German princes autonomy in return for their support.

■ The Empire of Otto the Great, ca. 963. The Ottonian Empire included not only Germany, but also Slavic lands to the east and disputed regions such as Lorraine to the west.

The Papacy.   The early successes of this imperial program created the seeds of its own destruction. Imperial efforts to reform the Church resulted in a second, competing claimant to universal authority: the papacy. In the later tenth and early eleventh centuries, emperors had intervened in papal elections, deposed and replaced corrupt popes, and worked to ensure that bishops and abbots would be educated, competent churchmen. The most effective reformer was Emperor Henry III (1039–1056), who undertook to reform the Church both in Germany and in Rome. When three rivals claimed the papacy, Henry called a synod, or meeting of bishops, which deposed all three and installed the first of a series of German popes. The most impressive was Henry's own cousin, Leo IX (1049–1054), who traveled widely in France, Germany, and Italy. Leo condemned simony, the practice of buying Church offices, and fostered monastic reforms such as that of Cluny.

He also encouraged the efforts of a group of young reformers drawn from across Europe.

Investiture and Reform.   In the next decades these new, more radical reformers began to advocate a widespread renewal of the Christian world, led not by emperors but by popes. These reformers pursued an ambitious set of goals. They sought to reform the morals of the clergy and in particular to eliminate married priests. They tried to free churches and monasteries from lay control both by forbidding lay men and women from owning churches and monasteries and by eliminating simony. They particularly condemned **lay investiture,** the practice by which kings and emperors appointed bishops and invested them with the symbols of their office. Finally, they insisted that the pope, not the emperor, was the supreme representative of God on earth and as such had the right to exercise a universal sovereignty.

Every aspect of the reform movement met with strong opposition throughout Europe. Emperor Henry IV (1056–1106) clashed head-on with Pope Gregory VII (1073–1085) over the emperor's right to appoint and to install or invest bishops in their offices. This investiture controversy changed the face of European political history. For the first time, public opinion played a crucial role in politics, and for the first time the idea of the separate spheres of church and state began to emerge in European political theory.

In the end, the conflict weakened both the empire and the papacy. In 1075, the emperor Henry IV, supported by many German bishops, attempted to depose Gregory. In return, Gregory excommunicated and deposed Henry, freed the German nobility from their obligations to him, and encouraged them to rebel. As anti-imperial strength grew, Henry took a desperate gamble. Crossing the Alps in the dead of winter in 1077, he arrived before the castle of Canossa in northern Italy, where Gregory was staying. Dressed as a humble penitent, Henry stood in the snow, asking the pope for forgiveness and reconciliation. As a priest, the pope could not refuse, and he lifted the excommunication. Once more in power, Henry resumed appointing bishops. In 1080, Gregory again excommunicated and deposed Henry, but this time the majority of the German nobles and bishops remained loyal to the emperor, and Henry marched on Rome. Deserted by most of his clergy, Gregory fled to southern Italy and died in Salerno in 1085.

Henry did not long enjoy his victory. Gregory's successors rekindled the opposition to Henry and even convinced Henry's own son to join in the revolt. The conflict ended only in 1122, when Emperor Henry V (1106–1125) and Pope Calixtus II (1119–1124) reached an agreement known as the Concordat of Worms, which differentiated between the royal and spiritual spheres of authority and allowed the emperors a limited role in episcopal election and investiture. This compromise changed the nature of royal rule in the empire, weakening the emperors and contributing to the long-term decline of royal government in Germany.

The decline that began with the investiture controversy continued as emperors abandoned political power north of the Alps to pursue their ambitions in Italy. Frederick I Barbarossa (1152–1190) gained the support of the German princes for his largely futile efforts in northern Italy by granting them extraordinary privileges. His successors continued his policy of focusing on Italy with no better success. In 1230, Frederick II (1215–1250) conceded to each German prince sovereign rights in his own territory. From the thirteenth to the nineteenth centuries, these princes ruled their territories as independent states, leaving the office of emperor a hollow title.

The investiture controversy ultimately compromised the authority of the pope as well as that of the emperor. First, the series of compromises beginning with the Concordat of Worms established the potent Western idea of separate spheres of authority for secular and religious government. Second, although in the short run popes were able to exercise enormous political influence, from the thirteenth century they were increasingly unable to make good their claims to absolute authority.

The Pinnacle of Papal Power.   Papal power was based on more than Scripture. Over the centuries, the popes had acquired large amounts of land in central Italy and in the Rhone Valley, which formed the nucleus of the papal states. Moreover, in every corner of Europe, bishops and clergy were, at least in theory, agents of papal programs. Church courts also claimed jurisdiction over all clerics, regardless of the nature of the legal problem, and over all baptized Christians in such fundamental issues as legitimacy of marriages, inheritances, and oaths.

During the pontificate of Innocent III (1198–1216), the papacy reached the height of its power. Innocent made and deposed emperors, excommunicated kings, summoned a crusade against heretics in the south of France, and placed whole countries such as England and France under interdict, that is, the suspension of all religious services, when rulers dared to contradict him. Still, he found time to support Francis of Assisi and Dominic and, in 1215, to call the Fourth Lateran Council, which culminated the reforms of the past century.

At the council, more than 1,200 assembled bishops and abbots, joined by great nobles from across Europe, defined fundamental doctrines such as the nature of the Eucharist, ordered annual confession of sins, and detailed procedures for the election of bishops. They also mandated a strict lifestyle for clergy and forbade their participation in judicial procedures in which accused persons had to undergo painful ordeals, such as grasping a piece of red-hot iron and carrying it a prescribed distance to prove their innocence. More ominously, the council also mandated that Jews wear special identifying markings on their clothing—a sign of the increasing hostility that Christians felt toward the Jews in their midst.

During the thirteenth century, the papacy continued to perfect its legal system and its control over clergy throughout Europe. However, politically the popes were unable to assert their claims to universal supremacy. This was true both in Italy, where the communes in the north and the kingdom of Naples in the south resisted direct papal control, and in the emerging kingdoms north of the Alps, where monarchs successfully intervened in Church affairs. The old claims of papal authority rang increasingly hollow. When Pope Boniface VIII (1294–1303) attempted to prevent the French king Philip IV (1285–1314) from taxing the French clergy, boasting that he could depose kings "like servants" if necessary, Philip proved him wrong. Philip's agents hired a gang of adventurers, who kidnapped the pope, plundered his treasury, and released him a broken, humiliated wreck. He died three weeks later. The French king who had engineered Boniface's humiliation represented a new political tradition: the medieval nation-state.

The Nation-States: France and England

The office of king was less pretentious than that of emperor. As the Carolingian world disintegrated, a variety of kingdoms had appeared in France, Italy, Burgundy, and Provence. Kingship was well established in England and northern Spain, and powerful chieftains were consolidating royal power at the expense of their aristocracies in Scandinavia, Poland, Bohemia, and Hungary. The claims of kings were much more modest than those of emperors or popes. Kings laid claim to a limited territory; they were only one of many representatives of God on earth; and finally, they were far from absolute rulers. During the tenth and eleventh centuries, the powers of

CHRONOLOGY
PROMINENT POPES AND RELIGIOUS FIGURES OF THE HIGH MIDDLE AGES

1049–1054*	Pope Leo IX
1073–1085	Pope Gregory VII
1088–1099	Pope Urban II
1098–1179	Hildegard of Bingen
1119–1124	Pope Calixtus II
1170–1221	Saint Dominic
1182–1226	Saint Francis of Assisi
1198–1216	Pope Innocent III
1225–1274	Saint Thomas Aquinas
1294–1303	Pope Boniface VIII

*Dates for popes are dates of reign.

justice, coinage, taxation, and military command, once considered public, had been usurped by aristocrats and nobles. Kings needed the support of these magnates, and often—as in the case of France—these dukes and counts were wealthier and more powerful than the kings. Still, between the tenth and fourteenth centuries, some monarchies, especially those of France and England, developed into powerful, centralized, and vigorous kingdoms. In the process they gave birth to what has become the modern state.

France: Biology, Bureaucracy, and Sanctity. In 987, when Hugh Capet was elected king of the West Franks, no one suspected that his successors would become the most powerful rulers of Europe, for they were relatively weak magnates whose only real power lay in the region between Paris and Orléans. The dukes of Normandy, descendants of Vikings whose settlement had been recognized by Frankish kings, ruled their duchy with an authority of which the kings could only dream. Less than a century later, Duke William of Normandy expanded his power even more by conquering England. In the twelfth century, the English kings ruled the Angevin Empire, a vast collection of hereditary lands on both sides of the English Channel. Other nobles, such as the counts of Flanders and the counts of Poitou, also seemed more impressive than the house of Hugh Capet. Nevertheless, under Hugh's successors, the kingdom of France became the most powerful monarchy in Europe and the center of European learning, architecture, and art.

The medieval French monarchy owed its creation in large part to biology and bureaucracy. Between 987 and 1314, every royal descendant of Hugh Capet (after whom the dynasty was called the Capetian) left a male heir—an extraordinary record for a medieval family. During the same period, by comparison, the office of emperor was occupied by men from no fewer than nine families. By simply outlasting the families of their great barons, the Capetian kings were able to absorb lands when other families became extinct. This success was not just the result of luck. Kings such as Robert the Pious (996–1031) and Louis VII (1137–1180) risked excommunication to divorce wives who had not produced male heirs. In 1152, Louis had his marriage to the richest heiress of the twelfth century, Eleanor of Aquitaine (1122–1204), annulled in part because she had given him no sons. With the annulment he also lost the chance to absorb her territories of Aquitaine and Poitou. A few months later, Eleanor married Count Henry of Anjou (1133–1189), who two years later became King Henry II of England. Imagine Louis's chagrin when Eleanor produced four sons with Henry, in the process making the English kings the greatest magnates in France.

The Capetians' long run of biological luck, combined with the practice of having a son crowned during his father's lifetime and thus being firmly established before his father's death, was only part of the explanation for the Capetian success. The Capetians also wisely used their position as conse-crated sovereigns to build a power base in the Ile de France (the region around Paris) and among the bishops and abbots of the kingdom and then to insist on their feudal rights as the lords of the great dukes and counts of France. It was this foundation that Louis VII's son Philip II (1180–1223) used to create the French monarchy.

Philip II was known to posterity as Augustus, or the aggrandizer, because through his ruthless political intrigue and brilliant organizational sense he more than doubled the territory he controlled and more than quadrupled the revenue of the French crown. Through marriage he acquired Vermandois, the Amienois, Artois, and Valois. He later absorbed Flanders and set the stage for the absorption of the great county of Toulouse by his son Louis VIII (1223–1226) in the aftermath of the crusade against the dualist Albigensian heretics launched by Pope Innocent III. Philip's greatest coup, however, was the confiscation of all the continental possessions of the English King John (1199–1216), the son of Henry II and Eleanor of Aquitaine. Although John was sovereign in England, as lord of Normandy, Anjou, Maine, and Touraine, he was technically a vassal of King Philip. When John married the fiancée of one of his continental vassals, the outraged vassal appealed to Philip in his capacity as John's lord. Philip summoned John to appear before the royal court, and when he refused to do so, Philip ordered him to surrender all of his continental fiefs. This meant war, and one by one, John's continental possessions fell to the French king. Philip's victory over John's ally the emperor Otto IV (1198–1215) at Bouvines in 1214 sealed the English loss of Normandy, Maine, Anjou, Poitou, and Touraine.

To govern these vast regions, Philip needed an effective administrative system. Using members of families from the old royal demesne, he set up administrative officials called *baillis* and *seneschals*, nonfeudal salaried agents who collected his revenues and represented his interests. The baillis in particular, who were drawn from commoner families and often had received their education at the University of Paris, were the foundation of the French bureaucracy, which grew in strength and importance through the thirteenth century. By governing the regions of France according to local traditions but always with an eye to the king's interest, these bureaucrats did more than anyone else to create a stable, enduring political system.

Philip's grandson Louis IX (1226–1270) fine-tuned this administrative machine and, through his own piety, endowed it with the aura of sanctity. Generous, brave, and capable, Louis took seriously his obligation to provide justice for the poor and protection for the weak. A disastrous crusade, the so-called Seventh Crusade (1248–1254), which ended in his capture and ransom in Egypt, convinced Louis that his failure was punishment for his sins and those of his government. When he returned to France, he dispatched investigators to correct abuses by baillis and other royal officials and restored property that had been unjustly confiscated by his father's agents during the Albigensian Crusade. In addition, he established a permanent central court in Paris to hear appeals from throughout the kingdom. In 1270, Louis attempted another crusade and died in an epidemic in Tunis. The goodwill and devotion that Louis won from his subjects were a precious heritage that benefited his successors for centuries.

The growth of royal power transformed the traditional role of the aristocracy. As the power and wealth of the French kings increased, the ability of the nobles to maintain their independence decreased. Royal judges undermined lords' control over the peasantry. Royal revenues enabled kings to hire warriors rather than relying on traditional feudal levies. At the same time, the increasing expenses of the noble lifestyle forced all but the wealthiest aristocrats to look for sources of income beyond their traditional estates. Increasingly, they found this in royal service. Thus, in the thirteenth century the nobility began to lose some of its independence to the state.

England: Conquest, Accounting, and Cooperation.

A very different path brought the English monarchy to a level of power similar to that of the French by the end of the thirteenth century. While France was made by a family and its bureaucracy, the kingdom that was originally forged by Alfred and his descendants was transformed by the successors of William the Conqueror.

When King Edward the Confessor (1042–1066) died, three claimants disputed the succession. Anglo-Saxon sources insist that Edward and his nobles had chosen Earl Harold Godwinson (ca. 1022–1066) over Duke William of Normandy and the Norwegian king Harold III (1045–1066). William insisted that Edward had designated him and that years before, when Earl Harold had been shipwrecked on the Norman coast and befriended by the duke, he had sworn an oath to assist William in gaining the crown. Harold of Norway and William sailed for England. Harold Godwinson defeated the Norwegian's army and killed the king, but he met his end shortly afterward on the bloody field of Hastings, and William the Conqueror secured the throne.

William's England was a small, insular kingdom that had been united by Viking raids little more than a century before. Hostile Celtic societies bordered it to the north and west. Still, it had important strengths. First, the king of the English was not simply a feudal lord, a first among equals—he was a sovereign. Second, Anglo-Saxon government had been participatory, with the freemen of each shire taking part in court sessions and sharing the responsibilities of government. Finally, the king had agents, or *reeves,* in each shire (shire reeves, or sheriffs) who were responsible for representing the king's interests, presiding over the local court, and collecting royal taxes and incomes.

This ability to raise money was the most important aspect of the English kingship for William the Conqueror and his immediate successors, who remained thoroughly continental in interest, culture, and language (the first English king to speak English fluently was probably King John). England was seen primarily as a source of revenue. To tap this wealth, the

Norman kings transformed rather than abolished Anglo-Saxon governmental traditions, adding Norman feudal bonds and administrative control to Anglo-Saxon kingship.

William preserved English government while replacing Anglo-Saxon officers with his continental vassals, chiefly Normans and Flemings. He rewarded his supporters with land confiscated from the defeated Anglo-Saxons, but he was careful to give out land only in fief. In contrast to continental practice, in which many lords owned vast estates outright, in England all land was held directly or indirectly by the king. Because he wanted to know the extent of his new kingdom and its wealth, William ordered a comprehensive survey of all royal rights. The recorded account, known as the Domesday Book, was the most extensive investigation of economic rights since the Merovingians abandoned the late Roman tax rolls.

William and his successors needed an efficient system of controlling England when they were away. To this end, they developed the royal court, an institution inherited from their Anglo-Saxon predecessors, into an efficient system of fiscal and administrative supervision. The most important innovation was the use of a large checkerboard, or exchequer, which functioned like a primitive computer to audit the returns of their sheriffs. Annual payments were recorded on long rolls of parchment called pipe rolls, the first continuous accounting system in Europe. These improved accounting methods produced the most efficient and prosperous royal administration in Europe.

In the first half of the twelfth century, almost two decades of warfare over the succession greatly weakened royal authority, but Henry II (1154–1189) reestablished central power by reasserting his authority over the nobility and through his legal reforms. Using his continental wealth and armies, he brought the English barons into line, destroyed private castles, and reasserted his rights to traditional royal incomes. He strengthened royal courts by expanding royal jurisdiction at the expense of Church tribunals and of the courts of feudal lords.

Henry's efforts to control the clergy led to one of the epic clashes of the investiture struggle. The archbishop of Canterbury, Thomas à Becket (ca. 1118–1170), although a personal friend of Henry, refused to accept the king's claim to jurisdiction over clergy. For six years, Becket lived in exile on the Continent and infuriated Henry by his stubborn adherence to the letter of Church law. He was allowed to return to England in 1170, but that same year he was struck down in his own cathedral by four knights eager for royal favor. The king did penance but, unlike the German emperors, ultimately preserved royal authority over the English Church.

Henry's program to assert royal courts over local and feudal ones was even more successful, laying the foundation for a system of uniform judicial procedures throughout the kingdom: the common law. In France, royal agents observed local legal traditions but sought always to turn them to the king's advantage. In contrast, Henry's legal system simplified and cut through the complex tangle of local and feudal jurisdictions concerning land law. Any free person could purchase, for a modest price, a letter, or writ, from the king ordering the local sheriff to impanel a jury to determine whether that person had been recently dispossessed of an estate, regardless of that person's legal right to the property. The procedure was swift and efficient. If the jury found for the plaintiff, the sheriff immediately restored the property, by force if necessary. While juries may not have meted out justice, they did resolve conflicts, and they did so in a way that protected landholders. These writs became enormously successful and expanded the jurisdiction of royal courts.

Henry's son John may have made the greatest contribution to the development of the English state by losing Normandy and most of his other continental lands. Loss of these territories forced English kings to concentrate on ruling England, not on their continental territories. Moreover, John's financial difficulties, brought about by his unsuccessful wars to recover his continental holdings, led him to such extremes of fiscal extortion that his barons, prelates, and the townspeople of London revolted. In June 1215, he was forced to accept the "great charter of liberties," or **Magna Carta,** a conservative feudal document demanding that he respect the rights of his vassals and of the burghers of London. The great significance of the document was its acknowledgment that the king was not above the law.

John and his weak, ineffective son Henry III (1216–1272), although ably served by royal judges, were forced by their failures to cede considerable influence to the great barons of the realm. Henry's son Edward I (1272–1307), a strong and effective king who conquered Wales, defended the remaining continental possessions against France, and expanded the common law, found that he could turn baronial involvement in government to his own advantage. By summoning his barons, bishops, and representatives of the towns and shires to participate in a "parley," or "parliament," he could raise more funds for his wars. Like similar Spanish, Hungarian, and German assemblies of the thirteenth century, these assemblies were occasions to consult, to present royal programs, and to extract extraordinary taxes for specific projects. They were also op-portunities for those who were summoned to petition the king for redress of grievances. However, since the growing wealth of the towns and countryside made their financial support essential, these groups came to anticipate that they had a right to be consulted and to consent to taxation.

Through a system of royal courts and justices employing local juries and a tradition of representative parliaments, this forced self-government, coupled with an exacting system of accounting, increased the power of the English monarchy. By 1300, France, with its powerful royal bureaucracy, and England, with its courts and accountants, were the most powerful states in the West.

CONCLUSION

By 1300, Europe had achieved a level of population density, economic prosperity, cultural sophistication, and political organization greater than at any time since the Roman Empire. Across Europe, a largely free peasantry cultivated a wide variety of crops, both for local consumption and for growing commercial markets, while landlords sought increasingly rational approaches to estate management and investment. In cities and ports, merchants, manufacturers, and bankers presided over an international commercial and manufacturing economy that connected Scandinavia to the Mediterranean Sea. In schools and universities, students learned the skills of logical thinking and disputation while absorbing the traditions of Greece and Rome in order to prepare themselves for careers in law, medicine, and government. In courts and palaces, nascent bureaucracies worked to expand the rule of law over recalcitrant nobles, to keep the peace, and to preserve justice. Finally, after almost a thousand years of political, economic, and intellectual isolation, western Europe had become once more a dominant force in world civilization.

QUESTIONS FOR REVIEW

1. How did the different social roles of peasants, knights, and clergymen interact and complement each other?
2. In what ways did life in the urban world pose a threat to the values and priorities of aristocrats and churchmen?
3. How were the pope and the Holy Roman Emperor both dependent on each other and in conflict?
4. Why would Europe's medieval kings ultimately be more successful than the Holy Roman Emperor or the papacy in establishing strong, centralized states?

KEY TERMS

chivalry, *p. 177*

Crusades, *p. 180*

demesne, *p. 176*

feudalism, *p. 179*

fief, *p. 178*

guilds, *p. 184*

lay investiture, *p. 189*

Magna Carta, *p. 193*

Scholastic method, *p. 185*

serfs, *p. 176*

three-field system, *p. 176*

universitas, *p. 185*

vassals, *p. 178*

DISCOVERING WESTERN CIVILIZATION ONLINE

You can obtain more information about the High Middle Ages at the websites listed below. See also the Companion Website that accompanies this text, www.ablongman.com/kishlansky, which contains an online study guide and additional resources.

General Websites

Medieval Women
georgetown.edu/labyrinth/subjects/women/women.html
Links to resources on medieval women.

Byzantine and Medieval Studies Links
www.fordham.edu/halsall/medweb/
Professor Paul Halsall's links to the medieval world.

The Countryside

Castles on the Web
www.castlesontheweb.com/
An entire website dedicated to castles, abbeys, and medieval churches.

Medieval Towns

Durham Cathedral and Castle
www.dur.ac.uk/~dla0www/c_tour/tour.html
A virtual tour of Durham's cathedral.

Paris at the Time of Philippe Auguste
www.philippe-auguste.com/uk/index.html
Medieval Paris at the end of the twelfth century.

Medieval Toledo
geocities.com/Athens/Academy/8636/Toledo.html
A site devoted to the city of Toledo in the Middle Ages with an emphasis on its Jewish history links to other related Spanish sites.

The Invention of the State

Les Capetiens-Les Croisades (Capetians to the Crusades)
philae.sas.upenn.edu/French/caroly.html
A hypertext site devoted to Capetian France (in French).

Medieval England
georgetown.edu/labyrinth/subjects/british_isles/england/england.html
The Labyrinth site with links to every aspect of medieval England.

Magna Carta
www.nara.gov/exhall/charters/magnacarta/magmain.html
A site devoted to the Magna Carta, including images of the charter itself.

Virtual Library: History: German History
www.erlangerhistorikerseite.de/heidelberg/gh/e3.html
Links to medieval Germany sites (in German).

SUGGESTIONS FOR FURTHER READING

The Countryside

Robert Bartlett, *The Making of Europe: Conquest, Colonization, and Cultural Change, 950–1350* (Princeton, NJ: Princeton University Press, 1993). A challenging study of European expansion.

Frederic Cheyette, *Ermengard of Narbonne* (Ithaca, NY: Cornell University Press, 2001). An evocative account of Provençal society in the eleventh and twelfth centuries.

Georges Duby, *The Chivalrous Society* (Berkeley: University of California Press, 1978). Essays on the French aristocracy by the leading medieval historian.

Georges Duby, *The Knight, the Lady, and the Priest: The Making of Modern Marriage in Medieval France* (New York: Pantheon Books, 1984). A short study of the conflict between lay and religious social values in medieval France.

John France, *Western Warfare in the Age of the Crusades, 1000–1300,* (Ithaca, NY: Cornell University Press, 1999). Warfare in the High Middle Ages.

Richard W. Kauper, *Chivalry and Violence in Medieval Europe* (Oxford: Oxford University Press, 2001). A comprehensive look at the relationship between chivalry and medieval violence.

Jonathan Riley-Smith, ed., *The Oxford Illustrated History of the Crusades* (Oxford: Oxford University Press, 2001). A comprehensive, collectively authored introduction to Crusade history.

Medieval Towns

Hilde De Ridder-Symoens, ed., *A History of the University in Europe, Vol. 1: Universities in the Middle Ages* (Cambridge: Cambridge University Press, 1991). A multi-authored comprehensive history of medieval universities to 1500.

Barbara A. Hanawalt and Kathryn L. Reyerson, eds., *City and Spectacle in Medieval Europe* (Minneapolis: University of Minnesota Press, 1994). Essays on urban ritual and culture in the Middle Ages.

P. J. Jones, *The Italian City-State: From Commune to Signoria* (Oxford, NY: Clarendon Press, 1997). Major survey of Italian urban history.

Robert S. Lopez, *The Commercial Revolution of the Middle Ages, 950–1350* (New York: Cambridge University Press, 1971). An excellent survey of medieval commercial history.

Joseph H. Lynch, *The Medieval Church: A Brief History* (London and New York: Longman, 1992). A short introduction to medieval Church history.

David Nicholas, *The Growth of the Medieval City* (New York: Addison-Wesley Longman, 1997). A survey of the diversity of medieval urban development from late antiquity to the 1330s.

The Invention of the State

Robert Bartlett, *England under the Norman and Angevin Kings, 1075–1225* (Oxford: Oxford University Press, 2000). A survey of England from the eleventh to thirteenth centuries.

Thomas N. Bisson, ed., *Cultures of Power: Lordship, Status, and Process in Twelfth-Century Europe* (Philadelphia: University of Pennsylvania Press, 1995). Important collection of essays on medieval lordship.

Jean Dunbabin, *France in the Making, 843–1180* (New York: Oxford University Press, 1985). Good overview of the formation of France.

Horst Fuhrmann, *Germany in the High Middle Ages, c. 1050–1200* (New York: Cambridge University Press, 1986). A fresh synthesis of German history by a leading German historian.

Bernard F. Reilly, *The Medieval Spains* (Cambridge: Cambridge University Press, 1993). Comprehensive survey of the social, political, and cultural history of the medieval Iberian peninsula.

Teofilo F. Ruiz, *From Heaven to Earth: The Reordering of Castilian Society, 1150–1350* (Princeton, NJ: Princeton University Press, 2004). An intelligent examination of the relationship between language and social and political change in Spain.

Joseph R. Strayer, *On the Medieval Origins of the Modern State* (Princeton, NJ: Princeton University Press, 1970). A very brief but imaginative account of medieval statecraft by a leading historian of French institutions.

For a list of additional titles related to this chapter's topics, please see www.ablongman.com/kishlansky.

Chapter 10

THE LATER MIDDLE AGES, 1300–1500

The Visual Record

WEBS OF STONE AND BLOOD

Like a delicate web of woven stone, the Gothic vaulting in the choir of Saint Vitus Cathedral in Prague encloses and unifies the sacred space over which it floats. In a similar manner, the great aristocratic families of the fourteenth and fifteenth centuries spun webs of estates, hereditary principalities, and fiefs across Europe. In art as in life, dynamic individuals reshaped the legacy of the past into new and unexpected forms.

In France, where Gothic architecture originated in the twelfth century, architects had long used stone springers and vaults, but only to emphasize verticality and lift the eyes of the faithful to the heavens. Through the thirteenth and fourteenth centuries, French architects vied with one another to raise their vaults ever higher but never rethought the basic premise of their design. Peter Parler (1330–1399), the architect of Saint Vitus, approached the design of his cathedral in a novel way. He used intersecting vaults not simply for height but to bind together the interior space of the edifice in a net of intersecting stone arches. This ability to rethink the architectural heritage of the past marked Peter Parler as the greatest architectural genius of the fourteenth century. Emperor Charles IV (1355–1378), the head of the most successful web-spinning aristocratic family of the late Middle Ages, recognized Parler's talent and enlisted him in making the Bohemian capital one of the most splendid cities of Europe.

Along with his innovations in architecture, Peter Parler also opened new directions in sculpture. Again breaking with French tradition, in which sculptors sought to present their subjects as ideal types, Parler concentrated on realism and individual portraiture in his work. The carved heads of Bohemia's kings, queens, prelates, and princes that peer down from the ambulatory of Saint Vitus are real people with their blemishes, their virtues, and their vices marked in their faces. Parler's own portrait bust also appears among those of kings and queens.

Parler was 23 when Charles IV, then king of Bohemia and soon to be Holy Roman Emperor, invited him to complete his great Prague cathedral, which had been begun by a French architect and modeled on the great cathedrals of France. With Charles's patronage, Parler modified the building program to incorporate his original vision of architecture and portraiture. He went on to direct the construction of churches, bridges, and towers in Prague and throughout Bohemia. Within a generation, Parler's students had spread his refinement of Gothic architecture and sculpture throughout the Holy Roman Empire. Parler, the weaver of stone, and Charles, the weaver of politics, were emblematic of their age.

Looking Ahead

This chapter explores the tensions, crises, and creativity of Parler's age. It examines the rise of Central Europe as a central stage of cultural and political action, follows the disasters of the Hundred Years' War, the Black Death, and the Great Schism, and reviews the religious, artistic, and literary creativity of the later Middle Ages. ➤

POLITICS AS A FAMILY AFFAIR

Like those of his architect, Charles's roots were in the Rhineland and his cultural inspiration was in France. The ancestral estates of his family, the house of Luxembourg, lay on the banks of the Moselle River. Between 1250 and 1350, the Luxembourg family greatly expanded its political and geographical powers by involving itself in the dynastic politics of the decaying Holy Roman Empire. During the fourteenth century, Charles of Luxembourg (later Emperor Charles IV) controlled a patchwork of lands that included Luxembourg, Brabant, Lusatia, Silesia, Moravia, Meissen, and Brandenburg. His daughter married Richard II of England. A son succeeded him as king of Bohemia, and another obtained the Hungarian crown.

Such fragmented and shifting territorial bases were typical of the great families of the fourteenth and fifteenth centuries. Everywhere, family politics threatened the fragile institutional developments of the thirteenth century, but this was especially true in the empire. Aristocrats competed for personal power and used public office, military command, and taxing power for private ends. What mattered was neither territorial boundaries nor political divisions but marriage alliances, kinship, and dynastic ambitions.

The Struggle for Central Europe

In addition to the Luxembourgs, four other similarly ambitious families competed for dominance in the empire. First were the Wittelsbachs, the Luxembourgs' chief competitors. The Wittelsbachs had originated in Bavaria but had since spread across Europe. In the west, the Wittelsbachs had acquired Holland, Hainaut, and Frisia; in the east, they temporarily held Tyrol and Brandenburg. Next were the Habsburgs, allies of the Luxembourgs, who had begun as a minor comitial family in the region of the Black Forest. They expanded eastward, acquiring Austria, Tyrol, Carinthia, and Carniola. When Rudolf I of Habsburg (1273–1291) was elected emperor in 1273, Otakar II, king of Bohemia (1253–1278) and head of the powerful Premysl family, dismissed Rudolf as "poor." Compared with the Premysls, perhaps he was. At its height, the Premysl family controlled not only Bohemia but also Moravia, Austria, and a miscellany of lands stretching from Silesia in the north to the Adriatic Sea. Finally, the house of Anjou, descendants of Charles of Anjou, the younger brother of the French king Louis IX, who had become king of Naples, created a similar eastern network. Charles's son Charles Robert secured election as king of Hungary in 1310. His son Louis (1342–1382) added the crown of Poland (1370–1382) to the Hungarian crown of Saint Stephen. The protracted wars and maneuvers that these families conducted for dominance in the empire resembled nothing so much as the competition that had taken place three centuries earlier for dominance in feudal France.

Eastern Expansion.   For over a century, not only great princes but also monks, adventurers, and simple peasants streamed into the kingdoms and principalities of eastern Europe. Since the early thirteenth century, the Teutonic orders had used the sword to spread Christianity along the Baltic coast. By the early fourteenth century, these knight-monks had conquered Prussia and the coast as far east as the Narva River, now well within Russia, where they reached the borders of the Christian principality of Novgorod. The pagan inhabitants of these regions had to choose between conversion and expulsion. When they fled, their fields were turned over to land-hungry German peasants. Long wagon trains of pioneers snaked their way across Germany from the Rhineland, Westphalia, and Saxony to this new frontier. There they were able to negotiate advantageous contracts with their new lords, guaranteeing them greater freedom than they had known at home.

By the fifteenth century, religious and secular German lords had established a new agrarian economy, modeled on western European estates, in regions that were previously unoccupied or sparsely settled by the indigenous Slavic peoples. This economy specialized in the cultivation of grain for export to the west. Each fall, fleets of hundreds of ships sailed from Gdansk and Riga to the ports of the Netherlands, England, and France. Returning flotillas carried Flemish cloth and tons of salt, for preserving food, as far as Novgorod. The influx of Baltic grain into Europe caused a decline in domestic grain prices and a corresponding economic slump for landlords throughout the fourteenth and fifteenth centuries.

Central European Kingdoms.   Farther south, the Christian kingdoms of Poland, Bohemia, and Hungary beckoned different sorts of westerners. Newly opened silver and copper mines in Bohemia, Silesia, southern Poland, and Hungarian Transylvania needed skilled miners, smelters, and artisans. Many were recruited from the overpopulated regions of western Germany. East-west trade routes developed to export these metals, giving new life to the Bohemian towns of Prague and Brno, the Polish cities of Kraków and Lwów, and Hungarian Buda and Bratislava. Trade networks reached south to the Mediterranean via Vienna, the Brenner Pass, and Venice. To the north, trade routes extended to the Elbe River and the trading towns of Lübeck and Bremen. The Bavarian towns of Augsburg, Rothenburg, and Nuremberg flourished at the western end of this network. To the east, Lwów became a trading center connecting southern Russia with the west.

The wealth of eastern Europe, its abundant land, and its relative freedom attracted both peasants and merchants. The promise of profitable marriages with eastern royalty drew ambitious aristocrats. Continually menaced by one another and by the aggressive German aristocracy to the west, the royal families of Poland, Hungary, and Bohemia were eager to make marriage alliances with powerful aristocratic families from farther afield. Through such a marriage, for example, Charles

MAP DISCOVERY

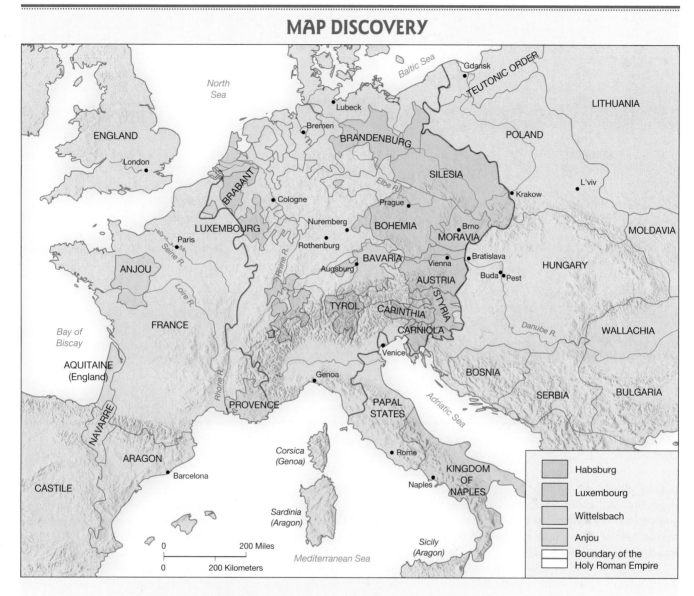

Central and Eastern Europe, ca. 1378

Examine this complex map of rival dynasties in fourteenth-century Europe. How do you explain the discontinuous territorial holdings of these great competing families? To what extent could the regions of the Holy Roman Empire be considered a state in 1378? Based on the text discussion, where might the Habsburgs be expected to extend and consolidate their power in the east?

Robert of Anjou became king of Hungary after the extinction of that realm's ancient royal dynasty. Similarly, Charles Robert's son Louis inherited the Polish crown in 1370 after the death of Casimir III, the last king of the Polish Piast dynasty. Nobles of the eastern European kingdoms were pleased to confirm the election of such outsiders. The elections prevented powerful German nobles from claiming succession to the Bohemian, Hungarian, and Polish thrones. At the same time, the families of the western European aristocracy did not have sufficiently strong local power bases to challenge the autonomy of the eastern nobility.

Charles IV (1347–1378) was typical of these restless dynasts. His grandfather, Emperor Henry VII (1308–1313), had arranged for his son John of Luxembourg to marry Elizabeth (d. 1330), the Premysl heiress of Bohemia, and thus acquire the Bohemian crown in 1310. John was king in name only. He spent most of his career fighting in the dynastic wars of the empire and of France. However, by mastering the intricate

GENEALOGY
THE FRENCH AND ENGLISH SUCCESSIONS

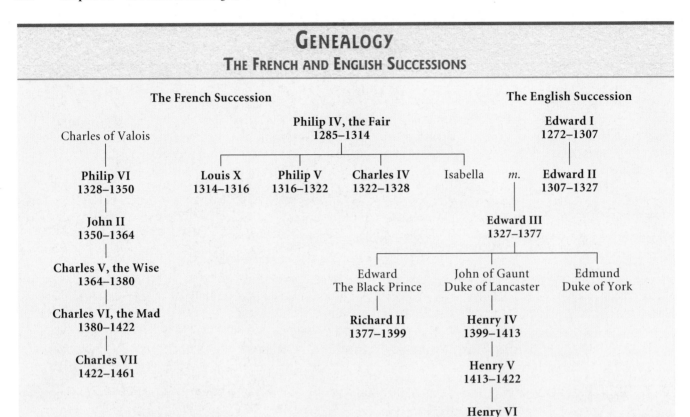

The French Succession

Charles of Valois

Philip IV, the Fair
1285–1314

Philip VI
1328–1350

Louis X
1314–1316

Philip V
1316–1322

Charles IV
1322–1328

Isabella   *m.*

John II
1350–1364

Charles V, the Wise
1364–1380

Charles VI, the Mad
1380–1422

Charles VII
1422–1461

The English Succession

Edward I
1272–1307

Edward II
1307–1327

Edward III
1327–1377

Edward
The Black Prince

John of Gaunt
Duke of Lancaster

Edmund
Duke of York

Richard II
1377–1399

Henry IV
1399–1413

Henry V
1413–1422

Henry VI
1422–1461

politics of the decaying Holy Roman Empire, he arranged the deposition of the Wittelsbach emperor Louis IV (1314–1347) and secured the election of Charles as king of the Romans, that is, heir of the empire, in 1346. The following year the Bohemian crown passed to Charles.

Although born in Prague, Charles had spent most of his youth in France, where he was deeply influenced by French culture. On his return to Prague in 1333, however, he rediscovered his Czech cultural roots. As king of Bohemia, he worked to make Prague a cultural center by combining French and Czech traditions. He imported artisans, architects, and artists to transform and beautify his capital. In 1348, he founded a university in Prague, the first in the empire, modeled on the University of Paris. Keenly interested in history, Charles provided court historians with the sources necessary to write their histories of the Bohemian kingdom.

Charles took a more active role in this cultural renewal than perhaps any European king since Alfred of England, fostering a literary renaissance in both Latin and Czech. Although he had forgotten his native Czech during his long stay in France, he soon learned to read and write it as well as French, German, Italian, and Latin. He authored a number of religious texts, fostered the use of the Czech language in religious services, and initiated a Czech translation of the Bible. He even composed his own autobiography, perhaps the first lay person to do so in medieval Europe.

The effects of Charles's cultural policies were far-reaching—but in directions he never anticipated. His interests in Czech culture and religious reform bore unexpected fruit during the reign of his son Sigismund, king of Germany (1410–1437), Bohemia (1419–1437), and Hungary (1387–1437) and Holy Roman Emperor (1433–1437). During Sigismund's reign, Czech religious and political reformers came into open conflict with the powerful German-speaking minority at the University of Prague. Led by the theologian Jan Hus (ca. 1372–1415), this reform movement ultimately challenged the authority of the Roman Church and became the direct predecessor of the great Reformation of the sixteenth century.

Even while building up his beloved city of Prague, Charles was dismantling the Holy Roman Empire. By the fourteenth century, the title of emperor held little political importance, although as an honorific title it was still bitterly contested by the great families of the empire. Charles sought to end such disputes and at the same time to solidify the autonomy of the kingdoms such as Bohemia against the threats of future imperial candidates. In 1356, he issued the **Golden Bull,** an edict that officially recognized what had long been the reality, namely, that the various German princes and kings were autonomous rulers. The bull also established the procedure by which future emperors would be elected. Thereafter, the emperor was chosen by seven great princes of the empire without the consultation or interference of the pope—a tradition of interference that dated to the coronation of Charlemagne. The procedure made disputed elections less likely, but it acknowledged that the office itself was less significant.

The same process that sapped the power of the emperor also reduced the significance of the princes. The empire fragmented into a number of large kingdoms and duchies such as Bohemia, Hungary, Poland, Austria, and Bavaria in the east and over 1,600 autonomous principalities, free towns, and sovereign bishoprics in the west. The inhabitants of these territories, often ruled by foreigners who had inherited sovereign powers through marriage, organized themselves into estates—political units of knights, burghers, and clergy—to present a united front in dealing with their prince. The princes, in turn, did not enjoy any universally recognized right to rule and were forced to negotiate with their estates for any powers they actually enjoyed.

The disintegration of the empire left political power east of the Rhine widely dispersed for over 500 years. While this meant that Germany did not become a nation-state until the nineteenth century, decentralization left late medieval Germany as a fertile region of cultural and constitutional creativity. In this creative process, the office of emperor played no role. After the Habsburg family definitively acquired the imperial office in 1440, the office of emperor ceased to have any role in Germany. Rather, the office became one of the building blocks of the great multinational Habsburg empire of central Europe, an empire that survived until 1918.

A Hundred Years of War

The political map of western Europe was no less a patchwork quilt of family holdings than was the empire. In the Iberian Peninsula, power struggles and futile wars engaged the three Christian monarchies of Castile, Aragon, and Portugal. Only with the marriage of Ferdinand of Aragon and Isabella of Castile in 1469 did something like a unified Spain begin to emerge from this world of family rivalries.

Similar struggles threatened to overwhelm the feudal monarchies of France and England in the fourteenth and fifteenth centuries. In both kingdoms, weakening economic climates and demographic catastrophe exacerbated dynastic crises and fierce competition.

Three long-simmering disputes triggered the series of campaigns collectively termed the **Hundred Years' War.** The first issue was conflicting rights in Gascony in southern France. Since the mid-thirteenth century, the kings of England had held Gascony as a fief of the French king. Neither monarchy was content with this arrangement, and for the next 75 years, kings quarreled constantly over sovereignty in the region.

The second point of contention was the close relationship between England and the Flemish cloth towns, which were the primary customers for English wool. Early in the fourteenth century, Flemish artisans rose up in a series of bloody revolts against the aristocratic cloth dealers who had long mo-

nopolized power. The count of Flanders and the French king supported the wealthy merchants; the English sided with the artisans.

The third dispute concerned the royal succession in France. Charles IV (1322–1328), the son of Philip IV, the Fair, died without an heir. The closest descendant of a French king was the grandson of Philip the Fair, King Edward III of England (1327–1377). However, Edward was the son of Philip's daughter Isabella. The French aristocracy, which did not want an English king to inherit the throne and unite the two kingdoms, pretended that according to ancient Frankish law, the crown could not pass through a woman. Instead, they preferred to give the crown to a cousin of the late king, Philip VI (1328–1350), who became the first of the Valois kings of France. At first, the English voiced no objection to Philip's accession, but in 1337, when the dispute over Gascony again flared up and Philip attempted to confiscate the region from his English "vassal" Edward III, the English king declared war on Philip. Edward's stated goal was not only to recover Gascony but also to claim the crown of his maternal grandfather.

Chivalry and Warfare. Though territorial and dynastic rivalries were the triggers that set off the war, its deeper cause was chivalry. The elites of Europe were both inspired by and trapped in a code of conduct that required them not only to maintain their honor by violence but also to cultivate violence to increase that honor. This code had been appropriate in a period of weak kingship, but by the late thirteenth century the growth of courts and royal power in France and in England left little room for private vengeance and vendettas. Nobles were now more often royal retainers than knights errant traveling about the countryside righting wrongs. Government was increasingly an affair of lawyers and bureaucrats, war an affair of professionals. Yet kings and nobles alike still agreed with the sentiment expressed by a contemporary poet: "The glory of princes is in their pride and in undertaking great peril." By the fourteenth century, only war provided sufficient peril.

Edward III of England and his rival Philip VI of France both epitomized the chivalrous knight. Both gloried in luxurious living and conspicuous consumption. Captivated by the romantic tales of King Arthur and the Round Table, in 1344 Edward organized a four-day-long round table celebration at which he entertained the most outstanding nobles in England with jousting contests, minstrels, and expensive gifts. A few years later, Edward organized the Order of the Garter, a select group of nobles who were to embody the highest qualities of chivalry. For a ruler like Edward, obsessed with knightly glory, war with France was the ideal way to win honor and fame.

In spite of his chivalric ideals, Edward was practical when it came to organizing and financing his campaigns. Philip shared Edward's ideals but lacked his rival's practicality and self-assurance. Before his elevation to the throne, Philip had been a valiant and successful warrior, fond of jousting, tournaments, and lavish celebrations. After his coronation he continued to act like a figure from a knightly romance, surrounding himself with aristocratic advisers who formed the most brilliant court of Europe, dispensing the royal treasure to his favorites, and dreaming of leading a great crusade to free the Holy Land. However, as the first French king in centuries who was elected rather than born into the right of succession, he treated the magnates from whose ranks he had come with excessive deference. He hesitated to press them for funds and deferred to them on matters of policy even while missing opportunities to raise other revenue from towns and merchants. Finally, although a competent warrior, Philip was no match in strategy or tactics for his English cousin.

Still, the sheer size and wealth of France should have made it the favorite in any war with England. Its population of roughly 16 million made it by far the largest and most densely populated kingdom in Europe. It was a major producer of cereal, wines, and cloth. The Flemish cloth towns, subdued by Philip in 1328, were the most industrialized area of Europe. England, by contrast, was a small, sparsely populated kingdom of under 5 million, and its economy was much less tied into international trade.

At the start of the war, Philip could rely on an income roughly three to five times greater than that of Edward. His greater income was matched by greater expenses, however, and he had no easy way to raise extraordinary funds for war. In contrast, the English king could use Parliament as an efficient source of war subsidies. Edward could also extract great sums from taxes on England's wool exports. Even after the invasion of France, Philip had to resort to manipulation of the coinage, confiscation of Italian bankers' property, and a whole range of nuisance taxes to finance his campaigns.

War was expensive. In spite of chivalrous ideals, nobles no longer fought as vassals of the king but as highly paid mercenaries. The nature of this service differed greatly on the two sides of the Channel. In France, the tactics and personnel had changed little since the twelfth century. The core of any army was the body of heavily armored nobles who rode into battle with their lords, supported by lightly armored knights. Behind them marched infantrymen recruited from towns and armed with pikes. Although the French also hired mercenary Italian crossbowmen, the nobles despised them and never used them effectively.

In contrast, centuries of fighting against Welsh and Scottish enemies had sharpened the English armies and their tactics. The great nobles continued to serve as heavily armored horsemen, but professional companies of foot soldiers raised by individual knights made up the bulk of the army. These professional companies consisted largely of pikemen and, most important, longbowmen. Although it was not as accurate as the crossbow, the English longbow had a greater range. Moreover, when massed archers fired volleys of arrows into enemy ranks, they proved extremely effective against enemy pikemen and even lightly armored cavalry.

English Successes.   The first real test of the two armies came at the Battle of Crécy in 1346. When an overwhelmingly superior French force advanced against the English army, the English massed their archers on a hill and rained arrows down on the French cavalry, which attacked in a glorious but suicidal manner. The English victory was total. By midnight they had repelled 16 assaults, losing only 100 men while killing over 3,000 French. The survivors, including Philip VI, fled in disorder. Strangely enough, the French learned nothing from the debacle. In 1356, Philip's successor John II (1350–1364) rashly attacked an English army at Poitiers and was captured. In 1415, the French blundered in a different way at Agincourt. This time, most of the heavily armored French knights dismounted and attempted to charge the elevated English position across a muddy field. Barely able to walk and unable to rise if they fell, all were captured. Out of fear that his numerically inferior army would be overwhelmed if the French recovered their breath, the English king ordered over 1,500 French nobles and 3,000 ordinary soldiers killed. English losses were fewer than 100.

Pitched battles were not the worst defeats for the French. More devastating were the constant raiding and systematic destruction of the French countryside by the English companies. The relief effort launched by Pope Benedict XII (1334–1342) in 1339 gives some idea of the scale of destruction. Papal agents, sent to aid victims of the English invasion, paid out over 12,000 pounds—the equivalent of one-third of the English annual royal income—to peasants in just one region of northern France.

Raiding and pillaging continued for decades, even during long truces between the French and English kings. During periods of truce, unemployed free companies of French and English mercenaries roamed the countryside, supporting themselves by banditry while awaiting the renewal of more formal hostilities. Never had the ideals of chivalric conduct been so far distant from the brutal realities of warfare.

The French kings were powerless to prevent such destruction, just as they were unable to defeat the enemy in open battle. Since the kings were incapable of protecting their subjects or winning in battle, the "silken thread binding together the kingdom of France," as one observer put it, began to unravel, and the kingdom that had been so painstakingly constructed by the Capetian monarchs began to fall apart. Not only did the English make significant territorial conquests, but the French nobles began behaving much like those in the Holy Roman Empire, carving out autonomous lordships. Private warfare and castle building, never entirely eradicated even by Louis IX and Philip IV, increased as royal government lost its ability to control the nobility. Whole regions of the kingdom slipped entirely from royal authority. Duke Philip the Good of Burgundy (1396–1467) allied himself with England against France and profited from the war to form a far-flung lordship that included Flanders, Brabant, Luxembourg, and Hainaut. By the time of his death, he was the most powerful ruler in Europe. Much of the so-called Hundred Years' War was actually a French civil war.

During this century of war, the French economy suffered even more than the French state. Trade routes were broken, and commerce declined as credit disappeared. French kings

■ The battle of Agincourt (1415) was one of the great battles of the Hundred Years' War. The heavily armored French cavalry met defeat at the hands of a much smaller force of disciplined English pikemen and longbowmen.

repeatedly seized the assets of Italian merchant bankers in order to finance the war. Such actions made the Italians, who had been the backbone of French commercial credit, extremely wary about extending loans in the kingdom. The kings then turned to French and Flemish merchants, extorting from them forced loans that dried up capital that might otherwise have been returned to commerce and industry. Politically and economically, France seemed doomed.

Joan of Arc and the Salvation of France.   The flower of French chivalry did not save France. Instead, at the darkest moment of the long and bloody struggle, salvation came at the hands of a simple peasant girl from the county of Champagne. By 1429, the English and their Burgundian allies held virtually all of northern France, including Paris. Now they were besieging Orléans, the key to the south. The heir to the French throne, the dauphin, was the weak-willed and uncrowned Charles VII (1422–1461). To him came Joan of Arc (1412–1431), an illiterate but deeply religious girl who bore an incredible message of hope. She claimed to have heard the voices of saints ordering her to save Orléans and have the dauphin crowned according to tradition at Reims.

Charles and his advisers were more than skeptical about this brash peasant girl who announced her divinely ordained mission to save France. Finally convinced of her sincerity, if not of her ability, Charles allowed her to accompany a relief force to Orléans. The French army, its spirit buoyed by the belief that Joan's simple faith was the work of God, defeated the English and ended the siege. This victory led to others, and on 16 July 1429, Charles was crowned king at Reims.

After the coronation, Joan's luck began to fade. She failed to take Paris, and in 1431 she was captured by the Burgundians, who sold her to the English. Eager to get rid of the troublesome girl, the English had her tried as a heretic. Charles made no move to save her, even though she had saved his kingdom. She was burned at the stake in Rouen on 30 May 1431.

Despite Joan's inglorious end, the tide had turned. The French pushed the English back toward the coast. In the final major battle of the war, fought at Formigny in 1450, the French used a new and telling weapon to defeat the English: gunpowder. Rather than charging the English directly, as they had done so often before, they mounted cannon and pounded the English to bits. Gunpowder completed the destruction of the chivalric traditions of warfare begun by archers and pikemen. By 1452, English continental holdings had been reduced to the town of Calais. The continental warfare of more than a century was over.

The English Wars of the Roses. Though war on the Continent had ended, warfare in England was just beginning. In some ways, the English monarchy had suffered even more from the Hundred Years' War than had the French. At the outset, English royal administration had been more advanced than that of the French. The system of royal agents, courts, and parliaments had created the expectation that the king could preserve peace and provide justice at home while waging successful and profitable wars abroad. As the decades dragged on without a decisive victory, the king came to rely on the aristocracy, enlisting its financial assistance by granting these magnates greater power at home.

War created powerful and autonomous aristocratic families with their own armies. Under a series of weak kings these families fought among themselves. Ultimately, they took sides in a civil war to determine the royal succession. For 30 years, from 1455 to 1485, supporters of the house of York, whose badge was the white rose, fought the rival house of Lancaster, whose symbol was the red rose. The English Wars of the Roses, as the conflict came to be called, finally ended in 1485, when Henry Tudor of the Lancastrian faction defeated his opponents. He inaugurated a new era as Henry VII (1485–1509), the first king of the Tudor dynasty.

LIFE AND DEATH IN THE LATER MIDDLE AGES

The violence and pageantry of late medieval life played out against a backdrop of extraordinary social upheaval. By the end of the thirteenth century, population growth in the West had strained available resources to the breaking point. All arable land was under cultivation, and even marginal moorland, rocky mountainsides, and plains were being pressed into service to feed a growing population. At the same time, kings and nobles demanded ever higher taxes and rents to finance their wars and extravagant lifestyles. The result was a precarious balance in which a late frost, a bad harvest, or hungry mercenaries could mean disaster. Part of the problem could be alleviated by importing grain from the Baltic or from Sicily, but this solution carried risks of its own. Transportation systems were too fragile to ensure regular supplies, and their rupture could initiate a cycle of famine, disease, and demographic collapse. Population began to decline slowly around 1300, and the downturn became catastrophic within 50 years. Between 1300 and 1450, Europe's population fell by more than 30 percent. It did not recover until the seventeenth century.

Dancing with Death

Between 1315 and 1317, the first great famine of the fourteenth century, triggered by crop failures and war, struck Europe. People died by the thousands. Urban workers, because they were chronically undernourished, were particularly hard hit. In the Flemish cloth town of Ypres, whose total population was less than 20,000, the town ordered the burial of 2,794 paupers' corpses within a five-month period. Although this was the greatest famine in medieval memory, it was not the last. The relatively prosperous Italian city of Pistoria, for example, recorded 16 different famines and food shortages in the fourteenth and fifteenth centuries. Disease accompanied famine. Crowded and filthy towns, opposing armies with their massed troops, and overpopulated countrysides provided fertile ground for the spread of infectious disease. Moreover, the greatly expanded trade routes of the thirteenth and fourteenth centuries, which carried goods and grain between East and West, also provided highways for deadly microbes. At Pistoria again, local chroniclers of the fourteenth and fifteenth centuries reported 14 years of sickness, fevers, epidemic, and plague.

Between 1347 and 1352, from one-half to one-third of Europe's population died from a virulent combination of bubonic, septicemic, and pneumonic plagues, known to history as the **Black Death.** The disease, carried by the fleas of infected rats, traveled the caravan routes from central Asia. It arrived in Messina, Sicily, aboard a merchant vessel in October 1347. From there the Black Death spread up the boot of Italy and then into southern France, England, and Spain. By 1349, it had reached northern Germany, Portugal, and Ireland. The following year the Low Countries, Scotland, Scandinavia, and Russia fell victim.

Plague victims died horribly. Soon after being bitten by an infected flea, they developed high fever, began coughing, and suffered excruciatingly painful swellings in the lymph nodes of the groin or armpits. These swellings were known as *buboes,* from which the disease took its name. In the final stages the victims began to vomit blood. The bubonic form of the disease usually killed within five days. The septicemic form, which attacked the blood, was swifter and deadlier. People infected by the airborne pneumonic form usually died in less than three days—in some cases, within a matter of hours.

Plague was all the more terrifying because its cause, its manner of transmission, and its cure were totally unknown until the end of the nineteenth century. Preachers saw the plague as divine punishment for sin. Ordinary people frequently accused Jews of causing it by poisoning drinking water. The medical faculty of Paris announced that it was the result of the conjunction of the planets Saturn, Jupiter, and Mars, which caused a corruption of the surrounding air.

Responses to the plague were equally varied. In many German towns, terrified Christian citizens looked for outside scapegoats and slaughtered the Jewish community. Cities, aware of the risk of infection although ignorant of its process, closed their gates and turned away outsiders. Individuals with means fled to country houses or locked themselves in their homes to avoid contact with others. Nothing worked. As devastating as the first outbreak of the plague was, its aftershocks were even more catastrophic. Once established in Europe, the disease continued to return roughly once each generation. The last outbreak of the plague in Europe was the 1771 epidemic in Moscow that killed 60,000.

MAP DISCOVERY

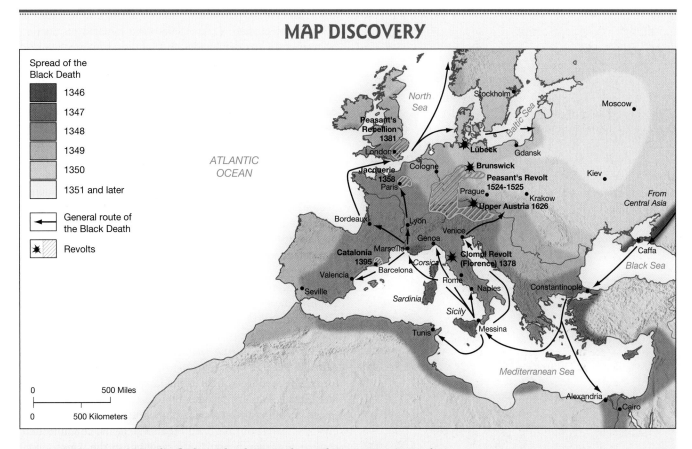

Spread of the Black Death and Peasant Revolts

How closely did the spread of the Black Death follow the medieval trade networks shown in the map on p. 183? What was the general direction and average annual speed of the disease's spread? Was the Black Death only a disaster to western Europe? Note the locations of peasant revolts. Based on the chapter discussion, what similarities and differences existed among the groups that revolted in the Later Middle Ages? Was there a relationship between the devastation of the plague and the outbreak of revolts?

The Black Death, along with other epidemics, famines, and war-induced shortages, affected western Europe much more than eastern Europe. The culminating effect of these disasters was a darker, more somber vision of life than that of the previous centuries. This vision found its expression in the Dance of Death, an increasingly popular image in art. Naked, rotting corpses dance with great animation before the living. The latter, depicted in the dress of all social orders, are immobile, surprised by death, reluctant but resigned.

Although no solid statistics exist from the fourteenth century, the plague certainly killed more people than all of the wars and famines of the century. It was the greatest disaster ever to befall Europe. The Black Death touched every aspect of life, hastening a process of social, economic, and cultural transformation that was already under way. The initial outbreak shattered social and economic structures. Fields were abandoned, workplaces stood idle, international trade was suspended. Traditional bonds of kinship, village, and even religion were broken by the horrors of death, flight, and failed expectations. "People cared no more for dead men than we care for dead goats," wrote one survivor. Brothers abandoned brothers, wives deserted husbands, and terror-stricken parents refused to nurse their own children.

Nothing had prepared Europe for this catastrophe. No teaching of the Church or its leaders could adequately explain it, and in spite of desperate attempts to fix the blame on Jews or strangers, no one but God could be held responsible. Survivors stood alone and uncertain before a new world. Across Europe, moralists reported a general lapse in traditional ethics, a breakdown in the moral codes. The most troubling aspect of this breakdown was what one defender of the old order termed "the plague of insurrection" that spread across Europe. This plague was brought on by the dimming of the hopes held by the survivors of the Black Death.

■ A page from the fourteenth-century psalter and prayer book of Bonne of Luxembourg, duchess of Normandy. The three figures of the dead shown here contrast with three living figures on the facing page of the psalter to illustrate a moral fable.

The Plague of Insurrection

Initially, even this darkest cloud had a silver lining. Lucky survivors of the plague soon found other reasons to rejoice. Property owners, when they finished burying their dead, discovered that they were far richer in land and goods. At the other end of the social spectrum, the plague had eliminated the labor surplus. Peasants were suddenly in great demand. For a time, at least, they were able to negotiate substantially higher wages and an improved relationship with landlords.

These hopes were short lived. The rise in expectations produced by the redistribution of wealth and the labor shortage created new tensions. Landlords sought laws forcing peasants to accept pre-plague wages and tightened their control over serfs to prevent them from fleeing to cities or other lords. At the same time, governments attempted to benefit from laborers' greater prosperity by imposing new taxes. In cities, where the plague had been particularly devastating, the demographic decline sharply lowered demand for goods and thus lowered the need for manufacturing and production of all

kinds. Like rural landowners, master craftsmen sought legislation to protect their incomes. New laws reduced production by restricting access to trades and increased masters' control over the surviving urban laborers. Social mobility, once a characteristic of urban life, slowed to a halt. Membership in guilds became hereditary, and young apprentices and journeymen had little hope of ever rising to the level of independent master craftsmen.

These new tensions led to violence when kings added their demands for new war taxes to the landlords' and masters' attempts to erase the peasants' and workers' recent gains. The first revolts took place in France, where peasants and townspeople, disgusted with the incompetence of the nobility in their conduct of the war against England, feared that their new wealth would be stolen from them by corrupt and incompetent aristocrats.

The Jacquerie.   In 1358, to ransom King John II from the English, the French government attempted to increase taxes on the peasantry. At the same time, local nobles increased their rents and demands. Peasants in the area of Beauvais, north of Paris, fearing that they would lose their modest gains of the previous ten years, rebelled against their landlords. The revolt—known as the **Jacquerie** for the archetypical French peasant, Jacques Bonnehomme—was a spontaneous outburst directed against the nobility, whom the peasants saw as responsible for all their ills. Without real leadership or program, peasants attacked as many nobles as they could find, killing men, women, and children and burning their homes and castles. The peasants' brutality deeply shocked the upper classes, whose own violence was constrained within the bounds of the chivalric code. Because the Church largely supported the power structure, the uprising was also strongly anticlerical. Churches were burned, and priests were killed. Success bred further attacks, and the disorganized army of peasants began to march south toward Paris, killing, looting, and burning everything associated with the despised nobility.

In the midst of this peasant revolt, Etienne Marcel (ca. 1316–1358), a wealthy Parisian cloth merchant, led an uprising of Parisian merchants, which sought to take control of royal finances and force fiscal reforms on the dauphin, the future Charles V. Although initially the rebels were primarily members of the merchant and guild elite, Marcel soon enlisted the support of the radical townspeople against the aristocracy. He even made overtures to the leaders of the Jacquerie to join forces. For a brief time it appeared that the aristocratic order in France might succumb. However, in the end, peasant and merchant rebels were no match for professional armies. The Jacquerie met its end at Meaux, outside Paris, where an aristocratic force cut the peasants to pieces. Survivors were systematically hunted down and hanged or burned alive. The Parisian revolt met a similar fate. Aristocratic armies surrounded the city and cut off its food supply. Marcel was assassinated, and the dauphin Charles regained the city.

The English Peasants' Revolt and Urban Uprisings.
The French revolts set the pattern for similar uprisings across Europe. Rebels were usually relatively prosperous peasants or townspeople whose economic situations were threatened by aristocratic attempts to turn back the clock to the period before the Black Death. In 1381, English peasants, reacting to new and hated taxes, rose in a less violent but more coordinated revolt known as the Great Rebellion. Peasant revolts took place in the northern Spanish region of Catalonia in 1395 and in Germany throughout the fourteenth and fifteenth centuries. The largest was the great Peasants' Revolt of 1524. Although always ruthlessly suppressed, European peasant uprisings continued until the peasant rebellion of 1626 in upper Austria. These outbursts indicated not necessarily the desperation of Europe's peasantry, but the new belief that they could change their lives for the better through united action.

Urban artisans imitated the example of their rural cousins. Although there had been some uprisings in the Flemish towns before the Black Death, revolts of townspeople picked up momentum in the second half of the fourteenth century. The town rebels were generally independent artisans and small tradesmen who wanted to break the control of the powerful guilds. The one exception to this pattern was the Ciompi revolt of 1378 in Florence, in which the wool workers forced recognition of two guilds of laborers alongside the powerful guilds of masters. The workers and artisans controlled city government until 1382, when mercenaries hired by the elite surrounded the workers' slums and crushed them in bloody house-to-house fighting. In spite of the brutal suppression and ultimate failure of popular revolts, they became permanent if intermittent features on the European social landscape. The legacy of the Jacquerie was seen 431 years later in the storming of the Bastille.

Living and Dying in Medieval Towns

Population decline, war, and class conflict in France and the Low Countries fatally weakened the vitality of the commercial and manufacturing system of northwestern Europe. These same events reduced the market for Italian goods and undermined the economic strength of the great Italian cities. The Hundred Years' War bankrupted many of Florence's greatest banking houses, such as the Bardi and Peruzzi, that lent to both French and English kings. Commercial activity declined as well. In the 1330s, Venice had sent between four and nine trading galleys to Flanders each year; by the 1390s, the city was sending only three to five. Genoa, which had earlier led in the trade with the cloth towns of the north, saw the economic activity of its port decline by roughly one-third to one-half during the same period. While Italians did not disappear from northern cities, they no longer held a near monopoly on northern trade. Events outside of Europe also led to the decline of Italian economic power. In the course of the fourteenth and fifteenth centuries, the Mongol Khanates gradually lost power or were absorbed into local traditions. In China,

adherents of the White Lotus sect, a millenarian, messianic offshoot of Buddhism, led the revolt that established the Ming dynasty. In western Asia, Tamerlane (1370–1405), a Muslim of Mongolian descent, briefly and brutally restored the Khanate, but after his death Turkish peoples divided his vast lands among tribal rulers. In Russia, the Duke Ivan I of Moscow (1328–1341) rose to power by persuading the Mongols to appoint him as the sole collector of tribute from the various Slavic states. A century later, his successor Prince Ivan III the Great (1462–1505) led a successful revolt against the remnants of Mongol rule, subjugated the other Russian princes to himself and assumed the title of tsar (or caesar). The disintegration of the Mongol Empire and the rise of new, aggressive kingdoms also caused disruptions of the Silk Route and Italian trade with China and India. Soon, Europeans would begin to look for alternative routes to the East.

Economic Shifts.   The setbacks of the Italians worked to the advantage of German towns in the disintegrating empire. Along the Baltic Sea, in Scandinavia, and in northern Germany, towns such as Lübeck, Lüneburg, Visby, Bremen, and Cologne formed a commercial and political alliance to control northern trade. During the second half of the fourteenth century this **Hanseatic League**—the word *hansa* means "company"—monopolized the northern grain trade and forced Denmark to grant its members exclusive rights to export Scandinavian fish throughout Europe. Hanseatic merchants established colonies from Novgorod to London to Bruges and even Venice. They carried dried and salted fish to Prague and supplied grain from Riga to England and France.

English towns also profited from the decline of Flanders and France. The population decline of the fourteenth century led many English landowners to switch from traditional farming to sheep raising, since pasturing sheep required few workers and promised cash profits. While surviving peasants were driven off the land and forced to beg for a living, lords produced more wool than ever before. However, instead of exporting the wool to Flanders to be made into cloth, the English began to make cloth themselves. Protected by high tariffs on imports and low duties on exports, England had become a major exporter of finished cloth by the middle of the fifteenth century.

Addressing Poverty and Crime.   The new social and economic circumstances of European towns accentuated the gulf between rich and poor. The streets and markets of fifteenth-century towns bustled with the sights and sounds of rich Hanseatic merchants, Italian bankers, and prosperous local tradesmen. The back alleys and squatter settlements on the edges of these towns teemed with a growing mass of desperate workers and their families. The combination of economic depression, plague, and rural crisis deepened the misery of the growing population of urban poor. Medieval towns responded by developing new means of public assistance and social control.

■ Breaking on the wheel was a particularly gruesome punishment inflicted on condemned criminals during the later Middle Ages. The criminal's broken limbs are threaded through the spokes of the wheel and tied with ropes. The mocking executioner holding leftover rope stands at the right. To the left are three seemingly sympathetic spectators.

Traditionally, charity, whether by individuals or organizations, had been a religious act that focused more on the soul of the giver than on the life of the recipient. Hospitals, for example, were all-purpose religious institutions providing lodging for pilgrims, the elderly, and the ill. By the fourteenth century, such pious institutions had become inadequate to deal with the increasing numbers of poor and ill. Towns began to assume control over a centralized system of public assistance. Although men and women who had taken religious vows staffed these institutions, city governments contributed to their budgets and oversaw their finances. Cities also attempted to rationalize the distribution of charity according to need and merit. Antwerp, for example, established a centralized relief service, which distributed badges to those deemed worthy of public assistance. Only people who wore the badges could receive food.

One consequence of poverty was increased crime, which led to repressive measures and harsh punishments. Traditionally, in much of Europe, crimes such as robbery, lar-

ceny, and even manslaughter had been punishable by fines and payments to the victim or the victim's heirs. Elsewhere, as in France and England, where corporal punishment had been the normal penalty for major crimes, hanging, blinding, and the loss of a hand or foot had been the most common punishments. During the later Middle Ages, gruesome forms of mutilation and execution became common for a long list of offenses. Petty larceny was punished with whipping, cutting off ears or thumbs, branding, or expulsion. In some towns, robbery of an amount over three pence was punished with death. Death by hanging might be replaced by more savage punishments such as breaking on the wheel. In this particularly brutal torture, the prisoner's limbs and back were first broken with a wagon wheel. Then the criminal was tied to the wheel and left on a pole to die. Drowning, boiling, burning, and burial alive, a particularly common punishment for women, were other frequently used methods of execution.

The frequency of such punishments increased with their severity. In Augsburg, until the middle of the thirteenth century, executions were so rare that the city did not even have a public executioner before 1276. However, in the following two centuries the city fathers increased executions in an attempt to combat a rising crime rate. In 1452, the skulls of 250 hanged persons were found in pits on the gallows hill. At the same time, the bodies of 32 thieves twisted in the wind above.

THE SPIRIT OF THE LATER MIDDLE AGES

In spite of the constant presence of death, Europeans of the later Middle Ages celebrated life with vigor, creativity, and a growing sense of individuality and independence. During the fourteenth century, the Church failed to provide unified leadership. The institutional division of the Church was paralleled by divisions over how to lead the proper Christian life. Many devout Christians developed independent lifestyles that were intended to bring them closer to God without reliance on the Church hierarchy. Some elaborated beliefs that the church branded as heresy. Others called into question the philosophical bases of theological speculation that had developed since the time of Abelard and Aquinas. Finally, the increasing pluralism of European culture gave rise to new literary traditions that both celebrated and criticized the medieval legacy of Christianity, chivalry, and social order.

The Crisis of the Papacy

The universal empire as well as its traditional competitor, the universal Church, declined in the later Middle Ages. The papacy never recovered from the humiliating defeat Pope Boniface VIII suffered at the hands of King Philip the Fair in 1303. The ecclesiastical edifice created by the thirteenth-century popes was shaken to its foundations, first by becoming a virtual appendage of the French monarchy and then by a dispute that for more than 40 years gave European Christians a choice between two, and finally three, claimants to the chair of Saint Peter.

In 1305, the College of Cardinals elected as pope the bishop of Bordeaux. The new pope, who took the name Clement V (1305–1314), was close to Philip IV of France and had no desire to meet the fate of his predecessor, Pope Boniface VIII. Therefore, Clement took up residence not in Rome but in the papal city of Avignon on the east bank of the Rhone River. Technically, Avignon was a papal estate within the Holy Roman Empire. Actually, with France just across the river, the pope at Avignon was under French control.

The Avignon Papacy.   For the next 70 years, French popes and French cardinals ruled the Church. The traditional enemies of France as well as religious reformers who expected leadership from the papacy looked on this situation with disgust. Critics such as the Italian poet Petrarch accused the Avignon popes and their courtiers of every possible crime and sin, but they were no worse than any other great lords of the fourteenth century. In pursuit of political and financial

rewards, they had simply lost sight of their roles as religious leaders.

The popes of Avignon were more successful in achieving their financial goals than in winning political power. Although they attempted to follow an independent course in international affairs, their French orientation eroded their influence in European politics, especially in the Holy Roman Empire. Pope John XXII (1316–1334), one of the most unpleasant and argumentative individuals ever to hold the chair of Peter, tried to block the election of the Wittelsbach Louis of Bavaria as emperor. Louis ignored the pope, invaded Italy, and was proclaimed emperor by the people of Rome. In 1338, the German electors solemnly declared that the imperial office was held directly from God and did not require papal confirmation—a declaration that was later upheld in the Golden Bull. No longer could the popes exert any direct influence in the internal affairs of Europe's states.

Frustrated politically, the Avignon popes concentrated on perfecting the legal and fiscal system of the Church and were enormously successful in concentrating the vast financial and legal power of the Church in the papal office. From the papal court, or *curia*, they created a vast and efficient central bureaucracy whose primary role was to increase papal revenues.

Revenues came from two main sources. The less lucrative but ultimately more critical source was the sale of **indulgences.** The Church had long taught that sinners who repented might be absolved of their sins and escape the fires of hell. However, they still had to suffer temporal punishment. This punishment, called penance, could take the form of fasting, prayer, or performance of some good deed. Having failed to do penance on earth, absolved sinners would have to endure a period in purgatory before they could be admitted to heaven. However, since the saints had done more penance than was required to make up for the temporal punishments due them, they had established a treasury of merit, a sort of spiritual bank account. The pope was the banker and could transfer some of this positive balance to repentant sinners in return for some pious act such as contributing money to build a new church. These so-called indulgences could be purchased for one's own use or to assist the souls of family members already in purgatory. Papal "pardoners" working on commission used high-pressure sales pitches to sell indulgences across Europe.

The second and major source of papal income was the sale of Church offices, or *benefices.* Popes claimed the right to appoint bishops and abbots to all benefices and to collect a hefty tax for the appointment. Papal appointees often acquired numerous offices and viewed them merely as sources of income, leaving pastoral duties, when they were performed at all, to hired local clergy.

The Great Schism.   In 1377, Pope Gregory XI (1370–1378) returned from Avignon to Rome but died almost immediately on arrival. Thousands of Italians, afraid that the cardinals would elect another Frenchman, surrounded the church where they were meeting and demanded an Italian pope. The terrified cardinals elected an Italian, who took the name Urban VI (1378–1389). Once elected, Urban attempted to reform the curia, but he did so in a most undiplomatic way, insulting the cardinals and threatening to appoint enough non-French bishops to their number to end French control of the curia. The cardinals soon left Rome and announced that because the election had been made under duress, it was invalid and Urban should resign. When he refused, they held a second election and chose a Frenchman, Clement VII (1378–1394), who took up residence in Avignon. The Church now had two heads, both with reasonable claims to the office.

The chaos created by this so-called **Great Schism** divided Western Christendom. In every diocese, when a bishop died, his successor had to be appointed by the pope. But by which pope? To whom did taxes go? Who received the income from the sale of indulgences or benefices? Did appeals in the Church courts go to Rome or to Avignon? More significantly, since each pope excommunicated the supporters of his opponent, everyone in the West was under a sentence of excommunication. Could anyone be saved?

Nothing in Church law or tradition offered a solution to this crisis. Nor did unilateral efforts to settle the crisis succeed. France twice invaded Italy in an attempt to eliminate Urban but failed both times. When Urban and Clement died, cardinals on both sides elected successors. By the end of the fourteenth century, France and the empire were exasperated with their popes, and even the cardinals were determined to end the stalemate.

Conciliarism.   Church lawyers argued that only a general council could end the schism. Both popes opposed **conciliarism** because it suggested that an assembly of the Church rather than the pope held supreme authority. However, in 1408, cardinals from both sides summoned a council in the Italian city of Pisa. The council deposed both rivals and elected a new pope. But this solution only made matters worse, since neither pope accepted the council's decision. Europe now had to contend with not two but three popes, each claiming to be the true successor of Saint Peter.

Six years later, the Council of Constance managed a final solution. There, under the patronage of the emperor-elect Sigismund (1410–1437), cardinals, bishops, abbots, and theologians from across Europe met to resolve the crisis. Their goal was not only to settle the schism but also to reform the Church to prevent a recurrence of such a scandal. The participants at Constance hoped to restructure the Church as a limited monarchy in which the powers of the pope would be controlled through frequent councils. The Pisan and Avignon popes were deposed. The Roman pope, abandoned by all of his supporters, abdicated. Before doing so, however, he formally convoked the council to preserve the tradition that a general council had to be called by the pope. Finally, the council elected as pope an Italian cardinal who was not aligned with any of the claimants. The election of the cardinal, who took the name of Martin V (1417–1431), ended the schism.

The relief at the end of the Great Schism could not hide the very real problems left by over a century of papal weakness. The prestige of the papacy had been permanently compromised. Everywhere, the Church had become more national in character. The conciliarist demand for control of the Church, which had ended the schism, lessened the power of the pope. Moreover, during the century between Boniface VIII and Martin V, new religious movements had taken root across Europe, movements that the political creatures who had occupied the papal office could neither understand nor control. The Council of Constance, which brought an end to the schism, also condemned Jan Hus, the leader of the Czech reform movement and the spiritual founder of the later Protestant reformation of the sixteenth century. The disintegration of the Church loomed ever closer as pious individuals turned away from the organized Church and sought divine help in personal piety, mysticism, or even magic.

Discerning the Spirit of God

When Joan of Arc first appeared before the dauphin in 1429, he feared that she was a witch. Only a physical examination by matrons, which determined that she was a virgin, persuaded him otherwise—witches were believed to have had intercourse with the devil. Everyone in the late Middle Ages was familiar with witches, saints, and heretics. Distinguishing among them was often a matter of perspective.

Witchcraft.   Accusations of witchcraft were relatively rare in the Middle Ages. The age of witch-hunts occurred later, in the sixteenth and seventeenth centuries. During the Middle Ages, magic existed in a wide variety of forms, but its definition was fluid, and its practitioners were not always considered evil. Alchemists and astrologers held honored places in society, while simple practitioners of folk religion, medicine, and superstition were condemned, particularly when they were poor women. Witches, believed to have made a contract with the devil, were condemned and persecuted as heretics. Only at the end of the fifteenth century, with the publication of the *Witches' Hammer,* a handbook for inquisitors, did the European witch craze begin in earnest. Earlier, authorities feared more those people who sought their own pacts not with the devil but with God.

Lay Piety.   Even as Europeans were losing respect for the institutional Church, people everywhere were seeking closer and more intimate relationships with God. Distrusting the formal institutions of the Church, lay persons and clerics turned to private devotions and to mysticism to achieve union with the divine. Most of these stayed within the Church. Others, among them many female mystics, maintained an ambiguous relationship with the traditional institutions of Christianity. A few, such as the Brethren of the Free Spirit, broke sharply with it.

In the fourteenth and fifteenth centuries, a great many pious lay men and women chose to live together to strive for spiritual perfection without entering established religious orders. The Brethren of the Common Life in the Rhineland and Low Countries dedicated themselves to preaching, charity, and a pious life. In the early fifteenth century, an unknown member of the Brethren wrote the *Imitation of Christ,* a book of spiritual direction that remains today the most widely read religious text after the Bible.

Christians of the later Middle Ages sought to imitate Christ and venerated the Eucharist, or communion wafer, which the Church taught was the actual body of Jesus. Male mystics focused on imitating Jesus in his poverty, his suffering, and his humility. Women developed their own form of piety, which focused not on wealth and power but on spiritual nourishment, particularly as provided by the Eucharist. For women mystics, radical fasting became preparation for the reception of the Eucharist, which was often described in highly emotional and erotic terms. After a long period of fasting, Lukardis of Oberweimar (d. 1309) had a vision in which Jesus appeared to her as a handsome youth and blew into her mouth. In the words of her biographer, "She was infused with such sweetness and such inner fruition that she felt as if drunk." From the age of 23, Catherine of Sienna (d. 1380) subsisted entirely on the Eucharist, cold water, and bitter herbs that she sucked and then spat out. For those and other pious women, fasting and devotion to the Eucharist did not mean rejection of the body. Rather, these were attempts to use their senses to approach perfect union with God, who was for them both food and drink.

Heresy and Revolt

Only a thin line separated the saint's heroic search for union with God from the heretic's identification with God. The radical Brethren of the Free Spirit believed that God was all things and that all things would return to God. Such pantheism denied the possibility of sin, punishment, and the need for salvation. Members of the sect were hunted down, and many were burned as heretics. The specter of the Inquisition, the ecclesiastical court system that was charged with ferreting out heretics, hung over all such communities.

John Wycliffe.   When unorthodox Christians were protected by secular lords, the ecclesiastical courts were powerless. This was the case with John Wycliffe (ca. 1330–1384), an Oxford theologian who attacked the doctrinal and political bases of the Church. He taught that the value of the sacraments depended on the worthiness of the priest administering them, that Jesus was present in the Eucharist only in spirit, that indulgences were useless, and that salvation depended on divine predestination rather than individual merit. Normally, these teachings would have led him to the stake. But he had also attacked the Church's right to wealth and luxury, an idea whose political implications pleased the English monarchy and nobility. Wycliffe's own exemplary manner of life and his teaching that the Church's role in temporal affairs should be severely limited made him an extremely popular figure in

England. Therefore he was allowed to live and teach in peace. Only under Henry V (1413–1422) were Wycliffe's followers, known as Lollards, vigorously suppressed by the state. Before this condemnation took place, however, Wycliffe's teachings reached the kingdom of Bohemia through the marriage of Charles IV's daughter Anne of Bohemia to the English king Richard II. Anne took with her to England a number of Bohemian clerics, some of whom studied at Oxford and absorbed Wycliffe's political and religious teachings, which they then took back to Bohemia.

Jan Hus.   In Prague, some of Wycliffe's less radical teachings took root among the theology faculty of the new university, where the leading proponent of Wycliffe's teachings was Jan Hus (1373–1415), an immensely popular young master and preacher. Although Hus rejected Wycliffe's ideas about the priesthood and the sacraments, he and other Czech preachers attacked indulgences and demanded a reform of Church liturgy and morals. They grafted these religious demands onto an attack on German dominance of the Bohemian kingdom. These attacks outraged both the Pisan pope John XXIII (1410–1415) and the Bohemian king Wenceslas IV (1378–1419), who favored the German faction. The pope excommunicated Hus, and the king expelled the Czech faculty from the university. Hus was convinced that he was no heretic and that a fair hearing would clear him. He therefore agreed to travel to the Council of Constance under promise of safe conduct from the emperor-elect Sigismund to defend his position. There, he was tried on a charge of heresy, convicted, and burned at the stake.

News of Hus's execution touched off a revolt in Bohemia. Unlike the peasant revolts of the past, however, this revolt had broad popular support throughout all levels of Czech society. Peasants, nobles, and townspeople saw the attack on Hus and his followers as an attack on Czech independence and national interest by a Church and an empire controlled by Germans. Soon a radical faction known as the Taborites was demanding the abolition of private property and the institution of a communal state. Although moderate **Hussites** and Bohemian Catholics combined to defeat the radicals in 1434, most of Bohemia remained Hussite through the fifteenth century. The sixteenth-century reformer Martin Luther declared himself a follower of Jan Hus.

Religious Persecution in Spain

Through the thirteenth century, even as kings of England and France expelled Jews from their kingdoms and as they were subjected to sporadic pogroms and massacres in Germany, Jews and Muslims were tolerated on the Iberian Penninsula. This fragile existence was shattered in the fourteenth and fifteenth centuries. The causes were complex: a declining economy, political unrest, Christian triumphalism as the reconquest moved into its last stages, and nascent nationalism all increased intercultural tensions. In 1391, mendicant friars inflamed Aragon with preaching against Jews and caused widespread violent attacks. Thereafter, in towns across Spain Christians rose up in arms against their Jewish neighbors in riots animated both by a hatred of Jews and a protest against the king. Thousands died and thousands more were forced to convert.

The Muslim population fared no better. In the fifteenth century, Muslims faced conversion or expulsion, first to Granada and, after that last Muslim principality fell in 1492, to North Africa. Those who resisted were hunted down, their villages destroyed, and their populations dispersed.

In time, even Muslim and Jewish converts (termed respectively *moriscos* and *conversos*) found that Christian baptism was not necessarily a protection. Most moriscos remained secretly faithful to Islam and were ruthlessly persecuted and expelled. Many conversos also continued to practice their faith in secret for generations. However, many descendants of Jewish converts became sincere Christians: their ranks included bishops, inquisitors, and even saints (such as Teresa of Ávila). Nevertheless, Spaniards became obsessed with fears of

CONVIVENCIA

By the High Middle Ages the position of Jews in western Europe was difficult. They had been expelled from England and from France. In Spain, under a system known as Convivencia, *or living together, they still enjoyed royal protection. However, as this text, known as* Las Siete Partidas, *issued in 1263 by King Alfonso X of Castile and in force through the fourteenth and fifteenth centuries shows, hostility, fueled by unfounded rumors of ritual murder, was making Jewish life increasingly precarious.*

Focus Questions

What beliefs and prejudices led to Christians' intolerance toward Jews? What protections did Jews receive from the king?

Jews should pass their lives among Christians quietly and without disorder, practicing their own religious rites, and not speaking ill of the faith of Our Lord Jesus Christ, which Christians acknowledge. Moreover, a Jew should be very careful to avoid preaching to, or converting any Christian, to the end that he may become a Jew, by exalting his own belief and disparaging ours. Whoever violates this law shall be put to death and lose all his property. And because we have heard it said that in some places Jews celebrated, and still celebrate Good Friday, which commemorates the Passion of Our Lord Jesus Christ, by way of contempt; stealing children and fastening them to crosses, and making images of wax and crucifying them, when they cannot obtain children; we order that, hereafter, if in any part of our dominions anything like this is done, and can be proved, all persons who were present when the act was committed shall be seized, arrested and brought before the king; and after the king ascertains that they are guilty, he shall cause them to be put to death in a disgraceful manner, no matter how many there may be.

We also forbid any Jew to dare to leave his house or his quarter on Good Friday, but they must all remain shut up until Saturday morning; and if they violate this regulation, we decree that they shall not be entitled to reparation for any injury or dishonor inflicted upon them by Christians.

Saturday is the day on which Jews perform their devotions, and remain quiet in their lodgings, and do not make

contracts or transact any business; and for the reason that they are obliged by their religion, to keep it, no one should on that day summon them or bring them into court. Wherefore we order that no judge shall employ force or any constraint upon Jews on Saturday, in order to bring them into court on account of their debts; or arrest them; or cause them any other annoyance; for the remaining days of the week are sufficient for the purpose of employing compulsion against them, and for making demands for things which can be demanded of them, according to law. Jews are not bound to obey a summons served upon them on that day; and, moreover, we decree that any decision rendered against them on Saturday shall not be valid; but if a Jew should wound, kill, rob, steal, or commit any other offense like these for which he can be punished in person and property, then the judge can arrest him on Saturday.

We also decree that all claims that Christians have against Jews, and Jews against Christians shall be decided and determined by our judges in the district where they reside, and not by their old men. And as we forbid Christians to bring Jews into court or annoy them on Saturday; so we also decree that Jews, neither in person, nor by their attorneys, shall have the right to bring Christians into court, or annoy them on this day. And in addition we forbid any Christian, on his own responsibility, to arrest wrong any Jew either in his person or property, but where he has any complaint against him he must bring it before our judges; and if anyone be so bold as to use violence against the Jews, or rob them of anything he shall return them double the value of the same.

Las Siete Partidas, tr. Samuel Parsons Scott (Chicago: Published for the Comparative Law Bureau of the American Bar Association by Commerce Clearing House, Inc., 1931).

anyone descended from Jews or Muslims and instituted legal sanctions against anyone who could not prove "purity of blood," that is, who might have Jewish or Muslim ancestors.

William of Ockham and the Spirit of Truth

The critical and individualistic approach that characterized religion during the later Middle Ages was also typical of the philosophical thought of the period. The delicate balance between faith and reason taught by Aquinas and other intellectuals in the thirteenth century disintegrated in the fourteenth. As in other areas of life, intellectuals questioned the basic suppositions of their predecessors, directing intellectual activity away from general speculations and toward particular, observable reality.

The person primarily responsible for this new intellectual climate was the English Franciscan William of Ockham (ca. 1300–1349). Excommunicated for his defense of radical poverty, Ockham joined the imperialist cause at the court of Emperor Louis IV. Imperial power, he argued, derived not from the pope but from the people. He believed that people should be free to determine their own form of government and to elect rulers. They should be able to make their choice directly, as in the election of the emperor by electors who represent the people, or implicitly, through continuing forms of government. In either case, Ockham believed, government should be entirely secular and that neither popes nor bishops nor priests should have any role. Ockham went still further. He denied the absolute authority of the pope, even in spiritual matters. Rather, Ockham argued, parishes, religious orders, and monasteries should send representatives to regional synods, which in turn would elect representatives to general councils. Ockham's ideas on Church governance offered the one hope for a solution to the Great Schism that erupted shortly after his death. The Council of Constance, which ended the schism, was the fruit of Ockham's political theory.

As radical as Ockham's political ideas were, his philosophical outlook was even more extreme and exerted a more direct and lasting influence. The Christian Aristotelianism that developed in the thirteenth century had depended on the validity of general concepts called universals, which could be analyzed through the use of logic. Aquinas and others who studied the eternity of the world, the existence of God, the nature of the soul, and other philosophical questions believed that people could reach general truths by abstracting universals from particular, individual cases. Ockham argued that universals were merely names, no more than convenient tags for discussing individual things. He stated that universals had no connection with reality and could not be used to reason from particular observations to general truths. This radical **nominalism** (from the Latin *nomen,* "name") thus denied that human reason could aspire to certain truth. For Ockham and his followers, philosophical speculation was essentially a logical, linguistic exercise, not a way to certain knowledge.

Just as Ockham's political theory dominated the later fourteenth century, his nominalist philosophy won over the philosophical faculties of Europe. Since he had discredited the value of Aristotelian logic to increase knowledge, the result was, on the one hand, a decline in abstract speculation and, on the other, a greater interest in scientific observation of individual phenomena. In the next generation, Parisian professors, trained in the tradition of Ockham, laid the foundation for scientific studies of motion and the universe that led to the scientific discoveries of the sixteenth and seventeenth centuries.

Vernacular Literature and the Individual

Just as the religious and philosophical concerns of the later Middle Ages developed within national frameworks and criticized accepted authority from the perspective of individual experience, so too did the vernacular (as opposed to Latin) literatures of the age begin to explore the place of the individual within an increasingly complex society. Across Europe, authors reviewed the traditional values of society with a critical eye, reworking and transforming traditional literary genres into statements both personal and profound.

Italy.   In Italy, a trio of Tuscan poets, Dante Alighieri (1265–1321), Petrarch (1304–1374), and Boccaccio (1313–1375), not only made Italian a literary language but composed in it some of the greatest literature of all time. Dante, the first and greatest of the three, wrote the *Divine Comedy* during the last years of his life.

The *Divine Comedy* is a view of the whole Christian universe, populated with people from antiquity and from Dante's own day. The poem is both a sophisticated summary of philosophical and theological thought at the beginning of the fourteenth century and an astute political commentary on his times. The poet sets this vision within a three-part poetic journey through hell (*Inferno*), purgatory (*Purgatorio*), and heaven (*Paradiso*). In each part, Dante adopts a poetic style appropriate to the subject matter. His journey through hell to witness the sufferings of the damned is described in brutal, immediate language. In purgatory, Dante meets sinners whose punishments will someday end. These he describes in a language of dreams, imagination, and nostalgic recollection. Paradise is portrayed in a symbolic language that is nonphysical and nonrepresentational. In the face of transcendent perfection, human imagery and poetry fail. In his final vision, he sees the reflected light of a mystical rose in which the saints are ranked. The *Divine Comedy* is Dante's personal summary of all that is good and bad in medieval culture and politics.

England.   Dante had set his great poem within a vision of the other world. Emerging English literature was more firmly rooted in contemporary society. William Langland (ca. 1330–1395) and Geoffrey Chaucer (ca. 1343–1400) both presented images of their social milieu. In *Piers Plowman,* Langland presents society from the perspective of the peasantry. Chaucer's work, *The Canterbury Tales,* is much more sophisticated and wide-ranging, weaving together the whole spectrum of late medieval literature and life.

CHRONOLOGY
THE LATER MIDDLE AGES, 1300–1500

1305–1377	Babylonian Captivity (Avignon papacy)
1337–1452	Hundred Years' War
1347–1352	Black Death spreads throughout Europe
1358	Jacquerie revolt of French peasants; Etienne Marcel leads revolt of Parisian merchants
1378	Ciompi revolt in Florence
1380	Death of Catherine of Siena
1378–1417	Great Schism divides Christianity
1381	Great Rebellion of English peasants
1409–1410	Council of Pisa
1414–1417	Council of Constance ends Great Schism
1415	Jan Hus executed
1431	Death of Joan of Arc
1455–1485	English Wars of the Roses

Chaucer placed his tales in the mouths of a group of 30 pilgrims traveling to the tomb of Thomas à Becket at Canterbury. The pilgrims represent different walks of life: a simple knight, a vulgar miller, a lawyer, a lusty widow, a merchant, a squire, a physician, a nun, her chaplain, and a monk, among others. The tales that they tell are drawn from folklore, Italian literature, the lives of the saints, courtly romance, and religious sermons. However, Chaucer played with the tales and their genres in the retelling. He used them to contrast or illuminate the persons and characters of their tellers as well as to comment in subtle and complex ways on the literary, religious, and cultural traditions of which they were part. In his mastery of the whole heritage of medieval culture and his independent use of this heritage, Chaucer proved himself the greatest English writer before Shakespeare.

France.   Much of Italian and English literature drew material and inspiration from French, which continued into the fifteenth century to be the language of courtly romance, projecting an unreal world of allegory and nostalgia for a glorious if imaginary past. Popular literature, which developed largely in the towns, often dealt with courtly themes but with a critical and more realistic eye.

In this literary world an extraordinary woman, who was widowed at 25, was able to earn a living for herself and her family with her pen. As a successful woman of letters,

Christine de Pisan (1364–ca. 1430) fought the stereotypical medieval image of women as weak, sexually aggressive temptresses. With wit and reason, she argued that women could be virtuous and showed the fallacies of traditional antifeminist preaching, poetry, and belief. In her *Hymn to Joan of Arc*, she saluted her famous contemporary for her accomplishments, bringing dignity to women, striving for justice, and working for peace in France. Christine's life and writing epitomized the new possibilities and new interests of the fifteenth century. They included an acute sense of individuality, a willingness to look for truth not in the clichés of the past but in actual experience, and a readiness to defend one's views with tenacity. Although an heir of the medieval world, Christine, like her contemporaries, already embodied the attitudes of a new age.

That new age was reflected in a second tradition in fifteenth-century France, that of realist poetry. Around 1453, just as the English troops were enduring a final battering from the French artillery, Duke Charles of Orléans (1394–1465) organized a poetry contest. Each contestant was to write a ballad that began with the contradictory line "I die of thirst beside the fountain." The duke, himself an outstanding poet, wrote an entry that embodied the traditional courtly themes of love and fortune:

> *I die of thirst beside the fountain,*
> *Shaking from cold and the fire of love;*
> *I am blind and yet guide the others;*
> *I am weak of mind, a man of wisdom;*
> *Too negligent, often cautious in vain,*
> *I have been made a spirit,*
> *Led by fortune for better or for worse.*

An unexpected and very different entry came from the duke's prison. The prisoner-poet, François Villon (1432–ca. 1464), was a child of the Paris streets, an impoverished student, a barroom brawler, a killer, and a thief. He was also the greatest realist poet of the Middle Ages, and his poetry won him release from prison. His entry read:

> *I die of thirst beside the fountain,*
> *Hot as fire, my teeth clattering,*
> *At home I am in an alien land;*
> *I shudder beside a glowing brazier,*
> *Naked as a worm, gloriously dressed,*
> *I laugh and cry and wait without hope,*
> *I take comfort and sad despair,*
> *I rejoice and have no joy,*
> *Powerful, I have no force and no strength,*
> *Well received, I am expelled by all.*

The duke focused on the sufferings of love, the thief on the physical sufferings of the downtrodden. The two poets represent the contradictory tendencies of literature in the later Middle Ages. The themes and ideas that were expressed ranged from the polished, traditional values of the aristocracy trying to maintain the ideals of chivalry in a new and changed world to the views of ordinary people, by turns reverent or sarcastic, joyful or despondent.

CONCLUSION

The legacy of the Middle Ages was a complex and ambiguous one. The thousand years of synthesis of classical, barbarian, and Christian traditions did not disappear. The bonds holding this world together were not yet broken. But the last centuries of the Middle Ages bequeathed a critical detachment from this heritage, expressed in the revolts of peasants and workers, the preaching of radical religious reformers, the poems of mystics and visionaries, and rising individualism.

QUESTIONS FOR REVIEW

1. What social and political forces prevented both the Holy Roman Emperors and the French kings from uniting the lands they ruled?
2. How did disease transform social relations in fourteenth-century Europe?
3. Why did a division in the papacy mean both political chaos and spiritual fear for Europeans?
4. How did the vernacular literature of Dante, Chaucer, and Christine de Pisan represent a departure from previous literary traditions?

KEY TERMS

Black Death, *p. 204*

conciliarism, *p. 210*

Golden Bull, *p. 200*

Great Schism, *p. 210*

Hanseatic League, *p. 207*

Hundred Years' War, *p. 201*

Hussites, *p. 211*

indulgences, *p. 209*

Jacquerie, *p. 206*

nominalism, *p. 213*

DISCOVERING WESTERN CIVILIZATION ONLINE

You can obtain more information about the Later Middle Ages at the websites listed below. See also the Companion Website that accompanies this text, www.ablongman.com/kishlansky, which contains an online study guide and additional resources.

Politics as a Family Affair

Web Gallery of Art: Bohemian School

www.kfki.hu/~arthp/tours/mini/Bohemian.html

Overview of art and architecture in Bohemia under the patronage of Charles IV.

The Hundred Years' War History Page

geocities.com/Wellesley/Veranda/1912/hundred/history.htm#top

A web page devoted to the Hundred Years' War.

Life and Death in the Later Middle Ages

Internet Resources on the Black Death

www.historyguide.org/ancient/death.html

An annotated list of web links to sites about the Great Plague of the fourteenth century.

The Spirit of the Later Middle Ages

Avignon: The Medieval and Papal Period

www.avignon.com/anglais/avi003.html

A brief introduction to Avignon and the papal palaces.

SUGGESTIONS FOR FURTHER READING

General Reading

Robert Bartlett, *The Making of Europe: Conquest, Colonization, and Cultural Change, 950–1350* (Princeton, NJ: Princeton University Press, 1993). A comparative study of Europe's expansion into the Celtic, Islamic, and Slavic worlds in the Later Middle Ages.

Johan Huizinga, *The Autumn of the Middle Ages,* trans. Rodney J. Payton and Ulrich Mammitzsch (Chicago: University of Chicago Press, 1996). An important new translation of the classic interpretation of culture and society in the Burgundian court in the Later Middle Ages.

Daniel Waley, *Later Medieval Europe: From Saint Louis to Luther* (London: Longman, 1985). A brief introduction with a focus on Italy.

Politics as a Family Affair

Richard W. Kaeuper, *Chivalry and Violence in Medieval Europe* (Oxford: Oxford University Press, 1999). A fine analysis of the complex relationship between chivalric ethos and the violence of aristocratic society in the Middle Ages.

Joachim Leuschner, *Germany in the Late Middle Ages* (Amsterdam: Elsevier, 1980). An introduction to late medieval German history.

Jean W. Sedlar, *East Central Europe in the Middle Ages, 1000–1500* (Seattle: University of Washington Press, 1994). A thematic introduction to the medieval history of the region that today comprises Poland, the Czech Republic, Slovakia, Hungary, Romania, Bulgaria, Albania, and the former Yugoslavia.

Life and Death in the Later Middle Ages

P. Dollinger, *The German Hansa* (Stanford, CA: Stanford University Press, 1970). A brief history of the Hansa intended for the nonspecialist.

Bronislaw Geremek, *The Margins of Society in Late Medieval Paris,* trans. Jean Birrell (Cambridge: Cambridge University Press, 1987). A landmark study of the urban poor in the Later Middle Ages.

Edward S. Hunt and James M. Murray, *A History of Business in Medieval Europe, 1200–1550* (Cambridge: Cambridge University Press, 1995). A brief and readable history of medieval business practice.

John Kelly, *The Great Mortality: An Intimate History of the Black Death* (London: Fourth Estate, 2005). A popular, well written account of the great fourteenth-century plague.

David Nicholas, *The Growth of the Medieval City: From Late Antiquity to the Early Fourteenth Century* (London, New York: Longman, 1997). A comprehensive survey of medieval towns.

Teofilo F. Ruiz, *Spanish Society 1400–1600* (Harlow: Longman, 2001). A sensitive and original survey of Spanish society at the end of the Middle Ages.

The Spirit of the Later Middle Ages

Renate Blumenfeld-Kosinski, ed., trans. Kevin Brownlee, *The Selected Writings of Christine De Pizan: New Translations, Criticism* (New York: Norton, 1997). A selection of de Pizan's works and of scholarship on her. The place to start for learning about her.

Eamon Duffy, *The Stripping of the Altars: Traditional Religion in England, 1400–1580* (New Haven: Yale University Press, 1992). A revisionist study of local religion at the end of the Middle Ages.

David A. Fein, *François Villon Reconsidered* (New York: Macmillan, 1997). Villon's poetry and his life examined by an authority.

Malcolm Lambert, *Medieval Heresy: Popular Movements from the Gregorian Reform to the Reformation,* 2nd ed. (Oxford: Blackwell, 1992). A comprehensive survey of heretical movements from the eleventh to the sixteenth centuries.

Caroline Walker Bynum, *Holy Feast and Holy Fast: The Religious Significance of Food to Medieval Women* (Berkeley: University of California Press, 1987). An imaginative and scholarly examination of the role of food in the spirituality of medieval women.

Scott L. Waugh and Peter D. Diehl, eds., *Christendom and Its Discontents: Exclusion, Persecution, and Rebellion, 1000–1500* (New York: Cambridge University Press, 1995). Important collection of essays on heresy and dissent in western Europe.

For a list of additional titles related to this chapter's topics, please see www.ablongman.com/kishlansky.

The Visual Record

A CIVIC PROCESSION

It is 25 April 1444, the day Venice celebrates its patron, Saint Mark, with a procession around the square that bears his name. Processions are a common form of civic ritual through which a community defines itself. This procession includes the religious orders (the white-clad brothers of the Confraternity of Saint John are passing before us now), the civic leaders seen just behind them, and an entire band filing by on the right. The procession is not staged, as a modern ceremony would be, and this difference is evident in the relaxed attitude of the ordinary citizens who gather in the middle of the square. In the lower left-hand corner, some friars are reading music; at the lower right, members of the confraternity carry their candles negligently.

Yet the painting, *The Procession of the Relic of the Holy Cross* (1496) by Gentile Bellini (ca. 1429–1507), was commissioned to commemorate a miracle rather than a civic procession. On the evening before Saint Mark's day, a visiting merchant and his son were touring the square when the boy accidentally fell and cracked his skull. The doctors who were called to treat him regarded the case as hopeless and advised the father to prepare for his son's death. The next morning, the Brothers of the Confraternity of Saint John paraded their relic, a piece of the true cross on which Jesus was crucified. The merchant (the red-clad figure kneeling just to the right of center where the line of brothers breaks) approached the golden altarpiece containing the relic, knelt, and prayed that Saint Mark would miraculously cure his son. The next day, the boy revived.

The Brothers of Saint John commissioned Bellini to commemorate this event. Bellini came from the most distinguished family of painters in Venice. His father, Jacopo, had studied in Florence and had brought both of his sons into his workshop when they were young boys. Until the age of 30, Gentile and his younger and more famous brother, Giovanni, worked on their father's commissions, learning the difficult craft of painting. Art was very much a family business in fifteenth-century Italy. The large workshops with their master and hordes of apprentices turned out vast canvases with assembly-line precision. The master was first and foremost a businessman who gained the commissions. He then created the composition and sketched it out; his skilled assistants, like the Bellini brothers, worked on the more complex parts; and young apprentices painted backgrounds.

Although *The Procession of the Relic of the Holy Cross* was designed to recreate a central moment in the history of the confraternity, it is not the confraternity that dominates the picture. Miracles were a part of civic life, and each town took pride in the special manifestations of heavenly care that had taken place within it. Thus it is Venice that is the centerpiece of Bellini's canvas. Dominating the painting is the Basilica of San Marco, with its four great horses over the center portico and the winged lion—the city's symbol—on the canopy above the horses. The procession emanates from the duke's palace to the right of the church, and the great flags of the city flutter everywhere. By the end of the fifteenth century, Venice was one of the greatest powers on earth, the center for international trade and finance. Home to the largest concentration of wealthy families anywhere in Europe, it could well afford the pomp and splendor of its processions.

Looking Ahead

The achievements of God and the achievements of humans blend together in Bellini's painting as they blended together in that era of remarkable accomplishments that historians call the Renaissance. In this chapter, we shall see how philosophy, art, architecture, and literature enjoyed a remarkable development in the Italian city-states and how Renaissance ideals were exported throughout the continent and came to define the age. ➤

RENAISSANCE SOCIETY

Perhaps the most surprising result of the Black Death was the way in which European society revived itself in the succeeding centuries. Even at the height of the plague, a spirit of revitalization was evident in the works of artists and writers. Petrarch (1304–1474), the great humanist poet and scholar, was among the first to differentiate the new age in which he was living from two earlier ones: the classical world of Greece and Rome, which he admired, and the subsequent Dark Ages, which he detested. This spirit of self-awareness is one of the defining characteristics of the **Renaissance**. "It is but in our own day that men dare boast that they see the dawn of better things," wrote Matteo Palmieri (1406–1475).

What was the Renaissance? A French word for an Italian phenomenon, *renaissance* literally means "rebirth." The word captures both the emphasis on humanity that characterized Renaissance thinking and the renewed fascination with the classical world. But the Renaissance was an age rather than an event. There is no moment at which the Middle Ages ended. Late medieval society was artistically creative, socially well developed, and economically diverse. Yet eventually, the pace of change accelerated, and it is best to think of the Renaissance as an era of rapid transitions. Encompassing the two centuries between 1350 and 1550, it passed through three distinct phases. The first, from 1350 to 1400, was characterized by a declining population, the uncovering of classical texts, and experimentation in a variety of art forms. The second phase, from 1400 to 1500, was distinguished by the creation of a set of cultural values and artistic and literary achievements that defined Renaissance style. The large Italian city-states developed stable and coherent forms of government, and the warfare between them gradually ended. In the final period, from 1500 to 1550, invasions from France and Spain transformed Italian political life, and the ideas and techniques of Italian writers and artists radiated to all points of the Continent. Though Renaissance ideas and achievements did spread throughout western Europe, they are best studied where they first developed: on the Italian peninsula.

Cities and Countryside

The Italian peninsula differed sharply from other areas of Europe in the extent to which it was urban. By the late Middle Ages, nearly one in four Italians lived in a town, in contrast to one in ten elsewhere. Not even the plague did much to change this ratio. By 1500, seven of the ten largest cities in the West were in Italy. Naples, Venice, and Milan, each with a population of more than 100,000, led the rest. But it was the numerous smaller towns, with populations nearer to 1,000, that gave the Italian peninsula its urban character. Cities dominated their regions economically, politically, and culturally and served as convenient centers of judicial and ecclesiastical power. The diversified activities of their inhabitants created vast concentrations of wealth, and Italy was the banking capital of the world.

Cities acted as central places around which a cluster of large and small villages was organized. Urban areas, especially the small towns, provided markets for the agricultural produce of the countryside and for the manufactured goods of the urban craft workers. This allowed for the specialization in agricultural and industrial life that increased both productivity and wages. Cities also caught the runoff of rural population, especially the surplus of younger sons and daughters who could not be accommodated on the farms. Cities grew by migration rather than by natural increase. Thus the areas surrounding a city were critical to its prosperity and survival. The urban system was a network of cities encompassed by towns encircled by rural villages. Florence, the dominant city in the region of Tuscany, exemplifies this relationship. Though it possessed two-thirds of its region's wealth, Florence contained only 14 percent of the regional population. The surrounding countryside was agriculturally rich, because marketing costs were low and demand for foodstuffs was high. Smaller cities channeled their local produce and trade to Florence.

Although cities may have dominated Renaissance Italy, by present standards they were small in both area and population. A person could walk across fifteenth-century Florence in less than half an hour. In 1427, its population was 37,000, only half its pre-plague size. Most Italian cities contained large fields for agricultural production, and within the outer walls of Florence were gardens and grain fields. Inside the inner city walls the people crowded together into tightly packed quarters. The intensity of the stench from raw sewage, rotting foodstuffs, and animals being brought to slaughter was equaled only by the din of hoofs and wooden cartwheels on the paving stones.

Urban populations were organized far differently than rural ones. On the farms the central distinctions involved ownership of land. Some farmers owned their estates outright and left them intact to their heirs. Others were involved in a sharecropping system by which absentee owners of land supplied working capital in return for half of the farm's produce. A great gulf in wealth separated owners from sharecroppers. Those who owned their land normally lived with surplus; those who sharecropped always lived on the margin of subsistence.

In the city, however, distinctions were based first on occupation, which largely corresponded to social position and wealth. Cities began as markets, and the privilege to participate in the market defined citizens. City governments provided protection for consumers and producers by creating monopolies through which standards for craftsmanship were maintained and profits for craftsmen were guaranteed. These monopolies were called guilds or companies. Each large city had its own hierarchy of guilds. At the top were the important manufacturing groups—clothiers, metalworkers, and the like. Just below them were bankers, merchants, and the administrators of civic and Church holdings. At the bottom were grocers, masons, and other skilled workers. Roughly speaking, all

MAP DISCOVERY

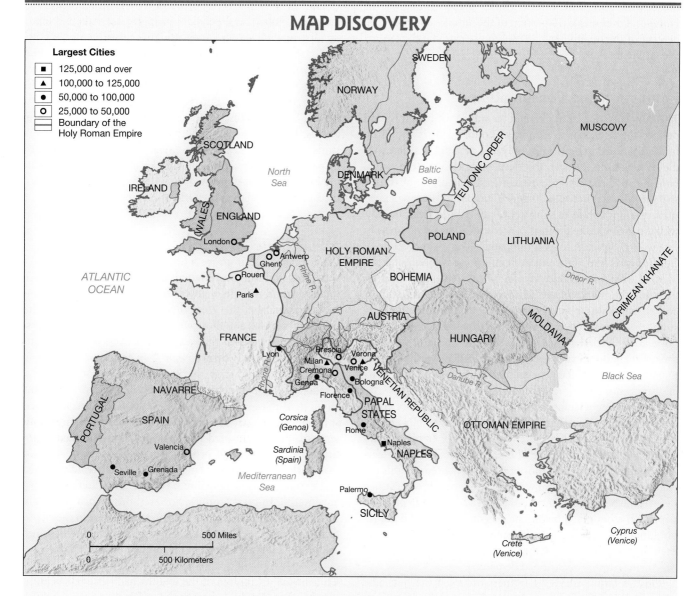

Legend

Largest Cities

- ■ 125,000 and over
- ▲ 100,000 to 125,000
- ● 50,000 to 100,000
- ○ 25,000 to 50,000
- ▭ Boundary of the Holy Roman Empire

Largest Cities in Western Europe, ca. 1500

Examine the locations of western Europe's largest cities at the beginning of the sixteenth century. Where were these cities concentrated? What was the least urbanized part of Europe? Based on this information, why do you suppose the Mediterranean Sea was considered the center of Europe? What was distinctive about the Holy Roman Empire?

of those within the guild structure, from bottom to top, lived comfortably. Yet the majority of urban inhabitants were not members of guilds. Many managed to eke out a living as wage laborers; many more were simply destitute. As a group, these poor people constituted as much as half of the entire population. Most depended on civic and private charity for their very survival.

The disparities between rich and poor were overwhelming. The concentration of wealth in the hands of an ever-narrowing group of families and favored guilds characterized every large city. One reason for this was the extreme instability of economic life. Prices and wages fluctuated wildly in response to local circumstance. After an epidemic of plague, wages climbed and the prices of consumer goods tumbled. A bad harvest sent food prices skyrocketing. Only those who could stockpile goods in times of plenty and consume them in times of want were safe. Capital was the key to continued wealth. Monopolies ensured the profitability of trade and manufacturing, but only those with sufficient capital could engage in either. In Florence, for example, 10 percent of the families controlled 90 percent of the wealth, with an even more extreme concentration at the top.

Production and Consumption

This concentration of wealth and the way in which it was used defined the Renaissance economy. Economic life is bound up in the relationship between supply and demand. The late medieval economy, despite the development of international banking and long-distance trade, was still an economy of primary producers: Between 70 and 90 percent of Europe's population was involved in subsistence agriculture. Even in Italy, which contained the greatest concentration of urban areas in the world, agriculture predominated. The manufacture of clothing was the only other significant economic activity. Most of what was produced was for local consumption rather than for the marketplace. The relationship between supply and demand was precisely measured by the full or empty stomach. Even in good times, more than 80 percent of the population lived at subsistence level with food, clothing, and shelter their only expenses. Therefore, when we discuss the market economy of the Renaissance, we are discussing the circumstances of the few rather than the many.

The defining characteristic of the early Renaissance economy was population change. Recurring waves of plague kept population levels low for more than a century. In the century between 1350 and 1450, one in every six years was characterized by an unusually high mortality rate. At the end of this period, Florence's population was only a quarter of what it had been at the beginning. This dramatic reduction in population depressed economic growth. The general economy did not revive until the sustained population increase toward the end of the fifteenth century. Until then, in both agriculture and manufacturing, supply outstripped demand.

On the farms, surviving farmers occupied the best land and enlarged their holdings. In the shops, finished products outnumbered the consumers who survived the epidemics. Overproduction meant lower prices for basic commodities, and the decline in population meant higher wages for labor. At the lowest levels of society, survivors found it easier to earn their living and even to create a surplus than had their parents. For a time the lot of the masses improved.

But for investors, such economic conditions meant that neither agriculture nor cloth making was particularly attractive. Expensive investments in land or equipment for sharecropping were paid off in inexpensive grain; high wages for the few surviving skilled workers brought a return in cheap cloth. In such circumstances, consumption was more attractive than investment, but it was not merely the perceived shortage of profitable investment opportunities that brought on the increase in conspicuous consumption during the fifteenth century. In the psychological atmosphere created by unpredictable, swift, and deadly epidemics, luxurious living seemed an appropriate response. Moreover, although tax rates increased, houses and personal property normally remained exempt, making luxury goods attractive investments.

For these reasons the production and consumption of luxuries soared. By the middle of the fourteenth century, Florence was known for its silks and jewelry as much as for its cloth. Venice became a European center for the glass industry, especially for the finely ground glass that was used in eyeglasses. Production of specialty crops such as sugar, saffron, fruits, and high-quality wine expanded. International trade increasingly centered on acquiring Eastern specialties, resulting in a serious outflow of gold and silver that enriched first the Byzantine and then the Ottoman emperors.

The Experience of Life

Luxury helped to improve a life that for rich and poor alike was short and uncertain. Renaissance children who survived infancy found their lives governed by parentage and by gender. In parentage, the great divide was between those who lived with surplus and those who lived at subsistence. The first category encompassed the wealthiest bankers and merchants down to those who owned their own farms or engaged in small urban crafts. The vast majority of urban and rural dwellers were members of the second category. About the children of the poor we know very little, other than that their survival was unlikely. If they did not die at birth or shortly afterward, they might be abandoned—especially if female—to the growing number of orphanages in the cities, waste away from lack of nutrition, or fall prey to ordinary childhood diseases. Eldest sons were favored; younger daughters were disadvantaged. In poor families, however, this favoritism meant little more than early apprenticeship to day labor in the city or farm labor in the countryside. Girls were frequently sent out as domestic servants far from the family home.

Childhood.   Children of the wealthy had better chances for survival than did children of the poor. For the better off, childhood might begin with "milk parents," in the home of the family of a wet nurse who would breast-feed the baby through infancy. Only the very wealthy could afford a live-in wet nurse, which would increase the child's chances of survival. Again, daughters were more likely to be sent far from home and least likely to have their nursing supervised. The use of wet nurses not only emancipated parents from the daily care of infants, it also allowed them to resume sexual relations. Nursing women refrained from sex in the belief that it affected their milk.

During the period between weaning and apprenticeship, Renaissance children lived with their families. A family's decisions to abandon children, to send them away from the household when very young, or to take in domestic servants were based on economic calculations. In the competition for scarce resources, the way in which children were managed might determine the survival of the family unit. Sons could expect to be apprenticed to a trade, probably between the ages

ON THE FAMILY

Leon Battista Alberti wrote a number of important tracts that set out the general principles of a subject, including On Architecture, *which was considered the basic text for 300 years. His writings on the family bring insight into the nature of a patriarchal, male-dominated institution.*

Focus Questions

According to Alberti, why is it important for men to look for an "honorable manner" when choosing a wife? What role would Alberti see the wife playing in a marriage?

They say that in choosing a wife one looks for beauty, parentage, and riches. . . . Among the most essential criteria of beauty in a woman is an honorable manner. Even a wild, prodigal, greasy, drunken woman may be beautiful of feature, but no one would call her a beautiful wife. A woman worthy of praise must show first of all in her conduct, modesty, and purity. Marius, the illustrious Roman, said in that first speech of his to the Roman people: "Of women we require purity, of men labor." And I certainly agree. There is nothing more disgusting than a coarse and dirty woman. Who is stupid enough not to see clearly that a woman who does not care for neatness and cleanliness in her appearance, not only in her dress and body but in all her behavior and language, is by no means well mannered? How can it be anything but obvious that a bad-mannered woman is also rarely virtuous? We shall consider elsewhere the harm that comes to a family from women who lack virtue, for I myself do not know which is the worse fate for a family, total celibacy or a single dishonored woman. In a bride, therefore, a man must first seek beauty of mind, that is, good conduct and virtue.

In her body he must seek not only loveliness, grace, and charm but must also choose a woman who is well made for bearing children, with the kind of constitution that promises to make them strong and big. There's an old proverb, "When you pick your wife, you choose your children." All her virtues will in fact shine brighter still in beautiful children. It is a well-known saying among poets: "Beautiful character dwells in a beautiful body." The natural philosophers require that a woman be neither thin nor very fat. Those laden with fat are subject to coldness and constipation and slow to conceive. They say that a woman should have a joyful nature, fresh and lively in her blood and her whole being. They have no objections to a dark girl. They do reject girls with a frowning black visage, however. They have no liking for either the undersized or the overlarge and lean. They find that a woman is most suited to bear children if she is fairly big and has limbs of ample length. They always have a preference for youth, based on a number of arguments which I need not expound here, but particularly on the point that a young girl has a more adaptable mind. Young girls are pure by virtue of their age and have not developed any spitefulness. They are by nature modest and free of vice. They quickly learn to accept affectionately and unresistingly the habits and wishes of their husbands.

From Leon Battista Alberti, *On the Family.*

---

of 10 and 13. Most, of course, learned the crafts of their fathers, but not necessarily in their father's shop. Sons inherited the family business and its most important possessions—tools of the trade or beasts of labor for the farm. Inheritance customs varied. In some places, only the eldest son received the equipment of the family occupation; in others, like Tuscany, all the sons shared it. Still, in the first 15 years of life, these most-favored children would have spent between one-third and one-half of their time outside the household in which they had been born.

Marriage and the Family.   Expectations for daughters centered on their chances of marriage. For a girl, dowry was everything. If a girl's father could provide a handsome one, her future was secure; if not, the alternatives were a convent, which would take a small bequest, or a match lower down the social scale, where the quality of life deteriorated rapidly. Daughters of poor families entered domestic service in order

to have a dowry provided by their masters. The dowry was taken to the household of the husband. There, the couple resided until they established their own separate family. If the husband died, it was to his parental household that the widow returned.

Women married in late adolescence, usually around the age of 20. Among the wealthy, marriages were perceived as familial alliances and business transactions rather than love matches. The dowry was an investment on which fathers expected a return, and while the bride might have some choice, it was severely limited. Compatibility was not a central feature in matchmaking. Husbands were, on the average, ten years older than their wives and likely to leave them widows. In the early fifteenth century, about one-fourth of all adult women in Florence were widows.

Men married later—near the age of 25 on the farms, nearer 30 in the cities because of the cost of setting up in trade or on the land. Late marriage meant long supervision under the watchful eye of father or master, an extended period between adolescence and adulthood. The reputation that Renaissance cities gained for homosexuality and licentiousness must be viewed in light of the advanced age at which males married. The level of sexual frustration was high, and its outlet in ritual violence and rape was also high. Many men, even with families, never succeeded in setting up separately from their fathers or older brothers.

Men came of age at 30 but were thought to be old by 50. Thus for men, marriage and parenthood took place in middle age rather than in youth. Valued all their lives more highly than their sisters, male heads of households were the source of all power in their domiciles, in their shops, and in the state. They were responsible for overseeing every aspect of the upbringing of their children. But their wives were essential partners who governed domestic life. Women labored not only at the hearth, but in the fields and shops as well. Their economic contribution to the well-being of the family was critical, both in the dowry they brought at marriage and in the labor they contributed to the household. If their wives died, men with young children remarried quickly. While there were many bachelors in Renaissance society, there were few widowers.

In most cases, death came suddenly. Epidemic diseases, of which plague was the most virulent, struck with fearful regularity. They struck harder at the young—children and adolescents, who were the majority of the population—and hardest in the summer months, when other viruses and bacteria weakened the population. Starvation was rare, less because of food shortage than because the seriously undernourished were more likely to succumb to disease than to famine. In urban areas, the government would intervene to provide grain from public storehouses at times of extreme shortage; in the countryside, large landholders commonly exercised the same function.

The Quality of Life

Although life may have been difficult during the Renaissance, it was not unfulfilling. Despite constant toil and frequent hardship, people of the Renaissance had reason to believe that their lives were better than those of their ancestors and that their children's lives would be better still. On the most basic level, health improved and, for those who survived plague, life expectancy increased owing to the relative surplus of grain throughout the fifteenth century and the wider variety of foods consumed. Bread remained the most widely consumed foodstuff, but there was more pork and lamb in the diet of ordinary people in the fifteenth century than there would be for the next 400 years. At the upper levels of society, sweet wine and citrus fruits helped to offset the lack of vegetables. This diversification of diet resulted from improvements in transportation and communication, which brought more goods and services to a growing number of towns in the chain that linked the regional centers to the rural countryside.

The towns and cities also introduced a new sense of social and political cohesiveness. The city was something to which people belonged. In urban areas, they could join social groups of their own choosing and develop networks of support that were not possible in rural environments. Blood relations remained the primary social group. Kin were the most likely source of aid in times of need, and charity began at home. Kin groups extended well beyond the immediate family, with both cousins and in-laws laying claim to the privileges of blood. The urban family could also depend on the connections of neighborhood. In some Italian cities, wealth or occupation determined housing patterns. In others, like Florence, rich and poor lived side by side and identified themselves with their small administrative unit and with their local church. Thus they could participate in relationships with others both above and below them in social scale. From their superiors they gained connections that helped their families; from their inferiors they gained devoted clients.

As in the Middle Ages, the Church remained the spatial, spiritual, and social center of people's lives. Though Renaissance society became more worldly in outlook, this worldliness took place within the context of an absorbing devotional life. There was not yet any separation between faith and reason. The Church provided explanations for both the mysterious and the mundane. The clergy performed the rituals of baptism, marriage, and burial that measured the passage of life. Religious symbols also adorned the flags of militia troops, the emblems of guilds, and the regalia of the city itself. The Church preserved holy relics that were venerated for their power to protect the city or to endow it with particular skills and resources. Through its holy days, as much as through its rituals, the Church helped to channel leisure activities into community celebrations.

A growing sense of civic pride and individual accomplishment were underlying characteristics of the Italian Renaissance, enhanced by the development of social cohesion and community solidarity that both Church and city-state fostered. It is commonly held that the Renaissance was both elitist and male dominated, that it was an experience separate from that of the society at large. There can be no question that it was the rich who commissioned works of art or that it was the highly skilled male artisans who executed them. But neither lived in a social vacuum. The Renaissance was not an event whose causes were the result of the efforts of the few or whose consequences were limited to the privileged. In fact, the Renaissance was not an event at all. Family values that permitted early apprenticeships in surrogate households and emphasized the continuity of crafts from one generation to the next made possible the skilled artists of the Renaissance cities. The stress on the production of luxury goods placed higher value on individual skills and therefore on excellence in workmanship. Church and state sought to express social values through representational art. One of the chief purposes of wall murals was to instruct the unlettered in religion, to help them visualize the central episodes in Christian history. The grandiose architecture and statuary that adorned central places were designed to enhance civic pride and communicate the protective power of public institutions.

RENAISSANCE ART

In every age, artistic achievement represents a combination of individual talent and predominant social ideals. Artists may be at the leading edge of the society in which they live, but it is the spirit of that society that they capture in word or song or image. Artistic disciplines also have their own technical development. Individually, Renaissance artists were attempting to solve problems about perspective and three-dimensionality that had defeated their predecessors. But the particular techniques or experiments that interested them owed as much to the social context as they did to the artistic one. For example, the urban character of Italian government led to the need for civic architecture, public buildings on a grand scale. The celebration of individual achievement led to the explosive growth of portraiture. Not surprisingly, major technological breakthroughs were achieved in both areas.

This relationship between artist and social context was especially important in the Renaissance, when artists were closely tied to the crafts and trades of urban society and to the demands of clients who commissioned their work. Although it was the elite who patronized art, it was skilled tradespeople who produced it. Artists normally followed the pattern of any craftsman: an apprenticeship begun as a teenager and a long period of training and work in a master's shop. This form of education gave the aspiring artist a practical bent and a keen appreciation for the business side of art. Studios were identified with particular styles and competed for commissions from clients, especially the Church. Wealthy individuals commissioned art as investments, as marks of personal distinction, and as displays of public piety. Isabella d'Este (1474–1539), one of the great patrons of Renaissance artists, wrote hundreds of letters specifying the details of the works she commissioned. She once sent an artist a thread of the exact dimensions of the pictures she had ordered. Demand for art was high. The vast public works projects needed buildings, the new piazzas (public squares) and palazzos (private houses) needed statuary, and the long walls of churches needed murals.

The survival of so many Renaissance masterpieces allows us to reconstruct the stages by which the remarkable artistic achievements of this era took place. Although advances were made in a variety of fields during the Renaissance, the three outstanding areas were architecture, sculpture, and painting. Modern artists would consider each a separate discipline, but Renaissance artists crossed their boundaries without hesitation. Not only could these artists work with a variety of materials, their intensive and varied apprenticeships taught them to apply the technical solutions of one field to the problems of another. Few Renaissance artists confined themselves to one area of artistic expression, and many created works of enduring beauty in more than one medium. Was Michelangelo's greatest achievement his sculpture of David, his paintings on the ceiling of the Sistine Chapel, or his design for the dome of Saint Peter's? Only a century of interdisciplinary cross-fertilization could have prepared the artistic world for such a feat.

An Architect, a Sculptor, and a Painter

The century that culminated in Michelangelo's extraordinary achievements began with the work of three Florentine masters who deeply influenced one another's development: Brunelleschi (1377–1446), Donatello (1386–1466), and Masaccio (1401–1428). In the Renaissance, the dominant artistic discipline was architecture. Buildings were the most expensive investment patrons could make, and the technical knowledge necessary for their successful construction was immense. The architect not only designed a building, he also served as its general contractor, construction supervisor, and inspector. Moreover, the architect's design determined the amount and the scale of the statuary and decorative paintings to be incorporated. By 1400, the Gothic style of building had dominated western Europe for over two centuries. Its characteristic pointed arches, vaulted ceilings, and slender spires had simplified building by removing the heavy walls that were formerly thought necessary to support great structures. Gothic construction permitted greater height, a characteristic that was especially desirable in cathedrals, which stretched toward the heavens. But although the buildings themselves were simplified, the techniques for erecting them became more complex. By the fifteenth century, architects had turned their techniques into an intricate style. They became obsessed by angular arches, elaborate vaultings and buttresses, and long, pointed spires.

It was Brunelleschi who decisively challenged the principles of Gothic architecture by recombining its basic elements with those of classical structures. Basing his designs on geometric principles, Brunelleschi reintroduced planes and spheres as dominant motifs. His greatest work was the dome on the cathedral in Florence, begun in 1420. His design for the dome was simple but bold. The circular windows are set inside a square of panels, which in turn are set inside a rectangle. Brunelleschi is generally credited with having been the first Renaissance artist to have understood and made use of perspective, though it was immediately put to more dramatic effect in sculpture and painting.

In sculpture, the survival of Roman and Hellenistic pieces, mostly bold and muscular torsos, conveyed the direct influence of classical art. Donatello translated these classical styles into more naturalistic forms. His technique is evident in the long, flowing robes in most of his works, sculpted in the natural fashion in which cloth hung. Donatello revived the freestanding statue, which demanded greater attention to human anatomy because it was viewed from many angles. He also led the revival of the equestrian statue, sculpting the Venetian captain-general Gattamelata for a public square in Padua. This enormous bronze horse and rider (1445–1450) relied on the standpoint of the viewer to achieve its overpowering effect. This use of **linear perspective** is also seen in Donatello's breathtaking altar scenes of the miracles of Saint Anthony in Padua, which resemble nothing so much as a canvas cast in bronze.

These altar scenes evince the unmistakable influence of the paintings of Masaccio. His frescoes in the Brancacci Chapel in Florence were studied and sketched by all of the great artists

■ Donatello's bronze statue *Judith Slaying Holofernes* symbolized the Florentines' love of liberty and hatred of tyranny.

of the next generation, who unreservedly praised his naturalism. What most claim the attention of the modern viewer are Masaccio's shading of light and shadow and his brilliant use of linear perspective to create the illusion that a flat surface has three dimensions. Masaccio's work depicted standard Christian themes, but always with a novel approach. In an adoration scene, he portrayed a middle-aged Madonna and a dwarfish baby Jesus; in a painting of Saint Peter paying tribute money, he used his own likeness as the face of one of the apostles. His two best-known works are the *Holy Trinity* (1425), which provides the classic example of the use of linear perspective, and the *Expulsion of Adam and Eve* (ca. 1427).

Renaissance Style

By the middle of the fifteenth century, a recognizable Renaissance style had triumphed. The outstanding architect of this period was Leon Battista Alberti (1404–1472), whose treatise *On Building* (1452) remained the most influential work on the subject until the eighteenth century. Alberti consecrated the geometric principles laid down by Brunelleschi and infused them with a humanist spirit. He revived the classical dictum that a building, like a body, should have an even number of supports and, like a head, an odd number of openings. This furthered precise geometric calculations in scale and design.

No sculptor challenged the preeminence of Donatello for another fifty years, but in painting there were many contenders for the garlands worn by Masaccio. The first was Piero della Francesca (ca. 1420–1492), who broke new ground in his concern for the visual unity of his paintings. From portraits to processions to his stunning fresco *The Resurrection* (ca. 1463), Piero concentrated on the most technical aspects of composition. Another challenger was Sandro Botticelli (1445–1510), whose classical themes, sensitive portraits, and bright colors set him apart from the line of Florentine painters with whom he studied. His mythologies of the *Birth of Venus* and *Spring* (ca. 1478) depart markedly from the naturalism inspired by Masaccio.

This concern with beauty and personality is also seen in the paintings of Leonardo da Vinci (1452–1519), whose creative genius embodied the Renaissance ideal of the "universal man." Leonardo's achievements in scientific, technical, and artistic endeavors read like a list of all of the subjects known during the Renaissance. His detailed anatomical drawings and the method he devised for rendering them, his botanical observations, and his engineering inventions (including models for a tank and an airplane) testify to his unrestrained curiosity. His paintings reveal a continuation of the scientific application of mathematics to matters of proportion and perspective. Leonardo's psychological portrait *La Gioconda* (1503–1506), popularly called the Mona Lisa, is quite possibly the best-known picture in the Western world.

From Brunelleschi to Alberti, from Masaccio to Leonardo da Vinci, Renaissance artists placed a unique stamp upon visual culture. By reviving classical themes, geometric principles, and a spirit of human vitality, they broke decisively from the dominant medieval traditions. Art became a source of individual and collective pride, produced by masters, but consumed by all. Cities and wealthy patrons commissioned great works of art for public display. New buildings rose everywhere, adorned with the statues and murals that still stand as a testimony to generations of artists.

Michelangelo

The artistic achievements of the Renaissance culminated in the creative outpourings of Michelangelo Buonarroti (1475–1564). Poet, sculptor, painter, and architect, Michelangelo imparted his genius to everything he touched. Uncharacteristically, he came from a family of standing in Florentine society. At the age of 14, over the opposition of his father, he was apprenticed to a leading painter and spent his spare time in Florentine churches, copying the works of Masaccio, among others.

In 1490, Michelangelo gained a place in the household of Lorenzo de Medici. He claimed to have taught himself sculpturing during this two-year period, a remarkable feat considering the skills required. In fact, what was unusual about Michelangelo's early development was that he avoided the long years of apprenticeship during which someone else's style was implanted on the young artist. In the Medici household he came into contact with leading Neoplatonists, who taught that humankind was on an ascending journey of perfectibility toward God. These ideas can be seen as one source of the heroic concept of humanity that Michelangelo brought to his work.

In 1496, Michelangelo moved to Rome, where his abilities as a sculptor brought him to the attention of Jacopo Galli, a banker. Galli commissioned a classical work for himself and procured another for a French cardinal, which became the *Pietà*. Although this was his first attempt at sculpting a work of religious art, Michelangelo would never surpass it in beauty or composition. The *Pietà* created a sensation in Rome, and by the time Michelangelo returned to Florence in 1501, at the age of 26, he was already acknowledged as one of the great sculptors of his day. He was immediately commissioned to work on an enormous block of marble that had been quarried nearly a half-century before and had defeated the talents of a series of carvers. He worked continuously for three years on his *David* (1501–1504), a piece that completed the union between classical and Renaissance styles.

Though Michelangelo always believed himself to be primarily a sculptor, his next outstanding work was in the field of painting. In 1508, Pope Julius II summoned Michelangelo to Rome and commissioned him to decorate the ceiling of the small ceremonial chapel that had been built next to the new papal residence. Michelangelo's plan was to portray, in an extended narrative, human creation and those Old Testament events that foreshadowed the birth of the Savior. First,

Michelangelo framed his scenes within the architecture of a massive classical temple. In this way, he was able to give the impression of having flattened the rounded surface on which he worked. Then, within the center panels, came his fresco scenes of the events of the creation and of human history from the Fall to the Flood. His representations were simple and compelling: the fingers of God and Adam nearly touching, Eve with one leg still emerging from Adam's side, and the half-human snake in the temptation are all majestically evocative.

The *Pietà*, the *David*, and the paintings of the Sistine Chapel were the work of youth. Michelangelo's crowning achievement, the building of Saint Peter's basilica in Rome, was the work of age. The base work of Saint Peter's had already been laid, and drawings for its completion had been made thirty years earlier by Donato Bramante. Michelangelo altered these plans in an effort to bring more light into the church and to provide a more majestic facade outside. His main contribution, however, was the design of the great dome, which centered the interior of the church on Saint Peter's grave. More than the height, it is the harmony of Michelangelo's design that creates the sense of the building thrusting upward like a Gothic cathedral of old. Michelangelo did not live to see the dome of Saint Peter's completed.

Renaissance art served Renaissance society, reflecting both its concrete achievements and its visionary ideals. This art was a synthesis of old and new, building on classical models, particularly in sculpture and architecture, but adding newly discovered techniques and skills. When Giorgio Vasari (1511–1574) came to write his *Lives of the Great Painters, Sculptors, and Architects* (1550), he found over 200 artists worthy of distinction. But Renaissance artists did more than construct and adorn buildings or celebrate and beautify spiritual life. Inevitably, their work expressed the ideals and aspirations of the society in which they lived—the new emphasis on learning and knowledge, on the here and now rather than the hereafter, and, most important, on humanity and its capacity for growth and perfection.

RENAISSANCE IDEALS

Renaissance thought went hand in glove with Renaissance art. Scholars and philosophers searched the works of the ancients to find the principles on which to build a better life. They scoured monastic libraries for forgotten manuscripts, discovering, among other things, Greek poetry, history, the works of Homer and Plato, and Aristotle's *Poetics*. Their rigorous application of scholarly procedures for the collection and collation of these texts was one of the most important contributions of the Renaissance intellectuals who came to be known as **humanists.** Humanism developed in reaction to an intellectual world that was centered on the Church and dominated by other-worldly concerns. Although humanism was by no means antireligious, it was thoroughly secular in outlook.

■ The creation of Adam and Eve, a detail from Michelangelo's frescoes on the ceiling of the Sistine Chapel. The Sistine frescoes had become obscured by dirt and layers of varnish and glue applied at various times over the years. In the 1980s, they were cleaned to reveal their original colors.

Humanists celebrated worldly achievements. Pico della Mirandola's *Oration on the Dignity of Man* (1486) is the best known of a multitude of Renaissance writings influenced by the discovery of the works of Plato. Pico believed that people could perfect their existence on earth because God had endowed humans with the capacity to determine their own fate. This emphasis on human potential found expression in the celebration of human achievement.

Thus humanists studied and taught the humanities, the skills of disciplines such as **philology,** the art of language, and **rhetoric,** the art of expression. Though they were mostly lay people, humanists applied their learning to both religious and secular studies. Although most reacted strongly against Scholasticism, they were heavily indebted to the work of medieval churchmen. Nor were they hostile to the Church. Petrarch, Bruni, and Alberti were all employed by the papal court at some time in their careers, as was Lorenzo Valla, the most influential of the humanists. Their interest in human

achievement and human potential must be set beside their religious beliefs. As Petrarch stated quite succinctly, "Christ is my God; Cicero is the prince of the language I use."

Humanists and the Liberal Arts

The most important achievements of humanist scholars centered on ancient texts. It was the humanists' goal to discover as much as had survived from the ancient world and to provide texts of classical authors that were as full and accurate as possible.

Studying the Classical World. Although much was already known of the Latin classics, few of the central works of ancient Greece had been recovered. Humanists preserved this heritage by reviving the study of the Greek language and by translating Greek authors into Latin. After the fall of Constantinople in 1453, Italy became the center for Greek studies as Byzantine scholars fled the Ottoman conquerors. Humanists also introduced historical methods in studying texts, establishing principles for determining which of many manuscript copies of an ancient text was the oldest, the most accurate, and the least corrupted by their copyists. This was of immense importance in studying the writings of the ancient Fathers of the Church, many of whose manuscripts had not been examined for centuries. The humanist emphasis on the humanistic disciplines fostered new educational ideals. Along with the study of theology, logic, and natural philosophy, which had dominated the medieval university, humanist scholars stressed the importance of grammar, rhetoric, moral philosophy, and history. They believed that the study of these "liberal arts" should be undertaken for its own sake. This gave a powerful boost to the ideal of the perfectibility of the individual that appeared in so many other aspects of Renaissance culture.

Humanists furthered the secularization of Renaissance society through their emphasis on the study of the classical world. The rediscovery of Latin texts during the late Middle Ages spurred interest in all things ancient. Petrarch, who is rightly called the father of humanism, revered the great Roman rhetorician Cicero above all others. Petrarch's emphasis upon language led to efforts to recapture the purity of ancient Latin and Greek, languages that had become corrupted over the centuries. The leading humanist in the generation after Petrarch was Leonardo Bruni (1370–1444), who was reputed to be the greatest Greek scholar of his day. He translated Plato and Aristotle and did much to advance mastery of classical Greek and foster the ideas of Plato.

Philology and Lorenzo Valla.

The study of the origins of words, their meaning, and their proper grammatical usage may seem an unusual foundation for one of the most vital of all European intellectual movements. But philology was, in fact, the humanists' chief concern. This can best be illustrated by the work of Lorenzo Valla (1407–1457). Valla was brought up in Rome, where he was largely self-educated, though according to the prescriptions of the Florentine humanists. Valla entered the service of Alfonso I, king of Naples, and applied his humanistic training to affairs of state. The kingdom of Naples bordered on the Papal States, and its kings were in continual conflict with the papacy. The pope asserted the right to withhold recognition of the king, a right that was based on the jurisdictional authority supposedly ceded to the papacy by the Emperor Constantine in the fourth century—the so-called Donation of Constantine. Valla settled the matter definitively. Applying historical and philological critiques to the text of the Donation, Valla proved that it could not have been written earlier than the eighth century, 400 years after Constantine's death. He mercilessly exposed words and terms that had not existed in Roman times, such as *fief* and *satrap,* and thus proved beyond doubt that the Donation was a forgery and papal claims based on it were without merit.

Civic Humanism.

Valla's career demonstrates the impact of humanist values on practical affairs. Although humanists were scholars, they made no distinction between an active and a contemplative life. A life of scholarship was a life of public service. This **civic humanism** is best expressed in the writings of Leon Battista Alberti (1404–1472), whose treatise *On the Family* (1443) is a classic study of the new urban values, especially prudence and thrift. Alberti extolled the virtues of "the fatherland, the public good, and the benefit of all citizens." An architect, a mathematician, a poet, a playwright, a musician, and an inventor, Alberti was one of the great virtuosi of the Renaissance.

Alberti's own life might have served as a model for the most influential of all Renaissance tracts, Castiglione's *The Courtier* (1528). Baldesar Castiglione (1478–1529) directed his lessons to the public life of the aspiring elite. It was his purpose to prescribe the characteristics that would make the ideal courtier, who was as much made as born. He prescribed every detail of the education necessary for the ideal state servant, from table manners to artistic attainments. Castiglione's perfect courtier was an amalgam of all that the elite of Renaissance society held dear. He was to be educated as a scholar, he was to be occupied as a soldier, and he was to serve his state as an adviser.

Renaissance Science

As the spirit of the Renaissance looked back to the classical world and ahead to the achievements that would come from the adaptation of ancient wisdom, so Renaissance scientific inquiry was focused in two directions. The first was text-based knowledge derived from recovered works mainly from classical Greece; the second was experiment-based knowledge achieved through observation. Texts dominated the life sciences, especially medicine and biology; experimentation enriched the physical sciences such as engineering and cartography. But it is important to realize that both ways of knowing blended together. Doctors were instructed by the classics but increasingly learned their anatomy by dissection. Navigators carried the works of Ptolemy on voyages of discovery but amended his maps and charts with what they found in practice.

The biological sciences were given new life by the recovery of the writings of Hippocrates and Galen. Medicine became a subject for learned inquiry and the medical school at Padua was considered the greatest in Europe. The work of Hippocrates concerned diagnosing common diseases and attempting to find treatments. Galen's studies of the human body, rediscovered, formed the basis for a new interest in anatomy and led to experiments in human dissection. Such experimentation improved knowledge of anatomy, which led to advances in setting broken bones and treating injuries. Galen taught that the body was composed of humors that corresponded to the four elements of life—earth, air, water, and fire. In the healthy body the humors were well mixed, but in the diseased body there was an imbalance. This explains why doctors attempted to cure disease by the use of leeches or the practice of "bleeding," cutting open a vein and allowing blood to run out. The extraction of blood was believed to aid in restoring the balance of the humors and thus the health of the body.

While the life sciences were advanced through attention to ancient texts, engineering developed through the experiences of Renaissance craftsmen and artists who were attempting to solve practical problems of proportion, stability, and height in the buildings, bridges, and ultimately domes that they built. Most of the important advances in engineering were actually made in the service of military ventures. The science of ballistics advanced through greater mathematical precision in studying the relationship between speed and trajectory in the shooting of artillery. Leonardo da Vinci attempted to apply a theory of mechanics to Renaissance warfare, and he made drawings for the creation of war machines such as tanks and flying machines such as airplanes, though, of course, neither were produced during his lifetime. But he was expert in building working models of machines, in advising princes on their fortifications, and suggesting improvements in the art of gunnery. All his contributions were made by experimentation rather than through text-based learning. Wherever he went, Leonardo built workshops to construct models and kept careful notebooks of the results of his trials. This spirit of experimentation would ultimately lead to the birth of a recognizably scientific method in the next century.

Machiavelli and Politics

At the same time that Castiglione was drafting a blueprint for the idealized courtier, Niccolò Machiavelli (1469–1527) was laying the foundation for the realistic sixteenth-century ruler. No Renaissance work has been more important or more controversial than Machiavelli's *The Prince* (1513). Its vivid prose, its epigrammatic advice—"men must either be pampered or crushed"—and its clinical dissection of power politics have attracted generation after generation of readers. With Machiavelli, for better or worse, begins the science of politics.

Machiavelli came from an established Florentine family. He entered state service and rose to the relatively important office of secretary to the Council of Ten, the organ of Florentine government that was responsible for war and diplomacy. Here, Machiavelli received his education in practical affairs. He was an emissary to Cesare Borgia during his consolidation of the Papal States at the turn of the century and carefully studied Borgia's methods. A tireless correspondent, Machiavelli began to collect materials for various tracts on military matters.

But as suddenly as he rose to his position of power and influence, he fell from it. The militia he had advocated and in part organized was soundly defeated by the Spaniards, and the Florentine republic fell. Machiavelli was summarily dismissed from office in 1512 and was imprisoned and tortured the following year. Released and banished from the city, he retired to a small country estate. Immediately, he began writing what became his two greatest works: *The Prince* (1513) and *The Discourses on Livy* (1519).

Machiavelli has left a haunting portrait of his life in exile, and it is important to understand how intertwined his studies of ancient and modern politics were.

> On the coming of evening, I return to my house and enter my study; and at the door I take off the day's clothing covered with mud and dust, and put on garments regal and courtly; and reclothed appropriately, I enter the ancient courts of ancient men, where, received by them with affection, I feed on that food which only is mine and which I was born for.

The Prince is a handbook for a ruler who would establish a lasting government. It attempts to set down principles culled from historical examples and contemporary events to aid the prince in attaining and maintaining power. By study of these precepts and by their swift and forceful application, Machiavelli believed, the prince might even control fortune itself. What made *The Prince* so remarkable in its day, and what continues to enliven debate over it, is that Machiavelli was able to separate all ethical considerations from his analysis. Whether this resulted from cynicism or from his own expressed desire for realism, Machiavelli uncompromisingly instructed the would-be ruler to be half human and half beast—to conquer neighbors, to murder enemies, and to deceive friends. Steeped in the humanist ideals of fame and *virtù*—a combination of virtue and virtuosity, of valor, character, and ability—he sought to reestablish Italian rule and place government on a stable scientific basis that would end the perpetual conflict among the Italian city-states.

The careers of Lorenzo Valla and Niccolò Machiavelli illustrate how humanists were able to bring the study of the liberal arts into the service of the state. Valla's philological studies had a vital impact on diplomacy; Machiavelli's historical studies were directly applicable to warfare. Humanists created a demand for learning that helps account for the growth of universities, the spread of literacy, and the rise of printing. They also created a hunger for knowledge that characterized intellectual life for nearly two centuries.

THE POLITICS OF THE ITALIAN CITY-STATES

Like studs on a leather boot, **city-states** dotted the Italian peninsula. They differed in size, shape, and form. Some were large seaports; others were small inland villages. Some cut wide swaths across the plains; others were tiny islands. The absence of a unifying central authority in Italy, resulting from the collapse of the Holy Roman Empire and the papal schism, allowed ancient guilds and confraternities to transform themselves into self-governing societies. By the beginning of the fifteenth century, the Italian city-states were the center of power, wealth, and culture in the Christian world.

This dominion rested on several conditions. First, their geographical position favored the exchange of resources and goods between East and West. A great circular trade encompassed the Byzantine Empire, the North African coastal states, and the Mediterranean nations of western Europe. The Italian peninsula dominated the circumference of that circle. Its port cities, Genoa and Venice especially, became great maritime powers through their trade in spices and minerals. Moreover, just beyond the peninsula to the north lay the vast and populous territories of the Holy Roman Empire. Their continuous need for manufactured goods, especially cloth and metals, was filled by long caravans that traveled from Italy through the Alps. Milan specialized in metal crafts. Florence was a financial capital as well as a center for the manufacture of fine luxury goods. Finally, the city-states and their surrounding areas were agriculturally self-sufficient.

Because of their accomplishments we tend to think of these Italian "city-states" as small nations. Even the term city-state implies national identity. Each city-state governed itself according to its own rules and customs, and each defined itself in isolation from the larger regional or tribal associations that had once prevailed. Italy was neither a nation nor a people.

The Five Powers

Although there were dozens of Italian city-states, by the early fifteenth century five had emerged to dominate the politics of the peninsula. In the south was the kingdom of Naples, the only city-state governed by a hereditary monarchy. Its politics were mired in conflicts over its succession. During the fourteenth century, Naples was ruled successively by French and Hungarian princes. The fifteenth century began with civil warfare between rival claimants of both nations, and it was not until the Spaniard Alfonso I of Aragon (1442–1458) secured the throne in 1443 that peace was restored and Naples and Sicily were reunited.

Bordering Naples were the Papal States, whose capital was Rome but whose territories stretched far to the north and lay

MAP DISCOVERY

Italy, 1494

Notice how Italy was organized into city-states at the end of the fifteenth century. Which were the largest city-states? Which city-states seem most susceptible to foreign invasion? Which states had the best positioning for trade? When the wars of Italy began in 1494 (discussed later in this chapter), France sided with Milan against Naples, Florence, and the Papal States. Based on the positions of the combatants, what do you think would have been the likeliest route for the French invasion? Which city-states could the French avoid fighting?

on both sides of the spiny Apennine mountain chain that extends down the center of the peninsula. Throughout the fourteenth and early fifteenth centuries the territories under the nominal control of the Church were largely independent and included such thriving city-states as Bologna, Ferrara, and Urbino. Even in Rome the weakened papacy had to contend with noble families for control of the city.

The three remaining dominant city-states—Florence, Milan, and Venice—were bunched together in the north. Florence, center of Renaissance culture, was one of the wealthiest cities of Europe before the devastations of the plague and the sustained economic downturn of the late fourteenth century. The city itself was inland, and its main waterway, the Arno, ran to the sea through Pisa, whose subjugation in 1406 was a turning point in Florentine history. Nominally, Florence was a republic, but during the fifteenth century it was ruled in effect by its principal banking family, the Medici.

To the north of Florence was the duchy of Milan, the major city in Lombardy. It, too, was landlocked, cut off from the sea by Genoa. But Milan's economic life was oriented northward to the Swiss and German towns beyond the Alps, and its major concern was preventing foreign invasions. The most warlike of the Italian cities, Milan was a despotism, ruled for nearly two centuries by the Visconti family.

The last of the five powers was the republic of Venice, which became the leading maritime power of the age. Until the fifteenth century, Venice was less interested in securing a landed empire than in dominating a seaborne one. The republic was ruled by a hereditary elite, headed by an elected **doge,** who was the chief magistrate of Venice, and a variety of small elected councils.

The political history of the Italian peninsula during the late fourteenth and early fifteenth centuries is one of unrelieved turmoil. Wherever we look, the governments of the city-states were threatened by foreign invaders, internal conspiracies, or popular revolts. In the 1370s, the Genoese and Venetians fought their fourth war in little more than a century, this one so bitter that the Genoese risked much of their fleet in an unsuccessful effort to conquer Venice itself. At the turn of the century, the Hungarian occupant of the throne of Naples invaded both Rome and Florence. Florence and Milan were constantly at war with each other. Nor were foreign threats the only dangers. In Milan, three Visconti brothers inherited power. Two murdered the third, and then the son of one murdered the other to reunite the inheritance. The Venetians executed one of their military leaders, who was plotting treachery. One or another Florentine family usually faced exile when governments there changed hands. Popular revolts channeled social and economic discontent against the ruling elites in Rome, Milan, and Florence. The revolt of the "Ciompi" (the wooden shoes) in Florence in 1378 was an attempt by poorly paid wool workers to reform the city's exclusive guild system and give guild protection to the wage laborers lower down the social scale. In Milan, an abortive republic was established in reaction against strong-arm Visconti rule.

By the middle of the fifteenth century, however, two trends were apparent amid this political chaos. The first was the consolidation of strong centralized governments within the large city-states. These took different forms but yielded a similar result: internal political stability. The return of the popes to Rome after the Great Schism restored the pope to the head of his temporal estates and began a long period of papal dominance over Rome and its satellite territories. In Milan, one of the great military leaders of the day, Francesco Sforza (1401–1466), seized the reins of power after the failure of the Visconti line. The succession of King Alfonso I in Naples ended a half century of civil war. In both Florence and Venice, the grip of the political elite over high offices was tightened by placing greater power in small advisory councils and, in Florence, by the ascent to power of the Medici family. In sum, this process is known as the rise of signorial rule. The rise of the signories made possible the second development of this period: the establishment of a balance of power within the peninsula.

It was the leaders of the Italian city-states who first perfected the art of diplomacy. Constant warfare necessitated continual alliances, and by the end of the fourteenth century the large city-states had begun the practice of keeping resident ambassadors at the major seats of power. This provided leaders with accurate information about the conditions of potential allies and enemies. Diplomacy was both an offensive and a defensive weapon. This was especially so because the city-states hired their soldiers as contract labor. These mercenary armies, whose leaders were known as *condottieri,* from the name of their contract, were both expensive and dangerous to maintain. If they did not bankrupt their employers, they might desert them or, even worse, turn on them. Thus Francesco Sforza, the greatest *condottiere* of the fifteenth century, gained power in Milan. Sforza's consolidation of power in Milan initially led to warfare, but ultimately it formed the basis of the Peace of Lodi (1454). This established two balanced alliances, one between Florence and Milan and the other between Venice and Naples. These states, along with the papacy, pledged mutual nonaggression, a policy that lasted for nearly 40 years.

The Peace of Lodi did not bring peace. It only halted the long period in which the major city-states struggled against one another. Under cover of the peace, the large states continued the process of swallowing up their smaller neighbors and creating quasi-empires. Civilian populations were overrun, local leaders were exiled or exterminated, tribute money was taken, and taxes were levied. Each of the five states either increased its mainland territories or strengthened its hold on them. Venice and Florence especially prospered.

Venice: A Seaborne Empire

Water shaped the destiny of Venice. Facing the Adriatic Sea, the city is formed by a web of lagoons. Through its center snakes the Grand Canal, whose banks were lined with buildings that celebrated its civic and mercantile power. At the

Piazza San Marco stood the vast palace of the doge, elected leader of the republic, and the Basilica of Saint Mark, a domed church built in the Byzantine style. At the Rialto were the stalls of bankers and moneylenders. Here, too, were the auction blocks for the profitable trade in European slaves, east European serfs, and battlefield captives who were sold into service to Egypt or Byzantium.

Venice owed its prosperity to trade rather than conquest. Its position at the head of the Adriatic permitted access to the raw materials of both East and West. The rich Alpine timberland behind the city provided the hardwoods necessary for shipbuilding. The inhabitants of the hinterland were steady consumers of grain, cloth, and the new manufactured goods—glass, silk, jewelry, and cottons—that came pouring onto the market in the late Middle Ages.

But the heart of Venetian success lay in the way in which it organized its trade and its government. The key to Venetian trade was its privileged position with the Byzantine Empire. Venice had exchanged with the Byzantines military support for tax concessions that gave Venetian traders a competitive edge in the spice trade with the East. The spice trade was so lucrative that special ships were built to accommodate it. These galleys were constructed at public expense and doubled as the Venetian navy in times of war. By controlling these ships, the government strictly regulated the spice trade. Rather than allow the wealthiest merchants to dominate it, as they did in other cities, Venice specified the number of annual voyages and sold shares in them at auction based on a fixed price. This practice allowed big and small merchants to gain from the trade and encouraged all merchants to find other trading outlets.

Like its trade, Venetian government was also designed to disperse power. Although it was known as the Most Serene Republic, Venice was not a republic in the sense that we use the word; it was rather an oligarchy—a government by a restricted group. Political power was vested in a Great Council whose membership had been fixed at the end of the thirteenth century. All males whose fathers enjoyed the privilege of membership in the Great Council were registered at birth in the Book of Gold and became members of the Great Council when they came of age. From the body of the Great Council, which numbered about 2,500 at the end of the fifteenth century, was chosen the Senate, a council about one-tenth the size, whose members served a one-year term. It was from the Senate that the true officers of government were selected: the doge, who was chosen for life, and members of a number of small councils, who administered affairs and advised the doge. Members of these councils were chosen by secret ballot in an elaborate process by which nominators were selected at random. Terms of office on the councils were extremely short in order to limit factionalism and to prevent any individual from gaining too much power. Though small groups exercised more power in practice than they should have in theory, the Venetian oligarchy was never troubled by either civil war or popular rebellion.

With its mercantile families firmly in control of government and trade, Venice created a vast overseas empire in the East during the thirteenth and fourteenth centuries. Naval supremacy allowed the Venetians to offer protection to strategic outposts in return for either privileges or tribute. But in the fifteenth century, Venice turned westward. In a dramatic reversal of its centuries-old policy, it began a process of conquest in Italy itself. There were several reasons for this new policy. First, the Venetian navy was no longer the unsurpassed power that it once had been. The Genoese wars had drained resources, and the revival of the Ottoman Turks in the East posed a growing threat that ultimately resulted in the fall of Constantinople (1453) and the end of Venetian trading privileges. Outposts in Dalmatia and the Aegean came under assault from both the Turks and the king of Hungary, cutting heavily into the complicated system by which goods were circulated by Venetian merchants. It was not long before Portuguese competition affected the most lucrative of all the commodities traded by the Venetians: pepper. Perhaps more important, mainland expansion offered new opportunities for Venice. Not all Venetians were traders, and the new industries that were being developed in the city could readily benefit from control of mainland markets. Most decisive of all, opportunity was knocking. In Milan, Visconti rule was weakening, and the Milanese territories were ripe for picking.

Venice reaped a rich harvest. From the beginning of the fifteenth century to the Peace of Lodi, the Most Serene Republic engaged in unremitting warfare. Its successes were remarkable. It pushed out to the north to occupy all the lands between the city and the Habsburg territories; it pushed to the east until it straddled the entire head of the Adriatic; and it pushed to the west almost as far as Milan itself. The western conquests, in particular, brought large populations under Venetian control, which, along with their potential as a market, provided a ready source of taxation. By the end of the fifteenth century, the mainland dominions of Venice were contributing nearly 40 percent of the city's revenue at a cost far smaller than that of the naval empire a century earlier.

Florence: Spinning Cloth into Gold

Florentine prosperity was built on banking and wool. Beginning in the thirteenth century, Florentine bankers were among the wealthiest and most powerful in the world. Initially, their position was established through support of the papacy in its long struggle with the Holy Roman Empire. Florentine financiers established banks in all the capitals of Europe and the East. In the Middle Ages, bankers served more functions than simply handling and exchanging money. Most were also tied to mercantile adventures and underwrote industrial activity. So it was in Florence that international bankers purchased high-quality wool to be manufactured into the world's finest woven cloth.

The activities of both commerce and cloth manufacture depended on external conditions, and so the wealth of

■ A view of Florence in 1490.

Florence was potentially unstable. In the mid-fourteenth century, instability came with the plague that devastated the city. Nearly 40 percent of the entire population was lost in the single year 1348, and recurring outbreaks continued to ravage the survivors. Loss of workers and markets seriously disrupted manufacturing. By 1380, cloth production had fallen to less than a quarter of pre-plague levels. On the heels of plague came wars. The property of Florentine bankers and merchants abroad was an easy target, and in this respect the wars with Naples at the end of the fourteenth century were particularly disastrous. Thirty years of warfare with Milan, interrupted by only a single decade of peace (1413–1423), resulted in total bankruptcy for many of the city's leading commercial families. More significant, the costs of warfare created a massive public debt. Every Florentine of means owned shares in this debt, and the republic was continually devising new methods for borrowing and staving off crises of repayment. Small wonder that the republic turned for aid to the wealthiest banking family in Europe, the Medici.

As befitted a city whose prosperity was based on manufacturing, Florence had a strong guild tradition. The most important guilds were associated with banking and cloth manufacture, but they included the crafts and food processing trades as well. Only guild members could participate in government, electing the nine *Signoria* who administered laws, set tax rates, and directed foreign and domestic policy. Like that of Venice, Florentine government was a republican oligarchy, and like Venice, it depended on rotated short periods in office and selections by lot to avoid factionalism. But Florence had a history of factionalism that was longer than its history of republican government. Its formal structures were occasionally altered so that powerful families could gain control of the real centers of political power, the small councils and emergency assemblies through which the Signoria governed. Conservative leadership drawn from the upper ranks of Florentine society guided the city through the wars of the early fourteenth century. But soon afterward, the leaders of its greatest families—the Albizzi, the Pazzi, and the Medici—again divided Florentine politics into factions.

The ability of the Medici to secure a century-long dynasty in a government that did not have a head of state is just one of the mysteries surrounding the history of this remarkable family. Cosimo de Medici (1389–1464) was one of the richest men in Christendom when he returned to the city in 1434 after a brief exile. His leading position in government rested on supporters who were able to gain a controlling influence on the Signoria. Cosimo built his party carefully, banishing his Albizzi enemies, recruiting followers among the craftsmen he employed, and even paying delinquent taxes to maintain his voters' eligibility. Most important, emergency powers were invoked to reduce the number of citizens qualified to vote for the Signoria until the majority were Medici backers.

Cosimo was a great patron of artists and intellectuals. He collected books and paintings, endowed libraries, and spent lavishly on his own palace, the Palazzo Medici. Cosimo's position as an international banker brought him into contact with the heads of other Italian city-states, and it was his personal relationship with Francesco Sforza that finally ended the Milanese wars and brought about the Peace of Lodi.

Cosimo's grandson, Lorenzo (1449–1492), held strong humanist values instilled in him by his mother, Lucrezia Tornabuoni, who organized his education. He brought

Michelangelo and other leading artists to his garden; he brought Pico della Mirandola and other leading humanists to his table. Lorenzo's power was based on his personality and reputation. His diplomatic abilities were the key to his survival. Almost immediately after Lorenzo came to power, Naples and the papacy began a war with Florence, a war that was costly to the Florentines in both taxation and lost territory. In 1479, Lorenzo traveled to Naples and personally convinced the Neapolitan king to sign a separate treaty. This restored the Italian balance of power and ensured continued Medici rule in Florence.

There is some doubt whether Lorenzo should be remembered by the title "the Magnificent" that was bestowed on him. His absorption in politics came at the expense of the family's commercial enterprises, which were nearly ruined during his lifetime. Branch after branch of the Medici bank closed as conditions for international finance deteriorated, and the family fortune dwindled. Moreover, the emergency powers that Lorenzo invoked to restrict participation in government changed forever the character of Florentine republicanism, irredeemably corrupting it. There is no reason to accept his enemies' judgment that Lorenzo was a tyrant, but the negative consequences of his rule cannot be ignored. In 1494, two years after Lorenzo's death, the peninsula was plunged into the wars that turned it from the center of European civilization into a satellite region.

The End of Italian Hegemony, 1450–1527

In the course of the Renaissance, western Europe was Italianized. For a century, the city-states dominated the trade routes that connected East and West. Italian manufactures, such as Milanese artillery, Florentine silk, and Venetian glass, were prized above all others. The ducat and the florin, two Italian coins, were universally accepted in an age when every petty prince minted his own. The peninsula exported culture in the same way that it exported goods. Humanism quickly spread across the Alps, aided by the recent invention of printing (which the Venetians soon dominated), and Renaissance standards of artistic achievement were known worldwide and everywhere imitated. The city-states shared their technology as well. The compass and the navigational chart, projection maps, double-entry bookkeeping, eyeglasses, the telescope— all profoundly influenced what could be undertaken. In this spirit, Christopher Columbus, a Genoese seaman, successfully crossed the Atlantic under the Spanish flag, and Amerigo Vespucci, a Florentine merchant, gave his name to the newly discovered continents.

Political and Military Unrest.   But it was not in Italy that the rewards of such achievement were enjoyed. There, the seeds of political turmoil and military imperialism, combined with the rise of the Ottoman Turks, were to reap a not unexpected harvest. Under the cover of the Peace of Lodi, the major city-states had scrambled to enlarge their mainland empires. By the end of the fifteenth century, they eyed one another warily. Each expected the others to begin a peninsulawide war for hegemony and took the steps that ultimately ensured the contest. Each shared the dream of recapturing the glory that was Rome. Long years of siege and occupation had militarized the Italian city-states. Venice and Florence balanced their budgets on the backs of their captured territories, Milan had been engaged in constant war for decades, and even the papacy was militarily aggressive.

The Italian Decline.   The disunited Italians were not able to meet the challenge of the most remarkable military leader of the age, the Ottoman prince Mehmed II (1451–1481), who conquered Constantinople and Athens and threatened Rome itself. The rise of the Ottomans (whose name is derived from Osman, their original tribal leader) is one of the most compelling stories in world history. Little more than a warrior tribe at the beginning of the fourteenth century, 150 years later the Ottomans had replaced stagnant Byzantine rule with a virile and potent empire. First, they gobbled up the towns and cities in a wide arc around Constantinople. Then they fed on the Balkans and the eastern kingdoms of Hungary and Poland. By 1400, they were a presence in all the territory that stretched from the Black Sea to the Aegean; by 1450, they were its master.

Venice was most directly affected by the Ottoman advance. Not only was its favored position in eastern trade threatened, but during a prolonged war at the end of the fifteenth century the Venetians lost many of their most important commercial outposts. Ottoman power closed off the markets of eastern Europe, and by 1480, Venetian naval supremacy was a thing of the past.

Successive popes pleaded in vain for holy wars to halt the advance of the Ottoman Turks. The fall of Constantinople in 1453 was an event of epochal proportions for Europeans; many believed that it foreshadowed the end of the world. Yet it was Italians rather than Ottomans who plunged the peninsula into the wars from which it never recovered.

The Wars of Italy (1494–1529) began when Naples, Florence, and the Papal States united against Milan. At first this alliance seemed little more than another shift in the balance of power. But rather than call on Venice to redress the situation, the Milanese leader, Ludovico Sforza, sought help from the French. An army of French cavalry and Swiss mercenaries, led by Charles VIII of France (1483–1498), invaded the peninsula in 1494. With Milanese support, the French swept all before them. Florence was forced to surrender Pisa, a humiliation that led to the overthrow of the Medici and the establishment of French sovereignty. The Papal States were next to be occupied, and within a year Charles had conquered Naples without engaging the Italians in a single significant battle. Unfortunately, the Milanese were not the only ones who could play at the game of foreign alliances. The Venetians and the pope united and called on the services of King Ferdinand of Aragon and the Holy Roman Emperor. Italy was now a battleground in what became a total European war for dynastic supremacy. The city-states used their foreign allies to settle old scores and to extend their own mainland empires. At the turn of the century, Naples was dismembered. In 1509, the pope conspired to organize the most powerful combination of forces yet known against Venice. All of the mainland possessions of the Most Serene Republic were lost, but by a combination of good fortune and skilled diplomacy, Venice itself survived. Florence was less fortunate, becoming a pawn first of the French and then of the Spanish. The final blow to Italian hegemony was the sack of Rome in 1527 by German mercenaries.

CONCLUSION

The sense of living in a new age, the spirit of human achievement, and the curiosity and wonderment of writers and artists all characterized the Renaissance. The desire to recreate the glories of Rome was not Machiavelli's alone. It could be seen in the palaces of the Italian aristocracy, in the papal rebuilding of the Holy City, and in the military ambitions of princes. But the legacy of empire, of "ancient and heroic pride," had passed out of Italian hands.

QUESTIONS FOR REVIEW

1. What social and cultural conditions were peculiar to the Italian peninsula, and how might those conditions have contributed to the Renaissance?
2. What were the principal characteristics of the Renaissance style in the visual arts?
3. What is humanism, and why was the study of languages so important to the humanists?
4. In what ways did the ideas of Niccolò Machiavelli reflect the reality of politics in the city-states of Renaissance Italy?

KEY TERMS

city-states, *p. 230*

civic humanism, *p. 229*

condottieri, p. 232

doge, *p. 232*

humanists, *p. 227*

linear perspective, *p. 226*

philology, *p. 228*

Pietà, p. 227

Renaissance, *p. 220*

rhetoric, *p. 228*

DISCOVERING WESTERN CIVILIZATION ONLINE

You can obtain more information about the Italian Renaissance at the websites listed below. See also the Companion Website that accompanies this text, www.ablongman.com/kishlansky, which contains an online study guide and additional resources.

Renaissance Society

NM's Creative Impulse: Renaissance

www.history.evansville.net/renaissa.html#Resources

A site of links to a wide array of subjects relating to the era of the Renaissance. A good starting point.

The Florentine Republic

www.mega.it/eng/egui/epo/secrepu.htm

The history of the Florentine Republic with links to major tourist attractions and buildings. Brief biographies of important Florentine citizens can also be found.

Renaissance Art

Renaissance Art

www.anu.edu.au/ArtHistory/renart/pics.art/index_1.html

A pictorial guide to the major artists of the Italian Renaissance and their works. Thumbnail representations lead to links on specific pieces.

Leon Battista Alberti—Great Buildings Online

www.greatbuildings.com/architects/Leon_Battista_Alberti.html

A page devoted to Alberti's architecture with a brief biography and links to pictures.

Michelangelo Buonarroti

www.mega.it/eng/egui/pers/micbuon.htm

A website devoted to Michelangelo with a variety of links to text and images of Renaissance Florence.

WebMuseum: The Italian Renaissance (1420–1600)

www.ibiblio.org/wm/paint/tl/it-ren/

Reproductions of Renaissance art, with accompanying text.

SUGGESTIONS FOR FURTHER READING

General Reading

P. Burke, *Culture and Society in Renaissance Italy* (Princeton, NJ: Princeton University Press, 1999). A good introduction to social and intellectual developments.

Paul Grendler, ed., *Encyclopedia of the Renaissance* (New York: Scribners, 1999). A valuable reference work for all aspects of the Renaissance.

Denys Hay, *The Italian Renaissance* (Cambridge, England: Cambridge University Press, 1977). The best first book to read, an elegant interpretive essay.

Renaissance Society

Carlo Cipolla, *Before the Industrial Revolution: European Society and Economy, 1000–1700,* 3rd ed. (New York: W. W. Norton, 1994). A sweeping survey of social and economic developments across the centuries.

J. R. Hale, *Renaissance Europe: The Individual and Society* (Berkeley: University of California Press, 1978). A lively study that places the great figures of the Renaissance in their social context.

D. Herlihy and C. Klapisch-Zuber, *Tuscans and Their Families* (New Haven, CT: Yale University Press, 1985). A difficult but rewarding study of the social and demographic history of Florence and its environs.

Margaret L. King, *Women of the Renaissance* (Chicago: University of Chicago Press, 1991). A study by a leading women's historian.

Renaissance Art

Michael Baxandall, *Painting and Experience in Fifteenth-Century Italy* (Oxford, England: Oxford University Press, 1972). A study of the relationship between painters and their patrons and of how and why art was produced.

Anthony Grafton, *Leon Battista Alberti: Master Builder of the Italian Renaissance* (New York: Hill and Wang, 2000). A lucid biographical study of a truly renaissance man.

Frederick Hartt, *History of Italian Renaissance Art* (Englewood Cliffs, NJ: Prentice-Hall, 1974). The most comprehensive survey, with hundreds of plates.

Howard Hibbard, *Michelangelo* (New York: Harper & Row, 1974). A compelling biography of an obsessed genius.

Lisa Jardine and Jerry Brotton, *Global Interests: Renaissance Art Between East and West* (Ithaca, NY: Cornell University Press, 2000). A bold argument about Renaissance art and its relation to Ottoman culture.

Michael Levey, *Early Renaissance* (London: Penguin, 1967). A concise survey of art, clearly written and authoritative.

Linda Murray, *High Renaissance and Mannerism* (London: Thames & Hudson, 1985). The best introduction to late Renaissance art.

Renaissance Ideals

Hans Baron, *The Crisis of the Early Italian Renaissance* (Princeton, NJ: Princeton University Press, 1966). One of the most influential intellectual histories of the period.

George Holmes, *The Florentine Enlightenment,* 2nd ed. (Oxford: Clarendon Press, 1992). A new edition of the best study of intellectual developments in Florence.

Quentin Skinner, *Machiavelli* (Oxford: Oxford University Press, 1981). A brief but brilliant biography.

The Politics of the Italian City-States

Gene Brucker, *Florence, The Golden Age 1138–1737* (Berkeley: University of California Press, 1998). The best single-volume introduction to Florentine history with excellent illustrations.

J. R. Hale, *Florence and the Medici* (London: Thames & Hudson, 1977). A compelling account of the relationship between a city and its most powerful citizens.

Frederic C. Lane, *Venice: A Maritime Republic* (Baltimore, MD: Johns Hopkins University Press, 1973). A complete history of Venice that stresses its naval and mercantile developments.

Lauro Martines, *Power and Imagination: City-States in Renaissance Italy* (New York: Alfred A. Knopf, 1979). An important interpretation of the politics of the Italian powers.

Eugene F. Rice, Jr., *The Foundations of Early Modern Europe, 1460–1559,* 2nd ed. (New York: W. W. Norton, 1994). The best short synthetic work.

Charles Stinger, *The Renaissance in Rome* (Bloomington, IN: University of Indiana Press, 1998). A thorough account of one of the great ages in the history of Rome.

For a list of additional titles related to this chapter's topics, please see www.ablongman.com/kishlansky.

12

THE EUROPEAN EMPIRES

The Visual Record

ASTRIDE THE WORLD

Henry VIII lived large. He was a bear of a man, famed for his ability to hunt all day while wearing out a pack of trained horses, for his prowess in wrestling bouts, including one with King Francis I of France, and, of course, for having six wives. His accomplishments as leader were equally impressive. Bequeathed a surplus by his father, Henry spent lavishly in an attempt to restore England to European prominence. He allied with Spain to fight France and with France to fight Spain and ran an expensive but futile campaign to be elected Holy Roman Emperor. He sponsored humanist thinkers and brought them to his court from all over Europe. He also encouraged the new learning at the Universities of Oxford and Cambridge and during his reign one of the classic works of English literature, Sir Thomas More's *Utopia,* was written. Henry's generals decisively defeated the Scots, England's troublesome northern neighbor, and his ministers successfully completed the integration of Wales into the English crown.

In 1532, when his attempt to secure an annulment of his first marriage failed, Henry dissolved England's ties to the Church of Rome declaring that "this realm of England is an Empire"—the first statement of British imperial ambition. He had Parliament declare him Supreme Head of the Church in England and then helped himself to the vast holdings of the Catholic religious orders—perhaps as much as a third of all of the land in England. Though Henry VIII shared his plunder with his loyal nobility and gentry, the lion's share was his. Henry's own religious beliefs remained shrouded in mystery, but he guided his nation toward the Protestantism that would bloom under his son Edward VI and his daughter Elizabeth I.

Henry VIII has passed through the ages as the very symbol of a monarch, an image captured by the German portrait painter Hans Holbein. His great skill was in rendering subjects true to life and his paintings of the Henrician court and its leading members, such as Thomas More and Thomas Cromwell, rival the works of Italian Renaissance portraiturists. But none were more memorable than the artist's numerous studies of Henry himself. Holbein was able to capture both the ferocity and the grandeur of the king.

Ironically, one of Holbein's most powerful and most famous portraits of Henry did not survive the seventeenth century. Part of a mural that Holbein painted in Henry's Whitehall Palace in 1537, the original work was lost when the palace burned in 1698. However, Holbein's followers had copied the grand painting, and earlier sketches of it by Holbein himself also survived, and so we still have a strong visual record of Holbein's vision of the king. The image shown here is a vibrant copy of the Whitehall Palace original, painted on oak panels, likely in the mid-sixteenth century. In this portrait, Henry stands with straight legs suggesting the solidity of tree trunks, one arm bent at the elbow as if in defiance of all comers. There is not even a suggestion of doubt as the king thrusts out his chest and fixes the viewer with a penetrating

stare. The artist represents the sumptuousness of Henry's court in the monarch's clothing. Fabric literally encases him, flowing in folds and gathers of intricate design and the costliest material. Furs drape over his doublet and elaborately embroidered red cloak. Enormous rubies bedeck not only his great gold chain, but his hat and vest, running down both sleeves, all to create an overwhelming sense of opulence. Even the protruding codpiece is meant to convey the potency of a king who had finally sired a male heir. Every detail conveys the impression of a monarch at the height of his power.

Looking Ahead

This image of Henry VIII is among the most recognizable from an age of monarchy that began in the sixteenth century and coincided with the consolidations of nations in western Europe and their expansion into all corners of the globe. Everywhere small principalities and kingdoms were absorbed by their larger and more powerful neighbors, and Europe's military might was on display as far east as India and as far west as Peru. Though England played but a small part in a century dominated by Spain and France, even its monarch could believe that he bestrode the world like a colossus. ➤

EUROPEAN ENCOUNTERS

The sixteenth century was an age of exploration. Knowledge bequeathed from the past created curiosity about the present. Technological change made long sea voyages possible, and the demands of commerce provided incentives. Ottoman expansion on the southern and eastern frontiers of the Continent threatened access to the goods of the East on which Europeans had come to rely. Spices were rare and expensive, but they were not merely luxuries. They had many practical uses. Some acted as preservatives, others as flavorings to make palatable the rotting foodstuffs that were the fare of even the wealthiest Europeans. Some spices were used as perfumes to battle the noxious gases that rose from urban streets and invaded homes and workplaces. The drugs of the East, the nature of which we can only guess at, helped to soothe chronic ill health. The demand for all of these "spices" continued to rise at a greater rate than their supply.

To pay for the spices, Western gold and silver flowed steadily eastward. As supplies of precious metals dwindled, economic growth in Europe slowed. Throughout the fifteenth century, ever-larger amounts of Western specie were necessary to purchase ever-smaller amounts of Eastern commodities. Europe faced a severe shortage of gold and silver, a shortage that threatened its standard of living and its prospects for economic growth. The search was on for new sources of gold.

Africa and a Passage to India

It was the Portuguese who made the first dramatic breakthroughs in exploration and colonization. Perched on the southwestern tip of Europe, Portugal was an agriculturally poor and sparsely populated nation. Among its few marketable commodities were fish and wine. However, the Portuguese had long sailed the Atlantic, where they had established bases in the Azores and Madeira islands. Their small ships, known as **caravels,** were ideal for ocean travel, and their navigators were among the most skillful in the world. Yet they were unable to participate in the lucrative Mediterranean trade in bullion and spices until the expanding power of the Ottomans threatened the traditional eastern sea routes.

Prince Henry the Navigator. In the early fifteenth century, the Portuguese gained a foothold in northern Africa and used it to stage voyages along the continent's unexplored western coast. Like most explorers, the Portuguese were motivated by a mixture of faith and greed. Establishing southern bases would enable them to surround their Muslim enemies while also giving them access to the African bullion trade. The Portuguese navigator Bartolomeu Dias (ca. 1450–1500) summarized these goals succinctly: "To give light to those who are in darkness and to grow rich." Under the energetic leadership of Prince Henry the Navigator (1394–1460), the Portuguese pushed steadily southward. Prince Henry studied navigational techniques, accumulated detailed accounts of voyages, and encouraged the creation of accurate maps of the African coastline.

Prince Henry's systematic program paid off in the next generation. By the 1480s, Portuguese outposts had reached almost to the equator, and in 1487, Bartolomeu Dias rounded the tip of Africa and opened the eastern African shores to Portuguese traders. The aim of these enterprises was access to Asia rather than Africa. Dias might have reached India if his crew had not mutinied and forced him to return home. A decade later, Vasco da Gama (ca. 1460–1524) rounded the Cape of Good Hope and crossed into the Indian Ocean. When he returned to Lisbon in 1499, laden with the most valuable spices of the East, Portuguese ambitions were achieved. Larger expeditions followed, one of which, blown off course, touched the South American coast of Brazil, which was soon subsumed within the Portuguese dominions.

The Beginnings of the Slave Trade. The exploration of the African coast also brought the Portuguese into contact with Muslim traders who had developed connections between North Africa and the middle of the continent. They bartered for gold, ivory, and exotic spices, exchanging colorful cloth, metalwork, and other manufactured goods. They also bartered for slaves. Slavery was a common feature of the cultures that interacted in Africa. Europeans had used slaves in ancient times and had developed a theory that justified slavery by capture. Muslims were dependent upon them for their armies and bought many slaves from European sources. Africans enslaved those who were captured in tribal wars and sold them out of Africa, first to Muslim traders and then to the Portuguese. The popes who granted Portugal a monopoly on European trade in Africa also sanctioned the trade in African slaves upon the condition that those enslaved had not converted to Christianity.

The slave trade began almost immediately. At first African slaves were imported to Europe as a curiosity and were purchased by wealthy families. But the discovery of the Azores and the Canary Islands provided a much more valuable use for the enslaved Africans. Their ability to labor in intense heat fitted them for agricultural work in the new sugar fields that were being developed in these Atlantic islands. By the 1470s it was estimated that over a thousand African slaves a year were being imported into Portugal and that a significant percentage of those were sold to Spanish masters who also saw their value in farming. Originally, the slaves were purchased either from Muslim traders or directly from African tribal leaders. Horses became the preferred medium of exchange, and Prince Henry the Navigator financed the trade until his death. Thereafter, the right to trade in slaves was sold to private entrepreneurs, who were less scrupulous. Soon the Portuguese were simply conducting raids on coastal villages to capture as many Africans as they could cram on to their boats.

In these early decades, slaves were viewed as just another trading commodity and valued only in regard to their profit. Ships were still small, voyages still risky, and capital still

MAP DISCOVERY

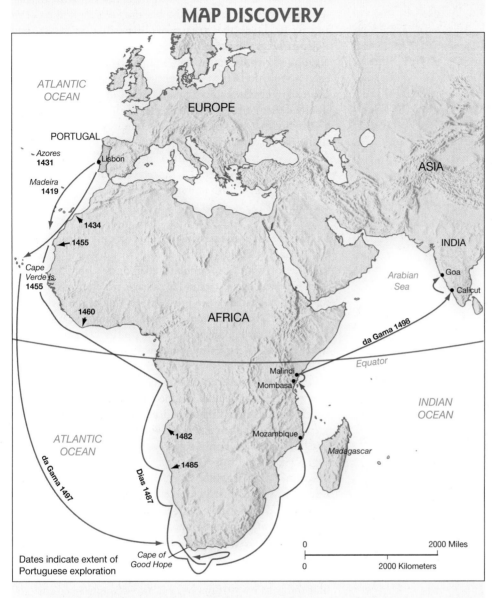

Portuguese Explorations

Examine the routes of the Portuguese explorers. What was their strategy of exploration? How long did it take for explorers to round the tip of Africa? What was the ultimate goal of Portuguese seafarers?

The Asian Trade. Building on their experience in West Africa, the Portuguese came to the East as traders rather than as conquerors. They developed a policy of establishing military outposts to protect their investments and subduing native populations only when necessary. Throughout the East, the Portuguese took advantage of local feuds to gain allies, and they established trading compounds that were easily defensible. By the beginning of the sixteenth century, the Portuguese Empire spanned both the eastern and western coasts of Africa and the western shores of India. Most important, the Portuguese controlled Ceylon and Indonesia, the precious Spice Islands from which came cloves, cinnamon, and pepper. Almost overnight, Lisbon became one of the trading capitals of the world, tripling in population between 1500 and 1550.

Mundus Novus

While the bulk of Portuguese resources were devoted to the Asian trade, those of the Spanish kingdom came to be concentrated in the New World. Though larger and richer than its western neighbor, Spain had been segmented into a number of small kingdoms and principalities and divided between Christians and Muslims. Not until the end of the fifteenth century, when the crowns of Aragon and Castile were united and the Muslims were expelled from Granada, could the Spanish concentrate their resources. By then they were far behind in establishing commercial enterprises. With Portugal dominating the African route to India, Queen Isabella of Castile was persuaded by a Genoese adventurer, Christopher Columbus (ca. 1446–1506), to take an interest in a western route. That interest resulted in one of the greatest accidents of history.

Christopher Columbus. Like all well-informed people of his day, Columbus believed the world was round. He

scarce. The agricultural use of African slaves was limited by the small amount of commercial agriculture undertaken by Europeans. The Portuguese held a monopoly on transporting slaves from Africa, but the trade soon centered in Seville where Italians dominated it. This was a significant, if unplanned development. Seville would soon become the center of the Spanish overseas empire, and the Spanish colonies in America would soon become the destination for most of the African slaves bought by Europeans.

■ This sixteenth-century map of Java and the Moluccas shows European traders bartering for spices. At the upper left, a ship laden with the rich cargo sails for markets in Europe.

calculated that a westward course would be shorter and less expensive than the path that the Portuguese were breaking around Africa—but he was wrong. He misjudged the size of the globe by a quarter and the distance of the journey by 400 percent. Columbus sailed westward into the unknown in 1492, and on 12 October he landed in the Bahamas, on an island that he named San Salvador. He had discovered a *Mundus Novus*, a New World.

Initially, Columbus's discovery was a disappointment. He had gone in search of a western passage to the Indies and he had failed to return to Spain laden with Eastern spices. Despite his own belief that the islands he had discovered lay just off the coast of Japan, it was soon apparent that he had found an altogether unknown landmass. Columbus's own explorations and those of his successors continued to focus on discovering a route to the Indies. This was all the more imperative once the Portuguese succeeded in finding the passage

around Africa. Rivalry between the two nations intensified after 1500, when the Portuguese began exploring the coast of Brazil. In 1494, the **Treaty of Tordesillas** had confined Portugal's right to the eastern route to the Indies as well as to any undiscovered lands east of an imaginary line fixed west of the Cape Verde Islands. This entitled Portugal to Brazil. The Spanish received whatever lay west of the line. At the time, few doubted that Portugal had the better of the bargain.

But Spanish-backed explorations soon proved the value of the newly discovered lands. In 1513, Vasco Núñez de Balboa (1475–1517) crossed the Isthmus of Panama and became the first European to view the Pacific Ocean. The discovery of this ocean refueled Spanish ambitions to find a western passage to the Indies.

Ferdinand Magellan. In 1519, Ferdinand Magellan (ca. 1480–1521), a Portuguese mariner in the service of Spain, set sail in pursuit of Columbus's goal of reaching the Spice Islands by sailing westward. His voyage, which he did not live to complete, remains the most astounding of the age. After making the Atlantic crossing, Magellan resupplied his fleet in Brazil. Then his ships began the long southerly run toward the tip of South America, though he had no idea of the length of the continent. After suppressing mutinies and overcoming shipwrecks and desertions, Magellan finally found the straits that still bear his name. By the time Magellan entered the Pacific, he had already lost two ships and much of his crew.

When Magellan finally reached land, first in the Marianas and then in the Philippines, the crew fell prey to natives more aggressive than those they had met in South America. Magellan's foolhardy decision to become involved in a local war cost him his life. It was left to his navigator, Sebastian Elcano (ca. 1476–1526), to complete the journey. In 1522, three years and one month after setting out, Elcano returned to Spain with a single ship and eighteen survivors of the crew of 280. But in his hold were spices of greater value than the cost of the expedition. His return provided practical proof that the world was round, but it also demonstrated that the vastness of the Pacific Ocean made a western passage to the Indies uneconomical. The circumnavigation of Magellan and Elcano brought to an end the first stage of the Spanish exploration of the New World. In 1529, the Spanish crown relinquished its claims to the Spice Islands to the Portuguese for a cash settlement. By then, trading spices was less alluring than mining gold and silver.

The Spanish Conquests

The exploits of Hernando Cortés (1485–1547) opened the next stage of Spanish discovery. The Spanish colonized the New World along the model of their reconquest of Spain. Individuals were given control over land and the people on it in return for military service. The interests of the crown were threefold: to convert the natives to Christianity, to extend sovereignty over new dominions, and to gain profit from the venture. The colonial entrepreneurs had a singular interest: to grow rich. Most of the colonizers came from the lower orders of Spanish society. Even the original captains and governors were drawn from groups, such as younger sons of the nobility, that would have had little opportunity for rule in Castile.

Many of the protective measures taken by the crown to ensure orderly colonization and fair treatment of the natives were ineffective in practice. During the first decades of the sixteenth century, Spanish captains and their followers subdued the Indian populations of the Caribbean Islands and put them to work on the agricultural haciendas they had carved out for themselves. As early as 1498, Castilian women began arriving in the New World. Their presence helped to change the character of the settlement towns from wild frontier gar-

risons to civilized settlements. Some of the women ultimately inherited huge estates and participated fully in the forging of Spanish America.

Life on the hacienda, however, did not always satisfy the ambitions of the Spanish colonizers. Hernando Cortés was one such conquistador. Having participated in the conquest of Cuba, Cortés sought an independent command to lead an expedition into the hinterland of Central America, where a fabulous empire was rumored to exist. Having gathered a force of 600 men, Cortés sailed across the Gulf of Mexico in 1519 and established a fort at Vera Cruz, where he garrisoned 200 men. He then sank his boats so that none of his company could turn back. With 400 soldiers, he marched 250 miles

THE HALLS OF MONTEZUMA

Bernal Díaz del Castillo (ca. 1492–1581) was one of the soldiers who accompanied Hernando Cortés on the conquest of the Aztecs. Díaz wrote The True History of the Conquest of New Mexico *to refute what he regarded as inaccurate accounts of the conquest. In this passage, he describes the Aztec gods from a Christian point of view and shows how difficult it was for the Europeans to understand the different cultures they were encountering.*

Focus Questions

Díaz describes the Aztec gods as devils and idols. What does this reveal about the Europeans' way of thinking? Why would Cortés want to see Montezuma's gods, and why does Montezuma show them to him?

Then Cortés said to Montezuma . . . "Your Highness is indeed a great prince, and it has delighted us to see your cities. Now that we are here in your temple, will you show us your gods?"

Montezuma replied that he would first have to consult with his priests. After he had spoken with them, he bade us enter a small tower room, a kind of hall where there were two altars with very richly painted planks on the ceiling. On each altar there were two giant figures, their bodies very tall and stout. The first one, to the right, they said was Uichilobos, their god of war. It had a very broad face with monstrous, horrible eyes, and the whole body was covered with precious stones, gold, and pearls that were stuck on with a paste they make in this country out of roots. The body was circled with great snakes made of gold and precious stones, and in one hand he held a bow and in the other some arrows. A small idol standing by him they said was his page; he held a short lance and a shield rich with gold and precious stones. Around the neck of Uichilobos were silver Indian faces and things that we took to be the hearts of these Indians, made of gold and decorated with many precious blue stones.

There were braziers with copal incense, and they were burning in them the hearts of three Indians they had sacrificed that day. All the walls and floor were black with crusted blood, and the whole place stank.

To the left stood another great figure, the height of Uichilobos, with the face of a bear and glittering eyes made of their mirrors, which they call *tezcal*. It was decorated with precious stones the same as Uichilobos, for they said that the two were brothers. This Tezcatepuca was the god of hell and had charge of the souls of the Mexicans. His body was girded with figures like little devils, with snakelike tails. The walls were so crusted with blood and the floor was so bathed in it that in the slaughterhouses of Castile there was no such stink. They had offered to this idol five hearts from the day's sacrifices. . . .

Our captain said to Montezuma, half laughingly, "Lord Montezuma, I do not understand how such a great prince and wise man as yourself can have failed to come to the conclusion that these idols of yours are not gods, but evil things—devils is the term for them. . . ."

The two priests with Montezuma looked hostile, and Montezuma replied with annoyance, "Señor Malinche, if I had thought that you would so insult my gods, I would not have shown them to you. We think they are very good, for they give us health, water, good seedtimes and weather, and all the victories we desire. We must worship and make sacrifices to them. Please do not say another word to their dishonor."

From Bernal Díaz, *The True History of the Conquest of New Mexico* (1552–1568).

through steamy jungles and over rugged mountains before glimpsing the first signs of the great Aztec civilization. The Aztec Empire was a loose confederation of native tribes that the Aztec had conquered during the previous century. It was ruled by the emperor Montezuma II (1502–1520) from his capital at Tenochtitlán, a marvelous city built of stone and baked clay in the middle of a lake. Invited to an audience with the Aztec emperor, Cortés and his men saw vast stores of gold and silver.

The conquest of the Aztecs took nearly a year and remains an overwhelming feat of arms. Nearly 100,000 natives from the tribes that the Aztecs had conquered supported the Spanish assault. Cortés's cavalry terrified the Aztecs, who had never seen either horses or iron armaments. Cortés also benefited from the Aztec practice of taking battlefield captives to be used in religious sacrifices. This allowed many Spanish soldiers who would otherwise have been killed to be rescued and to fight again.

By 1522, Cortés was master of an area larger than all of Spain. But the cost in native lives was staggering. In 30 years, a population of approximately 25 million had been reduced to fewer than 2 million. Most of the loss was due to exposure to European diseases such as smallpox, typhoid, and measles, against which the indigenous peoples had no immunity. Their labor-intensive system of agriculture could not survive the rapid decrease in population, and famine followed pestilence.

This tragic sequence was repeated everywhere the Europeans appeared. In 1531, Francisco Pizarro (ca. 1475–1541) conquered the Peruvian empire of the Incas, vastly extending the territory under Spanish control. A huge silver mine was discovered in 1545 at Potosí in what is now southern Bolivia, and the gold and silver that poured into Spain in the next quarter century helped to support Spanish dynastic ambitions in Europe. During the course of the sixteenth century, over 200,000 Spaniards migrated across the ocean. Perhaps one in ten were women, who married and set up families. Succeeding generations created huge haciendas built with the forced labor of black African slaves, who proved better able to endure the rigors of mining and farming than did the native peoples.

The Legacy of the Encounters

By the seventeenth century, long-distance trade had begun to integrate the regions of the world into a single marketplace. Slaves bought in Africa mined silver in South America. The bullion was shipped to Spain, where it was distributed across Europe. Most went to Amsterdam to settle Spanish debts, Dutch bankers having replaced the Italians as the paymasters of Europe. From Holland, some of the silver traveled east to the Baltic Sea, the Dutch lifeline, where vital stores of grain and timber were purchased for home consumption. Even more of this silver was carried to Asia to buy spices in the Spice Islands, cottons in India, or silk in China. Millions of ounces flowed from America to Asia via the European trading

routes. On the return voyage, Indian cottons were traded in Africa to purchase slaves for the South American silver mines.

Gold, God, and Glory. Gold, God, and glory neatly summarized the motives of the European explorers. The gold of Africa and the silver of South America enriched the Western nations. Christian missions arose wherever the European empires touched down: among Africans, Asians, and Amerindians. And glory there was in plenty. The feats of the great discoverers were recounted in story and song.

Yet many technological problems had to be overcome. Advances in navigational skills, especially in dead reckoning and later in calculating latitude from the position of the sun, were essential preconditions for covering the distances that were to be traveled. Ship designs became more sophisticated. The magnetic compass and the astrolabe were indispensable tools. Better maps and charts fueled both ambitions and abilities. It was a mapmaker who named the newly found continents after Amerigo Vespucci (1451–1512), the Italian explorer who voyaged to Brazil for the Portuguese. It may have been an accident that Columbus found the New World, but it was no coincidence that he was able to land in the same place three more times.

Nor was it happenstance that European forces conquered the peoples they encountered in both east and west. Generations of warfare against Muslims had honed the skills of Christian warriors. European ships were sturdily built and armed with cannons that could be used on land or at sea. Soldiers were well-equipped and battle-tested. Military leaders were trained and experienced in the arts of siege and the tactics of divide and conquer.

The Columbian Exchange. The encounters between Europeans and native Americans were a cultural and intellectual event of the first magnitude, likely stirring the imaginations of native tribesmen as much as those of European writers. But it was also an ecological and biological event with enormous consequences—a transfer of microbes, animals, and plants known as the **Columbian Exchange.**

The mixing of populations that had historically remained separate had effects that no one could have foreseen. First and foremost were issues of public health. When the Spanish explorers arrived in the Caribbean islands, they carried agents of common diseases such as measles, smallpox, and influenza that raged in European population centers and killed many thousands each year but to which survivors carried a lifetime immunity. The native populations of the Americas endured their first exposure to these diseases all at once and millions succumbed in the first half-century of contact. Similarly, it was believed that Europeans first contracted the venereal disease syphilis through sexual encounters with American women. Though experts still debate whether syphilis originated in the New World, there was an epidemic of the disease in western Europe after the explorers returned home.

Disease was not the only unanticipated exchange that resulted from the encounters. On their ships the Spanish ex-

MAP DISCOVERY

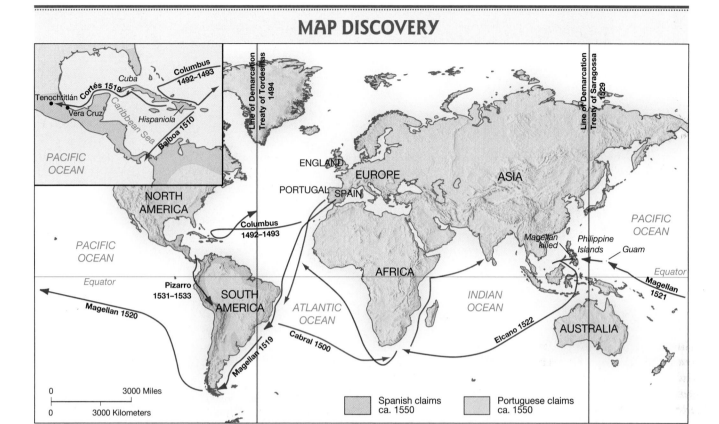

Claims of Spain and Portugal to Overseas Empires

Examine the voyages of discovery and the claims to overseas empires. How did Portuguese and Spanish exploration differ? What was the effect of the Treaty of Tordesillas on their travel and claims? Why was it believed at the time that Portugal was the more powerful empire?

---

plorers brought horses, pigs, cows, and other domesticated animals unknown in the Americas. Not only did these new animals change patterns of work among the native populations, but they also changed dietary customs. Pork and beef gradually entered the diet of those who traded with the colonists and ultimately into that of the general population.

Nor was the exchange one-sided. Beginning in the 1550s, European naturalists catalogued thousands of unknown species, a small number of which were suited to the different climates and soils of Europe. Among the most important of these species were a number of foodstuffs that ultimately had a transforming effect on the European diet. A small yellow fruit from the Americas took root in southern Italy, where the hot sun and rich clay provided a perfect growth environment. The Italians called it *pomodoro*—the yellow apple—but the native Americans called it *tomato*. Central Europe proved a welcoming place to grow another South American plant, the potato—a food so nutritious that laborers could nearly survive on it alone. It was to become a staple of the German diet

and later was to be both a boon and a bane in Ireland. South American chili peppers found their market in Hungary, where they were dried and powdered to be used as a condiment called paprika. Even the French found their diet enhanced by products of the New World; the popular cocoa bean, after generations of refinement, was used to make chocolate.

European Reflections. Riches and converts, power and glory, all came in the wake of exploration. But in the process of discovering new lands and new cultures, Europe also learned something of its own aspirations. Early Portuguese voyagers went in quest of the mythical Prester John, a saintly figure who was said to rule a heaven on earth in the middle of Africa. The first children born on Madeira were named Adam and Eve, though this slave plantation of sugar and wine was an unlikely Garden of Eden. The optimism of those who searched for the fountain of youth in the Florida swamps was not only that they would find it there, but that a long life was worth living. Contact with the cultures of the New World also

■ Contact with cultures of the New World forced Europeans into a different way of thinking about the old world. In this detail from *The Cognoscenti*, a seventeenth-century Flemish painting, English scholars and navigators examine European encounters with new lands and new cultures.

forced a different kind of thinking about life in the old one. The supposed customs of strange lands provided the setting for one of the great works of English social criticism, Sir Thomas More's *Utopia* (1516).

Europe also discovered and revealed a darker side of itself in the age of exploration. Accompanying the boundless optimism and assertive self-confidence that made so much possible was a tragic arrogance and callous disregard toward native peoples. Portuguese travelers described Africans as "dog-faced, dog-toothed people, satyrs, wild men, and cannibals." Such attitudes helped to justify enslavement. Though they encountered heritages that were in some ways richer than their own, few Westerners harbored any appreciation of them. The Portuguese spice trade did not depend on da Gama's indiscriminate bombardment of the port of Calicut. In this and other unfortunate episodes the destruction was wanton. It revealed the rapaciousness, greed, and cruelty of many European conquerors. These were the impulses of the Crusades rather than of the Renaissance.

GEOGRAPHICAL TOUR
Europe in 1500

Just as the map of the world was changing as a result of the voyages of discovery, so the map of Europe was changing as a result of the activities of princes. The early sixteenth century was the age of the prince, the first great stage of nation building that would last for the next 300 years. The **New Monarchies,** as they are sometimes called, consolidated territories that were divided culturally, linguistically, and historically. The states of Europe are political units that were forged by political means: by diplomacy, by marriage, and most com-

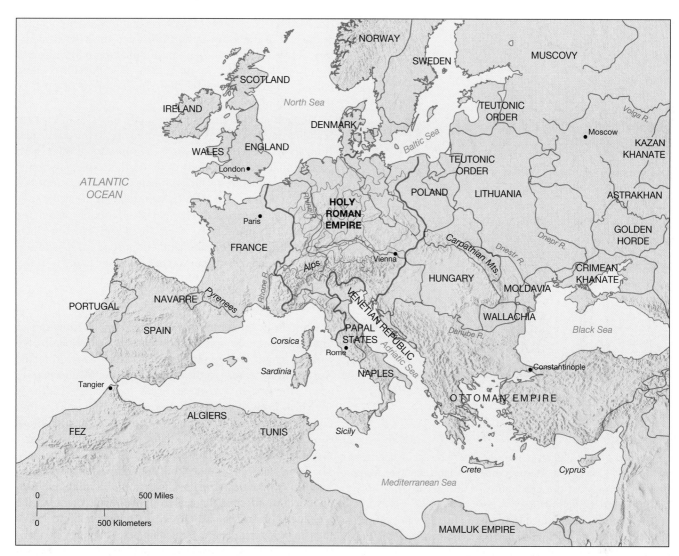

■ **Map A. Europe in 1500.** While the western part of Europe had taken on its modern features, central and eastern Europe continued to change their boundaries.

monly by war. The national system that we take for granted when thinking about Europe is a relatively recent development. Before we can observe its beginnings, we must first have a picture of Europe as it existed in 1500 (see **Map A**). At that time it was composed of nearly 500 distinct political units.

Europe is a concept rather than a clear-cut geographical unit. The vast plain that stretches from the Netherlands to the steppes of Russia presents few natural barriers to migration. Tribes had been wandering across this plain for thousands of years, slowly settling into the more fertile lands to practice their agriculture. Only in the south did geographical forces stem the flow of humanity. The Carpathian Mountains created a basin for the settlement of Slavic peoples that ran down to the Black Sea. The Alps provided a boundary for French, Germanic, and Italian settlements. The Pyrenees defined the Iberian peninsula, with a mixture of African and European peoples.

Boundaries of Eastern Europe

In the east, three great empires had created the political geography that could be said to define a European boundary: the Mongol, the Ottoman, and the Russian. During the early Middle Ages, Mongol warriors had swept across the Asian steppes and conquered most of central and southern Ukraine. By the sixteenth century, the Mongol Empire was disintegrating, its lands divided into a number of separate states called khanates. The khanate of the Crimea, with lands around the northern shores of the Black Sea, created the southeastern border of Europe (see **Map B**).

The Ottoman territories defined the southern boundary. By 1450, the Ottomans controlled all of Byzantium and Greece, dominating from the Black Sea to the Aegean. Fifty years later, they had conquered nearly all the lands between the Aegean and the Adriatic Seas. A perilous frontier was

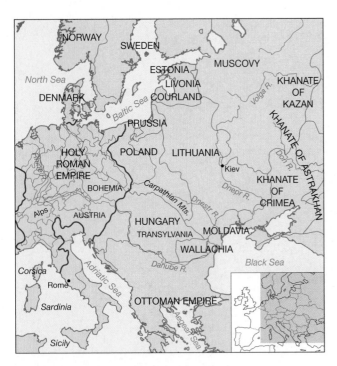

■ **Map B. Eastern Europe Before the Consolidation of Russia.** The duchy of Lithuania had reached the height of its power and stretched from the Baltic to the Black Sea.

established on the Balkan peninsula. There the principalities of Moldavia, Wallachia, Transylvania, and Hungary (see **Map B**) held out against the Ottomans for another quarter of a century before being overrun.

The Russian state defined the eastern boundary of Europe. Russia, too, had been a great territorial unit of the Middle Ages, centered at Kiev in the west and stretching eastward into Asia. The advance of the Mongols in the thirteenth century had contracted the eastern part of Russia. Its western domains had disintegrated under the practice of dividing the ruling prince's inheritance among his sons. In 1500, Europe reached as far east as the principality of Muscovy. There the heritage of East and West mingled. In some periods of history, Russia's ties with the West were most important; at other times, Russia retreated into isolation from Europe.

The northern borders of eastern Europe centered on the Baltic Sea, one of the most important trading routes of the early modern era (see **Map B**). On the northern coasts lay the Scandinavian nations of Sweden, Norway, and Denmark. These loosely confederated nations had a single king throughout the fifteenth century. Denmark, the southernmost of the three, was also the richest and most powerful. On the southern side of the Baltic lay the dominions of the Teutonic Knights, physically divided by the large state of Poland-Lithuania. The Teutonic territories, in the valuable Baltic region of Prussia, had been colonized by German crusaders in the thirteenth century.

Poland-Lithuania comprised an enormous territory that stretched the length of Europe from the Baltic to the Black Sea

(see **Map B**). The crowns of these two nations had been joined at the end of the fourteenth century, and their dynastic history was tied up with the nations of Bohemia and Hungary to their west and south. At the end of the fifteenth century, Poland, Lithuania, Bohemia, and Hungary were all ruled by the same family, the Jagiellons.

Mongols and Ottomans to the south, Russians in the east, Scandinavia in the north, Poland-Lithuania in the center, and Hungary in the west—such were the contours of the eastern portion of Europe. Its lands were, on the whole, less fertile than those farther west, and its climate was more severe. It was a sparsely populated region. Its wealth lay in the Baltic fisheries, in the Hungarian and Bohemian silver mines, and in the enormous Russian forests, where wood and its by-products were plentiful. Except in the southern portions of Poland and central Bohemia, the region was agriculturally poor.

Central Europe

The middle of the continent was defined by the Holy Roman Empire and was occupied almost entirely by Germanic peoples. In length, the empire covered the territory from the North and Baltic seas to the Adriatic and the Mediterranean, where the Italian city-states were located. In width, it stretched from Bohemia to Burgundy. Politically, central Europe comprised a bewildering array of principalities, church lands, and free towns. By the end of the fifteenth century, the Holy Roman Empire was an empire in name only. The large states of Brandenburg, Bohemia, and Bavaria resembled the political units of the east. In the south, the Alps provided an effective physical boundary, which allowed the archduchy of Austria and the Swiss Confederation to follow their own separate paths. Stretching across the center of the empire, from the Elbe River to the North Sea, were a jumble of petty states. Great cities such as Nuremberg and Ulm in the south, Bremen and Hamburg in the north, and Frankfurt and Cologne in the west were free municipalities. Large sections of the northwestern part of the empire were governed by the Church through resident bishops. Further to the west were the prosperous Low Countries: Holland and its port of Amsterdam, Brabant and its port of Antwerp. In the southwest, the empire extended in some places as far as the Rhone River and included the rich estates of Luxembourg, Lorraine, and Burgundy (see **Map C**).

The riches of the empire made it the focal point of Europe. Nearly 15 million people lived within its borders. Its agriculture varied from the olive- and wine-producing areas in the southwest to the great granaries in its center. Rich mineral deposits and large reserves of timber made the German lands industrially advanced. The European iron industry was centered here, and the empire was the arms manufacturer for the western world. The empire was also a great commercial center, heir to the Hanseatic League of the Middle Ages, and its merchants were replacing the Italians as the leading international bankers.

Like the empire, the Italian peninsula was divided into a diverse collection of small city-states (see **Map C**). During the

■ **Map C. Central Europe.** This map of central Europe shows the boundaries of the Holy Roman Empire.

course of the fifteenth century, five of these had emerged as most powerful (see Chapter 11). In the north were the duchy of Milan, Florence, and Venice. In the south was Rome, spiritual center of Catholicism and residence of the pope. Papal lands stretched far to the north of Rome, and wars to defend or expand them were Roman as well as papal ventures. The kingdom of Naples, the breadbasket of the Mediterranean, occupied the southernmost part of Italy and included the agriculturally rich island of Sicily.

Western Europe

The Iberian peninsula, the French territories, and the British Isles formed the westernmost borders of Europe (see **Map D**). Separated from France in the north by the Pyrenees, and surrounded by the Atlantic Ocean and the Mediterranean Sea on the west and east, the Iberian peninsula was most influenced by the fact that it is separated from North Africa only by the easily navigable Strait of Gibraltar. During the Middle Ages, the peninsula was overrun by North African Muslims, whom the Spanish called Moors. From the eighth to the fifteenth centuries, Iberian history was dominated by the **reconquista,** the recapture and re-Christianization of the conquered terri-

tories. This reconquest was finally completed in 1492, when the Moors were pushed out of Granada and the Jews were expelled from Spain. At the end of the fifteenth century, the Iberian peninsula contained several separate kingdoms. The most important were Portugal on the western coast; Aragon with its Mediterranean ports of Barcelona and Valencia; and Castile, the largest of the Iberian states (see **Map D**). The marriage of King Ferdinand of Aragon and Queen Isabella of Castile in 1469 had joined the crowns of Aragon and Castile, but the two kingdoms remained separate.

The remnants of ancient Gaul were also favored by a maritime location, with coasts on the Mediterranean and the Atlantic. Britain was less than thirty miles from France across the English Channel. Toward the end of the fifteenth century, France was still divided into many smaller fiefs. The royal domain centered on Paris and extended to Champagne in the east and Normandy in the west (see **Map D**). South of this area, however, from Orléans to Brittany, were principalities that had long been contested between England and France. Nor was the rich central plain yet integrated into the royal domain. Agriculturally, French lands were the richest in Europe. France enjoyed both Mediterranean and Atlantic climates, which suited the growing of the widest variety of foodstuffs.

■ **Map D. Western Europe.** Western Europe was already consolidated into nation-states.

Its population of approximately 13 million was second only to that of the Holy Roman Empire.

Across the Channel lay Britain (comprising England, Scotland, and Wales) and Ireland (see **Map D**). Britain had been settled by an array of European colonizers—Romans, Danes, Angles, and Saxons—before being conquered in the eleventh century by the French Normans. From that time, it was protected by the rough waters of the English Channel and the North Sea and developed a distinct cultural and political heritage. Wales to the west and Scotland to the north were still separate nations at the beginning of the sixteenth century. Both were mountainous lands with harsh climates and few natural advantages. They were sparsely populated. Though Ireland, too, was sparsely populated, it contained several rich agricultural areas that were especially suited for dairying and grazing.

In 1500, Europe exhibited a remarkable diversity of political and geographical forms. Huge states in the east, tiny principalities in the center, and emerging nations in the west seemingly had little in common. There was as yet no state system, and there was no clear group of dominant powers. The western migration of the Germanic peoples appeared to be over, but their consolidation was as yet unimagined. The Iberians struggled to expel the Moors, the Hungarians to hold back the Ottomans. Everywhere one looked were fragmentation and disarray. Yet in less than half a century the largest empire yet known in the West would be formed. States would be consolidated and dynasties established all over the continent. And with the rise of the state would come the dream of dominion, an empire over all of Europe.

————————————————————————————————— ■

THE FORMATION OF STATES

Machiavelli identified the prince as the agent of change in the process of state formation. He believed that the successful prince could bring unity to his lands, security to his borders, and prosperity to his subjects. The unsuccessful prince brought nothing but ruin.

A process as long and as complex as the formation of a state, however, depends on more than the will of an individual. Factors such as geography, population, and natural resources are all important. So, too, are the structures through which human activity is channeled. The ways in which families are organized and wealth is transmitted from generation to generation can result in large estates with similar customs or small estates with varying ones. The manner in which social groups are formed and controlled can mean that power is centralized or dispersed. The beliefs of ordinary people and the way they practice them can define who is a part of a community and who is apart from it. All these elements and many others affected the way in which European states began to take shape at the end of the fifteenth century. Despite these complexities, we should not lose sight of the simple truth of Machiavelli's observations. In the first stages of the consolidation of European nations the role of the prince was crucial.

Indeed, in the middle of the fifteenth century there were many factors working against the formation of large states in Europe. The most obvious involved simple things such as transportation and communication. The distance that could be covered quickly was very small. In wet and cold seasons, travel was nearly impossible. Large areas were difficult to control and to defend. Communication was not only subject to the hazards of travel. Distinct languages or dialects, a principal feature of small states, contributed to separate cultures. Customary practices, common ancestry, and shared experiences helped to define a sense of community through which small states defined themselves.

To these natural forces that acted to maintain the existence of small units of government were added invented ones. To succeed, a prince had to establish supremacy over a number of rivals. For the most part, states were inherited. In some places it was customary to follow the rule of primogeniture, inheritance by the eldest son. In others, estates were split among sons or among children of both sexes. Some traditions, like the French, excluded inheritance through women; others, like the Castilian, treated women's claims as equal to men's. Short lives meant prolonged disputes about inheritance. Rulers had to defend their thrones from rivals with strong claims to legitimacy.

Rulers also had to defend themselves from the ambitions of their mightiest subjects. The constant warfare of the European nobility was one of the central features of the later Middle Ages. To avoid resort to arms, princes and peers entered into all manner of alliances, using their children as pawns and the marriage bed as the chessboard. Rulers also faced independent institutions within their states, powerful organizations that had to be won over or crushed. By the end of the fifteenth century, the long process of taming the Church was about to enter a new stage. Fortified towns presented a different problem. They possessed both the labor and the wealth necessary to raise and maintain armies. They also jealously guarded their privileges. Rulers who could not tax their towns could not rule their state. Finally, most kingdoms had assemblies representing the propertied classes, especially in matters of taxation. Some, like the English Parliament and the Spanish Cortes, were strong; others, like the Imperial Diet and the French Estates-General, were weak. But everywhere, they posed an obstacle to the extension of the power of princes.

In combination, these factors slowed and shaped the process of state formation. But neither separately nor together were they powerful enough to overcome it. The fragmentation of Europe into so many small units of government made some consolidation inevitable; and as the first large states took shape, the position of smaller neighbors grew ever more precarious.

This was especially true by the end of the fifteenth century because of the increase in the destructive power of warfare. Technological advances in cannonry and in the skills of gunners and engineers made medieval fortifications untenable. The fall of Constantinople was as much a military watershed as it was a political one. Gunpowder decisively changed battlefield tactics. It made heavy armor obsolete and allowed for the development of a different type of warfare. Lightly armored horses and riders not only could inflict more damage on one another, but were now mobile enough to be used against infantry. Infantry armed with long pikes or small muskets became the crucial components of armies that were growing ever larger. Systems of supply were better, sources of small arms were more available, and the rewards of conquest were more tangible. What could not be inherited or married could be conquered.

Eastern Configurations

The interplay of factors that encouraged and inhibited the formation of states is most easily observed in the eastern parts of Europe. There the different paths taken by Muscovy and Poland-Lithuania stand in contrast. At the beginning of the sixteenth century, the principality of Muscovy was the largest European political unit. Muscovy had established itself as the heir to the ancient state of Russia through conquest, shrewd political alliances, and the good fortune of its princes to be blessed with long reigns. Muscovy's growth was phenomenal. Under Ivan III, "the Great" (1462–1505), Muscovy expanded to the north and west. During a long series of wars it annexed Novgorod and large parts of Livonia and Lithuania. Between 1460 and 1530, Muscovy increased its territory by 1.5 million square miles.

A number of factors led to the rise of Muscovy. First, external threats had diminished. The deterioration of the Mongol empire, which had dominated south-central Russia, allowed Ivan to escape the yoke of Mongol rule that the Russian princes had worn for centuries. Second, the fall of Constantinople made Muscovy the heir to eastern Christendom, successor to the Roman and Byzantine empires. Ivan's marriage to Sophia, niece of the last emperor of Byzantium, cemented this connection. Sophia brought both Italian craftsmen and Byzantine customs to the Russian court, helping Ivan open his contacts with the wider world. Third, Ivan the Great was fortunate in having no competitors for his throne. He was able to use other social groups to help administer the new Muscovite territories without fear of setting up a rival to power.

Ivan extended the privileges of his nobility and organized a military class, the members of which received land as a reward for their fidelity. He also developed a new theory of sovereignty that rested on divine rather than temporal power. Traditionally, Russian princes ruled their lands by patrimony. They owned both estates and occupants. Ivan the Great extended this principle to cover all lands to which there was an ancient Russian claim and combined it with the religious authority of the Orthodox Church. Both he and his successors ruled with the aid of able Church leaders, who were normally part of the prince's council.

Ivan the Terrible.   What made the expansion of Muscovy so impressive is that land once gained was never lost. The military and political achievements of Ivan the Great were furthered by his son Vasili and his more famous grandson Ivan IV, "the

Terrible" (1533–1584). Ivan IV defeated the Mongols on his southeastern border and incorporated the entire Volga basin into Muscovy. But his greatest ambition was to gain a port on the Baltic Sea and establish a northern outlet for commerce. His objective was to conquer Livonia, but in nearly three decades of warfare between Muscovy and Poland-Lithuania, with whom Livonia had allied itself, Muscovy's territorial victories fell short of the real prize. Furthermore, Ivan's northern campaigns seriously weakened the defense of the south. In 1571, the Crimean Tatars advanced from their territories on Muscovy's southwestern border and inflicted a powerful psychological blow when they burned the city of Moscow. Although the Tatars were eventually driven off Muscovite soil, expansion in both north and south was at an end for the next 75 years.

By the reign of Ivan IV, Muscovite society was divided roughly into three groups: the hereditary nobility, known as the boyars; the military service class; and the peasantry, who were bound to the land. There was no large mercantile presence in Muscovy, and its urban component remained small. The boyars, who were powerful landlords of great estates, owed little to the tsar. They inherited their lands and did not necessarily benefit from expansion and conquest. Members of the military service class, on the other hand, were bound to the success of the crown. Their military service was a requirement for the possession of their estates, which were granted out of lands gained through territorial expansion. Gradually, the new military service class grew in power and prestige, largely at the expense of the older boyars. Ivan IV used members of the military service class as legislative advisers and elevated them in his parliamentary council (the Zemsky Sobor), which also contained representatives of the nobility, clergy, and towns.

Unlike his grandfather, Ivan IV had an abiding mistrust of the boyars. They had held power when he was a child, and it was rumored that his mother had been poisoned by them. It was his treatment of the boyars that earned him the nickname "the Terrible." During his brutal suppression of supposed conspiracies, several thousand families were massacred by Ivan's own orders and thousands more by the violent excesses of his agents. He also forcibly relocated boyar families. This practice made the boyars' situation similar to that of the military service class, whose members owed their fortunes to the tsar. For the first time the boyars were required to perform military service to the tsar.

All of these measures contributed to the breakdown of local networks of influence and power and to a disruption of local governance. But they also made possible a system of central administration, one of Ivan IV's most important achievements. Ivan IV promoted the interests of the military service class over those of the boyars, but he did not destroy the nobility. New boyars were created, especially in conquered territories, and these new families owed their positions and loyalty to the prince. Both boyars and the military benefited from Ivan's policy of binding the great mass of people to the land. Russian peasants had few political or economic rights in comparison to Western peasants. The right of peasants to move from the estate of one lord to that of another was suspended, all but binding the peasantry to the land. This serfdom made possible the prolonged absence of military leaders from their estates and contributed to the creation of the military service class. But it also made imperative the costly system of coercing agricultural and industrial labor. In the long term, serfdom retarded economic development by removing the incentive for large landholders to make investments in commerce or to improve agricultural production.

Poland-Lithuania. The growth of an enlarged and centralized Muscovy stands in contrast to the experiences of Poland-Lithuania during the same period. At the end of the fifteenth century, Casimir IV (1447–1492) ruled the kingdom of Poland and the grand duchy of Lithuania. His son Wladislaw II ruled Bohemia (1471–1516) and Hungary (1490–1516). Had the four states been permanently consolidated, they could have become an effective barrier to Ottoman expansion in the south and Russian expansion in the east. But the union of crowns did not mean the union of states or the dominance of any one state.

While the Polish-Lithuanian monarchs enjoyed longevity similar to that of the Muscovites, those who ruled Hungary and Bohemia were not so fortunate. By the sixteenth century, a number of claimants to both crowns existed, and the competition was handled by diplomacy rather than war. The formal union of the Polish and Lithuanian crowns in 1569 also involved the decentralization of power and the strengthening of the rights of the nobility in both countries. In the end, the states split apart. The Russians took much of Lithuania; the Ottomans took much of Hungary. Bohemia, which in the fifteenth century had been ruled more by its nobles than by its king, was absorbed into the Habsburg territories after 1526.

There were many reasons why a unified state failed to develop in east-central Europe. First, wars with the Ottomans and the Russians absorbed resources. Second, the princes faced rivals to their crowns. Though Casimir IV was able to place his son on the thrones of both Bohemia and Hungary, he managed to do so against the powerful claims of the Habsburg princes, who continued to intrigue against the Jagiellons. These contests for power necessitated concessions to leading citizens, which decreased the princes' ability to centralize their kingdoms or to effect real unification among them. The nobility of Hungary, Bohemia, and Poland-Lithuania all developed strong local interests that increased over time. War, rivalries for power, and a strong nobility prevented any one prince from dominating this area as the princes of Muscovy dominated theirs.

The Western Powers

As in the east, there was no single pattern to the consolidation of the large western European states. They, too, were internally fragmented and externally imperiled. While England had to overcome the ruin of decades of civil war, France and Spain faced the challenges of invasion and occupation. Each nation formed its state differently: England by administrative centralization, France by good fortune, and Spain by dynastic marriage. Yet in 1450, few imagined that any one of these states would succeed.

The Taming of England. Alone among European states, England suffered no threat of foreign invasion during the fifteenth century. This island fortress might easily have become the first consolidated European state were it not for the ambitions of the nobility and the weakness of the crown. For 30 years, the English aristocracy fought over the spoils of a helpless monarch. The Wars of the Roses (1455–1485) were as much a free-for-all among the English peerage as they were a contest for the throne between the houses of Lancaster and York. At their center was an attempt by the dukes of York to wrest the crown from the mad and ineffective Lancastrian king Henry VI (1422–1461). All around the edges was the continuation of local and family feuds that had little connection to the dynastic struggle.

Three decades of intermittent warfare had predictable results. The houses of Lancaster and York were both destroyed. Edward IV (1461–1483) succeeded in gaining the crown for the house of York, but he was never able to wear it securely. When he died, his children, including his heir, Edward V (1483), were placed in the protection of their uncle Richard III (1483–1485). It was protection that they did not survive. The two boys disappeared, reputedly murdered in the Tower of London, and Richard declared himself king. Richard's usurpation led to civil war, and he was killed by the forces of Henry Tudor at the battle of Bosworth Field in 1485. By the end of the Wars of the Roses, the monarchy had lost both revenue and prestige, and the aristocracy had stored up bitter memories for the future.

It was left to Henry Tudor to deal with the power of the nobility and the poverty of the monarchy. No English monarch had held secure title to the throne for over a century. Henry Tudor, as Henry VII (1485–1509), put an end to this dynastic instability at once. He married Elizabeth of York, in whose heirs would rest the legitimate claim to the throne. Their children were indisputable successors to the crown. He also began the long process of taming his overmighty subjects. Traitors were hanged, and turncoats were rewarded. He and his son Henry VIII (1509–1547) adroitly created a new peerage, which soon was as numerous as the old feudal aristocracy. These new nobles owed their titles and loyalty to the Tudors. They were favored with offices and spoils and were relied on to suppress both popular and aristocratic rebellions.

The financial problems of the English monarchy were not so easily overcome. In theory and practice, an English king was normally supposed to live "of his own," that is, by relying on the revenues from his own estates rather than on payments from his subjects. The English landed classes had established the principle that only on extraordinary occasions were they to be required to contribute to the maintenance of government. This principle was defended through their representative institution, the Parliament. When the kings of England wanted to tax their subjects, they had first to gain the assent of Parliament. Though

Parliaments did grant requests for extraordinary revenue, especially for national defense, they did so grudgingly. The English landed elites were not exempt from taxation, but they were able to control the amount of taxes they paid.

Since the king was dependent on the efficient management of his own estates, English state building required the growth of centralized institutions that could oversee royal lands and collect royal customs. Gradually, medieval institutions such as the Exchequer were supplanted by newer organs that were better able to adjust to modern methods of accounting, record keeping, and enforcement. Henry VII sent ministers to view and value royal lands. He ordered the cataloging and collection of feudal obligations in order to squeeze as much as possible from a not very juicy inheritance. His financial problems limited both domestic and foreign policy.

Not until the middle of the next reign was the English monarchy again solvent. As a result of his dispute with the papacy, Henry VIII confiscated the enormous wealth of the Catholic church and, with one stroke, solved the Crown's monetary problems (see Chapter 13). But the real contribution that Henry and his chief minister, Thomas Cromwell (ca. 1485–1540), made to forming an English state was the way in which this windfall was administered. Cromwell accelerated the process of centralizing government that had begun under Edward IV. He divided administration according to its functions by creating separate departments of state, modeled on courts. These new departments were responsible for record keeping, revenue collection, and law enforcement. Each had a distinct jurisdiction and a permanent trained staff. Cromwell coordinated the work of these distinct departments by expanding the power of the Privy Council, which included the heads of these administrative bodies. Through a long evolution, the Privy Council came to serve as the king's executive body. Cromwell also saw the importance of Parliament as a legislative body. Through Parliament, royal policy could be turned into statutes that had the assent of the political nation. If Parliament was well managed, issues that were potentially controversial could be defused. Laws passed by Parliament were more easily enforced locally than were proclamations issued by the king.

The Unification of France. The forces working against the consolidation of a French state were formidable. France was surrounded by aggressive and powerful neighbors with whom it was frequently at war. Its greatest nobles were semi-independent princes who were constant rivals for the throne. French people were primarily loyal to their province and viewed the pretensions of the monarchy with deep suspicion. France was also splintered by profound regional differences. The north and south were divided by culture and by language (the *langue d'oc* in the south and the *langue d'oil* in the north).

The first obstacles to unification that were overcome were the external threats to French security. For over a century the throne of France had been contested by the kings of England. The so-called Hundred Years' War, which was fought intermittently between 1337 and 1453, originated in a dispute over the inheritance of the French crown and English possessions in Gascony in southern France (see Chapter 10). The war was fought on French soil, and by the early fifteenth century, English conquests in north central France extended from Normandy to the borders of the Holy Roman Empire.

The struggle between the kings of England and the kings of France allowed French princes and dukes, who were nominally vassals of the king, to enhance their autonomy by making their own alliances with the highest bidder. When the English were finally driven out of France in the middle of the fifteenth century, the kings of France came into a weakened and divided inheritance.

Nor was England the only threat to the security of the French monarchy. On France's eastern border, in a long arching semicircle, were the estates of the dukes of Burgundy. The kings of France and the dukes of Burgundy shared a common ancestry: both were of the House of Valois. But the two branches of the family grew apart. The original Burgundian inheritance was in the southeast, centered at Dijon. A good marriage and good fortune brought to the first duke the rich northern province of Flanders. For the next hundred years, the aim of the dukes of Burgundy was to unite their divided estates. While England and France were locked in deadly embrace, Burgundy systematically grew, absorbing territory from both the Holy Roman Empire and France. The conquest of Lorraine finally connected the ducal estates in one long, unbroken string. The power of Burgundy threatened its neighbors in all directions. Both France and the empire were too weak to resist its expansion, but the confederation of Swiss towns to the southwest of Burgundy was not. In a series of stunning military victories, Swiss forces repelled the Burgundians from their lands and demolished their armies. Charles the Bold, the last Valois duke of Burgundy, fell at the Battle of Nancy in 1477. His estates were quickly dismembered. France recovered its ancestral territories, including Burgundy itself, and through no effort of its own was now secure on its eastern border.

The king who was most associated with the consolidation of France was Louis XI (1461–1483). He inherited an estate that had been exhausted by warfare and civil strife. More by chance than by plan, he vastly extended the territories under the dominion of the French crown and, more important, subdued the nobility. Louis XI was as cunning as he was peculiar. In an age in which royalty was expressed through magnificence, Louis sported an old felt hat and a well-worn coat. His enemies constantly underestimated his abilities, which earned him the nickname "the Spider." But during the course of his reign, Louis XI gradually won back what he had been forced to give away. Years of fighting both the English and each other left the ranks of the French aristocracy depleted. As blood spilled on the battlefields, the stocks of fathers and sons ran low. Estates to which no male heirs existed fell forfeit to the king. In this manner, the crown absorbed Anjou and Maine in the northwest and Provence in the south. More important, Louis XI ultimately obtained control of the two greatest independent fiefs, Brittany and Orléans, by marrying his son Charles to the heiress of Brittany and his daughter Jeanne to the heir of Orléans. When, in 1527, the lands of the duke of Bourbon fell to the crown, the French monarch ruled a unified state.

The French experience demonstrated how a state could be formed without the designs of a great leader. Neither Louis XI nor his son Charles VIII (1483–1498) was a nation builder. Louis's main objective was always to preserve his estate. His good fortune saved him from the consequences of many ill-conceived policies. But no amount of luck could make up for Louis's failure to obtain the Burgundian Low Countries for France after the death of Charles the Bold in 1477. The marriage of Mary of Burgundy to Maximilian of Habsburg was one of the great turning points in European history. It initiated a struggle for control of the Low Countries that endured for over two centuries.

These long years of war established the principle of royal taxation, which was so essential to the process of state building in France. This enabled the monarchy to raise money for defense and for consolidation. Because of the strength of the nobles, most taxation fell only on the commoners, the so-called third estate. The *taille* was a direct tax on property from which the nobility and clergy were exempt. The *gabelle* was a consumption tax on the purchase of salt in most parts of the kingdom, and the *aide* was a tax on a variety of commodities, including meat and wine. These consumption taxes were paid by all members of the third estate, no matter how poor they might be. Although there was much complaint about taxes, the French monarchy established a broad base for taxation and a high degree of compliance long before any other European nation.

Along with money went soldiers, needed to repel the English and to defend the crown against rebels and traitors. Again the French monarchy was the first to establish the principle of a national army, raised and directed from the center but quartered and equipped regionally. From the nobility were recruited the cavalry, from the towns and countryside the massive infantry. Fortified towns received privileges in return for military service to the king. Originally, towns were required to provide artillery, but constant troubles with the nobility had led the kings of France to establish their own store of heavy guns. The towns supplied small arms, pikes, and swords and later pistols and muskets. By the beginning of the sixteenth century, the French monarch could raise and equip an army of his own.

The Marriages of Spain.   Before the sixteenth century there was little prospect of a single nation emerging on the Iberian peninsula. North African Muslims, called Moors, occupied the province of Granada in the south; the stable kingdom of Portugal dominated the western coast. The Spanish peoples were divided among a number of separate states. The two most important were Castile, the largest and wealthiest kingdom, and Aragon, which was composed of a number of quasi-independent regions, each of which maintained its own laws and institutions. Three religions and four languages (not including dialects) widened these political divisions. And the different states had different outlooks. Castile was, above all, determined to rid itself of the Moors in Granada and to convert to Christianity its large Jewish population. Aragon played in the high-stakes game for power in the Mediterranean. It claimed sovereignty over Sicily and Naples and exercised it whenever it could.

A happy teenage marriage brought together the unhappy kingdoms of Castile and Aragon. When Ferdinand of Aragon and Isabella of Castile secretly exchanged wedding vows in 1469, both their homelands were rent by civil war. In Castile, Isabella's brother Henry IV (1454–1474) struggled unsuccessfully against the powerful Castilian nobility. In Aragon, Ferdinand's father, John II (1458–1479), faced a revolt by the rich province of Catalonia on one side and the territorial ambitions of Louis XI of France on the other. Joining the heirs together increased the resources of both kingdoms.

Ferdinand took an active role in the pacification of Castile, while Castilian riches allowed him to defend Aragon from invasion. In 1479, the two crowns were united, and the Catholic monarchs, as they were called, ruled the two kingdoms jointly. But the unification of the crowns of Castile and Aragon was not the same as the formation of a single state. Local privileges were zealously guarded, especially in Aragon, where the representative institutions of the towns, the Cortes, were aggressively independent. The powerful Castilian nobility never accepted Ferdinand as their king and refused him the crown after Isabella's death.

But Ferdinand and Isabella (1479–1516) took the first steps toward forging a Spanish state. Their most notable achievement was the final recovery of the lands that had been conquered by the Moors. For centuries the Spanish kingdoms had fought against the North African Muslims who had conquered large areas of the southern peninsula. The reconquista was characterized by short bursts of warfare followed by long periods of wary coexistence. By the middle of the fifteenth century, the Moorish territory had been reduced to the province of Granada. The final stage of the reconquista began in 1482 and lasted for a decade. It was waged as a holy war and was financed in part by grants from the pope and the Christian princes of Europe. In 1492, Granada finally fell, and the province was absorbed into Castile.

The reconquista played an important part in creating a national identity for the Christian peoples of Spain. To raise men and money for the war effort, Ferdinand and Isabella mobilized their nobility and town governments and created a central organization to oversee the invasion. The conquered territories were used to reward the men who had aided the effort, though the crown maintained control and jurisdiction over most of the province. But the idea of the holy war also had a darker side and an unanticipated consequence. The Jewish population that had lived peacefully in Castile and Aragon became another object of hostility. Many Jews had risen to prominence in government and in skilled professions. Others, who had accepted conversion to Christianity and were known as conversos, had become powerful figures in church and state.

Both groups were now attacked. The conversos fell prey to a special church tribunal created to examine their sincere devotion to Catholicism. This was the **Spanish Inquisition,** which, though it used traditional judicial practices—torture to gain confessions, public humiliation to show contrition, and burnings at the stake to maintain purity—used them on a scale never before seen. Thousands of conversos were killed, and many more families had their wealth confiscated to be used for the reconquista. In 1492, the Jews were expelled from Spain. Though the reconquista and the expulsion of the Jews inflicted great suffering on victims and incalculable loss to the Castilian economy, both events enhanced the prestige of the Catholic monarchs.

The joint presence of Ferdinand and Isabella in the provinces of Spain was symbolic of the unity they strove to achieve. Ferdinand made Castilian the official language of government in Aragon and even appointed Castilians to Aragonese posts. He and Isabella actively encouraged the intermarriage of the two aristocracies and the expansion of the number of wealthy nobles who held land in both kingdoms. Nevertheless, these measures did not unify Spain or erase the centuries-long tradition of hostility among the diverse Iberian peoples.

It was left to the heirs of Ferdinand and Isabella to forge together the Spanish kingdoms, and the process was a painful one. The hostility to a foreign monarch that both the Castilian nobility and the Aragonese towns had shown to Ferdinand and Isabella increased dramatically at the accession of their grandson Charles V (1516–1556), who had been born and raised in the Low Countries, where he ruled over Burgundy and the Netherlands. Through a series of dynastic accidents, Charles was heir to the Spanish crown with its possessions in the New World and to the vast Habsburg estates that included Austria. Charles established his rule in Spain gradually. For a time he was forced to share power in Castile and to suppress a disorganized aristocratic rebellion.

Because of his foreign obligations, Charles was frequently absent from Spain. During those periods he governed through regents and royal councils that did much to centralize administration. Though Castile and Aragon had separate councils, they were organized similarly and had greater contact than before. Charles V realized the importance of Spain, especially of Castile, in his empire. He established a permanent bureaucratic court, modeled on that of Burgundy, and placed able Spaniards at the head of its departments. This smoothed over the long periods when Charles was abroad, especially the 13 years between 1543 and 1556.

The most important factor in uniting the Spanish kingdoms, however, was the fact that Charles V brought Spain to the forefront of European affairs in the sixteenth century. Spanish prowess, whether in arms or in culture, became a source of national pride that helped to erode regional identity.

■ Flemish tapestry showing Isabella and Ferdinand attended by courtiers and ladies-in-waiting.

Gold and silver from the New World helped to finance Charles's great empire, and he achieved nearly all of the ancient territorial ambitions of the Spanish kingdoms. In Italy, he prosecuted Aragonese claims to Sicily and Naples. In the north, he held on firmly to the kingdom of Navarre, which had been annexed by Ferdinand, and secured Spain's border with France. In the south, he blocked off Ottoman and Muslim expansion. The reign of Charles V ushered in the dawn of Spain's golden age.

THE DYNASTIC STRUGGLES

The formation of large states throughout Europe led inevitably to conflicts among them. Long chains of marriages among the families of the European princes meant that sooner or later the larger powers would lay claim to the same inheritances and test the matter by force. Thus the sixteenth century was a period of almost unrelieved general warfare in Europe. Advances in technology made war more efficient and more expensive—and also more horrible. The use of artillery against infantry increased the number of deaths and maiming injuries, as did the replacement of the arrow by the bullet. As the size of armies increased, so did casualties. The slaughter of French nobility at Pavia in 1525 was the largest in a century; the Turkish sultan, Suleiman the Magnificent, recorded the burial of 24,000 Hungarian soldiers after the battle of Mohacs in 1526.

Power and Glory

The frequency with which offensive war was waged in the sixteenth century raises a number of questions about the militaristic values of the age. Valor remained greatly prized—a Renaissance virtue inherited from the crusading zeal and chivalric ideals of the Middle Ages. Princes saw valor as a personal attribute and sought to do great deeds. Ferdinand of Aragon and Francis I (1515–1547) of France won fame for their exploits in war. Charles the Bold and Louis II of Hungary were less fortunate. Their battlefield deaths led to the breakup of their states. Wars were fought to further the interests of princes rather than the interests of national sovereignty or international Christianity. They were certainly not fought in the interests of their subjects. States were an extension of a prince's heritage. The wars of the sixteenth century were dynastic wars.

The New Monarchs waged war and defended their territories in new ways. Internal security depended on locally raised forces or hired mercenaries. Both required money, which was becoming available in unprecedented quantities as a result of the increasing prosperity of the early sixteenth century and the windfall of gold and silver from the New World. Professional soldiers, of whom the Swiss and Germans were the most noteworthy, sold their services to the highest bidders. Developments in transport and supply enabled campaigns to take place far from the center of a state. Finally, communications were improving. The need for knowledge about potential rivals or allies had the

effect of expanding the European system of diplomacy. Resident agents were established in all the European capitals, and they had a decisive impact on war and peace. Their dispatches formed the most reliable source of information about the strengths of armies or the weaknesses of governments, about the births of heirs or the deaths of princes.

Personality also played a part in the international warfare of the early sixteenth century. The three most consistent protagonists—Charles V, Francis I, and Henry VIII—were of similar age and outlook. Each came unexpectedly to his throne in the full flush of youth, eager for combat and glory. The three were self-consciously rivals, each jealous of the others' successes, each triumphant in the others' failures. As the three monarchs aged together, their youthful wars of conquest matured into strategic warfare designed to maintain a continental balance of power.

The Italian Wars

The struggle for supremacy in Europe in the sixteenth century pitted the French house of Valois against the far-flung estates of the Habsburg Empire. Yet the wars took place in Italy. The rivalries among the larger Italian city-states proved to be fertile ground for the newly consolidated European monarchies. Both French and Spanish monarchs had remote but legitimate claims to the kingdom of Naples in southern Italy. In 1494, the French king, Charles VIII, took up an invitation from the ruler of Milan to intervene in Italian affairs. His campaign was an unqualified, if fleeting, success. He marched the length of the peninsula, overthrew the Medici in Florence, forced the pope to open the gates of Rome, and finally seized the crown of Naples. The occupation was accomplished without a single great battle and lasted until the warring Italian city-states realized that they had more to fear from the French than from one another. Once that happened, Charles VIII beat a hasty retreat. But the French appetite for Italian territory was not sated. Soon a deal was struck with Ferdinand of Aragon to divide the kingdom of Naples in two. All went according to plan until these thieves fell out among themselves. In the end, Spain wound up with all of Naples, and France was left with nothing but debts and grievances.

Therefore, when Francis I came to the French throne and Charles V came to the Spanish, Naples was just one of several potential sources of friction. Not only had Ferdinand betrayed the French in Naples, he had also broken a long-standing peace on the Franco-Spanish border by conquering the independent but French-speaking kingdom of Navarre. Francis could be expected to avenge both slights. Charles, on the other hand, was the direct heir of the dukes of Burgundy. From his childhood he longed for the restoration of his ancestral lands, including Burgundy itself, which had been gobbled up by Louis XI after the death of Charles the Bold. Competition between Francis and Charles became all the more ferocious when Charles's grandfather, the Holy Roman Emperor Maximilian I (1486–1519), died in 1519. Both monarchs launched a vigorous campaign for the honor of succeeding him.

Charles V, who now inherited the Habsburg lands in Austria and Germany, succeeded to this eminent but empty dignity. His election as Holy Roman Emperor not only aggravated the personal animosity among the monarchs, but added another source of conflict in Italy. When Louis XII (1498–1515) had succeeded to the throne of France, he had laid claim to the duchy of Milan through an interest of his wife's, though he was unable to enforce it. Francis I proved more capable. In 1515, he stunned all of Europe by crushing the vaunted Swiss mercenaries at the battle of Marignano. But the duchy of Milan was a territory under the protection of the Holy Roman Emperor, and it soon appealed for imperial troops to help repel the French invaders. Milan was strategically important to Charles V because it was the vital link between his Austrian and Burgundian possessions. Almost as soon as he took up the imperial mantle, Charles V was determined to challenge Francis I in Italy.

The key to such a challenge was the construction of alliances among the various Italian city-states and most especially with England, whose aid both Charles and Francis sought to enlist in the early 1520s. Henry VII had found foreign alliances a ready source of cash, and he was always eager to enter into them as long as they did not involve raising armies and fighting wars. Henry VIII was made of sterner stuff. He longed to reconquer France and to cut a figure on the European scene. Despite the fact that his initial continental adventures had emptied his treasury without fulfilling his dreams, Henry remained eager for war. He was also flattered to find himself the object of attention of both Valois and Habsburg emissaries. Charles V made two separate trips to London, and Henry crossed the Channel in 1520 to meet Francis I in one of the gaudiest displays of conspicuous consumption that the century would witness, appropriately known as the Field of the Cloth of Gold.

The result of these diplomatic intrigues was an alliance between England and the Holy Roman Empire. English and Burgundian forces would stage an invasion of northern France, while Spanish and German troops would again attempt to dislodge the French from Italy. The strategy worked better than anyone could have imagined. In 1523, Charles's forces gained a foothold in Milan by taking the heavily fortified town of Pavia. Two years later, Francis was ready to strike back. At the head of his own royal guards, he massed Swiss mercenaries and French infantry outside Pavia and made ready for a swift assault. Instead, a large imperial army arrived to relieve the town, and in the subsequent battle, the French suffered a shattering defeat. Francis I was captured.

The victory at Pavia, which occurred on Charles V's twenty-fifth birthday, seemingly made him master of all of Europe. His ally Henry VIII urged an immediate invasion and dismemberment of France and began raising an army to spearhead the attack. But Charles's position was much less secure than it appeared. The Ottomans threatened his Hungarian territories, and the Protestants threatened his German lands. He could not afford a war of conquest in France. His hope now was to reach an agreement with Francis

■ Jean Clouet, *Portrait of Francis I* (sixteenth century). Rivalry between Francis and Charles V plunged Europe into decades of war.

I for a lasting European peace, and for this purpose the French king was brought in captivity to Madrid. Charles's terms, however, led not to peace but to 30 years of warfare.

Charles demanded that Burgundy be returned to him. Though Francis was hardly in a position to bargain, he held out on this issue for as long as possible and secretly prepared a disavowal of the final agreement before it was made. By the Treaty of Madrid in 1526, Francis I yielded Burgundy and recognized the Spanish conquest of Navarre and Spanish rule in Naples. The agreement was sealed by the marriage of Francis to Charles's sister, Eleanor of Portugal. But marriage was not sufficient security for such a complete capitulation. To secure his release from Spain, Francis was required to leave behind as hostages his seven-and eight-year-old sons until the treaty was fulfilled. For three years the children languished in Spanish captivity.

No sooner had he set foot on French soil than Francis I renounced the Treaty of Madrid. Despite the threat that this posed to his children, Francis argued that the terms had been extracted against his will, and he even gained the sanction of the pope for violating his oath. Setting France on a war footing, he began seeking new allies. Henry VIII, disappointed with the meager spoils of his last venture, switched sides. So, too, did a number of Italian city-states, including Rome. Most important, Francis I entered into an alliance with the Ottoman sultan, Suleiman the Magnificent (1520–1566), whose armies were pressing against the southeastern borders of the Holy Roman Empire. In the year following Pavia, the Ottomans secured an equally decisive triumph at Mohacs, which cut Hungary in two and threatened Vienna, the eastern capital of the Habsburg lands. Almost overnight, Charles V had been turned from hunter into hunted. The Ottoman threat demanded immediate attention in Germany, the French and English were preparing to strike in the Low Countries, and the Italian wars continued. In 1527, Charles's unpaid German mercenaries stormed through Rome, sacked the papal capital, and captured the pope. Christian Europe was mortified.

The struggle for European mastery ground on for decades. The Treaty of Cateau-Cambrésis in 1559 brought to a close 60 years of conflict. In the end, the French were no more capable of dislodging the Habsburgs from Italy than were the Habsburgs of forcing the Ottomans out of Hungary. The great stores of silver that poured into Castile from the New World were consumed in the fires of continental warfare. In 1557, both France and Spain declared bankruptcy to avoid foreclosures by their creditors. For the French, the Italian wars were disastrous. They seriously undermined the state's financial base, eroded confidence in the monarchy, and thinned the ranks of the ruling nobility. The adventure begun by Charles VIII in search of glory brought France nearly to ruin. It ended with fitting irony. After the death of Francis I, his son Henry II (1547–1559) continued the struggle. Henry never forgave his father for abandoning him in Spain, and he sought revenge on Charles V, who had been his jailer. He regarded the Treaty of Cateau-Cambrésis as a victory and celebrated it with great pomp and pageantry. Among the feasts and festivities were athletic competitions for the king's courtiers and attendants. Henry II entered the jousting tournament and there was killed.

CONCLUSION

Charles V died in his bed. The long years of war made clear that the dream to dominate Europe could only be a dream. He split apart his empire and granted to his brother, Ferdinand I (1558–1564), the Austrian and German lands and the mantle of the Holy Roman Empire. To his son, Philip II (1556–1598) he ceded the Low Countries, Spain and the New World, Naples, and his Italian conquests. In 1555, Charles abdicated all of his titles and retired to a monastery to live out his final days. The cares of an empire that had once stretched from Peru to Vienna were lifted from his shoulders. Beginning with his voyage to Castile in 1517, he had made ten trips to the Netherlands, nine to Germany, seven to Italy, six to Spain, four to France, two to England, and two to Africa. "My life has been one long journey," he told those who witnessed him relinquish his crowns. On 21 September 1558, he rested forever.

QUESTIONS FOR REVIEW

1. What impulses in European society were revealed by the global exploration and conquests of the Portuguese and the Spanish?
2. What qualities characterized the New Monarchies and what are some of the best examples of such princely states?
3. How and why did the experience of political and territorial unification differ in England, France, and Spain?
4. How did war between the great European monarchies contribute to unity within each?

KEY TERMS

caravels, *p. 240*

Columbian Exchange, *p. 244*

New Monarchies, *p. 246*

reconquista, *p. 249*

Spanish Inquisition, *p. 254*

Treaty of Tordesillas, *p. 242*

DISCOVERING WESTERN CIVILIZATION ONLINE

You can obtain more information about the European empires at the websites listed below. See also the Companion Website that accompanies this text, www.ablongman.com/kishlansky, which contains an online study guide and additional resources.

European Encounters
Discoverers Web
www.win.tue.nl/cs/fm/engels/discovery/
A site devoted to all ages of discovery with maps, short biographies, and time lines. There are links to the writings of Columbus, Cortés, and others of the early voyagers.

The Columbus Navigation Homepage
www.minn.net/~keithp/
Everything you ever wanted to know about Christopher Columbus.

1492: An Ongoing Voyage
www.loc.gov/exhibits/1492
A Library of Congress online exhibit on the causes and consequences of European exploration and expansion.

Christopher Columbus—A Culinary History
www.castellobanfi.com/features/story_3.html
A site devoted to the food and drink associated with a long ocean voyage in the fifteenth century.

Medieval Sourcebook: Exploration and Expansion
www.fordham.edu/halsall/sbook1z.html
Dozens of primary sources relating to the voyages of discovery.

The Formation of States
Henry VIII: Intrigue in the Tudor Court
www.archsoc.com/games/Henry.html
A board game that teaches both history and strategy.

SUGGESTIONS FOR FURTHER READING

General Reading

David Nicholas, *The Transformation of Europe 1300–1600* (New York: Oxford University Press, 1999). A comprehensive survey that emphasizes continuities between the sixteenth century and the preceding period.

Eugene Rice, *The Foundations of Early Modern Europe, 1460–1559,* 2nd ed. (New York: Norton, 1994). An outstanding synthesis.

European Encounters

C. R. Boxer, *The Portuguese Seaborne Empire, 1415–1825* (London: Hutchinson, 1968). The best history of the first of the explorer nations.

J. H. Elliott, *The Old World and the New, 1492–1650* (Cambridge: Cambridge University Press, 1970). A brilliant look at the reception of knowledge about the New World by Europeans.

Felipe Fernandez-Armesto, *Columbus* (Oxford: Oxford University Press, 1991). The best of the recent studies. Reliable, stimulating, and up-to-date.

Anthony Pagden, *Lords of All the World: Ideologies of Empire in Spain, Britain and France, c. 1500–c. 1800* (New Haven, CT: Yale University Press, 1995). A fresh look at the ideas behind the European encounter with the New World.

Hugh Thomas, *Rivers of Gold: The Rise of the Spanish Empire* (London: Widenfeld & Nicholson, 2004). A breathtaking retelling of Spain's New World Empire.

Geographical Tour—Europe in 1500: The Age of the New Monarchies

N. J. G. Pounds, *An Historical Geography of Europe, 1500–1800* (Cambridge: Cambridge University Press, 1990). A remarkable survey of the relationship between geography and history.

Daniel Waley, *Later Medieval Europe* (London: Longman, 1985). A good brief account.

The Formation of States

S. B. Chrimes, *Henry VII* (Berkeley: University of California Press, 1972). A traditional biography of the first Tudor.

Robert O. Crummey, *The Formation of Muscovy, 1304–1613* (London: Longman, 1987). The best one-volume history.

Norman Davies, *God's Playground: A History of Poland, Vol. 1, The Origins to 1795* (New York: Columbia University Press, 1982). The best treatment in English of a complex history.

Bernard Guenée, *States and Rulers in Later Medieval Europe* (London: Basil Blackwell, 1985). An engaging argument about the forces that helped shape the state system in Europe.

Henry Kamen, *The Spanish Inquisition: A Historical Revision* (New Haven, CT: Yale University Press, 1998). The best recent assessment of the power and activities of the Inquisition.

Paul M. Kendall, *Louis XI: The Universal Spider* (New York: Norton, 1971). A highly entertaining account of an unusual monarch.

John Lynch, *Spain, 1516–1598: From Nation State to World Empire* (Cambridge, MA: Blackwell, 1994). A valuable and expert survey.

J. H. Shennan, *The Origins of the Modern European State, 1450–1725* (London: Hutchinson, 1974). An analytic account of the rise of the state.

The Dynastic Struggles

J. R. Hale, *War and Society in Renaissance Europe* (Stroud, England: Sutton, 1998). Assesses the impact of war on the political and social history of early modern Europe.

William Maltby, *The Reign of Charles V* (New York: Palgrave, 2002). The most recent study of one of Europe's great emperors.

David Potter, *A History of France, 1460–1560* (London: Macmillan, 1995). A reliable survey that connects medieval and early modern developments.

J. J. Scarisbrick, *Henry VIII* (New Haven: Yale University Press, 1997). The definitive biography.

For a list of additional titles related to this chapter's topics, please see www.ablongman.com/kishlansky.

Chapter 13

THE REFORM OF RELIGION

CHAPTER OUTLINE

The Visual Record

SOLA SCRIPTURA

"In the beginning was the Word, and the Word was with God, and the Word was God." In no other period of European history was this text of the apostle John so appropriate. In the early sixteenth century, Europeans developed an insatiable appetite for hearing and reading the Bible. Scriptures rolled off printing presses in every shape and form, from the great vellum tomes of Gutenberg, pictured here, to pocket Bibles that soldiers carried into battle. They came in every imaginable language. Before 1500 there were 14 complete Bibles printed in German, four each in Italian, French, and Spanish, one in Czech, and even one in Flemish. There were hundreds more editions in Latin, the official Vulgate Bible first translated by Saint Jerome in the fourth century. Separate sections, especially the Psalms and the first books of the Old Testament, were also printed by the thousands. When Martin Luther began his own German translation of the Bible in 1522, it immediately became an international bestseller. In 25 years, it went into 430 editions. It is estimated that 1 million German Bibles were printed in the first half of the sixteenth century, at a time when Europe had a German-speaking population of about 15 million people, 90 percent of whom were illiterate.

Bible owning was no fad. It was but one element in a new devotional outlook that was sweeping the Continent and would have far-reaching consequences for European society during the next 150 years. A renewed spirituality was to be seen everywhere. It was expressed in a desire to change the traditional practices and structures of the Roman Church. It was expressed in a desire to have learned and responsible ministers to tend to the needs of their parishioners. It was expressed in a desire to establish godly families, godly cities, and godly kingdoms. Sometimes it took the form of sarcasm and bitter denunciations; sometimes it took the form of quiet devotion and pious living. It came from within the Roman Church as much as from without.

The inspiration for reform was based on the Word of God. Scholars, following humanist principles, worked on biblical translations in an attempt to bring a purer text to light. Biblical commentary dominated the writings of churchmen as never before. Woodcut pictures depicting scenes from the life of Jesus or from the Old Testament were printed in untold quantities for the edification of the unlettered. For the first time, common people could, in their own dwellings, contemplate representations of the lives of the saints. Many of the Bibles that were printed in the vernacular—that is, in the languages spoken in the various European states rather than in Latin—were interleaved with illustrations of the central events of Christian history. Preachers spoke to newly aware audiences and relied on

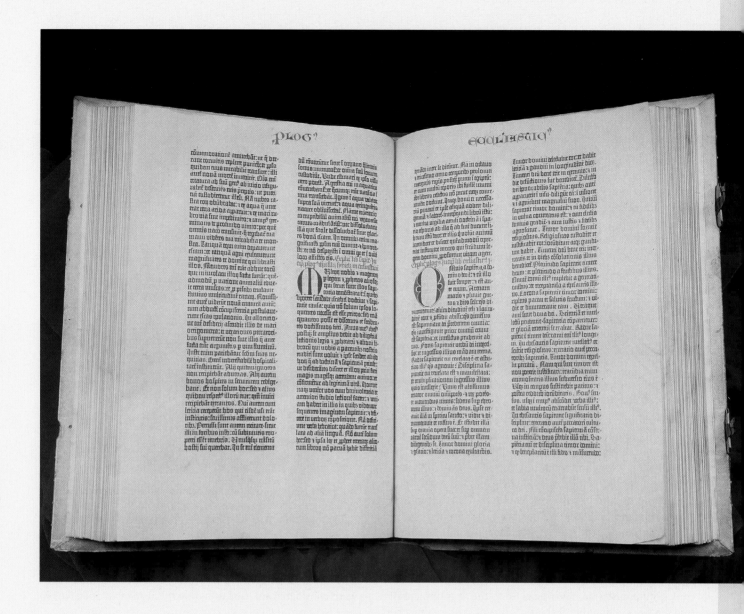

biblical texts to draw out their message. Study groups, especially in urban areas, proliferated so that the literate could read and learn together. Bible reading became a part of family life, one that mothers and fathers could share with their children and their servants.

Looking Ahead

Sola scriptura—*by the word alone—became the battle cry of religious reform. As we will see in this chapter, in the early* decades of the sixteenth century Europeans experienced one of the greatest of all religious rebirths: the Protestant Reformation. The **Reformation** was a movement to purify the Catholic Church that resulted in the creation of new religions denominations in Europe collectively known as Protestants from their protest against Roman Catholic practices. But the Catholic Church experienced its own renewal as well. Figures such as Luther, Calvin, and Ignatius of Loyola were part of the most remarkable generation of religious leaders since the foundation of Christianity. ➤

THE INTELLECTUAL REFORMATION

In the early sixteenth century, reformers throughout western Europe preached new ideas about religious doctrine and religious practice. At first these ideas took the form of a sustained critique of the Roman Catholic Church, but they soon developed a momentum of their own. Some reformers remained within traditional Catholicism; others moved outside and founded new Protestant churches. Wherever this movement for religious reform, whether Catholic or Protestant, appeared, it was fed by new ideas. And the rapid communication of new ideas was made possible by the development of printing, which appeared in Germany in the late fifteenth century and spread across Europe in the succeeding decades. Yet printing was as much a result as a cause of the spread of ideas. The humanist call for a return to the study of the classics and for the creation of accurate texts, first heard in Italy, aroused scholars and leaders in all of the European states. Their appetite for manuscripts exhausted the abilities of the scribes and booksellers who reproduced texts. Printing responded to that demand.

The Print Revolution

The development of printing did not cause religious reform, but it is difficult to see how reform would have progressed in its absence. The campaign to change the doctrine and practice of Catholicism was waged through the press, as millions of flyers and pamphlets were distributed across Europe to spread the new ideas. One third of all books sold in Germany between 1518 and 1525 were written by Martin Luther.

Printing, one of the true technological revolutions in western history, was not invented. It developed as a result of progress made in allied industries, especially papermaking and goldsmithing. Scholars and university students needed copies of manuscripts. Their need led to the development of a trade in bookselling that flourished in almost every university town. The process of reproduction was slowed by difficulties in obtaining the sheepskins and calfskins on which the manuscripts were written. In the early fifteenth century, copyists began to substitute paper made from linen rags for the expensive vellum skins. A number of German craftsmen experimented with using movable metal type to make exact reproductions of manuscripts on paper. In the 1450s in Mainz, Johannes Gutenberg (ca. 1400–1468) and his partners succeeded and published their famous Bibles.

The association of early printing with goldsmithing resulted from the high level of technical skill that was necessary to create the hard metal stamps from which the softer metal type was produced. Printing was an expensive business. The investment in type and in paper was considerable. Only the press itself was cheap; any corn or wine press could be used to bring the long, flat sheets of paper down on a wooden frame filled with ink-coated metal type. Booksellers initially put up the capital needed to cast the stamps, mold the type, and buy

■ An early German print shop. The man at the left operates the screw press while an apprentice (right) stacks the printed sheets. The man in the back is setting type for the next impression.

the paper. They bound the printed pages and found the markets to distribute them. At first, sales were slow. Printed books were considered inferior to handwritten manuscripts. Nor at first were printed books less expensive. Buying a Bible such as those printed by Gutenberg was a major investment, equivalent to purchasing a house today. Many printing shops quickly went bankrupt as they misjudged their markets and were unable to pay back their loans.

Still, once it was begun, printing spread like wildfire. By 1480, over 110 towns had established presses, most in Italy and Germany. After that the pace quickened. By the beginning of the sixteenth century, Venice and Paris were the centers of the printing industry; the Paris presses produced over 300 new titles annually. Most of the early printed works were either religious or classical. Bibles, church service books, and the commentaries of the Church Fathers were most common. Cicero topped the list of classical authors.

Printing rapidly came to be a basic part of life. In the first 40 years after the presses were first set up, perhaps as many as 20 million books were produced and distributed. Printing changed the habits of teachers and students, the way in which the state conducted its business, and the methods of legal training and legal proceedings. Compilations of laws could now be widely distributed and more uniformly enforced. Printing had a similar effect on the development of scientific study. The printing press popularized the discoveries of the New World and contributed to the reproduction of more accurate charts and maps, which in turn facilitated further discovery. Printing also helped to standardize language by frequent repetition of preferred usage and spelling. Perhaps most important, printing created an international intellectual community whose ideas could be dispersed the length and breadth of the Continent. The printing press enhanced the value of ideas and of thinking. Nothing could be more central to the reform of religion.

Christian Humanism

Many of the ideas that spread across Europe as the result of the printing revolution originated in Italian humanism (see Chapter 11). The revival of classical literature, with its concern for purity in language and eloquence in style, was one of the most admired achievements of the Renaissance. Students from all over Europe who descended on Italian universities to study medicine and law came away with strong doses of philology, rhetoric, moral philosophy, and the other liberal arts. By the beginning of the sixteenth century, the force of humanism was felt strongly in northern and western Europe, where it was grafted onto the traditional theological teaching. The combination was a new and powerful intellectual movement known as **Christian humanism.**

The humanism of the north differed from that of the Italian city-states. Although the Italian humanists were certainly Christian, they were interested in secular subjects, especially in mastering classical languages and translating classical texts. Italian humanists had established techniques for the recovery of accurate texts and had developed principles for compiling the scholarly editions that now poured forth from the printing presses. Christian humanists applied these techniques to the study of the authorities and texts of the Church. Most of the new humanists had been trained in Italy, where they devoted themselves to the mastery of Greek and Latin. They had imbibed the idea that scholars, using their own critical faculties, could establish the authority of texts and the meaning of words. Building on the patient work of their predecessors and the advantages offered by printing, this new generation of humanists brought learning to educated men and women throughout Europe.

Christian humanism was a program of reform rather than a philosophy. It aimed to make better Christians through better education. Humanists were especially interested in the education of women. Thomas More (1478–1535) raised his daughters to be among the educated elite of England. Renowned women scholars held places at Italian universities. Humanist educational principles posed an implicit challenge to Roman Catholicism. Schools had once been the monopoly of the Church, which used them to train clergymen. Literacy

itself had been preserved over the centuries so that the gospel could be propagated.

By the sixteenth century these purposes had been transformed. Schools now trained many people who were not destined for careers in the Church, and literacy served the needs of the state, the aristocracy, and the merchant classes. More important, as the humanists perfected their techniques of scholarship, the Church continued to rely on traditional methods of training and traditional texts. The dominant manner of teaching at the schools and universities was known as Scholasticism. Passages of biblical texts were studied through the commentaries of generations of Church Fathers. Rote memorization of the opinions of others was more highly valued than critical thinking. Argument took place by formal disputation of questions on which the Fathers of the Church disagreed. The Vulgate Bible was used throughout western Christendom. It was now a thousand years old.

The Humanist Movement

Many humanist criticisms of Church teaching focused on its failure to inspire individuals to live a Christian life. Humanist writers were especially scathing about popular practices that bordered on superstition, such as pilgrimages to holy places or the worship of relics from the early history of the Church. Such beliefs became the butt of popular humor: "If the fragments [of the Lord's Cross] were joined together they would seem a full load for a freighter. And yet the Lord carried his whole cross." Christian humanists wanted to inspire Christians. As the great Dutch humanist Desiderius Erasmus observed, "To be learned is the lot of only a few; but no one is unable to be a Christian, no one is unable to be pious."

Christian humanism was an international movement. The humanists formed the elite of the intellectual world of the sixteenth century, and their services were sought by princes and peers as well as by the most distinguished universities. In fact, the New Monarchs supported the humanists and protected them from their critics. Marguerite of Navarre, sister of Francis I, was an accomplished writer who frequently interceded on behalf of the leading French humanists. Ferdinand of Aragon, Henry VIII, and the Holy Roman Emperors Maximilian I and Charles V all brought humanists to their courts and aided their projects. Maria of Hungary and Mary and Elizabeth Tudor were trained in humanist principles and participated in humanist literary achievements.

The centerpiece of humanist reforms was the translation of Christian texts. Skilled in Greek and Latin, informed by scholars of Hebrew and Aramaic, humanist writers prepared new editions of the books of the Bible and of the writings of the early Church Fathers. The Polyglot (literally "many languages") Bible that was produced in 1522 at the University of Alcala took a team of scholars 15 years to complete. They rigorously compared texts of all known biblical manuscripts and established the principle that inconsistencies among Latin manuscripts were to be resolved by reference to Greek texts and difficulties in Greek texts by reference to Hebrew texts. The result was six volumes that allowed scholars to compare the texts. The Old Testament was printed in three parallel columns of Hebrew, Latin Vulgate, and Greek. The New Testament was printed in double columns of Greek and Vulgate. The Greek edition of the Bible and its establishment as a text that was superior to the Vulgate caused an immediate sensation throughout humanist and Church circles.

The Wit of Erasmus

Though the Polyglot Bible contained the first completed Greek edition of the New Testament, it was not the first published one. That distinction belongs to the man whose name is most closely associated with the idea of Christian humanism: Desiderius Erasmus of Rotterdam (ca. 1466–1536). Orphaned at an early age, Erasmus was educated by the Brothers of the Common Life, a lay brotherhood that specialized in schooling children and preparing them for a monastic life. Marked out early by his extraordinary intellectual gifts, Erasmus entered a monastery and was then allowed to travel to pursue his studies, first in France and then in England.

In England, Erasmus learned of new techniques for instructing children both in classical knowledge and in Christian morals, and he became particularly interested in the education of women. While in England, Erasmus composed a short satire, *In Praise of Folly* (1509), a work that became one of the first best sellers. He also came to realize the importance of recovering the texts of the early Church Fathers.

At the age of 30, Erasmus began the arduous task of learning ancient Greek and devoted his energies to a study of the writings of Saint Jerome, the principal compiler of the Vulgate, and to preparing an edition of the Greek texts of the Bible. Erasmus's translation of the New Testament and his edition of the writings of Saint Jerome both appeared in 1516.

Erasmus devoted his life to restoring the direct connection between the individual Christian and the textual basis of Christian doctrine. Although he is called the father of biblical criticism, Erasmus was not a theologian. He was more interested in the practical impact of ideas than in the ideas themselves. His scathing attacks on the Scholastics, popular superstition, and the pretensions of the traditionalists in the Church and the universities all had the same goal: to restore the experiences of Christ to the center of Christianity. His sarcastic indictment of theologians in his book *In Praise of Folly* illustrates his irreverent attitude toward men of the church:

> As for theologians, perhaps the less said the better on this gloomy and dangerous theme, since they are a style of man who show themselves exceeding supercilious and irritable unless they can heap up six hundred conclusions about you and force you to recant; and if you refuse, they promptly brand you as a heretic—for it is their custom to terrify by their thunderings those whom they dislike.

Though his patrons were the rich and his language was Latin, Erasmus also hoped to reach men and women lower down the social order, those whom he believed the Church had failed to educate. "The doctrine of Christ casts aside no age, no sex, no fortune or position in life. It keeps no one at a distance."

THE LUTHERAN REFORMATION

On the surface, the Roman Catholic Church appeared to be as strong as ever at the beginning of the sixteenth century. Yet everywhere in Europe, the cry was for reform: Reform the venal papacy and its money-sucking bishops; reform the ignorant clergy, the sacrilegious priests, the fallen nuns, and the wayward friars. Wherever one turned, one saw abuses. Parish livings were sold to the highest bidder to raise money. This was simony. Rich appointments were given to the kinsmen of powerful Church leaders rather than to those who were most qualified. This was nepotism. Individual clergymen accumulated numerous positions whose responsibilities they could not fulfill. This was pluralism. Some priests who took the vow of chastity lived openly with their concubines. Some mendicants who took the vow of poverty dressed in silk and ate from golden plates.

The Spark of Reform

Europe was becoming more religious. The signs of religious fervor were everywhere. Cities hired preachers to expound the gospel. Pilgrims to the shrines of saints clogged the roadways every spring and summer. Rome remained the greatest attraction, but pilgrims covered the Continent. The shrine of the apostle Saint James at Compostela in Spain was believed to cure the ill. Endowments of masses for the dead increased. Henry VII of England provided money for 10,000 masses to be said for his soul. Even city merchants might bequeath funds for several hundred masses. In the chantries, where such services were performed, there were neither enough priests nor enough altars to supply the demand.

People wanted more from the Church than the Church could possibly give them. Humanists condemned visits to the shrines as superstitious; pilgrims demanded that the relics be made more accessible. Reformers complained of pluralism; the clergy complained that they could not live on the salary of a single office. Civic authorities demanded that the established Church take greater responsibility for good works; the pope demanded that civic authorities help to pay for them.

Contradiction and paradox dominated the movements for reform. Though the most vocal critics of the Church complained that its discipline was too lax, for many ordinary people its demands were too rigorous. The obligations of penance and confession weighed heavily on them. Church doctrine held that sins had to be washed away before the souls of the dead could enter heaven. Until then, they suffered in purgatory. Sins were cleansed through penance, the performance of acts of contrition assigned after confession. But the ordeal of confession kept many people away. "Have you skipped Mass?

Have you dressed proudly? Have you thought of committing adultery? Have you insulted or cursed your parents?" These were just a few of the uncomfortable questions that priests were instructed to pose in confession. In towns, merchants were asked about their trading practices, shopkeepers about the quality of their goods. Magistrates were questioned about their attitudes to the clergy, intellectuals about their attitudes to the pope. It is hardly surprising that the sale of **indulgences** became a popular substitute for penance and confession.

The Sale of Indulgences

An indulgence was a portion of the treasury of good works performed by righteous Christians throughout the ages. Indulgences could be granted to people who wanted to atone for their sins. Strictly speaking, an indulgence supplemented penance rather than substituted for it. It was effective only for the contrite—for sinners who repented of their sins. But as the practice of granting indulgences spread, this subtle distinction largely disappeared. The living bought indulgences to cleanse the sins of the dead, and some even bought indulgences in anticipation of sins they had not yet committed.

By the sixteenth century, to limit abuses by local church authorities, only the pope, through his agents, could grant indulgences. Popes used special occasions to offer an indulgence for pilgrimages to Rome or for contributions to special papal projects. Other indulgences were licensed locally, usually at the shrines of saints or at churches that contained relics.

The indulgence controversy was a symptom rather than a cause of the explosion of feelings that erupted in the small German town of Wittenberg in 1517. In that year the pope was offering an indulgence to help finance the rebuilding of

■ An anonymous caricature of Johann Tetzel, whose sale of an indulgence inspired Martin Luther's Ninety-five Theses. Tetzel answered with 122 theses of his own but was rebuked and disowned by the Catholics.

Saint Peter's Basilica in Rome. The pope chose Prince Albert of Brandenburg (1490–1545) to distribute the indulgence in Germany, and Albert hired the Dominican friar Johann Tetzel (ca. 1465–1519) to preach its benefits.

Martin Luther Challenges the Church

Enthusiasm for the indulgence spread to the neighboring state of Saxony, where the ruler, Frederick III, the Wise (1463–1525), banned its sale. Frederick's great collection of relics carried their own indulgences, and Tetzel offered unwelcome competition. But Saxons flocked into Brandenburg to make their purchases, and by the end of October, Tetzel was not very far from Wittenberg Castle, where Frederick's relics were housed. On All Saints' Day the relics would be opened to view, and with the harvest done, one of the largest crowds of the year would gather to see them. On the night before, Martin Luther (1483–1546), a professor of theology at Wittenberg University, posted on the door of the castle church ninety-five theses attacking indulgences and their sale.

In so doing, Luther was following the Scholastic tradition of disputation, in which scholars presented propositions, or theses, for open debate with all comers. Luther's theses were controversial, but they were meant to be. Only circumstance moved Luther's theses from the academic to the public sphere. Already there was growing concern among clergy and theologians about Tetzel's blatant sale of indulgences. Hordes of purchasers believed that they were buying unconditional remission of sin. Individual priests and monks began to sound the alarm: an indulgence without contrition was worthless.

Luther's theses focused this concern and finally communicated it beyond the walls of the Church and the university. The theses were quickly translated into German and spread throughout the Holy Roman Empire. Prospective buyers of indulgence became wary; past purchasers became angry. But Prince Albert and the pope needed the income. They could not stand by while sales collapsed and anticlerical and antipapal sentiment grew.

Martin Luther's Faith

Although he was only an obscure German professor, Martin Luther was not a man to challenge lightly. In his youth he had studied for a career in law, but against his father's wishes he entered an Augustinian monastery and was ordained a priest in 1507. He received his doctorate at the university in Wittenberg and was appointed to the theology faculty in 1512. An outstanding teacher, Luther began to be picked for administrative posts and became overseer of 11 Augustinian monasteries. His skills in disputation were widely recognized, and he was sent to Rome to argue a case on behalf of his order. He fulfilled each task beyond expectation.

In all outward appearances, Luther was successful and contented, but beneath this tranquil exterior lay a soul in torment. Despite his devotion, he could not erase his sense of sin;

he could not convince himself that he could achieve the righteousness God demanded of him.

Knowledge of his salvation came to Luther through study. His internal agonies led him to ponder over and over again the biblical passages that described the righteousness of God. In the intellectual tradition in which he had been trained, that righteousness was equated with law. The righteous person either followed God's law or was punished by God's wrath. It was this understanding that tormented him. "I thought that I had to perform good works till at last through them Jesus would become a friend and gracious to me." But no amount of good works could overcome Luther's feelings of guilt for his sins. Almost from the moment he began lecturing in 1512, he searched for the key to the freedom of his own soul.

Even before he wrote his Ninety-five Theses, Luther had made the first breakthrough by a unique reading of the writings of Saint Paul. "I pondered night and day until I understood the connection between the righteousness of God and the sentence 'The just shall live by faith.' Then I grasped that the justice of God is the righteousness by which through grace and pure mercy, God justifies us through faith. Immediately I felt that I had been reborn and that I had passed through wide open doors into paradise!" Finally he realized that the righteousness of God was a gift freely given to the faithful. To receive God's righteousness, one had only to believe in God's infinite mercy. It was this belief that fortified Luther during his years of struggle with both civil and Church powers.

Over the next several years, Luther refined his spiritual philosophy and drew out the implications of his newfound beliefs. His religion was shaped by three interconnected tenets. First came justification by faith alone—*sola fide.* An individual's everlasting salvation came from faith in God's goodness rather than from the performance of good works. Sin could not be washed away by penance, and it could not be forgiven by indulgence. Second, faith came only through the knowledge and contemplation of the Word of God—*sola scriptura.* All that was needed to understand the justice and mercy of God was contained in the Bible. Reading the Word, hearing the Word, expounding on and studying the Word—this was the path to faith and through faith to salvation. Third, all who believed in God's righteousness and had achieved their faith through the study of the Bible were equal in God's eyes. The priesthood included all believers. Each followed his or her own calling and found his or her own faith through Scripture. Ministers and preachers could help others to learn God's Word, but they could not confer faith.

Luther's ideas posed a fundamental challenge to the Roman Catholic Church, but it was not Luther alone who initiated the reform of religion. His obsession with salvation was based on the same impulse that had made indulgences so popular. Justification by faith alone provided an alternative to the combination of works and faith that many Roman Catholics found too difficult to fulfill. Luther's insistence that faith comes only through the study of the Word of God was facilitated by the new learning and the invention of printing. The printing press prepared the ground for the dissemination

of his ideas as much as it disseminated them. This was a contribution of the Renaissance. Luther's hope for the creation of a spiritual elite, confirmed in their faith and confident of their salvation, readily appealed to the citizens of hundreds of German towns who had already made of themselves a social and economic elite. This was a contribution of the growth of towns. The idea of the equality of all believers meant that all were equally responsible for fulfilling God's commandments. This set secular rulers on an equal footing with the pope at a moment in Western history when rulers were already challenging papal power in matters of both church and state. This was a contribution of the formation of states. For all his painful soul-searching, Luther embodied the culmination of changes of which he was only dimly aware.

From Luther to Lutheranism

The first to feel the seriousness of Luther's challenge to the established order was the reformer himself. The head of Luther's order, a papal legate, and finally the Emperor Charles V all called for Luther to recant his views on indulgences. Luther was excommunicated by Pope Leo X in 1521 and ordered by Charles V to appear before the diet, or assembly, in Worms, Germany, in April of that year. There he gave the same infuriating reply: If he could be shown the places in the Bible that contradicted his views, he would gladly change them. Charles V declared Luther an enemy of the empire. In both Church and state he was now an outlaw.

In fact, during the three years between the posting of his theses and his appearance before the emperor, Luther came to conclusions that were much more radical than his initial attack on indulgences. He came to believe that the papacy was a human rather than a divine invention. Therefore he denounced both the papacy and the general councils of the Church. In his *Address to the Christian Nobility of the German Nation* (1520) he called on the princes to take the reform of religion into their own hands.

But Luther had attracted powerful supporters as well as powerful enemies. Prince Frederick III of Saxony consistently intervened on his behalf, and the delicate international situation forced Luther's chief antagonists to move more slowly than they might have wished. The pope hoped first to keep Charles V off the imperial throne and then to maintain a united front with the German princes against him. Charles V, already locked in his lifelong struggle with the French, needed German military support and peace in his German territories. These factors consistently played into Luther's hands.

While the pope and the emperor were otherwise occupied, Luther refined his ideas and won important converts. As time passed, Luther's reputation grew, not only in Germany, but all over Europe. Between 1517 and 1520, he published 30 works, all of which achieved massive sales. Luther's individual accomplishments were remarkable, but what turned his theology into a movement, which after 1529 came to be known as Protestantism, was the support he received among German princes and within German cities.

Princes and Cities.   Individual princes turned to Luther's theology for several reasons. First and foremost was sincere religious conviction. Second were political and economic factors. As German princes worked to centralize their administrations, protect themselves from predatory neighbors, and increase their revenues, they felt the burden of papal exactions. Taxes and gifts flowed south to a papacy dominated by Italians. Luther's call for civil rulers to lead their own churches meant that civil rulers could keep their own revenues.

The Reformation spread particularly well in the German cities, especially those to which the emperor had granted the status of freedom from the rule of any prince. The cities had long struggled with the tension of the separate jurisdictions of state and Church. Much urban property was owned by the Church and so was exempt from taxation and law enforcement, and the clergy constituted a significant proportion of urban populations. Reformed religion stressed the equality of clergy and laity and thus the indisputable power of civil authorities. Paradoxically, it was because the cities contained large numbers of priests that Luther's ideas reached the cities quickly. Many of his earliest students served urban congregations and began to develop doctrines and practices that, though based on Luther's ideas, were adapted to the circumstances of city life. The reform clergy became integrated into the life of the city in a way that the Catholic clergy had not. They married the daughters of citizens, became citizens themselves, and trained their children in the guilds. Moreover, the imperial free cities were also centers of the printing trade and home to many of the most noted humanists who were initially important in spreading Luther's ideas.

Luther's message held great appeal for the middle orders in the towns. While it was necessary for the leader of a state to support reform if it was to survive, in the cities it was the petty burghers, lesser merchants, tradespeople, and artisans who led the movements that ultimately gained the approval of city governments. These groups resented the privileges given to priests and members of religious orders who paid no taxes and were exempt from the obligations of citizenship. The level of anticlericalism, always high in Germany, was especially acute in cities that were suffering economic difficulties. Pressure from ordinary people and petty traders forced town leaders into action. The evangelism of reforming ministers created converts and an atmosphere of reform. Support from members of the ruling oligarchy both mobilized these pressures and capitalized on them. Town governments secured their own autonomy over the Church, tightening their grip on the institutions of social control and enhancing the social and economic authority of their members. Once they became Protestant, city governments took over many of the functions of the religious houses, often converting them into schools or hostels for the poor. Former monks were allowed to enter trades. Former nuns were encouraged to marry. Luther himself married an ex-nun after the dissolution of her convent.

The Appeal for Women.   Religious reform appealed to women as well as men, but it affected them differently. Noblewomen were among the most important defenders of Protestant reformers, especially in states in which the prince opposed it. Marguerite of Navarre (1492–1549), sister of Francis I, frequently intervened with her brother on behalf of individual Lutherans who fell afoul of Church authorities. She created her own court in the south of France and stocked it with both humanists and Protestants. Her devotional poem, *Mirror of the Sinful Soul* (1533), inspired women reformers and was translated into English by Elizabeth I. Mary of Hungary (1505–1558) played a similar role in the Holy Roman Empire. Sister of both Charles V and Ferdinand I, queen of Hungary, and later regent of the Netherlands, she acted as patron to Hungarian reformers. Though Mary was more humanist than Protestant, Luther dedicated an edition of Psalms to her, and she read a number of his works. Her independent religious views infuriated both of her brothers. Bona, wife of Sigismund I of Poland, was especially important in eastern reform. An Italian by birth, Bona (1493–1558) was a central figure in spreading both Renaissance art and humanist learning into Poland. She became one of the largest independent landowners in the state and initiated widespread agricultural and economic reforms. Her private confessor was one of Poland's leading Protestants.

Luther's reforms also appealed to women who were not so highly placed in society. The doctrine of the equality of all believers put men and women on an equal spiritual footing even if it did nothing to break the male monopoly of the ministry. In the private sphere, family life became the center of faith when salvation was removed from the control of the Church. Luther's marriage led him to a deeper appreciation of the importance of the wife and mother in the family's spirituality.

By following humanist teaching on the importance of educating women of the upper orders and by encouraging literacy, the reformers did much that was uplifting. Girls' schools were founded in a number of German cities, and townswomen could use their newly acquired skills in their roles as shopkeepers, family accountants, and teachers of their children. But there were losses as well as gains. The attack on the worship of saints and especially of the Virgin Mary removed female images from religion. Protestantism was male-dominated in a way that Catholicism was not. Moreover, the emphasis on reading the Bible tended to reinforce the image of women as weak and inherently sinful. The dissolution of the convents took away the one institution that valued women's gender and allowed them to pursue a spiritual life outside marriage.

The Spread of Lutheranism

By the end of the 1520s, the empire was divided between cities and states that accepted reformed religion and those that adhered to Roman Catholicism. Large German communities across northern Europe, mostly founded as trading outposts, became focal points for the penetration of reformist ideas. In Livonia, the Teutonic Knights established a Lutheran form of worship that soon took hold all along the shores of the Baltic.

Lutheran-inspired reformers seized control of the Polish port city of Gdansk, which they held for a short time, and neighboring Prussia officially established a Lutheran church. Polish translations of Luther's writings were disseminated into Poland-Lithuania, and Protestant communities were established as far south as Krakow.

Merchants and students carried Luther's ideas into Scandinavia, but there the importance of political leaders was crucial. Christian III (1534–1559) of Denmark had been present at the Diet of Worms when Luther made his famous reply to Charles V. Christian was deeply impressed by the reformer, and after a ruinous civil war he confiscated Catholic Church property in Denmark and created a reformed religion under Luther's direct supervision.

Paradoxically, Lutheranism came to Sweden as part of an effort to throw off the yoke of Danish dominance. When Gustav I Vasa (1523–1560) led a successful uprising against the Danes and became king of Sweden, he encouraged the spread of Protestant ideas. The result was a more gradual establishment of Lutheranism in Sweden than in Denmark. Lutheranism flourished in Scandinavia, where it remains the dominant religion to this day.

As important as Protestant ideas were in northern and central Europe, they proved most fertile in the Swiss towns of the empire. Here was planted the second generation of reformers, theologians who drew radical new conclusions from Luther's insights. In the east, Huldrych Zwingli (1484–1531) brought reformed religion to the town of Zurich. Educated at the University of Basel and deeply influenced by humanist thought early in his career, Zwingli was a preacher among the Swiss mercenary troops that fought for the empire. In 1516, he met Erasmus in Basel and, under his influence, began a study of the Greek writings of the Church Fathers and of the New Testament. Zwingli was also influenced by reports of Luther's defiance of the pope, for his own antipapal views were already developing.

MAP DISCOVERY

Intensity of green represents the approximate strength of Lutheranism

The Spread of Lutheranism

Observe the extent of Lutheranism across Europe in the sixteenth century. Where was Lutheranism concentrated? Notice how Lutheranism swept through entire states. How was Europe divided between Protestants and Catholics?

Perhaps most decisively for his early development, Zwingli was stricken by plague in 1519. In his life-and-death struggle he came to a profoundly personal realization of the power of God's mercy.

These experiences became the basis for the reform theology that Zwingli preached in Zurich. He believed that the Church had to recover its earlier purity and to reject the innovations in practices that successive popes and general councils had brought in. He stressed the equality of believers, justification by faith alone, and the sufficiency of the gospel as authority for church practice. He attacked indulgences, penance, clerical celibacy, prayers to the Virgin, statues and images in churches, and a long list of other practices. He regarded the Mass as a commemorative event rather than one that involved the real presence of Christ. His arguments were so effective that the town council adopted them as the basis for a reform of religion.

The principles that Zwingli preached quickly spread to neighboring Swiss states. Practical as well as theological, Zwingli's reforms were carried out by the civil government with which he allied himself. This was not the same as the protection that princes had given to Lutherans. Rather, in the places that came under Zwingli's influence, there was an important integration of church and state. He stressed the divine origins of civil government and the importance of the magistrate as an agent of Christian reform: "A church without the magistrate is mutilated and incomplete." This theocratic idea—that the leaders of the state and the leaders of the church were linked—became the basis for further social and political reform.

THE PROTESTANT REFORMATION

By the middle of the 1530s, Protestant reform had entered a new stage. Luther did not intend to form a new religion; his struggle had been with Rome. His religion was one of protest.

Most of his energy was expended in attack and counterattack. The second generation of reformers faced a different task. The new reformers were the church builders who had to systematize doctrine for a generation that had already accepted religious reform. Their challenge was to draw out the logic of reformed ideas and to create enduring structures for reformed churches. The problems they faced were as much institutional as doctrinal. How was the new church to be governed in the absence of the traditional hierarchy? How could discipline be enforced when members of the reformed community went astray? What was the proper relationship between the community of believers and civil authority? Whatever the failings of the Roman Catholic Church, it had ready answers to these critical questions.

Geneva and Calvin

The Reformation came late to Geneva. In the sixteenth century, Geneva was under the dual government of the duchy of Savoy and the Catholic bishop of the town, who was frequently a Savoy client. The Genevans also had their own town council, which traditionally struggled for power against the bishop. By the 1530s the council had gained the upper hand. The council confiscated Church lands and institutions, secularized the Church's legal powers, and forced the bishop and most of his administrators to flee the city. War with Savoy in-

THE ETERNAL DECREE

John Calvin was born in France but led the Reformation in the Swiss town of Geneva. He was one of the leaders of the second generation of reformers, whose task was to refine the structure of church doctrine. Calvinism was propounded in the Institutes of the Christian Religion *(1534), from which this section on the doctrine of predestination is taken.*

Focus Questions
According to Calvin, why is everyone contaminated by sin? What power do humans have over their spiritual destiny?

We must be content with this—that such gifts as it pleased the Lord to have bestowed upon the nature of man he vested in Adam; and therefore when Adam lost them after he had received them, he lost them not only from himself but also from us all. . . . Therefore from a rotten root rose up rotten branches, which sent their rottenness into the twigs that sprang out of them; for so were the children corrupted in their father that they in turn infected their children. . . .

And the apostle Paul himself expressly witnesseth that therefore death came upon all men, because all men have

sinned and are wrapped in original sin and defiled with the spots thereof. And therefore the very infants themselves, since they bring with them their own damnation from their mothers' womb, are bound not by another's but by their own fault. For although they have not as yet brought forth the fruits of their own iniquity, yet they have the seeds thereof inclosed within them; yea, their whole nature is a certain seed of sin, therefore it cannot but be hateful and abominable to God. . . .

Predestination we call the eternal decree of God, whereby he has determined with himself what he wills to become of every man. For all are not created to like estate; but to some eternal life and to some eternal damnation is foreordained. Therefore as every man is created to the one or the other end, so we say that he is predestinate either to life or to death.

From John Calvin, *Institutes of the Christian Religion.*

■ This painting depicts a Calvinist service in Lyon, France, in 1564. The men and women are segregated, and the worshippers are seated according to rank. An hourglass times the preacher's sermon.

evitably followed, and Geneva would certainly have been crushed into submission except for its alliance with neighboring Bern, a potent military power among the Swiss towns.

Geneva was saved and was free to follow its own course in religious matters. In 1536, the adult male citizens of the city voted to become Protestant. But there was as yet no reformer in Geneva to establish a Protestant program and no clear definition of what that program might be.

Martin Luther had started out to become a lawyer and ended up a priest. John Calvin started out to become a priest and ended up a lawyer. The difference tells much about each man. Calvin (1509–1564) was born in France, the son of a bishop's secretary. His education was based on humanist principles, and he learned Greek and Hebrew, studied theology, and received a legal degree from the University of Orléans. Around the age of 20 he converted to Lutheranism. Francis I was determined to root Protestants out of France, and Calvin fled Paris. Persecution of Protestants continued in France, and one of Calvin's close friends was burned for heresy. These events left an indelible impression on Calvin. In 1535, he left France for Basel, where he wrote and published the first edition of *Institutes of the Christian Religion* (1536), a defense of French Protestants against persecution. Calvin returned briefly to France to wind up his personal affairs and then decided to settle in Strasbourg, where he could retire from public affairs and live out his days as a scholar.

To Calvin, providence guided all human action. He could have no better evidence for this belief than what happened next. War between France and the empire clogged the major highways to Strasbourg. Soldiers constantly menaced travelers, and Protestants could expect the worst from both sides. Therefore Calvin and his companions detoured through Geneva, where Guillaume Farel (1489–1565), one of Geneva's leading Protestant reformers, persuaded Calvin to remain in Geneva and lead its reformation.

Calvin's greatest contributions to religious reform came in church structure and discipline. He had studied the writings of the first generation of reformers and accepted without question justification by faith alone and the biblical foundation of religious authority. Like Luther and Zwingli, he believed that salvation came from God's grace. But more strongly than his predecessors, he believed that the gift of faith was granted only to some and that each individual's salvation or damnation was predestined before birth. The doctrine of **predestination** was a traditional one, but Calvin emphasized it differently and brought it to the center of the problem of faith. "Many are called but few are chosen," Calvin quoted from the Bible. Those who were predestined to salvation were obliged to govern; those who were predestined to damnation were obliged to be governed.

Calvin structured the institution of the Genevan church in four parts: the pastors, who preached the Word to their congregations; the doctors, who studied and wrote; the deacons, who oversaw the institutions of social welfare, such as hospitals and schools, run by the church; and finally the elders of the church, who governed the church in all moral matters. They were the most controversial part of Calvin's establishment and the most fundamental. They had the power to discipline. Chosen from among the elite of the city, the 12 elders enforced the strict Calvinist moral code that extended into all aspects of private life. Sexual offenses were the most common. Adultery and fornication were vigorously suppressed, and prostitutes, who had nearly become a recognized guild in the early sixteenth century, were expelled from Geneva.

The structure that Calvin gave to the Genevan church soon became the basis for reforms throughout the Continent. The Calvinist church was self-governing, independent of the state, and therefore capable of surviving and even flourishing in a hostile environment. Expanded in several subsequent editions, *The Institutes of the Christian Religion* became the most influential work of Protestant theology. It had begun as an effort to extend Protestantism to Calvin's homeland, and waves of Calvinist-educated pastors returned to France in the midsixteenth century and established churches along Calvinist lines. Calvinism spread north to the Low Countries, where it became the basis for Dutch Protestantism, and east, where it flourished in Lithuania. It reached places untouched by Luther and revitalized reform where Lutheranism had been suppressed. Perhaps its greatest impact was in Britain, where the reformation took place not once but twice.

The English Reformation

The king of England wanted a divorce. Henry VIII had been married to Catherine of Aragon (1485–1536) as long as he had been king, and she had borne him no male heir to carry on his line. She had given birth to six children and endured several miscarriages, yet only one daughter, Mary, survived. Henry came to believe that this was God's punishment for his marriage. Catherine had been married first to Henry's older brother, who had died as a teenager, and there was at least one scriptural prohibition against marrying a brother's wife. A papal dispensation had been provided for the marriage; now Henry wanted a papal dispensation for an annulment. For three years his case ground its way through the papal courts. Catherine of Aragon was the aunt of the Emperor Charles V, and the emperor had taken her side in the controversy. With imperial power in Italy at its height, the pope was content to hear all of the complex legal and biblical precedents argued at leisure.

By 1533, Henry could wait no longer. He had already impregnated Anne Boleyn (ca. 1507–1536), one of the ladies-in-waiting at his court, and for the child—which Henry was certain would be a boy—to be legitimate, a marriage would have to take place at once. Legislation was prepared in Parliament to prevent papal interference in the decisions of England's courts, and Thomas Cranmer (1489–1556), archbishop of Canterbury, England's highest ecclesiastical officer,

agreed to annul Henry's first marriage and celebrate his second. This was the first step in a complete break with Rome. Under the guidance of Thomas Cromwell (ca. 1485–1540), the English Parliament passed statute after statute that made Henry supreme head of the Church in England and owner of its vast wealth. Monasteries were dissolved, and a Lutheran service was introduced. On 7 September 1533, Anne Boleyn gave birth not to the expected son, but to a daughter, the future Queen Elizabeth I.

The Church of England.   Henry's reformation was an act of state, but the English Reformation was not. There was an English tradition of dissent from the Roman Church that stretched back to the fourteenth century. Anticlericalism was especially virulent in the towns, where citizens refused to pay fees to priests for performing services such as burial. And humanist ideas flourished in England, where Thomas More, John Colet, and a host of others supported both the new learning and its efforts to reform spiritual life. Luther's attack on ritual and the Mass and his emphasis on Scripture and faith echoed the lost Lollard program and found many recruits in London and the northern port towns.

Protestantism grew slowly in England because it was vigorously repressed. Like Francis I and Charles V, Henry VIII viewed actual attacks on the established church as potential attacks on the established state. Henry had earned the title Defender of the Faith from the pope in 1521 for authoring an attack on Luther. The first published English translation of the New Testament, made by William Tyndale in 1525, had to be smuggled into England. As sensitivity to the abuses of the Church grew and Lutheran ideas spread, official persecution sharpened.

Henry's divorce unleashed a groundswell of support for religious change. The king's own religious beliefs remained a secret, but Anne Boleyn and Thomas Cromwell sponsored Lutheran reforms, and Thomas Cranmer put them into practice. Religion was legislated through Parliament, and the valuable estates of the Church were sold to the gentry. These practices found favor with both the legal profession and the landed elites and made Protestantism more palatable among these conservative groups. It was in the reign of Edward VI (1547–1553), Henry's son by his third wife, that the central doctrinal and devotional changes were made. Church service was now conducted in English, and the first two English prayer books were created. The Mass was reinterpreted along Zwinglian lines and became the Lord's Supper, the altar became the communion table, and the priest became the minister. Preaching became the center of the church service, and concern about the education of learned ministers resulted in commissions to examine and reform the clergy.

Beginning in the 1530s, state repression turned against Catholics. Those who would not swear the new oaths of allegiance or recognize the legality of Henry VIII's marriage suffered for their beliefs as the early Protestants had suffered for theirs. Thomas More and over 40 others paid with their lives for their opposition. An uprising in the north in 1536, known as the Pilgrimage of Grace, was suppressed, but Catholicism continued to flourish in England, surviving underground during the reigns of Henry and Edward and reemerging under Mary I (1553–1558).

The Successors of Henry VIII.   Mary Tudor, the first woman to rule England, held to the Catholic beliefs in which her mother, Catherine of Aragon, had raised her, and she vowed to bring the nation back to her mother's church. She reestablished papal sovereignty, abolished Protestant worship, and introduced a crash program of education in the universities to train a new generation of priests. The one thing that Mary could not achieve was restoration of monastic properties and Church lands. They had been scattered irretrievably, and any attempt at confiscation from the landed elite would surely have been met with insurrection. Catholic retribution for the blood of their martyrs was not long in coming. Cranmer and three other bishops were burned for heresy.

Nearly 800 Protestants fled the country rather than suffer a similar fate. These Marian exiles, as they came to be called, settled in a number of reformed communities, Zurich, Frankfurt, and Geneva among them. There they imbibed the second generation of Protestant ideas, especially Calvinism, and from there they began a propaganda campaign to keep reformed religion alive in England. It was the Marian exiles who were chiefly responsible for the second English reformation, which began in 1558 when Mary died and her half-sister, Elizabeth I (1558–1603), came to the throne.

Under Elizabeth, England returned to Protestantism, but not the Protestantism that had come before. Even the most advanced reforms during Edward's reign now seemed too moderate for the returning exiles. Against Elizabeth's wishes, the English church adopted the Calvinist doctrine of predestination and the simplification (but not wholesale reorganization) of the structure of the church. But it did not become a model of thoroughgoing reformation. The Thirty-nine Articles (1563) continued the English tradition of compromising points of disrupted doctrine and of maintaining traditional practices wherever possible.

The Reformation of the Radicals

Schism breeds schism. That was the stick with which Catholic Church and civil authorities beat Luther from the beginning. By attacking the authority of the established church and flouting the authority of the established state, he was fomenting social upheaval. But he insisted that his own ideas buttressed rather than subverted authority, especially civil authority under whose protection he had placed the Church. As early as 1525, peasants in Swabia appealed to Luther for support in their social rebellion. They based some of their most controversial demands, such as the abolition of tithes and labor service, on biblical authority. Luther instructed the rebels to lay down their arms and await their just rewards in heaven. But Luther's ideas had a life of their own. He clashed with Erasmus over free will and with Zwingli over the Mass. Toward the end of his life he felt that he was holding back the floodgates against the second generation of Protestant thinkers. Time and again, serious reformers wanted to take one or another of his doctrines further than he was willing to go himself. The water was seeping in everywhere.

The most dangerous threat to the establishment of an orthodox Protestantism came from groups who were described, not very precisely, as **Anabaptists.** Though this label—which means, literally, "baptism again"—identified people who practiced adult baptism, it was mainly used to tar religious opponents with the brush of extremism. Anabaptists appeared in a number of German and Swiss towns in the 1520s. Taking seriously the doctrine of justification by faith, Anabaptists argued that only believers could be members of the true church of God. Because baptism was the sacrament through which entry into the church took place, Anabaptists reasoned that it was a sacrament for adults rather than infants. But infant baptism was a core doctrine for both Catholics and Protestants. It symbolized the acceptance of Christ, and without it, eternal salvation was impossible. It was a practical doctrine. Unbaptized infants who died could not be accepted in heaven, and infant mortality was appallingly common.

Thus the doctrine of Anabaptism posed a psychological as well as a doctrinal threat to the reformers. But the practice of adult baptism paled in significance compared to many of the other conclusions that religious radicals derived from the principle of *sola scriptura*—by the Word alone. Some groups argued the case that since true Christians were only those who had faith, all others must be cast out of the church. These true Christians formed small separate sects. Many believed that their lives were guided by the Holy Spirit, who directed them from within. Some went further and denied the power of civil authority over true believers. Some argued for community of goods among believers and rejected private property. Others literally followed passages in the Old Testament that suggested polygamy and promiscuity.

Wherever they settled, these small bands of believers were persecuted to the brutal extent of the laws of heresy. Catholics burned them, Protestants drowned them, and they were stoned and clubbed out of their communities. There was enough substance in their ideas and enough sincerity in their patient sufferings that they continued to recruit followers as they were driven from town to town, from Germany into the Swiss cities, and from Switzerland into Bohemia and Hungary.

There, on the eastern edges of the empire, the largest groups of Anabaptists finally settled. Though all practiced adult baptism, only some held goods in common or remained pacifist. Charismatic leaders such as Balthasar Hubmaier (1485–1528) and Jacob Hutter (d. 1536) spread Anabaptism to Moravia in southern Bohemia, where they converted a number of nobles to their views. They procured land for their communities, which came to be known as the Moravian Brethren. Independent groups existed in England and throughout northwest Europe, where Menno Simons (1496–1561), a Dutch Anabaptist, spent his life organizing bands of followers who came to be known as Mennonites.

THE CATHOLIC REFORMATION

Like a rolling wave, Protestant reform washed across Europe, but the rock of the Roman Catholic Church endured. Though pieces of the universal church crumbled away in northern Germany, Switzerland, Bohemia, Scandinavia, England, and Scotland, the dense mass remained in southern Germany, Italy, Poland-Lithuania, Spain, France, and Ireland. Catholics felt the same impulses toward a more fulfilling religious life as Protestants and complained of the same abuses of clerical, state, and papal powers. But the Catholic response was to reform the church from within. A new personal piety was stressed, which led to the founding of additional spiritual orders. The ecclesiastical hierarchy became more concerned with pastoral care and initiated reforms of the clergy at the parish level. The challenge of converting other peoples, Asians and Amerindians especially, led to the formation of missionary orders and to a new emphasis on preaching and education. Protestantism itself revitalized Catholicism.

The Spiritual Revival

The quest for individual spiritual fulfillment dominated later medieval Roman Catholicism. Erasmus, Luther, and Zwingli were all influenced by a Catholic spiritual movement known as the **New Piety.** It was propagated in Germany by the Brethren of the Common Life, a lay organization that stressed the importance of personal meditation on the life of Christ. *The Imitation of Christ* (1427), the central text of the New Piety, commonly attributed to Thomas à Kempis (1379–1471), was among the most influential works of the later Middle Ages. The Brethren taught that a Christian life should be lived according to Christ's dictates as expressed in the Sermon on the Mount. They instructed their pupils to lead a simple ascetic life with personal devotion at its core. These were the lessons that the young Erasmus found so liberating and the young Luther so stifling.

The New Piety, with its emphasis on a simple personal form of religious practice, was a central influence on Christian humanism. It is important to realize that humanism developed within the context of Catholic education and that many churchmen embraced the new learning and supported educational reform or patronized works of humanist scholarship. The Polyglot Bible was organized by Cardinal Jiménez de Cisneros (1436–1517), archbishop of Toledo and primate of Spain. The greatest educational reformer in England, John Colet (1467–1519), was dean of Saint Paul's, London's cathedral church. Without any of his famed irony, Erasmus dedicated his Greek Bible to the pope. The leading Christian humanists remained within the Catholic Church even after many of their criticisms had formed the basis of Protestant reforms.

This combination of piety and humanism imbued the ecclesiastical reforms initiated by Church leaders. Cardinal Jiménez de Cisneros, who also served as inquisitor-general of the Spanish Inquisition, undertook a wide-ranging reorganization of Spanish religious life in the late fifteenth century. Though not every project was successful, Jiménez de

Cisneros's program took much of the sting out of Protestant attacks on clerical abuse, and there was never a serious Protestant movement in Spain.

The most influential reforming bishop was Gian Matteo Giberti (1495–1543) of Verona. Using his own frugal life as an example, Giberti rigorously enforced vows, residency, and the pastoral duties of the clergy. He founded almshouses to aid the poor and orphanages to house the homeless. In Verona, Giberti established a printing press, which turned out editions of the central works of Roman Catholicism, especially the writings of Augustine.

The most important indication of the reforming spirit within the Roman Church was the foundation of new religious orders in the early sixteenth century. Devotion to a spiritual life of sacrifice was the chief characteristic of the lay and clerical orders that had flourished throughout the Middle Ages. In one French diocese, the number of clergy quadrupled in the last half of the fifteenth century. Although the number of entrants to the traditional orders of Franciscans and Dominicans did not rise as quickly, the growth of lay communities such as the Brethren of the Common Life attested to the continuing appeal of Catholic devotionalism.

Devotionalism was particularly strong in Italy, where a number of new orders received papal charters. The Capuchins were founded by the Italian peasant Matteo de Bascio (ca. 1495–1552). He sought to follow the strictest rule of the life of Saint Francis of Assisi, a path that even the so-called Observant Franciscans had found too arduous. In contrast, the Theatines were established by a group of well-to-do Italian priests who also wanted to lead a more austere devotional existence than was to be found in the traditional orders. Like the Capuchins, they accepted a life of extreme poverty, in which even begging was only a last resort.

In Spain, Saint Teresa of Ávila (1515–1582) led the reform of the Carmelites. She believed that women had to withdraw totally from the world around them to achieve true devotion. Against the wishes of the male superiors of her order, she founded a convent to put her beliefs into practice and began writing devotional tracts such as *The Way of Perfection* (1583). In 1535, Angela Merici (ca. 1474–1540) established the Ursulines, one of the most original of the new foundations, composed of young unmarried girls who remained with their families but lived chaste lives devoted to the instruction of other women.

Loyola's Pilgrimage

At first glance, Saint Ignatius Loyola (1491–1556) seems an unlikely candidate to lead one of the most vital movements for religious reform in the sixteenth century. The thirteenth child of a Spanish noble family, Loyola trained for a military life in the service of Castile. In 1521, he was one of the garrison defenders when the French besieged Pamplona. A cannonball shattered his leg, and he was carried home for a long enforced convalescence. There, he slowly and carefully read the only books in the castle: a life of Christ and a history of the saints. His reading inspired him. Before, he had sought glory and renown in battle. But when he compared the truly heroic deeds of the saints to his own vainglorious exploits, he decided to give his life over to spirituality.

Loyola was not a man to do things by halves. He resolved to model his life on the sufferings of the saints about whom he had read. He renounced his worldly goods and endured a year-long regimen of physical abstinence and spiritual nourishment in the town of Manresa. He deprived himself of food and sleep for long periods and underwent a regimen of seven hours of daily prayer, supplemented by nearly continuous religious contemplation. "But when he went to bed great enlightenment, great spiritual consolations often came to him, so that he lost much of the time he had intended for sleeping." During this period of intense concentration he first began to have visions, which later culminated in a mystical experience in which Christ called Loyola directly to his service.

Like Luther, Loyola was tormented by his inability to achieve grace through penance, but unlike Luther he redoubled his efforts. At Manresa, Loyola encountered the *Imitation of Christ,* which profoundly influenced his conversion. He recorded the techniques he used during this vigil in *The Spiritual Exercises,* which became a handbook for Catholic devotion. In 1523, crippled and barefoot, he made a pilgrimage to Jerusalem. He returned to Spain intent on becoming a priest.

By this time, Loyola had adopted a distinctive garb that attracted both followers and suspicion. Twice, the Spanish ecclesiastical authorities summoned him to be examined for heresy. In 1528, he decided to complete his studies in

■ Rubens's (1577–1640) *The Miracles of Saint Ignatius Loyola.* Founder of the Society of Jesus, Loyola prepared his Jesuit recruits for an active, rather than a contemplative, life.

France, where he and a small group of friends eventually decided to form a brotherhood after they became priests. They devoted themselves to the cure of souls and took personal vows of poverty, chastity, and obedience to the pope. On a pilgrimage to Rome, Loyola and his followers again attracted the attention of ecclesiastical authorities. Loyola explained his mission to them and in 1540 won the approval of Pope Paul III to establish a new holy order, the Society of Jesus.

Loyola's Society was founded at a time when the spiritual needs of the Church were being extended beyond the confines of Europe. Loyola volunteered his followers, who came to be

known as Jesuits, to serve in the remotest parts of the world. One disciple, Francis Xavier (1506–1552), made converts to Catholicism in the Portuguese port cities in the East and then in India and Japan. Other Jesuits became missionaries to the New World, where they offered Christian consolation to the Amerindian communities. By 1556, the Society of Jesus had grown from 10 to 1,000, and Loyola had become a full-time administrator in Rome.

Loyola never abandoned the military images that had dominated his youth. He enlisted his followers in military terms. The Jesuits were "soldiers of God" who served "beneath the banner of the Cross." Loyola's most fundamental innovation in these years was the founding of schools to train recruits for his order. Jesuit training was rigorous. Since they were being prepared for an active rather than a contemplative life, Jesuits were not cloistered during their training. Jesuit schools were opened to the laity, and lay education became one of the Jesuits' most important functions. Loyola lived to see the establishment of nearly a hundred colleges and seminaries and the spread of his order throughout the world. He died while at prayer.

The Counter-Reformation

The Jesuits were both the culmination of one wave of Catholic reform and the advance guard of another. They combined the piety and devotion that stretched from medieval mysticism through humanism, diocesan reforms, and the foundations of new spiritual orders. But they also represented an aggressive Catholic response that was determined to meet Protestantism head on and repel it—the **Counter-Reformation.** This was the Church militant. Old instruments such as the Inquisition were revived, and new weapons such as the Index of Prohibited Books were forged. But the problems of fighting Protestantism were not only those of combating Protestant ideas. Like oil and water, politics and religion failed to combine. Emperor Charles V and the hierarchy of the German church demanded thoroughgoing reform of the Catholic Church; the pope and the hierarchy of the Italian church resisted the call. As head of the Catholic Church, the pope was distressed by the spread of heresy in the lands of the empire. As head of a large Italian city-state, the pope was consoled by the weakening of the power of his Spanish rival. Brothers in Christ, pope and emperor were mortal enemies in everything else. Throughout the Catholic states of Germany came the urgent cry for a reforming council of the Church. But the voices were muffled as they crossed the Alps and made their way down the Italian peninsula.

At the emperor's instigation, the first serious preparations for a general council of the Church were made in the 1530s. The papacy warded it off. The complexities of international diplomacy were one factor—the French king was even less anxious to bring peace to the empire than the pope was—and the complexities of papal politics were another. The powers of a general council in relation to the powers of the papacy had never been clarified. After the advent and spread of Protestantism, successive popes had little reason to believe that in this gravest crisis of all, a council would be mindful of papal prerogatives. In fact, Catholic reformers were as bitter in their denunciations of papal abuses as Protestants were. The second attempt to arrange a general council of the Church occurred in the early 1540s. Again the papacy warded it off.

These factors ensured that when a general council of the Church finally did meet, its task would not be an easy one. The northern churches, French and German alike, wanted reforms of the papacy; the papacy wanted a restatement of orthodox doctrine. Many princes whose states were divided

CHRONOLOGY	
THE REFORMATION AND THE COUNTER-REFORMATION	
1517	Luther writes his Ninety-five Theses
1521	Luther is excommunicated and declared an enemy of the empire; Henry VIII receives title Defender of the Faith
1523	Zwingli expounds his faith in formal disputation
1533	Henry VIII divorces Catherine of Aragon, marries Anne Boleyn, and breaks with the Church of Rome
1536	Calvin publishes *Institutes of the Christian Religion*
1540	Loyola receives papal approval for Society of Jesus
1545–1563	Council of Trent
1553	Mary I restores Catholicism in England
1563	Elizabeth I enacts the Thirty-nine Articles, which restores Protestantism to England

among Catholics and Protestants wanted compromises that might accommodate both. Ferdinand I, king of Bohemia, saw the council as an opportunity to bring the Hussites back into the fold. Charles V and the German bishops wanted the leading Protestant church authorities to offer their own compromises on doctrine that might form a basis for reuniting the empire. The papacy wanted traditional church doctrine reasserted.

The general council of the Church that finally met in Trent from 1545 to 1563 thus had nearly unlimited potential for disaster. It began in compromise—Trent was an Italian town under the government of the emperor—but ended in total victory for the views of the papacy. For all of the papacy's seeming weaknesses (the defections of England and the rich north German territories cut into papal revenues, and Italy was under Spanish occupation) an Italian pope always held the upper hand at the council. Fewer than one-third of the delegates came from outside Italy. The French looked on the council suspiciously and played only a minor role, and the emperor forbade his bishops to attend after the council moved to Bologna.

Yet for all of these difficulties, the councillors at Trent made some real progress. They corrected a number of abuses, of which the sale of indulgences was the most substantive. They formulated rules for the better regulation of parish

MAP DISCOVERY

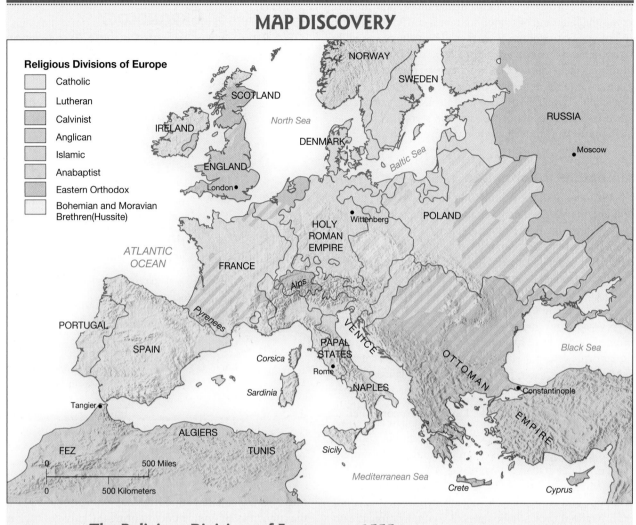

Religious Divisions of Europe

- Catholic
- Lutheran
- Calvinist
- Anglican
- Islamic
- Anabaptist
- Eastern Orthodox
- Bohemian and Moravian Brethren (Hussite)

The Religious Divisions of Europe, ca. 1555

Which was the largest religious denomination by the middle of the sixteenth century? Which states were most at risk of internal religious warfare? Notice the difference in the ways in which Lutheranism and Calvinism spread. Where did Catholicism remain untouched by the new religions?

priests and stressed the obligation of priests and bishops to preach to their congregations. They ordered seminaries to be founded in all dioceses where there was not already a university so that priests could receive sufficient education to perform their duties. They prepared a new modern and uniform Catholic service and centralized and updated the Index of Prohibited Books to include Protestant writings from all over the Continent.

The Council of Trent made no concessions to Protestants, moderate or radical. The councillors upheld justification by faith and works over justification by faith alone. They con-

firmed the truth of Scripture and the traditions of the Church against Scripture alone. They declared the Vulgate to be the only acceptable text of the Bible and encouraged vast bonfires of Greek and Hebrew Scriptures in an effort to undo the great scholarly achievements of the humanists. They reaffirmed the seven sacraments and the doctrine of the miracle of the Eucharist. They upheld clerical celibacy. The redefinition of traditional Roman Catholicism drew the doctrinal lines clearly and ended decades of confusion. But it also meant that the differences between Catholics and Protestants could now be settled only by the sword.

The Empire Reacts

Warfare dominated the reform of religion almost from its beginning. The burnings, drownings, and executions by which both Catholics and Protestants attempted to maintain religious purity were but raindrops compared to the sea of blood that was shed in sieges and on battlefields beginning in the 1530s. The Catholic divisions were clear. The empire continued to be engaged in the west with its archenemy, France, and in the south with the ever-expanding Ottoman Empire. Charles V needed not only peace within his own German realms, but positive support for his offensive and defensive campaigns. He could never devote his full resources to suppressing Protestant dissent.

Yet there was never a united Protestant front to suppress. The north German towns and principalities that accepted Lutheranism in the 1520s had had a long history of warfare among themselves. Princes stored up grievances from past wars and contested inheritances; cities stored up jealousies from commercial rivalries and special privileges. Added to this was the division between Luther and Zwingli over doctrinal issues that effectively separated the German and Swiss components of the Reformation from each other.

Although both the Protestant and the Catholic sides were internally weak, it was the greater responsibilities of Charles V that allowed for the uneasy periods of peace. Each pause gave the Protestant reformers new life. Lutheranism continued to spread in the northern part of the empire, Zwinglian reform in the south. Charles V asked the papacy to convoke a general council and the Protestants to stop evangelizing in new territories. But Protestant leaders were no more capable of halting the spread of the Reformation than were Catholics. Thus each violation of each uneasy truce seemed to prove treachery. In 1546, just after Luther's death, both sides raised armies in preparation for renewed fighting. In the first stage of war, Charles V scored a decisive victory, capturing the two leading Protestant princes and conquering Saxony and Thuringia, the homeland of Lutheran reform.

Charles V's greatest victories were always preludes to his gravest defeats. The remaining Protestant princes were driven into the arms of the French, who placed dynastic interests above religious concerns. Again Europe was plunged into general conflict, with the French invading the German states from the west, the Turks from the south, and the Protestant princes from the north. Charles V, now an old and broken man, was forced to flee through the Alps in the dead of winter and was brought to the bargaining table soon after. By the Peace of Augsburg in 1555 the emperor agreed to allow the princes of Germany to establish the religion of their people. Protestant princes would govern Protestant states, and Catholic princes would govern Catholic states. The Peace of Augsburg ended 40 years of religious struggle in Germany.

CONCLUSION

In 1547, the then-victorious Charles V stood at the grave of Martin Luther. He had been buried in the shadow of the church in which he had been baptized, and now other shadows darkened his plot. Imperial troops were masters of all Saxony and were preparing to turn back the religious clock in Luther's homeland. The emperor was advised to have the body exhumed and burned, to carry out 25 years too late the Edict of Worms that had made Luther an outlaw from Church and state. But Charles V was no longer the self-confident young emperor who had been faced down by the Saxon monk on that long-ago day. Popes had come and gone, and his warrior rivals, Francis I and Henry VIII, were both dead. Charles alone survived. He had little stomach for the petty revenge that he might now exact on the man who, more than any other, had ruined whatever hope there might have been for a united empire that was dominant over all of Europe. "I do not make war on dead men," Charles declared as he turned away from the reformer's grave. But the ghosts of Luther and Zwingli, of Calvin and Ignatius of Loyola were not so easily laid. For another century they would haunt a Europe that could do nothing else but make war on dead men.

QUESTIONS FOR REVIEW

1. How did humanism prepare the way for the Reformation?
2. What motivated Martin Luther?
3. What were the differences between the reforming ideas of Luther, Zwingli, and Calvin?

4. How did the Catholic Church respond to the challenges posed by the Protestant Reformation?

KEY TERMS

Anabaptists, *p. 272*

Christian humanism, *p. 263*

Counter-Reformation, *p. 275*

indulgences, *p. 265*

New Piety, *p. 273*

predestination, *p. 270*

Reformation, *p. 261*

sola fide, p. 266

sola scriptura, p. 261

DISCOVERING WESTERN CIVILIZATION ONLINE

You can obtain more information about the reform of religion at the websites listed below. See also the Companion Website that accompanies this text, www.ablongman.com/kishlansky, which contains an online study guide and additional resources.

The Lutheran Reformation

Lutherstadt Wittenberg, Martin Luther
www.wittenberg.de/e/seiten/personen/luther.html
A site devoted to Martin Luther and the city of Wittenberg. Texts of the famous Ninety-five Theses and other of Luther's writings as well as pictures of locations associated with the Lutheran reformation.

The Protestant Reformation

The Reformation Guide
www.educ.msu.edu/homepages/laurence/reformation/index.htm
The Reformation guide is the best starting place for information about all aspects of the Protestant Reformation. Dozens of links to follow.

Discovery and Reformation
www.wsu.edu/~dee/REFORM/REFORM.HTM
A primarily text-based site created by Washington State University, with profiles of key individuals and explanations of the issues at stake.

Project Wittenberg
www.iclnet.org/pub/resources/text/wittenberg/wittenberg-home.html
The home page of Project Wittenberg, containing a large number of texts (including hymns) by Luther and other Reformers.

Tudor History
tudorhistory.org/
A site with links to a variety of subjects relating to England under the Tudors. Biographies of the kings and queens, bibliographies, maps, and documents.

Reformation Picture Gallery
www.mun.ca/rels/hrollmann/reform/pics/pics.html
Contemporary pictures of leading reformers and the places associated with the Protestant Reformation. Excellent reproductions, especially from woodcuts.

Internet Modern History Sourcebook: Reformation Europe
www.fordham.edu/halsall/mod/modsbook02.html
Sources for both the Reformation and Counter-Reformation with links to other valuable sites.

SUGGESTIONS FOR FURTHER READING

General Reading

Owen Chadwick, *The Reformation* (London: Penguin Books, 1972). An elegant and disarmingly simple history of religious change.

Diarmaid MacCulloch, *The Reformation* (London: Viking, 2003). A vastly impressive survey of the Reformation from a leading scholar.

Steven Ozment, *The Age of Reform, 1250–1550* (New Haven, CT: Yale University Press, 1980). An important interpretation of an epoch of religious change.

The Intellectual Reformation

E. Eisenstein, *The Printing Revolution in Early Modern Europe* (Cambridge: Cambridge University Press, 1983). An abridged edition of a larger work that examines the impact of printing upon European society.

Adrian Johns, *The Nature of the Book: Print and Knowledge in the Making* (Chicago: University of Chicago Press, 1998). A major new synthesis with an unusual interpretation.

R. W. Scribner, *For the Sake of Simple Folk* (Cambridge: Cambridge University Press, 1994). A study of the impact of the Reformation on common people. Especially good on the iconography of reform.

James Tracy, *Erasmus of the Low Countries* (Berkeley, CA:, 1996). A brief biography of the great Dutch humanist.

The Lutheran Reformation

Roland Bainton, *Here I Stand* (New York: New American Library, 1968). The single most compelling biography of Luther.

Bernd Moeller, *Imperial Cities and the Reformation* (Durham, NC: Labyrinth Press, 1982). A central work that defines the connection between Protestantism and urban reform.

Heiko Oberman, *Luther: Man Between God and the Devil* (New York: Doubleday, 1992). English translation of one of the best German biographies of Luther. Sets Luther within the context of late medieval spirituality.

G. R. Potter, *Huldrych Zwingli* (New York: St. Martin's Press, 1984). A difficult but important study of the great Swiss reformer.

Lyndal Roper, *The Holy Household: Women and Morals in Reformation Augsburg* (Oxford: Oxford University Press, 1991). The best work to show the impact of the Reformation on family life and women.

R. W. Scribner, *The German Reformation* (Atlantic Highlands, NJ: Humanities Press, 1986). An excellent introduction, especially to the social history of the Reformation.

The Protestant Reformation

William Bousma, *John Calvin* (Oxford: Oxford University Press, 1988). A study that places Calvin within the context of the social and intellectual movements of the sixteenth century.

Claus-Peter Clasen, *Anabaptism, A Social History, 1525–1618* (Ithaca, NY: Cornell University Press, 1972). An important study of the Anabaptist movement.

A. G. Dickens, *The English Reformation,* 2nd ed. (London: Batsford, 1989). The classic study of reform in England.

J. J. Scarisbrick, *Henry VIII* (Berkeley: University of California Press, 1968). The classic biography of the larger-than-life monarch.

The Catholic Reformation

Jean Delumeau, *Catholicism Between Luther and Voltaire* (Philadelphia: Westminster Press, 1977). An important reinterpretation of the Counter-Reformation.

Carlos Eire, *From Madrid to Purgatory* (Cambridge: Cambridge University Press, 1995). A brilliant study of the Spanish culture of death during the Counter-Reformation.

W. W. Meissner, *Ignatius of Loyola: The Psychology of a Saint* (New Haven, CT: Yale University Press, 1994). A searching study of the founding spirit of the Counter-Reformation.

John W. O'Malley, *Trent and All That: Renaming Catholicism in the Early Modern Era* (Cambridge, MA: Harvard University Press, 2000). A re-examination of Catholicism in the century surrounding the Council of Trent.

A. D. Wright, *The Counter-Reformation* (New York: St. Martin's Press, 1984). A comprehensive survey.

For a list of additional titles related to this chapter's topics, please see www.ablongman.com/kishlansky.

Chapter 14

EUROPE AT WAR, 1555–1648

The Visual Record

THE MASSACRE OF THE INNOCENTS

"War is one of the scourges with which it has pleased God to afflict men," wrote Cardinal Richelieu (1585–1642), the French minister who played no small part in spreading the scourge. War was a constant of European society and penetrated to its very core. It dominated all aspects of life. It enhanced the power of the state, it defined gender roles, it consumed lives and treasure and commodities ravenously. War affected every member of society from combatants to civilians. There were no innocent bystanders. Grain in the fields was destroyed because it was food for soldiers; houses were burned because they provided shelter for soldiers. Civilians were killed for aiding the enemy or holding out against demands for their treasure and supplies. Able-bodied men were taken forcibly to serve as conscripts, leaving women to plant and harvest as best they could.

Neither the ancient temple nor the Roman costume can conceal the immediacy of the picture shown here. It is as painful to look at now as it was when it was created over 350 years ago. Painted by Nicolas Poussin (1594–1665) at the height of the Thirty Years' War, *The Massacre of the Innocents* remains a horrifying composition of power, terror, and despair. The cruel and senseless slaughter of the innocent baby that is about to take place is echoed throughout the canvas. In the background between the executioner's legs can be seen a mother clasping her own child tightly and anticipating the fall of the sword. In the background on the right, another mother turns away from the scene and carries her infant to safety. In the foreground strides a mother holding her dead child. She tears at her hair and cries in anguish. To a culture in which the image of mother and child—of Mary and Jesus—was one of sublime peacefulness and joy, the contrast could hardly have been more shocking.

The picture graphically displays the cruelty of the soldier, the helplessness of the child, and the horror of the mother. By his grip on the mother's hair and his foot on the baby's throat, the warrior shows his brute power. The mother's futile effort to stop the sword illustrates her powerlessness. She scratches uselessly at the soldier's back. Naked, the baby boy raises his hands as if to surrender to the inevitable, as if to reinforce his innocence.

To study Europe at war, we must enter a world of politics and diplomacy, of issues and principles, of judgment and error. There can be no doubt that the future of Europe was

decisively shaped by this century of wholesale slaughter, during which dynastic and religious fervor finally ran its course. The survival of Protestantism, the disintegration of the Spanish empire, the rise of Holland and Sweden, the collapse of Poland and Muscovy, the fragmentation of Germany—these were all vital transformations the consequences of which would be felt for centuries. We cannot avoid telling this story, untangling its causes, narrating its course, and revealing its outcome. But neither should we avoid facing its reality. Look again at the painting by Poussin.

Looking Ahead

As we will see in this chapter, warfare in the seventeenth century decisively reshaped power relations of families and states. Protestantism survived after nearly a century of military challenge and the power of the great Habsburg dynasty was finally crushed. In its place rose France, England, and Holland, and a new chapter of European conflict began. ➤

THE CRISES OF THE WESTERN STATES

"Un roi, une foi, une loi"—"One king, one faith, one law." This was a prescription that members of all European states accepted without question in the sixteenth century. Society was an integrated whole, equally dependent on monarchical, ecclesiastical, and civil authority for its effective survival. A European state could no more tolerate the presence of two churches than it could the presence of two kings. But the Reformation had created two churches. The coexistence of Catholics and Protestants in a single realm posed a stark challenge to accepted theory and traditional practice.

The problem proved intractable because it admitted only one solution: total victory. There could be no compromise for several reasons. Religious beliefs were profoundly held. Religious controversy was more than a life-and-death struggle: it was a struggle between everlasting life and eternal damnation. Doomed, too, was the practical solution of toleration. To the modern mind, toleration seems so logical that it is difficult to understand why it took over a century of bloodshed before it came to be grudgingly accepted by the most bitterly divided countries. But toleration was not a practical solution in a society that admitted no principle of organization other than one king, one faith.

The French Wars of Religion

No wars are more terrible than civil wars. The loss of lives and property is staggering, but the loss of communal identity is greater still. Generations pass before societies recover from their civil wars. Such was the case with the **French wars of religion.**

The Spread of Calvinism and Religious Division. Protestantism came late to France. Not until after Calvin reformed the Church in Geneva and began to export his brand of Protestantism did French society begin to divide along religious lines. By 1560 there were over 2,000 Protestant congregations in France, and their membership totaled nearly 10 percent of the French population. Calvin and his successors achieved their greatest following among the middle ranks of urban society: merchants, traders, and artisans. They also found a receptive audience among aristocratic women, who eventually converted their husbands and children.

However, the wars of religion were brought on by more than the rapid spread of Calvinism. Equally important was the vacuum of power that had been created when Henry II (1547–1559) died in a jousting tournament. Surviving Henry were his extraordinary widow, Catherine de Médicis, three daughters, and four sons, the oldest of whom, Francis II (1559–1560), was only 15 years old. Under the influence of his beautiful young wife, Mary, Queen of Scots, Francis allowed Mary's relatives, the Guise family, to dominate the great offices of state and to exclude their rivals from power. The Guises controlled the two most powerful institutions of the state: the army and the Church.

Catherine de Médicis (1519–1598), the wife of Henry II of France, was the real power behind the throne during the reigns of her sons Charles IX (1560–1574) and Henry III (1574–1589). Her overriding concern was to ensure her sons' succession and to preserve the power of the monarchy.

The Guises were staunchly Catholic, and among their enemies were the Bourbons, princes of the blood with a direct claim to the French throne but also a family with powerful Protestant members. The revelation of a Protestant plot to remove the king from Paris provided the Guises with an opportunity to eliminate their most potent rivals. The Bourbon duc de Condé, the leading Protestant peer of the realm, was sentenced to death. But five days before Condé's execution, Francis II died, and Guise power evaporated. The new king, Charles IX (1560–1574), was only 10 years old and firmly under the grip of his mother, Catherine de Médicis, who now declared herself regent of France.

Civil War.   Condé's death sentence convinced him that the Guises would stop at nothing to gain their ambitions. Force would have to be met with force. Protestants and Catholics alike raised armies, and in 1562, civil war ensued. Once the wars began, the leading Protestant peers fled the court, but the position of the Guises was not altogether secure. Henry Bourbon, king of Navarre, was the next in line to the throne should Charles IX and his two brothers die without male heirs. Henry had been raised in the Protestant faith by his mother, Jeanne d'Albret, whose own mother, Marguerite of Navarre, was among the earliest protectors of the **Huguenots,** as the French Calvinists came to be called.

The inconclusive nature of the early battles might have allowed for the pragmatic solution by Catherine de Médicis had it not been for the assassination of the duc de Guise in 1563 by a Protestant fanatic. This act added a personal vendetta to the religious passions of the Catholic leaders. They encouraged the slaughter of Huguenot congregations and openly planned the murder of Huguenot leaders. Protestants gave as good as they got. In open defiance of Valois dynastic interests, the Guises courted support from Spain, while the Huguenots imported Swiss and German mercenaries to fight in France. Noble factions and irreconcilable religious differences were pulling the government apart.

The Saint Bartholomew's Day Massacre. By 1570, Catherine was ready to attempt another reconciliation. She announced her plans for a marriage between her daughter Margaret and Henry of Navarre, a marriage that would symbolize the spirit of conciliation between the crown and the Huguenots. The marriage was to take place in Paris during August 1572. The arrival of Huguenot leaders from all over France to attend the marriage ceremony presented an opportunity of a different kind to the Guises and their supporters. If leading Huguenots could be assassinated in Paris, the Protestant cause might collapse, and the truce that the wedding signified might be turned instead into a Catholic triumph.

Saint Bartholomew was the apostle whom Jesus described as a man without guile. Ironically, it was on his feast day that the Huguenots who had innocently come to celebrate Henry's marriage were led like lambs to the slaughter. On 24 August 1572 the streets of Paris ran red with Huguenot blood. Although frenzied, the slaughter was inefficient. Henry of Navarre and a number of other important Huguenots escaped the carnage and returned to their urban strongholds. In the following weeks the violence spread from Paris to the countryside, and thousands of Protestants paid for their beliefs with their lives.

One King, Two Faiths

The Saint Bartholomew's Day Massacre was a transforming event in many ways. In the first place, it prolonged the wars. A whole new generation of Huguenots now had an attachment to the continuation of warfare: their fathers and brothers had been mercilessly slaughtered. By itself, the event was shocking enough; in the atmosphere of anticipated reconciliation created by the wedding, it screamed out for revenge. And the target for retaliation was no longer limited to the Guises and their followers. By accepting the results of the massacre, the monarchy sanctioned it and spilled Huguenot blood on itself. For more than a decade, Catherine de Médicis had maintained a distance between the crown and the leaders of the Catholic movement. That distance no longer existed.

The Theory of Resistance.   After Saint Bartholomew's Day, Huguenot theorists began to develop the idea that resistance to a monarch whose actions violated divine commandments or civil right was lawful. For the first time, Huguenot writers provided a justification for rebellion. Perhaps most importantly, a

■ Painting of the Saint Bartholomew's Day Massacre. The massacre began in Paris on 24 August 1572, and the violence soon spread throughout France.

genuine revulsion against the massacres swept the nation. A number of Catholic peers now joined with the Huguenots to protest the excesses of the crown and the Guises. These Catholics came to be called the *politiques,* from their desire for a practical settlement of the wars. They were led by the duke of Anjou, who was next in line to the throne when Charles IX died in 1574 and Henry III (1574–1589) became king.

Against them, in Paris and a number of other towns, the Catholic League was formed, a society that pledged its first allegiance to religion. The League took up where the Saint Bartholomew's Day Massacre left off, and the slaughter of ordinary people who professed the wrong religion continued. Matters grew worse in 1584 when the duke of Anjou died. With each passing year it was becoming apparent that Henry III would produce no male heir. After the duke's death, the Huguenot Henry of Navarre was the next in line for the throne. Catholic Leaguers talked openly of altering the royal succession and began to develop theories of lawful resistance to monarchical power. By 1585, when the final civil war began—the war of the three Henrys, named for Henry III, Henry Guise, and Henry of Navarre—the crown was in the weakest possible position. Paris and the Catholic towns were controlled by the League, and the Protestant strongholds were controlled by Henry of Navarre. King Henry III could not abandon his capital or his religion, but neither could he gain control of the Catholic party. The extremism of the Leaguers kept the politiques away from court; and without the politiques there could be no settlement.

In December 1588, Henry III summoned Henry Guise and Guise's brother to a meeting in the royal bedchamber. There, they were murdered by the king's order. The politiques were blamed for the murders—revenge was taken on a number of them—and Henry III was forced to flee his capital. He made a pact with Henry of Navarre, and together royalist and Huguenot forces besieged Paris. All supplies were cut off from the city, and only the arrival of a Spanish army prevented its fall. In 1589, Catherine de Médicis died, her ambition to reestablish the authority of the monarchy in shambles, and in the same year a fanatic priest gained revenge for the murder of the Guises by assassinating Henry III.

Henry IV.   Now Henry of Navarre came into his inheritance. But after nearly 30 years of continuous civil war, it was certain that a Huguenot could never rule France. If Henry was to become king of all France, he would have to become a Catholic king. It is not clear when Henry made the decision to accept the Catholic faith—"Paris is worth a Mass," he reportedly declared—but he did not announce his decision at once. Rather, he strengthened his forces, tightened his bonds with the politiques, and urged his countrymen to expel the Spanish invaders. He finally made his conversion public and in 1594 was crowned Henry IV (1589–1610). A war-weary nation was willing to accept him.

In 1598, Henry proclaimed the **Edict of Nantes,** which granted limited toleration to the Huguenots. It was the culmination of decades of attempts to find a solution to the existence of two religions in one state. It was a compromise that satisfied no one, but it was a compromise that everyone could accept. "One king, two faiths" was as apt a description of Henry IV as it was of the settlement. Yet neither Henry's conversion nor the Edict of Nantes stilled the passions that had spawned and sustained the French wars of religion. Sporadic fighting between Catholics and Huguenots continued, and fanatics on both sides fanned the flames of religious hatred. Henry IV survived 18 attempts on his life before he was finally felled by an assassin's knife in 1610, but by then he had established the monarchy and brought a semblance of peace to France.

The World of Philip II

While France was caught up in religious strife, Spain, by the middle of the sixteenth century, had achieved the status of the greatest power in Europe. The dominions of Philip II (1556–1598) of Spain stretched from the Atlantic to the Pacific; his continental territories included the Netherlands in the north and Milan and Naples in Italy. In 1580, Philip became king of Portugal, uniting all the states of the Iberian peninsula. With the addition of Portugal's Atlantic ports and its sizable fleet, Spanish maritime power was now unsur-

CHRONOLOGY	
THE FRENCH WARS OF RELIGION	
1559	Death of Henry II
1560	Protestant duc de Condé sentenced to death
1562	First battle of wars of religion
1563	Catholic duc de Guise assassinated; Edict of Amboise grants limited Protestant worship
1572	Saint Bartholomew's Day Massacre
1574	Accession of Henry III
1576	Formation of Catholic League
1584	Death of duc d'Anjou makes Henry of Navarre heir to throne
1585	War of the three Henrys
1588	Duc de Guise murdered by order of Henry III
1589	Catherine de Médicis dies; Henry III assassinated
1594	Henry IV crowned
1598	Edict of Nantes

MAP DISCOVERY

Habsburg Lands at the Abdication of Charles V

Notice how dispersed were the states controlled by Charles V when he abdicated the throne in 1556. Why do you think he divided his empire between his son Philip II and his brother Ferdinand I? What made it possible for the Netherlands to revolt from Spanish control?

habitat for Calvinist preachers, who made converts across the entire social spectrum. As Holy Roman Emperor, Charles V may have made his peace with Protestants, but as king of Spain he had not. Charles V had maintained the purity of the Spanish Catholic Church through a careful combination of reform and repression.

Philip II intended to pursue a similar policy in the Low Countries. With papal approval, he initiated a scheme to reform the hierarchy of the Church by expanding the numbers of bishops, and he invited the Jesuits to establish schools for orthodox learning. Simultaneously, he strengthened the power of the Inquisition and ordered the enforcement of the decrees of the Council of Trent. The Protestants sought the protection of their local nobles, who, Catholic or Protestant, had their own reasons for opposing the strict enforcement of heresy laws. Provincial nobles and magistrates resented both the policies that were being pursued and the fact that they disregarded local autonomy. Town governors and noblemen refused to cooperate in implementing the new laws.

passed. Philip saw himself as a Catholic monarch fending off the spread of heresy. He came to the throne at just the moment that Calvinism began its rapid growth in northern Europe and provided the impetus for the greatest crisis of his reign: the revolt of the Netherlands.

Though Philip's father, Charles V, amassed a great empire, he had begun only as the duke of Burgundy. Charles's Burgundian inheritance encompassed a diverse territory in the northwestern corner of Europe. The 17 separate provinces of this territory were called the Netherlands, or the Low Countries, because of the flooding that kept large portions of them under water. The Netherlands, one of the richest and most populous regions of Europe, was an international leader in manufacturing, banking, and commerce. In the southern provinces, French was the background and language of the inhabitants; in the northern ones, Germans had settled, and Dutch was spoken.

The Low Countries had accepted the Peace of Augsburg in a spirit of conciliation in which it was never intended. Here, Catholics, Lutherans, Anabaptists, and Calvinists peaceably coexisted. As in France, this situation changed dramatically with the spread of Calvinism. The heavy concentration of urban populations in the Low Countries provided the natural

The Revolt of the Netherlands

The passive resistance of nobles and magistrates was soon matched by the active resistance of the Calvinists. Unable to enforce Philip's policy, Margaret of Parma, his half-sister, whom Philip had made regent, agreed to a limited toleration. But in the summer of 1566, before this toleration could be put into effect, bands of Calvinists unleashed a storm of iconoclasm in the provinces, breaking stained glass windows and statues of the Virgin and the saints, which they claimed were idolatrous. Helpless in the face of determined Calvinists and apathetic Catholics, local authorities could not protect Church property. Iconoclasm gave way to open revolt. Fearing social rebellion, even the leading Protestant noblemen took part in suppressing these riots.

Rebellion and War. In Spain, the events in the Netherlands were treated for what they were: open rebellion. Despite the fact that Margaret had already restored order, Philip II was determined to punish the rebels and enforce the

CHRONOLOGY
REVOLT OF THE NETHERLANDS

1559	Margaret of Parma namedregent of the Netherlands
1566	Calvinist iconoclasm begins revolt
1567	Duke of Alba arrives in Netherlands and establishes Council of Blood
1568	Protestant Count Egmont executed
1572	Protestants capture Holland and Zeeland
1573	Alba relieved of his command
1576	Sack of Antwerp; Pacification of Ghent
1581	Catholic and Protestant provinces split
1585	Spanish forces take Brussels and Antwerp
1609	Twelve Years' Truce

heresy laws. A large military force under the command of the duke of Alba (1507–1582) was sent from Spain as an army of occupation. Alba lured leading Protestant noblemen to Brussels, where he publicly executed them in 1568. He also established a military court to punish participants in the rebellion, a court that came to be called the Council of Blood. The Council handed down over 9,000 convictions, 1,000 of which carried the death penalty. As many as 60,000 Protestants fled beyond Alba's jurisdiction. Alba next made an example of several small towns that had been implicated in the iconoclasm. He allowed his soldiers to pillage the towns at will before slaughtering their entire populations and razing them to the ground. By the end of 1568, royal policy had gained a sullen acceptance in the Netherlands, but for the next 80 years, with only occasional truces, Spain and the Netherlands were at war.

The Protestants Rebel. Alba's policies had driven Protestants into rebellion, and this forced the Spanish government to maintain its army by raising taxes from the provinces that had remained loyal. Soon the loyal provinces were also in revolt, not over religion but over taxation and local autonomy. Tax resistance and fear of an invasion from France left Alba unprepared for the series of successful assaults Protestants launched in the northern provinces during 1572. The Protestant generals established a permanent base in the north-western provinces of Holland and Zeeland. By 1575, they had gained a stronghold that they would never relinquish. Prince William of Orange (1533–1584) assumed the leadership of the two provinces, which were now united against the tyranny of Philip's rule.

Spanish government was collapsing all over the Netherlands. William ruled in the north, and the States-General, a parliamentary body composed of representatives from the separate provinces, ruled in the south. Margaret of Parma had resigned in disgust at Alba's tactics, and Alba had been relieved of his command when his tactics failed. No one was in control of the Spanish army. The soldiers, who had gone years with only partial pay, now roamed the southern provinces looking for plunder. Brussels and Ghent had both been targets, and in 1576 the worst atrocities of all occurred when mutinous Spanish troops sacked Antwerp. Over 7,000 people were slaughtered, and nearly one-third of the city burned to the ground.

The "Spanish fury" in Antwerp effectively ended Philip's rule over his Burgundian inheritance. The Protestants had established a permanent home in the north. The States-General had established its ability to rule in the south, and Spanish policy had been totally discredited. To achieve a settlement, the Pacification of Ghent of 1576, the Spanish government conceded local autonomy in taxation, the central role of the States-General in legislation, and the immediate withdrawal of all Spanish troops from the Low Countries. This rift among the provinces was soon followed by a permanent split. In 1581, one group of provinces voted to depose Philip II while a second group decided to remain loyal to him. Philip II refused to accept the dismemberment of his inheritance or to recognize the independent Dutch state that now existed in Holland.

Meanwhile, Protestant England under Elizabeth I (1558–1603) had sided with the Dutch Protestants opposing Philip II. During Elizabeth's reign, England and Spain entered a long period of hostility. English pirates raided Spanish treasure ships returning to Europe, and Elizabeth covertly aided both French and Dutch Protestants. Finally, in 1588, Philip decided to invade England. A great fleet set sail from the Portuguese coast to the Netherlands, where a large Spanish army was waiting to be conveyed to England.

The **Spanish Armada** comprised over 130 ships, many of them the pride of the Spanish and Portuguese navies. They were bigger and stronger than anything possessed by the English, whose forces were largely merchant vessels hastily converted for battle. But the English ships were faster and more easily maneuverable in the unpredictable winds of the English Channel. They also carried guns that could easily be reloaded for multiple firings, whereas the Spanish guns were designed to discharge only one broadside before hand-to-hand combat ensued. With these advantages, the English were able to prevent the Armada from reaching port in the Netherlands and to destroy many individual ships as they were blown off course.

Throughout the 1580s and 1590s, Spanish military expeditions attempted to reunite the southern provinces and to conquer the northern ones. But Spanish successes in the south were outweighed by the long-term failure of their objectives in the north. In 1609, Spain and the Netherlands concluded the Twelve Years' Truce, which tacitly recognized the existence

■ The defeat of the immense armada that Philip II sent to invade England in 1588 dealt a serious blow to Spain's standing in Europe.

of the state of Holland. By the beginning of the seventeenth century, Holland was not only an independent state; it was one of the greatest rivals of Spain and Portugal.

THE STRUGGLES IN EASTERN EUROPE

In eastern Europe, dynastic struggles outweighed the problems created by religious reform. Muscovy remained the bulwark of Eastern Orthodox Christianity, immune from the struggles over the Roman faith. Protestantism did spread into Poland-Lithuania, but its presence was tolerated by the Polish state. The spread of dissent was checked not by repression, but by a vigorous Catholic reformation led by the Jesuits. The domestic crises in the East were crises of state rather than of the Church. In Muscovy, the disputed succession that followed the death of Ivan the Terrible plunged the state into anarchy and civil war. Centuries of conflict between Poland-Lithuania and Muscovy came to a head with the Poles' desperate gamble to seize control of their massive eastern neighbor. War between Poland-Lithuania and Muscovy inevitably dominated the politics of the entire region. The Baltic states, most notably Sweden, soon joined the fray.

Kings and Diets in Poland

Until the end of the sixteenth century, Poland-Lithuania was the dominant power in the eastern part of Europe. It was economically healthy and militarily strong. Through its Baltic ports, especially Gdansk, Poland played a central role in international commerce and a dominant role in the northern grain trade. The vast size of the Polish state made defense difficult, and during the course of the sixteenth century it had lost lands to Muscovy in the east and to the Crimean Tatars in the south. But the permanent union with Lithuania in 1569 and the gradual absorption of the Baltic region of Livonia more than compensated for these losses. Matters of war and peace, of taxation, and of reform were placed under the strict supervision of the Polish Diet, a parliamentary body that represented the Polish landed elite. The diet also carefully controlled religious policy. Roman Catholicism was the principal religion in Poland, but the state tolerated numerous Protestant and Eastern creeds. In the Warsaw Confederation of 1573, the Polish gentry vowed "that we who differ in matters of religion will keep the peace among ourselves."

The biological failure of the Jagiellon monarchy in Poland ended that nation's most successful line of kings. Without a natural heir, the Polish nobility and gentry, who officially

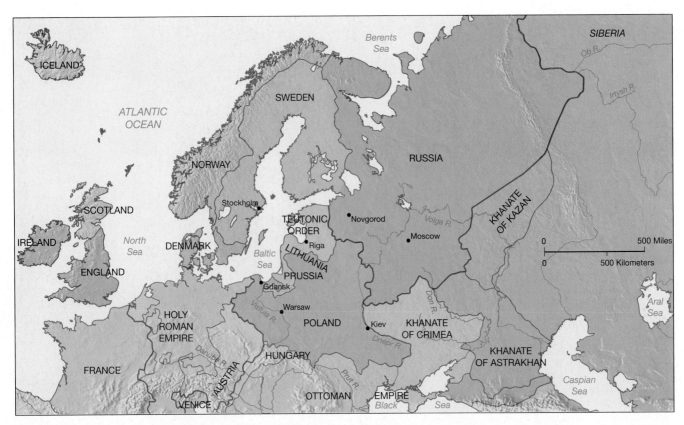

■ Eastern Europe (ca. 1550) after the consolidation of Russia and the growth of Poland. The eastern part of Europe was still sparsely populated and economically underdeveloped.

elected the monarch, had to peddle their throne among the princes of Europe. When Sigismund III (1587–1632) was elected to the Polish throne in 1587, he was also heir to the crown of Sweden. Sigismund accepted the prohibitions against religious repression outlined in the Warsaw Confederation, but he actively encouraged the establishment of Jesuit schools, the expansion of monastic orders, and the strengthening of the Roman Catholic Church.

All of these policies enjoyed the approval of the Polish ruling classes. But the diet would not support Sigismund's efforts to gain control of the Swedish crown, which he inherited in 1592 but from which he was deposed three years later. If Sigismund triumphed in Sweden, all Poland would get was a part-time monarch. The Polish Diet consistently refused to give the king the funds necessary to invade Sweden successfully. Nevertheless, Sigismund mounted several unsuccessful campaigns against the Swedes that sapped Polish money and manpower.

Muscovy's Time of Troubles

The wars of Ivan the Great and Ivan the Terrible in the fifteenth and sixteenth centuries were waged to secure agricultural territory in the west and a Baltic port in the north. Both objectives came at the expense of Poland-Lithuania. But after the death of Ivan the Terrible in 1584, the Muscovite state began to disintegrate. For years it had been held together only by

conquest and fear. Ivan's conflicts with the boyars, the hereditary nobility, created an aristocracy that was unwilling and unable to come to the aid of Ivan's successors. By 1601, the crown was plunged into a crisis of legitimacy known as the **Time of Troubles.** Ivan had murdered his heir in a fit of anger and left his half-witted son to inherit the throne. This led to a vacuum of power at the center as well as a struggle for the spoils of government. Private armies ruled great swaths of the state, and pretenders to the crown—all claiming to be Dimitri, the lost brother of the last legitimate tsar—appeared everywhere. Ambitious groups of boyars backed their own claimants to the throne. So, too, did ambitious foreigners who eagerly sought to carve up Muscovite possessions.

Muscovy's Time of Troubles was Poland's moment of opportunity. While Muscovy floundered in anarchy and civil war, Poland looked to regain the territory that it had lost to Muscovy over the previous century. Sigismund abandoned war with Sweden to intervene in the struggle for the Russian crown. Polish forces crossed into Muscovy, and Sigismund's generals backed one of the strongest of the false Dimitris, but their plan to put him on the throne failed when he was assassinated. Sigismund used the death of the last false Dimitri as a pretext to assert his own claim to the Muscovite crown. More Polish forces poured across the frontier. In 1610, they took Moscow, and Sigismund proclaimed himself tsar, intending to unite the two massive states.

The Russian boyars, so long divided, now rose against the Polish enemy. The Polish garrison in Moscow was starved into submission, and a native Russian, Michael Romanov (1613–1645), was chosen tsar by an assembly of landholders, the Zemsky Sobor. He made a humiliating peace with the Swedes—who had also taken advantage of the Time of Troubles to invade Muscovy's Baltic provinces—in return for Swedish assistance against the Poles. Intermittent fighting continued for another 20 years. In the end, Poland agreed to peace and a separate Muscovite state but only in exchange for large territorial concessions.

The Rise of Sweden

Sweden's rise to power during the seventeenth century was as startling as it was swift. Until the Reformation, Sweden had been part of the Scandinavian confederation ruled by the Danes. Although the Swedes had a measure of autonomy, they were very much a junior partner in Baltic affairs. Denmark controlled the narrow sound that linked the Baltic Sea with the North Sea, and its prosperity derived from the tolls it collected on imports and exports. When, in 1523, Gustav I Vasa led the uprising of the Swedish aristocracy that ended Danish domination, he won the right to rule over a poor, sparsely populated state with few towns or developed seaports. The Vasas ruled Sweden in conjunction with the aristocracy. Although the throne was hereditary, the part played by the nobility in elevating Gustav I Vasa (1523–1560) gave the nobles a powerful voice in Swedish affairs. Through the council of state, known as the Rad, the Swedish nobility exerted a strong check on the monarch.

Sweden's aggressive foreign policy began accidentally. When in the 1550s the Teutonic Knights found themselves no longer capable of ruling in Livonia, the Baltic seaports that had been under their dominion scrambled for new alliances. Muscovy and Poland-Lithuania were the logical choices, but the town of Reval, an important outlet for Russian trade near the mouth of the Gulf of Finland, asked Sweden for protection. After some hesitation, since the occupation of territory on the southern shores of the Baltic would involve great expense, Sweden fortified Reval in 1560. A decade later, Swedish forces captured Narva, farther to the east, and consolidated Sweden's hold on the Livonian coast. By occupying the most important ports on the Gulf of Finland, Sweden could control a sizable portion of the Muscovite trade. As the Swedes secured the northern Livonian ports, more of the Muscovy trade moved to the south and passed through Riga, which would have to be captured or blockaded if the Swedes were to control commerce in the eastern Baltic.

Sigismund's aggressive alliance with the Polish Jesuits had persuaded the Swedish nobility that he would undermine their Lutheran church, and Sigismund was deposed in favor of his uncle Charles IX (1604–1611). War between Sweden and Poland resulted from Sigismund's efforts to regain the Swedish crown, and the Swedes used the opportunity to blockade Riga and to occupy more Livonian territory. The

■ The Rise of Sweden. For the only time in its history, Sweden acquired territories on the European mainland.

Swedish navy was far superior to any force that the Poles could assemble, but on land, Polish forces were masters. The Swedish invasion force suffered a crushing defeat and had to retreat to its coastal enclaves. The Poles now had an opportunity to retake all of Livonia, but, as always, the Polish Diet was reluctant to finance Sigismund's wars. Furthermore, Sigismund had his eyes on a bigger prize. Rather than follow up its Swedish victory, Poland invaded Muscovy.

Meanwhile, the blockade of Riga and the assembly of a large Swedish fleet in the Baltic threatened Denmark. The Danes continued to claim sovereignty over Sweden and took the opportunity of the Polish-Swedish conflict to reassert it. In 1611, under the energetic leadership of the Danish king Christian IV (1588–1648), Denmark invaded Sweden from both the east and the west. The Danes captured the towns of Kalmar and Alvsborg and threatened to take Stockholm. To end the Danish war, Sweden accepted humiliating terms in 1613, renouncing all claims to the northern coasts and recognizing Danish control of the Arctic trading route.

Paradoxically, these setbacks became the springboard for Swedish success. Fear of the Danes led both the English and the Dutch into alliances with Sweden. These countries all shared Protestant interests, and the English were heavily committed to the Muscovy trade, which was still an important part of Swedish commerce. Fear of the Poles had a similar effect on Muscovy. In 1609, the Swedes agreed to send 5,000 troops to Muscovy to help repel the Polish invasion. In return, Muscovy agreed to cede to Sweden its Baltic possessions. This was accomplished in 1617 and gave Sweden complete control of the Gulf of Finland.

In 1611, during the middle of the Danish war, Charles IX died and was succeeded by his son Gustavus Adolphus (1611–1632), one of the leading Protestant princes of his day. Gustavus's greatest skills were military, and he inherited an ample navy and an effective army. Unlike nearly every other European state, Sweden raised its forces from its own citizens. Gustavus introduced new weapons such as the light mobile gun and reshaped his army into standard-size squadrons and regiments, which were easier to administer and deploy.

The calamitous wars that Gustavus inherited from his father occupied him during the early years of his reign. He was forced to conclude the humiliating peace with the Danes in 1613 and to go to war with the Russians in 1614 to secure the Baltic coastal estates that had been promised in 1609. Gustavus's first military initiative was to resume war with Poland to force Sigismund to renounce his claim to the Swedish throne. In 1621, Gustavus landed in Livonia and in two weeks captured Riga, the capstone of Sweden's Baltic ambitions. Occupation of Riga increased Swedish control of the Muscovy trade and deprived Denmark of a significant portion of its customs duties. Gustavus now claimed Riga as a Swedish port and successfully demanded that ships sailing from there pay tolls to Sweden rather than Denmark. By the mid-seventeenth century, Sweden ranked among the leading Protestant powers.

THE THIRTY YEARS' WAR, 1618–1648

In time, the isolated conflicts that dotted the corners of Europe were joined together. In 1609, Spain and the Dutch Republic had signed a truce that was to last until 1621. In over 40 years of nearly continuous fighting, the Dutch had carved out a state in the northern Netherlands. They used the truce to consolidate their position and increase their prosperity. Spain had reluctantly accepted Dutch independence, but Philip III (1598–1621), like his father before him, never abandoned the objective of recovering his Burgundian inheritance. By the beginning of the seventeenth century, Philip had good reasons for hope. Beginning in the 1580s, Spanish forces had reconquered the southern provinces of the Netherlands. The prosperous towns of Brussels, Antwerp, and Ghent were again under Spanish control, and they provided a springboard for another invasion.

The Twelve Years' Truce gave Spain time to prepare for the final assault. During this time, Philip III attempted to resolve all of Spain's other European conflicts so that he could then give full attention to a resumption of the Dutch war. Circumstance smiled on his efforts. In 1603, the pacific James I (1603–1625) came to the English throne. Secure in his island state, James I desired peace among all Christian princes. He quickly concluded the war with Spain that had begun with the

attempted invasion of the Spanish Armada, and he entered into negotiations to marry his heir to a Spanish princess. In 1610, the bellicose Henry IV of France was felled by an assassin's knife. French plans to renew war with Spain were abandoned with the accession of the eight-year-old Louis XIII (1610–1643). The **Thirty Years' War** was about to begin.

Bohemia Revolts

The Peace of Augsburg had served the German states well. The principle that the religion of the ruler was the religion of the state complicated the political life of the Holy Roman Empire, but it also pacified it. Though rulers had the right to enforce uniformity on their subjects, in practice many of the larger states tolerated more than one religion. By the beginning of the seventeenth century, Catholicism and Protestantism had achieved a rough equality within the German states, symbolized by the fact that of the seven electors who chose the Holy Roman Emperor, three were Catholic, three were Protestant, and the seventh was the emperor himself, acting as king of Bohemia. This situation was not unwelcome to the leaders of the Austrian Habsburg family who succeeded Emperor Charles V. By necessity, the eastern Habsburgs were more tolerant than their Spanish kinfolk. The head of their house was elected king of Bohemia and king of Hungary, both states with large Protestant populations.

A Fatal Election. In 1617, Mathias, the childless Holy Roman Emperor, began making plans for his cousin, Ferdinand Habsburg, to succeed him. Ferdinand was a very devout and very committed Catholic. To ensure a Catholic majority among the electors, the emperor relinquished his Bohemian title and pressed for Ferdinand's election as the new king of Bohemia. The Protestant nobles of Bohemia forced the new king to accept the strictest limitations on his political and religious powers, but once elected, Ferdinand had not the slightest intention of honoring the provisions that had been thrust on him. His opponents were equally strong willed. When Ferdinand violated Protestant religious liberties, a group of noblemen marched to the royal palace in Prague in May 1618, found two of the king's chief advisers, and hurled them out of an upper-story window.

The Defenestration of Prague, as this incident came to be known, initiated a Protestant counteroffensive throughout the Habsburg lands. Fear of Ferdinand's policies led to Protestant uprisings in Hungary as well as Bohemia. The men who seized control of the government declared Ferdinand deposed and the throne vacant. But they had no candidate to accept their crown. Whatever their religion, princes were always uneasy about the overthrow of a lawful ruler. Whoever came to be called king of Bohemia in place of Ferdinand would have to face the combined might of the Habsburgs. When Emperor Mathias died in 1619, Ferdinand succeeded to the imperial title as Ferdinand II (1619–1637), and Frederick V, one of the Protestant electors, accepted the Bohemian crown.

WAR IS HELL

No source has better captured the brutality of the Thirty Years' War than the novel Simplicissimus *(1669). In a series of loosely connected episodes, the hero (whose name means "the simplest of the simple") is snatched from his village to serve in marauding armies whose confrontations with local villagers are usually more horrifying than the episode narrated here.*

Focus Questions

How do the peasants respond to the troopers' actions? What does this passage suggest about the breadth of the average villager's experience?

These troopers were even now ready to march, and had the pastor fastened by a rope to lead him away. Some cried, "Shoot him down, the rogue!" Others would have money from him. But he, lifting up his hands to heaven, begged, for the sake of the Last Judgment, for forbearance and Christian compassion, but in vain; for one of them rode down and dealt him such a blow on the head that he fell flat, and commended his soul to God. Nor did the remainder of the captured peasants fare any better. But even when it seemed these troopers, in their cruel tyranny, had clean lost their wits, came such a swarm of armed peasants out of the wood, that it seemed a wasps'-nest had been stirred. And these began to yell so frightfully and so furiously to attack with sword and musket that all my hair stood on end; and never had I been at such a merrymaking before: for the peasants of the Spessart and the Vogelsberg are as little wont as are the Hessians and men of the Sauerland and the Black Forest to let themselves be crowed over on their own dunghill. So away went the troopers, and not only left behind the cattle they had captured, but threw away bag and baggage also, and so cast all their booty to the winds lest themselves should become booty for the peasants: yet some of them fell into their hands. This sport took from me well-nigh all desire to see the world, for I thought, if 'tis all like this, then is the wilderness far more pleasant.

From Hans Von Grimmelshausen, *The Adventurous Simplicissimus.*

Frederick V, the "Winter King."

Frederick was a sincere but weak Calvinist whose credentials were much stronger than his abilities. His mother was a daughter of Prince William of Orange and his wife, Elizabeth, was a daughter of James I of England. It was widely believed that Elizabeth's resolution that she would "rather eat sauerkraut with a king than roast meat with an elector" decided the issue. No decision could have been more disastrous for the fate of Europe. Frederick ruled a geographically divided German state known as the Palatinate. One hundred miles separated the two segments of his lands, but both were strategically important. The Lower Palatinate bordered on the Catholic Spanish Netherlands and the Upper Palatinate on Catholic Bavaria.

Once Frederick accepted the Bohemian crown, he was faced with a war on three fronts. Ferdinand II had no difficulty enlisting allies to recover the Bohemian crown, since he could pay them with the spoils of Frederick's lands. Spanish troops from the Netherlands occupied the Lower Palatinate, and Bavarian troops occupied the Upper Palatinate. Frederick, by contrast, met rejection wherever he turned. Neither the Dutch nor the English would send more than token aid; both had advised him against breaking the imperial peace. The Lutheran princes of Germany would not enter into a war between Calvinists and Catholics, especially after Ferdinand II promised to protect the Bohemian Lutherans.

At the Battle of the White Mountain in 1620, Ferdinand's Catholic forces annihilated Frederick's army. Frederick and Elizabeth fled to Denmark, and Bohemia was left to face the wrath of Ferdinand, the victorious king and emperor. The retribution was horrible. Mercenaries who had fought for Ferdinand II were allowed to sack Prague for a week. Elective monarchy was abolished, and Bohemia became part of the hereditary Habsburg lands. Free peasants were enserfed and subjected to imperial law. Nobles who had supported Frederick lost their lands and their privileges. Calvinism was repressed and thoroughly rooted out, consolidating forever the Catholic character of Bohemia. Frederick's estates were carved up, and his rights as elector were transferred to the Catholic duke of Bavaria. The Battle of the White Mountain was a turning point in the history of central Europe, for it forced all Protestant nations to arm for war.

The War Widens

For the Habsburgs, religious and dynastic interests were inseparable. Ferdinand II and Philip III of Spain fought for their beliefs and for their patrimony. Their victory gave them more than they could have expected. Ferdinand swallowed up Bohemia and strengthened his position in the empire. Philip gained possession of a vital link in his supply route between Italy and the Netherlands. Spanish expansion threatened France. The occupation of the Lower Palatinate placed a ring of Spanish armies around France from the Pyrenees to the Low Countries. The French too searched for allies. But French

CHRONOLOGY
THE THIRTY YEARS' WAR

1618	Defenestration of Prague
1619	Ferdinand Habsburg elected Holy Roman Emperor; Frederick of the Palatinate accepts the crown of Bohemia
1620	Catholic victory at battle of the White Mountain
1621	End of Twelve Years' Truce; war between Spain and Netherlands
1626	Danes form Protestant alliance under Christian IV
1627	Spain declares bankruptcy
1630	Gustavus Adolphus leads Swedish forces into Germany
1631	Sack of Magdeburg; Protestant victory at Breitenfeld
1632	Protestant victory at Lützen; death of Gustavus Adolphus
1635	France declares war on Spain
1640	Portugal secedes from Spain
1643	Battle of Rocroi; French forces repel Spaniards
1648	Peace of Westphalia

opinion remained divided over which was the greater evil: Spain or Protestantism.

The Danes Respond.   Frederick, now in Holland, refused to accept the judgment of battle. He lobbied for a grand alliance to repel the Spaniards from the Lower Palatinate and to restore the religious balance in the empire. Though his personal cause met with little sympathy, his political logic was impeccable, especially after Spain again declared war on the Dutch. A grand Protestant alliance—secretly supported by the French—brought together England, Holland, a number of German states, and Denmark. It was the Danes who led this potentially powerful coalition. In 1626, a large Danish army under the command of King Christian IV engaged imperial forces on German soil. But Danish forces could not match the superior numbers and the superior leadership of the Catholic mercenary forces under the command of the ruthless and brilliant Count Albrecht von Wallenstein (1583–1634). In 1629, the Danes withdrew from the empire and sued for peace.

If the Catholic victory at the White Mountain in 1620 threatened the well-being of German Protestantism, the Catholic triumph over the Danes threatened its survival. More powerful than ever, Ferdinand II was determined to turn the religious clock back to the state of affairs that had existed when the Peace of Augsburg was concluded in 1555. He demanded that all lands that had then been Catholic but had since become Protestant must now be returned to the Catholic fold. He also proclaimed that because the Peace of Augsburg made no provision for the toleration of Calvinists, they would no longer be tolerated in the empire. These policies together constituted a virtual revolution in the religious affairs of the German states, and they proved impossible to impose. Ferdinand succeeded in only one thing: he united Lutherans and Calvinists against him. Moreover, the costs of the war were heavy even for the victors. Wallenstein, who had over 130,000 men in arms, would no longer take orders from anyone, and Ferdinand II was forced to dismiss him from service.

Protestant Gains.   In 1630, King Gustavus Adolphus of Sweden decided to enter the German conflict to protect Swedish interests. While Gustavus Adolphus struggled to construct his alliance, imperial forces continued their triumphant progress. In 1631, they besieged, captured, and put to the torch the town of Magdeburg. Perhaps three-fourths of the 40,000 inhabitants of the town were brutally slaughtered. The sack of Magdeburg marked a turning point in Protestant fortunes. It gave the international Protestant community a unifying symbol that enhanced Gustavus's military efforts. Brandenburg and Saxony joined Gustavus Adolphus, allowing him to open a second front in Bohemia. In the autumn of 1631, this combination overwhelmed the imperial armies. Gustavus won a decisive triumph at Breitenfeld, while the Saxons occupied Prague.

Gustavus Adolphus lost no time in pressing his advantage. While Ferdinand II pleaded with Wallenstein to again lead the imperial forces, the Swedes marched west to the Rhine, easily conquering the richest of the Catholic cities and retaking the Lower Palatinate. In early 1632, Protestant forces plundered Bavaria, but Wallenstein resumed his command and chose to chase the Saxons from Bohemia rather than the Swedes from Bavaria. Not until the winter of 1632 did the armies of Gustavus and Wallenstein finally meet. At the Battle of Lützen, the Swedes won the field but lost their beloved king. Wounded in the leg, the back, and the head, Gustavus Adolphus died. In less than two years he had decisively transformed the course of the war and the course of Europe's future. Protestant forces now occupied most of central and northern Germany.

The Long Quest for Peace

The final stages of the war involved the resumption of the century-old struggle between France and Spain. When the Twelve Years' Truce expired in 1621, Spain again declared war on the Dutch. Dutch naval power was considerable, and the Dutch took the war to the far reaches of the globe, attacking

Portuguese settlements in Brazil and in the East and harassing Spanish shipping on the high seas. In 1628, the Dutch captured the entire Spanish treasure fleet as it sailed from the New World. Spain had declared bankruptcy in 1627, and the loss of the whole of the next year's treasure from America exacerbated an already catastrophic situation.

These reversals, combined with the continued successes of Habsburg forces in central Europe, convinced Louis XIII and his chief minister, Cardinal Richelieu, that the time for active involvement in European affairs was now at hand. Throughout the early stages of the war, France had secretly aided anti-Habsburg forces. Gustavus Adolphus's unexpected success dramatically altered French calculations. Now it was evident that the Habsburgs could no longer combine their might, and Spanish energies would be drained off in the Netherlands and central Europe. The time had come to take an open stand. In 1635, France declared war on Spain.

■ Gustavus Adolphus of Sweden, shown at the battle of Breitenfeld in 1631. The battle was the first important Protestant victory of the Thirty Years' War. Gustavus died on the battlefield at Lützen in the following year.

France took the offensive first, invading the Spanish Netherlands. In 1636, a Spanish army struck back, pushing to within 25 miles of Paris before it was repelled. Both sides soon began to search for a settlement, but pride prevented them from laying down their arms. Spain toppled first. Its economy in shambles and its citizens in revolt over high prices and higher taxes, it could no longer maintain its many-fronted war. The Swedes again defeated imperial forces in Germany. The Dutch destroyed much of Spain's Atlantic fleet in 1639, and the Portuguese rose up against the union of crowns that had brought them nothing but expense and the loss of crucial portions of their empire. In 1640, the Portuguese regained their independence. In 1643, Spain gambled once more on a knockout blow against the French. But at the Battle of Rocroi, exhausted French troops held out, and the Spanish invasion failed.

By now, the desire for peace was universal. Most of the main combatants had long since perished: Philip III, ever optimistic, in 1621; Frederick V, an exile to the end, in 1632; Gustavus Adolphus, killed at Lutzen in the same year; Wallenstein, murdered by order of Ferdinand II in 1634; Ferdinand himself in 1637; and Louis XIII in 1643, five days before the French triumph at Rocroi. Those who succeeded them did not have the same passions, and after so many decades the longing for peace was the strongest emotion on the Continent.

In 1648 a series of agreements, collectively known as the Peace of Westphalia, established the outlines of the political geography of Europe for the next century. Its focus was on the Holy Roman Empire, and it reflected Protestant successes in the final two decades of war. Sweden gained further territories on the Baltic, making it master of the north German ports. France, too, gained in territory and prestige. It kept the vital towns in the Lower Palatinate through which Spanish men and matériel had moved, and though it did not agree to come to terms with Spain immediately, France's fear of encirclement was at an end. The Dutch gained statehood through official recognition by Spain and through the power they had displayed in building and maintaining an overseas empire.

Territorial boundaries were reestablished as they had existed in 1624, giving the Habsburgs control of both Bohemia and Hungary. The independence of the Swiss cantons was now officially recognized as were the rights of Calvinists to the protection of the Peace of Augsburg, which again was to govern the religious affairs of the empire. Two of the larger German states were strengthened as a counterweight to the emperor's power. Bavaria was allowed to retain the Upper Palatinate, and

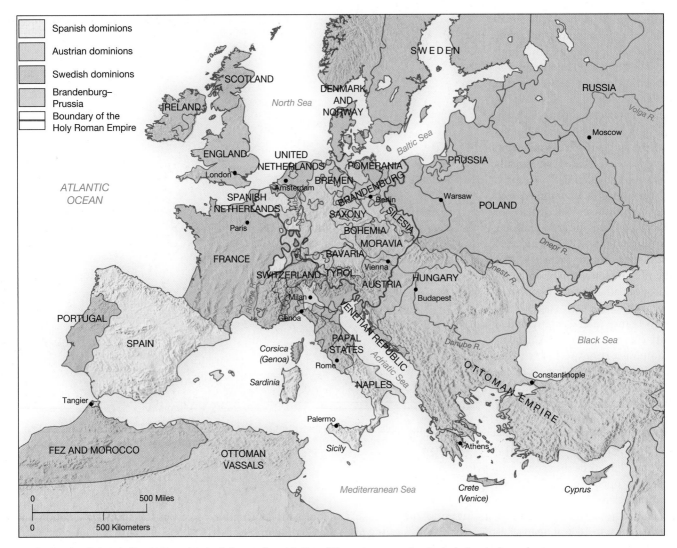

■ The Peace of Westphalia, 1648, recognized the new boundaries of European states that included an independent Portugal and the United Netherlands. It also recognized the growth of the Ottoman Empire into the Balkans.

Brandenburg, which ceded some of its coastal territory to Sweden, gained extensive territories in the east. The emperor's political control over the German states was also weakened. German rulers were given independent authority over their states and the imperial diet, rather than the emperor, was empowered to settle disputes. Thus weakened, future emperors ruled in the Habsburg territorial lands with little ability to control, or influence, or even arbitrate German affairs. The judgment that the Holy Roman Empire was neither holy, nor Roman, nor an empire was now irrevocably true.

CONCLUSION

The Peace of Westphalia put the pieces of the map of European states back together. Protestantism and Catholicism now coexisted, and there was to be little further change in the geography of religion. The northwest of Europe—England,

Holland, Scandinavia, and the north German states—was Protestant; the south was Catholic. The empire of the German peoples was now at an end, and the Austro-Hungarian empire was at a beginning. Holland and Sweden had become international powers; Spain and Denmark faded from prominence. Muscovy began a long period of isolation from the West as it attempted to restore a semblance of government to its people.

The costs of the century of nearly continuous warfare were horrific. The population of Germany fell from 15 million in 1600 to 11 million in 1650. The armies brought destruction of all kinds in their wake. Plague again raged in Europe; the town of Augsburg lost 18,000 inhabitants in the early 1630s. Famine, too, returned to a continent that 50 years earlier had been self-sufficient in grain. The war played havoc with all of the economies that it touched. Inflation, devaluation of coinage, and huge public and private debts were all directly attributable to the years of fighting. Furthermore, the toll taken on the spirit of generations that never knew peace is incalculable.

QUESTIONS FOR REVIEW

1. How was Henry IV able to bring peace to France after decades of civil war?
2. What were the political and religious connections between the Armada launched against England by Philip II and the revolt of the Netherlands?
3. How did Sweden rise to become one of Europe's great powers in the first half of the seventeenth century?
4. How did religion help spark and spread the Thirty Years' War?
5. What were the effects of the Peace of Westphalia on political arrangements in the heart of Europe?

KEY TERMS

Edict of Nantes, *p. 284*

French wars of religion, *p. 282*

Huguenots, *p. 283*

politiques, *p. 284*

Spanish Armada, *p. 286*

Thirty Years' War, *p. 290*

Time of Troubles, *p. 288*

DISCOVERING WESTERN CIVILIZATION ONLINE

You can obtain more information about Europe at war at the websites listed below. See also the Companion Website that accompanies this text, www.ablongman.com/kishlansky, which contains an online study guide and additional resources.

The Crises of the Western States

Internet Modern History Sourcebook: Early Modern West
www.fordham.edu/halsall/mod/modsbook1.html#Conflict
Links to documents on the French wars of religion, the invasion of the Spanish Armada, and the Thirty Years' War.

WebMuseum: The Northern Renaissance (1500–1615)
www.ibiblio.org/wm/paint/tl/north-ren/
Links to pictures and portraits from the late sixteenth and early seventeenth centuries.

Pieter Bruegel the Elder: *The Triumph of Death*
www.ibiblio.org/wm/paint/auth/bruegel/death.jpg
A web page depicting Peter Brueghel's *Triumph of Death,* one of the most evocative paintings of the destruction wrought by warfare in early modern Europe.

The Thirty Years' War, 1618–1648

The Avalon Project: Treaty of Westphalia
www.yale.edu/lawweb/avalon/westphal.htm
The full text of the Treaty of Westphalia that ended the Thirty Years' War.

SUGGESTIONS FOR FURTHER READING

General Reading

M. S. Anderson, *The Origins of the Modern European State System, 1494–1618* (London: Longman, 1998). A survey of developments stressing war and diplomacy across all of Europe.

Jan de Vries, *The European Economy in an Age of Crisis* (Cambridge: Cambridge University Press, 1976). A comprehensive study of economic development, including long-distance trade and commercial change.

J. H. Elliott, *Europe Divided, 1559–1598* (New York: Harper & Row, 1968). An outstanding synthesis of European politics in the second half of the sixteenth century.

Geoffrey Parker, *Europe in Crisis, 1598–1648* (London: William Collins and Sons, 1979). Compelling study of European states in the early seventeenth century.

The Crises of the Western States

Susan Brigden, *New Worlds, Lost Worlds: The Rule of the Tudors, 1485–1603* (New York: Viking, 2001). The latest volume in the new Penguin History of Britain series.

J. A. Guy, *Tudor England* (Oxford: Oxford University Press, 1988). A magisterial survey by the leading scholar of Tudor England.

Henry Kamen, *Spain, 1469–1714* (London: Longman, 1983). A thorough survey with valuable interpretations.

Robert Kingdon, *Myths about the St. Bartholomew's Day Massacres, 1572–76* (Cambridge, MA: Harvard University Press, 1988). A study of the impact of a central event in the history of France.

R. J. Knecht, *The French Civil Wars, 1562–1598* (New York: Pearson Education, 2000). A compact survey of the religious, social, and political dimensions of the conflicts that raged in France through the second half of the sixteenth century.

John Lynch, *Spain, 1516–1598: From Nation State to World Empire* (Cambridge, MA: Blackwell, 1994). An expert survey.

Garrett Mattingly, *The Armada* (Boston: Houghton Mifflin, 1959). Still the classic account, despite recent reinterpretations.

Geoffrey Parker, *The Dutch Revolt* (London: Penguin Books, 1977). An outstanding account of the tangle of events that comprised the revolts of the Netherlands.

Geoffrey Parker, *Philip II* (Boston: Little, Brown, 1978). The best introduction.

Michael Roberts, *Gustavus Adolphus and the Rise of Sweden* (London: English Universities Press, 1973). A highly readable account of Sweden's rise to power.

C. V. Wedgwood, *William the Silent, William of Nassau, Prince of Orange, 1533–1584* (New York: Norton, 1968). A stylish biography.

Alison Weir, *Elizabeth the Queen* (London: J. Cape, 1998). A lively biography of the great queen.

The Struggles in Eastern Europe

David Kirby, *Northern Europe in the Early Modern Period: The Baltic World, 1492–1772* (London: Longman, 1990). The best single volume on Baltic politics.

S. F. Platonov, *The Time of Troubles* (Lawrence: University Press of Kansas, 1970). A good narrative of the disintegration of the Muscovite state.

Michael Roberts, *The Swedish Imperial Experience* (Cambridge: Cambridge University Press, 1979). Reflections on Swedish history by the preeminent historian of early modern Sweden.

The Thirty Years' War

J. H. Elliott, *Richelieu and Olivares* (Cambridge: Cambridge University Press, 1984). A comparison of statesmen and statesmanship in the early seventeenth century.

Peter Limm, *The Thirty Years' War* (London: Longman, 1984). An excellent brief survey with documents.

Geoffrey Parker, ed., *The Thirty Years' War*, 2nd ed. (London: Routledge, 1997). A revised edition of the standard survey of the conflict.

For a list of additional titles related to this chapter's topics, please see www.ablongman.com/kishlansky**.**

Chapter 15

THE EXPERIENCES OF LIFE IN EARLY MODERN EUROPE, 1500–1650

The Visual Record

HAYMAKING

It is summer in the low countries. The trees are full, the meadows are green, and bushes hang heavy with fruit. The day has dawned brightly for haymaking. Yesterday, the long meadow was mowed. Today, the hay will be gathered, and the first fruits and vegetables of the season will be harvested. From throughout the village, families come together in labor. Twice each summer, the grass is cut, dried, and stacked. Some of it will be left in the fields for the animals until autumn; some will be carried into large lofts and stored for the winter.

This scene of communal farming was repeated with little variation throughout Europe in the sixteenth century. The village we are viewing is fairly prosperous. We can see at least three horses (still a luxury for farmers) and a large wheeled cart. The houses of the village also suggest comfort. The one at the far right is typical. It contains one floor for living and a loft for storage. The chimney separates a kitchen in the back from the long hall where the family works, sleeps, and entertains itself. The bed—it is not uncommon for there to be only one for the whole family—is probably located near the fireplace. It will be restuffed with straw after the harvest. The spinning wheel probably stands near the single window, which is covered by oiled animal skin, since glass is still much too expensive for use in rural housing. The long end of the hall, farthest from heat and light, will be home to the family's animals once winter sets in. But now, in summer, it is a luxurious space where children can play or parents can claim a little privacy.

The church, easily distinguished by its steeple and arched doorway, is made of brick. The steeple has 16 windows, probably all set with expensive glass and some even with stained glass. The church would have been built over several generations at considerable cost to the villagers. Even the most prosperous houses in the far meadow are all made of timber and thatch, and only the village well, in the middle of the picture, and the chimneys of the houses show any other sign of brick.

In the center of the scene are a large number of laborers. Four men with pitchforks load the cart while two women sweep the hay that falls back into new piles. Throughout the field, men and women, distinguished only by their clothing, rake hay into large stacks for successive loadings of the cart. At least 25 individuals work at these tasks. Men perform the heaviest work of loading the haycart and hammering the scythes; men and women share all the other work. Although no children appear in the scene, some are undoubtedly at work picking berries and beans.

The scenes of physical labor remind us that the life of ordinary people in the sixteenth century was neither romantic nor despondent, neither quaint nor primitive. It had its own joys and sorrows, its own triumphs and failures. Inevitably, we compare it to our experiences and contrast it to our comforts. By our standards, a sixteenth-century prince endured greater material hardships than a twentieth-century slum resident. There was no running water, no central heating, no lavatories, no electricity. There was no relief for toothache, headache, or numbing pain. Travel was dangerous and exhausting. There was no protection from the open air, and many nights were spent on the bare ground. Waiting for winds to sail was more tedious and uncertain than waiting for planes to fly. Entertainment was sparse and the court jester was no match for ipod or the DVR. But though we cannot help but be struck by these differences, we must not judge life in sixteenth-century Europe by our own standard of living. We must exercise our historical imagination if we are to appreciate the conditions of early modern European society.

Looking Ahead

In this chapter, we will examine the social and economic conditions of early modern European society, dominated as it was by extreme change, and often, hardship. We will see how population growth put pressure on the European economy and how the rich became richer as food prices rose. We will also see how European governments were overwhelmed by changes they could only dimly perceive. ➤

ECONOMIC LIFE

There was no typical sixteenth-century European. Language, custom, geography, and material conditions separated people in one place from those in another. Contrasts between social groups were more striking still. A Muscovite boyar had more in common with an English nobleman than either had with his own country's peasants. A Spanish goldsmith and a German brass maker lived remarkably similar lives when compared with the life of a shepherd anywhere in Europe. No matter how carefully historians attempt to distinguish between country and town life, between social or occupational groups, or between men and women, they are still smoothing out edges that are very rough, turning individuals into aggregates, and sacrificing the particular for the general.

One distinctive sixteenth-century experience that all groups shared, though they could only dimly perceive it, was change. In general, one generation improved on the situation of the last. Agriculture increased; more land was cleared, more crops were grown, and better tools were crafted. On the negative side, irreplaceable resources were lost as more trees were felled, more soil was eroded, and more fresh water was polluted. These changes and dynamic transformations in economic and social conditions affected everyday life in the sixteenth century.

Rural Life

In the sixteenth century, as much as 90 percent of the European population lived on farms or in small towns in which farming was the principal occupation. Villages were small and relatively isolated. They might range in size from a hundred families, as was common in France and Spain, to fewer than 20 families, which was the average size of Hungarian villages. These villages, large or small, prosperous or poor, were the bedrock of the sixteenth-century state. Surplus peasant population fed the towns' insatiable need for laborers and the crowns' for soldiers. The manor, the parish, and the rural administrative district were the institutional infrastructures of Europe. Each organized the peasantry for its own purposes. Manorial rents supported the lifestyle of the nobility; parish tithes supported the works of the Church; and local taxes supported the power of the state. Rents, tithes, and taxes easily absorbed more than half of the wealth produced by the land.

To survive on what remained, the village community had to be self-sufficient. In good times, there was enough to eat and some to save for the future. Hard times meant hunger and starvation. One in every three harvests was bad; one in every five was disastrous. Between one-fifth and one-half of the grain harvested had to be saved as seed for the next planting season. When hunger was worst, people faced the agonizing choice of eating or saving their "seed corn."

The Sixteenth-Century Household. Hunger and cold were the constant companions of the average European. In Scandinavia and Muscovy, winter posed as great a threat to survival as starvation did. Everywhere in Europe, homes were inadequate shelter against the cold and damp. Most were built of wood and roofed in thatch. Inside walls were patched with dried mud, and windows were few and narrow. Piled leaves or straw covered the ground and acted as insulation. The typical house was one long room with a stone hearth at the end. The hearth provided both heat and light and belched forth soot and smoke through a brick chimney.

People had relatively few household possessions. The essential piece of furniture was the wooden chest, which was used for storage. A typical family could keep all of its belongings in the chest, which could then be buried or carried away in time of danger. The chest had other uses as well. Its flat top served as a table or bench or a raised surface on which food could be placed. Tables and stools were becoming more common during the sixteenth century, though chairs were still a great luxury. In areas in which spinning, weaving, or other domestic skills were an important part of the family's economy, a long bench was propped against the wall, usually beneath a window. Bedsteads were also becoming more common as the century wore on. They raised the straw mattresses off the ground, keeping them warmer and drier. All other family possessions related to food production. Iron spits and pots, or at least metal rings and clamps for wooden ones, were treasured goods that were passed from generation to generation. Most other implements were wooden. Long-handled spoons, boards known as trenchers used for cutting and eating, and one large cup and bowl were the basic stock of the kitchen. The family ate from the long trencher and passed the bowl and cup. Knives were essential farm tools that doubled for kitchen and mealtime duty, but forks were still a curiosity.

The scale of life was small, and its pace was controlled by nature: up at dawn, asleep at dusk, long working hours in summer, short ones in winter. For most people, the world was bounded by the distance that could be traveled on foot. Those who stayed all their lives in their rural villages may never have seen more than a hundred other people at once. Their wisdom, handed down through generations, was of the practical experience that was necessary to survive the struggle with nature.

Reliance on Agriculture. Peasant life centered on agriculture. Technology and technique varied little across the Continent, but there were significant differences depending on climate and soil. Across the great plain, the breadbasket that stretched from the Low Countries to Poland-Lithuania, the most common form of crop growing was still the three-field rotation system. In this method, winter crops such as wheat or rye were planted in one field; spring crops such as barley, peas, or beans were planted in another; and the third field was left fallow. More than 80 percent of what was grown on the farm was consumed on the farm. In most parts of Europe, wheat was a luxury crop, sold at market rather than eaten at home. Wheat bread was prized for its taste, texture, and white color. Rye and barley were the staples for peasants. These grains were cheaper to grow, had higher yields, and could be brewed as well as baked. Most was baked into the coarse black bread that was the mainstay of the peasant diet. Two to three pounds a day for an adult male was an average allotment when grain was readily available. Beer and gruels of grain and skimmed milk or water flavored with fruit juice supplemented peasant fare. In one form or another, grain provided over 75 percent of the calories in a typical diet.

The warm climate and dry weather of Mediterranean Europe favored a two-crop rotation system. With less water and stronger sunlight, half the land had to be left fallow each year to restore its nutrients. Here, fruit, especially grapes and olives, was an essential supplement to diet. With smaller cereal crops, wine replaced beer as a beverage. The fermentation of grapes and grain into wine and beer also provided convenient ways of storing foodstuffs. Wine and olive oil were also luxury products and were most commonly exchanged for meat, which was less plentiful on southern European farms.

Animal husbandry was the main occupation in the third agricultural area of Europe, the mountainous and hilly regions. Sheep, the most common animal, provided the raw material for almost all clothing. Their skins were used for parchment and as window coverings, and they were a ready source of inexpensive meat. In western Europe, their wool was the main export of both England and Spain. Sheep could graze on land that was unsuitable for grain growing, and they could be sheared twice a year to provide a surplus of wool. Pigs were prevalent in woodland settlements. They foraged for food and were kept, like poultry, for slaughter. Oxen were essential as draft animals. In the dairying areas of Europe, cattle produced milk, cheese, and butter; in Hungary and Bohemia, the great breeding center of the Continent, they were raised for export; almost everywhere else, they were used as beasts of burden.

Most agricultural land was owned not by those who worked it, but by lords who let it out in various ways. The land was still divided into manors, and the manor lord, or

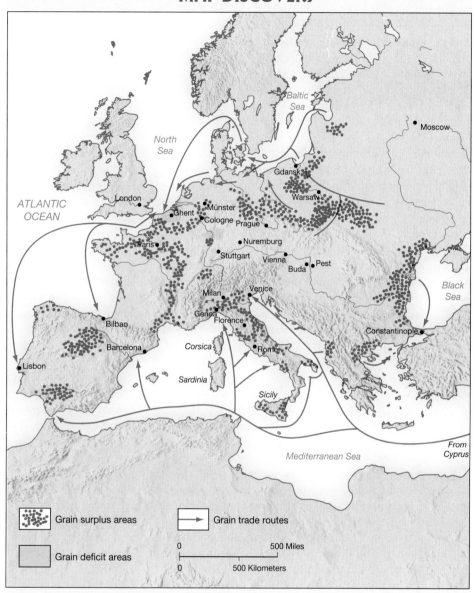

MAP DISCOVERY

Grain Supply and Trade in Sixteenth-Century Europe

Where were the breadbaskets of Europe located? What was the relationship between urban areas and grain supply? How did grain move from suppliers to consumers?

seigneur, was still responsible for maintaining order, administering justice, and arbitrating disputes. Lords were not necessarily individual members of the nobility; in fact, the lords were more commonly the Church or the state. In western Europe, peasants generally owned between one-third and one-half of the land they worked; eastern European peasants owned little if any land. But by the sixteenth century, almost all peasants enjoyed security of tenure on the land they worked. In return for various forms of rents, they used the land as they saw fit and could hand it down to their children. Rents were only occasionally paid in coin, though money rents became more common as the century progressed. More frequently, the lord received a fixed proportion of the land's yield or received labor from the peasant. Labor service was being replaced by monetary payments in northern and western Europe, but it continued in the east. German and Hungarian peasants normally owed two or three days' labor on the lord's estate each week, while Polish peasants might owe as much as four days. Labor service tied the peasants to the land they worked. Eastern European peasants were less mobile than peasants in the west, and as a result, towns were fewer and smaller in the east.

Though the land in each village was set out in large fields so that crops could be rotated, families owned their own pieces within the field, usually in scattered strips. There were also large common fields used as pasture, as well as common woodlands where animals foraged, fuel was gathered, and game was hunted. Villagers disputed frequently over rights to sticks and branches of trees and over the number of sheep or cows that could be grazed in the meadows, especially when resources were scarce.

Farm work was ceaseless toil. Six or seven times a year, farmers tilled the fields to spread animal manure below the surface of the soil. Although most villages possessed metal plows, the team of draft animals was the single essential component for farming. The births of foals and calves were more celebrated events than the births of children; the death of an ox or a horse was a catastrophe. Calamities lurked everywhere, from rain and drought to locusts and crows. Most farms could support only one family at subsistence level, and excess sons and daughters had to fend for themselves, either through marriage in the village or by migration to a town.

Town Life

In the country, people worked to the natural rhythm of the day and season. In the town, the bell tolled every hour. In the summer, the laborers gathered at the town gates at four in the morning, in the winter at seven. The bell signaled the time for morning and afternoon meals as well as the hour to lay down tools and return home. Wages were paid for hours worked—seven in winter, as many as sixteen in midsummer.

The Heart of Commerce. In all towns, an official guild structure organized and regulated labor. Rules laid down the requirements for training, the standards for quality, and the conditions for exchange. Only those who were officially sanctioned could work in trades, and each trade could perform only specified tasks.

While the life of the peasant community turned on self-sufficiency, that of the town turned on interdependence. The town was one large marketplace in which the circulation of goods dictated the residents' survival. Men and women in towns worked as hard as people on farms, but town dwellers generally received a more varied and more comfortable life in return. This is not to suggest that hunger and hardship were unknown in towns. Urban poverty was endemic and grew worse as the century wore on. In most towns, as much as one quarter of the entire population might be destitute, living on casual day labor, charity, or crime. But the institutional network of support for the poor and homeless was stronger. The urban poor fell victim more often to disease than to starvation.

Towns were distinguished by the variety of occupations that existed within them. The preparation and exchange of food dominated small market towns. Peasants would bring in their finest produce for sale and exchange it for vital manufactured goods such as iron spits or pots for cooking. In smaller towns, there was as much barter as sale; in larger places, money was exchanged for commodities. Women dominated the food trades in most market towns, trading, buying, and selling in the shop fronts that occupied the bottom story of their houses. In these small towns, men divided their time between traditional agricultural pursuits—there were always garden plots and even substantial fields attached to towns— and manufacturing. Almost every town made and distributed to the surrounding area some special product that drew to the town the wealth of the countryside.

The Work Force. In larger towns, the specialization of labor was more intense, and wage earning was more essential. Large traders dominated the major occupations such as baking, brewing, and cloth manufacture, leaving distribution in the hands of the family economy, where there might still be a significant element of bartering. Piecework handicrafts became the staple for less prosperous town families, who prepared raw materials for the large manufacturers or finished products before their sale. Metalworking or glassworking normally took place in one quarter of the town, brewing or baking in another. Each craft required long years of technical training, which was handed down from parents to children.

In large towns there were also specialized trades that women performed. There were 55 midwives in Nuremberg in the middle of the sixteenth century, and a board of women chosen from among the leading families of the town supervised their work. Nursing the sick also seems to have been an exclusively female occupation. So, too, was prostitution, which was officially sanctioned in most large towns in the early sixteenth century. There were official brothels, which were subject to taxation and government control. Public bathhouses served as unofficial brothels for the upper ranks of urban society. They, too, were regulated, especially after the first great epidemic of venereal disease in the early sixteenth century.

Most town dwellers, however, lived by unskilled labor. The most lucrative occupations were strictly controlled, so people who flocked to towns in search of employment usually hired themselves out as day laborers, hauling and lifting goods onto carts or boats or delivering water and food. After the first decades of the century, the supply of laborers exceeded the demand, and town authorities were constantly attempting to expel the throngs of casual workers. The most fortunate of such workers might succeed in becoming servants.

Domestic service was a critical source of household labor. Even families who were on the margins of subsistence employed servants to undertake innumerable household tasks, which allowed parents to pursue their primary occupations. Domestics were not apprentices, though they might aspire to become apprentices to the trade followed in the family with whom they lived. If they had kinship bonds in the town, apprenticeship was a likely outcome. But more commonly, domestics remained household servants, frequently changing employers in hope of more comfortable housing and better food.

Just as towns grew by the influx of surplus rural population, they sustained themselves by the import of surplus agricultural production. Most towns owned vast tracts of land, which they leased to peasants or farmed by hired labor. The town of Nuremberg controlled 25 square miles of forest and farmlands; the region around Toledo was inhabited by thousands of peasants who paid taxes and rents to city landlords. All towns had municipal storehouses of grain to preserve their inhabitants from famine during harvest failures. The diet of even a casual laborer would have been envied by an average peasant. Male grape pickers in Stuttgart received meat, soup, vegetables, wine, and beer; females got soup, vegetables, milk, and bread. In addition they received their wages. It is hardly surprising that towns were enclosed by thick walls and defended by armed guards.

Economic Change

Over the course of the sixteenth century, the European population increased by about one-third, much of the growth taking place in the first 50 years. Rough estimates suggest the rise to have been from about 80 million to 105 million. Patterns of growth varied by region. The population of the eastern part of Europe seems to have increased more steadily across the century, whereas in western Europe there was a population explosion in the early decades. The population of France may have doubled between 1450 and 1550, from 10 million to 20 million, before the wars of religion reversed the trend at the end of the century. The population of England nearly doubled between 1500 and 1600 from more than 2 million to more than 4 million. Europe had finally recovered from the devastation of the Black Death, and by 1600 its population was greater than it had ever been. Demographic growth was even more dramatic in the cities. In 1500, only four cities had populations greater than 100,000; in 1600, there were eight. Fifteen large cities more than doubled their populations. London experienced a phenomenal 400 percent increase.

The rise in population dramatically affected the lives of ordinary Europeans. In the early part of the century, the first phase of growth brought prosperity. Because there was uncultivated land that could be plowed and enough commons and woodlands to be shared, population increase was a welcome development. Even when rural communities began to reach their natural limits, opportunity still existed in the burgeoning towns and cities. At first the cycle was beneficial. Surplus on the farms led to economic growth in the towns. Growth in the towns meant more opportunities for people on the farms. The first waves of migrants to the towns found opportunity everywhere. Apprenticeships were easy to find, and the shortage of casual labor kept wages at a decent rate. For a short while, rural families could send their younger sons and daughters to the towns and could purchase a few luxury goods for themselves.

This window of opportunity could not remain open forever. With more mouths to feed, more crops had to be planted, and new fields were carved from less fertile areas. In some villages, land was taken from the woodlands or scrublands that were used for animal forage and domestic fuel. In Spain, the land that was reclaimed came at the expense of land used for sheep grazing. This damaged both the domestic and foreign wool trade. It also reduced the amount of fertilizer that was available for enriching the soil. In England and the Low Countries, large drainage projects were undertaken to reclaim land for crops. In the east, so-called forest colonies sprang up, clearing space in the midst of woodlands for new farms.

By midcentury the window of opportunity shut more firmly on people who were attempting to enter the urban economy. Town governments tightened apprenticeship requirements. Guilds raised fees for new entrants and designated only a small number of places where their goods could be purchased. Most apprenticeships were limited to patrimony: one son for each full member. Such restrictions meant that newly arrived immigrants could enter only the less profitable small crafts.

As workers continued to flood into the towns, real wages began to fall, not only among the unskilled but throughout the workforce. A black market in labor developed to take advantage of the surplus population. In terms of purchasing power, the wages of a craftsman in the building trade in England fell by half during the sixteenth century. Peasants in the French region of Languedoc who hired out for farm labor lost 56 percent of their purchasing power during the century. Grape pickers, among the least skilled agricultural laborers, endured declines up to 300 to 400 percent.

The fall in real wages took place against a backdrop of inflation that has come to be called the **Price Revolution.** Over the course of the century, cereal prices increased between fivefold and sixfold, and prices of manufactured goods increased between twofold and threefold. Most of the rapid increase came in the second half of the century, a result of both population growth and the import of precious metals from the New World. Sixteenth-century governments understood little

MAP DISCOVERY

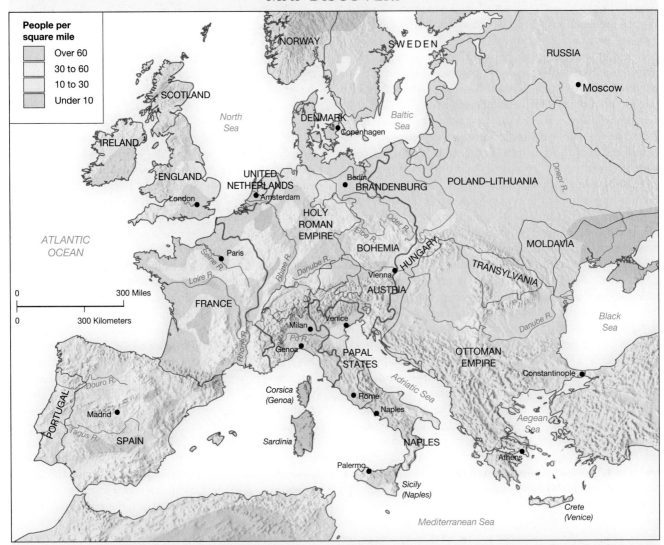

People per square mile

- Over 60
- 30 to 60
- 10 to 30
- Under 10

Population Density in Europe, ca. 1600

Which were the most populated parts of Europe at the beginning of the seventeenth century? Which were the least populated? What was the relationship between population and access to water routes?

about the relationship between money supply and prices. Gold and silver from America flooded the international economy, raising commodity prices. As prices rose, so did the deficits of the state, which was the largest purchaser of both agricultural and manufactured goods. With huge deficits, states began to devalue their coins in the mistaken belief that this would lower their debt. But debased coinage resulted in still higher prices, and higher prices resulted in greater debt. The Price Revolution was felt throughout the Continent and

played havoc with government finances, international trade, and the lives of ordinary people.

A 500 percent inflation in agricultural products over a century is not much by modern standards. Compounded, the rate averages less than 2 percent a year. But the Price Revolution did not take place in a modern society or within a modern market economy. In the sixteenth century, this level of rising prices disrupted everything. In the Spanish town of Seville, almost all buildings were rented on 99-year leases to the families who lived and worked in them. This was a fairly common practice throughout Europe. It meant that a landlord who rented a butcher shop and living quarters in 1501 could not raise the rent until 1600! Similarly, lords frequently held the right to purchase agricultural produce at specified prices. That system, similar to today's commodity market, helped both lords and peasants plan ahead, but it assumed steady prices.

Therefore, an enduring increase of prices created profound social dislocation and threw into turmoil all groups and sections of the European economy. Some people became destitute; others became rich beyond their dreams. The towns were particularly hard hit, for they exchanged manufactured goods for food and so suffered when grain prices rose faster than those of other commodities. Landholders who derived their income from rents were squeezed; those who received payment in kind reaped a windfall of more valuable agricultural goods. As long as ordinary peasants consumed what they raised, the nominal value of commodities did not matter. But if some part of their subsistence was obtained by labor, they were in grave peril.

There was now an enormous incentive to produce a surplus for market and to begin to specialize in particular grains that were in high demand. Every small scrap of land that individual peasant families could bring under cultivation would now yield foodstuffs that could be exchanged for manufactured goods that had been unimaginable luxuries a generation earlier. The tendency for all peasants to hold roughly equivalent amounts of land abruptly ceased. The fortunate could now become prosperous by selling their surplus. The unfortunate found ready purchasers for their strips and common rights.

The beneficial cycle now turned vicious. Those who had sold out and left the land looking for prosperity in the towns were forced to return to the land as agrarian laborers. In western Europe, they became the landless poor, seasonal migrants without the safety net of rooted communal life. In eastern Europe, labor service enriched the landed nobility, who were able to sell vast stores of grain in the export market. Poland-Lithuania became a major supplier of cereals to northern Europe. But agricultural surplus from the east could not make up for the great shortfall in the west. By the end of the sixteenth century, the western European states faced a crisis of subsistence.

SOCIAL LIFE

The basic assumption of sixteenth-century European society was inequality. The group, rather than the individual, was the predominant unit in society. The first level of the social order was the family and the household, then came the village or town community, and finally the gradations of ranks and orders of society at large. Each group had its own place in the social order, and each performed its own essential function. Society was the sum of its parts.

This traditional social organization was severely tested over the course of the sixteenth century. Economic change reshaped ideas of mobility and drew sharper distinctions between rural and urban life. The growth of towns challenged beliefs about the primacy of agricultural production and the subordinate nature of trade and commerce. The rise to new wealth and prominence of some social groups challenged traditional elites' hold on power and prestige. The transformation of landholding patterns in the villages challenged the stability of rural communities. The rising numbers of poor people challenged the institutions of charitable relief and posed the threat of crime and disorder. Eventually, these developments led to bloody confrontations between social groups.

Social Constructs

Hierarchy was the dominant principle of social organization in the sixteenth century. The hierarchy of masters, journeymen, and apprentices dominated trades; trades themselves existed in a hierarchy. Civic government was a hierarchy of officials led by the elite of councillors and mayors. Among the peasants was the hierarchy of freeholder, laborer, and leaseholder, as well as the more flexible social hierarchy among the ancient and prosperous families and the newer and struggling ones. The family itself was hierarchically organized, with the wife subordinate to her husband, the children to their parents, and the apprentices and servants to their master and mistress. Hierarchy was a principle of orderliness that helped to govern social relations. It is tempting to approach hierarchy through wealth, but the ranks of the nobility cannot be explained by gradations of wealth among nobles, and there were many rich town dwellers who were not members of the governing elite.

Status rather than wealth determined the social hierarchy of the sixteenth century. It conferred privileges and exacted responsibilities according to rank. Status was everywhere apparent. It was confirmed in social conventions such as bowing and hat doffing. In towns and cities, the clothing people were allowed to wear, even the foods they were allowed to eat, reflected status. Status was signified by titles, not just in the ranks of the nobility, but even in ordinary communities of masters and mistresses, goodmen and goodwives, squires and ladies, the English equivalents of a wide variety of European titles. The acceptance of status was an everyday, unreflective act. Inequality was an unquestioned fact of life.

Images that people used to describe both the natural world and their social world reinforced the functional nature of hierarchy. The most elaborate image was that of the **Great Chain of Being,** a description of the universe in which everything had a place, from God at the top to inanimate objects such as rocks and stones at the bottom. Complex accounts of the Chain listed the nine orders of angels, the multiple ranks of humans, even the degrees of animals and plants, from which lions emerged as kings of the jungle. For ordinary people, the Great Chain of Being expressed the belief that all life was interconnected, that every link was a part of a divinely ordered universe and was as necessary as every other.

The second metaphor that was used to describe society stressed this notion of interdependency even more strongly. This was the image of the Body Politic, in which the head ruled, the arms protected, the stomach nourished, and the feet labored. In the state, the king was the head, the church was the soul, the nobles were the arms, the artisans were the hands, and the peasants were the feet. Like the Chain of Being, the Body Politic was a profoundly conservative concept of social organization that precluded the idea of social mobility.

Social Structure

The Great Chain of Being and the Body Politic were static concepts of social organization. But in the sixteenth century, European society was in a state of dynamic change. Fundamentally, all European societies were divided between nobles and commoners, though relationships between the two orders differed from place to place.

The Nobles.   Nobility was a legal status that conferred certain privileges on its holders and passed by inheritance from one generation to the next. Each rank had its own privileges, and each was clearly demarcated from the next. The coat of arms was a universally recognized symbol of rank and family connection. Though various systems of title were in use across the Continent, the hierarchy of prince, duke, earl, count, and baron was roughly standard.

Because rulers conferred these titles on individuals, elevating some to higher ranks and others from commoner to no-

ble, the nobility was a political order as well as a social one. Political privileges were among the nobility's most important attributes. In many countries, the highest offices of the state and the military were reserved for members of the nobility. Noblemen were also granted rights of political participation in the deliberative bodies of the state. In England, the peerage was defined as all those who were summoned to the House of Lords. In most parts of central Europe, the nobility alone composed the diets that advised the monarch.

Finally, members of the nobility held economic privileges, a result both of their rank and of their role as lords on the lands they owned. In almost every state, the nobility was exempt from most kinds of taxation. The interests of the nobles conflicted directly with those of the ruler, and the larger the number of tax exemptions for the nobility, the stronger was its power in relation to the monarch. Tax exemptions of the nobility were most extensive in eastern and central Europe. There, the crowns were elective rather than hereditary, allowing the nobles to bargain their support. As Polish agriculture developed into an export industry, exemption from internal tolls and customs gave the nobility a competitive advantage over merchants in the marketing of goods. The nobility in western Europe enjoyed fewer immunities but not necessarily less valuable ones.

Privileges implied obligations. Initially, the nobility was the warrior caste of the state, and its primary obligations were to raise, equip, and lead troops into battle. Much of the great wealth that nobles possessed was at the service of the ruler during times of war, and war was a perpetual activity. By the sixteenth century, the military needs of the state had far surpassed the military power of its nobility. Warfare had become a national enterprise that required central coordination. Nobles became administrators as much as warriors, though it is fair to say that many did both. The French nobility came to be divided into the nobility of the sword and the nobility of the robe—that is, warriors and officeholders.

Nobles also had the obligation of governing at both the national and the local level. At the discretion of the ruler, they could be called to engage in any necessary occupation, no matter how disruptive to their economic or family affairs. They administered their estates and settled the disputes of their tenants. In times of want, they were expected to provide for the needy. The obligation of good lordship was implicitly understood, if not always explicitly carried out, between lord and peasant.

Town Elite and Gentry.   The principal distinction in sixteenth-century society was between lord and commoners, but it was not the only one. A new social group was emerging in the towns—a group that had neither the legal nor the social privileges of nobility but performed many of the same functions. The towns remained a separate unit of social orga-

■ Georges de La Tour, *The Fortune Teller*. In the painting, which serves as a warning to the naive about the wicked ways of the world, a fashionably dressed young innocent is drawn into the snare of the wily fortune teller.

nization in most states, enjoying many of the same political and economic privileges as the nobility. Representatives of the towns met with the nobles and the king and were the most important part of the national deliberative assemblies, like the English Parliament or the French estates. Towns were granted legal rights to govern their own citizens, to engage in trade, and to defend themselves by raising and storing arms. Though they paid a large share of most taxes, towns also received large tax concessions.

As individuals, members of the town elite held no special status in society at large. Some were among the richest people in the state, but they had to devise their own systems of honor and prestige. In Venice, the *Book of Gold* distinguished the local elite from the ranks of ordinary citizens. In France and Spain, some of the highest officers of leading towns were granted noble status. In England, wealthy guild members could become knights, a rank just below noble status. German burghers, as prosperous townsmen were called, remained caught between noble and common, despised from above because they worked with their hands, envied from below for their wealth and comfort. In Wurtenberg, the nobility withdrew from the towns and sought the status of free knights.

In rural society the transformation of agricultural holdings in many places also created a group that fit uncomfortably between lords and commoners. The accumulation of larger and larger estates, by purchase from the nobility, the state, or the church, made lords—in the sense of landowners with tenants—of many who were not lords in rank. They received rents and dues from their tenants, administered their estates, and preserved the so-called moral economy that sustained the peasants during hard times. In England, this group came to be known as the gentry, and there were parallel groups in Spain, France, and the Holy Roman Empire. The gentry aspired to the privileges of the nobility. In England, members of the gentry had the right to have a coat of arms and could be knighted. But knighthoods were not hereditary and did not confer membership in the House of Lords. In Spain, the caballeros and hidalgos gained noble privileges but were still of lower status than the grandees.

Social stratification also marked rural communities. In many German villages, a principal distinction was made between those who held land in the ancient part of the settlement—the Esch—and those who held land in those areas into which the village had expanded. The Esch was normally the best land. But interestingly, the holders of the Esch were tied to the lord of the estate, while holders of the less desirable lands were free peasants. Here, freedom to move from place to place was less valued than was the right to live in the heart of the village.

Just the opposite set of values prevailed in English villages, where freeholders were in the most enviable position. They led the movements to break up the common fields for planting and were able to initiate legal actions against their lord. Whenever village land was converted to freehold, unfree tenants would go into debt to buy it. Increasingly, French peasants came to own the land they farmed. They protested

against the very title of villein, claiming that its older association with serfdom discouraged others from trading with those so labeled. The distinction between free and unfree went even further in Muscovy, where thousands of starving laborers sold themselves into slavery.

In towns, the order of rank below the elite pertained as much to the kind of work that one performed as it did to the level at which the work was undertaken. The critical division in town life was between those who had the freedom of the city—citizens—and those who did not. Citizenship was restricted to membership in certain occupations and was closely regulated. It could be purchased, but most citizenship was earned by becoming a master in one of the guilds. Only males could be citizens. In Germany, the feminine equivalent for the word that denoted a male citizen meant prostitute! But women who were married to citizens enjoyed their husbands' privileges, and widows of citizens could pass the privileges to their new husbands when they remarried.

Social Change

In the sixteenth century, social commentators believed that change was transforming the world in which they lived. In 1600, a Spanish observer blamed the rise of the rich commoners for the ills of the world. An Englishman commenting on the rise of the gentry could give no better definition of its status than to say that a gentleman was one who lived like a gentleman. In France, the challenge that the new nobility of the robe posed to the old nobility of the sword poisoned relations between these two segments of the ruling elite. The military service class in Muscovy, who were of more use to the Muscovite princes than the traditional landed nobility, posed an even greater threat to the privileges of the boyars.

The New Rich. Pressures on the ruling elites of European society came from above as well as below. The expansion of the state and the power of the prince frequently came as a result of direct conflict with the nobility. Only in east central Europe did the consolidation of the state actually enhance the privileges of the traditional noble orders, and these were areas in which towns were small and urban elites were weak.

Many factors promoted social change during the course of the sixteenth century. First, population increase necessitated an expansion of the ruling orders. With more people to govern, there had to be more governors who could perform the military, political, and social functions of the state. Second, opportunities to accumulate wealth expanded dramatically with the Price Revolution. Traditionally, wealth was calculated in land and tenants rather than in the possession of liquid assets such as gold and silver. But with the increase in commodity prices, surplus producers could rapidly improve their economic position. Moreover, state service became a source of unlimited riches. The profits to be made from tax collecting, officeholding, or the law could easily surpass those to be made from landholding. And the newly rich clamored for privileges.

The New Poor. Social change was equally apparent at the bottom of the social scale, but here it could not be so easily absorbed. The continuous growth of population created a group of landless poor who squatted in villages and clogged the streets of towns and cities. Rough estimates suggest that as many as one-quarter of all Europeans were destitute. This was a staggering figure in great cities, amounting to tens of thousands in London or Paris.

Traditionally, local communities cared for their poor. Widows, orphans, and the handicapped, who would normally constitute over half of the poor in a village or town, were viewed as the "deserving poor," worthy of the care of the community through the Church or private almsgiving. Catholic communities such as Venice created a system of private charity that paralleled the institutions of the Church. Though Protestant communities took charity out of the control of the Church, they were no less concerned about the plight of the deserving poor. In England a special tax, the poor rate, supported the poor. Perhaps the most elaborate system of all existed in the French town of Lyon. There, all the poor were registered and given identity cards. Each Sunday, they would receive a week's worth of food and money. Young girls were provided with dowries, and young boys were taught crafts. But this enlightened system was for the deserving poor only.

Charity was an obligation of the community, but as the sixteenth century wore on, the number of destitute people grew beyond the ability of the local community to care for them. Many of those who now begged for alms fell outside the traditional categories of the deserving poor. They were men and women who were capable of working but incapable of finding more than occasional labor. They left their native communities in search of employment and thus forfeited their claims on local charity. Most wound up in the towns and cities, where as strangers they had no claim on local charity. Poor mothers abandoned their newborn infants on the steps of foundling hospitals or the houses of the rich.

The problem of crime complicated the problems of poverty and vagrancy. Increasing population and increasing wealth equaled increasing crime; the addition of the poor to the equation aggravated the situation. The poor, outsiders to the community without visible means of support, were the easiest targets of official retribution. Throughout the century, numerous European states passed vagrancy laws. In England, the poor were whipped from village to village until they were returned home. Both Venetian and Dutch vagrants were regularly rounded up for galley service. Vagrants in Hungary were sold into slavery. Sexual offenses were criminalized, especially bastardy, since the birth of illegitimate children placed an immediate burden on the community. Prostitutes, who had long been tolerated and regulated in towns, were now persecuted. Rape increased. Capital punishment was reserved for the worst crimes—murder, incest, and grand larceny being most common—but, not surprisingly, executions were carried out mostly on outsiders to the community.

■ *Feeding the Hungry*, by Cornelius Buys, 1504. A maidservant is doling out small loaves to the poor and the lame at the door of a wealthy person's home. The poor who flocked to the towns were often forced to rely on charity to survive.

Peasant Revolts

The economic and social changes of the sixteenth century had serious consequences. Most telling was the upswing of violent confrontations between peasants and their lords. Across Europe and with alarming regularity, peasants took up arms to defend themselves from what they saw as violations of traditional rights and obligations. Peasant revolts were not hunger riots. Though they frequently occurred in periods of want, they were not desperate attacks against warehouses or grain silos. Nor did those who took part in the revolts form an undisciplined mob. Most revolts chose leaders, drew up petitions of grievances, and organized the rank and file into a semblance of military order. Leaders were literate—drawn more commonly from among the lower clergy or minor gentry than from the peasantry—political demands were moderate, and tactics were sophisticated. But peasant revolts so profoundly threatened the social order that they were met with the severest repression.

Agrarian Changes.   It is essential to realize that while peasants revolted against their lords, at bottom their anger and frustration were caused by agrarian changes that could be neither controlled nor understood. As population increased and market production expanded, many of the traditional rights and obligations of lords and peasants became oppressive. One example is that of forest rights. On most estates the forests surrounding a village belonged to the lord. Commonly, the village had its own woodlands in which animals foraged and fuel and building material were available. As population increased, new land was put under the plow, and grain fields pressed up against the forest. There were more animals in the village, and some of them were let loose to consume the young sprouts and saplings. Soon there was not enough food for the wild game that was among the lord's most valuable property. So the game began to feed on the peasants' crops, which were now placed so appetizingly close to the forests. It was a capital crime for a peasant to kill wild game, but neither could the peasants allow the game to consume their crops.

A similar conflict arose over enclosing crop fields. An **enclosure** was a device—normally a fence or hedge that surrounded an area—to keep a parcel of land separate from the planted strips of land owned by the villagers. It could be used for grazing animals or raising a specialty crop for the market. But an enclosure destroyed the traditional form of village agriculture whereby decisions on which crops to plant were made communally. It became one of the chief grievances of the English peasants. But while enclosures broke up the old field system in many villages, they were a logical response to the transformation of land ownership that had already taken place. As more and more land was accumulated by fewer and fewer families, it made less and less sense for them to work widely scattered strips all over the village. If a family could consolidate its holdings by swaps and sales, it could gain an estate that was large enough to be used for both crops and grazing. An enclosed estate allowed wealthy farmers to grow more luxury crops for market or to raise only sheep on a field that had once been used for grain.

Enclosure was a process that both lord and rich peasant undertook, but it drove the smallholders from the land and was thus a source of bitter resentment for the poorer peasants. It was easy to protest the greed of the lords who, owning the most land, were the most successful enclosers. But enclosures

resulted more from the process whereby villages came to be characterized by a very small elite of large landholders and a very large mass of smallholders and landless poor. It was an effect rather than a cause.

From Hungary to England, peasant revolts brought social and economic change into sharp relief. A call for a crusade against Ottoman advances in 1514 provided the opportunity for Hungarian peasants to revolt against their noble landlords. Thousands dropped their plowshares and grasped the sword of a holy war. But, in fact, war against the Ottomans did not materialize. Instead, the mobilized peasants, under the leadership of disaffected army officers and clergymen, issued grievances against the labor service that they owed to their lords as well as numerous violations of customary agricultural practices. Their revolt turned into a civil war and was crushed with great brutality. In eastern England, Ket's Rebellion centered on peasant opposition to enclosure. The rebels occupied Norwich, the second largest city in the realm, but their aspirations were for reform rather than revolution. They, too, were crushed by well-trained forces.

Uprising in Germany.   The complexity of these problems is perhaps best revealed in the series of uprisings that are known collectively as the German Peasants' War. It involved tens of thousands of peasants, and it combined a whole series of agrarian grievances with an awareness of the new religious spirit preached by Martin Luther. Luther condemned both lords and peasants—the lords for their rapaciousness, the peasants for their rebelliousness. Though he had a large following among the peasants, his advice that earthly oppressions be passively accepted was not followed. The Peasants' War was directed against secular and ecclesiastical lords, and the rebels attacked both economic and religious abuses. The combination of demands, such as the community's right to select its own minister and the community's right to cut wood freely, attracted a wide following in the villages and small towns of southern and central Germany. The printed demands of the peasantry, the most famous of which was the Twelve Articles of the Peasants of Swabia (1525), helped to spread the movement far beyond its original bounds. The peasants organized themselves into large armies led by experienced soldiers, but ultimately, movements that refused compromise were ruthlessly crushed.

At base, the demands of the peasantry addressed the agrarian changes that were transforming German villages. Population growth was creating more poor villagers who could only hire out as laborers but who demanded a share of common grazing and woodlands. Because the presence of these poor people increased the taxable wealth of the village, they were advantageous to the lord. But the strain they placed on resources was felt by both the subsistence and surplus farmers. Tensions within the village were all the greater in that the landless members were the kin of the landed. If they were to be settled properly on the land, then the lord would have to let the village expand. If they were to be kept on the margins of subsistence, then the more prosperous villagers would have to be able to control their numbers and their conduct. In either case, the peasants needed more direct responsibility for governing the village than existed in their traditional relationship with their lord. Therefore, the peasants of Swabia demanded release of the village peasantry from the status of serfs. They wanted to be allowed to move off the land, to marry out of the village without penalty, and to be free of the death taxes that further impoverished their children. They also wanted stable rents fixed at fair rates, a limit placed on labor service, and a return to the ancient customs that governed relations between lords and peasants. All of these proposals were backed by an appeal to Christian principles of love and charity. They were profoundly conservative.

The demands of the German peasants reflected a traditional order that no longer existed. In many places, the rents and tithes that the peasants wanted to control no longer belonged to the lords of the estates. They had been sold to town corporations or wealthy individuals who purchased them as an investment and expected to realize a fair return. Most tenants did enjoy stable and fixed rents, but only on their traditional lands. As they increased their holdings, perhaps to keep another son in the village or to expand production for the market, they were faced with the fact that rents were higher and land was more expensive than it had been before. Marriage fines, death duties, and labor service were oppressive, but they balanced the fact that traditional rents were very low. In many east German villages, peasants willingly increased their labor service for a reduction in their money rents. It was hardly likely that they could have both. If the peasants were being squeezed, and there can be little doubt that they were, it was not only the lords who were doing the squeezing. The Church took its tenth, the state increased its exactions, and the competition for survival and prosperity among the peasants themselves was ferocious. Peasants were caught between the jaws of an expanding state and a changing economy. When they rebelled, the jaws snapped shut.

PRIVATE AND COMMUNITY LIFE

The great events of the sixteenth century—the discovery of the New World, the consolidation of states, the increasing incidence and ferocity of war, and the reform of religion—all had a profound impact on the lives of ordinary people. However slowly and intermittently these developments penetrated to isolated village communities, they were inextricably bound up with the experiences and world view of all Europeans.

The Family

Sixteenth-century life centered on the family, the primary kinship group. European families were predominantly nuclear, composed of a married couple and their children. In western Europe, a small number of families contained the adult siblings of the family head, uncles and aunts who had not yet established their own families. This pattern was more common in the east, especially in Hungary and Muscovy, where taxation was based on households and thus encouraged extended families. Yet, however families were composed, kinship had a wider orbit than just parents and children. In-laws, step relations, and cousins were considered part of the kin group and could be called on for support in a variety of contexts from charity to employment and business partnerships. In towns, such family connections created large and powerful clans.

In a different sense, family was lineage, the connections between preceding and succeeding generations. This was an important concept among the upper ranks of society, in which ancient lineage, genuine or fabricated, was a valued component of nobility. Even in peasant communities, however, lineage existed in the form of the strips in the field that were passed from generation to generation and named for the family that owned them.

The family was also an economic unit. It was the basic unit for the production, accumulation, and transmission of wealth. Occupation determined the organization of the economic family. Every member of the household had his or her own functions that were essential to the survival of the unit. Tasks were divided by gender and by age, but there was far more intermixture than is traditionally assumed. On farms, women worked at nearly every occupation with the exception of mowing and plowing. In towns, they were vital to the success of shops and trades, though they were denied training in the skilled crafts. As laborers, they worked in the town fields—for little more than half the wages of men performing the same tasks—and in carrying and delivering goods and materials. Children contributed to the economic vitality of the household from an early age.

Finally, the family was the primary unit of social organization. It was in the family that children were educated and the social values of hierarchy and discipline were taught. Authority in the family was strictly organized in a set of three overlapping categories. At the top was the husband, head of the household, who ruled over his wife, children, and servants. All members of the family owed obedience to the head. Children owed obedience to their parents, male or female. Similarly, servants owed obedience to both master and mistress. Male apprentices were under the authority of the wife, mother, and mistress of the household. The importance of the family as a social unit was underscored by the fact that people who were not attached to families attracted suspicion in sixteenth-century society. Single men were often viewed as potential criminals, single women as potential prostitutes.

Though the population of Europe was increasing in the sixteenth century, families were not large. Throughout northern and western Europe, the size of the typical family was two adults and three or four children. Late marriages and breastfeeding helped to control family size. The first restricted the number of childbearing years; the second increased the space between pregnancies. Women married around age 25, men slightly later. Most women could expect about 15 fertile years and seven or eight pregnancies if neither they nor their husbands died in the interim. Only three or four children were likely to survive beyond the age of ten. In her fertile years, a woman was constantly occupied with infants. If she used a wet nurse, as many women in the upper ranks of society did, then she was likely to have 10 or 12 pregnancies during her fertile years and correspondingly more surviving children. Constant pregnancy and child care may help explain some of the gender roles that men and women assumed in the sixteenth century. Biblical injunctions and traditional stereotypes help explain others. Whether a woman was pregnant or not, her labor was a vital part of the domestic economy, especially until the first surviving children were strong enough to assume their share. The woman's sphere was the household. On the farm, she was in charge of the preparation of food, the care of domestic animals, the care and education of children, and the manufacture and cleaning of the family's clothing. In towns, women supervised the shop that was part of the household. They sold goods, kept accounts, and directed the work of domestics or apprentices.

The man's sphere was the public one: the fields in rural areas, the streets in towns. Men plowed, planted, and did the heavy reaping work of farming. They made and maintained essential farm equipment and had charge of the large farm animals. They marketed surplus produce and made the few purchases of equipment or luxury goods. Men performed the labor service that was normally due the lord of the estate, attended the local courts in various capacities, and organized the affairs of the village. In towns, men engaged in heavy labor, procured materials for craft work, and marketed their product if it was not sold in the household shop. Only men could be citizens of the towns or full members of most craft guilds, and only men were involved in civic government.

This separation of men and women into the public and the domestic spheres meant that marriage was a blending of complementary skills. Each partner brought to the marriage essential knowledge and abilities that were fundamental to the economic success of the union. Except in the largest towns, nearly everyone was married for at least a part of his or her life. Remarriage was more common for men than for women, however, because a man continued to control the family's property after the death of his wife, whereas a widow might have only a share of it after bequests to children or provisions for apprentices.

While male roles were constant throughout the life cycle, as men trained for and performed the same occupations from childhood to death, female roles varied greatly depending on

■ Jan Vermeer's *The Milkmaid* (1658–1660) shows a domestic servant absorbed in her household tasks. Homes were sparsely furnished, though this family was rich enough to possess a table, an earthenware bowl and jug, and a footstove that held hot coals (seen on the floor behind the maid).

the situation. While under the care of fathers, masters, or husbands, women worked in the domestic sphere; once widowed, they assumed the public functions of head of household. Many women inherited shops or farmland; most became responsible for the placement and training of their children. But because of the division of labor on which the family depended and because of the inherent social and economic prejudices that segregated public and domestic roles, widows were particularly disadvantaged.

Communities

The family was part of a wider community. On the farm, this community was the rural village; in the town, it was the ward, quarter, or parish in which the family lived. Community life must not be romanticized. Interpersonal violence, lawsuits, and feuds were common in both rural and urban communities. Like every other aspect of society, the community was socially and economically stratified, gender roles were segregated, and resources were inequitably divided. But the community was also the place where people found their social identity. It provided marriage partners for its families, charity for its poor, and a local culture for all of its inhabitants.

Identities and Customs. The two basic forces that tied the rural community together were the lord and the priest. The lord set conditions for work and property ownership that necessitated common decision making on the part of the village farmers. The lord's presence, commonly in the form of an agent, could be both a positive and a negative force for community solidarity. Use of the common lands, the rotation of labor service, and the form in which rents in kind were paid were all decisions that had to be made collectively. Village leadership remained informal, though in some villages, headmen or elders bargained with the lord's agent or resolved petty disputes among the villagers. Communal agreement was also expressed in communal resistance to violations of custom or threats to the moral economy. All these forms of negotiation fused individual families into a community. So, too, in a different way did the presence of the parish priest or minister, who attended all the pivotal events of life—birth, marriage, and death. The church was the only common building of the community; it was the only space that was not owned outright by the lord or an individual family. The scene of village meetings and ceremonies, it was the center of both spiritual and social life. The parish priest served as a conduit for all the news of the community and the focal point for the village's festive life.

Communities were also bound together by their own social customs. In rural parishes, there was the annual perambulation, a walk around the village fields that usually occurred before planting began. It was led by the priest, who blessed the fields as the village farmers followed.

In towns, ceremonial processions were far more elaborate. Processions might take place on saints' days in Catholic communities or on anniversaries of town liberties. The order of the march, the clothing worn by the participants, and the objects displayed reflected the strict hierarchies of the town's local organizations.

Weddings and Festivals. Not all ceremonial occasions were so formal. The most common ceremony was the wedding, a public event that combined a religious rite and a community procession with feasting and festivity. It took different forms in different parts of Europe and in different social groups. Many couples were engaged long before they were married, and in many places it was the engagement that was most important to the individuals and the wedding that was most important to the community. Traditional weddings involved the formal transfer of property, an important event in rural communities where the ownership of strips of land or common rights concerned everyone. The bridal dowry and the groom's inheritance were formally exchanged during the wedding, even if both were small. The public procession, "the marriage in the streets," as it was sometimes called in towns, proclaimed the union throughout the community.

Other ceremonies were equally important in creating a shared sense of identity within the community. In both town and countryside, the year was divided by a number of festivals that defined the rhythm of toil and rest. They coincided with both the seasonal divisions of agricultural life and the central events of the Christian calendar. Christmas and Easter were probably the most widely observed Christian holidays, but **Carnival,** which preceded Lent, was a frenzied round of feasts and parties that resulted in a disproportionate number of births nine months later. The twelve days of Christmas were only loosely attached to the birth of Jesus and were even abolished by some Protestant churches. The rites of May, which celebrated the rebirth of spring, were filled with sexual play among the young adults of the community. All Hallows' Eve was a celebration for the community's dead, whose spirits were believed to wander the village on that night, visiting kin and neighbors.

In addition to feasting, dancing, and play, festivals often included sports, such as soccer or wrestling, which served to channel aggressions. At such times, village elders would also arbitrate disputes, and marriage alliances or property transactions would be arranged.

Festivals further cemented the political cohesion of the community. Seating arrangements signaled the hierarchy of the community, and public punishment of offenders reinforced deference and social and sexual mores. Youth groups or the village women might band together to shame a promiscuous woman or to place horns on the head of a cuckolded husband. These forms of community ritual worked not only to punish offenders but also to reinforce the social and sexual values of the village as a whole.

Popular Beliefs and the Persecution of Witches

Ceremony and festival are reminders that sixteenth-century Europe was still a preliterate society. Despite the introduction of printing and the millions of books that were produced during the period, the vast majority of Europeans conducted their affairs without the benefit of literacy. Outside a small circle of intellectuals, there was little effective knowledge about either human or celestial bodies. The mysteries of the sun, moon, and stars were as deep as those of health and sickness. But this does not mean that ordinary people lived in a constant state of terror and anxiety. They used the knowledge they did have to form a view of the universe that conformed to their experiences and responded to their hopes.

Magical Practices. These beliefs blended Christian teaching and folk wisdom with a strong strain of magic. Popular belief in

magic could be found everywhere in Europe, and it operated in much the same way as science does today. Only skilled practitioners could perform magic. It was a technical subject that combined expertise in the properties of plants and animals with theories about the composition of human and heavenly bodies. It had its own language, a mixture of ancient words and sounds with significant numbers and catch phrases. Magicians specialized. Alchemists worked with rocks and minerals, astrologers with the movement of the stars. Witches were thought to understand the properties of animals especially well.

Magical practices appealed to people at all levels of society. The wealthy favored astrology and paid handsomely to

THE DEVIL'S DUE

Evidence of the supernatural world abounded for the people of premodern Europe. Natural disasters such as plague and human disasters such as war promoted fear of witchcraft. When the world seemed out of balance and the forces of good retreated before the forces of evil, people sought someone to blame for their troubles. Witches were an obvious choice. Accused witches were most commonly women on the margins of society. Once brought before the authorities, many admitted their traffic with Satan, especially under torture. The Witch Hammer is a set of detailed instructions for the rooting out of witches, including procedures to induce their confessions.

Focus Questions

What is the point of torture, punishment, or investigation? Is the suspected witch seen as being in control of his or her magic?

The method of beginning an examination by torture is as follows: First, the jailers prepare the implements of torture, then they strip the prisoner (if it be a woman, she has already been stripped by other women, upright and of good report). This stripping is lest some means of witchcraft may have been sewed into the clothing—such as often, taught by the Devil, they prepare from the bodies of unbaptized infants, [murdered] that they may forfeit salvation. And when the implements of torture have been prepared, the judge, both in person and through other good men zealous in the faith, tries to persuade the prisoner to confess the truth freely; but, if he will not confess, he bids attendants make the prisoner fast to the strappado or some other implement of torture. The attendants obey forthwith, yet with feigned agitation. Then, at the prayer of some of those present, the prisoner is loosed again and is taken aside and once more persuaded to confess, being led to believe that he will in that case not be put to death.

But if, neither by threats nor by promises such as these, the witch cannot be induced to speak the truth, then the jailers must carry out the sentence, and torture the prisoner according to the accepted methods, with more or less of severity as the delinquent's crime may demand. And, while

he is being tortured, he must be questioned on the articles of accusation, and this frequently and persistently, beginning with the lighter charges—for he will more readily confess the lighter than the heavier. And, while this is being done, the notary must write down everything in his record of the trial—how the prisoner is tortured, on what points he is questioned, and how he answers.

And note that, if he confesses under the torture, he must afterward be conducted to another place, that he may confirm it and certify that it was not due alone to the force of the torture.

But, if the prisoner will not confess the truth satisfactorily, other sorts of tortures must be placed before him, with the statement that, unless he will confess the truth, he must endure these also. But, if not even thus he can be brought into terror and to the truth, then the next day or the next but one is to be set for a *continuation* of the tortures—not a *repetition,* for they must not be repeated unless new evidence be produced. . . .

And during the interval, before the day assigned, the judge, in person or through approved men, must in the manner above described try to persuade the prisoner to confess, promising her (if there is aught to be gained by this promise) that her life shall be spared.

The judge shall see to it, moreover, that throughout this interval guards are constantly with the prisoner, so that she may not be left alone; because she will be visited by the Devil and tempted into suicide.

From *The Witch Hammer.*

discover which days and months were the most auspicious for marriages and investments. The poorest villagers sought the aid of herbalists to help control the constant aches and pains of daily life. Sorcerers and wizards were called on in more extreme circumstances, such as a threatened harvest or matters of life and death. These magicians competed with the remedies offered by the Church. Special prayers and visits to the shrines of particular saints were believed to have similar curative value. Magical and Christian beliefs were often practiced simultaneously. In some French villages, for example, four-leaf clovers were considered especially powerful if they were found on a particular saint's day. It was not until the end of the century, when Protestant and Catholic leaders condemned magical practices and began a campaign to root them out, that magic and religion came into conflict.

Magical practices served a variety of purposes. Healing was the most common, and many "magical" brews were effective remedies for the minor ailments for which they were prescribed. Most village magicians were women because it was believed that women had unique knowledge and understanding of the body. Magic was also used for predictive purposes. Certain charms and rituals were believed to have the power to affect the weather, the crops, and even human events. As always, affairs of the heart were as important as those of the stomach. Magicians advised the lovesick on potions and spells that would gain them the object of their desires. Finally, it was believed that magic had the power to alter the course of nature and could be used for both good and evil purposes.

The Witch Craze. Magic for evil was black magic, or witchcraft. Witches were believed to possess special powers that put them into contact with the devil and the forces of evil, which they could then use for their own purposes. Belief in the prevalence of good and evil spirits was Christian as well as magical. But the Church had gradually consigned the operation of the devil to the afterlife and removed his direct agency from earthly affairs. Beginning in the late fifteenth century, Church authorities began to prosecute large numbers of suspected witches. By the end of the sixteenth century, there was a continentwide witch craze. Confessions were obtained under torture, as were further accusations.

Witches were usually women, most often unmarried or widowed. In a sample of more than 7,000 cases of witchcraft prosecuted in early modern Europe, over 80 percent of the defendants were women. There is no clear explanation for why women fulfilled this important and powerful role. Belief in women's special powers over the body through their singular ability to give birth is certainly one part of the explanation, for many stories about the origins of witches suggest that they were children fathered by the devil and left to be raised by women. This sexual element of union with the devil and the common belief that older women were sexually aggressive combined to threaten male sexual dominance. Witches were also believed to have peculiar physical characteristics. A group of Italian witches, male and female, were distinguished by hav-

ing been born with a caul, that is, a membrane around their heads that was removed after birth. Accused witches were strip-searched to find the devil's mark, which might be any bodily blemish. Another strand of explanation lies in the fact that single women existed on the fringes of society, isolated and exploited by the community at large. Their occult abilities thus became a protective mechanism that gave them a function within the community while they remained outside it.

It is difficult to know how important black magical beliefs were in ordinary communities. Most of the daily magic that was practiced was a mixture of charms, potions, and prayers that mingled magical, medical, and Christian beliefs. Misfortunes that befell particular families or social groups were blamed on the activities of witches. The campaign of the established churches to root out magic was directed largely against witches. The churches transposed witches' supposed abilities to communicate with the devil into the charge that they worshiped the devil. Because there was such widespread belief in the presence of diabolical spirits and in the capabilities of witches to control them, Protestant and Catholic church courts could easily find witnesses to testify in support of the charges against individual witches. Over 100,000—perhaps several times that many—condemned witches in Europe were burned, strangled, drowned, or beheaded. Yet wherever sufficient evidence exists to understand the circumstances of witchcraft prosecutions, it is clear that the community itself was under some form of social or economic stress rather than that there was any increase in the presence or use of witches.

CONCLUSION

Population growth, economic diversification, and social change characterized life in sixteenth-century Europe. It was a century of extremes. The poor were getting poorer, and the rich were getting richer. The early part of the century has been called the golden age of the peasantry; the later part has been called the crisis of subsistence. At all levels of the social scale, the lives of grandparents and grandchildren were dramatically different. For surplus producers, the quality of life improved throughout the century. The market economy expanded. Agricultural surplus was exchanged for more land and a wider variety of consumer goods. Children could be given an education, and domestic and agricultural labor was cheap and plentiful. For subsistence producers, the quality of life eroded. In the first half of the century, their diet contained more meat than it would for the next 300 years. Their children could be absorbed on new farms or sent to towns where there was a shortage of both skilled and unskilled labor. But gradually, the outlook turned bleak. The land could support no more new families, and the towns needed no more labor. As wages fell and prices rose, peasants in western Europe were caught between the crushing burdens of taxation from lord, state, and church and the all-too-frequent catastrophes of poor harvests, epidemic disease, and warfare. In eastern Europe, the peasantry was tied to the land in a new serfdom, which provided minimum subsistence in return for the loss of freedom and opportunity. When peasants anywhere rose up against these conditions, they were cut down and swept away like new-mown hay. The witch hunts of the sixteenth and early seventeenth centuries reflected troubled times, a pervasive misogyny, and a misguided effort to eliminate the cause of the troubles.

QUESTIONS FOR REVIEW

1. What physical forces and social customs shaped the everyday life of Europe's rural population?
2. What was the nature of demographic change in the sixteenth century, and what was its impact on the European economy?
3. How are the terms "stratification," "hierarchy," and "status" useful for understanding social relations in early modern Europe?
4. How were the different roles of men and women within the family reflected in the different lives of men and women in the wider community?

KEY TERMS

Carnival, *p. 312*

enclosure, *p. 309*

Great Chain of Being, *p. 305*

Price Revolution, *p. 303*

seigneur, *p. 302*

DISCOVERING WESTERN CIVILIZATION ONLINE

You can obtain more information about life in early modern Europe at the websites listed below. See also the Companion Website that accompanies this text, www.ablongman.com/kishlansky, which contains an online study guide and additional resources.

Social Life

Internet Modern History Sourcebook: Everyday Life in Premodern Europe

www.fordham.edu/halsall/mod/modsbook04.html

A site with links to sources, pictures, and accounts of everyday life in early modern Europe. A good place to start.

Modern History Sourcebook: Social Conditions in 17th Century France

www.fordham.edu/halsall/mod/17france-soc.html

Documents illustrating social conditions in early modern France.

Private Life

Witchcraft

www.kenyon.edu/projects/margin/witch.htm

A site with links to sources concerning European witchcraft.

Also includes suggestions for further reading and a brief overview of the subject.

Witches and Witchcraft

Womenshistory.about.com/cs/witches

This site offers historical information about witches and witchcraft in Europe and America and includes links to related sites.

Life in Tudor England

englishhistory.net/tudor/tudorlife.html

Part of a comprehensive site on Tudor England, this section on life in Tudor England offers information on topics including food and drink, pastimes and entertainment, and mental illness.

SUGGESTIONS FOR FURTHER READING

General Reading

Peter Burke, *Popular Culture in Early Modern Europe* (New York: Harper & Row, 1978). A lively survey of cultural activities among the European populace.

Henry Kamen, *European Society, 1500–1700* (London: Hutchinson, 2000). A general survey of European social history.

Peter Laslett, *The World We Have Lost: Further Explored* (New York: Scribners, 1984). One of the pioneering works on the family and population history of England.

Economic Life

Judith Bennett, *Ale, Beer, and Brewsters: Women's Work in a Changing World* (Oxford: Oxford University Press, 1996). An important study of the role of women in one of the most traditional trades.

Fernand Braudel, *Civilization and Capitalism: The Structures of Everyday Life* (New York: Harper & Row, 1981). Part of a larger work filled with fascinating detail about the social behavior of humankind during the early modern period.

Emmanuel Le Roy Ladurie, *The French Peasantry, 1450–1660* (London: Scholar Press, 1987). A complex study of the lives of the French peasantry.

Peter Musgrave, *The Early Modern European Economy* (New York: St. Martin's Press, 1999). A multidimensional survey of economic life.

Social Life

Yves-Marie Bercé, *Revolt and Revolution in Early Modern Europe* (New York: St. Martin's Press, 1987). A study of the structure of uprisings throughout Europe by a leading French historian.

Natalie Zemon Davis, *Women on the Margins: Three Seventeenth-Century Lives* (Cambridge, MA: Harvard University Press, 1995). Three short and stimulating biographies of early modern European women by a leading historian of popular culture.

Jonathan Dewald, *The European Nobility 1400–1800* (Cambridge: Cambridge University Press, 1996). An outstanding survey based on a wide range of sources.

Edward Muir, *Ritual in Early Modern Europe* (Cambridge: Cambridge University Press, 1997). A fascinating account of the transformations in concepts of time and the body in early modern Europe.

Barry Reay, *Popular Cultures in England, 1550–1750* (New York: Addison Wesley Longman, 1998). A sound and insightful thematic survey.

E. M. W. Tillyard, *The Elizabethan World Picture* (New York: Harper & Row, 1960). The classic account of the social constructs of English society.

Private Life

Roger Chartier, ed., *A History of Private Life, Vol. 3, Passions of the Renaissance* (Cambridge, MA: Harvard University Press, 1989). A lavishly illustrated study of the habits, mores, and structures of private life from the fifteenth to the eighteenth centuries.

Stuart Clark, *Thinking with Demons: The Idea of Witchcraft in Early Modern Europe* (Oxford: Oxford University Press, 1997). A sensitive reading of the sources for the study of witchcraft.

Beatrice Gottlieb, *The Family in the Western World from the Black Death to the Industrial Age* (Oxford: Oxford University Press, 1994). An outstanding introduction to the transformations in the lives of families.

R. A. Houston, *Literacy in Early Modern Europe* (London: Longman, 1988). How literacy and education became part of popular culture from 1500 to 1800.

Brian Levack, *The Witch-Hunt in Early Modern Europe* (London: Longman, 1987). A study of the causes and meaning of the persecution of European witches in the sixteenth and seventeenth centuries.

R. Muchembled, *Popular Culture and Elite Culture in France, 1400–1750* (Baton Rouge: Louisiana State University Press, 1985). A detailed treatment of the practices of two conflicting cultures.

Steven Ozment, *Ancestors: The Loving Family in Old Europe* (Cambridge, MA: Harvard University Press, 2001). A brief and accessible survey by a leading historian, making a spirited defense of early modern family life against historians who have portrayed the premodern family in grim terms.

D. Underdown, *Revel, Riot, and Rebellion* (Oxford: Oxford University Press, 1985). An engaging study of popular culture and its relationship to social and economic structures in England.

Merry E. Wiesner, *Women and Gender in Early Modern Europe* (Cambridge: Cambridge University Press, 1993). The best introduction to European women's history.

For a list of additional titles related to this chapter's topics, please see www.ablongman.com/kishlansky.

Chapter 16

THE ROYAL STATE IN THE SEVENTEENTH CENTURY

CHAPTER OUTLINE

The Visual Record

FIT FOR A KING

Behold Versailles, the greatest palace of the greatest king of the greatest state in seventeenth-century Europe. Everything about it was stupendous, a reflection of the grandeur of Louis XIV and of France. Sculptured gardens in dazzling geometric forms stretched for acres, scenting the air with exotic perfumes. Nearly as beautiful as the grounds were the 1,400 fountains, especially the circular basins of Apollo and Latona, the sun god and his mother. The hundreds of water jets that sprayed at Versailles defied nature as well as the senses, for the locale was not well-irrigated and water had to be pumped through elaborate mechanical works all the way from the Seine. Gardens and fountains provided the setting for the enormous palace with its hundreds of rooms for both use and show. Five thousand people, one tenth of whom served the king alone, inhabited the palace. Thousands of others flocked there daily. Most lived in the adjacent town, which had grown from a few hundred people to over 40,000 in a single generation. The royal stables quartered 12,000 horses and hundreds of carriages. The cost of all of this magnificence was equally astounding, estimated to be over 100 million French pounds. Louis XIV ordered the official receipts burned.

Like the marble of the palace, nature itself was chiseled to the requirements of the king. Forests were pared to make leafy avenues or trimmed to conform to the geometric patterns of the gardens. In spring and summer, groves of orange trees grown in tubs were everywhere; in winter and fall they were housed indoors at great expense. Life-size statues and giant carved urns lined the carefully planned walkways that led to breathtaking views or sheltered grottoes. A cross-shaped artificial canal, more than a mile long, dominated the western end of the park.

Despite all the extravagance, the palace was so uncomfortable to live in that Louis had a separate chateau built on the grounds as a quiet retreat. His wife and his mistresses complained constantly of accommodations in which all interior comforts had been subordinated to the external facade of the building. Versailles was a seat of state as well as the home of the monarch, and it is revealing that the private was sacrificed to the public.

Soldiers, artisans, and the merely curious clogged the three great avenues that led from Paris to the palace. When the king dined in public, hordes of Parisians drove out for the spectacle, filing past the monarch as if he were an exhibit at a museum. The site itself was

poorly drained, and the stench of sewage was particularly noxious in the heat and the rain. Even the gardens were too vast to be enjoyed. In the planted areas, the smell of flowers was overpowering while the acres of mown lawn proved unattractive to an aristocracy little given to physical exercise. In these contrasts of failure amid achievement, Versailles stands as an apt symbol of its age: a gaudy mask to hide the wrinkles of the royal state.

Versailles expressed the contradictions of its age. The seventeenth century was an era when the rich got richer and the poor got poorer. It was a time when the monarchical state expanded its power and prestige even as it faced grave challenges to its very existence. It was an epoch of unrelenting war amid a nearly universal desire for lasting peace.

Looking Ahead

The great palaces of European absolute monarchs were designed to intimidate those who visited them. They were the representation of royal power at its apex. As we will learn in this chapter, not since Rome's emperors were at the height of their glory had power been more concentrated in the hands of rulers, and what they had consolidated over centuries they now had to protect against competing dynasties or rebellious subjects. ➤

THE RISE OF THE ROYAL STATE

The wars that dominated the early part of the seventeenth century had a profound impact on the western European states. Not only did they cause terrible suffering and deprivation, but they also demanded efficient and better-centralized states to conduct them. War was both a product of the European state system and a cause of its continued development. As armies grew in size, their material needs grew in volume. As the battlefield spread from state to state, defense became government's most important function. More and more power was absorbed by the monarch and his chief advisers; more and more of the traditional privileges of aristocracy and of towns were eroded. At the center of these rising states, particularly in western Europe, were the king and his court. In the provinces were tax collectors and military recruiters.

Divine Kings

In the early sixteenth century, monarchs treated their states and their subjects as personal property. Correspondingly, rulers were praised in personal terms, for their virtue, their wisdom, or their strength. By the early seventeenth century, the monarchy had been transformed into an office of state. Now rulers embodied their nation, and, no matter what their personal characteristics, they were held in awe because they were monarchs.

Thus, as rulers lost direct personal control over their territory, they gained indirect symbolic control over their nation. This symbolic power was manifested everywhere. By the beginning of the seventeenth century, monarchs had permanent seats of government attended by vast courts of officials, place seekers, and servants. They no longer moved from place to place with their vast entourages. The idea of the capital city emerged, with Madrid, London, and Paris as the models. Here, the grandiose style of the ruler stood proxy for the wealth and glory of the nation. Great display bespoke great pride and strength.

Portraits of rulers conveyed the central message. Elizabeth I was depicted astride a map of England or clutching a rainbow and wearing a gown woven of eyes and ears to signify her power to see and hear her subjects. The Flemish artist Sir Anthony van Dyck (1599–1641) created powerful images of three generations of Stuart kings of England. Diego Velázquez (1599–1660) was court painter to Philip IV of Spain. His series of equestrian portraits of the Habsburgs—kings, queens, princes, and princesses—exude the spirit of the seventeenth-century monarchy, the grandeur and pomp, the power and self-assurance. Peter Paul Rubens (1577–1640) represented 21 separate episodes in the life of Marie de Médicis, queen regent of France.

Monarchy was also glorified in literature. National history, particularly of recent events, enjoyed wide popularity. Its avowed purpose was to draw the connection between the past and the present glories of the state. A popular French history of the period was entitled *On the Excellence of the Kings and the Kingdom of France.* Francis Bacon (1561–1626), who is remembered more as a philosopher and scientist, wrote a laudatory history of England's Henry VII, founder of the Tudor dynasty.

In England, the seventeenth century was a period of renaissance. Poets, playwrights, historians, and philosophers gravitated to the English court. Ben Jonson (1572–1637), a commoner whose wit and talent brought him to court, made his mark by writing and staging masques, light entertainment

■ Queen Elizabeth I of England. This portrait was commissioned by Sir Henry Lee to commemorate the queen's visit to his estate at Ditchley. Here the queen is the very image of Gloriana—ageless and indomitable.

that included music, dance, pantomime, and acting. Jonson's lavish productions, with sets designed by the great architect Inigo Jones (1573–1652), were frequently staged at Christmastime and starred members of the court as players. The masques took for their themes the grandeur of England and its rulers.

Shakespeare and Kingship.

Many of the plays of William Shakespeare (1564–1616) also dealt with monarchy. Like Jonson, Shakespeare came from an ordinary family and began his career as an actor and producer of theater. He soon began to write as well as direct his plays, and his company, the King's Players, received royal patronage. He set many of his plays at the courts of princes, and even comedies such as *Measure for Measure* (1604) and *The Tempest* (1611) centered on the power of the ruler to dispense justice and to bring peace to his subjects. Shakespeare's history plays focused entirely on the character of kings. In *Richard II* (1597) and *Henry VI* (three parts, 1591–1594), Shakespeare exposed the harm that weak rulers inflicted on their states, while in *Henry IV* (two parts, 1598–1600) and *Henry V* (1599) he highlighted the benefits to be derived from strong rulers. In Shakespeare's tragedies, a flaw in the ruler's personality brought harm to the world around him. In *Macbeth* (1606) this flaw was ambition; in *Hamlet* (1602) it was irresolution. Shakespeare's concentration on the affairs of rulers helped to reinforce their dominating importance in the lives of all of their subjects.

Monarchy and Law.

The political theory of the **divine right of kings** further enhanced the importance of monarchs. This theory held that the institution of monarchy had been created by God and that the monarch functioned as God's representative on earth. One clear statement of divine right theory was actually written by a king, James VI of Scotland, who later became King James I of England (1603–1625). In *The True Law of Free Monarchies* (1598), James reasoned that God had placed kings on earth to rule and had charged them with the obligations "to minister justice; to establish good laws; and to procure peace." God would also judge them in heaven for their transgressions.

The idea of divine origin of monarchy was uncontroversial, and it was espoused not only by kings. The French Estates-General, for example, in 1614 agreed that "the king is sovereign in France and holds his crown from God only." This sentiment echoed the commonplace view of French political theorists. The greatest writer on the subject, Jean Bodin (1530–1596), called the king "God's image on earth." In *The Six Books of the Commonwealth* (1576), Bodin defined the essence of the monarch's power: "The principal mark of sovereign majesty is essentially the right to impose laws on subjects generally without their consent."

Kings were nevertheless bound by the law of nature and the law of nations. They could not deprive their subjects of their lives, their liberties, or their property without due cause established by law. As one French theorist held, "While the kingdom belongs to the king, the king also belongs to the kingdom." Wherever they turned, kings were instructed in the duties of kingship.

The Court and the Courtiers

In reality, the day-to-day affairs of government had grown beyond the capacity of any monarch to handle them. The expansion in the powers of the western states absorbed more officials than ever. At the beginning of the sixteenth century, the French court of Francis I employed 622 officers; at the beginning of the seventeenth century, the court of Henry IV employed over 1,500. Yet the difference was not only in size. Members of the seventeenth-century court were becoming servants of the state as well as of the monarch.

Expanding the court was one of the ways in which monarchs co-opted potential rivals within the aristocracy. In return, those who were favored received royal grants of titles, lands, and income. As the court expanded, so did the political power of courtiers. Royal councils—a small group of leading officeholders who advised the monarch on state business—grew in significance. The council assumed management of the government and soon began to advocate policies for the monarch to adopt.

Yet the court still revolved around the monarch. The monarch appointed, promoted, and dismissed officeholders at will. As befitted this type of personal government, most monarchs chose a single individual to act as a funnel for private and public business. This was the "favorite," whose role combined varying proportions of best friend, right-hand man, and hired gun. Some favorites, such as the French Cardinal Richelieu and the Spanish Count-Duke Olivares, were able to transform themselves into chief ministers. Others, like the English Duke of Buckingham, simply remained royal companions. Favorites lasted only as long as they retained their influence with the monarch. Richelieu claimed that it was "more difficult to dominate the four square feet of the king's study than the affairs of Europe." The parallel careers of Richelieu, Olivares, and Buckingham neatly illustrate the dangers and opportunities of the office.

Cardinal Richelieu (1585–1642), a younger son of a minor French noble family, trained for the law and then for a position that his family owned in the Church. He was made a cardinal in 1622. After skillful participation in the meeting of the Estates-General of 1614, Richelieu was given a court post through the patronage of Queen Marie de Médicis, mother of Louis XIII. The two men made a good match. Louis XIII hated the work of ruling, and Richelieu loved little else.

Though Richelieu received great favor from the king—he became a duke and amassed the largest private fortune in France—his position rested on his managerial abilities. Richelieu never enjoyed a close personal relationship with his monarch, and he never felt that his position was secure. In 1630, Marie de Médicis turned against him, and he was very nearly ousted from office. His last years were filled with suppressing plots to undermine his power or to take his life.

A GLIMPSE OF A KING

Louis de Rouvroy, duc de Saint-Simon, spent much of his career at the court of Louis XIV. His Memoires *provide a fascinating study of life at Versailles, as well as poison pen portraits of the king and his courtiers. Here he describes some habits of the king.*

Focus Questions

How does the king maintain his power over the nobles? Why does so much in this political system depend on personal skills and self-presentation?

He always took great pains to find out what was going on in public places, in society, in private houses, even family secrets, and maintained an immense number of spies and tale-bearers. These were of all sorts; some did not know that their reports were carried to him; others did know it; there were others, again, who used to write to him directly, through channels which he prescribed; others who were admitted by the backstairs and saw him in his private room. Many a man in all ranks of life was ruined by these methods, often very unjustly, without ever being able to discover the reason; and when the King had once taken a prejudice against a man, he hardly ever got over it. . . .

No one understood better than Louis XIV the art of enhancing the value of a favour by his manner of bestowing it; he knew how to make the most of a word, a smile, even of a glance. If he addressed any one, were it but to ask a trifling question or make some commonplace remark, all eyes were turned on the person so honored; it was a mark of favour which always gave rise to comment. . . .

He loved splendour, magnificence, and profusion in all things, and encouraged similar tastes in his Court; to spend money freely on equipages and buildings, on feasting and at cards, was a sure way to gain his favour, perhaps to obtain the honour of a word from him. Motives of policy and something to do with this; by making expensive habits the fashion, and, for people in a certain position, a necessity, he compelled his courtiers to live beyond their income, and gradually reduced them to depend on his bounty for the means of subsistence.

From duc de Saint-Simon, *Memoires.*

The Count-Duke Olivares (1587–1645) was a younger son of a lesser branch of a great Spanish noble family. By the time he was 20, he had become a courtier with a title, a large fortune, and, most unusually, a university education. Olivares became the favorite of King Philip IV (1621–1665). He was elevated to the highest rank of the nobility and used his closeness to the monarch to gain court appointments for his relatives and political supporters.

But he was more interested in establishing political policy than in building a court faction. His objective was to maintain the greatness of Spain, and he attempted to further the process of centralizing Spanish royal power, which was not very advanced. Olivares's plans for a nationally recruited and financed army ended in disaster. His efforts at tax reform went unrewarded. He advocated the aggressive foreign policy that mired Spain in the Thirty Years' War and the eighty years of war in the Netherlands. As domestic and foreign crises mounted, Philip IV could not resist the pressure to dismiss his chief minister. In 1643, Olivares was removed from office; two years later, physically exhausted and mentally deranged, he died.

The Duke of Buckingham (1592–1628) was also a younger son but was not of the English nobility. He received the aimless education of a country gentleman, spending several years in France learning the graces of fashion and dancing. He was reputedly one of the handsomest men in Europe, and his looks and charm eventually brought him to the attention of

Queen Anne, the wife of James I. She recommended Buckingham for a minor office that gave him frequent access to the king, and in less than seven years he rose from commoner to duke, the highest rank of the English nobility.

Along with his titles, Buckingham acquired political power. He assumed a large number of royal offices, among them Admiral of the Navy, and placed his relatives and dependents in many others. Buckingham took his obligations seriously. He began a reform of naval administration, for example, but his rise to power was so sudden that he found enemies at every turn. These increased dramatically when James I died in 1625, but Buckingham still managed to become the favorite and chief minister of the new king, Charles I (1625–1649). With Charles I firmly behind him, his accumulation of power and patronage proceeded unabated, as did the enmity he aroused. In 1628, Buckingham was assassinated by a discontented naval officer. While Charles I wept inconsolably at the news, ordinary Londoners drank to the health of Buckingham's killer.

The Drive to Centralize Government

Richelieu, Olivares, and Buckingham met very different ends, but they shared a common goal: to extend the authority of the monarch over his state and to centralize his control over the machinery of governance. One of the chief means by which kings and councilors attempted to expand the authority of the state was through the legal system.

Administering justice was one of the sacred duties of the monarchy. The complexities of ecclesiastical, civil, and customary law gave trained lawyers an essential role in government. As the need for legal services increased, royal law courts multiplied and expanded. In France, the Parlement of Paris, the main law court of the state, became a powerful institution that contested with courtiers for the right to advise the monarch.

In Spain the *letrados*—university-trained lawyers who were normally members of the nobility—were the backbone of royal government. Formal legal training was a requirement for many of the administrative posts in the state. In Castile, members of all social classes frequently used the royal courts to settle personal disputes. The expansion of a centralized system of justice thus joined the interests of subjects and the monarchy.

In England, central courts situated in the royal palace of Westminster grew, and the lawyers and judges who practiced in them became a powerful profession. They were especially active in the House of Commons of the English Parliament, which, along with the House of Lords, had extensive advisory and legislative powers. More important than the rise of the central courts, however, was the rise of the local ones. The English crown extended royal justice to the counties by granting legal authority to members of the local social elite. These justices of the peace, whose position can be traced to medieval times, became agents of the crown in their own localities. Justices were given power to hear and settle minor cases and to imprison people who had committed serious offenses until the assizes, the semiannual sessions of the county court.

Assizes combined the ceremony of rule with its process. Royal authority was displayed in a great procession to the courthouse that was led by the judge and the county justices, followed by the grand and petty juries of local citizens who would hear the cases and finally by the carts carrying the prisoners to trial. Along with the legal business that was performed, assizes were occasions for edifying sermons, typically on the theme of obedience. Their solemnity, marked by the black robes of the judge, the Latin of the legal proceedings, and the public executions, served to instill a sense of the power of the state in the throngs of ordinary people who witnessed them.

Efforts to integrate center and locality extended to more than the exercise of justice. The monarch also needed officials who could enforce royal policy in localities where the special privileges of groups and individuals remained strong. By the beginning of the seventeenth century, the French monarchy had begun to rely on new central officials known as **intendants** to perform many of the tasks of the provincial governors. Cardinal Richelieu expanded the use of the intendants, and by the middle of the century they had become a vital part of royal government.

The Lords Lieutenant were a parallel institution created in England. Unlike every other European state, England had no national army. Every English county was required to raise, equip, and train its own militia. Lords Lieutenant were in charge of these trained bands. The lieutenants were chosen from the greatest nobles of the realm, but they delegated their work to members of the local gentry, large landholders who took on their tasks as a matter of prestige rather than profit. Perhaps not surprisingly, the English military was among the weakest in Europe, and nearly all its foreign adventures ended in disaster.

Efforts to centralize the Spanish monarchy could not proceed so easily. The separate regions over which the king ruled maintained their own laws and privileges. Attempts to apply Castilian rules or implant Castilian officials always drew opposition from other regions. In 1625, Olivares proposed a plan to help unify Spain and solve the dual problems of military manpower and military finance. After 1621, Spain was fighting in the Netherlands and Germany. Olivares called for a Union of Arms to which all the separate regions of the empire, including Mexico, Peru, Italy, and the dominions in Iberia, would contribute. Olivares was able to establish at least the principle of unified cooperation, but not all of the Iberian provinces were persuaded to contribute. Catalonia stood on its ancient privileges and refused to grant either troops or funds.

The Taxing Demands of War

More than anything else, the consolidation of the state was propelled by war, which required increased governmental powers of taxation. Perhaps half of all revenue of the western states went to finance war. To maintain its military forces, the state had to squeeze every penny from its subjects. Old taxes had to be collected more efficiently, and new taxes had to be introduced and enforced. Such unprecedented demands for money on the part of the state were always resisted. The privileged challenged the legality of levying taxes; the unprivileged tried to avoid paying them.

The economic hardships caused by the ceaseless military activity touched everyone. Those in the direct path of battle had little left to feed themselves, let alone to provide to the state. The disruption of the delicate cycle of planting and harvesting devastated local communities. Armies plundered ripened grain and trampled seedlings as they moved through fields. The conscription of village men and boys removed vital skills and labor from the community. Peasants were squeezed by the armies for crops, by the lords for rents, and by the state for taxes.

In fact, the inability of the lower orders of European society to finance a century of warfare was clear from the beginning. In Spain and France, much wealth was beyond the reach of traditional royal taxation. The nobility and many of the most important towns had long enjoyed exemption from basic taxes on consumption and wealth. European taxation was regressive, falling most heavily on those who were least able to pay. Rulers and subjects alike recognized the inequities of the system, and regime after regime considered overhauling the national tax system but ultimately settled for new emergency levies. Nevertheless, the fiscal crisis that the European wars provoked did result in an expansion of state taxation.

Military spending also increased in England. War with Ireland in the 1590s and with Spain between 1588 and 1604 depleted the reserves that the crown had obtained when Henry VIII dissolved the monasteries. Disastrous wars against France and Spain in the 1620s provoked fiscal crisis for a monarchy that had few direct sources of revenue. While the great wealth of the kingdom was in land, the chief sources of revenue for the crown were in trade. In the early seventeenth century, customs duties became a lucrative source of income when the judges ruled that the king could determine which commodities could be taxed and at what rate.

Because so much of the crown's revenues derived from commerce and because foreign invasion could come only from the sea, the most pressing military need of the English monarchy was for naval defense. Even during the Armada crisis, the largest part of the English fleet had been made up of private merchant ships pressed into service through the emergency tax of Ship Money. This was a tax on each port town to hire a merchant ship and fit it out for war. In the 1630s, Charles I revived Ship Money and extended it to all English localities.

Still, no matter how much new revenue was provided for war finance, more was needed. New taxes and increased rates of traditional taxation created suffering and a sense of grievance throughout the western European states. Opposition to taxation was not based on greed. The state's right to tax was not yet an established principle. Monarchs received certain forms of revenue in return for grants of immunities and privileges to powerful groups in their state. The state's efforts to go beyond these restricted grants was viewed as theft of private property. In the Ship Money case, challengers argued that the king had no right to such demands except in a case of national emergency. The king argued that such an emergency existed, since pirates were attacking English shipping. But if Charles I did not make a convincing claim for national emergency, the monarchs of France and Spain, the princes of Germany, and the rulers of the states of eastern Europe all did.

Throughout the seventeenth century, monarchy was consolidating its position as a form of government. The king's authority came from God, but his power came from his people. By administering justice, assembling armies, and extracting resources through taxation, the monarch ruled as well as governed. The richer and more powerful the king, the more potent was his state. His subjects began to identify themselves as citizens of a nation and to see themselves in distinction to other nations.

THE CRISES OF THE ROYAL STATE

The expansion of the functions, duties, and powers of the state in the early seventeenth century was not universally welcomed in European societies. The growth of central government came at the expense of local rights and privileges held by organized bodies such as the Church and the towns or by individuals such as provincial officials and aristocrats. The state proved to be a powerful competitor for the meager surplus produced on the land. As rents and prices stabilized in the early seventeenth century, after a long period of inflation, taxation increased, especially with the gathering momentum of the Thirty Years' War. State exactions burdened all segments of society. Peasants lost the small benefit that rising prices had conferred on producers. The surplus that parents had once passed on to children was now taken by the state. Local officials, never altogether popular, came to be seen as parasites and provided easy targets for peasant rebellions. Larger landholders, whose prosperity depended on rents and services from an increasingly impoverished peasantry, suffered along with their tenants. Even the great magnates were appalled by the state's insatiable appetite.

It was not only taxation that aroused opposition. Social and economic regulation meant more laws, more lawyers, and more agents of enforcement. State regulation was disruptive and expensive at a time when the fragile European economy was in decline. The early seventeenth century was a time of hunger in most of western Europe. Subtle changes in climate reduced the length of growing seasons and the size of crops. Bad harvests in the 1620s and 1640s left disease and starvation in their wake. And the wars ground on.

By the middle of the seventeenth century, a Europe-wide crisis was taking shape. Bread riots and tax revolts had become increasingly common in the early seventeenth century. As the focus of discontent moved from local institutions to the state, the forms of revolt and the participants also changed. Members of the political elite began to formulate their own grievances against the expansion of state power. A theory of resistance, first developed in the French wars of religion, came to be applied to political tyranny and posed a direct challenge to the idea of the divine right of kings. By the 1640s, all of these forces converged, and rebellion exploded across the Continent. In Spain, the ancient kingdoms of Catalonia and Portugal asserted their independence from Castilian rule; in France, members of the aristocracy rose against a child monarch and his regent. In Italy, revolts rocked Naples and Sicily. In England, a constitutional crisis gave way to civil war and then to the first political revolution in European history.

The Need to Resist

Europeans lived more precariously in the seventeenth century than in any period since the Black Death. One benchmark of crisis was population decline. In the Mediterranean, the Spanish population fell from 8.5 million to 7 million, and the Italian population from 13 million to 11 million. The ravages of the Thirty Years' War were most clearly felt in central Europe. Germany lost nearly one-third of its people; Bohemia lost nearly half. England, the Netherlands, and France were hardest hit in the first half of the century and only gradually recovered by 1700. Population decline had many causes, and

EUROPEAN POPULATION DATA (IN MILLIONS)							
Year	**1550**	**1575**	**1600**	**1625**	**1650**	**1675**	**1700**
England	3.0	—	4.0	4.5	—	5.8	5.8
France	—	20.0	—	—	—	—	19.3
Italy	11.0	13.0	13.0	13.0	12.0	11.5	12.5
Russia	9.0	—	11.0	8.0	9.5	13.0	16.0
Spain	6.3	—	7.6	—	5.2	—	7.0
All Europe	85.0	95.0	100.0	100.0	80.0	90.0	100.0

direct casualties from warfare were only a very small component. The indirect effects of war—the disruption of agriculture and the spread of disease—were far more devastating. Spain alone lost half a million people at the turn of the century and another half million between 1647 and 1652. Severe outbreaks of plague hit England in 1625 and in 1665, and France endured three consecutive years of epidemics from 1629 to 1631.

All sectors of the European economy from agriculture to trade stagnated or declined in the early seventeenth century, but peasants were hardest hit. The surplus from good harvests did not remain in rural communities to act as a buffer for bad ones. Tens of thousands died during the two great subsistence crises in the late 1620s and the late 1640s.

Acute economic crisis led to rural revolt. As the French peasants reeled from visitations of plague, frost, and floods, the French state was raising the taille, the tax on basic commodities that fell most heavily on the lower orders. A series of French rural revolts in the late 1630s protested tax increases. The *Nu-Pieds* ("barefooted") rose against changes in the salt tax; other peasants rose against new levies on wine. These revolts typically began with the murder of a local tax official, the organization of a peasant militia, and the recruitment of local clergy and notables. The rebels forced temporary concessions from local authorities but never achieved lasting reforms. Each revolt ended with the reimposition of order by the state. In England, the largest rural protests, such as the Midland Revolt of 1607, centered on opposition to the enclosure of grain fields and their conversion to pasture.

The most spectacular popular uprisings occurred in Spanish-occupied Italy. In the spring of 1647, in the Sicilian city of Palermo, violence broke out in the wake of a disastrous harvest, rising food prices, and relentless taxation. As grain prices rose, the city government subsidized the price of bread, running up huge debts in the process. When the town governors could no longer afford the subsidies, they decided to reduce the size of the loaf rather than increase its price. The women of the city rioted when the first undersized loaves were placed on sale, and soon the entire city was in revolt. Commoners who were not part of the urban power structure led the revolt, and for a time they achieved the abolition of Spanish taxes on basic foodstuffs. Their success provided the model for a similar uprising in Naples, the largest city in Europe. The revolt began in 1647 after the Spanish placed a tax on fruit. A crowd gathered in protest, burned the customs house, and murdered several local officials. The rebels again achieved the temporary suspension of Spanish taxation. But neither of the Italian urban revolts could attract support from the local governors or the nobility. Both uprisings were eventually crushed.

The Right to Resist

Rural and urban revolts by members of the lower orders of European society were doomed to failure. Not only did the state control vast military resources, but it could count on the loyalty of the governing classes to suppress local disorder. Only when disgruntled local elites joined the angry peasants did the state face a genuine crisis. Traditionally, aristocratic rebellion was sparked by rival claimants to the throne. By the early seventeenth century, however, hereditary monarchy was too firmly entrenched to be threatened by aristocratic rebellions. When Elizabeth I of England died without an heir, the throne passed to her cousin, James I, without even a murmur of discontent. In France, the assassination of Henry IV in 1610 left a child on the throne, yet it provoked little more than intrigue over which aristocratic faction would advise him. The principles of hereditary monarchy and the divine right of kings laid an unshakable foundation for royal legitimacy. But if the monarch's right to rule could no longer be challenged, was the method of rule equally unassailable? Were subjects bound to their sovereign in all cases whatsoever?

Resistance Theory. Luther and Calvin had preached a doctrine of passive obedience. Magistrates ruled by divine will and must be obeyed in all things, they argued. Both left a tiny crack in the door of absolute submission, however, by recognizing the right of lesser magistrates to resist their superiors if divine law was violated. During the French civil wars, a broader theory of resistance began to develop. In attempting to defend themselves from accusations that they were rebels, a number of Huguenot writers responded with an argument that accepted the divine right of kings but maintained that kings were placed on earth by God to uphold piety and justice. When they failed to do so, lesser magistrates were obliged to resist them. Because God would not institute tyranny, oppressive monarchs could not be acting by divine right. Therefore, the king who violated divine law could be punished. In the most influential of these writings, *A Defense of Liberty Against Tyrants* (1579), Philippe Duplessis-Mornay (1549–1623) took the critical next step and argued that the king who violated the law of the land could also be resisted.

In the writings of both the French Huguenots and the Dutch Protestants there remained strict limits to this right to resist. These authors accepted divine right theory and restricted resistance to other divinely ordained magistrates.

Logic soon drove the argument further. If it was the duty of lesser magistrates to resist monarchical tyranny, why was it not the duty of all citizens to do so? This question was posed by the Jesuit professor Juan de Mariana (1536–1624) in *The King and the Education of the King* (1598). Since magistrates were first established by the people and then legitimated by God, magistrates were nothing other than the people's representatives. If it was the duty of magistrates to resist the tyranny of monarchs, Mariana reasoned, then it must also be the duty of every individual citizen. "If the sacred fatherland is falling into ruins, he who tries to kill the tyrant will be acting in no ways unjustly."

In his defense of the English Revolution, the great English poet John Milton (1608–1674) built on traditional resistance theory. Kings were instituted by the people to uphold piety and justice. Lesser magistrates had the right to resist monarchs. An unjust king forfeited his divine right and was to be punished like any ordinary citizen. In *The Tenure of Kings and Magistrates* (1649), Milton expanded on the conventional idea that society was formed by a covenant, or contract, between ruler and ruled. The king, in his coronation oath, promised to uphold the laws of the land and to rule for the benefit of his subjects. The subjects promised to obey. Failure to meet obligations—by either side—broke the contract.

Resistance and Rebellion. By the middle of the seventeenth century, resistance theory provided the intellectual justification for a number of attacks on monarchical authority. In 1640, simultaneous rebellions in the ancient kingdoms of Portugal and Catalonia threatened the Spanish monarchy. The Portuguese successfully dissolved the rather artificial bonds that had been created by Philip II and resumed their separate national identity. Catalonia, the easternmost province of Spain, which Ferdinand of Aragon had brought to the union of crowns in the fifteenth century, presented a more serious challenge. Throughout the 1620s, Catalonia, with its rich Mediterranean city of Barcelona, had consistently rebuffed Olivares's attempts to consolidate the Spanish provinces. The Catalan Cortes—the representative institution of the towns—refused to make even small contributions to the Union of Arms or to successive appeals for emergency tax increases. Catalonian

leaders feared that these demands were only an entering wedge. They did not want their province to go the way of Castile, where taxation was as much an epidemic as was plague.

Catalonia resisted demands for contributions to the Spanish military effort, but soon the province was embroiled in the French war, and Olivares was forced to bring troops into Catalonia. The presence of the soldiers and their conduct inflamed the local population. In the spring of 1640, an unconnected series of peasant uprisings took place. Soldiers and royal officials were slain, and the Spanish viceroy of the province was murdered. But the violence was not directed only against outsiders. Attacks on wealthy citizens raised the specter of social revolt.

It was at this point that a peasant uprising broadened into a provincial rebellion. The political leaders of Barcelona sanctioned the rebellion and decided to lead it. They declared that Philip IV had violated the fundamental laws of Catalonia and that in consequence their allegiance to the crown of Spain was dissolved. They turned to Louis XIII of France, offering him sovereignty if he would preserve their liberties. In fact, the Catalonians simply exchanged a devil they knew for one they did not. The French happily sent troops into Barcelona to repel a Spanish attempt to crush the rebellion. Now two armies occupied Catalonia. The Catalan rebellion lasted for 12 years. When the Spanish finally took Barcelona in 1652, both rebels and ruler were exhausted from the struggle.

The revolt of the Catalans posed a greater external threat to the Spanish monarchy than it did an internal one. In contrast, the French **Fronde,** an aristocratic rebellion that began in 1648, was more directly a challenge to the underlying authority of the state. It too began in response to fiscal crises brought on by war. Throughout the 1640s, the French state, tottering on the edge of bankruptcy, had used every means of creative financing that its ministers could devise. Still, it was necessary to raise traditional taxes and to institute new ones. The first tactic revived peasant revolts, especially in the early years of the decade; the second led to the Fronde.

The Fronde was a rebellion against the regency government of Louis XIV (1643–1715), who was only four years old when he inherited the French throne. His mother, Anne of Austria (1601–1666), ruled as regent with the help of her Italian adviser, Cardinal Mazarin (1602–1661). In the circumstances of war, agricultural crisis, and financial stringency, no regency government was going to be popular, but Anne and Mazarin made the worst of a bad situation. They initiated new taxes on officeholders, Parisian landowners, and the nobility. Soon all three groups united against them, led by the Parlement of Paris, the highest court in the land, in which new decrees of taxation had to be registered. When the Parlement refused to register a number of the new taxes proposed by the government and soon insisted on the right to control the crown's financial policy, Anne and Mazarin struck back by having a number of Parlement members arrested. But in 1648, barricades went up in Paris, and the court, along with the nine-year-old king, fled the capital. Quickly, the Fronde—which took its name from the slingshots that children used to hurl stones at carriages—became an aristocratic revolt aimed not at the king but at his advisers. Demands for Mazarin's resignation, the removal of the new taxes, and greater participation in government by nobles and Parlement were coupled with profuse statements of loyalty to the king.

The duc de Condé, leader of the Parisian insurgents, courted Spanish aid against Mazarin's forces, and the cardinal was forced to make concessions to prevent a Spanish invasion of France. The leaders of the Fronde agreed that the crown must overhaul its finances and recognize the rights of the administrative nobility to participate in formulating royal policy. But they had no concrete proposals to accomplish either aim. Nor could they control the deteriorating political situation in Paris and a number of provincial capitals, where urban and rural riots followed the upper-class attack on the state. The catastrophic winter of 1652, with its combination of harvest failure, intense cold, and epidemic disease, brought the crisis to a head. Louis XIV was declared old enough to rule, and his forces recaptured Paris, where he was welcomed as a savior. The Fronde accomplished little other than to demonstrate that the French aristocracy remained an independent force in politics. Like the Catalonian revolt, it revealed the fragility of the absolute state on the one hand, yet its underlying stability on the other.

The English Civil War

The most profound challenge to monarchical authority in the seventeenth century took place in England. In 1603, James I succeeded his cousin Elizabeth I without challenge. He was not a lovable monarch, but he was capable, astute, and generous. His principal difficulties were that he was Scottish and that he succeeded a legend. Elizabeth I had ruled England successfully for over forty years. As the economy soured and the state tilted toward bankruptcy in the 1590s, the queen remained above criticism. She sold off royal lands worth thousands of pounds and ran up huge debts at the turn of the century. Yet the gleaming myth of the glorious virgin queen was not the least bit tarnished, and when she died, the general population wept openly.

At first, James I endeared himself to the English gentry and aristocracy by showering them with the gift of social elevation. On his way to London from Scotland, the first of the Stuart kings knighted thousands of gentlemen. But he showered favor equally on his own countrymen, members of his royal Scottish court who accompanied him to England. A strong strain of ethnic prejudice combined with the disappointed hopes of English courtiers to generate immediate hostility to the new regime. Though he relied on Elizabeth's most trusted ministers to guide state business, James was soon plunged into financial and political difficulties. He never escaped from either.

Charles I. James's financial problems resulted directly from the fact that the tax base of the English monarchy was undervalued. For decades the monarchy had staved off a crisis by selling lands that had been confiscated from the Church in the mid-sixteenth century. But this solution reduced the Crown's long-term revenues and made it dependent on extraordinary grants of taxation from Parliament. Royal demands for money were met by parliamentary demands for political reform. The most significant, in 1628, during the reign of Charles I, led to the formulation of the Petition of Right, which restated the traditional English freedoms from arbitrary arrest and imprisonment (habeas corpus), from nonparliamentary taxation, and from the confiscation of property by martial law.

Religious problems mounted on top of economic and political difficulties. **Puritans** were demanding thoroughgoing church reforms. One of the most contentious issues raised by some Puritans was the survival in the Anglican Church of the Catholic hierarchy of archbishops and bishops. These Puritans demanded the abolition of this episcopal form of government and its replacement with a presbyterial system

■ Charles I by Daniel Myrtens. The antagonism between Charles and Parliament sparked a civil war in England.

similar to that in Scotland, in which congregations nominated their own representatives to a national assembly. Neither James I nor his son, Charles I, opposed religious reform, but to achieve their reforms, they strengthened episcopal power. In the 1620s, Archbishop William Laud (1573–1645) rose to power in the English church by espousing a Calvinism so moderate that many denied it was Calvinism at all. Laud preached the beauty of holiness and strove to reintroduce decoration in the church and a formal decorum in the service. One of Laud's first projects after he was appointed archbishop of Canterbury was to establish a consistent divine service in England and Scotland by creating new prayer books.

It fell to the unfortunate dean of St. Giles Cathedral in Edinburgh to introduce the new Scottish prayer book in 1637. The reaction was immediate: Someone threw a stool at his head, and dozens of women screamed that "popery" was being brought to Scotland. Citizens rioted, and the clergy and the nobility resisted the use of the new prayer book. To Charles I the opposition was rebellion, and he began to raise forces to suppress it. But the Scots fought back, and by the end of 1640 an army of Charles's Scottish subjects had successfully invaded England.

Now the fiscal and political problems of the Stuart monarchs came into play. For 11 years, Charles I had managed to live from his own revenues. He had accomplished this by a combination of economy and the revival of ancient feudal rights that struck hard at the governing classes. He levied fines for unheard-of offenses, expanded traditional taxes, and added a brutal efficiency to the collection of revenue. While these expedients sufficed during peacetime, they could not support an army and war. Charles I was again dependent on grants from Parliament, which he reluctantly summoned in 1640.

The Long Parliament.   The **Long Parliament,** which met in November 1640 and sat for thirteen years, saw little urgency in levying taxes to repel the Scots. After all, the Scots were resisting Laud's religious innovations, and many Englishmen agreed that they should be resisted. Parliament proposed a number of constitutional reforms that Charles I reluctantly accepted. The Long Parliament would not be dismissed without its own consent. In the future, Parliaments would be summoned once in every three years. Due process in common law would be observed, and the ancient taxes that the Crown had revived would be abolished.

At first, Charles I could do nothing but bide his time and accept these assaults on his power and authority. Once he had crushed the Scots, he would be able to bargain from a position of strength. But as the months passed, it became clear that Parliament had no intention of providing him with money or forces. By the end of 1641, Charles's patience had worn thin. He bungled an attempt to arrest the leaders of the House of Commons, but he successfully spirited his wife and children out of London. Then he too left the capital and headed north, where, in the summer of 1642, he raised the royal standard and declared the leaders of Parliament rebels and traitors. England was plunged into civil war.

There were strong passions on both sides. Parliamentarians believed that they were fighting to defend their religion, their liberties, and the rule of law. Royalists believed that they were

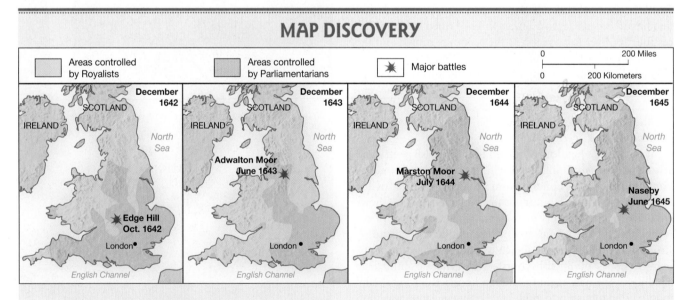

MAP DISCOVERY

English Civil War

How would you describe the geographical divisions at the beginning of the war in 1642? Who appears to have been winning the war by December 1643? How did the war progress between 1644 and 1645?

fighting to defend their monarch, their church, and social stability. After nearly three years of inconclusive fighting, Parliament won a decisive victory at Naseby in June 1645 and brought the war to an end the following summer. The king was in captivity, bishops had been abolished, a Presbyterian church had been established, and limitations were placed on royal power. All that was necessary to end three years of civil war was the king's agreement to abide by the judgment of battle.

But Charles I had no intention of surrendering either his religion or his authority. Despite the rebels' successes, they could not rule without him, and he would concede nothing as long as opportunities to maneuver remained. In 1647 there were opportunities galore. The war had proved ruinously expensive to Parliament. It owed enormous sums to the Scots, to its own soldiers, and to the governors of London. Each of these elements had its own objectives in a final settlement of the war, and they were not altogether compatible. London feared the parliamentary army, unpaid and camped dangerously close to the capital. The Scots and the English Presbyterians in Parliament feared that the religious settlement that had already been made would be sacrificed by those known as Independents, who desired a more decentralized church. The Independents feared that they would be persecuted just as harshly by the Presbyterians as they had been by the king. In fact, the war had settled nothing.

The English Revolutions

Charles I happily played both ends against the middle until the army decisively ended the game. In June 1647, parliamentary soldiers kidnapped the king and demanded that Parliament pay their arrears, protect them from legal retribution, and recognize their service to the nation. Those in Parliament who opposed the army's intervention were impeached, and when London Presbyterians rose up against the army's show of force, troops moved in to occupy the city. The civil war, which had come so close to resolution in 1647, had now become a military revolution. Religious and political radicals flocked to the army and encouraged the soldiers to support their programs and to resist disbandment. New fighting broke out in 1648, as Charles encouraged his supporters to resume the war. But forces under the command of Sir Thomas Fairfax (1612–1671) and Oliver Cromwell (1599–1658) easily crushed the royalist uprisings in England and Scotland. The army now demanded that Charles I be brought to justice for his treacherous conduct both before and during the war. When the majority in Parliament refused, still hoping to reach an accommodation with the king, the soldiers again acted decisively. In December 1648, army regiments were sent to London to purge the two houses of Parliament of those who opposed the army's demands. The remaining members, contemptuously called the Rump Parliament, voted to bring the king to trial for his crimes against the liberties of his subjects. On 30 January 1649, Charles I was executed, and England was declared to be a commonwealth. The monarchy and the House of Lords were abolished, and the nation was to be governed by what was left of the membership of the House of Commons.

Oliver Cromwell.   For four years, the members of the Rump Parliament struggled with proposals for a new constitution, achieving little. In 1653, Oliver Cromwell, with the support of the army's senior officers, forcibly dissolved the Rump and became the leader of the revolutionary government. At first he ruled along with a Parliament that had been handpicked from among the supporters of the commonwealth. When Cromwell's Parliament proved no more capable of governing than had the Rump, a written constitution, The Instrument of Government (1653), established a new polity. Cromwell was given the title Lord Protector, and he was to rule along with a freely elected Parliament and an administrative body known as the council of state.

Cromwell was able to smooth over conflicts and hold the revolutionary cause together through the force of his own personality. He was a devout Puritan who had opposed the arbitrary policies of Charles I and who believed in a large measure of religious toleration for Christians. Though many urged him to accept the crown of England and begin a new monarchy, Cromwell steadfastly held out for a government in which fundamental authority resided in Parliament. Until his death he defended the achievements of the revolution.

But a sense that only a single person could effectively rule a state remained strong. When Cromwell died in 1658, his oldest son Richard was proposed as the new lord protector, but Richard had very little experience in either military or civil affairs. Nor did he have the sense of purpose that was his father's greatest source of strength. Without an individual to hold the movement together, the revolution fell apart. In 1659, the army again intervened in civil affairs, dismissing the recently elected Parliament and calling for the restoration of the monarchy. After a period of negotiation in which the king agreed to a general amnesty with only a few exceptions, the Stuarts were restored when Charles II (1649–1685) took the throne in 1660.

Twenty years of civil war and revolution had their effect. Parliament became a permanent part of civil government. Royal power over taxation and religion was curtailed, though in fact Parliament proved more vigorous in suppressing religious dissent than the monarchy ever was. England was to be a reformed Protestant state, though there remained much dispute about what constituted reform. Absolute monarchy had become constitutional monarchy with the threat of revolution behind the power of Parliament and the threat of anarchy behind the power of the Crown.

The Glorious Revolution.   The threats of revolution and of anarchy proved potent in 1685 when James II (1685–1688) came to the throne. A declared Catholic, James attempted to use his power of appointment to foil the constraints that Parliament imposed on him. He elevated Catholics to leading posts in the military and in the central government and began a campaign to pack a new Parliament with his supporters. This

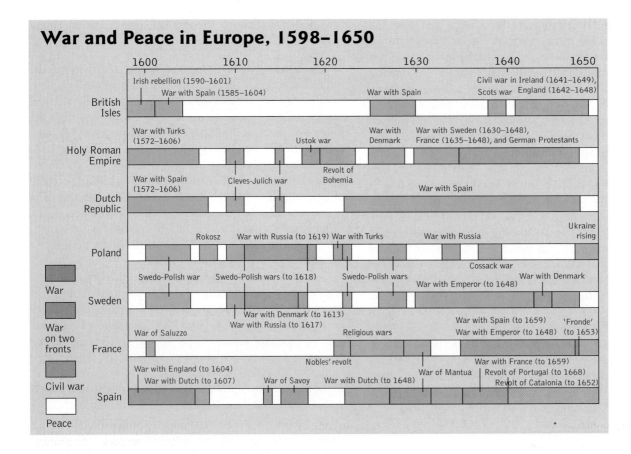

War and Peace in Europe, 1598–1650

proved to be too much for the governing classes, which entered into negotiations with William, prince of Orange, who was the husband of Mary Stuart, James's eldest daughter. In 1688, William landed in England with a small force. Without support, James II fled to France, the English throne was declared vacant, and William and Mary were proclaimed king and queen of England. There was little bloodshed and little threat of social disorder, and the event soon came to be called the **Glorious Revolution.** Its achievements were set down in the Declaration of Rights (1689), which was presented to William and Mary before they took the throne. The declaration reasserted the fundamental principles of constitutional monarchy as they had developed over the previous half-century. Security of property and the regularity of Parliaments were guaranteed. The Toleration Act (1689) granted religious freedom to nearly all groups of Protestants. The liberties of the subject and the rights of the sovereign were to be in balance.

The events of 1688 in England reversed a trend toward increasing power on the part of the Stuarts. This second episode of resistance resulted in the development of a unique form of government, which, a century later, spawned dozens of imitators. John Locke (1632–1704) was the theorist of the Revolution of 1688. He was heir to the century-old debate on resistance, and he carried the doctrine to a new plateau. In *Two Treatises on Government* (1689), Locke developed the contract theory of government. Political society was a compact that individuals entered into freely for their own well-being. It was designed to maintain each person's natural rights:

life, liberty, and property. Natural rights were inherent in individuals; they could not be given away. The contract between rulers and subjects was an agreement for the protection of natural rights. When rulers acted arbitrarily, they were to be deposed by their subjects, preferably in the relatively peaceful manner in which James II had been replaced by William III.

The efforts of European monarchies to centralize their power came at the expense of the Church, the aristocracy, and the localities. It was a difficult struggle that took place over decades. In France, the Fronde was an aristocratic backlash; in Spain, the revolt of the Catalans pitted the Castilian crown against a proud ethnic province. In England, the excesses of monarchy were succeeded by the excesses of parliamentary rule. But the lesson that the English ruling elites learned was that for a nation to enjoy the benefits of a powerful central authority, it was necessary to restrain that authority. The Revolution of 1688 helped to create a constitutional balance between ruler and ruled.

THE ZENITH OF THE ROYAL STATE

The midcentury crises tested the mettle of the royal states. Over the long term, the seventeenth-century crises had two different consequences. First, they provided a check to the exercise of royal power. Fear of recurring rebellions had a chilling effect on policy, especially taxation. Reforms of financial administration, long overdue, were one of the themes of the later seventeenth century. Even as royal government strengthened itself, it remained concerned about the impact of its policies. The memory of rebellion also served to control the ambitions of factious noblemen and town oligarchies.

If nothing else, these episodes of opposition to the rising royal states made clear the universal desire for stable government, which was seen as the responsibility of both subjects and rulers. By the second half of the seventeenth century, effective government was the byword of the royal state. The natural advantages of monarchy had to be merged with the interests of the citizens of the state and their desires for wealth, safety, and honor. After so much chaos and instability the monarchy had to be elevated above the fray of day-to-day politics to become a symbol of the nation's power and glory.

In England, Holland, and Sweden a form of constitutional monarchy developed in which rulers shared power, in varying degrees, with other institutions of state. In England it was Parliament; in Holland, the town oligarchies; in Sweden, the nobility. But in most other states in Europe there developed a pure form of royal government known as **absolutism.** Absolute monarchy revived the divine right theories of kingship and added to them a cult of the personality of the ruler. Absolutism was practiced in states as dissimilar as Denmark, Brandenburg-Prussia, and Russia. It reached its zenith in France under Louis XIV, the most powerful of the seventeenth-century monarchs.

The Nature of Absolute Monarchy

Locke's theory of contract provided one solution to the central problem of seventeenth-century government: how to balance the monarch's right to command and the subjects' duty to obey. By establishing a constitutional monarchy, in which power was shared between the ruler and a representative assembly of subjects, England found one path out of this thicket. But it was not a path that many others could follow.

The English solution was most suited to a state that was largely immune from invasion and land war. Constitutional government required a higher level of political participation of citizens than did absolute monarchy. Greater participation meant greater freedom of expression, greater toleration of religious minorities, and greater openness in the institutions of government. All were dangerous. The price that England paid was a half-century of governmental instability.

The alternative to constitutional monarchy was absolute monarchy. It, too, found its leading theorist in England. Thomas Hobbes (1588–1679), in his greatest work, *Leviathan* (1651), argued that before civil society had been formed, humans had lived in a savage state of nature, "in a war of every man against every man." This was a ghastly condition without morality or law. People came together to form a government for the most basic of all purposes: self-preservation. Without government they were condemned to a life that was "solitary, poor, nasty, brutish, and short." To escape the state of nature, individuals pooled their power and granted it to a ruler. The terms of the Hobbesian contract were simple. Rulers agreed to

rule; subjects agreed to obey. When the contract was intact, people ceased to live in a state of nature. When it was broken, they returned to it. With revolts, rebellions, and revolutions erupting in all parts of Europe, Hobbes's state of nature never seemed very far away.

For most states of Europe in the later seventeenth century, absolute monarchy became not only a necessity but an ideal. The consolidation of power in the hands of the divinely ordained monarch, who, nevertheless, ruled according to principles of law and justice, was seen as the perfect form of government.

The main features of absolute monarchy were all designed to extend royal control. As in the early seventeenth century, the person of the monarch was revered. Courts grew larger and more lavish in an effort to enhance the glory of the monarchy and thereby of the state. "*L'état, c'est moi*" ("I am the state"), Louis XIV was supposed to have said. As the king grew in stature, his competitors for power all shrank. Large numbers of nobles were herded together at court under the watchful eye of monarchs who now ruled rather than reigned. The king shed the cloak of his favorites and rolled up his own sleeves to manage state affairs. Representative institutions were weakened or cast aside. Monarchs needed standing armies trained in the increasingly sophisticated arts of war, so the military was expanded and made an integral part of the machinery of government. The military profession developed within nations, gradually replacing mercenary adventurers who fought for booty rather than for duty.

Yet the absolute state was never as powerful in practice as it was in theory. Nor did it ever exist in its ideal shape. Absolutism was always in the making, never quite made. Its success depended on a strong monarch who knew his own will and could enforce it. It depended on unity within the state, on the absence or ruthless suppression of religious or political minorities. The absolute ruler needed to control information and ideas to limit criticism of state policy. Ultimately, the absolute state rested on the will of its citizens to support it.

Absolutism in the East

Frederick William, the Great Elector of Brandenburg-Prussia (1640–1688), made highly effective use of the techniques of absolutism. In 1640, he inherited a scattered and ungovernable collection of territories. The nobility, known as *die Junker*, enjoyed immunity from almost all forms of direct taxation, and the towns had no obligation to furnish either men or supplies for military operations beyond their walls.

When Frederick William attempted to introduce an excise—the commodity tax on consumption that had so successfully financed the Dutch Revolt and the English Revolution—he was initially rebuffed. But military emergency overcame legal precedents. By the 1650s, Frederick William had established the excise in the towns, though not in the countryside.

With the excise as a steady source of revenue, the Great Elector set about forming one of the most capable and best disciplined standing armies of the age. He organized one of the first departments of war to oversee all of the details of the creation of his army, from housing and supplies to the training of young officer candidates. This department was also responsible for the collection of taxes. By integrating military and civilian government, Frederick William established an efficient state bureaucracy that was particularly responsive in times of crisis. The creation of the Prussian army was the force that led to the creation of the Prussian state.

The same materials that forged the Prussian state led to the transformation of Russia. Soon after the young Tsar Peter I, known later as "the Great" (1682–1725), came to the throne, he realized that he could compete with the western states only by learning to play their game.

Like Frederick William, Peter concentrated on military reform. He understood that if Russia was to flourish in a world dominated by war and commerce, it would have to reestablish its hold on the Baltic ports. This meant dislodging the Swedes from the Russian mainland and creating a fleet to protect

Russian trade. Neither goal seemed likely. The Swedes were one of the great powers of the age, constant innovators in battlefield tactics and military organization. Peter studied their every campaign. His first wars against the Swedes ended in humiliating defeats, but with each failure came a sharper sense of what was needed to succeed.

First Peter introduced a system of conscription and created a standing army. He unified the military command at the top and stratified it in the field. He established promotion based on merit and established military schools to train cadets for the next generation of officers.

Finally, in 1709, Peter realized his ambitions. At the battle of Poltava, the Russian army routed the Swedes, wounding King Charles XII, annihilating his infantry, and capturing dozens of his leading officers. After the battle of Poltava, Russia gradually replaced Sweden as the dominant power in the Baltic.

As an absolute ruler, Peter the Great's power was unlimited, but it was not uncontested. He secularized the Russian

MAP DISCOVERY

Expansion of Russia Under Peter the Great

Notice the extent of the Russian Empire in 1689 and territory added by Peter the Great. What was important about the new territory? What was the role of the battle of Poltava in expanding the empire? The route of Peter's trip to western Europe is marked here. Why did he travel where he did? Based on the chapter discussion, what impact did his trip have on the way he ruled his empire?

Orthodox church, subjecting it to state control and confiscating much of its wealth. He broke the old military service class, which attempted a coup d'état when he was abroad in the 1690s. By the end of his reign, the Russian monarchy was among the strongest in Europe.

The Origins of French Absolutism

Nowhere was absolutism as successfully implanted as in France. Louis XIII (1610–1643) was only eight years old when he came to the throne, and he grew slowly into his role under the tutelage of Cardinal Richelieu. It was Richelieu's vision that stabilized French government. As chief minister, Richelieu saw clearly that France's survival and prosperity depended on strengthening royal power. He preached a doctrine of *raison d'état* ("reason of state"), in which he placed the needs of the nation above the privileges of its most important groups. Richelieu saw three threats to stable royal government: the Huguenots, the nobles, and the most powerful provincial governors.

Richelieu took measures to control all three. The power of the nobles was the most difficult to attack. The nobles' long tradition of independence from the crown had been enhanced by the wars of religion. The ancient aristocracy, the nobility of the sword, felt themselves to be in a particularly vulnerable position. Their world was changing, and their traditional roles were becoming obsolete. Professional soldiers replaced them at war, professional administrators at government. Mercantile wealth threatened their economic superiority, and the growth of the nobility of the robe—lawyers and state officials—threatened their social standing. They were hardly likely to take orders from a royal minister such as Richelieu.

To limit the power of local officials, Richelieu used intendants to examine their conduct and to reform their administration. He made careful appointments of local governors and brought more regions under direct royal control. Against the Calvinists, who were called Huguenots in France, Richelieu's policy was more subtle. He was less interested in challenging their religion than their autonomy. In 1627, when the English sent a force to aid the Huguenots against the government, Richelieu and Louis XIII abolished the Huguenots' privileges altogether. They were allowed to maintain their religion but not their special status. Finally, in 1685, Louis XIV revoked the Edict of Nantes, which had guaranteed civil and religious rights to the Huguenots. All forms of Protestant worship were outlawed, and the ministers who were not hunted down and killed were forced into exile. Despite a ban on Protestant emigration, over 200,000 Huguenots fled the country, many of them carrying irreplaceable skills with them to Holland and England in the west and to Brandenburg in the east.

Richelieu's program was a vital prelude to the development of absolute monarchy in France. The cardinal did not act without the full support of Louis XIII, but there can be no doubt that Richelieu was the power behind the throne. Louis XIII hated the business of government and even neglected his principal responsibility of providing the state with an heir. For years, he and his wife slept in separate palaces, and only a freak rainstorm in Paris forced him to spend a night with the queen, Anne of Austria, in 1637. It was the night of the conception of Louis XIV. Louis XIII and Richelieu died within six months of each other in 1642–1643, and the nation again endured the turmoil of a child king.

Louis le Grand

Not quite five years old when he came to the throne, Louis XIV was tutored by Cardinal Jules Mazarin (1602–1661), Richelieu's successor as chief minister. Mazarin was more ruthless and less popular than his predecessor, but like Richelieu, he was an excellent administrator.

The King and His Ministers.   In order to pacify the rebellious nobility of the Fronde, who opposed Mazarin's power, Louis XIV was declared to have reached his majority at the age of 13. But it was not until Mazarin died ten years later, in 1661, that the king began to rule.

Louis was blessed with able and energetic ministers. The two central props of his state—money and might—were in the hands of dynamic men, Jean-Baptiste Colbert (1619–1683) and the Marquis de Louvois (1639–1691). Colbert, to whom credit belongs for the building of the French navy, the reform of French legal codes, and the establishment of national academies of culture, was Louis's chief minister for finance. Colbert's fiscal reforms were so successful that in less than six years a debt of 22 million French pounds had become a surplus of 29 million. Colbert achieved this astonishing feat not by raising taxes but by increasing the efficiency of their collection. Until Louis embarked on his wars, the French state was solvent.

To Louvois, Louis's minister of war, fell the task of reforming the French army. During the Fronde, royal troops were barely capable of defeating the makeshift forces of the nobility. By the end of the reign, the army had grown to 400,000, and its organization had been thoroughly reformed.

Louis XIV furthered the practice of relying on professional administrators to supervise the main departments of state and to offer advice on matters of policy. He built on the institution of the intendant that Richelieu had developed with so much success. Intendants were now a permanent part of government, and their duties expanded from their early responsibilities as coordinators and mediators into areas of policing and tax collection. It was through the intendants that the wishes of central government were made known in the provinces.

The Court of Versailles.   Though Louis XIV was well served, it was the king himself who set the tone for French absolutism. "If he was not the greatest king he was the best actor of majesty that ever filled the throne," wrote an English observer. The acting of majesty was central to Louis's rule. His residence at Versailles was the most glittering court of Europe. When the court and king moved there permanently in 1682, Versailles became the envy of the Continent. But behind the imposing facade of Versailles stood a well-thought-out plan for domestic and international rule.

■ This Hyacinthe Rigaud portrait of Louis XIV in his coronation robes shows the splendor of *Le Roi Soleil* (the Sun King), who believed himself to be the center of France as the sun is the center of the solar system.

Louis XIV attempted to tame the French nobles by requiring their attendance at his court. Louis established a system of court etiquette so complex that constant study was necessary to prevent humiliation. While the nobility studied decorum, they could not plot rebellion. Leading noblemen of France rose at dawn so that they could watch Louis be awakened and hear him speak his first words. Dozens followed him from hall to gallery and from gallery to chamber as he washed, dressed, prayed, and ate. There was no greater concern than the king's health, unless it was the king's mood, which was as changeable as the weather.

During Louis's reign, France replaced Spain as the greatest nation in Europe. Massive royal patronage of art, science, and thought brought French culture to new heights. The French language replaced Latin as the universal European tongue. France was the richest and most populous European state, and Louis's absolute rule finally harnessed these resources to a single purpose. France became a commercial power rivaling the Netherlands, a naval power rivaling England, and a military power without peer. It was not only for effect that Louis took the image of the sun as his own. In court, in the nation, and throughout Europe, everything revolved around him.

Louis XIV made his share of mistakes. His aggressive foreign policy ultimately bankrupted the crown. But without doubt, his greatest error was to persecute the Huguenots. As an absolute ruler, Louis regarded the Huguenots, with their separate communities and distinct forms of worship, as an affront to his authority. Supporters of the monarchy celebrated the revocation of the Edict of Nantes in 1685 as an act of piety. But the persecution of the Huguenots was a social and political disaster for France. The Huguenots who fled to other Protestant states spread stories of atrocities that stiffened European resolve against Louis. Those who remained became an embittered minority who pulled at the fabric of the state at every chance. Nor did the official abolition of Protestantism have much effect on its existence. Against these policies the Huguenots held firmly to their beliefs. There were well over one million French Protestants, undoubtedly the largest religious minority in any state. Huguenots simply went underground, practicing their religion secretly and gradually replacing their numbers. No absolutism, however powerful, could succeed in eradicating religious beliefs.

CONCLUSION

Louis XIV gave his name to the age that he and his nation dominated, but he was not its only towering figure. The Great Elector, Peter the Great, Louis the Great—so they were judged by posterity—all had forged nations for a new age. Their style of rule showed the royal state at its height, still revolving around the king but more and more dependent on permanent institutions of government that followed their own imperatives. The absolute state harnessed the economic and intellectual resources of the nation to the political will of the monarch, who ruled by incorporating vital elements of the state into the process of government. In England, the importance of the landholding classes was recognized in the constitutional powers of Parliament. The rights of the monarch were balanced against the liberties of the subject. In Prussia, the military power of the Junker was asserted through command in the army, the most important institution of the state. In France, Louis XIV co-opted many nobles at his court, while he made use of a talented pool of lawyers, clergymen, and administrators in his government. A delicate balance existed between the will of the king and the will of the state, a balance that would soon lead these Continental powers into economic competition and military confrontation.

QUESTIONS FOR REVIEW

1. How did war in the seventeenth century contribute to the creation of more powerful monarchical states?
2. What religious and political ideas were developed to justify resistance to monarchical authority?
3. What political and religious problems combined to bring England to civil war, and what results did the conflict produce in English government?
4. How did rulers such as Frederick William of Brandenburg, Peter the Great, or Louis XIV, and theorists such as Hobbes, justify absolute monarchical power?

KEY TERMS

absolutism, *p. 331*

divine right of kings, *p. 321*

Fronde, *p. 326*

Glorious Revolution, *p. 330*

intendants, *p. 323*

Long Parliament, *p. 328*

Puritans, *p. 327*

DISCOVERING WESTERN CIVILIZATION ONLINE

You can obtain more information about the royal state in the seventeenth century at the websites listed below. See also the Companion Website that accompanies this text, www.ablongman.com/kishlansky, which contains an online study guide and additional resources.

The Crises of the Royal State

Internet Modern History Sourcebook: Constitutional States

www.fordham.edu/halsall/mod/modsbook06.html

Links to sources relating to the reign of Charles I and the revolution against him.

The Execution of Charles I

www.baylor.edu/BIC/WCIII/Essays/charles.1.html

Excerpts from primary sources describing the execution of Charles I.

The Zenith of the Royal State

Baroque Living History Society: L'Age d'Or & Kirke's Lambs

www.kipar.org/

A site on the Golden Age of France in the seventeenth century but with extensive links to English and Dutch materials on a variety of subjects.

Chateau de Versailles

www.chateauversailles.fr/en

The website of Versailles, with views of the gardens and rooms inside the palace. (Version of site in English.)

Creating French Culture

www.loc.gov/exhibits/bnf/bnf0005.html

The Library of Congress's exhibition on the Age of Absolutism shows manuscripts, medals, and portraits of leading figures at the French court.

SUGGESTIONS FOR FURTHER READING

General Reading

Perry Anderson, *Lineages of the Absolutist State* (London: NLB Books, 1974). A sociological study of the role of absolutism in the development of the Western world.

Euan Cameron, ed., *Early Modern Europe: An Oxford History* (Oxford, New York: Oxford University Press, 1999). Valuable essays by leading historians with well-chosen topics and illustrations.

Thomas Munck, *Seventeenth-Century Europe, 1598–1700* (New York: St. Martin's Press, 1990). A comprehensive survey.

David Sturdy, *Fractured Europe 1600–1721* (Oxford: Blackwell, 2002). A thorough survey of the complex military and political events of the long seventeenth century.

The Rise of the Royal State

Yves-Marie Bercé, *The Birth of Absolutism* (London: Macmillan, 1996). A history of France from the reign of Louis XIV to the eve of the Revolution by a leading historian of France.

J. H. Elliott, *Richelieu and Olivares* (Cambridge: Cambridge University Press, 1984). A brilliant dual portrait.

J. H. Elliott and Jonathan Brown, *A Palace for a King* (New Haven, CT: Yale University Press, 1980). An outstanding work on the building and decorating of a Spanish palace.

Graham Parry, *The Golden Age Restor'd* (New York: St. Martin's Press, 1981). A study of English court culture in the reigns of James I and Charles I.

The Crises of the Royal State

Jonathan Israel, ed., *The Anglo-Dutch Moment* (Cambridge: Cambridge University Press, 1991). Essays by an international team of scholars on the European dimensions of the Revolution of 1688.

M. A. Kishlansky, *A Monarchy Transformed* (London: Penguin Books, 1996). A narrative survey of a remarkable era.

G. Parker and L. Smith, eds., *The General Crisis of the Seventeenth Century* (London: Routledge & Kegan Paul, 1978). A collection of essays on the problem of the general crisis.

Quentin Skinner, *The Foundations of Modern Political Thought,* 2 vols. (Cambridge: Cambridge University Press, 1978). A seminal work on the history of ideas from Machiavelli to Calvin.

W. A. Speck, *The Revolution of 1688* (Oxford: Oxford University Press, 1988). The best single volume on the event that transformed England into a global power.

Lawrence Stone, *The Causes of the English Revolution* (New York: Harper & Row, 1972). A vigorously argued explanation of why England experienced a revolution in the mid-seventeenth century.

The Zenith of the Royal State

Joseph Bergin, *The Rise of Richelieu* (New Haven, CT: Yale University Press, 1991). A fascinating portrait of a consummate politician.

Peter Burke, *The Fabrication of Louis XIV* (New Haven, CT: Yale University Press, 1992). A compelling account of a man and a myth.

Paul Dukes, *The Making of Russian Absolutism* (London: Longman, 1982). A thorough survey of Russian history in the seventeenth and eighteenth centuries.

Nicholas Henshall, *The Myth of Absolutism: Change and Continuity in Early Modern European Monarchy* (London: Longman, 1992). A searching examination of the problem of absolutism in the western European states.

Vasili Klyuchevsky, *Peter the Great* (London: Random House, 1958). A classic work, still the best study of Peter.

H. W. Koch, *A History of Prussia* (London: Longman, 1978). A comprehensive study of Prussian history, with an excellent chapter on the Great Elector.

Geoffrey Parker, *The Military Revolution* (Cambridge: Cambridge University Press, 1988). A lucid discussion of how power was organized and deployed in the early modern state.

John Wolf, *Louis XIV* (New York: Norton, 1968). An outstanding biography of the Sun King.

For a list of additional titles related to this chapter's topics, please see www.ablongman.com/kishlansky.

SCIENCE AND COMMERCE IN EARLY MODERN EUROPE

The Visual Record

REMBRANDT'S LESSONS

By the early seventeenth century, interest in scientific investigation had spread out from narrow circles of specialists to embrace educated men and women. One of the more spectacular demonstrations of new knowledge was public dissection, which by law could be performed only on the corpses of criminals. Here the secrets of the human body were revealed both for those who were in training as physicians and for those who had the requisite fee and a strong stomach. Curiosity about the human body was becoming a mark of education. Pictures drawn on the basis of dissections filled the new medical texts like the one on the stand at the feet of the corpse in *The Anatomy Lesson of Dr. Nicolaes Tulp* (1632) by Rembrandt van Rijn (1606–1669).

The painting was commissioned by members of the Amsterdam company of surgeons, the physicians' guild of the early seventeenth century. Rembrandt was to compose the picture so that each of the sitters (whose names are written on the paper one of them holds in his hand), as well as Dr. Tulp, would appear as if he alone were the subject of a portrait. Rembrandt succeeded beyond expectation. Each individual stands out from the group, yet the drama of the scene unifies them. Rembrandt froze the action as Dr. Tulp was demonstrating how the gesture he was making with his left hand looked in the dissected arm of the cadaver.

The Anatomy Lesson established the 25-year-old Rembrandt as one of the most gifted painters in Amsterdam. The group portrait, which Rembrandt brought to new levels of expression, was becoming a favorite genre. It was used to celebrate the leaders of Dutch society, who, unlike the leaders of most other European states, were not princes and aristocrats, but merchants, guild officials, and professionals. Rembrandt captured a spirit of civic pride in his group portraits. Here it was the surgeons' guild; later it would be the leaders of the cloth merchants' guild; another time a militia company.

Like the leaders of the surgeons' guild who commissioned their own portrait, the Dutch Republic swelled with pride in the seventeenth century. Its long war with Spain was finally

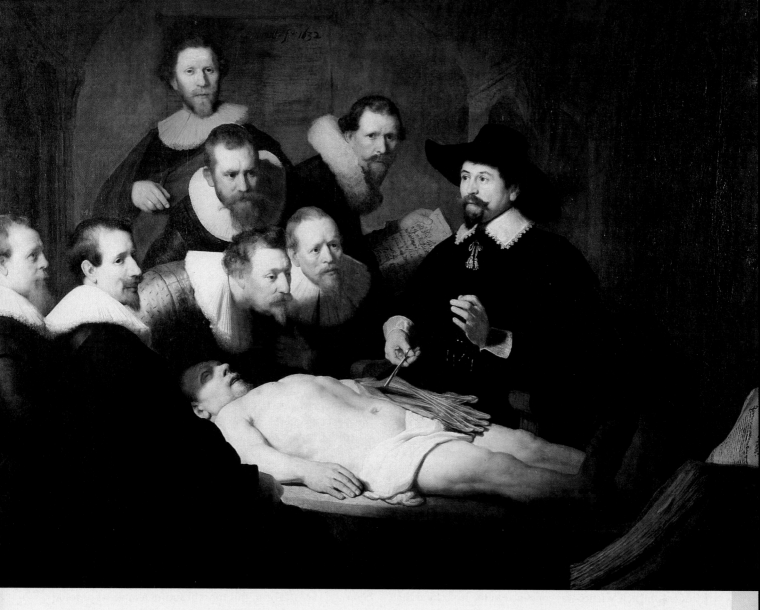

over, and the new state was flourishing. Its ships traveled to all parts of the globe. Bankers and merchants were the backbone of the Dutch Republic. Yet this republic of merchants was also one of the great cultural centers of the Continent. In the burgeoning port of Amsterdam, the fastest-growing city in Europe, artists, philosophers, and mathematicians lived in close proximity. The free exchange of ideas made Amsterdam home to people who had been exiled for their beliefs. The Dutch practiced religious toleration as no one else did. Catholics, Protestants, and Jews all were welcomed and allowed to pursue their own paths without persecution.

Looking Ahead

Freedom of thought and freedom of expression helped develop a new spirit of scientific inquiry, like that portrayed in The Anatomy Lesson of Dr. Nicolaes Tulp. *As this chapter will show, maritime nations such as Holland and England took full advantage of scientific and technological discovery to expand their overseas trade and enrich their citizens. Although much of the new science was seemingly abstract, its practical applications ultimately fueled a new commercial spirit and a new European economy.* ➤

THE NEW SCIENCE

The emergence of the new science challenged the intelligentsia's most basic assumptions and beliefs. Men dropping balls from towers or peering at the skies through a glass claimed that they had disproved thousands of years of certainty about the nature of the universe. New discoveries seemed to loosen the moorings of everything that educated people thought they knew about their world. Although common sense told them that the sun moved from east to west while the earth stood still, the new science insisted that the earth was in constant motion and that it revolved around the sun.

The **scientific revolution** was the opening of a new era in European history. After two centuries of classical revival, European thinkers had finally come up against the limits of ancient knowledge. Ancient wisdom had served Europeans well, but now the certainties of the past were being called into question. The explanations of the universe and the natural world that had been advanced by Aristotle and codified by his followers no longer seemed adequate. Breaking the hold of Aristotelianism, however, was no easy task. A full century was to pass before even learned people would accept the proofs that the earth revolved around the sun. Even then, the most famous of them—Galileo—had to recant these views or be condemned as a heretic.

The two essential characteristics of the new science were that it was materialistic and mathematical. Its materialism was contained in the realization that the universe was composed of matter in motion. This meant that the stars and planets were made not of some perfect ethereal substance but of the same matter that was found on the earth. They were therefore subject to the same rules of motion as were earthly objects. The mathematics of the new science was contained in the realization that calculation had to replace common sense as the basis for understanding the universe. Mathematics itself was transformed with the invention of logarithms, analytic geometry, and calculus. Scientific experimentation took the form of measuring repeatable phenomena. When Galileo attempted to develop a theory of acceleration, he rolled a brass ball down an inclined plane and recorded the time and distance of its descent one hundred times before he was satisfied with his results.

The new science was a Europe-wide movement. The spirit of scientific inquiry flourished everywhere among the educated. The main contributors to astronomy were a Pole, a Dane, a German, and an Italian. The founder of medical chemistry was Swiss; the best anatomist was Belgian. England contributed most of all—the founders of modern chemistry, biology, and physics. By and large, these scientists operated outside the traditional seats of learning at the universities. Though most were university-trained and not a few taught the traditional Aristotelian subjects, theirs was not an academic movement. Rather, it was a public one that was made possible by the printing press. Once published, findings became building blocks for scientists throughout the Continent and from one generation to the next. Many discoveries were made in the search for practical solutions to ordinary problems, and what was learned fueled advances in technology and the natural sciences. The new science gave seventeenth-century Europeans a sense that they might finally master the forces of nature.

Heavenly Revolutions

Aristotle had presented a view of the physical world that coincided with a view of the spiritual and moral one. The heavens were unchangeable, and therefore they were better than the earth. The sun, moon, and planets were all faultless spheres, unblemished and immune from decay. Their motion was circular because the circle was the perfect form of motion. The earth was at the center of the universe because it was the heaviest planet and because it was at the center of the Great Chain of Being, between the underworld of spirits and the upperworld of gods. The Aristotelian worldview was thus easily incorporated into Christianity. Aristotle's description of the heavens as being composed of a closed system of crystalline rings that held the sun, moon, and planets in their circular orbits around the earth left room for God and the angels to reside just beyond the last ring.

In the 1490s, Nicolaus Copernicus (1473–1543) came to the Polish University of Krakow, where the latest astronomical theories were vigorously debated. He became fascinated by astronomy and puzzled by the debate over planetary motion. Copernicus believed, like Aristotle, that the simplest explanations were the best. If the sun was at the center of the universe and the earth was simply another planet in orbit, then many of the most elaborate explanations of planetary motion were unnecessary. "At rest, in the middle of everything is the sun," Copernicus wrote in *On the Revolutions of the Heavenly Spheres* (1543). "For in this most beautiful temple who would place this lamp in another or better position than that from which it can light up the whole thing at the same time?" Because Copernicus accepted most of the rest of the traditional Aristotelian explanation, especially the belief that the planets moved in perfect circles, his sun-centered universe was only slightly better at predicting the position of the planets than the traditional earth-centered one, but Copernicus's idea stimulated other astronomers to make new calculations.

Brahe and Kepler. Under the patronage of the king of Denmark, Tycho Brahe (1546–1601) built a large observatory to study planetary motion. In 1572, Brahe discovered a nova, a brightly burning star that was previously unknown. This discovery challenged the idea of an immutable universe composed of crystalline rings. In 1577, the appearance of a comet cutting through the supposedly impenetrable rings punched another hole in the old cosmology. Brahe's own views were a hybrid of old and new. He believed that all planets but the earth revolved around the sun and that the sun and the planets revolved around a fixed earth. To demonstrate this theory, Brahe and his students compiled the largest and most accurate mathematical tables of planetary motion yet known. From this research, Brahe's pupil, Johannes Kepler (1571–1630), one of the great mathematicians of the age, formulated laws of planetary motion. Kepler discovered that planets orbited the sun in an elliptical rather than a circular path. This accounted for their movements nearer to and farther from the earth. He further demonstrated that there was a precise mathematical relationship between the speed with which a planet revolved and its distance from the sun. Kepler's findings supported the view that the solar system was heliocentric and that the heavens, like the earth, were made of matter that was subject to physical laws.

Galileo. What Kepler demonstrated mathematically, the Italian astronomer Galileo Galilei (1564–1642) confirmed by observation. With a telescope that he had created by using magnifying lenses and a long tube, Galileo saw parts of the heavens that had never been dreamt of before. In 1610, he discovered four moons of Jupiter, proving conclusively that not all heavenly bodies revolved around the earth. He observed the landscape of the earth's moon and described it as being full of mountains, valleys, and rivers. It was of the same imperfect form as the earth itself. He even found spots on the sun, which suggested that it, too, was composed of ordinary matter. Many of Galileo's scientific discoveries had to do with motion—he was the first to posit a law of inertia—but his greatest contribution to the new science was his popularization of the Copernican theory.

As news of his experiments and discoveries spread, Galileo became famous throughout the Continent, and his support for heliocentrism became a celebrated cause. In 1616, the Roman Catholic Church cautioned him against promoting his views. In 1633, a year after publishing *A Dialogue Between the Two Great Systems of the World*, the Inquisition tried Galileo and forced him to recant the idea that the earth moves. He spent the rest of his life under house arrest. But Galileo insisted that there was nothing in the new science that was anti-Christian. He rejected the view that his discoveries refuted the Bible, arguing that the Bible was often difficult to interpret and that nature was another way in which God revealed himself.

The Natural World

The new science originated from a number of traditions that were anything but scientific. Inquiry into nature and the environment grew out of the discipline of natural philosophy and was nurtured by spiritual and mystical traditions. Much of the most useful medical knowledge had come from the studies of herbalists; the most reliable calculations of planetary motion had come from astrologers. Though the first laboratories and observatories were developed in aid of the new science, practice in them was as much magical as experimental. The modern emphasis on experimentation and empirical observation developed only gradually. What was new about the new

■ Andreas Cellarius created this artistic depiction of the solar system in the late seventeenth century. The chart portrays the heliocentric universe described by Copernicus and Galileo and the elliptical orbits of the planets posited by Kepler. An outsized earth is shown in four different positions as it orbits the sun.

science was the determination to develop systems of thought that could help humans to understand and control their environment. There was a greater openness and spirit of cooperation about discoveries than in the past, when experiments were conducted secretly and results were kept hidden away.

Neoplatonism and the New Scientists.

Aristotelianism was not the only philosophical system to explain the nature and composition of the universe. During the Renaissance, the writings of Plato attracted a number of Italian humanists, most notably Marsilio Ficino (1433–1499) and Pico della Mirandola (1463–1494). In Florence, they taught Plato's theory that the world was composed of ideas and forms, which were hidden by the physical properties of objects. These Neoplatonic humanists believed that the architect of the universe possessed the spirit of a geometrician and that the perfect disciplines were music and mathematics. These elements of Neoplatonism created an impetus for the mathematically based studies of the new scientists. They were especially important among the astronomers, who used both calculation and geometry in exploring the heavens. But they also served to bolster the sciences of alchemy and astrology. **Alchemy** was the use of fire in the study of metals, an effort to find the essence of things through their purification. Whereas medieval alchemists mostly attempted to find gold and silver as the essence of lead and iron, the new experimentation focused on the properties of metals in general. Astrology was the study of the influence of the stars on human behavior, calculated by planetary motion and the harmony of the heavenly spheres. Astrologers made careful calculations based on the movement of the planets and were deeply involved in the new astronomy. The Neoplatonic emphasis on mathematics also supported a variety of mystical sciences based on numerology. These were efforts to predict events from the combination of particular numbers.

Paracelsus.

The Swiss alchemist Paracelsus (1493–1541) studied alchemy before becoming a physician. Though he worked as a doctor, his true vocation was alchemy, and he conducted innumerable experiments that were designed to extract the essence of particular metals. Paracelsus taught that all matter was composed of combinations of three principles: salt, sulfur, and mercury. This view replaced the traditional belief in the four elements of earth, water, fire, and air.

The Paracelsian system transformed ideas about chemistry and medicine. Paracelsus rejected the theory that disease was caused by an imbalance in the humors of the body—the standard view of Galen, the great Greek physician of the second century C.E. Instead, Paracelsus argued that each disease had its own cause, which could be diagnosed and remedied. Whereas traditional doctors treated disease by bloodletting or sweating to correct the imbalance of humors, Paracelsus prescribed the ingestion of particular chemicals, especially distilled metals such as mercury, arsenic, and antimony, and he favored administering them at propitious astrological moments.

Boyle and Chemistry.

Although established physicians and medical faculties rejected Paracelsian cures and methods, his influence spread among ordinary practitioners. It ultimately had a profound impact on the studies of Robert Boyle (1627–1691), an Englishman who helped to establish the basis of the science of chemistry. Boyle devoted his energies to raising the study of medical chemistry above that of merely providing recipes for the cure of disease. He worked carefully and recorded each step in his experiments. Boyle's first important work, *The Sceptical Chymist* (1661), attacked both the Aristotelian and Paracelsian views of the basic components of the natural world. Boyle rejected both the four elements and the three principles. Instead, he favored an atomic explanation in which matter "consisted of little particles of all sizes and shapes." Changes in these particles, which would later be identified as the chemical elements, resulted in changes in matter. Boyle's most important experiments were with gases—a word that Paracelsus invented. Boyle formulated the relationship between the volume and pressure of a gas (Boyle's Law), and he invented the air pump.

Medical Science.

The new spirit of scientific inquiry also affected medical studies. The study of anatomy through dissection had helped the new scientists to reject many of the descriptive errors in Galen's texts. The Belgian doctor Andreas Vesalius (1514–1564) published the first modern set of anatomical drawings in 1543. But accurate knowledge of the composition of the body did not mean better understanding of its operation. One of the greatest mysteries was how blood moved through the vital organs. William Harvey (1578–1657), an Englishman who had received his medical education in Italy, was interested in the anatomy of the heart. He examined hearts in more than forty species before concluding that the heart worked like a pump and that the valves of the heart chambers allowed the blood to flow in only one direction. He concluded that the blood was pumped by the heart and circulated throughout the entire body.

Sir Isaac Newton.

The greatest of all English scientists was the mathematician and physicist Sir Isaac Newton (1642–1727), who brought together the various strands of the new science. He revived the mystical notions of attraction and repulsion and merged the astronomers and astrologers, the chemists and alchemists. Newton was the first to understand the composition of light, the first to develop a calculus, the first to build a reflecting telescope. He made stunning contributions to the sciences of optics, physics, astronomy, and mathematics. His magnum opus, *Mathematical Principles of Natural Philosophy* (1687), is one of the most important scientific works ever composed. Newton offered a solution to the following problem: If the world was composed of matter in motion, what was motion?

Though Galileo had first developed a theory of inertia—the idea that a body at rest stays at rest—most materialists believed that motion was inherent in objects. In contrast, Newton believed that motion was the result of the interaction of objects and that it could be calculated mathematically. From his experiments he formulated the concept of force and his famous laws of motion: (1) that objects that are at rest or in uniform linear motion remain in such a state unless acted on by an external force; (2) that changes in motion are proportional to force; and (3) that for every action there is an equal and opposite reaction. From these laws of motion, Newton advanced one step further: If the world was no more than matter in motion and if all motion was subject to the same laws, then the movement of the planets could be explained in the same way as the movement of an apple falling from a tree. There was a mathematical relationship between attraction and repulsion—a universal gravitation, as Newton called it—that governed the movement of all objects. Newton's theory of gravity joined Kepler's astronomy and Galileo's physics. The mathematical, materialistic world of the new science was now complete.

Science Enthroned

By the middle of the seventeenth century, the new science was firmly established throughout Europe. Royal and noble patrons supported the enterprise by paying some of the costs of equipment and experimentation. Royal observatories were created for the astronomers, colleges of physicians for the doctors, laboratories for the chemists. Both England and France established royal societies of learned scientists. The French Académie des Sciences (1666) was composed of 20 salaried scientists and an equal number of students, divided among the different branches of scientific learning. The English Royal Society (1662) boasted some of the greatest minds of the age. It was there that Newton first made public his most important discoveries. Scientific bodies were also formed outside the traditional universities. These were the so-called mechanics colleges, such as Gresham College in London, where the practical applications of mathematics and physics were taught.

The establishment of learned scientific societies and practical colleges fulfilled part of the program advocated by Sir Francis Bacon (1561–1626), one of the leading supporters of scientific research in England. In *The Advancement of Learning* (1605), Bacon proposed a scientific method through inductive, empirical experimentation. Bacon believed that experiments should be carefully recorded so that results were both reliable and repeatable, and in his numerous writings he stressed the practical impact of scientific discovery.

Bacon's support for the new science contrasts markedly with the stance taken by the Roman Catholic Church. Embattled by the Reformation and the wars of religion, the Church regarded the new science as another heresy. Not only did it confound ancient wisdom and contradict Church teachings, but it was also a lay movement that was neither directed nor controlled from Rome. Galileo's trial slowed the momentum of scientific investigation in Catholic countries and starkly posed the conflict between authority and knowledge. Nevertheless, the Church's stand was based on more than narrow self-interest. Ever since Copernicus had pub-

lished his views, a new skepticism had emerged among European intellectuals. Every year new theories competed with old ones, and dozens of contradictory explanations for the most common phenomena were advanced and debated. The skeptics concluded that nothing was known and nothing was knowable. Their position led inevitably to the most shocking of all possible views: atheism.

But the new science was not necessarily an attack on established religion. Few of the leading scientists saw a contradiction between their studies and their faith. Still, by the middle of the century, attacks on the Church were increasing, and some people blamed the new science for them. Therefore, it was altogether fitting that one of the leading mathematicians of the day should provide the method for harmonizing faith and reason.

René Descartes (1596–1650) was trained in one of the best Jesuit schools in France before taking a law degree in 1616. He entered military service in the Dutch Republic and, after the outbreak of the Thirty Years' War, joined the Duke of Bavaria's army. Descartes was keenly interested in mathematics, and during his military travels he met and was tutored by a leading Dutch mathematician. In 1619, he dreamt of discovering the scientific principles of universal knowledge. After this dream, Descartes returned to Holland and began to develop his system. He was on the verge of publishing his views when he learned of Galileo's condemnation. Reading Galileo's *Dialogue Between the Two Great Systems of the World*, Descartes discovered that he himself shared many of Galileo's opinions and had worked out mathematical proofs for them, but he refrained from publishing until 1637, when he brought out the *Discourse on Method*.

In the *Discourse on Method*, Descartes demonstrated how skepticism could be used to produce certainty. He began by declaring that he would reject everything that could not be clearly proven beyond doubt. Thus he rejected the material world, the testimony of his senses, and all known or imagined opinions. He was left only with doubt. But what was doubt if not thought, and what was thought if not the workings of his mind? The only thing of which he could be certain, then, was that he had a mind. Thus his famous formulation: "I think, therefore I am." From this first certainty came another, the knowledge of perfectibility. He knew that he was imperfect and that a perfect being had to have placed that knowledge within him. Therefore a perfect being—God—existed.

Descartes's philosophy, known as **Cartesianism,** rested on the dual existence of matter and mind. Matter was the material world, which was subject to the incontrovertible laws of mathematics. Mind was the spirit of the creator. Descartes was one of the leading mechanistic philosophers, believing that all objects operated in accord with natural laws. He invented analytic geometry and made important contributions to the sciences of optics and physics on which Newton would later build. But his proof that the new science could be harmonized with the old religion was his greatest contribution.

Astronomy, chemistry, biology, and physics all had their modern origins in the seventeenth century. Because thinking about the natural world was integrated, discoveries in one discipline made possible breakthroughs in another. Though many of the pathbreaking discoveries of the new scientists would not find practical use for centuries, the spirit of discovery had a great impact in an age of commerce and capital. The quest for mathematical certainty and prime movers led directly to improvements in agriculture, mining, navigation, and industrial activity. The new sense of control over the material world provided a new optimism for generations of Europeans and bolstered the desire to expand commerce at home and abroad.

EMPIRES OF GOODS

Under the watchful eye of the European states, a worldwide marketplace for the exchange of commodities had been created. First the Dutch and then the English had established monopoly companies to engage in exotic trades in the East. The Spanish and Portuguese, then the English and French had

established colonial dependencies in the Atlantic, which they carefully nurtured in hope of economic gain. Protected trade had flourished beyond the wildest dreams of its promoters. Luxury commodities became staples; new commodities became luxuries. Trade enhanced the material life of all European peoples, though it came at great cost to the Asians, Africans, and Latin Americans whose labor and raw materials were converted into the new crazes of consumption.

Though long-distance trade was never as important to the European economy as was inland and intracontinental trade, its development in the seventeenth and eighteenth centuries had a profound impact on lifestyles, economic policy, and ultimately warfare. The first great commercial power, the Dutch, owed their achievements to innovative techniques, rational management, and a social and cultural environment that supported mercantile activities. Dutch society was freer than any other, open to new capital, new ventures, and new ideas. The Dutch developed the innovative concept of the **entrepôt,** a place where goods were brought for storage before being exchanged. They

MAP DISCOVERY

Dutch Trade Routes, ca. 1650

The Dutch were the greatest commercial nation of the seventeenth century. According to the trade routes shown here, how would you describe the extent of Dutch trade? Why are there so many trading centers in the East? Based on information provided in the chapter, what were some of the major goods exchanged in the various trade regions? Why did the Dutch not secure major colonial possessions (orange-shaded areas) in the East?

pioneered in finance by establishing the Bank of Amsterdam in 1609. They led in shipbuilding by developing as early as 1570 the flyboat, a long flat-hulled vessel that was designed specifically to carry bulky cargoes such as grain. They traded around the globe with the largest mercantile fleet yet known. Because the Dutch dominated the European economy, the French and English began to pass laws to eliminate Dutch competition. The English banned imports that were carried in Dutch ships; the French banned Dutch products. Both policies cut heavily into Dutch superiority, and both ultimately resulted in commercial warfare. By the end of the seventeenth century, England and France surpassed the Dutch.

The Marketplace of the World

By the sixteenth century, all the major trading routes had already been opened. The Spanish moved back and forth across the Atlantic; the Dutch and Portuguese sailed around the tip of Africa to the Indian Ocean. The Baltic trade connected the eastern and western parts of Europe as Danes, Swedes, and Dutch exchanged Polish and Russian raw materials for English and French manufactured goods. The Mediterranean was still a vital artery of intercontinental trade, but its preeminent role was diminishing. In 1600, almost three-quarters of the Asian trade was still land-based, much of it carried through the Middle East to the Mediterranean. A century later, nearly all Asian trade was carried directly to western Europe by Dutch and English vessels. Commercial power was shifting to the northern European states just as dramatically as military and political power.

The Evolution of Long-Distance Travel. The technology that was associated with commerce achieved no major breakthroughs to compare with the great transformations of the fifteenth century, when new techniques of navigation made transatlantic travel possible. There continued to be improvements, however. The new astronomical findings were a direct aid to navigation, as were the recorded experiences of so many practiced sea travelers. The materials that were used to make and maintain ships improved with the importation of pitch and tar from the east and with the greater availability of iron and copper from Scandinavia. The single most important innovation in shipbuilding was the Dutch flyboat, which helped traders gain maximum profit from their journeys to the Baltic. Flyboats sacrificed speed and maneuverability for economy and capacity. They carried no heavy armaments and so were well adapted to the serene Baltic trade.

Innovation, organization, and efficient management were the principal elements of what historians have called the commercial revolution. Concerted efforts to maximize opportunities and advantages accounted for the phenomenal growth in the volume and value of commercial exchange. One of the least spectacular and most effective changes was the replacement of bilateral trade with **triangular trade.** In bilateral trade, the surplus commodities of one community were exchanged for those of another. For communities with few desirable commodities, bilateral trade meant the exchange of precious metals for

goods; and throughout much of the sixteenth and early seventeenth centuries, bullion was by far the most often traded commodity. Triangular trade created a larger pool of desirable goods. British manufactured goods could be traded to Africa for slaves, the slaves could be traded in the West Indies for sugar, and the sugar could be consumed in Britain. Moreover, the merchants who were involved in shifting these goods from place to place could achieve profits on each exchange. Indeed, their motive in trading could now change from dumping surplus commodities to matching supply and demand.

The New Forms of Banking. Equally important were the changes made in the way trade was financed. Because states, cities, and even individuals could stamp their own precious metal, there were hundreds of different European coins with different nominal and metallic values. The influx of American silver further destabilized an already unstable system of exchange. The Bank of Amsterdam was created in 1609 to establish a uniform rate of exchange for the various currencies that were traded in that city. From this useful function developed transfer banking, or giro banking, a system that had been invented in Italy. In giro banking, various merchant firms held money on account and issued bills of transfer from one to another. This transfer system meant that merchants in different cities did not have to transport their precious metals or endure long delays in having their accounts settled.

Giro banking also aided the development of bills of exchange, an early form of checking. Merchants could conclude trades by depositing money in a given bank or merchant house and then having a bill drawn for the sum they owed. Bills of exchange were especially important in international trade, as they made large-scale shipments of precious metals to settle trade deficits unnecessary. By the end of the seventeenth century, bills of exchange had become negotiable; that is, they could pass from one merchant to another without being redeemed. Thus a Dutch merchant could buy French wines in Bordeaux with a bill of exchange drawn on an account in the Bank of Amsterdam. The Bordeaux merchant could then purchase Spanish oranges and use the same bill of exchange as payment. There were two disadvantages to this system: Ultimately, the bill had to return to Amsterdam for redemption, and when it did, the account on which it was drawn might be empty.

The establishment of the Bank of England in 1694 overcame such difficulties. The Bank of England was licensed to issue its own bills of exchange, or bank notes, which were backed by the revenue from specific English taxes. This security of payment was widely sought after, and the Bank of England soon became a clearinghouse for all kinds of bills of exchange. The bank would buy in bills at a discount, paying less than their face value, and pay out precious metal or their own notes in exchange.

The effects of these and many other small-scale changes in business practice helped to fuel prolonged growth in European commerce. It was the European merchant who made this growth possible, accepting the risks of each individual transaction and building up small pools of capital from which successive transactions could take place. Most mercantile ventures were conducted by individuals or families and were based on the specialized trade of a single commodity. Trade offered high returns because it entailed high risks. The long delays in moving goods and their uncertain arrival, the unreliability of agents and the unscrupulousness of other traders, and the inefficiencies in transport and communication all weighed heavily against success. Merchants who succeeded did so less by luck than by hard work. They used family members to receive shipments. They lowered shipping costs by careful packaging. They lowered protection costs by securing their trade routes. Financial publications lowered the costs of information. Ultimately, lower costs meant lower prices. For centuries, luxury goods dominated intercontinental trade, but by the eighteenth century, European merchants had created a world marketplace in which the luxuries of the past were the common fare of the present.

Consumption Choices

As long-distance trade became more sophisticated, merchants became more sensitive to consumer tastes. Low-volume, high-quality goods such as spices and silks, which were the preserve of the largest trading companies, had reached saturation levels by the early seventeenth century. The price of pepper, the most used of all spices, fell nearly continuously after 1650. Triangular trade allowed merchants to provide a better match of supplies and demands. The result was the rise to prominence of a vast array of new commodities, which not only continued the expansion of trade but also reshaped diet, lifestyles, and patterns of consumption. New products came from both the East and the West. Dutch and English incursions into the Asian trade provoked competition with the Portuguese and enlarged the range of commodities that were shipped back to Europe. An aggressive Asian triangle was created in which European bullion bought Indonesian spices that were exchanged for Persian silk and Chinese and Japanese finished goods. In the Atlantic, the English were quick to develop both home and export markets for a variety of new or newly available products.

The New Commodities. The European trade with Asia had always been designed to satisfy consumer demand rather than to exchange surplus goods. Europeans manufactured little that was desired in Asia, so the chief commodity imported to the East was bullion: tons of South American silver, perhaps one-third of all that was produced. In return came spices, silk, coffee, jewels, jade, porcelain, dyes, and a wide variety of other exotic goods. By the middle of the seventeenth century, the Dutch dominated the spice trade; they obtained a virtual monopoly over cinnamon, cloves, nutmeg, and mace and carried the largest share of pepper. Each year, Europeans consumed perhaps one million pounds of the four great spices and seven million pounds of pepper. Both Dutch and the English competed for preeminence in the silk trade. The Dutch concentrated on Chinese silk, which they used mostly

in trade with Japan. The English established an interest in lower-quality Indian silk spun in Bengal.

The most important manufactured articles imported from the East to Europe were the lightweight, brightly colored Indian cottons known as calicoes. Until the middle of the seventeenth century, cotton and cotton blended with silk were used in Europe only for wall hangings and table coverings. The material, which was soft and smooth to the touch, soon replaced linen for use as underwear and close-fitting garments among the well-to-do. The fashion quickly caught on, and the Dutch, who were first to realize the potential of the cotton market, began to export calicoes throughout the Continent. The English and French followed suit, establishing their own trading houses in India and bringing European patterns and designs with them for the Asians to copy.

Along with the new apparel from the East came new beverages. Coffee, which was first used in northern Europe in the early seventeenth century, had become a fashionable drink by the end of the century. Coffee houses sprang up in the major urban areas of northern Europe. As a basic beverage and import commodity, coffee was surpassed in importance only by tea. While coffee drinking remained the preserve of the wealthy, tea consumption spread throughout European society. It was probably most important in England, where the combination of Chinese tea and West Indian sugar created a phenomenal growth in consumption. In 1706, England imported 100,000 pounds of tea. By the end of the century the number had risen to over 15 million pounds. The English imported most of this tea directly from China, where an open port had been established at Canton. Tea soon became the dominant cargo of the large English merchant ships coming from Asia. Some manufactured goods would be brought to India on the outward voyage, but once the ships had loaded the green and black teas, they sailed directly home. Almost all tea was purchased with bullion, since the Chinese had even less use for European goods than did other Asians. Not until the discovery that the Chinese consumed large quantities of opium, which was grown in India and Southeast Asia, did a triangular trade develop.

Colonial Trade: The Demand for Sugar. The success of tea was linked to the explosive growth in the development of sugar in Europe's Atlantic colonies. The Portuguese found Brazil's hot, humid climate to be well suited for cultivation of the cane plants. The island of Barbados became the first English sugar colony. The planters modeled their development on Brazil, where African slaves were used to plant, tend, and cut the giant canes from which the sugar was extracted. Hot, sweet tea quickly became a popular drink throughout English society. By 1700, the English were sending home over 50 million pounds of sugar besides what they were shipping directly to the North American colonies.

The African Slave Trade. The triangular trade of manufactures—largely reexported calicoes—to Africa for slaves, who were exchanged in the West Indies for sugar, became the dominant form of English overseas trade. Colonial production depended on the enforced labor of hundreds of thousands of Africans. Gold and silver, tobacco, sugar, rice, and indigo were all slave crops. Africans were enslaved by other Africans and then sold to Europeans to be used in the colonies. More than six million black slaves were imported into the Americas during the course of the eighteenth century. Although rum and calicoes were the main commodities exchanged for slaves, the Africans who dominated the slave trade organized a highly competitive market. Every colonial power participated in this lucrative trade. More than three million slaves were imported into the Portuguese colony of Brazil; by the end of the eighteenth century, the sugar island of Saint Domingue held 500,000 slaves and only 35,000 French inhabitants. The English, with their sugar colonies of Barbados and Jamaica and their tobacco colonies of Virginia and Maryland, ultimately came to control the slave trade. The prosperous economies of Newport, Rhode Island, and the English port of Liverpool were built entirely on the slave trade, as were hundreds of plantation fortunes.

The new commodities flooded into Europe from all parts of the globe. By the middle of the eighteenth century, tea, coffee, cocoa, gin, and rum were among the most popular beverages. These were all products that had been largely unknown a century earlier. Tea and sugar passed from luxury to staple in little more than a generation, and the demand for both products continued to increase. To meet it, the European trading powers needed to create and maintain a powerful and efficient mercantile system.

Dutch Masters

For the nearly 80 years between 1565 and 1648 that the Dutch were at war, they grew ever more prosperous. While the economies of most other European nations were sapped by warfare, the Dutch seemed to draw strength from their interminable conflict with the Spanish empire. They did have the advantage of fighting defensively on land and offensively on sea. Land war was terribly costly to the aggressor, which had to raise large armies, transport them to the site of battles or sieges, and feed them while they were there. The defender simply had to fortify strong places, keep its water routes open to secure supplies, and wait for the weather to change. Sea war—or piracy, depending on one's viewpoint—required much smaller outlays for men and matériel and promised the rewards of captured prizes. The Dutch became expert at attacking the Spanish silver fleets, singling out the slower and smaller vessels for capture. The Dutch also benefited from the massive immigration into their provinces of Protestants who had lived and worked in the southern provinces. The immigrants brought vital skills in manufacturing and large reserves of capital for investment in Dutch commerce.

Though the Dutch Republic comprised seven separate political entities, with a total population of about two million, the province of Holland was preeminent among them. Holland contained more than one-quarter of this population, and its trading port of Amsterdam was one of the great cities of Europe. The city had grown from a mid-sized urban community of 65,000 in 1600 to a metropolis of 170,000 50 years later. The port was one of the busiest in the world, for it was

■ This diagram shows how slaves were packed into cargo holds for the notorious Middle Passage to the Americas. The plan was a model of efficiency, for slave traders sought to maximize profits.

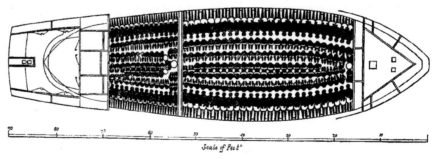

built to be an entrepôt. Vast warehouses and docks lined its canals. Visitors were impressed by Amsterdam's bustle, cleanliness, and businesslike appearance. The central buildings were the Bank and the Exchange, testimony to the dominant activities of the residents.

The Dutch dominated all types of European trade. They handled more English coal than England, more French wine than France, more Swedish iron than Sweden. Dutch ships outnumbered all others in every important port of Europe. Goods were brought to Amsterdam to be redistributed throughout the world. Dutch prosperity rested first on the Baltic trade. Even after it ceased to expand in the middle of the seventeenth century, the Baltic trade made up over one-quarter of all of Holland's commercial enterprise. The Dutch also were the leaders in the East Indian trade throughout the seventeenth century. They held a virtual monopoly on the sale of exotic spices and the largest share of the pepper trade. Their imports of cottons and especially of porcelain began new consumer fads that soon resulted in the development of European industries. Dutch potteries began to produce china, as lower-quality ceramic goods came to be known. Dutch trade in the Atlantic was of less importance, but the Dutch did have a colonial presence in the New World, controlling a number of small islands and the rapidly growing mainland settlement of New Netherland. Yet the Dutch still dominated the secondary market in tobacco and sugar, becoming the largest processor and refiner of these important commodities.

In all of these activities, the Dutch acted as merchants rather than as consumers. Unlike most other Europeans, they regarded precious metal as a commodity like any other and took no interest in accumulating it for its own sake. This attitude enabled them to pioneer triangular trading and develop the crucial financial institutions that were necessary to expand their overseas commerce. The Dutch were not so much innovators as improvers. They saw the practical value in Italian accounting and banking methods and raised them to new levels of efficiency. They made use of marine insurance to help diminish the risks of mercantile activity. Their legal system favored the creation of small trading companies by protecting individual investments. The European stock and commodity markets were centered in Amsterdam. By the 1670s, over 500 commodities were traded on the Amsterdam exchange, and even a primitive futures market had evolved for those who wanted to speculate.

There were many explanations for the unparalleled growth of this small maritime state into one of the greatest of European trading empires. Geography and climate provided one impetus; the lack of sufficient foodstuffs provided another. Yet there were cultural characteristics as well. One was the openness of Dutch society. Even before the struggle with Spain, the northern provinces had shown a greater inclination toward religious toleration than had most parts of Europe. Amsterdam became a unique center for religious and intellectual exchange. European Jews flocked there, as did Catholic dissidents such as Descartes. They brought with them a wide range of skills and knowledge

along with capital that could be invested in trade. By the middle of the seventeenth century, the Dutch Republic enjoyed a reputation for cultural creativity that was the envy of the Continent. A truly extraordinary school of Dutch artists led by Rembrandt celebrated this new state born of commerce with vivid portrayals of its people and its prosperity.

Mercantile Organization

Elsewhere in Europe, trade was the king's business. The wealth of the nation was part of the prestige of the monarch, and its rise or fall was part of the crown's power. In all European states except the Dutch Republic, the activities of merchants were scorned by both the landed elite and the salaried bureaucrats. Yet the activities of the mercantile classes took on increasing importance for the state for two reasons. First, imported goods, especially luxuries, were a noncontroversial target for taxation. Customs duties and excise taxes grew all over Europe. Second, the competition for trade was seen as a competition between states rather than between individual merchants. Trading privileges involved special arrangements with foreign powers, arrangements that recognized the sovereign power of European monarchs. In this way, trade could bring glory to the state.

Mercantilism. The competition for power and glory derived from the theory of **mercantilism,** a set of assumptions about economic activity that were commonly held throughout Europe and that guided the policies of almost every government. Mercantilists believed that the wealth of a nation resided in its stock of precious metal and that economic activity was a zero-sum game. In other words, they believed that there was a fixed amount of money, a fixed amount of commodities, and a fixed amount of consumption. What one country gained, another lost. If England bought wine from France and paid £100,000 in precious metal for it, then England was £100,000 poorer and France was £100,000 richer. If one was to trade profitably, it was absolutely necessary to wind up with a surplus of precious metal. Therefore, it was imperative that governments regulate trade so that the stocks of precious metal were protected from the greed of the merchants. The first and most obvious measure of protection was to prohibit the export of coin except by license, a prohibition that was absolutely unenforceable and was violated more often by government officials than by merchants.

These ideas about economic activity led to a variety of forms of economic regulation. The most common was the **monopoly,** a grant of special privileges in return for both financial considerations and an agreement to abide by the rules set out by the state. Some monopolies were granted by the crown as a reward for past favors or to purchase future support. Monopolists usually paid considerable fees for their rights, but they could make capital investments with the expectation of long-term gains. This advantage was especially important in attracting investors for risky and expensive ventures such as long-distance trade. Monopolists also benefited the economy as a whole by increasing productive investment at a time when most capital was being used to purchase land, luxury goods, or offices.

The East India Companies. Two monopoly companies, the English and the Dutch East India Companies, dominated the Asian trade. The English East India Company, founded in 1600 with a capital of £30,000, was given the exclusive right to the Asian trade and immediately established itself throughout the Indian Ocean. The Dutch East India Company was formed two years later with ten times the capital of its English counterpart. By the end of the century, the Dutch company employed over 12,000 people. Both companies were **joint-stock companies,** a new form of business organization. Subscribers owned a percentage of the total value of the company, based on the number of shares they bought, and were entitled to a distribution of profits on the same basis. Shares could be exchanged without the breakup of the company as a whole. Both Amsterdam and London soon developed stock markets to trade the shares of monopoly companies.

Both East India companies were remarkably good investments. The Dutch East India Company paid an average dividend of 18 percent for over 200 years. The value of English East India Company shares rose fivefold in the second half of the seventeenth century alone. Few other monopoly companies achieved a record comparable to those of the East India companies. Companies that failed included the English Royal African Company, founded in 1672 to provide slaves for the Spanish colonies, and the French East Indian and African Companies. The Dutch and English companies were successful because they were able to lower the costs of protecting their ships and cargoes.

Protective Trade Regulations. Monopolies were not the only form of regulation in which seventeenth-century governments engaged. For states with Atlantic colonies, regulation took the form of restricting markets rather than traders. In the 1660s, the English government, alarmed at the growth of Dutch mercantile activity in the New World, passed a series of **Navigation Acts** designed to protect English shipping. Colonial goods—primarily tobacco and sugar—could be shipped to and from England only in English boats. If the French wanted to purchase West Indian sugar, they could not simply send a ship to the English colony of Barbados loaded with French goods and exchange them for sugar. Rather, they had to make their purchases from an English import-export merchant, and the goods had to be unloaded in an English port before they could be reloaded to be shipped to France. As a result of these protective measures, the English reexport trade skyrocketed. In the year 1700, reexports amounted to nearly 40 percent of all English commerce. With such a dramatic increase in trading, all moved in English ships, shipbuilding boomed, and English ports and coastal towns enjoyed heightened prosperity. For a time, colonial protection proved effective.

ENCOUNTERING PIRATES

The increase in commercial shipping and long-distance trade also meant an increase in assaults at sea. Pirates were a constant threat in the Mediterranean where they were based on the Barbary coast of North Africa and were not unknown as far afield as the English Channel. Pirates had a reputation for ruthlessness and cruelty that far surpassed any of their actual deeds. They were a popular subject for travelers' tales, short fiction, and poetry. Even in the eighteenth century they were associated with buried treasure and deserted islands. This account is from a French sea captain whose ship is accosted on the high seas.

Focus Questions
How did the sailors first defend themselves? What did they fear about the pirates?

Meanwhile the seitie [a type of boat favored by Mediterranean pirates] had got to within musket-shot of us, and without firing at us she sent over her boat with six men in it dressed like Provencals each with a hat on his head. When they were close enough to be heard they asked us who we were and where we were bound. . . . I shouted to them not to come any closer or I would shoot at them, so they returned to their ship where I had observed several Moorish turbans. I told the crew not to fire without my or-

der. And at that moment they all wept and lamented, saying: "Farewell liberty! What will become of our wives and children?" So I said: "We must defend ourselves. Let us commend ourselves to God and the Holy Virgin. If we escape, let us promise to have masses said and to walk barefoot to the first place where we find a church." We sang the *Salve Regina* rather quietly, and I saw that my men were very discouraged, so I stove in the end of a barrel of powder at my cabin doorway, stuck a lighted length of match in the end of my pistol and said in an angry voice: "God Almighty, if anyone fails in his duty, I'll kill him and set the match to this powder. Better to die than end up a slave to these cruel savages."

From Jean Doublet, *Encounter with a Barbary Pirate* (1682).

The French entered the intercontinental trade later than their North Atlantic rivals, and they were less dependent on trade for their subsistence. French protectionism was as much internal as colonial. Of all the states of Europe, only France could satisfy its needs from its own resources. Achieving such self-sufficiency, however, required coordination and leadership. In the 1670s, Louis XIV's finance minister, Jean-Baptiste Colbert (1619–1683), developed a plan to bolster the French economy by protecting it against European imports. First Colbert followed the English example of restricting the reexport trade by requiring that imports come to France either in French ships or in the ships of the country from which the goods originated. In addition, he used tariffs to make imported goods unattractive in France. He sponsored a drive to increase French manufacturing, especially of textiles, tapestries, linens, glass, and furniture. To protect the investments in French manufacturing, enormous duties were placed on the import of similar goods manufactured elsewhere. The Venetian glass industry, for example, suffered a serious blow from Colbert's tariffs. English woolen manufacturers were also damaged, and the English sought retaliatory measures. At the same time, the English had already begun to imitate this form of protection. In the early eighteenth century, England attempted to limit the importation of cotton goods from India to prevent the collapse of the domestic clothing industry.

The Navigation Acts and Colbert's program of protective tariffs were directed specifically against Dutch reexporters. The Dutch were the acknowledged leaders in all branches of commerce in the seventeenth century. There were many summers when there were more Dutch vessels than English ships in London Harbor. In the 1670s, the Dutch merchant fleet was probably larger than the English, French, Spanish, Portuguese, and German fleets combined. Restrictive navigation practices were one way to combat an advantage that the Dutch had built through heavy capital investment and by breaking away from the prevailing theories about the relationship between wealth and precious metals. English and French economic protectionism cut heavily into the Dutch trade, and ultimately, both the English and French overtook the Dutch. But protectionism had its price. Just as the dynastic wars were succeeded by the wars of religion, the wars of religion were succeeded by the wars of commerce.

THE WARS OF COMMERCE

The belief that there was a fixed amount of trade in the world was still strong in the late seventeenth century. One country's gains in trade were another's losses. Competition for trade was part of the struggle by which the state grew powerful. It was not inevitable that economic competition would lead to warfare, but restrictive competition was another matter.

Thus the scramble for colonies in the seventeenth century led to commercial warfare in the eighteenth. As the English gradually replaced the Dutch as the leading commercial nation, so the French replaced the English as the leading competitor. Their struggles for the dominance of world markets brought European warfare to every corner of the globe.

The Mercantile Wars

Commercial warfare in Europe began between the English and the Dutch in the middle of the seventeenth century. Both had established aggressive overseas trading companies in the Atlantic and in Asia. In the early seventeenth century, the Dutch were the undisputed leaders. Their carrying capacity and trade monopolies were the greatest in the world. Yet the English were rising quickly. Their Atlantic colonies began to produce valuable new commodities such as tobacco and sugar, and their Asian trade was expanding decade after decade. Conflict was inevitable, and the result was three naval wars fought between 1652 and 1674. (See "The West and the Wider World: The Nutmeg Wars," pp. 352–353.)

The Dutch had little choice but to strike out against English policy, but they also had little chance of overall success. Their spectacular naval victory in 1667, when the Dutch fleet surprised many English warships at port and burned both ships and docks at Chatham, obscured the fact that Dutch commercial superiority was slipping. In 1664, the English conquered New Netherland on the North American mainland and renamed it New York. With this defeat, the Dutch lost their largest colonial possession. The wars were costly to both states, nearly bankrupting the English crown in 1672. Anglo-Dutch rivalry was finally laid to rest after 1688, when William of Orange, stadtholder of Holland, became William III (1689–1702), king of England.

The Anglo-Dutch commercial wars were just one part of a larger European conflict. Dutch commerce was as threatening to France as it was to England, though in a different way. Under Colbert, France pursued a policy of economic independence. The state supported internal industrial activity through the financing of large workshops and the encouragement of new manufacturing techniques. To protect French products, Colbert levied punitive tariffs on Dutch imports; these tariffs severely depressed both trade and manufacture in Holland. Though the Dutch retaliated with restrictive tariffs of their own—in 1672 they banned the import of all French goods for an entire year—the Dutch economy depended on free trade. The Dutch had much more to lose than did France in a battle of protective tariffs.

The battle that Louis XIV had in mind, though, was more deadly than one of tariffs. Greedily, he eyed the Spanish Netherlands—to which he had a weak claim through his Habsburg wife—and believed that the Dutch stood in the way of his plans. The Dutch had entered into an alliance with the English and Swedes in 1668 to counter French policy, and Louis was determined to crush them in retaliation. He successfully bought off both of Holland's supposed allies, providing cash pensions to the kings of England and Sweden in return for England's active participation and Sweden's passive neutrality in the impending war. In 1672, Louis's army, over 100,000 strong, invaded the Low Countries and swept all before them. Only the opening of the dikes by the Dutch prevented the French from entering the province of Holland itself.

The French invasion coincided with the third Anglo-Dutch war, and the United Provinces found themselves besieged on land and sea. Their international trade was disrupted, their manufacturing industries were in ruins, and their military budget skyrocketed. Only able diplomacy and skillful military leadership prevented their total demise. A separate peace was made with England; Spain, whose sovereign territory had been invaded, entered the war on the side of the Dutch, as did a number of German states. Louis's hope for a lightning victory faded, and the war settled into a series of interminable sieges and reliefs of fortified towns. The Dutch finally persuaded France to come to terms in the Treaty of Nijmegen (1678–1679). While Louis XIV retained a number of the territories he had taken from Spain, his armies withdrew from the United Provinces, and he agreed to lift most of the commercial sanctions against Dutch goods. The first phase of mercantile warfare was over.

The Wars of Louis XIV

It was Louis XIV's ambition to restore the ancient Burgundian territories to the French crown and to provide secure northern and eastern borders for his state. Pursuit of these aims involved him in conflicts with nearly every other European state. Spain had fought for 80 years to preserve the Burgundian inheritance in the Low Countries. By the Peace of Westphalia (1648), the northern portion of this territory became the United Provinces, while the southern portion remained loyal to the crown and became the Spanish Netherlands. This territory provided a barrier between Holland and France that both states attempted to strengthen by establishing fortresses and bridgeheads at strategic places. In the east, Louis eyed the duchies of Lorraine and Alsace and the large swath of territory farther south known as Franche-Comté. The Peace of Westphalia had granted France control of a number of imperial cities in these duchies, and Louis aimed to link them together. All of these territories were ruled by Habsburgs: Alsace and Lorraine by the Austrian Holy Roman Emperor, Franche-Comté by the Spanish king.

The Balance of Power.

In the late seventeenth century, ambassadors and ministers of state began to develop the theory of a **balance of power** in Europe. This was a belief that no state or combination of states should be allowed to become so powerful that its existence threatened the peace of the others. Behind this purely political idea of the balance of power lay a theory of collective security that knit together the European state system. French expansion in either direction not only threatened the other states that were directly involved but also posed a threat to European security in general.

Louis showed his hand clearly enough in the Franco-Dutch war that had ended in 1679. Though he withdrew his forces from the United Provinces and evacuated most of the territories he had conquered, by the Treaty of Nijmegen France absorbed Franche-Comté as well as portions of the

Spanish Netherlands. Louis began plotting his next adventure almost as soon as the treaty was signed. War finally came in 1688, when French troops poured across the Rhine to seize Cologne. A united German empire led by Leopold I, archduke of Austria, combined with the maritime powers of England and Holland, led by William III, to form the Grand Alliance, the first of the great balance of power coalitions. In fact, the two sides proved to be so evenly matched that the Nine Years' War (1688–1697) settled very little, but it did demonstrate that a successful European coalition could be formed against France. It also signified the permanent shift in alliances that resulted from the Revolution of 1688 in England. Although the English had allied with France against the Dutch in 1672, after William became king he persuaded the English Parliament that the real enemy was France. Louis's greatest objective, to secure the borders of his state, had withstood its greatest test. He might have rested satisfied but for the vagaries of births, marriages, and deaths.

Like his father, Louis XIV had married a daughter of the king of Spain. Philip IV had married his eldest daughter to Louis XIV and a younger one to Leopold I of Austria, who subsequently became the Holy Roman Emperor (1658–1705). Before he died, Philip finally fathered a son, Charles II (1665–1700), who attained the Spanish crown at the age of four but was mentally and physically incapable of ruling his vast empire. For decades, it was apparent that there would be no direct Habsburg successor to the Spanish empire. Louis XIV and Leopold I both had legitimate claims to an inheritance that would have irreversibly tipped the European balance of power.

The War of the Spanish Succession.

As Charles II grew increasingly feeble, efforts to find a suitable compromise to the problem of the Spanish succession were led by William III, who, as stadtholder of Holland, was vitally interested in the fate of the Spanish Netherlands and, as king of England, was equally interested in the fate of the Spanish American colonies. In the 1690s, two treaties of partition were drawn up. The first achieved near universal agreement but was nullified by the death of the German prince who was to inherit the Spanish crown. The second, which would have given Italy to Louis's son and everything else to Leopold's son, was opposed by Leopold, who had neither naval nor commercial interests and who claimed most of the Italian territories as imperial fiefs.

All of these plans had been made without consulting the Spanish, who wanted to maintain their empire intact. To this end, they devised a brilliant plan. Charles II bequeathed his entire empire to Philip of Anjou, the younger grandson of Louis XIV, with two stipulations: that Philip renounce his claim to the French throne and that he accept the empire intact, without partition. If he—or, more to the point, his grandfather, Louis XIV—did not accept these conditions, the empire would pass to Archduke Charles, the younger son of Leopold I. Such provisions virtually ensured war between France and the empire unless compromise between the two

The West and the Wider World
THE NUTMEG WARS

A seed about the size of an acorn connected Portugal, Holland, and England to a small string of islands in the Pacific Ocean and to the eastern seaboard of North America. It created a series of trading wars among the European powers in the seventeenth century and resulted in a number of trade treaties with the leaders of the Banda Islands, in what is now Indonesia. East and West became linked as great European sailing ships made port at the juncture of the Indian and Pacific Oceans in search of the seeds of the tree *Myristica Fragrans,* which grew only on the Banda Islands and which had the singular virtue of producing two rare spices greatly prized by Europeans: mace and, especially, nutmeg.

Flimsy in appearance, the seeds of the *Myristica Fagrans* could be harvested with no greater effort than the shaking of its branches. The husk of the seed pod yielded the delicate spice mace that was used in cookery and as a base for fragrances. The pod itself after husking, drying, and cracking yielded the nutmeg, a versatile spice (some think it is the distinctive ingredient in Coca Cola) that experienced a craze in the first decades of the seventeenth century. Its use as a flavoring was long known in China and South Asia and it had entered the Mediterranean in small quantities through the efforts of Muslim traders. But once the Portuguese started importing it in bulk, around twenty tons a year by the middle of the sixteenth century, merchants and apothecaries began to tout its other virtues. Its fragrance was a desirable mask for the acrid odors of ordinary life when applied either to the skin or a piece of linen. Its exotic origins suggested mystical power. By the end of the century, when the Dutch entered the trade and annual imports grew toward 100 tons, nutmeg was widely believed to be an aphrodisiac, and since aphrodisiacs work on the mind rather than the body, what was believed was all that mattered. Demand

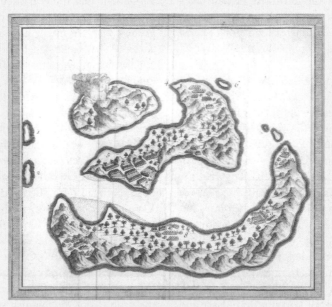

■ Engraving of the Banda Islands, based on a sixteenth-century map by Theodore de Bry.

rose and supply fell. By the beginning of the seventeenth century, when the English contested Dutch supremacy in global trade, the two nations were bringing back a staggering 200 to 250 tons from the Bandas. By then nutmeg was a wonder drug indeed, believed capable of curing ailments from headache to the sweating sickness associated with plague. What cost a tenth of a penny a pound on the island docks of the South Seas sold in a London or an Amsterdam shop for 7000 times that amount. Small wonder that the greatest trading companies in the world were pooling resources to outfit ships to sail for nutmeg.

Indeed, nutmeg was so valuable to Europeans in the seventeenth century that their quest to obtain it led three nations to dispatch their merchants on eighteen-month journeys from which most never returned. If they did not perish during the long sea voyage around the horn of Africa, along the Coromandel Coast of India, and past the great pepper island of Java, they were imperiled by barely submerged razor-sharp volcanic rocks that guarded the Banda Islands on which the trees flourished. Shifting trade winds also made the islands inaccessible six months a year. Only those with good guides or good luck laid anchor there. If the merchants survived the dangers of nature, then they faced those of man. Every European captain claimed his nation held exclusive trading rights to these miraculous seeds, and in the open waters of the Pacific Ocean might made right. More than one great sailing ship had its hull punctured by cannon balls, its mast burned by flaming arrows, its crew killed or scuttled by rival merchants.

Even to reach an island port in safety was no guarantee of success. The indigenous peoples were fierce, capable, and resolutely independent. As one Englishman described them, the Bandanese were "men warlike and agile, strong and valiant . . . courteous and affable . . . full of contention amongst themselves, but generally united against the common enemy." Though the islands were small, they were not unified politically. Each village contained its own governing council, which meant that trade was very much a local affair. The Bandanese granted "exclusive" trading rights as often as possible and

352

■ Engraving of a massacre of Dutch soldiers by the Bandanese.

placidly watched the Europeans squabble over them. In the long months during which the traders waited for the winds to shift so they could depart, misunderstandings and misdeeds were resolved lethally.

The growing popularity of nutmeg in the West and the evolution of trade with European merchants had an enormous impact on the Banda Islands. Though the Bandanese used nutmeg in their cooking, the abundant resource was hardly considered a prized commodity. Until the Portuguese arrived, most nutmeg was carried off the islands in small boats and bartered for ceramics, metalwork, and agricultural products. The Portuguese attempted to control the nutmeg trade as well as to convert local leaders, many of whom were Muslim, to Christianity. While the Portuguese greatly increased the amount of nutmeg that was gathered and shipped, their attempts to prevent the traditional barter trade and to win religious converts led to near constant conflict with the locals. Thus, when the Dutch arrived in 1599 and dispersed the Portuguese fleet, they were welcomed by the Bandanese and were allowed to build a fort where they could store bags of seed and await return voyages.

The Bandanese soon tired of the Dutch as well. By now the islanders had become more sophisticated traders, securing guns, powder, and shot in return for bags of nutmeg, and their conflicts with the Dutch occasionally turned into pitched battles. In 1609, the Bandanese massacred 46 Dutchman; in 1616, the Dutch invaded Ay Island and slaughtered hundreds of indigenous people. In this environment of conflict, the arrival of the English seemed the answer to a prayer, and local Bandanese leaders entered into contracts to provide these new European visitors with as much nutmeg as they could carry away in exchange for weapons. Just as the leaders had hoped,

the Dutch and the English began to fight each other, the English insisting that the commerce of the seas was open to everyone, the Dutch that they held monopoly rights to nutmeg.

The Dutch were the greater power, and they soon drove the English from all but one of the Banda islands, the small island of Rhun. In 1619, the European nations signed a treaty granting each the territory they held but it had little effect in Banda. The Dutch began a systematic depopulation of the smaller islands, invaded Rhun, and cut down all of its nutmeg trees. In 1621, they assaulted the English fort that was now inhabited by the Bandanese and killed anyone who did not flee into the mountains. Most of the islanders were captured and sold into slavery, replaced in turn by other South Asian slaves.

Not only had the Dutch gained control of the nutmeg trade, they now controlled the nutmegs as well. They offered land on the islands to any Dutch trader who would settle there. Again, in violation of their treaty with the English, they invaded Rhun and destroyed whatever new growth had occurred there. In retaliation, the English attacked a Dutch island outpost half a world away, the set-

tlement of New Amsterdam. In 1667, the two European powers settled their differences with an exchange. The English turned over the Banda island of Rhun, the Dutch the American island of Manhattan. Wily Dutch traders had once purchased it for the derisory sum of $24 worth of trinkets. Now their government traded it away for a volcanic rock where nutmeg would no longer grow, and they were convinced they had gotten the better of the deal. The linking of East and West in seventeenth-century global trade networks had enormous consequences. In the case of nutmeg, the search for seeds had led to half a century of fighting among the Europeans, the decimation of the population of Banda, and Dutch domination of the spice.

....

QUESTIONS FOR DISCUSSION

Why did Europeans come to the Pacific islands? How did the organization of Bandanese society create conflict for the Portuguese and Dutch? How did the Bandanese manage to maintain their freedom for half a century after the first Europeans arrived? What was the Dutch solution to threats to their nutmeg monopoly?

....

powers could be reached. Before terms could even be suggested, however, Charles II died, and Philip V (1700–1746) was proclaimed king of Spain and its empire.

Thus the eighteenth century opened with the War of the Spanish Succession (1702–1714). Emperor Leopold rejected the provisions of Charles's will and sent his troops to occupy Italy. Louis XIV confirmed the worst fears of William III when he provided his grandson with French troops to "defend" the Spanish Netherlands. William III revived the Grand Alliance and initiated a massive land war against the combined might of France and Spain. The allied objectives were twofold: to prevent the unification of the French and Spanish thrones and to partition the Spanish empire so that both Italy and the Netherlands were ceded to Austria. Louis XIV's objective was simply to preserve as much as possible of the Spanish inheritance for the house of Bourbon.

William III died in 1702 and was succeeded by Anne (1702–1714). John Churchill (1650–1722), Duke of Marlborough and commander-in-chief of the army, continued William's policy. England and Holland again provided most of the finance and sea power, but the English also provided a land army that was nearly 70,000 strong. Prussia joined the Grand Alliance, and disciplined Prussian troops helped to offset the addition of the Spanish army to Louis's forces. Churchill defeated French forces in 1704 at Blenheim in Germany and in 1706 at Ramillies in the Spanish Netherlands. France's military ascendancy was over.

Efforts to negotiate a peace settlement took longer than the war itself. The Austrians had taken control of Italy, the English and Dutch had secured the Spanish Netherlands, and the French had been driven back beyond the Rhine. The Allies believed that they could now impose any treaty they pleased on Louis XIV and, along with concessions from France, attempted to oust his grandson, Philip V, from the Spanish throne. This proved impossible to achieve, though it took more than five years to learn the lesson. By then the European situation had taken another strange twist. Both the emperor Leopold and his oldest son had died. Now Leopold's younger son, Archduke Charles, inherited the empire as Charles VI (1711–1740) and raised the prospect of an equally dangerous combined Austrian-Spanish state.

Between 1713 and 1714, a series of treaties at Utrecht settled the War of the Spanish Succession. Spanish possessions in Italy and the Netherlands were ceded to Austria; France abandoned all its territorial gains east of the Rhine and ceded its North American territories of Nova Scotia and Newfoundland to England. England also acquired from Spain Gibraltar, on the southern coast of Spain, and the island of Minorca in the Mediterranean. Both were strategically important to English commercial interests. English intervention in the Nine Years' War and the War of the Spanish Succession did not result in large territorial gains, but it did result in an enormous increase in English power and prestige. Over the next 30 years, England would assert its own imperial claims.

The Colonial Wars

The Treaty of Utrecht (1713–1714) ushered in almost a quarter century of peace in western Europe. Austrian rule in the Netherlands and Italy remained a major irritant to the

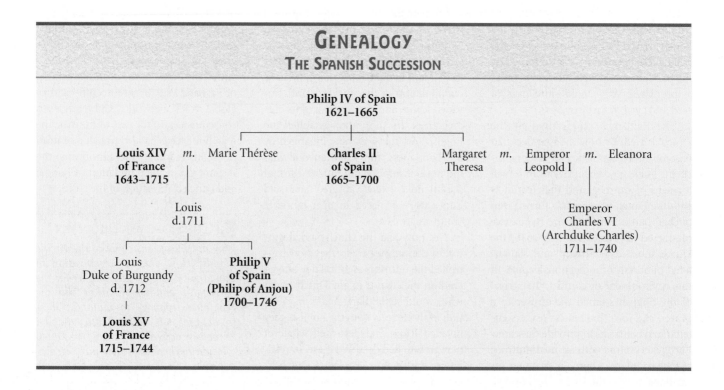

GENEALOGY
THE SPANISH SUCCESSION

Philip IV of Spain
1621–1665

Louis XIV   *m.*   Marie Thérèse   **Charles II**   Margaret   *m.*   Emperor   *m.*   Eleanora
of France   **of Spain**   Theresa   Leopold I
1643–1715   1665–1700

                        Louis   Emperor
                        d.1711   Charles VI
                                                                                              (Archduke Charles)
                                                                                              1711–1740

Louis   **Philip V**
Duke of Burgundy   **of Spain**
d. 1712   **(Philip of Anjou)**
                              1700–1746

Louis XV
of France
1715–1744

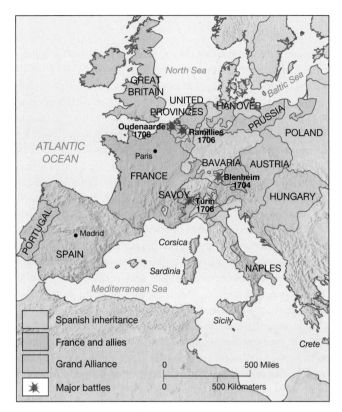

■ War of the Spanish Succession. The great British victories in this war were in the Spanish Netherlands and the Holy Roman Empire. They established Britain as a great power.

practice. Tariffs on imports and customs duties on British goods provided a double incentive for smuggling.

France emerged as Britain's true colonial rival. In the Caribbean, the French had the largest and most profitable of the West Indian sugar islands, Saint Domingue (modern-day Haiti). In North America, France not only held Canada but also laid claim to the entire continent west of the Ohio River. The French did not so much settle their colonial territory as occupy it. They surveyed the land, established trading relations with the Native Americans, and built forts at strategic locations. The English, in contrast, had developed fixed communities, which grew larger and more prosperous by the decade. France decided to defend its colonies by establishing an overseas military presence. Regular French troops were shipped to Canada and installed in Louisbourg, Montreal, and Quebec. The British responded with

Spanish, but Spain was too weak to do more than sulk and snarl. The death of Louis XIV in 1715 quelled French ambitions for a time and even led to an Anglo-French accord, which guaranteed the preservation of the settlement reached at Utrecht. Peace allowed Europe to rebuild its shattered economy and resume the international trade that had been so severely disrupted over the last 40 years. The Treaty of Utrecht had resolved a number of important trading issues, all in favor of Great Britain, as England was known after its union with Scotland in 1707. In addition to receiving Gibraltar and Minorca from Spain, Britain was granted the monopoly to provide slaves to the Spanish American colonies and the right to send one trading ship a year to them. In the East and in the West, Britain was becoming the dominant commercial power in the world.

Part of the reason for Britain's preeminence was the remarkable growth of its Atlantic colonies. Like every other colonial power, the British held a monopoly on their colonial trade. They were far less successful than were the Spanish and French in enforcing the notion that colonies existed only for the benefit of the parent country, but the English Parliament continued to pass legislation aimed at restricting colonial trade with other nations and other nations' colonies. Like most other mercantile restrictions, these efforts were stronger in theory than in

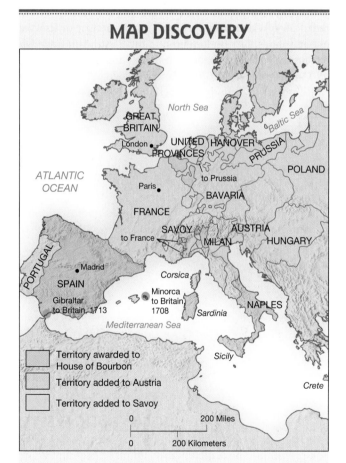

The Treaty of Utrecht

What critical gains did Britain make as a result of the 1714 Treaty of Utrecht? Notice the extent of Austria after the treaty. What problems were the Austrian government most likely to face? What did Savoy gain?

troops of their own and sent an expeditionary force to clear the French from the Ohio River Valley. This action was the immediate cause of the Seven Years' War (1756–1763).

Although the Seven Years' War had a bitter Continental phase, it was essentially a war for empire between the English and the French. There were three main theaters: the North American mainland, the West Indian sugar plantations, and the eastern coast of India. All over the globe, the British won smashing victories. The British navy blockaded the water route to Canada and ultimately captured Montreal and Quebec. After some initial successes, the French were driven back west across the Mississippi River, and their line of fortresses in the Ohio Valley fell into English hands. The English took all the French sugar islands except Saint Domingue. British success in India was equally complete. The French were chased from their major trading zone, and English dominance was secured.

By the end of the Seven Years' War, Britain had become a global imperial power. In the Peace of Paris (1763), France ceded all of Canada in exchange for the return of its West Indian islands. British dominion in the East Indian trade was recognized and led ultimately to British dominion in India itself. In less than a century, France's ascendancy was broken, and Europe's first modern imperial power had been created.

CONCLUSION

European commercial expansion was the first step in a long process that would ultimately transform the material life of all human beings. The quest for new commodities led to the sophistication of transportation, marketing, and distribution—all vital developments for agricultural changes in the future. The ability to move large quantities of goods from place to place and to exchange them at different parts of the globe laid the foundation for organized manufacturing. The practical impact of scientific discovery, as yet only dimly glimpsed, would soon spur the transformation of handicrafts into industries. In the eighteenth century, the material world was still being conquered, and the most unattractive features of this conquest were all too plainly visible. Luxuries for the rich were won by the labors of the poor and the enslaved. (For a discussion of eighteenth-century culture and society, see Chapter 19.) The greed of merchants and the glory of princes made an unholy alliance that resulted in warfare around the globe.

As intercontinental trade made the world grow smaller and increasingly interdependent, the scientific revolution made the universe larger and reduced the earth from its traditional status as the central point of reference to being just one of a family of planets orbiting the sun.

QUESTIONS FOR REVIEW

1. What was new about the methods and ideas of Copernicus, Brahe, Kepler, and Galileo, and why were they threatening to Catholic doctrine?
2. In what ways did the new science build upon traditional ideas associated with alchemy and astrology? In what ways was it a departure?
3. What new technologies, trading practices, and financial devices assisted the expansion of long-distance trading?
4. Why were the Dutch especially well-suited to participate in the worldwide expansion of European commerce?
5. How did the governments of the various European nations promote their own commercial interests?

KEY TERMS

alchemy, *p. 342*

balance of power, *p. 351*

Cartesiansim, *p. 343*

entrepôt, *p. 344*

joint-stock companies, *p. 349*

mercantilism, *p. 348*

monopoly, *p. 348*

Navigation Acts, *p. 349*

scientific revolution, *p. 340*

triangular trade, *p. 345*

DISCOVERING WESTERN CIVILIZATION ONLINE

You can obtain more information about science and commerce in early modern Europe at the websites listed below. See also the Companion Website that accompanies this text, www.ablongman.com/kishlansky, which contains an online study guide and additional resources.

The New Science

Internet Modern History Sourcebook: Scientific Revolution

www.fordham.edu/halsall/mod/modsbook09.html

Links to sources and other sites dealing with the scientific revolution.

The Art of Renaissance Science

www.crs4.it/Ars/arshtml/arstoc.html

An interesting site dealing with the relations between Renaissance art and early modern science.

Sir Isaac Newton

www-gap.dcs.st-and.ac.uk/
~history/Mathematicians/Newton.html

A miscellany of material on Sir Isaac Newton.

The Galileo Project

es.rice.edu/ES/humsoc/Galileo/

A site devoted to Galileo that contains pictures of his instruments and guides to his experiments.

Empires of Goods

Trade Products in Early Modern History

www.bell.lib.umn.edu/Products/Products.html

A site describing the new products introduced to Europe during the period of global expansion.

Holland Museums

www.hollandmuseums.nl/

An online gallery of Dutch art, with text available in English.

History House: Tulipomania

www.historyhouse.com/in_history/tulip/

The story of tulip mania in seventeenth-century Holland.

SUGGESTIONS FOR FURTHER READING

General Reading

Jeremy Black, *The Rise of the European Powers, 1679–1793* (New York: Edward Arnold, 1990). A look at diplomatic history from an English point of view.

Jan de Vries, *The European Economy in an Age of Crisis* (Cambridge: Cambridge University Press, 1976). A comprehensive study of economic development, including long-distance trade and commercial change.

K. H. D. Haley, *The Dutch in the Seventeenth Century* (London: Thames and Hudson, 1972). A well-written and well-illustrated history of the golden age of Holland.

A. Rupert Hall, *The Revolution in Science, 1500–1750* (London: Longman, 1983). The best introduction to the varieties of scientific thought in the early modern period. Detailed and complex.

Derek McKay and H. M. Scott, *The Rise of the Great Powers, 1648–1815* (London: Longman, 1983). An outstanding survey of diplomacy and warfare.

The New Science

H. F. Cohen, *The Scientific Revolution* (Chicago: University of Chicago Press, 1994). The history of the idea of the scientific revolution and of the events that comprised it.

Stillman Drake, *Galileo* (New York: Hill and Wang, 1980). A short but engaging study of the great Italian scientist.

Margaret C. Jacob, *The Cultural Meaning of the Scientific Revolution* (New York: Alfred A. Knopf, 1988). Scientific thought portrayed in its social context.

Lisa Jardine, *Ingenious Pursuits: Building the Scientific Revolution* (New York: Anchor Books, 1999). A new study emphasizing the technical contexts of the scientific revolution and interactions between its major figures.

Londa Schiebinger, *The Mind Has No Sex? Women in the Origins of Modern Science* (Cambridge, MA: Harvard University Press, 1990). The role of women in the scientific revolution.

Steven Shapin, *The Scientific Revolution* (Chicago: University of Chicago Press, 1996). An excellent brief introduction.

Richard Westfall, *The Construction of Modern Science: Mechanisms and Mechanics* (Cambridge: Cambridge University Press, 1977). A survey of scientific developments from Kepler to Newton. A good introduction to both mechanics and mathematics.

Richard Westfall, *The Life of Isaac Newton* (Cambridge: Cambridge University Press, 1993). The best short biography.

Empires of Goods

J. N. Ball, *Merchants and Merchandise: The Expansion of Trade in Europe* (London: Croom Helm, 1977). A good overview of European overseas economies.

K. N. Chaudhuri, *The Trading World of Asia and the English East India Company* (Cambridge: Cambridge University Press, 1978). A brilliant account of the impact of the Indian trade on both Europeans and Asians.

Philip Curtin, *The Atlantic Slave Trade* (Madison: University of Wisconsin Press, 1969). A study of the importation of African slaves into the New World, with the best estimates of the numbers of slaves and their destinations.

Ralph Davis, *The Rise of the Atlantic Economies* (Ithaca, NY: Cornell University Press, 1973). A nation-by-nation survey of the colonial powers.

Jonathan Israel, *Dutch Primacy in World Trade, 1585–1740* (Oxford: Oxford University Press, 1989). The triumph of Dutch traders and techniques written by the leading authority.

Joseph Miller, *Way of Death: Merchant Capitalism and the Angolan Slave Trade, 1730–1830* (Madison: University of Wisconsin Press, 1988). An illuminating portrait of the eighteenth-century slave trade, with an unforgettable account of the slave voyages.

Sidney Mintz, *Sweetness and Power* (New York: Viking Press, 1985). An anthropologist explores the lure of sugar and its impact on Western society.

Simon Schama, *The Embarrassment of Riches* (New York: Alfred A. Knopf, 1987). A social history of the Dutch Republic that explores the meaning of commerce in Dutch society.

The Wars of Commerce

Jeremy Black, *A System of Ambition? British Foreign Policy, 1660–1793* (London: Longman, 1991). The best survey of Britain's international relations during the long eighteenth century.

A. C. Carter, *Neutrality or Commitment: The Evolution of Dutch Foreign Policy, 1667–1795* (London: Edward Arnold, 1975). A tightly written study of the objectives and course of Dutch diplomacy.

Paul Langford, *The Eighteenth Century, 1688–1815* (New York: St. Martin's Press, 1976). A reliable guide to the growth of British power.

J. A. Lynn, *The Wars of Louis XIV, 1667–1714* (London: Longman, 1999). A comprehensive study by a leading military historian of France.

Richard Pares, *War and Trade in the West Indies, 1739–1763* (Oxford: Oxford University Press, 1936). A blow-by-blow account of the struggle for colonial supremacy in the sugar islands.

For a list of additional titles related to this chapter's topics, please see www.ablongman.com/kishlansky.

Chapter 18

THE BALANCE OF POWER IN EIGHTEENTH-CENTURY EUROPE

The Visual Record

A DASHING OFFICER

From the middle of the seventeenth century, Britain was a great sea-faring power. Its navy, built up during the reign of Charles I and the rule of Oliver Cromwell, challenged the Dutch for imperial supremacy in the east and the Spanish for colonial supremacy in the west. Louis XIV actually paid the British government a subsidy to remain neutral in his commercial and territorial wars and even attempted to rent British ships on occasion. The British flag flew on seas worldwide and it would not be long before Britannia ruled the waves. But beginning at the end of the seventeenth century, Great Britain also became a feared landed military power. Under its Dutch king, William III, British armies successfully held the French at bay in the Nine Years' War and inflicted defeat upon them in the brutal War of the Spanish Succession (1702–1714). British generals, such as the Duke of Marlborough, became European-wide celebrities, their feats the subject of story, song, and painting.

Britain's rise to military greatness was as swift as it was unexpected and it lasted for more than one hundred years. The titanic struggle with France dominated the lives of four successive generations and was not finally concluded until the Battle of Waterloo in 1815. Throughout the eighteenth century, the military was present in British society in a way in which it never had been before or would be again. A society that had openly condemned the concept of a standing army now gave way to one in which the presence of uniformed officers was everywhere. Where younger sons had once gone into the church, now they joined the guards. Where the impoverished and luckless had once migrated to London, now they took the King's shilling, as voluntary enlistment was called. The excess agricultural populations of Scotland and Ireland, once doomed to hunger and starvation, now became the raw materials for the greatest fighting men Europe had known.

One indication of the new prominence given soldiers was the painting of their portraits by the most talented artists of the day. This portrait of Captain Robert Orme was painted by Sir Joshua Reynolds, founder and first president of the Royal Academy and one of the greatest portrait artists of the age. Reynolds revived the long tradition of English portrait painting that had reached its height with the Fleming Van Dyck and the German Kneller. But Reynolds was no foreign import. He was born and raised in Devonshire, learned his trade by painting sailors at Plymouth Docks, and even sailed on a naval expedition. Reynolds's military portraits capture that spirit of patriotism, of strength, and of courage that the British expected from their officers. Captain Orme, a member of the prestigious Coldstream Guards, is portrayed in a

moment of action, his stead foaming and winded, the message that he carries admitting of no delay. Slaughter rages behind him. In his haste, his hair has come undone and his extended right arm suggests that he is about to mount and gallop away. But in his pause there is a great stillness and confidence. His gaze is suffused with reassurance, the jaw solid, the eyes piercing. This is the image of flesh and blood that carried Britain to its greatness in the wars of the eighteenth century.

Looking Ahead

The balance of power established by the European monarchies in the eighteenth century was achieved on the battle-field. As we shall see in this chapter, in Russia, Prussia, and Austria, noblemen flocked to military service and the military portion of national economies multiplied dramatically. In the east, her neighbors three times carved up Poland. In the west, the continuing struggle between France and Britain resulted in the destabilization of French society that prepared the way for the French Revolution. In the Atlantic, Britain casually lost its North American colonies in a war it fought half-heartedly for a prize it no longer appreciated. ➤

GEOGRAPHICAL TOUR
A Grand Tour of Europe in 1714

In the eighteenth century, young noblemen from every European nation completed their education by taking a grand tour. Usually in company with a tutor, they would visit the palaces, castles, and churches of their neighboring countries, learn a little of the language, and mingle with others of their class who were engaged in a similar experience. Noblemen who took the grand tour in the second decade of the century witnessed the redrawing of Europe's political map as well as a new balance of power among the European states.

The political geography of Europe was reorganized at the beginning of the eighteenth century by two treaties. The Treaty of Utrecht (1713–1714) created a new Europe in the west, and the Treaty of Nystad (1721) did the same in the east.

Both agreements reflected the dynamics of change that had taken place over the previous century. The rise of France on the Continent and of Britain's colonial empire around the globe were facts that could no longer be ignored. The decline of Sweden and Poland and the emergence of Russia as a great power were the beginning of a long-term process that would continue to dominate European history.

All of that could be seen on a map of Europe in the early eighteenth century (see **Map A**). France's absorption of Alsace and encroachments into Lorraine would be bones of contention between the French and Germans for two centuries and would ultimately contribute to the outbreak of World Wars I and II. The political footballs of the Spanish Netherlands and Spanish Italy, now temporarily Austrian, continued to be kicked around until the nationalist movements of the nineteenth century gave birth to Belgium, Luxembourg, and a united Italy. The emergence of Brandenburg-Prussia on the north German coast and the

■ **Map A. Europe in 1714.** This map shows Europe as established by the Treaty of Utrecht.

gradual decline in the power of the Holy Roman Emperor were both vital to the process that created a unified Germany and a separate Austria. In the southeast, the slow but steady reconquest of the Balkans from Ottoman dominion restored the historic southern border of the Continent. The inexorable expansion of Russia was also already apparent.

Expansion of Western Europe

Perhaps the most obvious transformation in the political geography of western Europe was the expansion of European power around the globe.

Colonies in the Americas. In the Atlantic, Spain remained the largest colonial power, controlling all of Mexico and Central America, the largest and most numerous of the Caribbean islands, North America from Colorado to California (as well as Florida), and most of South America (see **Map B**). The other major colonial power in the region was Portugal, which held the richly endowed colony of Brazil.

■ **Map B. The Americas.** Much of the American continents was still uncharted with most settlements in the coastal areas.

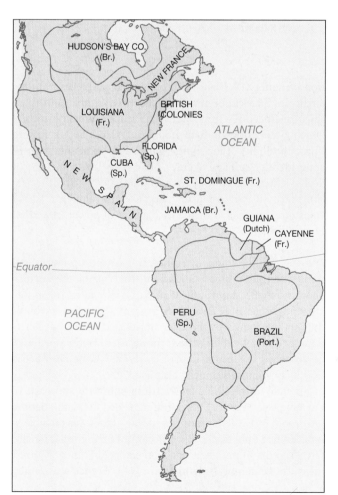

In North America, the French and British shared the eastern half of the continent (see **Map B**). The French controlled most of it. They had landed first in Canada and then slowly made their way down the Saint Lawrence River. New France, as their colonial empire was called, was a trading territory, and it expanded along the Great Lakes and the Ohio, Missouri, and Mississippi Rivers all the way to the Gulf of Mexico. France also claimed the territory of Louisiana, named for Louis XIV, which stretched from New Orleans to Montana. The British settlements ranged along the Atlantic seaboard from Maine to Georgia. Unlike the French, the British settled their territory and were interested in expansion only when their population, which was doubling every 25 years, outgrew its resources. By the early eighteenth century, the ports of Boston, New York, Philadelphia, and Charleston were thriving commercial centers.

Colonies in the Far East. Europeans managed their eastern colonial territories differently than they did those in the Atlantic. Initially, the Portuguese and the Dutch had been satisfied with establishing trading factories—coastal fortresses in Africa and Asia that could be used as warehouses and defended against attack. But in the seventeenth century, the European states began to take control of vital ports and lucrative islands (see **Map C**). Here, the Dutch were the acknowledged leaders, replacing the Portuguese, who had begun the process at the end of the sixteenth century. Holland held, by force or in conjunction with local leaders, all the Spice Islands in the Pacific. The Dutch also occupied both sides of the Malay Peninsula and nearly all the coastal areas of the islands in the Java Sea. Dutch control of Ceylon was strategically important for its Indian trade. Compared to the Dutch, all other European states had only a minor territorial presence in the

■ **Map C. India and the East Indies.** The famous Spice Islands were still controlled by the Dutch while the British gained footholds on both coasts of India.

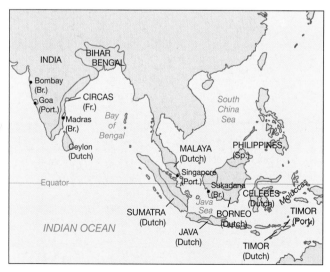

East, with the exception of Spain, which still controlled the Philippines. The British had limited their eastern outposts to trading establishments. Through these they maintained a significant presence in India. During the eighteenth century, the British began to colonize the Indian subcontinent directly (see **Map C**).

Great Britain.   Imperial expansion was the most obvious change in the geopolitical boundaries of Europe, but it was not the only one. A brief tour of the western states after the Treaty of Utrecht reveals some others. In 1707, England and Scotland formally joined together to form Great Britain (see **Map D**). In addition to its eastern and western colonies, Britain had also gained control of Gibraltar at the foot of Spain and the island of Minorca in the Mediterranean (see **Map E**). Both territories were strategically important to British commerce.

The Low Countries.   Across the English Channel were the Low Countries, now permanently divided between the United Provinces in the north, led by Holland, and the provinces in the south that had remained loyal to the Spanish crown in the sixteenth century (see **Map D**). By 1714, the golden age of the Dutch was over. They lost their predominance in European trade to France and much of their eastern empire to Britain. The Spanish Netherlands, the original Burgundian inheritance, were now being slowly dismembered. Since the acces-

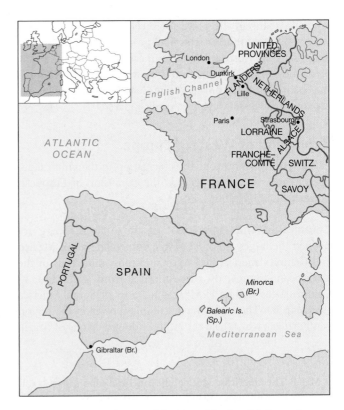

■ **Map E. France and Spain.** The War of the Spanish Succession permanently separated France and Spain.

■ **Map D. Great Britain and the Low Countries.** Great Britain and the Low Countries were the two leading European commercial nations.

sion of Louis XIV, France had plucked small pieces from the territories that had been contested between France and Spain since the fifteenth century. Between French aggression and the Dutch occupation of such important places as Ghent and Ypres, the ability of the southern provinces to maintain a separate identity suffered a grave blow. The Treaty of Utrecht dealt a still graver blow by assigning sovereignty over this territory to Austria, ostensibly because the emperor was a Habsburg, but really because the balance of power in western Europe demanded it.

France.   To the south lay France, still the most powerful nation in Europe despite its losses in the War of the Spanish Succession (see **Map E**). By 1714, Louis XIV had broken forever the danger of Spanish encirclement. Louis had methodically set out to occupy those territories that were strategically necessary to defend his state from invasion. In the northeast, he absorbed the duchy of Bar. In the north, he absorbed a healthy portion of Flanders. He pushed the eastern boundary of his state to the Rhine by overrunning Alsace and parts of Lorraine (see **Map E**). Strasbourg remained French under the settlement of 1714, testimony to the fact that it was possible to hold France only at the western banks of the Rhine. Finally, farther to the south, Louis had won and held Franche-Comté, once the center of Burgundy. In 1714, France was larger, stronger, and better able to defend its borders than ever before. It was also exhausted.

Spain.   As France expanded, Spain contracted. Less than two centuries earlier, a Spanish king had dreamed of being monarch over all of Europe. Now a French Bourbon sat on the great Habsburg throne, and Spain was slowly being sliced to pieces. By 1714, the European territories of the Spanish empire had been reduced to Iberia itself (see **Map E**). However, the loss of its European empire ultimately proved to be a blessing in disguise for Spain, which now entered a new and unexpected phase of growth and influence.

The Empire.   The center of Europe remained occupied by the agglomeration of cities, bishoprics, principalities, and small states known collectively as the Holy Roman Empire but now more accurately called the German empire (see **Map F**). There were still over 300 separate jurisdictions, most of them vulnerable to preying neighbors such as Louis XIV. Bavaria in the south and Saxony, Brandenburg, and Hanover in the north were among the most important of the large states, with the added twist that Hanover was now ruled by the king of Great Britain. The emperor, now officially prohibited from in-

■ **Map F. The Holy Roman Empire.** It was still a conglomeration of towns, principalities, and bishoprics, but increasingly the empire was losing political and administrative control over its lands.

terference in the internal administration of the large states, was less dominant in German affairs than he had been before the Thirty Years' War.

Increasingly, Habsburg power centered on Austria, Bohemia, and Hungary (see **Map F**). This was especially true during the reign of Leopold I (1655–1705). Withstanding threats on all sides, Leopold was able to expand his state to the west and south and bring Austria into the ranks of the great European powers. Such an outcome could hardly have been foreseen in 1683, when the Ottomans besieged Vienna itself and only the arrival of 70,000 Polish-led troops saved the city from falling. From that time forward, Austrian forces scored stunning victories. By 1699, almost all of Hungary had been retaken by Austria; with the Treaty of Passarowitz in 1718, Austria gained the rest of Hungary and Serbia. The Treaty of Utrecht had already granted Austria control of the Netherlands, Lombardy, and Naples, making the Austrian Habsburgs rulers of a European empire (see **Map F**).

Austria's Italian possessions included the vast southern territories of Naples (including Sicily after 1720) and the rich industrial area surrounding Milan in the north. Alongside the Austrian territories a number of independent city-states, including Venice and Genoa, continued to flourish on the Italian peninsula. The grand duchy of Tuscany, with its great city of Florence, and the Papal States had expanded over the course of the seventeenth century, absorbing their smaller neighbors until both were large, consolidated territories (see **Map F**). To the west of the Italian states was the duchy of Savoy (see **Map F**), which grew and prospered. After the War of the Spanish Succession, Savoy was counted among the victors, though it had fought on both sides. Duke Victor Amadeus II became a king when he received the island of Sicily, which he exchanged with Austria for Sardinia in 1720 (see **Map F**).

Thus the Treaty of Utrecht signaled a new configuration of political power. England, France, Prussia, and Austria were the ascending powers; Holland and Spain were the declining ones. Italy and the southern Netherlands were the bones over which the biggest dogs fought. This was western Europe in 1714.

Realignment in Eastern Europe

In eastern Europe it was the Treaty of Nystad (1721), which ended the Great Northern War (1700–1721), that fixed the political geography. Here the emerging powers were Russia and Prussia; those in decline were Sweden and Poland. The critical factor in eastern European politics remained access to the sea. Gaining control of outlets to the Baltic Sea in the north and the Black Sea in the south was the central motivation for the long years of war fought among the eastern states.

Russia.   The expansion of Russia is one of the central events in European history, and the early eighteenth century is its pivotal period. During the long years of social and economic recovery after the death of Ivan the Terrible in 1584, Russia had been easy prey for its powerful neighbors Sweden and Poland. Through a series of wars and political pacts, Russia had ceded most of its Baltic territories to Sweden and had relinquished land and population in the west to Poland. Peter the Great (1682–1725) set out to reclaim what had been lost. As a result of the Great Northern War, Russia regained the eastern Baltic coastline from the southeastern end of Finland to Riga in the west (see **Map G**). Russia now controlled all of the vital Baltic ports in the east. Peter built a new capital, Saint Petersburg, on the Gulf of Finland and laid the foundation for the Russian navy.

Sweden. What Russia gained, Sweden lost (see **Map G**). At the height of its power in the middle of the seventeenth century, Sweden had dominated the Baltic. It had occupied all of Finland, controlled the important eastern coast of Norway, and gained a foothold in Germany. But Sweden's century-long rise to power was followed by a rapid period of decline. As a result of the Great Northern War, Sweden lost all of its German territories. Those on the North Sea went to Hanover; those on the Baltic went to Prussia. Livonia, Estonia, and the eastern provinces were returned to Russia, but Sweden was able to hold on to its vital gains from the Danes. Sweden had built its own window to the west at Göteborg on the North Sea, and from there it could carry on direct trade with Britain and the Netherlands.

Prussia. Since the end of the Thirty Years' War, Brandenburg-Prussia, a domain of the Holy Roman Empire, had been growing steadily (see **Map G**). From the capital at Berlin the princes of Brandenburg directed the accumulation of small neighboring German lands: Magdeburg and Halle to the southwest, a piece of Pomerania to the northeast. Brandenburg expanded in every direction, but it could do little to join itself to the kingdom of Prussia. A huge swath of Poland separated the two. In the eighteenth century, the determination to expand and close the gap dominated Prussian history.

Poland. This aim meant eventual conflict with Poland, which, despite its political weakness, was one of the largest territories in Europe (see **Map G**). On its southern border it held back Ottoman expansion, while on its eastern border it held back the Russians. Its great port of Gdansk on the Baltic dominated the grain and timber trade with northern Europe as well as local Baltic commerce between Scandinavia and the mainland. Sweden and Russia controlled Poland politically, helping to nominate its elected kings and ensuring that its decentralized form of aristocratic government kept it weak. By the beginning of the eighteenth century, it was a helpless giant ready to be toppled.

Thus a potent Prussia and Russia and a prostrate Poland characterized the realignment of the eastern portion of Europe. At the same time, the separation between east and west was narrowing. Prussia's German orientation and the westernization of Russia led to closer ties with the west.

■ **Map G. Russia and Sweden.** Sweden's age of territorial expansion was over by the beginning of the eighteenth century.

THE RISE OF RUSSIA

At the beginning of the eighteenth century, Russia was scarcely of concern to the rest of Europe. Peter the Great changed that. The Treaty of Nystad had confirmed the magnitude of his victory over the Swedes in the Great Northern War. The change created consternation in the courts of Europe. Little was known about the Russian ruler or his state. Letters from European merchants stationed in Moscow were the main source of Western knowledge about the vast Muscovite empire. What little mercantile contact there was between Russia and the West was conducted entirely by westerners, who were allowed to live in Moscow in a separate ghetto called "German-town."

Peter the Great sought greater contact with western Europe. Twice he visited Europe to discover the secrets of western prosperity and might. He arranged marriages between the closest heirs to his throne, including his son Alexis, and the sons and daughters of German princes and dukes. By 1721, he had established 21 separate foreign embassies. The sons of the Russian gentry and nobility were sent to the west—sometimes forcibly—to further their education and to learn to adapt to western outlooks. Peter recruited foreign engineers and gunners to serve in his army, foreign architects to build his new capital at Saint Petersburg, foreign scholars to had come from Byzantium rather than Rome, thus giving Russian Christianity an eastern flavor. Its Asian territories mixed the influence of Mongols and Ottomans; its southern borders met Tatars and Cossacks. While most European states were racially and ethnically homogeneous, Russia was a loose confederation of diverse peoples. Yet the western states posed the greatest threat to Russia in the seventeenth century, and it was to the West that Peter, like his father before him, turned his attention.

Nearly all of Peter's reforms—economic, educational, administrative, social, military—were aimed at enhancing military efficiency rather than civil progress. In his 30 years of active rule, there was only one year—1724—during which he was not at war. Vital reforms such as the poll tax (1724), which changed the basis of taxation from the household to the individual adult male, had enormous social consequences. The new policy of taxing individuals officially erased whole social classes. A strict census, taken (and retaken) to inhibit tax evasion, became the basis for further governmental encroachments on the tsar's subjects. Yet the poll tax was designed not for any of these purposes but to increase tax revenue for war. Similarly, the establishment of compulsory, lifetime military service, which was required of the landowning classes (the nobility and gentry), was undertaken to provide officers and state servants for an expanding military machine.

Although Peter's reforms were developed from little other than military necessity, they constituted a fundamental transformation in the life of all Russian people. The creation of a gigantic standing army and an entirely new navy meant conscription of the Russian peasantry on a grand scale. In a ten-year period of the Great Northern War, the army absorbed 330,000 conscripts, most of whom never returned to their homes. Military service was not confined to the peasantry. Traditionally, the rural gentry raised and equipped the local conscript forces and gave them what training they could. Most of the gentry lived on estates that had been granted to them along with the resident peasants as a reward for their military contributions. Peter the Great intensified the obligations of the gentry. Not only were they to serve the state for life, but they were to accompany their regiments to the field and lead them in battle. When too old for active military service, they were to perform administrative service in the new departments of state.

The expansion of military forces necessitated an expansion of military administration as well. Peter's first innovation was the creation of the Senate, a group of nine senior administrators who were to oversee all aspects of military and civil government. The Senate became a permanent institution of government led by an entirely new official, the Procurator-General, who presided over its sessions and could propose legislation as well as oversee administration. From the Senate emanated 500 officials known as the fiscals, who traveled throughout the state looking for irregularities in tax assessment and collection. They quickly developed into a hated and feared internal police force.

Peter's efforts to reorganize his government went a step further in 1722, when he issued the **Table of Ranks.** This was an official hierarchy of the state that established the social position or

■ This portrait of Peter the Great by his court painter Louis Caravaque pays homage to Peter's intense interest in naval matters. Ships flying English, Dutch, Danish, and Russian flags prepare for maneuvers under his command.

head the new state schools, and foreign administrators to oversee the new departments of state. He borrowed freely from Europe and adapted sensibly. If necessary, he would drag his country kicking and screaming into the modern world.

By 1721, Russia was recognized all over Europe as an emerging power. The Russian navy, built mostly by foreigners, was now capable of protecting Russian interests and defending important ports such as Riga and Saint Petersburg. Even the Dutch, who had long plotted the decline of Swedish might, now became nervous. It was therefore unsettling that the Russian ruler now wanted to be recognized as an emperor.

The Reforms of Peter the Great

Peter the Great was not the first Russian tsar to attempt to borrow from the West. The process had been under way for decades. The opening of the northern port of Archangel in 1584 led to direct contact with British and Dutch traders, who brought new ideas and useful products. But Russia was a vast state, and Europe was only one of its neighbors. Russia's religion rank of individuals. It was divided into three categories: military service, civil service, and owners of landed estates. Each category contained 14 ranks, and it was decreed that every person who entered the hierarchy did so at the bottom and worked his way up. The creation of the Table of Ranks demonstrated Peter's continued commitment to merit as a criterion for advancement. This standard had been shown in the military, where officers were promoted on the basis of service and experience rather than birth or background. Equally important was Peter's decision to make the military service the highest of the three categories. This reversed the centuries-old positions of the landed aristocracy and the military service class. Though the old nobility also served in the military and continued to dominate state service, the Table of Ranks opened the way for the infusion of new elements into the Russian elite.

Many of the men who were able to advance in the Table of Ranks did so through attendance at the new institutions of higher learning that Peter founded. His initial educational establishments were created to further the military might of the state. The Colleges of Mathematics, Engineering, and Artillery, which became the training grounds for his army officers, were all founded during the Great Northern War. Peter was also interested in liberal education, and he had scores of Western books translated into Russian. He had a press established in Moscow to print original works, including the first Russian newspaper. He decreed that a new, more Westernized alphabet replace the one used by the Russian Orthodox church and that books be written in the vernacular rather than in the formal literary language of religious writers. He also introduced Arabic numerals into official accounting records.

In all of these ways and more, Peter the Great transformed Russia, but the changes did not come without cost. The traditions of centuries were not easily broken. Intrigue against Peter led first to confrontation with the old military elite and later to conflict with his only son, Alexis. It remains unclear whether the plot with which Alexis was connected actually existed or was a figment of Peter's imagination, but it is abundantly clear that Alexis's death in 1718 from torture plunged the state into a succession crisis in 1725. In the end, the great costs of westernization were paid by the masses of people, who benefited little from the changes.

Life in Rural Russia

At the beginning of the eighteenth century, nearly 97 percent of the Russian people lived on the land and practiced agriculture. Their lifestyles and farming methods had changed little for centuries. A harsh climate and low yields characterized Russian agriculture. One-third of the annual harvests during the eighteenth century were poor or disastrous, yet throughout the century, state taxation was making ever larger demands on the peasantry. During Peter's reign alone, direct taxation increased by 500 percent.

The theory of the Russian state was one of service, and the role of Russian peasants was to serve their master. The law code of 1649 formalized a process that had been under way for over a century whereby peasants lost status and became the property of their landlords. During the next century, laws curtailed the ability of peasants to move freely from one place to another, eliminated their right to hold private property, and abolished their freedom to petition the tsar against their masters. At the same time that landlords increased their hold over peasants, the state increased its hold over landlords. They were made responsible for the payment of taxes owed by their peasants and for the military service due from the peasants. By the middle of the eighteenth century, over half of all peasants—6.7 million adult males by 1782—had become serfs, the property of their masters, without any significant rights or legal protection.

If serfs made up the bottom half of the Russian peasantry, there were few advantages to being in the top half among the state peasants. State peasants lived on lands owned by the monarchy itself. Like the serfs, state peasants were subject to the needs of the state for soldiers and workers. Forced labor was used in all of Peter's grandiose projects. Saint Petersburg was built by the backbreaking labor of peasant conscripts.

Many Russian peasants developed a philosophy of submission and a rich folk culture that valued a stubborn determination to endure. For those who would no longer bend to the knout—the heavy leather whip that was the omnipresent enforcer of obedience—only flight or rebellion remained. Hundreds of thousands of serfs fled to state-owned lands in hope of escaping the cruelties of individual landlords. Although severe penalties were imposed for aiding runaway serfs, in fact most state overseers and many private landlords encouraged runaways to settle on their lands. In their social and economic conditions, eighteenth-century Russian peasants were hardly distinguishable from medieval European serfs.

The Enlightened Empress Catherine

Of all the legacies of Peter the Great, perhaps the one of most immediate consequence was that government could go on without him. During the next 37 years, six tsars ruled Russia, "three women, a boy of twelve, an infant, and a mental weakling," as one commentator acidly observed. Although each succession was contested, the government continued to function smoothly, and Peter's territorial conquests were largely maintained. Russia also experienced a remarkable increase in population during this period. Between 1725 and 1762, the population grew from 13 to 19 million, a jump of nearly one-half in a single generation. This explosion of people dramatically increased the wealth of the landholding class, whose members reckoned their status by the number of serfs they owned.

The expansion of the economic resources of the nobility was matched by a rise in their legal status and political power. This period was sarcastically dubbed "the emancipation of the nobility," a phrase that captures not only the irony of the growing gap between rich and poor but also the contrast between the social structures of Russia and those of western Europe. In return for their privileges and status, Peter the Great extended the duties that the landowning classes owed to the state. By granting unique rights, such as the ownership of serfs, to the descendants of the old military service class, Peter had forged a Russian nobility. However, lifetime service was the price of nobility.

To gain and hold the throne, each succeeding tsar had to make concessions to the nobles to win their loyalty. The requirement of service to the state was gradually weakened until finally, in 1762, the obligation was abolished entirely.

Catherine's Accession.

The abolition of compulsory service was not the same as the abolition of service itself. In fact, the end of compulsory service enabled Catherine II, the Great (1762–1796), to enact some of the most important reforms of her reign. Her first two acts as empress—having her husband, Peter III, murdered and lowering the salt tax—strengthened her position.

Catherine was a dynamic personality who alternately captivated and terrified those with whom she came into contact. She was influenced on the one hand by the new French ideas of social justice and the nobility of the human race and on the other by the traditional Russian ideas of absolute rule over an enserfed and subhuman population. Catherine handled these contrasting dimensions of her rule masterfully, gaining abroad the reputation as the most enlightened of European monarchs and at home the sincere devotion of her people.

The most important event in the early years of Catherine's reign was the establishment of a legislative commission to review the laws of Russia. Catherine herself wrote the *Instruction* (1767) by which the elected commissioners were to operate. She borrowed her theory of law from the French jurist Baron de Montesquieu (1689–1755) and her theory of punishment from the Italian reformer Cesare Beccaria (1738–1794). Among other things, Catherine advocated the abolition of capital punishment, torture, serf auctions, and the breakup of serf families by sale. Few of these radical reforms were ever put into practice.

In 1775, Catherine restructured local government. Russia was divided into 50 provincial districts, each with a population of between 300,000 and 400,000 inhabitants. Each district was to be governed by both a central official and elected local noblemen. This reform was modeled on the English system of justices of the peace. In 1785, Catherine issued the Charter of the Nobility, a formal statement of the rights and privileges of the noble class. The charter incorporated all the gains the nobility had made since the death of Peter the Great, but it also instituted the requirements for local service that had been the basis of Catherine's reforms. District councils with the right to petition the tsar directly became the centerpiece of Russian provincial government.

Catherine's reforms did little to enhance the lives of the vast majority of her people. She took no effective action to end serfdom or to soften its rigors. In fact, by grants of state land, Catherine gave away 800,000 state peasants, who became serfs. So, too, did millions of Poles who became her subjects after the partition of Poland in 1793 and 1795.

Pugachev's Revolt.

Popular discontent fueled the most significant uprising of the century, Pugachev's Revolt (1773–1775), which took place during Catherine's reign. Emelyan Pugachev (1726–1775) was a Cossack who had been a military adventurer in his youth. Disappointed in his career, he made his way to the Ural Mountains, where he recruited Asian tribesmen and laborers who were forced to work in the mines. By promising freedom and land ownership, he drew peasants to his cause. In 1773,

CHILDHOOD TRAUMAS

Catherine the Great left a fascinating account of her early years, which is in sharp contrast to her reputation for ruthlessness as a ruler.

Focus Questions
What kinds of attention did Catherine's parents show her? What is the significance of the fact that Catherine tells the story of her coughing attack just after describing her parents' treatment of her?

My father, whom I saw very seldom, considered me to be an angel, my mother did not bother much about me. She had had, eighteen months after my birth, a son whom she passionately loved, whereas I was merely tolerated and often repulsed with violence and temper, not always with justice. I was aware of all this, but not always able to understand what I really felt about it.

At the age of seven I was suddenly seized with a violent cough. It was the custom that we should kneel every night and every morning to say our prayers. One night as I knelt and prayed I began to cough so violently that the strain caused me to fall on my left side, and I had such sharp pains in my chest that they almost took my breath away.

Finally, after much suffering, I was well enough to get up and it was discovered, as they started to put on my clothes, that I had in the meantime assumed the shape of the letter *Z*: my right shoulder was much higher than the left, the backbone running in a zigzag and the left side falling in.

From Catherine the Great, *Memoirs* (1755).

Pugachev declared himself to be Tsar Peter III, the murdered husband of Catherine II. He began with small raiding parties against local landlords and military outposts and soon gained the allegiance of tens of thousands of peasants. In 1774, with an army of nearly 20,000, Pugachev took the city of Kazan and threatened to advance on Moscow. It was another year before state forces could effectively control the rebellion. Finally, Pugachev was betrayed by his own followers and sent to Moscow, where he was executed.

During the reigns of Peter and Catherine the Great, Russia was transformed into an international power. Saint Petersburg, a window to the West, attracted many of Europe's leading luminaries. At court, French was spoken, the latest fashions were worn, and the newest ideas for economic and educational reform were aired. The Russian nobility mingled comfortably with its European counterparts, while the military service class developed into bureaucrats and administrators. Although court society glittered, for millions of peasants the quality of life was no better at the end of the campaign of westernization than it had been at the beginning.

THE TWO GERMANIES

The Thirty Years' War, which ended in 1648, initiated a profound transformation of the Holy Roman Empire. Warfare had devastated imperial territory and left a legacy of political consequences. There were now two empires—a German and an Austrian—though both were ruled by the same person. In the German territories, whether Catholic or Protestant, the Holy Roman Emperor was more a constitutional monarch than the absolute ruler he was in Austria. The larger states such as Saxony, Bavaria, and Hanover made their own political alliances despite the jurisdictional control that the emperor claimed to exercise. Most decisively, so did Brandenburg-Prussia. By the beginning of the eighteenth century, the electors of Brandenburg had become the kings of Prussia, and Prussian military power and efficient administrative structure became the envy of its German neighbors.

The Austrian empire was composed of Austria and Bohemia, the Habsburg hereditary lands, and as much of Hungary as could be controlled. Austria remained the center of the still-flourishing Counter-Reformation and a stronghold of Jesuit influence. The War of the Spanish Succession, which gave the Habsburgs control of the southern Netherlands and parts of Italy, brought Austria an enhanced role in European affairs. Austria remained one of the great powers of Europe and the leading power in the Holy Roman Empire, despite the rise of Prussia. Indeed, from the middle of the eighteenth century the conflict between Prussia and Austria was the defining characteristic of central European politics.

The Rise of Prussia

The transformation of Brandenburg-Prussia from a petty German principality to a great European power was one of the most significant developments of the eighteenth century.

Frederick William, the Great Elector (1640–1688), had begun the process of forging Brandenburg-Prussia into a power in its own right by building a large and efficient military machine. At the beginning of the eighteenth century, Prussia was on the winning side in both the War of the Spanish Succession and the Great Northern War. When the battlefield dust had settled, Prussia possessed Pomerania and the Baltic port of Stettin. It was now a recognized power in eastern Europe.

Frederick William I.   Frederick William I (1713–1740) and his son Frederick II, the Great (1740–1786), turned this promising beginning into an astounding success. A devout Calvinist, Frederick William I deplored waste and display. The reforms he initiated were intended to subordinate both aristocracy and peasantry to the needs of the state and to subordinate the needs of the state to the demands of the military.

Because of its exposed geographical position, Prussia's major problem was to maintain an efficient and well-trained army during peacetime. Security required a constant state of military preparedness, yet the relaxation of military discipline and the desertion of troops to their homes inevitably followed the cessation of hostilities. Frederick William I solved this problem by integrating the economic and military structures of his state. First he appointed only German officers to command his troops, eliminating mercenaries. Then he placed these noblemen at the head of locally recruited regiments. Each adult male in every district was required to register for military service in the regiment of the local landlord. These reforms dramatically increased the effectiveness of the army by shifting the burden of recruitment and training to the localities.

Yet despite all the attention that Frederick William I lavished on the military—by the end of his reign, nearly 70 percent of state expenditures went to the army—his foreign policy was largely pacific. In fact, his greatest achievements were in civil affairs, reforming the bureaucracy, establishing a sound economy, and raising state revenues. Through generous settlement schemes and by welcoming Protestant and Jewish refugees, Frederick William was able to expand the economic potential of these eastern territories. Frederick William I pursued an aggressive policy of land purchase to expand the royal domain, and the addition of so many new inhabitants in Prussia further increased his wealth. While the major western European powers were discovering deficit financing and the national debt, Prussia was running a surplus.

Frederick the Great.   Financial security was vital to Frederick the Great's success. Father and son had quarreled bitterly throughout Frederick's youth, and most observers expected that out of spite, Frederick would tear down all that his father had built up. He and his father were cast in the same mold, however, with the unexpected difference that Frederick was the more ruthless and ambitious. With his throne, Frederick II inherited the fourth largest army in Europe and the richest treasury. He wasted no time in putting both to use. His two objectives were to acquire the Polish corridor of West

Prussia that separated his German and Prussian territories and the agriculturally and industrially rich Austrian province of Silesia to the southeast of Berlin. Just months after his coronation, Frederick conquered Silesia, which soon came to dominate the Prussian economy.

It was Frederick's military prowess that earned him the title "the Great." However, his achievements went beyond the military arena. More than his father, Frederick II forged an alliance with the Prussian nobility, integrating the nobles into a unified state. A tightly organized central administration, which depended on the cooperation of the local nobility, directed both military and bureaucratic affairs. At the center, Frederick worked tirelessly to oversee his government. Whereas Louis XIV had proclaimed, "I am the state," Frederick the Great announced, "I am the first servant of the state." He codified the laws of Prussia, abolished torture and capital punishment, and instituted agricultural techniques imported from the states of western Europe. By the end of Frederick's reign, Prussia had become a model for bureaucratic organization, military reform, and enlightened rule.

Austria Survives

Austria was the great territorial victor in the War of the Spanish Succession, acquiring both the Netherlands and parts of Italy. Austrian forces recaptured a large part of Hungary from the Turks, thereby expanding Austria's territory to the south and the east. Charles VI (1711–1740), hereditary ruler of Austria and Bohemia, king of Hungary, and Holy Roman Emperor of the German nation, was recognized as one of Europe's most potent rulers—but appearances were deceptive. The apex of Austrian power and prestige had already passed, and Austria's rivals in eastern Europe, Russia, and Prussia were on the rise.

Decentralized Rule. The difficulties facing Austria ran deep. The Thirty Years' War had made the emperor more an Austrian monarch than an imperial German ruler. On the Austrian hereditary estates, the Catholic Counter-Reformation continued unabated, bringing with it the benefits of Jesuit education, cultural revival, and the religious unity that was necessary to motivate warfare against the Ottomans. But these benefits came at a price. Perhaps as many as 200,000 Protestants fled Austria and Bohemia, taking their skills and capital with them. For centuries the vision of empire had dominated Habsburg rule. This meant that the Austrian monarchy was a multiethnic confederation of relatively autonomous lands loosely tied together by loyalty to a single head. Hungary even elected the Habsburg emperor its king in a separate ceremony. Therefore it was hard for Austria to centralize in the same way as had Prussia.

Austria was predominantly rural and agricultural. Less than 5 percent of the population lived in towns of 10,000 or more; less than 15 percent lived in towns at all. The landed aristocracy exploited serfs to the maximum. Not only were serfs required to give labor service three days a week (and up to six days a week during planting and harvest times), but the nobility maintained a full array of feudal privileges, including the right to mill all grain and brew all beer. When serfs married, when they transferred property, even when they died, they paid taxes to their lord. As a result, they had little left to give the state. In consequence, the Austrian army was among the smallest and poorest of the major powers, despite the fact that it had the most active enemies along its borders.

Lack of finance, lack of human resources, and lack of governmental control were not the only problems facing Charles VI. With no sons to succeed him, Charles feared that his hereditary and elective states would go their separate ways after his death and that the great Habsburg monarchy would end. For 20 years, his abiding ambition was to gain recognition for the principle that his empire would pass intact to his daughter, Maria Theresa. He expressed the principle in a document known as the **Pragmatic Sanction,** which stated that all Habsburg lands would pass intact to the eldest heir, male or female. Charles VI made concession after concession to gain acceptance of the Pragmatic Sanction. But the leaders of Europe licked their lips at the prospect of a dismembered Austrian empire.

Maria Theresa. In 1740, soon after Maria Theresa (1740–1780) inherited the imperial throne, Frederick of Prussia invaded the rich Austrian province of Silesia and attracted allies for an assault on Vienna. Faced with Bavarian, Saxon, and Prussian armies, Maria Theresa appeared before the Hungarian estates, accepted their crown, and persuaded them to provide her with an army capable of halting the allied advance. Though she was unable to reconquer Silesia, Hungarian aid helped her to hold the line against her enemies.

The loss of Silesia, the most prosperous part of the Austrian domains, signaled the need for fundamental reform. The new eighteenth-century idea of building a state replaced the traditional Habsburg concern with maintaining an empire. Maria Theresa and her son Joseph II (1780–1790) began the process of transformation. For Austria, state building meant first the reorganization of the military and civil bureaucracy to clear the way for fiscal reform. As in Prussia, a central directory was created to oversee the collection of taxes and the disbursement of funds. Maria Theresa personally persuaded her provincial estates both to increase taxation and to extend it to the nobles and the clergy. Although her success was limited, she finally established royal control over the raising and collection of taxes.

Maria Theresa also improved the condition of the Austrian peasantry. She established the doctrine that the "peasant must be able to support himself and his family and pay his taxes in time of peace and war." She limited labor service to two days per week and abolished the most burdensome feudal dues. Joseph II ended serfdom altogether. The new Austrian law codes guaranteed peasants' legal rights and established their ability to seek redress through the law. Joseph II hoped to extend reform even further. In the last years of his life, he

■ Maria Theresa and her family. Eleven of Maria Theresa's 16 children are posed with the empress and her husband, Francis of Lorraine. Standing next to his mother is the future emperor Joseph II.

The Politics of Power

Frederick the Great's invasion of Silesia in 1740 was callous and cynical. Since the Pragmatic Sanction bound him to recognize Maria Theresa's succession, Frederick calculatingly offered her a defensive alliance in return for which she would simply hand over Silesia. It was an offer she should not have refused. Though Frederick's action initiated the War of the Austrian Succession, he was not alone in his desire to shake loose parts of Austria's territory. Soon nearly the entire Continent became embroiled in the conflict.

The War of the Austrian Succession.   The War of the Austrian Succession (1740–1748) resembled a pack of wolves stalking its injured prey. It quickly became a major international conflict involving Prussia, France, and Spain on one side and Austria, Britain, and Holland on the other. Spain joined the fighting to recover its Italian possessions, Saxony claimed Moravia, France entered Bohemia, and the Bavarians moved into Austria from the south. With France and Prussia allied, it was vital that Britain join with Austria to maintain the balance of power. Initially, the British did little more than subsidize Maria Theresa's forces, but once France renewed its efforts to conquer the Netherlands, both Britain and the Dutch Republic joined in the fray.

That the British cared little about the fate of the Habsburg empire was clear from the terms of the treaty that they dictated at Aix-la-Chapelle (Aachen) in 1748. Austria recognized Frederick's conquest of Silesia as well as the loss of parts of its Italian territories to Spain. France, which the British had always regarded as the real enemy, withdrew from the Netherlands in return for the restoration of a number of colonial possessions. The War of the Austrian Succession made Austria and Prussia permanent enemies and gave Maria Theresa a crash course in international diplomacy. She learned firsthand that self-interest rather than loyalty underlay power politics.

The Seven Years' War.   This lesson was reinforced in 1756, when Britain and Prussia entered into a military accord at the beginning of the Seven Years' War (1756–1763). Prussian expansion and duplicity had already alarmed both Russia and France, and Frederick II feared that he would be squeezed from both the east and the west. He could hardly expect help from Maria Theresa, so he made overtures to the British, whose interests in protecting Hanover, the hereditary estates of their German-born king, outweighed their prior commitments to Austria. Frederick's actions drove France into the arms of both the Austrians and the Russians, and an alliance that included the German state of Saxony was formed in defense. Thus was initiated a diplomatic revolution in which France and Austria became allies after 300 years as enemies.

Once again, Frederick the Great took the offensive, and once again, he won his risk against the odds. His attack on Saxony and Austria in 1756 brought a vigorous response from the Russians, who interceded on Austria's behalf with a massive army. Three years later, at the battle of Kunersdorf,

abolished obligatory labor service and ensured that all peasants kept one-half of their income before paying local and state taxes. Such a radical reform met a storm of opposition and was abandoned at the end of Joseph's reign.

The reorganization of the bureaucracy, the increase in taxation, and the social reforms that created a more productive peasantry revitalized the Austrian state. The efforts of Maria Theresa and Joseph II to overcome provincial autonomy worked better in Austria and Bohemia than in Hungary. The Hungarians declined to contribute at all to state revenues, and Joseph II took the unusual step of refusing to be crowned king of Hungary so that he would not have to make any concessions to Hungarian autonomy. He even imposed a tariff on Hungarian goods sold in Austria. More seriously, parts of the empire had already been lost before the process of reform could begin. Prussia's seizure of Silesia was the hardest blow of all. Yet in 1740, when Frederick the Great and his allies had swept down from the north, few would have predicted that Austria would survive.

Frederick suffered the worst military defeat of his career when the Russians shattered his armies. In 1760, his forces were barely one-third of the size of those massed by his opponents, and it was only a matter of time before he was fighting defensively from within Prussia.

In 1762, Russian Empress Elizabeth died. She was succeeded by her nephew, the childlike Peter III, a German by birth who worshipped Frederick the Great. When Peter came to the throne, he immediately negotiated peace with Frederick, abandoning not only his allies but also the substantial territorial gains that the Russian forces had made within Prussia. It was small wonder that the Russian military leadership joined in the coup d'état that brought Peter's wife, Catherine, to the throne in 1762. With Russia out of the war, Frederick was able to fend off further Austrian offensives and to emerge with his state, including Silesia, intact.

The Seven Years' War did little to change the boundaries of the German states, but it had two important political results. The first was to establish beyond doubt the status of Prussia as a major power and a counterbalance to Austria in central Europe. The existence of the dual Germanies, one led by Prussia and the other by Austria, was to have serious consequences for German unification in the nineteenth century and the two world wars in the twentieth. The second result of the Seven Years' War was to initiate a long period of peace in eastern Europe. Both Prussia and Austria were financially exhausted from two decades of fighting. Both states needed a breathing spell to initiate administrative and economic improvements, and the period following the Seven Years' War witnessed the sustained programs of internal reforms for which Frederick the Great, Maria Theresa, and Joseph II were famous in the decades following 1763.

The Partitions of Poland. Peace among the eastern European powers did not mean that they abandoned their territorial ambitions. All over Europe, absolute rulers reformed their bureaucracies, streamlined their administrations, increased their sources of revenue, and built enormous standing armies—except in Poland, that is. There, the autonomous power of the nobility remained as strong as ever. No monarchical dynasty was ever established, and each elected ruler not only confirmed the privileges of the nobility but usually was forced to extend them. In the Diet, the Polish representative assembly, small special-interest groups could bring legislative business to a halt by exercising their veto power. Given the size of Poland's borders, its army was pathetically inadequate, and the Polish monarchy was helpless to defend its subjects from the destruction on all sides.

In 1764, Catherine the Great and Frederick the Great combined to place one of Catherine's former lovers on the Polish throne and to turn Poland into a weak dependent. Russia and Prussia had different interests in Poland's fate. For Russia, Poland represented a vast buffer state that kept the German powers at a distance from Russia's borders. It was more in Russia's interest to dominate Polish foreign policy than to conquer its territory. For Prussia, Poland looked like another helpless flower, "to be picked off leaf by leaf," as Frederick observed. Poland seemed especially appealing because Polish territory, including the Baltic port of Gdansk, separated the Prussian and Brandenburg portions of Frederick's state.

By the 1770s, the idea of carving up Poland was being actively discussed in Berlin, Saint Petersburg, and Vienna. In 1772, the three great eastern powers struck a deal. Russia would take a large swath of the grain fields of northeast Poland, which included over one million people; Frederick would unite his lands by seizing West Prussia; and Austria would gain both the largest territories, including Galicia, and the greatest number of people, nearly two million Polish subjects.

In half a century, the balance of power in central Europe had shifted decisively. Prussia's absorption of Silesia and parts of Poland made it a single geographical entity as well as a great economic and military power. Austria fought off an attempt to dismember its empire and went on to participate in the partition of Poland. From one empire there were now two states, and the relationship between Prussia and Austria would dominate central Europe for the next century.

■ This engraving by Le Mire is called "The Cake of the Kings: First Partition of Poland, 1773." The monarchs of Russia, Austria, and Prussia join in carving up Poland. The Polish king is clutching his tottering crown.

THE GREATNESS OF GREAT BRITAIN

By the middle of the eighteenth century, Great Britain had become the leading power of Europe. It had won its spurs in Continental and colonial wars. Britain was unsurpassed as a naval power, able to protect its far-flung trading empire and to make a show of force in almost any part of the world. Perhaps more impressively, for a nation that did not support a large standing army, British soldiers had won decisive victories in the European land wars. Until the American Revolution, Britain came up a winner in every military venture it undertook. In addition, Britain enjoyed economic preeminence. British colonial possessions in the Atlantic and Indian Oceans poured consumer products into Britain for export to the European marketplaces. (See "The West and the Wider World: The British Raj in India," pp. 376–377.) The manufacturing industries that other European states attempted to create with huge government subsidies flourished in Britain through private enterprise.

British military and economic power was supported by a unique system of government. In Britain, the nobility served the state through government. The British constitutional system, devised in the seventeenth century and refined in the eighteenth, shared power between the monarchy and the ruling elite through the institution of Parliament. Central government integrated monarch and ministers with chosen representatives from the localities. Such integration not only provided the Crown with the vital information it needed to formulate national policy, but also eased acceptance and enforcement of government decisions. Government was seen as the rule of law, which, however imperfect, was believed to operate for the benefit of all. The relative openness of the British system hindered diplomatic and colonial affairs, in which secrecy and rapid changes of direction were often the monarch's most potent weapons. These weaknesses came to light most dramatically during the struggle for independence waged by Britain's North American colonists.

The British Constitution

The British Constitution was a patchwork of laws and customs that was gradually sewn together. Many of its greatest innovations came about through circumstance rather than design, and circumstance continued to play an essential role in its development in the eighteenth century. At the apex of the government stood the king, not an absolute monarch like his European counterparts, but not necessarily less powerful for having less arbitrary power. The British people revered monarchy and the monarch. The theory of mixed government depended on the balance of interests represented by the monarchy, the aristocracy in the House of Lords, and the people in the House of Commons. The monarch, as the actual and symbolic leader of the nation and the Supreme Head of the Church of England, was still regarded as divinely ordained and a special gift to the nation. Allegiance to the Anglican Church thus intensified allegiance to the king.

The partnership between the Crown and the representative body was best expressed in the idea that the British government was composed of King-in-Parliament. Parliament consisted of three separate organs: monarch, lords, and commons. Though each existed separately as a check on the potential excesses of the others, parliamentary government could operate only when the three functioned together. The king was charged with selecting ministers, initiating policy, and supervising administration. The two houses of Parliament were charged with raising revenue, making laws, and presenting subjects' grievances to the Crown.

The British gentry dominated the Commons, occupying over 80 percent of the 558 seats in any session. Most of these members also served as unpaid local officials in the counties, as justices of the peace, captains of the local militias, or collectors of local taxes. They came to Parliament not only as representatives of the interests of their class, but as experienced local governors who understood the needs of both Crown and subject.

Nevertheless, the Crown had to develop methods to coordinate the work of the two houses of Parliament and facilitate the passage of governmental programs. The king and his ministers began to use the deep royal pockets of offices and favors to bolster their friends in Parliament. Not only were those employed by the Crown encouraged to find a place in the House of Commons, but those who had a place in Parliament were encouraged to take employment from the Crown. Despite its potential for abuse, this was a political process that integrated center and locality, and at first it worked rather well. Men with local standing were brought into central offices, where they could influence central policymaking while protecting their local constituents. These officeholders, who came to be called *placemen,* never constituted a majority of the members of Parliament. They formed the core around which eighteenth-century governments operated, but it was a core that needed direction and cohesion. Such leadership and organization were the essential contribution of eighteenth-century politics to the British Constitution.

Parties and Ministers

Although parliamentary management was vital to the Crown, it was not the Crown that developed the basic tools of management. Rather, these techniques originated within the political community itself, and their usefulness was only slowly grasped by the monarchy. The first and, in the long term, most important tool was the party system. Political **parties** initially developed in the late seventeenth century around the issue of the Protestant succession. Those who opposed James II because he was a Catholic attempted to exclude him from inheriting the Crown. They came to be called by their opponents **Whigs,** which meant "Scottish horse thieves." Those who supported James's hereditary rights but who also supported the Anglican Church came to be called by their opponents **Tories,** which meant "Irish cattle rustlers."

The Whigs supported a Protestant monarchy and a broad-based Protestantism. They attracted the allegiance of large numbers of dissenters, heirs to the Puritans of the seventeenth century who practiced forms of Protestantism different from that of the Anglican Church. The struggle between Whigs and Tories was less a struggle for power than one for loyalty to their opposing viewpoints. As the Tories tended to oppose the succession of Prince George of Hanover and the Whigs to support it, it was no mystery which party would find favor with George I (1714–1727). Moreover, as long as there was a pretender to the British throne—another rebellion took place in Scotland in 1745 led by the grandson of James II—the Tories continued to be tarred with the brush of disloyalty.

The division of political sympathies between Whigs and Tories helped to create a set of groupings to which parliamentary leadership could be applied. A national rather than a local or regional outlook could be used to organize support for royal policy as long as royal policy conformed to that national outlook. The ascendancy of the Whigs enabled George I and his son George II (1727–1760) to govern effectively through Parliament, but at the price of dependence on the Whig leaders. Though the monarch had the constitutional freedom to choose his ministers, realistically he could choose only Whigs and practically none but the Whig leaders of the House of Commons. Fortunately for the first two Georges, they found a man who was able to manage Parliament but desired only to serve the Crown.

Sir Robert Walpole (1676–1745), who came from a gentry family in Norfolk, was an early supporter of the Hanoverian succession. Once George I was securely on the throne, Walpole became an indispensable leader of the House of Commons. An excellent public speaker, he relished long working days and the details of government, and he understood better than anyone else the intricacies of state finance. Walpole became First Lord of the Treasury, a post that he transformed into first minister of state. From his treasury post, Walpole assiduously built a Whig parliamentary party. He carefully dispensed jobs and offices, using them as bait to lure parliamentary supporters. Walpole's organization paid off both in the passage of legislation desired by the Crown and at the polls, where Whigs were returned to Parliament time and again.

From 1721 to 1742, Walpole was the most powerful man in the British government. His long tenure in office was as much a result of his policies as of his methods of governing. He brought a measure of fiscal responsibility to government by establishing a fund to pay off the national debt. In foreign policy, he pursued peace with the same fervor that both his predecessors and his successors pursued war. The long years of peace brought prosperity to both the landed and merchant classes, but they also brought criticism of Walpole's methods. His use of government patronage to build his parliamentary party was attacked as corruption. So too were the ways in which the pockets of Whig officeholders were lined. During his last decade in office, Walpole struggled to survive. His attempt to extend the excise tax on colonial goods nearly led to his loss of office in 1733. His refusal to respond to the clamor for continued war with Spain in 1741 finally led to his downfall.

Walpole's 20-year rule established the pattern of parliamentary government. The Crown needed a "prime" minister who was able to steer legislation through the House of Commons. It also needed a patronage broker who could take control of the treasury and dispense its largess in return for parliamentary backing. Walpole's personality and talents had combined these two roles. Thereafter, they were divided. Those who had grown up under Walpole had learned their lessons well. The Whig monopoly of power continued unchallenged for nearly another 20 years. The patronage network that Walpole had created was vastly extended by his Whig successors. Even minor posts in the customs or the excise offices were exchanged for political favor, and only those approved by the Whig leadership could claim them. The cries of corruption grew louder, and in London a popular radicalism developed in opposition to the Whig oligarchy. The outcry was taken up as well in the North American colonies, where two million British subjects champed at the bit of imperial rule.

CHRONOLOGY
THE NEW EUROPEAN POWERS

1707	England and Scotland unite to form Great Britain
1713–1714	Peace of Utrecht ends War of the Spanish Succession (1702–1714)
1714	British Crown passes to house of Hanover
1721	Treaty of Nystad ends Great Northern War (1700–1721)
1721–1742	Sir Robert Walpole leads British House of Commons
1722	Peter the Great of Russia creates Table of Ranks
1740	Frederick the Great of Prussia invades Austrian province of Silesia
1748	Treaty of Aix-la-Chapelle ends War of the Austrian Succession (1740–1748)
1756–1763	Seven Years' War pits Prussia and Britain against Austria, France, and Russia
1773–1775	Pugachev's Revolt in Russia
1774	Boston Tea Party
1775	American Revolution begins
1785	Catherine the Great of Russia issues Charter of the Nobility

The West and the Wider World
THE BRITISH RAJ IN INDIA

In the middle of the eighteenth century, the focus of the British Empire shifted from west to east. Up to that point, Britain had only been a bit player in the scramble for the spice trade and had lost the competition for nearly all of the Caribbean and South American commodities, but it had managed to claim much of the Atlantic seaboard of the inhospitable North American continent. There, English, Scots, and Irish settled colonies and built villages and towns. Thousands and then tens of thousands of Britons had made the transatlantic journey throughout the seventeenth century seeking their fortunes in the wilderness. By the middle of the eighteenth century, British North America was a flourishing society that provided a ready market for manufactured and luxury commodities. Over 25 percent of all British exports went to North America, nearly £31 million by 1740.

By contrast, English ventures in the East had resulted in only one success: the right of the East India Company to trade in India. The Mughal emperors granted this right in the early seventeenth century, as much a slight to the Portuguese as a favor to the English. Here, a classic mercantile venture was established. A few hundred Englishmen were placed in forts that contained warehouses for the accumulation of Asian goods and that kept the Westerners largely segregated from the indigenous population. English trade in India grew slowly. Each year the company would send its fleet of ships to be laden with the merchandise that had been collected from the hinterland. Purchases were made mostly with bullion that was carried to India by the company's expedition. Brightly colored cottons called chintzes, porcelain,

woven carpets, spices, and tea were the most highly prized goods, with tea becoming the most profitable by the beginning of the eighteenth century. The English had taken up residence on the east coast of India where they estab-

■ Oudh watercolor (1782) of British colonial administrator Warren Hastings with a servant. Hastings was the first governor-general of all India, 1773–1784.

lished their largest base at Calcutta, and it was not long before those who stayed behind became involved in the lucrative trans-Asian trade, especially with China.

Company employees supplemented their meager wages by using their privileged position to exchange Indian goods for Chinese goods. The Indian commodity most prized in China was the drug opium because its production was illegal in China. Other company members traded with Persia, the great Middle Eastern Empire whose contacts with India went back centuries. In this way, British products such as North American tobacco made their way around the globe. Trading on their own accounts while awaiting the arrival of the company's annual fleet, English merchants in India could make enormous fortunes. If they were lucky enough to survive the perils of Eastern climes and diseases they could return to Britain as wealthy men, "nabobs" in eighteenth-century parlance, belittled for the source of their wealth but tolerated for its quantity.

The British went to India to trade and stayed to rule. The Raj (a Hindi word for kingdom) came about accidentally and by degrees. At the beginning no one would have thought that India could have been conquered and few thought that it could be ruled. It was governed throughout the seventeenth century by the Mughals, Persians who had fled marauding Afghans and who had slowly expanded their power until they established a capital at Agra, where one of their emperors built a palace for his wife known ever after as the Taj Mahal. The Mughals created a magnificent court and were protected by an efficiently trained army. In the areas that they controlled directly they extracted a tax on land—the dirwani—from the entire peasant population. But their hold over the South Asian subcontinent was precarious and ever shifting. Most of India was ruled by independent princes known as nawabs. They paid a cash tribute to the Mughals when they had to but otherwise fiercely guarded their independence. The East India Company was treated similarly. They had been granted trading rights in return for an annual payment, but unlike the nawabs they had no incentive to weaken Mughal power.

This arrangement worked smoothly until the 1760s. By then the India trade had become essential to the English economy and the number of Englishmen living in company forts in Bengal had grown to number in the thousands. To protect their large investment and their teeming warehouses, the company employed former British military officers and soldiers and equipped them with the latest armaments. Not surprisingly, company leaders were drawn into local disputes where their power was often decisive. As Mughal influence declined, British prestige rose and inevitably a clash occurred. It began not between the British and the Indians, but between the British and the French, the other European nation with a strong presence in India. Wars in Europe that pitted Britain against France expanded to become world wars throughout their colonial empires.

In India, it was the military brilliance of a young cavalry officer, Robert Clive, that eventually led to British dominance and the expulsion of the French in the 1760s. Clive was simply an employee of the East India Company and not an agent of the British government. His actions were designed to protect the company's trading factories—the French had captured Madras in the 1740s—and defend its employees. But British successes made the Mughals wary. In 1756, Mughal forces besieged and captured Calcutta, the most important British trading settlement. The city's governor fled the town and those officials captured by the Mughals were imprisoned in the local jail known descriptively as the Black Hole. The imprisonment of Englishmen in the Black Hole of Calcutta demanded retribution, and Clive inflicted it. Not only did his forces recapture Calcutta, but Clive also connived to oust the Mughal em-

■ In this painting by Edward Penny (1773), Robert Clive is shown receiving a grant from a nawab of Bengal.

peror and have him replaced by a rival willing to reconfirm all of Britain's trading rights and also to grant it political control over the province of Bengal. As if he were a local ruler, Clive was offered the dirwani—the right to collect local taxes from the entire population. It was an offer he could not refuse.

It was also the most poisoned of all chalices for the British. Quickly and inevitably, the East India Company was drawn into governing Bengal and soon other provinces of India as well. The yield from the dirwani changed the balance of trade in Asia dramatically. Now it was the British who were exporting bullion and creating a drain on the local Indian economy. On the other hand, the company needed to send thousands of administrators east to

protect their rights and to offer government to the tangle of feuding religious, ethnic, and class interests. Shares of the company's stock declined while the cost of administering an empire rose. After the American War of Independence, it was in India that British imperial interest and efforts were focused, forging a relationship quite different from the trading partnership with which it had begun.

QUESTIONS FOR DISCUSSION

What was Britain's initial interest in India? What European nation challenged this interest? How did the British East India Company come to rule the province of Bengal and other Indian provinces? How did these developments change Britain's relationship with India?

America Revolts

Britain's triumph in the Seven Years' War (1756–1763) had come at great financial cost to the nation. At the beginning of the eighteenth century, the national debt stood at £14 million; by 1763 it had risen to £130 million. Then, as now, the cost of world domination was staggering. George III (1760–1820) came to the throne with a taste for reform and a desire to break the Whig stranglehold on government. He was to have limited success on both counts. In 1763, the king and his ministers agreed that reform of colonial administration was long overdue. Such reform would have the twin benefit of shifting part of the burden of taxation from Britain to North America and of making the commercial side of colonization pay.

This was sound thinking all around, and in due course, Parliament passed a series of duties on goods imported into the colonies, including glass, wine, coffee, tea, and most notably sugar. The so-called Sugar Act (1764) was followed by the Stamp Act (1765), a tax on printed papers such as newspapers, deeds, and court documents. Both acts imposed taxes in the colonies similar to those that already existed in Britain. Accompanying the acts were administrative orders designed to cut into the lucrative black market trade. The government instituted new rules for searching ships and transferred authority over smuggling from the local colonial courts to Britain's Admiralty courts. Though British officials could only guess at the value of the new duties imposed, it was believed that with effective enforcement, £150,000 would be raised. All this would go toward paying the vast costs of colonial administration and security.

British officials were perplexed when these mild measures met with a ferocious response. Assemblies of nearly every colony officially protested the Sugar Act and petitioned for its repeal. Riots followed passage of the Stamp Act. Tax collectors were hounded out of office, their resignations precipitated by threats and acts of physical violence. In Massachusetts, mobs that included political leaders in the colony razed the homes of the collector and the lieutenant-governor. However much the colonists might have regretted the violence that was done, they believed that an essential political principle was at stake. It was a principle of the freedom of an Englishman.

At their core, the American colonists' protests underscored the vitality of the British political system. The Americans argued that they could not be taxed without their consent and that their consent could come only through representation in Parliament. Since there were no colonists in Parliament, Parliament had no jurisdiction over the property of the colonists. Taxation without representation was tyranny. There were a number of subtleties to this argument that were quickly lost as political rhetoric and political action heated

■ The First British Empire (ca. 1763). The empire was the result of commercial enterprise and Britain's military successes.

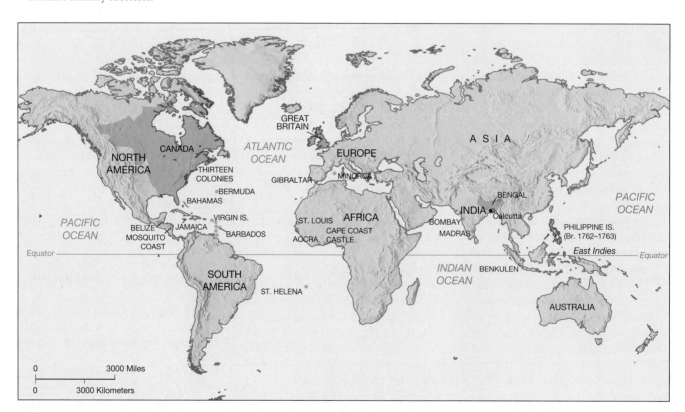

up. First, the colonists did tax themselves through their own legislatures, and much of that money paid the costs of administration and defense. Second, as a number of pamphleteers pointed out, no one in the colonies had asked the British government to send regiments of the army into North America. The colonists had little reason to put their faith in British protection. Hard-fought colonial victories were tossed away at European negotiating tables, while the British policy of defending Indian rights in the Ohio Valley ran counter to the settlers' interests. When defense was necessary, the colonists had proven themselves both able and cooperative in providing it. A permanent tax meant a permanent army, and a standing army was as loathed in the colonies as it was in Britain.

The passion generated in the colonies over the issue of taxation without parliamentary representation was probably no greater than that generated in Britain. For the British, the principle at issue was parliamentary sovereignty. Once the terms of debate had been so defined, it was difficult for either side to find a middle ground.

Parliamentary moderates managed repeal of the Stamp Act and most of the clauses of the Sugar Act, but they also joined in passing the **Declaratory Act** (1766), which stated unequivocally that Parliament held sovereign jurisdiction over the colonies "in all cases whatsoever." This claim became more and more difficult to sustain as colonial leaders began to cite the elements of resistance theory that had justified the Revolution of 1688. Then the protest had been against the tyranny of the king; now it was against the tyranny of Parliament. American propagandists claimed that a conspiracy existed to deprive the colonists of their property and rights, to enslave them for the benefit of special interests and corrupt politicians.

The techniques of London radicals who opposed parliamentary policy were adopted by colonists. Newspapers were used to whip up public support; boycotts brought ordinary people into the political arena; public demonstrations such as the Boston Tea Party (1774) were carefully designed to intimidate; and mobs were occasionally given free rein. Violence was met by violence, and in 1775, full-scale fighting was under way. Eight years later, Britain withdrew from a war it could not win, and the American colonies were left to govern themselves.

CONCLUSION

By the end of the third quarter of the eighteenth century, Europe had a new political configuration. A continent that had once been dominated by a single power—Spain in the sixteenth century and France in the seventeenth—was now dominated by a state system in which alliances among several great powers held the balance. Despite the loss of its American colonies, Great Britain had proved to be the most potent of the states. Its victories over the French in the Seven Years' War and over France and Prussia in the War of the Austrian Succession secured its position. However, this position could be maintained only through alliances with the German states, either Prussia or Austria. The rise of Prussia provided a counterweight to French domination of the Continent. Though these two states became allies in the middle of the century, the ambitions of their rulers made them natural enemies, and it would not be long before French and Prussian armies were again pitted against each other. France, still the wealthiest and most populous of European states, had slumbered through the eighteenth-century reorganization. The legacies of Louis XIV took a long time to reach fruition. He had claimed glory for his state, giving the French people a sense of national identity and national destiny but causing enormous social and economic dislocation. Thus the mid-eighteenth century was to be an age of the greatest literary and philosophical achievement for France, but the late eighteenth century was to witness the greatest social upheaval that Europe had ever known.

QUESTIONS FOR REVIEW

1. What were the great powers of Europe in the eighteenth century and in what ways was there a balance of power among them?
2. What did Peter I and Catherine II of Russia accomplish during their reigns that justifies the title "the Great"?
3. How was the tiny state of Brandenburg-Prussia able to make itself into one of Europe's major powers, and what did that mean for the Austrian empire?
4. How did Britain's theory of mixed government and its parliamentary party system assist its rise to become Europe's great imperial power?
5. How and why did the balance of power shift during the eighteenth century?

KEY TERMS

Declaratory Act, *p. 379*

parties, *p. 374*

Pragmatic Sanction, *p. 371*

Table of Ranks, *p. 367*

Tories, *p. 374*

Whigs, *p. 374*

DISCOVERING WESTERN CIVILIZATION ONLINE

You can obtain more information about the balance of power in eighteenth-century Europe at the websites listed below. See also the Companion Website that accompanies this text, www.ablongman.com/kishlansky, which contains an online study guide and additional resources.

The Rise of Russia

Russia
www.english.upenn.edu/~jlynch/FrankenDemo/Places/russia.html
A site detailing the history of Russia from the time of Peter the Great. Links to the building of St. Petersburg.

Modern History Sourcebook: Catherine the Great
www.fordham.edu/halsall/mod/18catherine.html
Sources from the reign of Catherine the Great.

The Two Germanies

Friedrich II, the Great (1712–1786)
www.hfac.uh.edu/gbrown/philosophers/leibniz/FriedrichGreat/FriedrichGreat.html
A hyper-linked biographical essay on Frederick the Great of Prussia.

The Greatness of Great Britain

The American Revolution
www.revolution.h-net.msu.edu/
A site with extensive links to all aspects of the American Revolution.

Declaring Independence: Drafting the Documents
www.loc.gov/exhibits/declara/declara1.html
An online exhibit at the Library of Congress on the drafting of the Declaration of Independence.

SUGGESTIONS FOR FURTHER READING

General Reading

M. S. Anderson, *Europe in the Eighteenth Century, 1713–1783,* 3d ed. (London: Longman, 1987). A country-by-country survey of political developments.

Jeremy Black, *Europe and the World 1650–1830* (New York: Routledge, 2002). An intelligent survey of Europe in a wider perspective.

David Kirby, *Northern Europe in the Early Modern Period* (London: Longman, 1991). Political history from a Baltic perspective, with excellent chapters on Sweden and Russia.

Nicholas Riasanovsky, *A History of Russia* (New York: Oxford University Press, 1993). The best one-volume history of Russia.

Geographical Tour: Europe in 1714

Derek McKay and H. M. Scott, *The Rise of the Great Powers* (London: Longman, 1983). An outstanding survey of diplomacy and warfare.

The Rise of Russia

John T. Alexander, *Catherine the Great: Life and Legend* (Oxford: Oxford University Press, 1989). A lively account of the public and private life of the Russian Empress.

M. S. Anderson, *Peter the Great* (London: Thames and Hudson, 1978). A well-constructed, comprehensive biography.

Paul Dukes, *The Making of Russian Absolutism, 1613–1801* (London: Longman, 1982). An extensive survey of the Russian monarchy in its greatest period.

Lindsey Hughes, *Russia in the Age of Peter the Great* (New Haven: Yale University Press, 1998). A detailed, thematically organized reappraisal of Russia in the era of Peter's reign.

The Two Germanies

Reed S. Browning, *The War of the Austrian Succession* (London: Macmillan, 1995). A comprehensive history of a complicated event.

David Fraser, *Frederick the Great: King of Prussia* (New York: Allen Lane, 2001). The latest biography.

J. Gagliardo, *Germany Under the Old Regime* (London: Longman, 1991). The best single-volume history.

H. W. Koch, *A History of Prussia* (London: Longman, 1978). A study of the factors that led to Prussian dominance of Germany.

C. A. Macartney, *Maria Theresa and the House of Austria* (Mystic, CT: Verry Inc., 1969). Still the best introductory study.

The Greatness of Great Britain

Bernard Bailyn, *The Ideological Origins of the American Revolution* (Cambridge, MA: Harvard University Press, 1967). A brilliant interpretation of the underlying causes of the break between Britain and the North American colonies.

Jeremy Black, *Britain as a Military Power* (London: UCL Press, 1999). A reliable survey of military developments in Britain.

John Brewer, *The Sinews of Power: War, Money, and the English State, 1688–1783* (Cambridge, MA: Harvard University Press, 1990). An influential and clearly written book on the fiscal and military innovations that underwrote English power in the eighteenth century.

J. C. D. Clark, *English Society, 1688–1832* (Cambridge: Cambridge University Press, 1985). A bold reinterpretation of the most important features of English society.

Linda Colley, *Britons* (New Haven, CT: Yale University Press, 1992). A lively account of how a nation was forged from Welsh, Scots, and English and how unity and diversity intermixed.

Paul Langford, *A Polite and Commercial People: England 1727–1783* (Oxford: Oxford University Press, 1989). The standard survey in the Oxford history series.

Gordon Wood, *The Radicalism of the American Revolution* (New York: Alfred A. Knopf, 1992). How the ideals of the American Revolution shaped an emerging nation.

For a list of additional titles related to this chapter's topics, please see www.ablongman.com/kishlansky.

19

CULTURE AND SOCIETY IN EIGHTEENTH-CENTURY EUROPE

The Visual Record

HAPPY FAMILIES

"Happy families are all alike," wrote Lev Tolstoy in the nineteenth century, when the idea of a happy family was already a cliché. Such an idea would never have occurred to his eighteenth-century forebears. For them the happy family was doubly new—new in the change in the relationships within the family and new in the stress on happiness itself. Personal happiness was an invention of the Enlightenment, the result of novel attitudes about human aspirations and human capabilities. "Happiness is a new idea in Europe," wrote Louis de Saint-Just (1767–1794). It emerged in response to the belief that what was good brought pleasure and what was evil brought pain. Happiness, both individual and collective, became the yardstick by which life was measured. This meant a reorientation in personal conduct and, most of all, a reorientation of family life. Especially for people with an economic cushion, a pleasurable family life was essential. Husbands and wives were to become companions, filled with romantic love for each other and devoted to domestic bliss. Children were to be doted on, treated not as miniature adults to be lectured and beaten, but as unfilled vessels into which all that was good was to be poured.

Were ever a couple more in love than the husband and wife depicted in *A Visit to the Wet Nurse* by Jean-Honoré Fragonard (1732–1806)? The man clasps his wife's arm to his cheek, she lays her hand on his shoulder. Their sighs are almost audible! Together, they admire the fruit of their love: the baby asleep in the cradle. They have come together to see how the wet nurse is caring for their child. Doubtless it was they who provided the rather opulent bassinet, which contrasts sharply with the other furniture in the room, and the linens and pillows into which the baby has nestled.

At the beginning of the eighteenth century, the use of a wet nurse was still common among the families of the French bourgeoisie, the class to which this couple—judging from their clothes—undoubtedly belongs. As time moved on, however, more and more mothers began to nurse their babies themselves. In part, this change was a response to the higher mortality rate among infants sent out to wet nurses. The unsanitary environment of the towns ran a close race with the neglect that many wet nurses showed their charges. But a wet nurse who could be supervised, that is, one who lived near enough to

be visited but far enough away from the town to enjoy wholesome air, might be the best of both worlds.

But there are two families in this picture, and they are hardly alike. At first glance, the wet nurse looks like an old woman. It is shocking to realize that she cannot be much older than thirty, an age beyond which wealthy families would not hire her for fear either that she would not have much milk or that it would be sour. The two younger children are undoubtedly hers, the youngest probably just weaned so that all of her milk would go to the baby. The wet nurse also spins to earn a little extra.

Looking Ahead

Like much else in the eighteenth century, the world of the family was divided between high and low. As we shall see in this chapter, it was developments in the middle that were most characteristic of eighteenth-century social and cultural developments. The spirit of Enlightenment was spreading from the elites throughout all social ranks, improving education, health, and social welfare. The rapid growth of the bourgeoisie, or the middle class, enhanced the quality of life for tens of thousands and transformed values in the most basic institutions of society. ➤

EIGHTEENTH-CENTURY CULTURE

The eighteenth century spawned a rich and costly culture. Decorative architecture, especially interior design, reflected the increasing sociability of the aristocracy. Entertainment, especially music, became a central part of aristocratic culture. The string quartet made its first appearance in the eighteenth century, and chamber music enjoyed unparalleled popularity.

Musical entertainments in European country houses were matched by the literary and philosophical entertainments of the urban salons. The salons, especially in Paris, blended the aristocracy and bourgeoisie with the leading intellectuals of the age. At formal meetings, papers on scientific or philosophical topics were read and discussed. At informal gatherings, new ideas were examined and exchanged. The most influential thinkers of the day presented the ideas of the **Enlightenment,** a new European outlook on religion, society, and politics.

The Enlightenment

The Enlightenment was less a set of ideas than it was a set of attitudes. At its core was a critical questioning of traditional institutions, customs, and morals. In 1762, the French philosopher Jean-Jacques Rousseau (1712–1778) published one of the most important works on social theory, *The Social Contract,* which opened with the gripping maxim "Man is born free and everywhere he is in chains." But most of the great thinkers of the Enlightenment were not so much philosophers as savants, knowledgeable popularizers whose skills were in simplifying and publicizing a hodgepodge of new views.

In France, Enlightenment intellectuals were called **philosophes** and claimed all the arts and sciences as their purview. *The Encyclopedia* (35 volumes, 1751–1780), edited by Denis Diderot (1713–1784), was one of the greatest achievements of the age. Entitled the *Systematic Dictionary of the Sciences, Arts, and Crafts,* it attempted to summarize all acquired knowledge and to dispel all imposed superstitions. There was no better definition of a philosophe than that given to them by one of their enemies: "Just what is a philosophe? A kind of monster in society who feels under no obligation towards its manners and morals, its proprieties, its politics, or its religion. One may expect anything from men of their ilk."

The Enlightenment was by no means a strictly French phenomenon. Its greatest figures included the Scottish economist Adam Smith (1723–1790), the Italian legal reformer Cesare Beccaria (1738–1794), and the German philosopher Immanuel Kant (1724–1804). In France, it began among antiestablishment critics; in Scotland and the German states it

■ During the Enlightenment, salons showcased the most influential thinkers of the day. Here, a lecture is being given at the house of Madame Geoffrin.

flourished in the universities; and in Prussia, Austria, and Russia it was propagated by the monarchy. The Enlightenment began in the 1730s and was still going strong a half-century later, when its attitudes had been absorbed into the mainstream of European thought.

No brief summary can do justice to the diversity of enlightened thought in eighteenth-century Europe. Because it was an attitude of mind rather than a set of shared beliefs, there are many contradictory strains to follow. In his famous essay *What Is Enlightenment?* (1784), Immanuel Kant described it simply as freedom to use one's own intelligence. "I hear people clamor on all sides: Don't argue! The officer says: Don't argue, drill! The tax collector says: Don't argue, pay. The pastor says: Don't argue, believe." To all of them, Kant replied: "Dare to know! Have the courage to use your own intelligence."

The Spirit of the Enlightenment

In 1734, a small book entitled *Philosophical Letters Concerning the English Nation* appeared in France. Its author, Voltaire (1694–1778), who had spent two years in Britain, demonstrated again and again the superiority of the British. They practiced religious toleration and were not held under the sway of a venal clergy. They valued people for their merits rather than their birth. Their political constitution was a marvel—"The English nation is the only one on earth that has succeeded in controlling the power of kings by resisting them." They made national heroes of their scientists, poets, and philosophers. In all of this, Voltaire contrasted British virtue with French vice. He attacked the French clergy and nobility directly and the French monarchy implicitly. Not only did he praise the genius and accomplishments of Sir Isaac Newton above those of René Descartes, but he also graphically contrasted the Catholic Church's persecution of Descartes with the British state's celebration of Newton.

Voltaire.   In France, Voltaire's book *Philosophical Letters* was officially banned and publicly burned, and a warrant was issued for his arrest. The *Philosophical Letters* dropped like a bombshell on the moribund intellectual culture of the Church and the universities and burst open the complacent, self-satisfied Cartesian world view. The book ignited a movement that would soon spread to nearly every corner of Europe.

Born in Paris in 1694 into a bourgeois family with court office, François-Marie Arouet, who later took the pen name Voltaire, was educated by the Jesuits, who encouraged his poetic talents and instilled in him an enduring love of literature. He was a difficult student, especially as he had already rejected the core of the Jesuits' religious doctrine. He was no less difficult as he grew and began a career as a poet and playwright. It was not long before he was imprisoned in the Bastille for penning verses that maligned the honor of the regent of France. When released from prison, he insulted a nobleman, who retaliated by having his servants publicly beat Voltaire. Voltaire issued a challenge for a duel, a greater insult than the first, given his low birth. He was again sent to the Bastille and was

released only on the promise that he would leave the country immediately.

Thus Voltaire found himself in Britain, where he spent two years learning English and writing plays. When he returned to Paris in 1728, it was with the intention of popularizing Britain to Frenchmen. He wrote and produced a number of plays and began writing the *Philosophical Letters,* a work that not only secured his reputation but also forced him into exile at the village of Cirey, where he moved in with the Marquise du Châtelet (1706–1749).

The Marquise du Châtelet, though only 27 at the time of her liaison with Voltaire, was one of the leading advocates of Newtonian science in France. She built a laboratory in her home and introduced Voltaire to experimental science. While she undertook the immense challenge of translating Newton into French, Voltaire worked on innumerable projects: poems, plays, philosophical and antireligious tracts (which she wisely kept him from publishing), and histories. It was one of the most productive periods of his life, and when the Marquise du Châtelet died in 1749, Voltaire was crushed.

Then older than 50, Voltaire began his travels. He was invited to Berlin by Frederick the Great, but the relationship between these two great egotists was predictably stormy and resulted in Voltaire's arrest in Frankfurt. Finally allowed to leave Prussia, Voltaire eventually settled in Geneva, where he quickly became embroiled in local politics and was asked to leave.

Voltaire was tired of wandering and tired of being chased. He was also deeply affected by the tragic earthquake in Lisbon in 1755, when thousands of people attending church services were killed. Optimism in the face of such a senseless tragedy was no longer possible. His black mood was revealed in *Candide* (1759), which was to become his enduring legacy. *Candide* introduced the ivory-tower intellectual Dr. Pangloss, the overly optimistic Candide, and the very practical philosophy "We must cultivate our own garden."

Voltaire's greatest contribution to Enlightenment attitudes was probably his capacity to challenge all authority. He held nothing sacred. He questioned his own paternity and the morals of his mother; he lived openly with the Marquise du Châtelet and her husband; and he spoke as slightingly of kings and aristocrats as he did of his numerous critics. At the height of the French Revolution, Voltaire's body was removed from its resting place in Champagne and taken with great pomp to Paris and interred in the Pantheon, where the heroes of the nation were put to rest. "Voltaire taught us to be free" was the slogan that the Parisian masses chanted during the funeral procession. It was an ending that was perhaps too solemn and conventional for one as irreverent as Voltaire. When the monarchy was restored after 1815, his bones were unceremoniously dumped in a lime pit.

Hume.   Some enlightened thinkers based their critical outlook on skepticism, the belief that nothing could be known for certain. When the Scottish philosopher David Hume (1711–1776) was accused of being an atheist, he countered the charge by saying that he was too skeptical to be certain that God did not exist. Hume's first major philosophical work, *A Treatise of Human Nature* (1739), made absolutely no impression on his contemporaries. Hume worked as a merchant's clerk, a tutor, and finally a private secretary. During these years he continued to write, publishing a series of essays on the subject of morality and rewriting his treatise into *An Enquiry Concerning Human Understanding* (1748), his greatest philosophical work.

Hume made two seminal contributions to Enlightenment thought. He exploded the synthesis of Descartes by arguing that neither matter nor mind could be proved to exist with any certainty. Only perceptions existed, either as impressions of material objects or as ideas. If human understanding was based on sensory perception rather than on reason, then there could be no certainty in the universe. Hume's second point launched a frontal attack on established religion. If there could be no certainty, then the revealed truths of Christian religion could have no basis. In his historical analysis of the origins of religion, Hume argued that "religion grows out of hope or fear." He attacked the core of Christian explanations that were based on either Providence or miracles by arguing that for anyone who understood the basis of human perception, it would take a miracle to believe in miracles.

Montesquieu. In 1749, Hume received in the mail a work from an admiring Frenchman, entitled *The Spirit of the Laws*. The sender was Charles-Louis de Secondat, Baron Montesquieu (1689–1755). Born in Bordeaux, he ultimately inherited both a large landed estate and the office of president of the Parlement of Bordeaux. His novel *Persian Letters* (1721) was a brilliant satire of Parisian morals, French society, and European religion all bound together by the story of a Persian despot who leaves his harem to learn about the ways of the world. The use of the Persian outsider allowed Montesquieu to comment on the absurdity of European customs in general and French practices in particular. The device of the harem allowed him to titillate his audience with exotic sexuality.

After this success, Montesquieu decided to sell his office and make the grand tour. He spent nearly two years in England, for which, like Voltaire, he came to have the greatest admiration. Back in Bordeaux, Montesquieu began to assemble his thoughts for a work of political theory. The two societies that he most admired were those of ancient Rome and present-day Britain, and he studied the forms of their government and the principles that animated them. *The Spirit of the Laws* was published in 1748, and despite its gargantuan size and densely packed examples, it was immediately recognized as a masterpiece. Catherine the Great of Russia kept it at her bedside, and it was the single most influential work for the framers of the United States Constitution.

In both *Persian Letters* and *The Spirit of the Laws*, Montesquieu explored how liberty could be achieved and despotism avoided. He divided all forms of government into republics, monarchies, and despotisms. Each form had its own peculiar spirit: virtue and moderation in republics, honor in monarchies, and fear in despotisms. Like each form, each spirit was prone to abuse and had to be restrained if republics were not to give way to vice and excess, monarchies to corruption, and despotisms to repression. Montesquieu classified regimes as either moderate or immoderate and, through the use of extensive historical examples, attempted to demonstrate how moderation could be maintained through rules and restraints, through the spirit of the law.

For Montesquieu, a successful government was one in which powers were separated and checks and balances existed within the institutions of the state. As befitted a provincial magistrate, he insisted on the absolute separation of the judiciary from all other branches of government. The law needed to be independent, impartial, and just. Montesquieu advocated that law codes be reformed and reduced mainly to regulate crimes against persons and property. Punishment should fit the crime but should be humane. Montesquieu was one of the first to advocate the abolition of torture. Like most Europeans of his age, he saw monarchy as the only realistic form of government, but he argued that for a monarchy to be successful, it needed a strong and independent aristocracy to restrain its tendency toward corruption and despotism. He based his arguments on the example of Britain, which he praised as the only state in Europe in which liberty resided.

Enlightened Education and Social Reform. Enlightened thinkers attacked established institutions, above all the Church. Most were **deists** who believed in the existence of God on rational grounds only. Following the materialistic ideas of the new science, deists believed that nature conformed to its own material laws and operated without divine intervention. God, in a popular Enlightenment image, was like a clockmaker who constructed the elaborate mechanism, wound it, and gave the pendulum its first swing. After that, the clock worked by itself. Deists were accused of being anti-Christian, and they certainly opposed the ritual forms of both Catholic and Protestant worship as well as the role of the Church in education, for education was the key to an enlightened view of the future.

Jean-Jacques Rousseau attacked the educational system. His tract on education, disguised as the romantic novel *Émile* (1762), argued that children should be taught by appealing to their interests rather than with strict discipline. Education was crucial because the Enlightenment was dominated by the idea of the British philosopher John Locke (1632–1704) that the mind was blank at birth, a *tabula rasa*—"white paper void of all characters"—and that it was filled up by experience. Contrary to the arguments of Descartes, Locke wrote, in *An Essay Concerning Human Understanding* (1690), that there were no innate ideas and no good or evil that was not conditioned by experience. For Locke, as for a host of thinkers after him, good and evil were defined as pleasure and pain. We do good because it is pleasurable, and we avoid evil because it is painful. Morality was a sense experience rather than a theological one. It was also relative rather than absolute. This was an observation that derived from increased interest in non-European cultures. Baron Montesquieu's *Persian Letters* was the most popular novel of a genre that described non-European societies that knew nothing of Christian morality.

By the middle of the eighteenth century, the pleasure/pain principle enunciated by Locke had come to be applied to the foundations of social organization. If personal good was pleasure, then social good was happiness. The object of government, in the words of the Scottish moral philosopher Francis Hutcheson (1694–1746), was "the greatest happiness of the greatest number." This principle was at the core of *Crimes and Punishments* (1764), Cesare Beccaria's pioneering work of legal reform. Laws were instituted to promote happiness within society. They had to be formulated equitably for both criminal and victim. Punishment was to act as a deterrent to crime rather than as retribution. Therefore Beccaria advocated the abolition of torture to gain confessions, the end of capital punishment, and the rehabilitation of criminals through the improvement of penal institutions. By 1776, happiness was established as one of the basic "rights of man," enshrined in the American Declaration of Independence as "life, liberty, and the pursuit of happiness."

It was in refashioning the world through education and social reform that the Enlightenment revealed its orientation toward the future. "Optimism" was a word invented in the eighteenth century to express this feeling of liberation from the weight of centuries of traditions. "This is the best of all possible worlds and all things turn out for the best" was the satirical slogan of Voltaire's *Candide*. But if Voltaire believed that enlightened thinkers had taken optimism too far, others believed that it had to be taken further still.

Progress, an idea that not all enlightened thinkers shared, was another invention of the age. It was expressed most cogently by the French philosopher the Marquis de Condorcet (1743–1794) in *The Progress of the Human Mind* (1795), in which he developed an almost evolutionary view of human development from a savage state of nature to a future of harmony and international peace.

The Impact of the Enlightenment

The influence of Enlightenment ideas was felt everywhere, even seeping to the lowest strata of society. Paradoxically, enlightened political reform took firmer root in eastern Europe, where the ideas were imported, than in western Europe, where they originated. It was absolute rulers who were most successful in borrowing Enlightenment reforms.

Enlightened ideas informed the eastern European reform movement that began around mid-century, especially in the areas of law, education, and the extension of religious toleration. Law reforms were influenced by the works of

CHRONOLOGY	
MAJOR WORKS OF THE ENLIGHTENMENT	
1690	*An Essay Concerning Human Understanding* (Locke)
1721	*Persian Letters* (Baron Montesquieu)
1734	*Philosophical Letters Concerning the English Nation* (Voltaire)
1739	*A Treatise of Human Nature* (Hume)
1740	*Pamela* (Richardson)
1748	*An Enquiry Concerning Human Understanding* (Hume); *The Spirit of the Laws* (Baron Montesquieu)
1751–1780	*Encyclopedia* (Diderot)
1759	*Candide* (Voltaire)
1762	*Émile; The Social Contract* (Rousseau)
1764	*Crimes and Punishments* (Beccaria)
1784	*What Is Enlightenment?* (Kant)
1795	*The Progress of the Human Mind* (Marquis de Condorcet)
1798	*An Essay on the Principles of Population* (Malthus)

Montesquieu and Beccaria. In Prussia and Russia, the movement to codify and simplify the legal system did not reach fruition in the eighteenth century, but in both places it was well under way. The Prussian jurist Samuel von Cocceji (1679–1755) initiated the reform of Prussian law and legal administration. Cocceji's project was to make the enforcement of law uniform throughout the realm, to prevent judicial corruption, and to produce a single code of Prussian law. The code, finally completed in the 1790s, reflected the principles of criminal justice articulated by Beccaria. In Russia, the Law Commission summoned by Catherine the Great in 1767 never did complete its work. Nevertheless, profoundly influenced by Montesquieu, Catherine attempted to abolish torture and to introduce the Beccarian principle that the accused was innocent until proven guilty. In Austria, Joseph II presided over a wholesale reorganization of the legal system. Courts were centralized, laws were codified, and torture and capital punishment were abolished.

Enlightenment ideas also underlay the efforts to improve education in eastern Europe. The religious orders, especially the Jesuits, were the most influential educators of the age, and the Enlightenment attack on them created a void that had to be filled by the state. Efforts at compulsory education were first undertaken in Russia under Peter the Great, but these were aimed at the compulsory education of the nobility. Catherine extended the effort to the provinces, attempting to educate a generation of Russian teachers. She was especially eager for women to receive primary schooling, although the prejudice against educating women was too strong to overcome. Austrian and Prussian reforms were more successful in extending the reach of primary education, even if its content remained weak.

Religious toleration was the area in which the Enlightenment had its greatest impact in Europe, though again this was most visible in the eastern countries. Freedom of worship for Catholics was barely whispered about in Britain, and neither France nor Spain was moved to tolerate Protestants. Nevertheless, within these parameters there were some important changes in the religious makeup of the western European states. In Britain, Protestant dissenters were no longer persecuted for their beliefs. By the end of the eighteenth century, the number of Protestants outside the Church of England was growing, and by the early nineteenth century, discrimination against such Protestants was all but eliminated. In France and Spain, relations between the national church and the papacy were undergoing a reorientation. Both states were asserting more independence—both theologically and financially—from Rome. The shift was symbolized by disputes over the role of the Jesuits, who were finally expelled from France in 1764 and from Spain in 1767.

In eastern Europe, enlightened ideas about religious toleration did take effect. Catherine the Great abandoned persecution of a Russian Orthodox sect known as the Old Believers. Prussia had always tolerated various Protestant groups, and with the conquest of Silesia it acquired a large Catholic population. Catholics were guaranteed freedom of worship; Frederick the Great even built a Catholic church in Berlin to symbolize this policy. Austria extended enlightened ideas about toleration furthest. Maria Theresa was a devout Catholic and actually increased religious persecution in her realm, but Joseph II rejected his mother's dogmatic position. In 1781, he issued the **Patent of Toleration,** which granted freedom of worship to Protestants and members of the Eastern Orthodox church. The following year he extended this toleration to Jews. Joseph's attitude toward toleration was as practical as it was enlightened. He believed that the revocation of the Edict of Nantes—which had granted limited toleration to Protestants—at the end of the seventeenth century had been an economic disaster for France, and he encouraged religious toleration as a means to economic progress.

Joseph's belief that religious toleration could promote economic progress was in keeping with the ferment of new ideas on economics in Europe. A science of economics was first articulated during the Enlightenment. A group of French thinkers known as the **physiocrats** subscribed to the view that land was wealth and thus argued that agricultural activity, especially improved means of farming and livestock breeding, should take first priority in state reforms. Because wealth came from land, taxation should be based only on land ownership, a principle that was coming into increased prominence, despite the opposition of the landowning class. Physiocratic ideas combined a belief in the sanctity of private property with the need for the state to increase agricultural output. Ultimately, the physiocrats, like the great Scottish economic theorist Adam Smith, came to believe that government should cease to interfere with private economic activity. They articulated the doctrine *laissez faire, laissez passer*—"let it be, let it go." The ideas of Adam Smith and the physiocrats, particularly the **laissez-faire** doctrine, ultimately formed the basis for nineteenth-century economic reform.

If the Enlightenment did not initiate a new era, it did offer a new vision, whether in Hume's psychology, Montesquieu's political science, Rousseau's sociology, or Smith's economic theory. All of these subjects, which have had such a powerful impact on contemporary life, had their modern origins in the Enlightenment. As the British poet Alexander Pope (1688–1744) put it, "Know then thyself, presume not God to scan / The proper study of mankind is man." Enlightened thinkers challenged existing ideas and existing institutions. A new emphasis on self and on pleasure led to a new emphasis on happiness. All three fed into the distinctively Enlightenment idea of self-interest. Happiness and self-interest were values that would inevitably corrode the old social order, which was based on principles of self-sacrifice and corporate identity. It was only a matter of time.

EIGHTEENTH-CENTURY SOCIETY

Eighteenth-century society was a hybrid of old and new. It remained highly stratified socially, politically, and economically. Birth and occupation determined wealth, privilege, and quality of life as much as they had in the past. But in the eighteenth century, the gulf between top and bottom was being filled by a thriving middle class, a **bourgeoisie,** as they were called in France. There were now more paths toward the middle and upper classes and more wealth to be distributed among people living above the level of subsistence, but at the top of society the nobility remained the privileged order in every European state.

The Nobility

Nobles were defined by their legal rights. They had the right to bear arms, the right to special judicial treatment, and the right to tax exemptions. In Russia, only nobles could own serfs; in Poland, only nobles could hold government office. In France and Britain, the highest court positions were always reserved for noblemen. Nobles dominated the Prussian army. The Spanish nobility, rich or poor, shunned all labor as a right of their heritage. Swedish and Hungarian noblemen had their own legislative chambers, just as the British had the House of Lords.

Though all who enjoyed these special rights were noble, not all nobles were equal. In many states, the noble order was subdivided into easily identifiable groups. The Spanish *grandees,* the upper nobility, were numbered in the thousands; the Spanish *hidalgos,* the lower nobility, were numbered in the hundreds of thousands. In Hungary, out of 400,000 noblemen, only about 15,000 belonged to the landed nobility, who held titles and were exempt from taxes. In England, the elite class was divided between the peers and the gentry. The peers held titles, were members of the House of Lords, and had a limited range of judicial and fiscal privileges. In the mid-eighteenth century there were only 190 British peers. The gentry, which numbered over 20,000, dominated the House of Commons and local legal offices but were not strictly members of the nobility. The French nobility was informally divided into the small group of peers known as the *Grandes,* whose ancient lineage, wealth, and power set them apart from all others; a rather larger service nobility whose privileges derived in one way or another from municipal or judicial service; and what might be called the country nobility, whose small estates and local outlook made their exemption from taxes vital to their survival.

These distinctions among the nobilities of the European states masked a more important one: wealth. As the saying went, "All who were truly noble were not wealthy, but all who were truly wealthy were noble." In the eighteenth century, despite the phenomenal increase in mercantile activity, wealth was still calculated in profits from the ownership of land, and it was the wealthy landed nobility who set the tone of elite life in Europe.

For the wealthy, aristocracy was becoming an international status. The influence of Louis XIV and the court of Versailles lasted for well over a century and spread to town and country life. Most nobles maintained multiple residences. The new style of aristocratic entertainment required more public space on the first floor, while the increasing demand for personal and familial privacy necessitated more space in the upper stories. The result was larger and more opulent homes. Here, the British elite led all others. To the expense of architecture was added the expense of decoration. New materials, such as West Indian mahogany, occasioned new styles, and both drove up costs. The high-quality woodwork and plastering that the English Adam brothers made fashionable was quickly imitated on the Continent. Only the Spanish nobility shunned country estates, preferring to reside permanently in towns.

The building of country houses was only one part of the conspicuous consumption of the privileged orders. Improvements in travel, in both transport and roads, permitted increased contact between members of the national elites. The stagecoach and canals made travel quicker and more enjoyable. The grand tour of historical sites continued to be used as a substitute for formal education. The grand tour was also a means of introducing the European aristocracies to each other. Whether it was a Russian noble in Germany or a Briton in Prussia, all spoke French and shared a common cultural outlook.

Much of that outlook was cultivated in the **salons,** a social institution begun in the seventeenth century by French women that gradually spread throughout the continent. In the salons, especially those in Paris, the aristocracy and the bourgeoisie mingled with the leading intellectuals of the age, examining and exchanging new ideas. It was in the salons that the impact of the Enlightenment, the great European intellectual movement of the eighteenth century, first made itself felt.

■ William Hogarth was famous for his satirical series paintings. *Marriage à la Mode,* ca. 1743, depicts the complicated negotiations between a wealthy merchant and an aristocrat for a marriage between their families and shows the progress of the arranged match to its end. In this scene of domestic disarray, second in the series, the marriage quickly proves to be a disaster.

The Bourgeoisie

Bourgeois is a French word, and it carried the same tone of derision in the eighteenth century that it does today. The bourgeois male was a man on the make, scrambling after money or office or title. The bourgeoisie provided the safety valve between the nobility and those who were acquiring wealth and power but who lacked the advantages of birth and position. They served vital functions in all European societies, dominating trade, both nationally and internationally. They made their homes in cities and did much to improve the quality of urban life. They developed their own culture and class identity and permitted successful individuals to enjoy a sense of pride and achievement.

In the eighteenth century, the bourgeoisie was growing in numbers and importance. Some of its members were able to pass into the nobility through the purchase of land or office. But for most, their own social group began to define its own values, which centered on the family and the home. Their homes became a social center for kin and neighbors, and their outlook on family life reflected new personal relationships.

Marriages were made for companionship as much as for economic advantage. Romantic love between husbands and wives was newly valued. So were children, whose futures came to dominate familial concern. Childhood was recognized as a separate stage of life and the education of children as one of the most important of parental concerns. The image of the affectionate father replaced that of the hard-bitten businessman; the image of the doting mother replaced that of the domestic drudge.

Urban Elites.   In the society of orders, nobility was the acid test. The world was divided into the small number of those who had it and the large number of those who did not. At the apex of the non-noble pyramid was the bourgeoisie, the elites of urban Europe whose place in the society of orders was ambiguous. *Bourgeois,* or *burgher,* simply meant "town dweller," but as a social group it had come to mean "wealthy town dweller." The bourgeoisie was strongest where towns were strongest: in western rather than in eastern Europe and in northern rather than southern Europe with the notable exception of Italy. Holland was the exemplar of a bourgeois republic. More than half of the Dutch population lived in towns, and there was no significant aristocratic class to compete for power. The Regents of Amsterdam were the equivalent of a European court nobility in wealth, power, and prestige, though not in the way in which they had accumulated their fortunes. The size of the bourgeoisie in various European states cannot be absolutely determined. At the end of the eighteenth century, the British middle classes probably constituted around 15 percent of the population, the French bourgeoisie less than 10 percent. By contrast, the Russian and Hungarian urban elites were less than 2 percent of the population of those states.

Like the nobility, the bourgeoisie constituted a diverse group. At the top were great commercial families engaged in the expanding international marketplace and reaping the profits of trade. In wealth and power they were barely distinguishable from the nobility. At the bottom were the so-called petite bourgeoisie: shopkeepers, craftsmen, and industrial employers. The solid core of the bourgeoisie was employed in trade, exchange, and service. Most were engaged in local or national commerce. Trade was the lifeblood of the city, for by itself the city could neither feed nor clothe its inhabitants. Most bourgeois fortunes were first acquired in trade. Finance was the natural outgrowth of commerce, and another segment of the bourgeoisie accumulated or preserved capital through the sophisticated financial instruments of the eighteenth century. While the very wealthy loaned directly to the central government or bought shares in overseas trading companies, most bourgeois participated in government credit markets. They purchased state bonds or lifetime annuities and lived on the interest. The costs of war flooded the urban credit markets with high-yielding and generally stable financial instruments. Finally, the bourgeoisie were members of the burgeoning professions that provided services for the rich. Medicine, law, education, and the bureaucracy were all bourgeois professions, for the cost of acquiring the necessary skills could be borne only by those who were already wealthy.

The bourgeoisie grew as European urbanization continued steadily throughout the eighteenth century. In 1600, only 20 European cities contained as many as 50,000 people; in 1700, that number had risen to 32, and by 1800 it has increased to 48. London, the largest city, had grown to 865,000 people, a remarkable feat considering that in 1665, over one-quarter of the London population died in the Great Plague. In such cities, the demand for lawyers, doctors, merchants, and shopkeepers was almost insatiable.

Besides wealth, the urban bourgeoisie shared another characteristic: mobility. The aspiration of the bourgeoisie was to become noble, either through office or by acquiring rural estates. In Britain, a gentleman was still defined by lifestyle: "All are accounted gentlemen in England who maintain themselves without manual labor." Many trading families left their wharves and countinghouses to acquire rural estates and live off rents. In France and Spain, nobility could still be purchased, though the price was constantly going up. For the greater bourgeoisie the transition was easy; for the lesser it was usually just beyond their grasp. The bourgeoisie did not only imagine their discomfort; they were made to feel it at every turn. Despised from above, envied from below, they were the subject of jokes, of theater, and of popular songs. They were the first victims in the shady financial dealings of the crown and court, the first casualties in urban riots. Their one consolation was that as a group they got richer and richer. And as a group they began to develop a distinctive culture that reflected their qualities and aspirations.

Bourgeois Values.   Although many members of the bourgeoisie aspired to noble status, others had no desire to wear the silks and furs that were reserved for the nobility or to attend the opening night at the opera decked in jewels and finery. In fact, such ostentation was alien to them. A real tension existed between the values of noble and bourgeois. The ideal noble was idle, wasteful, and ostentatious; the ideal bourgeois was industrious, frugal, and sober. When Louis XVI tried to make household economies in the wake of a financial crisis, critics said that he acted "like a bourgeois."

Even if the bourgeoisie did not constitute a class, they did share certain attitudes that constituted a culture. The wealthy among them participated in the new world of consumption, whether they did so lavishly or frugally. For those who aspired to more than their birth allowed, there was a loosening of the strict codes of dress that reserved certain fabrics, decorative materials, and styles to the nobility. Merchants and bankers could now be seen in colored suits or with pipings made of cloth of gold; their wives could be seen in furs and silks. They might acquire coaches and carriages to take them on the Sunday rides through the town gardens or to their weekend retreats in the suburbs. Parisian merchants, even master craftsmen such as clockmakers, were now acquiring suburban homes although they could not afford to retire to them for the summer months.

Increasingly, the bourgeoisie was also beginning to travel. In Britain, whole towns were established to cater to leisure travelers. The southwestern town of Bath, famous since Roman times for the soothing qualities of its waters, was the most popular of all European resort towns. Brighton, a seaside resort on the south coast, quadrupled in size in the second half of the eighteenth century. Bathing—what we would call swimming—either for health or for recreation, became a middle-class fad, displacing traditional fears of the sea.

Leisure and Entertainment.   Leisure activities of the bourgeoisie quickly became commercialized. Theaters and music halls proliferated. Voltaire's plays were performed before packed houses in Paris. In Venice, it was estimated that over 1,200 operas were produced in the eighteenth century. Public concerts were a mark of bourgeois culture, for the court nobility was entertained at the royal palaces or at great country houses.

Theater and concertgoing were part of the new attitude toward socializing that was one of the greatest contributions of the Enlightenment. Enlightened thinkers spread their views in the salons, and the salons soon spawned the academies, local scientific societies that, though led and patronized by provincial nobles, included large numbers of bourgeois members. The academies sponsored essay competitions, built up libraries, and became the local center for intellectual interchange. A less-structured form of sociability took place in the coffeehouses and tearooms that came to be a feature of even small provincial towns. In the early eighteenth century, there were over 2,000 London coffee shops where men—for the coffeehouse was largely a male preserve—could talk about politics, read the latest newspapers and magazines, and indulge their taste for this still-exotic beverage. Parisian clubs, called *societés,* covered a multitude of diverse interests. Literary *societés* were the most popular, maintaining their purpose by forbidding drinking, eating, and gambling on their premises.

Above all, bourgeois culture was literate culture. Wealth and leisure led to mental pursuits—if not always to intellectual ones. The proliferation of relatively cheap printed material had an enormous impact on the lives of those who were able to afford it. Holland and Britain were the most literate European societies and also, because of the absence of censorship, the centers of European printing. This was the first great period of the newspaper and the magazine. The first daily newspaper appeared in London in 1702; 80 years later, 37 provincial towns had their own newspapers, and the London papers were read all over Britain. Then, as now, the newspaper was as much a vehicle for advertisement as for news. News reports tended to be bland, avoiding controversy and concentrating on general national and international events. Advertising, by contrast, tended to be lurid, promising cures for incurable ills and the most exquisite commodities at the most reasonable prices.

For entertainment and serious political commentary the British reading public turned to magazines, of which there were over 150 separate titles by the 1780s. The most famous were *The Spectator,* which ran in the early part of the century and did much to set the tone for a cultured middle-class life, and the *Gentleman's Magazine,* which ran in the mid-century and was said to have had a circulation of nearly 15,000. The longest-lived of all British magazines was *The Ladies' Diary,* which continued in existence from 1704 to 1871 and doled out self-improvement, practical advice, and fictional romances in equal proportion.

The Ladies' Diary was not the only publication aimed at lettered bourgeois women. A growing body of both domestic literature and light entertainment was available to them. This included a vast number of teach-yourself books aimed at instructing women how best to organize domestic life or how to navigate the perils of polite society. Moral instruction, particularly on the themes of obedience and sexual fidelity, was also popular. But the greatest output directed toward women was in the form of fanciful romances, from which a new genre emerged. The novel first appeared in its modern form in the 1740s. Samuel Richardson (1689–1761) wrote *Pamela* (1740), the story of a maidservant who successfully resisted the advances of her master until he finally married her. The story tended to overshadow the overt moral message that was Richardson's original intention.

Family Life.   In the eighteenth century, a remarkable transformation in home life was under way, one that the bourgeoisie shared with the nobility: the celebration of domesticity. The image—and sometimes the reality—of the happy home, where love was the bond between husband and wife and between parents and children, came to dominate both the literary and visual arts. Only those who were wealthy enough to afford to dispense with women's work could partake of the new domesticity, and only those who had been touched by Enlightenment ideas could attempt to make the change. But where it occurred, the transformation in the nature of family life was one of the most profound alterations in eighteenth-century culture.

The first step toward the transformation of family relationships was in centering the conjugal family in the home. In the past, the family was a less important structure for most people than the social groups to which they belonged or the neighborhood in which they lived. Marriage was an economic partnership at one end and a means to carry on lineage at the other. Individual fulfillment was not an object of marriage, and this attitude could be seen among the elites in the high level of arranged marriages, the speed with which surviving spouses remarried, and the formal and often brutal personal relationships between husbands and wives.

Patriarchy was the dominant value within the family. Husbands ruled over wives and children, making all of the crucial decisions that affected both the quality of their lives and their futures. As late as the middle of the eighteenth century, a British judge established the "rule of thumb," which asserted that a husband had a legal right to beat his wife with a stick, but the stick should be no thicker than a man's thumb. It was believed that children were stained with the sin of Adam at birth and that only the severest upbringing could clean some of it away. Children were sent out first for wet-nursing, then at around the age of seven for boarding, either at school or in a trade, and finally into their own marriages.

This profile of family life began to change, especially in western Europe, during the second half of the eighteenth century. Though the economic elements of marriage remained strong, romantic and sexual attraction became a factor. Even in earlier centuries, parents did not simply assign a spouse to their children, but by the eighteenth century, adolescents themselves searched for their own marriage partners and exercised a strong negative voice in identifying unsuitable ones.

LOVE AND MARRIAGE

Frances Brooke (1724–1789) was one of the earliest women novelists in Britain, publishing her first novel, The History of Lady Julia Mandeville, *in 1763. Orphaned at an early age, she settled in London and earned her living as a translator, writer, and editor. Brooke also participated in the thriving magazine culture of mid-eighteenth-century London. In her essay periodical,* The Old Maid, *she addressed domestic and public issues through the voice of a fictional mouthpiece, "Mary Singleton, Spinster." In this excerpt from the first issue of the magazine, the "Old Maid" reflects on her personal history and the circumstances that led to her unmarried state.*

Focus Questions

How does the passage of time affect the Old Maid's recollections about her past? According to this selection, how do parents control the destiny of their children and heirs? What appears to be the role of love in eighteenth-century marriages?

I was born in the north of England, being the eldest daughter of an honest country justice, who having no children but me and a younger sister, proposed leaving his estate, a clear eight hundred a year, betwixt us. My sister married a neighboring gentleman, and I might perhaps have followed her example, having very good offers (upon my word it's true, I have several love letters by me, which I read once a year, on my birthday, by the help of spectacles) but unluckily, at the age of twenty three, I was addressed by a gentleman so very agreeable, and so passionately fond of me, that though he had not a shilling, I unknown to any body, partly from inclination, partly for fear the poor man should hang himself, which he often threatened, engaged myself to him. As it was impossible to get my father's consent, we agreed to wait till his death; and my lover, who was bred to no employment, went in the meantime to reside with an old relation, in a distant country, who had a good estate, and whose son had a friendship for him. After two years of expectation, during which my faithful admirer, who contrived to see me as often as the distance of the place, and his dependent situation would permit, had frequently pressed me to marry him privately, my father died.

Though my concern for his death was real, love soon dried up my tears: no one who is not as romantic as I then was can imagine the joy I felt at being able to give my lover such a proof of the disinterestedness of my passion: I sent a servant post with a letter full of fine sentimental rhapsodies which I am now convinced were very foolish, and received the following answer,

> Madam,
>
> I am sorry for your loss: I have also been so unhappy as to lose my uncle and cousin, who both died of the smallpox within this week: the excess of my grief, and the multiplicity of business I am at present engaged in, by being left heir to my uncle's estate, render it impossible for me to wait upon you. I am much obliged to you for the expressions of regard in your's [sic], and am sorry to tell you, my uncle when dying, insisted on my promise to marry Miss Wealthy, who was intended for my cousin. The will of the dead ought to be sacred therefore it is impossible for me to fulfill the engagement into which we, perhaps imprudently, entered. I expect from your known candor that you will do me the justice to believe no motive but the gratitude and respect I own to the memory of this dear relation, to whose generosity I am so much obliged, could make me give up the hope of being yours. I doubt not your good sense and religion will enable you to bear with becoming fortitude, a shock, which I have need of all the strength of manly reason to support. I sincerely wish you every happiness, and that you may whenever you marry, meet with a man more worthy of you . . .
> —J.C.

From *The Old Maid,* Number 1 (November 15, 1755).

Companionate Marriage.   The quest for compatibility, no less than the quest for romantic love, led to a change in personal relationships between spouses. The extreme formality of the past was gradually breaking down. Husbands and wives began spending more time with each other, developing common interests and pastimes. Their personal life began to change. For the first time, houses were built to afford the couple privacy from their children, their servants, and their guests. Rooms were designed for specific functions and were set off by hallways.

Couples had more time for each other because they were beginning to limit the size of their families. There were a number of reasons for this development, which again pertained only to the upper classes. For one thing, child mortality rates were declining among wealthy social groups. Virulent epidemic diseases like the plague, which knew no class lines, were gradually disappearing, and sanitation was improving. Bearing fewer children had an enormous impact on women's lives, reducing the danger of death and disablement in childbirth and giving women time to pursue domestic tasks. Many couples appear to have made a conscious decision to space births, though success was limited by the fact that the most common technique of birth control was coitus interruptus, or withdrawal.

New Attitudes Toward Children.   The transformation in the quality of relationships between spouses was mirrored by an even greater transformation in attitudes toward children. Childhood now took on a new importance for many reasons.

With the decline in mortality rates, parents could feel that their emotional investment in their children had a greater chance of fulfillment. Equally important were the new ideas about education, especially Locke's belief that the child enters into the world a blank slate whose personality is created through early education. This view placed a new responsibility on parents and gave them the concept of childhood as a stage through which individuals passed. This idea could be seen in the commercial sphere as well as in any other. In 1700, there was not a single shop in London that sold children's toys exclusively; by the 1780s, toy shops were everywhere. There were also shops that sold clothes specifically designed for children; children's clothes were no longer simply adult clothes in miniature. Most important of all was the development of materials for the education of children. This took place in two stages. At first, children's books were designed to help adults teach children. Later came books directed at children themselves with large print, entertaining illustrations, and nonsensical characters, usually animals that taught moral lessons.

The commercialization of childhood was, of course, directed at adults. The new books and games for children had to be purchased and used by parents as well. More and more mothers were devoting their time to their children. Among the upper classes, the practice of wet-nursing began to decline. Mothers wanted to nurture their infants both literally by breast-feeding and figuratively by teaching them. Children became companions to be taken on outings to the increasing number of museums or shows of curiosities.

■ *The Snatched Kiss,* or *The Stolen Kiss* (1750s), by Jean-Honoré Fragonard, was one of the "series paintings" popular in the late eighteenth century. A later canvas entitled *The Marriage Contract* shows the next step in the lives of the lovers.

The emergence of the bourgeoisie was one of the central social developments of the eighteenth century. The bourgeois culture, which emphasized a fulfilling home life, leisure pursuits, and literacy, soon came to dominate the values of educated society in general. But the population at large could not share this transformation of family life. Working women could afford neither the cost of instructional materials for their children nor the time to use them. Ironically, working women now began using wet nurses, once the privilege of the wealthy, because increasingly a working woman's labor was the margin of survival for her family. Working women enjoyed no privacy in the hovels in which they lived with large families in single rooms. Wives and children were still beaten by husbands and fathers. By the end of the eighteenth century, two distinct family cultures coexisted in Europe, one based on companionate marriage and the affective bonds of parents and children and the other based on patriarchal dominance and the family as an economic unit.

The Masses

Although more Europeans were surviving than ever before, with more food, more housing, better sanitation, and even better charities, there was also more misery. Those who would have succumbed to disease or starvation a century before now survived from day to day, beneficiaries—or victims—of increased farm production and improved agricultural marketing. The market economy organized a more effective use of land as large farming enterprises gobbled up smaller units, but it created a widespread social problem. The landless agrarian laborer of the eighteenth century was the counterpart of the sixteenth century wandering beggar. In the cities, the plight of the poor was as desperate as ever. Even the most openhearted charitable institutions were unable to cope with the massive increase in the poor. Thousands of mothers abandoned their children to the foundling hospitals, hoping that they would have a better chance of survival, even though hospital death rates were near 80 percent.

Despite widespread poverty, many members of the lower orders were able to gain some benefit from existing conditions. The richness of popular culture, signified by a spread of literacy into the lower reaches of European society, was one indication of this change. So, too, were the reforms urged by enlightened thinkers to improve basic education and to improve the quality of life in the cities. For that segment of the lower orders that could keep its head above water, the eighteenth century offered new opportunities and new challenges.

Breaking the Cycle. Of all the legacies of the eighteenth century, none was more fundamental than the steady increase in European population that began around 1740. This was not the first time that Europe had experienced sustained population growth, but it was the first time that such growth was not checked by a demographic crisis. In 1700, the European population is estimated to have been 120 million. By 1800, it had grown 50 percent to over 180 million, with regional variations in the growth rate. While France, Spain, and Italy expanded between 30 and 40 percent, Prussia doubled and Russia and Hungary may have tripled in number. Britain increased by 80 percent from about 5 to 9 million, but the rate of growth was accelerating. In 1695, the English population stood at 5 million. It took 62 years to add the next million and 24 years to add the million after that. In 1781, the population was 7 million, but it took only 13 years to reach 8 million and only 10 more years to reach 9 million. Steady population growth had continued without significant checks for more than half a century.

Ironically, the traditional pattern of European population found its theorist at the very moment that it was about to disappear. In 1798, Thomas Malthus (1766–1834) published *An Essay on the Principles of Population*. Reflecting on the history of European population, Malthus observed the cyclical pattern by which growth over one or two generations was checked by a crisis that significantly reduced population. From these lower levels, new growth began until it was checked and the cycle repeated itself. Because the number of people increased more quickly than did food supplies, the land could sustain only a certain level of population. When that level was near, the population became prone to a demographic check. Malthus divided population checks into two categories: positive and preventive. Positive checks were war, disease, and famine, all of which Malthus believed were natural, though brutal, means of population control. Preventive checks were the means by which societies could limit their growth to avoid the devastating consequences of positive checks. Celibacy, late marriages, and sexual abstinence were among the choices that Malthus approved, though abortion, infanticide, and contraception were also commonly practiced.

Patterns of Population. In the sixteenth and seventeenth centuries, the dominant pattern of the life cycle was high infant and child mortality, late marriages, and early death. All controlled population growth. Infant and child mortality rates were staggering; only half of those born reached the age of 10. Late marriage was the only effective form of birth control, given the strong social taboos against sexual relations outside marriage, for a late marriage reduced a woman's childbearing years. Women in western Europe generally married between the ages of 24 and 26; they normally ceased bearing children around the age of 40. But not all marriages lasted this 14- or 16-year span, since one or the other partner sometimes died. On average, the childbearing period for most women was 10 to 12 years, long enough to endure six pregnancies, which would result in three surviving children.

Three surviving children for every two adults would, of course, have resulted in a 50 percent rise in population in every generation. Celibacy was one limiting factor; urban death rates were another. Perhaps as much as 15 percent of the population in western Europe remained celibate either by entering religious orders that imposed celibacy or by lacking the personal or financial attributes necessary to marry. In the cities, rural migrants accounted for the appallingly high death rates. When we remember that the largest European cities were continuously growing—London from 200,000 in 1600 to 675,000 in 1750, Paris from 220,000 to 576,000, Rome from 105,000 to 156,000, Madrid from 49,000 to 109,000, Vienna from 50,000 to 175,000—then we can appreciate how many countless thousands of immigrants perished from disease, famine, and exposure before they could marry and have children. If urban perils were not enough, there were still the positive checks. Plagues carried away hundreds of thousands of people, wars halved populations of places in their path, and famine overwhelmed the weak and the poor.

The late seventeenth and early eighteenth centuries were a period of population stagnation if not actual decline. Not until the third or fourth decade of the eighteenth century did another growth cycle begin. It rapidly gained momentum throughout the Continent and showed no signs of abating after two full generations. Fertility was increasing as some women were marrying younger, thereby increasing their childbearing years. Illegitimacy rates were also rising.

But increasing fertility was only part of the picture. More significant was decreasing mortality. The positive checks of the past were no longer as potent. European warfare not only diminished in scale after the middle of the eighteenth century, it changed location as well. Rivalry for colonial empires removed the theater of conflict from European communities. So did the increase in naval warfare. As warfare abated, so did epidemic disease. The plague had all but disappeared from western Europe by the middle of the eighteenth century. The widespread practice of quarantine, especially in Hungary, which had been the crucial bridge between eastern and western epidemics, went far to eradicate the scourge of centuries.

Public health improvements also played a role in population increases. Urban sanitation was becoming more effective. Clean water supplies, organized waste and sewage disposal, and strict quarantines were increasingly part of urban regulations. The use of doctors and trained midwives helped to lower the incidence of stillbirth and decreased the number of women who died in childbirth. Almost everywhere, levels of infant and child mortality were decreasing. More people were being born, and more were surviving to adulthood. The result was renewed population growth. No wonder Malthus was worried.

Agricultural Improvements.   In the past, if warfare or epidemic diseases failed to check population growth, famine would have done the job. How the European economy conquered famine in the eighteenth century is a complicated story. There was no single breakthrough that accounts for the ability to feed the tens of millions of additional people who now inhabited the Continent. Holland and Britain used dynamic new agricultural techniques, but most European agriculture was still mired in the time-honored practices that had endured for centuries. Not everyone could be fed or fed adequately. Widespread famine might have disappeared, but slow starvation and chronic undernourishment had not. Hunger was more common at the end of the eighteenth century than at the beginning, and the nutritional content of a typical diet may have reached its lowest point in European history.

Nevertheless, Europe's capacity to sustain rising levels of population can be explained only in terms of agricultural improvement. Quite simply, European farmers were now producing more food and marketing it better. In the most advanced societies, this was a result of conscious efforts to make agriculture more efficient. In traditional open-field agriculture, communities quickly ran up against insurmountable obstacles to growth. The three-field crop rotation system left a significant proportion of land fallow each year, while the concentration on subsistence cereal crops progressively eroded the land that was in production. Common farming was only as strong as the weakest member of the community. There was little incentive for successful individuals to plow profits back into the land, through either the purchase of equipment or the increase of livestock.

Livestock was a crucial variable in agricultural improvement. As long as there was barely enough food for humans to eat, only essential livestock could be kept alive over the winter. Oxen, which were still the ordinary beasts of burden, and pigs and poultry, which required only minimal feed, were the most common. But few animals meant little manure, and without manure the soil could not easily be regenerated.

Around the middle of the seventeenth century, solutions to these problems began to appear. The first change was consolidation of landholdings so that traditional crop rotations could be abandoned. A second innovation was the introduction of **fodder crops,** some of which—such as clover—added nutrients to the soil, while others—such as turnips—were used to feed livestock. Better grazing and better winter feed increased the size of herds, and new techniques of animal husbandry, particularly crossbreeding, produced hardier strains. It was quite clear that the key to increased production lay in better fertilization, and by the eighteenth century, some European farmers had broken through the "manure barrier." Larger herds, the introduction of clover crops, the use of human waste from towns, and even the first experiments with lime as an artificial fertilizer were all part of the new agricultural methods.

The New Staples.   Along with the new crops that helped to nourish both soil and animals came new crops that helped to nourish people. Indian corn, or maize, was a staple crop for Native Americans and gradually came to be grown in most parts of western Europe. Maize not only had higher nutritional value than most other cereals, it also yielded more food per acre than did traditional grains. So, too, did the potato, which also entered the European diet from the New World. The potato grew in poor soil, required less labor, and yielded an abundant and nutritious harvest. It rapidly took hold in Ireland and parts of Prussia, from which it spread into eastern Europe. The potato allowed families to subsist on smaller amounts of land with less capital outlay.

It must be stressed, however, that these new developments involved only a very narrow range of producers. The new techniques were expensive, and knowledge of the new crops spread slowly. Change had to overcome inertia, intransigence, and fear of failure. The most important improvements in agricultural production were more traditional ones. Basically, there was an increase in the amount of land that was used for growing. In Russia, Prussia, and Hungary, hundreds of thousands of new acres came under the plow; in the west, drainage schemes and forest clearance expanded productive capacity.

There was also an upswing in the efficiency with which agricultural products were marketed. From the seventeenth century onward, market agriculture was gradually replacing subsistence agriculture in most parts of Europe. Market agriculture had the advantage of allowing specialization on farms. Single-crop farming enabled farmers to benefit from the peculiarities of their own soil and climate. They could then exchange their surplus for the range of crops they needed to subsist. Market exchange was facilitated by improved transportation and communication and above all by the increase in the population of towns, which provided demand. The new national and international trade in large quantities of grain evened out regional variations in harvests and went a long way toward reducing local grain shortages. The upkeep of

roads, the building of canals, and the clearing of waterways created a national lifeline for the movement of grain.

Finally, it is believed that the increase in agricultural productivity owed something to a change in climate that took place in the late eighteenth century. The European climate is thought to have been unusually cold and wet during the seventeenth century, and it seems to have gradually warmed during the eighteenth century.

The Plight of the Poor.   Incremental improvements in agriculture, transportation, and climate contributed to the most serious social problem of the eighteenth century: the dramatic population increase of poor people throughout Europe. There was grim irony in the fact that advances in the production and distribution of food and the retreat of war and plague allowed more people to survive from hand to mouth than ever before. Whereas their ancestors had succumbed to quick death from disease or starvation, they eked out a miserable existence of constant hunger and chronic pain with death at the end of a seemingly endless corridor.

It is impossible to gauge the number of European poor or to separate them into categories of greater and greatest misery. The truly indigent—the starving poor—probably made up 10 to 15 percent of most societies, perhaps as many as 20 million people throughout the Continent. They were most prevalent in towns but were an increasing burden on the countryside, where they wandered in search of agricultural employment. The wandering poor had no counterpart in eastern Europe, where serfdom kept everyone tied to the land, but the hungry and unsheltered certainly did. Yet the problem of poverty was not to be seen only among the destitute. In fact, the uniqueness of the poor in the eighteenth century is that they were drawn from social groups that even in the hungry times of the early seventeenth century had been successful subsistence producers.

It was easy to see why poverty was increasing. The relentless advance of population drove up the price of food and drove down the price of wages. In the second half of the eighteenth century, the cost of living in France rose by over 60 percent while wages rose by only 25 percent. In Spain, the cost of living increased by 100 percent while wages rose only 20 percent. Only in Britain did wages nearly keep pace with prices. Rising prices made land more valuable. At the beginning of the eighteenth century, as the first wave of population expansion hit western Europe, smallholdings began to decrease in size. The custom of partible inheritance, by which each son received a share of land, shrank the average size of a peasant holding below that necessary to sustain an average-size family, let alone a family that was growing larger. In one part of France it was estimated that 30 acres was a survival plot of land in good times. At the end of the seventeenth century, 80 percent of the peasants there owned less than 25 acres.

As holdings contracted, the portion of the family income that was derived from wage labor expanded. In such circumstances, males were more valuable than females, either as

■ The poverty of eighteenth-century London slums was a favorite subject of the English artist William Hogarth. *Gin Lane* depicts the London poor in alcoholic delirium, their only escape from the misery of their daily lives.

farmers or laborers, and there is incontrovertible evidence that European rural communities practiced female infanticide. In the end, however, it became increasingly difficult for the peasant family to remain on the land. Small freeholders were forced to borrow against future crops until a bad harvest led to foreclosure. Many were allowed to lease back their own lands, on short terms and at high rents, but most swelled the ranks of agricultural laborers, migrating during the planting and harvest seasons, suffering cruelly during winter and summer.

Emigration was the first logical consequence of poverty. In places where rural misery was greatest, such as Ireland, whole communities pulled up stakes and moved to America. Frederick the Great attracted hundreds of thousands of emigrants to Prussia by offering them land. But most rural migrants did not move to new rural environments. Rather, they followed the well-trodden paths to the cities. Many traditional domestic crafts were evolving into industrial activities. In the past, peasants supplemented their family income by processing raw materials in the home. Spinning, weaving, and sewing were common cottage industries in which the workers took in the work, supplied their own equipment, and were paid by the piece. Now, especially in the cloth trades, a new form of industrial activity was being organized. Factories, usually located in towns or larger villages, assembled workers together, set them at larger and more efficient machines, and paid them for their time rather than for their output. Families who were unable to support themselves from the land had no choice but to follow the movement of jobs.

Caring for the Poor. Neither state nor private charities could cope with the flood of poor immigrants. Hospitals, workhouses, and, more ominously, prisons were established or expanded to deal with them. Hospitals were residential asylums rather than places for health care. They took in the old, the incapacitated, and, increasingly, the orphaned young. Workhouses existed for those who were capable of work but incapable of finding it. In most places, workhouses, which were supposed to improve the values of the idle poor by keeping them busy, served only to improve the profits of the industrialists, who rented out workhouse inmates at below-market wages. Prisons grew with crime. There were spectacular increases in crimes against property in all eighteenth-century cities, and despite severe penalties that could include hanging for petty theft, more criminals were incarcerated than executed. Enlightened arguments for the reform of prisons and punishment tacitly acknowledged the social basis of most crime. As always, the victims of crime were mostly drawn from the same social backgrounds as the perpetrators. Along with all of their other troubles, it was the poor who were most commonly robbed, beaten, and abused.

Popular Culture. While many people endured unrelieved misery, others lived comfortably by the standards of the age, and almost everyone believed that things were better now than they had ever been before. Popular culture was a rich mixture of family and community activities that provided outlets from the pressures of work and the vagaries of fortune. It was no less sustaining to the population at large than was the purely literate culture of the elite and no less vital as a means of explanation for everyday events than the theories of the philosophers or the programs of the philosophes.

In fact, the line between elite and popular culture in the eighteenth century was a thin one. For one thing, there was still much mixing of social classes in both rural and urban environments. Occasions of display, such as festivals, village fairs, or religious holidays, brought entire communities together and reinforced their collective identities. Moreover, there were many shared elements between the two cultures. All over Europe, literacy was increasing. Nearly half of the inhabitants of France were literate by the end of the eighteenth century, as were perhaps 60 percent of the population in Britain. Men were more likely to have learned to read than women, as were inhabitants of urban areas. More than one-quarter of French women could read, a number that had doubled over the century. As the rates of female literacy rose, so did overall rates, for women took the lead in teaching children.

Popular literacy spawned popular literature in remarkable variety. Religious tracts were found throughout Europe. They contained stories of Catholic saints or Protestant martyrs or proverbs and prayers. Romances, the staple of lending libraries, were usually published and sold in inexpensive installments. The best-selling popular fiction, at least in western Europe, was melodramatic tales of knights and ladies from the age of chivalry.

Popular social activities continued to reflect the violent and even brutal nature of day-to-day existence. Village festivals were still the safety valve of youth gangs who enforced sexual morals by shaming husbands whose wives were unfaithful or women whose reputations were sullied. Many holidays were celebrated by sporting events that pitted inhabitants of one village against those of another. These almost always turned into free-for-alls in which broken bones were common and deaths were not unknown.

Even more popular were the so-called blood sports involving animals. Dogfighting and cockfighting are among those that still survive today. Less attractive to the modern mind were bearbaiting or bull running, in which the object was the slaughter of a large beast over a prolonged period of time. Blood sports were not confined to the masses—foxhunting and bullfighting were pastimes for the very rich—but they formed a significant part of local social activity.

So, too, did the tavern or alehouse, which in town or country was the site for local communication and recreation, where staggering amounts of alcohol were consumed. The increased use of spirits—gin, brandy, rum, and vodka—changed the nature of alcohol consumption in Europe. Wine and beer had always been drunk in quantities that we would find astounding, but these beverages were also an important part of people's diet. By contrast, the nutritional content of spirits was negligible. People drank spirits to get drunk, and drunkenness rose to new levels.

CONCLUSION

Eighteenth-century Europe was a society of orders that was gradually transforming itself into a society of classes. In other words, official ranks such as noble and commoner were giving way to a ranking by wealth or poverty. At the top, still vigorous, was the nobility. But the bourgeoisie was growing, and many of its members managed to pass into the nobility through the purchase of land or office. Opulence and poverty increased in step as the fruits of commerce and land enriched the upper orders while rising population im- poverished the lower ones. The rise of the new science and of Enlightenment ideas highlighted the contradictions. The attack on traditional authority, especially the Roman Catholic Church, was an attack on a conservative, static world view. Enlightenment thinkers looked to the future, to a new world shaped by reason and knowledge, a world that was ruled benevolently for the benefit of all human beings. Government, society, the individual—all could be improved if only the rubble of the past were cleared away. The Enlightment thinker could hardly have imagined how po- tent their vision would become.

QUESTIONS FOR REVIEW

1. What were the main elements of Enlightenment thought?
2. What social, moral, and religious traditions were challenged by the ideas of thinkers such as Voltaire, Hume, Montesquieu, and Rousseau?
3. How did the European nobility maintain its social eminence in the face of a new bourgeois culture created by an expand- ing middle class?
4. Why did Europe's population begin to grow so dramati- cally in the eighteenth century, and how did society re- spond to the challenges that it posed?

KEY TERMS

bourgeoisie, *p. 388*

deists, *p. 386*

Enlightenment, *p. 384*

fodder crops, *p. 395*

laissez-faire, *p. 388*

Patent of Toleration, *p. 388*

philosophes, *p. 384*

physiocrats, *p. 388*

salons, *p. 389*

DISCOVERING WESTERN CIVILIZATION ONLINE

You can obtain more information about culture and society in eighteenth-century Europe at the websites listed below. See also the Companion Website that accompanies this text, www.ablongman.com/kishlansky, which contains an online study guide and additional resources.

Eighteenth-Century Culture

NM's Creative Impulse: Enlightenment
www.history.evansville.net/enlighte.html
The best starting point for the culture and history of the age of Enlightenment.

Eighteenth-Century Resources
andromeda.rutgers.edu/~jlynch/18th/
A gateway to a wealth of sources on many different aspects of eighteenth-century culture.

Eighteenth-Century Studies
eserver.org/18th/
A list of links to a wide range of material relating to eigh- teenth-century literature and culture.

Internet Modern History Sourcebook: The Enlightenment
www.fordham.edu/halsall/mod/modsbook10.html
An outstanding collection of texts of Enlightenment writers.

Eighteenth-Century Society

The New Child: British Art and the Origins of Modern Childhood
www.bampfa.berkeley.edu/exhibits/newchild/
A site devoted to the nature of childhood in eighteenth-cen- tury Britain.

Voice of the Shuttle: Restoration and 18th Century
vos.ucsb.edu/browse.asp?id=2738
An inclusive page of links and resources for the study of English literature in the eighteenth century.

SUGGESTIONS FOR FURTHER READING

General Reading

T. C. W. Blanning, *The Culture of Power and the Power of Culture: Old Regime Europe 1660–1789* (New York: Oxford University Press, 2002). An outstanding example of the new cultural history.

William Doyle, *The Old European Order, 1660–1800,* 2d ed. (Oxford: Oxford University Press, 1992). An important essay on the structure of European societies and the ways in which they held together.

Henry Kamen, *Early Modern European Society* (New York: Routledge, 2000). A concise social history by a leading historian.

Eighteenth-Century Culture

A. J. Ayer, *Voltaire* (New York: Random House, 1986). A brief and vibrant study.

Robert Darnton, *The Forbidden Best-Sellers of Pre-Revolutionary France* (New York: W. W. Norton, 1995). A look at the underbelly of the Enlightenment that both provides gripping reading and makes us think about the Enlightenment in new ways.

John G. Gagliardo, *Enlightened Despotism* (New York: Thomas Y. Crowell, 1967). A sound exploration of the impact of Enlightenment ideas on the rulers of Europe, with emphasis on the east.

Norman Hampson, *The Enlightenment* (London: Penguin Books, 1982). The best one-volume survey.

Patrick Mauries, *Cabinets of Curiosities* (London: Thames and Hudson 2002). A fascinating account of collectors and collecting.

Daniel Roche, *France in the Enlightenment* (Cambridge, MA: Harvard University Press, 1998). A wide-ranging survey of everything from politics to popular culture.

Judith Sklar, *Montesquieu* (Oxford: Oxford University Press, 1987). A concise, readable study of the man and his work.

Eighteenth-Century Society: The Nobility

Jonathan Dewald, *The European Nobility, 1400–1800* (Cambridge: Cambridge University Press, 1996). An insightful survey.

Jerzy Lukowski, *The European Nobility in the Eighteenth Century* (New York: Palgrave MacMillan, 2003). Especially valuable for its treatment of eastern Europe.

Eighteenth-Century Society: The Bourgeoisie

John Brewer, *The Pleasures of the Imagination: English Culture in the Eighteenth Century* (London: HarperCollins, 1997). A fascinating study of the making of high culture in England.

Peter Earle, *The Making of the English Middle Class* (London: Methuen, 1989). The manners, mores, and mindset of the group that would come to dominate nineteenth-century Britain.

Jean-Louis Flandrin, *Families in Former Times* (Cambridge: Cambridge University Press, 1979). Strong on family and household organization.

Olwen Hufton, *The Prospect Before Her: A History of Women in Western Europe* (New York: Alfred Knopf, 1996). A survey of women's history that is particularly strong on the eighteenth century.

Simon Shama, *The Embarrassment of Riches* (Berkeley: University of California Press, 1987). The social life of Dutch burghers, richly portrayed.

Lawrence Stone, *The Family, Sex and Marriage in England, 1500–1800* (New York: Harper & Row, 1979). A controversial but extremely important argument about the changing nature of family life.

Eighteenth-Century Society: The Masses

Peter Burke, *Popular Culture in Early Modern Europe* (New York: Harper & Row, 1978). A wide survey of practices throughout the Continent.

Olwen Hufton, *The Poor in Eighteenth-Century France* (Oxford: Oxford University Press, 1974). A compelling study of the life of the poor.

E. A. Wrigley and R. S. Schofield, *The Population History of England* (Cambridge, MA: Harvard University Press, 1981). The most important reconstruction of a national population, by a team of researchers.

For a list of additional titles related to this chapter's topics, please see www.ablongman.com/kishlansky.

Chapter 20

THE FRENCH REVOLUTION AND THE NAPOLEONIC ERA, 1789–1815

The Visual Record

EIGHTEENTH-CENTURY REVOLUTION

In the second half of the eighteenth century, two separate revolutions toppled regimes on both sides of the Atlantic. In the first of the two great upheavals, the American Revolution, which lasted from 1775 to 1783, the 13 British colonies located along the Atlantic seaboard secured their independence from Great Britain. They formed themselves into the United States, a democratic republic with its own Declaration of Independence and Constitution. While the American Revolution was challenging British rule in the New World, France appeared to be ruled by a stable and powerful monarchy, one so secure in its reign that it was able to lend a helping hand to those colonists opposing England's king George III.

In the image shown here, entitled "Independence of the United States," the unknown artist is glorifying both the king of France, Louis XVI (1774–1791), and the American Revolution. Louis XVI, the king who would be guillotined by radical revolutionaries in 1793, is commemorated in the painting as a great man of revolution, more important by virtue of his position on the monument than even George Washington and Benjamin Franklin. Washington, whose name is misspelled as "Waginston," is not memorialized as father of his country. Instead, the inscription on the pedestal acknowledges Louis as the "Liberator" of America and the seas, an assertion that would have come as a surprise to the colonists struggling to cast off the British yoke. The memorial column itself is topped by images of the French monarchy including a globe with three fleurs-de-lis and the rooster of the French nation.

Next to the monument is the figure of America, symbolized by a half-naked "noble savage" draped in animal skins and feathers holding the scepter of power in his right hand and in his left hand a pole surmounted by a Phrygian cap of ancient Roman origins, which became popular in the French Revolution as the symbol of liberty. Under his left foot, America is trampling the British lion, next to the broken British trident symbolizing British failure both as a land and sea power.

The landscape is not a New England scene at all, but a tropical scene with palm trees, one of which is wrapped in a banner proclaiming, "In raising myself up, I make myself beautiful." The aura of the New World as an uncharted territory very different from Europe and the French countryside served both to idealize the American continent and to distance its revolution from the political experience of the French. In an exotic terrain, Louis XVI could appear as a "liberator," as unearned as the title might be.

INDÉPENDANCE DES ÉTATS-UNIS.

le 4 Juillet 1776, les Treize Colonies Confédérées ... connues depuis sous le nom d'Etats-Unis) sont ... éclarées, par le Congrès, libres et indépendantes. ... Gerard, porteur des pouvoirs de LOUIS XVI, Roi ... France, Benjamin Franklin, pour les États-Unis,

désastre accélère la Paix L'indépendance des ... États-Unis est reconnue par les Traités de Paix ... Pénétrés de reconnoissance pour les services que ... LOUIS XVI leur a rendus, les États-Unis ont de ... puis fait élever à Philadelphie un monument qui ...

The American Revolution was popular in France and attracted supporters including the French aristocrat and military man Marquis de Lafayette, who even went to the New World to fight in the revolutionary army and persuaded the French government to provide financial aid to the American cause.

Looking Ahead

The French Revolution began six years after the American War of Independence ended, and lasted for a decade. The French revolutionaries of 1789 shared many elements in common with their American counterparts, including an awareness of the writings of the same philosophers and intellectuals on both sides of the Atlantic whose works questioned existing institutions and traditions in favor of democracy, liberty, and equality. Yet to understand the Revolution in France, which, like its American predecessor, also embodied new ideas about government and citizenship, one must understand the distinctive nature of French society, economy, and politics in the 50 years or so preceding 1789 and the crisis in the Old Regime. As we shall see in this chapter, the resulting experiments with parliamentary government and representative and participatory democracy were deeply rooted in crises and practices of Old Regime France. While experimenting with democracy, France contended with internal violence and foreign wars. Until his defeat by the allied European powers, Napoleon was able to consolidate the French state through reform at home and victory abroad, and in so doing was both the heir of the Revolution and its destroyer. ➤

THE FRENCH REVOLUTION AND THE FALL OF THE MONARCHY

Those who lived through it were sure that there had never been a time like it before. The French Revolution, or the Great Revolution, as it was known to people alive at the time, was a period of creation and discovery. The ten years from 1789 to 1799 were punctuated by genuine euphoria and democratic transformations. But the French Revolution was also a time of violence and destruction. From the privileged elites who initiated the overthrow of the existing order to the peasants and workers, men and women, who railed against tyranny, the revolution touched every segment of society.

The revolution achieved most in the area of politics. The overthrow of absolutist monarchy brought with it new social theories, new symbols, and new behavior. The excitement of anarchy was matched by the terror of repression. In the search for a new order, competing political forms followed one after the other in rapid succession: constitutional monarchy, republic, oligarchy, and dictatorship.

At the end of the eighteenth century France was a state in trouble, but it was not alone. Revolutionary incidents flared up throughout Europe in the second half of the eighteenth century in the Netherlands, Belgium, and Ireland. Absolute authority was challenged and sometimes modified. Across the Atlantic, American colonists concerned with the principle of self-rule had thrown off the yoke of the British in the War of Independence. But none of the events, including the American Revolution, was so violent in breaking with the old order, so extensive in involving millions of men and women in political action, and so consequential for the political futures of other European states as was the French Revolution. The triumphs and contradictions of the revolutionary experiment in democracy mark the end of the old order and the beginning of modern history. Politics would never be the same again.

The Political and Fiscal Crisis of Eighteenth-Century France

The French monarchy was in a state of perpetual financial crisis across the eighteenth century. Louis XV, like his great-grandfather Louis XIV, ruled as an absolute monarch, but he lacked sufficient funds to run the state. He sought loans to meet his needs as well as to pay the interest on existing debts. Borrowing at high rates required the government to pay out huge sums in interest and service fees on the loans that were keeping it afloat. The outlays in turn piled the state's indebtedness ever higher, requiring more loans, and threatening to topple the whole financial structure of the state and the regime itself. The monarchy tried to reduce expenditures, but such attempts were limited by the necessity of maintaining an effective and costly army and navy because of wars on both the Continent and in the colonies.

The nadir of Louis XV's reign came in 1763, with the French defeat in the Seven Years' War. The defeat not only left France barren of funds, it also promoted further expenditures for strengthening the French navy against the superior British fleet. The king saw taxation as the only way out of the financial trap in which he now found himself.

But raising taxes was far from an easy undertaking, and it was one that required the support of the aristocracy. The heightened tensions between the monarch and the aristocracy found expression in various institutions, especially the parlements, which were the 13 sovereign courts in the French judicial system, with their seats in Paris and a dozen provincial centers. The magistrates of each parlement were members of the aristocracy, some of them nobles of recent origin and others of long standing, depending on the locale. Following the costly Seven Years' War, the parlements chose to exercise the power of refusal by blocking a proportional tax to be imposed on nobles and commoners alike. The magistrates resisted taxation, arguing that the king was attacking the liberty of his subjects by attempting to tax those who were exempt by virtue of their privileged status.

By challenging the king, the parlements became a battleground between the elite, who claimed that they represented the nation, and the king, who said the nation was himself. The king repeatedly attempted to neutralize the power of the parlements by relying instead on his own state bureaucracy, which was too weak for the task. The king's agents in the provinces, called intendants, were accountable directly to the central government. The intendants, as the king's men, and the magistrates who presided in the parlements represented contradictory claims to power. As the king's needs increased in the second half of the eighteenth century, the situation was becoming intolerable for those exercising power and those aspiring to rule in the name and for the good of the nation. The financial crisis provided the elite of notables, made up of both aristocrats and bourgeois, with the basis for asserting their own ascendancy to political power. Louis XV, who is often remembered for his cavalier prediction, "*Après moi, la déluge*," ("After me comes the flood,") indeed left a debt that swamped his grandson and successor Louis XVI. This tension between a growing debt that was undermining the monarchy and the increased ascendancy of an elite of nobles and bourgeois came to characterize the **Old Regime** in France.

When Louis XVI assumed the French throne in 1774, he was only 20 years old. He inherited a monarchy in a state of perpetual financial crisis. Not only did he inherit a trouble-ridden fiscal structure, but Louis XVI also made his own contributions to it, increasing the debt greatly by his involvement in the War of American Independence (1775–1783). Following the advice of a series of ministers, Louis sought structural solutions to the debt through a reformed fiscal policy, taxation, and other new sources of revenue, but each set of reforms offended different established interests. In the end, he resorted to an unusual but available step—the convening of the **Estates-General**—as a means of achieving reforms and providing financial stability for the state.

Historically, the Estates-General was the representative body of the three "estates," or social groups, of France—the clergy (the First Estate), the nobility (the Second Estate), and the commoners (the Third Estate). The **Third Estate** was composed of all those members of the realm who enjoyed no special privilege—28 million French people. The Estates-General had not been convened since 1614. Through this body and its duly chosen representatives, Louis XVI sought the consent of the nation to levy taxes. In the political organizing that took place in the winter of 1788–1789 the seeds of revolution were sown.

Convening the Estates-General

When Louis XVI announced in August 1788 that the Estates-General would meet at Versailles in May 1789, people from all walks of life hoped for some redress of their miseries. The king hoped that the clergy, nobility, and commoners would solve his fiscal problems. Every social group, from the nobles to the poorest laborers, had its own agenda and its own ideas about justice, social status, and economic well-being.

One in four nobles had moved from the bourgeoisie to the aristocratic ranks in the eighteenth century; two out of every three had been ennobled during the seventeenth or eighteenth centuries. Nobles had succeeded in expanding their

■ This cartoon depicts the plight of the French peasants. An old farmer is bowed down under the weight of the privileged aristocracy and clergy while birds and rabbits, protected by unfair game laws, eat his crops.

economic and social power and they now sought to preserve it. Furthermore, a growing segment of the nobility, influenced by Enlightenment ideas and the example of English institutions, was intent on increasing the political dominance of the aristocracy.

Members of the Third Estate, traditionally excluded from political and social power, were presented with the opportunity of expressing their opinions on the state of government and society. As commoners in the Third Estate, the bourgeoisie embraced within it a variety of professions, from bankers and financiers to businessmen, merchants, entrepreneurs, lawyers, shopkeepers, and artisans. Those who could not read stood in marketplaces and city squares or sat around evening fires and had the political literature read to them. Farmhands and urban laborers realized that they were participating in the same process as their social betters, and they believed they had a right to speak and be heard.

It was a time of great hope, especially for workers and peasants who had been buffeted by the rise in prices, decline in real wages, and the hunger that followed crop failures and poor harvests. There was new promise of a respite and a solution. Taxes could be discussed and changed, the state bureaucracy could be reformed—or better, abolished. Intellectuals discussed political alternatives in the salons of the wealthy. Nobles and bourgeois met in philosophical societies dedicated to enlightened thought. Commoners gathered in cafes to drink and debate. Although the poor often fell outside of the network of communication, they were not immune to the ideas that emerged. In the end, people of all classes had opinions and were more certain than ever of their right to express their ideas. Absolutism was in trouble, though Louis XVI did not know it, as people began to forge a collectively shared idea of politics. People now had a forum—the Estates-General—and a focus—the politics of taxation.

"If Only the King Knew."   In conjunction with the political activity and in scheduled meetings, members of all three estates drew up lists of their problems. This process took place in a variety of forums, including guilds and village and town meetings. The people of France drew up grievance lists—known as *cahiers de doléances*—that were then carried to Versailles by the deputies elected to the Estates-General. The grievance lists contained the collective outpouring of problems of each estate and are important for two major reasons. First, they made clear the similarity of grievances shared throughout France. Second, they indicated the extent to which a common political culture, based on a concern with political reform, had permeated different levels of French society. Both the privileged and the nonprivileged identified a common enemy in the system of state bureaucracy to which the monarch was so strongly tied. Although the king was still addressed with respect, new concerns with liberty, equality, property, and the rule of law were voiced.

"If only the king knew!" In that phrase, French men and women had for generations expressed their belief in the inevitability of their fate and the benevolence of their king.

They saw the king as a loving and wise father who would not tolerate the injustices visited on his subjects if only he knew what was really happening. In 1789, peasants and workers were questioning why their lives could not be better, but they continued to express their trust in the king. Combined with their old faith was a new hope. The peasants in the little town of Saintes recorded their newly formed expectations:

> Our king, the best of kings and father of a great and wise family, will soon know everything. All vices will be destroyed. All the great virtues of industriousness, honesty, modesty, honor, patriotism, meekness, friendliness, equality, concord, pity, and thrift will prevail and wisdom will rule supreme.

Those who opposed the revolution later alleged that the grievance lists proved the existence of a highly coordinated plot on the part of secret societies out to destroy the regime. They were wrong. Similarities in complaints, demands, and language proved the forging of a new political consciousness, not a conspiracy. Societies and clubs circulated "model" grievance lists among themselves, resulting in the use of similar forms and vocabulary. People were questioning their traditional roles and now had elected deputies who would represent them before the king. In the spring of 1789, a severe economic crisis that heightened political uncertainty swept through France. For a king expected to save the situation, time was running out.

The elected deputies arrived at Versailles at the beginning of May 1789 carrying in their valises and trunks the grievances of their estates. The opening session of the Estates-General took place in a great hall especially constructed for the event. The 1,248 deputies presented a grand spectacle as they filed to their assigned places to hear speeches by the king and his ministers. Contrasts among the participants were immediately apparent. Seated on a raised throne under a canopy at one end of the hall, Louis XVI was vested in full kingly regalia. On his right sat the archbishops and cardinals of the First Estate, strikingly clad in the pinks and purples of their offices. On his left were the richly and decorously attired nobility of the Second Estate. Facing the stage sat the 648 deputies of the Third Estate, dressed in plain black suits, stark against the colorful and costly costumes of the privileged. Members of the Third Estate had announced beforehand that they would not follow the ancient custom for commoners of kneeling at the king's entrance. Fired by the hope of equal treatment and an equal share of power, they had come to Versailles to make a constitution. The opening ceremony degenerated into a moment of confusion over whether members of the Third Estate should be able to wear their hats in the presence of the king. Many saw in the politics of clothing a tense beginning to their task.

The Crisis in Voting by Estate.

The tension between commoners and the privileged was aggravated by the unresolved issue of how the voting was to proceed. Traditionally, each of the three orders was equally weighted. The arrangement favored the nobility, who controlled the first two estates, since the clergy themselves were often noble.

The Third Estate was adamant in its demand for vote by head. The privileged orders were equally firm in insisting on vote by order. Paralysis set in, as days dragged into weeks and the estates were unable to act. The body that was to save France from fiscal collapse was hopelessly deadlocked.

Abbé Emmanuel Joseph Sieyès (1748–1836), a member of the clergy, emerged as the critical leader of the Third Estate. Sieyès had already established his reputation as a firebrand reformer with his eloquent pamphlet, "What Is the Third Estate?" published in January 1789. He understood that although eighteenth-century French society continued to be divided by law and custom into a pyramid of three tiers, these orders or estates were obsolete in representing social realities. The base of the pyramid was formed by the largest of the three estates, those who worked—the bourgeoisie, the peasantry, and urban and rural workers—and produced the nation's wealth. He argued that as long as the First and Second Estates did not share their privileges and rights, they were not a part of the French nation.

Under the influence of Sieyès and the reformist consensus that characterized their ranks, the delegates of the Third Estate decided to proceed with their own meetings. On 17 June 1789, joined by some sympathetic clergy, the Third Estate changed its name to the National Assembly as an assertion of its true representation of the French nation. Three days later, members of the new National Assembly found themselves locked out of their regular meeting room by the king's guard. Outraged by the insult, they moved to a nearby indoor tennis court, where they vowed to stay together for the purpose of writing a constitution. The event, known as the Oath of the Tennis Court, marked the end of the absolutist monarchy and the beginning of a new concept of the state that power resided in the people. The revolution had begun.

The Importance of Public Opinion.

The drama of Versailles, a staged play of gestures, manners, oaths, and attire, also marked the beginning of a far-reaching political revolution. Although it was a drama that took place behind closed doors, it was not one unknown to the general public. Throughout May and June 1789, Parisians trekked to Versailles to watch the deliberations and then they brought the news back to the capital. Deputies wrote home to their constituents to keep them abreast of events. Newspapers that reported daily on the wranglings and pamphleteers who analyzed them spread the news throughout the nation. Information, often conflicting, stirred up anxiety; news of conflict encouraged action.

The frustration and stalemate of the Estates-General threatened to put the spark to the kindling of urban unrest. The people of Paris had suffered through a harsh winter and spring under the burdens of high prices (especially of bread), limited supplies, and relentless tax demands. The rioting of the spring had for the moment ceased as people waited for their problems to be solved by the deputies of the Estates-General. The suffering of the urban poor was not new, but their ability to connect economic hardships with the politics at Versailles and to blame the government was. As hopes began to dim with the

MAP DISCOVERY

Boundaries, 1789

★ Revolutionary centers

Areas of the Great Fear, July – Aug. 1789

French boundaries, 1793

Counterrevolutionary activity

• Centers of counter-revoluntionary activity

Areas of insurrection

Revolutionary France

The French Revolution was not merely a Parisian phenomenon, as this map shows. Locate the revolutionary centers on the map. What feature is common to all of these centers? How do you explain their distribution throughout France? Pockets of insurrection and counter-revolution were scattered for the most part in the southeast and west. What did they have in common? What territories did France gain between 1789 and 1793 and why did it expand?

news of political stalemate, news broke of the creation of the National Assembly. It was greeted with new anticipation.

The Outbreak of Revolutionary Action in 1789

The king, who had temporarily withdrawn from sight following the death of his son at the beginning of June, reemerged to meet with the representatives of each of the three estates and propose reforms, including a constitutional monarchy. But Louis XVI refused to accept the now popularly supported National Assembly as a legitimate body, insisting instead that he must rely on the three estates for advice. He simply did not understand that the choice was no longer his to make. He summoned troops to Versailles and began concentrating soldiers in Paris. Civilians continually clashed with members of the military, whom they jostled and jeered. The urban crowds recognized the threat of repression that the troops represented. People decided to meet force with force. To do so, they needed arms themselves—and they knew where to get them.

The Storming of the Bastille. On 14 July 1789, the irate citizens of Paris stormed the Bastille, a royal armory that also served as a prison for a handful of debtors. The storming of the Bastille became the great symbol in the revolutionary legend of the overthrow of the tyranny and oppression of the Old Regime. But it is significant for another reason. It was an expression of the power of the people to take politics into their own hands. Parisians were following the lead of their deputies in Versailles. They had formed a citizen militia known as the National Guard, and they were prepared to defend their concept of justice and law.

The people who stormed the Bastille were not the poor, the unemployed, the criminals, or the urban rabble, as their detractors portrayed them. They were petty tradesmen, shopkeepers, and wage-earners, who considered it their right to seize arms in order to protect their interests. The Marquis de Lafayette (1757–1834), a noble beloved of the people because of his participation in the American Revolution, helped organize the National Guard. Under his direction, the militia adopted the tricolor flag as its standard. The tricolor combined the red and blue colors of the city of Paris with the white of the Bourbon royal family. It became the flag of the revolution, replacing the fleur-de-lis of the Bourbons. It is the national flag of France today.

The king could no longer dictate the terms of the constitution. By their actions, the people in arms had ratified the National Assembly. Louis XVI was forced to yield. The events in Paris set off similar uprisings in cities and towns throughout France. National guards in provincial cities modeled themselves after the Parisian militia. Government officials fled their posts and abandoned their responsibilities. Commoners stood ready to fill the power vacuum. But the revolution was not just an urban phenomenon: the peasantry had their own grievances and their own way of making a revolution.

Peasant Fear of an Aristocratic Plot.

The precariousness of rural life and the increase in population in the countryside contributed to the permanent displacement and destitution of a growing sector of rural society. Without savings and destroyed by poor harvests, impoverished rural inhabitants wandered the countryside looking for odd jobs and eventually begging to survive. All peasants endured common obligations placed on them by the crown and the privileged classes. A bewildering array of taxes afflicted peasants: they owed the tithe to the Church, land taxes to the state, and seigneurial dues and rents to the landlord. In some areas, peasants repaired roads and drew lots for military service. Dues affected almost every aspect of rural life. The labor of women was essential to the survival of the rural family. Peasant women sought employment in towns and cities as seamstresses and servants in order to send money back home to struggling relatives. Children, too, added their earnings to the family pot. In spite of various strategies for survival, the lives of more and more peasant families were disrupted by the end of the eighteenth century as they were displaced from the land.

News of the events of Versailles and then of the revolutionary action in Paris did not reassure rural inhabitants. By the end of June the hope of deliverance from crippling taxes and dues was rapidly fading. The news of the Oath of the Tennis Court and the storming of the Bastille terrified country folk, who saw the actions as evidence of an aristocratic plot that threatened sorely needed reforms. As information moved along postal routes in letters from delegates to their supporters, and as news was repeated in the Sunday market gatherings, distortions and exaggerations crept in. It seemed to rural inhabitants that their world was falling apart. Some peasants believed that Paris was in the hands of brigands

and that the king and the Estates-General were victims of an aristocratic plot. Rural vision, fueled by empty stomachs, was apocalyptic.

That state of affairs was aggravated as increasing numbers of peasants were pushed off the land to seek employment as transient farm laborers, moving from one area to another with the cycles of sowing and harvesting. Throughout the 1780s, the number of peasants without land was increasing steadily. Starving men, women, and children, filthy and poorly dressed, were frightening figures to villagers who feared that the same fate would befall them with the next bad harvest. As one landowner lamented, "We cannot lie down without fear, the nighttime paupers have tormented us greatly, to say nothing of the daytime ones, whose numbers are considerable."

Most peasants had lived in the same place for generations and knew only the confines of their own villages. They were uneasy about what existed beyond the horizon. Transients, often speaking strange dialects, disrupted and threatened the social universe of the village. In order to survive, wanderers often resorted to petty theft, stealing fruit from trees or food from unwatched hearths. Often traveling in groups, hordes of vagabonds struck fear into the hearts of farm workers, trampling crops and sleeping in open fields. Peasants were sure that the unfortunate souls were brigands paid by the local aristocracy to persecute a peasantry already stretched to the breaking point.

The Peasant Revolt.

Hope gave way to fear. Beginning on 20 July 1789, peasants in different areas of France reacted collectively throughout France, spreading false rumors of a great conspiracy. Fear gripped whole villages and in some areas spawned revolt. Just as urban workers had connected their economic hardships to politics, so too did desperate peasants see their plight in political terms. They banded together and marched to the residences of the local nobility, breaking into chateaux with a single mission in mind: to destroy all legal documents by which nobles claimed payments, dues, and services from local peasants. They drove out the lords and in some cases burned their chateaux, putting an end to the tyranny of the privileged over the countryside. The peasants had taken matters into their own hands. They intended to consign the last vestiges of aristocratic privilege to the bonfires of aristocratic documents.

The overthrow of privileges rooted in a feudal past was not as easy as that. Members of the National Assembly were aghast at the eruption of rural violence. They knew that to stay in power they had to maintain peace. They also knew that to be credible they had to protect property. Peasant destruction of seigneurial claims posed a real dilemma for the bourgeois deputies directing the revolution. If they gave in to peasant demands, they risked losing aristocratic support and undermining their own ability to control events. If they gave in to the aristocracy, they risked a social revolution in the countryside, which they could not police or repress. Liberal members of the aristocracy cooperated with the bourgeois leaders in finding a solution.

In a dramatic meeting that lasted through the night of 4 August 1789, the National Assembly agreed to abolish the principle of privilege. The peasants had won—or thought they had. In the weeks and months ahead, rural people learned that they had lost their own prerogatives—the rights to common grazing and gathering—and were expected to buy their way out of their feudal services. In the meantime, parliamentary action had saved the day: the deputies stabilized the situation through legislating compromise.

Women on the March.   Women participated with men in both urban and rural revolutionary actions. Acting on their own, women were responsible for one of the most dramatic events of the early years of the revolution: In October 1789, they forced the king and the royal family to leave Versailles for Paris to deal in person with the problems of bread supply, high prices, and starvation. Women milling about in the marketplaces of Paris on the morning of 5 October were complaining bitterly about the high cost and shortages of bread. The National Assembly was in session, and the National Guards were patrolling the streets of Paris. But the trappings of political change had no impact on the brutal realities of the marketplace.

Women were in charge of buying the food for their families. Every morning they stood in lines with their neighbors reenacting the familiar ritual. Some mornings they were turned away, told by the baker or his assistants that there was no bread. On other days they did not have enough coins in their purses to buy the staple of their diet. Women responsible for managing the consumption of the household were most directly in touch with the state of provisioning the capital. When they were unable to feed their families, the situation became intolerable.

So it was, on the morning of 5 October 1789, that 6,000 Parisian women marched out of the city and toward Versailles. They were taking their problem to the king with the demand that he solve it. Later in the day, Lafayette led the Parisian National Guard to Versailles to mediate events. The women were armed with pikes, the simple weapon available to the poorest defender of the revolution, and they were prepared to use them. The battle came early the next morning, when the women, now accompanied by revolutionary men, tired and cold from waiting all night at the gates of the palace, invaded the royal apartments and chased Marie Antoinette from her bedroom. Several members of the royal guards, hated by the people of Paris for alleged insults against the tricolor cockade, were killed by the angry crowd, who decapitated them and mounted their heads on pikes. A shocked Louis XVI agreed to return with the crowd to Paris. The crowd cheered Louis's

■ A contemporary print of the women of Paris advancing on Versailles. The determined marchers are shown waving pikes and dragging an artillery piece. The women were hailed as heroines of the revolution.

Depart des Heroines de Paris pour Versailles le 5 Octobre 1789.

decision, which briefly reestablished his personal popularity. But as monarch, he had been humiliated at the hands of women of the capital. Reduced to the roles of "the baker, the baker's wife, and the baker's son" by jeering crowds, the royal family was forced to return to Paris that very day. Louis XVI was now captive to the revolution, whose efforts to form a constitutional monarchy he purported to support.

Declaring Political Rights

"Liberty consists in the ability to do whatever does not harm another." So wrote the revolutionary deputies of 1789. Sounding a refrain similar to that of the American Declaration of Independence, the Declaration of the Rights of Man and Citizen appeared on 26 August 1789. The document amalgamated a variety of Enlightenment ideas drawn from the works of political philosophy, including those of Locke and Montesquieu. "Men are born and remain free and equal in rights. Social distinctions may be based only on common utility." Perhaps most significant of all was the attention given to property, which was declared a "sacred and inviolable," "natural," and "imprescriptible" right of man.

In the year of tranquility that followed the violent summer of 1789, the new politicians set themselves the task of creating institutions based on the principle of liberty and others embodied in the Declaration of the Rights of Man and Citizen. The result was the Constitution of 1791, a statement of faith in a progressive constitutional monarchy. A king accountable to an elected parliamentary body would lead France into a prosperous and just age. The constitution acknowledged the people's sovereignty as the source of political power. It also enshrined the principle of property by making voting rights dependent on property ownership. All men might be equal before the law, but by the Constitution of 1791 only wealthy men had the right to vote for representatives and hold office.

Civil Liberties.   All titles of nobility were abolished. In the early period of the revolution, civil liberties were extended to Protestants and Jews, who had been persecuted under the Old Regime. Previously excluded groups were granted freedom of thought, worship, and full civil liberties. More reluctantly, deputies outlawed slavery in the colonies in 1794. Slave unrest in Saint Domingue (modern-day Haiti) had coincided with the political conflicts of the revolution and exploded in rebellion in 1791, driving the revolutionaries in Paris to support black independence although it was at odds with French colonial interests. Led by Toussaint L'Ouverture (1743–1803), black rebels worked to found an independent Haitian state, which was declared in 1804. But the concept of equality with regard to race remained incompletely integrated with revolutionary principles, and slavery was reestablished in the French colonies in 1802.

Women's Rights.   Men were the subject of the newly defined rights. No references to women or their rights appear in the constitutions or the official Declarations of Rights.

Women's organizations agitated for an equitable divorce law, and divorce was legalized in September 1792. Women were critical actors in the revolution from its very inception, and their presence shaped and directed the outcome of events, as the women's march to Versailles in 1789 made clear. The Marquis de Condorcet (1743–1794), elected to the Legislative Assembly in 1791, was one of the first to chastise the revolutionaries for overlooking the political rights of women who, he pointedly observed, were half of the human race. "Either no individual of the human race has genuine rights, or else all have the same; and he who votes against the right of another, whatever the religion, color, or sex of that other, has henceforth abjured his own." Condorcet argued forcefully but unsuccessfully for the right of women to be educated.

The revolutionaries had declared that liberty was a natural and inalienable right, a universal right that was extended to all with the overthrow of a despotic monarch and a privileged elite. The principle triumphed in religious toleration. Yet the revolutionary concept of liberty foundered on the divergent claims of excluded groups—workers, women, and slaves—who demanded full participation in the world of politics. In 1792, revolutionaries confronted the contradictions inherent in their political beliefs of liberty and equality that were being challenged in the midst of social upheaval and foreign war. In response, the revolution turned to more radical measures to survive.

The Trials of Constitutional Monarchy

The disciplined deliberations of committees intent on fashioning a constitutional monarchy replaced the passion and fervor of revolutionary oratory. The National, or Constituent, Assembly divided France into new administrative units—*départements*—for the purpose of establishing better control over municipal governments. Along with new administrative trappings, the government promoted its own rituals. On 14 July 1790, militias from each of the newly created 83 départements of France came together in Paris to celebrate the first anniversary of the storming of the Bastille. A new national holiday was born and with it a sense of devotion and patriotism for the new France liberated by the revolution. In spite of the unifying elements, however, the newly achieved revolutionary consensus began to show signs of breaking down.

The Counterrevolution.   In February 1790, legislation dissolved all monasteries and convents, except for those that provided aid to the poor or that served as educational institutions. As the French church was stripped of its lands, Pope Pius VI (1775–1799) denounced the principles of the revolution. In July 1790, the government approved the Civil Constitution of the Clergy: priests now became the equivalent of paid agents of the state. By requiring an oath of loyalty to the state from all practicing priests, the National Assembly created a new arena for dissent. Catholics were forced to choose to embrace or reject the revolution. Many "nonjuring" priests who refused to take the oath went into hiding. The wedge driven between the Catholic Church and revolutionary France allowed a mass-based counterrevolution to emerge. Aristocratic émigrés who had fled the country because of their opposition to the revolution were languishing for lack of a popular base. From his headquarters in Turin, the king's younger brother, the Comte d'Artois, was attempting to incite a civil war in France. When the revolutionaries decided to attack the Church not just as a landed and privileged institution but also as a religious one, the counterrevolution rapidly expanded.

Late one night in June 1791, Louis XVI, Marie Antoinette, and their children disguised themselves as commoners, crept out of the royal apartments in the Tuileries Palace, and fled Paris. Louis intended to leave France to join royalist forces opposing the revolution at Metz. He got as far as Varennes, where he was captured by soldiers of the National Guard and brought back to a shocked Paris. The king had abandoned the revolution. Although he was not put to death for another year and a half, he was more than ever a prisoner of the revolution.

The Fiscal Crisis.   The defection of the king was certainly serious, but it was not the only problem facing the revolutionaries. Other problems plagued the revolutionary government, notably foreign war and the fiscal crisis, coupled with inflation. In order to establish its seriousness and legitimacy, the National Assembly had been willing in 1789 to absorb the debts of the Old Regime. The new government could not sell titles and offices, as the king had done to deal with financial problems, but it did confiscate Church property. In addition, it issued treasury bonds in the form of assignats in order to raise money. The assignats soon assumed the status of bank notes, and by the spring of 1790 they had become compulsory legal tender. Initially they were to be backed by land confiscated from the Church and sold by the state. But the need for money soon outran the value of the land available, and the government continued to print assignats according to its needs. Depreciation of French currency in international markets and inflation at home resulted. The revolutionary government found itself in a situation which in certain respects was worse than that experienced by Louis XVI before the calling of the Estates-General. Assignat-induced inflation produced a sharp decline in the fortunes of bourgeois investors living on fixed incomes. Rising prices meant increased misery for workers and peasants.

New counterrevolutionary groups were becoming frustrated with revolutionary policies. Throughout the winter and spring of 1791–1792, people rioted and demanded that prices be fixed, while the assignat dropped to less than half its face value. Peasants refused to sell crops for the worthless paper. Hoarding further drove up prices. Angry crowds turned to pillaging, rioting, and murder, which became more frequent as the value of the currency declined and prices rose.

Foreign war beginning in the fall of 1791 also challenged stability. Some moderate political leaders welcomed war as a blessing in disguise, since it could divert the attention of the masses away from problems at home and promote loyalty to the revolution. Others envisioned war as a great crusade to bring revolutionary principles to oppressed peoples throughout Europe. The king and queen, trapped by the revolution, saw war as their only hope of liberation. Louis XVI could be rightfully restored as the leader of a France defeated by the sovereigns of Europe. Some who opposed the war believed it would destabilize the revolution. France must solve its problems at home, they argued, before fighting a foreign enemy. Louis, however, encouraged those ministers and advisers eager for battle. In April 1792, France declared war against Austria.

Individuals, events, economic realities, and the nature of politics conspired against the success of the first constitutional experiment. The king's attempt to flee France in the summer of 1791 seriously wounded the attempt at compromise. Many feared that the goals of the revolution could not be preserved in a country at war and with a king of dubious loyalties.

EXPERIMENTING WITH DEMOCRACY, 1792–1799

The revolution was a school for the French nation. A political universe populated by individual citizens replaced the eighteenth-century world of subjects loyal to their king. The new construction of politics, in which all individuals were equal, ran counter to prevailing ideas about collective identities defined in guilds and orders. People on all levels of society learned politics by doing it. In the beginning, experience helped. The elites, both noble and bourgeois, had served in government and administration. But the rules of the game under the Old Regime had been very different, with birth and wealth determining power.

After 1789, all men were declared free and equal, in opportunity if not in rights. Men of ability and talent, who had served as middlemen for the privileged elite under the Old Regime, now claimed power as their due. Many of them were lawyers, educated in the rules and regulations of the society of orders. They experienced firsthand the problems of the exercise of power in the Old Regime, and they had their own ideas about reform. But the school of the revolution did not remain the domain of a special class. Women demanded their places but continued to be excluded from the political arena, though the importance of their participation in the revolution was indisputable. Workers talked of seizing their rights, but because of the inherent contradictions of representation and participation, experimenting with democracy led to outcomes that did not look very democratic at all.

The Revolution of the People

The first stage of the French Revolution, lasting from 1789 through the beginning of 1792, was based on liberty—the liberty to compete, to own, and to succeed. The second stage of the French Revolution, which began in 1792, took equality as its rallying cry. It was the revolution of the working people of French cities. The popular movement that spearheaded political action in 1792 was committed to equality of rights in a way not characteristic of the leaders of the revolution of 1789. Urban workers were not benefiting from the revolution, but they had come to believe in their own power as political beings. Organized on the local level into sections, artisans in cities identified themselves as **sans-culottes**—literally, those trousered citizens who did not wear knee breeches (*culottes*)—to distinguish themselves from the privileged elite.

Who constituted the popular movement? The self-designated sans-culottes were the working men and women of Paris. Some were wealthier than others, some were wage earners, but all shared a common identity as consumers in the marketplace. They hated the privileged (*les gros*), who appeared to be profiting at the expense of the people. The sans-culottes wanted government power to be decentralized, with neighborhoods ruling themselves through sectional organizations. As the have-nots, they were increasingly intent on pulling down the haves, and they translated the sense of vengeance into a new revolutionary justice. On 10 August 1792, the people of Paris stormed the Tuileries, chanting their demands for "Equality!" and "Nation!" The people tramped across the silk sheets of the king's bed and broke his fine furniture, reveling in the private chambers of the royal family. Love and respect for the king had vanished. What the people of Paris demanded was the right to vote and participate in a popular democracy. Working people were acting independently of other factions, and the bourgeois political leadership became quickly aware of the need to scramble to maintain order. When they invaded the Tuileries Palace on the morning of 10 August, the sans-culottes did so in the name of the people. They saw themselves as patriots whose duty it was to brush the monarchy aside. The people were now a force to be reckoned with and feared.

"Terror Is the Order of the Day"

Political factions characterized revolutionary politics from the start. The terms *Left* and *Right,* which came to represent opposite ends of the political spectrum, originated in a description of where people sat in the Assembly in relation to the podium. Political designations were refined in successive parliamentary bodies. The Convention was the legislative body elected in September 1792 that succeeded the Legislative Assembly and had as its charge determining the best form of government after the collapse of the monarchy. On 21 September 1792, the monarchy was abolished in France; on the following day the Republic, France's first, came into being. Members of the Convention conducted the trial of Louis XVI for treason and pronounced his sentence: execution by the guillotine in January 1793.

The various political factions of the Convention were described in terms borrowed from geography. The Mountain, sitting on the upper benches on the left, was made up of

members of the Jacobin Club (named for its meeting place in an abandoned monastery). The **Jacobins** were the most radical element in the National Convention, supporting democratic solutions and speaking in favor of the cause of people in the streets.

Jacobin Ascendancy. Both **Girondins,** the more moderate revolutionary faction, and Jacobins were from the middle ranks of the bourgeoisie, and both groups were dedicated to the principles of the revolution. Although they controlled the ministries, the Girondins began to lose their hold on the revolution and the war. The renewed European war fragmented the democratic movement, and the Girondins, unable to control violence at home, saw political control slipping away. They became prisoners of the revolution when 80,000 armed Parisians surrounded the National Convention in June 1793.

Girondin power had been eroding in the critical months between August 1792 and June 1793. A new leader was working quietly and effectively behind the scenes to weld a partnership between the popular movement of sans-culottes and the Jacobins. He was Maximilien Robespierre (1758–1794), leader of the Mountain and the Jacobin Club. Robespierre was typical of the new breed of revolutionary politician. Only 31 years old in 1789, he wrote mediocre poems and attended the local provincial academy to discuss the new ideas when he was not practicing law in his hometown of Arras. Elected to the Estates-General, he joined the Jacobin Club and quickly rose to become its leader. He was willing to take controversial stands on issues: unlike most of his fellow members of the Mountain—including his rival, the popular orator Georges-Jacques Danton (1759–1794)—he opposed the war in 1792. Although neither an original thinker nor a compelling orator, Robespierre discovered with the revolution that he was an adroit political tactician. He gained a following and learned how to manipulate it. It was he who engineered the Jacobins' replacement of the Girondins as leaders of the government.

Robespierre and the Reign of Terror. Robespierre's chance for real power came when he assumed leadership of the Committee of Public Safety in July 1793. Faced with the threat of internal anarchy and external war, the elected body, the National Convention, yielded political control to the 12-man Committee of Public Safety that ruled dictatorially under Robespierre's direction. The Great Committee, as it was known at the time, orchestrated the **Reign of Terror** (1793–1794), a period of systematic state repression that meted out justice in the people's name. Summary trials by specially created revolutionary tribunals were followed by the swift execution of the guilty under the blade of the guillotine.

Influenced by *The Social Contract* (1762) and other writings of Jean-Jacques Rousseau, Robespierre believed that sovereignty resided with the people. For him, individual wills and even individual rights did not matter when weighed against the will of the nation. The king was dead; the people were the new source of political power. Robespierre saw himself in the all-important role of interpreting and shaping the people's will. His own task was to guide the people "to the summit of its destinies." As he explained to his critics, "I am defending not my own cause but the public cause." As head of the Great Committee, Robespierre oversaw a revolutionary machinery dedicated to economic regulation, massive military mobilization, and a punitive system of revolutionary justice characterized by the slogan, "Terror Is the Order of the Day." Militant revolutionary committees and revolutionary tribunals were established throughout France to identify traitors and to mete out the harsh justice that struck hardest against those members of the bourgeoisie perceived as opponents of the government.

The guillotine became the symbol of revolutionary justice, but it was not the only means of execution. In Lyon, officials of the Reign of Terror had prisoners tied to stakes in open fields and fired on with cannons. In Nantes, a Parisian administrator of the new justice had enemies of the revolution chained to barges and drowned in the estuary of the Loire. The civil war, which raged most violently in the Vendée in the west of France, consisted often of primitive massacres that sent an estimated quarter of a million people to their deaths. The bureaucratized Reign of Terror was responsible for about 40,000 executions in a nine-month period, resulting in the image of the republicans as "drinkers of blood."

The Cult of the Supreme Being, a civic religion without priests or churches and influenced by Rousseau's ideas about nature, followed de-Christianization. The cathedral of Notre Dame de Paris was turned into the Temple of Reason, and the new religion established its own festivals to undermine the persistence of Catholicism. The cult was one indication of the Reign of Terror's attempt to create a new moral universe of revolutionary values.

Women Excluded. Women remained conspicuously absent from the summit of political power. After 1793, Jacobin revolutionaries, who had been willing to empower the popular movement of workers, turned against women's participation and denounced it. Women's associations were outlawed and the Society of Revolutionary Republican Women was disbanded. Olympe de Gouges, revolutionary author of the Declaration of the Rights of Woman and Citizen, was guillotined. Women were declared unfit for political participation, according to the Jacobins, because of their biological functions of reproduction and child-rearing. Rousseau's ideas about family policy were probably more influential than his political doctrines. His best-selling books, *La Nouvelle Héloise* (1761) and *Émile* (1762), which combined went into 72 editions before 1789, were moral works that transformed people's ideas about family life. Under his influence, the reading public came to value a separate and private sphere of domestic and conjugal values. Following Rousseau's lead, Robespierre and the Jacobins insisted that the role of women as mothers was incompatible with women's participation in the political realm.

The Thermidorian Reaction. By attacking his critics on both the Left and the Right, Robespierre undermined the support he needed to stay in power. He abandoned the alliance with the popular movement that had been so important in bringing him to power. Robespierre's enemies—and he had many—were able to break the identification between political power and the will of the people that Robespierre had established. As a result, he was branded a traitor by the same process that he had used against many of his own enemies. He saved France from foreign occupation and internal collapse, but he could not save democracy through terror. In the summer of 1794, Robespierre was guillotined. The Reign of Terror ceased with his death in the revolutionary month of Thermidor 1794.

The revolution did not end with the **Thermidorian Reaction,** as the fall of Robespierre came to be known, but his execution initiated a new phase. For some, democracy lost its legitimacy. The popular movement was reviled, and sans-culotte became a term of derision. Jacobins were forced underground. Price controls were abolished, resulting in extreme hardship for most urban residents. Out of desperation, in April 1795 the Jacobins and the sans-culottes renewed their alliance and united to demand "bread and the Constitution of 1793." The politics of bread had never been more accurately captured in slogan. Those who took to the streets in 1795 saw the universal manhood suffrage of the unimplemented 1793 constitution as the way to solve their economic problems. But their demands went unheeded; the popular revolution had failed.

The End of the Revolution

In the four years after Robespierre's fall, a new government by committee, called the Directory, appeared to offer mediocrity, caution, and opportunism in place of the idealism and action of the early years of the revolution. No successor to Robespierre stepped forward to command center stage. There were no heroes like Lafayette or the great Jacobin orator Georges-Jacques Danton to inspire patriotic fervor. Nor were there women like Olympe de Gouges to demand in the public arena equal rights for women. Most people, numbed after years of change, barely noticed that the revolution was over. Ordinary men in parliamentary institutions effectively did the day-to-day job of running the government. They tried to steer a middle path between royalist resurgence and popular insurrection. This nearly forgotten period in the history of the French Revolution was the fulfillment of the liberal hopes of 1789 for a stable constitutional rule.

The Directory, however, continued to be dogged by European war. A mass army of conscripts and volunteers had successfully extended France's power and frontiers. France expelled foreign invaders and annexed territories, including Belgium, while increasing its control in Holland, Switzerland, and Italy. But the expansion of revolutionary France was expensive and increasingly unpopular. Military defeats and the corruption of the Directory undermined government control. The Directory might have succeeded in the slow accretion of a

CHRONOLOGY
THE FRENCH REVOLUTION

August 1788	Louis XVI announces meeting of Estates-General to be held May 1789
5 May 1789	Estates-General convenes
17 June 1789	Third Estate declares itself the National Assembly
20 June 1789	Oath of the Tennis Court
14 July 1789	Storming of the Bastille
20 July 1789	Revolution of peasantry begins
26 August 1789	Declaration of the Rights of Man and Citizen
5 October 1789	Parisian women march to Versailles; force Louis XVI to return to Paris
February 1790	Monasteries, convents dissolved
July 1790	Civil Constitution of the Clergy
June 1791	Louis XVI and family attempt to flee Paris; are captured and returned
September 1791	France's First Constitution
April 1792	France declares war on Austria
10 August 1792	Storming of the Tuileries
22 September 1792	Revolutionary calendar implemented
January 1793	Louis XVI executed
July 1793	Robespierre assumes leadership of Committee of Public Safety
1793–1794	Reign of Terror
1794	Robespierre guillotined
1799	Napoleon overthrows the Directory and seizes power

parliamentary tradition, but reinstatement of **conscription** in 1798 met with widespread protest and resistance. No matter what their political leanings, people were weary. They turned to those who promised stability and peace.

In the democratic experiment at the heart of the second stage of the French Revolution, the sovereign will of the people permanently replaced the monarch's claim to divine right to rule. Yet with democracy came tyranny. The severe repression of the terror revealed the pressures that external war and civil unrest created for the new republic. The Thermidorian Reaction and the elimination of Robespierre as the legitimate interpreter of the people's will ushered in a period of conciliation, opportunism, and a search for stability. Ironically, the savior that France found to answer its needs for peace and a just government was a man of war and a dictator.

THE REIGN OF NAPOLEON, 1799–1815

The great debate that rages to this day about Napoleon revolves around the question of whether he fulfilled the aims of the French Revolution or perverted them. In his return to a monarchical model, Napoleon resembled the enlightened despots of eighteenth-century Europe. In a modern sense, he was also a dictator, manipulating the French people through a highly centralized administrative apparatus. He locked French society into a program of military expansion that depleted its human and material resources. Yet in spite of destruction and war, he dedicated his reign to building a French state according to the principles of the revolution.

Bonaparte Seizes Power

In 1795, a young, penniless, and unknown military officer moved among the wealthy and the beautiful of Parisian society and longed for fame. Already nicknamed at school "the Little Corporal" on account of his short stature, he was snubbed because of his background and ridiculed for his foreign accent. Yet within four years this young man had become the ruler of France.

Napoleon's Training and Experience. Napoleon Bonaparte (1769–1821) was a true child of the eighteenth century. He shared the philosophes' belief in a rational and progressive world. Napoleon was born into an Italian noble family in Corsica, which, until a few months before his birth, was part of the Republic of Genoa. He secured a scholarship to the French military school at Brienne, graduating in 1784. He then spent a year at the Military Academy in Paris and received a commission as a second lieutenant of artillery in January 1786.

The French Revolution changed everything for Napoleon. It made new posts available as aristocratic generals defected, and it created great opportunities for military men to test their mettle. Foreign war and civil war required military leaders who were devoted to the revolution. Forced to flee Corsica because he had sided with the Jacobins, Bonaparte crushed Parisian protesters who rioted against the Directory in 1795. The revolutionary wars had begun in 1792 as wars to liberate humanity in the name of liberty, equality, and fraternity. Yet concerns for power, territory, and riches replaced earlier French concerns with defense of the nation and of the revolution.

This aggrandizement was nowhere more evident than in the Egyptian campaign of 1798, in which Napoleon

MAP DISCOVERY

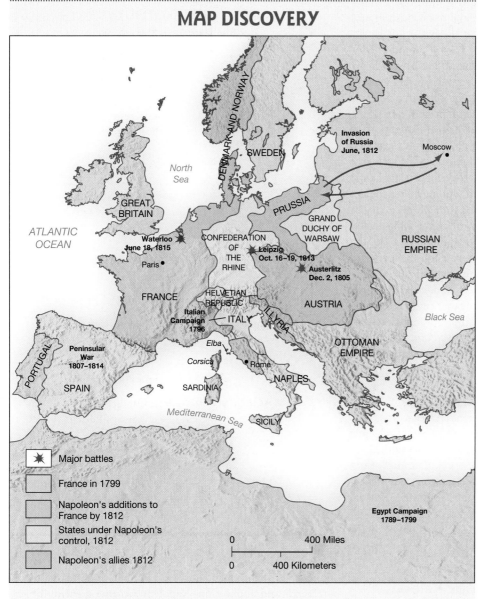

Major battles

France in 1799

Napoleon's additions to France by 1812

States under Napoleon's control, 1812

Napoleon's allies 1812

0   400 Miles
0   400 Kilometers

Napoleon's Empire

Note the expansion of France under Napoleon's rule. How much of western and central Europe did Napoleon control by 1812? Why did Great Britain remain outside of Napoleon's influence? Why were Prussia, Austria, Denmark, and Norway allies of France in 1812?

he extended French rule into central Italy, he became the embodiment of revolutionary values and energy.

Napoleon as First Consul. In 1799, Napoleon Bonaparte readily joined a conspiracy that pulled down the Directory, the government he had earlier preserved, and became the first consul of a triumvirate of consuls. Napoleon set out to secure his position of power by eliminating his enemies on the Left and weakening those on the Right. He guaranteed the security of property acquired in the revolution, a move that undercut royalists who wanted to return property to its original owners. Through policing forces and special criminal courts, law and order prevailed and civil war subsided. The first consul promised a balanced budget and appeared to deliver it. Bonaparte spoke of healing the nation's wounds, especially those opened by de-Christianization during the revolution. Realizing the importance of religion in maintaining domestic peace, Napoleon reestablished relations with the pope in 1801 by the Concordat, which recognized Catholicism as the religion of the French and restored the Roman Catholic hierarchy.

Napoleon's popularity as first consul flowed from his military and political successes and his religious reconciliation. He had come to power in 1799 by appealing for the support of the army. In 1802, Napoleon decided to extend his power by calling for a plebiscite in which he asked the electorate to vote him first consul for life. Public support was overwhelming. An electoral landslide gave Napoleon greater political power than any of his Bourbon predecessors had known.

Napoleon at War with the European Powers

Napoleon was at war or preparing for war during his entire reign. His military successes, real and apparent, before 1799 had been crucial in his bid for political power. By 1802, he had

Bonaparte headed an expedition whose goal was to enrich France by hastening the collapse of the Turkish Empire, crippling British trade routes, and handicapping Russian interests in the region. With Napoleon's highly publicized campaigns in Egypt and Syria, the war left the European theater and moved to the east, leaving behind the original revolutionary ideals.

The Egyptian campaign, which was in reality a disaster, made Napoleon a hero at home. His victories in the Italian campaign in 1796–1797 had launched his political career. As signed favorable treaties with both Austria and Great Britain. He appeared to deliver a lasting peace and to establish France as the dominant power in Europe. But the peace was short-lived. In 1803, France embarked on an 11-year period of continuous war. Under Napoleon's command, the French army delivered defeat after defeat to the European powers. Austria fell in 1805, Prussia fell in 1806, and the Russian armies of Alexander I were defeated at Friedland in 1807. In 1808, Napoleon invaded Spain to drive out British expeditionary forces intent on invading France. Spain became a satellite kingdom of France, although the conflict continued.

Britain was the one exception to the string of Napoleonic victories. Napoleon initially considered sending a French fleet to invade the island nation. Lacking the strength necessary to achieve this, he turned to economic warfare and blockaded European ports against British trade. Beginning in 1806, the **Continental System,** as the blockade was known, erected a structure of protection for French manufactures in all continental European markets. The British responded to the tariff walls and boycotts with a naval blockade that cut French commerce off from its Atlantic markets. The Continental System did not break the British economy, however, and the French economy did not flourish when faced with restricted resources and the persistence of a black market in smuggled goods.

Still, by 1810, Napoleon was master of the Continent. French armies had extended revolutionary reforms and legal codes outside France and brought with them civil equality and religious toleration. They had also drained defeated countries of their resources and had inflicted the horrors of war with armies of occupation, forced billeting, and pillage. Napoleon's empire extended across Europe, with only a diminished Austria, Prussia, and Russia remaining independent. He placed his relatives and friends on the thrones of the new satellite kingdoms of Italy, Naples, Westphalia, Holland, and Spain.

The First Empire and Domestic Reforms

Napoleon measured domestic prosperity in terms of the stability of his reign. Through the 1802 plebiscite that voted him first consul for life, Napoleon maintained the charade of constitutional rule while ruling as virtual dictator. In 1804, he abandoned all pretense and had himself proclaimed emperor of the French. He staged his own coronation and that of his wife Josephine at the cathedral of Notre Dame de Paris.

The Importance of Science and Economic Reforms. Secure in his regime, surrounded by a new nobility that he created on the basis of military achievement and talent, Napoleon set about implementing sweeping reforms in every area of government. He recognized the importance of science for both industry and war. The revolution had removed an impediment to the development of a national market by creating a uniform system of weights and measures—the metric system, which was established by 1799. Napoleon felt the need to go further. To ensure French predominance in scientific

CHRONOLOGY THE REIGN OF NAPOLEON	
1799	Napoleon establishes consulate, becomes first consul
1801	Napoleon reestablishes relations with pope, restores Roman Catholic hierarchy
1802	Plebiscite declares Napoleon first consul for life
1804	Napoleon proclaims himself Emperor of the French
1806	Continental System implemented
1808–1814	France engaged in Peninsular War with Spain
June 1812	Napoleon invades Russia
September 1812	French army reaches Moscow, is trapped by Russian winter
1813	Napoleon defeated at Battle of Nations at Leipzig
March 1814	Napoleon abdicates and goes into exile on island of Elba
March 1815	Napoleon escapes Elba and attempts to reclaim power
15 June 1815	Napoleon is defeated at Waterloo and exiled to island of Saint Helena

research and application, Napoleon became a patron of science, supporting important work in the areas of physics and chemistry. Building for the future, Napoleon made science a pillar in the new structure of higher education.

The Directory had restored French prosperity through stabilization of the currency, fiscal reform, and support of industry. Napoleon's contribution to the French economy was the much needed reform of the tax system. He authorized the creation of a central banking system. French industries flourished under state protection. The blockade forced the development of new domestic crops such as beet-sugar and indigo, which became substitutes for colonial products. Napoleon extended the infrastructure of roads, so necessary for the expansion of national and European markets.

The New Legal System.   Perhaps his greatest achievement was the codification of law, a task begun under the revolution. Combined with economic reforms, the new **Napoleonic Code** facilitated trade and the development of commerce by regularizing contractual relations and protecting property rights and equality before the law. The civil laws of the new code carved out a family policy characterized by hierarchy and subordination. Married women were neither independent nor equal to men in ownership of property, custody of children, and access to divorce. Women also lacked political rights. In the Napoleonic Code, women, like children, were subjected to paternal authority. The Napoleonic philosophy of woman's place is well captured in an anecdote told by Madame

Germaine de Staël (1766–1817), a leading intellectual of her day. On finding herself seated next to Napoleon at a dinner party, she asked him whom he considered the greatest woman, alive or dead. Napoleon responded, "The one who has had the most children."

Napoleon turned his prodigious energies to every aspect of French life. He encouraged the arts and created a police force. He had monuments built but did not forget about sewers. He organized French administrative life in a fashion that has

THE CIVIL CODE OF THE CODE NAPOLÉON (1804)

While still first consul, Bonaparte assembled a group of the country's leading legal specialists to replace the vast agglomeration of feudal, customary, and canon laws, all with their own courts and procedures, with a unified system based on Roman law. The Civil Code, *along with the* Criminal Code, *made up the* Code Napoléon, *and consisted of 2,281 articles intended to cover all aspects of civil life from birth to death, all civic aspects relating to family and property, contractual responsibilities, and civil liberties. A unified legal system became the basis for economic development and was arguably Napoleon's greatest achievement as ruler of France. The* Civil Code *replaced the Roman Catholic Church as having authority over marriage, and although divorce was permitted in the* Code, *it was outlawed in 1816 and not permitted again until 1884.*

Focus Questions

What rights do men enjoy in this passage that women do not? What are you able to conclude about the rights of married women who work?

Of the respective rights and duties of parent and children

212. Husband and wife owe each other fidelity, support, and assistance.

213. A husband owes protection to his wife; a wife owes obedience to her husband.

214. A wife is bound to live with her husband and to follow him wherever he deems proper to reside. The husband is bound to receive her, and to supply her with whatever is necessary for the wants of life, according to his means and condition.

215. A wife cannot sue in court without the consent of her husband, even if she is a public tradeswoman or if there is no community or she is separated as to property.

216. The husband's consent is not necessary when the wife is prosecuted criminally or in a police matter.

217. A wife, even when there is no community, or when she is separated as to property, cannot give, convey, mortgage, or acquire property, with or without consideration, without the husband joining in the instrument or giving his written consent.

218. If a husband refuses to allow his wife to sue in court, the Judge may grant the authorization.

219. If a husband refuses to allow his wife to execute an instrument, the wife can cause her husband to be summoned directly before the Tribunal of the First Instance of the common domicile, and such Tribunal shall grant or refuse its consent in the Judges' room after the husband has been heard or has been duly summoned.

220. A wife may, if she is a public tradeswoman, bind herself without the husband's consent with respect to what relates to her trade, and in that case she also binds her husband if there is a community of property between them. She is not considered a public tradeswoman if she merely retails the goods of her husband's business, but only when she has a separate business.

221. When a sentence has been passed upon a husband which carries with it a degrading corporal punishment, even if it has been passed by default, a wife, even of full age, cannot, during the continuance of the punishment, sue in court nor bind herself, unless she has been authorized by the Judge, who may in such cases grant the consent without the husband having been heard or summoned.

222. If a husband has been interdicted or is absent, the Judge may with proper knowledge of the case, authorize the wife to sue in court or to bind herself.

223. Any general authorization, even given by marriage contract, is only valid as to the management of the wife's property.

224. If the husband is a minor, the authorization of the Judge is necessary to the wife, either to sue in court or to bind herself.

225. A nullity based on the want of authorization can only be set up by the wife, the husband, or the heirs.

226. A wife can make a will without her husband's consent.

endured. In place of the popular democratic movement, he offered his own singular authority. In place of elections, clubs, and free associations, he gave France plebiscites and army service. To be sure, Napoleon believed in constitutions, but he thought they should be "short and obscure." For Napoleon, the great problem of democracy was its unpredictability. His regime solved that problem by eliminating choices.

Decline and Fall

Militarily, Napoleon went too far. The first cracks in the French facade began to show in the Peninsular War (1808–1814) with Spain, as Spanish guerrilla tactics proved costly for French troops. But Napoleon's biggest mistake occurred when he decided to invade Russia in June 1812.

The Invasion of Russia and the Battle of Nations.
Having decisively defeated Russian forces in 1807, Napoleon entered into a peace treaty with Tsar Alexander I that guaranteed Russian allegiance to French policies. But Alexander repudiated the Continental System in 1810 and appeared to be preparing for his own war against France. Napoleon seized the initiative, sure that he could defeat Russian forces once again. With an army of 500,000 men, Napoleon moved deep into Russia in the summer of 1812. The tsar's troops fell back in retreat, and when Napoleon and his men entered Moscow in September, they found a city in flames. The people of Moscow had destroyed their own city to deprive the French troops of winter quarters. Napoleon's men found themselves facing a severe Russian winter without overcoats, without supplies, and without food. The starving and frostbitten French army

was forced into retreat. Fewer than 100,000 men made it back to France.

The empire began to crumble. Britain, unbowed by the Continental System, remained Napoleon's sworn enemy. Prussia joined Great Britain, Sweden, Russia, and Austria in opposing France anew. In the Battle of Nations at Leipzig in October 1813, France was forced to retreat. Napoleon refused a negotiated peace and fought on until the following March, when the victorious allies marched down the streets of Paris and occupied the French capital. Deserted by his allies, Napoleon abdicated in April 1814 in favor of his young son, the titular king of Rome (1811–1832). When the allies refused to accept the young "Napoleon II," the French called on the Bourbon Louis XVIII and crowned him king. Napoleon was then exiled to the Mediterranean island of Elba.

Napoleon's Final Defeat: Waterloo.
Still, it was not quite the end for Napoleon. While the European heads of state sat in Vienna trying to determine the future of Europe and France's place in it, Napoleon returned from his exile on Elba. On 15 June 1815, Napoleon once again confronted the European powers in one of the most famous battles in history: Waterloo. With 125,000 loyal French forces, Napoleon seemed within hours of reestablishing the French empire in Europe, but the defeat of his forces was decisive. Napoleon's return proved brief, lasting only 100 days. He was exiled to the island of Saint Helena in the South Atlantic. For the next six years, Napoleon wrote his memoirs under the watchful eyes of his British jailors. He died a painful death on 5 May 1821 from what today is believed to have been cancer.

■ This 1835 painting by De Boisdenier depicts the suffering of Napoleon's Grand Army on the retreat from Moscow. The Germans were to meet a similar fate more than 100 years later when they invaded Russia without adequate supplies for the harsh winter.

CONCLUSION

The period of revolution and empire from 1789 to 1815 radically changed the face of France. A new, more cohesive elite of bourgeois and nobles emerged, sharing power based on wealth and status. Ownership of land remained a defining characteristic of both old and new elites. A new state bureaucracy, built on the foundations of the old, expanded and centralized state power.

The people as sovereign now legitimated political power. Napoleon at his most imperial never doubted that he owed his existence to the people. He channeled democratic forces into enthusiasm for empire. He learned his lessons from the failure of the Bourbon monarchy and the politicians of the revolution. For 16 years, Napoleon successfully reconciled the Old Regime with the new France. Yet he could not resolve the essential problem of democracy: the relationship between the will of the people and the exercise of political power. The picture in 1815 was not dramatically different from the situation in 1789. The revolution might be over, but changes fueled by the revolutionary tradition were just beginning. The struggle for a workable democratic culture recurred in France for another century and elsewhere in Europe through the twentieth century.

QUESTIONS FOR REVIEW

1. To what extent was the French nobility responsible for the crisis that destroyed the Old Regime?
2. How did commoners, men and women, transform a crisis of government into a revolution?
3. Why did the leaders of the revolution resort to a "reign of terror" and what effect did that have on the revolution?
4. What problems in France and beyond contributed to the rise of Napoleon?
5. What did Napoleon accomplish in France, and what brought about his fall?

KEY TERMS

cahiers de doléances, p. 403

conscription, p. 412

Continental System, p. 414

Estates-General, p. 402

Girondins, p. 410

Jacobins, p. 410

Napoleonic Code, p. 414

Old Regime, p. 402

Reign of Terror, p. 410

sans-culottes, p. 410

Thermidorian Reaction, p. 411

Third Estate, p. 402

DISCOVERING WESTERN CIVILIZATION ONLINE

You can obtain more information about the French Revolution and the Napoleonic Era at the websites listed below. See also the Companion Website that accompanies this text, www.ablongman.com/kishlansky, which contains an online study guide and additional resources.

The French Revolution and the Fall of the Monarchy

Creating French Culture

www.loc.gov/exhibits/bnf/bnf0001.html
Different aspects of French culture as a form of elite power from Charlemagne to Charles de Gaulle are presented by the Library of Congress. Most of the material is from the collections of the Bibliothèque Nationale de France.

Liberty, Equality, Fraternity: Explaining the French Revolution

Chnm.gmu.edu/revolution/
This site contains an extraordinary archive of key images, maps, songs, timelines, and texts from the French Revolution. The site is authored by Professors Lynn Hunt and Jack Censer, leading scholars in the field of French revolutionary history.

Chateau de Versailles

www.chateauversailles.fr/en/
Devoted to the history and images of Versailles, this site provides brief essays about the people and events significant to court culture during the seventeenth and eighteenth centuries. It also explores the role of Versailles in French culture after the French Revolution.

Experimenting with Democracy, 1789–1792

St. Just

history.hanover.edu/texts/stjust.html
Texts by St. Just, a close colleague of Robespierre and a member of the Committee of Public Safety, which orchestrated the Reign of Terror.

Modern History Sourcebook: Robespierre: The Supreme Being

www.fordham.edu/halsall/mod/robespierre-supreme.html

This site contains Robespierre's words on The Cult of the Supreme Being and links to other sites.

The Reign of Napoleon, 1799–1815

Internet Modern History Sourcebook: French Revolution

www.fordham.edu/halsall/mod/modsbook13.html

This site will direct students to the Modern History Sourcebook section of documents on the French Revolution, Napoleon, and the Napoleonic Wars.

Napoleon

www.napoleon.org/en/home.asp

Sponsored by the Foundation Napoleon for "the furtherance of study and research into the civil and military achievements of the First and Second Empires," this site is aimed at a nonacademic audience providing chronologies, essays, images and videos, and links to other sites on Napoleon.

SUGGESTIONS FOR FURTHER READING

The French Revolution and the Fall of the Monarchy

Keith Michael Baker, *Inventing the French Revolution* (Cambridge: Cambridge University Press, 1992). The author views the French Revolution as a basically political event that can only be understood in the context of the changing political culture of the eighteenth century, with special attention to the use of language and the role of public opinion as a political invention.

Roger Chartier, *The Cultural Origins of the French Revolution,* tr. Lydia G. Cochrane (Durham, NC: Duke University Press, 1991). Argues for the importance of the rise of critical modes of thinking in the public sphere in the eighteenth century and of long-term de-Christianization in shaping the desire for change in French society and politics.

William Doyle, *Origins of the French Revolution* (Oxford: Oxford University Press, 1988). An excellent introduction devoted to the historiography of the revolution since 1939, followed by an analysis of the breakdown of the Old Regime and the struggle for power.

François Furet and Denis Richet, *The French Revolution* (New York: Macmillan, 1970). Two experts on the French Revolution present a detailed overview of the period from 1789 to 1798.

Georges Lefebvre, *The Great Fear of 1789* (New York: Pantheon Books, 1973). This classic study analyzes the rural panic that swept through parts of France in the summer of 1789 as a distinct episode in the opening months of the revolution with its own internal logic.

Colin Lucas, ed., *Rewriting the French Revolution* (Oxford: Clarendon Press, 1991). Eight scholars present interpretations in the areas of social development, ideas, politics, and religion.

Daniel Roche, *The People of Paris* (Berkeley: University of California Press, 1987). An essay on popular culture in the eighteenth century in which the author surveys the lives of the Parisian popular classes—servants, laborers, and artisans—and examines their housing, furnishings, dress, and leisure activities.

D. M. G. Sutherland, *France, 1789–1815: Revolution and Counter-Revolution* (New York: Oxford University Press, 1986). An interpretation of the revolutionary period that stresses the struggle against counterrevolution and presents the revolution as a complex and contradictory process of social and political conflict over incompatible rights and privileges enjoyed by significant portions of the population.

Timothy Tackett, *Becoming a Revolutionary: The Deputies of the French National Assembly and the Emergence of a Revolutionary Culture* (Princeton: Princeton University Press, 1996). This collective biography of the cohort of deputies to the National Assembly demonstrates that their practical experience was distinct from that of the nobility.

Michel Vovelle, *The Fall of the French Monarchy* (Cambridge: Cambridge University Press, 1984). A social history of the origins and early years of the revolution, beginning with a brief examination of the Old Regime and paying special attention to social and economic changes initiated by the revolution, the role of the popular classes, and the creation of revolutionary culture.

Experimenting with Democracy, 1792–1799

Jack Censer and Lynn Hunt, *Liberty, Equality, Fraternity: Exploring the French Revolution* (University Park: Pennsylvania State University Press, 2001). This book is accompanied by a CD-ROM and provides a unique multimedia introduction to the French Revolution.

François Furet, *Interpreting the French Revolution* (Cambridge: Cambridge University Press, 1981). A series of essays challenging many of the assumptions about the causes and outcome of the revolution and reviewing its historiography.

Dominique Godineau, *The Women of Paris and Their French Revolution* (Berkeley: University of California Press, 1998). A compelling account on the lives of women revolutionaries. Godineau presents women's protests as a mass movement within the revolution.

Patrice Higonnet, *Goodness Beyond Virtue: Jacobins During the French Revolution* (Cambridge: Harvard University Press, 1998). The author considers the Jacobin politics as a model for modern democrats, not to be reduced to the tragedy of the Terror.

Michael L. Kennedy, *The Jacobin Clubs in the French Revolution, 1793–1795* (New York: Berghahn Books, 2000). The final volume of Kennedy's three-volume history of the Jacobin Club focusing on the period between May 1793 and August 1795.

Sara E. Melzer and Leslie Rabine, eds., *Rebel Daughters: Women and the French Revolution* (New York: Oxford University Press, 1992). Contributors from a variety of disciplines examine the importance of women in the French Revolution, with special attention to the exclusion of women from the new politics.

Albert Soboul, *The Sans-Culottes* (New York: Anchor, 1972). A study of the artisans who composed the core of popular political activism in revolutionary Paris.

The Reign of Napoleon, 1799–1815

Louis Bergeron, *France Under Napoleon* (Princeton, NJ: Princeton University Press, 1981). An analysis of the structure of Napoleon's regime, its social bases of support, and its opponents.

Jean Tulard, *Napoleon: The Myth of the Saviour* (London: Weidenfeld and Nicolson, 1984). In this biography of Napoleon, the Napoleonic Empire is presented as a creation of the bourgeoisie, who desired to end the revolution and consolidate their gains and control over the lower classes.

Isser Woloch, *Napoleon and His Collaborators: The Making of a Dictatorship* (New York: Norton, 2001). Woloch explains the success of Napoleon's regime in terms of the support of his civilian collaborators.

Isser Woloch, *The New Regime: Transformations of the French Civic Order* (New York: Norton, 1994). Woloch's study emphasizes the break of the new regime from the old, placing the institutions created or revamped after 1789 in the context of a new civic order and citizenship.

For a list of additional titles related to this chapter's topics, please see www.ablongman.com/kishlansky.

21

INDUSTRIAL EUROPE

The Visual Record

AN IRON FORGE

The key to **industrialization** was the replacement of muscle with machine. This demanded ingenuity on the part of inventors, capital on the part of investors, and adaptability on the part of workers. Whether in the cotton mills, where water-powered jennies allowed one worker to spin more than 100 had before, or in the pits, where engines allowed water to be drained and miners to dig deeper, machinery changed the nature of production and productivity. Technological innovation transformed the nature of work in Britain.

Although we think of industry in terms of factories, labor forces, and mass output, early industry developed within the context of individual producers. Families worked in cottages to spin and weave, iron was refined and shaped by the village smith. The initial stages of the Industrial Revolution involved changing the ways in which these small producers worked. Joseph Wright's depiction of *An Iron Forge* is a case in point, a family portrait that almost resembles a nativity scene except that the birth being celebrated is the machine forging of iron, the miracle product of the age.

Joseph Wright of Derby was born and bred in the English Midlands where the Industrial Revolution first began. He was fascinated by the scientific developments of his age and specialized in paintings that were technically accurate. *An Iron Forge* was one of a number of industrial scenes that Wright painted in the 1770s when advances in technology were changing the face of rural life. The small shop must have once been that of an ordinary blacksmith, but now it has been transformed into a forge. Outside of the picture a giant water wheel turns a rod that is attached to the drum in the bottom left-hand corner of the painting. The drum turns a shaft which lifts the heavy tilting hammer until it strikes the wooden beam above it. The hammer then falls with the force of its weight to strike the bar of iron that is held in place on the anvil by the iron forger's assistant. No human could swing so heavy a hammer or shape so large a bar of iron so easily. Every detail is precise, in imitation of the mechanical process. For example, the anvil sits in a pan filled with wooden chips which act as a cushion to absorb the shock of the hammer blows. The tiled floor and bricked walls absorb the flying sparks as the red-hot metal is molded into bars.

While the machinery is drawn precisely and the technology of the forge is represented accurately, it is the artist's imagination that creates the scene. Though the iron forger who gazes proudly upon his family is portrayed with huge, muscular arms and a powerful torso, he is not engaged in toil. He represents enlightened industry, able to stand above the backbreaking work that had previously been associated with smithing. Indeed, of the three workmen in the picture, only one is actually laboring and he is simply holding the tongs which keeps the iron in

place. It is the machine that labors—the drum turning, the cam lifting, the hammer falling—and the people who benefit—proud parents, healthy and happy children. All are the product, the artist seems to be saying, of the new industrialization.

Looking Ahead

As this chapter will discuss, industrialization began in Great Britain around forges like the one portrayed by Joseph Wright. It was the result of changes in agricultural practices that allowed for a larger population to be supported by fewer farmers. It was powered first by coal and its use in the production of iron and then by steam, which allowed for powerful engines to mechanize production. The steam engine also allowed for a revolution in transportation with the development of the railroads. Industrialization transformed every aspect of the British economy and soon spread throughout Europe. ➤

THE TRADITIONAL ECONOMY

For generation after generation, age after age, economic life was dominated by toil. Every activity was labor-intensive. Wood was chopped with an axe. Water was drawn from wells or dragged in buckets from the nearest stream. Everything that was consumed was pulled or pushed or lifted, and by the middle of the eighteenth century, nearly eight out of ten Europeans still tilled the soil.

Although the traditional economy was dominated by agriculture, an increasing amount of labor was devoted to manufacture. The development of a secure and expanding overseas trade created a worldwide demand for consumer goods. In the countryside, small domestic textile industries grew up. Families would take in wool for spinning and weaving to supplement their income from agriculture. When times were good, they would expend proportionately less effort in manufacturing; when times were bad, they would expend more. Their tasks were set by an entrepreneur who provided raw materials and paid the workers by the piece. Wages paid to rural workers were lower than those paid to urban laborers because rural workers' wages were not subject to guild restrictions and because they supplemented farm income. Though domestic industry increased the supply of manufactures, it demanded even more labor from an already overworked sector of the traditional economy.

By the eighteenth century, the process that would ultimately transform the traditional economy was already under way. It began with the **agricultural revolution** (discussed below), one of the great turning points in human history. Before it occurred, the life of every community and of every citizen was always a hostage of nature. The struggle to secure an adequate food supply was the dominant fact of life to which nearly all productive labor was dedicated. After the agricultural revolution, an inadequate food supply was a political rather than an economic fact of life. Fewer and fewer farmers were required to feed more and more people. In Britain, where nearly 70 percent of the population was engaged in agriculture at the end of the seventeenth century, less than 2 percent worked on farms at the end of the twentieth century. By the middle of the nineteenth century, the most advanced economies were capable of producing vast surpluses of basic commodities. The agricultural revolution was not an event, and it did not happen suddenly. It would not deserve the label "revolution" at all were it not for its momentous consequences: Europe's escape from the shackles of the traditional economy.

Rural Manufacture

By the end of the eighteenth century, the European population was reaching the point at which another check on its growth might be expected. Between 1700 and 1800, total European population had increased by nearly 50 percent, and the rate of growth was continuing to accelerate. This vast expansion of rural population placed a grave strain on agricultural production. Decade by decade, more families attempted to eke out an existence from the same amount of land. The gains made from intensive cultivation were now lost to overpopulation.

The crisis of overpopulation meant that not only were there more mouths to feed, there were more bodies to clothe. This increased the need for cloth and thus for spinners and weavers. Traditionally, commercial cloth production was the work of urban artisans, but the expansion of the marketplace and the introduction of new fabrics, especially cotton and silk, had eroded the monopoly of most of the clothing guilds. Merchants could sell as much finished product as they could find, and the teeming rural population provided a tempting pool of inexpensive labor for anyone who was willing to risk the capital to purchase raw materials. Initially, farming families took manufacturing work into their homes to supplement their income. Spinning and weaving were the most common occupations, and they were treated as occasional work, reserved for the slow times in the agricultural cycle. This was known as cottage industry. It was side-employment, less important and less valuable than the vital agricultural labor that all members of the family undertook.

But by the middle of the eighteenth century, cottage industry was developing in a new direction. As landholdings grew smaller, even good harvests did not promise subsistence to many families. This oversupply of labor was soon organized into the **putting-out system**, which mobilized the resources of the rural labor force for commercial production of large quantities of manufactured goods. The characteristics of the putting-out system were similar throughout Europe. The entrepreneur purchased raw materials, which were "put out" to the homes of workers, where the manufacture took place, most commonly spinning or weaving. The finished goods were returned to the entrepreneur, who sold them at a profit, with which he bought raw materials to begin the process anew.

Putting-out required only a low level of skill and inexpensive common tools. Rural families did their own spinning, and rural villages did their own weaving. Thus putting-out demanded little investment, in plant, equipment, or education. Nor did it inevitably disrupt traditional gender-based tasks in the family economy. Spinning was women's work, weaving was men's, and children helped at whichever task was under way.

As long as rural manufacture supplemented agricultural income, it was seen as a benefit for everyone involved—the entrepreneur, the individual worker, and the village community. But gradually, the putting-out system came to dominate the lives of many rural families. Spinning and weaving became full-time occupations for families that kept no more than a small garden. But without agricultural earnings, piecework rates became starvation wages, and families who were unable to purchase their subsistence were forced to rely on loans from the entrepreneurs who set them at work. Long hours in dank cottages performing endlessly repetitive tasks became the lot of millions of rural inhabitants. And their numbers increased annually. Whereas the sons of farmers

The Traditional Economy 423

MAP DISCOVERY

Percentage increase

- Over 80
- 60 – 79
- 40 – 59
- 20 – 39
- Under 20

Population Growth in Europe, 1800–1850

Notice which parts of Europe experienced the largest growth in population in the first half of the nineteenth century. Compare the rate of population growth in Spain and Norway and Sweden. Which grew faster? In which parts of Europe did the population increase the most during this period? What impact would you expect such growth to have on the agricultural economy? On the rate of industrialization?

employ, there was little incentive to seek more efficient techniques.

The Agricultural Revolution

The continued growth of Europe's population necessitated an expansion of agricultural output. In most places, this was achieved by intensifying traditional practices, bringing more land into production, and using more labor to work the land. But in the most advanced European economies, first in Holland and then in England, traditional agriculture underwent a long but dynamic transformation, an agricultural revolution. It was a revolution of technique rather than technology. Many of the methods that were to increase crop yields had been known for centuries but had never been practiced as systematically as they came to be from the seventeenth century onward and had never been combined with a commercial attitude toward farming. It was the owners' willingness and ability to invest capital in their land that transformed subsistence farming into commercial agriculture.

Enclosures. As long as farming was practiced in open fields, there was little incentive for individual landowners to invest in improvements to their scattered strips. Commercial agriculture was more suited to large estates than small ones and was more successful when the land could be utilized in response to market conditions rather than the necessities of subsistence. The consolidation of estates and the enclosure of fields were thus the initial steps in a long-term process of change.

In England, where enclosure was to become most advanced, it was already under way in the sixteenth century. Prosperous families had long been consolidating their strips in the open fields, and at some point, the lord of the manor and the members of the community agreed to carve up the common fields and make the necessary exchanges to consolidate everyone's

waited to inherit land before they formed their families, the sons of cottage weavers needed only a loom to begin theirs. They could afford to marry younger and to have more children, for children could contribute to manufacturing from an early age. Consequently, the expansion of the putting-out system contributed to overpopulation. The putting-out system was labor-intensive, and as long as there were ready hands to lands. Perhaps as much as three-quarters of the arable land in England was enclosed by agreement before 1760. Enclosure by agreement did not mean that the breakup of the open-field community was always a harmonious process. Riots before or after agreed enclosures were not uncommon. Poor farmers who had once enjoyed the right to use certain strips of land for cultivation and pasture often found themselves reduced to working as hired hands for larger landowners.

Opposition to enclosure by agreement led, in the eighteenth century, to enclosure by act of Parliament. Parliamentary enclosure was legislated by government, a government that was composed for the most part of large landowners. A commission would view the community's lands and divide them, usually by a prescribed formula. Between 1760 and 1815, more than 1.5 million acres of farmland were enclosed by act of Parliament. During the late eighteenth century, the Prussian and French governments emulated this practice by ordering large tracts of land enclosed.

The enclosure of millions of acres of land was one of the largest expenses of the new commercial agriculture. As hedging or fencing off the land and plowing up the commons proceeded, more and more agricultural activity become market-oriented. Single crops were sown in large enclosed fields and exchanged at market for the mixture of goods that had previously been grown in the village. Market production turned farmers' attention from producing a balance of commodities to increasing the yield of a single commodity.

Agricultural Innovations.   The first innovation was the widespread cultivation of fodder crops such as clover and turnips. Crops like clover restore nutrients to the soil as they grow, shortening the period in which land has to lie fallow. Moreover, farm animals grazing on clover or feeding on turnips return more manure to the land, further increasing its productivity. Turnip cultivation had begun in Holland and was brought to England in the sixteenth century. But it was not until the late seventeenth century that Viscount Charles "Turnip" Townshend (1675–1738) made turnip cultivation popular. Townshend and other large Norfolk landowners developed a new system of planting known as the four-course rotation, in which wheat, turnips, barley, and clover succeeded one another. This method kept the land in productive use, and both the turnip and clover crops were used to feed larger herds of animals.

The ability of farmers to increase their livestock was as important as their ability to grow more grain. Not only were horses and oxen more productive than humans—a horse could perform seven times the labor of a man while consuming only five times the food—but the animals also refertilized the land as they worked. Light fertilization of a single acre of arable land required an average of 25,000 pounds of manure. But animals competed with humans for food, especially during the winter months, when little grazing was possible. To conserve grain for human consumption, some livestock had to be slaughtered in the autumn. Therefore the development of the technique of meadow floating was a remarkable break-

through. By flooding low-lying land near streams in the winter, English and Dutch farmers could prevent the ground from freezing during their generally mild winters. When the water was drained, the land beneath it would produce an early grass crop on which the beasts could graze. This meant that more animals could be kept alive during the winter.

The relationship between animal husbandry and grain growing became another feature of commercial agriculture. In many areas, farmers could choose between growing grain and pasturing animals. When prices for wool or meat were relatively higher than those for grain, fields could be left in grass for grazing. When grain prices rose, the same fields could be plowed. Consolidated enclosed estates made this convertible husbandry possible. The decision to hire field workers or shepherds could be taken only by large agricultural employers.

Convertible husbandry was but the first step in the development of a true system of regional specialization in agriculture. Different soils and climates favored different uses of the land. In southern and eastern England, the soil was thin and easily depleted by grain growing. Traditionally, these light soil areas had been used almost exclusively for sheep rearing. On the other hand, the clay soils of central England, though poorly drained and hard to work, were more suited to growing grain. The new agricultural techniques reversed the pattern. The introduction of fodder crops and increased fertilization rejuvenated thin soils, and southeastern England became the nation's breadbasket. Large enclosed estates provided a surplus of grain throughout the eighteenth century. By the 1760s, England was exporting

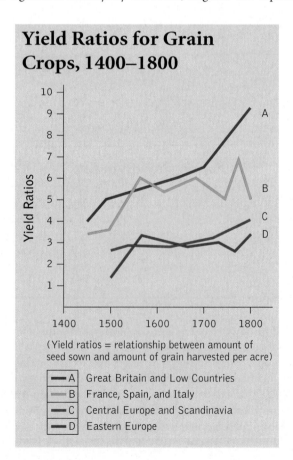

Yield Ratios for Grain Crops, 1400–1800

(Yield ratios = relationship between amount of seed sown and amount of grain harvested per acre)

A	Great Britain and Low Countries
B	France, Spain, and Italy
C	Central Europe and Scandinavia
D	Eastern Europe

enough grain to feed over half a million people. Similarly, the midland clays became the location of great sheep runs and cattle herds. Experiments in herd management, crossbreeding, and fattening all resulted in increased production of wool, milk, meat, leather, soap, and tallow for candles.

There can be no doubt about the benefits of the transformation of agricultural practices that began in Holland and England in the seventeenth century and spread slowly to all corners of the Continent over the next 200 years. Millions more mouths were fed at lower cost than ever before. In 1700, each person engaged in farming in England produced enough food for 1.7 people; in 1800, each produced enough for 2.5 people. Cheaper food allowed more discretionary spending, which fueled the demand for consumer goods, which in turn employed more rural manufacturers. But there are no benefits without costs. The transformation of agriculture was also a transformation in a way of life. The open-field village was a community; the enclosed estate was a business. The plight of the rural poor was tragic enough in villages of kin and neighbors, where face-to-face charity might be returned from one generation to the next. As landless laborers, however, the rural poor became fodder for the factories, the "dark satanic mills" that came to disfigure the land. For the destitute, charity was now bestowed on them in anonymous parish workhouses or by the good works of the comfortable middle class. In all of these ways the agricultural revolution changed the face of Europe.

THE INDUSTRIAL REVOLUTION IN BRITAIN

Like the changes in agriculture, the changes in manufacturing that began in Britain during the eighteenth century were more revolutionary in consequence than in development. A workforce that was predominantly agricultural in 1750 had become predominantly industrial a century later. A population that for centuries had centered on the south and east was now concentrated in the north and west. Liverpool, Manchester, Glasgow, and Birmingham mushroomed into giant cities. While the population of England grew by 100 percent between 1801 and 1851, from about 8.5 million to over 17 million, the populations of Liverpool and Manchester grew by over 1,000 percent.

It was the replacement of animal muscle by hydraulic and mineral energy that made this continued population growth possible. Water and coal drove machinery that dramatically increased human productivity. In 1812, one woman could spin as much thread as 200 women had in 1770. What was most revolutionary about the **Industrial Revolution** was the wave after wave of technological innovation and the hundreds of adjustments in technique that applied new ideas in one industry to another, that opened bottlenecks and solved problems.

The Industrial Revolution was a sustained period of economic growth and change brought about by the application of mineral energy and technological innovations to the process of manufacturing. It took place largely during the century between 1750 and 1850, though different industries moved at different paces and sustained economic growth continued in Britain until the First World War. It is difficult to define precisely the timing of the Industrial Revolution because, unlike a political event, an economic transformation does not happen all at once. Nor are new systems and inventions ever really new. Coal miners had been using rails and wheeled carriages to move ore since the seventeenth century; in the sixteenth century, "Jack of Newbury" had housed his cloth workers in a large shed. The one was the precursor of the railroad and the other was the precursor of the factory, but each preceded the Industrial Revolution by more than a century. Before 1750, innovations made their way slowly into general use, and after 1850 the pace of growth slowed appreciably. By then, Britain had a manufacturing economy, less than one-quarter of its labor force engaged in agriculture, and nearly 60 percent was involved in industry, trade, and transport.

Britain First

The Industrial Revolution occurred first in Britain, but even in Britain, industrialization was a regional phenomenon rather than a national one. Many areas of Britain remained untouched by innovations in manufacturing methods and agricultural techniques, though none remained unaffected by the prosperity that industrialization brought. This was the result of both national conditions and historical developments. When industrialization spread to the Continent, it took hold, as it had in Britain, in regions where mineral resources were abundant or where domestic manufacturing was a traditional activity. There was no single model for European industrialization, however often contemporaries looked toward Britain for the key to unlock the power of economic growth.

Water and Coal.   Among Britain's blessings, water was foremost. Britain was favored by an internal water system that tied inland communities together. In the eighteenth century, no place in Britain was more than 70 miles from the sea or more than 30 miles from a navigable river. Water transport was far cheaper than hauling goods overland; a packhorse could carry 250 pounds of goods on its back or move 100,000 pounds by walking alongside a river pulling a barge. Small wonder that river transport was one of the principal interests of merchants and traders. Beginning in the 1760s, private concerns began to invest in the construction of canals, first to move coal from inland locations to major arteries and then to connect the great rivers themselves. Over the next 50 years, several hundred miles of canals were built by authority of Navigation Acts, which allowed for the sale of shares to raise capital. In 1760, the Duke of Bridgewater (1736–1803) lived up to his name by completing the first great canal. Among the beneficiaries were the people of Manchester, where the price of coal was halved.

Coal was the second of Britain's natural blessings. Britain's reserves of wood, especially those near centers of population, were nearly depleted by the eighteenth century. Coal had been in use as a fuel for several centuries, it was abundant, and it was easily transported on water. The location of large coalfields along waterways was a vital condition of its early use. As canals and roadways improved, more inland coal was brought into production for domestic use. Yet it was in industry rather than in the home that coal was put to its greatest use. Here again, Britain was favored, for large seams of coal were also located near large seams of iron.

Economic Infrastructure. The factors that contributed to Britain's early industrialization were not only those of natural advantage. Over the course of years, Britain had developed an infrastructure for economic advancement. The transformation of domestic handicrafts to industrial production depended as much on the abilities of merchants as on those of manufacturers. The markets for domestic manufacturing had largely been overseas, where British merchants built up relationships over generations. Export markets were vital to the success of industrialization as production grew dynamically, and most ventures needed a quick turnaround of sales to reinvest their profits in continued growth. Equally important, increased production meant increased demand for raw materials: Swedish bar iron for casting, Egyptian and American cotton for textiles, Oriental silk for luxuries. The expansion of shipping mirrored the expansion of the economy, tripling during the eighteenth century to over one million tons of cargo capacity.

The expansion of shipping, agriculture, and investment in machines, plant, and raw material all required capital. Not only did capital have to exist, but it had to be made productive. Profits in agriculture, especially in the south and east, had somehow to be shifted to investment in industry in the north and west. The wealth of merchants, which flowed into London, had to be redistributed throughout the economy. Short-term investments had to give way to long-term financing. At the end of the seventeenth century, the creation of the Bank of England had begun the process of constructing a reliable banking system. The Bank of England dealt almost entirely with government securities, but it also served as a bill broker. It bought the debts of reputable merchants at a discount in exchange for Bank of England notes. Bank of England notes could then be exchanged between merchants, and this increased the liquidity of the English economy, especially in London. It also became the model for provincial banking by the middle of the eighteenth century. In 1700, there were just 12 provincial banks; by 1790, there were nearly 300.

Though the banking system was vital to large enterprises, in fact the capital for most industry was raised locally, from kin and neighbors, and it grew by plowing profits back into the business. At least at the beginning, manufacturers were willing to take risks and to work for small returns to ensure the survival and growth of their business.

Minerals and Metals

The Industrial Revolution could not have occurred without coal. It was the black gold of the eighteenth century, the fuel that fed the furnaces and turned the engines of industrial expansion. The coal produced by one miner generated as much energy as 20 horses. Coal mining was the first capital-intensive industry in Britain and was already well developed by the seventeenth century. Only the very wealthy could afford to invest in coal mining, and the largest English coalfields were owned by landed families of means who were able to invest agricultural profits in mining.

Early Coal Mining. The technical problems of coal mining grew with demand. As surface seams were exhausted it became necessary to dig deeper shafts, to lower miners farther underground, and to raise the coal greater heights to the surface. Underground mining was extremely dangerous, however, and in addition to frequent cave-ins, miners struggled against inadequate ventilation and light.

But by far the most difficult mining problem was water. As pits were sunk deeper, they reached pools of groundwater, which enlarged as the coal was stripped away from the earth. The pit acted like a riverbed and was quickly filled. Water drainage presented the greatest obstacle to deep-shaft mining. Women and children could carry the water out in large skin-lined baskets, which were attached to a winding wheel and pulled up by horses. Primitive pumps, also horse-powered, had been devised for the same purpose. Neither method was efficient or effective when shafts sank deeper. In 1709, Thomas Newcomen (1663–1729) introduced a steam-driven pump, which enabled water to be sucked through a pipe directly from the pit bottom to the surface. Though the engine was expensive to build and needed tons of coal to create the steam, it could raise the same amount of water in a day as 2,500 humans, and within 20 years of its introduction there were 78 engines draining coal and metal mines in England.

Innovations like Newcomen's engine helped to increase coal output at just the time that it became needed as an industrial fuel. Between 1700 and 1830, coal production increased tenfold, despite the fact that deeper and more difficult seams were being worked. Eventually, the largest demand for coal came from the iron industry. In 1793, just two ironworks consumed as much coal as the entire population of Edinburgh. Like coal mining, iron making was both capital- and labor-intensive, requiring expensive furnaces, water-powered bellows, and mills in which forged iron could be slit into rods or rolled into sheets. Iron making depended on an abundance of wood, for it took the charcoal derived from ten acres of trees to refine one ton of iron ore. Because each process in the making of iron was separate, furnaces, forges, and mills were located near their own supplies of wood. The shipping of the bulky ore, pig iron, and bar iron added substantially to its cost.

The great innovations in the production of iron came with the development of techniques that allowed for the use of coal rather than wood charcoal in smelting and forging. As early as 1709, Abraham Darby (ca. 1678–1717), a Quaker nail maker, experimented with smelting iron ore with coke, coal from which most of the gas has been burned off. Iron coking greatly reduced the cost of fuel in the first stages of production, but because most ironworks were located in woodlands

■ Women and children often labored in horrible conditions that were cramped, lacked fresh air, and offered little sunlight.

rather than near coal pits, the method was not widely adopted. Moreover, although coke made from coal was cheaper than charcoal made from wood, coke added its own impurities to the iron ore. Nor could it provide the intense heat needed for smelting without a large bellows. The cost of the bellows offset the savings from the coke until James Watt (1736–1819) invented a new form of steam engine in 1775.

The Steam Engine.   Like most innovations of the Industrial Revolution, James Watt's steam engine was an adaptation of existing technology. Although Watt is credited with the invention of the condensing steam engine, one of the seminal creations in human history, the success of his work depended on the achievements of numerous other people. An instrument maker in Glasgow, Watt was asked to repair a model of a Newcomen engine and immediately realized that it would work more efficiently if there were a separate chamber for the condensation of the steam. Though his idea was sound, Watt spent years attempting to implement it. He did not succeed until he became partners with the Birmingham iron maker and manufacturer Matthew Boulton (1728–1809). At Boulton's works, Watt found craft workers who could make precision engine valves, and at the foundries of John Wilkinson (1728–1808) he found workers who could bore the cylinders of his engine to exact specifications. Watt later designed the mechanism to convert the traditional up-and-down motion of the pumping engine into rotary motion, which could be used for machines and ultimately for locomotion.

Watt's engine received its first practical application in the iron industry. Wilkinson became one of the largest customers for steam engines, using them for pumping, moving wheels, and ultimately increasing the power of the blast of air in the forge. Increasing the heat provided by coke in the smelting and forging of iron led to the transformation of the industry. In the 1780s, Henry Cort (1740–1800), a naval contractor, experimented with a technique for using coke as fuel in removing the impurities from pig iron. The iron was melted into puddles and stirred with rods. The gaseous carbon that was brought to the surface burned off, leaving a purer and more malleable iron than even charcoal could produce. Because the

iron had been purified in a molten state, Cort reasoned, it could be rolled directly into sheets rather than first being made into bars. He erected a rolling mill adjacent to his forge and combined two separate processes into one.

Puddling and rolling had an immediate impact on iron production. Charcoal was no longer needed. From mineral to workable sheets, iron could be made entirely with coke, so ironworks moved to the coalfields. Forges, furnaces, and rolling machines were brought together and powered by steam engines. By 1808, output of pig iron had grown from 68,000 to 250,000 tons and that of bar iron from 32,000 to 100,000 tons.

Cotton Is King

Traditionally, British commerce was dominated by the woolen cloth trade, in which techniques of production had not changed for hundreds of years. During the course of the seventeenth century, new fabrics appeared on the domestic market, particularly linen, silk, and cotton. It was cotton that captured the imagination of the eighteenth-century consumer, especially brightly colored, finely spun Indian cotton.

Domestic Industries.   Spinning and weaving were organized as domestic industries. Work was done in the home on small, inexpensive machines to supplement the income from farming. Even the widespread development of full-time domestic manufacturers did not satisfy the increased demand for cloth. Limited output and variable quality characterized British textile production throughout the early part of the eighteenth century. The breakthrough came with technological innovation. Beginning in the mid-eighteenth century, a series of new machines dramatically increased output and, for the first time, allowed English textiles to compete with Indian imports.

The first innovation was the flying shuttle, invented by John Kay (1704–1764) in the 1730s. A series of hammers drove the shuttle, which held the weft, through the stretched warp on the loom. The flying shuttle allowed weavers to work alone rather than in pairs, but it was adopted slowly, for it increased the demand for spun thread, which was already in short supply. The

■ In the eighteenth century, a number of British inventors patented new machines that transformed the British textile industry and marked the beginning of the Industrial Revolution. Among the inventions was the spinning jenny, invented by James Hargreaves in 1764, and named for his daughter. The jenny, which permitted the spinning of a number of threads at the same time, made possible the automatic production of cotton thread.

spinning bottleneck was opened by James Hargreaves (d. 1778), who devised a machine known as the jenny. The jenny was a wooden frame containing a number of spindles around which thread was drawn by means of a hand-turned wheel. The first jennies allowed for the spinning of eight threads at once, and improvements brought the number to more than 100. Jennies replaced spinning wheels by the tens of thousands. The jenny was a crucial breakthrough in redressing the balance between spinning and weaving, though it did not solve all problems. Jenny-spun thread was not strong enough to be used as warp, which continued to be wheel spun.

The need to provide stronger warp threads was ultimately solved by the development of the water frame. It was created in 1769 by Richard Arkwright (1732–1792), whose name was also to be associated with the founding of the modern factory system. Arkwright's frame consisted of a series of water-power-driven rollers, which stretched the cotton before spinning. These stronger fibers could be spun into threads that were suitable for warp, and English manufacturers could finally produce an all-cotton fabric. It was not long before another innovator realized that the water frame and the jenny could be combined into a single machine, one that would produce an even finer cotton yarn than that made in India. The mule, so named because it was a cross between a frame and a jenny, was invented by Samuel Crompton (1753–1827).

It was the decisive innovation in cotton cloth production. By 1811, ten times as many threads were being spun on mules as on water frames and jennies combined.

The original mules were small machines that could be used for domestic manufactures. But increasingly, the mule followed the water frame into purposely built factories, where it became larger and more expensive. The need for large rooms to house the equipment and the need for a ready source of running water to power it provided an incentive for the creation of factories where manufacturers could maintain control over the quality of products through strict supervision of the workforce.

Cotton Factories.   Richard Arkwright constructed the first cotton factories in Britain, all of which were designed to house water frames. The organization of the cotton industry into factories was one of the pivotal transformations in economic life. Domestic spinning and weaving took place in agricultural villages; factory production took place in mill towns. The location of the factory determined population movements, and from the first quarter of the eighteenth century onward, a great shift toward the northeast of England took place. Moreover, the character of the work itself changed. The operation of heavy machinery reversed the traditional gender-based tasks. Mule spinning became men's work; hand-loom weaving was taken over by women. The mechanization of weaving took longer than that of spinning because of difficulties in perfecting a power loom and because of opposition to its introduction by workers known as Luddites, who organized machine-breaking riots in the 1810s. The Luddites attempted to maintain the traditional organization of their industry and the independence of their labor. For a time, hand-loom weavers managed to survive by accepting lower and lower piece rates. But their competition was like that of a horse against an automobile. In 1820, there were over 250,000 hand-loom weavers in Britain; by 1850, the number was fewer than 50,000. Weaving as well as spinning became factory work.

The transformation of cotton manufacture had a profound effect on the overall growth of the British economy. It increased shipping because the raw material had to be imported, first from the Mediterranean and then from America. American cotton, especially after 1794, when American inventor Eli Whitney (1765–1825) patented his cotton gin, fed a nearly insatiable demand. In 1750, Britain imported less than five million pounds of raw cotton; a century later, the volume had grown to 588 million pounds. And to each pound of raw cotton, British manufacturers added the value of their technology and of their labor. By the mid-nineteenth century, nearly half a million people earned their living from cotton, which alone accounted for over 40 percent of the value of all British exports. Cotton was undeniably the king of manufactured goods.

The Iron Horse

The first stage of the Industrial Revolution in Britain was driven by the production of consumer goods. Pottery, cast-iron tools, clocks, toys, and textiles, especially cottons, were all manufactured in quantities that had been unknown in the early eighteenth century. These products fed a ravenous market at home and abroad. The greatest complaint of industrialists was that they could not get enough raw materials or fuel, nor could they ship their finished products fast enough to keep up with demand. Transportation was becoming a serious stumbling block to continued economic growth. Even with the completion of the canal network that linked the major rivers and improvement in highways and tollways, raw materials and finished goods moved slowly.

It was the need to ship increasing amounts of coal to foundries and factories that provided the spur for the development of railways. Ever since the seventeenth century, coal had been moved from the seam to the pit on rails, constructed first of wood and later of iron. Broad-wheeled carts pulled by horses ultimately ran from the seam to the dock. By 1800, there were perhaps 300 miles of iron rail in British mines. In the same year, Watt's patent on the steam engine expired, and inventors began to apply the engine to a variety of mechanical tasks.

Richard Trevithick (1771–1833) was the first to experiment with a steam-driven carriage. George Stephenson (1781–1848), who is generally recognized as the father of the modern railroad, made a vital improvement in engine power by increasing the steam pressure in the boiler and exhausting the smoke through a chimney. In 1829, he won a £500 prize with his engine "the Rocket," which pulled a load three times its own weight at a speed of 30 miles per hour and could actually outrun a horse.

The First Railways. In 1830, the first modern railway, the Manchester-to-Liverpool line, was opened. Like the Duke of Bridgewater's canal, it was designed to move coal and bulk goods, but surprisingly, its most important function came to be moving people. In its first year, the Manchester-Liverpool line carried over 400,000 passengers, who generated double the revenue derived from freight. Investors in the Manchester-Liverpool line, who pocketed a comfortable 9.5 percent when government securities were paying 3.5 percent, learned quickly that links between population centers were as important as those between industrial sites. The London-Birmingham and London-Bristol lines were both designed with passenger traffic in mind. Railway building was one of the great boom activities of British industrialization. By 1835, Parliament had passed 54 separate acts establishing over 750 miles of railways. By 1852, over 7,500 miles of track were in use.

From Goods to Passengers. By the 1850s, coal was the dominant cargo shipped by rail, and the speedy, efficient service continued to drive prices down. The iron and steel industries were modernized on the back of demand for rails, engines, and cast-iron seats and fittings. In peak periods—and railway building was a boom-and-bust affair—as much as one-quarter of the output of the rolling mills went into domestic railroads, and much more went into continental systems. The railways also consumed massive amounts of bricks for beddings, sidings, and especially bridges, tunnels, and stations. Finally, the railways were a leading employer of labor, surpassing the textile mills in peak periods.

Most of all, the railroads changed the nature of people's lives. Whole new concepts of time, space, and speed emerged to govern daily activities. The cheap railway excursion was born to provide short holidays or even daily returns. Over six million people visited London by train to view the **Crystal Palace Exhibition** in 1851, a number equivalent to one-third of the population of England and Wales. By speeding all forms of communication, the railways brought people together and helped to develop a sense of national identity.

Entrepreneurs and Managers

The Industrial Revolution in Britain was not simply invented. Too much credit is given to a few breakthroughs, and too little is given to the ways in which they were improved and dispersed. The Industrial Revolution was an age of gadgets when people believed that new was better than old and that there was always room for improvement. "The age is running mad after innovation," the English moralist Dr. Johnson wrote. "All the business of the world is done in a new way; men are hanged in a new way." Societies for the advancement of knowledge sprang up all over Britain. Journals and magazines

■ Honoré Daumier (1808–1879), *The Third-Class Carriage.* Daumier captured a human condition
peculiar to the modern era: "the lonely crowd."

promoted new ideas and techniques. Competitions were held
for the best invention of the year, and prizes were awarded for
agricultural achievements. Practical science rather than pure
science was the hallmark of industrial development.

Yet technological innovation was not the same as industrialization. A vital change in economic activity took place in the organization of industry. Putters-out, with their circulating capital
and hired laborers, could never make the economies necessary
to increase output and quality while simultaneously lowering
costs. This was the achievement of industrialists, producers who
owned workplace, machinery, and raw materials and who invested fixed capital by plowing back their profits. Industrial enterprises came in all sizes and shapes. As late as 1840, fewer than
10 percent of the cotton mills employed more than 500 workers.
Most were family concerns with under 100 employees, and
many of them failed. There were over 30,000 bankruptcies in the
eighteenth century, testimony both to the risks of business and
the willingness of entrepreneurs to take them.

To survive against these odds, successful industrialists had
to be both entrepreneurs and managers. As entrepreneurs

they raised capital, almost always locally from relatives,
friends, or members of their church. Quakers were especially
active in financing each other's enterprises. The industrial entrepreneur also had to understand the latest methods for
building and powering machinery and the most up-to-date
techniques for performing the work. One early manufacturer
claimed "a practical knowledge of every process from the cot-
ton-bag to the piece of cloth." Finally, entrepreneurs had to
know how to market their goods. In these functions, industrial entrepreneurs developed logically from putters-out.

But industrialists also had to be managers. The most difficult
task was organization of the workplace. Most gains in productivity were achieved through the specialization of function. The
processes of production were divided and subdivided until
workers performed a basic task over and over. The education of
the workforce was the industrial manager's greatest challenge.
Workers had to be taught how to use and maintain their machines and disciplined to apply themselves continuously. At least
at the beginning, it was difficult to staff the factories. Many employed children as young as the age of seven from workhouses

or orphanages, who, though cheap to pay, were difficult to train and discipline. It was the manager's task to break old habits of intermittent work, indifference to quality, and petty theft of materials. Families were preferred to individuals, for then parents could instruct and supervise their children. There is no reason to believe that industrial managers were more brutal masters than were farmers or that children were treated better in workhouses than in mills. Labor was a business asset, what was sometimes called "living machinery," and its control with carrots and sticks was the industrial manager's chief concern.

Who were the industrialists who transformed the traditional economy? Because British society was relatively open, they came from every conceivable background: dukes and orphans, merchants and salespeople, inventors and improvers. Though some went from rags to riches, like Richard Arkwright, who was the thirteenth child of a poor barber, it was extremely difficult for a laborer to acquire the capital necessary to set up a business. Wealthy landowners were prominent in capital-intensive aspects of industries, for example owning ironworks and mines, but few established factories. Most industrialists came from the middle classes, which comprised only one-third of the British population but provided as many as two-thirds of the first generation of industrialists. These included lawyers, bankers, merchants, and people who were already engaged in manufacturing, as well as tradespeople, shopkeepers, and self-employed craft workers. The career of every industrialist was unique, as a look at two—Josiah Wedgwood and Robert Owen—will show.

Josiah Wedgwood. Josiah Wedgwood (1730–1795) was the thirteenth child of a long-established English potting family. He worked in the potteries from childhood, but a deformed leg made it difficult for him to turn the wheel. Instead, he studied the structure of the business. His head teemed with ideas for improving ceramic manufacturing, but it was not until he was 30 that he could set up on his own and introduce his innovations. These encompassed both technique and organization, the entrepreneurial and managerial sides of his business.

Wedgwood developed new mixtures of clays that took brilliant colors in the kiln and new glazes for both "useful" and "ornamental" ware. He was repelled by the disorder of the traditional pottery, with its waste of materials, uneven quality, and slow output. When he began his first works, he divided the making of pottery into distinct tasks and separated his workers among them. He invested in schools to help train young artists, in canals to transport his products, and in London shops to sell them. Wedgwood was a marketing genius. He named his famed cream-colored pottery Queen's ware and made special coffee and tea services for leading aristocratic families. He would then sell replicas by the thousands. In less than 20 years, Wedgwood pottery was prized all over Europe, and Wedgwood's potting works were the standard of the industry.

Robert Owen. Robert Owen (1771–1858), the son of a small tradesman, was apprenticed to a clothier at the age of

10. As a teenager he worked as a shop assistant in Manchester, where he audaciously applied for a job as manager of a cotton mill. At 19, he was supervising 500 workers and learning the cotton trade. Owen was immediately successful, increasing his workers' output and introducing new materials to the mill. In 1816, he entered a partnership to purchase the New Lanark mill in Scotland.

Owen found conditions in Scotland much worse than those in Manchester. Over 500 workhouse children were employed at New Lanark, where drunkenness and theft were endemic. Owen believed that to improve the quality of work, one had to improve the quality of the workplace. He replaced old machinery with new, reduced working hours, and instituted a monitoring system to check theft. To enhance life outside the factory, he established a high-quality company-run store, which plowed its profits into a school for village children.

Owen was struck by the irony that in the mills, machines were better cared for than humans. He thought that with the same attention to detail that had so improved the quality of commodities, he could make even greater improvements in the quality of life. He prohibited children under the age of 10 from mill work and instituted a ten-hour day for child labor. His local school took infants from one year old, freeing women to work and ensuring each child an education. Owen instituted old-age and disability pensions, funded by mandatory contributions from workers' wages. Taverns were closed, and workers were fined for drunkenness and sexual offenses. In the factory and the village, Owen established a principle of communal regulation to improve both the work and the character of his employees. New Lanark became the model of the world of the future, and each year, thousands of people made an industrial pilgrimage to visit it.

The Wages of Progress

Robert Owen ended his life as a social reformer. His efforts to improve the lot of his workers at New Lanark led to experiments to create ideal industrial communities throughout the world. He founded cooperative societies, in which all members shared in the profits of the business, and supported trade unions in which workers could better their lives. His followers planted colonies in which goods were held in common and the fruits of labor belonged to the laborers. Owen's agitation for social reform was part of a movement that produced results of lasting consequence. The **Factory Act (1833)** prohibited factory work by children under the age of nine, provided two hours of daily education, and effectively created a 12-hour day in the mills until the Ten Hours Act (1847). The Mines Act (1842) prohibited women and children from working underground.

Nor was Owen alone in dedicating time and money to the improvement of workers' lives. The rapid growth of unplanned cities exacerbated the plight of people who were too poor and overworked to help themselves. Conditions of housing and sanitation were appalling even by nineteenth-century standards. *The Report on the Sanitary Condition of the Laboring Population in Britain* (1842), written by Edwin

Chadwick (1800–1890), so shocked Parliament and the nation that it helped to shift the burden of social reform to the government. The Public Health Act (1848) established boards of health and the office of medical examiner. The Vaccination Act (1853) and the Contagious Diseases Act (1864) attempted to control epidemics.

The movement for social reform began almost as soon as industrialization. The Industrial Revolution initiated profound changes in the organization of British society. Cities sprang up from grain fields almost overnight. The lure of steady work and high wages prompted an exodus from rural Britain and spurred an unremitting boom in population. In 1750, about 15 percent of the population lived in urban areas; by 1850, about 60 percent did. Industrial workers married younger and produced more children than their agricultural counterparts. For centuries, women had married in their middle twenties, but by 1800, age at first marriage had dropped to 23 for the female population as a whole and to nearly 20 in the industrial areas. This was in part because factory hands did not have to wait until they inherited land or money and in part because they did not have to serve an apprenticeship. Early marriage and large families also signified a belief that things were better now and would be even better soon.

Expansion of Wealth.   The Industrial Revolution brought a vast expansion of wealth and a vast expansion of people to share it. Agricultural and industrial change made it possible to support comfortably a population over three times that of the seventeenth century, when it was widely believed that England had reached the limits of expansion. Despite the fact that population doubled between 1801 and 1851, per capita income rose by 75 percent, which means that had the population remained stable, per capita income would have increased by a staggering 350 percent. At the same time, untold millions of pounds had been sunk into canals, roads, railways, factories, mines, and mills.

But the expansion of wealth is not the same as the improvement in the quality of life, for wealth is not equally distributed. An increase in the level of wealth may mean only that the rich are getting richer more quickly than the poor are getting poorer. Similarly, economic growth over a century involved the lives of several generations, which experienced different standards of living. One set of parents may have sacrificed for the future of their children; another may have mortgaged it. Moreover, economic activity is cyclical. Trade depressions, like those induced by the War of 1812 and the American Civil War, which interrupted cotton supplies, could have disastrous short-term effects. The Great Hunger of the 1840s was a time of agrarian crisis and industrial slump. The downturn of 1842 threw 60 percent of the factory workers in the town of Bolton out of work at a time when there was neither unemployment insurance nor a welfare system. Finally, quality of life cannot be measured simply in economic terms. People with more money to spend may still be worse off than their ancestors, who may have preferred leisure to wealth or independence to the discipline of the clock.

There are no easy answers to the quality-of-life question. It seems clear that in the first stages of industrialization, only the wealthy benefited economically, though much of their increased wealth was reinvested in expansion. Under the impact of population growth, the Napoleonic wars, and regional harvest failure, real wages seem to have fallen from the levels reached in the 1730s. Industrial workers were not substantially better off than agricultural laborers when the high cost of food and rent is considered. But beginning around 1820, there is convincing evidence that the real wages of industrial workers were rising, despite the fact that more and more work was semiskilled and unskilled machine-minding and more of it was being done by women, who were generally paid only two-thirds as much as men. Thus, in the second half of the Industrial Revolution, both employers and workers saw a bettering of their economic situation. This was one reason why rural workers flocked to the cities to take the lowest-paid and least desirable jobs in the factories.

Social Costs.   But economic gain had social costs. The first was the decline of the family as a labor unit. In both agricultural and early industrial activity, families labored together. Workers would not move to mill towns without the guarantee of a job for all members of their family, and initially, they could drive a hard bargain. The early factories preferred family labor to workhouse conscripts, and it was traditional for children to work beside their parents, cleaning, fetching, or assisting in minding the machines. Children provided an essential part of family income, and the youngest children were the agency of care for infirm parents. Paradoxically, it was the agitation for improvement in the conditions of child labor that spelled the end of the family work unit. At first, young children were barred from the factories, and older ones were allowed to work only a partial adult shift. Though reformers intended that schooling and leisure be substituted for work, the separation of children from parents in the workplace ultimately made possible the substitution of teenagers for adults, especially as machines replaced skilled human labor. The individual worker now became the unit of labor, and during economic downturns it was adult males with their higher salaries who were laid off first.

The decline of the family as a labor unit was matched by other changes in living conditions when rural dwellers migrated to cities. Many rural habits were unsuited to both factory work and urban living. The tradition of "Saint Monday," for example, was one that was deeply rooted in the pattern of agricultural life. Little effort was expended at the beginning of the work week, and progressively more was expended toward the end. Sunday leisure was followed by Monday recovery, a slow start to renewed labor. The factory demanded constant application, six days a week. Strict rules were enforced to keep workers at their stations and their minds on their jobs. More than efficiency was at stake. Early machines were not only crude, they were dangerous, with no safety features to cover moving parts. Maiming accidents were common in the early factories, the fault of both workers and machines. Similarly, industrial workers entered the world of the cash economy. Most agricultural workers were used

EXPLOITING THE YOUNG

The condition of child laborers was a concern of English legislators and social reformers from the beginning of industrialization. Most of the attention was given to factory workers, and most legislation attempted to regulate the age at which children could begin work, the number of hours they could be made to work, and the provision of schooling and religious education during their leisure. It was not until the mid-1840s that a parliamentary commission was formed to investigate the condition of child labor in the mines. In this extract, the testimony of the child is confirmed by the observations of one of the commissioners.

Focus Questions

How does Mr. Franks's account differ from Ellison Jack's own? Why do you think Ellison offers information about her level of literacy and knowledge of the Bible?

Ellison Jack, 11-years-old girl coal-bearer at Loanhead colliery, Scotland: I have been working below three years on my father's account; he takes me down at two in the morning, and I come up at one and two next afternoon. I go to bed at six at night to be ready for work next morning: the part of the pit I bear in the seams are much on the edge. I have to bear my burthen up four traps, or ladders, before I get to the main road which leads to the pit bottom. My task is four or five tubs: each tub holds 4G cwt. I fill five tubs in twenty journeys.

I have had the strap when I did not do my bidding. Am very glad when my task is wrought, as it sore fatigues. I can read, and was learning the writing; can do a little; not been at school for two years; go to kirk occasionally, over to Lasswade: don't know much about the Bible, so long since read.

R. H. Franks, Esq., the sub-commissioner: A brief description of this child's place of work will illustrate her evidence. She has first to descend a nine-ladder pit to the first rest, even to which a shaft is sunk, to draw up the baskets or tubs of coals filled by the bearers; she then takes her creel (a basket formed to the back, not unlike a cockle-shell flattened towards the neck, so as to allow lumps of coal to rest on the back of the neck and shoulders), and pursues her journey to the wall-face, or as it is called here, the room of work. She then lays down her basket, into which the coal is rolled, and it is frequently more than one man can do to lift the burden on her back. The tugs or straps are placed over the forehead, and the body bent in a semicircular form, in order to stiffen the arch.

"Child Labor in the Coal Mines," Testimony to the Parliamentary Investigative Committee (1842).

to being paid in kind and to barter exchange. Money was an unusual luxury that was associated with binges of food, drink, and frivolities. This made adjustment to the wage packet as difficult as adjustment to the clock. Cash had to be set aside for provisions, rent, and clothing. On the farm, the time of a bountiful harvest was the time to buy durable goods; in the factory, "harvest time" was always the same.

Such adjustments were not easy, and during the course of the nineteenth century a way of life passed from England forever. For some, its departure caused profound sorrow; for others, it was an occasion of good riddance. A vertically integrated society in which lord of the manor, village worthies, independent farmers, workers, and servants lived together interdependently was replaced by a society of segregated social classes. By the middle decades of the nineteenth century, a class of capitalists and a class of workers had begun to form and had begun to clash. The middle classes abandoned the city centers and built exclusive suburban communities in which to raise their children and insulate their families. Conditions in the cities deteriorated under the pressure of overcrowding, lack of sanitation, and the absence of private investment. The loss of interaction between these different segments of society had profound effects on the struggle to improve the quality of life for everyone. Leaders of labor saw themselves as fighting against profits, greed, and apathy; leaders of capital saw themselves as battling drunkenness, sloth, and ignorance. Between these two stereotypes there was little middle ground.

THE INDUSTRIALIZATION OF THE CONTINENT

Though Britain took the first steps along the road to an industrial economy, it was not long before other European nations followed. There was intense interest in "the British miracle," as it was dubbed by contemporaries. European ministers, entrepreneurs, even heads of state visited British factories and mines in the hope of learning the key industrial secrets that would unlock the prosperity of a new age. The Crystal Palace exhibition of manufacturing and industry, held in London in 1851, was the occasion for a Continent-wide celebration of the benefits of technology. By then, many European nations had begun the transformation of their own economies and had entered a period of sustained growth.

There was no single model for the industrialization of the continental states. Contemporaries continually made comparisons with Britain, but in truth the process of British industrialization was not well suited to any part of the Continent but the coal-rich regions in Belgium and the Rhineland. Nevertheless, all of Europe benefited from the British experience. No one else had to invent the jenny, the mule, or the steam engine. Therefore, although industrialization began later on the Continent, it could progress more quickly. France and Germany were building a railroad system within years of Britain, despite the fact that they had to import most of the technology, raw materials, and engineers.

Britain shaped European industrialization in another way. Its head start made it very difficult for follower nations to compete against British commodities in the world market. This meant that European industrialization would be directed first and foremost to home markets, where tariffs and import quotas could protect fledgling industries. Though European states were willing to import vital British products, they placed high duties on British-made consumer goods and encouraged higher-cost domestic production. Britain's competi-

tive advantage demanded that European governments become involved in the industrialization of their countries, financing capital-intensive industries, backing the railroads, and favoring the establishment of factories.

European industrialization was therefore not the thunderclap that occurred in Britain. In France, it was a slow, accretive development that took advantage of traditional skills and occupations and gradually modernized the marketplace. In Germany, industrialization had to overcome the political divisions of the empire, the economic isolation of the petty states, and the wide dispersion of vital resources. Regions rather than states industrialized in the early nineteenth century, and parts of Austria, Italy, and Spain imported machinery and techniques and modernized their traditional crafts. But most of these states and most of the eastern part of Europe remained tied to a traditional agrarian-based economy that provided neither labor for industrial production nor purchasing power for industrial goods. These areas quickly became sources for raw materials and primary products for their industrial neighbors.

MAP DISCOVERY

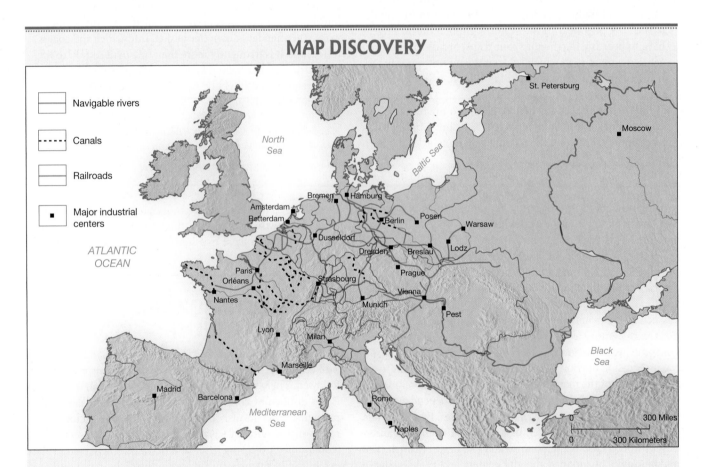

Industrial Revolution on the Continent

What were the least industrial parts of Europe outside of Great Britain? In what directions did the major railroads run? How did the progress of industrialization in continental Europe compare with that in Britain? What impact did industrialization have on Spain and Italy?

France: Industrialization Without Revolution

The experience of France in the nineteenth century demonstrates that there was no single path in industrialization. Each state blended its natural resources, historical experiences, and forms of economic organization in unique combinations. While some mixtures resulted in explosive growth, as in Britain, others made for steady development, as in France.

French industrialization was keyed to domestic rather than export markets and to the application of new technology to a vast array of traditional crafts. France possessed a pool of highly skilled and highly productive labor, a manufacturing tradition that was oriented toward the creation of high-quality goods, and consumers who valued taste and fashion over cost and function. While the British dominated the new mass market for inexpensive cottons and cast-iron goods, a market with high sales but low profit margins, the French were producing luxury items whose scarcity kept both prices and profits high.

Two decisive factors determined the nature of French industrialization: population growth and the French Revolution.

Slow Growth.   From the early eighteenth to the mid-nineteenth century, France grew slowly. In 1700, the French population stood at just under 20 million; in 1850, it was under 36 million, a growth rate of 80 percent. In contrast, Germany grew 135 percent, from 15 to 34 million, and England grew 300 percent, from 5 to 20 million, during the same period. Nevertheless, France remained the most populous nation in western Europe, second on the Continent only to Russia. Because of its moderate population growth, France was not pressured by the force of numbers to abandon its traditional agricultural methods, nor did it face a shortage of traditional supplies of energy. Except during crop failures, French agriculture could produce to meet French needs, and more than enough wood remained for domestic and industrial use.

The Impact of the French Revolution.   The consequences of the French Revolution are less clear. Throughout the eighteenth century, the French economy performed at least as well as had the British and better in many areas. French overseas trade had grown spectacularly until it was checked by military defeat in the Seven Years' War (1756–1763). French agricultural output increased steadily, while French rural manufactures flourished. A strong guild tradition still dominated urban industries, and although it restricted competition and limited growth, it also helped to maintain standards for the production of high-quality goods that made French commodities so highly prized throughout the world. The revolution disrupted every aspect of economic life. Some of its outcomes were unforeseen and unwelcome. For example, Napoleon's Continental System, which attempted to close European markets to Britain, resulted in a shipping war, which the British won decisively and which eliminated France as a competitor for overseas trade in the mid-nineteenth century. But other outcomes were the result of direct policies, even if their impact could not have been entirely predicted. Urban guilds and corporations were abolished, opening trades to newcomers but destroying the close-knit groups that trained skilled artisans and introduced innovative products. Similarly, the breakup of both feudal and common lands to satisfy the hunger of the peasantry had the effect of maintaining a large rural population for decades.

Despite the efforts of the central government, there had been little change in the techniques used by French farmers over the course of the eighteenth century. French peasants clung tenaciously to traditional rights that gave even the smallest landholder a vital say in community agriculture. Landlords were predominantly absentees, less interested in the organization of their estates than in the dues and taxes that could be extracted from them. Therefore the policies of successive revolutionary governments strengthened the hold of small peasants on the land. With the abolition of many feudal dues and with careful family planning, smallholders could survive and pass a meager inheritance on to their children. French agriculture was able to supply the nation's need for food, but it could not release large numbers of workers for purely industrial activity.

Stages of Industrial Progress.   French industrial growth was constrained on the one hand by the relatively small numbers of workers who could engage in manufacturing and on the other by the fact that a large portion of the population remained subsistence producers, cash-poor and linked only to small rural markets. Throughout the eighteenth century, the French economy continued to be regionally segregated rather than nationally integrated. The size of the state inhibited a highly organized internal trade, and there was little improvement of the infrastructure of transportation. Though some British-style canals were built, canals in Britain were built to move coal rather than staple goods, and France did not have much coal to move. Manufacturing concerns were still predominantly family businesses whose primary markets were regional rather than international. There was no national capital market until the mid-nineteenth century, and there were precious few regional ones.

It was not until midcentury that sustained industrial growth became evident in France. This was largely the result of the construction of railroads on a national plan, financed in large part by the central government. Whereas in Britain the railways took advantage of a national market, in France they created one. They also gave the essential stimulation to the modernization of the iron industry, of machine making, and of the capital markets.

The disadvantages of being on the trailing edge of economic change were mitigated for a time by conventional practices of protectionism. Except in specialty goods, agricultural produce, and luxury products, French manufacturers could not compete with either British or German commodities. Had France maintained its position as a world trader, this comparative disadvantage would have been devastating. But defeat in the wars of commerce had led to a drawing inward of French economic effort. Marseilles and Bordeaux, once bustling centers of European trade, became provincial backwaters in the nineteenth century. But the internal market was still strong enough to support industrial growth, and domestic commodities could be protected by prohibitive tariffs, especially against British textiles, iron, and, ironically, coal.

While France achieved industrialization without an industrial revolution, it also achieved economic growth within the context of its traditional values. Agriculture may not have modernized, but the ancient village communities escaped the devastation that modernization would have brought. The orderly progression of generations of farming families characterized rural France until the shattering experiences of the Franco-Prussian War (1870) and the First World War (1914–1918). Nor did France experience the mushroom growth of new cities, with all of their problems of poverty, squalor, and homelessness. Slow population growth ameliorated the worst of the social diseases of industrialization, while traditional rural manufacturing softened the transformation of a way of life.

Germany: Industrialization and Union

The process of industrialization in Germany was dominated by the historic divisions of the empire of the German peoples. Before 1815, there were over 300 separate jurisdictional units within the empire, and after 1815 there were still more than 30. These included large advanced states such as Prussia, Austria, and Saxony as well as small free cities and the personal enclaves of petty nobles who had guessed right during the Napoleonic wars. Political divisions had more than political impact. Each state clung tenaciously to its local laws and customs, which favored its citizens over outsiders. Merchants who lived near the intersection of separate jurisdictions could find themselves liable for several sets of tolls to move their goods and several sets of customs duties for importing and exporting them. These would have to be paid in different currencies at different rates of exchange according to the different regulations of each state. Small wonder that German merchants exhibited an intense localism, preferring to trade with members of their own state and supporting trade barriers against others. Such obstacles had a depressing effect on the economies of all German states but pushed with greatest weight against the manufacturing regions of Saxony, Silesia, and the Rhineland.

Agriculture.   Most of imperial Germany was agricultural land that was suited to a diversity of uses. The mountainous regions of Bavaria and the Austrian alpine communities practiced animal husbandry. There was a grain belt in Prussia, where the soil was poor but the land was plentiful, and one in central Germany in which the soil was fertile and the land was densely occupied. The Rhine Valley was one of the richest in all of Europe and was the center of German wine production. While English farmers were turning farms into commercial estates, German peasants were learning how to make do with less land.

Agricultural estates were organized differently in different parts of Germany. In the east, serfdom still prevailed. Peasants were tied to the land and its lord and were responsible for labor service during much of the week. Methods of cultivation were traditional, and neither peasants nor lords had much incentive to adopt new techniques. In central Germany, the long process of commuting labor service into rents was nearly complete by the end of the eighteenth century. The peasantry was not yet free, as a series of manorial relationships still tied them to the land, but they were no longer mere serfs. Finally, western Germany was dominated by free farmers who either owned or leased their lands and who had a purely economic relationship with their landlords. The restriction of peasant mobility in much of Germany posed difficulties for the creation of an industrial workforce. As late as 1800, over 80 percent of the German population was engaged in agriculture, a proportion that would drop slowly over the next half century.

Though Germany was well endowed with natural resources and skilled labor in a number of trades, it had not taken part in the expansion of world trade during the seventeenth century, and the once bustling Hanseatic ports had been far outdistanced by the rise of the Atlantic economies. The principal exported manufacture was linen, which was expertly spun and woven in Saxony and the Prussian province of Silesia. The linen industry relied on the putting-out system and some factory spinning, especially after the introduction of British mechanical innovations. But even the most advanced factories were still being powered by water, and so they were located in mountainous regions where rapidly running streams could turn the wheels. Neither linens nor traditional German metal crafts could compete on the international markets, but they could find a wider market within Germany if only the problems of political division could be resolved.

The Zollverein.   The problems of political division were especially acute for Prussia after the reorganization of European boundaries in 1815. Prussian territory now included the coal- and iron-rich Rhineland provinces, but a number of smaller states separated these areas from Prussia's eastern domain. Each small state exacted its own tolls and customs duties whenever Prussian merchants wanted to move goods from one part of Prussia to the other. Such movement became more common in the nineteenth century as German manufacturing began to grow in step with its rising population. Between 1815 and 1865, the population of Germany grew by 60 percent, to over 36 million. This was an enormous internal market, nearly as large as France, and the Prussians resolved to make it a unified trading zone by creating a series of alliances with smaller states, known as the **Zollverein** (1834). The Zollverein was not a free trade zone, like the British Empire, but rather a customs union in which member states adopted the liberal Prussian customs regulations. Every state was paid an annual portion of receipts based on its population, and every state—except Prussia—increased its revenues as a result. Prussia gained the ability to move goods and materials from east to west. It also forced Hanover and Saxony into the

Zollverein and kept its powerful rival Austria out. Prussia's economic union soon proved to be the basis for the union of the German states.

The creation of the Zollverein was vital to German industrialization. It permitted the exploitation of natural advantages, such as plentiful supplies of coal and iron, and it provided a basis for the building of railroads. Germany was a follower nation in the process of industrialization. Seeking to learn from England, it brought British equipment and engineers to Germany, and German manufacturers sent their children to England to learn the latest techniques in industrial management. Friedrich Engels (1820–1895) worked in a Manchester cotton factory, where he observed the appalling conditions of the industrial labor force and wrote *The Condition of the Working Class in England* (1845). Steam engines were installed in German coal mines, if not in factories, and the process of puddling revolutionized iron making, though most iron was still smelted with charcoal rather than coke. Coal was plentiful in Prussia, but it was found at the eastern and western extremities of Germany. Therefore the railroads were the key to tapping German industrial potential. Here, they were a cause rather than a result of industrialization. The agreements that were hammered out in the creation of the Zollverein made possible the planning necessary to build single rail lines across the boundaries of numerous states.

Germany imported most of its engines directly from Britain and so adopted the standard British gauge for its system. As early as 1850, there were over 3,500 miles of rail in Germany, with important roads linking the manufacturing districts of Saxony and the coal and iron deposits of the Ruhr. Twenty years later, Germany was second only to Britain in the amount of track that had been laid and opened. By then, Germany was no longer simply a follower. German engineers and machinists, trained in Europe's best schools of technology, were turning out engines and rolling stock second to none. And the railroads transported a host of high-quality manufactures, especially durable metal goods that came to carry the most prestigious trademark of the late nineteenth century: "Made in Germany."

The Lands That Time Forgot

Nothing better demonstrates the point that industrialization was a regional rather than a national process than a survey of the states that did not develop industrial economies by the middle of the nineteenth century. These states ranged from the Netherlands, which was still one of the richest areas in Europe, to Spain and Russia, which were the poorest. Also included were Austria-Hungary, the states of the Italian peninsula, and Poland. In all of these nations there was some industrial progress. The Bohemian lands of Austria contained a highly developed spinning industry; the Spanish province of Catalonia produced more cotton than Belgium; and the Basque region was rich in iron and coal. Northern Italy mechanized its textile production, particularly silk spinning, while in the regions around both Moscow and Saint Petersburg, fac-

tories were run on serf labor. Nevertheless, the economies of all these states remained nonindustrial and, except that of the Netherlands, dominated by subsistence agriculture.

There were many reasons why these states were unable to develop their industrial potential. Some, such as Naples and Poland, were simply underendowed with resources; others, such as Austria-Hungary and Spain, faced difficulties of transport and communications that could not easily be overcome. Spain's modest resources were located on its northern and eastern edges, while a vast arid plain dominated the center. To move raw materials and finished products from one end of the country to the other was a daunting task, made more difficult by a lack of waterways and the rudimentary condition of Spanish roads. Two-thirds of Austria-Hungary was either mountains or hills, a geographic feature that presented obstacles that not even the railroads could easily solve. But there was far more than natural disadvantage behind the failure of these parts of Europe to move in step with the industrializing states. Their social structure, agricultural organization, and commercial policies all hindered the adoption of new methods, machines, and modes of production.

The leaders of traditional economies maintained tariff systems that insulated their own producers from competition. But protection was sensible only when it protected rather than isolated. Inefficiently produced goods of inferior quality were the chief results of the protectionist policies of the follower nations. Failure to adopt steam-powered machines made traditionally produced linens and silks so expensive that smuggling occurred on an international scale. Though these goods might find buyers in domestic markets, they could not compete in international trade, and one by one the industries of the follower nations atrophied. The economies that remained traditionally organized came to be exploited for their resources by those that had industrialized. Traditional agriculture could not produce the necessary surplus of either labor or capital to support industry, and industry could not economize sufficiently to make manufactured goods cheap enough for a poor peasantry.

There was more than irony in the fact that one of the first railroads built on the Continent was built in Austria but designed to be powered by horses rather than engines. The first railways in Italy linked royal palaces to capital cities; those in Spain radiated from Madrid and bypassed most centers of natural resources. In these states, the railroads were built to move the military rather than passengers or goods. They were state-financed, were occasionally state-owned, and almost always lost money. They were symbols of the industrial age, but in these states they were symbols without substance.

CONCLUSION

The industrialization of Europe in the eighteenth century was an epochal event in human history. The constraints on daily life that nature imposed were loosened for the first time. No longer did population growth in one generation mean famine in the next. No longer was it necessary for the great majority of people to toil in the fields to earn their daily bread. Manufacture replaced agriculture as humanity's primary activity, though the change was longer and slower than the burst of industrialization that took place in the first half of the nineteenth century. For the leaders, Britain especially, industrialization brought international eminence. British achievements were envied, British inventors were celebrated, and Britain's constitutional and social organization was lauded. A comparatively small island nation

had become the greatest economic power in Europe. Industrialization had profound consequences for economic life, but its effects ran deeper than that. The search for new markets would result in the conquest of continents; the power of productivity unleashed by coal and iron would result in the first great arms race. Both would reach fruition in World War I, the first industrial war. For better or worse, we still live in the industrial era that began in Britain in the middle of the eighteenth century.

QUESTIONS FOR REVIEW

1. Why did early manufacturing develop in the countryside, and what effect did that have on manufacturing practices and social relations?
2. In what ways were the ideas about organization of manufacturers such as Josiah Wedgwood and Robert Owen as significant as new technology in the development of industry in Britain?

3. How did British society address some of the changes in peoples' lives that were brought about by industrialization?
4. How did industrialization on the Continent differ from industrialization in England?
5. Why did some nations develop little industry at all?

KEY TERMS

agricultural revolution, p. 422

Crystal Palace Exhibition, *p. 429*

Factory Act (1833), *p. 431*

industrialization, *p. 420*

Industrial Revolution, *p. 425*

putting-out system, *p. 422*

Zollverein, *p. 436*

DISCOVERING WESTERN CIVILIZATION ONLINE

You can obtain more information about industrial Europe at the websites listed below. See also the Companion Website that accompanies this text, www.ablongman.com/kishlansky, which contains an online study guide and additional resources.

The Industrial Revolution in Britain

Reminiscences of James Watt
www.history.rochester.edu/steam/hart/
A nineteenth-century account of the life of James Watt and his role as inventor of the steam engine with links to the history of the steam engine.

Women in World History Curriculum: Industrial Revolution
www.womeninworldhistory.com/lesson7.html
Sponsored by Women in World History Curriculum, this site details the plight of working women in industrial England.

Child Labour in the 19th Century
www.spartacus.schoolnet.co.uk/IRchild.main.htm
This site chronicles child labor in Britain, including life in the factory and first-hand experiences.

The Industrialization of the Continent

Modern History Sourcebook: Tables Illustrating the Spread of Industrialization
www.fordham.edu/halsall/mod/indrevtabs1.html
Charts and statistics about industrialization in Europe.

Internet Modern History Sourcebook: Industrial Revolution
www.fordham.edu/halsall/mod/modsbook14.html
An outstanding collection of documents on the Industrial Age with links.

SUGGESTIONS FOR FURTHER READING

General Reading

T. S. Ashton, *The Industrial Revolution* (Oxford: Oxford University Press, 1997). A compelling brief account of the traditional view of industrialization.

Niall Ferguson, *The Cash Nexus: Money and Power in the Modern World, 1700–2000* (New York: Basic Books, 2001). A transnational history of the role of finance in the making of the modern world.

Jordan Goodman and Katrina Honeyman, *Gainful Pursuits: The Making of Industrial Europe, 1600–1914* (London: Edward Arnold, 1988). A brief overview of the entire process of industrialization.

The Traditional Economy

Richard Brown, *Society and Economy in Modern Britain, 1700–1850* (London: Routledge, 1991). A comprehensive survey.

J. D. Chambers and G. E. Mingay, *The Agricultural Revolution* (London: Batsford, 1966). The classic survey of the changes in British agriculture.

The Industrial Revolution in Britain

N. F. R. Crafts, *British Economic Growth During the Industrial Revolution* (Oxford: Oxford University Press, 1986). A highly quantitative study by a new economic historian arguing the case that economic growth was slow in the early nineteenth century.

François Crouzet, *The First Industrialists* (Cambridge: Cambridge University Press, 1985). An analysis of the social background of the first generation of British entrepreneurs.

Martin Daunton, *Progress and Poverty: An Economic and Social History of Britain, 1700–1850* (Oxford: Oxford University Press, 1995). The best single-volume survey on the Industrial Revolution and its effects on British society.

Phyllis Deane, *The First Industrial Revolution*, 2d ed. (Cambridge: Cambridge University Press, 1979). The best introduction to the technological changes in Britain.

Richard Price, *British Society, 1680–1880: Dynamism, Containment, and Change* (New York: Cambridge University Press, 1999). A new argument about the nature of British society in the age of the Industrial Revolution.

John Rule, *The Vital Century: England's Developing Economy, 1714–1815* (London: Longman, 1992). A comprehensive survey of the British economy.

E. P. Thompson, *The Making of the English Working Class* (New York: Random House, 1966). A brilliant and passionate study of the ways laborers responded to the changes brought about by the industrial economy.

The Industrialization of the Continent

W. O. Henderson, *The Rise of German Industrial Power* (Berkeley: University of California Press, 1975). A chronological study of German industrialization that centers on Prussia.

Tom Kemp, *Industrialization in Nineteenth-Century Europe*, 2d ed. (London: Longman, 1985). Survey of the process of industrialization in the major European states.

Sidney Pollard, *Peaceful Conquest* (Oxford: Oxford University Press, 1981). Argues the regional nature of industrialization throughout western Europe.

Roger Price, *The Economic Transformation of France* (London: Croom Helm, 1975). A study of French society before and during the process of industrialization.

Wolfgang Schivelbusch, *The Railway Journey* (Berkeley: University of California Press, 1986). A social history of the impact of railways, drawn from French and German sources.

Clive Trebilcock, *The Industrialization of the Continental Powers, 1780–1914* (London: Longman, 1981). A complex study of Germany, France, and Russia.

For a list of additional titles related to this chapter's topics, please see www.ablongman.com/kishlansky**.**

Chapter 22

POLITICAL UPHEAVALS AND SOCIAL TRANSFORMATIONS, 1815–1850

The Visual Record

POTATO POLITICS

Vegetables have histories too. But none has a more interesting history in the West than the humble potato. First introduced to northern Europe from the Andean highlands of South America at the end of the sixteenth century, it rapidly became a staple of peasant diets from Ireland to Russia. The potato's vitamins, minerals, and high carbohydrate content provided a rich source of energy to Europe's rural poor. It was simple to plant, it required little or no cultivation, and it did well in damp, cool climates. Best of all, it could be grown successfully on the smallest plots of land. One acre could support a family of four for a year.

In his painting *Planting Potatoes,* the French painter Jean-François Millet (1814–1875) depicts the peasants in a reverent posture, bowing as field laborers might in prayer (as they do in Millet's more sentimental work, *The Angelus*). The couple's baby sleeps swaddled in a basket shaded by the tree. Millet, the son of a wealthy peasant family, understood well the importance of the potato in the peasant family diet.

But the fleshy root not only guaranteed health; it also affected social life. Traditionally, peasants had delayed marrying and starting families because of the unavailability of land. Now the potato allowed peasants who had only a little land to marry and have children earlier. In peasant homes where family members did putting-out work for local entrepreneurs, potato cultivation drew little labor away from the spinning wheel and loom. It permitted prosperous farmers to devote more land to cash crops, since only a small portion was required to feed a family. Most commonly, however, the potato was the single crop grown by most Irish farm workers. As the sole item of diet, it provided life-sustaining nutrients and a significant amount of the protein so necessary for heavy labor. The Irish adult male ate an average of twelve to fourteen pounds of cooked potatoes a day—a figure that may seem preposterous to us today.

Proverbs warned peasants against putting all their eggs in one basket, but no folk wisdom prepared the Irish for the potato disaster that struck them. In 1845, a fungus from America destroyed the new potato crop. Although peasants were certainly accustomed to bad harvests and crop failures, they had no precedent for the years of blight that followed. From 1846 to 1850, famine and the diseases resulting from it—scurvy,

dysentery, cholera, and typhus fever—killed over a million people in what became known as the Great Hunger. Within five years the Irish population was reduced by almost 25 percent.

The Irish potato famine has been called the "last great European natural disaster," but it was as much a social and political disaster as a natural one. The government of the United Kingdom of Great Britain and Ireland seemed powerless to stop the famine. The repeal of protective trade barriers to allow the Irish to buy cheaper grain was of no help to the penniless farmers, and although emergency work relief and soup kitchens were briefly offered, they were withdrawn when a banking crisis hit England. The workhouses created under the Irish Poor Law system were not intended to deal with such disasters. Mass deaths and mass graves were the inevitable result.

Looking Ahead

As the wealth of European societies expanded in the nineteenth century, so did the number of those who lived on the edge, poised between unemployment and starvation. The Irish Great Hunger was the most striking example of the problem that plagued all Western societies in the first half of the nineteenth century: what to do with the poor. In this chapter, we shall see that while the boundaries of European nations were redefined following the Napoleonic Wars in order to create stability, the economic hardships of peasants and workers continued to plague and disrupt European societies internally. The new ideologies of the first half of the nineteenth century grappled with the challenge of reshaping state and society. But social inequities continued to fuel protest and revolution between 1815 and 1850 and pulled down governments across Europe. ➤

GEOGRAPHICAL TOUR
Europe in 1815

Peasants like those depicted by Millet in his painting *Planting Potatoes* seldom traveled beyond their own villages. Of course, all that changed with Napoleon's quest for empire. Napoleon placed in motion large armies of peasants and workers crisscrossing the continent, and no one state on its own had been able to defeat his conscript armies. In the end, those combined powers who were victorious in defeating Napoleon's empire learned a lesson on the territorial and political interdependence of Europe. They now saw the whole of Europe as one entity and conceived of peace in terms of a general European security.

The primary goal of the leaders of Russia, Austria, Prussia, and France who met in 1815 was to devise the most stable ter-ritorial arrangement possible. That goal entailed redrawing the map of Europe (see **Map A**). During the negotiations, traditional claims of the right to rule came head to head with new ideas about stabilization. The equilibrium that was established in 1815 made possible a century-long European peace. Conflicts erupted, to be sure, but they took on the characteristics of the new system that was constructed at Vienna in 1815.

The Congress of Vienna

In 1814, representatives of the victorious Allies agreed to convene in the Austrian capital of Vienna for the purposes of mopping up the mess created in Europe by French rule and restoring order to European monarchies.

The central actors whose personalities dominated the **Congress of Vienna** were the Austrian minister of foreign affairs Prince Klemens von Metternich (1773–1859), the British foreign secretary Viscount Castlereagh (1769–1822), the

■ **Map A. Europe, 1815.** In a series of treaties following Napoleon's defeat, the European powers redrew the map of Europe to create the most stable territorial arrangement and ensure European security. At the center of Europe stood the German confederation, outlined here in red.

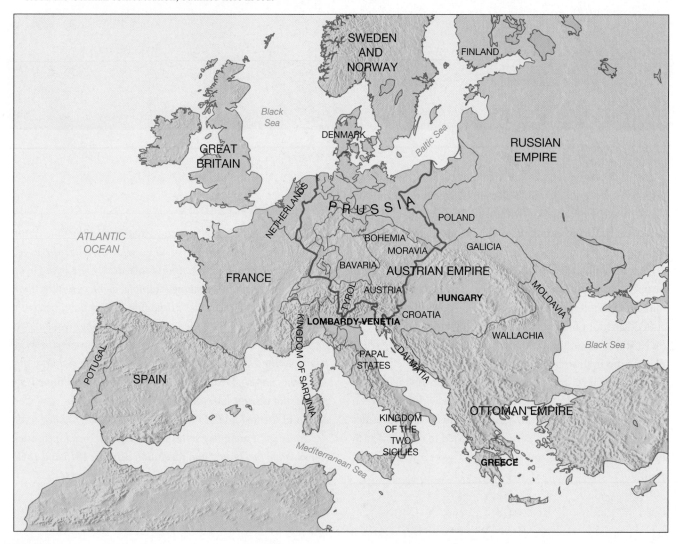

■ **Map B. France, 1815.** In determining the borders of France, European heads of state were torn between the need to punish and control France and the importance of reconciliation with France for a stable Europe. The Second Peace of Paris of November 1815 permitted France to return to the borders of 1790 and to resume its role as one of the Great Powers.

the 1792 boundaries, which included Avignon, Venaissin, parts of Savoy, and German and Flemish territories, none of which had belonged to France in 1789.

Even after the hundred-day return of Napoleon, the "Usurper," the Second Peace of Paris of November 1815 somewhat less generously declared French frontiers to be restricted to the boundaries of 1790 (see **Map B**) and exacted from France an indemnity of 700 million francs. An army of occupation consisting of 150,000 troops was also placed on French soil at French expense but was removed ahead of schedule in 1818.

New Territorial Arrangements.   The dominant partnership of Austria and Britain at the Congress of Vienna resulted in treaty arrangements that served to restrain the ambitions of Russia and Prussia. No country was to receive territory without giving up something in return, and no one country was to receive enough territory to make it a present or future threat to the peace of Europe. To contain France, some steps taken before the Congress of Vienna were ratified or expanded. In June 1814, the Low Countries had been set up as a unitary state as a buffer against future French expansion on the Continent and a block to the revival of French sea power. The new Kingdom of the Netherlands (see **Map C**), created out of the former Dutch Republic and the

French minister of foreign affairs Charles Maurice de Talleyrand (1754–1838), the Russian tsar Alexander I (1801–1825), and the Prussian king Frederick William III (1797–1840). In spite of personal eccentricities and occasionally outright hostilities among Europe's leaders, all shared a concern with reestablishing harmony in Europe.

Settling with France.   Because of the concern with establishing harmony at the time of Napoleon's defeat, the peace that was enforced against France was not a punitive one. After Napoleon's abdication in 1814, the Four Powers decided that leniency was the best way to support the restored Bourbon monarchy. After 1793, royalist émigrés referred to the young son of the executed Louis XVI as Louis XVII, although the child died in captivity and never reigned. In 1814, the Great Powers designated the elder of the two surviving brothers of Louis XVI as the appropriate candidate for the restored monarchy. Because of the circumstances of his restoration, the new king, Louis XVIII (1814–1815, 1815–1824), bore the ignominious image of returning "in the baggage car of the Allies." Every effort was made not to weigh him down with a harsh settlement. The First Peace of Paris, signed by the Allies with France in May 1814, had established French frontiers at

■ **Map C. Kingdom of the Netherlands.** As a buffer on France's northernmost border, the new Kingdom of the Netherlands was a forced union of two regions with different languages and religions. The union lasted only until 1831 when the southern provinces revolted to form Belgium.

■ **Map D. Italian Peninsula, 1815.** Austria gained major territorial concessions on the Italian peninsula. The Austrian Empire now included Lombardy and Venetia. Austria was also influential throughout the peninsula in the Papal States, the three small duchies (Tuscany, Parma, Modena), and the Kingdom of the Two Sicilies.

■ **Map E. German Confederation.** The league of German states created in 1815 replaced the Holy Roman Empire. The 39 states, of which 35 were monarchies and 4 were free cities, existed to ensure the independence of its member states and support in case of external attack. The member states of Austria and Prussia lay partially outside of the confederation.

Austrian Netherlands, was placed under the rule of William I (1815–1840). The Catholic southern provinces were thus uneasily reunited with the Protestant northern provinces, regions that had been separated since the Peace of Westphalia in 1648. Great Britain gave William I of the Netherlands two million pounds to fortify his frontier against France. The reestablishment of a monarchy that united the island kingdom of Sardinia with Piedmont and that included Savoy, Nice, and part of Genoa contained France on its southeast border (see **Map D**). To the east, Prussia was given control of the left bank of the Rhine. Switzerland was reestablished as an independent confederation of cantons. Bourbon rule was restored in Spain on France's southwestern border.

Austria's power was firmly established in Italy, through either outright territorial control or influence over independent states (see **Map D**). The Papal States were returned to Pope Pius VII (1800–1823), along with territories that had been Napoleon's Cisalpine Republic and the Kingdom of Italy. The Republic of Venice was absorbed into the Austrian Empire. Lombardy and the Illyrian provinces on the Dalmatian coast were likewise restored to Austria. The Italian duchies of Tuscany, Parma, and Modena were placed under the rule of Habsburg princes.

After the fall of Napoleon, the Allies made no attempt to restore the Holy Roman Empire. Napoleon's Confederation of the Rhine, which organized the majority of German territory under French auspices in 1806, was dissolved. In its place, the lands once divided into 300 petty states in central Europe were reorganized into 38 states in the German Confederation (see **Map E**). The German Confederation was intended as a bulwark against France, not to serve any nationalist or parliamentary function. The 38 states, along with Austria as the thirty-ninth, were represented in a new Federal Diet at Frankfurt, dominated by Austrian influence.

All of these changes were the result of carefully discussed but fairly uncontroversial negotiations. The question of Poland was more problematic. Successive partitions by Russia, Austria, and Prussia in 1772, 1793, and 1795 had completely dismembered the land that had been Poland. Napoleon had reconstituted a small portion of Poland as the grand duchy of Warsaw. The Congress of Vienna's dilemma was what to do with this Napoleonic creation and with Polish territory in general. Fierce debate over Poland threatened to shatter congressional harmony (see **Map F**).

Tsar Alexander I of Russia argued for a large Poland that he intended to be fully under his influence. Frederick William III of Prussia contended that if a large Poland were to be created,

■ **Map F. Poland, 1815.** An independent kingdom in name only, Poland was under the influence of Russia. Prussia carved off Posen, and Austria maintained control of Galicia. Krakow was defined by treaty as an independent republic.

■ **Map G. Saxony.** In 1806, Saxony had sided with France against Prussia and remained allies with the French for the remainder of the wars. With Napoleon's defeat in 1815, about 40 percent of Saxony became part of Prussia.

Prussia would expect compensation by absorbing Saxony (see **Map G**). Both Great Britain and France distrusted Russian and Prussian territorial aims. In the midst of the crisis over Poland, Talleyrand, the wily and brilliant French negotiator, persuaded Britain and Austria to sign a secret treaty with France to preserve an independent Polish territory. He then deliberately leaked news of the secret agreement of these powers to go to war, if necessary, to block Russian and Prussian aims. Alexander I and Frederick William III immediately backed down.

In the final arrangement, Prussia retained the Polish territory of Posen, and Austria kept the Polish province of Galicia (see **Map F**). Krakow, with its population of 95,000, was declared a free city. Finally, a kingdom of Poland, nominally independent but in fact under the tutelage of Russia, emerged from what remained of the grand duchy of Warsaw. It was a solution that benefited no one in particular and disregarded Polish wishes.

In addition to receiving Polish territories, Prussia gained two-fifths of the kingdom of Saxony (see **Map G**) as well as territory on the left bank of the Rhine, the duchy of Westphalia, and Swedish Pomerania. With these acquisitions, Prussia doubled its population to around 11 million people. The Junkers, the landed class of east Prussia, reversed many of the reforms of the Napoleonic period. The new territories that

Prussia gained were rich in waterways and resources but geographically fragmented. The dispersal of holdings that was intended to contain Prussian power in central Europe spurred Prussia to find new ways of uniting its markets. In this endeavor, Prussia constituted a future threat to Austrian power over the German Confederation.

In Scandinavia, Russia's conquest of Finland was acknowledged by the members of the Congress. In return, Sweden acquired Norway from Denmark. Unlike Austria, Prussia, and Russia, Great Britain made no claim to territories at the Congress. Having achieved its aim of containing France, its greatest rival for dominance on the seas, Britain returned the French colonies it had seized in war. For the time being, the redrawing of the territorial map of Europe had achieved its pragmatic aim of guaranteeing the peace. It was now left to a system of alliances to preserve that peace.

The Alliance System

Only by joining forces had the European powers been able to defeat Napoleon, and the necessity of a system of alliances was recognized even after the battles were over. Two alliance pacts dominated the post-Napoleonic era: the renewed Quadruple Alliance and the Holy Alliance.

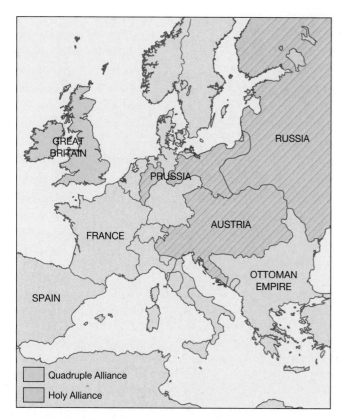

CHRONOLOGY
THE ALLIANCE SYSTEM

May 1814	First Peace of Paris
23 September 1814–9 June 1815	Congress of Vienna
26 September 1815	Formation of the Holy Alliance
20 November 1815	Second Peace of Paris; Formation of the Quadruple Alliance
November 1818	Quadruple Alliance expands to include France in Quintuple Alliance
1823	French restoration of Bourbon Monarchy in Spain

■ **Map H. Quadruple Alliance and Holy Alliance.** The Quadruple Alliance grew out of the need of the Great Powers to create a stable Europe, and had as its initial impulse the creation of a buffer against a future French threat. Austria, Great Britain, Prussia, and Russia entered into the agreement as the basis for defining the balance of power in Europe. In the Holy Alliance, Russia, Austria, and Prussia entered an accord to treat each other according to the precepts of the Christian religion. Unlike the Quadruple Alliance, the Holy Alliance served as a justification for repression against dissent.

The **Quadruple Alliance** (see **Map H**), signed by the victorious powers of Great Britain, Austria, Russia, and Prussia in November 1815, was intended to protect Europe against future French aggression and to preserve the status quo. In 1818, having completed its payment of war indemnities, France joined the pact, which then became the **Quintuple Alliance.** The five powers promised to meet periodically over the next 200 years to discuss common problems and to ensure the peace.

The **Holy Alliance** (see **Map H**) was the brainchild of Alexander I and was heavily influenced by his mystical view of international politics. In this pact, the monarchs of Prussia, Austria, and Russia agreed to renounce war and to protect the Christian religion. The Holy Alliance spoke of "the bonds of a true and indissoluble brotherhood . . . to protect religion, peace, and justice." Russia was able to give some credibility to the alliance with the sheer size of its army. Career diplomats were aware of the hollowness of the Holy Alliance as a treaty arrangement, but it did indicate the will-ingness of Europe's three eastern autocracies to intervene in the affairs of other states.

The concept of Europe acting as a whole, through a system of periodic conferences, marked the emergence of a new diplomatic era. However, conflict was inherent in the commitment of parliamentary governments to open consultation and the need for secrecy in diplomacy. Dynastic regimes sought to intervene in smaller states to buoy up despots. That certainly seemed to be the case in 1822, when the European powers met to consider restoring the Bourbon monarchy in Spain. The British, acting as a counterbalance to revolutionary tendencies, refused to cooperate and blocked united action by the Alliance. France took military action on its own in 1823, restored King Ferdinand VII, and abolished the Spanish constitution.

In both the Congress of Vienna and the system of alliances that succeeded it, European nations aimed to establish a balance of power that recognized legitimate rulers and preserved the peace. The upheaval of the French Revolution and the revolutionary and Napoleonic wars had made clear that the interdependence of nations was a guarantee of survival. Europe's statesmen hoped that by keeping the peace abroad, domestic peace would follow.

THE NEW IDEOLOGIES

After 1815, the world was changing in many ways. As national boundaries were being redefined, the ways in which Europeans regarded their world was also being transformed. Steam-driven mechanical power in production and transportation steadily replaced human and animal power. In deference to what it was replacing, the new mechanical force was measured in units of horsepower. The new technology challenged old values; new definitions of worth emerged from the changing world of work. The fixed, castelike distinctions of the old aristocratic world were under attack or in disarray. Western intellectuals struggled to make sense of the new age and their place in it.

The political and economic upheavals of the first half of the nineteenth century encouraged a new breed of thinkers to search for ways to explain the transformations of the period. Before midcentury, Europeans witnessed one of the most intellectually fertile periods in the history of the West. This era gave birth to new ideologies—liberalism, nationalism, romanticism, conservatism, and socialism—that came to shape the ideas and institutions of the present day.

The New Politics of Preserving Order

European states had been dealing with war for over two decades. Now they faced the challenge of peace. The revolution and Napoleon had not only meant military engagements; they had also brought the force of revolutionary ideas to the political arena, and these ideas did not retire from the field after Waterloo. Nor did treaties restore an old order, despite their claims. Governments throughout Europe had to find new ways to deal with the tension between state authority and individual liberty. Conservative and liberal thinkers took very different paths in the pursuit of political stability.

Conservatism. **Conservatism** represented a dynamic adaptation to a social system in transition. In place of individualism, conservatives stressed the established institutions of European society; in place of reason and progress, conservatives advocated gradual, evolutionary growth and social stability. They opposed an abrupt break with tradition. Liberty, argued British statesman Edmund Burke (1729–1797) in *Reflections on the Revolution in France* (1790), must emerge out of the gradual development of the old order, not its destruction. On the Continent, conservatives Louis de Bonald (1754–1840) and Joseph de Maistre (1753–1821) defended the monarchical principle of authority against the onslaught of revolutionary events.

Conservatism took a reactionary turn in the hands of the Austrian statesman Prince Klemens von Metternich. The Carlsbad decrees of 1819 are a good example of the "Metternich system" of espionage, censorship, and university repression in central Europe, which sought to eliminate any constitutional or nationalist sentiments that had arisen during the Napoleonic period. The German Confederation approved the decrees against free speech and civil liberties and set up mechanisms to root out "subversive" university students. Students who had taken up arms in the Wars of Liberation (1813–1815) against France had done so in hopes of instituting liberal and national reforms. Metternich's system aimed at uprooting these goals. Student fraternities were closed, and police became a regular fixture in the university. Political expression was driven underground for at least a decade. Metternich set out to crush liberalism, constitutionalism, and parliamentarianism in central Europe.

Liberalism. The term *liberal* was first used in a narrow, political sense to indicate the Spanish party of reform that supported the constitution modeled on the French document of 1791. But the term assumed much broader connotations in the first half of the nineteenth century as its appeal spread among the European middle classes. Two main tenets of **liberalism** asserted the freedom of the individual and the corruptibility of authority. As a political doctrine, liberalism built on Enlightenment rationalism and embraced the right to vote, civil liberties, legal equality, constitutional government, parliamentary sovereignty, and a free market economy. Liberals firmly believed that less government was better government and that noninterference would produce a harmonious and well-ordered world. They also believed that human beings were basically good and reasonable and needed freedom in which to flourish. The sole end of government should be to promote that freedom.

Liberal thinkers grappled with the political conflicts of the revolutionary period and the economic disruptions brought on by industrialization. The Great Revolution at the end of the eighteenth century spawned a vast array of liberal thought in France. Republicans, Bonapartists, and constitutional monarchists cooperated as self-styled "liberals," who shared a desire to preserve the gains of the revolution while ensuring orderly rule. Liberal ideas also influenced a variety of political movements in the United States, including those demanding the liberation of slaves and the extension of legal and political rights to women.

By the mid-nineteenth century, liberal thinking constituted a dominant strain in British politics. Jeremy Bentham (1748–1832) founded **utilitarianism,** a fundamentally liberal doctrine that argued for "the greatest happiness of the greatest number" in such works as *Introduction to the Principles of Morals and Legislation.* Bentham believed that government could achieve positive ends through limited and "scientific" intervention. John Stuart Mill (1806–1873) forged his own brand of classical liberalism in his treatise *On Liberty* (1859). Mill went beyond existing political analyses to apply economic doctrines to social conditions in *Principles of Political Economy* (1848). He espoused social reform for the poor and championed the equality of women and the necessity of birth control. David Ricardo (1772–1823), in *Principles of Political Economy and Taxation* (1817), outlined his opposition to government intervention in foreign trade and elaborated his "iron law of wages," which contended that wages would stabilize at the subsistence level. Increased wages would cause the working classes to increase, and the resulting competition in the labor market would drive wages down to the subsistence level.

Romanticism and Change

Unlike liberalism and conservatism, which were fundamentally political ideologies, **romanticism** designated a variety of literary and artistic movements throughout Europe that spanned the period from the late eighteenth century to the

■ *Liberty Leading the People* (1831) by Eugène Delacroix captures the spirit of the French romantics, who looked upon revolutionary action as a way to achieve union with the spirit of history.

mid-nineteenth century. One could be a liberal and a romantic just as easily as one could be a conservative and a romantic.

The Romantic World View.   Above all, in spite of variations, romantics shared similar beliefs and a common view of the world. Among the first romantics were the English poets William Wordsworth (1770–1850) and Samuel Taylor Coleridge (1772–1834), whose collaborative *Lyrical Ballads* (1798) exemplified the iconoclastic romantic idea that poetry was the result of "the spontaneous overflow of powerful feelings," rather than a formal and highly disciplined intellectual exercise. Romantics in general rebelled against the confinement of classical forms and refused to accept the supremacy of reason over emotions.

Intellectuals, Artists, and Freedom.   By rooting artistic vision in spontaneity, romantics endorsed a concept of creativity based on the supremacy of human freedom. The artist was valued in a new way as a genius through whose insight and intuition great art was created. Intuition, as opposed to scientific learning, was endorsed as a valid means of knowing. Building on the work of the eighteenth-century philosopher Immanuel Kant (1724–1804), romanticism embraced subjective knowledge. Inspiration and intuition took the place of reason and science in the romantic pantheon of values.

Germaine de Staël (1766–1817), whose writings influenced French political theory after 1815, is often hailed as the founder of French romanticism. She wrote histories, novels, literary criticism, and political tracts that opposed the tyranny of Napoleonic rule. Like many other romantics, she was greatly influenced by the writings of Jean-Jacques Rousseau, and through him she discovered that "the soul's elevation is born of self-consciousness." The recognition of the subjective meant for de Staël that women's vision was as essential as men's for the flowering of European culture.

The supremacy of emotions over reason found its way into the works of the great romantic composers of the age: Louis Hector Berlioz (1803–1869), the French composer who set Faust's damnation to music; Polish virtuoso Frédéric Chopin (1810–1849); and Hungarian concert pianist Franz Liszt (1811–1886). Artists such as J. M. W. Turner (1775–1851), the English landscape painter, and Eugène Delacroix (1798–1863), the leader of the French romantic school in painting, shared a rebellious experimentation with color and a rejection of classical conventions and forms.

In the postrevolutionary age of the years between 1815 and 1850, romanticism claimed to be no more than an aesthetic stance in art, letters, and music, a posture that had no particular political intent. Yet its validation of the individual as opposed to the caste or the estate was a revolutionary doctrine that helped to define a new political consciousness.

Reshaping State and Society

As another legacy of the French Revolution, the concept of the nation as a source of collective identity and political allegiance became a political force after 1815. Just as nationalism put the needs of the people at the heart of its political doctrine, so did socialism focus on the needs of society and especially of the poor.

Nationalism.   In its most basic sense, nationalism before 1850 was the political doctrine that glorified the people united against the absolutism of kings and the tyranny of foreign oppressors. The success of the French Revolution and the spread of Napoleonic reforms boosted nationalist doctrines, which were most fully articulated on the Continent. In Germany, Johann Gottfried von Herder (1744–1803) rooted national identity in German folk culture. *The Fairy Tales* (1812–1814) of the brothers Jacob Ludwig Grimm (1785–1863) and Wilhelm Carl Grimm (1786–1859) had a similar national purpose. The brothers painstakingly captured in print the German oral tradition of peasant folklore. The philosophers Johann Fichte (1762–1814) and Georg Wilhelm Friedrich Hegel (1770–1831) emphasized the importance of the state. There was a new concern with history, as nationalists sought to revive a common cultural past.

In the period between 1830 and 1850, many nationalists were liberals and many liberals were nationalists. The nationalist yearning for liberation meshed with the liberal political program of overthrowing tyrannical rule. Giuseppe Mazzini (1805–1872) represented the new breed of liberal nationalist. A less-than-liberal nationalist was political economist Georg Friedrich List (1789–1846), who formulated a statement of economic nationalism to counter the liberal doctrines of David Ricardo. Arguing that free trade worked only for the wealthy and powerful, List advocated a program of protective tariffs for developing German industries. British free trade, he perceived, was merely economic imperialism in disguise. List was one of the few nationalists who did not wholeheartedly embrace liberal economic doctrines. Beyond ideology and po-

litical practices, nationalism began to capture the imagination of groups who resented foreign domination. Expanding state bureaucracies did little to tame the centrifugal forces of nationalist feeling and probably exacerbated a desire for independence in eastern and central Europe, especially in the Habsburg-ruled lands.

Nationalists valued the authenticity of the vernacular and folklore over the language and customs imposed by a foreign ruler. Herder and the brothers Grimm were German examples of the romantic appreciation of the roots of German culture. While French romantics emphasized the glories of their revolutionary heritage, German romantics stressed the importance of history as the source of one's identity. By searching for the self in a historic past, and especially in the Middle Ages, they glorified their collective cultural identity and national origins.

Socialism.   Socialists rejected the world as it was. Socialism, like other ideologies of the first half of the nineteenth century, grew out of the changes in the structure of daily life and the structure of power. There were as many stripes of socialists as there were of liberals, nationalists, and conservatives.

Socialist thinkers in France theorized about alternative societies in which wealth would be more equitably distributed. To Henri de Saint-Simon (1760–1825) the accomplishments and potential of industrial development represented the highest stage in history. In a perfect and just society, productive work would be the basis of all prestige and power. The elite of society would be organized according to the hierarchy of its productive members, with industrial leaders at the top.

Like Saint-Simon, the French social theorist Pierre Joseph Proudhon (1809–1865) recognized the social value of work. But unlike Saint-Simon, Proudhon refused to accept the dominance of industrial society. Proudhon gained national prominence with his ideas about a just society, free credit, and equitable exchange. In his famous pamphlet *What Is Property?* (1840), Proudhon answered, "Property is theft." However, this statement was not an argument for the abolition of private ownership. Proudhon reasoned that industrialization had destroyed workers' rights, which included the right to the profits of their own labor. In attacking "property," in its meaning of profits amassed from the labor of others, Proudhon was arguing for a socialist concept of limited possession—people had the right to own only what they had earned from their own labor—and for a potentially anarchist concept of limited government—people had the right to rule themselves.

At least one socialist believed in luxury. Charles Fourier (1772–1837), an unsuccessful traveling salesman, devoted himself to the study and improvement of society and formulated one of the most trenchant criticisms of industrial capitalism. In numerous writings between 1808 and his death, this eccentric, solitary man put forth his vision of a utopian world organized into units called phalanxes that took into account their members' social, sexual, and economic needs. With a proper mix of duties, everyone in the phalanx would work only a few hours a day. In Fourier's scheme, work was not naturally abhorrent, but care had to be taken to match temperaments with tasks. Women and men fulfilled themselves and found pleasure and gratification through work. People would be paid according to their contributions in work, capital, and talent. In Fourier's phalanxes, every aspect of life would be organized communally, although neither poverty nor property would be eliminated. Education would help to dispel discord, and rich and poor would learn to live together in perfect harmony.

Charles Fourier's work, along with that of Saint-Simon and Proudhon, became part of the tradition of utopian thinking that can be traced back to Thomas More in the sixteenth century. Because he believed in the ability of individuals to shape themselves and their world, Fourier intended his critique of society to be a blueprint for living. Fourier's followers set up communities in his lifetime—40 phalanxes were established in the United States alone—but because of financial frustrations and petty squabbling, all of them failed.

The emancipation of women was an issue acknowledged by socialists as well as liberals. Some social reformers, including Fourier, put the issue of women's freedom at the center of their plans to redesign society. Other social reformers joined with conservative thinkers in arguing that women must be kept in their place, which was in the home.

Socialists, along with other ideologues in the decades before the middle of the nineteenth century, were aware of how rapidly their world was changing. Many believed that a revolution that would eliminate poverty and the sufferings of the working class was at hand. Followers of Saint-Simon, Proudhon, and Fourier all hoped that their proposals and ideas would change the world and prevent violent upheaval. Not all social critics were so sanguine.

In January 1848, two young men, one a philosopher living in exile and the other a businessman working for his father, began a collaboration that would last a lifetime with the publication of a short tract entitled **The Communist Manifesto.** Karl Marx (1818–1883) and Friedrich Engels (1820–1895) described the dire situation of the working classes throughout the 1840s. The growing poverty and alienation of the **proletariat,** the propertyless masses, the authors promised, would bring to industrialized Europe a class war against the capitalists. Exploited workers were to prepare themselves for the moment of revolution by joining with each other across national boundaries: "Workers of the world unite. You have nothing to lose but your chains." In light of subsequent events, the *Manifesto* appears to be a work of great predictive value. But neither Marx nor Engels could know that the hour of revolution was at hand.

Intellectuals and reformers hoped with the force of their ideas to reshape the world in which they lived. The technology of industrial production informed people's values and required a new way of looking at the world. Liberals, nationalists, romantics, conservatives, and socialists addressed the challenges of a changing economy in a political universe buffeted by democratic ideas. Rather than providing neat answers, ideologies fueled actions, and often violent protest and revolution erupted in the streets.

PROTEST AND REVOLUTION

For European societies that had remained stable, if not stagnant, for centuries, the changes in the first half of the nineteenth century were undoubtedly startling and disruptive. New factories created the arena for exploitation and misery. More people than ever before lived in cities, and national populations faced the prospect of becoming urban. Urban congestion brought crime and disease; patterns of consumption demonstrated beyond dispute that people were not created equal. A new European society that challenged existing political ideas and demanded new political formulations was in the process of emerging.

Causes of Social Instability

The fabric of stability began unraveling throughout Europe beginning in the 1820s. The forces of order reacted to protest with repression everywhere in Europe. Yet armed force proved inadequate to contain the demands for political participation and the increased political awareness of whole segments of the population. Workers, the middle class, and women's political organizations now demanded, through the vote, the right to govern themselves.

Urban Miseries. In 1800, two of every one hundred Europeans lived in a city. By 1850, the number of urban dwellers per hundred had jumped to five and was rising rapidly. England, where one of every two inhabitants lived in a city, had become an urban society by midcentury. London was the fastest-growing city in Europe.

Massive internal migration caused most urban growth. People from the same rural areas often lived together in the same urban neighborhoods and even in the same boardinghouses. Irish emigrants, for example, crowded together in the "Little Dublin" section of London. Until midcentury, many migrants returned to their rural homes for the winter when work, especially in the building trades, was scarce in the city. Young migrant women who came to the city to work as servants sent money home to support rural relatives or worked to save a nest egg—or dowry—in order to return to the village permanently. Before 1850, 20 percent of the workers in London were domestics, and most of these were women.

Despite the neighborhood support networks that migrants constructed for themselves, the city was not always a hospitable place. Workers were poorly paid, and women workers were more poorly paid than men. When working women were cut free of the support of home and family, uncounted numbers were forced into part-time prostitution to supplement meager incomes. More and more women resorted to prostitution as a means of surviving in times of unemployment. It is conservatively estimated that there were 34,000 prostitutes in Paris in 1850 and 50,000 in London. Increased prostitution created an epidemic of venereal diseases, especially syphilis, for which there was no cure until the twentieth century.

Urban crime also grew astronomically, thefts accounting for the greatest number of crimes. Social reformers identified poverty and urban crowding as causes of the increase in criminal behavior. In 1829, both Paris and London began to create modern urban police forces to deal with the challenges to law and order. Crime assumed the character of disease in the minds of middle-class reformers. Statisticians and social scientists, themselves a new urban phenomenon, produced massive theses on social hygiene, lower-class immorality, and the unworthiness of the poor. The pathology of the city was widely discussed. Always at the center of the issue was the "social question": the growing problem of what to do with the poor.

The "Social Question." State-sponsored work relief expanded after 1830 for the deserving poor: the old, the sick, and children. Able-bodied workers who were idle were regarded as undeserving and dangerous, regardless of the causes of their unemployment. Performance of work became an indicator of moral worth, as urban and rural workers succumbed to downturns in the economic cycle. Those who were unable to work sought relief, as a last resort, from the state. What has been called "a revolution in government" took place in the 1830s and 1840s, as legislative bodies increased regulation of everything from factories and mines to prisons and schools.

Some argued, as in the case of the Irish famine, that the government must do nothing to intervene because the problem would correct itself, as Thomas Malthus had predicted 40 years earlier, through the "natural" means of famine and death that would keep population from outgrowing available resources and food supplies. The Irish population, one of the poorest in Europe, had indeed doubled between 1781 and 1841, and for Malthusians the Irish famine was the fulfillment of their vision that overpopulation would be corrected by war, disease, or famine. Poverty was a social necessity; by interfering with it, this first group insisted, governments could only make matters worse.

Others contended that poverty was society's problem, not a law of nature. Therefore, it was the social responsibility of the state to take care of its members. The question of how to treat poverty, or "the social question" as it came to be known among contemporaries, underlay many of the protests and reforms of the two decades before 1850 and fueled the revolutionary movements of 1848. Parliamentary legislation attempted to improve the situation of the poor and especially the working class in the 1830s and 1840s.

In 1833, British reformers turned their attention to the question of child labor. Parliament passed the Factory Act of 1833, which prohibited the employment of children under nine years of age and restricted the work week of children between the ages of 9 and 13 to 48 hours. No child in this age group could work more than nine hours a day. Teenagers between 13 and 18 years of age could work no more than 69 hours a week. By modern standards these "reformed" workloads present a shocking picture of the heavy reliance on child labor. The British Parliament commissioned investigations, compiled in the "Blue Books," that reported the abusive treatment of men, women, and children in factories. Similar studies existed for French and Belgian industry.

The British legislation marked an initial step in state intervention in the workplace. Additional legislation over the next three decades further restricted children's and women's labor in factories and concerned itself with improvement of conditions in the workplace. At bottom the social question was: What was the state's responsibility in caring for its citizens?

■ This 1834 engraving from *The Oracle of Health* shows the brutal treatment of children working in an English textile factory. The meager wages of children were often necessary for the survival of their families.

The Revolutions of 1830

Few Europeans who were alive in 1830 remembered the age of revolution from 1789 to 1799. Yet the legends were kept alive from one generation to the next. Secret political organizations perpetuated Jacobin republicanism. Mutual-aid societies and artisan associations preserved the rituals of democratic culture. A revolutionary culture seemed to be budding in the student riots in Germany and in the revolutionary waves that swept across southern and central Europe in the early 1820s. Outside Manchester, England, in August 1819, a crowd of 80,000 people gathered in St. Peter's Field to hear speeches for parliamentary reform and universal male suffrage. The cavalry swept down on them in a bloody slaughter that came to be known as the **Peterloo massacre,** a bitter reference to the Waterloo victory four years before.

Poor harvests in 1829 followed by a harsh winter left people cold, hungry, and bitter. Misery fueled social protest, and the convergence of social unrest with long-standing political demands touched off apparently simultaneous revolutions all over Europe. Governmental failures to respond to local grievances sparked the revolutions of 1830. Highly diverse groups of workers, students, lawyers, professionals, and peasants rose up spontaneously to demand a voice in the affairs of government.

The French Revolution of 1830.   In France, the late 1820s was a period of increasing political friction. Charles X (1824–1830), the former comte d'Artois, had never resigned himself to the constitutional monarchy accepted by his brother and predecessor, Louis XVIII. When Charles assumed the throne in 1824, he dedicated himself to a true restoration of kingship as it existed before the revolution. To this end, he realigned the monarchy with the Catholic Church and undertook several unpopular measures, including approval of the death penalty for people who were found guilty of sacrilege. The king's bourgeois critics, heavily influenced by liberal ideas about political economy and constitutional rights, sought increased political power through their activities in secret organizations and in public elections. The king responded to his critics by relying on his ultraroyalist supporters to run the government. In May 1830, the king dissolved the Chamber of Deputies and ordered new elections. The elections returned a liberal majority that was unfavorable to the king. Charles X retaliated with what proved to be his last political act, the Four Ordinances, in which he censored the press, changed the electoral law to favor his own candidates, dissolved the newly elected chamber, and ordered new elections.

Opposition to Charles X might have remained at the level of political wrangling and journalistic protest had it not been for the problems plaguing the people of Paris. A severe winter in France had driven food prices up by 75 percent. The king underestimated the extent of hardship and the political volatility of the population. Throughout the spring of 1830, prices continued to rise and Charles continued to blunder. In a spontaneous uprising in the last days of July 1830, workers took to the streets of Paris. The revolution that they initiated spread rapidly to towns and the countryside, as people throughout France protested the cost of living, hoarding by grain merchants, tax collection, and wage cuts. In "three glorious days" the restored Bourbon regime was pulled down, and Charles X fled to England.

The people fighting in the streets demanded a republic, but they lacked organization and political experience. Liberal bourgeois politicians quickly filled the power vacuum. They presented Charles's cousin, the duc d'Orléans, as the savior of France and the new constitutional monarch. This July Monarchy, born of a revolution, put an end to the Bourbon Restoration. Louis-Philippe, the former duc d'Orléans, became king of the French. The charter that he brought with him was, like its predecessor, based on restricted suffrage, with property ownership a requisite for voting.

Unrest in Europe.   Popular disturbances did not always result in revolution. In Britain, rural and town riots erupted over grain prices and distribution, but no revolution followed. German workers broke their machines to protest low wages and loss of control of the workplace, but no prince was displaced. In Switzerland, reformers found strength in the French revolutionary example. Ten Swiss cantons granted liberal constitutions and established universal manhood suffrage, freedom of expression, and legal equality.

In southern Europe, Turkish overlords ruled Greece as part of the Ottoman Empire. The longing for independence smoldered in Greece throughout the 1820s as public pressure to support the Greeks mounted in Europe. Greek insurrections were answered by Turkish retaliations throughout the Ottoman Empire. The sultan of Turkey had been able to call on his vassal, the pasha of Egypt, to subdue Greece. In response, Great Britain, France, and Russia signed the Treaty of London in 1827, pledging intervention on behalf of Greece. In a joint effort, the three powers defeated the Egyptian fleet. Russia declared war on Turkey the following year, seeking territorial concessions from the Ottoman Empire. Following the Russian victory, Great Britain and France joined Russia in declaring Greek independence. The concerted action of the three powers in favor of Greek independence was neither an endorsement of liberal ideals nor a support of Greek nationalism. The British, French, and Russians were reasserting their commitment, made at the Congress of Vienna, to territorial stability.

Belgian Independence.   The overthrow of the Bourbon monarch in France served as a model for revolution in other parts of Europe. In the midst of the Greek crisis the Belgian provinces revolted against the Netherlands. The Belgians' desire to have their own nation struck at the heart of the Vienna settlement. Provoked by a food crisis similar to that in France, Belgian revolutionaries took to the streets in August 1830. Belgians protested the deterioration of their economic situation and made demands for their own Catholic religion, their own language, and constitutional rights. Bitter fighting on the barricades in Brussels ensued, and the movement for freedom and independence spread to the countryside.

The Great Powers disagreed about what to do. Russia, Austria, and Prussia were all eager to see the revolution crushed. France, having just established the new regime of the July Monarchy, and Great Britain, fearing the involvement of the central and eastern European powers in an area where Britain had traditionally had interests, were reluctant to intervene. A provisional government in Belgium set about the task of writing a constitution. All five great powers recognized Belgian independence, with the proviso that Belgium was to maintain the status of a neutral state.

The Forgotten Revolutions.   Russia, Prussia, and Austria were convinced to accept Belgian independence because they were having their own problems in eastern and southern Europe. Revolution erupted in Warsaw when Polish army cadets and university students revolted in November 1830 to demand independence and a constitution. Landed aristocrats and gentry helped to establish a provisional government but soon split over how radical reforms should be. Polish peasants refused to support either landowning group. Within the year, Russia brought in 180,000 troops to crush the revolution and reassert its rule over Poland.

In February 1831, the Italian states of Modena and Parma rose up to throw off Austrian domination of northern Italy. The revolutionaries were ineffective against Austrian troops. Revolution in the Papal States resulted in French occupation that lasted until 1838 without serious reforms. Nationalist and republican yearnings were driven underground, kept alive there in the Young Italy movement under the leadership of Giuseppe Mazzini.

Although the revolutions of 1830 are called "the forgotten revolutions" of the nineteenth century, they are important for several reasons. First, they made clear to European states how closely tied together were their fates. True to the principles of the Vienna settlements of 1815, European leaders preserved the status quo and maintained the balance of power. Revolutions in Poland and Italy were contained by Russia and Austria without interference from the other powers. Where adaptation was necessary, as in Greece and Belgium, the Great Powers were able to compromise on settlements, even though the solutions ran counter to previous policies. Heads of state were willing to use the forces of repression to stamp out protest. The international significance of the revolutions reveals a second important aspect of the events of 1830: the vulnerability of international politics to domestic instability.

Finally, the 1830 revolutions exposed a growing awareness of politics at all levels of European society. If policies in 1830 revealed a shared consciousness of events and shared values among ruling elites, the revolutions disclosed a growing awareness among the lower classes of the importance of politics in their daily lives. In a dangerous combination, workers and the lower classes throughout Europe were politicized, yet they continued to be excluded from political power.

Reform in Great Britain

The right to vote had been an issue of contention in the revolutions of 1830 in western Europe. Only the Swiss cantons enforced the principle of one man, one vote. The July Revolution in France had doubled the electorate, but still only a tiny minority of the population (less than 1 percent) enjoyed the vote. Universal male suffrage had been mandated in 1793 during the Great Revolution but not implemented. Those in power believed that the wealthiest property owners were best qualified to govern, in part because they had the greatest stake in politics and society. One also needed to own property to hold office, since those who served in parliaments received no salary.

The Rule of the Land.   Landowners also ruled Britain. Migration to cities had depleted the population of rural areas, but the electoral system did not adjust to these changes. Large towns had no parliamentary representation, while dwindling county electorates maintained their parliamentary strength. Areas that continued to enjoy representation greater than that justified by their population were dubbed "rotten boroughs" or "pocket boroughs" to indicate a corrupt and antiquated

■ This English cartoon of 1832 is titled *The Clemency of the Russian Monster.* It shows Nicholas I in the guise of a bear with menacing teeth and claws addressing the Poles after crushing their rebellion against Russian rule.

'Gentlemen,' says Nicholas I, the bear, to the Polish revolutionaries of 1830, 'I know that you wish to address me; but to spare you from delivering a pack of lies, I desire that you hold your tongues.' The Polish rebellion of 1830–31 was brutally suppressed by the Russians. However, this brutality reinforced Polish national sentiment (the Poles rebelled again in 1863) and engaged the sympathy of the West for the Poles—as this English cartoon shows. (2)

electoral system. In general, urban areas were grossly underrepresented, as the wealthy few controlled county seats. Liberal reformers tried to rectify the electoral inequalities by reassigning parliamentary seats on the basis of density of population.

After much parliamentary wrangling and popular agitation, the **Great Reform Bill of 1832** proposed a compromise. Although the vast majority of the population still did not have the vote, the new legislation strengthened the industrial and commercial elite in the towns, enfranchised most of the middle class, opened the way to social reforms, and encouraged the formation of political parties. In the 1830s, new radical reformers, disillusioned with the 1832 reform bill because it strengthened the power of a wealthy capitalist class, argued that democracy was the only answer to the problems plaguing British society.

The Chartist Movement.

In 1838, a small group of labor leaders, including representatives of the London Working Men's Association, an organization of craft workers, drew up a document known as the People's Charter. The single most important demand of the charter was that all men must have the vote. In addition, Chartists petitioned for a secret ballot, salaries for parliamentary service, elimination of property qualifications to run for office, equal electoral districts, and annual elections.

Chartism blossomed in working-class towns and appeared to involve all members of the family. Women organized Chartist schools and Sunday schools in radical defiance of local church organizations. Many middle-class observers were sure that the moment for class war and revolutionary upheaval had arrived. The government responded with force to the perceived threat of armed rebellion and imprisoned a number of Chartist leaders. The final moment for Chartism occurred in April 1848, when 25,000 Chartist workers, inspired by revolutionary events on the Continent, assembled in London to march on the House of Commons. They carried a newly signed petition demanding the enactment of the terms of their charter. In response, the government deputized nearly 200,000 "special" constables in the streets. These deputized private citizens were London property owners and skilled workers who were intent on holding back a revolutionary rabble. Tired, cold, and rain-soaked, the Chartist demonstrators disbanded. No social revolution took place in Great Britain, and the dilemma of democratic representation was deferred.

Workers Unite

The word *proletariat* entered European languages before the mid-nineteenth century to describe those workers afloat in the labor pool who owned nothing, not even the tools of their labor, and who were becoming appendages to the new machines that dominated production.

Luddism.

Mechanization deprived skilled craftworkers of control of the workplace. In Great Britain, France, and Germany, groups of textile workers destroyed machines in protest. Machine-breakers tyrannized parts of Great Britain from 1811 to 1816 in an attempt to frighten masters. The movement was known as Luddism after its mythical leader, Ned Ludd. Workers damaged and destroyed property for more control over the work process, but such destruction met with severe repression. From the 1820s to the 1850s, sporadic but intense outbursts of machine-breaking occurred in continental Europe. Skilled workers, fearing that they would be pulled down into the new proletariat because of mechanization and the increased scale of production, organized in new ways after 1830.

Uprisings and strikes in France increased dramatically from 1831 to 1834 and favored the destruction of the monarchy and the creation of a democratic republic. Many French craft workers grew conscious of themselves as a class and embraced a socialism that was heavily influenced by their own traditions and contemporary socialist writings. Republican socialism spread throughout France by means of a network of traveling journeymen and tapped into growing economic hardship and political discontent with the July Monarchy. Government repression drove worker organizations underground in the late 1830s, and secret societies proliferated.

Women in the Workforce.

Women were an important part of the workforce in the industrializing societies. Working men were keenly aware of the competition with cheaper female labor in the factories. Women formed a salaried workforce in the home, too. To produce cheaply and in large quantities, some manufacturers turned to subcontractors for the simpler tasks in the work process. These new middlemen contracted out work such as cutting and sewing to needy women, who were often responsible for caring for family members in their homes.

Cheap female labor, paid by the piece, allowed employers to profit by keeping overhead costs low and by driving down the wages of skilled workers. Trade unions opposed women's work both in the home and in the factories. Women's talents, union leaders explained, were more properly devoted to domestic chores. Unions argued that their members should earn a wage "sufficient to support a wife and children." Unions consistently excluded women workers from their ranks.

French labor leader Flora Tristan, speaking not only as a worker but also as a wife and mother, had a very different answer for those who wanted to remove women from the workplace and assign them to their "proper place" in the home. She recognized that working women needed to work in order to support themselves and their families. Tristan told audiences in Europe and Latin America that the emancipation of women from their "slave status" was essential if the working class as a whole was to enjoy a better future.

Working women's only hope, according to Tristan, lay in education and unionization. She urged working men and women to join together to lay claim to their natural and inalienable rights. In some cases, working women formed their own organizations, like that of the Parisian seamstresses who

FLORA TRISTAN AND THE RIGHTS OF WORKING WOMEN

Flora Tristan (1803–1844) was a feminist and socialist who in the 1830s was actively involved in efforts to reintroduce divorce and to abolish the death penalty. She made her greatest political efforts for the creation of an international union of workers. The education of women was, Tristan asserted, essential for the success and prosperity of the working class. She toured slums in England and traveled across France on lecture tours to promote workers' unions and the education of women. The excerpt below is taken from her important book, L'Union Ouvrière, 1843. *Tristan's argument for women's education is based not only on the claims of women to basic human rights, but on her assertion that educated women held the key to the betterment of families, the working class, and the whole society.*

Focus Questions

Why is education so important in Tristan's justification of women's rights? Would you describe Tristan as a reformer or a revolutionary?

. . . [I]t is imperative, in order to improve the intellectual, moral, and material condition of the working class, that women of the lower classes be given a rational and solid education, conducive to the development of their good inclinations, so that they may become skillful workers, good mothers, capable of raising and guiding their children, and of tutoring them in their school work, and so that they may act as moralizing agents in the life of the men on whom they exert an influence from the cradle to the grave.

Do you begin to understand, you, men, who cry shame before even looking into the question, why I demand rights for woman? Why I should like her to be placed on a footing of absolute equality with man in society, and that she should be so by virtue of the legal right every human being brings at birth?

I demand rights for women because I am convinced that all the misfortunes in the world result from the neglect and contempt in which woman's natural and inalienable rights have so far been held. I demand rights for woman because

it is the only way she will get an education, and because the education of man in general and man of the lower classes in particular depends on the education of woman. I demand rights for woman because it is the only way to obtain her rehabilitation in the Church, the law, and society, and because this preliminary rehabilitation is necessary to achieve the rehabilitation of the workers themselves. All the woes of the working class can be summed up in these two words: poverty and ignorance, ignorance and poverty. Now, I see only one way out of this labyrinth: begin by educating women, because women have the responsibility of educating male and female children. . . .

As soon as the dangerous consequences of the development of the moral and physical faculties of women—dangerous because of women's current slave status—are no longer feared, woman can be taught with great care so as to make the best possible use of her intelligence and work. Then, you, men of the lower classes, will have as mothers skillful workers who earn a decent salary, are educated, well brought up, and quite capable of raising you, of educating you, the workers, as is proper for free men. You will have well brought up and well educated sisters, lovers, wives, friends, with whom daily contacts will be most pleasant for you. Nothing is sweeter or more agreeable to a man's heart than the sensible and gracious conversation of good and well educated women.

joined together to demand improved working conditions. On the whole, however, domestic workers in the home remained isolated from other working women, and many women in factories feared the loss of their jobs if they engaged in political activism. The wages of Europe's working women remained low, often below subsistence level.

Revolutions Across Europe, 1848–1850

Europeans had never experienced a year like 1848. Beginning soon after the ringing in of the New Year, revolutionary fervor swept through nearly every European country. By year's end, regimes had been created and destroyed. France, Italy, the German states, Austria, Hungary, and Bohemia were shaken to their foundations. Switzerland, Denmark, and Romania ex-

perienced lesser upheavals. Great Britain had survived reformist agitation, and famine-crippled Ireland had endured a failed insurrection.

Hindsight reveals warning signs in the two years before the 1848 cataclysm. Beginning in 1846, a severe famine racked Europe. Lack of grain drove up prices. An increasing percentage of disposable income was spent on food for survival. Lack of spending power severely damaged markets and forced thousands of industrial workers out of their jobs. The famine hurt everyone—the poor, workers, employers, and investors—as recession paralyzed the economy.

The food crisis took place in a heavily charged political atmosphere. Throughout Europe during the 1840s, middle and lower classes had intensified their agitation for democracy. Chartists in Great Britain argued for a wider electorate.

Bourgeois reformers in France campaigned for universal manhood suffrage. The movement was known as the "banquet" campaign because its leaders attempted to raise money by giving speeches at subscribed dinners. In making demands for political participation, those who were agitating for the vote necessarily criticized those who were in power. Freedom of speech and freedom of assembly were demanded as inalienable rights. The food crisis and political activism were the ingredients of an incendiary situation.

In addition to a burgeoning democratic culture, growing demands for national autonomy based on linguistic and cultural claims spread through central, southern, and eastern Europe. Although the revolts in Poland in 1846 failed, they encouraged similar movements for national liberation among Italians and Germans. Even in the relatively homogeneous nation of France, concerns with national mission and national glory grew among the regime's critics. National unity was primarily a middle-class ideal. Liberal lawyers, teachers, and businessmen from Dublin to Budapest to Prague agitated for separation from foreign rule. Austria, with an empire formed of numerous ethnic minorities, had the most to lose. Since 1815, Metternich had been ruthless in stamping out nationalist dissent. By the 1840s, nationalist claims were assuming a cultural legitimacy that was difficult to dismiss or ignore.

France Leads the Way.   The events in France in the cold February of 1848 ignited the conflagration that swept Europe. On 22 February, bourgeois reformers had staged their largest banquet to date in Paris in support of extension of the vote. City officials became nervous at the prospect of thousands of workers assembling for political purposes and canceled the scheduled banquet. This was the spark that touched off the powder keg. In a spontaneous uprising, Parisians demonstrated against the government's repressive measures. Skilled workers took to the streets not only in favor of the banned banquet but also with the hope that the government would recognize the importance of labor to the social order. Shots were fired; a demonstrator was killed. The French Revolution of 1848 had begun.

Events moved quickly. The National Guard, a citizen militia of bourgeois Parisians, defected from Louis-Philippe. Many army troops that were garrisoned in Paris crossed the barricades to join revolutionary workers. The king attempted some reform, but it was too little and too late. Louis-Philippe fled. The Second Republic was proclaimed at the insistence of the revolutionary crowds on the barricades. The Provisional Government, led by the poet Alphonse de Lamartine (1790–1869), included members of both factions of political reformers of the July Monarchy: moderates who sought constitutional reforms and an extension of the suffrage and radicals who favored universal manhood suffrage and social programs to deal with poverty and work. Only the threat of popular violence held this uneasy alliance together.

The people fighting in the streets had little in common with the bourgeois reformers who assumed power on 24 February. Workers made a social revolution out of a commitment to their right to work, which would replace the right to property as the organizing principle of the new society. Only one member of the new Provisional Government was a worker, and he was included as a token symbol of the intentions of the new government. The government acknowledged the demand of the right to work and set up two mechanisms to guarantee workers' relief. First, a commission of workers and employers was created to act as a grievance and bargaining board and to settle questions of common concern in the workplace. Headed by the socialist Louis Blanc (1811–1882) and known as the Luxembourg Commission, the worker-employer parliament was an important innovation but accomplished little other than deflecting workers' attention away from the problems of the Provisional Government. The second measure was the creation of "national workshops" to deal with the problems of unemployment in Paris. Workers from all over France poured into Paris with the hope of finding jobs. However, the workshops had a residency requirement that even Parisians had difficulty meeting. As a result, unemployment skyrocketed. Furthermore, the government was going bankrupt trying to support the program. The need to raise taxes upset peasants in the provinces. National pressure mounted to repudiate the programs of the revolution.

French workers were too weak to dominate the revolution. The government recalled General Louis Cavaignac (1802–1857) from service in Algeria to maintain order. In a wave of armed insurrection, Parisian workers rebelled in June of 1848. Using troops from the provinces who had no identification with the urban population and employing guerrilla techniques he had mastered in Algeria, Cavaignac put down the uprising. The Second Republic was placed under the military dictatorship of Cavaignac until December, when presidential elections were scheduled.

Revolutions in Central and Eastern Europe.   France was not alone in undergoing revolution in 1848. Long-suppressed desires for civil liberties and constitutional reforms erupted in widespread popular disturbances in Prussia and the German states. Fearing a war with France and unable to count on Austria or Russia for support, the princes who ruled Baden, Württemberg, Hesse-Darmstadt, Bavaria, Saxony, and Hanover followed the advice of moderate liberals and acceded quickly to revolutionary demands. In Prussia, King Frederick William IV (1840–1861) preferred to use military force to respond to popular demonstrations. Only in mid-March 1848 did the Prussian king yield to the force of the revolutionary crowds building barricades in Berlin by ordering his troops to leave the city and by promising to create a national Prussian assembly. The king was now a prisoner of the revolution.

MAP DISCOVERY

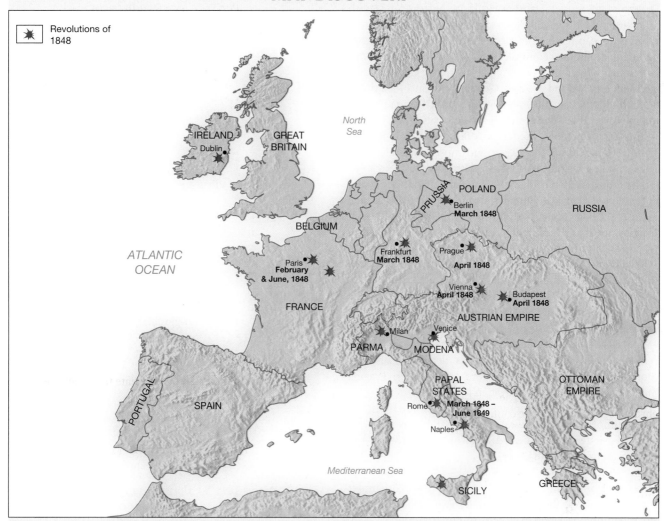

The Revolutions of 1848

In less than a generation, a second major wave of revolutions swept across Europe from west to east in 1848. What were the centers of revolutionary action in 1848 and what was their relationship to the seats of political power? How do you explain the timing of the eastern trajectory of successive revolutions? How did the map of Europe change as a result of these revolutions?

Meanwhile, the collapse of absolute monarchy in Prussia gave further impetus to a constitutional movement among the liberal leaders of the German states. The governments of all the German states were invited to elect delegates to a national parliament in Frankfurt. The Frankfurt parliament, which was convened in May 1848, had as its dual charge the framing of a constitution and the unification of Germany. It was composed, for the most part, of members of the middle class, with civil servants, lawyers, and intellectuals predomi-

nating. In spite of the principle of universal manhood suffrage, there was not a single worker among the 800 men who were elected. To most parliamentarians, who were trained in universities and shared a social and cultural identity, nationalism and constitutionalism were inextricably related.

As straightforward as the desire for a German nation appeared to be, it was complicated by two important facts. First, there were non-German minorities living in German states. What was to be done with the Poles, Czechs, Slovenes, Italians, and Dutch in a newly constituted and autonomous German nation? Second, there were Germans living outside the German states under Habsburg rule in Austria, in Danish Schleswig and Holstein, in Posen (Poznan), in Russian Poland, and in European Russia. How were they to be included within the linguistically and ethnically constituted German nation? After much wrangling over a "small" Germany that excluded Austrian Germans and a "large" Germany that included them, the Frankfurt parliament opted for the small-Germany solution in March 1849. The crown of the new nation was offered to the unpredictable Frederick William IV of Prussia (1840–1861), head of the largest and most powerful of the German states. Unhappy with his capitulation to the revolutionary crowd in March 1848, the Prussian king refused to accept a "crown from the gutter." He had his own plans to rule over a middle-European bloc, but not at the behest of liberal parliamentarians. The attempt to create a German nation crumbled with his unwillingness to lead.

Revolution in Austrian-dominated central Europe was concentrated in three places: Vienna, Budapest, and Prague. By April 1848, Metternich had fallen from power, and the Viennese revolutionaries had set up a constituent assembly. In Budapest, the initial steps of the patriot Lajos Kossuth (1802–1894) toward establishing a separate Hungarian state seemed equally solid, as the Magyars defeated Habsburg troops. Habsburg armies were more successful in Prague, where they crushed the revolution in June 1848.

In December 1848, Emperor Ferdinand I (1835–1848), whose authority had been weakened irreparably by the overthrow of Metternich, abdicated in favor of his 18-year-old nephew, Franz Josef I (1848–1916).

Italian Nationalism.   The Habsburg empire was also under siege in Italy, where the Kingdom of the Two Sicilies, Tuscany, and Piedmont declared new constitutions in March 1848. Championed by Charles Albert of Piedmont, Venice and Lombardy rose up against Austria. Nationalist sentiments had percolated underground in the Young Italy movement, founded in 1831 by Giuseppe Mazzini. Mazzini (1805–1872), a tireless and idealistic patriot, favored a democratic revolution. In spite of a reputation for liberal politics, Pope Pius IX (1846–1878) lost control of Rome and was forced to flee the city. Mazzini became head of the Republic of Rome, created in February 1849.

The French government decided to intervene to protect the pope's interests and sent in troops to defeat the republicans. One of Mazzini's disciples, Giuseppe Garibaldi (1807–1882), returned from exile in South America to undertake the defense of Rome. Garibaldi was a capable soldier who had learned the tactics of guerrilla warfare by joining independence struggles in Brazil and Argentina. Although his legion of poorly armed patriots and soldiers of fortune, known from their attire as the Red Shirts, waged a valiant effort to defend the city from April to June 1849, they were no match for the

CHRONOLOGY PROTEST AND REVOLUTION	
August 1819	Peterloo Massacre
1824	Charles X assumes French throne
1827	Treaty of London to support liberation of Greece
July 1830	Revolution in Paris; creation of July Monarchy under Louis-Philippe
August 1830	Revolution in Belgium
November 1830	Revolution in Poland
1831–1838	Revolutions in Italian states
1831–1834	Labor protests in France
1832	Britain's Great Reform Bill
1838	Drawing up the first People's Charter in Britain
1846	Beginning of food crisis in Europe; revolts in Poland
1846–1848	Europe-wide movements for national liberation
February 1848	Revolution in France; overthrow of the July Monarchy; proclamation of the French Second Republic and creation of Provisional Government
March 1848	Uprisings in some German states; granting of a constitution in Prussia
March 1848– June 1849	Revolutions in Italy
April 1848	Revolutions in Vienna, Budapest, Prague
May 1848	Frankfurt Assembly
June 1848	Second revolution in Paris, severely repressed by army troops under General Cavaignac
December 1848	Presidential elections in France; Louis Napoleon wins

highly trained French army. French troops restored Pius IX as ruler of the Papal States.

Meanwhile, from August 1848 to the following spring, the Habsburg armies fought and finally defeated each of the revolutions throughout the Austrian Empire. Austrian success can be explained in part because the various Italian groups of Piedmontese, Tuscans, Venetians, Romans, and Neapolitans lacked coordination and central organization. Both Mazzini and Pius IX had failed to provide the focal point of leadership necessary for a successful national movement. By the fall of 1849, Austria had solved the problems in its own capital and with Italy and Hungary by military dominance. Austria understood that a Germany united under Frederick William IV of Prussia would undermine Austrian dominance in central Europe.

Europe in 1850. In 1850, Austrians threatened the Prussians with war if they did not give up their plans for a unified Germany. In November of that year, Prussian ministers signed an agreement with their Austrian counterparts in the Moravian city of Olmutz. The convention became known as "the humiliation of Olmutz" because Prussia was forced to accept Austrian dominance or go to war. In every case, military force and diplomatic measures prevailed to defeat the national and liberal movements within the German states and the Austrian Empire.

By 1850, a veneer of calm spread over central Europe. In Prussia, the peasantry was emancipated from feudal dues, and a constitution, albeit conservative and based on a three-class system, was established. Yet beneath the surface was the deeper reality of Austrian decline and Prussian challenge. The great Habsburg Empire had needed to call on outside help from Russia to defeat its enemies within. The imperial giant was again on its feet, but for how long? In international relations, Austria's dominance in the German Confederation had diminished, as Prussia assumed greater political and economic power.

The 1848 revolutions spelled the end to the concert of Europe as it had been defined in the peace settlement of 1815. The European powers were incapable of united action to defend established territorial interests.

The revolutions of 1848 failed in part because of the irreconcilable split between moderate liberals and radical democrats. The participation of the masses had frightened members of the middle classes who were committed to moderate reforms that did not threaten property. In France, working-class revolutionaries had attempted to replace property with labor as the standard of status. Property triumphed. In the face of more extreme solutions, members of the middle class were willing to accept the increased authority of existing rule as a bulwark against anarchy. In December 1848, Prince Louis Napoleon, nephew of the former emperor, was elected president of the Second Republic by a wide margin. The first truly modern French politician, Louis Napoleon managed to appeal to everyone—workers, bourgeois, royalists, and peasants—by making promises that were vague or unkeepable. Severe repression forced radical protest into hiding. The new Bonaparte bided his time until the moment in 1851 when he seized absolute power.

Similar patterns emerged elsewhere in Europe. In Germany, the bourgeoisie accepted the dominance of the old feudal aristocracy as a guarantee of law and order. Repressive government, businessmen were sure, would restore a strong economy. The attempts in 1848 to create new nations based on ethnic identities were in shambles by 1850.

Nearly everywhere throughout Europe, constitutions had been systematically withdrawn with the recovery of the forces of reaction. With the French and Swiss exceptions, the bids for the extension of the franchise failed. The propertied classes remained in control of political institutions. Radicals willing to use violence to press electoral reforms were arrested, killed, or exiled. There seemed to be no effective opposition to the rise and consolidation of state power. The 1848 revolutions have been called a turning point at which modern history failed to turn. Contemporaries wondered how so much action could have produced so few lasting results.

CONCLUSION

The perception that nothing had changed was wrong. The revolutions of 1848 and subsequent events galvanized whole societies to political action. Conservatives and radicals alike turned toward a new realism in politics. Governments could no longer ignore economic upheavals and social dislocations if they wanted to survive. Revolutionaries also learned that the state could wield powerful forces of repression. The state wielded powerful forces of violence against which nationalists, socialists, republicans, and liberals had all been proved helpless. Organizing, campaigning, and lobbying were newly learned political skills, as was outreach across class lines—from bourgeoisie to peasantry—around common political causes. In these ways, 1848 was a turning point in the formation of a modern political culture.

QUESTIONS FOR REVIEW

1. What problems did European peacemakers confront at the Congress of Vienna and how did they attempt to resolve the problems?
2. How did industrialization change European families?
3. In what ways were liberalism and nationalism compatible with each other; how were they in conflict?
4. What are the connections between various ideologies—for instance, liberalism, romanticism, or socialism—and the revolutions of 1830 and 1848?

KEY TERMS

chartism, *p. 454*

The Communist Manifesto, p. 450

Congress of Vienna, *p. 442*

conservatism, *p. 447*

Great Reform Bill of 1832, *p. 454*

Holy Alliance, *p. 446*

liberalism, *p. 447*

Peterloo Massacre, *p. 451*

proletariat *p. 450*

Quadruple Alliance, *p. 446*

Quintuple Alliance, *p. 446*

romanticism, *p. 447*

utilitarianism, *p. 447*

DISCOVERING WESTERN CIVILIZATION ONLINE

You can obtain more information about political upheavals and social transformations between 1815 and 1850 at the websites listed below. See also the Companion Website that accompanies this text, www.ablongman.com/kishlansky, which contains an online study guide and additional resources.

Geographical Tour: Europe in 1815

Internet Modern History Sourcebook: Conservative Order

www.fordham.edu/halsall/mod/modsbook16.html

The site provides documents, discussions, and bibliographies on the Congress of Vienna and charts the development of conservative thought.

The New Ideologies

McMaster University Archive for the History of Economic Thought

socserv.mcmaster.ca/econ/ugcm/3ll3

A site for texts in modern economic theory.

Internet Modern History Sourcebook: Liberalism

www.fordham.edu/halsall/mod/modsbook18.html

A collection of links to primary documents and bibliographies on liberalism.

Internet Modern History Sourcebook: Nationalism

www.fordham.edu/halsall/mod/modsbook17.html

The Nationalism Project

www.nationalismproject.org/

These sites provide links to primary documents and bibliographies of nationalism.

Internet Modern History Sourcebook: Romanticism

www.fordham.edu/halsall/mod/modsbook15.html

This site provides links to primary texts on romantic philosophy and literature.

Voice of the Shuttle

vos.ucsb.edu/index.asp

This comprehensive database for humanities research provides links to general resources, criticism, and primary texts. Type "Romantics" into the search function for resources on romantic philosophy and literature.

Marxist Internet Archive: Marxist Writers

www.marxists.org/archive/index.htm

The site provides translated texts of Marx and Engels as well as other prominent Social Democrats and Communists.

Protest and Revolution

Child Labour in the 19th Century

www.spartacus.schoolnet.co.uk/IRchild.htm

A collection of biographies of reformers and promoters of child labor laws, electronic texts of major child labor legislation, and excerpts from primary sources concerning child labor in nineteenth-century Britain.

The Emancipation of Women: 1750–1920

www.spartacus.schoolnet.co.uk/women.htm

The site contains links to biographies of major figures, essays on the major organizations and societies, and electronic texts of the women's movement in Britain.

Internet Modern History Sourcebook: 1848

www.fordham.edu/halsall/mod/modsbook19.html

The site provides documents, discussions, bibliographies and other links on the revolutions of 1848.

SUGGESTIONS FOR FURTHER READING

Geographical Tour: Europe in 1815

Tim Chapman, *The Congress of Vienna: Origins, Processes, and Results* (New York: Routledge, 1998). A brief, comprehensive survey of how the European powers victorious

against Napoleon redrew Europe's frontiers. It follows the impact of the settlement to its demise in the twentieth century.

Robert Gildea, *Barricades and Borders, Europe 1800–1914* (Oxford: Oxford University Press, 1996). A synthetic overview of economic, demographic, political, and international trends in European society.

Robin Okey, *The Habsburg Monarchy: From Enlightenment to Eclipse* (New York: St. Martin's Press, 2001). An informative survey of Austrian rule from the mid-eighteenth century to the end of World War I, which contains an annotated bibliography and materials drawn from historiographic material in Magyar, Serbo-Croat, Czech, and other eastern European language sources.

The New Ideologies

Jonathan Beecher, *Charles Fourier: The Visionary and His World* (Berkeley: University of California Press, 1986). An intellectual biography that traces the development of Fourier's theoretical perspective and roots it firmly in the social context of nineteenth-century France.

Craig Calhoun, *The Question of Class Struggle: Social Foundations of Popular Radicalism During the Industrial Revolution* (Chicago: University of Chicago Press, 1982). Presents popular protest of eighteenth- and early nineteenth-century England as the reaction of communities of artisans defending their traditions against encroaching industrialization.

Gareth Stedman Jones, *Languages of Class: Studies in English Working Class History, 1832–1982* (Cambridge: Cambridge University Press, 1983). A series of essays, on topics such as working-class culture and Chartism, that examine the development of class consciousness.

William H. Sewell, Jr., *Work and Revolution in France: The Language of Labor from the Old Regime to 1848* (Cambridge: Cambridge University Press, 1980). Traces nineteenth-century working-class socialism to the corporate culture of Old Regime guilds through traditional values, norms, language, and artisan organizations.

Denis Mack Smith, *Mazzini* (New Haven, CT: Yale University Press, 1994). Mazzini is presented as an important force in legitimizing Italian nationalism by associating it with republicanism and the interests of humanity.

Edward P. Thompson, *The Making of the English Working Class* (New York: Pantheon Books, 1963). A classic in social history that spans the late eighteenth to mid-nineteenth centuries in examining the social, political, and cultural contexts in which workers created their own identity and put forward their own demands.

Protest and Revolution

Maurice Agulhon, *The Republican Experiment, 1848–1852* (Cambridge: Cambridge University Press, 1983). Traces the Revolution of 1848 from its roots to its ultimate failure in 1852 through an analysis of the republican ideologies of workers, peasants, and the bourgeoisie.

Clive Church, *Europe in 1830: Revolution and Political Change* (London: Allen & Unwin, 1983). Considers the origins of the 1830 revolutions within a wider European crisis through a comparative analysis of European regions.

R. J. W. Evans and Hartmut Pogge von Strandmann, eds., *The Revolutions in Europe, 1848–1849: From Reform to Reaction* (Oxford: Oxford University Press, 2000). A focused collection of articles on the mid-nineteenth-century collapse of authority across Europe.

Alan J. Kidd, *State, Society, and the Poor in Nineteenth-Century England* (New York: St. Martin's Press, 1999). This volume is part of the *Social History in Perspective* series; it provides an overview of poverty in industrializing England, the role of the poor laws, public welfare, and charitable organizations in the nineteenth century.

Catherine J. Kudlick, *Cholera in Post-Revolutionary Paris: A Cultural History* (Berkeley: University of California Press, 1996). Examines the cultural values of ruling elites and demonstrates the role disease played in shaping political life and class identity in nineteenth-century France.

Patricia O'Brien, *The Promise of Punishment: Prisons in Nineteenth-Century France* (Princeton: Princeton University Press, 1982). An overview of the creation of the penitentiary system in nineteenth-century France and the rise of the new science of punishment, criminology, and the eventual appearance of alternatives to the penitentiary system.

Redcliffe N. Salaman, *The History and Social Influence of the Potato,* revised impression edited by J. G. Hawkes (Cambridge: Cambridge University Press, 1985). The classic study of the potato. A major portion of the work is devoted to the potato famine.

Jonathan Sperber, *Revolutionary Europe, 1780–1850* (New York: Longman, 2000). Considers the revolutions of 1848 within the context of economic and social changes rooted in Old Regime politics and society and from the perspective of the twenty-first century.

For a list of additional titles related to this chapter's topics, please see www.ablongman.com/kishlansky**.**

23

STATE BUILDING AND SOCIAL CHANGE IN EUROPE, 1850–1871

The Visual Record

THE BIRTH OF THE GERMAN EMPIRE

Although not ordinarily a fanciful man, Otto von Bismarck (1815–1898) wrote to his wife that he imagined himself a midwife assisting at a momentous birth. The birth in his day-dream was the **Proclamation of the German Empire** on 21 January 1871. As the Prussian statesman stood in the Versailles Palace outside Paris on that fateful day, surrounded by German aristocrats, he could not forget the years of struggle and planning—the precarious pregnancy, so to speak—that had preceded this joyous event.

The newly established Second Reich, successor to the Holy Roman Empire (962–1806), united the German states into a single nation. The unification had involved years of foreign wars and diplomatic maneuverings. The placid, glossy scene painted by Anton von Werner (1843–1915) hardly suggests Bismarck's strong emotions on this momentous day. The richly marbled and mirrored room, the site of the birth of the German Empire, figures as prominently in the tableau as the uniformed princes and aristocrats, who, with sabers, helmets, and standards raised, cheer the new emperor. The choice of the Hall of Mirrors as the meeting place for the German princes was intended as an assertion of German superiority in Europe. The great hall, after all, had been built by Louis XIV to reflect and glorify the power of absolutist France. Here, the kings of France had presided over lavish ceremonies and opulent receptions. Here, Napoleon I had honored his generals, victorious in conquering central Europe. Here, not long before, Napoleon III had danced on the parqueted floors with Queen Victoria of Britain. And now, here meet the representatives of the German princes who successfully combined forces to defeat the French Second Empire in only six weeks of war in the fall of 1870, to complete the French humiliation.

The painting shows King William I of Prussia on the dais, flanked by his son Crown Prince Frederick William, and his son-in-law, Friedrich I, the Grand Duke of Baden, whose upraised hand signals the cheer for the new emperor. At the foot of the steps, like a loyal retainer, stands the self-described midwife, Otto von Bismarck, who is singled out in his pure white uniform. Yet there is something amiss. The new German emperor stands to one side of the canvas while Bismarck commands its center. If most eyes of the cheering princes turn to the emperor, ours are pulled to the chancellor of the new reich. In both hands, Bismarck holds both the document proclaiming the empire and his Prussian military helmet. The artist has shown that it was Bismarck's event, for it was Bismarck who crafted a united Germany.

Bismarck created this new "state of princes," the German Empire, through "iron and blood"—force and military conquest—and not by democratic means. Conservative state building succeeded in unifying Germany where the liberal ideology of representative government had failed.

To Bismarck's left, in profile facing the emperor, stands Count Helmuth von Moltke (1800–1891), head of the Prussian General Staff and the man responsible for reorganizing the Prussian army with Bismarck's support. Medals for bravery and service to his sovereign adorn Moltke's chest. With one foot forward, Moltke is a man of action, almost caught in midstride, a man ready to move into the future.

Looking Ahead

In this chapter, we will examine the period between 1850 and 1871, when unification of territories was an important part of the process of building a nation in both Germany and Italy.

Successful statesmen were diplomats who used alliances to further national interests. They were also realists willing to use force to further national interests. The existing nation-states of France, Great Britain, and Russia, with little in common save their commitment to progress, pursued different paths to state reform and consolidation of national power.

The changing values and force of new ideas so evident in the political realm also characterized the changing world of the home and family. Just as realism was a dominant force in politics, realism in arts and sciences became a means of promoting material progress. With the convergence of these changes in a variety of realms, Europeans witnessed the birth of the modern age in the third quarter of the nineteenth century. ➤

BUILDING NATIONS: THE POLITICS OF UNIFICATION

The revolutions of 1848 had occurred in a period of political experimentation. Radicals enlisting popular support had tried and failed to reshape European states for their own nationalist, liberal, and socialist ends. Governments in Paris, Vienna, Berlin, and a number of lesser states had been swept away as revolutions created a power vacuum but no durable solutions. To fill that vacuum, a new breed of politicians emerged in the 1850s and 1860s, men who understood the importance of the centralized nation-state and the need of reforms from above. They shared a new realism about means and ends, and about using foreign policy successes to further domestic programs.

The Crimean War

In 1849 and 1850, Russia had fulfilled its role as policeman of Europe by supporting Austria against Hungary and Prussia. Yet Russia was not merely content to keep the peace; it sought greater power to the south in the Balkans. The narrow straits connecting the Black Sea with the Aegean Sea were controlled by the Ottoman Empire. Russia hoped to benefit from Ottoman weakness caused by internal conflicts and gain control of the straits as an outlet for the Russian fleet to the Mediterranean.

At the center of the hope for Ottoman disintegration lay the **Eastern Question,** the term that was used in the nineteenth century to designate the problems surrounding the European territories controlled by the Ottoman Empire. Each of the Great Powers—Russia, Great Britain, Austria, Prussia, and France—hoped to benefit territorially from the collapse of Ottoman control. In 1853, Great Power rivalry over the Eastern Question created an international situation that led to war.

In 1853, the Russian government demanded that the Turkish government recognize Russia's right to protect Greek Orthodox believers in the Ottoman Empire. The Turkish government refused Russian demands, and the Russians ordered troops to enter the Danubian principalities of Moldavia and Wallachia, which were held by the Turks.

In October 1853, the Turkish government, counting on support from Great Britain and France, declared war on Russia. Russia easily prevailed over its weaker neighbor to the south. In a four-hour battle, a Russian squadron destroyed the Turkish fleet off the coast of Sinope. Tsar Nicholas I (1825–1855) drew up the terms of a settlement with the Ottoman Empire and submitted them to Great Britain and France for review.

The two western European powers, fearing Russian aggrandizement at Turkish expense, responded by declaring war on Russia on 28 March 1854, a date that marked a new phase in the Crimean War. The Italian kingdom of Sardinia also joined the war against Russia in January 1855, hoping to make its name militarily and win recognition for its aim to unite Italy into a single nation. Although Great Britain, France, and the Italian state of Sardinia did not have explicit economic in-

terests, they were motivated by ambition, prestige, and rivalry in the Balkans.

British and French troops landed in the Crimea, the Russian peninsula extending into the Black Sea, in September 1854, with the intention of capturing Sevastopol, Russia's heavily fortified chief naval base on the Black Sea. The allies laid siege to the fortress at Sevastopol, which fell on 11 September 1855 after 322 days of battle. The defeated Russians abandoned Sevastopol, blew up their forts, and sank their own ships. Facing the threat of Austrian entry into the war, Russia agreed to preliminary peace terms.

In the Peace of Paris of 1856, Russia relinquished its claim as protector of Christians in Turkey. The British gained the neutralization of the Black Sea. The mouth of the Danube was returned to Turkish control, and an international commission was created to oversee safe navigation on the Danube. The Danubian principalities were placed under joint guarantee of the powers, and Russia gave up a small portion of Bessarabia. In 1861, the principalities were united in the independent nation of Romania.

The Crimean War had dramatic and enduring consequences. Russia ceased to play an active role in European affairs and turned toward expansion in central Asia. Its withdrawal opened up the possibility for a move by Prussia in central Europe.

Unifying Italy

The Kingdom of Sardinia, meanwhile, was leading the drive for Italian reunification. Italy had not been a single political entity since the end of the Roman Empire in the west in the fifth century. The movement to reunite Italy culturally and politically was known as the *Risorgimento* (literally, "resurgence").

Cavour's Political Realism. In 1848, both Giuseppe Mazzini's Young Italy movement and Giuseppe Garibaldi's Red Shirts had sought a united republican Italy achieved through direct popular action, but they had failed. It took a politician of aristocratic birth to recognize that Mazzini's and Garibaldi's model of revolutionary action was doomed against the powerful Austrian military machine. Mazzini was a moralist. Garibaldi was a fighter. But Camillo Benso di Cavour (1810–1861) was an opportunistic politician and a realist.

As premier of Sardinia from 1852 to 1859 and again in 1860–1861, Cavour was well placed to launch his campaign for Italian unity. The Kingdom of Sardinia, whose principal state was Piedmont, had made itself a focal point for unification efforts. Its king, Carlo-Alberto (1831–1849), had stood alone among Italian rulers in opposing Austrian domination of the Italian peninsula in 1848 and 1849. Severely defeated by the Austrians, he was forced to abdicate. He was succeeded by his son Victor Emmanuel II (1849–1861), who had the good sense to appoint Cavour as his first minister. From the start, Cavour undertook liberal administrative measures that included tax reform, stabilization of the currency, improvement of the railway system, the creation of a transatlantic steamship system, and the support of private enterprise. With these pro-

■ The Unification of Italy. By 1860, the majority of the Italian "boot" was under the rule of Piedmont-Sardinia. By 1870, the unification was complete.

grams, Cavour created for Sardinia the dynamic image of progressive change. He involved Sardinia in the Crimean War, thereby securing its status among the European powers.

Most important, however, was Cavour's alliance with France against Austria in 1858. The alliance was quickly followed by an arranged provocation against the Habsburg monarchy. Austria declared war in 1859 and was easily defeated by French forces in the battles of Magenta and Solferino. The peace settlement joined Lombardy to the Piedmontese state.

Cavour's approach was not without its costs. His partnership with a stronger power meant sometimes following France's lead, and the need to cajole French support meant enriching France with territorial gain in the form of Nice and Savoy. However, Sardinia got more than it gave up. In the summer of 1859, revolutionary assemblies in Tuscany, Modena, Parma, and the Romagna, wanting to eject their Austrian rulers, voted in favor of union with the Piedmontese. By April 1860, these four areas of central Italy were under Victor Emmanuel II's rule. Sardinia had doubled in size to become the dominant power on the Italian peninsula.

Southern Italians took their lead from events in central Italy and, in the spring of 1860, initiated disorders against the rule of King Francis II (1859–1861) of Naples. Uprisings in Sicily inspired Giuseppe Garibaldi to return from his self-im-

posed exile to organize his own army of Red Shirts, known as the Thousand, who liberated Sicily and then crossed to the Italian mainland to expel Francis II from Naples. Garibaldi next turned his attention to the liberation of the Holy City, where a French garrison protected the pope.

As Garibaldi's popularity as a national hero grew, Cavour became alarmed at the competition in uniting Italy and took secret steps to block the advance of the Red Shirts and their leader. To seize the initiative, Cavour directed the Piedmontese army into the Papal States. After defeating the pope's troops, Cavour's men crossed into the Neapolitan state and scored important victories against forces loyal to the king of Naples. Cavour proceeded to annex southern Italy for Victor Emmanuel II, using plebiscites to seal the procedure.

A King for a United Italy.   At this point, in 1860, Garibaldi yielded his own conquered territories to Sardinia, making possible the declaration of a united Italy under Victor Emmanuel II, who reigned as king of Italy from 1861 to 1878.

The new king of Italy was now poised to acquire Venetia, which was under Austrian rule, and Rome, which was ruled by Pope Pius IX, and Victor Emmanuel devoted much of his foreign policy in the 1860s to these ends. In 1866, when Austria lost a war with Prussia, Italy struck a deal with the victor and gained control of Venetia. When Prussia prevailed against France in

■ In this British cartoon of 1860, Garibaldi surrenders his power to Victor Emmanuel II, king of Piedmont-Sardinia (soon to be king of a united Italy). The caption reads "Right Leg in the Boot at Last."

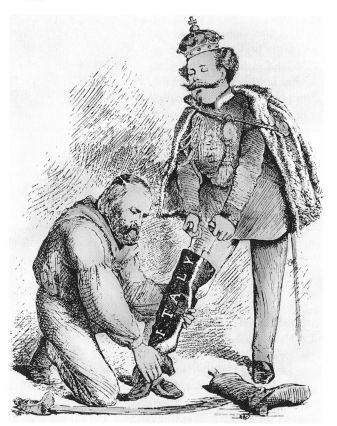

1870, Victor Emmanuel took over Rome. The boot of Italy, from top to toe, was now a single nation. The pope remained in the Vatican, opposed to an Italy united under King Victor Emmanuel II.

Unifying Germany

In this age of realistic politicians, Prussian statesman Otto von Bismarck (1815–1898) emerged as the supreme practitioner of **realpolitik,** the ruthless use of any means, including illegal and violent ones, to advance a country's interests. Bismarck was a Junker, an aristocratic estate-owner from east of the Elbe River, who entered politics in 1847. In the 1850s, he became aware of Prussia's future in the center of Europe; he saw that the old elites must be allied with the national movement to survive.

Prussia's Seven Weeks' War with Austria. In 1850, Prussia had been forced to accept Austrian dominance in central Europe or go to war. Throughout the following decade, however, Prussia systematically undermined Austrian power and excluded Austria from German economic affairs. In 1862, at the moment of a crisis provoked by the king over military reorganization, Bismarck became minister-president of the Prussian cabinet and foreign minister. He overrode the parliamentary body, the Diet, by reorganizing the army without a formally approved budget. In 1864, he constructed an alliance between Austria and Prussia for the purpose of invading Schleswig, a predominantly German-speaking territory controlled by the king of Denmark. Within five days of the invasion, Denmark yielded the duchies of Schleswig and Holstein, now to be ruled jointly by Austria and Prussia.

Counting on the neutrality of France and Great Britain, the support of Sardinia, and good relations with Russia, Bismarck promoted a crisis between Austria and Prussia over management of the formerly Danish territories and led his country

MAP DISCOVERY

The Unification of Germany

In this map, regard the diversity in size and type of political entities that were combined to form the new state of Germany. What annexation did the War of 1866 make possible? How did the peace settlement with France affect the creation of the German state? Why was the North German Confederation so important in determining the formation of the new German Empire?

into war with Austria in June 1866. In this Seven Weeks' War, Austrian forces proved to be no match for the better-equipped and better-trained Prussian army. Bismarck dictated the terms of the peace, excluding Austria from a united, Prussian-dominated Germany. In 1867, in response to pressures from the subject nationalities, the Habsburg Empire transformed itself into a dual monarchy of two independent and equal states under one ruler, who would be both the emperor of Austria and the king of Hungary. In spite of the reorganization, the problem of nationalities persisted, and ethnic groups began to agitate for total independence from imperial rule.

The Franco-Prussian War. Bismarck's biggest obstacle to German unification was laid to rest with Austria's defeat. The south German states continued to resist the idea of Prussian dominance, but growing numbers of people in Baden, Württemberg, Bavaria, and the southern parts of Hesse-Darmstadt recognized the value of uniting under Prussian leadership.

Many French observers were troubled by the Prussian victory over Austria and were apprehensive about what a united Germany might portend for the future of French dominance in Europe. Napoleon III attempted unsuccessfully to contain Prussian ambitions through diplomatic maneuverings. Instead, France found itself stranded without important European allies. In the spring of 1870, Bismarck seized the initiative and provoked a crisis with France. The issue of succession to the Spanish throne provided the pretext. On 13 July 1870, the Prussian king (later Emperor William I) sent a message to Napoleon III reporting a meeting with the French ambassador. Bismarck skillfully edited this "Ems Dispatch" to suggest that the French ambassador had insulted the Prussian king, then leaked news of the incident to the press in both countries.

As a direct result of this contrived misunderstanding, France declared war on Prussia in July 1870. As Bismarck hoped, the southern German princes immediately sided with the Prussian king. Unlike the Germans, who were well prepared for war, the French had not coordinated deployment with the new technology of the railroad. Although French troops had the latest equipment, they were sent into battle without instructions on how to use it. And they were outnumbered almost two to one. All these factors combined to spell disaster for the French. Within a matter of weeks it was obvious that France had lost the Franco-Prussian War. The path was now clear for the declaration of the German Empire in January 1871.

Prussian Dominance of United Germany. In unifying Germany, Bismarck built on the constitution of the North German Confederation formed in 1867, which guaranteed Prussian dominance. Bismarck used the bureaucracy as a mainstay of the emperor. The new **Reichstag**—the national legislative assembly—was to be elected by means of universal male suffrage, but it was not sovereign, and the chancellor was accountable only to the emperor.

The United States: Civil War and Reunification

In the 1860s, another crisis in state building was resolved across the Atlantic. The United States cemented political unity through the use of force in its Civil War (1861–1865). The president of the United States, Abraham Lincoln (1809–1865), mobilized the superior resources of the industrial Northern states against the heavily agrarian, slave-owning South. The United States worked to achieve national unity and territorial integrity in another sense through ongoing expansion westward by eliminating and subduing Native American peoples.

With the emancipation of the slaves, republican democracy appeared to triumph in the United States. Newly created European nation-states followed a different path: Plebiscites were manipulated by those in power in Italy, and a neo-absolutism emerged in Germany. Yet the Civil War in the United States and the successful bids for unification in Italy and Germany shared remarkable similarities. In all three countries, wars eventually resulted in a single national market and a single financial system without internal barriers. Unified national economies, particularly in Germany and the United States, paved the way for significant economic growth and the expansion of industrial power.

Nationalism and Force

The personification of nation-states was one of the great achievements of statesmen throughout Europe between 1850 and 1870. The language and symbols they put in place created the nation itself, a new political reality whose forms contained a modern political consciousness. The nation-state became an all-knowing being whose rights had to be protected, whose destiny had to be assured.

The nation was above all a creation that minimized or denied real differences in dialect and language, regional loyalties, local traditions, and village identities. No power was acknowledged to exist above the nation-state, and no power could sanction the nation's actions but itself. Force was an acceptable alternative to diplomacy. Violence and nationalism were inextricably linked in the unification of both Italy and Germany in the third quarter of the nineteenth century.

National unification had escaped the grasp of liberals and radicals between 1848 and 1850 with the failure of revolutionary and reform movements. In the 1850s and 1860s, those who were committed to radical transformations worked from within the existing system. The new realists subordinated liberal nationalism to conservative state-building. Under newly dynamic conservative leadership, military force would validate what intellectuals and idealistic revolutionaries had not been able to legitimate through ideological claims.

REFORMING EUROPEAN SOCIETY

After the revolutions of 1848, government repression silenced radical movements throughout Europe. But repression could not maintain social harmony and promote growth and prosperity. In the third quarter of the nineteenth century, Europe's leaders recognized that reforms were needed to build dynamic and competitive states. Three different models for social and political reform developed in France, Great Britain, and

Russia after 1850. All three sets of reforms took place in unified nation-states. The three societies had little in common with each other ideologically, but all reflected a commitment to progress and an awareness of the state's role and responsibility in achieving it.

The Second Empire in France, 1852–1870

One model was that of France, where the French emperor worked through a highly centralized administrative structure and with a valued elite of specialists to achieve social and economic transformation.

Napoleon III. Under Napoleon III's direction the Second Empire achieved economic expansion and industrial development. A new private banking system enabled the pooling of investors' resources to finance industrial expansion. Napoleon III and his advisers believed that prosperity was the answer to all social problems. Between 1852 and 1860, the government supported a massive program of railroad construction. Jobs multiplied, and investment increased. Agriculture expanded as railroad lines opened new markets. The rich got richer, but the extreme poverty of the first half of the nineteenth century was diminishing. Brutal misery in the city and countryside did not disappear, but on the whole, the standard of living increased as wages rose faster than prices.

Rebuilding Paris. The best single example of the energy and commitment of the imperial regime was the rebuilding of the French capital. Before midcentury, Paris was one of the most unsanitary, crime-ridden, and politically volatile capitals in Europe. Within 15 years it had been transformed into a city of lights, wide boulevards and avenues, monumental vistas, parks, and gardens. Poor districts were cleared to make way for the elegant apartment buildings of the Parisian bourgeoisie. As workers from all over France migrated to the capital in search of jobs, the population nearly doubled, increasing by just under one million in the 1850s and 1860s. Wide, straight Parisian avenues served as an international model that was copied in Mexico City, Brussels, Madrid, Rome, Stockholm, and Barcelona between 1870 and 1900.

The Foreign Policy of the Second Empire. Just as a new Paris would make France a center of Western culture, Napoleon III intended his blueprint for foreign policy to restore France to its pre-1815 status as the greatest European power. By involving France in both the Crimean War and the war for Italian unification, Napoleon III returned France to adventurous foreign policies, acquired Nice and Savoy from Sardinia, and reversed the settlements of 1815.

French construction of the Suez Canal between the Red Sea and the Mediterranean created tensions with Great Britain, which was protective of its own dominance in the Mediterranean and the Near East. Nevertheless, the free trade agreement between the British and the French in 1860 was a landmark in overseas policy and a commitment to liberal economic policies.

The Second Empire's involvement in Mexico was a fiasco. The Mexican government had been chronically unable to pay its foreign debts, and France was Mexico's largest creditor. Napoleon III hoped that by intervening in Mexican affairs, he could strengthen ties with Great Britain and Spain, to whom the Mexicans also owed money. With the backing of Mexican conservatives who opposed Mexican president Benito Juárez (1806–1872), Napoleon III supported the Austrian archduke Maximilian (1832–1867) as emperor of Mexico. After he was crowned in 1863, the new Mexican emperor struggled to rule in an enlightened manner, but he was stymied from the beginning by his ineptitude and lack of popular support. Following the recall of the 34,000 French troops that, at considerable expense, were keeping Maximilian's troubled regime in place, Maximilian was captured and executed by a firing squad in the summer of 1867. The Mexican disaster damaged the prestige of Napoleon III's regime in the international arena, and in 1870 the humiliatingly rapid defeat of French imperial forces in the Franco-Prussian War ended the experiment in liberal empire.

The Victorian Compromise

Great Britain provided another model of reform, which was fostered through liberal parliamentary democracy. In government by "amateurs," with local rather than a highly centralized administration, British legislation alternated between a philosophy of freedom and one of protection. But reforms were always hammered out by parliamentary means with the support of a gradually expanding electorate.

Parliamentary Reforms. In contrast to France, Britain enjoyed apparent social harmony without revolution and without civil war. The relative calm of British society in the middle of the nineteenth century owed much to the fact that Great Britain had an enormously productive capitalist economy of sustained growth.

The stability and calm were undoubtedly exaggerated, however, for Great Britain at midcentury had its share of serious social problems. British slums rivaled any in Europe. Poverty, disease, and famine ravaged the kingdom. Social protests of the 1840s raised fears of upheavals similar to those in continental Europe. Yet Great Britain avoided a revolution. One explanation for the relative calm lay in Britain's parliamentary tradition, which emphasized liberty as the birthright of English citizens and was able slowly to adapt to the demands of an industrializing society. The great compromise of Victorian society was the reconciliation of industrialists' commitment to unimpeded growth with the workers' need for the state's protection.

As part of a pattern of slow democratization, the Reform Bill of 1832 gave increased political power to the industrial and manufacturing bourgeoisie, who joined a landed aristocracy and merchant class. But the property qualification meant that

■ William Gladstone rides in an omnibus in this painting titled *One of the People*, by Alfred Morgan. This mode of transport was thought of as a social leveler because all classes of people could afford the fares.

only 20 percent of the population could vote. In 1867, under conservative leadership, a second reform bill was introduced. Approval of this bill doubled the electorate, giving the vote to a new urban population of shopkeepers, clerks, and workers. In 1884, farm laborers were enfranchised. Women, however, remained barred from voting until after World War I.

Gladstone and Disraeli.
The lives and careers of two men, William Ewart Gladstone (1809–1898) and Benjamin Disraeli (1804–1881), exemplify the particular path the British government followed in maintaining public peace. Rivals and political opponents, both men served as prime ministers and both left their mark on the age.

William Gladstone was a classical liberal who believed in free enterprise and opposed state intervention. Good government, according to Gladstone, should remove obstacles to talent, competition, and individual initiative but should interfere as little as possible in economy and society. Gladstone's first term as prime minister (1868–1874) significantly advanced the British liberal state. Taking advantage of British prosperity, Gladstone abolished tariffs, cut defense expenditures, lowered taxes, and sponsored sound budgets. He furthered the liberal agenda by disestablishing the Anglican Church in Ireland in 1869. The Anglican Church had been the source of great resentment to the vast majority of Irish Catholics, who had been forced to pay taxes to support the Protestant state church.

Gladstone reformed the army and the civil service. His government introduced the secret ballot. Finally, the Liberal party stressed the importance of education for an informed electorate and passed an education act that aimed to make elementary schooling available to everyone. These reforms added up to a liberal philosophy of government. Liberal government was above all an attack on privilege. It sought to remove restraints on individual freedom and foster opportunity and talent.

During these years, another political philosophy—conservatism—also left its mark on British government. Under the flamboyant leadership of Benjamin Disraeli, the Conservative party, trusting the state to correct and protect, supported state intervention and regulation on behalf of the poor and disadvantaged. Disraeli sponsored the Factory Act of 1875, which set a maximum of 56 hours on the factory work week. The Public Health Act established a sanitary code. The Artisans Dwelling Act defined minimum housing standards. Probably the most important conservative legislation was the Trade Union Act, which permitted picketing and other peaceful labor tactics.

Disraeli championed protection against free trade. Unlike the Liberals, he insisted on the importance of traditional institutions such as the monarchy, the House of Lords, and the Church of England. His work in organizing a national party machinery facilitated the adaptation of the parliamentary system to mass politics. His methods of campaigning and building a mass base of support were used by successful politicians regardless of political persuasion.

As the intersecting careers of Gladstone and Disraeli demonstrate, the British model combined free enterprise with intervention and regulation. The clear issues and the clear choices of the two great parties—Liberal and Conservative—dominated parliamentary life after midcentury. In polarizing parliamentary politics, they also invigorated it.

The terms "liberal" and "conservative" hold none of the meaning today that they did for men and women in the nineteenth century. Classical liberalism has little in common with its twentieth-century counterpart, which favors an active, interventionist state. Disraeli is a far more likely candidate for the twentieth-century liberal label than is Gladstone, Britain's leading nineteenth-century liberal statesman.

Reforming Russia

Russia offered a third model for reform in the nineteenth century. Like Britain, Russia had avoided revolution at midcentury and hoped to preserve social peace. Yet the Russian model for reform stood in dramatic contrast to Britain's. Russia was an unreformed autocracy in which the tsar held absolute power. Without a parliament, without a constitution, and without civil liberties for his subjects, the Russian ruler governed through a bureaucracy and a police force. Economically, Russia was a semifeudal agrarian state with a class of privileged aristocrats supported by serf labor on their estates.

A Serf-Holding Nation. For decades—since the reign of Alexander I (1801–1825)—the tsars and their advisers realized that they were out of step with developments in western Europe. An awareness was growing that serfdom was uncivilized and morally wrong, as critics compared the Russian practice with the atrocities of American slavery. Among the European powers, only Russia remained a serf-holding nation. Russian serfs were tied to the land and owed dues and labor services in return for the lands they held. Peasant protests mounted, attracting public attention to the plight of the serfs. But in spite of growing moral concern, there were many reasons to resist the abolition of serfdom. How were serf-holders to be compensated for the loss of labor power? What was to be the freed serfs' relationship to the land?

Alexander II and the Emancipation of the Serfs. Hesitation about abolition evaporated with the Russian defeat in the Crimean War. The new tsar, Alexander II (1855–1881), viewed Russia's inability to repel an invasion force on its own soil as proof of its backwardness. Russia had no railroads and was forced to transport military supplies by carts to the Crimea. It took three months to provision troops; the enemy could do so in three weeks. Liberating the serfs would permit a well-trained reserve army to exist without fear of rebellion and would also create a system of free labor, so necessary for industrial development.

In March 1861, the tsar signed the emancipation edict that liberated 52 million serfs. Serfdom was eliminated in Poland three years later. Alexander II, who came to be known as the "Tsar-Liberator," compromised between landlord and serf by allotting land to freed peasants while requiring from the former serfs redemption payments that were spread out over a period of 49 years. To guarantee repayment, the land was granted not directly to individual peasants but to the village commune (*mir*), which was responsible for collecting redemption payments. The peasant paid the state in installments; the state reimbursed the landowner in the form of interest-bearing bonds and redemption certificates. Neither serf nor landholder benefited from these financial arrangements; the real winner in the abolition of serfdom was the state, which expanded its bureaucratic hierarchy and financial infrastructure.

The Great Reforms. The tsar introduced a vast array of "Great Reforms"—emancipating the serfs, creating local parliamentary bodies (*zemstvos*), reorganizing the judiciary, modernizing the army—yet Russia was not sufficiently liberalized or democratized to satisfy the critics of autocracy. Between 1860 and 1870, a young generation of intelligentsia, radical intellectuals who were influenced by the rhetoric of revolution in western Europe, protested against the existing order, traveling from village to village to educate the peasants and in some cases to attempt to radicalize them.

The Populist Movement. The radicals paid dearly for their commitment to populism when they were subjected to mass trials and repression in the late 1870s. Some of these critics fled into exile to reemerge as revolutionaries in western Europe, where they continued to oppose the tsarist regime and helped to shape the tradition of revolution and dissent in Western countries. Other educated men and women who remained in Russia chose violence as the only effective weapon against absolute rule. Terrorists who called themselves "Will of the People" decided to assassinate the tsar; in the "emperor hunt" that followed, numerous attempts were made on the tsar's life.

In response to attempts on his life and the assassination of public officials, which were intended to cripple the central regime, Alexander II put the brakes on reform in the second half of his reign. The Great Reforms could not be undone, however, and had set in motion sweeping economic and social changes. The state encouraged capitalist growth and witnessed the rise of a professional middle class and the formation of an embryonic factory proletariat. Yet reforms had increased expectations for an equally dramatic political transformation that failed to materialize. In the end, the Will of the People movement succeeded in its mission. In St. Petersburg in 1881, a terrorist bomb killed Alexander II, the Tsar-Liberator.

The Politics of Leadership

Political modernization was not achieved in Russia; and in western and central Europe, modern politics emerged only after 1850. Until that time, traditional political institutions had prevailed. When faced with revolutionary upheavals, regimes aimed for stability and preservation of their control. Only after 1850 did political leaders emerge who understood the world of politics and directed it to their own ends. Three statesmen typified the new approach to the public world of power: Camillo di Cavour, Otto von Bismarck, and Louis Napoleon.

The Demise of Royal Authority.

In old-regime Europe, power flowed downward from the monarch, who was perched atop a hierarchically organized social system that is often depicted as a pyramid. In the first half of the nineteenth century, men and women learned that those in power could be questioned. The good of the people was the primary justification for government. Power now flowed upward from the citizens to their appointed and elected representatives. The new power brokers were those who could control and direct the flow, not merely be carried along or swept away by it. These were realists in the same tradition as Machiavelli and reflected the new political culture of the nineteenth century. They understood the importance of public opinion, which they used as a tool for the shaping of consensus, the molding of support. They also appreciated the power of the press.

The Supremacy of the Nation-State.

The new political men also shared, to varying degrees, a disregard for traditional morality in decision making. The nation-state was the supreme justification for all actions. Realpolitik meant that statesmen had to think in terms of military capability, technological dominance, and the acceptable use of force. In the gamesmanship of statecraft, they were risk takers.

However, modern European statesmen did not share a common ideological outlook. Cavour leaned toward liberal ideas, while Bismarck was unquestionably conservative, and Louis Napoleon held a blend of liberal and conservative views. Yet these leaders enacted similar policies and sponsored similar legislation to strengthen and promote their states.

CHANGING VALUES AND THE FORCE OF NEW IDEAS

Just as the political world was undergoing transformation, the social, material, and intellectual world was also changing. As feminist thinkers struggled against entrenched prejudice against women, other thinkers brought new insights to the

MISTRESS OF THE HOUSE

Mrs. Beeton's Book of Household Management *was first published in 1861 and in less than a year sold 60,000 copies. Isabella Beeton was 23 years old when the book first appeared and she died at the age of 28 before she saw its vast success as one of the most published and reissued guidebooks of all time. The book is filled with practical advice on a wide variety of subjects ranging from wet-nursing, care of a sick child, etiquette, fashion, and cooking. Mrs. Beeton also provided a strong rationale for the importance of the domestic sphere in the modern world. The sections below are from Chapter 1, "The Mistress."*

Focus Questions

What is Mrs. Beeton's purpose in using military and business comparisons to describe the housewife's role? What is Mrs. Beeton's view of servants and of the mistress' responsibility as their manager? Why is an orderly household so important to the author?

As with the commander of an army, or the leader of any enterprise, so it is with the mistress of a house. Her spirit will be seen through the whole establishment; and just in proportion as she performs her duties intelligently and thoroughly, so will her domestics follow her path. Of all those acquirements, which more particularly belong to the feminine character, there are none which take a higher rank, in our estimation, than such as enter into a knowledge of household duties; for on these are perpetually dependent the happiness, comfort, and well-being of a family. . . .

Early rising is one of the most essential qualities which enter into good Household Management, as it is not only the parent of health, but of innumerable other advantages. Indeed, when a mistress is an early riser, it is almost certain that her house will be orderly and well-managed. On the contrary, if she remain in bed till a late hour, then the domestics, who, as we have before observed, invariably partake somewhat of their mistress's character, will surely become sluggards. To self-indulgence all are more or less disposed, and it is not to be expected that servants are freer from fault than the heads of houses. The great Lord Chatham thus gave his advice in reference to this subject:— "I would have inscribed on the curtains of your bed, and the walls of your chamber, 'If you do not rise early, you can make progress in nothing.'"

From Mrs. Isabella Beeton, *The Book of Household Management* (1861).

study of human society, some of which worked to impede women's progress toward equality. The third quarter of the nineteenth century opened an era that was especially rich in creativity in the natural and applied sciences.

The Politics of Homemaking

Industrialization had separated the workplace from the home, which was now glorified as a comfortable refuge from the harsh outside world. In 1870, an article in a popular Victorian magazine asserted, "Home is emphatically man's place of rest, where his wife is his friend who knows his mind, where he may be himself without fear of offending, and relax the strain that must be kept out of doors: where he may feel himself safe, understood, and at ease." Managing this domestic haven and her children was the middle-class woman's task, and "home economics" was invented during this period to help her organize her work.

This ideal of domestic order and tranquility was beyond the reach of the vast majority of the population. Working-class wives and mothers often had to earn wages if their families were to survive. In 1866, women constituted a significant percentage of the French labor force, including 45 percent of all textile workers. At the height of the rhetoric about the virtues of domesticity, as many as 40 percent of married Englishwomen worked in mills in industrial areas such as Lancashire. Others performed piecework in their homes so that they could care for their children.

Many middle-class women protested against the ideology that confined them to the domestic sphere. Earlier in the century, the great novelist Jane Austen had to keep a piece of muslin work on her writing table in the family drawing room to cover her papers lest visitors detect evidence of literary activity. In the next generation, Florence Nightingale refused to accept the embroidery and knitting to which she was assigned at home. Middle-class women's demands for equal treatment became more persistent after 1870. Patterns of behavior changed within the family, and they were not fixed immutably in social practice. Woman's place and woman's role proved to be much-disputed questions in the new politics of homemaking.

Realism in the Arts

Realism in the arts and literature was a rejection of romantic idealism and subjectivity. The realist response to the disillusionment with the political failures of the post-1848 era characterized a wide array of artistic and literary endeavors. Realists depicted the challenges of urban and industrial growth by confronting the alienation of modern life.

The Social World of the Artist. The term *realism* was first used to describe the paintings of Gustave Courbet (1819–1877). In *The Artist's Studio* (1855), Courbet portrayed himself surrounded by the intellectuals and political figures of his day. He may have been painting a landscape, but contemporary political life crowded in; a starving Irish peasant and her child crouch beneath the easel. Of his unrelenting canvases, none more fittingly portrays the harsh realism of bourgeois life than the funeral ceremony depicted in *Burial at Ornans* (1849–1850) or better depicts the brutality of workers' lives than *Stone Breakers* (1849).

Other artists shared Courbet's desire to reject the conventions prevailing in the art world in favor of portraying reality

■ Gustave Courbet (1819–1877), *Burial at Ornans.* This painting portrays the harsh realm of a bourgeois funeral ceremony.

in its natural and social dimensions. Jean-François Millet's paintings of peasants and workers (see p. 441) sought for a truth deeper than a surface beauty. Realist artists often strove to make a social commentary by capturing scenes from the daily life of the poor that would not have been considered fit subjects for art a generation before.

Realist Novels.   After midcentury, idealization in romantic literature yielded to novels depicting the objective and unforgiving social world. Through serialization in journals and newspapers, fiction reached out to mass audiences, who obtained their "facts" about modern life through stories that often cynically portrayed the monotony of daily existence. In *Hard Times* (1854), set in the imaginary city of Coketown, Charles Dickens (1812–1870) created an allegory that exposed the sterility and soullessness of industrial society.

In *Madame Bovary* (1856), Gustave Flaubert (1821–1880), the great French realist novelist, recounts the story of a young country doctor's wife whose desire to escape from the boredom of her provincial existence leads her into adultery and eventually results in her destruction. Flaubert was put on trial for obscenity and violating public morality with his tale of the unrepentant Emma Bovary. Mary Ann Evans (1819–1890), writing under the pseudonym George Eliot, was also concerned with moral choices and responsibilities in her novels, including *Middlemarch* (1871–1872), a tale of idealism disappointed by the petty realities of provincial English life.

The problem of morality in the realist novel is nowhere more apparent than in the works of the Russian writer, Fyodor Dostoyevsky (1821–1881), whose protagonists wrestle with a universe where God no longer exists and where they must shape their own morality. The impoverished student Raskolnikov in *Crime and Punishment* (1866) justifies his brutal murder of an old woman that occurs in the opening pages of the novel. Realist art and literature addressed an educated elite public but did not flinch before the unrelenting poverty and harshness of contemporary life. The morality of the realist vision lay in depicting the social evils for what they were: failures of a smug and progressive middle class.

The New World of Photography.   Nineteenth-century photography was the result of wedding art and science. Although various techniques made it possible to capture images and landscapes on paper in the early decades of the nineteenth century, Louis Daguerre (1789–1851) can be credited as a pioneer in the photographic process with the invention of the daguerreotype in 1839. Daguerre was both a French scene painter and a physicist, and he brought both his sensibilities and scientific training to the process of capturing images on silver-coated copper plates treated with iodine vapor.

The fascination with photography in the nineteenth century can be observed in its use for portraits by growing numbers of ordinary people, just as in an earlier time the wealthy and powerful sat for oil portraits. In addition, the camera, still a cumbersome object, was used for country landscapes, urban landmarks, and recording the horrors and glory of battle.

■ Calotype of the Adamson family, ca. 1844, by pioneer photographers Robert Adamson (shown at far right) and David Octavius Hill of Scotland. The new technology of photography enabled middle-class families to have their portraits taken, a luxury once available only to those wealthy enough to commission artists.

Within a generation, cameras altered the way people understood the world around them and how they recorded human life. An increasing emphasis on the real world, reflected in literature, art, and discoveries in science was fueled by the altered worldview and the new consciousness that photography made possible.

Charles Darwin and the New Science

Science had a special appeal for a generation of Europeans disillusioned with the political failures of idealism in the revolutions of 1848. It was not an age of great scientific discovery, but rather one of synthesis of previous findings and their technological applications. Science was, above all, to be useful in promoting material progress.

The preeminent scientist of the age, Charles Darwin (1809–1882), was a great synthesizer. As a young man, he sailed around the world on the *Beagle* (1831–1836) as the ship's naturalist, collecting specimens and fossils. His greatest finds were in South America and especially on the Galapagos Islands. He spent the next 20 years of his life writing about his observations. The result, *On the Origin of Species by Means of Natural Selection* (1859), was a book that changed the world.

Darwin's argument was a simple one: Life forms originate in struggle and perpetuate themselves through struggle. The outcome of this struggle was determined by **natural selection,** or what came to be known as "survival of the fittest." Better-adapted individuals survived; others died out. Competition between species and within species produced a dynamic model of organic evolution and progress based on struggle. Darwin did not use the word "evolution" in the original edition, but a positivist belief in an evolutionary process permeated the text. Force explained the past and would guarantee the future, as the fittest survived. The general public found these ideas to be applicable to a whole range of human endeavors and to theories of social organization.

Karl Marx and the Science of Society

Another iconoclastic thinker of this creative period was Karl Marx (1818–1883). "Just as Darwin discovered the law of development of organic nature, Marx discovered the law of development of human history." So spoke Friedrich Engels (1820–1895), longtime friend of and collaborator with Karl Marx, over Marx's grave. The son of a Prussian lawyer, Marx had rejected the study of the law to become a philosopher. As a brilliant young scholar, Marx developed a materially grounded view of society. In 1844, he joined forces with Friedrich Engels, a wealthy German businessman whose father owned factories in Manchester, England. Engels had just written *The Condition of the Working Class in England in 1844,* an exposé of the social costs of industrialization. Marx and Engels found that they were kindred spirits, both moved by the struggles of the poor and the economic exploitation of workers.

The philosophy of Marx and Engels was built on a materialist view of society in which human beings were defined not by their souls but by their labor. Labor was a struggle to transform nature by producing commodities useful for survival. Building on this fundamental concept of labor, Marx and Engels saw society as being divided into two camps: those who owned property and those who did not. For Marx, every social system was divided into classes and carried within it the seeds of its own destruction. In a world of commerce and manufacturing, the capitalist bourgeoisie exploited labor for low wages; they were the new aristocracy against whom workers would eventually rebel.

Marx was more than an observer; he was a critic of capitalism who espoused revolutionary change. His labor theory of value was the wedge that he drove into the self-congratulatory rhetoric of the capitalist age. Labor was the source of all value, he argued, yet the bourgeois employers denied workers the profit of their work by refusing to pay them a decent wage. Instead, they pocketed the profits. He believed workers were separated, or alienated, from the product of their labor. But more profoundly, in his view of a capitalist system, all workers were alienated from the creation that made them human; they were alienated from their labor.

The force of Karl Marx's ideas mobilized thousands of contemporaries who were aware of the injustices of capitalism. Few thinkers have left a more lasting legacy than Karl Marx, which has survived distortion, opposition, and criticism from ideologues and scholars. Marx was a synthesizer who combined economics, philosophy, politics, and history in a wide-ranging critique of industrial society.

Marxism spread across Europe as workers responded to its message. Political parties coalesced around Marxist beliefs and programs, and Marxists were beginning to be heard in associations of workers. In London in 1864, they helped to found the International Working Men's Association, an organization of workers dedicated to "the end of all class rule." The promise of a common association of workers transcending national boundaries became a compelling idea to those who envisioned the end of capitalism. In 1871, Marx and his followers turned to Paris for proof that the revolution was at hand.

A New Revolution?

Soundly defeated on 2 September 1870, Napoleon III and his fighting force of 100,000 men became Prussia's prisoners of war. With the emperor's defeat, the Second Empire collapsed. But even with the capture of Napoleon III, the city of Paris refused to capitulate. The dedication of Parisians to the ongoing war with the Prussians was evident from the first. The regime's liberal critics in Paris seized the initiative to proclaim France a republic. If a corrupt and decadent empire could not save the nation, then France's Third Republic could.

The Siege of Paris.   In mid-September 1870, two German armies surrounded Paris and began a siege that lasted for over four months. Bismarck's troops were intent on bringing the city to its knees not by fighting but by cutting off its vital supply lines. By November, food and fuel were dwindling, and Parisians were facing starvation. Undaunted, they began to eat dogs, cats, and rats. Soon horses disappeared from the streets, and the zoo was depleted of animals.

Despite food and fuel shortages, the proud Parisians fought on. The Germans began a steady bombardment of the city beginning in January 1871. Although Parisians continued to resist through three weeks of shelling, the rest of France wanted an end to the war. The Germans agreed to an armistice to allow French national elections. French citizens outside Paris repudiated the war and returned an overwhelmingly conservative majority to seek peace. Thus the siege came to an end, but it left deep wounds that continued to fester.

CHRONOLOGY
STATE BUILDING AND SOCIAL CHANGE

1853–1856	Crimean War
1859	Austria declares war on Kingdom of Sardinia; France joins forces with Italy
1860	Piedmont-Sardinia annexes duchies in central Italy; France gains Nice and Savoy
3 March 1861	Emancipation of Russian serfs
14 March 1861	Kingdom of Italy proclaimed with Victor Emmanuel II as king
1861–1865	American Civil War
1863	Maximilian crowned emperor of Mexico
1863	Prussians and Austrians at war with Denmark
1866	Seven Weeks' War between Austria and Prussia; Italy acquires Venetia
1867	Emperor Maximilian executed
July 1870	Franco-Prussian War begins
2 September 1870	French Second Empire capitulates with Prussian victory at Sedan
20 September 1870	Italy annexes Rome
18 January 1871	German Empire proclaimed
March–May 1871	Paris Commune

The Paris Commune.   Parisians felt betrayed by the rest of France. Through four months in a besieged city, they had sacrificed, suffered, and died. The war was over, but Paris was not at peace. The new national government, safely installed outside Paris at Versailles, attempted in March 1871 to disarm the Parisian citizenry by using army troops. Parisian men, women, and children poured into the streets to protect their cannons and to defend their right to bear arms. In the fighting that followed, the Versailles troops were driven from the city, and Paris was under siege again.

The spontaneity of the March uprising was soon succeeded by organization. Citizens rallied to the idea of the city's self-government and established the **Paris Commune,** as other French cities followed the capital's lead. Parisians were still at war, not against a foreign enemy but against the rest of France. The defense of the commune lasted for 72 days. Armed women formed their own fighting units, the city council regulated labor relations, and neighborhoods ruled themselves. The short-lived Paris Commune ended in May 1871, as government troops reentered the city and brutally crushed it. In one "Bloody Week," 25,000 Parisians were massacred, and 40,000 others were arrested and tried. Such reprisals inflamed radicals and workers all over Europe. The example of the commune became a rallying cry for revolutionary movements throughout the world and inspired the future leaders of the Russian revolutionary state.

The commune was important at the time, but not as a revolution. It offered two lessons: First, it demonstrated the power of patriotism. Competing images of the nation were at stake, one Parisian and the other French, but no one could deny the power of national identity to inspire a whole city to suffer and to sacrifice. Second, the commune made clear the power of the state. No revolutionary movement could succeed without controlling the massive forces of repression that were at the state's command. The commune had tried to recapture a local, federal view of the world but failed to take sufficient account of the power of the state that it opposed.

CONCLUSION

Western societies had crossed the threshold into the modern age in the third quarter of the nineteenth century. Strong states from Great Britain to Russia were committed to creating and preserving the conditions of industrial expansion. The machine age, railroads, and metallurgy were spreading industrial development much more widely through western and central Europe than had been possible before 1850. Italians and Prussians, in attempting to join the ranks of nation-states, realized that the goal of a strong nation could be achieved only with industrial development and social reforms.

State building in Western societies went hand in hand with growth in the social responsibilities of government. The national powers that would dominate world politics and economy in the twentieth century all underwent modernizing transitions in the 1860s. These included the United States, France, Great Britain, and Germany. The Austrian Empire, too, undertook programs to modernize its government and economy, and the Russian Empire established social reforms of unparalleled dimensions. New nations came into existence in this period through the limited use of armed force. With the establishment of the German Empire, Otto von Bismarck, the most realistic of politicians, was intent on preserving the peace in Europe by balancing the power of the great European states. Europeans prided themselves on being both modern and realistic in the third quarter of the nineteenth century. Peace was possible if it was armed and vigilant. Reform, not revolution, many were sure, was the key to the future progress of European societies.

QUESTIONS FOR REVIEW

1. How did the process of creating nation-states in Germany and Italy differ?
2. What social and political circumstances explain the different reforms undertaken in France, Britain, and Russia?
3. How did industrialization change women's lives, and how did such changes depend on a woman's social class?
4. What were the connections between Darwin's ideas about nature and Marx's ideas about society?
5. What forces inspired the creation of the Paris Commune, and what did its fate suggest about the possibility of revolution in the late nineteenth century?

KEY TERMS

Eastern question, *p. 464*

natural selection, *p. 474*

Paris Commune, *p. 475*

Proclamation of the German Empire, *p. 462*

realism, *p. 472*

realpolitik, *p. 466*

Reichstag, *p. 467*

Risorgimento, *p. 464*

zemstvos, p. 470

DISCOVERING WESTERN CIVILIZATION ONLINE

You can obtain more information about state building and social change in Europe between 1850 and 1871 at the websites listed below. See also the Companion Website that accompanies this text, www.ablongman.com/kishlansky, which contains an online study guide and additional resources.

Building Nations: The Politics of Unification

The Crimean War (1853–1856)
www.hillsdale.edu/oldacademics/history/war/19Crim.htm
Electronic texts of officers' and soldiers' accounts of the battles of the Crimean War.

Internet Modern History Sourcebook: 19th Century Italy
www.fordham.edu/halsall/mod/modsbook23.html
This site focuses on documents relating to the unification of Italy and the Risorgimento.

Modern History Sourcebook: Documents of German Unification, 1848–1871
www.fordham.edu/halsall/mod/germanunification.html
This site provides translations of major primary documents concerning the unification of Germany.

Reforming European Society

The Victorian Web
www.victorianweb.org
A comprehensive collection of links to Victorian England.

Age of Liberalism: 1848–1914
campus.northpark.edu/history/WebChron/WestEurope/LiberalAge.html
A collection of links to chronologies for the "Age of Liberalism," 1848–1914.

Internet Modern History Sourcebook: Russian Revolution
www.fordham.edu/halsall/mod/modsbook39.html
This site, a repository for links to the Russian Revolution, provides links to documents on nineteenth-century tsarist Russia.

Changing Values and the Force of New Ideas

Florence Nightingale
www.kings.edu/womens_history/florence.html
Annotated bibliography of literature on Florence Nightingale.

The Eighteenth Brumaire of Louis Napoleon
csf.colorado.edu/psn/marx/Archive/1852-18brum/
Electronic text of Karl Marx's *Eighteenth Brumaire of Napoleon.*

1851 Project: The Great Exhibition
www.nal.vam.ac.uk/projects/1851.html
This site draws upon the collection of the National Library of Art in London to chronicle the Great Exhibition of 1851.

The Darwin Page
web.clas.ufl.edu/users/rhatch/pages/02-TeachingResources/readingwriting/darwin/05-DARWIN-PAGE.html
Web page of Professor Robert Hatch of the University of Florida, which provides links to bibliographies, texts, and other resources on Charles Darwin.

Paris Commune Archive
dwardmac.pitzer.edu/Anarchist_Archives/pariscommune/Pariscommunearchive.html
A Pitzer College political studies site providing summaries of the major players and events of the Paris Commune as well as an extensive bibliography.

Internet Women's History Sourcebook
www.fordham.edu/halsall/women/womensbook.html
This section of the Modern History Sourcebook focuses on women's history from antiquity to the present. The subchapter on modern European women's history provides links to texts on the structure of working women's lives as well as texts on feminism and the suffrage movement.

SUGGESTIONS FOR FURTHER READING

Building Nations: The Politics of Unification

Derek Beales, *The Risorgimento and the Unification of Italy* (London: Allen & Unwin, 1982). Drawing a distinction between unification and national revival, Beales situates the period of unification within the larger process of cultural and political revival.

David Blackbourn, *The Long Nineteenth Century: A History of Germany, 1780–1918* (New York: Oxford University Press, 1998). This book examines the emergence of Germany from the late eighteenth century through the First World War in terms of politics, economics, and culture.

John A. Davis, ed., *Italy in the Nineteenth Century, 1796–1900* (New York: Oxford University Press, 2000). The essays of nine specialists provide an historical analysis of Italian society, politics, and culture.

Dieter Langewiesche, *Liberalism in Germany* (Princeton, NJ: Princeton University Press, 2000). This study traces the roots of German liberalism to the late eighteenth century and emphasizes the role of individual German states, with a special chapter on the local influences on the formation of the nation-state between 1815 and 1860.

Lucy Riall, *The Italian Risorgimento: State, Society, and National Unification* (New York: Routledge, 1999). Riall examines the historiography of Italian unification and presents the turbulent period of "resurgence" as a turning point in Italian history.

Denis Mack Smith, *Cavour* (London: Weidenfeld and Nicolson, 1985). Smith contrasts Cavour and his policies with those of Garibaldi and Mazzini and considers the challenge of regionalism to the unification process.

Reforming European Society

Jane Burbank and David Ransel, eds., *Imperial Russia: New Histories for the Empire* (Bloomington: Indiana University Press, 1998). A collection of essays using new methodologies for understanding Russian history in the eighteenth and nineteenth centuries.

Judith Flanders, *Inside the Victorian Home: A Portrait of Domestic Life in Victorian England* (New York: W.W. Norton & Co., 2004). This examination of the daily lives of ordinary people reconstructs the drudgery of Victorian domesticity and "the different mental world" of that era.

Catherine Hall, Keith McClelland, and Jane Rendall, *Defining the Victorian Nation: Class, Race, Gender and the British Reform Act of 1867* (Cambridge: Cambridge University Press,

2000). This co-authored study presents a cultural, social, and gender history of the extension of the vote in 1867, accompanied by strong bibliographic aids.

Sudhir Hazareesingh, *From Subject to Citizen: The Second Empire and the Emergence of Modern French Democracy* (Princeton, NJ: Princeton University Press, 1998). In showing the relationship between the local and the national, the author provides a reevaluation of the emergence of republican citizenship in the Second Empire.

Margaret Homans, *Royal Representations: Queen Victoria and British Culture, 1837–1876* (Chicago: University of Chicago Press, 1998). Victoria is examined as a monarch, a symbol, and a wife and mother as a key to British culture.

Alain Plessis, *The Rise and Fall of the Second Empire, 1852–1871,* tr. Jonathan Mandelbaum (Cambridge: Cambridge University Press, 1985). Discusses the Second Empire as an important transitional period in French history, when the conflict was between traditional and modern values in political, economic, and social transformations.

Changing Values and the Force of New Ideas

Jenni Calder, *The Victorian Home* (London: B. T. Batsford, 1977). A cultural and social history of Victorian domestic life in which the author describes both bourgeois and working-class domestic environments.

Bonnie G. Smith, *Ladies of the Leisure Class: The Bourgeoises of Northern France in the Nineteenth Century* (Princeton, NJ: Princeton University Press, 1981). Explores the impact of industrialization on the lives of bourgeois women in northern France and demonstrates how the cult of domesticity emerged in a particular community.

Robert Tombs, *The Paris Commune, 1871* (London: Longman, 1999). A synthetic overview of the events of the commune and their impact on the course of French and European history.

Martha Vicinus, *Independent Women: Work and Community for Single Women, 1850–1920* (Chicago: University of Chicago Press, 1985). Chronicles the choices that Victorian women made to live outside the norms of marriage and domesticity in various women's communities, including sisterhoods, nursing communities, colleges, boarding schools, and settlement houses.

For a list of additional titles related to this chapter's topics, please see www.ablongman.com/kishlansky.

Chapter 24

THE CRISIS OF EUROPEAN CULTURE, 1871–1914

The Visual Record

SPEEDING TO THE FUTURE

"We want to demolish museums and libraries." These are the words not of an anarchist or a terrorist but of a poet. The Italian writer Emilio Marinetti (1876–1944) endeavored, symbolically at least, through the power of his pen, to destroy the citadels of Western culture at the beginning of the twentieth century. Marinetti was not alone in wanting to pull down all that preserved art and learning in the West. Joined by other artists and writers who called themselves **futurists,** Marinetti represented a desire to break free of the past. By shocking complacent bourgeois society with their art, futurists hoped to fashion a new and dynamic civilization. Although they were a small group with limited influence, their concerns were shared by a growing number of intellectuals who judged European culture to be in the throes of a serious moral and cultural crisis. Futurist ideas also reflected the growing preoccupation with the future common among European men and women who spurned the value of tradition.

The futurist painter Umberto Boccioni (1882–1916) captures an aspect of the dynamic intensity of this changing world in his *Riot in the Galleria* (1910). The painting is set in front of a respectable, Italian coffee shop frequented by well-dressed middle-class men and women. In a flurry of light and shadow, a rush of figures moves toward two women engaged in a brawl at center. That the brawlers are female underscores the irrationality of the incident; yet the brawl itself is not what compels our attention. Rather, it is the movement of the crowd, like moths to a flame, that Boccioni intends us to see. The objects in motion are little more than vibrations in space, faceless and indistinguishable as individuals. The crowd does not walk or run. It appears instead to be in flight. The crowd moves without forethought, attracted by the violence and the possibility of participating in it. Those on the periphery who have not yet joined the frenzy look as though they too will soon be swept into the action.

In the violence of the riot we are shown beauty of movement that surpasses that of an orderly waltz. Boccioni uses the warm glow of the electric lights, symbol of the modern age, to illuminate a "new reality." Golden tones, warm oranges and rosy hues, shadowed in delicate purples, create a mosaic whose beauty in the play of color is strangely at odds with the theme of the two brawling figures who activate the crowd. There is no meaning beyond the movement.

Riot in the Galleria reflects the early twentieth-century preoccupation with change. European society seemed to many contemporaries to be moving into an abyss, a world of tu-

multuous change but one without values. Technology was transforming Europe with breakneck speed. New forms of communication and transportation—the telephone, the wireless telegraph, the bicycle, the automobile, the airplane—were obliterating traditional understandings of time and space. The cinema and the X-ray altered visual perception and redefined the ways in which people saw the world around them. Science undermined how people thought about themselves by challenging moral and religious values as hollow and meaningless. The natural sciences threw into doubt the existence of a creator.

Like the political revolutionaries of an earlier age, futurist artists issued manifestoes. They sought the liberation of the human spirit from a world that could no longer be understood or controlled. Liberation could be achieved only through immersion in mass society and rapid change. Ironically, Boccioni met his death in 1916 as a soldier in the war that he welcomed as a purifying event.

Looking Ahead

As Europe passed from the nineteenth to the twentieth century, the new, grand scale of industrial production and po-

litical life was matched by the emergence of mass society. As this chapter will discuss, the need for regulation and control in mass democracy challenged the liberal, nineteenth-century emphasis on individual rights and parliamentary rule in Great Britain, Germany, France, and Austria. Mass democracy drew new social groups, workers and peasants, into the political arena, but it also continued to exclude others, including women, ethnic minorities, and Jews, whose pursuit of inclusion further challenged parliamentary forms.

The sciences and the new scientific study of society known as the social sciences contributed to attempts to understand how the physical world functioned, its predictability, and its improvement through technological and applied advances in knowledge. A new consciousness shaped ideas about family life, gender roles, and patterns of consumption as Europeans entered the twentieth century. ➤

EUROPEAN ECONOMY AND THE POLITICS OF MASS SOCIETY

Between 1871 and 1914 the scale of European life was radically altered. Industrial society had promoted largeness as the norm, as growing numbers of people worked under the same roof. Large-scale heavy industries fueled by new energy sources dominated the economic landscape. Great Britain, the leader of the first phase of the Industrial Revolution of the eighteenth century, slipped in prominence as an industrial power at the end of the nineteenth century, as Germany and the United States devised successful competitive strategies of investment, protection, and control.

Regulating Boom and Bust

The organization of factory production throughout Europe and the proximity of productive centers to distribution networks meant ever greater concentration of populations in urban areas. Like factories, cities were getting bigger at a rapid rate and were proliferating in numbers. With every passing year, fewer people remained on the land, and those who stayed were increasingly linked to cities and tied into national cultures by new transportation and communications networks.

The Need for Regulation.
Between 1873 and 1895, an epidemic of slumps battered the economics of European nations. These slumps, characterized by falling prices, downturns in productivity, and declining profits, did not strike European nations simultaneously, nor did they affect all countries with the same degree of severity. But the slumps of the late nineteenth century and the boom period of intense economic expansion from 1895 to 1914 did teach industrialists, financiers, and politicians one important lesson: Alternating booms and busts in the business cycle were dangerous and had to be regulated. Workers and their families suffered even more as the job market periodically shrank.

Too much of a good thing brought on the steady deflation of the last quarter of the nineteenth century. In the world economy there was an overproduction of agricultural products—a sharp contrast to the famines that had ravaged Europe only 50 years earlier. Overproduction resulted from two new factors in the world economy: technological advances in crop cultivation and the low cost of shipping and transport, which had opened European markets to cheap agricultural goods from the United States, Canada, and Argentina. The drop in food prices affected purchasing power in other sectors and resulted in long-term deflation and unemployment.

Financiers, politicians, and businessmen dedicated themselves to eliminating the boom-and-bust phenomenon, which they considered dangerous. The application of science and technology to industrial production required huge amounts of capital. The two new sources of power after 1880, petroleum and electricity, could be developed only with heavy capital investment. Large mechanized steel plants were too costly for small family firms of the scale that had industrialized textile production so successfully earlier in the century. Heavy machinery, smelting furnaces, buildings, and transport were all beyond the means of the small entrepreneur.

To raise the capital necessary for the new heavy industry at the end of the nineteenth century, firms had to look outside themselves to the stock market, banks, or the state to find adequate capital resources. But investors and especially banks refused to invest without guarantees on their capital. Because investment in heavy industry meant tying up capital for extended periods of time, banks insisted on safeguards against falling prices. The solution that they demanded was the elimination of uncertainty through the regulation of markets.

Cartels.
Regulation was achieved through the establishment of **cartels,** combinations of firms in a given industry united to fix prices and to establish production quotas. Cartels were agreements among big firms intent on controlling markets and guaranteeing profits. Trusts were another form of collaboration that resulted in the elimination of unprofitable businesses. Firms joined together horizontally within the same industry; for example, all steel producers agreed to fix prices and set quotas. Or they combined vertically by controlling all levels of the production process from raw materials to the finished product and all other ancillary products necessary to or resulting from the production process. Firms in Great Britain, falling behind in heavy industry, failed to form cartels and for the most part remained in private hands. But heavy industry in Germany, France, and Austria, to varying degrees, sought regulation of markets and prices through international cartels.

Banks, which had been the initial impetus behind the transformation to a regulated economy, in turn formed consortia to meet the need for greater amounts of capital. A consortium, paralleling a cartel, was a partnership among banks, often international in character, in which interest rates and the movement of capital were regulated by mutual agreement. The state, too, played an important role in directing the economy. In capital-poor Russia, the state used indirect taxes on the peasantry to finance industrialization and railway construction at the end of the nineteenth century. Russia also needed to import capital, primarily from France after 1887.

Throughout Europe, nation-states protected domestic industries by erecting tariff barriers against foreign goods. Only Great Britain among the major powers stood by a policy of free trade. Europe was split into two tiers—the haves and have-nots: those countries with a solid industrial core and those that had remained unindustrialized. This division had a geographic character, the north and west of Europe being heavily developed and capitalized and the southern and eastern parts of Europe remaining heavily agricultural. For both the haves and have-nots, tariff policies were an attractive form of regulation by the state to protect established industries and to nurture industries that were struggling for existence.

Challenging Liberal England

Great Britain experienced the transformation in political organization and social structure before other European nations. But after 1870, changes in politics influenced by the scale of the new industrial society spread to every European country. The policies that the emerging mass society generated were making clearer the contradictions inherent in the ideal of democracy. Mass demands were pushing aside the liberal emphasis on individual rights valued by parliamentary governments everywhere.

Great Britain had avoided revolution and social upheaval in the nineteenth century. Its strong parliamentary tradition was based on a homogeneous ruling elite. Aristocrats, businessmen, and financial leaders shared a common educational background in England's elitist educational system of public schools and the universities of Oxford and Cambridge. Schooling produced a common outlook and common attitudes toward parliamentary rule, whether in the Conservative or the Liberal party, and guaranteed a certain stability in policies and legislation.

Trade Unions.   In the 1880s, issues of unemployment, public health, housing, and education challenged the attitudes of Britain's ruling elite and fostered the advent of independent working-class politics. Between 1867 and 1885, extension of

suffrage increased the electorate fourfold. Protected by the markets of its empire, the British economy did not experience the roller-coaster effect of recurrent booms and busts after 1873. But after 1900, wages stagnated as prices continued to rise, and workers responded by supporting militant trade unions.

Trade unions, drawing on a long tradition of working-class associations, were all that stood between workers and the economic dislocation caused by unemployment, sickness, or old age. In addition, new unions of unskilled and semiskilled workers flourished, beginning in the 1880s and 1890s. A Scottish miner, James Keir Hardie (1856–1915), attracted national attention as the spokesman for a new political movement, the Labour party, whose goal was to represent workers in Parliament. In 1892, Hardie was the first independent working man to sit in the House of Commons. Hardie and his party convinced trade unions that it was in their best interests to support Labour candidates instead of Liberals in parliamentary elections after 1900. By 1906, the new Labour party had 29 seats in Parliament. Intellectuals now joined with trade unionists in demanding public housing, better public sanitation, municipal reforms, and improved pay and benefits for workers.

Parliamentary Reforms.   The existence of the new Labour party pressured Conservatives and Liberals to develop more enlightened social programs. After 1906, under threat of losing votes to the Labour party, the Liberal party heeded the pressures for reform. The "new" Liberals supported legislation to strengthen the right of unions to picket peacefully. Led by

■ A union leader addresses striking British coal miners in 1912. Labor unions became increasingly militant after the turn of the century as rising unemployment and declining real wages cut into the gains of the working class.

David Lloyd George (1863–1945), who was chancellor of the exchequer, Liberals sponsored the National Insurance Act of 1911. The act provided compulsory payments to workers for sickness and unemployment benefits.

In order to gain approval to pay for this new legislation, Lloyd George recognized that Parliament itself had to be renovated. The Parliament Bill of 1911 reduced the House of Lords, dominated by Conservatives resistant to proposed welfare reforms, from its status as equal partner with the House of Commons. Commons could and now did raise taxes without the consent of the House of Lords to pay for new programs that benefited workers and the poor.

Extraparliamentary Protest. Social legislation did not silence unions and worker organizations. Between 1910 and 1914, waves of strikes broke over England. Coal miners, seamen, railroad workers, and dockers protested against stagnant wages and rising prices.

The high incidence of strikes was a consequence of growing distrust of Parliament and of a regulatory state bureaucracy responsible for the social welfare reforms. Labour's voice grew more strident. The Trade Unions Act of 1913 granted unions legal rights to settle their grievances with management directly. Only the outbreak of war in 1914 ended the possibility of a general strike by miners, railwaymen, and transport workers. The question of Irish home rule also plagued Parliament. In Ulster in northern Ireland, army officers of Protestant Irish background threatened to mutiny. In addition, women agitating for the vote shattered parliamentary complacence. The most advanced industrial nation, with its tradition of peaceful parliamentary rule, had entered the age of mass politics.

Political Struggles in Germany

During his reign as chancellor of the German Empire (1871–1890), Otto von Bismarck formed shrewd alliances that hampered the development of parliamentary government. He repeatedly and successfully blocked the emergence of fully democratic participation. In Germany, all males had the right to vote, but the German parliament, the Reichstag, enjoyed only restricted powers in comparison to the British Parliament. Bismarck's objective remained always the successful unification of Germany, and he promoted cooperation with democratic institutions and parties only as long as that goal was enhanced.

Bismarck and the German Parliament. Throughout the 1870s, the German chancellor collaborated with the German liberal parties in constructing the legal codes, the monetary and banking system, the judicial apparatus, and the railroad network that pulled the new Germany together. Bismarck backed German liberals in their antipapal campaign, in which the Catholic Church was depicted as an authority in competition with the German nation-state. The anti-Church campaign, launched in 1872, was dubbed the *Kulturkampf* ("struggle for civilization") because its supporters contended that it was a battle waged in the interests of humanity.

The legislation of the *Kulturkampf* expelled Jesuits from Germany, removed priests from state service, attacked religious education, and instituted civil marriage. Many Germans grew concerned about the social costs of such widespread religious repression, and the Catholic Center party increased its parliamentary representation by rallying Catholics as a voting bloc in the face of state repression. With the succession of a new pontiff, Leo XIII (1878–1903), Bismarck negotiated a settlement with the Catholic Church, cutting his losses and bringing the *Kulturkampf* to a halt.

The Social Democrat Party. Bismarck's repressive policies also targeted the Social Democratic party. The Social Democrats were committed to a Marxist critique of capitalism and to international cooperation with other socialist parties. Seeing them as a threat to stability in Germany and in Europe as a whole, Bismarck set out to smash them. In 1878, using the opportunity for repression presented by two attempts on the emperor's life, Bismarck outlawed the fledgling Socialist party. The Anti-Socialist Law forbade meetings among socialists, fund-raising, and distribution of printed matter. Nevertheless, individual Social Democratic candidates stood for election in this period and learned quickly how to work with middle-class parties to achieve electoral successes. By 1890, Social Democrats had captured 20 percent of the electorate and controlled 35 Reichstag seats in spite of Bismarck's anti-Socialist legislation.

Throughout the 1880s, as his ability to manage Reichstag majorities declined and as Socialist strength steadily mounted, Bismarck grew disenchanted with universal manhood suffrage. Beginning in 1888, the chancellor found himself at odds with the new emperor Wilhelm II (1888–1918) over his foreign and domestic policies. The young emperor dismissed Bismarck in March 1890 and abandoned the chancellor's anti-Socialist legislation. The Social Democratic party became the largest Marxist party in the world and, by 1914, the largest single party in Germany. During the period when the Social Democratic movement was outlawed, Bismarck and Wilhelm II used social welfare legislation to win mass support, including accident insurance, sick benefits, and old age and disability benefits. But such legislation did not undermine the popularity of socialism, nor did it attract workers away from Marxist programs, as the electoral returns demonstrated.

In the end, the Reichstag failed to defy the absolute authority of Emperor Wilhelm II, who was served after 1890 by a string of ineffectual chancellors. Despite its constitutional forms, Germany was ruled by a state authoritarianism in which the bureaucracy, the military, and various interest groups exercised influence over the emperor. A high-risk foreign policy that had a mass appeal was one way to circumvent a parliamentary system incapable of decision making.

Constitutional solutions had been short-circuited in favor of authoritarian rule.

Political Scandals and Mass Politics in France

The Third Republic in France had an aura of the accidental about its origins and of the precarious about its existence. Yet appearances were misleading. Founded in 1870 with the defeat of Napoleon III's empire by the Germans, the Third Republic claimed legitimacy by placing itself squarely within the revolutionary democratic tradition.

Creating Citizens. The Third Republic successfully worked toward the creation of a national community based on a common identity of citizens. Compulsory schooling, one of the great institutional transformations of French government in 1885, socialized French children in common values, patriotism, and identification with the nation-state. Old ways, local dialects, superstitious practices, and peasant insularity dropped away or were modified under the persistent pressure of a centralized curriculum of reading, writing, arithmetic, and civics. Compulsory service in the army for the generation of young men of draft age served the same end of communicating national values to a predominantly peasant population. Technology also accelerated the process of shaping a national citizenry, as railroad lines tied people together and new and better roads made distances shrink.

A truly national and mass culture emerged in the period between 1880 and 1914. French people were not necessarily more political, but they were political in a new way that enabled them to identify their own local interests with national issues.

The Boulanger Affair. A political crisis, known as the Boulanger Affair, temporarily threatened the stability of the republic and served as a good indication of the extent of the transformation in French political life at the end of the nineteenth century.

As minister of war, General Georges Boulanger (1837–1891) became a hero to French soldiers when he undertook needed reforms of army life. He won over businessmen by leading troops against strikers. Above all, he cultivated the image of a patriot ready to defend France's honor at any cost. But Boulanger was a shallow man who owed his success to a carefully orchestrated publicity campaign that made him the most popular man in France by 1886.

Boulanger's potential in the political arena attracted the attention of right-wing backers, including monarchists who hoped eventually to restore kingship to France. By 1889, Boulanger was able to amass enough national support to frighten the defenders of parliamentary institutions. The charismatic general ultimately failed in his bid for power and fled the country because of allegations of treason. But he left in his wake an embryonic mass movement on the Right that operated outside the channels of parliamentary institutions.

The Dreyfus Affair. A very different kind of crisis began to take shape in 1894 with the controversy surrounding the trial of Captain Alfred Dreyfus (1859–1935) that came to be known simply as "the Affair." Dreyfus was an Alsatian Jewish army officer who was accused of selling military secrets to the Germans. His trial for treason served as a lightning rod for xenophobia—the hatred of foreigners, especially Germans—and anti-Semitism, the hatred of Jews. Dreyfus was stripped of his commission and honors and sentenced to solitary confinement for life on Devil's Island, a convict colony off French Guiana in South America.

Illegal activities and outright falsifications by Dreyfus's superiors to secure a conviction came to light in the mass press and divided the nation. Those who supported Dreyfus's innocence, the pro-Dreyfusards, were for the most part on the left of the political spectrum and spoke of the republic's duty to uphold justice and freedom. The anti-Dreyfusards were associated with the traditional institutions of the Catholic Church and the army and considered themselves to be defending the honor of France.

The Affair represented the ability of an individual to seek redress against injustice. On the national level, the Affair represented an important transformation in the nature of French political life. Existing parliamentary institutions had been found wanting. They were unable to cope with the mass politics stirred up by Dreyfus's conviction. The newspaper press vied with parliament and the courts as a forum for investigation and decision making.

The crises provoked by Boulanger's attempt to gain power and the Dreyfus Affair demonstrated the major role of the press and the importance of public opinion in exerting pressure on the system of government. The press emerged as a myth-maker in shaping and channeling public opinion. Émile Zola (1840–1902), the great French novelist, spearheaded the pro-Dreyfusard movement with his damning article *"J'accuse!"* ("I Accuse!"), in which he pointed to the military and the judiciary as the "spirits of social evil" for persecuting an innocent man. The article appeared in a leading French newspaper and was influential in securing Dreyfus's eventual exoneration and the discovery of the real culprit, one of Dreyfus's colleagues on the general staff. The Third Republic was never in danger of collapsing, but it was transformed. The locus of power in parliament was challenged by pressure groups outside of it.

Defeating Liberalism in Austria

In the 1870s, the liberal values of the bourgeoisie dominated the Austro-Hungarian Empire. The Habsburg monarchy had adjusted to constitutional government, which was introduced throughout Austria in 1860. Faith in parliamentary government based on a restricted suffrage had established a tenuous foothold. After setbacks of 1848 and the troublesome decade of the 1860s, when Prussia had trounced Austria and Bismarck had routed the hope of an Austrian-dominated

German Empire, the Austrian bourgeoisie counted on a peaceful future with a centralized multinational state dedicated to order and progress.

By 1900, however, the urban and capitalist middle class that ruled Austria by virtue of a limited suffrage based on property had lost ground to new groups that were essentially anticapitalist and antiliberal in their outlook. The new groups were peasants, workers, urban artisans and shopkeepers, and the colonized Slavic peoples of the empire. Bourgeois politics and laissez-faire economics had offered little or nothing to these varied groups, who were now claiming the right of participation. Mass parties were formed based on radical pan-Germanic feeling, anticapitalism that appealed to peasants and artisans, hatred of the Jews shared by students and artisans, and nationalist aspirations that attracted the lower middle classes.

The political experiences of Great Britain, Germany, France, and Austria between 1871 and 1914 make clear the common challenges confronting western parliamentary systems in a changing era of democratic politics. In spite of variations, each nation experienced its own challenge to liberal parliamentary institutions, and each shaped its own responses to a new international phenomenon—the rise of the masses as a political force.

OUTSIDERS IN MASS POLITICS

By the end of the nineteenth century, a faceless, nameless electorate had become the basis of new political strategies and a new political rhetoric. A concept of class identification of workers was devalued in favor of interest-group politics in which lobbies formed around single issues to pressure European governments. But the apparently all-inclusive concept of mass society continued to exclude some groups: women, ethnic minorities, and Jews. Women and ethnic minorities learned to incorporate strategies and techniques of politics and organization that permitted them to challenge the existing political system. Others, including anarchists, rejected both the organizational techniques of mass society and the values of the nation-state. Outsiders, then, were both those intent on being integrated into mass politics and those who sought its destruction.

Feminists and Politics

Women's drive for emancipation had been a recurrent motif of European political culture throughout the nineteenth century. In the areas of civil liberties, legal equality with men, and economic autonomy, only the most limited reforms had been enacted. The glorification of domesticity was a kind of recognition of women's unique contribution to society, but it was also a means of keeping women "in their place."

Women's Rights.   European women who worked outside of the family were paid one-third to one-half of what men earned for the same work. In Great Britain, women did not enjoy equal divorce rights until the twentieth century. In France, married women had no control over their own incomes; all their earnings were considered their husband's private property. From the Atlantic to the Urals, women were excluded from economic and educational opportunities.

Growing numbers of women, primarily from the middle classes, began calling themselves "feminist," a term that was coined in France in the 1830s. The new feminists throughout western Europe differed from earlier generations in their willingness to organize mass movements and to appropriate the techniques of interest-group politics. The first international congress of women's rights, held in Paris in 1878, initiated an era of international cooperation and exchange among women's organizations. Women's groups now positioned themselves for sustained political action.

Movements for the Vote.   The lessons of the new electoral politics were not lost on feminists seeking women's emancipation through the vote. Leaders like Hubertine Auclert (1848–1914) in France and Emmeline Pankhurst (1858–1928) in Great Britain recognized the need for a mass base of support. If women's organizations were to survive as competing interest groups, they needed to form political alliances, control their own newspapers and magazines, and keep their cause before the public eye.

There was a growing willingness on the part of a variety of women's organizations to use mass demonstrations, rallies, and violent tactics. No movement operated more effectively in this regard than the British suffrage movement. In 1903, a group of eminently respectable middle-class and aristocratic British women formed the Women's Social and Political Union (WSPU). At the center of the movement was Emmeline Pankhurst, a middle-aged woman of frail and attractive appearance who had a will of iron and a gift for oratory. Mrs. Pankhurst and her two daughters, Christabel (1880–1958), a lawyer by training, and Sylvia (1882–1960), an artist, succeeded in keeping women's suffrage before the British public and brought the plight of British women to international attention.

Women's demands for political power were the basis of an unheralded revolution in Western culture. In Great Britain, the decade before the Great War of 1914 was a period of profound political education for women seeking the vote. An unprecedented 250,000 women gathered in Hyde Park in 1908 to hear more about female suffrage. Laughed at by men, ridiculed in the press, and taunted in public demonstrations, women activists refused to be quiet and to know their place.

European women did not gain the right to vote easily. In France and Germany, moderate and left-wing politicians opposed extension of the vote to women because they feared that women would strengthen conservative candidates. Many politicians thought that women were not "ready" for the vote and that they should receive it only as a reward—an unusual concept in democratic societies. Not until 1918 were British women granted limited suffrage, and not until 1928 did they gain voting rights that were equal to those of men. Only after war and revolution was the vote extended to other women in the West: Germany in 1918, the United States in 1920, and France at the end of World War II.

Women and Social Reform.   Not all activist women saw the right to vote as the solution to women's oppression. Those who agitated for social reforms for poor and working-class women parted ways with the militant suffragists. Sylvia Pankhurst, for example, left her mother and sister to their political battles to work for social reform in London's poverty-stricken East End. Women socialists were concerned with working-class women's "double oppression" in the home and in the workplace. Working-class women, most notably in Germany, united feminism with socialism in search of a better life.

The women's movements of the period from 1871 to 1914 differed socially and culturally from nation to nation. Yet there is a sense in which the women's movements constituted an international phenomenon. The rise in the level of women's political consciousness occurred in the most advanced Western countries almost simultaneously and had a predominantly middle-class character. In spite of concerted

CONSTANCE LYTTON

Civil disobedience by British women demanding the right to vote often led to their arrest. In protest, incarcerated suffragettes went on hunger strikes to publicize their cause. The British government responded with a brutal policy of force-feeding of prisoners. Constance Lytton, a British aristocrat and suffragette, recounts here the agony of being forcibly fed in prison. Her own health was seriously weakened by the experience.

Focus Questions

How did Constance Lytton express civil disobedience? Why was the government intent on force-feeding women incarcerated in this way, a practice not common with other prisoners?

[The prison's senior medical officer] urged me to take food voluntarily. I told him that was absolutely out of the question, that when our legislators ceased to resist enfranchising women then I should cease to resist taking food in prison. . . . I offered no resistance to being placed in position, but lay down voluntarily on the plank bed. Two of the wardresses took hold of my arms, one held my head and one my feet. One wardress helped to pour the food. The doctor leant on my knees as he stooped over my chest to get at my mouth. I shut my mouth and clenched my teeth. . . . The doctor offered me the choice of a wooden or steel gag; he explained elaborately, as he did on most subsequent occasions, that the steel gag would hurt and the wooden one not, and he urged me not to force him to use the steel gag. But I did not speak nor open my mouth, so that after playing about for a moment or two with the wooden one he finally had recourse to the steel. He seemed annoyed at my resistance and he broke into a temper as he plied my teeth with the steel implement. . . . The pain of it was intense and at last I must have given way for he got the gag between my teeth, when he proceeded to turn it much more than necessary until my jaws were fastened wide apart, far more than they could go

naturally. Then he put down my throat a tube which seemed to me much too wide and was something like four feet in length. The irritation of the tube was excessive. I choked the moment it touched my throat until it had got down. Then the food was poured in quickly; it made me sick a few seconds after it was down and the action of the sickness made my body and legs double up, but the wardresses instantly pressed back my head and the doctor leant on my knees. The horror of it was more than I can describe. I was sick over the doctor and wardresses, and it seemed a long time before they took the tube out. As the doctor left he gave me a slap on the cheek, not violently, but, as it were, to express his contemptuous disapproval, and he seemed to take for granted that my distress was assumed. . . . I had been sick over my hair, which, though short, hung on either side of my face, all over the wall near my bed, and my clothes seemed saturated with it, but the wardresses told me they could not get me a change that night as it was too late, the office was shut. I lay quite motionless, it seemed paradise to be without the suffocating tube, without the liquid food going in and out of my body and without the gag between my teeth. Before long I heard the sounds of the forced feeding in the next cell to mine. It was almost more than I could bear, it was Elsie Howey, I was sure. When the ghastly process was over and all quiet, I tapped on the wall and called out at the top of my voice, which wasn't much just then, "No surrender," and there came the answer past any doubt in Elsie's voice. "No surrender."

From Constance Lytton, *Prisons and Prisoners* (1914).

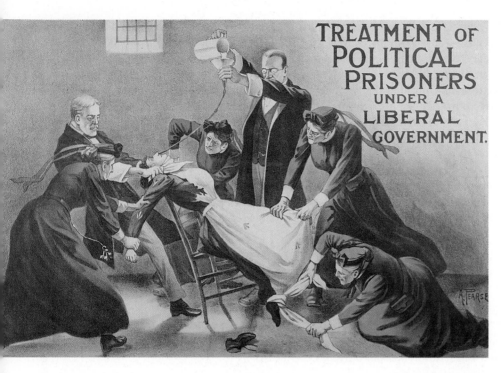

■ This British suffragette poster, published by the Women's Social and Political Union, graphically depicts the extreme methods used to force-feed women prisoners. A prison guard pulls back the prisoner's head, others hold down her arms and legs, and another ties her foot to the chair. A doctor holds a hose through which he forces gruel into the woman's nose.

efforts, however, women remained on the outside of societies that excluded them from political participation, access to education, and social and economic equality.

The Jewish Question and Zionism

Two million eastern European Jews migrated westward between 1868 and 1914 in search of peace and refuge. Seventy thousand settled in Germany. Others continued westward, stopping in the United States. Another kind of Jewish migration took place in the nineteenth century: the movement within nations of Jews from rural to urban areas. In eastern Europe, Jewish migrations coincided with downturns in the economic cycle, and Jews became scapegoats for the high rates of unemployment and high prices that seemed to follow in their wake. Most migrants were peddlers, artisans, or small shopkeepers who were seen as threatening to small businesses. Differing in language, culture, and dress, they were viewed as alien in every way.

Anti-Semitism.   The term **anti-Semitism,** meaning hostility to Jews, was first used in 1879 to give a pseudoscientific legitimacy to bigotry and hatred. Persecution was a harsh reality for Jews in eastern Europe at the end of the nineteenth century. In Russia, Jews could not own property and were restricted to living in certain territories, areas referred to as "the Pale." Organized massacres, or **pogroms,** in Kiev, Odessa, and Warsaw followed the assassination of Tsar Alexander II in 1881 and occurred again after the failed Russian revolution of 1905. Russian authorities blamed the Jews, who were perennially perceived as outsiders, for the assassination and revolu-

tion and the social instability that followed them. Pogroms resulted in the death and displacement of tens of thousands of eastern European Jews.

In western Europe, Jews considered themselves to be assimilated into their national cultures, identifying with their nationality as much as with their religion. Austrian and German Jews were granted full civil rights in 1867 on the principle that citizens of all religions enjoyed full equality. In France, Jews had been legally emancipated since the end of the eighteenth century. But the western and central European politics of the 1890s had a strong dose of anti-Semitism. Demagogues such as Georg von Schönerer (1842–1921) of Austria were capable of whipping up a frenzy of riots and violence against Jews. Western and central European anti-Semitism assumed a new level of virulence at the end of the nineteenth century.

Fear of the Jews was connected with hatred of capitalism. In France and Germany, Jews controlled powerful banking and commercial firms that became the targets of blame in hard times. Upwardly mobile sons of Jewish immigrants entered the professions of banking, trading, and journalism. They were also growing in numbers as teachers and academics. In the 1880s, more than half of Vienna's physicians (61 percent in 1881) and lawyers (58 percent of barristers in 1888) were Jewish. Their professional success only heightened tensions and condemnations of Jews as an "alien race." Anti-Semitism served as a violent means of mobilizing mass support, especially among the groups that felt threatened by capitalist concentration and large-scale industrialization. For anti-Semitic Europeans, Jews embodied the democratic, liberal, and cosmopolitan tendencies of the new culture that they were consciously rejecting in their new political affiliations.

MAP DISCOVERY

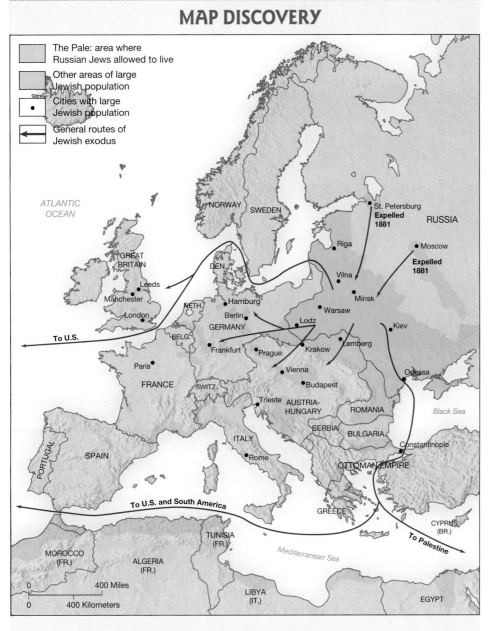

Legend:
- The Pale: area where Russian Jews allowed to live
- Other areas of large Jewish population
- Cities with large Jewish population
- General routes of Jewish exodus

Jewish Migration

Persecution and expulsions drove two million Jews out of Russia and eastern Europe between 1868 and 1914. Some settled in central Europe, while others traveled to Palestine and the Americas. According to this map, what features do the areas of large Jewish population have in common? What are the major general routes of Jewish exodus? Based on the chapter discussion, why did Jews migrate into and out of the Pale in western Russia? What were the major stopover points in the Jewish migrations to the south and west?

mothers was not the answer. Jews needed their own nation, it was argued, since they were a people without a nation. Zionism was the solution to what Jewish intellectuals called "the Jewish problem." Zion, the ancient homeland of biblical times, would provide a national territory, and a choice, to persecuted Jews. Zionism became a Jewish nationalist movement dedicated to the establishment of a Jewish state.

Theodor Herzl (1860–1904), an Austrian Jew born in Budapest, was the founder of **Zionism** in its political form. As a student in Vienna, he encountered discrimination, but his commitment to Zionism developed as a result of his years as a journalist in Paris. Herzl observed the anti-Semitic attacks in republican France that were provoked by the scandals surrounding the misappropriation of funds by prominent French politicians and business leaders during the failed French attempt to build a Panama canal and the divisive conflict over the Dreyfus Affair in the 1890s. He came to appreciate how deeply embedded anti-Semitism was in European society, and he despaired of the ability of corrupt parliamentary governments to uproot it. In *The Jewish State* (1896), Herzl concluded that Jews must have a state of their own. Under his direction, Zionism developed a world organization with the aim of establishing a Jewish homeland in Palestine.

Jews began emigrating to Palestine. With the financial backing of Jewish donors such as the French banker Baron de Rothschild, nearly 90,000 Jews had established settlements there by 1914. Calculated to tap a common Jewish identification with an ancient heritage, the choice of Palestine as a homeland was controversial from the beginning, and the problems arising from the choice have persisted to the present day.

Zionism. A Jewish leadership emerged in central and western Europe that treated anti-Semitism as a problem that could be solved by political means. For the generation at the end of the nineteenth century, the assimilation of their fathers and

■ Maurycy Minkowski, *After the Pogrom* (ca. 1910). Minkowski's works depict Jewish life in Poland before the Russian Revolution. In this painting he expertly captured the weariness, hopelessness, and fear of the refugees who have interrupted their flight to rest. The sense of isolation and dislocation evoked in the painting may derive from the deaf and mute artist's personal perception of profound separation and detachment.

Some Jewish critics of Zionism thought that a separate Jewish state would prove that Jews were not good citizens of their respective nation-states and would exacerbate hostilities toward Jews as outsiders. Yet Zionism had much in common with the European liberal tradition, because it sought in the creation of a nation-state for Jews the solution to social injustice. Zion, the Jewish nation in the Middle East, was a liberal utopia for the Jewish people. Zionism learned from other mass movements of the period the importance of a broad base of support. By the time of the First Zionist Congress, held in Basel, Switzerland, in 1897, it had become a truly international movement. Zionism did not achieve its goals before World War I, and the Jewish state of Israel was not recognized by the world community until 1948.

Workers and Minorities on the Margins

Changes in the scale of political life paralleled the rise of heavy industry and the increasing urbanization of European populations. New industrial and financial leaders assumed positions among Europe's ruling elite. A new style of politics brought new political actors into the public arena at the beginning of the twentieth century. Extraparliamentary groups grew in influence and power and exerted pressure on the political process. The politics of mass society made clear the contradictions inherent in democracy. Propaganda, the ability to control information, became the avenue to success.

There was no single anarchist doctrine, but the varieties of **anarchism** all shared a hope in a future free from constraints. Mikhail Bakunin (1814–1876), a member of the Russian nobility, became Europe's leading anarchist spokesman. Bakunin was a man of revolutionary action who espoused the use of violence to achieve individual liberation. He believed that all existing institutions must be swept away before ownership of production could be collectivized. Bakunin broke with Marx, whom he considered a "scientific bourgeois socialist," out of touch with the mass of workers.

In 1892, the trial in Paris of a bomb-throwing anarchist named Ravachol attracted great public attention. He and other French anarchists had captured the popular imagination with their threats to destroy bourgeois society by bombing private residences, public buildings, and restaurants. Ravachol's terrorist deeds represented the extreme rejection of participation in electoral politics. The public was frightened—but also fascinated. Ravachol opposed the state and the capitalist economy as the dual enemy that could be destroyed only through individual acts of random physical violence. For his crimes he was condemned to death and publicly executed.

The best-known anarchists of the late nineteenth century were those, like Ravachol, who engaged in terrorist assassinations and bombings. Although not all anarchists were terrorists intent on destruction, all shared a desire for a revolutionary restructuring of society. Most anarchists were loners. They dreamed of the collapse of the capitalist system with its exploitation and inequality and of the emergence of a society based on personal freedom, autonomy, and justice. Anarchists spurned the Marxist willingness to organize and participate in parliamentary politics. They disdained the tyranny of new organizations and bureaucracies that worked for gradual reforms at the expense of principles of justice.

Bakunin's successor in international anarchist doctrine was also a Russian of aristocratic lineage: Prince Pyotr Kropotkin

(1842–1921). Kropotkin united communism and anarchism, arguing that goods should be communally distributed, "from each according to his ability, to each according to his needs," a principle that Louis Blanc had expressed earlier. On the basis of his own empirical observations, Kropotkin argued that competition and dominance were not laws of nature and instead stressed human interdependence.

Anarchism had special appeal to workers in trades that were staggering under the blows of industrial capitalism. Calling themselves anarcho-syndicalists, artisans—especially in France—were able to combine local trade union organization with anarchist principles. But, unlike union movements in the industrialized countries of Great Britain and Germany, French trade unions remained small, weak, and local. The contrast between the Labour party in Great Britain and the German Social Democrats on the one hand and the French anarcho-syndicalists on the other highlighted the split between advanced industrial countries and less-developed areas of Europe, where an artisan class was attempting to preserve autonomy and control.

The problems of disaffected groups in general intensified before 1914. Anarchists and anarcho-syndicalist workers deplored the centralization and organization of mass society. Yet anarchism posed no serious threat to social stability because of the effectiveness of policing in most European states. As Friedrich Engels observed at the turn of the century, random violence directed against politics and the economy was no match for the repressive forces at the command of the nation-state. The politics of mass society excluded diverse groups, including women, Jews, and ethnic minorities, from participation. Yet the techniques, values, and organization of the world of politics remained available to all these groups. It was the outbreak of war in 1914 that silenced, temporarily at least, the challenge of these outsiders.

SHAPING THE NEW CONSCIOUSNESS

Both science and art contributed to the new world view that emerged in western society in the late nineteenth century. Not only was the European imagination opened up to new influences from the culture and aesthetics of other lands, but Europeans developed a critique of traditional values and rationalist thought from within through new developments in philosophy and science.

The Authority of Science

New scientific disciplines claimed to study society with methods similar to those applied to the study of bacilli and the atom. A traditional world of order and hierarchy gave way to a new way of perceiving reality. The discoveries of science had ramifications that extended beyond the laboratory, the hospital, and the classroom.

Discoveries in the Physical Sciences.   Scientific discoveries in the last quarter of the nineteenth century pushed outward the frontiers of knowledge. In physics, James Clerk

Maxwell (1831–1879) discovered the relationship between electricity and magnetism. Maxwell showed mathematically that an oscillating electric charge produces an electromagnetic field and that such a field radiates outward from its source at a constant speed—the speed of light. His theories led to the discovery of the electromagnetic spectrum, comprising radiation of different wavelengths, including X-rays, visible light, and radio waves. This discovery had important practical applications for the development of the electrical industry and led to the invention of radio and television. Within a generation, the names of Edison, Westinghouse, Marconi, Siemens, and Bell entered the public realm.

Discoveries in the physical sciences succeeded one another with great rapidity. The periodic table of chemical elements was formulated in 1869. Radioactivity was discovered in 1896. Two years later, Marie Curie (1867–1934) and her husband Pierre (1859–1906) discovered the elements radium and polonium. At the end of the century, Ernest Rutherford (1871–1937) identified alpha and beta rays in radioactive atoms. Building on the new discoveries, Max Planck (1858–1947), Albert Einstein (1879–1955), and Niels Bohr (1885–1962) dismantled the classical physics of absolute and determined principles and left in its place modern physics based on relativity and uncertainty. In 1900, Planck propounded a theory that renounced the emphasis in classical physics on energy as a wave phenomenon in favor of a new "quantum theory" of energy as emitted and absorbed in minute, discrete amounts.

In 1905, Albert Einstein formulated his special theory of relativity, in which he established the relationship of mass and energy in the famous equation $E = mc^2$. In 1916, he published his general theory of relativity, a mathematical formulation that created new concepts of space and time. Einstein disproved the Newtonian view of gravitation as a force and instead saw it as a curved field in the time-space continuum created by the presence of mass. No one at the time foresaw that applying Einstein's theory that a particle of matter could be converted into a great quantity of energy would unleash the most destructive human-made power in history: the atomic and hydrogen bombs, which Einstein, a pacifist, lived to see developed.

Achievements in Biology.   Though the discoveries in the physical sciences were the most dramatic, the biological sciences, too, witnessed great breakthroughs. Research biologists dedicated themselves to the study of disease-causing microbes and to the chemical bases of physiology. French chemist Louis Pasteur (1822–1895) studied microorganisms to find methods of preventing the spread of diseases in humans, animals, and plants. He developed methods of inoculation to provide protection against anthrax in sheep, cholera in chickens, and rabies in animals and humans.

The pace of breakthroughs in biological knowledge and medical treatment was staggering. The malaria parasite was isolated in 1880. The control of diseases such as yellow fever contributed to improvement in the quality of life. Knowledge

The West and the Wider World
AFRICAN ART AND EUROPEAN ARTISTS

The limited definition of civilization held by the Western world for more than a millennium began to broaden in the late nineteenth century. Anthropologists studying non-Western cultures argued that the social structure, habits, beliefs, and products of communities elsewhere in the world formerly dismissed as primitive or exotic were, in their own way, as complex and evolved as those based on European tradition. In the late nineteenth century, the world view of Europeans was expanded by two characteristic European institutions: world fairs and public museums. European countries and the United States hosted international exhibitions such as the London Great Exhibition of 1851 and the Chicago Columbian Exposition of 1893 that introduced art and cultural artifacts from all over the world to a mass public audience. Curiosity led to awareness, and gave way to growing appreciation and understanding of the cultures of different continents. For example, European exposure to the art forms and costumes of the Far East changed European style and painting in the second half of the nineteenth century. The discovery of Japanese painting, wood-block prints, and calligraphy provided an important influence on the new direction of European impressionists and postimpressionists. Japanese design was incorporated into the work of such leading Western artists as Edgar Degas and James Whistler.

No less important was the artistic influence of Africa, portrayed as the "dark continent" and the "white man's burden" by colonizing forces (see Chapter 25), on leading lights of the European art world. Pablo Picasso encountered African carvings for the first time as a young man in the ethnographic collections of the Trocadéro Museum in Paris. The Spanish artist was so fascinated by the directness and strength of the African aesthetic that he was inspired to abandon all traces of traditional form in his work and seek a new means of expression. In one of his best known works from the early twentieth century, *Les Desmoiselles d'Avignon* (1907, France, Figure 1), Picasso used the formula of African masks to cover the faces of the two women on the right of the canvas. Mask-like features were incorporated into the faces of the three women to the left. The denial of natural appearance in these women is coupled with the denial of a similar Western art convention, the illusion of three-dimensional space. Picasso fragments the planes of the background and the planes of some of the bodies, breaking them into the jagged slabs that would become the hallmark of Cubism. Picasso knew little about the cultural significance of the African masks he so admired and collected; he saw them as emblems of primitivism, appropriate for the spirit of danger and mystery he wanted to convey in a portrait of Avignon prostitutes. He saw in African art the point of departure and the

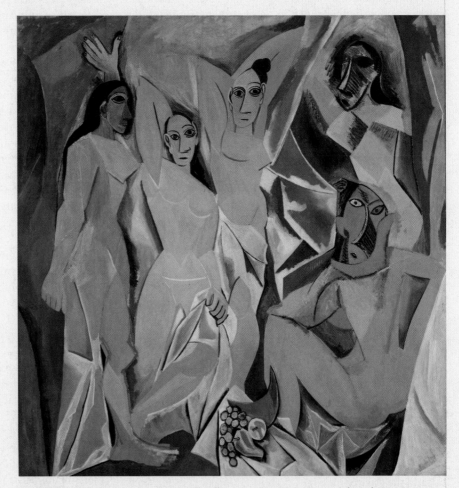

■ Figure 1. Pablo Picasso, *Les Demoiselles d'Avignon* (1907). Museum of Modern Art, New York/Art Resource, NY/© The Estate of Pablo Picasso/Artists Rights Society (ARS), New York

source of inspiration for a new and radical art in the West.

The dynamic of cultural exchange in the arts flowed in both directions. While leading European artists such as Picasso were forging new art forms by appropriating an African art aesthetic identified as primitive, African artists were borrowing and incorporating Western-inspired forms into their art. See this staff finial from the Kongo (ca. 16th–19th century, Figure 2) of an ivory figure representing a Kongo man, indicated by his broken teeth and beardless chin, with blue eyes and dressed in Western clothing. Wooden staffs topped with ivory carvings symbolized power and status to Kongo peoples. This particular figure, reddened by pigment and use, embodies the further status conferred by Western hat, high-collared jacket, and earring

typical of the earliest Westerners to trade in Africa. The man's garb positions him in a new wider world, associating Westernization with power and progress.

The Mami Wata cult of west Africa demonstrates another kind of cultural intersection. Images of this foreign water spirit seen here in a mask of the Guro peoples from the Ivory Coast in the mid-twentieth century (Figure 3) record the layering of ideas and aesthetics from abroad. Her posture and her attribute of the coiling snake have been traced back to a German color lithograph of an East Indian snake charmer, circulated throughout the Ivory Coast in the late nineteenth century. Here the Mami Wata figure is superimposed on the top of a beautiful and colorful tribal mask, demonstrating the graceful coexistence of cultures and influences. The combination of the Mami Wata icon with the traditional African mask, similar to those collected by Picasso, is intended to connote a particular spiritual force of imported ideas and influences. The cult of Mami Wata has endured through the twentieth century, and her image is associated with more than a dozen cultures from Senegal to Tanzania. Dressed according to modern Western standards, Mami Wata's form has continued to change with the times. Her iconography is a dynamic one that continues to develop.

Beyond form and content, one of the major differences that should be noted in considering the dynamic between the West and the wider world of African art is the presence of the individual artist in the Western aesthetic. We know *Les Desmoiselles d'Avignon* as

■ Figure 3. Mask with carving of Mami Wata, foreign water spirit (mid-20th century, Ivory Coast).

the work of the great artist Pablo Picasso, but in the African examples considered here, no artist's name was recorded. We know the art by the region and the community in which it was produced. The African emphasis on the role of the community in the production of art is quite different from the Western glorification of the individual artist and his or her creative act.

QUESTIONS FOR DISCUSSION

What African art form influenced Picasso, and how did his use of it lead to changes in Western art? What symbols did African artists in the same period import from the West and from other cultures? What qualities did Picasso attempt to convey by using African art forms? And what qualities did African artists recognize in appropriating Western symbols?

■ Figure 2. Staff finial of the Kongo peoples (ca. 16th–19th century).

burst the bounds of disciplines, and new fields developed to accommodate new concerns. Research in human genetics, a field that was only starting to be understood, was begun in the first decade of the twentieth century. The studies of Austrian botanist Gregor Mendel (1822–1884) in the crossbreeding of peas in the 1860s led to the Mendelian laws of inheritance.

Applied Knowledge.   Biological discoveries resulted in new state policies. Public health benefited from new methods of prevention and detection of diseases caused by germs. A professor at the University of Berlin, Rudolf Virchow (1821–1902), discovered the relationship between microbes, sewage, and disease that led to the development of modern sewer systems and pure water for urban populations. Biochemistry, bacteriology, and physiology promoted a belief in social progress through state programs. After 1900, health programs to educate the general public spread throughout Europe.

Discoveries that changed the face of the twentieth century proliferated in a variety of fields. This was a time of firsts in all directions: airplane flights and deep-sea expeditions, based on technological applications of new discoveries, pushed out boundaries of exploration above the land and below the sea. In 1909, the same year that work began in human genetics, U.S. explorer Robert E. Peary (1856–1920) reached the North Pole. In that year, too, plastic was first manufactured, under the trade name Bakelite. Irish-born British astronomer Agnes Mary Clerke (1842–1907) did pioneering work in the new field of astrophysics. Ernest Rutherford proposed a new spatial reality in his theory of the nuclear structure of the atom, which stated that the atom can be divided and consists of a nucleus with electrons revolving around it.

Establishing the Social Sciences

Innovations in the social sciences paralleled the drama of discovery in the biological and physical sciences. The "scientific" study of society purported to apply the methods of observation and experimentation to human interactions. After 1870, sociology, economics, history, psychology, anthropology, and archaeology took shape at the core of new social scientific endeavors. But just as scientific advances could be applied to destructive ends, so, too, did the social sciences promote inequities and prejudices in the Western world.

Economics.   The social scientific study of economics came to the aid of businessmen. The neoclassical economic theory of Alfred Marshall (1842–1924) and others recognized the centrality of individual choice in the marketplace while dealing with the problem of how businesses can know they have produced enough to maximize profits. Economists who were concerned with how individuals responded to prices devised a theory of marginal utility, by which producers could calculate costs and project profits on the basis of a pattern of response of consumers to price changes.

Psychology and Human Behavior.   "Scientific" psychology developed in a variety of directions. Wilhelm Wundt (1832–1920) established the first laboratory devoted to psychological research in Leipzig in 1879. From his experiments he concluded that thought is grounded in physical reality. The Russian physiologist Ivan Pavlov (1849–1936) won fame with a series of experiments demonstrating the conditioned reflex in dogs. Sigmund Freud (1859–1939) greatly influenced the direction of psychology with his theory of personality development and the creation of psychoanalysis, the science of the unconscious. Freudian probing of the unconscious was a model that was greatly at odds with the behavioral perspective of conditioned responses based on Pavlov's work.

Émile Durkheim (1858–1917), regarded as the founder of modern sociology, studied suicide as a social phenomenon. He pitted sociological theory against psychology and argued that deviance was the result not of psychic disturbances but of environmental factors and hereditary forces.

Heredity became a general explanation for behavior of all sorts. Everything from poverty, drunkenness, and crime to a declining birthrate could be attributed to biologically determined causes. For some theorists, this reasoning teetered on the edge of racism and ideas about "better blood." Science changed the way people thought and the way they lived. It improved the quality of life by defeating diseases, improving nutrition, and lengthening life span. But scientific knowledge was not without its costs. Scientific discoveries led to new forces of destruction. Scientific ideas challenged moral and religious beliefs. Science was invoked to justify racial and sexual discrimination. Traditional values and religious beliefs also did combat with the new god of science, with philosophers proclaiming that God was dead. Not least of all, science and the progress it promised came under attack by those like Friedrich Nietzsche (1844–1900), the German philosopher who questioned rational values as well as the emphasis on religion in Western thought.

The "New Woman" and the New Consciousness

As women continued to be excluded from national political participation, the right to vote was gradually being extended to all men in western Europe, regardless of property or social rank. New scientific ideas colluded with political prejudices to justify denying women equal rights. The natural sciences had a formative impact on prevailing views of gender relations and female sexuality and were used to prove women's inferiority.

Biology and Woman's Destiny.   In *The Descent of Man* (1871), Charles Darwin had concluded that the mental power of men was higher than that of women. French physiologist Paul Broca (1824–1880), a contemporary of Darwin, countered in 1873 that the skull capacity of the two sexes was very similar and that a case for inferiority could not be based on measurement. But Broca was atypical. Most scientific opinion argued in favor of female frailty and inferiority. These "scientific" arguments justified excluding women from educational opportunities and from professions such as medicine and law. There was also a generalized fear in Western societies that women who tried to exceed their "natural" abilities would damage their reproductive functions and neglect their nurturing roles.

The New Woman.   In this age of scientific justification of female inferiority, the "new woman" emerged. All over Europe the feminist movement had demanded social, economic, and political progress for women. But the "new woman" phenomenon exceeded the bounds of the feminist movement and can be described as a general cultural phenomenon. The "new woman" was characterized by intelligence, strength, and sexual desire—in every way man's equal.

The new woman's pursuit of independence included control over her own body. Margaret Sanger (1879–1966), an American, advocated birth control to help women take charge of their reproductive lives. She was arrested several times for her activities but helped to get laws passed that allowed doctors to disseminate information about birth control. Annie Besant (1847–1933) played a similar role in Great Britain. Aletta Jacobs (1849–1929), the first woman to practice medicine in Holland, opened a contraceptive clinic in 1882. By 1900, sexuality and reproduction were openly connected to discussions of women's rights.

Art and the New Age

In the last quarter of the nineteenth century, the world of art in western Europe and the United States was characterized by new discoveries, new subjects, and new modes of expression. At least a half dozen major and distinct art movements caught the imagination of artists and the general public. Beginning in the 1860s, impressionist painters led the way in rebelling against the conventions of the formal painting of the academic salons. Choosing unlikely subjects such as railway stations and haystacks in the works of Claude Monet (1840–1926), impressionists made a revolution in capturing on canvas the nature of light and atmosphere. Post-impressionists in the 1880s and 1890s built on the insights of their impressionist colleagues but went in new and less predictable directions, as exemplified in the work of Paul Cezanne (1839–1906), Vincent Van Gogh (1853–1890), and Henri Rousseau (1844–1910). Pointillism, well exemplified in the work of Georges Seurat (1859–1891), also followed the discoveries of the impressionists by using tiny dots to convey light and a spectrum of color.

All the art of this period also had certain features in common. The artists reflected the values and mores of a changing society in their work, both in their choice of subject matter and their choice of perspective. They were also influenced by breakthroughs in science and technology that allowed the understanding of how light worked through the new realism of the photographic medium and new discoveries in physics and the science of the material world. New knowledge about non-Western cultures and Europeans' widening view of the world also influenced artistic subjects and styles (see "The West and the Wider World: African Art and European Artists," pp. 490–491). The new art movements of the late nineteenth century also indicated a dramatic shift in the class base of art out of the salons of the elite and the aristocracy and into the venues of middle class life—the home, the public spheres of the café, the theater, and the railway station.

CONCLUSION

The pace of change in society and culture was accelerating in the years leading up to World War I. By 1914, many Europeans felt threatened by all these changes and new ideas. Elitist politicians devised schemes to exploit new opportunities; intellectuals talked of the possibility, even the desirability, of new manipulative dictatorships; and idealist dreams of democracy collided with the realities of mass politics. As the press fanned flames of controversy, social unrest seemed likely. Even the notion of retreat to a tranquil home and hearth was threatened by angry feminist activists. Imperialism also reached its culmination in the years 1870 to 1914 as the more powerful Western countries vied with each other for the possession of colonial territories.

QUESTIONS FOR REVIEW

1. Why did European economies run through cycles of boom and bust in the late nineteenth century, and how did European governments attempt to regulate the economy?
2. What challenges did liberal ideals and institutions confront in England, Germany, France, and Austria?
3. What social forces brought women and others into the new mass politics of the late nineteenth century?
4. What new ideas were being generated in psychology and the social sciences at the turn of the century, and what impact did that have on the way Europeans thought about gender relations?

KEY TERMS

| anarchism, *p. 488* | cartels, *p. 480* | pogroms, *p. 486* |
| anti-Semitism, *p. 486* | futurists, *p. 478* | Zionism, *p. 487* |

DISCOVERING WESTERN CIVILIZATION ONLINE

You can obtain more information about the crisis of European culture between 1871 and 1914 at the websites listed below. See also the Companion Website that accompanies this text, www.ablongman.com/kishlansky, which contains an online study guide and additional resources.

European Economy and the Politics of Mass Society

Encyclopaedia of British History: Socialism
www.spartacus.schoolnet.co.uk/socialism.htm
This is a fairly comprehensive site on the English labor movement, including texts, biographies of major figures, and other links.

Habsburg Source Texts Archive
www2.h-net.msu.edu/~habsweb/sourcetexts
Sponsored by the H-Net Discussion list HABSBURG, this site provides electronic texts relating to the creation of the Dual Monarchy.

Outsiders in Mass Politics

The Emancipation of Women: 1750–1920
www.spartacus.schoolnet.co.uk/women.htm
This site contains links to biographies of major figures, essays on the major organizations and societies, and electronic texts of the women's movement in Britain.

The Genesis Project
www.genesis.ac.uk
This mapping project on women's history research sources is provided by the Women's Library of London and the Research Support Libraries Programme.

Shaping the New Consciousness

Sigmund Freud and the Freud Archives
users.rcn.com/brill/freudarc.html
An exhaustive collection of links to archives, electronic texts, bibliographies, and other resources on Freud and the history of psychoanalysis.

Internet History of Science Sourcebook
www.fordham.edu/halsall/science/sciencesbook.html
A comprehensive collection of links to primary source materials, Websites, and bibliographies on major scientists, discoveries, and theories in the nineteenth century.

Art History Resources: 19th-Century Art & 20th-Century Art
witcombe.sbc.edu/ARTHLinks5.html
witcombe.sbc.edu/ARTH20thcentury.html
The first web page contains numerous links on the artists, styles, and schools of art in the nineteenth century, including impressionism, post-impressionism, and symbolism. The second page includes links to resources on art and artists of the twentieth century.

SUGGESTIONS FOR FURTHER READING

European Economy and the Politics of Mass Society

Edward Arnold, ed., *The Development of the Radical Right in France: From Boulanger to Le Pen* (New York: St. Martin's Press, 2000). Part I examines Boulangism, Socialism, anti-Semitism, right-wing working-class politics, and roots of right-wing radicalism.

Martin P. Johnson, *The Dreyfus Affair* (New York: St. Martin's Press, 1999). A concise and comprehensive overview of the Affair as a defining event in French history.

Kevin Repp, *Reformers, Critics, and the Paths of German Modernity, 1890–1914* (Cambridge, MA: Harvard University Press, 2000). The author looks at the reformers, intellectuals, and activists who shaped the modernist movement in Germany.

Outsiders in Mass Politics

June Purvis and Sandra Stanley Holton, eds., *Votes for Women* (New York: Routledge, 2000). The editors have brought together a collection of essays that reappraise the history of British suffragism by examining the activities of various women's groups and individuals from the nineteenth century to the interwar period.

Richard Stites, *The Women's Liberation Movement in Russia: Feminism, Nihilism, and Bolshevism, 1860–1930* (Princeton, NJ: Princeton University Press, 1978). Situates the Russian women's movement within the contexts of both nineteenth-century European feminism and twentieth-century communist ideology and traces its development from the early feminists through the rise of the Bolsheviks to power. Includes a discussion of the Russian Revolution's impact on the status of women.

Sophia A. van Wingerden, *The Women's Suffrage Movement in Britain, 1866–1928* (New York: St. Martin's Press, 1999). A chronological overview of the history of the British suffrage movement.

Shaping the New Consciousness

Geoffrey Crossick and Serge Jaumain, eds., *Cathedrals of Consumption: The European Department Store, 1850–1939* (Aldershot, England: Ashgate Publishing, 1999). A collection of articles about the creation of department stores in different European countries from the perspectives of culture, consumption, gender, and urban life.

Theodore M. Porter, *The Rise of Statistical Thinking, 1820–1900* (Princeton, NJ: Princeton University Press, 1986). This work traces the origins of modern statistical innovation of the early 1900s and shows the interdependence of the natural and social sciences.

Vanessa Schwartz, *Spectacular Realities: Early Mass Culture in Fin-de-Siécle Paris* (Berkeley: University of California Press, 1998). This work examines the formation and emergence of mass urban culture in late nineteenth-century Paris.

John Tosh, *A Man's Place: Masculinity and the Middle-Class Home in Victorian England* (New Haven, CT: Yale University Press, 1999). This work examines the roles of men in the private world of the domestic sphere and argues that Victorian masculinity was constructed not only in terms of work and male associations but also in terms of the home.

For a list of additional titles related to this chapter's topics, please see www.ablongman.com/kishlansky.

Chapter 25

EUROPE AND THE WORLD, 1870–1914

The Visual Record

THE POLITICS OF MAPMAKING

Before people knew how to write, they drew maps. Yet in 1885, only one-ninth of the land surface of the earth had been surveyed. Within the next decade, however, centuries-old ignorance diminished as cartographers, surveyors, and compilers fanned out around the globe to probe peninsulas and chart continents. By 1900, every continent, including Antarctica, had been explored and its measure taken.

This great leap forward in knowledge did not produce a standardized and uniform map of the world. State officials argued for the primacy of their own national traditions, symbols, colors, and units of measurement, and they blocked attempts at standardization. Mapmakers from Europe and the United States began to gather regularly at international conventions with the goal of devising a uniform map of the world that would satisfy everyone. Their attempts failed repeatedly.

One particular meeting in Paris in 1875 chose the meter as the standard unit of measurement for the world map. Supporters argued that the meter could provide mapmakers with a common language, easily understood and easily divisible. The British countered with yards and miles, unscientifically developed units of measurement to which they had been committed for centuries. Mapmakers who acknowledged the logic of the meter could not agree on which prototype meter should be taken as standard, though most agreed that the meter should be measured in reference to the arc of the meridian.

However, the prime meridian, the place on a map that indicates zero longitude, was itself not a fixed phenomenon. The debate over where the prime meridian should be located is a perfect example of the politics of mapmaking. Unlike the equator, which is midway between the north and south poles, zero longitude can be drawn anywhere. As a result, maps of different national origins located the prime meridian to enhance their own claims to importance. Paris, Philadelphia, and Beijing were just three of the sites for zero longitude on nineteenth-century maps.

Uniformity, the cartographers insisted, would have advantages for everyone. Not least of all, a standardized map would make standardized timekeeping easier. Standard time could be calculated according to zones of longitude. Germany had five different time zones in 1891. In France, every city had its own time taken from solar readings. The United States had over 200 time zones from one coast to the other. In industrial societies

with railroad timetables and legal contracts, time had to be controlled, and it had to be exact. Time had to be standardized. Specialists proposed that the Royal Observatory in Greenwich, England, was the best place to locate the prime meridian in order to calculate a standard time system. The French balked, insisting on Paris as the only candidate for the designation. In the end, there was compromise. The metric system prevailed as the standard for measurement, and the prime meridian passed through the Royal Greenwich Observatory, where standard time was calculated for most of the globe. All of this was possible for the first time only at the end of the nineteenth century, and the key to standardization was determined by geopolitical dominance. Great Britain, the most powerful imperial power, became the starting point for measuring time and space.

The accompanying map provides a dramatic example of the conquest of territories by the British Empire in 1886. The inset map in the upper right shows the extent of British territories a century earlier, and so the map demonstrates the growth of the empire. The figures at the borders of the map include both the colonizers (British prospectors, explorers, military men) and the colonized (native men and women of various conquered territories), all looking toward the figure of Brittania sitting atop the "world."

Looking Ahead

This chapter begins by considering the territorial arrangements and conflicts within Europe between 1870 and 1914 that created a new kind of foreign policy based on mutual interests and national vulnerabilities. The chapter then turns to European rivalries in the global arena and the territorial and market expansion into Africa and Asia that characterized the new imperialism. Finally, the chapter considers how imperial encounters changed both the colonized and the colonizer and produced interdependent markets and a new world economy. ➤

THE EUROPEAN BALANCE OF POWER, 1870–1914

Geopolitics, or the politics of geography, is based on the recognition that certain areas of the world are valuable for political reasons. The term, first used at the end of the nineteenth century, described a process well under way in international relations. Between 1870 and 1914, European states were locked in a competition within Europe for dominance and control. Geopolitics combined with rising nationalist movements in southern Europe and the Ottoman Empire to create a mood of increasing confrontation among Europe's great powers. The European balance of power that Bismarck had so carefully crafted began to disintegrate with his departure from office in 1890. By 1914, a Europe divided into two camps was no longer the sure guarantee of peace that it had been a generation earlier.

Upsetting the European Balance of Power

The map of Europe had been redrawn in the two decades after 1850. By 1871, Europe consisted of the Big Five—Britain, France, Germany, Austria-Hungary, and Russia—and a handful of lesser states. The declaration of the German Empire in 1871 and the emergence of Italy with Rome as its capital in 1870 unified numerous disparate states. Although not always corresponding to linguistic and cultural differences among Europe's peoples, national boundaries appeared to be fixed, with no country aspiring to territorial expansion at the expense of its neighbors. But the creation of the two new national units of Germany and Italy had legitimized nationalist aspirations and the militarism necessary to enforce them.

The Three Emperors' League.   Under the chancellorship of Otto von Bismarck, Germany led the way in forging a new alliance system based on the realistic assessment of power politics within Europe. In 1873, Bismarck joined together the three most conservative powers of the Big Five—Germany, Austria-Hungary, and Russia—into the Three Emperors' League. Consultation about mutual interests and friendly neutrality were the cornerstones of this alliance. Identifying one's enemies and choosing one's friends in this new configuration of power came in large part to depend on geographic weaknesses. The Three Emperors' League was one example of the geographic imperatives driving diplomacy. Bismarck was determined to banish the specter of a two-front war by isolating France on the Continent.

Each of the Great Powers had a vulnerability, a geographic Achilles' heel. Germany's vulnerability lay in its North Sea ports. German shipping along its only coast could easily be bottlenecked by a powerful naval force. Such an event, the Germans knew, could destroy their rapidly growing international trade. What was worse, powerful land forces could encircle Germany. As Britain's century-old factories slowly became obsolete under peeling coats of paint, Germany enjoyed

the advantages of a latecomer to industrialization, forced to start from scratch by investing in the most advanced machinery and technology. The German Reich was willing to support industrial expansion, scientific and technological training, and social programs for its workers. Yet as Germany surged forward to seize its share of world markets, it was acutely aware that it was hemmed in on the Continent. Germany could not extend its frontiers the way Russia had to the east. German gains in the Franco-Prussian war in Alsace and Lorraine could not be repeated without risking greater enmity. German leaders saw the threat of encirclement as a second geographic weakness. Bismarck's awareness of these geographic facts of life prompted his engineering of the Three Emperors' League in 1873, two years after the founding of the German Empire.

Austria-Hungary was Europe's second largest landed nation and the third largest in population. The same factors that had made it a great European power—its size and its diversity—now threatened to destroy it. The ramshackle empire of Europe was weakened by the centrifugal forces of linguistic and cultural diversity, by nationalities clamoring for independence and self-rule, and by an unresponsive political system. Austria-Hungary remained backward agriculturally and unable to respond to the industrial challenge of western Europe. It seemed most likely to collapse from social and political pressures.

Russia's vulnerability was reflected in its preoccupation with maintaining free access to the Mediterranean Sea. Russia, clearly Europe's greatest landed power, was vulnerable because it could be landlocked by frozen or blockaded ports. The ice that crippled its naval and commercial vessels in the Baltic Sea drove Russia east through Asia to secure another ice-blocked port on the Sea of Japan at Vladivostok in 1860 and to seek ice-free Chinese ports. Russia was equally obsessed with protecting its warm-water ports on the Black Sea. Whoever controlled the strait of the Bosporus controlled Russia's grain export trade, on which its economic prosperity depended.

The Ottoman Empire.   Another great decaying conglomeration was the Ottoman Empire, bridging Europe and Asia. Politically feeble and on the verge of bankruptcy, the Ottoman Empire with Turkey at its core comprised a vast array of ethnically, linguistically, and culturally diverse peoples. In the hundred years before 1914, increasing social unrest and nationalist bids for independence had plagued the Ottoman Empire. As was the case with the Habsburgs in Austria-Hungary, the Ottomans maintained power with increasing difficulty over these myriad ethnic groups struggling to be free. The Ottoman Empire, called "the sick man of Europe" by contemporaries, found two kinds of relations sitting at its bedside: those who would do anything to ensure its survival, no matter how weak, and those who hoped to hasten its demise. Fortunately for the Ottoman Empire, rivalry among its enemies helped to preserve it.

The Ottomans had already seen parts of their holdings lopped off in the nineteenth century. Britain had acquired

■ A *Punch* cartoon shows European leaders trying to keep the lid on the simmering kettle of Balkan crises.

Cyprus, Egypt, Aden, and Sudan from the Ottomans. Germany insinuated itself into Turkish internal affairs and financed the Baghdad Railway in an attempt to link the Mediterranean to the Persian Gulf. Russia acquired territories on the banks of the Caspian Sea and had plans to take Constantinople. But it was the volatile Balkan Peninsula that threatened to upset the European power balance. The Balkans appeared to be ripe for dismemberment. Internally, the Slavs sought independence from their Habsburg and Turkish oppressors. External pressures were equally great, with each of the major powers following its own political agenda.

The Instability of the Alliance System

The system of alliances formed between and among European states was guided by two realities of geopolitics: the tension between France and Germany and Russia's fear of becoming landlocked.

Franco-German Tensions. A major destabilizing factor in the European balance of power was the tension between

France and Germany. France had lost its dominance on the Continent in 1870–1871, when it was easily defeated by Prussia at the head of a nascent German Empire. With its back to the Atlantic, France faced the smaller states of Belgium, Luxembourg, Switzerland, and Italy and the industrially and militarily powerful Germany. France had suffered the humiliation of losing territory to Germany—Alsace and Lorraine in 1871—and was well aware of its continued vulnerability. Geopolitically, France felt trapped and isolated and in need of powerful friends as a counterweight to German power.

Russian Aspirations and the Congress of Berlin. Ostensibly, Russia had the most to gain from the extension of its frontiers and the creation of pro-Russian satellites. It saw that by championing pan-Slavic nationalist groups in southeastern Europe, it could greatly strengthen its own position at the expense of the two great declining empires, Ottoman Turkey and Austria-Hungary. Russia hoped to draw the Slavs into its orbit by fostering the creation of independent states in the Balkans. A Serbian revolt began in two Ottoman provinces, Bosnia and Herzegovina, in 1874. International opinion pressured Turkey to initiate reforms. Serbia declared war on Turkey on 30 June 1876; Montenegro did the same the next day. Britain, supporting the Ottoman Empire because of its trading interests in the Mediterranean, found itself in a delicate position of perhaps condemning an ally when it received news of Turkish atrocities against Christians in Bulgaria. Prime Minister Disraeli insisted that Britain was bound to defend Constantinople because of British interests in the Suez Canal and India. While Britain stood on the sidelines, Russia, with Romania as an ally, declared war against the Ottoman Empire. The war was quickly over; Russia captured all of Armenia and forced the Ottoman sultan, Abdul Hamid II (1842–1918), to sue for peace on 31 January 1878.

Although Great Britain was not largely landlocked as were Germany and Russia, the British had some reason to fear a possible naval blockade. And although the question of Irish home rule was a nationalities problem for Britain, it paled in comparison with Austria-Hungary's internal challenge. As an island kingdom, however, Great Britain relied on imports for its survival. The first of the European nations to become an urban and industrial power, Britain was forced to do so at the expense of its agricultural sector. It could not feed its own people without importing foodstuffs. Britain's geographic vulnerability was its dependence on access to its empire and the maintenance of open sea lanes. Britain saw its greatest menace as coming from the rise of other sea powers—notably Germany.

Bismarck, a seemingly disinterested party acting as an "honest broker," hosted the peace conference that met at Berlin. The British succeeded in blocking Russia's intentions for a Bulgarian satellite and keeping the Russians from taking Constantinople. Russia abandoned its support of Serbian nationalism, and Austria-Hungary occupied Bosnia and Herzegovina. The peace that was concluded at the 1878

Congress of Berlin disregarded Serbian claims, thereby ensuring continuing conflict over the nationalities question.

The Berlin Congress also marked the emergence of a new estrangement among the Great Powers. Russia felt betrayed by Bismarck and abandoned in its alliance with Germany. Bismarck in turn cemented a Dual Alliance between Austria-Hungary and Germany in 1879 that survived until the collapse of the two imperial regimes in 1918. The Three Emperors' League was renewed in 1881 with stipulations regarding the division of the spoils in case of a war against Turkey.

In 1882, Italy was asked to join the Dual Alliance with Germany and Austria-Hungary, thus converting it into the **Triple Alliance,** which prevailed until the beginning of World War I in 1914. Germany, under Bismarck's tutelage, signed treaties with Italy, Russia, and Austria-Hungary and established friendly terms with Great Britain. However, a new Balkan crisis in 1885 shattered the illusion of stable relations.

Hostilities erupted between Bulgaria and Serbia. Russia threatened to occupy Bulgaria, but Austria stepped in to prevent Russian domination of the Balkans, thus threatening the alliance of the Three Emperors' League. Russia was further angered by German unwillingness to support its interests against Austrian actions in the Balkans. Germany maintained relations with Russia in a new Reinsurance Treaty drawn up in 1887, which stipulated that each power would maintain neutrality should the other find itself at war. Bismarck now walked a fine line, balancing alliances and selectively disclosing the terms of secret treaties to nonsignatory countries with the goal of preserving the peace. His successor described Bismarck as the only man who could keep five glass balls in the air at the same time.

Bismarck was dismissed from the chancellorship in 1890 by the Kaiser Wilhelm II, a long-time enemy of Bismarck who came to the throne in 1888. Germany now found itself unable to juggle all the glass balls. Under Wilhelm II, Germany allowed the arrangement with Russia to lapse. Russia, in turn, allied itself with France in 1894. Also allied with Great Britain, France had broken out of the isolation that Bismarck had intended for it two decades earlier. The **Triple Entente** came into existence following the Anglo-Russian understanding of 1907. Now it was the Triple Entente of Great Britain, France, and Russia against the Triple Alliance of Germany, Austria-Hungary, and Italy.

There was still every confidence that these two camps could balance each other and preserve the peace. But from 1908 to 1909 the unresolved Balkan problem threatened to topple Europe's precarious peace. Against Russia's objections, Austria-Hungary annexed Bosnia and Herzegovina, the provinces it had occupied since 1878. Russia supported Serbia's discontent over Austrian acquisition of these predominantly Slavic territories that Serbia believed should be united with its own lands. Unwilling to risk a European war at this point, Russia was ultimately forced to back down under German pressure. Germany had to contend with its great

CHRONOLOGY	
EUROPEAN CRISES AND THE BALANCE OF POWER	
1871	German Empire created
1873	Three Emperors' League: Germany, Austria-Hungary, and Russia
1874	First Balkan crisis: Serbian revolt in Bosnia and Herzegovina
1875	Russo-Turkish War
1876	Serbia declares war on Turkey; Montenegro declares war on Turkey
1878	Congress of Berlin
1879	Dual Alliance: Germany and Austria-Hungary
1881	Three Emperors' League renewed
1882	Triple Alliance: Germany, Austria-Hungary, and Italy
1885	Second Balkan crisis: Bulgaria versus Serbia
1887	Reinsurance Treaty between Germany and Russia
1894	Russia concludes alliance with France
1907	Triple Entente: Great Britain, France, and Russia
1908	Austria-Hungary annexes Bosnia and Herzegovina
1912	Third Balkan crisis: Italy versus Turkey
1913	War erupts between Serbia and Bulgaria

geopolitical fear: hostile neighbors, France and Russia, on its western and eastern frontiers.

A third Balkan crisis erupted in 1912 when Italy and Turkey fought over the possession of Tripoli in North Africa. The Balkan states took advantage of this opportunity to increase their holdings at Turkey's expense. This action quickly involved Great Power interests once again. A second war broke out in 1913 over Serbian interests in Bulgaria. Russia backed Serbia against Austro-Hungarian support of Bulgaria. The Russians and Austrians prepared for war, while the British and Germans urged peaceful resolution. Although hostilities ceased, Serbian resentment toward Austria-Hungary over its frustrated nationalism was greater than ever. Britain, in its backing of Russia, and Germany, in its support of Austria-Hungary, were enmeshed in alliances that could involve them in a military confrontation.

THE NEW IMPERIALISM

The concept of empire was certainly not invented by Europeans in the last third of the nineteenth century. Before 1870, European states had controlled empires. The influence of Great Britain stretched beyond the limits of its formal holdings in India and South Africa. Russia held Siberia and central Asia, and France ruled Algeria and Indochina. Older empires, such as Spain, had survived from the sixteenth century, but as hollow shells. What, then, was new about the "new imperialism" practiced by England, France, and Germany after 1870?

In part, the **new imperialism** was the acquisition of territories on an intense and unprecedented scale. Industrialization created the tools of transportation, communication, and domination that permitted the rapid pace of global empire building. Above all, the new imperialism meant domination by the industrial powers over the nonindustrial world. The United States also participated in the new imperialism, less by territorial acquisition than by developing an "invisible" empire of trade and influence in the Pacific. The forms of imperialism may have varied from nation to nation, but the basically unequal relationship between an industrial power and an undeveloped territory did not.

Only nation-states commanded the technology and resources that were necessary for the new scale of imperialist expansion. Rivalry among a few European nation-states—notably, Great Britain, France, and Germany—was a common denominator that set the standards by which these nations and other European states gained control of the globe by 1900. Why did the Europeans create vast empires? Were empires built for economic gain, military protection, or national glory? Questions about motives may obscure common features of the new imperialism. Industrial powers sought to take over nonindustrial regions, not in isolated areas but all over the globe. In the attempt, they necessarily competed with one another, successfully adapting the resources of industrialism to the needs of conquest.

The Technology of Empire

For Europeans at the end of the nineteenth century, the world had definitely become a smaller place. Technology based on steam, iron, and electricity—the great forces of western industrialization—were responsible for shrinking the globe. Technology not only allowed Europeans to accomplish tasks and to mass-produce goods efficiently, but it also altered the previous conception of time and space.

Steam, which powered factories, proved equally efficient as an energy source in transportation. Great iron steamships fu-

eled by coal replaced the smaller, slower, wind-powered, wooden sailing vessels that had plied the sea for centuries. Steamships could carry large cargoes of people and goods and could meet schedules as precisely as railroads could. Just as the imperial Romans had used their network of roads to link far-flung territories to the capital, Europeans used sea-lanes to join their colonies to the home country.

Until 1850, Europeans ventured no farther on the African continent than its coastal areas. Now the installation of coal-burning boilers on smaller boats permitted navigation of previously uncharted rivers. Steam power made exploration and migration possible and greatly contributed to knowledge of terrain, natural wealth, and resources. Smaller, steam-powered vessels also increased European inland trade with China, Burma, and India.

Engineering Empire. While technology improved European mobility on water, it also literally moved the land. To accommodate the new iron- and then steel-hulled ships, harbors were deepened and canals were constructed. One of the greatest engineering feats of the century was the construction of a hundred-mile-long canal across the Isthmus of Suez in Egypt. Completed in 1869, the Suez Canal joined the Mediterranean and Red Seas and created a new, safer trade route to the East. No longer did trading vessels have to make the long voyage around Africa's Cape of Good Hope. The French built the Suez Canal under the supervision of Ferdinand de Lesseps (1805–1894), a diplomat with no technical or financial background who was able to promote construction because of concessions he received from Said Pasha of Egypt. The canal could accommodate ships of all sizes. Great Britain purchased a controlling interest in the Suez Canal in 1875 to benefit its trade with India.

De Lesseps later presided over the initial construction of the Panama Canal in the Western Hemisphere. The combination of French mismanagement, bankruptcy, and the high incidence of disease among work crews enabled the United States to acquire rights to the Panama project and complete it by 1914. Fifty-one miles long, the Panama Canal connected the Atlantic and Pacific Oceans across the Isthmus of Panama by a waterway containing a series of locks. Now the passage from the Atlantic to the Pacific took less than eight hours—significantly less time than the various overland routes or the voyage around the tip of South America. Both the Suez and Panama Canals saved travel time, which meant higher profits.

Technology also increased the speed of communication. In 1830, it took about two years for a person who sent a letter from Great Britain to India to receive a reply. In 1850, steam-powered mail boats shortened the time required for the same round-trip correspondence to about two or three months. But the real revolution in communication came through electricity. Thousands of miles of copper telegraph wire laced countries together; insulated underwater cables linked continents to each other. By the late nineteenth century, a vast telegraph network connected Europe to every major area of the world. In 1870, a telegram from London to Bombay arrived in a matter of hours, instead of months, and a response could be received back in London on the same day. Faster communications extended power and control throughout empires. Now Europeans could communicate immediately with their distant colonies, dispatching troops, orders, and supplies. This communication network eliminated the problem of overextension that had plagued Roman imperial organization in the third century. For the first time, continents that Europeans had discovered five centuries earlier were brought into daily contact with the West.

Medical Advances.

Technological advances in other areas helped to foster European imperialism in the nineteenth century. Advances in medicine allowed European men and women to penetrate disease-laden swamps and jungles. After 1850, European explorers, traders, missionaries, and adventurers carried quinine pills. The bitter-tasting derivative of cinchona-tree bark, **quinine** was discovered to be an effective treatment for malaria. This treatment got its first important test during the French invasion of Algeria in 1830, and it allowed the French to stay healthy enough to conquer that North African country between 1830 and 1847. David Livingstone (1813–1873) and Henry M. Stanley (1841–1904) were just two of the many explorers who crossed vast terrains and explored the waterways of Africa after malaria, the number one killer of Europeans, had been controlled.

Europeans carried the technologies of destruction as well as survival with them into less-developed areas of the world. New types of firearms that were produced in the second half of the nineteenth century included breech-loading rifles, repeating rifles, and machine guns. The new weapons gave the advantages of both accurate aim and rapid fire. The spears of African warriors and the primitive weaponry of Chinese rebels were no match for sophisticated European arms, which permitted their bearers to lie down while firing and to remain undetected at distances of up to half a mile.

The new technology did not cause the new imperialism. The Western powers used technological advances as a tool for establishing their control of the world. Viewed as a tool, however, the new technology does explain how vast areas of land and millions of people were conquered so rapidly.

Motives for Empire

If technology was not the cause but only a tool, what explains the new imperialism of the late nineteenth century? There are no easy or simple explanations. Individuals made their fortunes overseas, and heavy industries such as the Krupp firm in Germany prospered with the expansion of state-protected colonies. Yet many colonies were economically worthless. Tunisia and Morocco, acquired for their strategic and political

importance, constituted an economic loss for the French, who poured more funds into their administration than they were able to extract. Each imperial power held one or more colonies whose costs outweighed the return. Yet this does not mean that some Europeans were simply irrational in their pursuit of empire and glory.

Economics.

The test for economic motivation cannot simply be reduced to a balance sheet of debits and credits; in the end, an account of state revenues and state expenditures provides only a static picture of the business of empire. Even losses cannot be counted as proof against the profit motive in expansion. In modern capitalism, profits, especially great profits, are often predicated on risks. Portugal and Italy took great risks and failed as players in the game in which the great industrial powers called the shots. Prestige through the acquisition of empire was one way of keeping alive in the game. Imperialism was influenced by business interests, market considerations, and the pursuit of individual and national fortunes. Not by accident did the great industrial powers control the scramble and dictate the terms of expansion. Nor was it merely fortuitous that Great Britain, the nation that provided the model for European expansion, dedicated itself to the establishment of a profitable worldwide network of trade and investment. Above all, the search for investment opportunities, whether railroads in China or diamond mines in South Africa, lured Europeans into a world system that challenged capitalist ingenuity and imagination. Acquiring territory was only one means of protecting investments. But other benefits were associated with the acquisition of territory that cannot be reduced to economic terms, and those too must be considered.

Geopolitics.

Statesmen influenced by geopolitical concerns recognized the strategic value of certain lands. France, for example, occupied thousands of square miles of the Sahara to protect its interests in Algeria.

Other territory was important because of its proximity to sea routes. Egypt had significance for Great Britain not because of its inherent economic potential but because it allowed the British to protect access to lucrative markets in India through the Suez Canal. Beginning in 1875, the British purchased shares in the canal. By 1879, Egypt was under the informal dual rule of France and Great Britain. The British used the deterioration of internal Egyptian politics to justify their occupation of the country in 1882. Protected access to India also accounted for Great Britain's maintenance of Mediterranean outposts, its acquisition of territory on the east coast of Africa, and its occupation of territory in southern Asia.

A third geopolitical motive for annexation was the necessity of having fueling bases throughout the world for coal-powered ships. Islands in the South Pacific and the Indian Ocean were acquired primarily to serve as coaling stations for the great steamers carrying manufactured goods to colonial ports and returning with foodstuffs and raw materials. Ports along the southern rim of Asia served the same purpose. The need to protect colonies, fueling ports, and sea-lanes led to the creation of naval bases like those on the Red Sea at Djibouti by the French, in southeast Asia at Singapore by the British, and in the Hawaiian Islands at Honolulu by the Americans.

In turn, the acquisition of territories justified the increase in naval budgets and the size of fleets. Britain still had the world's largest navy, but by the beginning of the twentieth century, the United States and Germany had entered the competition for dominance of sea-lanes. Japan expanded its navy as a vehicle for its own claims to empire in the Pacific.

The politics of geography was land- as well as sea-based. As navies grew to protect sea-lanes, armies expanded to police new lands. Between 1890 and 1914, military expenditures of Western governments grew phenomenally; war machines doubled in size. Governments became consumers of heavy industry; their predictable participation in markets for armaments and military supplies helped to control fluctuations in the business cycle and to reduce unemployment at home. A side effect of the growing importance of geopolitics was the increased influence of military and naval leaders in foreign and domestic policy making.

Nationalism.   Many European statesmen in the last quarter of the nineteenth century gave stirring speeches about the importance of empire as a means of enhancing national prestige. In his Crystal Palace speech of 1872, Benjamin Disraeli, British prime minister in 1868 and from 1874–1880, put the challenge boldly to the British:

> I appeal to the sublime instinct of an ancient people. . . . The issue is not a mean one. It is whether you will be content to be a comfortable England, modelled and moulded upon Continental principles and meeting in due course an inevitable fate, or whether you will be a great country, an imperial country, a country where your sons, when they rise, rise to paramount positions and obtain not merely the esteem of their countrymen but command the respect of the world.

■ Great Britain originally opposed construction of the Suez Canal but soon recognized its crucial role in the route to India. In this cartoon, *The Lion's Share*, British Prime Minister Disraeli purchases a controlling interest in the Suez Canal Company from the khedive of Egypt. The British lion in the foreground guards the key to India, the symbol of the canal.

THE LION'S SHARE.

"GARE À QUI LA TOUCHE!"

National prestige was not an absolute value but one that was weighed relatively. Possessing an empire may have meant "keeping up with the Joneses," as it did for smaller countries such as Italy. Imperial status was important to a country like Portugal, which was willing to go bankrupt to maintain its territories. But prestige without economic power was the form of imperialism without its substance. Nation-states could, through the acquisition of overseas territories, gain bargaining chips to be played at the international conference table. In this way, smaller nations hoped to be taken seriously in the system of alliances that preserved the balance of power in Europe.

Western newspapers deliberately fostered the desire for the advancement of national interests. Newspapers competed for readers, and their circulations often depended on the passions they aroused. Filled with tales calculated to titillate and enter-tain, and with advertisements promising miracle cures, newspapers wrested foreign policy from the realm of the specialist and transformed politics into another form of entertainment. The drama and vocabulary of sporting events, whose mass appeal as a leisure activity also dates from this era, were now applied to imperialist politics. Whether it was a rugby match or a territorial conquest, readers backed the "home" team, disdained the opposition, and competed for the thrill of victory. This marked quite a change for urban dwellers whose grandparents worked the land and did not look beyond the horizon of their home villages. Newspapers forged a national consciousness whereby individuals identified with collective causes that they did not fully comprehend. Some observed what was happening with a critical eye, identifying a deep-seated need in modern men and women for excitement in their lives.

Joseph Chamberlain's Speech to the Birmingham Relief Association

Joseph Chamberlain (1836–1914) was an English businessman and statesman and, from 1873 to 1876, the mayor of one of Great Britain's leading industrial cities, Birmingham. He was a national advocate for an expansionist colonial policy as the means of keeping his country strong. On 22 January 1894, with no regard for African people, he spoke before a community group to convince them that British imperialism helped the working class.

Focus Questions

What are the motives evoked by Chamberlain to justify colonial expansion? How does he appeal to the patriotism of the English working classes?

Believe me, if in any one of the places [in Africa] to which I have referred any change took place which deprived us of that control and influence of which I have been speaking, the first to suffer would be the working-men of this country. Then, indeed, we should see a distress which would not be temporary, but which would be chronic, and we should find that England was entirely unable to support the enormous population which is now maintained by the aid of her foreign trade. If the working-men of this country understand, as I believe they do—I am one of those who have had good reason through my life to rely upon their intelligence and shrewdness—if they understand their own interests, they will never lend any countenance to the doctrines of those politicians who never lose an opportunity of pouring contempt and abuse upon the brave Englishmen, who, even at this moment, in all parts of the world are carving out new dominions for Britain, and are opening up fresh markets for British commerce, and laying out fresh fields for British labour. [Applause.] If the Little Englanders[i] had their way, not only would they refrain from taking the legitimate opportunities which offer for extending the empire and for securing for us new markets, but I doubt whether they would even take the pains which are necessary to preserve the great heritage which has come down to us from our ancestors. [Applause.]

When you are told that the British pioneers of civilisation in Africa are filibusters[ii], and when you are asked to call them back, and to leave this great continent to the barbarism and superstition in which it has been steeped for centuries, or to hand over to foreign countries the duty which you are unwilling to undertake, I ask you to consider what would have happened if 100 or 150 years ago your ancestors had taken similar views of their responsibility? Where would be the empire on which now your livelihood depends? We should have been the United Kingdom of Great Britain and Ireland; but those vast dependencies, those hundreds of millions with whom we keep up a mutually beneficial relationship and commerce would have been the subjects of other nations, who would not have been slow to profit by our neglect of our opportunities and obligations. [Applause.]

From Joseph Chamberlain, M.P., *Foreign and Colonial Speeches* (1897).
[i] Britain's anti-imperialists.
[ii] Persons engaged in private military actions against a foreign government.

Information conveyed in newspapers shaped opinion, and opinion, in turn, could influence policy. Leaders had to reckon with this new creation of "public opinion." In a typical instance, French newspaper editors promoted feverish public outcry for conquest of the Congo by pointing out the need to revenge British advances in Egypt. "Colonial fever" was so high in France in the summer of 1882 that French policy makers were pressured to pursue claims in the Congo basin without adequate assessment or reflection. As a result, the French government evicted Belgians and Portuguese from the northern Congo territory and enforced questionable treaty claims rather than risk public censure for appearing weak and irresolute.

Public opinion was certainly influential, but it could be manipulated. In Germany, the government often promoted colonial hysteria through the press to advance its own political ends. Chancellor Otto von Bismarck used his power over the press to support imperialism and to influence electoral outcomes in 1884. His successors were deft at promoting the "bread and circuses" atmosphere that surrounded colonial expansion to direct attention away from social problems at home and to maintain domestic stability.

The printed word was also manipulated in Britain during the Boer War (1899–1902), critics asserted, by business interests to keep public enthusiasm for the war effort high. J. A. Hobson (1858–1940), himself a journalist and theorist of imperialism, denounced the "abuse of the press" in his hard-hitting *Psychology of Jingoism* (1901), which appeared while the war was still being waged. Hobson recognized **jingoism** as the appropriate term for the "inverted patriotism whereby the love of one's own nation is transformed into hatred of another nation, and [into] the fierce craving to destroy the individual members of that other nation."

Jingoism was not a new phenomenon in 1900, nor was it confined to Britain. Throughout Europe, a mass public appeared increasingly willing to support conflict to defend national honor. Xenophobia, hatred of foreigners, melded with nationalism, both nurtured by the mass press, to put new pressures on the determination of foreign policy. Government elites, who formerly operated behind closed doors far removed from public scrutiny, were now accountable in new ways to faceless masses. Even in autocratic states such as Austria-Hungary, the opinion of the masses was a powerful political force that could destroy individual careers and dissolve governments.

Every nation in Europe had its jingoes, those who were willing to risk war for national glory. Significantly, the term "jingo" was coined in 1878 during a British showdown with the Russians over Turkey. The sentiment was so strong that "the Russians shall not have Constantinople" that the acceptability of war was set to music:

> *We don't want to fight,*
> *But, by jingo, if we do,*
> *We've got the men,*
> *We've got the ships,*
> *We've got the money too.*

This was the most popular music-hall song in Britain that year, and long after the crisis had faded, the tune and its lyrics lingered.

To varying degrees, all of these factors—economics, geopolitics, and nationalism—motivated the actions of the three great imperialist powers—Britain, France, and Germany—and their less-powerful European neighbors. The same reasons account for the global aspirations of non-European nations such as the United States and Japan. None of these powers acted independently; each was aware of what the others were doing and tailored its actions accordingly. Imperialism followed a variety of patterns but always with a built-in component of emulation and acceleration. It was both a cause and a proof of a world system of states in which the actions of one nation affected the others.

The nineteenth-century liberal belief in progress encouraged Europeans to impose their beliefs and institutions on captive millions. After all, industrial society had given Europe the technology, the wealth, and the power to tame nature and dominate the world. Imperialists moralized that they had not only the right but also the duty to develop the nonindustrialized world for their own purposes.

THE SEARCH FOR TERRITORY AND MARKETS

Most western Europeans who read about the distant regions that their armies and political leaders were bringing under control regarded these new territories as little more than entries on a great tally sheet or as distinctively colored areas on a map. The daily press recorded the numbers of square miles acquired and the names of the peoples in the occupied territories, and that was that. Few Europeans looked on imperialism as a relationship of power between two parties and, like all relationships, one influenced by both partners. Fewer still understood or appreciated the distinctive qualities of the conquered peoples.

The areas that European imperialism affected varied widely in their political organization. Large states existed in some parts of Africa; elsewhere, states were small or even nonexistent. Whatever the situation, however, Europeans, filled with the racist prejudices of the period, considered African governmental institutions too ineffectual to produce the economic change and growth of trade they then wanted. Military takeover and direct rule by European officials seemed the only feasible way to establish empire in Africa and extract the goods and labor these officials sought. In Asia, by contrast, societies such as India and China were territorially large and had efficient institutions of government dominated by established political hierarchies. Although they were more difficult to conquer, their leaders were more likely to cooperate with the imperial powers because their own interests were often similar to those of the Westerners. For these reasons, European empire builders pursued a variety of models: formal military empires (as in Africa), informal empires (as in China), or formal but indirect rule over hierarchical societies (as in India). The United States provided yet another model, one that relied on hegemonic influence as well as outright control.

The Scramble for Africa: Diplomacy and Conflict

In the mid-1860s, a committee of the British Parliament recommended that Britain withdraw from the scattering of small colonies it possessed in West Africa, arguing that they were costly anachronisms in an era of free trade. Just 30 years later, in 1898, the president of France, in commenting on French policies of the previous 20 years, remarked that "We have behaved like madmen in Africa, having been led astray by irre-

■ A contemporary cartoon characterized King Leopold of the Belgians as a monstrous snake crushing the life out of the black population of the Congo Free State. The territory was under the personal rule of the Belgian king from 1885 to 1908.

IN THE RUBBER COILS.

sponsible people called the 'colonialists.'" The "mad" event that had altered the political landscape of Africa was the so-called **scramble for Africa,** a partitioning of Africa that is usually considered as extending from around 1875 to around 1912. By its end, Europeans controlled virtually all Africa.

One cannot detect one single reason for the scramble as it actually took place on the ground. Africa is a large and complex continent, and the reasons for which Europeans pursued specific pieces of African territory were similarly complex. The explanations for the acquisition of a given colony, therefore, depend largely on the historical context of that particular case. In certain areas, such as the West African Sudanic and Sahara desert zones, ambitious French military men sought to advance their careers by carving out grand colonies. The existence of valuable minerals motivated the scramble for the area now called Zimbabwe, the Zambian/Zairian copper belt, and other areas. Along the West African coast, chronic disputes between traders working in an economy soured by a deterioration in the terms of trade seemed to require European annexation. Some colonies, such as present-day Uganda and Malawi, were created to please missionaries already working there. Britain took Egypt, and France occupied Djibouti for strategic reasons. As often as not, as in Mozambique, Tanzania, Namibia, and Botswana, some Europeans seized areas to keep other Europeans from doing the same thing. Only Ethiopia escaped the European grasp.

The Drive for Markets and Profits.   An important factor influencing imperialist expansion was the economic downturn in Europe that lasted from 1873 until 1896. This downturn, coupled with Germany's fast rise to economic power during the 1870s and 1880s, was deeply unsettling to many Europeans. Protectionist policies springing from new economic anxieties eroded earlier faith in free trade, and many Europeans became keen to acquire African territory just in case it should turn out to be useful in the long run. Even Britain, long the major champion of free trade, became ever more protectionist and imperialistic as the century neared its end.

Historians generally agree that the person who provided the catalyst for the scramble was Leopold II, king of the Belgians (1865–1909). His motive was greed. Early in 1876, Leopold read a report about the Congo River basin that claimed that it was "mostly a magnificent and healthy country of unspeakable richness" that could in "from 30 to 36 months begin to repay any enterprising capitalist." Leopold, an ambitious and frustrated king ruling over a small country, went to work at once to acquire this area, one-third the size of the United States, for himself. Cloaking himself in the mantle of philanthropy and asserting that all he desired was to stamp out the remnants of the East African slave trade, he organized the International African Association in late 1876.

His association soon established stations on the region's rivers and robbed the people of much valuable ivory. Meanwhile, Leopold himself skillfully lobbied for formal recognition of his association's right to rule the Congo basin. France and Portugal, also covetous of the area, objected, and after much diplomatic wrangling, an international conference was finally held in Berlin in late 1884 to decide the question. The Berlin Conference was important not only because it yielded the Congo basin to Leopold as the Congo Free State, but also because it laid down the ground rules for the recognition of other colonial claims in Africa. No longer would merely planting a flag in an area be considered adequate to establish sovereignty; instead, the creation of a real presence calculated to produce "economic development" would be needed. If by panicking the European states, Leopold's actions began the scramble, the Berlin Conference organized and structured it. However, it is clear in retrospect that the scramble would have occurred even without Leopold II's greedy intervention.

European Agreements and African Massacres.

In dividing Africa, the European states were remarkably cooperative. Although Britain did threaten Portugal with war in 1890 in a dispute about the area around Lake Malawi, and although it appeared for a while that Britain and France were headed toward armed conflict in 1898 over control of the headwaters of the Nile, peaceful diplomatic settlements were always worked out. Deals that traded one piece of territory for another were common, and peace was maintained. Diplomats did not consider Africa worth a European war.

Yet despite the importance of diplomatic compromise among European states during the scramble, every instance of European expansion in Africa, no matter what its specific motive, was characterized by a readiness to shoot Africans. With Hiram Maxim's invention in 1884 of a machine gun that could fire eleven bullets per second, and with the banning by the Brussels Convention of 1890 of the sale of modern weapons to Africans, the military advantage passed overwhelmingly to the imperialists. As the British poet Hilaire Belloc (1870–1953) tellingly observed,

> *Whatever happens, we have got*
> *The Maxim Gun, and they have not.*

The conquest of "them" became more like hunting than warfare. In 1893, for example, in Zimbabwe, 50 Europeans, using only six machine guns, killed 3,000 Ndebele people in less than two hours. In 1897, in northern Nigeria, a force of 32 Europeans and 500 African mercenaries defeated the 31,000-man army of the emir of Sokoto. Winston Churchill, reporting on the battle of Omdurman in the Sudan in 1898, summed up well the nature of such warfare:

> The [British] infantry fired steadily and stolidly, without hurry or excitement, for the enemy were far away and the officers careful. Besides the soldiers were interested in the work and took great pains. . . . And all the time out on the plain on the other side bullets were shearing through flesh, smashing and splintering bone; blood spouted from terrible wounds; valiant men were

struggling on through a hell of whistling metal, exploding shells, and spurting dust—suffering, despairing, dying.

After five hours of fighting, the numbers killed were 20 Britons, 20 Egyptian allies, and over 11,000 Sudanese.

Ethiopia as Exception.

One exception to the general rule of easy conquest was Ethiopia. The history of the country illustrates the importance of guns in the dynamics of the scramble. In the middle of the nineteenth century, the emperor of Ethiopia possessed little more than a grand title. Yet while the empire had broken down into its ethnic and regional components, the dream of a united empire was still alive. It was pursued by the emperors of the time, Amharic-speakers with their political base on the fertile plateau that constituted the heartland of the country. In their successful efforts to rebuild the empire, they relied increasingly on modern weapons imported from Europe and stockpiled.

By the early 1870s, however, the emperor realized that his achievements in rebuilding the empire were endangered not merely by the resistance of those whom he was then trying to force into his empire, but, more ominously, by the outside world, especially by Egypt to the north and the Sudan to the west. Furthermore, the opening of the Suez Canal in 1869 had made the Red Sea and its surrounding areas attractive not only to Egypt but also to European countries eager to protect their trade routes to Asia. By the end of the 1870s, as the scramble for Africa was seriously getting under way, France, Britain, and Italy all became interested in acquiring land in the region. After Britain occupied Egypt in 1882, France took Djibouti (1884) and Italy seized Eritrea (1885), both on the Red Sea.

The emperor, Menelik II (1889–1913), realized that he could exploit rival European interests in the area by playing off one European power against the others to obtain the weapons he needed for expanding his empire's boundaries. He therefore gave certain concessions to France in return for French weapons. Italy, upset at the growing French influence, offered weapons as well, and Menelik accepted them. Russia and Britain joined in. More and more modern weapons flowed into Ethiopia during the 1870s and 1880s and into the early 1890s, and Menelik steadily strengthened his ability both to suppress internal dissent and to block foreign encroachment.

Then, in the early 1890s, Menelik's strategy of balancing one European power against another began to unravel. In 1889, he had signed the Treaty of Wichale with Italy, granting it certain concessions in return for more arms shipments. Italy then claimed that Ethiopia had thus become an Italian protectorate and moved against Menelik when he objected. By 1896, Italy was ready for a major assault on the Ethiopian army, heady with the confident racism of the time that it could defeat the "primitive" Ethiopians with ease. General Oreste Baratieri (1841–1901), the commander of Italy's 18,000-man army in Eritrea, was wisely cautious, however, understanding that modern weapons functioned the same way whether they were fired by Africans or Italians. Knowing that Menelik's army of some 100,000 troops had very long supply lines, Baratieri decided to wait until Menelik could no longer supply his troops with food. Then, he assumed, Menelik's soldiers would simply disappear, and the Italians would walk in. But the prime minister of Italy, Francesco Crispi (1819–1901), wanted a quick, glorious victory to enhance his political reputation and ordered Baratieri to send his army into battle at once. Hopelessly outnumbered, the Italians lost over 8,000 men on 1 March 1896 at the decisive battle of Adowa. With its army destroyed and its artillery lost to the Ethiopians, Italy had no choice but to negotiate a peace.

France and Britain soon ratified Italy's acceptance of Ethiopia as a sovereign state with its greatly expanded imperial boundaries. As a consequence of its victory at Adowa—and attesting to the crucial importance of modern weaponry for survival in late nineteenth-century Africa—Ethiopia was the only African country aside from the U.S. quasi-colony of Liberia that Europeans did not occupy in the scramble for Africa. After 1896, Menelik, with his access to modern weapons assured by his country's international recognition, successfully continued his campaigns to extend his control over the Ethiopian empire's subordinate peoples.

Gold, Empire Building, and the Boer War

Europeans were as willing to shoot white Africans as they were black Africans during the scramble as they seized land and resources. In South Africa, for example, the British engaged in a long war over possession of the world's largest supply of gold with a group of white Africans, the Afrikaners, or Boers, settlers of Dutch and French Huguenot background who had developed their own unique identity during the eighteenth and early nineteenth centuries.

Afrikaner Rule. After the Great Trek (1837–1844), in which a large number of Afrikaners had withdrawn from British control by leaving the Cape Colony, the British had grudgingly recognized the independence of the Orange Free State and the Transvaal, the Afrikaner republics in the interior, in a series of formal agreements. The British complacently believed that the Afrikaners, economically weak and geographically isolated, could never challenge British preeminence in the region. Two events of the mid-1880s shattered their complacence. First, in 1884, Germany, Britain's greatest international competitor, inserted itself into the region by annexing Namibia as part of the scramble. The British, aware that the Germans and the Afrikaners were sympathetic to each other, worried about the German threat to their regional hegemony and economic prospects.

Britain's War in South Africa. British fear of the Germans was redoubled in 1886 when, in the Transvaal Republic, in the Witwatersrand area, the world's largest

deposits of gold were discovered. A group of British diamond mine owners who had grown rich exploiting the Kimberley diamond fields after their discovery in 1867 moved in quickly to develop the Witwatersrand's gold, which, because it lay deep in the ground, could be mined only with the investment of large amounts of capital. The best-known of these investors was Cecil Rhodes (1853–1902), a businessman and Cape Colony politician who was intent on expanding his wealth through an extension of British power to the north. Rhodes and his colleagues quickly identified Afrikaner governmental policies on agriculture, tariffs, and labor control as major impediments to profitable gold production. Therefore, in 1895 they organized, with the connivance of members of the British government, an attempt to overthrow the Afrikaner government of the Transvaal. This attempt, led by Dr. L. S. Jameson (1853–1917), Rhodes's lieutenant, involved the invasion of the Transvaal by British South African police and came to be known as the Jameson Raid. It was faultily executed, however, and, to Rhodes's utter humiliation, it failed.

The failure of the Jameson Raid prompted the British government to send a new agent, Alfred Milner (1854–1925), to the area in 1897. An ardent advocate of expanding the British Empire and of keeping German influence in the region to a minimum, and well aware of the importance of gold to Britain's financial position in the world, Milner was determined to push the Afrikaners into uniting with the British in South Africa, through either diplomacy or war. By 1899 it was clear that war was inevitable, and in October, British demands provoked a declaration of war from the Afrikaners. The British confidently expected to have the war over by Christmas, but the Afrikaners carried out a guerrilla war against inept British generals, and the so-called Boer War dragged on and on.

The British eventually sent 350,000 troops to South Africa, but these forces, even when reinforced by thousands of African auxiliaries, could not decisively defeat the 65,000 Afrikaner fighting men. Casualties were high on both sides, not merely from the fighting, but also because typhus epidemics broke out in the concentration camps in which the British interned Afrikaner women and children as they pursued their scorched-earth policies in the countryside. By the war's end, 25,000 Afrikaners, 22,000 British imperial troops, and 12,000 black Africans had died. Britain had also suffered great international criticism for having treated white Afrikaners as if they were black Africans.

In April 1902, the British accepted the conditional surrender of the Afrikaners. The British annexed the Afrikaner republics to the empire and took the opportunity to make the gold industry efficient. But they promised the Afrikaners that no political decisions regarding the majority black African population's political role in a future South Africa would be taken before returning governmental power to the Afrikaners. This crucial concession ensured that segregation would remain the model for race relations in South Africa throughout the twentieth century.

When World War I broke out in 1914, the scramble for Africa was over, and the map of the continent was colored in imperial inks. France had secured the largest chunk, some four million square miles of mostly tropical forests and deserts. Britain had the second largest empire, richer in minerals and agricultural potential than France's. Germany proudly possessed two West African colonies, Togo and Cameroon, as well as Namibia in southern Africa and Tanganyika in East Africa. Belgium had been forced to assume control over Leopold II's Congo in 1908 after scandals made his continued control unacceptable. Portugal had finally consolidated its feeble hold on Angola, Mozambique, and Portuguese Guinea. Italy had colonies in Libya, Eritrea, and Somalia, while Spain was left with some bits of coast. Only Ethiopia and Liberia were politically independent. Now that they had conquered Africa, the colonial powers had to face the

MAP DISCOVERY

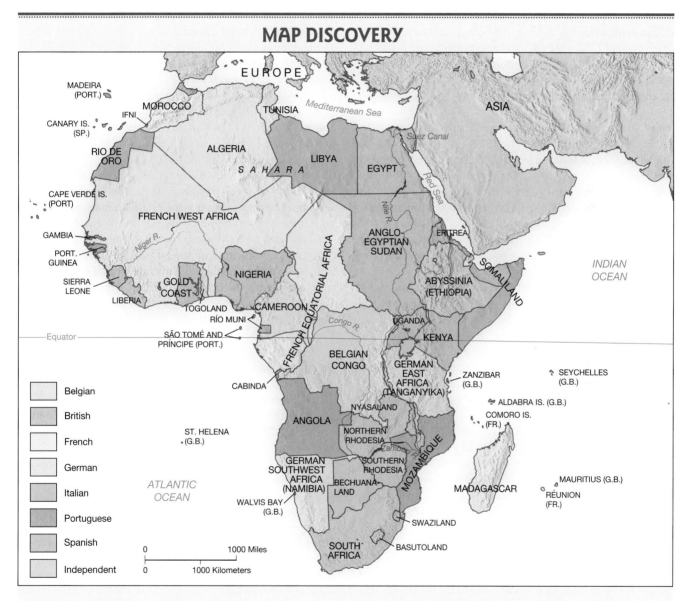

Africa, 1914

By 1914, the map of Africa emerged as a colorful patchwork indicating competing European interests. Do you perceive any patterns in the way the seven European nations laid claim to territory? What were the geopolitical imperatives that motivated the British to seek a swathe of territory from north to south? What are the only two states in 1914 not under the control or oversight of European powers? Based on the chapter discussion, how do you explain why they were exceptions?

issue of how their new colonies could be made to pay. And the conquered Africans had to face the issue of how they might regain their political and economic independence.

Imperialism in Asia

During the first half of the nineteenth century, strong Asian powers had grown stronger. China increased its control over inner Asian territories; Vietnam and Siam, predecessor to modern Thailand, enhanced their powers in southeast Asia. By the end of the nineteenth century, Asian political dynasties had suffered reversals. China had been permanently weakened in inner Asia; Vietnam had fallen under French colonial rule; Siam had lost half its territories. India had long constituted an important part of the British Empire. By contrast, Japan became an aggressive power, itself an imperial presence.

India. The British Parliament proclaimed that on New Year's Day, 1877, Queen Victoria (1837–1901) would add the title of empress of India to her many honors. India, the great jewel in the imperial crown, was a land Victoria had never seen. The queen's new title, not universally popular in Britain and unnoticed by most famine-stricken Indian peasants, in fact changed nothing about the way the British ruled India. Yet it was more than merely a symbolic assertion of dominance over a country that had long been controlled by the British.

India was the starting point of all British expansion, and it stood at the center of British foreign policy. To protect its sea routes to India and to secure its Indian markets, Britain acquired territories and carved out concessions all over the world. Devised by Prime Minister Benjamin Disraeli to flatter an aging monarch, the new title of empress was really a calculated warning to Russia, operating on India's northern frontier in Afghanistan, and to France, busily pursuing its own interests in Egypt.

Formal British rule in India began in 1861 with the appointment of a viceroy, who was assisted by legislative and executive councils. Both of these bodies included some Indian representatives. British rule encountered the four main divisions of the highly stratified Hindu society. At the top were Brahmans, the learned and priestly class, followed by the warriors and rulers, then the farmers and merchants, and finally by the peasants and laborers. On the outside existed the untouchables, a fifth division that was intended to perform society's most menial tasks. Rather than disrupt this divisive caste system, the British found it to their advantage to maintain the status quo.

The special imperial relationship originated in the seventeenth century, when the British East India Company, a joint-stock venture free of government control, began limited trading in Indian markets. The need for regulation and protection firmly established British rule by the end of the eighteenth century. Conquest of the Punjab in 1849 brought the last in-

dependent areas under British control. Throughout this period, Britain invested considerable overseas capital in India, and in turn India absorbed one-fifth of total British exports. The market for Indian cotton, for centuries exported to Asia and Europe, collapsed under British tariffs, and India became a consumer of cheap Lancashire cotton. The British also exploited India's agriculture, salt, and opium production for profit.

China. At the end of the eighteenth century, the British traded English wool and Indian cotton for Chinese tea and textiles. But Britain's thirst for Chinese tea grew, while Chinese demand for English and Indian textiles slackened. Britain discovered that Indian opium could be used to balance the trade deficit created by tea. British merchants and local Chinese officials, especially in the entry port of Canton, began to expand their profitable involvement in a contraband trade in opium. The British East India Company held a monopoly over opium cultivation in Bengal. Opium exports to China mounted phenomenally—from 200 chests in 1729 to 40,000 chests in 1838. By the 1830s, opium was probably Britain's most important crop in world markets. The British prospered as opium was pumped into China faster than tea was flowing out. Chinese buyers began paying for the drug with silver.

Concerned with the sharp rise in addiction, the accompanying social problems, and the massive outflow of silver, the Chinese government reacted. As Chinese officials saw it, they were exchanging their precious metal for British poison. Addicts were threatened with the death penalty. In 1839, the Chinese government destroyed British opium in the port of Canton, touching off the Opium War (1839–1842).

Between 1842 and 1895, China fought five wars with foreigners and lost all of them. Defeat was expensive, as China had to pay costs to the winners. Before the end of the century, Britain, France, Germany, and Japan had managed to establish major territorial advantages in their **spheres of influence,** sometimes through negotiation and sometimes through force. By 1912, over 50 major Chinese ports had been handed over to foreign control as "treaty ports." British spheres included Shanghai, the lower Yangzi, and Hong Kong. France maintained special interests in South China. Germany controlled the Shandong peninsula. Japan laid claim to the northeast.

Spheres of influence grew in importance at the beginning of the twentieth century, when foreign investors poured capital into railway lines, which needed treaty protection from competing companies. Railways furthered foreign encroachment and opened up new territories to foreign claims. As one Chinese official explained it, the railroads were like scissors that threatened to cut China into many pieces. Foreigners established no formal empires in China, but the treaty ports certainly signaled both informal rule and indisputable foreign dominance.

Treaty ports were centers of foreign residence and trade, where rules of **extraterritoriality** applied. This meant that

CHRONOLOGY
THE NEW IMPERIALISM IN AFRICA AND ASIA

1837–1844	Great Trek
1839–1842	Opium War
1869	Suez Canal completed
1884	Berlin Conference held to regulate imperialism in Africa
1886	Gold discovered in the Transvaal Republic
1894–1895	Sino-Japanese War
1896	Battle of Adowa
1899–1902	Boer War
1900	Boxer Rebellion
1904–1905	Russo-Japanese War

foreigners were exempt from Chinese law enforcement and that, although present on Chinese territory, they could be judged only by officials of their own countries. Extraterritoriality was a privilege not just for diplomats but for every foreign national. It implied both a distrust of Chinese legal procedures and a cultural arrogance about the superiority of Western institutions. It also provoked resentment and growing antiforeign sentiments among the Chinese.

To preserve extraterritoriality and maintain informal empires, the European powers appointed civilian representatives known as consuls. Often merchants themselves—in the beginning unpaid in their posts—and consuls acted as the chieftains of resident merchant communities, judges in all civil and criminal cases, and spokesmen for the commercial interests of the home country. They clearly embodied the commercial intentions of Western governments. Initially, they stood outside the diplomatic corps; later, they were consigned to its lower ranks. Consuls were brokers for commerce and interpreted the international commercial law that was being forged. Consulates spread beyond China as Western nations used consuls to protect their own interests. In Africa, consuls represented the trading concerns of European governments and were instrumental in the transition to formal rule.

Southeast Asia and Japan. European nations pursued imperialist endeavors elsewhere in Asia, acquired territories on China's frontiers, and took over states that had formerly paid tribute to the Chinese Empire. The British acquired Hong Kong (1842), Burma (1886), and Kowloon (1898). The Russians took over the Maritime Provinces in 1858. The

French made gains in Indochina (Annam and Tonkin) in 1884 and extended control over Laos in 1893 and Cambodia in 1884. Thailand was the only country in southeast Asia to escape direct control by the Western powers. Yet it was forced to yield territory it once controlled and to accept the treaty port system with its tariffs and extraterritoriality.

The Sino-Japanese War of 1894–1895 revealed Japan's intentions to compete as an imperialist power in Asia. The modernized and westernized Japanese army easily defeated the ill-equipped and poorly led Chinese forces. As a result, Japan gained the island of Taiwan. Pressing its ambitions on the continent, Japan locked horns with Russia over claims to the Liaodong peninsula, Korea, and south Manchuria. Following its victory in the Russo-Japanese War of 1904–1905, Japan expanded into all of these areas, annexing Korea outright in 1910. The ease with which the small Asian nation had defeated the Russian giant and contributed to the heightening of anti-imperialist sentiments in China sent a strong message to the West.

The Imperialism of the United States

The United States provided another variation on imperial expansion. Its westward drive across the North American continent, beginning at the end of the eighteenth century, established the United States as an imperial power in the Western Hemisphere. By 1848, the relatively young American nation stretched over 3,000 miles from one ocean to the other. It had met the opposition and resistance of the Native Americans with armed force, decimated them, and "concentrated" the survivors in assigned territories, and later on reservations.

At the end of the nineteenth century, the United States, possessing both the people and the resources for rapid industrial development, turned to the Caribbean and the Pacific islands in pursuit of markets and investment opportunities. By acquiring stepping stones of islands across the Pacific Ocean in the Hawaiian Islands and Samoa, it secured fueling bases and access to lucrative east Asian ports. And by intervening repeatedly in Central America and building the Panama Canal, the United States had established its hegemony in the Caribbean by 1914. Growing in economic power and hegemonic influence, both Japan and the United States had joined the club of imperial powers and were making serious claims against European expansion.

RESULTS OF A EUROPEAN-DOMINATED WORLD

Europeans fashioned the world in their own image, but in the process, Western values and Western institutions underwent profound and unintended transformations. Family values were articulated in an imperialist context, and race emerged as a key factor in culture. The discovery of new lands, new cultures, and new peoples altered the ways in which European women and men regarded themselves and viewed their place in the world. With the rise of new contenders for power—the United States and Japan—and growing criticism about the morality of capitalism, the Western world was not as predictable in 1914 as it had appeared in 1870.

A World Economy

Imperialism produced an interdependent world economic system with Europe at its center. Industrial and commercial capitalism linked the world's continents in a communications and transportation network that would have been unimaginable in earlier ages. As a result, foreign trade increased from 3 percent of world output in 1800 to 33 percent by 1913. The greatest growth in trade occurred in the period from 1870 to 1914, as raw materials, manufactured products, capital, and men and women were transported across seas and continents by those seeking profits.

Meeting Western Needs.   Most trading in the age of imperialism still took place among European nations and North America. But entrepreneurs in search of new markets

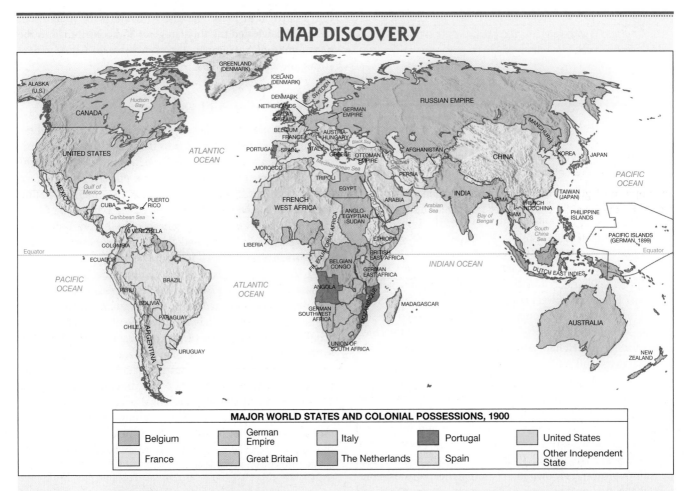

MAP DISCOVERY

MAJOR WORLD STATES AND COLONIAL POSSESSIONS, 1900

Belgium	German Empire	Italy
France	Great Britain	The Netherlands

Portugal · United States · Spain · Other Independent State

World Colonial Holdings

The European powers, great and small, competed with each other for world empires and world influence between 1870 and 1914. In terms of territory occupied, which nation held the largest global empire? What is the meaning of the expression, "The sun never sets on the British Empire"? Based on what you have read in the chapter, how do you explain the fact that the Netherlands held colonies in southeast Asia and Latin America, but had no holdings in Africa? How did the United States become an imperial power in this period? How do you explain the locations of U.S. colonial acquisitions?

and new resources saw in Africa and Asia opportunities for protected exploitation. New markets were created in nonindustrialized areas of the world to meet the needs of Western producers and consumers. European landlords and managers trained Kenyan farmers to put aside their traditional agricultural methods and to grow more "useful" crops such as coffee, tea, and sugar. The availability of cheaper British textiles of inferior quality drove Indian weavers away from their hand-looms. Chinese silk producers changed centuries-old techniques to produce silk thread and cloth that was suited to the machinery and mass-production requirements of the French. Trade permitted specialization but at the choice of the colonizer, not the colonized. World production and consumption were being shaped to suit the needs of the West.

Investment Abroad. Capital in search of profits flowed out of the wealthier areas of Europe into the nonindustrialized regions of Russia, the Balkans, and the Ottoman Empire, where capital-intensive expenditures (on railways, for instance) promised high returns. Capital investment in overseas territories also increased phenomenally as railroads were built to gain access to primary products. Great Britain led in overseas investment with loans abroad greater than those of its five major competitors—France, Germany, Holland, the United States, and Belgium—combined.

The City of London had become the world's banker, and the adoption of gold as the standard for exchange for most European currencies by 1874 further facilitated the operation of a single, interdependent trading and investment system. Britain remained the world's biggest trading nation, with half of its exports going to Asia, Africa, and South America and the other half to Europe and the United States. But Germany was Britain's fastest-growing competitor, with twice as many exports to Europe and expanding overseas trade by 1914. The United States had recently joined the league of the world's great trading nations and was running a strong third in shares of total trade.

Foreign investments often took the form of loans to governments or to enterprises that were guaranteed by governments. Investors might be willing to take risks, but they also expected protection, as did merchants and industrialists trading in overseas territories. Together, trade and investment interests exerted considerable pressure on European states for control through acquisition and concessions. The vast amounts of money involved help to explain the expectations of state involvement and the reasons why international competition, rivalry, and instability threatened to lead to conflict and to war.

Race and Culture

The West's ability to kill and conquer as well as to cure was, as one Victorian social observer argued, proof of its cultural superiority. Every colonizing nation had its spokesmen for the "civilizing mission" to educate and to convert African and Asian "heathens." Cultural superiority was only a short step from arguments for racial superiority. Prompted by the U.S. involvement in the Philippines, the British poet Rudyard Kipling (1865–1936) characterized the responsibilities of the advanced West as "the White Man's burden." The smug and arrogant attitude of his poem about the white man's mission revealed a deep-seated and unacknowledged racism toward peoples considered "half-devil and half-child." Race and culture were collapsed into each other. If Westerners were culturally superior, as they claimed, they must be racially superior as well. The "survival of the fittest" came to justify conquest and subjugation as "laws" of human interaction and, by extension, of relations among nations.

Women and Imperialism

Ideas about racial and cultural superiority were not confined to books by pseudoscientists and to discussions among policy makers. Public discussions about marriage, reproduction, motherhood, and child-rearing reflected new concerns about furthering "the imperial race"—that is, white Westerners. Women throughout Western societies were advised by reformers, politicians, and doctors to have more children and instructed to take better care of them. "Children [are] the most valuable of imperial assets," one British doctor lectured his readers. Healthy young men were needed in the colonies, they were told, to defend Western values. State officials paid greater attention to infant mortality at the end of the nineteenth century, set up health programs for children, and provided young women with training in home management, nutrition, and child care.

In the poem "The White Man's Burden," Kipling advised, "Send forth the best ye breed." All over Europe, newly formed associations and clubs stressed the need for careful mate selection. In Britain, Francis Galton (1822–1911) founded eugenics, the study of genetics for the purpose of improving inherited characteristics of the race. Imperialism, the propagandists proclaimed, depended on mothers, women who would nurture healthy workers, strong soldiers and sailors, and intelligent and capable leaders. High infant mortality rates and poor health of children were attributed directly to maternal failings, not to environmental factors or poverty. Kaiser Wilhelm II stressed that German women's attention to the "three Ks"—*Kinder, Küche, Kirche* ("children, kitchen, church")—would guarantee a race of Germans who would rule the world. British generals and French statesmen publicly expressed similar sentiments.

Some European women participated directly in the colonizing experience. As missionaries and nurses, they supported the civilizing mission. As wives of officials and managers, they were expected to embody the gentility and values of Western culture. Most men who traded and served overseas did so unaccompanied by women. But when women were present in any numbers, as they were in India before 1914, they were expected to preserve the exclusivity of Western communities.

Ecology and Imperialism

Ecology—the relationship and adjustment of human groups to their environment—was affected by imperial expansion, which dislocated the societies that it touched. Early explorers had disrupted little as they arrived, observed, and then moved on. The missionaries, merchants, soldiers, and businessmen who came later required the inhabitants with whom they came into contact to change their thinking and behavior. In some cases, dislocation resulted in material improvements, better medical care, and the introduction of modern technology. For the most part, however, the initial ecological impact of the imperialist was negative. Western men and women carried diseases to people who did not share their immunity. Traditional village life was destroyed in rural India, and African societies disintegrated under the European onslaught. Resistance existed everywhere, but in Africa, as we have seen, only the Ethiopians succeeded in keeping out foreigners. In East Asia, parts of China were subject to foreign influence, while Japan, after being forcibly opened to Western commerce, soon developed imperialist ambitions of its own. Missionaries, merchants, and purveyors of Western culture and technology flocked to all these places to enlighten the natives—and occasionally to learn from them.

Education of native populations had as its primary goal the improvement of administration and productivity in the colonies. When foreigners ruled indirectly through existing indigenous hierarchies, they often created corrupt and tyrannical bureaucracies that exploited natives. The indirect rule of the British in India was based on a pragmatic desire to keep British costs low.

When Asian and African laborers started producing for the Western market, they became dependent on its fluctuations. Victimized for centuries by the vagaries of weather, they now had to contend with the instability and cutthroat competition of cash crops in world markets. Men and women migrated from place to place in the countryside and from the countryside to newly formed cities. Such migrations necessarily affected family life, as individuals married later because they lacked the resources to set up households. Many women, cut free of their tribes (as was the case in Nairobi), turned to prostitution—literally for pennies—as a means of survival.

Some European countries used their overseas territories as dumping grounds for criminals. Imitating the earlier example of the British in Australia, the French developed Guiana and New Caledonia as prison colonies in the hope of solving their social problems at home by exporting undesirables.

Critiquing Capitalism

One consequence of imperialism was the critique of capitalism it produced. Critics who condemned it as exploitative and racist saw imperialism as an expression of problems that were inherent in capitalism. In 1902, J. A. Hobson (1858–1940) published *Imperialism, A Study,* in which he argued that underconsumption and surplus capital at home drove Western industrial countries overseas in search of a cure for these economic ills. Rather than solving the problems by raising workers' wages and thereby increasing their consumption power and creating new opportunities for investment in home markets, manufacturers, entrepreneurs, and industrialists sought higher profits abroad. Hobson considered these business interests "economic parasites," making large fortunes at the expense of national interests.

In the midst of world war, the future leader of the Russian revolution, Vladimir Ilyich Ulyanov (1870–1924)—or, to use his revolutionary name, Lenin—added his own critique of capitalism. He did not share Hobson's belief that capitalism was merely malfunctioning in its imperialist endeavors. Instead, Lenin argued in *Imperialism, the Highest Stage of Capitalism* (1916) that capitalism was inherently and inevitably imperialistic. Because he was sure that Western capitalism was in the process of effecting its own destruction, Lenin called World War I the final "imperialist war."

Critics, historians, and economists have since pointed out that both works are marred by errors and omissions. Yet they stand at the beginning of almost a century of debate over the morality and economic feasibility of imperialism. Hobson as a liberal and Lenin as a Marxist highlighted the connections between social problems at home—whether in late Victorian England or in prerevolutionary Russia—and economic exploitation abroad. Yet if electoral results and the popular press are any indication, Europeans not only accepted but warmly embraced the responsibilities of empire.

CONCLUSION

From the very beginning of the competition for territories and concessions, no European state could act in Africa or Asia without affecting the interests and actions of its rivals at home. The African scramble made clear how interlocking the system of European states was after 1870. The development of spheres of influence in China underlined the value of world markets and international trade for the survival and expansion of Western nations.

A balance of power among states guaranteed national security and independence until the end of the nineteenth century. But between 1870 and 1914, industrialization, technology, and accompanying capital formation created vast economic disparities. Conflict and disequilibrium challenged European stability and balance. Ultimately, it was the politics of geography on the European continent, not confrontations in distant colonies, that polarized the European states into two camps. Despite the unresolved conflicts pervading all of these crises, European statesmen prided themselves on their ability to settle disputes through reason and negotiation. Yet, it was the problems at home in Europe, not abroad in the colonies, that were to exacerbate geopolitical vulnerabilities and detonate a conflict far worse than the world had ever seen.

QUESTIONS FOR REVIEW

1. What geopolitical factors made the European balance of power so unstable around the turn of the century?
2. What social, political, and economic forces encouraged the nations of Europe to create overseas empires in the late nineteenth century?
3. How and why did European imperialism differ in Africa and Asia?
4. How did imperial expansion around the globe transform the lives of Europeans at home?

KEY TERMS

extraterritoriality, *p. 510*

geopolitics, *p. 498*

jingoism, *p. 505*

new imperialism, *p. 501*

quinine, *p. 502*

scramble for Africa, *p. 506*

spheres of influence, *p. 510*

Triple Alliance, *p. 500*

Triple Entente, *p. 500*

DISCOVERING WESTERN CIVILIZATION ONLINE

You can obtain more information about Europe and the world between 1870 and 1914 at the websites listed below. See also the Companion Website that accompanies this text, www.ablongman.com/kishlansky, which contains an online study guide and additional resources.

The European Balance of Power, 1870–1914

Internet Modern History Sourcebook: World War I

www.fordham.edu/halsall/mod/modsbook38.html

This site is part of a larger site on World War I primary and secondary sources, but it contains a section on the developments among the Great Powers from the 1870s to 1914.

The New Imperialism

Internet Modern History Sourcebook: Imperialism

www.fordham.edu/halsall/mod/modsbook34.html

A comprehensive site of links arranged by continent to primary source materials and bibliographies on imperialism.

Colonialism and Postcolonialism: Selected Biographies

landow.stg.brown.edu/post/misc/bibl.html

Another site of links to bibliographies on colonialism and postcolonialism.

European Imperialism

www.winsor.edu/library/euroimpe.htm

This site is sponsored by the Winsor School and contains an extensive list of links by region on European imperialism.

The European Search for Territory and Markets

Francophone Africa: Bibliographies

www.hum.port.ac.uk/slas/francophone/bibliographies.htm

A collection of bibliographies on the partition of Africa and the impact of colonization in Africa.

South African War Virtual Library

www.bowlerhat.com.au/sawvl/

A virtual library of essays, photos, and further links on the Boer War.

China: A Traveling Exhibit, 1903–1904

www.chinaexhibit.org

A virtual museum exhibit of photographs taken in 1903 of the Chinese countryside after the Boxer Rebellion.

SUGGESTIONS FOR FURTHER READING

The European Balance of Power, 1870–1914

Norman Rich, *Great Power Diplomacy, 1814–1914* (New York: McGraw-Hill Higher Education, 1992). This work surveys diplomatic activities from the end of the Napoleonic Wars to the eve of World War I.

Alan Sked, *The Decline and Fall of the Habsburg Empire, 1815–1918* (London: Longman, 1989). An overview of the Habsburg Empire's history from Metternich to World War I.

The author interprets the various historiographical debates over the collapse of Habsburg rule. Rather than treating the late empire as a case of inevitable decline, the book examines the monarchy as a viable institution within a multinational state.

The New Imperialism

Antoinette Burton, ed., *After the Imperial Turn: Thinking With and Through the Nation* (Durham, NC: Duke University Press, 2003). This collection provides a critical cultural analysis of nationalism and imperialism by showing the inadequacies of the nation as an analytic category.

David Cannadine, *Ornamentalism: How the British Saw Their Empire* (New York: Oxford University Press, 2001). The author approaches the history of the British Empire as interconnected with the history of the British nation and considers this "entire interactive system" in terms of a social construction and social perceptions.

Michael W. Doyle, *Empires* (Ithaca, NY: Cornell University Press, 1986). Nineteenth-century imperialism is placed in a broad historical context that emphasizes a comparative perspective of the European imperial experience.

Richard Drayton, *Nature's Government: Science, Imperial Britain, and the "Improvement" of the World* (New Haven, CT: Yale University Press, 2000). A fascinating examination of the role scientists, and especially botanists, played as partners with bureaucratic government in British imperial expansion.

Daniel R. Headrick, *The Tentacles of Progress: Technology Transfer in the Age of Imperialism, 1850–1940* (New York: Oxford University Press, 1988). Argues that the transfer of technology to Africa and Asia by the Western imperial powers produced colonial underdevelopment.

Robert H. MacDonald, *The Language of Empire: Myths and Metaphors of Popular Imperialism, 1880–1918* (Manchester, England: Manchester University Press, 1994). In studying the new metaphors of imperialism, the author examines the role of mythmakers, such as Rudyard Kipling, and popular fiction in shaping imperial perceptions and experiences. The author argues that the very shaping of language about non-European lands and peoples helped determine the form empire took in Great Britain.

The Search for Territory and Markets

Winfried Baumgart, *Imperialism: The Idea and Reality of British and French Colonial Expansion, 1880–1914* (New York: Oxford University Press, 1982). Principally concerned with the motives that led to imperial expansion, the author argues that the motives were many and that each action must be studied in its specific social, political, and economic context.

Raymond F. Betts, *The False Dawn: European Imperialism in the Nineteenth Century* (Oxford: Oxford University Press, 1976). Explores the ideology of empire and the process of cultural transmission through colonial institutions.

Eric Hobsbawm, *The Age of Empire, 1875–1914* (New York: Pantheon, 1987). A wide-ranging interpretive history of the late nineteenth century that spans economic, social, political, and cultural developments.

Thomas Pakenham, *The Scramble for Africa* (New York: Random House, 1991). A narrative history of how Europeans subdivided Africa among themselves.

Results of a European-Dominated World

Tony Ballantyne, *Orientalism and Race: Aryanism in the British Empire* (New York: Palgrave, 2002). Ballantyne traces how the idea of an Aryan race became an important feature of British imperial culture in the nineteenth century.

Johannes Fabian, *Language and Colonial Power: The Appropriation of Swahili in the Former Belgian Congo* (Cambridge: Cambridge University Press, 1986). Demonstrates how colonial power was exercised in the Belgian Congo through the study of the growth of Swahili as a lingua franca. The author pays particular attention to the uses of Swahili in industrial and other work situations.

Leila Tarazi Fawaz and C. A. Bayly, eds., *Modernity and Culture: From the Mediterranean to the Indian Ocean* (New York: Columbia University Press, 2002). This collection of essays demonstrates how cities in this vast region were increasingly cosmopolitan loci for a new kind of modernity that responded to political, economic, social, and cultural change.

Anne McClintock, *Imperial Leather: Race, Gender, and Sexuality in the Colonial Contest* (New York: Routledge, 1995). By using novels, diaries, advertisements, and other sources, the author demonstrates the relationship between images of domestic life and an ideology of imperial domination and focuses on the role of women in the colonial experience.

Paul B. Rich, *Race and Empire in British Politics* (Cambridge: Cambridge University Press, 1986). An intellectual history of ideas about race in the imperial tradition. Focusing on the years between 1890 and 1970, the author examines the political dimensions of race and race ideology in British society.

For a list of additional titles related to this chapter's topics, please see www.ablongman.com/kishlansky**.**

Chapter 26
WAR AND REVOLUTION, 1914–1920

The Visual Record

SELLING THE GREAT WAR

Advertising is a powerful influence in modern life. The leaders of European nations discovered its power in the years of world war from 1914 to 1918. When death counts mounted, prices skyrocketed, and food supplies dwindled, the frenzy and fervor for the war flagged. Then governments came to rely more heavily on the art of persuasion. For the first time in history, war had to advertise.

Political leaders came to realize that the advertising techniques developed by business leaders in the early years of the twentieth century could be useful. Governments took up the "science" of selling—not products but the idea of war. Citizens had to be persuaded to join, to fight, to work, to save, and to believe in the national war effort. Warring nations learned how to organize enthusiasm and how to mobilize the masses in support of what proved to be a long and bloody conflict.

The German poster shows a dramatic appeal to women to support war work. A stern soldier whose visage and bearing communicate strength and singleness of purpose is backed up by an equally determined young woman. She is in the act of handing him a grenade as she stands with him, facing the unseen enemy. The poster reminds us of the centrality of women's work to the waging of a new kind of war in the twentieth century.

The battlefront had to be backed up by a "home front"—a term that was used for the first time in the Great War—of working men, women, and even children.

Early war posters stressed justice and national glory. Later, as weariness with the war spread, the need for personal sacrifice became the dominant theme. Look at the sad female figure rising from a sea of suffering and death in the second poster. The woman, both goddesslike and vulnerable, symbolizes Great Britain. She is making a plea for action, seeking soldiers for her cause. This appeal for volunteers for the armed forces was unique to Great Britain, where conscription was not established until 1916. The dark suffering and death in the water, lapping at her robes, are reflected in her eyes. She evinces a fierce determination as she exhorts, "Take up the sword of justice." In February 1915, Germany declared the waters around the British

TAKE UP THE
SWORD OF JUSTICE

Isles to be a war zone. All British shipping was subject to attack as well as neutral merchant vessels, which were attacked without warning. In May 1915, the *Lusitania* was sunk, taking with it over 1,000 lives, including those of 128 Americans. The poster frames an illuminated horizon where a ship that is probably the *Lusitania* goes down. We need not read a word to understand the call to arms against the perfidy of an enemy who has killed innocent civilians. The female figure's determined jaw, clenched fist, and outstretched arms communicate the nobility of the cause and the certainty of success.

Civilians had to be mobilized for two reasons. First, soldiers at the front had to be constantly replenished from civilian reserves. Second, the costs of the war in food, equipment, and productive materials were so high that civilian populations had to be willing to endure great hardships to produce supplies for soldiers at the front. Nations at war used advertising to coordinate civilian and military contributions to a common cause.

Looking Ahead

The European governments proudly "selling" war to their citizens in 1914 expected quick victories. Instead, they experienced a prolonged global war, costly in human life and material destruction, stretching out over four devastating years. Military technology and timetables called the tune in a defensive war fought from the trenches with sophisticated weapons capable of maiming and killing in new ways. The intervention of the United States and German defeat preceded a peace that reshaped Europe as a whole in fundamental ways. In the case of Russia, the war signaled political and social collapse and a revolution of unprecedented scale. ➤

THE WAR EUROPE EXPECTED

In 1914, Europe stood confidently at the center of the world. Covering only 7 percent of the earth's surface, Europe dominated the world's trade and was actively exporting both its goods and its culture all over the globe. The values of nineteenth-century liberalism permeated the self-confident world view of European men and women in 1914. They assumed that they could discover the rules that governed the world and use them to fashion a better civilization.

Many Europeans took stability and harmony for granted as preconditions for progress; yet they also recognized the usefulness of war. No one expected or wanted a general war, but liberal values served the goals of limited war, just as they had justified imperial conquest. Statesmen decided that there were rules to the game of war that could be employed in the interests of statecraft. Science and technology also served the interests of war. Statesmen and generals were sure that modern weapons would prevent a long war. Superiority in armed force became a priority for European states seeking to protect the peace.

The beginning of the modern arms race resulted in "armed peace" as a defense against war. Leaders nevertheless expected and planned for a short and limited war. Previous confrontations among European states had been limited in duration and destruction, as in the case of Prussia and France in 1870, or confined to peripheries, as squabbles among the Great Powers in Africa indicated. The alliance system was expected to defend the peace by defining the conditions of war.

As international tensions mounted, the hot summer days of 1914 were a time of hope and glory. The hope was that war, when it came, would be "over by Christmas." The glory was the promise of ultimate victory in the "crusade for civilization" that each nation's leaders held out to their people. When war did come in 1914, it was a choice, not an accident. Yet it was a choice that Europeans did not understand, one whose limits they could not control. Their unquestioned pride in reason and progress that ironically had led them to this war did not survive the four years of barbaric slaughter that followed.

Separating Friends from Foes

At the end of the nineteenth century, the world appeared to be coming together in a vast international network linked by commerce and finance. A system of alliances based on shared interests also connected states to one another. After 1905, the intricate defensive alliances between and among the European states maintained the balance of power between two blocs of nations and helped to prevent one bloc from dominating the other. Yet by creating blocs, alliances identified foes as well as friends. On the eve of the war, France, Great Britain, and Russia stood together in the Triple Entente. Since 1882, Germany, Austria-Hungary, and Italy had joined forces in the Triple Alliance. Other states allied with one or the other of these blocs in pacts of mutual interest and protection. Throughout the world, whether in North Africa, the Balkans, or Asia, the power of some states was intended to balance the

■ European Alliances on the Eve of World War I. Alliance systems divided Europe into two great blocs with few countries remaining neutral.

power of others. Yet the balance of power did not exist simply to preserve the peace. It existed to preserve a system of independent national societies—nation-states—in a precarious equilibrium. Gains in one area by one bloc had to be offset by compromises in another area to maintain the balance. Nations recognized limited conflict as a legitimate means of preserving equilibrium.

The alliance system of blocs reflected the growing impact of public opinion on international relations. Statesmen had the ability to manipulate the newspaper images of allies as good and rivals as evil. But controlling public opinion served to lock policy makers into permanent partnerships and "blank checks" of support for their allies. Western leaders understood that swings in public opinion in periods of crisis could hobble their efforts to act in the nation's best interest. Permanent military alliances with clearly identified "friends" therefore took the place of more fluid arrangements.

Because of treaty commitments, no country expected to face war alone. Alliances that guaranteed military support permitted weak nations to act irresponsibly, with the certainty that they would be defended by their more powerful partners. France and Germany were publicly committed to their weaker allies, Russia and Austria-Hungary, respectively, in supporting imperialist ambitions in the Balkans from which they themselves derived little direct benefit. The interlocking system of defensive alliances was structured to match strength against strength—France against Germany, for example—thereby making a prolonged war more likely than would be the case if a weak nation confronted a strong enemy. At base, the alliance system stood as both a defense against war and an invitation to it.

Military Timetables

As Europe soon discovered, military timetables restricted a country's options at times of conflict. The crisis of the summer of 1914 revealed the extent to which politicians and statesmen had come to rely on military expertise and strategic considerations for decisions. Military general staffs assumed increasing importance in state policy making. War planners became powerful as war was accepted as an alternative to negotiation. Germany's military preparations are a good example of how war strategy exacerbated crises and prevented peaceful solutions.

The Schlieffen Plan.   Alfred von Schlieffen (1833–1913), the Prussian general and chief of the German General Staff from 1891 to 1905 who developed the war plan, understood little about politics but spent his life studying the strategic challenges of warfare. His war plan was designed to make Germany the greatest power on the Continent. The **Schlieffen Plan,** which he set before his fellow officers in 1905, was bold and daring: in the likely event of war with Russia, Germany would launch a devastating offensive against France. Schlieffen reasoned that France, with its strong military forces, would come to the aid of its ally, Russia. Russia, lacking a modern transportation system, could not mobilize as rapidly as France.

Russia also had the inestimable advantage of the ability to retreat into its vast interior. If Germany were pulled into a war with Russia, its western frontier would be vulnerable to France, Russia's powerful ally. The Schlieffen Plan recognized that France would have to be defeated before Germany could turn its forces eastward against Russia. The Schlieffen Plan thus committed Germany to a war with France, regardless of particular circumstances. Furthermore, with its strategy of invading the neutral countries of Belgium, Holland, and Luxembourg in order to defeat France in six weeks, the plan would have ignored the rights of the neutral countries.

Russia's Mobilization Plan and the French Plan XVII. Germany was not alone in being driven by military considerations. Russian military strategists planned full mobilization if war broke out with Austria-Hungary, which was menacing the interests of Russia's ally Serbia. Russia foresaw the likelihood that Germany would come to the aid of Austria-Hungary. Russia knew, too, that because of its primitive railway network, it would be unable to mobilize troops rapidly. To compensate for this weakness, Russian leaders planned to mobilize *before* war was declared. German military leaders had no choice in the event of full Russian mobilization but to mobilize their own troops immediately and to urge the declaration of war. Once a general mobilization was under way on both sides, conflict could hardly be avoided. Mobilization would mean war.

Like the Schlieffen Plan, the French Plan XVII called for the concentration of troops in a single area with the intention of decisively defeating the enemy. The French command, not well informed about German strengths and strategies, designated Alsace and Lorraine for the immediate offensive against Germany in the event of war. Plan XVII left Paris exposed to the German drive through Belgium that the Schlieffen Plan proposed.

Military leaders throughout Europe argued that if their plans were to succeed, speed was essential. Delays to consider peaceful solutions would cripple military responses. Diplomacy bowed to military strategy. When orders to mobilize went out, armies would be set on the march. Like a row of dominoes falling with the initial push, the two alliance systems would be at war.

Assassination at Sarajevo

A teenager with a handgun started the First World War. On 28 June 1914, in Sarajevo, the sleepy capital of the Austro-Hungarian province of Bosnia, Gavrilo Princip (1895–1918), a 19-year-old Bosnian Serb, repeatedly pulled the trigger of his Browning revolver, killing the designated heir of the Habsburg throne, Archduke Franz Ferdinand, and his wife, Sophie. Princip belonged to the Young Bosnian Society, a group of students, workers, a few peasants, Croats, Muslims, and intellectuals who wanted to free Slavic populations from Habsburg control. Princip was part of a growing movement of South Slavs struggling for national liberation from Austria-Hungary.

Struggle over control of the Balkans had been a longstanding issue that had involved all the major European powers for decades. As Austria-Hungary's ally since 1879, Germany was willing to support Vienna's showdown in the Balkans as a way of stopping Russian advances in the area. The alliance with Germany gave Austria-Hungary a sense of security and confidence to pursue its Balkan aims. Germany had its own plans for domination of the Continent and feared that a weakened Austria-Hungary would undermine its own position in central Europe. Independent Balkan states to the south and east were also a threat to Germany's plans. German leaders hoped that an Austro-Serbian war would remain localized and would strengthen their ally, Austria-Hungary. While Austria-Hungary had Germany's support, Serbia was backed by a sympathetic Russia favoring nationalist movements in the Balkans. Russia had, in turn, been encouraged by France, its ally by military pact since 1894, to take a firm stand in its struggle with Austria-Hungary for dominance among Balkan nationalities.

The interim of five weeks between the assassination of the Archduke Ferdinand and the outbreak of the war was a period of intense diplomatic activity. The assassination gave Austria-Hungary the excuse it needed to bring a troublesome Serbia into line. On 23 July 1914, Austria-Hungary issued an ultimatum to Serbia and secretly decided to declare war regardless of the Serbs' response. The demands were so severe that, if met, they would have stripped Serbia of its independence. Austria's aim was to destroy Serbia. In spite of a conciliatory, although not capitulatory, reply from Serbia to its ultimatum, Austria-Hungary declared war on the Balkan nation on 28 July 1914. Russia mobilized two days later. Germany mobilized in response to the Russian action and declared war on Russia on 1 August and on France on 3 August. France had begun mobilizing on 30 July, when its ally, Russia, entered the war.

Great Britain briefly attempted to mediate a settlement in the Austro-Serbian conflict, but once France declared war, the domino effect of the alliance system was triggered. On 4 August, after Germany had violated Belgian neutrality in its march to France, Great Britain honored its treaty obligations and declared war on Germany. Great Britain entered the war because it judged that a powerful Germany could use ports on the English Channel to invade the British Isles. Italy alone of the major powers remained for the moment outside the conflict. Although Italy was allied with Germany and Austria-Hungary, its own aspirations in the Balkans kept it from fighting for the Austrian cause in 1914.

Self-interest, fear, and ambition motivated the Great Powers in different ways in the pursuit of war. The international diplomatic system that had worked so well to prevent war in the preceding decades now enmeshed European states in interlocking alliances and created a chain reaction. The Austro-Serbian war of July 1914 became a Europe-wide war within a month.

A NEW KIND OF WARFARE

The expectation of a speedy war of decisive victories and domestic glory drove European leaders and their populations to embrace armed conflict as an acceptable means of mediating grievances in 1914. The peace that had been preserved from the end of the nineteenth century to 1914 was a precarious one indeed, predicated as it was on military timetables that planned for war and alliance systems that guaranteed that local disagreements would become international conflicts. The international mechanisms for keeping the peace led directly to war and guaranteed that once war broke out, it would not remain limited and local.

Early in the war, the best-laid plans of political and military leaders collapsed. First, Europe got a war that was not limited but spread quickly throughout Europe and became global. Switzerland, Spain, the Netherlands, and all of Scandinavia remained neutral, but every other European nation was pulled into the war. In August 1914, Japan cast its lot with the **Allies,** as the Triple Entente came to be known, and in November, the Ottoman Empire joined the **Central Powers** of Germany and Austria-Hungary. In the following year, Italy joined the war, not on the side of its long-term treaty partners, Germany and Austria-Hungary, but on the side of the Allies, with the expectation of benefiting in the Balkans from Austrian defeat. Bulgaria joined Germany and Austria-Hungary in 1915, seeking territory at Serbia's expense. By the time the United States joined the fray in 1917, the war had become a world war.

The second surprise for the European powers was that they did not get a preventive war of movement or one of short duration. Within weeks that pattern had given way to what promised to be a long and costly war of attrition. The war started as German strategists had planned, with German victory in battle after battle. The end seemed near. But in less than a month, the war changed in ways that no one had predicted. Technology was the key to understanding the change and to explaining the surprises.

Technology and the Trenches

In nineteenth-century European warfare, armies had relied on mobile cavalry and infantry units whose greatest asset was speed. Rapid advance had been decisive in the Prussian victory over the French in 1870, which had resulted in the formation of the German Empire.

Digging In. Soldiers of the twentieth century were also trained for a moving war, high maneuverability, and maximum territorial conquest. Yet after the first six weeks of battle, soldiers found themselves having to dig ditches and fight from fixed positions. Soldiers on both sides shoveled out trenches four feet deep, piled up sandbags, mounted their machine guns, and began to fight an unplanned, defensive war.

The front lines of Europe's armies in the west wallowed in the trenches that ran from the English Channel to the Swiss frontier. The British and French on one side and the Germans on the other fought each other with machine guns and mortars, backed up by heavy artillery to the rear. Strategists on both sides believed that they could break through enemy lines. As a result, the gruesome monotony of trench warfare was punctuated periodically by infantry offensives in which large concentrations of artillery caused immense bloodshed. Ten million men were killed in this bizarre and deadly combination of old and new warfare. The glamour of battle that attracted many young men disappeared quickly in the daily reality of living in mud with rats and constantly facing death. The British poet Wilfred Owen (1893–1918) wrote shortly before his own death in battle about how the soldier next to him had been shot in the head, soaking Owen in blood: "I shall feel again as soon as I dare, but now I must not."

New Weapons.   The invention of new weaponry and heavy equipment had transformed war, but some old ways persisted.

ALL QUIET ON THE WESTERN FRONT

Eyewitness accounts described the horrors of the new trench warfare. But no one captured the war better than the German novelist Erich Maria Remarque (1898–1970), who drew on his own wartime experiences in All Quiet on the Western Front. *Published in 1928 and subsequently translated into 25 languages, this powerful portrayal of the transformation of a school boy into a soldier indicts the inhumanity of war and pleads for peace. Stressing the camaraderie of fighting men and sympathy for the plight of the enemy soldier, Remarque also underscored the alienation of a whole generation—the lost generation of young men who could not go home again after the war.*

Focus Questions

In the final paragraph, the narrator tells us his age. Would you have guessed his age from the opening three paragraphs? How does the narrator's description of his generation transcend enemy lines?

Attack, counter-attack, charge, repulse—these are words, but what things they signify! We have lost a good many men, mostly recruits. Reinforcements have again been sent up to our sector. They are one of the new regiments, composed almost entirely of young fellows just called up. They have had hardly any training, and are sent into the field with only a theoretical knowledge. They do know what a hand-grenade is, it is true, but they have very little idea of cover, and what is most important of all, have no eye for it. A fold in the ground has to be quite eighteen inches high before they can see it.

Although we need reinforcement, the recruits give us almost more trouble than they are worth. They are helpless in this grim fighting area, they fall like flies. Modern trench-warfare demands knowledge and experience; a man must have a feeling for the contours of the ground, an ear for the sound and character of the shells, must be able to decide beforehand where they will drop, how they will burst, and how to shelter from them.

The young recruits of course know none of these things. They get killed simply because they hardly can tell shrapnel from high-explosive, they are mown down because they are listening anxiously to the roar of the big coal-boxes falling in the rear, and miss the light, piping whistle of the low spreading daisy-cutters. They flock together like sheep instead of scattering, and even the wounded are shot down like hares by the airmen.

Their pale turnip faces, their pitiful clenched hands, the fine courage of these poor devils, the desperate charges and attacks made by the poor brave wretches, who are so terrified that they dare not cry out loudly, but with battered chests, with torn bellies, arms and legs only whimper softly for their mothers and cease as soon as one looks at them.

Their sharp, downy, dead faces have the awful expressionlessness of dead children. . . .

I am young, I am twenty years old; yet I know nothing of life but despair, death, fear, and fatuous superficiality cast over an abyss of sorrow. I see how peoples are set against one another, and in silence, unknowingly, foolishly, obediently, innocently slay one another. I see that the keenest brains of the world invent weapons and words to make it yet more refined and enduring. And all men of my age, here and over there, throughout the whole world see these things; all my generation is experiencing these things with me. What would our fathers do if we suddenly stood up and came before them and proffered our account? What do they expect of us if a time ever comes when the war is over? Through the years our business has been killing;—it was our first calling in life. Our knowledge of life is limited to death. What will happen afterwards? And what shall come out of us?

From Erich Maria Remarque, All Quiet on the Western Front.

In their bright blue coats and red trousers, French and Belgian infantrymen made easy targets. Cavalry units, though largely outmoded, survived even as the railroad made the mobilization, organization, and deployment of mass armies possible. Specialists were needed to control the new war machines that heavy industry had created.

The shovel and the machine gun transformed war. The machine gun was not new in 1914, but its strategic value was not fully appreciated before then. The British had used the Maxim machine gun in Africa, but strategists failed to ask how such a destructive weapon would work against an enemy that was equally armed with machine guns instead of spears. Military strategists continued to plan an offensive strategy when the weaponry developed for massive destruction had pushed them into fighting a defensive war from the trenches. Both sides resorted to concentration of artillery, increased use of poison gas, and unrestricted submarine warfare in desperate attempts to break the deadlock caused by meeting armed force with force.

The new emphasis on total victory drove the Central Powers and the Allies to grisly new inventions. Late in the war, the need to break the deadlock of trench warfare ushered in the airplane and the tank. Neither was decisive in altering the course of the war, although the airplane was useful for reconnaissance and for limited bombing and the tank promised the means of breaking through defensive lines. Chlorine gas was first used in warfare by the Germans in 1915. Mustard gas, which was named for its distinctive smell and which caused severe blistering, was introduced two years later. The Germans were the first to use flamethrowers, which were especially effective against mechanized vehicles with vulnerable fuel tanks. Barbed wire, invented in the American Midwest to contain farm animals, became an essential aspect of trench warfare as it marked off the no-man's-land between combatants and prevented surprise attacks.

The technology that had been viewed as a proof of progress was now channeled toward engineering new instruments of death. Some new weapons gave rise to their antidotes; for example, the invention of deadly gas was followed soon after by the invention of gas masks. Each side was capable of matching the other's ability to devise new armaments. Deadlocks caused by technological parity forced both sides to resort to desperate concentrations of men and weaponry that resulted not in decisive battles but in ever-escalating casualty rates. As they improved their efficiency at killing, the European powers were not finding a way to end the war.

The German Offensive

German forces seized the offensive in the west and invaded neutral Belgium at the beginning of August 1914. The Belgians resisted stubbornly but unsuccessfully. Belgian forts were systematically captured, and Brussels, the capital, fell under the German advance on 20 August. After the fall of Belgium, German military might swept into northern France with the intention of defeating the French in six weeks.

Germany on Two Fronts. In the years preceding the war, the German General Staff, unwilling to concentrate all of their troops in the west, had modified the Schlieffen Plan by committing divisions to Germany's eastern frontier. The absence

■ A typical World War I trench. Millions of soldiers lived amid mud, disease, and vermin, awaiting death from enemy shells. After the French army mutiny in 1916, the troops wrung the concession from their commanders that they would not have to charge German machine guns while armed only with rifles.

of the full German fighting force in the west did not appreciably slow the German advance through Belgium. Yet the Germans had underestimated both the cost of holding back the French in Alsace-Lorraine and the difficulty of maneuvering German forces and transporting supplies in an offensive war. Eventually, unexpected Russian advances in the east also siphoned off troops from the west. German forces in the west were so weakened by their offensive that they were unable to swing west of Paris, as planned, and instead chose to enter the French capital from the northeast by crossing the Marne River. This shift exposed the German First Army on its western flank and opened up a gap on its eastern flank.

The First Battle of the Marne. Despite an initial pattern of retreat and a lack of coordination of forces, Allied French and British troops were ready to take advantage of the vulnerabilities in the German advance. In a series of battles between 6 and 10 September 1914 that came to be known as the First Battle of the Marne, the Allies counterattacked and advanced into the gap. The German army was forced to drop back. In the following months, each army tried to outflank the other in what has been called "the race to the sea." By late fall, it was clear that the battles from the Marne north to the border town of Ypres in northwest Belgium near the English Channel had ended an open war of movement on the western front. Soldiers now dug in along a line of battle that changed little in the long three and a half years until March 1918.

The Allies gained a strategic victory in the First Battle of the Marne by resisting the German advance in the fighting that quickly became known as the "miracle" of the Marne. The legend was further enhanced by true stories of French troops being rushed from Paris to the front in taxicabs. Yet the real significance of the Marne lay in the severe miscalculations of military leaders and statesmen on both sides, who had expected a different kind of war. They did not understand that the new technology made a short war unlikely. Nor did they understand the demands that this new kind of warfare would make on civilian populations. Those Parisian taxi drivers foreshadowed how other European civilians would be called on again and again to support the war in the next four years.

"I don't know what is to be done—this isn't war." So spoke Lord Horatio Kitchener (1850–1916), one of the most decorated British generals of his time. He was not alone in his bafflement over the stalemate of trench warfare at the end of 1914. By that time, Germany's greatest fear, a simultaneous war on two fronts, had become a grim reality. The Central Powers were under siege, cut off from the world by the great battlefront in the west and by the Allied blockade at sea. The rules of the game had changed, and the European powers settled in for a long war.

War on the Eastern Front

War on Germany's eastern front was a mobile war, fought over vast distances. The Russian army was the largest in the world. Yet it was crippled from the outbreak of the war by inadequate supplies and poor leadership. At the end of August 1914, the smaller German army, supported by divisions drawn from the west, delivered a devastating defeat to the Russians in the one great battle on the eastern front. At Tannenberg the entire Russian Second Army was destroyed, and about 100,000 Russian soldiers were taken prisoner. Faced with this humiliation, General Aleksandr Vasilievich Samsonov (1859–1914), head of the Russian forces, committed suicide on the field of battle.

The German general Paul von Hindenburg (1847–1934), a veteran of the Franco-Prussian war of 1870, had been recalled from retirement to direct the campaign against the Russians because of his intimate knowledge of the area. Assisted by Quartermaster General Erich Ludendorff (1865–1937), Hindenburg followed the stunning victory of Tannenberg two weeks later with another devastating blow to Russian forces at the Masurian Lakes.

The Russians were holding up their end of the bargain in the Allied war effort, but at great cost. They kept the Germans busy and forced them to divert troops to the eastern front, weakening the German effort to knock France out of the war. In the south, the tsar's troops defeated the Austro-Hungarian army at Lemberg in Galicia in September. This Russian victory gave Serbia a temporary reprieve. But by mid-1915, Germany had thrown the Russians back and was keeping Austria-Hungary propped up in the war. By fall, Russia had lost most of Galicia, the Polish lands of the Russian Empire, Lithuania, and parts of Latvia and Belorussia to the advancing enemy. These losses amounted to 15 percent of Russia's territory and 20 percent of its population. The Russian army staggered, with over one million soldiers taken as prisoners of war and at least as many killed and wounded.

The Russian army, as one of its own officers described it, was being bled to death. Russian soldiers were poorly led into battle or not led at all because of the shortage of officers. Munitions shortages meant that soldiers often went into battle without rifles, armed only with the hope of scavenging arms from their fallen comrades. Despite these difficulties, the Russians, under the direction of General Aleksei Brusilov (1853–1926), commander of the Russian armies in the southern part of the eastern front, remarkably managed to throw back the Austro-Hungarian forces in 1916 and almost eliminated Austria as a military power. Russia's near destruction of the Austrian army benefited Russia's allies tremendously. To protect its partner, Germany was forced to withdraw eight divisions from Italy, alleviating the Allied situation in the Tyrol, and twelve divisions from the western front, providing relief for the French at Verdun and the British at the Somme. In addition, Russia sent troops to the aid of a new member of the Allied camp, Romania, an act that probably further weakened Brusilov's efforts. In response to Brusilov's challenge, the Germans established control over the Austrian army, assigning military command of the coalition to General Ludendorff. But this was the last great campaign on the eastern front and Russia's last show of strength in the Great War.

War on the Western Front

Along hundreds of miles of trenches, the French and British tried repeatedly to expel the Germans from northern France and Belgium. Long periods of inactivity were punctuated by orgies of heavy bloodletting. The German phrase, "All quiet on the western front," was used in military communiques to describe those periods of uneasy calm before the next violent storm.

Verdun.   Military leaders on both sides hoped for a decisive breakthrough that would win the war. In 1916, the Allies

MAP DISCOVERY

World War I

The Central Powers were in the unenviable position of fighting wars on two major fronts. The inset shows the stabilized western front of trench warfare in northern France and Belgium. Why did warfare focus in the west in this area, and why did it bog down for such a long period along this front? How did warfare along the eastern front differ, and why did the eastern front cover a much greater expanse? You will note the major battles in western and eastern Europe and the Ottoman Empire. Why was none of these battles decisive in ending the war? Were the British naval blockade and the German submarine war zone effective? Finally, note the reduced Russian territory as a result of the Treaty of Brest-Litovsk. Why was Russia willing to agree to such a loss of land to Germany before the war ended?

planned a joint strike at the Somme, a river in northern France that flowed west into the English Channel, but the Germans struck first at Verdun, a small fortress city in northeast France. By concentrating great numbers of troops, the Germans outnumbered the French five to two. As General Erich von Falkenhayn (1861–1922), chief of the General Staff of the German army from 1914 to 1916, explained it, the German purpose in attacking Verdun was "to bleed the French white by virtue of our superiority in guns."

On the first day of the battle, one million shells were fired. The battlefield was a living hell as soldiers stumbled across corpse after corpse. Against the German onslaught, French troops were instructed to hold out, though they lacked adequate artillery and reinforcements. General Joseph Joffre (1852–1931), commander-in-chief of the French army, was unwilling to divert reinforcements to Verdun.

The German troops advanced easily through the first lines of defense. But the French held their position for ten long, horrifying months of continuous mass slaughter from February to December 1916. General Henri Philippe Pétain (1856–1951) bolstered morale by constantly rotating his troops such that most of the French army—259 of 330 infantry battalions—saw action at Verdun. Nearly starving and poorly armed, the French stood alone in the bloodiest offensive of the war. Attack strategy backfired on the Germans as their own death tolls mounted.

Pétain and his flamboyant general Robert Georges Nivelle (1856–1924) were both hailed as heroes for fulfilling the instruction to their troops: "They shall not pass." Falkenhayn fared less well and was dismissed from his post. Yet no real winners emerged from the scorched earth of Verdun, where observers could see the nearest thing to desert created in Europe. Verdun was a disaster. The French suffered over half a million total casualties. German casualties were almost as high. A few square miles of territory had changed hands back and forth. In the end, no military advantage was gained, though almost 700,000 lives had been lost. Verdun demonstrated that an offensive war under these conditions was impossible.

The Somme.   Still, new offensives were devised. The British went ahead with their planned offensive on the Somme in July 1916. For an advance of seven miles, 400,000 British and 200,000 French soldiers were killed or wounded. German losses brought the total casualties of this offensive to one million men. Despite his experience at Verdun, French general Robert Nivelle planned his own offensive in the Champagne region in spring 1917. Nivelle's offensive resulted in 40,000 deaths, and he was dismissed. The French army was falling apart; mutiny and insubordination were everywhere.

The British believed that they could succeed where the French had failed. Under General Douglas Haig (1861–1928), the commander-in-chief of British expeditionary forces on the Continent, the British launched an attack in Flanders through the summer and fall of 1917. Known as the Passchendaele offensive, named for the village and ridge in whose "porridge of mud" much of the fighting took place, this campaign resulted in almost 400,000 British soldiers slaughtered for insignificant ter-

ritorial gain. The Allies and the Germans finally recognized that "going over the top" in offensives was not working and could not work. The war must be won by other means.

War on the Periphery

Recognizing the stalemate in the west, the Allies attempted to open up other fronts where the Central Powers might be vulnerable. In the spring of 1915, the Allies were successful in convincing Italy to enter the war on their side by promising that it would receive, at the time of the peace, the South Tyrol and the southern part of Dalmatia and key Dalmatian islands, which would assure Italy's dominance over the Adriatic Sea. By thus capitalizing on Italian antagonism toward Austria-Hungary over control of this territory, the Allies gained 875,000 Italian soldiers for their cause. Although these Italian troops were in no way decisive in the fighting that followed, Great Britain, France, and Russia saw the need to build up Allied support in southern Europe to reinforce Serbian attempts to keep Austrian troops beyond its borders. The Allies also hoped that by pulling Germans into this southern front, some relief might be provided for British and French soldiers on the western front.

Germany, in turn, was well aware of the need to expand its alliances beyond Austria-Hungary if it was to compete successfully against superior Allied forces. Trapped as they were to the east and west, the Central Powers established control over a broad corridor stretching from the North Sea through central Europe and down through the Ottoman Empire to the Suez Canal, which was so vital to British interests.

In the Balkans, where the war had begun, the Serbs were consistently bested by the Austrians. By late 1915, the Serbs were knocked out of the war, having lost one-sixth of their population through war, famine, and disease. The promise of booty persuaded Bulgaria to join Germany and Austria-Hungary. Over the next year and a half, the Allies responded by convincing Romania and then Greece to join them.

War in the Ottoman Empire.   The theater of war continued to expand. Although the Ottoman Empire had joined the war in late 1914 on the side of the Central Powers, its own internal difficulties attenuated its fighting ability. As a multinational empire consisting of Turks, Arabs, Armenians, Greeks, Kurds, and other ethnic minorities, it was plagued by Turkish misrule and Arab nationalism. Hence the Ottoman Empire was the weakest link in the chain of German alliances. Yet it held a crucial position. The Turks could block shipping of vital supplies to Russia through the Mediterranean and Black Seas. Coming to the aid of their Russian ally, a combined British and French fleet attacked Turkish forces at the strait of the Dardanelles in April 1915. In the face of political and military opposition, First Lord of the Admiralty Winston Churchill (1874–1965) supported the idea of opening a new front by sea. Poorly planned and mismanaged, the expedition was a disaster. When the naval effort in the German-mined strait failed, the British foolishly decided to land troops on the Gallipoli peninsula, which extends from the southern coast of

European Turkey. There British soldiers were trapped on the rocky terrain, unable to advance against the Turks, unable to fall back. Gallipoli was the first large-scale attempt at amphibious warfare. The Australian and New Zealand forces (ANZACs) showed great bravery in some of the most brutal fighting of the war. Critics in Britain argued that the only success of the nine-month campaign was its evacuation.

Britain sought to protect its interests in the Suez Canal. Turkish troops menaced the canal effectively enough to terrify the British into maintaining an elaborate system of defense in the area and concentrating large troop reinforcements in Egypt. War with the Ottoman Empire also extended battle into the oil fields of Mesopotamia and Persia. This attempt at a new front was initially a fiasco for the British and Russian forces that threatened Baghdad. The Allies proceeded not only without plans but also without maps. They literally did not know where they were going. Eventually, British forces recovered and took Baghdad in 1917, while Australian and New Zealand troops captured Jerusalem. The tentacles of war spread out, following the path of Western economic and imperial interests throughout the world.

War at Sea.   Most surprising of all was the indecisive nature of the war at sea. The great battleships of the British and German navies avoided confrontation on the high seas. The only major naval battle of the Great War, the Battle of Jutland in the North Sea, took place in early 1916. Each side inflicted damage on the other but, through careful maneuvering, avoided a decisive outcome to the battle. Probably the enormous cost of replacing battleships deterred both the British and the Germans from risking their fleets in engagements on the high seas. With the demands for munitions and equipment on the two great land fronts of the war, neither side could afford to lose a traditional war at sea. Instead, the British used their seapower as a policing force to blockade German trade and strangle the German economy.

The German navy, much weaker than the British, relied on a new weapon, the submarine, which threatened to become decisive in the war at sea. During the first months of the war, submarines were used for reconnaissance, but their battle potential became apparent in 1915. Undergoing technological improvements throughout the war, *Unterseebooten,* or U-boats, as German submarines were called, torpedoed six million tons of Allied shipping in 1917. With cruising ranges as high as 3,600 miles, German submarines attacked Allied and neutral shipping as far away as off the shore of the United States and the Arctic supply line to Russia. Outraged neutral powers considered the Germans to be in violation of international law. The Germans also rejected the requirements of warning an enemy ship and boarding it for investigation as too dangerous for submarines, which were no match for battleships above water. The Allies invented depth charges and mines that were capable of blowing German submarines out of the water. These weapons, combined with the use of the convoy system in the Atlantic and the Mediterranean, produced a successful blockade and antisubmarine campaign that put an end to the German advantage.

ADJUSTING TO THE UNEXPECTED: TOTAL WAR

The Great War differed from all previous European experiences and expectations of armed conflict. Technological advances, equally matched on both sides, introduced a war of attrition, defensive and prolonged. Nineteenth-century wars generally lasted six to eight weeks, were confined to one locale, and were determined by a handful of battles marked by low casualties. Such wars had nothing in common with the long, dirty, lice-infested reality of trench warfare with no end in sight to the slaughter.

The period from 1914 to 1918 marked the first time in history that the productive activities of entire populations were

■ Crew on the deck of a German World War I submarine at sea.

directed toward a single goal: military victory. The Great War became a war of peoples, not just of armies. This unexpected war of attrition required civilian populations to adjust to a situation in which what went on at the battlefront transformed life on the home front. For this reason the Great War became known as history's first *total* war.

Adjusting to the revolutionary concept of **total war,** governments intervened to centralize and control every aspect of economic life. The scale of production and distribution of war-related materials that victory required was unprecedented. To persuade civilians to suffer at home for the sake of the war, leaders pictured the enemy as an evil villain who must be defeated at any cost. The sacrifice required for a total war made total victory necessary. And total victory required an economy that was totally geared to fighting the war.

Mobilizing the Home Front

While soldiers were fighting on the eastern and western fronts, businessmen and politicians at home were creating bureaucratic administrations to control wages and prices, distribute supplies, establish production quotas, and, in general, mobilize human and material resources. The Allies and Central Powers organized civilians of all ages and both sexes to work for the war.

Women's Roles. Women played an essential role on the home front. They had never been isolated from the experiences and hardships of war, but they now found new ways to support the war effort. In cities, women went to work in munitions factories and war-related industries that had previously employed only men. Women filled service jobs, from firefighters to trolley-car conductors, jobs that were essential to the smooth running of industrial society and that men had left vacant. On farms, women literally took up the plow, as both men and horses were requisitioned for the war effort.

By 1918, 650,000 French women were working in war-related industries and in clerical positions in the army, and they had counterparts all over Europe. In Germany, two out of every five munitions workers were women. In Great Britain, the number of women workers jumped from 250,000 at the beginning of the war to five million by the war's end. Women also served in the auxiliary units of the armed services in the clerical and medical corps. In eastern European nations, women entered combat as soldiers. Although most women were displaced from their wartime jobs with the return of men after the armistice, they were as important to the war effort as were the men fighting at the front.

Government Controls. In the first months of the war, the private sector had been left to its own devices, with nearly disastrous results. Shortages, especially of shells, and bottlenecks in production threatened military efforts. Governments were forced to establish controls and to set up state monopolies to guarantee the supplies necessary to wage war. In Germany, industrialists Walter Rathenau (1867–1922) and Alfred

Hugenberg (1865–1951) worked with the government. By the spring of 1915, they had eliminated the German problem of munitions scarcity. France was in trouble six weeks after the outbreak of the war: it had used up half of its accumulated munitions supplies in the First Battle of the Marne. German occupation of France's northern industrial basin further crippled munitions production. Through government intervention, France improvised and relocated its war industries. The British government became involved in production, too, by establishing in 1915 the first Ministry of Munitions under the direction of David Lloyd George (1863–1945). Distinct from the Ministry of War, the Ministry of Munitions was to coordinate military needs with the armaments industry.

In a war that leaders soon realized would be a long one, food supplies assumed paramount importance. As the war pulled men off the farms, production declined. Germany, dependent on food imports and isolated from the world market by the Allied blockade, introduced rationing five months after the outbreak of the war. Other Continental nations followed suit. Government agents set quotas for agricultural producers. Armies were fed and supplied at the expense of domestic populations. Great Britain, which enjoyed a more reliable food supply by virtue of its sea power, did not impose food rationing until 1917.

Silencing Dissent

The strains of total war were becoming apparent. Two years of sacrificing and, in some areas, starving began to take their toll among soldiers and civilians on both sides. With the lack of decisive victories, war weariness was spreading. Work stoppages and strikes, which had virtually ceased with the outbreak of war in 1914, began to increase rapidly in 1916. Between 1915 and 1916 in France, the number of strikes by dissatisfied workers increased by 400 percent. Underpaid and tired workers went on strike, staged demonstrations, and protested exploitation. Labor militancy also intensified in the British Isles and Germany. Women were often in the forefront of these protests throughout Europe. Social peace between unions and governments was no longer held together by patriotic enthusiasm for war.

Politicians, too, began to rethink their suspension of opposition to government policies as the war dragged on. Dissidents among European socialist parties regained their prewar commitment to peace. Most Socialists had enthusiastically supported the declarations of war in 1914. By 1916, the united front that political opponents had presented against the enemy was crumbling under growing demands for peace.

In a total war, unrest at home guaranteed defeat. Governments knew that all opposition to war policies had to be eliminated. In a dramatic extension of the police powers of the state, among both the Allies and the Central Powers, criticism of the government became treason. Censorship was enforced. Propaganda became more virulent. Anyone who spoke for peace was no better than the enemy. The governments of every warring nation resorted to harsh measures.

Parliamentary bodies were stripped of power, civil liberties were suspended, and democratic procedures were ignored. The civilian governments of Premier Georges Clemenceau (1841–1929) in France and Prime Minister Lloyd George in Great Britain resorted to rule by emergency police power to repress criticism. Under Generals von Hindenburg and Ludendorff in Germany, military rule became the order of the day. Nowhere was government as usual possible in total war.

Every warring nation also sought to promote dissension among the populations of its enemies. Germany aided the Easter Rebellion in Ireland in 1916 in the hope that the Irish demand for independence would damage British fighting strength and morale. Germany also supported separatist movements among minority nationalities in the Russian Empire and was responsible for returning the avowed revolutionary V. I. Lenin under escort to Russia in April 1917. The British engaged in similar tactics. The British foreign secretary Arthur Balfour (1848–1930) worked with Zionist leaders in 1917 in drawing up the **Balfour Declaration,** which promised to "look with favor" on the creation of a Jewish homeland in Palestine. The British thereby encouraged Zionist hopes among central European Jews, with the intent of creating difficulties for German and Austrian rulers. Similarly, the British encouraged Arabs to rebel against Turks with the same promise of Palestine.

THE RUSSIAN REVOLUTION AND ALLIED VICTORY

For the Allies, 1917 began with a series of crises. Under the hammering of one costly offensive after another, French morale had collapsed and military discipline was deteriorating. A combined German-Austrian force had eliminated the Allied states of Serbia and Romania. The Italians experienced a military debacle at Caporetto and were effectively out of the war. The peril at sea had increased with the opening of unrestricted U-boat warfare against Allied and neutral ships.

Two events proved decisive in 1917 in determining the course of the war: the collapse of the Russian army and the entry of the United States. Russia, in the throes of domestic revolution, ceased to be an effective opponent, and Germany was able to concentrate more of its resources in the west, fight a one-front war, and utilize the foodstuffs and raw materials of its newly acquired Russian territories to buoy its home front. The war had gone from a stalemate to a state of crisis for both sides. Every belligerent state was experiencing war weariness, and pressures to end the war increased everywhere. Attrition was not working. Attacks were not working. Every country suffered from strikes, food riots, military desertions, and mutinies. Defeatism was everywhere on the rise.

Revolution in Russia

In order to understand Russia's withdrawal from the war, it is important to understand that Russia's ruler, Tsar Nicholas II (1894–1917), presided over an empire in the process of mod-

ernization with widening social divisions in 1914. Nicholas believed that a short, successful war would strengthen his monarchy against the domestic forces of change. Little did Nicholas know, when he committed Russia to the path of war instead of revolution, that he had guaranteed a future of war *and* revolution. He was delivering his nation up to humiliating defeat in global war and a devastating civil war. His own days were numbered, with his fate to be determined at the hands of a Marxist dictatorship.

The Last Tsar.   In 1914, Russia was considered backward by the standards of Western industrial society. Russia still recalled a recent feudal past. The serfs had been freed in the 1860s, but the nature of the emancipation exacerbated tensions in the countryside and peasant hunger for land. Russia's limited, rapid industrialization in the 1880s and 1890s was an attempt to catch up with Great Britain, France, and Germany as a world industrial power. But the speed of such change brought with it severe dislocations, especially in the industrial city of Moscow and the capital, St. Petersburg.

In 1905, the workers of St. Petersburg protested hardships due to cyclical downturns in the economy. On a Sunday in January 1905, the tsar's troops fired on a peaceful mass demonstration in front of the Winter Palace, killing and wounding scores of workers, women, and children who were appealing to the tsar for relief. The event, which came to be known as Bloody Sunday, set off a revolution that spread to Moscow and the countryside. In October 1905, the regime responded to the disruptions with a series of reforms that legalized political parties and established the Duma, or national parliament. Peasants, oppressed by their own burdens of taxation and endemic poverty, launched mass attacks on big landowners throughout 1905 and 1906. The government met workers and peasants' demands with a return to repression in 1907. In the half-decade before the Great War, the Russian state stood as an autocracy of parliamentary concessions blended with severe police controls.

What workers had learned in 1905 was the power and the means of independent organization. Factory committees, trade unions, and *soviets,* or elected workers' councils, proliferated. Despite winning a grant of legal status after 1906, unions gained little in terms of ability to act on behalf of their members. Unrest among factory workers revived on the eve of the Great War, a period of rapid economic growth and renewed trade-union activity. Between January and July 1914, Russia experienced 3,500 strikes. Although economic strikes were considered legal, strikes that were deemed political were not. With the outbreak of war, all collective action was banned as politically dangerous. Protest stopped, but only momentarily. The tsar certainly weighed the workers' actions in his decision to view war as a possible diversion from domestic problems.

Russia was less prepared for war than any of the other belligerents. Undoubtedly, it had more soldiers than other countries, but it lacked arms and equipment. Problems of provisioning such a huge fighting force placed great strains on the domestic economy and on the workforce. Under government coercion to meet the needs of war, industrial output doubled between 1914 and 1917, while agricultural production plummeted. The tsar, who unwisely insisted on commanding his own troops, left the government in the hands of his wife, the Tsarina Alexandra, a German princess by birth, and her eccentric peasant-priest adviser, Rasputin. Scandal, sexual innuendo, and charges of treason surrounded the royal court. The incompetence of a series of unpopular ministers further eroded confidence in the regime.

In the end, the war sharpened long-standing divisions within Russian society. Led by exhausted and starving working women, poorly paid and underfed workers toppled the regime in the bitter winter of March 1917. This event was the beginning of a violent process of revolution and civil war. The tsar abdicated, and all public symbols of the tsardom were destroyed. The banner bearing the Romanov two-headed eagle was torn down; in its place, the Red Flag, the international symbol of revolution, flew over the Winter Palace.

Dual Power. With the tsar's abdication, two centers of authority replaced autocracy. One was the Provisional Government, appointed by the Duma and made up of progressive liberals led by Prince Georgi Lvov (1861–1925), prime minister of the new government, who also served as minister of the interior. Aleksandr Kerenski (1881–1970), the only Socialist in the Provisional Government, served as minister of justice. The members of the new government hoped to establish constitutional and democratic rule.

The other center of authority was the soviets—committees or councils elected by workers and soldiers and supported by radical lawyers, journalists, and intellectuals in favor of socialist self-rule. Party organization and ideological consensus were generally lacking among the soviets, which were quite heterogeneous. The Petrograd Soviet was the most prominent among the councils. (In 1914, the name of St. Petersburg had been changed to the Russian "Petrograd.") This duality of power was matched by duality in policies and objectives and guaranteed a short-lived and unstable regime.

The problems facing the new regime soon became apparent as revolution spread to the provinces and to the battlefront. Peasants, who made up 80 percent of the Russian population, accepted the revolution and demanded land and peace. Without waiting for government directives, peasants began seizing the land. Peasants tried to alleviate some of their suffering by hoarding what little they had. The food crisis of winter persisted throughout the spring and summer, as bread lines lengthened and prices rose. Workers in cities gained better working conditions and higher wages. But wage increases were invariably followed by higher prices that robbed workers of their gains. Real wages declined.

In addition to the problems of land and bread, the war itself presented the new government with other insurmountable difficulties. Hundreds of thousands of Russian soldiers at the front deserted the war, having heard news from home of peasant land grabs and rumors of a new offensive planned for July. The Provisional Government, concerned with Russia's territorial integrity and its position in the international system, continued to honor the tsar's commitments to the Allies by participating in the war. By spring 1917, six to eight million Russian soldiers had been killed, wounded, or captured. The Russian army was incapable of fighting.

The Provisional Government tried everything to convince its people to carry on with the war. In the summer of 1917, the Women's Battalion of Death, composed exclusively of female recruits, was enlisted into the army. Its real purpose, officials admitted, was to "shame the men" into fighting. The all-female unit, like its male counterparts, experienced high losses; 80 percent of the force suffered casualties. The Provisional Government was caught in an impossible situation. It could not withdraw from the war, but neither could it fight. Continued involvement in the lost cause of the war blocked any consideration of social reforms.

While the Provisional Government was trying to deal with the calamities, many members of the intelligentsia, Russia's educated class, whom the tsar had exiled for their political beliefs, now rushed back from western Europe to take part in the great revolutionary experiment. During the months between February and July 1917, theorists of all stripes put their cases before the people, but it was the Marxists, or Social Democrats, who had the greatest impact on the direction of the revolution.

The Social Democrats believed that there were objective laws of historical development that could be discovered. Russia's future could be understood only in terms of the present situation in western Europe. Like Marxists in the West, the Russian Social Democrats split over how best to achieve a socialist state. The more moderate majority, the Mensheviks (meaning "minority"), wanted to work through parliamentary institutions and were willing to cooperate with the Provisional Government. A smaller faction—despite its name—calling themselves **Bolsheviks** (meaning "majority") dedicated themselves to preparation for a revolutionary upheaval. After April 1917, the Bolsheviks refused to work with the Provisional Government and organized themselves to take control of the Petrograd Soviet.

Lenin and the Opposition to War. The leader of the Bolsheviks was Vladimir Ilyich Ulyanov (1870–1924). Best known by his revolutionary name, Lenin, he had just returned from Switzerland to reassume leadership. Forty-seven years old at the time of the revolution, Lenin had spent most of his life in exile or in prison. More a pragmatist than a theoretician, he argued for a disciplined party of professional revolutionaries, a vanguard who would lead the peasants and workers in a socialist revolution against capitalism. In contrast to the Mensheviks, he argued that the time was ripe for a successful revolution and that it could be achieved through the soviets. Since they represented peasants and workers, he argued, they provided the democratic majority base needed for a true Marxist revolution.

Immediately on arrival in Petrograd, Lenin threw down the gauntlet to the Provisional Government. In his **April Theses** he promised the Russian people peace, land, and bread. The war must be ended immediately, he argued, because it represented an imperialist struggle that was benefiting

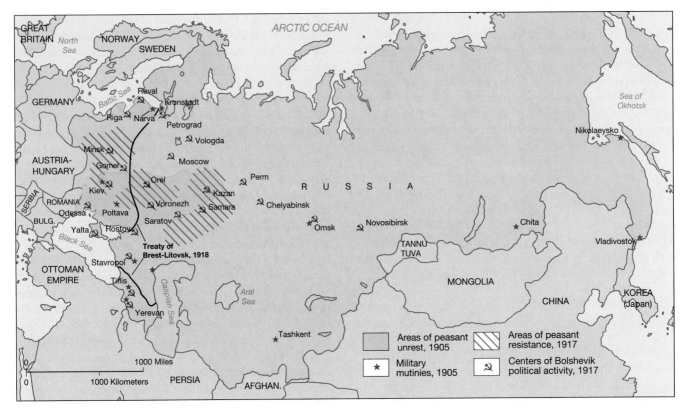

■ Revolution and Civil War in Russia, 1914–1920. Revolutionary and civil unrest was greatest in those areas of Russia
with the greatest concentrations of peasants. Kulaks, the more prosperous peasants, were severely repressed for resisting the requisitioning of food after 1918.

capitalists. Russia's duty was to withdraw and wait for a world
revolution. This was more than rhetoric on Lenin's part. His
years in exile in the West and news of mutinies and worker
protests convinced him that a Europe-wide revolution was
imminent. His revolutionary policies on land were little more
than endorsements of the seizures already taking place all over
Russia. Even his promises of bread had little substance. But on
the whole, the April Theses constituted a clear critique of the
policies of the Provisional Government.

Dissatisfaction with the Provisional Government increased
as the war dragged hopelessly on and bread lines lengthened.
In the midst of these calamities a massive popular demonstration erupted in July 1917 against the Provisional Government
and in favor of the soviets, which excluded the upper classes
from voting. The Provisional Government responded with repressive force reminiscent of the tsardom. The July Days were
proof of the growing influence of the Bolsheviks among the
Russian people. Although the Bolshevik leadership had withdrawn support for the demonstrations at the last moment,
Bolshevik rank-and-file party members strongly endorsed the
protest. Indisputably, Bolshevik influence was growing in the
soviets despite repression and persecution of its leaders. Lenin
was forced to flee to Finland.

As a result of the July Days, Kerenski, who had been heading
the Ministry of Justice, was named prime minister and continued the Provisional Government's moderate policies. To protect

the government from a coup on the right, Kerenski permitted
the arming of the Red Guards, the workers' militia units of the
Petrograd Soviet. The traditional chasm between the upper and
lower classes was widening as the policies of the Provisional
Government conflicted with the demands of the soviets.

The October Revolution.   The second revolution came in
November (October in the Russian calendar). This time it was
not a spontaneous street demonstration but the seizure of the
Russian capital by the Red Guards of the Petrograd Soviet. The
revolution was carefully planned and orchestrated by Lenin and
his vanguard of Bolsheviks, who now possessed majorities in the
soviets in Moscow, Petrograd, and other industrial centers.
Having returned surreptitiously from Finland, Lenin moved
through the streets of Petrograd disguised in a curly wig and
head bandages, watching the Red Guard seize centers of communication and public buildings. The military action was
directed by Lev Bronstein, better known by his revolutionary
name, Leon Trotsky (1879–1940). The Bolshevik chairman of
the Petrograd Soviet, Trotsky used the Red Guard to seize political control and arrest the members of the Provisional
Government. Kerenski escaped and fled the city.

The takeover was achieved with almost no bloodshed and
was immediately endorsed by an All-Russian Congress of
Soviets, which consisted of representatives of local soviets
from throughout the nation who were in session amid the

CHRONOLOGY
THE RUSSIAN REVOLUTION

January–July 1914	Protests and strikes
30 July 1914	Russia enters World War I
March 1917	First Russian Revolution: Abdication of Tsar Nicholas II
March 1917	Creation of Provisional Government
April 1917	Bolsheviks take control of Petrograd
July 1917	Massive demonstration against Provisional Government; Lenin is forced to flee Russia
November 1917	Bolsheviks and Red Guards seize political control in what comes to be known as the October Revolution
March 1918	Russia withdraws from World War I and signs Treaty of Brest-Litovsk
July 1918	Tsar Nicholas II and family are executed

takeover of the capital. A Bolshevik regime under Lenin now ruled Russia. Tsar Nicholas II and the royal family were executed by Bolshevik revolutionaries in July 1918.

The Treaty of Brest-Litovsk. Lenin immediately set to work to end the Great War for Russia. After months of negotiation, Russia signed a separate peace with the Germans in March 1918 in the **Treaty of Brest-Litovsk.** By every measure, the treaty was a bitter humiliation for the new Soviet regime. The territorial losses sustained were phenomenal. In a vast amputation, Russia was reduced to the size of its Muscovite period: it recognized the independence of the Ukraine, Georgia, and Finland; it relinquished its Polish territories, the Baltic States, and part of Byelorussia to Germany and Austria-Hungary; it handed over other territories on the Black Sea to Turkey. Lenin believed that he had no choice: he needed to buy time in order to consolidate the revolution at home, and he hoped for a socialist revolution in Germany that would soften the results of the treaty.

The Treaty of Brest-Litovsk was judged a betrayal, not only outside Russia among the Allied powers, but also inside Russia among some army officers who had sacrificed much for the tsar's war. To those military men, the Bolsheviks were no more than German agents who held the country in their sway.

To deal with the anarchy caused by the fratricidal struggle, Lenin had to strengthen the government's dictatorial elements at the expense of its democratic ones. The new Soviet state used state police to suppress all opposition. The dictatorship of the proletariat yielded to the dictatorship of the repressive forces.

In the course of the civil war, Lenin was no more successful than Kerenski and the Provisional Government had been in solving the problems of food supplies. Human costs of the civil war were high, with more than 800,000 soldiers dead on both sides and two million civilian deaths from dysentery and diseases caused by poor nutrition. Industrial production ceased, and people fled towns to return to the countryside.

The United States Enters the Great War

The Allies longed for the entry of the United States into the war. Although the United States was a neutral country, it had become an important supplier to the Allies from early in the war. American trade with the Allies had jumped from $825 million in 1914 to $3.2 billion in 1916. American bankers also made loans and extended credit to the Allies to the amount of $2.2 billion. The United States had made a sizable investment in the Allied war effort, and its economy was prospering.

Beginning with the sinking of the *Lusitania* in 1915, German policy on the high seas had incensed the American public. Increased U-boat activity in 1916 led President Woodrow Wilson (1856–1924) to issue a severe warning to the Germans to cease submarine warfare. However, the Germans were desperate, and the great advantage of submarines was in sneak attacks, a procedure that was against the international rules that required a warning. Germany initiated a new phase of unrestricted submarine warfare on 1 February 1917, when the German ambassador informed the U.S. government that U-boats would sink on sight all ships, including passenger ships, even those that were neutral and unarmed.

The United States Declares War. German machinations in Mexico were also revealed on 25 February 1917, with the interception of a telegram from Arthur Zimmermann (1864–1940), the German foreign minister. The telegram communicated Germany's willingness to support Mexico's recovery of "lost territory" in New Mexico, Arizona, and Texas in return for Mexican support of Germany in the event of U.S. entry into the war. American citizens were outraged. On 2 April 1917, Wilson, who had won the presidential election of 1916 on the promise of peace, asked the U.S. Congress for a declaration of war against Germany.

The entry of the United States was the turning point in the war, tipping the scales dramatically in favor of the Allies. The United States contributed its naval power to the large Allied convoys that formed to protect shipping against German attacks. In a total war, control and shipment of resources had become crucial issues, and it was in these areas that the U.S. entry gave the Allies indisputable superiority. The United States also sent "over there" tens of thousands of conscripts fighting with the American Expeditionary Forces under the leadership of General John "Black Jack" Pershing (1860–1948). They reinforced British and French troops and gave a vital boost to morale.

The U.S. government was new to the business of coordinating a war effort, but it displayed great ingenuity in creating a wartime bureaucracy that increased a small military establishment of 210,000 soldiers to 9.5 million young men registered before the beginning of summer 1917. By July 1918, the Americans were sending a phenomenal 300,000 soldiers a month to Europe. By the end of the war, two million Americans had traveled to Europe to fight in the war.

The U.S. entry is significant not just because it provided reinforcements, fresh troops, and fresh supplies to the beleaguered Allies. From a broader perspective, it marked a shift in the nature of international politics: Europe could no longer handle its own affairs and settle its own differences without outside help.

U.S. troops, although numerous, were not well trained, and they relied on France and Great Britain for their arms and equipment. But the Germans were aware that they could not hold out indefinitely against this superior Allied force. Austria-Hungary was effectively out of the war. Germany had no replacements for its fallen soldiers, but it was able to transfer troops from Russia, Romania, and Macedonia to the west. Realizing that its only chance of victory lay in swift action, the German high command decided on a bold measure: one great, final offensive that would knock the combined forces of Great Britain, France, and the United States out of the war once and for all by striking at a weak point and smashing through enemy lines. It almost worked.

German Defeat.   Known as the Ludendorff offensive, after the general who devised it, the final German push began in March 1918. Secretly amassing tired troops from the eastern front who had been pulled back after the Russian withdrawal, the Germans counted on the element of surprise to enable them to break through a weak sector in the west. On the first day of spring, Ludendorff struck. The larger German force gained initial success against weakened British and French forces. Yet in spite of breaches in defense, the Allied line held. The Allied Supreme Commander, General Ferdinand Foch (1851–1929), coordinated the war effort that withstood German offensives throughout the spring and early summer of 1918.

The final drive came in mid-July. More than one million German soldiers had already been killed, wounded, or captured in the months between March and July. German prisoners of war gave the French details of Ludendorff's plan. The Germans, now exposed and vulnerable, were placed on the defensive. The German army was rapidly disintegrating. On the other side, tanks, plentiful munitions, and U.S. reinforcements fueled an Allied offensive that began in late September. The German army retreated, destroying property and equipment as it went. With weak political leadership and indecision in Berlin, the Germans held on until early November. The end finally came after four years of war. On 11 November 1918, an armistice signed by representatives of the German and Allied forces took effect.

CHRONOLOGY
FIGHTING THE GREAT WAR

1905	Development of the Schlieffen Plan
28 June 1914	Assassination of Archduke Franz Ferdinand and his wife, Sophie
28 July 1914	Austria-Hungary declares war on Serbia
30 July–4 August 1914	Russia, France, Britain, and Germany declare war in accordance with system of alliances
August 1914	Germany invades Belgium
6–10 September 1914	First Battle of the Marne
1915	Germany introduces chlorine gas
April 1915–January 1916	Gallipoli Campaign
May 1915	Sinking of the *Lusitania*
February–December 1916	Battle at Verdun
1917	First use of mustard gas
2 April 1917	United States enters war
March 1918	Russia withdraws
11 November 1918	Armistice

The war had dragged on for slightly more than four years with great destruction and loss of life on both sides. Of the 70 million who were mobilized, about one in eight were killed. Battlefields of scorched earth and mud-filled ditches, silent at last, scarred once-fertile countrysides as grim memorials to history's first total war. In the end, only the entry of the United States into the war on the side of the Allies brought an end to the misery and bloodletting. The task of settling the peace now loomed.

SETTLING THE PEACE

In the aftermath of war, the task of the victors was to devise a settlement that would guarantee peace and stabilize Europe. Russia was excluded from the negotiations because of its withdrawal from the Allied camp in 1917, but much of what happened in the peace settlements reflected concern with the challenge of revolution that the new Soviet Russia represented. A variety of goals marked the peace talks: the idealistic desire to create a better world, the patriotic pursuit of self-defense, the commitment to self-determination of nations (the right of a people to determine their own form of government), and the fixing of blame for the outbreak of the war. In the end, the peace treaties satisfied none of these goals. Meanwhile, Russia's new leaders carefully watched events in the West, looking for opportunities that might permit them to extend their revolution to central Europe.

From January to June 1919, an assembly of nations convened in Paris to draw up the new European peace. Although the primary task of settling the peace fell to the Council of Four—Premier Georges Clemenceau of France, Prime Minister David Lloyd George of Great Britain, Prime Minister Vittorio Emanuele Orlando of Italy, and President Woodrow Wilson of the United States—small states, newly formed states, and non-European states, Japan in particular, joined in the task of forging the peace. The states of Germany, Austria-Hungary, and Soviet Russia were excluded from the negotiating tables where the future of Europe was to be determined.

Wilson's Fourteen Points

President Wilson, who captured international attention with his liberal views on the peace, was the central figure of the conference. He was firmly committed to the task of shaping a better world. Before the end of the war, he had proclaimed the **Fourteen Points** as a guideline to the future peace and as an appeal to the people of Europe to support his policies. Believing that secret diplomacy and the alliance system were responsible for the events leading up to the declaration of

war in 1914, he put forward as a basic principle "open covenants of peace, openly arrived at." Other points included the reduction of armaments, freedom of commerce and trade, self-determination of peoples, and a general association of nations to guarantee the peace. The Fourteen Points were, above all, an idealistic statement of the principles for a good and lasting peace. Point 14, which stipulated "mutual guarantees of independence and territorial integrity" through the establishment of the League of Nations, was endorsed by the peace conference. The League of Nations, which the United States refused to join in spite of Wilson's advocacy, was intended to arbitrate all future disputes among states and to keep the peace.

Georges Clemenceau of France was motivated primarily by a concern for his nation's security. France had suffered the greatest losses of the war in both human lives and property destroyed. To prevent a resurgent Germany, Clemenceau supported a variety of measures to cripple Germany as a military force on the Continent. Germany was disarmed. The territory west of the Rhine River was demilitarized, with occupation by Allied troops to last for a period of 15 years. With Russia unavailable as a partner to contain Germany, France supported the creation of a series of states in eastern Europe carved out of former Russian, Austrian, and German territory. Wilson supported these new states out of a concern for self-determination of peoples. Clemenceau supported them for reasons of French security.

Much time and energy were devoted to redrawing the map of Europe. New states were created out of the lands of three failed empires. On the basis of self-determination, Finland,

■ The representatives of the victorious Allies at Versailles: (left to right) David Lloyd George of Great Britain, Vittorio Orlando of Italy, Georges Clemenceau of France, and Woodrow Wilson of the United States.

Latvia, Estonia, Lithuania, Poland, Czechoslovakia, Austria, Hungary, and Yugoslavia were all granted nation-state status. However, the rights of ethnic and cultural minorities were violated in some cases because of the impossibility of redrawing the map of Europe strictly according to the principle of self-determination. In spite of good intentions, every new nation had its own national minority, a situation that held the promise of future troubles.

Treaties and Territories

The peace conference produced separate treaties with each of the defeated nations: Austria, Hungary, Turkey, Bulgaria, and Germany. The Austria settlement acknowledged the funda-mental disintegration of the Austrian Empire, recognizing an independent Czechoslovakian republic and preparing the way for a fusing of Croatia, Dalmatia, Bosnia and Herzegovina with the Kingdom of Serbia, into the nation of Yugoslavia. Hungary and Poland also emerged as independent nations thanks to territorial losses by Germany and Austria Hungary. Bulgaria lost territory on the Aegean Sea to Greece, and Yugoslavia assumed control of Bulgarian holdings in Macedonia. Romania gained Hungarian and Bulgarian territory.

In the Middle East, a separate treaty acknowledged Great Britain's mandate in Palestine, Mesopotamia, and Transjordan; and France's mandate in Syria. Hejaz emerged as an independent state. Many aspects of the postwar settlement affecting Turkey and the Middle East were renegotiated in the early 1920s, but British and French gains were preserved, and Hejaz remained as an independent state.

In November 1917, the British affirmed its support of the creation in Palestine of a national home for the Jewish people. This affirmation, known as the Balfour Declaration, was made by Lord Balfour on behalf of "His Majesty's Government" and was considered as a violation of promises made to the Arabs during the war that they would be given control of Palestine in return for supporting the Allied war effort. Although Arab rulers were given control of British mandates, and Prince Faisal assumed the title of king of Iraq, Arab resentment festered as increased numbers of European Jews moved into Palestine and Arab hopes for the creation of an Arab kingdom were dashed.

Amidst these other treaty negotiations, the treaty signed with Germany on 28 June 1919, known as the **Treaty of Versailles,** dealt exclusively with defeated Germany. In that treaty, signed in the great Versailles palace outside of Paris, the Allies imposed blame for the war on Germany and its expansionist aims in the famous War Guilt Clause. According to that clause, the war was Germany's fault, and Germany

■ Europe After World War I. The need for security on the Continent led France to support a buffer zone of new nations between Russia and Germany, carved out of the former Austrian Empire. German territory along the French border was demilitarized out of the same concern for protection.

must be made to pay. According to the treaty, "compensation will be made by Germany for all damage done to the civilian population of the Allies and their property by the aggression of Germany by land, by sea and from the air." Reparations, once the price of defeat, were now exacted as compensation for damages inflicted by a guilty aggressor.

The principle of punitive reparations was included in the German settlement. Germany learned it had to make a down payment of $5 billion against a future bill of $32 billion; had to hand over a significant proportion of its merchant ships, including all vessels of more than 1,600 tons; had to lose all German colonies; and had to deliver coal to neighboring countries. In addition, Germany lost the territory gained from Russia in 1918; returned Alsace and Lorraine to France; ceded territory to Belgium and eventually to Lithuania; and gave up parts of Prussia with large Polish populations. Furthermore, Germany lost control of the Saar, a coal-producing region, to France for fifteen years; and the German Baltic port of Danzig was declared an international "free city." By stripping Germany of key resources, territory and population, its ability to pay reparations was also weakened. These harsh clauses dictated by the determination of German war guilt, more than any other aspect of the peace settlement, came to haunt the Allies in the succeeding decades.

In the end, no nation obtained what it wanted from the peace settlement. The defeated nations believed that they had been badly abused. The victorious nations were aware of the compromises they had reluctantly accepted. Cooperation among nations was essential if the treaty was to work successfully. It had taken the combined resources, not only of France and the British Empire but also of Russia with its vast population and the United States with its great industrial and financial might, to defeat the power of Germany and the militarily ineffective Austro-Hungarian Empire. A new and stable balance of power depended on the participation of Russia, the United States, and the British Empire. But Russia was excluded from and hostile to the peace settlement, the United States was uncommitted to it, and the British Empire declined to guarantee it. All three Great Powers backed off from their European responsibilities at the end of the war. By 1920, all aspects of the treaty, but especially the reparations clause, had been questioned and criticized by the very governments that had written and accepted them. The search for a lasting peace had just begun.

CONCLUSION

By every measure, the Great War was disastrously expensive. Some European nations suffered more than others, but all endured significant losses of life, property, and productive capacity. The cost in human lives was enormous. In western Europe, 8.5 million were dead; total casualties amounted to 37.5 million. France lost 20 percent of its men between the ages of 20 and 44, Germany lost 15 percent, and Great Britain lost 10 percent. The war also resulted in huge losses in productive capacity. National economies buckled under the weight of foreign debts and resorted to a variety of methods to bail themselves out, including taxes, loans, and currency inflation. The people of Europe continued to pay for the war long after the fighting had ended.

The big winner in the war was the United States, which was now a creditor nation holding billions of dollars of loans to the Allies and operating in new markets established during the war. The shift was not a temporary move but a structural change. The United States now took its place as a Great Power in the international system. The world of 1914 was gone. What was to replace it was still very much in flux. To the east, Russia was engaged in a vast experiment of building a new society. In the west, the absence of war was not peace.

QUESTIONS FOR REVIEW

1. Why did so many in Europe look forward to war by the summer of 1914, and what had they done to bring it about?
2. How and why did the Great War differ so much from the expectations of both the generals and the majority of Europeans?
3. What is total war, and what made World War I the first such war in history?
4. In what ways did the Great War contribute to revolution in Russia?
5. How was peace at last achieved, and what were the terms of that peace?

KEY TERMS

Allies, *p. 522*

April Theses, *p. 531*

Balfour Declaration, *p. 530*

Bolsheviks, *p. 531*

Central Powers, *p. 522*

Fourteen Points, *p. 535*

Schlieffen Plan, *p. 521*

soviets, *p. 530*

total war, *p. 529*

Treaty of Brest-Litovsk, *p. 533*

Treaty of Versailles, *p. 536*

DISCOVERING WESTERN CIVILIZATION ONLINE

You can obtain more information about war and revolution between 1914 and 1920 at the websites listed below. See also the Companion Website that accompanies this text, www.ablongman.com/kishlansky, which contains an online study guide and additional resources.

The War Europe Expected

Photos and Posters of the Great War

www.geocities.com/SoHo/Gallery/8054

These are sites of posters, photos, and art of World War I.

A New Kind of Warfare

Military History: World War I (1914–1918)

wps.cfc.dnd.ca/links/milhist/wwi.html

Sponsored by Canadian Forces College, this site provides an extensive set of links about World War I with emphasis on military history.

Adjusting to the Unexpected: Total War

World War I: Trenches on the Web

www.worldwar1.com/

This site on World War I is sponsored by the History Channel.

The Great War (1914–1918)

www.pitt.edu/~pugachev/greatwar/ww1.html

A comprehensive site containing primary text, summaries, and photos of the major events in World War I.

The War Poems & Manuscripts of Wilfred Owen

www.hcu.ox.ac.uk/jtap/warpoems.htm

This site contains 57 of Wilfred Owen's war poems.

The Russian Revolution and Allied Victory

Russian Revolution Resources

www.historyguide.org/europe/rusrev_links.html

This site provides electronic texts in English of Lenin and Trotsky and several other links to sites on the Russian Revolution.

Settling the Peace

The Versailles Treaty

history.acusd.edu/gen/text/versaillestreaty/vercontents.html

This site is devoted to the Versailles Treaty, including the text of all articles of the treaty.

SUGGESTIONS FOR FURTHER READING

The War Europe Expected

Keith Robbins, *The First World War* (Oxford: Oxford University Press, 1984). The author explores the major cultural, political, military, and social developments between 1914 and 1918, including the course of the land war and modes of warfare.

Jeffrey Verhey, *The Spirit of 1914: Militarism, Myth, and Mobilization in Germany* (Cambridge: Cambridge University Press, 2000). The author captures the fervor and patriotism that surrounded the August experiences and the declaration of war and chronicles the survival of the memory of the "spirit of 1914" in the postwar period.

A New Kind of Warfare

Roger Chickering, *Imperial Germany and the Great War, 1914–1918* (Cambridge: Cambridge University Press, 1998). The author offers a synthetic treatment of the history of the war and its impact on German society.

Frans Coetzee and Marilyn Shevin-Coetzee, eds., *Authority, Identity and the Social History of the Great War* (Providence: Berghahn Books, 1995). Recognizing that 1914 marks the be-

ginning of the twentieth century, contributors examine the variety of national responses involved in waging total war and stress the interrelatedness of the home fronts and the battlefronts in affecting individual lives and identities.

Mark Cornwall, *The Undermining of Austria-Hungary: The Battle for Hearts and Minds* (New York: St. Martin's Press, 2000). This study presents extensive research on how propaganda was used by and against Austria-Hungary as a weapon of war.

Paul Fussell, *The Great War and Modern Memory* (New York: Oxford University Press, 2000). This twenty-fifth anniversary edition is a cultural history of World War I that treats the patterns and tendencies in war literature within the framework of a literary tradition.

John Keegan, *The First World War* (New York: Alfred A. Knopf, Inc., 1998). Keegan offers the definitive military history of the war based on diaries, letters, and reports, and in so doing illuminates the origins and progress of the war and the experience of the combatants.

Hew Strachan, ed., *The Oxford Illustrated History of the First World War* (Oxford: Oxford University Press, 1998). This extensively illustrated volume contains 23 chapters on key themes in the history of the Great War covering military issues, the home front, and the role of propaganda.

Adjusting to the Unexpected: Total War

Roger Chickering and Stig Förster, eds., *Great War, Total War: Combat and Mobilization on the Western Front, 1914–1918* (Cambridge: Cambridge University Press, 2000). In a collection of specialist essays, the authors consider the nineteenth-century origins of total industrialized warfare in search of a consensus on what constitutes total war.

Claire A. Culleton, *Working-Class Culture, Women, and Britain, 1914–1921* (New York: St. Martin's Press, 1999). A cultural and social history of British working-class women's experiences.

Belinda J. Davis, *Home Fires Burning: Food, Politics, and Everyday Life in World War I Berlin* (Chapel Hill: University of North Carolina Press, 2000). This thorough study examines the actions of women, especially poorer women, in Berlin during the war and the impact they had on politics and policy.

Patrick Fridenson, ed., *The French Home Front, 1914–1918* (Providence: Berg Publishers, 1992). The collection of articles demonstrates that unity on the home front concealed deep divisions, which led to open resistance and a redefined political universe at the end of the war.

Susan R. Grayzel, *Women's Identities at War: Gender, Motherhood, and Politics in Britain and France During the First World War* (Chapel Hill: University of North Carolina Press, 1999). A carefully documented cultural history of women's roles in World War I on the French and British home fronts.

Aviel Roshwald and Richard Stites, eds., *European Culture in the Great War: The Arts, Entertainment, and Propaganda, 1914–1918* (Cambridge: Cambridge University Press, 1999). This volume encompasses Europe to include western and eastern Europe and the South Slavic lands and examines the relationship between culture and politics during the war.

Jay Winter, Geoffrey Parker, and Mary Habeck, eds., *The Great War and the Twentieth Century* (New Haven, CT: Yale University Press, 2000). This volume of essays by leading scholars contributes to a comparative history of total war in the twentieth century.

The Russian Revolution and Allied Victory

Jane Burbank, *Intelligentsia and Revolution: Russian Views of Bolshevism, 1917–1922* (New York: Oxford University Press, 1982). The author examines the thinking of Russian intellectuals from the beginnings of revolution to the consolidation of Bolshevik power.

Sheila Fitzpatrick, *The Russian Revolution, 1917–1932* (Oxford: Oxford University Press, 1982). An analysis of the October Revolution of 1917 from the perspective of Stalinist society. The February and October revolutions of 1917, the civil war, and the economic policies of the 1920s are treated as various aspects of a single revolutionary movement.

Jane McDermid and Anna Hillyar, *Midwives of the Revolution: Female Bolsheviks and Women Workers in 1917* (Athens, OH: Ohio University Press, 1999). This work provides a good overview of the importance of women's actions in the Russian Revolution.

Settling the Peace

Manfred E. Boemeke, Gerald D. Feldman, Elisabeth Glaser, eds., *The Treaty of Versailles: A Reassessment After 75 Years* (Cambridge: Cambridge University Press, 1998). The volume is a synthetic reappraisal of the peace treaty, divergent peace aims, and postwar context in which it was developed.

David Stevenson, *The First World War and International Politics* (Oxford: Oxford University Press, 1988). A study of the global ramifications of World War I, this work traces the development of war aims on both sides, the reasons peace negotiations failed, and why compromise proved elusive.

For a list of additional titles related to this chapter's topics, please see www.ablongman.com/kishlansky.

Chapter 27

THE EUROPEAN SEARCH FOR STABILITY, 1920–1939

The Visual Record

THE HARSH LESSONS OF HYPERINFLATION

For many who survived the horrors of the Great War, worse disruptions were in store. Inflation, like combat, wreaked havoc with people's lives. During the war, prices had doubled in Great Britain, the United States, Germany, Canada, and Japan. Prices had tripled in France and Sweden; in Italy, they had quadrupled. But all of that was nothing compared to what happened after the war in Germany, Austria, Hungary, Poland, and Russia. Inflation was so great, with prices increasing astronomically—by tens of thousands of times as much—that a new term had to be created for the runaway inflation: hyperinflation. As prices reached staggering heights, currencies collapsed. In Germany in 1918, one prewar gold mark was worth two paper marks; by 1923, it took one billion paper marks to match a single gold mark in value. The currency was worthless.

In war it is important to identify the enemy. So too with hyperinflation did people seek out the adversary. The German expressionist artist George Grosz (1893–1959) was renowned for portraying the decadence and corruption of bourgeois society in the 1920s. In the painting shown here entitled *The Pillars of Society,* Grosz caricatured postwar Germany as composed of corrupt judges, greedy businessmen, mercenary militarists, and hypocritical pacifists.

Many believed that the postwar republican government of Germany was to blame because it had accepted a harsh peace treaty and made reparations payments. Socialists and Communists were singled out for special disdain. Jewish politicians, bankers, and financiers became scapegoats for Germany's economic problems. Confidence in the state evaporated. Inflation began in Germany during the war as the government printed money rather than levying taxes to pay off war debts. After the war, inflation continued because big business, in need of new capital, and organized labor, in search of jobs, benefited from it. The inflation was further aggravated by depreciation of the currencies in central and eastern European countries. The Allied demands for reparations payments further undermined confidence in the mark. The result was that double-digit inflation turned into hyperinflation in the spring of 1922. When the French army occupied the Ruhr and the German government printed money to subsidize the miners and trainmen who were conducting passive resistance, inflation became astronomical.

More and more paper money came into circulation without any corresponding increase in the amount of goods and services. As the value of money plummeted, prices soared. A handful of apples cost cartloads of paper currency—hundreds of billions of marks—at the

height of the inflation in the summer of 1923. People were paid twice a day so that they could rush to stores during their breaks and spend their earnings before their money became worth even less. Working people were malnourished; the unemployed starved. Only one in three German workers was fully employed by the end of 1923. With soaring prices, people lost security and stability just as surely as if they had been in a military upheaval.

Looking Ahead

In this chapter, we begin with a geographical tour of Europe that allows us to consider how economic and security issues *fueled national and territorial tensions. The Germans blamed the French for their reparations demands and their invading troops for the plight of Germany. Hyperinflation had extremely negative repercussions for democracy, as extremists on both the left and right blamed their liberal political leaders. When the Great Depression that began in 1929 hit European economies, the fear of new inflation prevented governments from using deficit spending to bring back prosperity. In Italy and Germany, fascist dictatorships promised solutions to all economic problems. People, having grown cynical and defiant through suffering, sought security in extraordinary and extrademocratic solutions.* ➤

GEOGRAPHICAL TOUR
Europe After 1918

The armistice that ended World War I in 1918 did not stop the process of social upheaval and transformations challenging attempts to restore order throughout Europe (see **Map A**). In 1918, parts of war-torn Europe faced the possibility of revolution. Russia, where revolution had destroyed tsardom, expectantly watched revolutionary developments in countries from the British Isles to eastern Europe. The Bolshevik leaders of Russia's revolution counted on the capitalist system to destroy itself. But that did not happen. By 1921, revolutions had been brutally crushed in Berlin, Munich, and Budapest. The Soviets, meanwhile, had won the civil war against those who opposed the Revolution and survived the intervention of the British, French, Japanese, and Americans. But the new Russian regime was diplomatically isolated and in a state of almost total economic collapse.

In 1917–1918, the United States had played a significant and central role in the waging of war and in the pursuit of peace. Under President Woodrow Wilson, who urged his country to guarantee European security and guide Europe's future, the American nation seemed promising as an active and positive force in international politics. By 1921, however, the United States had retreated to a position not of isolation, but of selective involvement. With one giant, Russia, devastated and isolated, and the other, the United States, reluctant, Europeans faced an uncertain future.

New Nation-States, New Problems

Before World War I, east-central Europe was a region divided among four great empires: the Ottoman, the Habsburg, the Russian, and the German. Under the pressure of defeat, those empires collapsed into their component national parts, and

■ **Map A. Europe After 1918.** The peace settlement dismantled the four great empires in Europe—the Ottoman, Habsburg, Russian, and German—and created new sovereign states.

territories. Romania swelled, fed on a diet of settlement concessions.

The Instability of Self-Determination.   World War I victor nations hoped that the new political geography of Europe would stabilize European affairs; they could not have been more wrong. They erred in their calculations in important ways. First, many of the new states were internally unstable precisely because of the principle of national self-determination, the idea that nationalities had the right to rule themselves. Honoring the rights of nationalities was simple in the abstract, but application of the principle proved complicated and at times impossible. Religious, linguistic, and ethnic diversity abounded, and recognizing one nationality often meant ignoring the rights of other ethnic groups. In Czechoslovakia, for example, the Czechs dominated the Slovaks and the Germans, even though the Czechs were fewer in number. Ethnic unrest plagued all of eastern Europe. Minority tensions weakened and destabilized the fragile governments.

Creating cohesive national economic units proved to be an insurmountable task for newly formed governments and administrations that lacked both resources and experience. Low productivity, unemployment, and overpopulation characterized most of east-central Europe. Attempts to industrialize and to develop new markets confronted many obstacles. Much of the land was farmed on a subsistence basis. What agricultural surplus was created was difficult to sell abroad. East-central Europeans, including Poles, Czechs, Yugoslavs, and Romanians, all tied to France through military and political commitments, were excluded from western European markets and were isolated economically from their treaty allies. Economic ties with Germany endured in ways that perpetuated economic dependence and threatened future survival.

Border Disputes.   Common borders produced tensions over territories. The peace settlements made no one happy. Poland quarreled with Lithuania, and Czechoslovakia vied with Poland over territorial claims. Poland, as was noted in Chapter 26, actually went to war with Russia for six months in 1920 in an effort to reclaim the Ukraine and expand its borders to what they had been more than a century earlier. The Bolsheviks counterattacked and tried to turn the conflict into a revolutionary war to spread communism to central Europe. The Poles turned the Russians back, and the Treaty of Riga, signed in March 1921, gave Poland much, but not all, of the territory it claimed. The treaty also left the Soviets with yet one more grievance against western capitalists in general and Poland in particular.

Hungary, having lost the most territory in World War I, held the distinction of having the greatest number of territorial grievances against its neighbors—Czechoslovakia, Romania, and Yugoslavia. Yugoslavia made claims against Austria. Bulgaria sought territories controlled by Greece and Romania. Ethnicity, strategic considerations, and economic

■ **Map B. East-Central Europe.** A dozen sovereign states were created in East-Central Europe in the hope that they would serve as an independent buffer between Russia and Germany and guarantee peace.

when the dust of the peace treaties had settled, the region had been molded into a dozen sovereign states (see **Map A**). The victorious Allies hoped that independent states newly created from fragments of empire would buffer Europe from the spread of communism westward and the expansion of German power eastward.

A swath of new independent states cut through the center of Europe. Finland had acquired its independence from Russia in 1917. Estonia, Latvia, and Lithuania, also formerly under Russian rule, comprised the now independent Baltic states (see **Map B**). After more than a century of dismemberment among three empires, Poland became a single nation again. Czechoslovakia was carved out of former Habsburg lands. Austria and Hungary shriveled to small independent states. Yugoslavia was pieced together from a patchwork of

■ **Map C. Germany.** France hoped to hem Germany in, according to the terms of the peace settlement. France regained from Germany the territories of Alsace and Lorraine that France had lost in the Franco-Prussian War in 1870. In the 1920s, the French began building massive fortifications, known as the Maginot Line, along its frontier with Germany.

needs motivated claims for territory. Disputes festered, fed by the intense nationalism that prevented the cooperation necessary for survival.

Germany, the Soviet Union, and Italy further complicated the situation with their own territorial claims against their east-central European neighbors. The new German government refused to accept the loss to Poland of Upper Silesia (see **Map C**) and the "Polish Corridor" that severed East Prussia from the rest of Germany. Russia refused to forget its losses to Romania, Poland, Finland, and the Baltic states. Italy, too weak to act on its own, nevertheless dreamed of expansion into Yugoslavia, Austria, and Albania. The redefined borders of eastern and central Europe produced animosity and the seeds of ongoing conflict. The new states of eastern Europe stood as a picket fence between Germany and Russia, a fence that held little promise of guaranteeing the peace or of making good neighbors.

German Recovery

From defeat, Germany, the most populous nation in western Europe, with 60 million people, emerged strong. In 1919, the German people endorsed a new liberal and democratic gov-

ernment, the **Weimar Republic,** so named for the city in which its constitution had been written. The new constitution was unusually progressive, with voting rights for women and extensive civil liberties for German citizens. Because World War I had not been fought in Germany, German transportation networks and industrial plants had escaped serious damage. Its industry was fed by raw materials and energy resources unsurpassed anywhere in Europe outside Russia.

Territorial Advantages and Goals. In east-central Europe, Germany had actually benefited from the dismantling of the Habsburg Empire and the removal of Poland and the Baltic states from Russian control. Replacing its formerly large neighbor to the east were weak states that were potentially susceptible to Germany's influence. Because the governments of east-central Europe feared communism, they were not likely to ally with the Soviet state. The existence of the small buffer states left open the possibility of German collaboration with Russia, since the two large nations might be able to negotiate their interests in the area.

On its western frontier, Germany's prospects were not so bright. Alsace and Lorraine had been returned to France (see **Map C**). From German territory a demilitarized zone had been created in the Rhineland. The Saar district was under the protection of League of Nations commissioners, and the Saar coal mines were transferred to French ownership until 1935, when a plebiscite returned the region to Germany.

Germany's primary foreign policy goal was revision of the treaty settlements of World War I. German statesmen sought liberation of the Rhineland from foreign military occupation, return of the Saar basin, and recovery of the Corridor and Upper Silesia from Poland.

German leaders set economic recovery as the basis of their new foreign policy. In 1922, Germany signed the Treaty of Rapallo with Russia, a peacetime partnership that shocked the western powers. Economics motivated the new Russo-German alliance; German industry needed markets, and the Russians needed loans to reconstruct their economy. Both states wanted to break out of the isolation imposed on them by the victors of World War I. However, Germany quickly learned that markets in Russia were limited and that hopes for recovery depended on financial cooperation with western Europe and the United States. At the end of 1923, Gustav Stresemann (1878–1929) assumed direction of the German Foreign Ministry and began to implement a conciliatory policy toward France and Britain. By displaying peaceful intentions, he hoped to secure U.S. capital for German industry and win the support of the West for the revision of the peace settlement.

The Locarno Treaties. Stresemann joined his French and British counterparts, Aristide Briand (1862–1932) and Austen Chamberlain (1863–1937), in fashioning a series of treaties at Locarno, Switzerland, in 1925. In a spirit of cooperation, Germany, France, and Belgium promised never again to go to war against each other and to respect the demilitarized zone that separated them. Britain and Italy "guaranteed" the borders of all three countries and assured the integrity of the demilitarized zone. The treaties initiated an atmosphere of good will, a "spirit of Locarno," that heralded a new age of security and nonaggression.

However, Germany did not renounce its ambitions in eastern Europe. Stresemann expected Germany to recover the territory that had been lost to Poland. He also knew that Germany must rearm and expand to the east. From the early 1920s until 1933, Germany secretly rearmed in violation of the Treaty of Versailles treaty agreements. Under cover, it rebuilt its army and trained its soldiers and airmen on Russian territory. In violation of the Treaty of Versailles, Germany planned to be once again a great power with the same rights as other European countries.

France's Search for Security

Having learned the harsh lessons of 1870–1871 and 1914–1918, France understood well the threat posed by a united, industrialized, and well-armed Germany. During the years immediately after World War I, France deeply distrusted Germany. France had a smaller population at 40 million people and lower industrial production than Germany. France was devastated by the war, and Germany was not. Even though France had the best-equipped army in the world in 1921, French leaders knew that without the support of Great Britain and the United States, France could not enforce the Treaty of Versailles and keep Germany militarily weak.

The Americans and the British refused to conclude a long-term peacetime alliance with the French. In search of allies on the Continent, therefore, France committed itself to an alliance in the east with Poland and the Little Entente nations of Czechoslovakia, Romania, and Yugoslavia. Treaties with these four states gave France some security in the event of an attack, but the treaties were also liabilities because France would have to fight to defend east-central Europe.

To keep Germany militarily and economically weak, the French attempted to enforce the Treaty of Versailles fully and completely in 1921–1923. They were willing to do so alone if necessary. In 1923, the French army invaded the Ruhr district of Germany and occupied it with the intention of collecting reparations payments. But the Ruhr invasion served only to isolate France further from its wartime allies. In 1924–1925, France decided to cooperate with the United States and Great Britain rather than continue a policy of enforcing the treaty alone and attempting to keep Germany weak. France withdrew its army from the Ruhr and some troops from the Rhineland. It agreed to lower German reparations payments. In addition, by signing the Locarno treaties, France cooperated with the Anglo-American policy that rejected the use of military force against Germany and promoted German economic recovery.

French anxiety about security continued. Nothing indicated the nature of this anxiety more clearly than the construction, beginning in the late 1920s, of the Maginot Line, a system of defensive fortifications between Germany and France (see **Map C**).

Throughout the 1920s, French political leaders tried to engage Great Britain in guaranteeing the security of France and Europe. The British agreed to defend France and Belgium against possible German aggression. However, they stopped short of promising to defend Poland and Czechoslovakia. After settling this matter at Locarno, Britain largely reverted to its prewar pattern of withdrawing from continental Europe and concentrating its attention on the demands of its global empire.

The United States in Europe

The Treaty of Versailles marked the demise of European autonomy. American intervention had boosted French and British morale during the crucial months of 1917. In providing financial help, ships, troops, and supplies, the United States had rescued the Allied powers. After the war, a balance of power in Europe could not be maintained without outside help. Germany had been defeated, but if it recovered, France and Britain alone would probably not be able to contain it. Security and peace now depended on the presence of the United States to guarantee a stable balance of power in Europe and to defend Western hegemony in the world.

However, the United States was unwilling to assume a new role as political leader of Europe and mediator of European conflict. It refused to sign a joint peace, arranging instead a separate peace with Germany. It also refused to join the League of Nations. Following the war, the League had been devised as an international body of nations committed, according to Article 10 of its covenant, to "respect and preserve as against external aggression the territorial integrity and existing political independence" of others. Germany was excluded from membership until 1926; and the Union of Soviet Socialist Republics (USSR) was denied entry until 1934. Otherwise, the League of Nations claimed a global membership. But the absence of U.S. support and the lack of any machinery to enforce its decisions undermined the possibility of the League's long-term effectiveness. Hopes that the international body could serve as a peacekeeper collapsed in 1931 with the League's failure to deal with the crisis of Japanese aggression against Manchuria.

Efforts at comprehensive international cooperation like the League of Nations did not overcome the problem of competitive nations, nor did the Kellogg-Briand Pact, which was signed by 23 nations in 1928. Named for U.S. Secretary of State Frank B. Kellogg (1856–1937) and French foreign minister Aristide Briand, who devised the plan, the pact renounced war. In the atmosphere of the 1920s, a time of hope and caution, the agreement carried all the weight of an empty gesture.

CRISIS AND COLLAPSE IN A WORLD ECONOMY

In 1918, the belligerent nations—winners and losers alike—had big bills on their hands. Although nations at war had borrowed abroad and from their own populations through the sale of war bonds, private citizens could not provide all the money needed to finance four years of war.

International Loans and Trade Barriers

France borrowed from Great Britain. Both Great Britain and France took loans from the United States. When these sources proved insufficient, they printed more money. Because more money had claims on the same amount of national wealth, the money in circulation was worth less. When the people who had purchased war bonds were then paid off with depreciated currency, they lost real wealth. Inflation had the same effect as taxation. The people had less wealth, and the government had less debt.

The United States, for the first time in history the leading creditor nation in the world, had no intention of wiping the slate clean by forgiving war debts. Nor did it intend to accept repayment in less-valuable postwar currencies; loans were tied to gold. Britain, France, and Belgium counted on reparations from Germany to pay their war debts and to rebuild their economies. Reparations were calculated on the basis of the damages Germany had inflicted on the Allies. The postwar Reparations Commission determined that Germany owed the victors 132 billion gold marks ($33 billion) to be paid in annual installments of 2 billion gold marks ($500 million) plus 26 percent of the value of German exports.

For the German people and for German leaders, reparations were an unacceptable, punitive levy that mortgaged the prosperity of future generations. Germany, too, wanted to recover from the years of privation of the war. Substantial reparations payments would have transferred real wealth from Germany to the Allies. Transferring wealth would have cut into any increase in the German standard of living in the 1920s, and it would have diminished the investment needed to make the German economy grow. Instead, the German government printed huge amounts of currency. The mark collapsed and world currencies were endangered.

With financial disaster looming, the British and Americans decided to intervene. A plan had to be devised that would permit Germany to prosper while funneling payments to France, which depended on reparations for its own recovery and for its war debt payments to the United States. In 1924, the U.S. banker Charles G. Dawes (1865–1951), along with a group of international financial experts appointed by the Allied governments, devised a solution to the reparations problem. The Dawes Plan aimed to end inflation and restore economic prosperity in Germany by giving Germany a more modest and realistic schedule of payments and by extending a loan from U.S. banks to get payments started.

As important as reparations and war debts are in any understanding of the Western world in the 1920s, they cannot be considered in isolation. Debtor nations, whether Allies paying back loans to the United States or defeated nations paying reparations to the victors, needed to be able to sell their goods in world markets. They saw trade as the principal way to accumulate enough national income to pay back what they owed and to prosper domestically without burying their citizens under a mountain of new taxes.

If trade was to be the stepladder out of the financial hole of indebtedness, open markets and stable currencies were its rungs. Yet the Republican political leaders in the United States insisted on high tariffs to protect domestic goods against imports, and high tariffs prevented Europeans from selling in the United States and earning the dollars they needed to repay war debts.

While blocking imports, the United States planned to expand its own exports to world markets, especially to Europe. The problem for U.S. exporters, however, was the instability of European currencies in the first half of the 1920s. All over Europe, governments allowed inflation to rise with the expectation that depreciating currencies would make their goods cheaper in world markets and hence more salable.

Depreciating European currencies on the one hand meant an appreciating dollar on the other. For the "grand design" of U.S. trade expansion, a strong dollar was no virtue. More and more German marks, British pounds, and French francs had to be spent to purchase U.S. goods. The result was that fewer U.S. exports were sold in European markets. Because two-thirds of Germany's long-term credits came from the United States, Germany's fate was directly linked to the fortunes of U.S. financial centers. Conversely, the soundness of U.S. banks depended on a solvent Germany, which now absorbed 18 percent of U.S. capital exports.

Despite the scaled-down schedule of the Dawes Plan, reparations remained a bitter pill for German leaders and the German public to swallow. In 1929, U.S. bankers devised another plan under the leadership of businessman Owen D. Young (1874–1962), chairman of the board of General Electric. Although the Young Plan initially transferred $100 million to Germany, Germans saw the twentieth century stretching before them as year after year of nothing but humiliating reparations payments. To make matters worse, after 1928, U.S. private loans shriveled in Germany as U.S. investors sought the higher yields of a booming stock market at home.

Europe as a whole made rapid progress in manufacturing production during the second half of the decade and by 1929 had surpassed its prewar (1913) per capita income. Yet structural weaknesses were present. The false security of a new gold standard masked the instability and interdependence of currencies. Low prices prevailed in the agricultural sector, keeping the incomes of a significant segment of the population depressed. But the low rate of long-term capital investment was obscured in the flurry of short-term loans, whose disappearance in 1928 spelled the beginning of the end for European recovery. The protectionist trade policy of the United States conflicted with its insistence on repayment of war debts. Germany's resentment over reparations was in no way alleviated by the Dawes and Young repayment plans. The irresponsibility of U.S. speculation in the stock market pricked the bubble of prosperity. None of these factors operated in isolation to cause the collapse that began in 1929. Taken together, however, they caused a depression of previously unimagined severity in the international economic system.

The Great Depression

In the history of the Western world the year 1929 has assumed mythic proportions. During one week in October of that year, the stock market in the United States collapsed. This crash set off the **Great Depression** in an international economic system that was already plagued with structural problems. It also marked the beginning of a long period of worldwide economic stagnation and depression.

Dependence on the American Economy.   A confluence of factors made Europe and the rest of the world vulnerable to reversals in the U.S. economy. Heavy borrowing and reliance on U.S. investment throughout the 1920s contributed to the inherent instability of European economies. Even Great Britain, itself a creditor, relied on short-term loans, but "borrowing short and lending long" proved to be disastrous when loans were recalled. Excessive lending and leniency were fatal mistakes of creditor nations, especially the United States. When, in the summer of 1929, U.S. investors turned off the tap of the flow of capital to search for higher profits at home, a precarious situation began to get worse.

A depression is a severe downturn marked by sharp declines in income and production, as buying and selling slow to a crawl. Depressions were not new in the business cycles of modern economies, but the Great Depression was more serious in extent and duration than any depression before or since. The bottom was not reached until three years after it began. In 1932, one in four American workers was without a job. One in three banks had closed its doors. People lost their homes, unable to pay their mortgages; farmers lost their land, unable to earn enough to survive. The great prosperity of the 1920s had vanished overnight.

The plight of the United States rippled through world markets. Americans stopped buying foreign goods. The Smoot-Hawley Tariff Act, passed by the U.S. Congress in 1930, created an impenetrable tariff fortress against agricultural and manufactured imports. The major trading nations of the world, including Great Britain, enacted similar protectionist measures. U.S. investment abroad dried up.

European nations tried to stanch the outward flow of capital and gold by restricting the transfer of capital abroad.

■ This poster for the October 1931 British general election reflects the National Government's concern over mass unemployment and industrial stagnation. The coalition National Government swamped the opposition Labour Party, taking 556 Parliament seats to Labour's 51.

Nevertheless, large amounts of foreign-owned gold ($6.6 billion from 1931 to 1938) were deposited in U.S. banks. In 1931, President Herbert Hoover supported a moratorium on the payment of reparations and war debts. The moratorium, combined with the pooling of gold in the United States, led to a run on the British pound sterling in 1931 and the collapse of Great Britain as one of the world's great financial centers.

Political Repercussions.   The gold standard disappeared from the international economy, never to return. So did reparations payments and war debts when the major nations of Europe met without the United States at a special conference held in Lausanne, Switzerland, in 1932. Something else died at the end of the 1920s: confidence in a self-adjusting economy, an "invisible hand" by which the business cycle would be

CHRONOLOGY
INTERNATIONAL POLITICS

1919	Creation of the League of Nations
1920	War between Poland and Russia
1921	Treaty of Riga
1922	Germany and Russia sign Treaty of Rapallo
1923	French and Belgian troops invade the Ruhr district
1924	Dawes Plan
1925	Locarno Treaties
1928	Kellogg-Briand Pact
1929	Young Plan
October 1929	Collapse of the U.S. stock market; beginning of the Great Depression
1935	Saar region returned to German control
1936	Germany stations troops in the Rhineland in violation of the Treaty of Versailles

righted. In 1932–1933 the Depression reached its nadir and became a global phenomenon.

In the decade after the Great War, peace settlements did not promote a stable, international community. Instead, self-determination of peoples created new grounds for national rivalries in eastern Europe, and prewar animosities persisted. The economic interdependence of nation-states through an international system of reparations payments and loans increased the vulnerability of governments to external pressures. With the collapse of world markets and the international finance system in 1929, political stability and international cooperation seemed more elusive than ever.

THE SOVIET UNION'S SEPARATE PATH

In the 1920s, the Soviet state was also faced with solving its economic problems. Lenin's successor, Joseph Stalin (1879–1953), obliged the Soviet people to achieve in a single generation what it had taken western Europe a century and a half to accomplish.

The Soviet Regime at the End of the Civil War

Echoing Karl Marx, the Bolshevik leader Lenin declared that the revolution and the civil war had been won in the name of "the dictatorship of the proletariat." The hammer and sickle on the Soviet flag represented the united rule of workers and peasants. But at the end of the civil war in 1921, the Bolsheviks, not the people, were in charge.

The small industrial sector was in total disarray by 1921. Famine and epidemics in 1921–1922 killed and weakened more people than the Great War and the civil war combined. The countryside had been plundered to feed the Red and White armies. The combination of empty promises and a declining standard of living left workers and peasants frustrated and discontented. Urban strikes and rural uprisings defied short-term solutions. The proletarian revolutionary heroes of 1917 were rejecting the new Soviet regime. The Bolshevik Party now faced the task of restoring a country exhausted by war and revolution.

At the head of the Soviet state was Lenin, the first among equals in the seven-man Politburo. The Central Committee of the Communist Party decided "fundamental questions of policy, international and domestic," but in reality the Politburo, the inner committee of the Central Committee, held the reins of power. The broad-based revolutionary coalition had, by the end of World War I, given way to one-party rule.

Among the Politburo seven, three men in particular attempted to leave their mark on the direction of Soviet policy: Leon Trotsky (1879–1940), Nikolai Bukharin (1888–1938), and Joseph Stalin (1879–1953). The great drama of Soviet leadership in the 1920s revolved around how the most brilliant (Trotsky) and the most popular (Bukharin) failed at the hands of the most shrewdly political (Stalin).

In the debate over the direction economic development should take, proposals ranged from a planned economy totally directed from above to an economy controlled from below. In 1920–1921, Leon Trotsky, at that time people's commissar of war, favored a planned economy based on the militarization of labor. Trade unions opposed such a proposal and argued for a share of control over production. Lenin, however, favored a proletarian democracy and supported unions that were organized independently of state control.

The controversy was resolved in the short run at the Tenth Party Congress in 1921, when Lenin chose to steer a middle course between trade union autonomy and militarization by preserving the unions and at the same time insisting on the state's responsibility for economic development. His primary goal was to stabilize Bolshevik rule in its progress toward socialism. He recognized that nothing could be achieved without the peasants. As a result, Lenin found himself embracing a new economic policy that he termed a "temporary retreat" from Communist goals.

The New Economic Policy, 1921–1928

In 1921, Lenin ended the forced requisitioning of peasant produce, which had been in effect during the civil war. In its place, peasants were to pay a tax in kind, that is, a fixed portion of their yield, to the state. Peasants in turn were permitted to reinstate private trade on their own terms. Party leaders accepted this shift in policy because it held the promise of

■ As members of the Politburo, Leon Trotsky (left), Nikolai Bukharin (center), and Joseph Stalin (right) each tried to direct Soviet economic policy. Only the politically shrewd Stalin would emerge victorious.

prosperity, so necessary for political stability. Lenin's actions to return the benefits of productivity to the economy, combined with those of the peasants to reestablish markets, created the **New Economic Policy (NEP)** that emerged in the spring and summer of 1921.

Bukharin's Role. It remained for Nikolai Bukharin, the youngest of the top Bolshevik leaders, to give shape and substance to the economic policy that allowed Russian producers to engage in some capitalist practices. Bukharin tackled Russia's single greatest problem: How could Russia, crippled by poverty, find enough capital to industrialize? Insisting on the need for long-term economic planning, Bukharin counted on a prosperous and contented peasantry as the mainstay of his policy. He also hoped to attract foreign investment in Soviet endeavors as a way of ensuring future productivity.

Bukharin appreciated the importance of landholding to Russian peasants and defended a system of individual farms and private accumulation. Agriculture would operate through a market system, and the peasants would have the right to control their own surpluses. Rural prosperity would generate profits that could be used for gradual industrial development. Bukharin's policy stood in stark contrast to Stalin's later plan to feed industry by starving the agricultural sector.

Collective and large-scale farming had to be deferred indefinitely to reconcile the peasantry to the state—a policy profoundly at odds with the programs of the Communist state to pull down the capitalist system and establish socialism. In 1924, the tax in kind was replaced with a tax in cash. With this shift, the state procured grain through commercial agencies and cooperative organizations instead of directly from the peasants. The move toward Western capitalist models seemed more pronounced than ever to critics of the NEP.

Beginning in 1922, Lenin suffered a series of strokes that virtually removed him from power by March 1923. When he died on 21 January 1924, the Communist leadership split over the ambiguities of the NEP. The backward nature of agriculture did not permit the kind of productivity that the NEP policy makers anticipated. Cities demanded more food as their populations swelled with the influx of unskilled workers from rural areas. In 1927, peasants held back their grain. The Soviet Union was then experiencing a series of foreign policy setbacks in the West and in China, and Bolshevik leaders spoke of an active anti-Soviet conspiracy by the capitalist powers, led by Great Britain. The Soviet state lowered the price of grain, thereby squeezing the peasantry. The war scare, combined with the drop in food prices, soon led to an economic crisis.

Stalin Takes Charge. By 1928, the NEP was in trouble. Stalin, general secretary of the Communist Party of the Soviet Union, saw his chance. Under his supervision, the state intervened to prevent peasants from disposing of their own grain surpluses. The peasants responded to requisitioning by hoarding their produce and violent rioting. Bukharin and the NEP were in danger. Stalin exploited the internal crisis and external dangers to eliminate his political rivals. Stalin's rival Trotsky had been expelled from the Communist Party in November 1927 on charges that he had engaged in antiparty activities. Banished from Russia in 1929, Trotsky eventually found refuge in Mexico, where he was assassinated in 1940 at Stalin's command.

Bukharin's popularity in the party also threatened Stalin's aspirations. Bukharin was dropped from the Politburo in 1929. He was arrested in 1937 and was tried and executed for alleged treasonous activities the following year. The fate that befell Trotsky and Bukharin was typical of that which afflicted anyone who stood in the way of Stalin's pursuit of dictatorial control. Beneath his apparently colorless personality, Stalin was a dangerous man of great political acumen, a ruthless, behind-the-scenes politician who controlled the machinery of the party to his own ends and was not averse to using violence to achieve them.

Stalin's Rise to Power

Joseph Stalin was born Iosif Vissarionovich Dzhugashvili in 1879. His self-chosen revolutionary name, Stalin, means "steel" in Russian and is as good an indication as any of his opinion of his own personality and will. Stalin, the man who ruled the Soviet Union as a dictator from 1928 until his death in 1953, was not a Russian. He was from Georgia, and he spoke Russian with an accent. Georgia, an area between the Black and Caspian seas, had been annexed by the expanding Russian empire in 1801.

As the only surviving child of his parents, Stalin endured a childhood of brutal poverty. With his mother's support, he nevertheless received an education and entered a seminary. His schooling gave him the opportunity to learn about revolutionary socialist politics. At the turn of the century, Georgia had a strong Marxist revolutionary movement that opposed Russian exploitation. Iosif dropped out of the seminary in 1899 to engage in underground Marxist activities, and he soon became a follower of Lenin.

Stalin's association with Lenin kept him close to the center of power after the October Revolution of 1917. First as people's commissar for nationalities (1920–1923) and then as general secretary of the Central Committee of the Communist Party (1922–1953), Stalin showed natural talent as a political strategist. His familiarity with non-Russian nationalities was a great asset in his dealings with the ethnic diversity and unrest in the vast Soviet state. Unlike other party leaders, who had lived in exile in western Europe before the revolution, Stalin had little knowledge of the West.

After Lenin's death in 1924, Stalin shrewdly bolstered his own reputation by orchestrating a cult of worship for Lenin. In 1929, Stalin used the occasion of his fiftieth birthday to fashion for himself a reputation as the living hero of the Soviet state. Icons, statues, busts, and images of all sorts of both Lenin and Stalin appeared everywhere in public buildings, schoolrooms, and homes. Stalin systematically began eliminating his rivals so that he alone stood unchallenged as Lenin's true successor.

The First Five-Year Plan

The cult of Stalin coincided with the First Five-Year Plan (1929–1932), which launched Stalin's program of rapid industrialization. Between 1929 and 1937, the period covered by the first two five-year plans (truncated because of their proclaimed success), Stalin laid the foundation for an urban industrial society in the Soviet Union. By brutally squeezing profits out of the agricultural sector, Stalin managed to increase heavy industrial production between 300 and 600 percent.

Stalin committed the Soviet Union to rapid industrialization as the only way to preserve socialism. The failure of revolutionary movements in western Europe meant that the Soviet Union must preserve "socialism in one country," the slogan of the political philosophy that justified Stalin's economic plans. Stalin made steel the idol of the new age. The Soviet state needed heavy machinery to build the future. An industrial labor force was created virtually overnight as peasant men and women were placed at workbenches and before the vast furnaces of modern metallurgical plants. The number of women in the industrial workforce tripled in the decade after 1929. Heavy industrial production soared between 1929 and 1932.

When he first began to deal with the grain crisis of 1928, Stalin did not intend collective agriculture as a solution. But by the end of 1929, the increasingly repressive measures instituted by the state against the peasants had led both to **collectivization** and to the deportation of *kulaks,* the derisive term for wealthy peasants that literally means "tight-fisted ones." Stalin achieved forced collectivization by confiscating land and establishing collective farms run by the state. Within a few months, half of all peasant farms were collectivized. By 1938, private land was virtually eliminated. The state set prices, controlled distribution, and selected crops with the intention of ensuring a steady food supply and freeing a rural labor force for heavy industry. More as a publicity ploy than as a statement of fact, the First Five-Year Plan was declared a success after only three years. It was a success in one important sense: It did lay the foundations of the Soviet planned economy, in which the state bureaucracy made all decisions about production, distribution, and prices.

Collectivization meant misery for the 25 million peasant families who suffered under it. At least five million peasants died between 1929 and 1932. Collectivization ripped apart the fabric of village life, destroyed families, and sent homeless peasants into exile. Some peasants retaliated by destroying their own crops and livestock. Ultimately, the peasants were to bear the chief burdens of industrialization.

The Comintern, Economic Development, and the Purges

In addition to promoting its internal economic development, the Soviet Union had to worry about survival in a world of capitalist countries.

After the Bolshevik revolution in 1917, Lenin had fully expected that other socialist revolutions would follow throughout the world. But as the prospects for world proletarian revolution evaporated, Soviet leaders sought to protect their revolutionary country from the hostile capitalist world through diplomacy. The end of the Allied intervention in Russia allowed the Bolshevik state to initiate diplomatic relations with the West, beginning with the Treaty of Rapallo signed with Germany in 1921. By 1924, all the major countries of the world—except the United States—had established diplomatic relations with the Soviet Union. In 1928, the Soviet Union cooperated in the preparation of a world disarmament conference to be held in Geneva and joined western European powers in a commitment to peace. The United States and the Soviet Union exchanged ambassadors for the first time in 1933.

The Comintern.   In addition to diplomatic relations, the Soviet state in 1919 encouraged various national Communist parties to form an association for the purpose of promoting and coordinating the coming world revolution. This Communist International, or Comintern, was based in Moscow and included representatives from 37 countries by 1920. As it became clear that a world revolution was not imminent, the Comintern concerned itself with the ideologi-

cal purity of its member parties. Under Lenin's direction, the Soviet Communist Party determined policy for all the member parties.

From 1924 to 1929, Bukharin and Stalin shared the view that the Comintern should promote the unity of working classes everywhere and should cooperate with existing worker organizations. In 1929, however, Stalin argued that advanced capitalist societies were teetering on the brink of new wars and revolutions. As a result, the Comintern must seek to sever the ties between Communist parties and social democratic parties in other countries to prepare for the revolutionary struggle. Stalin purged the Comintern of dissenters, and he decreed a policy of noncooperation in Europe from 1929 to 1933. As a result, socialism in Europe was badly split between Communists and democratic socialists, greatly facilitating the triumph of fascist movements, especially Nazism in Germany.

The Second Five-Year Plan, announced in 1933, succeeded in reducing the Soviet Union's dependence on foreign imports, especially in the areas of heavy industry, machinery, and metal works. The basic physical plant for armaments production was in place by 1937, and resources continued to be shifted away from consumer goods to heavy industrial development. This industrial development and the collectivization of agriculture brought growing urbanization. By 1939, one in three Soviet people were living in cities, compared to one in six in 1926. In his commitment to increased production, Stalin introduced into the workplace incentives and differential wage scales that were at odds with the principles and programs of the original Bolshevik revolution. Stricter discipline was enforced; absenteeism was punished with severe fines or loss of employment. Workers who exceeded their quotas were rewarded and honored.

The Great Purge.   Amid this rapid industrialization, Stalin inaugurated the **Great Purge,** actually a series of purges lasting from 1934 through 1938. People whom Stalin believed to be his opponents—real and imagined, past, present, and future—were labeled "class enemies." The most prominent of them were given show trials. They were intimidated and tortured into false confessions of crimes against the regime and condemned to death or imprisonment. Stalin wiped out the Bolshevik old guard and all potential opposition within the Communist Party to his personal rule. Probably 300,000 people were put to death, among whom were engineers, managers, technologists, and officers of the army and navy. In addition, seven million people were placed in labor camps. The purges dealt a severe blow to the command of the army and resulted in a shortage of qualified industrial personnel, slowing industrial growth. But Stalin now had unquestioned control of the Party and the country.

Coerced and planned industrial growth brought with it a top-heavy and often inefficient bureaucracy, and that bureaucracy ensured that the Soviet Union was the most highly centralized of the European states. The growing threat of war posed by Nazi Germany meant an even greater diversion of

CHRONOLOGY
THE SOVIET UNION'S SEPARATE PATH

November 1917	Bolsheviks and Red Guard seize power
1919	Creation of the Communist International (Comintern)
1920	Legalization of abortion and divorce
1921	End of the civil war
1921	Introduction of the New Economic Policy
3 April 1922	Stalin becomes secretary general of the Communist party
21 January 1924	Lenin dies
1924–1929	Comintern policy of "Unity of the Working Classes"
1927	Dissatisfied peasants hoard grain
November 1927	Trotsky expelled from Communist party
1928	Stalin introduces grain requisitioning
November 1929	Bukharin expelled from Politburo
1929	Introduction of First Five-Year Plan and the collectivization of agriculture
1929–1933	Comintern policy of noncooperation with Social Democratic parties
1933–1937	Second Five-Year Plan
1934–1938	Great Purge
1936	Abortion declared illegal
1938	Third Five-Year Plan

resources from consumer goods to war industries, beginning with the Third Five-Year Plan in 1938.

Women and the Family in the New Soviet State

The building of the new Soviet state exacted particularly high costs from women. Soviet women had been active in the revolution from the beginning. Lenin and the Bolshevik leaders were committed to the liberation of women, who, like workers, were considered to be oppressed under capitalism. Lenin denounced housework as "barbarously unproductive, petty, nerve-wracking, stultifying, and crushing drudgery." In its early days, the Soviet state pledged to protect the rights of mothers without narrowing women's opportunities or restricting women's role to the family.

After the October Revolution of 1917, the Bolsheviks passed a new law establishing equality for women within marriage. In 1920, abortion was legalized. New legislation established the right to divorce and removed the stigma from illegitimacy. Communes, calling themselves "laboratories of revolution," experimented with sexual equality. Russian women were enfranchised in 1917, the first women in a major country to win this right in national elections. The Russian Revolution went further than any revolution in history toward the legal liberation of women within such a short span of time.

These advances, as utopian as they appeared to admirers in western European countries, did not deal with the problems that the majority of Russian women faced. Bolshevik legislation did little to address the economic hardships of peasant and factory women. Although paid maternity leaves and nursing breaks were required by law, these guarantees became a source of discrimination against women workers, who were the last hired and first fired by employers trying to limit expenses. Divorce legislation was hardly a blessing for women with children, since men incurred no financial responsibility toward their offspring in terminating a marriage. Even as legislation was being passed in the early days of the new Soviet state, women were losing ground in the struggle for equal rights and independent economic survival.

By the early 1930s, reforms affecting women were in trouble, largely because of a plummeting birthrate, which alarmed Soviet planners. In 1936, women's right to choose to end a first pregnancy was revoked. In the following decade, all abortions were made illegal. Homosexuality was declared a criminal offense. The family was glorified as the mainstay of the socialist order, and the independence of women was challenged as a threat to Soviet productivity. While motherhood was idealized, the Stalinist drive to industrialize could not dispense with full-time women workers.

Women's double burden in the home and workplace became heavier during Stalin's reign. Most Russian women held full-time jobs in the factories or on the farms. They also worked what they called a "second shift" in running a household and taking care of children. In the industrialized nations of western Europe, the growth of a consumer economy lightened women's labor in the home to some extent. In the Soviet Union, procuring the simplest necessities was women's work that required waiting in long lines for hours. Lack of indoor plumbing meant that women spent hours hauling water for their families at the end of a working day. In such ways, rapid industrialization exacted its special price from Soviet women.

In the 1920s and 1930s, the search for stability and prosperity took the Soviet Union down a very different path from that of the states of western Europe. Rejecting an accommodation with a market economy, Stalin committed the Soviet people to planned rapid industrialization that was accomplished through mass repression and great human suffering and relied on a massive state bureaucratic system.

THE RISE OF FASCIST DICTATORSHIP IN ITALY

Throughout western Europe, parliamentary institutions, representative government, and electoral politics offered no ready solutions to the problems of economic collapse and the political upheaval on the left and the right. **Fascism** promised what liberal democratic societies failed to deliver: a way out of the economic and political morass. Ruling by means of dictatorship by a charismatic leader, fascism promised an escape from parliamentary chaos, party wranglings, and the threat of communism. It also promised order and security.

Fascism sounded very like socialism. In the Soviet Union, Bolshevik leaders reassured their people that socialism was the only way of dealing with the weaknesses and inequities of the world capitalist system that had been laid bare in the world war. Fascists employed similar language in their initial condemnations of the capitalist economy and liberal political institutions and values.

The word *fascism* is derived from the Latin *fasces,* the name for the bundle of rods with an ax head carried by the magistrates of the Roman Empire. Fascism was rooted in the mass political movements of the late nineteenth century, which emphasized nationalism, antiliberal values, and a politics of the irrational. The electoral successes of the German variant—National Socialism or **Nazism**—were just beginning in the late 1920s. In the same period, fascist movements appeared in England, Hungary, Spain, and France. But none was more successful than the fascist experiment in Italy.

Mussolini's Italy

Italy was a poor nation. Although Italy was one of the victorious Allies in World War I, Italians felt that their country had been betrayed by the peace settlement of 1919 by being denied the territory and status it deserved. A recently created electoral system based on universal manhood suffrage had produced parliamentary chaos and ministerial instability. People were beginning to doubt the parliamentary regime's hold on the future. It was under these circumstances that the Fascist Party, led by Benito Mussolini (1883–1945), entered politics in 1920 by attacking the large Socialist and Popular (Catholic) parties.

The Rise of Mussolini.   Mussolini had begun his political career as a Socialist. He had been arrested numerous times for Socialist political activities and placed under state surveillance. An ardent nationalist, he volunteered for combat in World War I and was promoted to the rank of corporal. Injured in early 1917 by an exploding shell detonated during firing practice, he returned to Milan to continue his work as editor of *Il Populo d'Italia* ("The People of Italy"), the newspaper he founded in 1914 to promote Italian participation in the war.

Mussolini yearned to be the leader of a revolution in Italy, and he recognized the persuasive power of the printed word. Emphasizing nationalist goals and vague measures of socioeconomic transformation, Mussolini identified a new enemy for Italy: Bolshevism. He organized his followers into a highly disciplined Fascist Party, which quickly developed its own national network.

Many Fascists were former socialists and war veterans like Mussolini who were disillusioned with postwar government. They dreamed of Italy as a great world power, as it had been in the days of ancient Rome. Their enemies were not only the Communists with their international outlook but also the big businesses and unions. Panicky members of the lower middle classes sought security against the economic uncertainties of inflation and were willing to endorse violence to achieve it. Near civil war erupted as Italian Communists and Fascists clashed violently in street battles in the early 1920s. The Fascists entered the national political arena and succeeded on the local level in overthrowing city governments.

The March on Rome.   On 28 October 1922, the Fascists, still a minority party, undertook their famous March on Rome, which followed similar Fascist takeovers in Milan and Bologna. Mussolini's followers occupied the capital. King Victor Emmanuel III invited Mussolini to form a government. Nationalist conservatives fully expected to be able to use the Fascists for their own ends. The accession of the new premier, however, marked the beginning of the end of parliamentary government and the emergence of Fascist dictatorship and institutionalized violence. Rising unemployment and severe inflation contributed to the politically deteriorating situation that helped to bring Mussolini to power.

Destruction and violence became fascism's most successful tools for securing political power. *Squadristi,* armed bands of Fascist thugs, attacked their political enemies, both Catholic and Socialist, destroyed private property, dismantled the printing presses of adversary groups, and generally terrorized both rural and urban populations. By the end of 1922, Fascists could claim a following of 300,000 members who endorsed the new politics of intimidation.

The Fascists also used intimidation to secure votes. One outspoken Socialist critic of Fascist violence, Giacomo

Matteotti, was murdered by Mussolini's subordinates in 1924. The deed threatened the survival of Mussolini's government as 150 Socialist, Liberal, and Popular party deputies resigned in protest. Mussolini chose this moment to consolidate his position by arresting and silencing his enemies. Within two years, Fascists were firmly in control, monopolizing politics, suppressing a free press, creating a secret police force, and transforming social and economic policies. Mussolini made Italy into a one-party dictatorship.

Dealing with Big Business and the Church.   In 1925, the Fascist Party entered into an agreement with Italian industrialists that gave industry a position of privilege protected by the state in return for its support. Mussolini presented this partnership as the end to class conflict, but in fact it ensured the dominance of capital and the control of labor and professional groups.

A corrupt bureaucracy run on bribes orchestrated the new relationship between big business and the state. In spite of official claims, Fascist Italy was hurt by the Great Depression. A large rural sector masked the problems of high unemployment by absorbing an urban workforce that was without jobs. Corporatism, a system of economic self-rule by interest groups, was a sham promoted on paper by Benito Mussolini that had little to do with the dominance of the Italian economy by big business. By lending money to Italian businesses that were on the verge of bankruptcy, the government acquired a controlling interest in key industries, including steel, shipping, heavy machinery, and electricity.

Mussolini, himself an atheist, recognized the importance of the Catholic Church in securing his regime. In 1870, when Italy was unified, the pope was deprived of his territories in Rome. This event, which became known as the "Roman Question," proved to be the source of ongoing problems for Italian governments. In February 1929, in the Lateran Treaty and the accompanying Concordat, Mussolini granted the pope sovereignty over the territory around St. Peter's Basilica and the Vatican. The treaty also protected the role of the Catholic Church in education and guaranteed that Italian marriage laws would conform to Catholic dogma.

By 1929, as the Great Depression loomed, *Il Duce* ("the leader"), as Mussolini preferred to be called, was at the height of his popularity and power. Apparent political harmony had been achieved by ruthlessly crushing fascism's opponents. The agreement with the pope, which restored harmony with the Church, was matched by a new sense of order and accomplishment in Italian society and the economy.

Mussolini's Plans for Empire

As fascism failed to initiate effective social programs, Mussolini's popularity plummeted. In the hope of boosting his sagging image, Il Duce committed Italy to a foreign policy of imperial conquest.

Italy had conquered Ottoman-controlled Libya in North Africa in 1911. Now, in October 1935, Mussolini's troops invaded Ethiopia. Using poison gas and aerial bombing, the Italian army defeated the forces of Ethiopian emperor Haile Selassie (1930–1974). European democracies cried out against the wanton attack, but Mussolini proclaimed Ethiopia an Italian territory.

The invasion of Ethiopia exposed the inability of the League of Nations to stop such flagrant violations. Great Britain and France protested Italy's conquest, and a rift opened up between these two western European nations and Italy. Mussolini had distanced himself from Nazi Germany, and he was critical of Hitler's plans for rearmament. Now, however, in light of the disapproval of Britain and France, Mussolini turned to Germany for support. In October 1936, Italy and Germany concluded a friendship alliance. In May 1939, in an agreement known as the Pact of Steel, Germany and Italy drew closer, each agreeing to offer support to the other in any offensive or defensive war.

Mussolini pursued other imperialist goals within Europe. The small Balkan nation of Albania entered into a series of agreements with Mussolini beginning in the mid-1920s that made it dependent financially and militarily on Italian aid. By 1933, Albanian independence had been thoroughly undermined. In order not to be outdone by Hitler, who was at the time dismantling Czechoslovakia, Mussolini invaded and annexed Albania in April 1939.

HITLER AND THE THIRD REICH

Repeated economic, political, and diplomatic crises of the 1920s buffeted Germany's internal stability. Most Germans considered reparations to be an unfair burden that should be resisted in every way possible. The German government did not actually promote inflation to avoid paying reparations, but it did do so to avoid a postwar recession, revive industrial production, and maintain high employment. But in 1923, the moderate inflation that stimulated the economy spun out of control into destructive hyperinflation.

The fiscal problems of the Weimar Republic obscure the fact that in the postwar period, Germany experienced real economic growth. German industry advanced, productivity was high, and German workers flexed their union muscles to secure better wages. Weimar committed itself to large expenditures for social welfare programs, including unemployment insurance. By 1930, social welfare was responsible for 40 percent of all public expenditures, compared to 19 percent before the war. All these changes, apparently fostering the well-being of the German people, aggravated the fears of German big businessmen, who resented the trade unions and the perceived trend toward socialism. The lower middle classes also felt cheated and economically threatened by inflation.

Growing numbers of Germans expressed disgust with parliamentary democracy. The Great Depression dealt a staggering blow to the Weimar Republic in 1929 as U.S. loans were withdrawn and German unemployment skyrocketed. By 1930, the antagonisms among the parties were so great that the parliament was no longer effective in ruling Germany. As chancellor from 1930 to 1932, Centrist leader Heinrich Brüning (1885–1970) tried to break this impasse by overriding the Weimar constitution. This move opened the door to enemies of the republic, and Brüning was forced to resign.

Hitler's Rise to Power

Adolf Hitler knew how to exploit the Weimar Republic's weaknesses for his own political ends. He denounced the reparations. He made a special appeal to Germans who saw their savings disappearing, first in inflation and then in the depression. He promised a way out of economic hardship and the reassertion of Germany's claim to status as a world power.

Just as Stalin was born a Georgian and not an ethnic Russian, Adolf Hitler (1889–1945) was born an Austrian outside the German fatherland he came to rule. Hitler came from a middle-class family with social pretensions. Aimlessness and failure marked Hitler's early life. Denied admission to architecture school, he took odd jobs to survive. When war broke out in 1914, he volunteered immediately for service in the German army. Wounded and gassed at the front, he was twice awarded the Iron Cross for bravery in action.

The army provided Hitler with a sense of security and direction. The peace that followed determined his commitment to a career in politics. Hitler profoundly believed in the stab-in-the-back legend: Germany had not lost the war; it had been defeated from within, stabbed in the back by communists, socialists, liberals, and Jews. The Weimar Republic signed the humiliating Treaty of Versailles and continued to betray the German people by taxing wages to pay reparations. His highly distorted and false view of the origins of the Republic and its policies was the basis for his demand that the "Weimar System" be abolished and replaced by a Nazi regime.

The Beer Hall Putsch of 1923. In 1923, Hitler, now leading a small National Socialist German Workers party, the Nazis, attempted to seize control of the Munich municipal government. This effort, known as the Beer Hall Putsch, failed, and Hitler served nine months of a five-year sentence in prison. There he began writing the first volume of his autobiography, *Mein Kampf* ("My Struggle"). In this turgid work, he condemned the decadence of Western society and singled out for special contempt Jews, Bolsheviks, and middle-class liberals. From the Munich episode, Hitler learned that he could succeed against the German republic only from within, by coming to power legally. By 1928, he had a small party of about 100,000 Nazis. Modifying his anticapitalist message, Hitler appealed to the discontented small farmers and tailored his nationalist sentiments to a frightened middle class.

■ Adolf Hitler salutes a huge crowd of Hitler Youth at a rally. The mass meetings were used by the Nazi mythmakers to enhance Hitler's image as the savior of Germany.

Hitler as Chancellor.   Adolf Hitler became chancellor of Germany in January 1933 by legal, constitutional, and democratic means. The Nazi party received its heaviest support from farmers, small businessmen, civil servants, and young people. In the elections of 1930 and 1932 the voters made the Nazi party the largest party in the country—although not the majority one. President Paul von Hindenburg invited Hitler to form a government. Hitler claimed that Germany was on the verge of a Communist revolution, and he persuaded Hindenburg and the Reichstag to consent to a series of emergency laws, which the Nazis used to establish themselves firmly in power. Legislation outlawed freedom of the press and public meetings and approved the use of violence against Hitler's political enemies, particularly the Socialists and the Communists. Within two months after Hitler came to office, Germany was a police state, and Hitler was a legal dictator who could issue his own laws without having to gain the consent of either the Reichstag or the president. After carrying out this "legal revolution," the Nazis abolished all other political parties, established single-party rule, dissolved trade unions, and put their own people into state governments and the bureaucracy.

Many observers at the time considered the new Nazi state to be a monolithic structure, ruled and coordinated from the center. However, this was not an accurate observation. Hitler actually issued few directives. Policy was set by an often chaotic jockeying for power among rival Nazi factions. Hitler's political alliance with traditional conservative and nationalist politicians, industrialists, and military men helped to give the state created by Adolf Hitler, which he called the **Third Reich,** a claim to legitimacy based on continuity with the past. (The First Reich was the medieval German Empire; the Second Reich was the German Empire created by Bismarck in 1871.)

The first of the paramilitary groups that were so important in orchestrating violence to eliminate Hitler's enemies was the Sturmabteilung (SA), or the storm troopers, under Ernst Röhm (1877–1934). Röhm helped Hitler achieve electoral victories by beating up political opponents on the streets and using other thuglike tactics. The SA, also known as Brown Shirts, adopted a military appearance for their terrorist operations. By the beginning of 1934, the SA had 2.5 million members, vastly outnumbering the regular army of 100,000 soldiers.

Heinrich Himmler (1900–1945) headed an elite force within the SA called the Schutzstaffel (SS), or protection squad. SS members wore black uniforms and menacing skull-and-crossbones insignia on their caps. Himmler seized control of political policing and emerged as Röhm's chief rival. In 1934, with the assistance of the army, Hitler and the SS purged the SA and executed Röhm, thereby making the SS Hitler's exclusive elite corps, entrusted with carrying out his extreme programs and responsible later for the greatest atrocities of the Second World War.

Nazi Goals

Hitler identified three organizing goals for the Nazi state: *Lebensraum* ("living space"), rearmament, and economic recovery. The goals were the basis of the new foreign policy

Hitler forged for Germany, and they served to fuse that foreign policy with the domestic politics of the Third Reich. All three were based on Hitler's version of social Darwinism—that the German race was the fittest and would survive and prosper at the expense of others.

Living Space.   Key to Hitler's world view was the concept of *Lebensraum,* living space, by which he considered it the right and the duty of the German master race to be the world's greatest empire, one that would endure for a thousand years. Hitler first stated his ideals about living space in *Mein Kampf,* in which he argued that superior nations had the right to expand into the territories of inferior states. Living space meant for him German domination of central and eastern Europe at the expense of Slavic peoples. Germany had to annex territories, and Hitler's primary target was what he called "Russia and her vassal border states."

Rearmament.   Hitler greatly escalated the secret rearmament of Germany begun by his Weimar predecessors in violation of the Treaty of Versailles. He withdrew Germany from the League of Nations and from the World Disarmament Conference, signaling a new direction for German foreign policy. In 1935, he publicly renounced the Treaty of Versailles and declared that Germany was rearming. The following year, he openly defied the French and moved German troops into the demilitarized Rhineland. In 1933, the German state was illicitly spending one billion Reichsmarks on arms, a figure that climbed to 30 billion by 1939.

Hitler knew that preparation for war would require full economic recovery. One of Germany's great weaknesses in World War I had been its dependence on imports of raw materials and foodstuffs. To avoid a repetition of this problem, Hitler instituted a program of autarky, or economic self-sufficiency, by which Germany aimed to produce everything that it consumed. He encouraged the efforts of German industry to develop synthetics for petroleum, rubber, metals, and fats.

Economic Recovery.   The state pumped money into the private economy, creating new jobs and achieving full employment after 1936, an accomplishment that was unmatched by any other European nation. Recovery was built on armaments as well as consumer products. The Nazi state's concentration of economic power in the hands of a few strengthened big businesses. The victims of corporate consolidation were the small firms that could no longer compete with government-sponsored corporations such as the chemical giant I. G. Farben.

In 1936, Hitler introduced his Four-Year Plan, which was dedicated to the goals of full-scale rearmament and economic self-sufficiency. Before the third year of the Four-Year Plan, however, Hitler was aware of the failure to develop sufficient synthetic products to meet Germany's needs. But if Germany could not create substitutes, it could take over territories that provided the products Germany lacked. Hitler was committed to territorial expansion from the time he came to power. He rearmed Germany for that purpose. When economists and generals cautioned him, he refused to listen. Instead, he removed his critics from their positions of power and replaced them with Nazis who were loyal to him.

Propaganda, Racism, and Culture

To reinforce his personal power and to sell his program for the total state, Hitler created a Ministry of Propaganda under Joseph Goebbels (1897–1945), a former journalist and Nazi Party district leader in Berlin. Goebbels was a master of manipulating emotions in mass demonstrations. Flying the flag and wearing the swastika signified identification with the Nazi state. With his magnetic appeal, Hitler inspired and manipulated the devotion of hundreds of thousands of those who heard him speak. Leni Riefenstahl, a young filmmaker working for Hitler, made a documentary of a National Socialist Party rally at Nuremberg. In scenes of swooning women and cheering men, her film, called *Triumph of the*

NATIONAL INCOME OF THE POWERS IN 1937 AND PERCENTAGE SPENT ON DEFENSE

	National Income (billions of dollars)	Percentage Spent on Defense
United States	68	1.5
British Empire	22	5.7
France	10	9.1
Germany	17	23.5
Italy	6	14.5
USSR	19	26.4
Japan	4	28.2

Will, recorded the dramatic force of Hitler's rhetoric and his ability to move the German people. Hitler's public charisma masked a profoundly troubled and warped individual. Yet millions, including admirers in western Europe and the United States, succumbed to his appeal.

Targeting the Young and Women.   The Nazi total state also sought to regulate family life. Special youth organizations were created for boys and girls between the ages of 10 and 18. After passage of the Hitler Youth Law in 1936, boys were required to join the Hitler Youth, which indoctrinated them with nationalistic and military values. Girls had to join the League of German Girls, which was intended to mold them into worthy wives and mothers. Unmarried girls between the ages of 17 and 21 were eligible to join Faith and Beauty, a voluntary organization that taught mainly middle-class girls etiquette, dancing, fashion consciousness, and beauty care. A woman's natural function, Hitler argued, was to serve in the home. Education for women beyond the care of home and family was a waste. The German Women's Bureau under Gertrud Scholtz-Klink instructed adult women in their "proper" female duties. In an effort to promote large families, the state paid allowances to couples for getting married, subsidized families according to their size, and gave tax breaks to large families. Abortion and birth control were outlawed.

By 1937, the need for women workers conflicted with the goals of Nazi propaganda. With the outbreak of war in 1939, women were urged to work, especially in jobs such as munitions manufacture, formerly held by men. For working women with families, the double burden was a heavy one, as women were required to work long shifts—60-hour work weeks were not unusual—for low wages. Many women resisted entering the workforce if they had other income. At the beginning of 1943, as World War II was raging, female labor became compulsory.

Enemies of the State.   Nazi propaganda condemned everything foreign, including Mickey Mouse, who was declared an enemy of the state in the 1930s. Purging foreign influences meant purging political opponents, especially members of the Communist Party, who were rounded up and sent to concentration camps in Germany. Communism was identified as an international Jewish conspiracy to destroy the German *Volk* (people of Aryan descent). Nazi literature also identified "asocials," those who were considered deviant in any way, including homosexuals, who were likewise to be expelled. Euthanasia was used on the mentally ill and the developmentally disabled in the 1930s. Concentration camps were expanded to contain enemies of the state. Later, when concentration camps became sites of extermination and forced labor, gypsies, homosexuals, criminals, and religious offenders had to wear insignia of different colors to indicate their basis for persecution. The people who received the greatest attention for elimination from Nazi Germany, and then from Europe, were Jews.

Scapegoating Jews.   The first measures against the German Jews—their exclusion from public employment and higher education—began in 1933. In 1935, the Nuremberg Laws were enacted to identify Jews, to deprive them of their citizenship, and to forbid marriage and extramarital sexual relations between Jews and non-Jews. On the night of 9 November 1938, synagogues were set afire, and books and valuables owned by Jews were confiscated throughout Germany. Jews were beaten, about 91 were killed, and 20,000 to 30,000 were imprisoned in concentration camps. The night came to be called ***Kristallnacht*** ("night of broken glass"), which referred to the Jewish shop windows smashed by the Brown Shirts under orders from Goebbels. The government claimed that *Kristallnacht* was an outpouring of the German people's will. An atmosphere of state-sanctioned hatred prevailed.

In addition to anti-Semitism, Hitler also placed other racist theories at the core of his fascist ideology. "Experts" decided that sterilization was the surest way to protect "German blood." In 1933, one of the early laws of Hitler's new Reich decreed compulsory sterilization of "undesirables" to "eliminate inferior genes." The Nazi state decided who these "undesirables" were and forced the sterilization of 400,000 men and women.

The Third Reich delivered on its promises to end unemployment, to improve productivity, to break through the logjam of parliamentary obstacles, and to return Germany to the international arena as a contender for power. Yet Hitler's Nazi government ruled by violence, coercion, and intimidation. With a propaganda machine that glorified the leader and vilified groups singled out as scapegoats for Germany's problems, Hitler destroyed democratic institutions and civil liberties in his pursuit of German power.

DEMOCRACIES IN CRISIS

In contrast to the fascist mobilization of society and the Soviet restructuring of the economy, European democracies responded to the challenges of the Great Depression with small, tentative steps. France and Great Britain were less successful than Nazi Germany in meeting the problems of the Great Depression. France paid a high price for parliamentary stalemate and was still severely depressed on the eve of war in 1938–1939. Great Britain maintained a stagnant economy and stable politics under Conservative leadership. Internal dissension ripped Spain apart. Its civil war assumed broader dimensions as the Soviet Union, Italy, and Germany struggled over Spain's future while Europe's democratic nations stood by and accepted defeat.

The Failure of the Left in France

France's Third Republic, like most European parliamentary democracies in the 1930s, was characterized by a multiparty system. Genuine political differences often separated one

Adolf Hitler on "Racial Purity"

The purity of German blood was a recurrent theme in Hitler's speeches and writings from the beginning of his political career. In attacking both liberalism and socialism, Hitler offered racial superiority as the essence of the National Socialist "revolution." This speech, delivered in Berlin on 30 January 1937, lays out his attack on the concept of individual rights and humanity in favor of the folk community.

Focus Questions

In this diatribe, how does race function to promote the "folk" and to undermine the individual's rights? Is Hitler's goal here to create "a better understanding" among nations?

The most important plank in the National Socialist program is to abolish the liberal idea of the individual and the Marxist idea of humanity and to substitute for them the folk community rooted in the soil and held together by the bond of common blood. This sounds simple, but it involves a principle which has great consequences.

For the first time and in the first country our people are being taught to understand that, of all the tasks we have to face, the most noble and the most sacred for all mankind is the concept that each racial species must preserve the purity of blood which God has given to it.

The greatest revolution won by National Socialism is that it has pierced the veil which hid from us the knowledge that all human errors may be attributed to the conditions of the time and hence can be remedied, but there is one error that cannot be set right once it has been made by men—that is, the failure to understand the importance of keeping the blood and the race free from intermingling, and in this way to alter God's gift. It is not for human beings to discuss why Providence created different races. Rather it is important to understand the fact that it will punish those who pay no attention to its work of creation. . . .

I hereby prophesy that, just as knowledge that the earth moves around the sun led to a revolutionary change in the world picture, so will the blood-and-race doctrine of the National Socialist movement bring about a revolutionary change in our knowledge. . . . It will also change the course of history in the future.

This will not lead to difficulties between nations. On the contrary, it will lead to a better understanding between them. But at the same time it will prevent the Jews, under the mask of world citizenship, from thrusting themselves among all nations as an element of domestic chaos. . . .

The National Socialist movement limits its domestic activities to those individuals who belong to one people. It refuses to permit those of a foreign race to have any influence whatever on our political, intellectual, or cultural life. We refuse to give any members of a foreign race a dominant position in our national economic system.

In our folk community, which is based on ties of blood, in the results which National Socialism has obtained by training the public in the idea of this folk-community, lies the deepest reason for the great success of our Revolution.

party from another. The tendency to parliamentary stalemate was aggravated by the depression and by the increasingly extremist politics on both the Left and the Right in response to developments in the Soviet Union and Germany.

The belief of the French people in a private enterprise economy was shaken by the Great Depression, but no new unifying belief replaced it. Distrusting both the New Deal model of the United States and the Nazi response to depression politics, the Third Republic followed a haphazard, wait-and-see policy of insulating the economy, discouraging competition, and protecting favored interests in both industry and agriculture. France clung to the liberal belief in the self-adjusting mechanism of the market—and suffered greatly for it.

In 1936, an electoral mandate for change swept the Left into power. The new premier, Léon Blum (1872–1950), was a Socialist. Lacking the votes to rule with an exclusively Socialist government, Blum formed a coalition of Left and Center parties that were intent on economic reforms, known as the **Popular Front.** Before Blum's government could take power, a wave of strikes swept France, and the Popular Front was pushed to intervene. It promised wage increases, paid vacations, and collective bargaining to French workers. The reduced work week of 40 hours caused a drop in productivity, as did the short-lived one-month vacation policy. The government did nothing to prevent the outflow of investment capital from France. Higher wages failed to generate increased consumer demand because employers raised prices to cover their higher operating costs.

German rearmament, now publicly known, forced France into rearmament, which France could ill afford. Blum's government failed in 1937, with France still bogged down in a sluggish and depressed economy. The last peacetime government of the 1930s represented a conservative swing back to laissez-faire policies that put the needs of business above those of workers and brought a measure of revival to the French economy.

The radical Right drew strength from the Left's failures. Right-wing leagues and organizations multiplied, appealing to a frightened middle class. The failure of the Socialists, in turn, drove many sympathizers further to the Left to join the Communist Party. A divided France could not stand up to the foreign policy challenges of the 1930s posed by Hitler's provocations.

Muddling Through in Great Britain

Great Britain was hard hit by the Great Depression in the 1930s; only Germany and the United States experienced comparable economic devastation. The socialist Labour government of the years 1929 to 1931 under Prime Minister Ramsay MacDonald (1866–1937) was unprepared to deal with the 1929 collapse. It took a coalition of moderate groups from the three parties—Liberal, Conservative, and Labour—to address the issues of high unemployment, a growing government deficit, a banking crisis, and the flight of capital. The National Government (1931–1935) was a nonparty, centrist coalition whose members included Ramsay MacDonald, retained as prime minister, and Stanley Baldwin (1867–1947), a Conservative with a background in iron and steel manufacturing.

Slow Recovery. In response to the endemic crisis, the National Government took Britain off the international gold standard and devalued the pound. To protect domestic production, tariffs were established. The British economy showed signs of slow recovery, and the government survived the crisis. Moderates and classical liberals in Great Britain persisted in defending the nonintervention of the government in the economy, despite new economic theories, such as that of John Maynard Keynes (1883–1946), who urged government spending to stimulate consumer demand as the best way to shorten the duration of the depression.

The British Union of Fascists. Sir Oswald Mosley (1896–1980) promoted a fascist response to Britain's problems. In 1932, he founded the British Union of Fascists (BUF), consisting of goon squads and bodyguards. The BUF was opposed to free trade liberalism and communism alike. Like other European fascist organizations, BUF squads beat up their political opponents and began attacking Jews, especially eastern European émigrés living in London. Public alarm over increasingly inflammatory and anti-Semitic BUF rhetoric converged with parliamentary denunciation. Popular support for the group was already beginning to erode when the BUF was outlawed in 1936. By this time, anti-Hitler feeling was spreading in Great Britain. In Great Britain, the traditional party system prevailed not because of its brilliant solutions to difficult economic problems but because of the willingness of

moderate parliamentarians to cooperate and to adapt, however slowly, to the new need for economic transformation.

The Spanish Republic as Battleground

In 1931, Spain became a democratic republic after centuries of Bourbon monarchy and almost a decade of military dictatorship. In 1936, the voters of Spain elected a Popular

CHRONOLOGY	
THE RISE OF FASCISM AND DEMOCRACY IN CRISIS	
28 October 1922	Italian Fascists march on Rome
November 1923	Beer Hall Putsch in Munich
1924	Fascists achieve parliamentary majority in Italy
1929	Lateran Treaty between Mussolini and Pope Pius XI
1932	Nazi party is single largest party in German parliament
January 1933	Hitler becomes chancellor of Germany
30 June 1934	Purge of the SA leaves Hitler and the SS in unassailable position
March 1935	Hitler publicly rejects Treaty of Versailles and announces German rearmament
15 September 1935	Enactment of Nuremberg Laws against Jews and other minorities
3 October 1935	Italy invades Ethiopia
1936	Popular Front government elected in Spain
July 1936	Beginning of Spanish Civil War
October 1936	Rome-Berlin Axis Pact, an Italo-German accord
1936–1937	Popular Front government in France
27 April 1937	Bombing of the Spanish town of Guernica
9 November 1938	*Kristallnacht* initiates massive violence against Jews
March 1939	Fascists defeat the Spanish Republic
April 1939	Italy annexes Albania
May 1939	Pact of Steel between Germany and Italy

Front government. The Popular Front in Spain was more radical than its French counterpart. The property of aristocratic landlords was seized; revolutionary workers went on strike; the Catholic Church and its clergy were attacked. This social revolution initiated three years of civil war. On one side were the Republicans, the Popular Front defenders of the Spanish Republic and of social revolution in Spain. On the other side were the Nationalists, those who sought to overthrow the Republic: aristocratic landowners, supporters of the monarchy and the Catholic Church, and much of the Spanish army.

The Spanish Civil War began in July 1936 with a revolt against the Republic from within the Spanish army. It was led by General Francisco Franco (1892–1975), a tough, shrewd, and stubborn conservative nationalist allied with the Falange, the fascist party in Spain. The conflict soon became a bloody military stalemate, with the Nationalists led by Franco controlling the more rural and conservative south and west of Spain and the Republicans holding out in the cities of the north and east—Madrid, Valencia, and Barcelona.

Almost from the beginning, the Spanish Civil War was an international event. Mussolini sent "volunteer" ground troops to fight alongside Franco's forces. Hitler dispatched technical specialists, tanks, and the Condor Legion, an aviation unit, to support the Nationalists. The Germans regarded Spain as a testing ground for new equipment and new methods of warfare, including aerial bombardment. The Soviet Union intervened on the side of the Republic, sending armaments, supplies, and technical and political advisers. Because the people of Britain and France were deeply divided in their attitudes toward the war in Spain, the British government stayed neutral, and the government of France was unable to aid its fellow Popular Front government in Spain. Although individual Americans volunteered to fight with the Republicans, the U.S. government did not prevent the Texas Oil Company from selling oil to Franco's insurgents, nor did it block the Ford Motor Company, General Motors, and Studebaker from supplying them with trucks.

In response to the Spanish government's pleas for help, 2,800 American volunteers, among them college students, professors, intellectuals, and trade unionists, joined the loyalist army and European volunteers in defense of the Spanish Republic. Britons and antifascist émigrés from Italy and Germany also joined international brigades, which were vital in helping the city of Madrid hold out against the Nationalist generals. The Russians withdrew from the war in 1938, disillusioned by the failure of the French, British, and Americans to come to the aid of the Republicans. Madrid fell to the Nationalists in March 1939. The government that Franco established sent one million of its enemies to prison or concentration camps.

CONCLUSION

The fragile postwar stability of the 1920s crumbled under the pressures of economic depression, ongoing national antagonisms, and insecurity in the international arena. Europe after 1932 was plagued by the consequences of economic collapse, fascist success, and the growing threat of armed conflict. Parliamentary institutions were fighting and losing a tug-of-war with authoritarian movements. A fascist regime was in place in Italy. Dictatorships triumphed in Germany, Spain, and much of eastern and central Europe. Liberal parliamentary governments were threatened by the economic and social challenges of the postwar years.

The exclusion of the Soviet Union from Western internationalism exacerbated the crisis. The Bolshevik revolution had served as a political catalyst among workers in the West, attracting them to the possibility of radical solutions. That potential radicalization aggravated class antagonisms where mass politics prevailed and drove some political leaders to seek antidemocratic solutions in response to social unrest.

QUESTIONS FOR REVIEW

1. What problems for European stability were created or left unresolved by the armistice ending World War I?
2. What did Stalin's victory over Trotsky mean for economic development in the Soviet Union?
3. What is fascism, and why was it so alluring to Italians, Germans, and other Europeans?
4. How were rearmament, anti-Semitism, and economic self-sufficiency all part of Hitler's vision of *Lebensraum*?
5. Why did Europe's remaining democracies prove to be so frail during the 1930s?

KEY TERMS

collectivization, *p. 550*

fascism, *p. 552*

Great Depression, *p. 547*

Great Purge, *p. 551*

Kristallnacht, p. 557

Lebensraum, p. 555

Nazism, *p. 552*

New Economic Policy (NEP), *p. 549*

Popular Front, *p. 558*

Third Reich, *p. 555*

Weimar Republic, *p. 544*

DISCOVERING WESTERN CIVILIZATION ONLINE

You can obtain more information about the European search for stability between 1920 and 1939 at the websites listed below. See also the Companion Website that accompanies this text, www.ablongman.com/kishlansky, which contains an online study guide and additional resources.

Geographical Tour: Europe After 1918

League of Nations Statistical and Disarmament Documents

www.library.nwu.edu/govpub/collections/league/index.html
This is the home page of a project to digitize documents published by the League of Nations.

Internet Modern History Sourcebook: Age of Anxiety

www.fordham.edu/halsall/mod/modsbook40.html
A collection of links to electronic texts and materials on the interwar period, focusing on the cultural crisis in European and American societies as a result of World War I.

Internet Modern History Sourcebook: The Depression

www.fordham.edu/halsall/mod/modsbook41.html
Comprehensive collection of primary sources and links to materials on the Great Depression in Europe and the United States.

The Soviet Union's Separate Path

NEP: A Bibliography of Soviet and Western Literature

www.lib.duke.edu/ias/slavic/nep.htm
This site contains an exhaustive bibliography on Soviet history during the period of the New Economic Policy.

Revelations from the Russian Archives

www.loc.gov/exhibits/archives
A virtual exhibit by the Library of Congress on material from the secret archives of the Central Committee of the Communist Party of the USSR.

The Rise of Fascist Dictatorship in Italy

Internet Modern History Sourcebook: Fascism in Europe

www.fordham.edu/halsall/mod/modsbook42.html
This site refers to fascism in general, but it focuses on a speech of Mussolini and Spanish Civil War materials.

Hitler and the Third Reich

The National Socialist Era, 1933–1945

www.h-net.msu.edu/~german/gtext/nazi/index.html
This is a small collection of electronic texts relating to the rise of the Nazis, the creation of the Third Reich, and World War II.

Internet Modern History Sourcebook: Nazism

www.fordham.edu/halsall/mod/modsbook43.html
A collection of primary documents and links on the Weimar Republic and the rise of Nazism.

Third Reich Stamps

www.geocities.com/WallStreet/Exchange/5456/third.html
A website of stamps issued during the Third Reich with brief descriptions depicting the cultural values propagated by the Nazis.

Democracies in Crisis

Spanish Civil War Archive

dwardmac.pitzer.edu/anarchist_archives/spancivwar/
Spanishcivilwar.html
This site was created by a political studies professor at Pitzer College (see link for Paris Commune in Chapter 23) and contains essays, bibliography, and photographs.

SUGGESTIONS FOR FURTHER READING

Geographical Tour: Europe After 1918

Manfred E. Boemeke, Gerald Feldman, and Elisabeth Glaser, eds., *The Treaty of Versailles: A Reassessment After 75 Years* (Cambridge: Cambridge University Press, 1998). This collection of essays constitutes a reappraisal of the divergent peace aims of the United States, France, Germany, and Great Britain and a new understanding of the period of temporary stability created by the treaty after the war.

Igor Lukes, *Czechoslovakia Between Stalin and Hitler: The Diplomacy of Edvard Beneš in the 1930s* (New York: Oxford University Press, 1996). By examining the role of the Czech statesman Edvard Beneš, this book provides an important perspective on the Munich crisis of 1938 and of Czechoslovakia's fate in the battle between East and West.

Crisis and Collapse in a World Economy

Gerald Feldman, *The Great Disorder: Politics, Economy, and Society in the German Inflation, 1914–1924* (New York: Oxford University Press, 1993). Feldman's monumental study of the German inflation provides a detailed historical account of the economic conditions and monetary policy in Germany during and after the war.

The Soviet Union's Separate Path

Stephen F. Cohen, *Bukharin and the Bolshevik Revolution: A Political Biography, 1888–1938* (Oxford: Oxford University Press, 1980). This milestone work is a general history of the period, as well as a political and intellectual biography of Bukharin, "the last Bolshevik," who supported an evolutionary road to modernization and socialism and whose policies were an alternative to Stalinism.

Sheila Fitzpatrick, *Everyday Stalinism—Ordinary Life in Extraordinary Times: Soviet Russia in the 1930s* (New York: Oxford University Press, 1999). The author explores the rituals, family life, and institutions of the Stalinist era, what the author calls the "distinctive Stalinist habitat" of Russian urban life in the 1930s.

Arch Getty and Roberta Manning, *Stalinist Terror: New Perspectives* (Cambridge: Cambridge University Press, 1994). Leading revisionist scholars of the Stalinist period provide a reassessment of the regime.

Robert C. Tucker, *Stalin in Power: The Revolution from Above, 1928–1941* (New York: W.W. Norton & Company, 1992). The author portrays how Stalin deliberately chose terror, mass murder, forced resettlement, and prison camps as a means of enforcing "revolution from above."

Chris Ward, ed., *The Stalinist Dictatorship* (New York: Oxford University Press, 1998). A collection of leading Soviet scholars examine Stalin's character, his role within the Soviet Union, and how Stalinism was a lived experience.

The Rise of Fascist Dictatorship in Italy

MacGregor Knox, *Dictatorship, Foreign Policy, and War in Fascist Italy and Nazi Germany* (London: Cambridge University Press, 2000). Expanding on his earlier work on Mussolini's foreign policy, the author offers a comparative perspective of Italy's and Germany's moves from unification to militant dictatorships, the similar forces that shaped their creation, and the differences in expansionist zeal, military traditions, and fighting power.

Zeev Sternhell with Mario Sznajder and Maia Asheri, *The Birth of Fascist Ideology: From Cultural Rebellion to Political Revolution* (Princeton, NJ: Princeton University Press, 1994). Approaches fascism as an ideology rather than a social movement and argues that it was already fully formed before World War I.

Hitler and the Third Reich

Ian Kershaw, *Hitler, 1889–1936: Hubris* (New York: W.W. Norton & Company, 1998); and *Hitler, 1936–1945: Nemesis* (New York: W.W. Norton & Company, 2000). The definitive two-volume biography provides a history of Germany society through Hitler's extraordinary political domination.

Dieter Langewiesche, *Liberalism in Germany.* Translated by Christiane Banerji. (Princeton, NJ: Princeton University Press, 2000). This work traces the history of German liberalism from the early nineteenth century to post-1945 politics in West Germany as it was embodied in political movements, organizations, and values.

Bernd Widdig, *Culture and Inflation in Weimar Germany* (Berkeley: University of California Press, 2001). Through literary and filmic sources, the author provides a cultural analysis of a defining economic event in Germany history.

Democracies in Crisis

Ivan T. Berend, *Decades of Crisis: Central and Eastern Europe Before World War II* (Berkeley: University of California Press, 1998). The author offers a comprehensive overview of central and eastern Europe in the first half of the twentieth century and argues that the region "embarked on a historical 'detour'" in rejecting the parliamentary system and turning to nationalist authoritarian regimes.

John Hiden and Patrick Salmon, *The Baltic Nations and Europe: Estonia, Latvia, and Lithuania in the Twentieth Century* (London and New York: Longman, 1991). Surveys the development of the Baltic states in the twentieth century, discussing Baltic independence, the period between the wars, and the states' incorporation into the Soviet Union, as well as renewed efforts toward independence in the Gorbachev era.

Julian Jackson, *The Popular Front in France: Defending Democracy, 1934–1938* (Cambridge: Cambridge University Press, 1988). An in-depth study of Léon Blum's government, with a special emphasis on cultural transformation and the legacy of the Popular Front.

Michael Jackson, *Fallen Sparrows: The International Brigades in the Spanish Civil War* (Philadelphia: American Philosophical Society, 1994). A careful description of the members and activities of the International Brigades, which were organized under the direction of the Comintern to save the Spanish Republic.

Stanley G. Payne, *Fascism in Spain, 1923–1977* (Madison: The University of Wisconsin Press, 1999). The author presents a comprehensive history of Spanish fascism from its origins to the death of Franco.

Michael Richards, *A Time of Silence: Civil War and the Culture of Repression in Franco's Spain, 1936–1945* (Cambridge: Cambridge University Press, 1998). This work examines Spanish society during and after the Spanish Civil War in relation to Franco's policy of "moral and economic reconstruction" based on self-sufficiency.

For a list of additional titles related to this chapter's topics, please see www.ablongman.com/kishlansky.

28

GLOBAL CONFLAGRATION: WORLD WAR II, 1939–1945

The Visual Record

PRECURSOR OF WAR

Adolf Hitler's entry into Vienna, capital city of his native country of Austria, was planned as a media event. The accompanying photograph displays a triumphant Hitler leading what appears to be a parade on 14 March 1938. Standing in his open Mercedes in order to be visible to thousands of cheering Austrians and protected by thirteen police cars, Hitler was no less the conqueror. The motorcade of limousines moved slowly along the Ringstrasse, Vienna's most important street of monumental public buildings, greeted by wildly cheering crowds. The Nazi swastika fluttered on flagpoles and draped facades. The viewer is left to wonder how the flags and banners could have been manufactured and positioned over the course of a weekend to greet the Fuhrer's unannounced and "friendly visit." The independent nation of Austria had, overnight and with virtually no bloodshed, become part of the German Reich.

On the first page of *Mein Kampf,* Hitler had promised, "Germany-Austria must return to the great German mother-country, and not because of any economic considerations. . . . One blood demands one Reich." By 1938, Hitler had consolidated power at home by removing the non-Nazi conservatives from positions of power in Germany. Now he alone determined foreign policy. As a cornerstone of that policy, Hitler aimed to unite all German people in one nation by extending German control over territories including those not ethnically German, but which could provide "living space" and economic self-sufficiency for the German race. (See "Nazi Goals" in Chapter 27.) Becoming increasingly impatient, Hitler feared that Germany could fail to achieve its destiny as a world power by waiting too long to act. He became more aggressive and willing to use military force as he set out to remove, one by one, the obstacles to German domination of central Europe—Austria, Czechoslovakia, and Poland.

The annexation of Austria was the first step in Hitler's plans for conquest. Using the threat of invasion, Hitler intimidated the Austrian government into legalizing the Nazi party, which thereby brought pro-Nazis into the Austrian cabinet and German troops into the country. Many Austrians wanted to be joined to Germany; others had no desire to be led by Nazis. A rigged plebiscite in April 1938, organized by Goebbels's Propaganda

Ministry, delivered a 99.75 percent vote of approval in Austria for annexation by Germany. With the union of Austria and Germany, the Third Reich claimed a population of 80 million people as it prepared itself for a war to the east. What appeared to be a parade of pomp and circumstance in March 1938 was really the precursor of a terrible conflagration that would last for six years and claim 50 million lives around the globe.

Looking Ahead

This chapter considers the events leading to the outbreak of the war in 1939 and how collaboration and resistance developed across Europe as the German army advanced. Virulent racism played a central role in directing the war against Jews,

Slavs, and others identified as inferior by Nazi racial policies. The power of Soviet patriotism and bravery and the entry of the United States into the war ensured Allied victory. Allied cooperation gave way, however, even as the peace was being forged under the direction of the two superpowers. The dropping of the atom bomb on Japan hastened the war's end, but would taint the ensuing peace. ➤

AGGRESSION AND CONQUEST

The years between 1933 and 1939 marked a bleak period in international affairs when the British, the French, and the Americans were unwilling or unable to recognize the dire threat to world peace of Hitler and his Nazi state. The leaders of these countries did not comprehend Hitler's single-minded goal to extend German living space eastward as far as western Russia. They failed to understand the seriousness of the Nazi process of consolidation at home. Their preoccupation with the threat of communism also blinded them to the deadly reality of Hitler's threat, so they took no action against Hitler's initial acts of aggression. The war that began in Europe in 1939 eventually became a great global conflict that pitted Germany, Italy, and Japan—the **Axis Powers**—against the British Empire, the Soviet Union, and the United States—the Grand Alliance.

Even before war broke out in Europe, there was armed conflict in Asia. The rapidly expanding Japanese economy depended on Manchuria for raw materials and on China for markets. Chinese boycotts against Japanese goods and threats to Japanese economic interests in Manchuria led to a Japanese military occupation of Manchuria and the establishment of the Japanese puppet state of Manchukuo there in 1931–1932. When the powers of the League of Nations, led by Great Britain, refused to recognize this state, Japan withdrew from the League. Fearing that the Chinese government was becoming strong enough to exclude Japanese trade from China, Japanese troops and naval units began an undeclared war in China in 1937. Many important Chinese cities—Peking, Shanghai, Nanking, Canton, and Hankow—fell to Japanese forces. Relentless aerial bombardment of Chinese cities and atrocities committed by Japanese troops against Chinese civilians outraged Europeans and Americans. The governments of the Soviet Union, Great Britain, and the United States gave economic, diplomatic, and moral support to the Chinese government of Chiang Kai-shek. Thus the stage was set for a major military conflict in Asia and in Europe.

Hitler's Foreign Policy and Appeasement

For Hitler, a war against the Soviet Union for living space was inevitable. It would come, he told some of his close associates, in the years 1943–1945. However, he wanted to avoid fighting anew the war that had led to Germany's defeat in 1914–1918. In World War I, Germany fought on two fronts, and German soldiers, civilians, and resources were exhausted. In the next war, Hitler wanted to avoid fighting Great Britain while battling Russia. He convinced himself that the British would remain neutral if Germany agreed not to attack the British Empire. Would they not appreciate his willingness to abolish forever the menace of communism? Were they not Aryans also?

The Campaign Against Czechoslovakia.   Encouraged by his success in annexing Austria in 1938, Hitler provoked a crisis in Czechoslovakia in the summer of the same year. He demanded "freedom" for the German-speaking people of the Sudetenland area of Czechoslovakia. His main objective, however, was to smash the Czech state, the major obstacle in central Europe to the launching of an attack on living space farther east.

Western statesmen did not understand Hitler's commitment to destroying Czechoslovakia or his willingness to fight a limited war against the Czechs to do so. Britain, seeking to avoid war, sent Prime Minister Neville Chamberlain (1869–1940) to reason with Hitler. Believing that transferring the Sudetenland, the German-speaking area of Czechoslovakia, to Germany was the only solution—and one that would redress some of the wrongs done to Germany after World War I—Chamberlain convinced France and Czechoslovakia to yield to Hitler's demands.

Appeasement at Munich.   Chamberlain's actions were the result of British self-interest. British leaders agreed that their country could not afford another war like the Great War of 1914–1918. Defense expenditures had been dramatically reduced to devote national resources to improving domestic social services, protecting world trade, and fortifying Britain's global interests. Britain understood well its weakened position in its dominions. In the British hierarchy of priorities, defense of the British Empire ranked first, above defense of Europe, and Britain's commitment to western Europe ranked above the defense of eastern and central Europe.

Hitler's response to being granted everything he requested was to renege and issue new demands. His desire for war could not have been more transparent, nor could his unwillingness to play by the rules of diplomacy have been clearer. One final meeting was held at Munich to avert war. On 29 September 1938, one day before German troops were scheduled to invade Czechoslovakia, Mussolini and the French prime minister, Edouard Daladier (1884–1970), joined Hitler and Chamberlain at Munich to discuss a peaceful resolution to the crisis.

At Munich, Chamberlain and Daladier again yielded to Hitler's demands. The Sudetenland was ceded to Germany, and German troops quickly moved to occupy the area. The policy of the British and French was dubbed '**appeasement**' to indicate the willingness to concede to demands to preserve peace. Appeasement became a dirty word in twentieth-century European history, taken to mean weakness and cowardice. Yet Chamberlain was neither weak nor cowardly. His great mistake in negotiating with Hitler was assuming that Hitler was a reasonable man who, like all reasonable people, wanted to avoid another war.

Chamberlain thought that his mediation at Munich had won for Europe a lasting peace—"peace for our time," he reported. The people of Europe received Chamberlain's assessment with a sense of relief and shame—relief over what had been avoided, shame at having deserted Czechoslovakia. In fact, the policy of appeasement further destabilized Europe and accelerated Hitler's plans for European domination. Within months, Hitler cast aside the Munich agreement by annihilating Czechoslovakia. German troops occupied the western, Czech part of the state, including the capital of Prague. The Slovak eastern part became a German satellite. At the same time, Lithuania was pressured into surrendering Memel to Germany, and Hitler demanded control of Gdansk and the Polish Corridor. No longer could Hitler's goals be misunderstood.

Hitler's War, 1939–1941

In the tense months that followed the Munich meeting and the occupation of Prague, Hitler readied himself for war in western Europe. In May 1939, he formed a military alliance, the Pact of Steel, with Mussolini's Italy. Then Hitler and Stalin, previously self-declared enemies, shocked the West by joining their two nations in a pact of mutual neutrality, the Non-Aggression Pact of 1939. Opportunism lay behind Hitler's willingness to ally with the Communist state that he had denounced throughout the 1930s. A German alliance with the Soviet Union would, Hitler believed, force the British and the French to back down and to remain neutral while Germany conquered Poland—the last obstacle to a drive for expansion eastward—in a short, limited war. Stalin recognized the failure of the western European powers to stand up to Hitler. There was little possibility, he thought, of an alliance against Germany with the virulently anti-Communist Neville Chamberlain. The best Stalin could hope for was that the Germans and the Western powers would fight it out while the Soviet Union waited to enter the war at the most opportune moment. As an added bonus, Germany promised not to interfere if the Soviet Union annexed eastern Poland, Bessarabia, and the Baltic republics of Latvia and Estonia.

Finally recognizing Hitler's intent, the British and the French also signed a pact in the spring of 1939, promising assistance to Poland in the event of aggression. Tensions mounted throughout the summer as Europeans awaited the inevitable German aggression. On 1 September 1939, Germany attacked Poland, and by the end of the month the vastly outnumbered Poles surrendered. Although the German army needed no assistance, the Soviet Union invaded Poland ten days before its collapse, and Germany and the Soviet Union divided the spoils. Not trusting his alliance with Hitler, Stalin took measures to defend the Soviet Union against a possible German attack. The Soviet Union assumed military control in the Baltic states and demanded of Finland territory and military bases from which the city of Leningrad (formerly Petrograd) could be defended. When Finland refused, the Soviets invaded. In the snows of the "Winter War" of 1939–1940, the Finns initially fought the Soviet army to a standstill, much to the encouragement of the democratic West. However, the Finns were eventually defeated in March 1940.

War in Europe.   Hitler's war, the war for German domination of Europe, had begun. But it had not begun the way he intended. Great Britain and France, true to their alliance with Poland and contrary to Hitler's expectations, declared war on

■ A German motorized detachment rides through a bomb-shattered town during the Nazi invasion of Poland in 1939. The invasion saw the first use of the *blitzkrieg*—lightning war—in which air power and rapid tank movement combined for swift victory.

Germany on 3 September 1939, even though they were unable to give any help to Poland. In the six months after the fall of Poland, no military action took place between Germany and the Allies, because Hitler postponed offensives in northern and western Europe due to poor weather conditions. This strange interlude, which became known as "the phony war," was a period of suspended reality in which France and Great Britain waited for Hitler to make his next move. Civilian morale in France deteriorated among a population that still remembered the death and destruction that France had endured in the Great War. An attitude of defeatism germinated and grew before the first French soldier fell in battle.

With the arrival of spring, Germany attacked Denmark and Norway in April 1940. Then on 10 May 1940, Hitler's armies invaded the Netherlands, Belgium, and Luxembourg. By the

MAP DISCOVERY

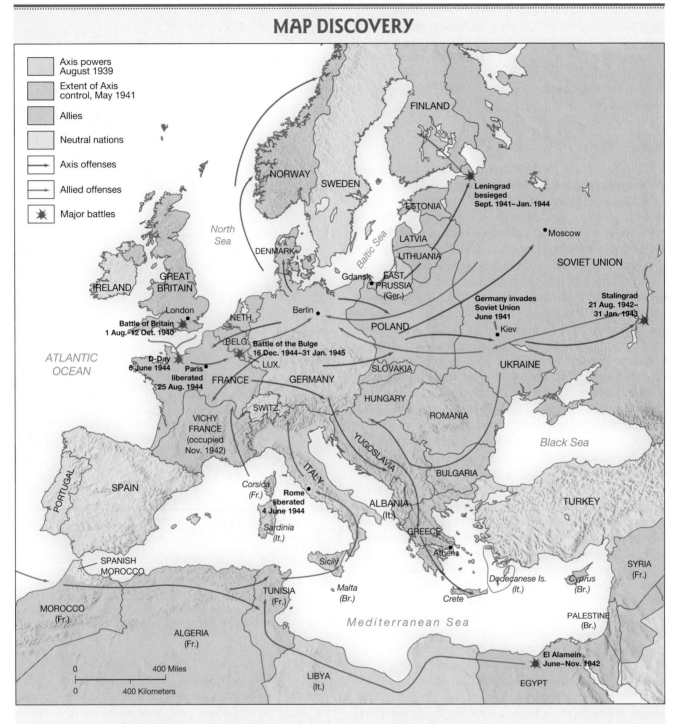

Axis powers
August 1939

Extent of Axis
control, May 1941

Allies

Neutral nations

Axis offenses

Allied offenses

Major battles

World War II in Europe

Note the movement of Axis armies in four different directions: north, south, east, and west. How
were the Axis forces able to sustain a multifront war? The Axis Powers controlled most of Europe
and north Africa by 1941. How do you explain the success of major Allied offensives?

third week of May, German mechanized forces were racing
through northern France toward the English Channel, cutting
off the British and Belgian troops and 120,000 French forces
from the rest of the French army. With the rapid defeat of

Belgium, these forces were crowded against the Channel and
had to be withdrawn from the beaches of Dunkirk. France,
with a large and well-equipped army, nevertheless relied on
Allied support and was in a desperate situation without it.

In France, the German army fought a new kind of war called *blitzkrieg* ("lightning war"), so named because of its speed. The British and the French had expected the German army to behave much as it had in World War I, concentrating its striking forces in a swing through coastal Belgium and Holland to capture Paris. French strategists believed that France was safe because of the hilly and forested terrain that they thought was impassable. They also counted on the protection of the fortress wall known as the Maginot Line that France had built in the interwar period. The Maginot Line stretched for hundreds of miles but was useless against mobile tank divisions that outflanked it. With stunning speed, Germany drove its tanks—panzers—through the French defenses at Sedan in eastern France.

The Fall of France. The French could have pinched off the advance of the overextended panzers, but the French army, suffering from severe morale problems, collapsed and was in retreat. On 17 June 1940, only weeks after German soldiers had stepped on French soil, Marshal Henri-Philippe Pétain, the great hero of the battle of Verdun in World War I, petitioned the Germans for an armistice. Three-fifths of France, including the entire Atlantic seaboard, was occupied by the German army and placed under direct German rule. In the territory that remained unoccupied, Pétain created a collaborationist government that resided at Vichy, a spa city in central France, and worked in partnership with the Germans for the rest of the war. Charles de Gaulle (1890–1970), a brigadier general who was opposed to the armistice, fled to London, where he set up a Free French government in exile.

The Battle of Britain. French capitulation in June 1940 followed Italian entry into the war on the side of Germany in the same month. The British were now alone in a war against the two Axis powers as Germany made plans for an invasion of the British Isles from across the English Channel. To prepare the way, the German air force under Reichsmarshal Hermann Göring (1893–1946) launched a series of air attacks against England, which became known as the Battle of Britain. The German air force first attacked British aircraft, airfields, and munitions centers and then shifted targets to major population centers such as London and industrial cities such as Coventry. Between 7 September and 2 November 1940, the city of London was bombed every night. Serious damage was inflicted on the city, and 15,000 people were killed.

Under the leadership of Winston Churchill the British resisted these attacks. Churchill had succeeded Chamberlain as prime minister in 1940. He was a master public speaker who, in a series of radio broadcasts, inspired the people of Britain with the historic greatness of the task confronting them: holding out against Nazism until the forces of the overseas British Empire and the United States could be marshaled to liberate Europe. The British Royal Air Force inflicted serious losses on German aircraft, while British industry was able to maintain steady production of planes, bombs, and armaments. Civilians endured the nightly destruction and air raids in

what Churchill termed Britain's "finest hour." Recognizing his lack of success in establishing air superiority over the Channel or in breaking the will of the British people, Hitler abandoned the Battle of Britain and canceled the invasion.

It was not in Great Britain but in the Balkans that Hitler was able to engage the British enemy and inflict serious losses. The British had a presence in the Greek peninsula, where their air units were deployed to support the valiant resistance of the Greeks against Italian aggression. In his original plans for a limited war, Hitler hoped to establish control over the Balkans by peaceful, diplomatic means. But Mussolini's disastrous attempt to achieve military glory by conquering Greece impelled Hitler to make his own plans to attack Greece. Using Bulgaria as the base of operations, Germany invaded Yugoslavia, whose government had been weakened by a recent military coup. The capital of Belgrade fell in April 1941. Internal ethnic enmity between the Croats and the Serbs led

■ The London Underground was pressed into service as a bomb shelter during the Battle of Britain.

to the mutiny of Croatian soldiers and the formation of an autonomous Croatian government in Zagreb that was favorably disposed to the Germans.

German troops then crossed the Yugoslav border into Greece, capturing the capital of Athens on 27 April 1941. German forces then turned their attention to the Greek island of Crete, where fleeing British soldiers sought refuge. In the first mass paratroop attack in history, the Germans rapidly subdued Crete, forcing the British to evacuate to Egypt. The British were routed and experienced humiliating defeat by the German blitzkrieg.

The Balkans were important to Hitler for a number of reasons. Half of Germany's wheat and livestock came from the countries of southeastern Europe. Romanian and Hungarian oil fields supplied Germany's only non-Russian oil. Greece and Yugoslavia were important suppliers of metal ores—including aluminum, tin, lead, and copper—so necessary for industry and the war effort.

The necessity of protecting resources, especially the Romanian oil fields, also gave the area geopolitical importance for Germany. Hitler was well aware of the strategic significance of controlling the Dardanelles in launching an attack against the Soviet Union. Potentially, the British lifeline to its empire could also be cut by control of the eastern Mediterranean.

Collaboration and Resistance

No one nation has ever controlled the Balkans, and Hitler understood that he must rule not by occupation but by collaboration. Collaboration made fewer demands on Germany's troops and resources, as Vichy collaboration in France made clear.

Some Balkan collaborators joined puppet governments out of an ideological commitment to fascism. They were hostile to communism and believed that Hitler's Nazism was far preferable to Stalin's communism. They saw in the German victory the chance to put their beliefs into practice. Some governments collaborated with the Germans out of national self-interest. The government of Hungary allied with Germany in the hope of winning back territory lost at the end of World War I, while Romania allied with the Soviet Union. The government of Slovakia was loyal to the Third Reich because Hitler had given it independence from the Czechs. A German puppet state was set up in the Yugoslav province of Croatia. Other collaborators were pragmatists who believed that by taking political office, they could negotiate with the German conquerors and soften the effects of the Nazi conquest on their people. Hitler had little affection for local ideological fascists and sometimes smashed their movements. He preferred to work with local generals and administrators.

Resistance against German occupation and collaborationist regimes took many forms. Resisters wrote subversive tracts, distributed them, gathered intelligence information for the Allies, sheltered Jews or other enemies of the Nazis, committed acts of sabotage, assassination or other violent acts, and carried on guerrilla warfare against the German army. Resisters ran the risk of endangering themselves and their families, who, if discovered, would be tortured and killed. Resistance movements developed most strongly after the German attack on the Soviet Union in 1941, when the Communist parties of occupied Europe formed the core of the violent resistance against the Nazi regime. Resistance grew stronger when the Germans began to draft young European men for work on German farms and in German factories. Many preferred to go underground rather than to Germany.

One of the great resistance fighters of the Second World War was Josip Broz (1892–1980), alias Tito. He was a Croatian communist and a Yugoslav nationalist. His partisans fought against Italian and German troops and kept ten or more German divisions tied up in Yugoslavia. Tito gained the admiration and the support of Churchill, Roosevelt, and Stalin. After liberation, Tito's organization won 90 percent of the vote in the Yugoslav elections, and he became the leader of the country in the postwar era. Resistance entailed enormous risks and required secrecy, moral courage, and great bravery. On the whole, however, the actions of resistance fighters seldom affected military timetables and did little to change the course of the war and Hitler's domination of Europe.

By the middle of 1941, Hitler controlled a vast continental empire that stretched from the Baltic Sea to the Black Sea and from the Atlantic Ocean to the Russian border. The German army occupied territories and controlled satellites, or Hitler relied on collaborationist governments for support. Having destroyed the democracies of western Europe, with the exception of Great Britain, Hitler's armies absorbed territory and marched across nations at rapid speed with technical and strategic superiority. But military conquest was not the only horror that the seemingly invincible Hitler inflicted on European peoples.

RACISM AND DESTRUCTION

War is hell, as the saying goes. But the horrors perpetrated in World War II exceeded anything ever experienced in Western civilization. In both the European and Asian theaters of battle, claims of racial superiority were invoked to justify inhuman atrocities. The Germans and Japanese used spurious arguments of racial superiority to fuel their war efforts. In Asia, the subjugation of inferior peoples became a rallying cry for conquest. But the Germans and the Japanese were not alone in using racist propaganda. The United States employed racial stereotypes to depict the inferiority of the enemy. They seized the property of Japanese-Americans living on the West Coast and interned them in "relocation" camps.

Nowhere, however, was the use of racism by the state more virulent than in Germany. Nazis used the phrase "the master race" to identify the human beings they considered worthy of living; those not worthy were designated "subhuman." Hatred of certain groups fueled both politics and war. Hitler promised the German people a purified Reich of Aryans "free of the Jews" and the racially and mentally inferior. Slavic peoples—Poles and Russians—he designated as subhumans who could be displaced in the search for *Lebensraum* and German destiny. With the war in eastern Europe, anti-Semitism changed from a policy of persecution and expropriation in the 1930s into a program of systematic extermination beginning in 1941.

Enforcing Nazi Racial Policies

Social policies that were erected on horrifying biomedical theories discriminated against a variety of social groups in the Third Reich. Beginning in 1933, police harassment of those identified as gypsies began in earnest. In 1936, the Nazi bureaucracy expanded to include the Reich Central Office against the Gypsy Nuisance, which assiduously maintained files on gypsies. Gypsies were subject to all racialist legislation and could be sterilized for their "inferiority" without any formal hearing process. In September 1939, even as the war was beginning, high-ranking Nazis planned the removal of 30,000 gypsies to Poland. Over 200,000 German, Russian, Polish, and Balkan gypsies were killed in the course of the war by internment in camps and by systematic extermination.

Nazi racial policies also singled out mixed-race children for special disgrace. Children born of white German mothers and black fathers were a consequence of the presence of French colonial troops from Senegal, Morocco, and Malaga, who were among the occupation forces in the Rhineland in the 1920s and 1930s. During both the Weimar Republic and the Nazi regime, the press attacked these children, who probably numbered no more than 500 to 800 individuals, as "Rhineland bastards." In 1937, without any legal proceedings, the Nazis sterilized them.

People who suffered from hereditary illnesses were also labeled a biological threat to the racial purity of the German people. State doctors devised illegitimate medical tests to establish who was feeble-minded and genetically defective. By treating the society of the Third Reich as one huge laboratory for the production of the racially fit and the "destruction of worthless life," categories were constructed according to subjective criteria that claimed scientific validation. Medical officials examined children, and those who were judged to be deformed were separated from their families and transferred to special pediatric clinics, where they were either starved to death or injected with lethal drugs. In the summer of 1939, the government organized euthanasia programs for adults and identified 65,000 to 70,000 Germans for death. The government required asylums to rank patients according to their race, state of health, and ability to work. These rankings were used to determine candidates for death. In Poland, mental patients were simply shot; in other places they were starved to death. The uncooperative, the sick, and the disabled were purged as racially undesirable.

The category covering the "asocial" was even broader than that covering hereditary illness. Under this designation, criminals, beggars, vagrants, and the homeless could be compulsorily sterilized. Alcoholics, prostitutes, and people with sexually transmitted diseases could be labeled asocial and treated accordingly. These forms of behavior were considered to be hereditary and determined by blood.

Nazi social policies likewise treated homosexuals as "community aliens." The persecution of homosexual men intensified after 1934, when any form of "same-sex immorality" became subject to legal prosecution. "Gazing and lustful intention" were left to the definition of the police and the courts. Criminal sentences could involve a term in a concentration camp. But because homosexuality was judged to be a sickness rather than an immutable biological trait, gays did not become the primary object of Nazi extermination policies that began to be enforced against the "biologically inferior." Treatment of homosexuality might involve psychoanalysis, castration, or indefinite incarceration in a concentration camp.

The badge of homosexual men in Nazi concentration camps during the war was a pink triangle. Although it is not clear how many homosexual men were actually killed by the Nazis, estimates run as high as 200,000. Officials of the Third Reich singled out homosexual men rather than lesbian women because the men's behavior was considered a greater threat to the perpetuation of the German race.

The Destruction of Europe's Jews

In 1933, when Hitler and the Nazis came to power, they did not have a blueprint for the destruction of Europe's Jews. The anti-Semitic policies of the Third Reich evolved incrementally in the 1930s and 1940s. After 1938, German civil servants expropriated Jewish property as rightfully belonging to the state. When the war began, Jews were rounded up and herded into urban ghettos in Germany and in the large cities of Poland. For a time, the German foreign ministry considered the possibility of deporting the more than three million Jews under German control to Madagascar, an island off the southeast coast of Africa. Until 1941, Nazi policies against the Jews were often uncoordinated and unfocused.

The Final Solution. Confinement in urban ghettos was the beginning of a policy of concentration that ended in annihilation. After identifying Jews, seizing their property, and confining them to ghettos, German authorities began to implement a step-by-step plan for extermination. There appears to have been no single order from Hitler that decreed what became known to German officials as the **Final Solution**—the total extermination of European Jews. But Hitler's recorded remarks make it clear that he knew and approved of what was being done to the Jews. A spirit of shared purpose permeated the entire administrative system from the civil service through the judiciary.

Administrative agencies competed to interpret Hitler's will. SS guards in the camps and police in the streets embraced Hitler's "mission" of destruction. To ensure that the whole process operated smoothly, a planning conference for the Final Solution was held for the benefit of state and party officials at Wannsee, a Berlin suburb, in January 1942. Reinhard Heydrich (1904–1942), head of the Sicherheitsdienst (SD), or Security Service of the SS, led the conference.

Mass racial extermination began with the German conquest of Poland, where both Jews and non-Jews were systematically

■ Seizing Jews in Warsaw. Nazi soldiers rounded up men, women, and children for "resettlement" in the east.

killed. It continued when Hitler's army invaded the Soviet Union in 1941. This campaign, known as Operation Barbarossa, set off the mass execution of eastern Europeans who were declared to be enemies of the Reich. The tactics of the campaign pointed the way to the Final Solution. To the Nazi leadership, Slavs were subhuman, and by extension, Russian Jews were the lowest of the low, even more despised than German Jews. Nazi propaganda had equated Jews with Communists, and Hitler had used the single word *Judeocommunist* to describe what he considered to be the most dangerous criminal and enemy of the Third Reich, the enemy who must be annihilated at any cost.

The executions were the work of the SS, the elite military arm of the Nazi Party. Special mobile murder squads of the SD under Heydrich were organized behind the German lines in Poland and Russia. Members of the army were aware of what the SS squads were doing and participated in some of the extermination measures. In the spring of 1941, Hitler ordered a massive propaganda campaign to be conducted among the armed forces. This campaign indoctrinated the army to believe that the invasion of the Soviet Union was more than a military campaign; it was a "holy war," a crusade that Germany was waging for civilization. SS chief Heinrich Himmler, probably responding to oral orders from Hitler, set about enforcing Hitler's threats with concrete extermination policies. Fearful that the SS would be outstripped by the regular army in Hitler's favor, Himmler exhorted his men to commit the worst atrocities.

Firing squads shot Russian victims en masse, then piled their bodies on top of one another in open graves. Reviewing these procedures for mass killings, Himmler—ever competitive with other Nazi agencies—suggested a more efficient means of exter-

mination that would require less labor power and would enhance the prestige of the SS. As a result, extermination by gas was introduced; the exhaust fumes of vans were piped into the enclosed cargo areas that served as portable gas chambers. In Poland, Himmler replaced the vans with permanent buildings housing gas chambers, which used Zyklon B, a gas developed for the purpose by the chemical firm I. G. Farben. The chambers could annihilate thousands of people at a time.

The Third Reich began erecting its vast network of death in 1941. The first extermination camp was created in Chelmno, Poland, where 150,000 people were killed between 1941 and 1944. The camps practiced systematic extermination of the groups that were deemed racially inferior, sexually deviant, and politically dangerous. The term **Holocaust** has been used to describe the mass slaughter of European Jews, most of which took place in five major killing centers in what is now Polish territory: Chelmno, Belzec, Sobibor, Treblinka, and Auschwitz. *Holocaust,* drawn from the Greek term for "burnt sacrifice," came to be used more generally after World War II to describe genocide and nuclear annihilation.

Many victims, transported for days in sealed railroad cars without food, water, or sanitation facilities, died before ever reaching the camps. Others died within months as forced laborers for the Reich. People of all ages were starved, beaten, and systematically humiliated. Guards taunted their victims verbally, degraded them physically, and tortured them with false hope. Having been promised clean clothes and nourishment, camp internees were herded into "showers" that dispensed gas rather than water. Descriptions of life in the camps reveal a systematized brutality and inhumanity on the part of the German,

Ukrainian, and Polish guards toward their victims. In all, 11 million people died by the extermination process—6 million Jews and almost as many non-Jews, including children, the aged, homosexuals, Slavic slave laborers, Soviet prisoners of war, Communists, members of the Polish and Soviet leadership, various resisters, gypsies, and Jehovah's Witnesses.

The words ARBEIT MACHT FREI ("Work Makes You Free") were emblazoned over the main gate at Auschwitz, the largest of the concentration camps. It was at Auschwitz that the greatest number of people died in a single place, including more than one million Jews. The healthy and the young were kept barely alive to work. Hard labor, starvation, and disease—especially typhus, tuberculosis, and other diseases that spread rapidly because of the lack of sanitation—claimed many victims.

On entering the camps, the sick and the aged were automatically designated for extermination because of their uselessness as a labor force. Many children were put to work, but some were designated for extermination. Many mothers chose to accompany their children to their deaths to comfort them in their final moments. Pregnant women, too, were considered useless in the forced labor camps and were sent immedi-

ately to the "showers." The number of German Jewish women who died in the camps was 50 percent higher than the number of German Jewish men. Starvation diets meant that women stopped menstruating. Because the Nazis worried that women of childbearing age would continue to reproduce, women who showed signs of menstruation were killed immediately. Women who were discovered to have given birth in the camp were killed, as were their infants. Family relations were completely destroyed, as inmates were segregated by sex. It soon became clear that even those who were allowed to live were intended only to serve the Nazis' short-term needs.

Resisting Destruction. The impossibility of any effective resistance was based on two essential characteristics of the process of extermination. First, the entire German state and its bureaucratic apparatus were involved in the policies, laws, and decrees of the 1930s that singled out victims while most other Germans stood silently by. There was no possibility of appeal and no place to hide. Those who understood early what was happening and who had enough money to buy their way out emigrated to safer places, including Palestine and the United

■ The Holocaust. The greatest loss of Jewish life in the Holocaust took place in Poland and the Soviet Union.

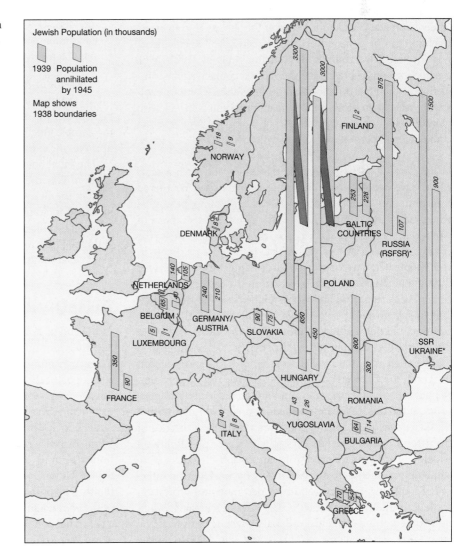

States. But most countries used immigration quotas to block the entry of German and eastern European refugees. Neither Britain nor the United States was willing to deal with a mass influx of European Jews. Jews in the occupied countries and the Axis nations had virtually no chance to escape. They were trapped in a society where all forces of law and administration worked against them.

A second reason for the impossibility of effective resistance was the step-by-step nature of the process of extermination, which meant that few understood the final outcome until it was too late. Initially, in the 1930s, many German Jews believed that things could get no worse and obeyed the German state as good citizens. Even the policy of removing groups from the ghetto militated against resistance because the hope was that sending 1,000 Jews to "resettlement" would allow the 10,000 Jews who remained behind to be saved. The German authorities deliberately cultivated misunderstanding of what was happening.

Isolated instances of resistance in the camps—rioting at Treblinka, for example—only highlight how impossible rebellion was for physically debilitated people in these heavily guarded centers. In April 1943, in the Warsaw ghetto, Jews organized a resistance movement with a few firearms and some grenades and homemade Molotov cocktails. Starvation, overcrowding, and epidemics made Warsaw, the largest of the ghettos, into an extermination camp. As news reached the ghetto that "resettlement" was the death warrant for tens of thousands of Polish Jews, armed rebellion erupted. It did not succeed in blocking the completion of the Final Solution against the Warsaw ghetto the following year, when the SS commandant proclaimed, "The Jewish Quarter of Warsaw is no more!" Polish and Russian Jews accounted for 70 percent of total Jewish deaths.

Who Knew?   It is impossible that killing on such a scale could have been kept secret. Along with those who ordered extermination operations, the guards and camp personnel who were involved in carrying out the directives were aware of what was happening. Those who brought internees to the camps, returning always with empty railroad cars, knew it, too. People who saw their neighbors disappearing believed for a time that they were being resettled in the east. But as news filtered back to central and western Europe, it was more difficult to sustain belief in this ruse. People who lived near the camps could not ignore the screams and the fumes of gas and burning bodies that permeated the environs of the camps.

Although it never publicly announced its extermination program, the German government convinced its citizens that the policies of the Nazi state could not be judged by ordinary moral standards. Official propaganda convinced millions that the Reich was the supreme good. Admitting the existence of the extermination program carried with it a responsibility on which few acted, perhaps out of fear of reprisals. There were some heroes, such as Raoul Wallenberg of Sweden, who interceded for Hungarian Jews and provided food and protection for Jews in the Budapest ghetto. The king of Denmark, when informed that the Nazis had ordered Danish Jews to wear the yellow star, stated that he and his family would also wear the yellow star as a "badge of honor." However, heroic acts were isolated and rare.

Collaborationist governments and occupied nations often cooperated with Nazi extermination policies. The French government at Vichy introduced and implemented a variety of anti-Jewish measures. All of this was done without German orders and without German pressure. By voluntarily identifying and deporting Jews, the Vichy government sent 75,000 men, women, and children to their deaths.

As the war dragged on for years, internees of the camps hoped and prayed for rescue by the Allies. But such help did not come. The U.S. State Department and the British Foreign Office had early and reliable information about the nature and extent of the atrocities. But they did not act.

The handful of survivors found by Allied soldiers who entered the camps after Germany's defeat presented a haunting picture of humanity. A British colonel who entered the camp at Bergen-Belsen in April 1945 gave a restrained account of what he found:

> As we walked down the main road of the camp, we were cheered by the internees, and for the first time we saw their condition. A great number were little more than living skeletons. There were men and women lying in heaps on both sides of the track. Others were walking slowly and aimlessly about, vacant expressions on their starved faces.

The sight of corpses piled on top of one another lining the roads, the piles of shoes, clothing, underwear, and gold teeth extracted from the dead shocked those who came to liberate the camps. One of the two survivors of Chelmno summed it up: "No one can understand what happened here."

The Final Solution was a perversion of every value of civilization. The international tribunal for war crimes that met in 1945 in the German city of Nuremberg attempted to mete out justice to the criminals who were responsible for the destruction of 11 million Europeans who had been labeled as demons and racial inferiors. History must record, even if it cannot explain, such inhumanity.

ALLIED VICTORY

At the end of 1941, the situation appeared grim for the British and their dominions and the Americans who were assisting them with munitions, money, and food. Hitler had achieved control of a vast land empire covering nearly all of continental Europe in the west, north, south, and center, as well as much of North Africa. This empire, which Hitler called his "New Order," included territories that were occupied and directly administered by the German army, satellites, and collaborationist regimes. It was fortified by alliances with Italy, the Soviet Union, and Japan. Hitler commanded the greatest fighting force in the world, one that had knocked France out of the war in a matter of weeks, brought destruction to British cities, and conquered Yugoslavia in 12 days. Much of the world was coming to fear German invincibility.

Then, in June 1941, Hitler's troops invaded the Soviet Union, providing the British with an ally. In December, the naval and air forces of Japan attacked U.S. bases in the Pacific, providing the British and the Russians with still another ally. What began as a European war became a world war. This was the war that Hitler did not want and that Germany could not win—a long, total war to the finish against three powers with inexhaustible resources: the British Empire, the Soviet Union, and the United States.

The Soviet Union's Great Patriotic War

Hitler had always considered the Soviet Union Germany's primary enemy. The 1939 Non-Aggression Pact with Stalin was no more than an expedient for Hitler. He rebuked a Swiss diplomat in 1939 for failing to grasp the central fact of his foreign policy:

> Everything I undertake is directed against Russia. If those in the West are too stupid and too blind to understand this, then I should be forced to come to an understanding with the Russians to beat the West, and then, after its defeat, turn with all my concentrated force against the Soviet Union.

Soviet Unpreparedness.   On 22 June 1941, when German armies marched into Russia, they found the large Soviet army totally unprepared for war. Stalin's purges in the late 1930s removed 35,000 officers from their posts by dismissal, imprisonment, or execution. Many of the men who replaced them were unseasoned in the responsibilities of leadership. The Russians had not expected the German attack to come so soon, and when the Germans did invade Russian territory, Stalin was so overwhelmed that he fell into a depression and was unable to act for days.

On 3 July 1941, in his first radio address after the attack, Stalin identified his nation with the Allied cause: "Our struggle for the freedom of our country will merge with the struggle of the peoples of Europe and America for their independence, for democratic liberties." He accepted offers of support from the United States and Great Britain. With France defeated and Great Britain crippled, the future of the war depended on Soviet fighting power and U.S. supplies.

German Offensive and Reversals.   Hitler's invasion of Russia involved three million soldiers from Germany and Germany's satellites, the largest invasion force in history. It stretched along an immense battlefront from the Baltic Sea to the Black Sea. Instead of exclusively targeting Moscow, the capital, the German army concentrated first on destroying Soviet armed forces and capturing Leningrad in the north and the oil-rich Caucasus in the south. In the beginning, the German forces advanced rapidly in a blitzkrieg across western Russia, where they were greeted as liberators in Ukraine. The Germans took 290,000 prisoners of war and massacred tens of thousands of others in their path through the Jewish settlements of western Russia.

Within four months, the German army had advanced to the gates of Moscow, but they concentrated their forces too late. The Red Army rallied to defend Moscow, as thousands of civilian women set to work digging trenches and antitank ditches around the city. The Soviet people answered Stalin's call for a scorched-earth policy by burning everything that might be useful to the advancing German troops. German troops had also burned much in their path, depriving themselves of essential supplies for the winter months ahead. The German advance was stopped, as the best ally of the Red Army—the Russian winter—settled in. The first snow fell at the beginning of October. By early November, German troops were beginning to suffer the harsh effects of an early and exceptionally bitter Russian winter.

Hitler promised the German people that "final victory" was at hand. So confident was Hitler of a speedy and decisive victory that he sent his soldiers into Russia wearing only light summer uniforms. Hitler's generals knew better and tried repeatedly to explain military realities to him. General Heinz Guderian (1888–1954), commander of the tank units, reported that his men were suffering frostbite, tanks could not be started, and automatic weapons were jamming in the subzero temperatures. Back in Germany, the civilian population received little accurate news of the campaign. They began to suspect the worst when the government sent out a plea for woolen blankets and clothing for the troops.

By early December, the German military situation was desperate. The Soviets, benefiting from intelligence information about German plans and an awareness that Japan was about to declare war on the United States, recalled fresh troops from the Siberian frontier and the border with China and Manchuria and launched a powerful counterattack against the poorly outfitted German army outside Moscow. Under the command of General Gyorgi Zhukov (1896–1974), Russian troops, dressed and trained for winter warfare, pushed the Germans back in retreat across the snow-covered expanses. By February, 200,000 German troops had been killed, 46,000 were missing in action, and 835,000 were casualties of battle and the weather. Thus the campaign cost the German army over one million casualties. It probably cost the Soviets twice that number of wounded, missing, captured, and dead soldiers. At the end of the Soviet counterattack in March, the German army and its satellite forces were in a shambles reminiscent of Napoleon's troops, who had been decimated 130 years earlier in the campaign to capture Moscow. An enraged Hitler dismissed his generals for retreating without his permission, and he himself assumed the position of commander-in-chief of the armed forces.

Hitler was not daunted by the devastating costs of his invasion of Russia. In the summer of 1942, he initiated a second major offensive, this time to take the city of Stalingrad. Constant bombardment gutted the city, and the Soviet army was forced into hand-to-hand combat with the German soldiers. But the German troops, once again inadequately supplied and unprepared for the Russian winter, failed to capture the city. The Battle of Stalingrad was over in the first days of February 1943. Of the original 300,000 members of the German Sixth Army, fewer than 100,000 survived to be taken prisoner by the Soviets.

Of those, only 5,000 returned to Germany in 1955, when German prisoners of war were repatriated.

Soviet Patriotism.   The Soviets succeeded by exploiting two great advantages in their war against Germany: the large Soviet population and their knowledge of Russian weather and terrain. There was a third advantage that Hitler ignored: the Soviet people's determination to sacrifice everything for the war effort. In his successive Five-Year Plans, Stalin had mobilized Soviet society with an appeal to fulfill and surpass production quotas. In the summer of 1941, as Hitler's troops threatened Moscow, Stalin used the same rhetoric to appeal to his Soviet "brothers and sisters" to join him in waging "the Great Patriotic War." The Russian people shared a sense of common purpose, sacrifice, and moral commitment in their loyalty to the nation.

The advancing Germans themselves intensified Soviet patriotism by torturing and killing tens of thousands of peasants who might have willingly cooperated against the Stalinist regime. Millions of Soviet peasants joined the Red Army. Young men of high school age were drafted into the armed forces. Three million women became wage earners for the first time as they replaced men in war industries. Women who remained on the land worked to feed the townspeople and the soldiers. Because the Red Army had requisitioned horses and tractors for combat, grain had to be sown and harvested by hand—and this often meant women's hands. Tens of thousands of Russians left their homes in western Russia to work for relocated Soviet industries in the Urals, the Volga region, Siberia, and Central Asia.

More than 20 million Soviet people—soldiers and civilians, men, women, and children—died in the course of World War II. In addition to those who were killed in battle, millions starved as a direct result of the hardships of war. In 1943, food was so scarce that seed for the next year's crops was eaten. One in every three men born in 1906 died in the war. But Soviet resistance did not flag.

The Great Patriotic War had a profound impact on Soviet views of the world and the Soviet Union's place in it. The Soviet Union sacrificed 10 percent of its population to the war effort and incurred well over 50 percent of all the deaths and casualties of the war. Few families escaped the death of members in the defense of the nation. Soviet citizens correctly considered that they had given more than any other country to defeat Hitler. For the Soviet people their suffering in battle made World War II the Soviet Union's war, and their sacrifice made possible the Allied victory.

The United States Enters the War

Victory still eluded the Allies in western Europe, where another nation, the United States, had now entered the fray. Although a neutral power, the United States began extending aid to the Allies after the fall of France in 1940. Since neither Britain nor the Soviet Union could afford to pay the entire cost of defending Europe against Hitler, the U.S. Congress passed the Lend-

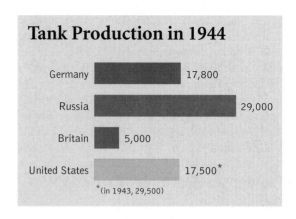

Tank Production in 1944

Germany	17,800
Russia	29,000
Britain	5,000
United States	17,500*

*(in 1943, 29,500)

Lease Act in 1941. This act authorized President Roosevelt to provide armaments to Great Britain and the Soviet Union without payment. America became "the arsenal of democracy." The United States and Britain sent 4,100 airplanes and 138,000 motor vehicles, as well as steel and machinery, to the Soviet Union for the campaign of 1943. In all, the United States pumped $11 billion worth of equipment into the Soviet war effort between 1941 and 1945. Stalin later told Roosevelt that the Soviet Union would have lost the war with Germany without the help of the Americans and the British.

Japan Attacks.   Before the United States entered the war, President Roosevelt and his advisers considered Germany, not Japan, to be America's primary target for a future war. The United States, aware that Japan wanted to expand its control over China and Southeast Asia, initially opposed this expansion through economic embargoes. The presence of the Soviet Union pressing eastward across Asia, coupled with the colonial presences in Asia of Great Britain, France, and the United States, severely constrained Japan's capacity to expand its frontiers and ensure its security. The war in western Europe and the German invasion of the Soviet Union in June 1941 meant that the Japanese could concentrate their attention farther south in China, Indochina, and Thailand. Japan's limited reserves of foreign currency and raw materials drew its attention to the oil and raw materials in Southeast Asia.

In September 1940, Japan joined forces with the Axis Powers of Germany and Italy in the Tripartite Pact, in which the signatories, promising mutual support against aggression, acknowledged the legitimacy of each other's expansionist efforts in Europe and Asia. Japanese-American relations deteriorated after the Japanese invasion of southern Indochina in July 1941. The United States insisted that Japan vacate China and Indochina and reestablish the open door for trade in Asia. However, the United States knew that it was only a matter of time until Japan attacked U.S. interests but was uncertain about where that attack would take place.

On Sunday morning, 7 December 1941, Japan struck at the heart of the U.S. Pacific Fleet, which was stationed at Pearl Harbor, Hawaii. The fleet was literally caught asleep at the switch: 2,300 people were killed, and eight battleships and nu-

PRESIDENT FRANKLIN ROOSEVELT'S REQUEST FOR A DECLARATION OF WAR ON JAPAN, 8 DECEMBER 1941

On 7 December 1941, the Japanese naval and air forces attacked the American naval base at Pearl Harbor in Hawaii, killing and wounding 3,457 military personnel and civilians. Most of the U.S. Pacific fleet was moored in Pearl Harbor, and it sustained severe damage to its naval vessels, battleships, and aircraft. U.S. military and political leaders were taken completely by surprise by the Japanese attack.

Focus Questions

Why is December 7, 1941, called a "day which will live in infamy"? How does Roosevelt's declaration of war reflect outrage over the "infamy"?

To the Congress of the United States:

Yesterday, December 7, 1941—a date which will live in infamy—the United States of America was suddenly and deliberately attacked by naval and air forces of the Empire of Japan.

The United States was at peace with that Nation and, at the solicitation of Japan, was still in conversation with its Government and its Emperor looking toward the maintenance of peace in the Pacific. Indeed, one hour after Japanese air squadrons had commenced bombing in Oahu, the Japanese Ambassador to the United States and his colleague delivered to the Secretary of State a formal reply to a recent American message. While this reply stated that it seemed useless to continue the existing diplomatic negotiations, it contained no threat or hint of war or armed attack.

It will be recorded that the distance of Hawaii from Japan makes it obvious that the attack was deliberately planned many days or even weeks ago. During the intervening time the Japanese Government has deliberately sought to deceive the United States by false statements and expressions of hope for continued peace.

The attack yesterday on the Hawaiian Islands has caused severe damage to American naval and military forces. Very many American lives have been lost. In addition, American ships have been reported torpedoed on the high seas between San Francisco and Honolulu.

Yesterday the Japanese Government also launched an attack against Malaya.

Last night Japanese forces attacked Hong Kong.

Last night Japanese forces attacked Guam.

Last night Japanese forces attacked the Philippine Islands.

Last night the Japanese attacked Wake Island.

This morning the Japanese attacked Midway Island.

Japan has, therefore, undertaken a surprise offensive extending throughout the Pacific area. The facts of yesterday speak for themselves. The people of the United States have already formed their opinions and well understand the implications to the very life and safety of our Nation.

As Commander-in-Chief of the Army and Navy I have directed that all measures be taken for our defense.

Always will we remember the character of the onslaught against us.

No matter how long it may take us to overcome this premeditated invasion, the American people in their righteous might will win through to absolute victory....

With confidence in our armed forces—with the unbounded determination of our people—we will gain the inevitable triumph—so help us God.

I ask that the Congress declare that since the unprovoked and dastardly attack by Japan on Sunday, December seventh, a state of war has existed between the United States and the Japanese Empire.

Franklin D. Roosevelt.

---

merous cruisers and destroyers were sunk or severely damaged. The attack crippled U.S. naval power in the Pacific as the U.S. Navy suffered its worst loss in history in a single engagement. The attack on Pearl Harbor led the United States immediately to declare war on Japan. In President Roosevelt's words, 7 December 1941 was "a date which will live in infamy."

In the next three months, Japan captured Hong Kong, Malaya, and the important naval base at Singapore from the British, taking 60,000 prisoners. In December 1941, the Japanese landed in Thailand and secured immediate agreement for Japanese occupation of strategic spots in the country. They then turned to the Malay peninsula, decisively defeating the British fleet off Malaya and pushing on the ground toward Singapore, which they conquered in February 1942. They conquered British Borneo in January, drove the Dutch from all of Indonesia but New Guinea, pushed U.S. forces in the Philippines into the Bataan peninsula, occupied Burma, and inflicted severe defeats on British, Dutch, and U.S. naval power in East Asia. U.S. General Douglas MacArthur (1880–1964) surrendered the Philippines to the Japanese on 2 January 1942 with the promise to return. With the armies of Germany deep in Russian territory, Australia faced the threat of a Japanese invasion.

■ A United States Army unit joins Allied forces at the beachheads of Normandy during Operation Overlord in 1944. The invasion began the opening of the second front that Stalin had been urging on the Allies since the German armies thrust into Russia in 1941.

Germany Declares War on the United States. Hitler praised the Japanese government for its action against the British Empire and against the United States and its "millionaire and Jewish backers." Germany, with its armies retreating from Moscow, nevertheless declared war on the United States on 11 December 1941. Hitler, in fact, considered that the United States was already at war with Germany because of its policy of supplying the Allies. Within days the United States, a nation with an army smaller than Belgium's, had gone from neutrality to a war in two theaters. Although militarily weak, the United States was an economic giant, commanding a vast industrial capacity and access to resources. The United States grew even stronger under the stimulus of war, increasing its production by 400 percent in two years. It now devoted itself to the demands of a total war and the unconditional surrender of Germany and then Japan.

Winning the War in Europe

The Allies did not always have the same strategies or concerns. President Roosevelt and Prime Minister Churchill had already discussed common goals in the summer of 1941 before U.S. entry into the war. The United States embraced the priority of the European war and the postponement of war in the Pacific. Stalin pleaded for the British and the Americans to open up a second front against Germany in western Europe to give his troops some relief and save Soviet lives. Anglo-American resources were committed to the Pacific to stop the Japanese advance, and the Americans and the British disagreed as to where a second front in Europe might be opened.

The second front came not in western Europe but in the Mediterranean. After the defeat of France in 1940 and the neutralization of the French navy in the Mediterranean, Italy saw a chance to extend its empire in North Africa. With a large army stationed in Libya, Ethiopia, Eritrea, and Italian Somaliland, Mussolini ordered a series of offensives against the Sudan, Kenya, British Somaliland, and Egypt. Most of the Italian advances had been reversed by the British, and 420,000 Italian troops, including African soldiers, were listed as casualties, compared to 3,100 British troops. Germany, however, having succeeded in invading Greece and Yugoslavia, turned its attention to aiding its Axis partner in trouble. In February 1941, Hitler sent General Erwin Rommel (1891–1944), a master strategist of tank warfare, to help the Italians take control of the Suez Canal by launching a counteroffensive in the North African war. Rommel's Axis troops succeeded in entering Egypt and driving the British east of the Egyptian border, thereby dealing the British a serious setback.

The British were simultaneously securing territories in Syria, Palestine, and Iraq to guarantee the oil pipelines of the Persian Gulf for the Allies. Between November 1941 and July 1942, the pendulum swung back and forth between Allied and

Axis forces in the Desert War, as the North African campaign came to be known. In August 1942 the Allied forces, now under the command of Bernard Montgomery (1887–1976), launched a carefully planned offensive at El Alamein, and Rommel was forced to retreat to Tunisia.

Now a joint U.S.-British initiative, the first of the war, landed troops in French Morocco and Algeria and advanced into Tunisia, attacking Rommel's Afrika Korps from behind. About 250,000 German and Italian soldiers were taken prisoner, as the Axis powers were decisively defeated in May 1943. Although not a central theater of the war, North Africa provided British forces with important victories and served as a testing ground for the cooperation of Allied forces.

Because of British interests in the Mediterranean, Churchill insisted on a move from North Africa into Sicily and Italy. This strategy was put into effect in 1942. The Italian government withdrew from the war in September, but German troops carried on the fight in Italy. The Anglo-American invasion of Italy did little to alleviate Russian losses, and the Soviet Union absorbed almost the entire force of German military power until 1944. Stalin's distrust of his allies increased. Churchill, Roosevelt, and Stalin met for the first time in late November 1943 in Teheran, Iran. Roosevelt and Churchill made a commitment to Stalin to open a second front in France within six months. Stalin, in turn, promised to attack Japan to aid the United States in the Pacific. The great showdown of the global war was at hand.

On 6 June 1944, Allied troops under the command of the U.S. General Dwight D. Eisenhower (1890–1969) came ashore on the beaches of Normandy in the largest amphibious landing in history. In a daring operation identified by the code name Operation Overlord, 2.2 million U.S., British, and Free French forces, 450,000 vehicles, and 4 million tons of supplies poured into northern France. Allied forces broke through German lines to liberate Paris in late August. The Germans launched a last-ditch counterattack in late December 1944 in Luxembourg and Belgium. This Battle of the Bulge only slowed the Allied advance; in March 1945, U.S. forces crossed the Rhine into Germany. Hitler, meanwhile, refused to surrender and insisted on a fight to the death of the last German soldier. Members of Hitler's own High Command had tried unsuccessfully to assassinate him in July 1944. The final German defeat came in April 1945, when the Russians stormed the German capital of Berlin. Hitler, living in an underground bunker near the Chancellery building, committed suicide on 30 April 1945.

Japanese War Aims and Assumptions

Japan and the United States entered the Pacific war with very different understandings of what was at stake. Initially, the Japanese appealed to Southeast Asian leaders as the liberators of Asian peoples from Western colonialism and imperialism.

Japanese Hegemony in Asia. The approach struck a responsive chord as the Japanese established what they called the Greater East Asia Co-Prosperity Sphere. In November 1943, Burma's leader, Ba Maw, spoke warmly of Japan, but his welcome of the Japanese liberators did not last long. As he bluntly explained in his memoirs, "The brutality, arrogance, and racial pretensions of the Japanese militarists in Burma remain among the deepest Burmese memories of the war years; for a great many people in Southeast Asia these are all they remember of the war."

The Greater East Asia Co-Prosperity Sphere began in 1940 and lasted until the summer of 1945. This reorganization of east and southeast Asia under Japanese hegemony constituted a redefinition of world geography with Japan at the center. The Japanese fashioned a romanticized vision of the family living in harmony, all members knowing their places and enjoying the complementary division of responsibilities and reciprocities that made family life work smoothly. Behind this pleasant image lurked the reality of a brutal power structure forcing subject peoples to accept massively inferior positions in a world fashioned exclusively to satisfy Japanese desires and needs. The Japanese viewed southeast Asia principally as a market for Japanese manufactured goods, a source of raw materials, and a source of profits for Japanese capital invested in mining, rubber, and raw cotton. Plans were made for hydroelectric power and aluminum-refining facilities.

Wartime Japanese nakedly displayed their disdain for the people they conquered in southeast Asia. All subject peoples were to bow on meeting a Japanese, while at public assemblies a ritual bow in the direction of the Japanese emperor was required. This practice dismayed southeast Asians such as Indies Muslims or Philippine Catholics, who regarded Japanese emperor worship as pagan and presumptuous. Japanese holidays, such as the emperor's birthday, were enforced as Co-Prosperity Sphere holidays, and the calendar was reset to the mythical founding of the Japanese state in 660 B.C.E.

The Japanese were less brazen toward the Chinese in their rhetoric, in part because so much of Japanese, and indeed East Asian, civilization had its roots in China. However, Japanese aggression against the Chinese included one of the worst periods of destruction in modern warfare. When the Japanese took over the Nationalist capital of Nanjing in December 1937, 20,000 women were raped, 30,000 soldiers were killed, and another 12,000 civilians died in the more than six weeks of wanton terror inflicted by Japanese soldiers.

Japan's View of the West. With regard to Westerners, Japanese propaganda avoided labeling them as inferior. In part, this reflected Japan's economic and political emulation of the West since the late nineteenth century. Rather than denigrating Western people, the Japanese chose to elevate themselves as a people descended from divine origins. Stressing their unique mythical history gave the Japanese a strong sense of moral superiority, which perhaps led them to misread Westerners. For example, some Japanese mistakenly assumed that individual selfishness and egoism would make Americans and Europeans incapable of mobilizing for a long fight.

MAP DISCOVERY

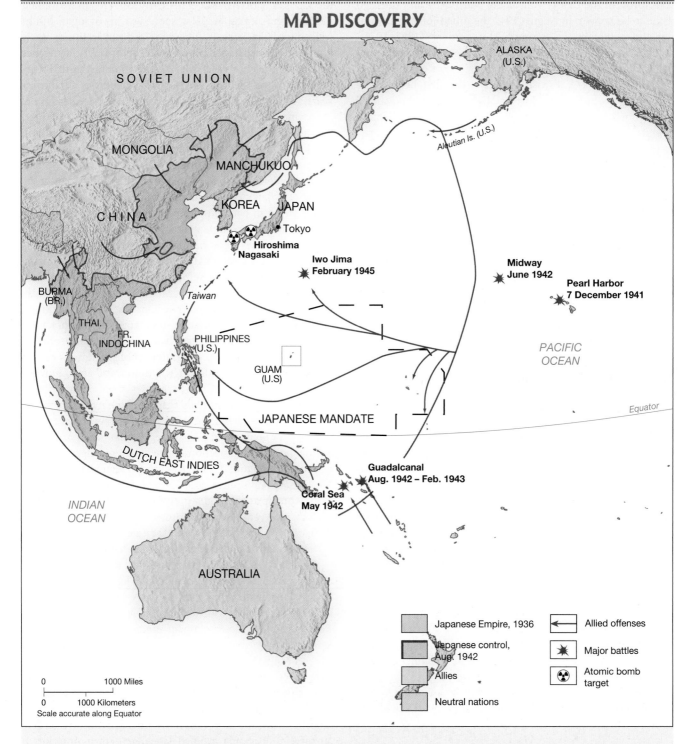

	Japanese Empire, 1936	←	Allied offenses
	Japanese control, Aug. 1942	✴	Major battles
	Allies	☢	Atomic bomb target
	Neutral nations		

0 — 1000 Miles
0 — 1000 Kilometers
Scale accurate along Equator

World War II in the Pacific, 1941–1945

Japan extended control throughout east and southeast Asia until the Japanese Empire reached its pinnacle in August 1942. Note the direction of major Allied offensives and the necessity of coordinated land, sea, and air offensives. Why were Hiroshima and Nagasaki chosen as atomic bomb targets?

Winning the War in the Pacific

The tide in the Pacific war began to turn when the planned Japanese invasion of Australia was thwarted. Fighting in the jungles of New Guinea, Australian and U.S. troops under the command of General Douglas MacArthur turned back the Japanese army. U.S. Marines did likewise with a bold landing at Guadalcanal and months of bloody fighting in the Solomon Islands. In June 1942, within six months of the attack on Pearl Harbor, U.S. naval forces commanded by Admiral Chester Nimitz (1885–1966) inflicted a defeat on the Japanese navy from which it could not recover. In the Battle of Midway, Japan lost four aircraft carriers, a heavy cruiser, over 300 airplanes, and 5,000 men. Midway was the Pacific equivalent of the Battle of Stalingrad.

In the summer of 1943, as the Soviet Union launched the offensive that was to defeat Germany, the United States began to move across the Pacific toward Japan. Nimitz and MacArthur conceived a brilliant plan in which U.S. land, sea, and air forces fought in a coordinated effort. With a series of amphibious landings, they hopped from island to island. Some Japanese island fortresses such as Tarawa were taken; others such as Truk were bypassed and cut off from Japanese home bases. With the conquest of Saipan in November 1944 and Iwo Jima in March 1945, the U.S. forces acquired bases from which B-29 bombers could strike at the Japanese home islands. In the summer of 1945, in the greatest air offensive in history, U.S. planes destroyed what remained of the Japanese navy, crippled Japanese industry, and mercilessly firebombed major population centers. The attack ended with the dropping of atomic bombs on the cities of Hiroshima and Nagasaki. The Japanese government accepted U.S. terms for peace and surrendered unconditionally on 2 September 1945 on the battleship *Missouri* in Tokyo Bay. Four months after the defeat of Germany, the war in Asia was over.

The Fate of Allied Cooperation: 1945

The costs of World War II in terms of death and destruction were the highest in history. An estimated 50 million lives had been lost, including those of 6 million Jews. Most of the dead were Europeans, and most of them were Russians and Poles. An unusually high incidence of civilian deaths distinguished the Second World War from previous wars: well over 50 percent of the dead were noncombatants. Deliberate military targeting of cities explains this phenomenon only in part. The majority of civilian deaths were the result of starvation, enslavement, massacre, and deliberate extermination.

Civilian Populations.   The psychological devastation of continual violence, deprivation, injury, and rape of survivors cannot be measured. Terrorizing citizens became an established means of warfare in the modern age. Another phenomenon not matched in the First World War emerged in 1945:

mass rape. The Soviet officer corps encouraged the advancing Russian army to use sexual violence against German women and girls. The Russians, treated brutally by Hitler's army, returned the savagery in their advance through eastern and central Europe. Rape became a means of direct retaliation. The Great Patriotic War reached its nadir in central Europe with collective rape as a form of war against civilians. In East Asia, victorious Japanese soldiers raped Chinese women as part of the spoils of war. Japanese military commanders also organized camps of "comfort women," unwilling young women who had been abducted from Korea, the Philippines, and other occupied areas to service the sexual "needs" of Japanese soldiers. Regardless of the country that was involved, victorious armies practiced rape against civilian populations as one of the unspoken aspects of conquest.

Material destruction was also great. Axis and Allied cities, centers of civilization and culture, were turned into wastelands by aerial bombing. The Germans bombed Rotterdam and Coventry. The British engineered the firebombing of Dresden. The German army destroyed Warsaw and Stalingrad. The United States leveled Hiroshima and Nagasaki. The nations of Europe were weakened after World War I; after World War II, they were crippled. Europe was completely displaced from the position of world dominance it had held for centuries. The United States alone was undamaged and stronger after the war than before, its industrial capacity and production greatly improved by the war.

The Big Three.   What would be the future of Europe? The leaders of the United States, Great Britain, and the Soviet Union—the **Big Three,** as they were called—met three times between 1943 and 1945: first at Teheran; then in February 1945 at Yalta, a Russian Black Sea resort; and finally in July and August 1945 at Potsdam, a suburb of Berlin. They coordinated their attack on Germany and Japan and discussed their plans for postwar Europe. After Allied victory, the governments of both Germany and Japan would be totally abolished and completely reconstructed. No deals would be made with Hitler or his successors; no peace would be negotiated with the enemy; surrender would be unconditional. Germany would be disarmed and de-Nazified, and its leaders would be tried as war criminals. The armies of the Big Three would occupy Germany, each with a separate zone, but the country would be governed as a single economic unit. The Soviet Union, it was agreed, could collect reparations from Germany. With Germany and Japan defeated, a United Nations organization would provide the structure for a lasting peace in the world.

Stalin expected that the Soviet Union would decide the future of the territories of eastern Europe that the Soviet army had liberated from Germany. This area was vital to the security of the war-devastated Soviet Union; Stalin saw it as a protective barrier against another attack from the west. The Big Three agreed that Romania, Bulgaria, Hungary,

CHRONOLOGY
WORLD WAR II

1937	Japan begins undeclared war on China
March 1938	Germany annexes Austria to the German Reich
29 September 1938	Chamberlain, Daladier, Mussolini, and Hitler meet at Munich conference
May 1939	Pact of Steel: military alliance between Italy and Germany
1939	Non-Aggression Pact between Germany and the Soviet Union
1 September 1939	Germany attacks Poland
3 September 1939	Great Britain and France declare war on Germany
April 1940	Germany attacks Denmark and Norway
May 1940	Germany invades the Netherlands, Belgium, Luxembourg, and then France
June 1940	Italy enters the war on the side of Germany
17 June 1940	French Marshal Pétain petitions Germany for an armistice and creates a collaborationist government at Vichy
September 1940	Japan, Germany, and Italy sign Tripartite Pact
September–November 1940	The Battle of Britain
22 June 1941	Germany invades the Soviet Union
1941	First extermination camp created in Chelmno, Poland
7 December 1941	Japan attacks Pearl Harbor; the following day, the United States declares war on Japan
11 December 1941	Germany declares war on the United States
January 1942	Wannsee Conference, where the Final Solution is planned
June 1942	Battle of Midway
September 1942	Italian government withdraws from the war
April 1943	Unsuccessful uprising in the Warsaw ghetto
November 1943	Churchill, Roosevelt, and Stalin meet at Teheran conference
6 June 1944	Allied forces land in northern France—D-Day
February 1945	Churchill, Roosevelt, and Stalin meet at Yalta
March 1945	American forces march into Germany
30 April 1945	Hitler commits suicide
July and August 1945	Churchill, Truman, and Stalin meet at Potsdam
6 August 1945	United States drops atomic bomb on Hiroshima
2 September 1945	Japan surrenders

Czechoslovakia, and Poland would have pro-Soviet governments. Since Soviet troops occupied these countries in 1945, there was little that the British and the Americans could do to prevent Russian control unless they wanted to go to war against the Soviet Union. Churchill realistically accepted this situation. But for Americans who took seriously the proclamations of President Roosevelt that their country had fought to restore freedom and self-determination to peoples oppressed by tyranny, Soviet power in eastern Europe was a bitter disappointment.

CONCLUSION

The war that broke out in 1939 was caused by German aggression, which the appeasement policies of the British failed to contain. Within two years, Hitler ruled continental western Europe by either occupation or collaboration. Although pockets of resistance existed, the activities of the resisters had little impact on the course of the war. Hitler undertook the destruction of Europe's Jewish population and attempted to eliminate other minorities deemed inferior by Nazi racial policies.

The year 1941 was a critical turning point in the war because of the German attack on its former ally, which brought Russia to the Allied cause. And in December of that same year, the Japanese attack on an American naval base in Hawaii brought the United States into the war. The war became a truly global conflagration. The Allies were able to coordinate the war effort on several fronts. American technology and resources proved critical in the Allied success. The dropping of two atom bombs also set the tone for determining the peace. And the ideological divide between East and West would sow the seeds of future dissension. With the defeat of Germany and Japan, the United States and the Soviet Union stood as the undisputed giants in world politics.

QUESTIONS FOR REVIEW

1. What factors made possible Hitler's diplomatic and military successes between 1933 and 1941?
2. Why did the Nazi regime believe that it needed to destroy the Jews, gypsies, and other outsiders, and how did it attempt to justify that policy?
3. How did Hitler's invasion of the Soviet Union and the entry of the United States into the war transform the military situation?
4. How did the Allies coordinate their efforts, and what factors strained relations between them?
5. How did the three Allied victors envision the future of Europe, and what steps did they take to ensure the peace?

KEY TERMS

appeasement, *p. 566*

Axis Powers, *p. 566*

Big Three, *p. 581*

blitzkrieg, p. 569

Final Solution, *p. 571*

Holocaust, *p. 572*

DISCOVERING WESTERN CIVILIZATION ONLINE

You can obtain more information about World War II at the websites listed below. See also the Companion Website that accompanies this text, www.ablongman.com/kishlansky, which contains an online study guide and additional resources.

Aggression and Conquest

The Avalon Project: Munich Pact 9/29/38
www.yale.edu/lawweb/avalon/imt/munich1.htm
Electronic text of the Munich agreements.

The Avalon Project: World War II Documents
http://www.yale.edu/lawweb/avalon/wwii/wwii.htm
An important collection of documents from the prewar years, the war years, and the subsequent peace settlements.

Racism and Destruction

United States Holocaust Memorial Museum
www.ushmm.org
Home page of the United States Holocaust Museum. The site contains a searchable online catalog of both documentary and photographic sources.

Simon Wiesenthal Center
www.wiesenthal.com
Home page of the Simon Wiesenthal Center and the Museum of Tolerance. It has an extensive collection of materials related to the Holocaust and anti-Semitism.

The Vidal Sassoon International Center for the Study of Antisemitism (SICSA)
sicsa.huji.ac.il/
This site contains an extensive bibliography on the Holocaust.

Allied Victory

Internet Modern History Sourcebook: World War II
www.fordham.edu/halsall/mod/modsbook45.html
A collection of primary source documents and links to materials on World War II.

World War II
www.archives.gov/digital_classroom/teaching_with_
documents.html#great_depression
War documents from the U.S. National Archives and
Research Administration.

Russian Photography Collection—War Photography
www.schicklerart.com/auto_exh/RPCWar
Images of World War II from the Soviet perspective.

Women Come to the Front
www.loc.gov/exhibits/wcf/wcf0001.html
A virtual exhibit by the Library of Congress on women journalists, photographers, and broadcasters during World War II.

SUGGESTIONS FOR FURTHER READING

Aggression and Conquest

Paul Kennedy, *The Realities Behind Diplomacy: Background Influences on British External Policy, 1865–1980* (London: Allen & Unwin, 1981). Essays dealing with the continuity of appeasement in British foreign policy across two centuries.

Ian Kershaw, *The Nazi Dictatorship* (London: Edward Arnold, 1985). A fine synthesis of key problems of interpretation regarding the Third Reich. Special attention is paid to the interdependence of domestic and foreign policy and the inevitability of war in Hitler's ideology.

Donald Cameron Watt, *How War Came: The Immediate Origins of the Second World War* (London: Heinemann, 1989). An international historian chronicles the events leading to the outbreak of the war.

Racism and Destruction

Renate Bridenthal, Atina Grossmann, and Marion Kaplan, eds., *When Biology Became Destiny: Women in Weimar and Nazi Germany* (New York: Monthly Review Press, 1984). A volume of essays pursuing common themes on the relation between sexism and racism in interwar and wartime Germany.

Raul Hilberg, *The Destruction of the European Jews,* 3 vols. (New York: Holmes and Meier, 1985). An exhaustive study of the annihilation of European Jews beginning with cultural precedents and antecedents. Examines step-by-step developments that led to extermination policies and contains valuable appendixes on statistics and a discussion of sources.

Charles S. Maier, *The Unmasterable Past: History, Holocaust, and German National Identity* (Cambridge, MA: Harvard University Press, 1988). A thoughtful discussion of the historical debate over the Holocaust and the comparative dimensions of the event. Especially valuable in placing the Holocaust within German history.

Michael R. Marrus, *The Holocaust in History* (New York: New American Library, 1987). A comprehensive survey of all aspects of the Holocaust, including the policies of the Third Reich, the living conditions in the camps, and the prospects for resistance and opposition.

Allied Victory

John Campbell, ed., *The Experience of World War II* (New York: Oxford University Press, 1989). This richly illustrated work provides an overview of the Second World War in both the Asian and European theaters in terms of origins, events, and consequences.

Akira Iriye, *The Origins of the Second World War in Asia and the Pacific* (London: Longman, 1987). Examines the events of the 1930s leading up to hostilities in the Pacific theater, with a special focus on Japanese isolation and aggression.

John Keegan, *The Second World War* (New York: Viking, 1990). Provides a panoramic sweep of "the largest single event in human history," with special attention to warfare in all its forms and the importance of leadership.

Gerhard L. Weinberg, *A World at Arms: A Global History of World War II* (New York: Cambridge University Press, 1994). An overview of the interactions among Germany, the Soviet Union, and Japan, which provides an integrated history of World War II with a helpful bibliographic essay.

For a list of additional titles related to this chapter's topics, please see www.ablongman.com/kishlansky.

Chapter 29

THE COLD WAR AND POSTWAR ECONOMIC RECOVERY: 1945–1970

The Visual Record

EUROPE IN RUINS

When the dust from the last bombs settled over Europe's cities, the balance sheets of destruction were tallied. Great cities including London, Cologne, Berlin, Stalingrad, and Warsaw incurred serious damage and human loss. Millions of refugees on the Continent found themselves homeless, having lost their loved ones, often all of their personal belongings, and the roofs over their heads. Millions more returned home from battlefronts and concentration camps to rubble, with wounds beyond healing. There were no jobs; there was nothing to eat. Peacetime rationing dipped below wartime levels. For many, the war was far gentler than the peace.

Warsaw in 1946 stands as a stark example of extreme destruction and of startling renewal. At the close of the war, Warsaw was an almost completely destroyed city, consisting of little more than dust, ashes, and the charred hulks of destroyed buildings, with no inhabitants, water, electricity, or sanitation. The scene here, captured by a photographer in early 1946, is not an isolated perspective but rather a landscape typical of Poland's capital after the war. By contrast with this image, Warsaw was recognized in the interwar period of the 1920s and 1930s as a metropolitan center of charm and culture, known for its artists and intellectuals and vibrant urban life.

Warsaw was annihilated not by an atomic bomb, but in stages over a five-year period by flamethrowers, tanks, and dynamite. Unrelenting aerial attacks by German planes against the city and its population systematically destroyed people and buildings in order to bring the civilian population to its knees. The Jewish ghetto was completely eliminated in 1943. The destruction, building by building, was premeditated and methodical. By the end of 1944, Warsaw was no more than a heap of rubble with almost 90 percent of its buildings destroyed. A large portion of its population was wiped out, and those who survived were in detention camps or in flight. Warsaw became known as "the vanished city."

But that is where the postwar story of recovery begins. With the liberation by the Red Army of what was left of the city, the Polish people almost immediately planned for the rebuilding of their capital, helped raise the necessary funds, and volunteered their labor to the great task. Women and children joined the men in clearing the rubble. Aid in the form of food, clothing, and shelter from organizations such as the United Nations Relief and Rehabilitation Administration supported the healing and rebuilding of Warsaw. Civilians

returned to the city. By 1951, the population reached 815,000, although still below its 1.3 million inhabitants in 1939.

In rebuilding Warsaw, the Polish people did not ignore the city's historic past by building a modern, postwar metropolis, as did the people of Frankfurt. Instead, they sought to reconstruct Warsaw as it had been in 1939 by recreating monuments and historic buildings in their original form. Often that required architects to consult unconventional sources, including paintings and postcards, in the absence of blueprints and plans. Palaces and castles were reborn, baroque buildings rose up, ornamental gardens were replanted, and ancient vistas and panoramas were brought back to life. The achievement of historical preservation was astounding. By 1951, a large part of the city had been rebuilt, perhaps one of the best examples of how Europeans met the postwar challenge of urban reconstruction and economic revival.

Looking Ahead

In this chapter, we shall see how, under the tutelage of the two superpowers, the United States and the Soviet Union, Europe diverged on two separate paths of reconstruction and economic integration after 1945. Europe dismantled its global empires. Cold war replaced the hot war of global conflagration. In the West and in the Eastern Bloc, different welfare state models emerged for the regulation and social distribution of economic expansion. Slowed prosperity in the late 1960s, combined with the growth of an independent youth culture, helped fuel protests in the East and the West. Dissent, prosperity, and rising and unmet consumer expectations characterized Western societies within twenty-five years—the span of a generation—after the end of World War II. ➤

587

THE ORIGINS OF THE COLD WAR

For victors and vanquished alike, the situation in Europe at the end of the Second World War was dire. Economies geared totally toward war efforts were incapable of the kind of reorientation needed to reconstruct markets and eliminate economic distress. Governments faced political crises as they attempted to restore or establish democratic principles. Moreover, Europe did not have the capital necessary to begin the process of rebuilding. Political disorganization reigned in Berlin, which was divided into sectors, in Germany, which was divided into zones, and in the former European empires, which were in the process of being dismantled. Even the winners were losers as survivors faced a level of human and material destruction unknown in the history of warfare. As one American military observer reported to his superiors in 1947, "Millions of people in the cities are slowly starving." Could Europe rise from these ashes and, if so, in what form?

Cold War conflict initially developed because of differing Russian and American notions regarding the economic reconstruction of Europe. The Soviet Union realized that American aid to Europe was not primarily a humanitarian program; it was part of an economic offensive in Europe that would contribute to the dominance of American capital in world markets. The United States recognized that the Soviet Union hoped to achieve its own recovery through outright control of eastern Europe.

The World in Two Blocs

With the cessation of the "hot" war that had ripped Europe apart from 1939 to 1945, the armies of the United States and the Soviet Union met on the banks of the Elbe River in 1945. Greeting each other as victors and allies, the occupying armies waited for direction on how to conduct the peace. Europe and Japan had been destroyed, leaving the United States and the Soviet Union as indisputably the two richest and strongest nations in the world.

The Soviets understood that they ran a sorry second to American military superiority—the United States was alone in possessing the atomic bomb—and to American wealth, which, measured in Gross National Product (GNP), was 400 percent greater than that of the Soviet Union. Stalin, nevertheless, committed the Soviet Union to an arms race in which he refused to accept American dominance. War had made the two superpowers wary allies; peace promised to make them once again active foes. In the three years that followed the war, a new kind of conflict emerged between the two superpower victors, a war deemed "cold" because of its lack of military violence, but a bitter war nonetheless.

The Cold War was rooted in the ideological opposition between communism and capitalist democracies, dominated by the two superpowers, the Soviet Union and the United States. It affected the entire world. Drawing on three decades of distrust between the East and the West, the Cold War was

related to the economic and foreign policy goals of both superpowers.

Winston Churchill captured the drama of the new international order in a speech he delivered in Missouri in 1946: "From Stettin in the Baltic to Trieste in the Adriatic an iron curtain has descended across the continent." The term **iron curtain** described graphically for many the new fate of Europe, rigidly divided between East and West, a pawn in the struggle of the superpowers.

The Division of Germany.   In central Europe, Cold War tensions first surfaced over the question of how to treat Germany. The United States and the Soviet Union had very different ideas about the future of their former enemy. In fostering economic reconstruction in Europe, the United States counted on a German economy transfused with American funds that would be self-supporting and stable. To the contrary, the Soviet Union, blaming Germany for its extreme

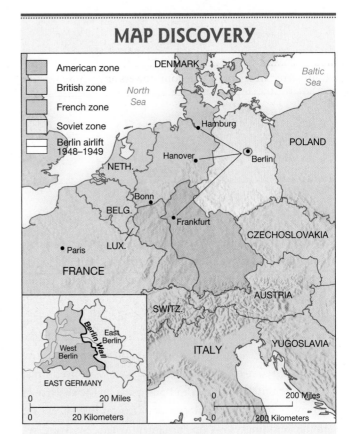

MAP DISCOVERY

The Division of Germany

Examine the division of Germany after World War II. Why did the four victor nations divide Germany into zones at the end of the war? How did Berlin come to be divided into two zones? What was the Soviet goal in blockading West Berlin, and why did the blockade fail?

destruction, was explicit in its demands: German resources must be siphoned off for Soviet reconstruction. Stricken as the Soviets were with 20 million dead, millions of homeless refugees in dire poverty, and 1,700 cities in ruins, commandeering German labor and stripping Germany of its industrial plant seemed to them only fair.

With Germany's defeat, its territory had been divided into four zones, occupied by American, Soviet, British, and French troops. An Allied Control Commission consisting of representatives of the four powers was to govern Germany as a whole in keeping with the decisions made at Yalta before the end of the war. As Soviet and American antagonisms over Germany's future deepened, however, Allied rule polarized between the East and the West, with the internal politics of each area determined by the ideological conflicts between communism and capitalist free enterprise.

Allied attempts to administer Germany as a whole faltered and failed in 1948 over a question of economic policy. The zones of the Western occupying forces (the United States, Great Britain, and France), now administered as a single unit, issued a uniform and stable currency that the Russians accurately saw as a threat to their own economic policies in Germany. The Soviets blockaded the city of Berlin, which, though behind the frontier of the Russian sector, was being administered in sectors by the four powers and whose western sector promised to become a successful enclave of Western capitalism. With the support of the people of West Berlin, the Allies responded by airlifting food and supplies into West Berlin for almost a year, defending it as an outpost that had to be preserved from the advance of communism. The Russians were forced to withdraw the blockade in the spring of 1949. The Berlin blockade hardened the commitment on both sides to two Germanys.

The two new states came into existence in 1949, their founding separated by less than a month. The Federal Republic of Germany (West Germany), within the American orbit, was established as a democratic parliamentary regime. Free elections brought the Christian Democrat Konrad Adenauer to power as chancellor. The German Democratic Republic (East Germany) was ruled as a single-party state under Walter Ulbricht, who took his direction from the Soviet Union. The division of Germany became a microcosm of the division of the world into two armed camps.

Eastern Europe and the Soviet Bloc.   With the support of local Communist parties, Soviet-dominated governments were established in Poland, Hungary, Bulgaria, and Romania in 1947. The following year, Czechoslovakia was pulled into the Soviet orbit. Czechoslovakia served as a significant marker in the development of Cold War confrontation. The tactics of the Communists in Czechoslovakia taught the West that coalition governments were unacceptable and undoubtedly hardened the resolve of U.S. policy makers in support of two Germanys. Needing the stability of peace, the Soviets saw in eastern Europe, hostile as the area may have been to forced integration, a necessary buffer against Western competition. The Soviet Union feared U.S. intentions to establish liberal governments and capitalist markets in the states bordering its own frontiers and viewed such attempts as a threat to Soviet interests. For those reasons, Stalin refused to allow free elections in Poland and, by force of occupying armies, annexed neighboring territories that included eastern Finland, the Baltic states, East Prussia, eastern Poland, Ruthenia, and Bessarabia. With the exception of East Prussia, the annexations were limited to territories that had once been part of tsarist Russia.

■ The Berlin airlift of 1948–1949 broke through the Soviet blockade of the city. Called "Operation Vittles," the airlift provided food and fuel for the beleaguered West Berliners. Here, children wait for the candy American pilots dropped in tiny parachute handkerchiefs. The Soviets ended the blockade in the spring of 1949.

MAP DISCOVERY

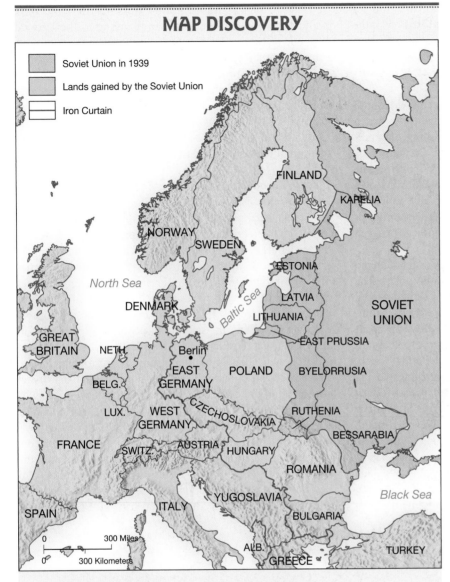

Soviet Union in 1939

Lands gained by the Soviet Union

Iron Curtain

The Soviet Union and the Soviet Bloc

Notice the boundary of the Soviet Union before 1939 and the territory it gained after World War II. Which countries in eastern Europe did the Soviet Union annex after the war and why? In other countries of eastern Europe the Soviet Union established economic and political control without annexation. Which countries constituted the Soviet bloc?

NATO and Other Treaty Alliances. With the aim of containing the USSR, a policy known as **containment,** the United States entered into a series of military alliances around the world. In order to provide mutual assistance should any member be attacked, the United States joined with Belgium, Britain, Canada, Denmark, France, Iceland, Italy, the Netherlands, Norway, and Portugal in 1949 to form the **North Atlantic Treaty Organization (NATO).** Greece and Turkey became members in 1952, West Germany in 1955, and

Spain in 1982. The potential military threat of the Soviet Union in Western Europe prompted the peacetime military alliance.

A challenge to Cold War power politics came from within the NATO alliance. General Charles de Gaulle, as president of the French Fifth Republic, rejected the straitjacket of American dominance in Western Europe and asserted his country's independent status by exploding the first French atomic bomb in 1960. Refusing to place the French military under an American general who served as Supreme Allied Commander for NATO, de Gaulle completely withdrew France from participation in NATO in 1966. He forged an independent French foreign policy, taking advantage of the loosening of bloc politics in the mid-1960s.

The Southeast Asia Treaty Organization (SEATO) in 1954 and the Baghdad Pact of 1955 (known as the Central Treaty Organization after 1959) followed. The United States strengthened its military presence throughout the period by acquiring 1,400 military bases in foreign countries for its own forces.

In 1955, Albania, Bulgaria, Romania, Czechoslovakia, Hungary, Poland, and East Germany joined with the Soviet Union to form a defensive alliance organization known as the **Warsaw Pact.** The USSR intended its Eastern European allies to serve as a strategic buffer zone against the NATO forces.

The Nuclear Club

The nuclear arms race began in earnest during World War II, well before the first atomic bomb was dropped in August 1945. The Germans, the Russians, and the British all had teams exploring the destructive possibilities of nuclear fission during the war, but the Americans had the edge in the development of the bomb. Stalin understood the political significance of the weapon and committed the Soviet Union to a breakneck program of development following the war.

The USSR ended the American monopoly and tested its first atomic bomb in 1949. Both countries developed the hydrogen bomb almost simultaneously in 1953. Space exploration by satellite was also deemed important in terms of the detection and deployment of bombs, and the Soviets pulled

■ The first hydrogen bomb test, on November 1, 1952, destroyed an entire island in the Pacific.

ahead in this area with the launching of the first satellite, *Sputnik I,* in 1957. Intercontinental ballistic missiles (ICBMs) followed, further accelerating the pace of nuclear armament.

The atomic bomb and thermonuclear weapons contributed greatly to the shape of Cold War politics. The incineration of Hiroshima and Nagasaki sent a clear message to the world about the power of total annihilation available to those who controlled the bombs. The threat of such total destruction made full and direct confrontation with an equally armed enemy impossible. Both the United States and the Soviet Union, the first two members of the **nuclear club,** knew that they had the capability of obliterating their enemy, but not before the enemy could retaliate. They also knew that the technology necessary for nuclear arms was available to any industrial power. By 1974, the nuclear club included Great Britain, France, the People's Republic of China, and India. Those countries joined the United States and the Soviet Union in spending the billions of dollars necessary every year to expand nuclear arsenals and to develop more sophisticated weaponry and delivery systems.

A new vocabulary transformed popular attitudes and values. *Missile gaps, deterrence, first strike, second strike, radioactive fallout,* and *containment* were all terms that heightened popular fears. Paranoia on both sides was encouraged by heads of state in their public addresses throughout the 1950s. Traitors were publicly tried while espionage was being sponsored by the state.

The Nuclear Test Ban Treaty of 1963, the first of its kind, banned tests in the atmosphere and inaugurated a period of lessening tensions between the Eastern and Western blocs. Arms limitation and nonproliferation were the subjects of a series of conferences between the United States and the Soviet Union in the late 1960s and pointed the way to limitations eventually agreed on in the next decade. The United Nations (UN), an organization created by the Allies immediately following World War II to take the place of the defunct League of Nations, established international agencies for the purpose of harnessing nuclear power for peaceful uses. By the early 1970s, both the United States and the Soviet Union recognized the importance of closer relations between the superpowers. The USSR and the United States had achieved nuclear parity. On the whole, however, the arms race persisted as a continuing threat in Cold War politics. The race required the dedication of huge national resources to maintain a competitive stance. Conventional forces, too, were expanded to protect Eastern and Western bloc interests.

Decolonization and the Cold War

No part of the globe escaped the tensions generated by the Cold War. By the end of the Second World War, European colonial empires had been weakened or destroyed by the ravages of battle, occupation, and neglect. Nationalist

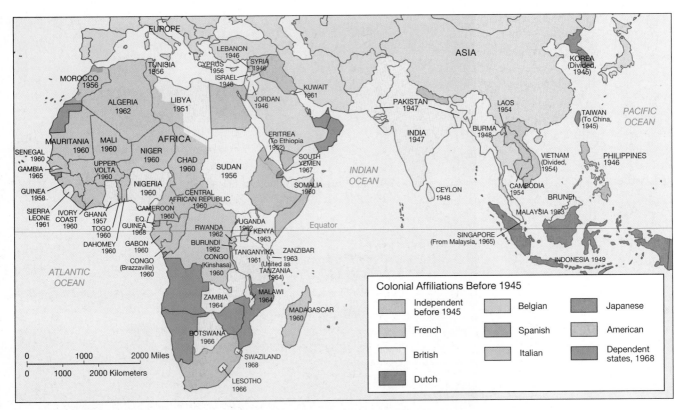

■ Decolonization. Few nations in Africa and south and southeast Asia were independent before 1945. Few remained dependent after 1968.

movements had been growing in power in the 1930s, and many nationalist leaders saw the war as a catalyst for independence. Former colonies were no longer directly controlled but, as newly independent countries, they had to contend with Cold War pressures to belong in one or the other superpower camp. Hence, **decolonization** often meant continued dependence.

Soviet leader Joseph Stalin limited the Soviet Union's foreign involvement following the Second World War to Communist regimes that shared borders with the USSR in Eastern Europe and Asia. But after Stalin's death in 1953, the Soviet Union turned to the **third world.** Former colonies played an important new role in the Cold War strategies with the accession to power of Nikita Khrushchev (1894–1971) in the mid-1950s. The Soviet Union abandoned its previous caution and assumed a global role in offering "friendship treaties," military advice, trade credits, and general support for attempts at national liberation in Asia, Africa, and Latin America. Both East and West took advantage of tribalism and regionalism, which worked against the establishment of strong central governments. Military rule and fragmentation often resulted. Instability and acute poverty continued to characterize former colonies after emancipation, regardless of whether the new leaders joined the communist or democratic camps.

Asia.   Great Britain knew that it no longer commanded the resources to control India, historically its richest colony, which under the leadership of Mohandas Gandhi (1869–1948) had been agitating for independence since 1920. Given the title of "Mahatma," or "great-souled," by his people, Gandhi advocated passive resistance to achieve independence. He sought to bring pressure on the colonizers by means of civil disobedience, boycotts, and public fasts instead of violence. The British granted self-government to India in 1946 with the proviso that if the bitter conflict between Hindus and Muslims was not settled by mutual agreement, Great Britain would decide on the division of power. As a result, Muslim and Hindu representatives agreed to the division of British India into the independent states of India and Pakistan in 1947. Ceylon (now Sri Lanka) and Burma (now Myanmar) achieved full independence in 1948.

In its march through Asia during the war, Japan had smashed colonial empires. Japan's defeat created a power vacuum that nationalist leaders were eager to fill. Civil wars erupted in China, Burma, Korea, and Indochina. In 1950, the United States and the United Nations intervened when North Korea attacked South Korea. Korea, formerly controlled by Japan, had been divided following the war as a result of the presence of Russian and American troops. Communist-dominated North Korea refused to accept the artificial boundary between it and Western-dominated South Korea. China, a Communist state following the victory of Mao Zedong (1893–1976) in 1949, intervened in the Korean conflict when American troops advanced on Chinese frontiers in October 1950. After three years of military stalemate, Korea was partitioned on the 38th parallel in 1953. The Soviet Union was not party to the conflict in Korea, but the United States considered China to be in the Soviet camp rather than an independent contender for power.

The United States was heavily committed as a military presence in Southeast Asia after the French withdrawal from Indochina following the French defeat at Dien Bien Phu in 1954. The North Vietnamese state was established under the French-educated leader Ho Chi Minh. South Vietnam was declared a republic, and the United States sponsored a regime that was considered favorable to Western interests. Arguing the domino theory—that one Southeast Asian country after another would fall like a row of dominoes to Communist takeover—the United States also intervened in Laos and Cambodia. Between 1961 and 1973, the United States committed American troops to a full-scale war—though officially termed only a military action—against Communist guerrilla forces throughout the region. After almost two decades of escalating involvement, in 1973 American troops were finally withdrawn from a war in Vietnam that they could not win.

Africa. The first wave of decolonization after 1945 had been in Asia, but it wasn't until the late 1950s and early 1960s that a second wave crested and crashed in Africa. Wartime experiences and rapid economic development fed existing nationalist aspirations and encouraged the emergence of mass political demands for liberation. A new generation of leaders, many of them educated in European institutions, moved from cooperation with home rule to demands for independence by the early 1960s. British Prime Minister Harold MacMillan (1894–1986) spoke of "the winds of change" in 1960, the year that proved to be a turning point in African politics. Britain and Belgium yielded their colonies. In 1960, Patrice Lumumba (1925–1961) became the first prime minister of the Republic of the Congo (present-day Democratic Republic of the Congo). White European rule continued in Rhodesia (now Zimbabwe) and South Africa, despite continued world pressure. African leader Kwame Nkrumah (1909–1972) of Ghana denounced the situation of African dependence as "neocolonialism" and called for a united Africa as the only means of resistance. He led Ghana in a policy of nonalignment in the Cold War. With Jomo Kenyatta (1894–1978) of Kenya, Nkrumah founded the Pan-African Federation, which promoted African nationalism.

The French, having faced what its officer corps considered a humiliating defeat in Indochina, held on against the winds of change in North Africa. France's problems in Algeria began in earnest in 1954 when Muslims seeking independence and self-rule revolted. Although the Algerian rebels successfully employed terrorist and guerrilla tactics, European settlers and the French army in Algeria refused to accept defeat. Facing

political collapse at home, the French, under the leadership of General Charles de Gaulle, ended the war and agreed to Algeria's independence, which was achieved in 1962.

The Middle East. The United States and the Soviet Union used aid to win support of "client" states in the Middle East. The withdrawal, sometimes under duress, of British and French rule in the Middle East and North Africa and the creation of the state of Israel in 1948 destabilized the area and created opportunities for new alliances. Egypt and Syria, for example, sought Soviet support against the new Israeli state, which had been formed out of the part of Palestine under British mandate since 1920 and which was dependent on U.S. aid.

Oil, an essential resource for rapid industrialization, was the object of Soviet politicking in Iran after World War II. Western oil companies, long active in the area, had won oil concessions in Iran in 1946, but such rights eluded the Soviets. In 1951, a nationalist Iranian government sought to evict Westerners by nationalizing the oil fields. The British blockaded Iranian trade in the Persian Gulf, and the newly formed American espionage organization, the Central Intelligence Agency (CIA), subverted the nationalist government and placed in power the shah of Iran, a leader favorable to American interests.

In 1956, a crisis came in Egypt. Egyptian President Gamal Abdel Nasser (1918–1970), a nationalist in power by virtue of a military coup d'état in 1952, oversaw the nationalization of the Suez Canal. British and French military forces attacked and were forced to withdraw by pressure from both the Soviet Union and the United States, which cooperated in seeking to avert a disaster. The Middle East, however, remained a Cold War powder keg, with Israeli and Arab nationalist interests and Soviet and American aid running on a collision course. The expansion of the Israeli state at the expense of its Arab neighbors further exacerbated tensions.

Latin America. The United States was also experiencing Cold War problems closer to home. In 1954, the CIA plotted the overthrow of Guatemala's leftist regime to keep Soviet influence out of the Western Hemisphere. In 1958, President Dwight D. Eisenhower sent his vice president, Richard M. Nixon, on a tour of Latin American countries. Crowds everywhere jeered the American vice president and hurled stones and eggs at his motorcade in response to U.S. policies. In 1959, a revolution in Cuba, an island nation only 90 miles off the American coast, resulted in the ejection of U.S. interests and the establishment of a Communist regime under the leadership of a young lawyer, Fidel Castro. In 1962, a direct and frightening confrontation occurred between the United States and the USSR over Soviet missile installations in Cuba. Following the Russian withdrawal from the island, both U.S. President John F. Kennedy and Soviet leader Nikita Khrushchev pursued a policy of *peaceful coexistence,* intent on averting nuclear confrontation. Both sides recognized how close they had come to mutual annihilation in the showdown over Cuba.

POSTWAR ECONOMIC RECOVERY IN EUROPE, JAPAN, AND THE SOVIET UNION

In contrast to the Soviet Union, the United States had incurred relatively light casualties in World War II. Because the fighting had not taken place on the North American continent, U.S. cities, farmlands, and factories were intact. As the chief producer and supplier for the Allied war effort, even before its entry into the conflict, the United States had benefited from the conflict in Europe and actually expanded its economic productivity during the war. In 1945, the United States was producing a full 50 percent of the world's GNP. Furthermore, the United States held two-thirds of the world's gold. A United States bursting with energy and prosperity was a real threat to the devastated Soviet Union. However, the United States knew that it lacked one important guarantee to secure its growth and its future prosperity: adequate international markets for its goods. The decade following the Great Depression of 1929 witnessed the search for a policy to expand U.S. markets. Both Europe and Japan were recognized as potential buyers for American goods, but both areas parried with protectionism to foster their own postdepression recovery.

The Economic Challenge

Economists judged that Europe would need at least 25 years to regain its prewar economic capacity. The worst was also feared: that Europe would never recover as a world economic power. Large-scale population movements made matters worse. Displaced persons by the millions moved across Europe. Just as the war had caused dislocation, so too did the peace create millions of refugees seeking asylum and a better life. The release of prisoners of war and slave workers imprisoned during the Third Reich strained already weak economies. Germans were expelled from territories that Germany had controlled before the war. Soviet expansionist policies forced others to flee Estonia, Latvia, and Lithuania. Jews who survived the concentration camps resettled outside Europe, primarily in Palestine and the United States.

European industrial production in 1945 was one-third of its level in 1938. Housing shortages existed everywhere. The transportation infrastructure was severely damaged: railways, roads, and bridges were in shambles all over Europe. Communications networks were in disarray. In some cases, industrial plants had not been as adversely affected as urban centers. Yet machinery everywhere had been worn out in wartime production, and replacement parts were nonexistent. German equipment was dismantled and seized by Soviet soldiers to be used in Russia in place of what the Germans had destroyed.

Agriculture, too, suffered severe reversals in wartime economies and was unable to resume prewar production in 1945. In general, European agriculture was producing at 50 percent of its prewar capacity. Livestock had been decimated during the war years—in France, for example, 50 percent of all farm animals had been killed—and it was estimated that restoring herds would take decades. Italy suffered greatly, with one-third of its overall assets destroyed. The scarcity of goods converged with ballooning inflation. Black markets with astronomical prices for necessities flourished, while currency rates plummeted. Everywhere the outlook was bleak. Yet in less than a decade, the situation was reversed. The solution came from outside of Europe.

The Economic Solution: The Marshall Plan

By the spring of 1947 it was clear to American policy makers that initial postwar attempts to stabilize European economies and promote world recovery were simply not working. The United States had, earlier in the same year, engineered emergency aid to Turkey and Greece, both objects of Soviet aspirations for control. President Truman articulated a doctrine bearing his name: "I believe that it must be the policy of the United States to support free people who are resisting attempted subjugation by armed minorities or by outside pressures." The aid emerged in an atmosphere of opposition between the United States and the Soviet Union over issues of territorial control in eastern and southern Europe. The Cold War coincided with and reinforced the U.S. need to reconstruct western Europe.

On 5 June 1947, Secretary of State George C. Marshall (1880–1959) delivered the commencement address at Harvard University. In his speech, Marshall introduced the European Recovery Act, popularly known as the **Marshall Plan,** through which billions of dollars in aid would be made available to European states, both in the east and in the west, provided that two conditions were met: (1) the recipient states had to cooperate with one another in aligning national economic policies and improving the international monetary system, and (2) they had to work toward breaking down trade barriers.

Participating countries included Austria, Belgium, Denmark, France, West Germany, Great Britain, Greece, Iceland, Italy, Luxembourg, the Netherlands, Norway, Sweden, Switzerland, and Turkey. The Soviet Union and eastern European countries were also eligible for aid under the original formulation. But the Soviets opposed the plan from the first, wary of U.S. intentions to extend the influence of Western capitalism. Soviet opposition encouraged members of the U.S. Congress, afraid of a Communist takeover in Europe, to support the plan.

The amount of U.S. aid to Europe was massive. More than $23 billion was pumped into western Europe between 1947 and 1952. By every measure, the Marshall Plan was judged a success in the West. American foreign aid restored western European trade and production while at the same time controlling inflation. Dean Acheson (1893–1971), Marshall's successor as secretary of state, described the plan in terms of "our duty as human beings" but nevertheless considered it "chiefly

THE MARSHALL PLAN

In the rituals that are part of graduation ceremonies, guest speakers often address the challenges of the future await-ing graduates. Not many commencement addresses change the world. The speech given by U.S. Secretary of State George C. Marshall at Harvard University in June 1947 was different. By pledging gifts in aid, the United States helped rebuild war-torn Europe and transform the world's economy.

Focus Questions

What does Marshall mean when he states that this policy is "directed not against any country or doctrine"? How does Marshall explain that the plan for economic recovery is not intended as charity?

The truth of the matter is that Europe's requirements for the next three or four years of foreign food and other es-sential products—principally from America—are so much greater than her present ability to pay that she must have substantial additional help or face economic, social, and political deterioration of a very grave character.

The remedy lies in breaking the vicious circle and restor-ing the confidence of the European people in the economic future of their own countries and of Europe as a whole. The manufacturer and the farmer throughout wide areas must be able and willing to exchange their products for currencies the continuing value of which is not open to question.

Aside from the demoralizing effect on the world at large and the possibilities of disturbances arising as a result of the desperation of the people concerned, the consequences to the economy of the United States should be apparent to all. It is logical that the United States should do whatever it is able to do to assist in the return of normal economic health in the world, without which there can be no political stability and no assured peace. Our policy is directed not against any country or doctrine but against hunger, poverty, desperation, and chaos. Its purpose should be the revival of a working economy in the world so as to permit the emergence of political and social conditions in which free institutions can exist. Such assistance, I am convinced, must not be on a piecemeal basis as various crises develop. Any assistance that this Government may render in the fu-ture should provide a cure rather than a mere palliative. Any government that is willing to assist in the task of recov-ery will find full cooperation, I am sure, on the part of the United States Government. Any government which maneu-vers to block the recovery of other countries cannot expect help from us. Furthermore, governments, political parties, or groups which seek to perpetuate human misery in order to profit therefrom politically or otherwise will encounter the opposition of the United States.

From Department of State Bulletin, 15 June 1947.

---

as a matter of national self-interest." Soviet critics and Western observers differed dramatically in describing self-interest and domination as the primary motives for the plan.

Western European Economic Integration

As significant as the gift of funds to European states undoubt-edly was, no less important was the whole administrative ap-paratus that American aid brought in its wake. In order to ex-pend available monies most effectively and comply with stipulations for cooperation and regulation, the states of west-ern Europe resorted to intensified planning and limited na-tionalization.

Planning for Recovery.   The ideas of intensified planning and limited nationalization were not new in the experience of European states. Regulation and state intervention dominated the formulation of economic policy. Special attention was given to workers' welfare through unemployment insurance, retirement benefits, public health, and housing policies.

European states recognized the need to provide a safety net for their citizens in order to avoid reexperiencing the disastrous depression and stagnation of the 1930s while attempting to rebuild their shattered economies.

It was the economic theory of John Maynard Keynes that influenced the planning process. His economic concepts had been applied successfully by neutral Sweden to its economic policies during the war, came into vogue throughout Europe in 1945, and triumphed in the postwar era. Keynes favored macroeconomic policies to increase productivity and argued for an active role for government in "priming the pump" of economic growth. The government should be responsible, ac-cording to Keynes, for the control and regulation of the econ-omy, with the goal of ensuring full employment for its people. Governments could and should check inflation and eliminate boom-and-bust cycles, incurring deficits by spending beyond revenues if necessary.

European Economic Cooperation.   U.S. foreign aid con-tributed mightily to the extension of central planning and the growth of the welfare state throughout western Europe. But money alone could not have accomplished the recovery that took place. The chief mechanism for administering Marshall Plan aid was the Office of European Economic Cooperation (OEEC). That master coordinating agency made the requirements for recovery clear. European states had to stabilize their own economies. Cooperation between the public and private sectors was intended to free market forces, modernize production, and raise productivity. Planning mechanisms, including transnational organizations and networks, resulted in the modernization of production and the assimilation of new techniques, new styles of management, and innovative business practices from the United States. The modernization of economies through centrally coordinated planning made Europe once again a major contender in the international economic arena.

The major exception to the establishment of central planning agencies and the nationalization of key industries was West Germany. Deciding against the British and French models of planned growth, the West Germans endorsed a free market policy that encouraged private enterprise while providing state insurance for all workers. What has been described as "a free enterprise economy with a social conscience" produced the richest economy in western Europe by the mid-1950s. The Krupp munitions and I. G. Farben chemical empires were successfully broken up into smaller units. Industries forced to start afresh benefited from the latest technology.

European integration, discussed before and during the war, received added impetus in the postwar period. The Marshall Plan reconciled western Europe with West Germany through economic cooperation, although that was by no means its original purpose.

Realizing that Europe as a region needed the cooperation of its member states if it was to contend in world markets, associations dedicated to integration began to emerge alongside economic planning mechanisms. The Council of Europe dealt with the "discussion of questions of common concern and by agreements and common action in economic, social, cultural, scientific, legal, and administrative matters and in the maintenance and further realization of human rights and fundamental freedoms." Although not itself a supranational institution with its own authority, the Council of Europe urged a federation among European states. Britain alone rejected all attempts to develop structures of loose intergovernmental cooperation.

Belgium, the Netherlands, and Luxembourg were the first European states to establish themselves as an economic unit—Benelux. Internal customs duties among the three states were removed, and a common external tariff barrier was erected. The Schuman Plan joined France and West Germany in economic cooperation by pooling all coal and steel resources, beginning in 1950. The creators of the plan, Jean Monnet (1888–1979) and Robert Schuman (1886–1963) of France, saw it as the first step toward the removal of all eco-

nomic barriers among European states and as a move toward eventual political integration. In 1951, the Netherlands, Belgium, Luxembourg, France, Italy, and West Germany formed the European Coal and Steel Community (ECSC). While constantly confronting domestic opposition on nationalist grounds, the ECSC succeeded in establishing a "common market" in coal and steel among its member states. In 1957, the same six members created the **European Economic Community (EEC)** and committed themselves to broadening the integration of markets. It was the beginning of what became known as the Common Market.

The Common Market aimed to establish among its member states a free movement of labor and capital, the elimination of restrictions on trade, common investment practices, and coordinated social welfare programs. National agricultural interests were to be protected. Great Britain was initially a vocal opponent of the Common Market and continued to defend its own trading relationship with its Commonwealth countries, eventually founding its own free trade association in 1959. In 1973, Great Britain became a member of the Common Market and joined with other European nations in defining common economic policies. The EEC meanwhile achieved the support of the United States in its transitional period, in which it had 15 years to accomplish its aims.

European union was a phenomenon of exclusion as much as inclusion. It sharpened antagonisms between the West and the East by its very success. While promoting prosperity, European economic unification favored concentration and the emergence of large corporations. Vast individual fortunes flourished under state sponsorship and the rule of the experts. National parliaments were sometimes eclipsed by new economic decision-making organizations that aimed to make western Europe into a single free trade area.

Japan's Recovery

Japanese economic challenges in the postwar era were similar to those of western Europe. As a defeated and occupied nation in 1945, Japan faced a grim future. U.S. aims for Asia were similar to those for Europe: American policy makers sought to create a multilateral system of world trade and preserve America's sphere of influence against Communist encroachment. The American general Douglas MacArthur was appointed the Supreme Commander for the Allied Powers and the head of occupation forces in Japan. His mission in Japan was to impose rapid economic change from above. The occupation government set out to erect institutions to promote political democratization and to eliminate militaristic institutions, official patronage, and censorship. Planning, both formal and informal, reshaped the economy as U.S. aid flowed into Japan during the late 1940s and early 1950s. The changes in Japan, as in western Europe, took place alongside growing American fears of communism in the region.

Japan turned its wartime devastation into an advantage by replacing destroyed factories with the latest technology, obtained by license from foreign firms. Through a combination of bureaucracy and patronage devoted to planned growth, Japan's GNP reached prewar levels by 1956. By 1968, Japan had turned defeat into triumph and stood as the third largest industrial nation in the world. Japanese growth paralleled the "economic miracle" of West Germany, with the Japanese economy growing at a rate three times faster than that of the United States between 1954 and 1967.

The abolition of the army and navy was a boon for the Japanese economy, since 16 percent of prewar GNP had been devoted to support of the military. Postwar demilitarization freed Japan of the financial exigencies of the arms race. Funds formerly used for arms now flowed into investment and new technology. (See "The West and the Wider World: Made in Japan," pp. 598–599.) Slowed population growth after 1948 and an increased volume of foreign trade contributed to Japanese prosperity. In the 1960s, Japan emerged as an affluent society undergoing a revolution in consumer durables, including televisions, washing machines, refrigerators, and automobiles.

Recipients of American aid surpassed U.S. goals. A multilateral system of world trade emerged out of the ashes of war. The effects of the Great Depression, which the world had been unable to shake throughout the 1930s, had been laid to rest by global war and its consequences.

The Soviet Path to Economic Recovery

The Soviet Union countered economic integration in the West with its own alliances and organizations. In 1949, the USSR established the Council for Mutual Economic Assistance, or **Comecon,** with bilateral agreements between the Soviet Union and eastern European states. Comecon was Stalin's response to the U.S. Marshall Plan in western Europe. Rather than providing aid, however, Comecon benefited the Soviet Union at the expense of its partners, seeking to integrate and control the economies of eastern Europe for Soviet gain. The Soviet Union implemented an expansion of its territorial boundaries as a way of reversing some of its drastic losses in the war. Above all, it wanted a protective ring of satellite states as security from attack from the West. Picking up territory from Finland, Poland, and parts of East Prussia and eastern Czechoslovakia; forcibly reincorporating the Baltic states of Estonia, Latvia, and Lithuania; and recovering Bessarabia, the Soviet Union succeeded in acquiring sizable territories. The Soviet state then began to dedicate itself to economic reconstruction behind a protective buffer of satellite states— Poland, East Germany, Czechoslovakia, Hungary, Romania, and Bulgaria—over which Soviet leaders exercised strong control. Yugoslavia and Albania chose to follow a more independent Communist path.

Under Stalin's direction, the Soviet Union concentrated all its efforts on reconstructing its devastated economy and, to that end, sought integration with eastern European states, whose technology and resources were needed for the rebuild-

ing of the Soviet state. U.S. dominance threatened the vital connection with eastern Europe that the Soviet Union was determinedly solidifying in the postwar years. In the years before his death in 1953, Joseph Stalin succeeded in making the Soviet Union a vital industrial giant second only to the United States. The Soviet economy experienced dramatic recovery after 1945, in spite of the severe damage inflicted on it during the war. The production of steel, coal, and crude oil skyrocketed under state planning. Heavy industry was the top priority of Soviet recovery, in keeping with prewar commitments to rapid modernization. In addition, the postwar Soviet economy assumed the new burdens of the development of a nuclear arsenal and an expensive program for the exploration of space. Stalin maintained the Soviet Union on the footing of a war economy, restricting occupational mobility and continuing to rely on forced-labor camps.

De-Stalinization.   In 1953, Stalin, who had ruled the Soviet Union for almost three decades, died. The vacuum that he left provoked a struggle for power among the Communist party leadership. It also initiated almost immediately a process of **de-Stalinization** and the beginnings of a thaw in censorship and repression. A growing urban and professional class expected improvements in the quality of life and greater freedoms after years of war and hardship. In 1956, at the Twentieth Party Congress, Nikita Khrushchev (1894–1971), as head of the Communist party, denounced Stalin as incompetent and cruel. After five years of jockeying for power among Stalin's former lieutenants, Khrushchev emerged victorious and assumed the office of premier in 1958.

De-Stalinization also took place in eastern Europe. Discontent over collectivization, low wages, and the lack of consumer goods fueled a latent nationalism among eastern European populations resentful of Soviet control and influence. Violence erupted in 1953 in East Berlin as workers revolted over conditions in the workplace, but it was quickly and effectively suppressed. Demands for reforms and liberalization in Poland also produced riots and changes in Communist party leadership. Wladislaw Gomulka (1905–1982), a Communist with a nationalist point of view who had survived Stalin's purges, aimed to take advantage of the power vacuum created by the departure of Stalinist leaders. Gomulka refused to back down in the face of severe Soviet pressure and the threat of a Soviet invasion to keep him from power. Elected as the first secretary of the Communist party in Poland, Gomulka sought to steer his nation on a more liberal course.

Hungarians followed suit with their demands for the withdrawal of Hungary from the Warsaw Pact. On 23 October 1956, inspired by the events in Poland, Hungarians rose up in anger against their old-guard Stalinist rulers. Imre Nagy (1896–1958), a liberal Communist, took control of the government, attempted to introduce democratic reforms, and relaxed economic controls. The Soviets, however, were unwilling to lose control of their sphere of influence in Eastern Bloc nations and

The West and the Wider World

MADE IN JAPAN

In the years following World War II a revolution was taking shape in manufacturing and marketing that would change the world. The revolution began in an unlikely place—war-crippled Japan—and it was all the more startling because, with the rise of Japanese industry, American and European producers were left behind in key electronics markets that came to symbolize the new consumption.

Japan's economic competitiveness commanded notice beginning in the late nineteenth century because it combined the new industrialization techniques of the West with traditional values of family and nation. The Japanese were influenced certainly by modes of production in the West and rapidly advanced their own productivity through the 1930s and the wartime economy.

With atomic destruction and military defeat many Japanese faced starvation and severe hardship. The Supreme Command of Allied Forces under General Douglas MacArthur brought in an occupying army whose emphasis was education and revitalization of the economy. Yet what happened in Japan after the war cannot be explained by the one-way transmission of ideas and institutions of a Western occupying force. When the occupation ended in 1952, Japan was already on its way to sustained high economic productivity through innovation, adaptability, and the application of its own cultural values to new management practices.

The rise of the Sony Corporation provides a good case study of the Japanese transformation. Sony's founders, according to the company's own history, were committed from the very beginning to capturing a mass consumer market and appropriating whatever tools available to do so. Working in less than optimum surroundings in an abandoned department store, Sony's founders stressed the importance of the team in production. After failed beginnings in rice cookers and heating pads but greater success with tape recorders, Sony struck on the radio and its potential in a mass market. Sony was the first to develop transistor radios for the home by applying a technology developed in the West and available to but not utilized by American and European producers. The Japanese company developed technical superiority and soon became a leader in the world market. The great success of Japanese industry resided in its ability to mass produce quality products at cheap prices.

How were the Japanese able to achieve such resounding success in the fifteen years following World War II? One way, of course, was by the appropriation of lessons learned in the West. Japanese industrial leaders visited the United States regularly, met with American business leaders, visited assembly lines, and studied management as a science. One American in particular, W. Edwards Deming, became a Japanese hero because of his seminars taught in Japan during the occupation on "statistical quality control." In 1960 the Japanese government created a prize in Deming's honor which is awarded annually to industries for their use of consumer research in improving the design of products and production. Sony,

■ Sony TR-55 from ca. 1955, Japan's first all transistor radio.

598

■ Toyota automobile construction at the Motomachi factory, Japan, ca. 1960s.

Matsushita, and Toyota are just a few of the industries that employed Deming's methods and those of other Western consultants who favored "total quality management." Such a total approach to the production process was not utilized by Western competitors until it was rediscovered in the West in the 1980s, thanks to Japan's success story.

In its unique culture of the workplace, the Japanese method put emphasis on the values of the individual worker and the importance of working in small teams. Management fully participated in production and respected employees' opinions and insights. The founders of Sony launched their enterprise immediately after the war by treating their employees like family, providing daily rice to them for their lunch breaks, and organizing joint recreation and vacations. Such emphasis on family

and the values of caring and responsibility for employees resonated strongly with Japanese culture and traditions. The emphasis in this new workplace culture was on the participation of the employees and the needs of the customers. Explicitly rejected was the Ford assembly-line model of mass-production as dehumanizing and destructive of quality in the goods produced. The Japanese innovators appropriated selectively from Western industrial theory and models and applied this knowledge to their own strategies.

So successful were the management innovations of the Japanese producers that Western industries began sending observers to study Japanese methods. Japanese auto producers in the United States at the present time use their own production methods based on Japanese cultural values with their

American employees. And industrialists from the European Union continue to send their business leaders to learn "the Japanese way." Perhaps no industry better demonstrates the two-way cultural exchange of ideas, institutions, and practices than consumer electronics in the global economy. Japan succeeded in dominating world markets because it understood that production and success must be rooted in the culture and values of its own people.

QUESTIONS FOR DISCUSSION

How did Japan develop new goods and new markets in the 1950s? Why was the mass-marketing of small electronics so well-suited to postwar Japan? In what ways did the United States and western Europe learn lessons from innovations in Japanese production?

to jeopardize their system of defense in the Warsaw Pact. Moscow responded to liberal experimentation in Hungary by sending tanks and troops into Budapest. Brutal repression and purges followed. The Hungarian experience in 1956 made clear that too much change too quickly would not be tolerated by the Soviet rulers. The thaw following Stalin's death had promoted expectations among eastern Europeans that a new era was dawning. The violent crushing of the Hungarian revolution was a reminder of the realities of Soviet control and the Soviet Union's defense priorities in eastern Europe.

The Soviet Standard of Living.

The Soviet Union's standard of living remained relatively low in the years when western Europe was undergoing a consumer revolution. Soviet consumption was necessarily stagnant, since profits were plowed back as investments in future heavy industrial expansion. In the Soviet Union and throughout the Eastern Bloc countries, women's full participation in the labor force was essential for recovery. In spite of their presence in large numbers in highly skilled sectors such as medicine, Soviet and Eastern Bloc women remained poorly paid, as did women in the West. Soviet men received higher salaries for the same work on the grounds that they had to support families.

The Soviet population was growing rapidly, from 170 million in 1939 to 234 million in 1967. Nikita Khrushchev promised the people lower prices and a shorter workweek, but in 1964, when he fell from power, Soviets were paying higher prices for their food than before. With a declining rate of development, the Soviet economy lacked the necessary capital to advance the plans for growth in all sectors. Defense spending nearly doubled in the short period between 1960 and 1968.

Eastern Bloc Economies and Dissent.

The nature of planned Soviet growth exacted heavy costs in the Eastern Bloc countries. Adhering to the Soviet pattern of heavy industrial expansion at the expense of agriculture and consumer goods, East Germany nearly doubled its industrial output by 1955, despite having been stripped of its industrial plants by the Soviet Union before 1948. Czechoslovakia, Bulgaria, Romania, and Yugoslavia all reported significant industrial growth in this period. Yet dislocations caused by collectivization and heavy defense expenditures stirred up social unrest in East Germany, Czechoslovakia, Poland, and Hungary. The Soviet Union responded with some economic concessions but on the whole stressed common industrial and defense pursuits, employing ideological persuasion and military pressure to keep its reluctant partners in line.

East Berlin in the late 1950s and early 1960s posed a particular problem for Communist rule. Unable to compete successfully in wages and standard of living with the capitalist western sector of the city, East Berlin saw increasing numbers of its population, especially the educated and professional classes, crossing the line to a more prosperous life. In 1961, the Soviet Union responded to the problem by building a wall that cordoned off the part of the city that it controlled. The **Berlin Wall** eventually stretched for 103 miles, with heavily policed crossing points, turrets, and troops and tanks facing each other across the divide that came to symbolize the Cold War.

The process of liberalization that had begun after Stalin's death and continued under Khrushchev certainly experienced its setbacks and reversals in the case of Budapest and Berlin. But in 1968 the policy of de-Stalinization reached a critical juncture in Czechoslovakia. Early in 1968, Alexander Dubcek,

■ Soviet tanks rumbled through Prague as troops from the Warsaw Pact countries invaded the Czechoslovakian capital in 1968, bringing an end to Alexander Dubcek's reform movement. Dubcek was rehabilitated in the liberalization of 1989 and elected chairman of the parliament.

Czech party secretary and a member of the educated younger generation of technocrats, had supported liberal reforms in Czechoslovakia that included decentralization of planning and economic decision making, market pricing, and market incentives for higher productivity and innovation. He acted on popular desire for nationalism, the end of censorship, and better working conditions. Above all, he called for democratic reforms in the political process that would restore rule to the people. Dubcek spoke of "socialism with a human face," although, unlike the Hungarians in 1956, he made no move to withdraw his country from the Warsaw Pact or to defy Soviet

CHRONOLOGY
COLD WAR AND ECONOMIC RECOVERY

1947	Marshall Plan starts U.S. aid to European countries; pro-Soviet governments established in Poland, Hungary, Bulgaria, and Romania
1948	Pro-Soviet government established in Czechoslovakia
1949	European states and United States form North Atlantic Treaty Organization (NATO); Federal Republic of Germany and German Democratic Republic established; Soviet Union creates Council for Mutual Economic Assistance (Comecon); Soviet Union tests its first atomic bomb
1950–1953	Korean War, ending with the partition of Korea
1953	United States and Soviet Union develop hydrogen bombs
1955	Formation of Warsaw Pact
1956	Hungarian uprising and subsequent repression by Soviet military forces
1957	The Netherlands, Belgium, Luxembourg, France, Italy, and West Germany form the European Economic Community (EEC), also called the Common Market; Soviet Union launches first satellite, *Sputnik I*
1961	Berlin Wall built
1961–1973	U.S. troops engaged in Vietnam
1962	Cuban missile crisis
1963	Soviet Union and United States sign Nuclear Test Ban Treaty
1968	Prague Spring uprising in Czechoslovakia, quelled by Soviet Union

leadership. Moscow nevertheless feared the erosion of obedience within the Eastern Bloc and the collapse of one-party rule in the Czech state and sent in thousands of tanks and hundreds of thousands of Warsaw Pact troops to Prague and other Czech cities to reestablish control. The Czechs responded with passive resistance in what became known as the **Prague Spring** uprising. The Soviet invasion made clear that popular nationalism was intolerable in an Eastern Bloc nation.

Alone among eastern European leaders, Marshal Tito of Yugoslavia resisted Soviet encroachment. As a partisan leader of the Communist resistance during World War II, Tito had earned the reputation as a war hero for his opposition to the Germans. Ruling Yugoslavia as a dictator after 1945, he refused to accede to Soviet directives to collectivize agriculture and to participate in joint economic ventures. For its defiance of Soviet supremacy, in 1948 Yugoslavia was expelled from the Cominform, the Soviet-controlled information agency that replaced the Comintern after 1943.

The slowed growth of the 1960s, the delay in development of consumer durables, and the inadequacy of basic foodstuffs, housing, and clothing were the costs that Eastern Bloc citizens paid for their inefficient and rigid planned economies dedicated to the development of heavy industry. In eastern Europe and the Soviet Union, however, poverty was virtually eliminated as the state subsidized housing, health care, and higher education, which were available to all.

THE WELFARE STATE AND SOCIAL TRANSFORMATION

The **welfare state,** a creation of the post–World War II era throughout Europe, grew out of the social welfare policies of the interwar period and out of the war itself. Welfare programs aimed to protect citizens through the establishment of a decent standard of living available for everyone. The experiences of the Great Depression had done much to foster concern for economic security. In France, the primary concern of the welfare state was the protection of children and the issue of family allowances. In Great Britain, as in Germany, emphasis was placed on unemployment insurance and health care benefits. Everywhere, however, the welfare state developed a related set of social programs and policies whereby the state intervened in the cycles of individual lives to provide economic support for the challenges of birth, sickness, old age, and unemployment.

Protection of the citizenry took varied forms according to Cold War politics. In the Warsaw Pact countries, the need to industrialize rapidly and to dedicate productive wealth to armament and military protection resulted in a nonexistent consumer economy in which the issues of quality of life and protection took a very different direction. Based on a concept of equal access to a minimum standard of living, welfare states did not treat all their members equally. Women were often disadvantaged in social welfare programs as family needs, men's rights, and the protection of children led to different national configurations.

Prosperity and Consumption in the West

Despite the different paths toward reconstruction following World War II, every western European nation experienced dramatic increases in total wealth. Per capita income was clearly on the rise through the mid-1960s, and there was more disposable wealth than ever before. Prosperity encouraged new patterns of spending based on confidence in the economy. That new consumerism, in turn, was essential to economic growth and future productivity.

The New Consumption.   The social programs of the welfare state played an important role in promoting postwar consumption. People began to relax about their economic futures, more secure because of the provisions of unemployment insurance, old-age pensions, and health and accident insurance. The state alleviated the necessity of saving for a rainy day by providing protection that had formerly been covered by the savings of workers. In the mid-1950s, all over western Europe, people began to spend their earnings, knowing that accidents, disasters, and sicknesses would be taken care of by the state. Western Europeans began to buy on credit, spending money they had not yet earned. That, too, was an innovation in postwar markets.

Welfare programs could be sustained only in an era of prosperity and economic growth, since they depended on taxation of income for their funds. Such taxation did not, however, result in a redistribution of wealth. Wealth remained in the hands of a few and became even more concentrated as a result of phenomenal postwar economic growth. In West Germany, for example, 1.7 percent of the population owned 35 percent of the society's total wealth.

Women's Wages.   Just as the welfare state did not redistribute wealth, it did not provide equal pay for equal work. In France, women who performed the same jobs as men received less pay. In typesetting, for example, women, who on average set 15,000 keystrokes per hour at the keyboards compared to 10,000 by men, earned 50 percent of men's salaries and held different titles for their jobs. Separate wage scales for women drawn up during the Nazi period remained in effect in West Germany until 1956. The skills associated with occupations performed by women were downgraded, as were their salaries. Women earned two-thirds or less of what men earned throughout western Europe. Welfare state revenues were a direct result of pay-scale inequities. Lower salaries for women meant higher profits and helped make economic recovery possible.

Family Strategies

The pressures on European women and their families in 1945 were often greater than in wartime. Severe scarcity of food, clothes, and housing required careful management. Women

who during the war held jobs in industry and munitions plants earned their own money and established their own independence. After the war, in victorious and defeated nations alike, women were moved out of the work force to make room for returning men. Changing social policies affected women's lives in the home and in the workplace and contributed to the politicization of women within the context of the welfare state.

Demography and Birth Control.   Prewar concerns with a declining birthrate intensified after World War II. In some European countries, the birthrate climbed in the years immediately following the war, an encouraging sign to observers who saw in the trend an optimistic commitment to the future after the cessation of the horrors of war. The situation was more complicated in France and the United States, where the birthrates began to climb even before the war was over. Nearly everywhere throughout Europe, however, the rise in the birthrate was momentary, with the United States standing alone in experiencing a genuine and sustained "baby boom" until about 1960. In Germany and in eastern Europe (Poland and Yugoslavia, for example), the costs of the war exacted heavy tolls on families long after the hostilities ended. On average, women everywhere were having fewer children by choice.

Technology had expanded the range of choices in family planning. In the early 1960s, the birth control pill became available on the European and American markets, primarily to middle-class women. Europeans were choosing to have smaller families. The drop in the birthrate had clearly preceded the new technological interventions that included intrauterine devices (IUDs), improved diaphragms, sponges, and more effective spermicidal creams and jellies. The condom, invented a century earlier, was now sold to a mass market. Information about their reproductive lives became more accessible to young women. Illegal abortions continued to be an alternative for women. Abortion was probably the primary form of birth control in the Soviet Union in the years following the war. Controversies, however, surrounded unhealthy side effects of the pill and the dangerous Dalkon shield, an IUD that had not been adequately tested before marketing and that resulted in the death or sterilization of thousands of women. Religious leaders also spoke out on the moral issues surrounding sexuality without reproduction. And in France and Italy, birth control information was often withheld from the public.

The Family and Welfare.   Concurrent with a low birthrate was a new valuing of family life and domestic virtues in the years after the war. Those who had lived through the previous 20 years were haunted by the memories of the Great Depression, severe economic hardships, destructive war, and the loss of loved ones. Women and men throughout western Europe and the United States embraced the centrality of the family to society, even if they did not opt for large families. Expectations for improved family life placed new demands on welfare state programs. They also placed increased demands on mothers, whose presence in the home was now seen as all-important for the proper development of the child.

Handbooks for mothers proliferated, instructing them in the "science" of child rearing. The best-seller, *Baby and Child Care,* by Dr. Benjamin Spock was typical of such guides.

European states implemented official programs to encourage women to have more children and to be better mothers. **Pronatalism,** as the policy was known, resulted from an official concern over low birthrates and a decline in family size. It is unlikely that pronatalism was caused by a fear of a decline in the labor force, since the influx of foreign workers, refugees from eastern Europe, and migrant laborers from poorer southern European nations provided an expanding labor pool. Other considerations about racial dominance and women's proper role seem to have affected the development of policies. In 1945, Lord Beveridge (1879–1960), the architect of the British welfare state, emphasized the importance of women's role "in ensuring the adequate continuance of the British race" and argued that women's place was in the home: "During marriage most women will not be gainfully employed. The small minority of women who undertake paid employment or other gainful employment or other gainful occupations after marriage require special treatment differing from that of single women."

Welfare state programs differed from country to country as the result of a series of different expectations of women as workers and women as mothers. Konrad Adenauer, chancellor of West Germany, spoke of "a will to children" as essential for his country's continued economic growth and prosperity. In Great Britain, the welfare system was built on the ideal of the mother at home with her children. With the emphasis on the need for larger families—four children was considered desirable in England—English society focused on the importance of the role of the mother. Family allowances determined by the number of children were tied to men's participation in the work force; women were defined according to their husbands' status. The state welfare system strengthened the financial dependence of English wives on their husbands.

In Great Britain, anxiety over the low birthrate was also tied to the debate over equal pay for women. Opponents of the measure argued that equal pay would cause women to forgo marriage and motherhood and should therefore be avoided. There was a consensus about keeping women out of the work force and paying them less in order to achieve that end.

The French system of *sécurité sociale* defined all women, whether married or single, as equal to men; unlike English women, all French women had the same rights of access to welfare programs as men. That may well have reflected the different work history of women in France and the recognition of the importance of women's labor for reconstruction of the economy. As a result, family allowances, pre- and post-natal care, maternity benefits, and child care were provided on the assumption that working mothers were a fact of life. French payments were intended to encourage large families and focused primarily on the needs of children. More and more women entered the paid labor force after 1945, and they were less financially dependent on their husbands than were their British counterparts.

Both forms of welfare state—the British that emphasized women's role as mothers and the French that accepted women's role as workers—were based on different attitudes about the nature of gender difference and equality. Women's political consciousness developed in both societies. The women's liberation movements of the late sixties and early seventies found their roots in the contradictions of differing welfare policies.

The Beginnings of Women's Protest.   The 1960s were a period of protest in Western countries as people demonstrated for civil rights and free expression. In Europe and America, protests against U.S. involvement in Vietnam began, emulating patterns of activism established in the movement for black civil rights. Pacifist and antinuclear groups united to "ban the bomb." Women participated in all of the movements, and by the end of the 1960s had begun to question their own place in organizations that did not acknowledge their claims to equal rights, equal pay, and liberation from the oppression of male society. A new critique began to form within the welfare state that indicated there were cracks in the facade.

One book in particular, written after World War II, captured the attention of many women who were aware of the contradictions and limitations placed on them by state and society. *The Second Sex* (1949), written by Simone de Beauvoir (1908–1986), a leading French intellectual, analyzed women's place in the context of Western culture. By examining the assumptions of political theories, including Marxism, in the light of philosophy, biology, history, and psychoanalysis, de Beauvoir uncovered the myths governing the creation of the female self. By showing how the male is the center of culture and the female is "other," de Beauvoir urged women to be independent and to resist male definitions. *The Second Sex* became the handbook of the women's movement in the 1960s.

A very different work, *The Feminine Mystique,* appeared in 1963. In that book, author Betty Friedan voiced the grievances of a previously politically quiescent group of women. Friedan was an American suburban homemaker and the mother of three children when she wrote about what she saw as the schizophrenic split in her own middle-class world between the reality of women's lives and the idealized image of the perfect homemaker. After World War II, women were expected to find personal fulfillment in the domestic sphere. Instead, Friedan found women suffering from the "sickness with no name" and the "nameless desperation" of a profound crisis in identity.

A new politics centering on women's needs and women's rights slowly took root. The feminist critique did not emerge as a mass movement until the 1970s. Youth culture and dissent among the young further influenced growing feminist discontent. But the agenda of protest in the sixties, reinforced by social policies, accepted gender differences as normal and natural.

Youth Culture and Dissent

Youth culture was created by outside forces as much as it was self-created. Socialized together in an expanding educational system from primary school through high school, the young came to see themselves as a social force. They were also socialized by marketing efforts that appealed to their particular interests as a group.

The prosperity that characterized the period from the mid-fifties to the mid-sixties throughout the West provided a secure base from which radical dissenters could launch their protests. The young people of the 1960s were the first generation to come of age after World War II. Although they had no memory themselves of the destruction of that war, they were reminded daily of the imminence of nuclear destruction in their own lives. The combination of the security of affluence and the insecurity of Cold War politics created a widening gap between the world of decision-making adults and the idealistic universe of the young. To the criticisms of parents, politicians, and teachers, the new generation responded that no one over 30 could be trusted.

New styles of dress and grooming were a rejection of middle-class culture in Europe and the United States. Anthropologists and sociologists in the 1960s began studying youth as if they were a foreign tribe. The "**generation gap**" appeared as the subject of hundreds of specialized studies. Adolescent behavior was examined across cultures. Sexual freedom and the use of drugs were subjected to special scrutiny. But, above all, it was the politics of the young that baffled and enraged many observers. When the stable base of economic prosperity began to erode as a result of slowed growth and inflation in the second half of the sixties—first in western Europe and then in the United States—frustrated expectations and shrinking opportunities for the young served as a further impetus for political action.

The Sexual Revolution. Increased emphasis on fulfillment through sexual pleasure was one consequence of the technological revolution in birth control devices, and it led to what has been called a revolution in sexual values in Western societies in the 1960s. The sexual revolution drew attention to sexual fulfillment as an end in itself. Women's bodies were displayed more explicitly than ever before in mass advertising in order to sell products from automobiles to soap. Sex magazines, sex shops, and movies were part of an explosion in the marketing of male sexual fantasies in the 1960s.

Sweden experienced the most far-reaching reforms of sexual mores in the 1960s. Sex education became part of every school's curriculum, contraceptive information was widely available, and homosexuality was decriminalized. Technology allowed women and men to separate pleasure from reproduction but did not alter men's and women's domestic roles. Pleasure was also separated from familial responsibilities, yet the domestic ideal of the woman in the home remained. Some women were beginning to question their exploitation in the sexual revolution. In the early 1970s, that issue became part of mass feminist protest.

The New Drug Culture. Just as sexuality was invested with new meaning within the context of protest, so was the use of drugs. Drug use was not new in history: through the ages drugs have been taken as painkillers or pleasure enhancers and used in religious and cultural rituals. Soldiers in nineteenth-century wars in Europe and America returned home addicted to opium and morphine, which they were given when treated for their wounds. In the 1960s, American soldiers in Vietnam turned to drugs as an escape from the horrors of war.

Drugs began to pervade Western cultures in seemingly harmless ways. At the end of the nineteenth century in the United States, the newly created Coca-Cola was originally made with cocaine, a drug derived from the coca shrub. Another ingredient in the soft drink formula was the kola nut, which contains the stimulant caffeine. In the 1950s and 1960s, chemical technology made possible the manufacture of syn-

■ Isle of Wight Festival, England, 1969. Open-air music festivals were a popular feature of the sixties—the era of pacifism, when young people experimented with sexual liberation, the drug culture, and Eastern mysticism.

thetic drugs. Pharmaceutical industries in Europe and the United States expanded by leaps and bounds with the mass marketing of amphetamines, barbiturates, and tranquilizers. Doctors prescribed the new drugs for a variety of problems from obesity to depression to sleeplessness. People discovered that the drugs had additional mood-altering effects.

Marijuana grew in popularity as a "recreational" drug, especially among college and university students in the 1960s. In fact, young people were the primary users of drugs of all sorts, including synthetic drugs such as the hallucinogen LSD (lysergic acid diethylamide). Hallucinogens were considered by their proponents to be mind-expanding drugs that permitted the achievement of new levels of consciousness. Drugs used by young people affluent enough to afford them served to widen the gap between the generations still further.

The Anti-War Movement and Social Protest.

Student protest, which began at the University of California at Berkeley in 1964 as the Free Speech movement, by the spring of 1968 had become an international phenomenon that had spread to other American campuses and throughout Europe and Japan. A common denominator of protest, whether in New York, London, or Tokyo, was opposition to the war in Vietnam. Growing numbers of intellectuals and students throughout the world condemned the U.S. presence in Vietnam as an immoral violation of the rights of the Vietnamese people and violent proof of U.S. imperialism.

Student protesters shared other concerns in addition to opposition to the war in southeast Asia. The growing activism on American campuses was aimed at social reform, student self-governance, and a recognition of the responsibilities of the university in the wider community. In West Germany, highly politicized radical activists, a conspicuous minority among the students at the Free University of Berlin, directed protest out into the wider society. Student demonstrations met with brutal police repression and violence, and rioting was common.

European students, more than their American counterparts, were also experiencing frustration in the classroom. European universities were unprepared to absorb the huge influx of students in the 1960s. The student–teacher ratio at the University of Rome, for example, was 200 to 1. In Italian universities in general, the majority of more than half a million students had no contact with their professors. The University of Paris was similarly overcrowded.

For the most part, student protest was primarily a middle-class phenomenon. In France, for example, only 4 percent of university students came from below the middle class. Higher education had been developed after World War II to serve the increased needs of a technocratic society. Instead of altering the social structure, which politically committed student protesters thought it should do, mass education served as a certifying mechanism for bureaucratic and technical institutions. Many of the occupations that students could look forward to were in dead-end service jobs or in bureaucratic posts.

Protest and the Economy.

Student dissent reflected the changing economy of the late 1960s. Inflation, which earlier in the decade had spurred prosperity, was spiraling out of control in the late sixties. In the advanced industrial countries of western Europe and later in the United States, the growth of the postwar period was slowing down. Economic opportunity was evaporating and jobs were being eliminated. One survey estimated that only one in three Italian university graduates in 1967 was able to find a job. The dawning awareness of shrinking opportunities in the workplace for students who had attained their degrees and been properly certified further aggravated student frustration and dissent. Anger about the uncertainties of their future mixed with the realization of the boredom of the careers that awaited them upon graduation.

By the late sixties, universities and colleges provided the students a forum for expressing their discontent with advanced industrial societies. In their protests, student activists rejected the values of consumer society. The programs and politics of the student protesters aimed to transform the world in which they lived. Student protesters in France chanted, *"Métro, boulot, dodo,"* a slang condemnation of the treadmill-like existence of those who spent their lives in a repetitive cycle of subway riding (*Métro*), mindless work (*boulot*), and sleep (*dodo*). The spirit of protest was expressed in the graffiti and posters that seemed to appear overnight on the walls of Paris.

In May 1968, French protest spread beyond the university when workers and managers joined students in paralyzing the French economy and threatening to topple the Fifth Republic. Between 7 and 10 million people went on strike in support of worker and student demands. White-collar employees and technicians joined blue-collar factory workers in the strike. Student demands, based on a thoroughgoing critique of the whole society, proved to be incompatible with the wage and consumption issues of workers. But the unusual, if short-lived, alliance of students and workers shocked those in power and induced reforms.

CONCLUSION

The division of the world into two camps framed the recovery of combatant nations dealing with the losses of World War II. The Cold War instilled fear in the populations who lived on both sides of the divide. Yet the Cold War also created the terms for stability following the upheaval of war. It promoted prosperity that preserved the long-term policies of both the United States and the Soviet Union in the twentieth century. The Soviet Union had buffered itself from the West by creating a ring of friendly nations on its borders and had continued its race to industrialize. The belief that the USSR had won the war for the Allies and the sense of betrayal that followed the war determined the outlook of grim distrust shared by postwar Soviet leaders who had survived the years from 1939 to 1945.

The United States, on the other hand, found itself playing the role of rich uncle in bankrolling the European recovery. Its long-term commitment to promoting its own economic interests by helping future trading partners led it also into playing the role of police officer throughout the world. The escalating war in Vietnam made America vulnerable to growing world criticism and to growing domestic discontent.

The gains of economic recovery began to unravel in the mid-1960s. The protests of 1968 were a response to changing economic conditions. In the West, rising expectations of consumer societies came up against the harsh realities of slowed growth. In the East, frustrated nationalism, the lack of consumer goods, and repressive conditions resulted in low morale, demonstrations, and outright conflict. After Stalin's death, resources were diverted to consumer goods, but there was little measurable improvement in the quality of life. By 1970, changing economies in both East and West affected the goals of the Cold War, still very much an organizing reality in the international arena. Created out of the aftermath of war, the Cold War now faced the challenges of prosperity both at home and abroad.

QUESTIONS FOR REVIEW

1. What did it mean for postwar European politics that the Continent was divided by an iron curtain?
2. What factors encouraged decolonization in the decades after World War II?
3. Why did western Europe's economy recover so rapidly, and how did that contribute to a gradual process of European economic integration?
4. How did the Soviet Union's strategy for recovery differ from that of western Europe?
5. What is the welfare state, and how did it transform the lives of ordinary Europeans?
6. What were some of the concerns that provoked protests from women, students, and others in the 1960s?

KEY TERMS

Berlin Wall, *p. 600*

Cold War, *p. 588*

Comecon, *p. 597*

containment, *p. 590*

decolonization, *p. 592*

de-Stalinization, *p. 597*

European Economic Community (EEC), *p. 596*

generation gap, *p. 604*

iron curtain, *p. 588*

Marshall Plan, *p. 594*

North Atlantic Treaty Organization (NATO), *p. 590*

nuclear club, *p. 591*

Prague Spring, *p. 601*

pronatalism, *p. 603*

third world, *p. 592*

Warsaw Pact, *p. 590*

welfare state, *p. 601*

DISCOVERING WESTERN CIVILIZATION ONLINE

You can obtain more information about the Cold War and postwar economic recovery at the websites listed below. See also the Companion Website that accompanies this text, www.ablongman.com/kishlansky, which contains an online study guide and additional resources.

The Origins of the Cold War

The Berlin Airlift: Documents, Images, History
www.trumanlibrary.org/whistlestop/study_collection/berlin_airlift/large/berlin_airlift.htm
A virtual exhibit with electronic texts on the Berlin Airlift as presented by the Harry S Truman Library and Museum.

Internet Modern History Sourcebook: A Bipolar World
www.fordham.edu/halsall/mod/modsbook46.html
A collection of primary source documents and links to the creation of the United Nations and the outbreak of the Cold War.

Cold War International History Project
www.wilsoncenter.org/index.cfm?fuseaction=topics.home&topic_id=1409
This site, sponsored by the Woodrow Wilson International Center for Scholars, provides a comprehensive list of primary documents and images, secondary sources, bibliographies, and working paper series on all aspects of the Cold War.

Soviet Archives Exhibit
www.ibiblio.org/expo/soviet.exhibit/entrance.html
A Soviet archive exhibit on the Cold War with images and electronic texts by the Library of Congress.

Postwar Economic Recovery in Europe, Japan, and the Soviet Union

Internet Modern History Sourcebook: Eastern Europe Since 1945
www.fordham.edu/halsall/mod/modsbook50.html
Two collections of links to primary sources and other sites on postwar western and eastern Europe.

The European Recovery: The Fiftieth Anniversary of the Marshall Plan
www.loc.gov/exhibits/marshall
A virtual museum exhibit with images and electronic primary and secondary texts on the Marshall Plan.

The Welfare State and Social Transformation

Internet Modern History Sourcebook: Modern Social Movements
www.fordham.edu/halsall/mod/modsbook56.html
A collection of primary source documents and links to sites on modern social movements including feminism, black power, and gay and lesbian rights.

The Sixties Project Home Page
lists.village.virginia.edu/sixties/
Web site of the Sixties Project, which brings together discussion lists, primary documents, bibliographies, museum exhibits, and personal testimonies about the 1960s and the Vietnam War from an exclusively American perspective.

Paris 1968 Posters
burn.ucsd.edu/paris.htm
A collection of posters of the 1968 protest movement in Paris.

SUGGESTIONS FOR FURTHER READING

The Origins of the Cold War

Franz Ansprenger, *The Dissolution of the Colonial Empires* (London: Routledge, 1989). An analysis of Europe's withdrawal from Asia and Africa following the Second World War, beginning with an examination of post–World War I imperialism.

Edward H. Judge and John W. Langdon, eds., *The Cold War: A History Through Documents* (New York: Prentice-Hall, 1998). Includes about 130 edited documents covering the period from 1945 to 1991.

Charles S. Maier, *In Search of Stability: Explorations in Historical Political Economy* (Cambridge: Cambridge University Press, 1987). Covers a wide variety of issues affecting twentieth-century Europe, including the foundation of American international economic policy after World War II and the conditions for stability in western Europe after 1945.

Bruce D. Porter, *The USSR in Third World Conflicts: Soviet Arms and Diplomacy in Local Wars, 1945–1980* (Cambridge: Cambridge University Press, 1984). A case study approach to the Soviet Union's changing postwar policies toward the third world that centers on local wars in Africa and the Middle East.

Postwar Economic Recovery in Europe, Japan, and the Soviet Union

Eric Hobsbawm, *The Age of Extremes: A History of the World, 1914–1991* (New York: Vintage Books, 1996). This volume covers what the author calls "the short twentieth century" from the outbreak of World War I to the fall of the Soviet Union. Of particular interest is the section on the 30 years following World War II, which the author sees as a "golden age" of extraordinary economic growth and social transformation.

Michael J. Hogan, *The Marshall Plan: America, Britain, and the Reconstruction of Western Europe* (Cambridge: Cambridge University Press, 1987). A thoroughly researched argument on the continuity of U.S. economic policy in the twentieth century. Hogan counters the belief that the Marshall Plan was merely a response to the Cold War.

Derek W. Urwin, *Western Europe Since 1945: A Political History,* 4th ed. (London: Longman, 1989). An updated general survey of postwar politics, with a special focus on the problems of reconstruction and the role of the resistance after 1945.

The Welfare State and Social Transformation

Simone de Beauvoir, *The Second Sex* (New York: Knopf, 1963). The author, one of France's leading intellectuals in the twentieth century, describes the situation of women's lives in the postwar West by placing them within the context of the history and myths governing Western culture.

Jane Jenson, "Both Friend and Foe: Women and State Welfare," *Becoming Visible: Women in European History,* ed.

Renate Bridenthal, Claudia Koonz, and Susan Stuard (Boston: Houghton Mifflin, 1987). This essay illuminates the mixed blessing of the welfare state for women after 1945 by focusing on the experiences of women in Great Britain and France.

Walter Laqueur, *Europe Since Hitler: The Rebirth of Europe* (New York: Penguin Books, 1982). Surveys politics, economy, society, and culture in order to explain Europe's postwar resurgence.

Susan Pederson, *Family, Dependence, and the Origins of the Welfare State: Britain and France, 1914–1945* (Cambridge: Cambridge University Press: 1994). Although this work covers the earlier period, the comparative approach to differing attitudes and policies provides an essential background to understanding family policy in postwar Europe.

Denise Riley, *War in the Nursery: Theories of the Child and Mother* (London: Virago Press, 1983). Treats social policies of postwar pronatalism within the context of the popularization of developmental and child psychologies in Europe, with special attention to Britain and the United States and an emphasis on the postwar period as a turning point in attitudes toward women and the family.

Mary Ruggie, *The State and Working Women: A Comparative Study of Britain and Sweden* (Princeton, NJ: Princeton University Press, 1984). A sociological study comparing the economic status of women in two European welfare states.

David Caute, *The Year of the Barricades: A Journey Through 1968* (New York: Harper & Row, 1988). More than its title suggests, this work is an overview of postwar youth culture on three continents. The politics of 1968 is featured, although other topics regarding the counterculture, lifestyles, and cultural ramifications are considered.

John R. Gillis, *Youth and History: Tradition and Change in European Age Relations, 1770–Present* (New York: Academic Press, 1981). Connects the history of European youth to broad trends in economic and demographic modernization over the past 200 years.

Margaret Mead, *Culture and Commitment: The New Relationships Between the Generations in the 1970s* (New York: Columbia University Press, 1978). This series of essays, written by one of America's premier anthropologists, explores the origins and consequences of the generation gap, with special attention to Cold War politics, historical conditions, and technological transformations.

For a list of additional titles related to this chapter's topics, please see www.ablongman.com/kishlansky.

Chapter 30

THE END OF THE COLD WAR AND NEW GLOBAL CHALLENGES, 1970 TO THE PRESENT

The Visual Record

THE BERLIN WALL COMES DOWN

The American poet Robert Frost captured a basic aspect of human nature when he wrote, "Good fences make good neighbors." The uneasy coexistence of Communist East Germany and liberal and capitalist West Germany reached a confrontation point 16 years after the end of World War II, with the building of a "fence"—the Berlin Wall. In August 1961, the wall, erected by the East German government under Soviet direction, bifurcated the former German capital and served its intended purpose of keeping East Germans confined behind it.

Why the wall? East Germany's chief problem in the 1950s was the exodus of over two million East Germans in search of a better life in the West. The flow of emigration throughout the 1950s turned into a torrent in the first eight months of 1961. The Berlin Wall was, more than anything else, erected to keep skilled and professional workers in East Germany. German leaders in the West continued to voice their long-term commitment to reunification, while East German leaders insisted on the independence and autonomy of their state.

Throughout its 28-year life, the Berlin Wall served as a chilling reminder of the great ideological divide between East and West in the Cold War. Cutting through neighborhoods, streets, and railway lines, the Berlin Wall also divided families in two. Yet the wall was porous, if even only slightly so. Passes could be authorized for holidays and special family events, funerals, weddings, and births so that East Berliners could visit their relatives. But long lines through checkpoints with passport and currency controls prevented circulation. Individuals attempting escape from East Berlin to the West were gunned down from watch towers along the wall. Consisting of over 90 miles of concrete slabs and barbed wire, the wall stood as a scar through the center of Berlin and around West Berlin. In 1963, President John F. Kennedy visited West Berlin and proclaimed in solidarity with citizens on both sides of the wall, "Ich bin ein Berliner" (I am a Berliner). In that same speech, Kennedy stated, "There are some who say that communism is the wave of the future. Let them come to Berlin." President Ronald Reagan used the occasion of his visit to West Berlin in 1987 to highlight the apparently increasing openness of the Soviet bloc.

Applications for authorized immigration to West Germany increased in the 1980s, and in 1984 East Germany allowed 30,000 citizens to emigrate to the West. Throughout the late 1980s, the emigration rate remained high, with an average exodus of 20,000 a year. With

Hungary's refusal to continue to block the passage of East Germans into West Germany, the floodgates were opened: 57,000 East Germans migrated via Hungary within a matter of weeks. In the face of angry demonstrations, Erich Honecker, head of the East German state, was forced to resign.

The new government opened the Berlin Wall on November 9, 1989, ending all restrictions on travel between East and West. The toppling of communism, already underway, was captured in that moment. Robert Frost wrote of good fences, but he concluded, "Something there is that doesn't love a wall." With the rise of democratic institutions, open markets, and civil liberties, the Cold War had come to an end.

Looking Ahead

By 1970, the postwar restrictions of a bipolar world were giving way to signs of republicanism, democracy, and self-rule. Some transformations were achieved with violence. Most notably, the history of ethnic differences led to war in the Balkans and the former Soviet republics. The United States was embroiled in conflicts throughout the Middle East. The place of the West in the global community continued to depend on social and gender inequalities. And a new kind of war based on the terrorism of civilian populations emerged as the weapon of choice of dispossessed groups around the globe. ➤

THE END OF THE COLD WAR AND THE EMERGENCE OF A NEW EUROPE

The Cold War, while it lasted from the post-1945 period to the late 1980s, provided a way of ordering the world. It served to divide friend from foe, to create spheres of economic interest, and to promote market relations among blocs of nations. Also, in a seemingly contradictory sense, it was a conflict that promoted stability and peace between the superpowers, no matter how uneasy. Yet chinks in the facade of Communist unity were already present by the mid-1960s, as we have seen in the previous chapter. As the Soviets faced growing discontent within the Soviet bloc, and as the nuclear threat made cooperation necessary, the bipolar security of the Cold War began to crumble.

The Brezhnev Doctrine and Détente

The use of military intervention to resolve the Czech crisis (Chapter 29) opened a new era governed by what came to be known as the **Brezhnev Doctrine.** Leonid Brezhnev (1906–1982), general secretary of the Communist party and head of the Soviet Union from 1966 to 1982, established a policy whereby the Soviet Union claimed the right to interfere in the internal affairs of its allies in order to prevent counterrevolution. Brezhnev was responsible for the decision to intervene in Czechoslovakia, arguing that a socialist state was obliged to take action in another socialist state if the survival of socialism was at stake. The Brezhnev Doctrine influenced developments in eastern Europe throughout the next decade. After 1968, rigidity and stagnation characterized the Soviet, East German, and Czechoslovakian governments, as well as Communist party rule in other eastern European states.

In the international arena, the Soviet Union had achieved nuclear parity. Now, from positions of equality, both sides expressed a willingness to negotiate. The 1970s became the decade of **détente,** a period of cooperation between the two superpowers. The Strategic Arms Limitation Treaty, known as SALT I, signed in Moscow in 1972, limited defensive antiballistic missile systems.

East–West relations after 1983 were characterized by less confrontation and more attempts at cooperation between the Soviet Union and the United States. The world political system itself appeared to have stabilized, with a diminution of conflict in the three main arenas of superpower competition—the third world, China, and western Europe. By the end of 1989, leaders in the East and West declared that the ideological differences that separated them were more apparent than real. They declared an end to the Cold War and sought a new and permanent détente.

The New Direction in Soviet Politics

By the mid-1980s, Soviet leaders were weighing the costs of increasing conflict within the Soviet bloc, which the Brezhnev Doctrine failed to control, and the promise of benefits from improved relations with the West. Growing dissent from intellectuals within the Soviet Union joined the voices of those from abroad who criticized Soviet repression. In response to the same forces of change, a different kind of leader was being forged in the ranks of the Communist party among a generation that favored more open political values and dynamic economic growth.

Typical of the new generation of political leaders was Mikhail Gorbachev, who was, above all, a technocrat, someone who could apply specialized technical knowledge to the problems of a stagnant Soviet economy. In 1985, the accession to power of Mikhail Gorbachev as general secretary ushered in a new age of openness.

As the youngest Soviet leader since Stalin, Gorbachev set in motion in 1985 bold plans for increased openness, which he called **glasnost,** and a program of political and economic restructuring, which he dubbed **perestroika.** The economic challenges that Gorbachev faced were enormous. Soviet citizens were better fed, better educated, and in better health than their parents and grandparents had been. Yet while economic growth continued throughout the postwar years, the rate of growth was slowing down in the 1970s. Some planners feared that the Soviet Union could never catch up to the United States, Japan, and West Germany. Soviet citizens were increasingly aware of the sacrifices and suffering that economic development had cost them in the twentieth century and of the disparities in the standards of living between the capitalist and communist worlds. Due to outmoded technology, declining older industries, pollution, labor imbalances, critical shortages of foodstuffs and certain raw materials, and a significant amount of hidden unemployment in unproductive industries, discontent became more widespread.

Gorbachev's programs between 1985 and 1988 promised more than they delivered. The promises were part of the problem since they created unmet expectations. Modest increases in output were achieved, but people's demands for food and consumer goods were rising faster than they could be met. The Soviet Union did not increase imports of consumer durables or food to meet the demand, nor did the quality of Soviet goods improve appreciably. Rising wages only gave workers more money that they could not or would not spend on Soviet products. The black market was a symbol both of the economic failures of the state and of the growing consumerism of Soviet citizens. Rather than purchase poorquality goods, Soviets chose to purchase foreign products at vastly inflated prices.

Although his economic reforms broke sharply with the centralized economy established by Stalin in the 1930s, Gorbachev candidly warned that he would not implement a consumption revolution in the near future. Many critics, including fellow communist Boris Yeltsin, believed that Gorbachev did not go far or fast enough with his economic reforms. Yet by 1989, many observers inside and outside the Soviet Union believed that a new age was at hand as the Soviet leader loosened censorship, denounced Stalin, and held the first free elections in the Soviet Union since 1917.

Reform in Eastern Europe

The Soviet example of restructuring and Gorbachev's calls for reforms and openness gave the lead to eastern Europe. In 1988, Gorbachev, speaking before the United Nations, assured the West that he would not prevent eastern European satellites from going their own way: "Freedom of choice is a universal principle," the Soviet head of state declared.

Poland and Grassroots Protest.   Poland's first free elections in 40 years were part of a vast mosaic of protest from which a pattern began to emerge in the spring of 1989. Poland, the most populous nation in eastern Europe, had played an important role in the Soviet bloc because of its strategic location as a corridor for supplies to the Soviet Union's 380,000 troops in East Germany. Yet its economy was never robust, and it had a 20-year history of worker protest and resistance. Throughout the 1970s, the Polish government, based on one-party rule, drew loans from abroad for investment in technology and industrial expansion. The government increased its foreign indebtedness rather than raise prices at home. In 1976, however, price increases were again decreed. A new wave of spontaneous strikes erupted, forcing the government to rescind the increases.

Poland's indebtedness to the West rose from $2.5 billion in 1973 to $17 billion in 1980. Poland was sinking into the mire of ever higher interest payments that absorbed the country's export earnings. At the beginning of July 1980, the government was forced yet again to raise food prices. Shipyard workers in Gdansk were ready, solidly organized in a new noncommunist labor union called **Solidarity** under the leadership of a politically astute electrician named Lech Walesa. The union staged a sit-down strike that paralyzed the shipyards. Union committees coordinated their activities from one factory to the next and succeeded in shutting down the entire economy. The government agreed to a series of union-backed reforms known as the Gdansk Accords, which, among other measures, increased civil liberties and acknowledged Solidarity's right to exist.

Within a year, Solidarity had an astounding 8 million members out of a population of 35 million. The Catholic Church lent important support to those who opposed Communist rule. Dissident intellectuals also cast their lot with the organized workers in demanding reforms. General Wojciech Jaruzelski became prime minister in February 1981, but the situation of shortages did not change appreciably. Jaruzelski attempted to curb the union's demands for democratic government and participation in management by harsh measures: he declared martial law on 13 December 1981. Jaruzelski was trying to save the Polish Communist party by using the Polish military to crack down on the dissidents. The Soviet response was to do nothing. Poland, as a result, was left to Polish rule.

Martial law in Poland produced military repression. Solidarity was outlawed and Walesa was jailed. The West did not lose sight of him: in 1983, the union leader was awarded the Nobel Peace Prize for his efforts. After years of negotiations and intermittent strikes, Solidarity was legalized once again in 1989. The economy was in dire straits, and Jaruzelski knew that he needed Solidarity's cooperation: he agreed to open elections. At the polls, Solidarity candidates soundly defeated the Communist party. Poland was the first country anywhere to turn a Communist regime out of office peacefully. Yet Poland did not pull out of the Warsaw Pact. As Lech Walesa explained in 1989 on West German television, "Poland cannot forget where it is situated. You know we are in the Warsaw Pact. That cannot be changed."

■ Strike leader Lech Walesa addresses shipyard workers in Gdansk, Poland, on 30 August 1980.

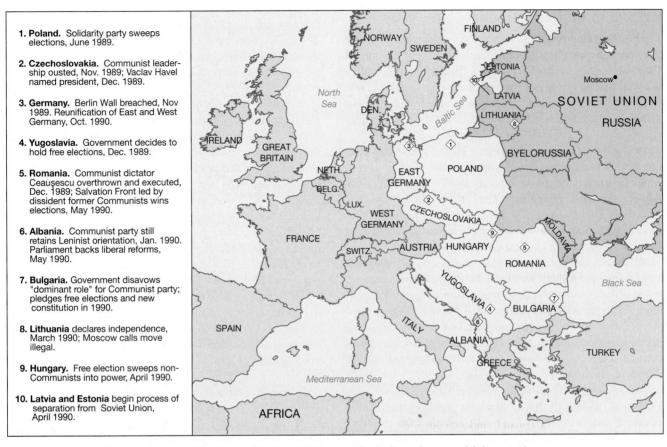

1. **Poland.** Solidarity party sweeps elections, June 1989.

2. **Czechoslovakia.** Communist leadership ousted, Nov. 1989; Vaclav Havel named president, Dec. 1989.

3. **Germany.** Berlin Wall breached, Nov 1989. Reunification of East and West Germany, Oct. 1990.

4. **Yugoslavia.** Government decides to hold free elections, Dec. 1989.

5. **Romania.** Communist dictator Ceauşescu overthrown and executed, Dec. 1989; Salvation Front led by dissident former Communists wins elections, May 1990.

6. **Albania.** Communist party still retains Leninist orientation, Jan. 1990. Parliament backs liberal reforms, May 1990.

7. **Bulgaria.** Government disavows "dominant role" for Communist party; pledges free elections and new constitution in 1990.

8. **Lithuania** declares independence, March 1990; Moscow calls move illegal.

9. **Hungary.** Free election sweeps non-Communists into power, April 1990.

10. **Latvia and Estonia** begin process of separation from Soviet Union, April 1990.

■ Events in Eastern Europe, 1989–1990. The events of 1989 and 1990 seemed to indicate that peaceful democratic change through free elections and liberal reforms would fill the void left by the collapse of communist rule.

The great challenge before the Solidarity government, as for the Communist regime that preceded it, was economic recovery. Inflation drove food prices up at the rate of 50 percent a month. The Polish government committed itself to freeing the zloty from state control and making it a convertible currency, one that could be bought and sold for other currencies on the international currency market, so that Polish goods could compete in world markets. Poland faced the task of earning enough foreign trade credits to alleviate its indebtedness and to justify foreign investment. In the mid-1990s, Poland continued its pursuit of a free market economy by attracting Western companies and corporations to open subsidiaries and to do business within its borders, as inflation slowed to a still high 20 to 30 percent, and a prosperous management class began emerging.

Hungary, Czechoslovakia, and Romania. In the same period as the Polish free elections, Hungary dismantled the barbed-wire fences on its Austrian border; all of its borders to the West were opened in September 1989. Unlike other eastern European countries, Hungary had begun experimenting cautiously with free markets and private control as early as the 1970s. As a result, Hungary was best positioned to engage in

serious trade with western Europe and made the most prosperous adjustment to democratic autonomy.

Czechoslovakia's revolution began with angry university students. Singing Czech versions of protest songs such as "We Shall Overcome," student protesters were reminiscent of the student activists of 1968. They tried to give flowers to police, who responded by bludgeoning the protesters. That spark touched off a mass movement that within days drove out the Czech Communist party. Idealism and growing public sympathy were on the side of the protesters. The dissident playwright Václav Havel, released from jail just before the demonstrations began, emerged as the leader of the democratic opposition and was elected president of the new government. He became a powerful spokesperson for democratic institutions and oversaw a relatively peaceful separation of the Czech Republic from Slovakia. All of the countries underwent what were considered "velvet revolutions," characterized by a lack of violence and an apparently smooth passage to a new order and the achievement of independence.

The year 1989 did not end, however, without bloody upheaval. Romania under communist dictator Nicolae Ceaucescu appeared to be pursuing a peaceful path. It had evaded its military responsibilities in the Warsaw Pact; it alone

CHRONOLOGY
THE VELVET REVOLUTIONS

1989	Free elections in Poland lead to the ouster of the Communist regime
September 1989	Hungary opens its borders to the West
November 1989	German Democratic Republic lifts travel restrictions between East and West Germany; the Berlin Wall comes down
December 1989	Václav Havel elected president of Czechoslovakia
July 1990	Havel reelected as president of the Czech and Slovak Federated Republic
1990	Boris Yeltsin elected president of the Russian Republic
1990	Gorbachev ends the Communist party's monopoly of power
1990	Lech Walesa elected president of Poland
October 1990	Federal Republic of Germany and German Democratic Republic reunited
December 1991	Eleven former Soviet republics form Commonwealth of Independent States (CIS); Mikhail Gorbachev resigns, and the Soviet Union is dissolved

of the member states had refused to participate in the Czechoslovakian intervention of 1968. Yet Romania was a state that could not tolerate internal protest. In December 1989, Ceaucescu ordered his troops to fire on demonstrators. Thousands of men, women, and children were killed and buried unceremoniously in mass graves. The slaughter set off a revolution in which Ceaucescu and his wife and co-ruler, Elena, were captured, tried, and executed by a firing squad. They were charged with genocide—the slaughter of 64,000 people—and the mismanagement of the economy. In the days that followed, Romanians spoke in the international media of their newly won freedom, as videotaped images of the slain leaders were broadcast to the world.

The Unification of Germany

The crumbling facade of Communist unity within the Soviet bloc was nowhere more evident than in East Germany. The German Democratic Republic (East Germany) and the German Federal Republic (West Germany), divided by the

victorious Allies following World War II, continued to develop after 1968 as two separate countries with different social, economic, and political institutions. On the surface, the differences seemed insurmountable. The erection of the Berlin Wall in 1961 (see The Visual Record, pp. 610–611) cutting the city in two stood as a continual reminder of the ideological divide between East and West.

In the 1980s, West Germany stood as an economic giant, second in foreign trade only to the United States and far ahead of Japan. East Germany also established itself as an important trading nation—fifteenth in the world in 1975. Nevertheless, citizens in East Germany were lured by the greater prosperity of the West. The lure proved too great in the 1980s and East Germany increasingly allowed its citizens to emigrate. The dismantling of the Berlin Wall in 1989 was symbolic of a greater opening of borders as greater numbers of East Germans chose the West.

An East Germany with open borders could no longer survive as its citizens poured into the promised land of the West in record numbers. The West German government intervened to assist East Germany in shoring up its badly faltering economy; the West German deutsche mark was substituted for the East German currency. Monetary union prefigured political unification. In October 1990, Germany became a single, united nation once again.

Germans represent the largest nationality in Europe west of Russia. Other Europeans feared the prospect of a united Germany, although publicly European leaders endorsed the principle of the self-determination of peoples. In addition, western Europeans were troubled by the impact a united Germany might have on plans for European unification in the European Union. Not least of all, Germans themselves feared reunification. Former East Germans were wary about marginalization and second-class citizenship, while West Germans worried that their poor cousins from the east would act as a brake on West Germany's sustained economic expansion. Nevertheless, Germany committed itself to a course of action to make of the German nation a unified people whose economy would continue to dominate European and world markets.

Russia and the New Republics

As eastern and central European nations were choosing self-rule and greater independence from the Soviet Union, the Soviet Union's own Communist party faced a dilemma. How could party rule and centralization be coordinated with the demands for freedom and autonomy that Gorbachev's own reforms fostered?

Aware of his precarious political position, Gorbachev appeared to retrench by increasing control over the media and by attempting to consolidate his base of power. As a result of the attempts, many believed that the regime was becoming authoritarian. Gorbachev was clearly walking a fine line in attempting to maintain stability, yet he was making no one happy—neither Communist party hard-liners nor Western-oriented supporters of capitalism.

Boris Yeltsin in Power.   The shocking end to the Gorbachev experiment came in August 1991. A quasi-military council of Communist hard-liners seized power in order to restore Communist rule and reverse democratic reforms. Gorbachev was taken prisoner in his vacation home in the Crimea. Soviet citizens from the Baltic republics to Siberia protested the takeover, and tens of thousands of Muscovites poured into the streets to defy the tanks and troops of the rebel government. Three people were killed outside Russia's parliament building, which had become a rallying point for the protesters. The timing of the coup was probably determined by the fact that Gorbachev was scheduled to sign a new union treaty with nine of the republics the day following his house arrest, which would have effectively broken up the Soviet empire.

Boris Yeltsin became a hero overnight, publicly defying the plotters, rallying popular support behind him, and helping convince Soviet army troops to disobey orders to attack the White House, as the parliament building in Moscow is called. After only two days, the coup d'état failed; Gorbachev returned to Moscow and banned the Communist party. Although Gorbachev retained his title of Soviet president, his prestige had been seriously damaged by the coup and by the challenge of Yeltsin's new dominance as a popular hero. In the national elections for the Congress of People's Deputies that followed, Boris Yeltsin, who had been dismissed as the head of the Moscow party in 1987, garnered 89 percent of the popular vote. As Yeltsin's star was on the rise, the Soviet Union was now in full collapse.

Economic Challenges.   Embarking on a drive toward westernization and playing catch-up with capitalist nations, liber-al reformers in Russia pressed after August 1991 for privatization of industry and the lifting of price controls. There was hope inside and outside Russia that the new state would easily enter the capitalist marketplace. The long lines in front of stores disappeared. But inflation ominously galloped to new heights, wiping out savings and pensions overnight. The black market, always in the shadows even in the most repressed of times, emerged boldly as a corrupt "mafia," and its people became the new business leaders of Russia. New markets relied on dollars, and neither banks nor police had the power to stem illegal activities. The combined crises of inflation and rule by a gangster elite weakened the barely emergent market economy and undermined the Russian ruble, whose value crashed in October 1994. While a new wealthy class was emerging, as many as 30 percent of the population had become indigent and lived below the poverty line. In 1996, the average monthly salary amounted to about $140 in its U.S. currency equivalent.

The Nationalities Problem.   A crucial element in understanding the end of the Soviet Union was the **nationalities problem** within its borders—the claim to self-determination made by Soviet minorities. The Soviet Union listed 102 separate nationalities in its 1979 census. Twenty-two of those nationalities had populations of one million or more people. That very diversity contributed to the disintegration of the Soviet Union from within. As Gorbachev supported the demands for self-determination in eastern Europe, he faced similar claims to autonomy in a growing number of Soviet republics. The nationalities problem proved to be even more challenging to Gorbachev's regime than the free market economy. In fact, the demands for more freedom in the marketplace went hand in hand with demands for greater cultural self-expression and political autonomy among minority nationalities.

■ The Big Mac comes to Moscow. McDonald's opened its first Soviet fast-food outlet in 1990, just a few blocks from the Kremlin. Muscovites stood in long lines for milkshakes, fries, and the "Bolshoi Mak."

The three major areas of nationalist conflict—Central Asia, Armenia, and the Baltic states—had been voicing grievances against the Soviet state since the 1920s. The protests of the 1980s differed from earlier outcries because a new and educated urban elite, formed after World War II, were now the protesters. Gorbachev's challenge was to harness their protests for autonomy without undermining the Communist party's authority, and to make the party the vehicle for the new social groups and their local needs. Because of the party's inability to accommodate these new political ends, Gorbachev ultimately failed.

Ethnic minorities, especially in the Soviet Baltic republics of Latvia, Lithuania, and Estonia, threatened the dominance of party rule in favor of immediate self-determination. Endorsing diversity of opinion, individual rights, and freedom as the bases of good government, Gorbachev now had to deal with vocal nationalities who took him at his word. Large-scale riots erupted in Lithuania over demands for nationalist rights. In 1988, Estonians demanded the right of veto over any law passed in Moscow. The Russian minority in Estonia protested attacks and prejudicial treatment in the Estonian republic. In the same year,

outright violence erupted in Azerbaijan as tens of thousands of Armenians took to the streets to demand the return of the Armenian enclave of Nagorno-Karabakh, incorporated into Azerbaijan in 1921. In the Azerbaijan capital of Baku, the center of Russia's oil-producing region, demonstrators demanded greater autonomy for their republic and the accountability of their deputies in Moscow. Violence between Azerbaijanis and Armenians resulted in 32 deaths and the displacement of tens of thousands. The state upheaval climaxed in December 1988, when an earthquake in Armenia killed 25,000 people. Soviet troops were placed in the area, ostensibly to deal with the aftermath of the natural disaster.

The Breakaway Republics Lead the Way.   One by one, all 15 of the Soviet republics proclaimed their independence, following the lead of the breakaway Baltic republics of Estonia, Lithuania, and Latvia. Having failed to agree on a new plan for union, Gorbachev and the leaders of ten republics transferred authority to an emergency State Council in September 1991 until a plan could be devised. By the end of

MAP DISCOVERY

Republics of the Soviet Union

The Soviet Union broke up into 15 independent nations, which embraced a variety of ethnic groups. Note the correspondence between ethnicity/language and independent nation status. What new republics have only one language? In the nation of Uzbekistan, how many ethnicities and languages are there? How many different ethnic groups remained in the new Russian state?

the year, the Soviet Union was faced with serious food shortages and was bankrupt, unable to pay its employees and dependent on the financial backing provided by Yeltsin as head of the Russian state. Rejecting all Soviet authority, Russia, Belarus, and Ukraine joined together in December 1991 to form the Commonwealth of Independent States (CIS). Eight other republics followed their lead. The Soviet Union thereby came to its end on 21 December 1991 with the resignation of Mikhail Gorbachev, who had become a man without a state to rule. Russian President Yeltsin moved into Gorbachev's Soviet presidential offices at the Kremlin.

Many issues remained unresolved. The new political organization did not address the endemic problems of economic hardship and left unanswered the questions of who would control the former Soviet Union's vast military machine, including its nuclear arsenal, and how trade networks and a stable monetary policy would be determined. Just as there were millions of Russians living beyond the borders of the Russian state with the rise of independent republics, there continued to be ethnic minorities within Russia who sought independence. Russia, on a smaller scale than its Soviet predecessor, was a federation of different ethnic minorities and a Russian majority population with no clear policy for autonomy or self-rule.

The year 1989 marked a watershed in the history of European politics. The beginnings of transformation were first signaled by the Soviet Union, followed by dramatic events in central and eastern Europe. The democratic tide appeared irreversible as symbols of freedom and cooperation proliferated throughout the former Warsaw Pact countries. One million people joined hands in a widely publicized event to form a 370-mile-long human chain that stretched across the Soviet Baltic republics of Estonia, Latvia, and Lithuania in protest against Soviet annexation in 1940. Other bodies defied borders, as in September 1989, when East Germans began a mass exodus into West Germany, voting with their feet for economic prosperity and democracy. Poland and Hungary opted for democratic regimes, and Bulgarians ended the 35-year reign of the dictator Todor Zhivkov and endorsed parliamentary government. Tens of thousands of Czech demonstrators in the capital city of Prague typified the peaceful "velvet revolution" of the democratic movement that swept through eastern and central Europe as they poured into the streets to sing songs about freedom and cheer their new heroes, dissidents persecuted and jailed under the former communist regime.

ETHNIC CONFLICT AND NATIONALISM

Yet freedom was not the only force unleashed with the collapse of communism. Ugly battles based on long-standing grievances erupted. Groups intent on autonomy and independence vied with each other over territories and borders.

Chechnya struggled to be free of Russian rule. The Balkans, where borders had been imposed at the end of World War I, erupted into genocidal strife that shocked the world.

In Bosnia, where a bloody war dragged on for years in the former Yugoslavia, the term **ethnic cleansing** laid bare the barbarity and genocide that were still very much a part of the Europe of the late twentieth century. The international arena seemed bereft of solutions to the troubling problem of borders at the beginning of the twenty-first century as terrorism and state repression defined the Chechen-Russian struggle.

The Chechen Challenge

In December 1994, Russia committed itself to a war with another of its ethnic minorities, the secessionist Chechens, who had declared themselves independent of Russia in 1991. The war was denounced in the international arena because of the Russian attacks against the civilian population. By the summer of 1996, Russia appeared to have lost the war and agreed to a truce, despite the fact that it possessed the largest army in Europe deployed against a much smaller opponent.

The development of a peace plan that would acknowledge Chechen autonomy within the Russian state was acceptable to the rebels, who saw the advantage of regrouping their forces and the need for a break in hostilities. But Kremlin officials expressed dismay that the move toward Chechen autonomy threatened "Russian territorial integrity."

In the summer of 1999, conflict again escalated into open warfare because of terrorist bombings in Moscow attributed to Chechen rebels. Affected by arguments of self-defense against terrorists, Russian popular opinion now turned in favor of repressing the Chechen bid for independence. Russia also had important economic motives for subduing the runaway republic, as Chechnya's location was central to the oil pipeline routes near the Caspian Sea. Several former Soviet states had begun building a new pipeline in the 1990s in order to circumvent the Russian supply and to sell directly to Western buyers.

In 2001, Russian president Vladimir Putin declared the war in Chechnya over. Yet violence continued. Following terrorist attacks in the United States on 11 September 2001, the Russians escalated their war against terrorism in Chechnya. The Chechens responded with terrorist tactics within the Russian state. Atrocities against Russian civilians escalated in 2004. Plane bombings on two flights leaving Moscow and the killing of 339 hostages held in a schoolhouse, half of whom were children, provoked global denunciation. Putin responded to these atrocities by limiting democracy and civil liberties, a move that unleashed popular discontent within Russia and criticism around the world.

War in the Balkans

Hopes for social transformation and liberal economic reforms were highest for Yugoslavia in 1989 with the waning of Soviet

A WOMAN REPORTER BEHIND THE LINES OF THE WAR IN CHECHNYA

Anne Nivat was the Moscow correspondent for the French daily newspaper Libération *in October 2000 when she interviewed the rebel president of Chechnya. Fluent in Russian and holding a doctorate in political science, Nivat traveled to southern Russia disguised as a Chechen woman to cover the war from the Chechen side. Her newspaper reports led to antiwar protests in Paris.*

Focus Questions

What indications does the Chechen rebel leader give that he sees guerrilla warfare within Chechnya as the best means of defeating Russia? What are his motives for opposition to the presence of Russian troops in Chechnya?

I finally find Maskhadov. He is wearing a military uniform with a pistol in his belt and appears to be in perfect health. Seated on a comfortable sofa in a "safe house," he seems relaxed and eager to share his thoughts on the situation in Chechnya. Outside, Russian armored vehicles pass through the autumn mist. Since he left Grozny the previous winter, the rebel president hasn't spent more than two consecutive days in any one spot. He usually communicates with his men and with the outside world by means of audiotapes. Few journalists take the trouble to hunt him down and interview him. In any case, he's very suspicious of the press. We talk for several hours over a meal of soup.

"The Russian intervention in Chechnya is about one year old. Where are we now?" I ask Maskhadov.

The fugitive leader answers simply: "As far as we're concerned, it all began on September 5, 1999, when the Russians bombed our country for the first time, and not on October 1. This time we're not so naïve to throw ourselves into all-out combat with the Russians, as we did in the first war. We know that's not the way to make any headway against their army. All we can do is mount a series [of] diversionary actions," he explains. "Our goal is not to halt their army but to conserve our own forces. While they occupy our territory—that is, while they remain inactive—their forces grow weaker, while ours get stronger. Our men are everywhere. The Russians know it, and yet they never mount an offensive. Their army is demoralized." . . .

Maskhadov is silent for a moment. He lets out a deep sigh. The Chechens, he admits, are tired of this war. "I recognize that the situation is difficult for the civilian population, which has become the target of the Russian army. I also regret that thousands of my countrymen have had to leave for Ingushetia or elsewhere. But each time I send out my representatives, they come back with the same message: 'Continue the fight. We're with you.' We can't afford to lose face, and the population knows it as well as I do. One way or another, the Russians will be forced to come to the negotiating table. I am constantly reminding Putin that he will be better off negotiating with me, as long as I am alive. It will be worse without me. And the Russians will leave in the end. Last time they led us to believe that they would never leave and then they disappeared. The worse thing would be if they stayed and we had to defend their troops here in Chechnya!" . . .

Maskhadov is enjoying our discussion. It is rare that he has the full attention of a member of the foreign press. He has a hard time tearing himself away, but he finally gets up to leave, followed by his Minister of Defense and two bodyguards. His old car starts up crankily. It carries him away to the edge of the forest. From there he will go on horseback to his camp.

From Anne Nivat, *Chienne de Guerre: A Woman Reporter Behind the Lines of the War in Chechnya,* translated by Susan Darnton (New York: Public Affairs Press, 2001), pp. 251–255.

power and the end of the Cold War. Yugoslavia, after all, was the success story of the Soviet bloc with open borders and its escape from the Stalinist grasp in 1948. Many Europeans believed it was moving toward a market economy with its liberal economic policies and trade agreements.

Yugoslavia was a federation of six people's republics, with Serbia, Croatia, and Bosnia and Herzegovina the three largest in descending order. In 1991, festering differences erupted in civil war between Serbs and Croats, as Serbian nationalists overran multiethnic Bosnia and Herzegovina in a bid for territorial aggrandizement of Serbia. Serbia and Croatia were more than long-standing rival enemies with a history of hostility that had been masked by their federated status in the Yugoslav state.

The History of Ethnic Differences. The divide between the Serbs and Croats was partly identified with religious differences—the Croats were historically Catholic, the Serbs Orthodox—but for the most part, their enmity was based on the competing claims over the South Slavic lands, Bosnia and Herzegovina, that were part of the former Ottoman and Austro-Hungarian Empires.

Conflicting territorial claims of the Serbs and Croatians were considerably exacerbated by two facts. First, a large number of Serbs lived in Croatia, and, of course, Croatians were present in the Serbian-claimed lands of Bosnia. Under Tito's rule, ethnic differences were held in check. After 1991, land claims were considerably complicated by the mixed population of Bosnia and Herzegovina. Second, another group, neither Catholic nor Orthodox but Muslim, amounting to 9 percent of the population of the former Yugoslavia and a majority of the Bosnian population, got caught in the crossfire of the war between Serbs and Croats and became a target for massacre and atrocities by the Serbs.

In 1992, the Serbian army evicted 750,000 Muslim civilians from their homes in Bosnia. Serb forces also continued to bomb civilians in the Bosnian capital of Sarajevo. It later came to light that in 1992 Serb leaders had authorized a policy of ethnic cleansing—including concentration camps, rape, and starvation—against Muslims. In 1995, the Serb military was also responsible for the mass killings of Muslims from Srebrenica. Such barbarity contributed heavily to forging a strong sense of national identity among Bosnian Muslims, who controlled the Bosnian army and the presidency.

Beginning in 1992, Muslims from other parts of the world, including Afghanistan, Iran, Turkey, Pakistan, and Arab countries such as Egypt, volunteered to fight alongside the soldiers of the Bosnian army as Muslim holy warriors or *moujahedeen* against the Serb nationalists. Used as shock troops by Bosnia commanders, they quickly earned a reputation as fierce fighters who inspired religious fervor among the Bosnian army.

The United Nations placed forces in Bosnia on a peace-keeping mission, which allowed it to take neither side in the war. NATO intervened against the Serbian attempt to overrun Bosnia after the outbreak of hostilities, and in September 1995 NATO stepped up the bombing of Bosnian Serb military installations and Serbian-held positions in Bosnia with the policy of avoiding civilian targets.

The Dayton Peace Accords brokered by the United States brought Muslim, Croat, and Serb leaders together in Ohio in November and December 1995. As part of the commitment to the accord, the Clinton administration sent 20,000 U.S. troops to join the 60,000 NATO troops already present to help enforce the peace. The aim of the accords was to create a unified country in Bosnia while recognizing ethnic interests. The settlement called for a shared three-person presidency chosen by free elections. In the judgment of some Western diplomats, such an arrangement offered little hope of a stable and enduring peace.

Kosovo and the Ongoing Conflict in Eastern Europe.
Yet another arena of bloodshed opened up in 1998. Kosovo, one of the six former Yugoslav republics, had been known as the "autonomous province" of Serbia. With the breakup of Yugoslavia, there had been movement toward an independent Kosovo, and even talk of a "Greater Albania," which would reunify Albanians in Kosovo, western Macedonia, and Albania. Checking attempts at Kosovo independence, Serbia proceeded to strip it of its autonomous status after 1990. In addition, there was overwhelming evidence that the Serb state intended to drive more than one million Kosovo Albanians from the province. The Kosovo Liberation Army responded with guerrilla actions against the Serbs.

Civil rights abuses and atrocities against Kosovo Albanians by Kosovo Serbs shocked the world into action in 1998. On the night of 24 March 1999, NATO forces began attacking Serbian targets in Kosovo in a massive military campaign of air strikes that lasted for almost 11 weeks. The war, a first in NATO's history, marked a failure in its policy of deterrence. As the lead partner, the United States justified an unpopular war at home by promising not to commit ground troops in battle. The air war succeeded, and United Nations peace-keeping forces, including U.S. troops, entered Kosovo in June 1999. The Serbs were probably responsible for the deaths of at least 10,000 and the expulsion of 800,000 Kosovo Albanians. With the defeat of Serb forces, Kosovo Albanians took the place of their Serb oppressors and committed new atrocities, now under the nose of peace-keeping forces, with the aim of driving non-Albanians out of the province. Intolerance and the desire for revenge boded ill for the future of peace in the region.

The new Serbia remained a tightly controlled state economy. Privatization was unconstitutional in Serbia. Former communist officials continued to run things, as before, as feudal fiefdoms for the profit of a few. Bosnia had no economy at all, and foreign investors, so necessary for economic recovery and trade, avoided putting funds in a country lacking financial institutions and a market orientation. In 2002, Serbia and Montenegro, both part of the former Yugoslavia, began discussions that resulted in the formation of a federation of the two republics, the new state of Serbia and Montenegro, in 2003.

But Albania, a tiny nation of 3.5 million people, was in the worst economic shape of all at the end of the twentieth century. As the poorest nation, with the highest infant mortality rate and the lowest life expectancy rate in Europe, Albania faced the challenges of the post-communist era with its industrial infrastructure in ruins, its government in shambles, and its environment polluted. Without the authoritarian control of communist rule, Albania disintegrated into a primitive society ruled by bandits, blood feuds, and vendettas.

Other eastern European states also were riddled with ethnic troubles—including Czechs and Slovaks, the Hungarians and Romanians over the border region of Transylvania, and the Bulgarians and Turks in Bulgaria—but none of those disputes involved the degree of violence that had occurred in the Balkans.

THE WEST IN THE GLOBAL COMMUNITY

The phenomenal growth and prosperity of western Europe came up against a new set of harsh realities in the 1970s with skyrocketing oil prices, inflation, and recession. Western

European nations saw greater cooperation as the best response in world markets dominated by the American superpower. A key component in achieving growth was not only the U.S. capital that helped fuel recovery, but also the availability to western European economies of a floating labor pool of workers from southern Europe and from former colonies in Asia and Africa. The permanent presence of foreign workers, many of them unemployed or erratically employed during the economic downturns of the 1970s and 1980s, came to be seen as a problem by welfare-state leaders and politicians of the New Right. Europe's new working class became the brunt of racist antagonism.

With the goal of reviving the economy in the 1980s, the 12 member states of the European Economic Community devoted themselves to making western Europe competitive as a bloc in world markets. They hoped that by uniting they could serve as a counterweight to American economic hegemony in the West. At the same time that Russian satellites in eastern Europe were breaking free of Soviet control and attempting to strike out on their own, the nations of western Europe were negotiating a new unity based on a single market and centralized policy making.

Europe, both east and west, seemed on the verge of a renaissance, united economically, committed to democratic institutions, and looking forward to the twenty-first century as a global power in its own right. Yet social and economic problems persisted, the costs of the welfare state rose, terrorism tyrannized democratic societies, and a new nationalism vied with cooperation across borders. The rosy vision of the West in a global community that many foresaw in 1990 seemed to have a cloudy future as the West faced the new century.

European Union and the American Superpower

In 1957, the founders of the European Economic Community, Robert Schuman and Jean Monnet, envisioned the idea of a United States of Europe. Both men perceived that Europe's only hope of competing in a new world system was through unity. The European Community (EC) had been created in 1967 by merging the three transnational European bodies—the European Coal and Steel Community, the European Economic Community, and the European Atomic Energy Community. It operated with its own commission, parliament, and council of ministers, though it had little real power over the operations of member states. In 1974, a European Council was created within the European Community, made up of heads of government who met three times a year. Almost since its inception, the European Community was committed to European integration.

The Politics of Oil.   The oil crisis of the 1970s encouraged isolationism among the members of the EC and eroded foreign markets, causing growing dependence on national suppliers and thereby undercutting the goals of the Common Market. As the crisis abated, competition and efficiency reemerged as priorities within the EC. Europeans were well aware that the United States and Japan had surged ahead after the 1973 crisis. The Common Market had been successful in promoting European growth and integration since 1958. Western European leaders realized that integration was the only defense against the permanent loss of markets and dwindling profits.

Toward a Single Europe.   In 1985, the EC negotiated the Single European Act, which by 1987 had been ratified by the parliamentary bodies of all the member nations. Final steps were initiated to establish a fully integrated market by 31 December 1992. The 12 members of the EC intended to eliminate internal barriers and to create a huge open market among the member states with common external tariff policies. In addition, the elimination of internal frontier controls with a single-format passport was intended to make travel easier and to avoid shipping delays at frontiers, thereby lowering costs. An international labor market based on standardized requirements for certification and interchangeable job qualifications would result. The easier movement of capital to areas where profitability was greatest was encouraged. All aspects of trade and communication, down to electrical plugs and sockets, had to be standardized. The goal behind the planning was to make the EC think and act as a single country. Supporters compared it to the 50 individual American states participating in one nation.

In 1989, there were 320 million European citizens of the 12 countries of the EC: the original Common Market six of France, West Germany, Belgium, the Netherlands, Luxembourg, and Italy were joined by Britain, Denmark, and Ireland in 1973, Greece in 1981, and Portugal and Spain in 1986.

Plans for European economic integration moved dramatically forward in October 1991 when the 12-nation European Community and the 7 nations of the European Free Trade Association (EFTA) joined forces to form a new common market to be known as the European Economic Area. The EFTA countries that joined forces with the EC included Austria, Finland, Iceland, Liechtenstein, Norway, Sweden, and Switzerland. Several of the EFTA nations announced plans to join the EC as well. The European Economic Area constituted the world's largest trading bloc, stretching from the Arctic Circle to the Mediterranean and consisting of about 380 million consumers. The nations of the EFTA agreed to abide by the EC's plans for economic integration and adopted the vast array of laws and regulations that governed the EC.

The European Union.   Meeting in Maastricht, the Netherlands, in December 1991, the heads of the 12 EC countries ratified a treaty momentous for the European Union. They agreed that a common currency, the **euro,** would replace the national currencies of eligible nations, and that a single central banking system, known as the European Monetary

Original EU member in 1992

Became member in 1995

Became member in 2004

0   500 Miles

0   500 Kilometers

■ European Union. The most stable and prosperous European nations formed the 12 original member states of the European Union in 1992, soon joined by three additional members. These members agreed to share a common currency, economic and social policies, and planning. In 2004, 10 new nations joined the EU.

Institute, would guide member nations in reducing inflation rates and budget deficits. Economic union would be reinforced by political union, with member states sharing a common European defense system and common social policies regulating immigration and labor practices. In that sense, the new **European Union** (EU) was intended as something more than the European Community (EC), which had been primarily an economic entity to promote free trade. In the words of French President François Mitterrand, the goals of the

European Union were: "One currency, one culture, one social area, one environment."

On 1 January 2002, Europeans in 12 of 15 member nations began using the new common currency, the euro. Since 1999 the euro had been a virtual currency, existing as a bookkeeping device. In 2002, the new hard currency replaced national monetary units including the French franc, the German mark, the Spanish peseta, the Greek drachma, and the Dutch guilder. Hailed as the European Union's boldest achievement, the new currency was intended to solidify the basis of integrated European markets and be competitive in international markets against the dollar. Within two months of the introduction of the euro, at the end of February 2002, the member nations of the European Union held a convention for the purpose of considering the creation of a Europe-wide constitution.

Many worried, however, that the long histories, traditions, and national identifications of the individual member states would stand in the way of a fully integrated and politically united Europe. Britain was the most reluctant of the member states at the prospect of European integration. British negotiators strongly resisted plans for monetary union because they feared losing national sovereignty rights. Nonetheless, Prime Minister Margaret Thatcher and her successor, John Major, solidly committed Great Britain to the EU. As Thatcher explained it: "Our destiny is in Europe." In addition to resisting monetary union, British public opinion polls reflected cynicism over the 1991 Maastricht negotiations and a social policy affecting working hours, minimum wages, and conditions of employment throughout Europe. Prime Minister Tony Blair continued to be committed to the European Union, although the British pursued a separate path to full membership.

The biggest expansion in the European Union came on 1 May 2004 when 10 new states, all from eastern Europe, became members of the EU. The inclusion of Cyprus, the Czech Republic, Estonia, Hungary, Latvia, Lithuania, Malta, Poland, Slovakia, and Slovenia now brought EU membership to 25. Some planners were wary about the prospect of including eastern European nations whose troubled economies, they feared, would dilute the economic strength of the EU. More optimistic predictions recognized the potential of an available labor pool and the possibility of new markets in the former Soviet bloc.

Originally intended to offset American dominance in European markets, in the 1990s the EU offered the opportunity of a closer economic relationship with the United States. The EU became the largest customer for American products. In addition, Ford, IBM, Digital, Boeing, Unisys, Otis, General Electric, Pratt & Whitney, McDonnell Douglas, and Pacific Telesis were just a few of the American companies that entered into partnerships and joint ventures with EU firms. The possibility of the emergence of a truly global marketplace seemed, paradoxically, more likely with the creation of the EU and other regional associations throughout the world. By fostering market economies, economic competition, political stability of democratic institutions, as well as common political, economic, and social policies, the EU offered a counterbalance to the void filled by the end of the Cold War and the promise of peace based on productivity and trade.

A New Working Class: Foreign Workers

Foreign workers played an important role in the industrial expansion of western Europe beginning in the 1950s. Western European nations needed cheap, unskilled laborers. Great Britain, France, and West Germany were the chief labor-importing countries; their economic growth in the 1950s and 1960s had been made possible by readily available pools of cheap foreign labor. The chief labor-exporting countries included Portugal, Turkey, Algeria, Italy, and Spain, whose sluggish economic performance spurred workers to seek employment opportunities beyond national borders. Great Britain also imported workers from the West Indies, Ireland, India, Pakistan, Africa, and southern Europe.

Migrant employment was by definition poorly paid, unskilled or semiskilled manual work. Foreign male workers found employment on construction sites all over western Europe. Foreign women worked in domestic service, personal care, and factories. Commonly, married men migrated without their families, with the goal of earning cash to send home to those left behind. Most immigrants who came looking for jobs carried with them the "myth of return," the belief that they would someday go back home. For the most part, however, foreign workers stayed in the host country. Irish workers were alone in returning to their home country.

Working Conditions and Rights. The lot of foreign workers was difficult and sometimes dangerous. Onerous and demanding labor was common. Foreign workers were often herded together in crowded living quarters, socially marginalized, and identified with the degrading work they performed. Foreign workers were frequently denied the rights of citizenship and subjected to the vagaries of legislation. In economic downturns they were the first to be laid off. Yet the obligations of foreign workers to send money back home to aged parents, spouses, children, and siblings persisted. Children who resided in the host country with their foreign-worker parents suffered from severe identity problems, experiencing discrimination in schools in the countries in which they were born and with which they identified. A rising incidence of violence among second-generation Algerian adolescents in France, for example, indicated tensions and a new kind of rebellion among migrant populations.

Women endured special problems within the foreign work force. Between 1964 and 1974, the majority of Portuguese immigrants to France came with families, but there were few social services to support them on their arrival. Dependable child care was either too expensive or unavailable to female workers with children. Increasing numbers of single women began migrating to western Europe independently of their households. Like men, they worked in order to send money back home.

Opposition and Restrictions. Opposition to the presence of foreign workers was often expressed in ultranationalist rhetoric and usually flared up in periods of economic reversals. Right-wing politicians sometimes complained that foreign workers deprived native workers of jobs. That argument seemed baseless, since many of the jobs filled by migrants were spurned by native workers as too menial, too poorly paid, or too physically demanding. Opposition to foreign

■ Indian immigrants in France sewing in a sweatshop. Immigrant workers in European countries took low-paying, menial jobs. They faced resentment from xenophobic native Europeans.

workers nonetheless became virulent. In 1986 in France, the xenophobic National Front campaigned on a platform of "France for the French" and captured 10 percent of the vote in national elections. Racism was out in the open in Western countries that had depended on a foreign labor force for their prosperity. Arab and black African workers in France resorted to work stoppages to protest police discrimination and identity controls that they likened to the yellow Stars of David that Jews had been required to wear in Nazi Germany. In 1996, the French government chartered planes to return undocumented Africans to Africa. Riots in Great Britain in 1980 and 1981, particularly in the London ghetto of Brixton, were motivated by racial discrimination against blacks, severe cuts in social welfare spending, and deteriorating working conditions.

The European Union attempted to impose uniform standards and quotas on immigration but these were often resisted by member nations. One reason they resisted was the lack of skilled workers to do certain jobs. For instance, at the beginning of the new century, Spain's economy was one of the fastest growing in western Europe. Yet Spain suffered labor shortages in the construction and agricultural sectors. Spanish employers relied heavily on illegal immigrants in spite of the fact that Spain had the highest unemployment rate in the European Union in the year 2000. Germany likewise suffered from high unemployment, yet sought increased numbers of professional workers from abroad because of the limited skills in the available pool of workers. A declining birth rate in western European countries also contributed to labor shortages and reliance on imported labor. On the whole, restrictions failed to achieve what they set out to do—remove foreign workers from Western countries by repatriation in spite of numerous policies to restrict and police illegal immigration.

The presence of foreign workers in European Union countries heightened racism and overt antagonism from a resurgent extreme Right. In the late 1980s, when movements for democratic freedom and human rights were being endorsed in eastern Europe, the problem of permanent resident "aliens" was without a solution in western Europe. Yet the need for cheap labor made the preservation of such a labor pool likely.

The issue of immigration became a prominent one in electoral campaigns throughout Europe in the 1990s. Opposition to the presence of foreign workers and concerns about protecting small business interests fueled ballot-box victories for the far right in Austria, the Netherlands, and France. In the first presidential election of the twenty-first century in France, the National Front candidate Jean-Marie Le Pen ran on the party's "France for the French" platform and garnered an unprecedented 18 percent of the electorate, giving pause to the democratic leadership of many European countries. In 2004, debate raged in the industrialized countries about how to deal with the apparently contradictory demands of high rates of endemic unemployment and labor shortages.

French Laws on Secularity. The presence of populations from north Africa and southern and eastern Europe in western Europe resulted in a clash of cultures, values, and religious beliefs. In France, Muslim girls began wearing veils and head scarves in school in growing numbers beginning in the late 1980s. Citing French laws on the separation of church and state, authorities ultimately banned all accessories and clothing that indicated religious affiliation, including crosses and yarmulkes. An amendment to the law in 2004 raised enforcement to the national level. The public debate about assimilation and citizenship reinforced the idea that citizenship required adherence to a common code and common cultural values. Although in the first week of school in September 2004 only 240 girls out of nearly 12 million students came to school wearing head scarves, the issue captured the attention of the world by exposing the tensions within Western societies caused by the influx of new, often foreign-born Muslim minorities.

Women's Changing Lives

During the last quarter of the twentieth century, the lives of Western women reflected dramatic social changes. Women were more educated than ever before. Access to institutions of higher learning and professional schools allowed women to participate in the work force in education, law, medicine, and business throughout the world, whether in France, the United States, or the Soviet Union. Women had been active in calling for the liberation of oppressed groups in the 1960s. Those activities served to heighten women's collective awareness of the disparities between their own situations and those of men in Western societies: women worked at home without pay; in the workplace, women received less pay than men for the same work.

In that period of increased educational and work opportunities, an international women's movement emerged. International conferences about issues related to women were media events in the 1970s. In 1975, the United Nations Conference on the Decade for Women was convened in Mexico City. Women activists believed that something more was needed than the conference, which was accused of seeking only to integrate women into existing social structures dominated by men. On 8 March 1976—International Women's Day—the International Tribunal of Crimes Against Women was convened in Brussels. Issues such as fertility and sexuality were at the center of the new politics of the women's movement, justified in the slogan, "The personal is political." Rape and abortion were problems of international concern. "Sisterhood is powerful!" gave way to a new organizing slogan, "International sisterhood is *more* powerful!"

Reforms and Political Action.   In Italy, political action by women yielded a new law in 1970 that allowed divorce under very restricted circumstances. Italian feminists used the legal system as a public forum. In France, the sale of contraceptives was legalized in 1968. French feminists, like their Italian counterparts, worked through the courts to make abortion legal: they achieved their goal in 1975. With the increasing integration of Europe in the 1990s, differing national practices in child care, health care, and gender parity were reviewed by the deliberative bodies of the European Union. Yet national differences of women's social and family roles still prevailed among European countries, including differences in education, health care, and reproductive rights.

The feminist movement created a new feminist scholarship that sought to incorporate women's experiences and perspectives into the disciplines of the humanities and the social sciences. Women's studies courses, which emphasized the history of women and their contributions to civilization, became part of university and college curricula throughout Europe and the United States. Reformers also attempted to transform language, which, they argued, had served as a tool of oppression.

In addition to promoting political action throughout Europe, issues of domestic violence, incest, and sexual orientation entered the political arena. In 1970, Western feminism was discovering that "socialism was not enough," and that women had to address problems of discrimination in terms of gender as much as class.

At the turn of the new century, feminists, student activists, environmentalists, and internationalists found common ground in the concerns of exploitation of a global work force, sweatshops, ecological devastation, and the pollution and exploitation of the environment. The biggest of these demonstrations occurred in Seattle, Washington, in November and December 1999, when thousands of protesters, women and men from around the world, converged for a week to protest the actions of the World Trade Organization and international corporations, perceived as prime culprits in global exploitation and pollution.

Terrorism: The "New Kind of War"

A new kind of warfare emerged globally as disfranchised groups rejected the avenues of cooperation and reform and instead chose violence as the sole means of achieving their political ends. The history of contemporary terrorism began after World War II. The creation of the state of Israel in part of the land of Palestine in 1948 led to conflict between the Israelis and the Palestinian Arabs, who refused to accept the new Jewish state. Israel's Arab neighbors went to war to support the Palestinians but were defeated by Israel in late 1948. Hundreds of thousands of Palestinians became refugees in neighboring Arab states, and Palestinian guerrillas decided that the best way to attack Israel and its protectors was with a global strategy of terrorist violence. The first Palestinian hijacking took place in the summer of 1968. Ejected from Jordan, Palestinian guerrillas set up their headquarters in Syria and Lebanon in order to continue their terrorist activities.

Another influence figured prominently in terrorism of the late twentieth century: Islamic fundamentalism. Muslim militants intent on waging a "holy war" for the oppressed could be found throughout the world in areas as different as Algeria, Bosnia and Herzegovina, France, and the Philippines. Muslim radicals in those and other countries shared a truly global commitment and were often heavily influenced by their formative volunteer experiences in the Afghan war of the 1980s. Conceiving of their mission as a holy one, they were able to form a series of loose connections with Muslims from other countries for the purposes of recruitment, training, and deployment of dedicated fighters. A taxi driver from Egypt, for example, who fought in the Afghan war was convicted for the 1993 bombing of New York's World Trade Center. Conspirators led by the convicted Egyptian cleric Omar Abdel

Rahman plotted to bomb the United Nations building, FBI headquarters in lower Manhattan, and the Lincoln and Holland tunnels linking Manhattan with New Jersey. The French blamed Afghan-trained Algerian Muslims for the 1994 Christmas Eve hijacking of an Air France airbus in which three passengers were killed in the initial shoot-out in Algiers.

Terrorists came from many nations and religious backgrounds. Peace-loving Muslims were maligned in Europe and the United States because of fundamentalists' actions. Following the 1995 bombing of the federal building in Oklahoma City, Arabs and Muslims across the United States were singled out for reprisals and intimidation until it was discovered that the Oklahoma City bombing was the act of domestic terrorists protesting U.S. government policies. The Oklahoma City attack, which terrorized the nation, fit the essential definition of the new terrorism as a violent act against innocent civilians for the purpose of undermining the power of the government.

Terrorism in the Last Quarter of the Twentieth Century.

By the late 1970s, a strategy of terrorist violence appealed to European revolutionaries intent on advancing a variety of political causes. Political killings became a tactic of choice for terrorists throughout the world. Victims were targeted by terrorists not because they merited any punishment themselves but as a means of attracting international attention to the terrorists' cause. Although motivated by different political agendas, terrorist groups often formed cooperative networks on an international basis, sharing training, weapons, and information. A small group of West German left-wing radicals known as the Red Army Faction executed key industrial, financial, and judicial leaders. The Red Army Faction was also responsible for a number of bombings, including that of the West German embassy in Stockholm. In Italy, a small group known as the Red Brigades was responsible for violent incidents, including the "kneecapping"—permanent crippling of people by shooting them in the knees—of leading Italian businessmen and the kidnapping and murder of the former Italian prime minister Aldo Moro. In 1981, the Red Brigades targeted the United States for their terrorist reprisals when they abducted an American general, James Dozier.

Western Europe served as an important arena for terrorist acts by non-European groups. To succeed—that is, to terrify mass populations—terrorists needed publicity. Terrorists relied on media exposure and claimed responsibility for acts only after they had been successfully completed. In September 1972, members of the Palestinian Black September movement kidnapped 11 Israeli athletes at the Olympic Games in Munich. An estimated 500 million people watched their televisions in horror as all 11 were slaughtered during an American sports broadcast. In a dramatic shoot-out, also televised, five of the terrorists died as well. Incidents such as the taking hostage of the OPEC oil ministers later in the decade in Vienna made urban populations aware of their vulnerability to gratuitous acts of violence. In 1979, 52 Americans were kidnapped from the American Embassy in Teheran and were held hostage for 444 days by a group of young Iranian revolutionaries who claimed to be battling against the "great Satan."

A recurrent pattern of terrorism prevailed throughout the 1980s with Israel and the United States often the targets of attacks. Incidents highlighted by international media coverage included: the attempted assassination of the pope in 1981 by a Turkish fascist; the blowing up of the U.S. Marine garrison in Beirut in 1983 by a Lebanese Shi'ite, whose act took the lives of 241 American soldiers as well as his own; the 1985 hijacking of a cruise ship, the *Achille Lauro,* by Palestinian ultranationalists, who killed one aged Jewish American passenger; and the bombing of TWA and El Al registration counters at two of Europe's busiest airports, in Rome and Vienna, in 1985. In December 1988, hundreds of people died when a Pan American plane on which a bomb had been planted exploded in flight over Lockerbie, Scotland. The bombing was probably in retaliation for the downing of an Iranian passenger airliner by the U.S. Navy in the Persian Gulf.

Terrorist activities against the United States escalated following the U.S. military action against Iraq in 1991 known as the Persian Gulf War. In February 1993, the explosion of a bomb planted in a small truck parked in the basement garage of the World Trade Center in New York killed six people, wounded a thousand, and did limited damage to the structure. Two terrorist attacks in Saudi Arabia in 1995 and 1996 killed 24 Americans. In August 1998, two major assaults against American embassies, one in Tanzania and the other in Kenya, killed 224 people and injured hundreds of others. In October 2000, a suicide attack against the USS *Cole* in the port of Aden took the lives of 17 sailors.

All of these attacks were attributed to the network of a single man, Osama bin Laden, a Saudi Arabian millionaire, who had been trained by the U.S. Central Intelligence Agency and who, between 1980 and 1989, had fought against the Russians in Afghanistan. In June 2001, bin Laden called on the Muslims of the world to mobilize themselves into a general **jihad,** or holy war, against their enemies. Three months after this call-to-arms, terrorists dealt their most extreme blow against the United States.

11 September 2001: A Turning Point.

On 11 September 2001, four U.S. passenger planes were hijacked and used as flying bombs in a coordinated action that targeted the World Trade Center in New York City and the Pentagon just outside of Washington, DC. Two of the four hijacked planes slammed into the twin towers of the World Trade Center, and a third plane hit its mark by diving into the Pentagon. The fourth plane crashed in a field in Pennsylvania, its suicide attack foiled by passengers who opposed their captors. More than 3,000 people were killed, thousands more were wounded, and the loss of property was unprecedented in the worst terrorist attack in history. The events horrified people around the world who understood that two symbols of American global financial and military dominance had been singled out in a carefully planned and executed mission of destruction. Once again, Osama bin Laden was identified as the mastermind of terrorist devastation. President George W.

Bush declared, in the wake of the terrorist attacks, that the United States was entering "a new kind of war," one not waged between nations but one whose stateless enemy would be sought out and hunted down. Terrorism had long plagued Europe and the Middle East, but the September 11 attacks marked the first time in history that an act of terrorist warfare by an external enemy took place on American soil. The event marked a turning point in the struggle against terrorism and a new focus in state security measures of Western governments. It also marked the beginning of a new war.

In October 2001, less than a month after the attacks, the United States and Great Britain undertook war in Afghanistan in pursuit of bin Laden, who was believed to have been harbored there by the Taliban, a fundamentalist Muslim ruling group. Though bin Laden was not captured, the Taliban was removed from power. In the fall of 2004, free elections were conducted throughout Afghanistan under the eyes of military observers for the nation's first elected president.

After September 11, the Americans and their allies in Europe and throughout the world joined forces in pledging to eradicate terrorism. Stringent security measures in airports and public places were instituted worldwide as nations faced harsh new political realities, including incidents of bioterrorism—germ warfare against civilians—in the months following the September terrorist attacks. When the European Union and the United States passed new laws and directives to combat terrorism, critics feared the curtailment of civil liberties. Such a curtailment in fact took place in Russia following terrorist incidents in the summer of 2004. Racist incidents against Muslims and Arabs mounted, even as European and American leaders stressed that

bin Laden and his network was a nonrepresentative and fanatical fringe within the Muslim world.

Throughout the post–September 11 era, Iraq and its leader Saddam Hussein continued to be singled out by the U.S. government as sympathetic to the terrorist cause and committed to developing "weapons of mass destruction." As a consequence of a United Nations' resolution, UN inspection teams entered Iraq in mid-November 2002 in a search for such weapons. None were found. In further pursuit of such weapons and with the intention of removing Hussein from power, President Bush ordered U.S. troops in coalition with British forces to lead an attack against Iraq in March 2003. Saddam Hussein was captured, but insurgent forces resisted the military occupation. Terrorist actions continued to take American and Iraqi lives as the American government attempted to rebuild the Iraqi economy during the peace. American involvement in this war was greatly unpopular and resulted in undermining Western alliances and increasing criticism of American foreign policy throughout the world.

Terrorism and Counterterrorism. Terrorism in the last quarter of the twentieth century was not a single movement but a wide variety of groups and organizations on both the left and right. Some organizations were Marxist; some were nationalist; some were Islamic fundamentalists. All defined the enemy as an imperialist and a colonizer. Industrial nations, especially the United States and Israel, were common targets of terrorist attacks. Terrorists all shared a vision of the world based on the commonly held belief that destruction of

■ This photograph captures the massive explosion caused when a second hijacked plane crashed into the World Trade Center in New York on 11 September 2001. The landmark twin towers were destroyed in the attack, and thousands of people were killed.

the existing order was the only way to bring about a more equitable system. Palestinian terrorists were willing to sacrifice their lives to ensure the establishment of an independent Palestinian state. In the case of bin Laden's fundamentalist Muslim terrorists, holy war was perceived as the only way to create an Islamic state free of Western influence and the corruption of a U.S.-dominated global economy.

Terrorists justified their violent actions in terms of the legitimacy of their cause. The Provisional Wing of the Irish Republican Army, for example, explained that it bombed crowds of Christmas shoppers in London as a means of uniting Northern Ireland with the Independent Irish Republic. Terrorists argued that just as resistance fighters in World War II had used bombs and assassinations as their means of fighting a more powerful enemy, they themselves were engaged in wars of liberation, revolution, and resistance and were using the only weapons at their disposal to fight great imperialist powers. Plastic explosives in suitcases, nearly impossible to detect by available technology, became the weapon of choice. If all was fair in war—and in World War II, both sides bombed innocent civilian victims in pursuit of victory—then, terrorists countered, they were fighting their war with the only weapons and in the only arena they had.

By the mid-1990s, it was clear that terrorism was an effective challenge to the tranquility of industrial nations. Modern terrorists were often able to evade policing and detection. Surveillance had not prevented terrorists from striking at airplanes and cruise ships. Yet terrorists accomplished little in the way of bringing about political change or solutions to problems.

West European governments often refused on principle to bargain with terrorists. Yet at times, European nations and the United States have been willing to negotiate for the release of kidnapped citizens. They have also been willing to use violence themselves against terrorists. Israel led the way in creating antiterror squads. In 1976, Israeli commandos succeeded in freeing captives held by pro-Palestinian hijackers of an Air France plane in Entebbe, Uganda. The following year, specially trained West German troops freed Lufthansa passengers and crew held hostage at Mogadishu, Somalia, on the east coast of Africa. The Arab kidnappers had hoped to bargain for the release of the imprisoned leaders of the Red Army Faction; the West German government refused. In 1986, the United States bombed Libya, long recognized as a training ground for international terrorist recruits, in retaliation for the bombing of a discotheque frequented by U.S. service personnel in West Germany. Israel bombed refugee camps to retaliate against Palestinian nationalists. The greatest mobilization in counterterrorist efforts came with U.S. leadership following the events of 11 September 2001. The goal of the "counterterrorism" was to undermine support for terrorists among their own people; its tactics and ends opened counterterrorism to the criticism that it was very similar to the terrorism it was opposing. In fact, torture of prisoners and interrogations in violation of the Geneva conventions at the hands of American soldiers and civilian personnel came to light in an Iraqi prison in the summer of 2004.

In spite of tactics of meeting violence with violence, the advanced industrial states of western Europe and the United States remained vulnerable to an invisible terrorist enemy. That elusive enemy could terrorize populations and incapacitate the smooth functioning of the modern industrial state. With the dawn of a new century, terrorism continued to threaten peace and paralyze security, at the very moment when people all over the globe celebrated the hope for a better world. After the large-scale terrorist attacks of 2001, the promise of a new and better world seemed, for many, to move further out of reach.

CONCLUSION

In 1970, Western nations had managed to put the destruction, hardship, and sacrifice of the Second World War behind them in the space of a single generation. Yet economic downturn and rising expectations of a better life continued to fuel protest and discontent. The escalating costs of nuclear parity were in conflict with the growing demands of consumer societies, and this conflict helped to end the Cold War. With the collapse of the Soviet Union, a period of new hope and international cooperation dawned.

The world of 1989 was now a world dominated by one superpower, the United States. It was also a world characterized by the rise of new political entities and the search for integration and stability in Europe. The Western world was undoubtedly a different place in the last quarter of the twentieth century from all that had gone before. But was the world really so transformed that one could speak of its being ordered in a different way? The iceberg of communism had melted. As democrats replaced dictators, some observers wondered if counterrevolution was waiting in the wings should the new capitalist experiments fail. In other countries, the dictators did not leave; they only changed their political allegiances. Proto-fascist and anti-Semitic groups became more vocal in the early 1990s amid the economic chaos.

One potentially unifying force was the marketplace. Democratic institutions seemed most stable in those countries with developed market economies. In the former Yugoslavia, for example, little had changed for the better since the fall of the communist regime. Russia itself suffered from a similar problem of economic readjustment and restructuring. Even where political reforms had been accomplished, economic reforms lagged behind or were nonexistent.

Western Europe and the United States realized the devastation that industrialization had wrought in their own countries after a century and a half of development, and were taking steps to control pollution and to clean up the air and the environment. Yet in eastern Europe, ecological concerns were considered a luxury as industries struggled uncontrolled to establish footholds in competitive markets. In spite of the emergence of a new world order of democratic states, many Europeans, both in the East and in the West, saw an uncertain future of misery and repression fueled as long as virulent nationalism remained unchecked.

Problems that plagued Western states in the modern era persisted. The triumph of the nation-state in the nineteenth century had carried the seeds of violence and destruction, as two world wars and countless local conflicts had proven. Democracy, likewise viewed as the best hope for a better world, struggled in new settings that lacked the institutions, the culture, and the experience of democratic values. Elected elites from Russia to Romania used positions of power for aggrandizement, both political and economic.

As the benefits of the welfare state in the West dwindled with slowed economic growth, the gap between the rich and the poor widened. The widening gulf characterized the new capitalist economies of the former Soviet bloc as well as those of the West. In the United States, the richest 1 percent of households controlled about 40 percent of the nation's wealth. In Germany, high-wage-earning families earned about two and a half times as much as low-wage workers. And the gap between rich and poor on a global scale yawned even wider into a gulf.

What lay ahead for Western societies? Would the third millennium be so different? Arthur Miller, the renowned American playwright, commented in the aftermath of the terrorist attacks of 11 September 2001, "It is so simple to destroy a city." Citizens of Western industrial societies had a new and shocking sense of their own vulnerability as they stood at the beginning of a new age of anxiety and fear. Symbols of civilization and economic achievement—skyscrapers and office buildings—could appear to melt in an instant, taking the lives of all those trapped inside. What was best in civilization at the beginning of the third millennium—selflessness, self-sacrifice, and willingness to help others in spite of personal cost—came face to face with mindless destruction and attacks on civilian populations but gave hope that the best values of civilization would prevail.

QUESTIONS FOR REVIEW

1. What caused the end of the Cold War?
2. How did the ideas of *glasnost* and *perestroika* help bring about the end of the Soviet Union?
3. How did the collapse of communist regimes in Russia and eastern Europe promote national and ethnic conflict?
4. What social, economic, and political forces contributed to German reunification?
5. How did the treaty signed by the nations of the European Community at Maastricht in 1991 create both hopes and fears of European unity?
6. How have democracy and nationalism come into conflict since 1989?
7. What nations and populations experienced terrorism in the late twentieth and early twenty-first centuries? What were the causes of terrorism and from what did terrorism derive its power?

KEY TERMS

Brezhnev Doctrine, *p. 612*
détente, *p. 612*
ethnic cleansing, *p. 618*
euro, *p. 621*
European Union (EU), *p. 622*
glasnost, *p. 612*
jihad, *p. 626*
nationalities problem, *p. 616*
perestroika, *p. 612*
Solidarity, *p. 613*

DISCOVERING WESTERN CIVILIZATION ONLINE

You can obtain more information about the end of the Cold War and new global challenges at the websites listed below. See also the Companion Website that accompanies this text, www.ablongman.com/kishlansky, which contains an online study guide and additional resources.

The End of the Cold War and the Emergence of a New Europe

Mikhail Sergeyevich Gorbachev
www.almaz.com/nobel/peace/1990a.html
A biography of Mikhail Gorbachev with electronic texts compiled by the Nobel Prize Internet Archive.

A Research Guide to Soviet History
www.unc.edu/depts/slavlib/html/guides/history_0.htm
A research guide to Soviet history sponsored by the University of North Carolina libraries.

Chronology of Russian History: Post-Soviet Period
www.departments.bucknell.edu/russian/chrono4.html
A chronology of Russian history since 1991 with links to additional resources.

Boris Yeltsin

www.cs.indiana.edu/hyplan/dmiguse/Russian/bybio.html
A chronology of Yeltsin's presidency with links to further materials on key events and personalities.

The Fall of the Berlin Wall 1989

www.remote.org/frederik/culture/berlin
A photo tour of the fall of the Berlin Wall supplemented by text from several German newspapers (in English).

A Concrete Curtain: The Life and Death of the Berlin Wall

www.wall-berlin.org/gb/berlin.htm
A virtual exhibit commemorating the tenth anniversary of the fall of the Berlin Wall with links to further readings.

Post–Soviet Russia: Library and Internet Resources

www.libraries.wright.edu/libnet/subj/pol/pls460.html
A research guide to post–Soviet Russian library and Internet resources sponsored by the Wright State University libraries.

Ethnic Conflict and Nationalism

International Helsinki Federation for Human Rights

www.ihf-hr.org/
Official website of the International Helsinki Federation for Human Rights, a nonprofit organization. This site is useful as a resource for the latest developments in the Balkans and in Chechnya from a human rights activist perspective.

Physicians for Human Rights: Chechnya Resources

www.phrusa.org/research/chechnya/chech_resources.html
Part of the Physicians for Human Rights official web page with links devoted to the conflict concerning Chechnya, including current newspaper and journal articles.

Bosnia Home Page at Caltech

www.its.caltech.edu/~bosnia/
This site provides links to essays and documents on the history of the disintegration of Yugoslavia and subsequent developments in the region.

Bosnia and Herzegovina Web Links

www.usip.org/library/regions/bosnia.html
The United States Institute of Peace provides links to web resources on the Balkan conflict and its resolution.

The West in the Global Community

History of European Integration Site

www.let.leidenuniv.nl/history/rtg/res1
This site provides primary source materials and bibliographies of the history of European integration. It also includes links to statistical data relating to the European Union and its organizations. It provides annotated links to the broader theme of Cold War history.

The New Europe@nationalgeographic.com

magma.nationalgeographic.com/ngm/0201/feature3/
This National Geographic feature on the New Europe includes articles, multimedia resources, and a downloadable map, as well as links to related sites.

The Terrorism Research Center

www.terrorism.com/index.shtml
The home page of the Terrorism Research Center. The site provides essays, documents, and links to additional materials on terrorism and political violence.

SUGGESTIONS FOR FURTHER READING

The End of the Cold War and the Emergence of a New Europe

Timothy Garton Ash, *In Europe's Name: Germany and the Divided Continent* (London: Jonathan Cape, 1993). An original and complex thesis that looks at German reunification from its origins in the 1970s.

Archie Brown, *The Gorbachev Factor* (New York: Oxford University Press, 1996). Traces Gorbachev's career and examines in detail his attempts to convert the Soviet Union into a social democratic variant of socialism.

Geoffrey Hosking, *The Awakening of the Soviet Union* (Cambridge, MA: Harvard University Press, 1990). Published in the midst of the dramatic changes taking place in the Soviet Union, this study emphasizes the social bases of reform and the challenges to Soviet leadership.

Michael Ignatieff, *Blood and Belonging: Journeys into the New Nationalism* (Toronto: Viking Press, 1993). A companion to a BBC television series, the volume provides a sophisticated exploration of expressions of nationalism throughout Europe.

Walter Laqueur, *The Dream That Failed: Reflections on the Soviet Union* (New York: Oxford University Press, 1994). This work recognizes the tenuous hold of capitalism in Russia and the possibility of a Communist party return.

Martin Malia, *The Soviet Tragedy: A History of Socialism in Russia, 1917–1991* (New York: Maxwell Macmillan International, 1994). A reevaluation by a leading Russian historian of the failure of communism.

Adam Michnik, *Letters from Freedom: Post–Cold War Realities and Perspectives* (Berkeley: University of California Press, 1998). Michnik, a journalist, politician, and writer imprisoned for his political views in the 1980s, is widely regarded as a hero in Poland today. This volume includes his articles, speeches, and interviews with leading European political figures and addresses the political realities of Europe after the end of the Cold War.

Joseph Rothschild, *Return to Diversity: A Political History of East Central Europe* (New York: Oxford University Press, 1989). A historical and analytical survey of Poland, Czechoslovakia, Hungary, Yugoslavia, Romania, Bulgaria, and Albania that appeared just before the great changes that swept through eastern Europe in 1989. Rothschild highlights the tensions between nationalist aspirations and Communist rule.

Henry Ashby Turner, Jr., *The Two Germanies Since 1945* (New Haven, CT: Yale University Press, 1987). A political history of the postwar division of Germany until 1987 that bridges a period the author contends was one of increasing involvement and underlying mutual interests between the two nations.

Ethnic Conflict and Nationalism

Richard Holbrooke, *To End a War* (New York: The Modern Library, 1998). The author offers a firsthand account of the intense diplomatic negotiations surrounding the Dayton Accords and a clear understanding of the problems plaguing Bosnia.

Tim Judah, *Kosovo: War and Revenge* (New Haven, CT: Yale University Press, 2000). Based on careful research, the author analyzes "the last great European war of the twentieth century."

Noel Malcolm, *Kosovo: A Short History* (New York: Harper Collins, 1999). The author is a historian who traces Kosovo's history to medieval times and challenges myths and debates about national origins.

Julie A. Mertus, *Kosovo: How Myths and Truths Started a War* (Berkeley: University of California Press, 1999). Having spent two years in Kosovo interviewing people affected by the conflict, the author offers an understanding of events from the perspective of the victims.

Michael A. Sells, *The Bridge Betrayed* (Berkeley: The University of California Press, 1996). The author stresses the role of religious nationalists, Serbian Orthodox and Croatian Roman Catholic, in waging a holy war resulting in genocide and destruction.

Susan L. Woodward, *Balkan Tragedy: Chaos and Dissolution After the Cold War* (Washington, DC: The Brookings Institution, 1995). This important study explains, in terms of the breakdown of political and civil order, why Yugoslavia disintegrated into ethnic hatreds so rapidly after 1989.

The West in the Global Community

Michael Emerson et al., *The Economics of 1992: The E.C. Commission's Assessment of the Economic Effects of Completing the Internal Market* (Oxford: Oxford University Press, 1988). A work replete with empirical data that give a comprehensive assessment of the potential impact of establishing a single internal market in the European Economic Community.

Mark Juergensmeyer, *The New Cold War? Religious Nationalism Confronts the Secular State* (Berkeley: The University of California Press, 1994). The author examines the growing significance of religious nationalism from a global perspective.

Geir Lundestad, *"Empire" by Integration* (New York: Oxford University Press, 1998). Provides a comprehensive overview of U.S. policy toward European integration.

Wolfgang Mommsen and Gerhard Hirschfeld, eds., *Social Protest, Violence and Terror in Nineteenth- and Twentieth-Century Europe* (London: Macmillan, 1982). Places terrorism within a historical context in Europe over a century and a half in a series of articles that takes a national case-history approach.

Richard E. Rubinstein, *Alchemists of Revolution: Terrorism in the Modern World* (New York: Basic Books, 1987). Examines the local root causes of terrorism in historical perspective and argues that terrorism is the social and moral crisis of a disaffected intelligentsia.

For a list of additional titles related to this chapter's topics, please see www.ablongman.com/kishlansky.

GLOSSARY

absolutism   Government in which power was consolidated in the hands of a divinely ordained monarch; typified by reverence for the monarch, weakening of representative institutions, and expansion of military.

agricultural revolution   Changes in the traditional agricultural system during the eighteenth century that included enclosure, introduction of fodder crops, intensified animal husbandry, and commercial market orientation.

alchemy   Study of metals in an effort to find their essence through purification. Medieval alchemists attempted to find precious metals such as silver and gold as the essence of base metals such as lead and iron.

Allies   In World War I, the United States, Great Britain, France, and Russia—the alliance that opposed and defeated the Central Powers of Germany and Austria-Hungary and their allies.

Anabaptists   Part of the radical Reformation, Protestant groups that varied in belief but agreed on the principle of adult baptism.

anarchism   A political movement based on rejection of extant political systems; most prominent in less industrialized Western nations.

anti-Semitism   Hostility toward and discrimination against Jews.

appeasement   British policy of making concessions to Germany in the 1930s in order to avoid war. It allowed Hitler to militarize the Sudetenland and eventually take all of Czechoslovakia.

April Theses   Lenin's promise to the Russian people and challenge to the Provisional Government to provide peace, land, and bread. These three issues became the rallying cries for the second Russian revolution and for the withdrawal of Soviet Russia from World War I.

Arians   During the early Christological controversies, followers of the Alexandrine theologian, Arius, who believed that Jesus was not equal to God the Father.

Axis Powers   In World War II, the alliance of Germany, Italy, and later Japan.

balance of power   Distribution of power among nations in alliances so that any one nation is prevented from dominating the others.

Balfour Declaration   The commitment by the British government issued in 1917 to support a Jewish homeland in Palestine.

Berlin Wall   Barrier built by East Germany in 1961 to halt an exodus of skilled professionals to the West; opened in 1989 as a prelude to the reunification of East and West Germany.

Big Three   The British, Soviet, and U.S. leaders who coordinated defeat of Germany and Japan in World War II and negotiated postwar settlements. Referred to Churchill, Stalin, and Roosevelt until 1945; Attlee, Stalin, and Truman by summer 1945.

Black Death   The virulent combination of bubonic, septicemic, and pneumonic plagues that destroyed between one third and one half of the population of Europe between 1347 and 1352.

blitzkrieg   "Lightning war"; the rapid advance accompanied by armored vehicles that typified the German military during World War II.

Bolsheviks   Radical faction of Marxist Social Democrats following a political theory based on necessity of violent revolution. The Bolsheviks came to power with Lenin in November 1917.

bourgeoisie   A French term referring to the commercial classes of Europe after the seventeenth century; primarily an urban class.

Brezhnev Doctrine   Policy of Soviet leader Leonid Brezhnev that approved the use of military intervention in the internal affairs of Soviet allies to prevent counterrevolution.

cahiers de doléances   Lists of grievances sent with representatives to the French Estates-General in 1789; demonstrated the existence of a widespread public political culture in France.

caliph   The successors of Muhammad who served as political and religious leaders of the Islamic world (see Umma).

capitularies   The written instructions for the implementation of royal directives at the local level produced by the clerics of the Carolingian court.

caravels   Small Portuguese ships developed in the fifteenth century that were ideal for ocean travel.

Carnival   One of the traditional sixteenth-century festivals, the feasts and carousing of which preceded the onset of Lent.

Carolingian Renaissance   The cultural revival of classical learning sponsored by the emperor Charlemagne. New schools and the copying of manuscripts were among its important achievements.

cartels   Combinations of firms in a given industry to fix prices and establish production quotas.

Cartesianism   Philosophy of René Descartes that rested on the dual existence of mind and matter, a principle that enabled the use of skepticism to create certainty.

Central Powers   Germany and Austria-Hungary during World War I.

chartism   An English working-class reform movement that flourished in the 1830s and 1840s and that demanded universal male suffrage (right to vote), payment for parliamentary service, equal electoral districts, and secret ballots.

chivalry   The ideals of knighthood, most notably fighting, that spread from northern France across Europe in the High Middle Ages.

Christian humanism   The application of the principles of humanistic education, particularly philology, to the documents of Christianity. It resulted in a program of reform through better education.

Christological controversies   The debate about the Christian Trinity (Father, Son, and Holy Spirit) and the relationship between humanity and divinity within it. It caused great division and conflict in the Church and society from the third to the fifth centuries.

city-states   Self-governing political units centered upon an urban area. During the fifteenth and sixteenth centuries, city-states took on various forms of government, including republics such as Venice and oligarchies such as Milan.

civic humanism   The use of humanistic training and education in the service of the state. Many humanists became advisers to princes or republican governments, holding high office and helping to establish policy.

Cold War   The diplomatic and ideological confrontation between the Soviet Union and the United States that began in the aftermath of World War II, dividing the world into two armed camps.

collectivization   Soviet plan under Stalin to create large communal state farms to replace private farms owned by peasants.

coloni   Tenant farmers who worked on the estates of wealthy landowners in the Roman Empire.

colonization   Process by which colonies, or new settlements with links to a parent state, are established.

Columbian Exchange   The transfer of microbes, animals, and plants in the encounters between Europeans and Native Americans during the age of exploration.

Comecon   The Council for Mutual Economic Assistance established in 1949 with bilateral agreements between the Soviet Union and eastern European states. Comecon was Stalin's response to the U.S. Marshall Plan in western Europe, but rather than providing aid it sought to integrate and control the economies of eastern Europe for Soviet gain.

The Communist Manifesto   A call to arms written in 1848 by Karl Marx and Frederich Engels in which they defined in general terms the class struggle in industrializing Europe.

conciliarism   The movement proposed by church lawyers in which only a general council of bishops could end the Great Schism.

condottiere   A mercenary military leader who sold his services and that of his private army to the highest bidder; used in the wars between the Italian city-states.

Congress of Vienna   A meeting of European powers after the Napoleonic wars in 1815; established a balance of power to preserve the status quo in post-revolutionary Europe.

conscription   Compulsory service of citizens in the army. France was the first modern state to enforce conscription. The ability to draft all able-bodied men was a key component in the Revolutionary and Napoleonic wars.

conservatism   Nineteenth-century ideology that favored tradition and stability and only gradual, or "organic," growth and change.

containment   Cold War policy of resisting the spread of Soviet communism.

Continental System   The economic boycott of England by Napoleon during the wars beginning in 1803.

Counter-Reformation   Catholic response to repel Protestantism.

Crusades   Religious wars of conquest directed against non-Christians and heretics in the eleventh through the thirteenth centuries.

Crystal Palace Exhibition   This international exhibition, held in London in 1851 in a specially built see-through exhibition hall, featured the greatest technological advances of the day and served as a spur for further industrialization.

culture   Those shared beliefs, values, customs, and practices that humans transmit from generation to generation through learning.

cuneiform   A form of writing from Mesopotamia characterized by wedge-shaped symbols pressed into wet clay tablets to record words.

Cynics   Followers of a Hellenistic Greek philosophy that rejected the world as the source of evil and unhappiness and advocated the reduction of possessions, connections, and pleasures to the absolute minimum.

Declaratory Act   A statute enacted in England in 1766 that stated that Parliament held sovereign jurisdiction over the North American colonies.

decolonization   Withdrawal of Western nations from colonies in Africa and Asia after World War II.

decurions   Members of the city councils in the Roman Empire. Initially, they were the backbone of the provincial elite but by the third and fourth centuries were crippled by their personal responsibility for provincial taxes.

deists   Those who believed that God created the universe but then did not intervene in its operation.

Delian League   League of Greek cities formed to drive out the Persian invaders. Its leader, Athens, turned it into its own empire.

demesne   Land kept by a medieval lord for his direct profit and worked a specified number of days each week by his peasants.

democracy   Form of government in which the citizens choose their leaders; began in Athens, Greece, in the fifth century B.C.E.

de-Stalinization   Process initiated by Nikita Khrushchev beginning in 1956 that reversed many of Stalin's repressive policies in the Soviet Union.

détente   From the French word meaning a relaxation in tension, cooperation between the two superpowers, the Soviet Union and the United States. This policy was characterized by improved U.S.-Soviet diplomatic relationships in the 1970s to lessen the possibility of nuclear war.

dictator   In the Roman Republic, an official who was granted unlimited power to rule the state for a period up to six months in a time of emergency. Sulla and Caesar both used the dictatorship for political ends.

diplomas   The records of royal grants and decisions produced by clerics in medieval courts.

divine rights of kings   Political theory that held that the institution of monarchy had divine origin and that the monarch functioned as God's representative on earth.

doge   Chief magistrate of the Venetian Republic who served for life.

Eastern Question   The question posed by the Great Powers about the future of the Ottoman territories.

Edict of Nantes   The proclamation by Henry IV of France granting limited toleration to Huguenots.

ekklesia   The assembly of all free male Athenian citizens.

emirs   Local military commanders who took control of provincial administration in the Islamic world at the expense of the caliphs by the tenth century.

empiricism   The philosophy propounded by Aristotle which rejected Plato's idea of abstract Forms in favor of practical observation and explanation, building general theories from particular data.

enclosure   In the eighteenth century, the closing off of common and public land within the open field system to foster private landholding.

Enlightenment   Philosophical and intellectual movement that began in Europe during the eighteenth century. The movement was characterized by a wave of new learning, especially in the sciences and mathematics, and the application of reason to solve society's problems.

entrepôt   A place where goods were brought for storage before being exchanged; a commercial concept originated by the Dutch.

Epicureans   Those who adhered to a Hellenistic Greek philosophy that the world was a random collection of atoms (atheistic and materialistic), and that one must pursue pleasure, but only in moderation as excess causes pain.

equestrians   In the early Roman Republic, the equestrians were one of the richest classes in the Roman army, those who could afford to maintain a horse. By the late republic, their role expanded into banking and commerce.

Estates-General   An official body assembled periodically by the medieval French state, consisting of representatives from three separate groups or "estates": those who prayed (the Church), those who fought (the aristocracy), and those who worked (commoners). Long in disuse by the monarch, it was convened by Louis XVI in 1789.

ethnic cleansing   Term introduced in the Balkan war of the 1990s to describe the systematic killing and forcible removal of one ethnic group by another.

ethnos   Large rural territorial units in the Dark Age and Archaic Greece focused around a central religious sanctuary and dominated by a local oligarchy, such as in Aetolia.

Etruscans   Peoples native to Italy who influenced the formation of the Roman state.

eunomia   The good order and obedience to the law which was the ideal of Sparta's militaristic society.

euro   Common currency of the European Union; accepted as common currency by all members of the European Union except the United Kingdom.

European Economic Community (EEC)   Formed in 1957 by Belgium, the Netherlands, Luxembourg, Italy, France, and West Germany to provide a single, integrated European market. Also known as the Common Market.

European Union (EU)   Formed in 1992 to succeed the European Community in terms of economic integration; members share defensive, social, and economic policies as well.

extraterritoriality   Exempted all foreigners in China from Chinese legal jurisdiction; practiced within foreign "spheres of influence" in China.

Factory Act (1833)   British Parliamentary legislation that prohibited factory work by children under age nine, provided two hours of daily education for factory children, and limited labor for adults to twelve hours each day.

fascism   Rooted in mass politics of the late-nineteenth century, a totalitarian political system that glorifies the state and subordinates the individual to the state's needs. First emerging in Italy after World War I, fascism appeared in virtually all European countries, but particularly Germany.

feudalism   Anachronistic term used by early modern lawyers to describe medieval relations of vassalage.

fief   A parcel of productive land along with the serfs and privileges attached to it granted by a lord to a knightly follower (vassal) in return for loyalty and military service.

Final Solution   The term used by the Third Reich to refer to the extermination of all people deemed unfit; resulted in the execution of 11 million men, women, and children, 6 million of them Jews.

First Triumvirate   Political alliance among Pompey, Crassus, and Caesar to share power in the Roman Republic.

fodder crops   Crops that were grown not for human consumption but to improve the nutrients in the soil. Some, such as turnips, were also used as animal feed.

Forms   In Plato's philosophy, the perfect ideal that underlies all worldly objects. In recollecting them from one's previous existence one communes with all that is good, true, and beautiful.

Fourteen Points   U.S. President Woodrow Wilson's idealistic set of guidelines drawn up as part of the peace process whose goal was to create a lasting peace after World War I.

French wars of religion   Violent clashes between French Catholics and Calvinists (Huguenots) from 1562–1598.

Fronde   An aristocratic revolution in France beginning in 1648 during the minority of Louis XIV, which was initiated by the tax policies of the minority government under Cardinal Mazarin.

futurists   Artists and intellectuals of the late nineteenth and early twentieth century who wanted to create a new culture free from traditional Western civilization. Futurists lionized technology, the masses, violence, and upheaval.

generation gap   The baby boom following World War II resulted in a generation that came of age in the 1960s. The gap refers to the divergence in values between a large cohort of adolescents and young adults and their parents that resulted in more liberal values and socio-cultural mores.

geopolitics   Politics of geography; based on recognition that certain areas of the world are valuable for political reasons.

Girondins   French revolutionary faction that was more moderate than the Jacobins.

glasnost   A Russian term meaning openness; one of the programs of reform initiated by Mikhail Gorbachev in the 1980s.

Glorious Revolution   Change of government in England in 1688–1689 when the Catholic monarch James II was replaced by the Dutch ruler William of Orange. Called "glorious" because it supposedly was accomplished without bloodshed.

Gnostics   An early Christian group that interpreted scripture as gnosis, or secret wisdom, and believed that Jesus had no human element. They were opposed by many bishops.

Golden Bull   The edict of emperor Charles IV in 1356 recognizing that German princes and kings were autonomous rulers.

Great Chain of Being   A hierarchic model of social organization common in the fifteenth and sixteenth centuries in which all parts of creation held a specific place in a divinely ordered universe.

Great Depression   Devastation of the global economy that began in 1929 with the U.S. stock market crash and lasted through the 1930s.

Great Purge   A series of executions between 1934 and 1938 in the Soviet Union that removed Joseph Stalin's political enemies.

Great Reform Bill of 1832   An extension of the right to vote in England to men of the middle class that resulted in a 50 percent increase in those eligible to vote.

Great Schism   The conflict (1378–1415) between two sets of rival popes based in Rome and Avignon that divided the loyalties of states and individuals across Europe.

guilds   Professional associations of merchants or artisans that offered protection of members and regulation of a particular trade or craft.

hadith   The written form of the Sunnah, practices established by the prophet Muhammad that guide the interpretation of the Qur'an.

Hanseatic League   A commercial and political alliance of northern German towns established in the late fourteenth century to monopolize the grain and fish trade of the Baltic Sea.

Hijra   In early Islam, the journey undertaken by Muhammad from Mecca to Medina in 622 in order to govern Medina and calm its internal political dissension.

Holocaust   During World War II, mass extermination of Jews by the Nazis under Adolph Hitler.

Holy Alliance   Prussia, Austria, and Russia, under the leadership of Tsar Alexander I, agreed to protect the peace and the Christian religion following the Congress of Vienna.

honestiores   The privileged classes of the later Roman Empire: senators, municipal gentry, and the military.

hoplites   In Archaic Greece, armed infantry soldiers.

Huguenots   French Calvinists led by Henry of Navarre. Huguenots were victims of the St. Bartholomew's Day Massacre, a slaughter of numerous Protestants in Paris in 1572 during the French wars of religion.

humanists   Scholars who studied and taught the humanities, the skills of disciplines such as philology—the art of language—and rhetoric—the art of expression; concentrated on ancient texts.

humiliores   The lower classes of the later Roman Empire whose status declined from the period of the *Pax Romana* and who suffered disproportionately from the tax increases of the period.

Hundred Years' War   A series of military engagements between England and France (1337–1452) over territorial and dynastic rivalries.

Hussites   Followers of Jan Hus who attacked the sale of indulgences and German political dominance in the kingdom of Bohemia. After his execution, they led a partially successful revolt.

iconoclasts   Breakers of icons; opponents of the mediating use of icons (religious images) in worship. Most emperors supported this faction in eighth- and early ninth-century Byzantium.

iconodules   Venerators of icons; the ecclesiastical faction that resisted the iconoclasts. Most of the people and lesser clergy were iconodules.

icons   Sacred images.

imperium   The powers conferred on magistrates by the Roman people: the supreme power to command, to execute the law, and to impose the death penalty.

indulgences   Remission of temporal punishment in Purgatory due to one's sins. Originally granted for performing pious acts, but later acquired through a grant to the church treasury. In the sixteenth century, indulgences were sold to raise money for the papacy; a critical issue in the Lutheran reform.

industrialization   Process by which production becomes mechanized.

Industrial Revolution   Sustained period of economic growth and change brought on by technological innovations in the process of manufacturing; began in Britain in the mid-eighteenth century.

intendants   Officials appointed by the central government in France to oversee the local administration of the regional aristocracy; a critical component of the centralization of the French state.

iron curtain   The term coined by former British Prime Minister Winston Churchill to describe the ideological divide between western and eastern Europe after World War II.

Jacobins   One of the political factions of the French National Convention that seized the initiative provided by the sans-culottes to take control of the radical revolution in the late eighteenth century; led by Maximilien Robespierre.

Jacquerie   The revolt of French peasants against the aristocracy and crown in 1358. It was part of the struggle for rights caused by the labor shortage after the Black Death.

jihads   Holy wars waged by Muslims against their religious enemies.

jingoism   Use of public opinion to stir support for one's own nation and hatred for another nation; used extensively by political leaders to justify imperial expansion.

joint-stock companies   Business enterprises that raise capital by selling shares to individuals who receive dividends on their investments.

kouros   Nude statues of young men that were a common subject in Archaic art. The stiff posture demonstrates the influence of Egyptian sculpture.

Kristallnacht   "Crystal night" in German; refers to the night of 9 November 1938 when mobs directed by the Nazis destroyed the homes, businesses, and synagogues of German Jews.

laissez-faire   An economic theory that required government to cease interference with private economic activity; Adam Smith and the physiocrats were its leading proponents.

lay investiture   The practice by which kings and emperors appointed bishops and invested them with the symbols of their office. It led to conflict between the papacy and the emperors in the eleventh century.

Lebensraum   "Living room"; one of Hitler's foreign policy objectives to extend the borders of Germany in eastern and central Europe.

liberalism   A political philosophy based on freedom of the individual and the corruptibility of authority; associated with constitutional reform in the first half of the nineteenth century.

Linear B   A syllabic form of writing from the late Greek Bronze Age which preserves the earliest known form of Greek. It was used by Mycenaean elites almost entirely for record keeping.

linear perspective   A technique developed in painting to give a flat surface the appearance of depth and dimension.

Long Parliament   An English Parliament that officially met from 1640 to 1653. It forced reforms under Charles I, defeated the royal armies during the English Civil War, and tried and executed the king.

maat   In Egyptian thought, the ideal state of the universe and of society which the pharaoh was supposed to uphold.

Magna Carta   The "great charter" limiting royal power that King John was forced to sign in 1215.

manses   Farms worked by slaves, serfs, and freemen in the Middle Ages.

Marchfield   The assembly of all free warriors in the early Germanic kingdoms in which the king's authority was all-powerful.

Marshall Plan   The U.S. economic aid program for European countries after World War II; intended to establish U.S. economic influence in European markets.

mercantilism   A popular state economy of the seventeenth century; involved bullionism, protective tariffs, and monopolies.

metics   The non-Athenian residents of Athens who comprised about half of the free population of the city. They were active in commerce and banking.

Minoan civilization   The culture of Crete in the Middle Bronze Age (2000–1550 B.C.E.) in which elites based at great palaces, such as Knossos, dominated the island politically, economically, and religiously.

minuscule   New style of handwriting developed in the Carolingian Renaissance to preserve texts; later adopted as standard script.

Mishnah   In Jewish law, the oral interpretation of the Torah (scripture) that was developed by the Pharisees and later developed into an extensive written body of legal interpretation.

missi dominici   Teams of counts and bishops that examined the state of each county in the Carolingian Empire on behalf of the king.

monasticism   The life of monks devoted to God, from the fourth century onward, either as part of communal organization or in solitary life. Monasticism began in Egypt as a rejection of the worldliness of civilization.

monopoly   Exclusive control of a market or industry; a form of economic regulation in which special privileges are granted in return for financial considerations and an agreement to abide by the rules set out by the state.

Mycenaean   Late Greek Bronze Age civilization that arose ca. 1600 B.C.E. at Mycenae and that encompassed the Greek mainland and parts of Asia Minor. Mycenaeans developed the Linear B script.

mystery cults   Religions that promised immediate, personal contact with a deity that would bring immortality.

Napoleonic Code   The recodification of French law carried out during Napoleon's reign.

nationalities problem   The existence of numerous ethnic minorities within the borders of the Soviet Union leading to demands for self-determination and political independence.

natural selection   A theory advanced by Charles Darwin that accounted for evolution of species; a realist scientific approach.

Navigation Acts   English economic legislation providing that colonial goods could only be shipped in English ships.

Nazism   National Socialism; German variant of fascism.

Neolithic era   The New Stone Age (8000–6500 B.C.E.) in which modern man developed agriculture and the first villages.

New Economic Policy (NEP)   A state-planned economic policy in the Soviet Union between 1921 and 1928; based on agricultural productivity, it required set payments from peasants; surpluses could be sold on the free market.

new imperialism   Imperialism practiced by European countries after 1870 that was, in essence, the domination by industrial powers over the nonindustrial world. Distinguished from the earlier acquisition of territory, new imperialism took a variety of forms including territorial occupations, colonization, exploitation of labor and raw materials, and development of economic spheres of influence.

New Monarchies   The more centralized European governments of western Europe created in the fifteenth and sixteenth centuries.

New Piety   An aspect of the Roman Catholic reform movement; originated among the Brethren of the Common Life with an emphasis on simplicity and more personalized religious practice.

nominalism   The doctrine of William of Ockham that argued that abstract terms or universals do not represent real existing things and that thus human reason could not aspire to certain truth.

North Atlantic Treaty Organization (NATO) An organization founded in 1949 the members of which signed a defense pact to protect those countries bordering the North Atlantic.

nuclear club The group of nations in possession of atomic weapons, originally consisting of the United States and the Soviet Union. By 1974, the nuclear club included Great Britain, France, the People's Republic of China, and India.

Old Regime The old order; political and social system of France in the eighteenth century before the French Revolution.

oligarchy Government by an elite few.

optimates The traditionalist Roman political faction that succeeded the Gracchi and sought to preserve the senatorial oligarchy against the populares.

Orthodox Christianity The official "right-teaching" faith of Constantinople as opposed to the heterodox peoples on the margins of the Byzantine Empire.

ostracism A practice in Athenian democracy by which anyone deemed to threaten the constitution could, by popular vote, be exiled for ten years without the loss of property.

Paleolithic era The Old Stone Age (600,000–10,000 B.C.E.) in which advanced primates developed into Neanderthals and also modern man. They hunted food or collected it by gathering.

Paris Commune Created in 1871 in the aftermath of the Franco-Prussian War; crushed by the national army after a brief struggle; symbol of revolution for radical politicians, including Marxists.

parties A form of political organization in which members of the British parliament divided into groups with identifiable interests. Whigs and Tories were the first political parties.

Patent of Toleration An edict of Joseph II of Austria in 1781 that granted freedom of worship to Protestants and members of the Greek Orthodox Church, in addition to Roman Catholics.

paterfamilias The male head of household in the Roman family. His power was absolute, including the power of life and death.

patricians Leaders of the gentes, or clans, in early Roman society.

Pax Romana The two centuries of peace and stability in the early Roman Empire inaugurated by the emperor Augustus.

perestroika A Russian term meaning restructuring; part of Mikhail Gorbachev's attempts to reform the Soviet government and economy in the 1980s.

Peterloo Massacre In August 1819, the English army troops policing a political crowd gathered near Manchester, England, lost control resulting in the deaths of 11 and the injury of hundreds of others.

phalanx A tightly ordered and well-disciplined body of elite Greek warriors in heavy armor that attacked in close formation with long spears.

philology The art of language; one of the most important aspects of humanist studies, based on models of ancient texts.

philosophes A French term for the intellectuals of the eighteenth-century Enlightenment. Voltaire, Diderot, and Condorcet were leading philosophes.

physiocrats A group of French thinkers who subscribed to the view that land was wealth and thus argued that improvements in agricultural activity should take first priority in state reforms.

pictograms The earliest form of writing in Mesopotamia, ca. 3500 B.C.E., in which pictures represented particular objects, such as animals.

Pietà A painting or sculpture of Mary mourning the dead Jesus. The most famous was carved by Michelangelo and is in St. Peter's Basilica.

plebs Families not organized into gentes, or clans, in early Roman society. The lower classes.

pogroms State-organized massacres of Jews.

polis The city-state of Archaic and Classical Greece, particularly found on the shores of the Aegean. A city formed the center of government (tyranny, oligarchy, or democracy) and of religious life with temples on its citadel (acropolis).

politiques During the sixteenth-century French wars of religion, a group of Catholics who joined with Huguenots to demand a practical settlement of the wars.

populares The Roman political faction that succeeded the Gracchi whose leaders appealed to the masses as a source of power.

Popular Front Socialist governments established in both France and Spain in the 1930s; the French version failed to solve the Great Depression and was voted out of office; the creation of a socialist republic in Spain initiated a civil war.

Pragmatic Sanction The document that attempted to secure the recognition of Maria Theresa as heiress to the Habsburg possessions of Charles VI.

Prague Spring Popular uprising and reform movement in 1968 Czechoslovakia, ended by Soviet invasion in August 1968.

predestination A fundamental principle of Calvin's theology: the belief that all Christians are predestined to either heaven or hell from the act of creation.

presbyters The priests of the early Christian tradition who were subordinated to bishops as hierarchy developed in the Church.

Price Revolution The dramatic price inflation of the fifteenth and sixteenth centuries; caused by monetary debasement and the influx of bullion from the New World.

princeps "First citizen"; the title assumed by the emperor Augustus to reassure public opinion by preserving the traditional constitutional forms.

Proclamation of the German Empire The creation in 1871 of the nation-state of Germany by uniting the 38 German states into a single national entity.

proletariat The industrial working class.

pronatalism State programs implemented after the Second World War to encourage women to have larger families.

Puritans English Protestants who sought to purify the Church of England of all traces of Catholicism.

putting-out system Mobilization of the rural labor force for commercial production of large quantities of manufactured goods; raw materials put out to homes of workers where manufacture took place.

Quadruple Alliance Pact signed in 1815 by the four powers who defeated Napoleon—Great Britain, Austria, Russia, and Prussia—for the purpose of protecting Europe against future French aggression.

Quintuple Alliance The Quadruple Alliance plus France, which joined the pact in 1818.

quinine An important nineteenth-century medical advance derived from cinchona that was an effective treatment for malaria; it permitted large numbers of Europeans to travel without risking death and disease.

realism An artistic and literary style that criticized industrialized society and rejected bourgeois concepts of morality.

realpolitik Pragmatic political theory advanced by Otto von Bismarck; ruthless pursuit by any means, including illegal and violent ones, in the interests of the state.

reconquista The Christian reconquest of the Iberian peninsula from the Spanish Muslims or Moors; completed in 1492 under Ferdinand and Isabella.

Reformation A movement to reform and purify the Catholic Church that resulted in the creation of new religious denominations in Europe collectively known as Protestants.

Reichstag   The national legislative body of the German Empire; elected by universal male suffrage.

Reign of Terror   The period from 1793 to 1794 when Maximilien Robespierre assumed leadership of the Committee of Public Safety and oversaw the revolutionary tribunals that sentenced about 40,000 people to execution.

Renaissance   A "rebirth" of classical learning and emphasis on humanity that characterized the period between 1350 and 1550.

rhetoric   The art of expression and persuasion.

Risorgimento   The nineteenth-century movement to reunite Italy.

romanticism   An artistic and literary tradition based on emotions rather than the intellect; rejection of classical traditions in favor of "nature"; often associated with nationalism.

salons   Informal social gatherings during the Enlightenment, frequently organized by women, in which topics of intellectual interest were discussed.

sans-culottes   Literally "those without knee-breeches"; working-class revolutionaries who initiated the radical stage of the French revolution in 1792.

Schlieffen Plan   The strategy of the German high command at the outset of World War I, predicated on knocking France out of the war.

Scholastic method   The combination of legal analysis from the new university at Bologna with Aristotelian logic established by Peter Abelard in the twelfth century to create the primary method of study in medieval universities.

scientific revolution   In the sixteenth and seventeenth centuries, a period of new scientific inquiry, experimentation, and discovery that resulted in a new understanding of the universe based on mathematical principles and led to the creation of the modern sciences, particularly astronomy and physics.

scramble for Africa   The colonization of Africa as part of the new imperialism. This domination of Africa by Germany, Britain, and France ended with the crisis at Fashoda.

Second Triumvirate   Alliance of Octavian, Mark Anthony, and Lepidus following the assassination of Julius Caesar to defeat the assassins and control the Roman Empire.

seigneur   Manor lord responsible for maintaining order, administering justice, and arbitrating disputes among tenants.

serfs   Peasants of degraded status and very limited legal rights who were dependent on the lords in the High Middle Ages. They formed the great bulk of the population.

Shi'ites   Muslims who follow the tradition that legitimate leadership of Islam can only come through the descendants of 'Ali, whom they regard as the last orthodox caliph.

sola fide   A fundamental principle of Luther's theology: justification of Christians by faith alone.

sola scriptura   By the Word alone; emphasis on scriptural authority in preference to the canons of the Church, a fundamental element of Luther's theology.

Solidarity   A non-communist Polish labor organization founded by Lech Walesa in the Gdansk shipbuilding yards; legalized in 1989 as a political movement, it won a victory in the first Polish democratic elections.

sophists   Professional teachers in fifth-century Greece who traveled from city to city instructing students, for a fee, in rhetoric, the art of persuasion.

soviets   Councils of workers in Russia formed after 1905 that became one center of power after the overthrow of the tsar; source of power for Lenin and Bolsheviks.

Spanish Armada   The Spanish fleet sent in 1588 to transport troops from the Low Countries for an invasion of England; defeated by the English fleets of Elizabeth I.

Spanish Inquisition   An ecclesiastical tribunal utilized to combat heresy and non-Christians; used by Ferdinand and Isabella against the conversos, or converted Jews of Spain.

spheres of influence   Diplomatic term used to connote territorial influence or control of weaker nations not necessarily occupied by the more powerful ones. The term was first used to explain one kind of control of western European powers in the 1800s during African imperialism, and was later used to describe European and Japanese territorial control and influence over markets in China at the end of the nineteenth century.

Stoics   Followers of the Hellenistic Greek philosophy propounded by Zeno, which teaches that orderliness is proper to the universe and that happiness derives from embracing one's divinely ordained role and unhappiness from rejecting it.

strategoi   Generals, the military commanders of themes in the Byzantine Empire. They were responsible for civil and military administration.

sunnah   In Islamic theology, the practices established by the prophet Muhammad. They were initially preserved by oral tradition.

Sunnis   The majority tradition of Islam that accepts that political succession should be based on consensus, the existing political order, and a leader's merits.

synod   A meeting of bishops called to debate Church policy, such as that at Whitby in 664, which established the customs of the Roman Church among Angles and Saxons.

Table of Ranks   Official state hierarchy in Russia under Peter the Great that established the social position or rank of individuals according to categories of military service, civil service, and ownership of landed estates.

tetrarchy   Rule by four; Diocletian's attempt to regulate the suggestion of the Roman Empire by dividing the empire into eastern and western parts, with both an augustus and a junior emperor, or caesar, ruling each part.

Thermidorian Reaction   Revolt beginning in July 1794 (the month of Thermidor) against the radicalism of the French Revolution, leading to the downfall and execution of Robespierre and the end of the Reign of Terror.

Third Estate   Branch of the French Estates-General consisting of the bourgeoisie and the working classes; separated from the other estates to form the National Assembly in 1789.

Third Reich   "The Third Empire"; Hitler's government, established after 1933.

third world   The former colonies of European and Asian imperialism; sought to separate themselves from European economic control after independence; operated in the United Nations as a nonaligned bloc.

Thirty Years' War   War lasting from 1618–1648.

three-field system   An efficient agricultural system in which one-third of the land was planted in autumn with wheat or rye, one-third remained fallow, and one-third was planted in spring with a crop that added nutrients to the soil.

Time of Troubles   The period of disruption within Russia following the death of Ivan the Terrible; only ended with the Polish invasion of Russia.

Torah   The body of law in Hebrew scripture.

Tories   Members of a political party in England that in the seventeenth century defended the principle of hereditary succession to the crown; in opposition to the Whigs. The Tories sought to preserve the traditional political structure and supported the authority of the Anglican church.

total war   War that requires mobilization of the civilian population in addition to the military; typified by centralized governments with limits on economy and civil rights.

Treaty of Brest-Litovsk   The Treaty between Russia and Germany signed in March 1918 whereby Soviet Russia withdrew from World War I.

Treaty of Tordesillas   A 1494 agreement that recognized Portugal's claims to Brazil, but gave all of the remainder of the New World to Spain.

Treaty of Versailles   Peace settlement with Germany at the end of World War I; included the War Guilt Clause fixing blame on Germany for the war and requiring massive reparations.

triangular trade   A three-way trade system during the seventeenth century involving the shipment, for example, of calicoes to Africa for slaves who were transported to the East Indies in exchange for sugar, which was shipped to Europe.

Triple Alliance   An alliance founded in 1882 between Germany, Austria-Hungary, and Italy at Germany's instigation for the purpose of securing mutual support on the European continent.

Triple Entente   Alliance founded in 1907 between France, Britain, and Russia. With the defection of Russia from the Three Emperors' League, it hemmed in Germany on both eastern and western borders.

tyrants   Rulers who had seized power illegally. Tyrannies replaced oligarchies in many *poleis* in Archaic Greece, such as at Corinth and Athens. The term did not have the negative connotations it does today, as many tyrants were popular leaders welcomed by their subjects.

Umma   The community of all believers in the Islamic faith. Initially, it was both a political and religious supertribe of Arabs.

universitas   The guilds of students that formed the first true universities from the twelfth century onward.

utilitarianism   Jeremy Bentham's philosophical plan to ensure social harmony through measurement of pleasure and pain or the greatest happiness of the greatest number; a liberal philosophy.

vassals   Knights sworn to fealty or loyalty to a lord; in return the lord granted the vassal a means of support, or fief.

Villanovans   Peoples of the first Iron Age culture in Italy (1000–800 B.C.E.), which was based in the north. They made iron tools and weapons and placed the ashes of their dead in large urns.

Warsaw Pact   Defensive alliance organization formed in 1955 by Albania, Bulgaria, Romania, Czechoslovakia, Hungary, Poland, East Germany, and the Soviet Union. The alliance served as a strategic buffer zone against NATO forces.

Weimar Republic   German government founded at the end of the First World War; used by German general staff as scapegoat for German defeat and harsh peace terms; overthrown in 1933.

welfare state   The tendency of post–World War II states to establish safety nets for citizens in areas of birth, sickness, old age, and unemployment.

wergeld   In Germanic society, the payment in reparation for crimes in place of blood vengeance. Tribal leaders used it to reduce internal hostilities.

Whigs   Members of a political party in England that in the seventeenth century supported the Protestant succession and a broad-based Protestantism and advocated a constitutional monarchy that limited royal power; in opposition to the Tories. The Whigs were later identified with social and parliamentary reform.

zemstvos   Local elected assemblies in Russia during the reign of Alexander II; representatives elected by landowners, townspeople, and peasants.

ziggurat   Babylonian tiered towers (or step-pyramids) from ca. 2000 B.C.E. that were dedicated to gods and stood near temples. They were among the most important buildings of Babylonian cities.

Zionism   A program initiated by Theodor Herzl to establish an independent Jewish state in Palestine.

Zollverein   A unified trading zone created by Prussia in which member states adopted the liberal Prussian customs regulations; an attempt to overcome the fragmented nature of the German economy.

CREDITS

DOCUMENT CREDITS

Chapter 1

"The Code of Hammurabi": From Pritchard, James B. *The Ancient Near East Anthology of Texts and Pictures.* Copyright © 1958 by Princeton University Press.

Chapter 2

Excerpt from "Hector and Andromache" from *The Iliad of Homer,* translated by Richmond Lattimore. Copyright © 1951 by the University of Chicago. Reprinted by permission of the University of Chicago Press.

Chapter 3

"The Two Faces of Athenian Democracy": Excerpts from Thucydides, *History of the Peloponnesian War,* translated by Rex Warner.

Chapter 4

"Polybius Describes the Sack of New Carthage": From Polybius, *Rise of the Roman Empire,* translated by Ian Scot-Kilvert.

Chapter 5

Excerpt from "The Reforms of Tiberius Gracchus" from *Roman Civilization, Vol. 1* by Naphtail Lewis and Meyer Reinhold. Copyright © 1951 Columbia University Press. Reprinted by permission.

Chapter 6

"Tacitus on the Germans": From Tacitus, *Germany.*

Chapter 7

The Qur'an: From the *Qur'an,* sura 2.

Chapter 8

"From Slave to Queen": Jo Ann McNamara, John E. Halborg, and George Whatley, "excerpts from 'Saint Bertilla, Abbess of Chelles'," in *Sacred Women of the Dark Ages.* Copyright, 1992 Duke University Press. All rights reserved. Used by permission of the publisher.

Chapter 9

"Pope Urban II Summons a Crusade": From *The First Crusade,* edited by Edward Peters. Copyright © 1971 University of Pennsylvania Press.

Chapter 10

"*Convivencia*": Excerpt from *Las Siete Partidas,* translated by Samuel Parson Scott. Chicago: Published for the Comparative Law Bureau of the American Bar Association by Commerce Clearing House, Inc. © 1931. All rights reserved. Reprinted by permission.

Chapter 11

"On the Family": From Leon Battista Alberti, "On the Family" in *The Family in Renaissance Florence* by Renee Watkins. Reprinted by permission of Renee Watkins.

Chapter 12

"The Halls of Montezuma": From Bernal Diaz, *The True History of the Conquest of New Spain,* in *The Bernal Diaz Chronicles,* translated and edited by Albert Idell, pp. 169–171.

Chapter 13

"The Eternal Decree": From John Calvin, *Institutes of the Christian Religion,* in *John Calvin, Selections from His Writings,* edited and with an introduction by John Dillenberger.

Chapter 14

"War is Hell": From Hans Jacob Cristoph Von Grimmelhausen, *The Adventurous Simplicissmus,* translated by A. T. S. Goodrick (1912).

Chapter 15

"The Devil's Due": From "Medieval Witchcraft" in *Translations and Reprints from the Original Sources of European History, Volume III,* published for the Department of History of the University of Pennsylvania, Philadelphia.

Chapter 16

"A Glimpse of a King": From *Memoirs of the Duke of Saint-Simon,* translated by Bayle St. John. (London: Swan Sonnonschein & Co., 1900).

Chapter 17

"Encountering Pirates": From Jean Doublet, *Encounter with a Barbary Pirate* (1682).

Chapter 18

"Childhood Traumas": From *The Memoirs of Catherine the Great,* edited by Dominique Maroger.

Chapter 19

"Love and Marriage": From *The Old Maid,* Number 1, by Frances Brooke, November 15, 1755.

Chapter 20

"The Civil Code of the Code Napoleon (1804)": From Henry Cachard, *The French Civil Code.* (London: Stevens and Sons, 1895).

Chapter 21

"Exploiting the Young": From "Child Labor in the Coal Mines," Testimony to the Parliamentary Investigative Committee (1842).

Chapter 22

"Flora Tristan": From "Flora Tristan" in *L'Union Ouvriere,* 3rd ed., (Paris and Lyons, 1843) as translated by Giselle Pincetl in *Harvest Quarterly,* 7 (Fall 1977). Reprinted by permission of Giselle Pincetl.

Chapter 23

"Mistress of the House": from *Mrs. Beeton's Book of Household Management,* 1861.

Chapter 24

"Constance Lytton": From Constance Lytton, *Prisons and Prisoners,* 1914.

Chapter 25

"Joseph Chamberlain's Speech to the Birmingham Relief Association": From Joseph Chamberlain, M. P., *Foreign and Colonial Speeches* (1897).

Chapter 26

"All Quiet on the Western Front": From Erich Maria Remarque, *All Quiet on the Western Front* (1928).

Chapter 27

"Adolf Hitler on Racial Purity": From "Racial Purity: Hitler Reverts to the Dominant Theme of the National Socialist Program" in *Hitler's Third Reich,* edited by Louis L. Snyder. Copyright © 1981 by Louis L. Snyder. Reprinted by permission of Rowman & Littlefield Publishing Group.

Chapter 28

"President Franklin Roosevelt's Request for a Declaration of War on Japan, 8 December 1941": From *World War II: Policy and Strategy* by Hans Adolf Jacobsen and Arthur J. Smith, Jr.

Chapter 29

"The Marshall Plan": From Department of State Bulletin, 15 June 1947.

Chapter 30

"A Woman Reporter Behind the Lines of the War in Chechnya": From *Chienne De Guerre: A Woman Reporter Behind the Lines of the War in Chechnya* by Ann Nivat, translated by Susan Damton. Copyright © 2001 by PublicAffairs. Reprinted by permission of PUBLICAFFAIRS, a member of Perseus Books, L.L. C.

PHOTO CREDITS

Introduction: 3 Photo Library International/Photo Researchers, Inc.
Chapter 1: 5 Augustin Ochsenreiter/South Tyrol Museum of Archaeology;
7 Kazuyoshi Nomachi/Pacific Press Service; **11** © The Trustees of the
British Museum; **16** The Metropolitan Museum of Art, Rogers Fund,
1931, (31.3.157) Photograph © 1983 The Metropolitan Museum of Art;
19 Erich Lessing/Art Resource, NY **Chapter 2: 25** William Francis Warden
Fund. Courtesy, The Museum of Fine Arts, Boston (63.473) Photograph
© 2007 Museum of Fine Arts, Boston; **28** Nimitallah/Art Resource, NY; **29**
Hirmer Verlag; **32** Scala/Art Resource, NY; **35** Hirmer Verlag; **39** Lee Boltin
Picture Library **Chapter 3: 44** (T) Scala/Art Resource, NY; **45** (B) Scala/Art
Resource, NY; **48** Réunion des Musées Nationaux/Art Resource, NY; **53**
Scala/Art Resource, NY; **57** Alinari/Art Resource, NY; **60** (T) Standing
Sakyamuni, Pakistan, Gandhara, probably Peshawar Area, Kushan Period
(1st century–320). Gray schist; H.119.7 cm © The Cleveland Museum of
Art. Gift of Morris and Eleanor Everett in memory of Flora Morris Everett
1972.43; **61** (B) The J. Paul Getty Museum, Los Angeles (Ms. Ludwig XV
9, fol. 43v); **63** Bridgeman-Giraudon/Art Resource, NY **Chapter 4: 69** A.
De Gregorio/Instituto Geografico de Agostini; **73** Hirmer Fotoarchiv,
Munich; **80** Bridgeman-Giraudon/Art Resource, NY; **83** Scala/Art
Resource, NY **Chapter 5: 86** (T) Scala/Art Resource, NY; **87** (B)
Nimatallah/Art Resource, NY; **88** Landesmuseum Mainz; **96** Erich
Lessing/Art Resource, NY; **101** Catacomb of Priscilla/Benedettine di
Priscilla/Pontificia Commissione di Archeologia Sacra, for Catacombe di
Priscilla; **106** © Biblioteca Apostolica Vaticana (Vatican) (Vat. lat. 2057 fol.
147, recto, Math 11a NS.10) **Chapter 6: 110** © The Trustees of the British
Museum (MME 1866,12-29,1); **111** British Museum; **113** Erich
Lessing/Art Resource, NY; **118** St. Peter's Vatican, Rome, Italy/Bridgeman
Art Library International **Chapter 7: 129** © SuperStock, Inc.; **130** Scala/Art
Resource, NY; **135** By Permission of the British library (Add MS 19352,
fol. 27v); **136** National Museum of China; **137** © Domkapitel Aachen,
Photo: Ann Münchow; **145** Istanbul University Library **Chapter 8: 153** ©
Domkapitel Aachen, Photo: Ann Münchow; **154** Fototeca Unione,
American Academy, Rome/Bridgeman Art Library International; **157**
British Museum/Eileen Tweedy/The Art Archive; **162** Bridgeman-
Giraudon/Art Resource, NY; **168** Universitets Oldsaksamling **Chapter 9:
174** Dagli Orti/The Art Archive; **175** Anders Blomquist/Lonely Planet
Images; **178** By Permission of the British Library (MS Harl. 4431. fol.
376); **184** By permission of the British Library (MS ROY 15 E III, fol.
269r); **186** Bildarchiv Preussischer Kulturbeseitz/Art Resource, NY; **187**
Scala/Art Resource, NY; **Chapter 10: 197** Erich Lessing/Art Resource, NY;
203 Lambeth Palace Library (MS.6,f.43); **206** The Metropolitan Museum
of Art, Cloisters Collection, 1969 (69.86) Photograph © 1991 The
Metropolitan Museum of Art; **208** Stadtarchiv Soest (Bestand A Nr. 2771)
Chapter 11: 219; 226; 228; 234 Scala/Art Resource, NY; **Chapter 12: 239**
Walker Art Gallery, National Museums Liverpool; **242** Bridgeman-
Giraudon/Art Resource, NY; **246** Reproduced by courtesy of the Trustees,
© The National Gallery, London; **255** Institut Amatller d'Art Hispanic;
257 Musée du Louvre, Paris/Bridgeman Art Library, London/©
SuperStock, Inc., **Chapter 13: 261** Library of Congress; **262** Private
Collection/Bridgeman Art Library; **265** Kunstsammlungen Der Veste
Coburg; **270** Geneva, Bibliothèque publique et universitaire, Départ.
iconographique; **274** Erich Lessing/Art Resource, NY **Chapter 14: 281**
Bridgeman-Giraudon/Art Resource, NY; **282** Art Resource, NY; **283**
François Dubois, Saint Bartholomew's Day, 1572–1584, oil on canvas, 94
cm × 154 cm, Musée Cantonal des Beaxu-Arts de Lausanne, Photo: J.-C.
Ducret, Musée Cantonal des Beaxu-Arts de Lausanne; **287** Erich
Lessing/Art Resource, NY; **293** Musée des Beaux-Arts de Strasbourg
(2.86.12970) **Chapter 15: 299** Roudnice Lobkowicz Collection/Bridgeman
Art Library; **306** La Tour, Georges de (1593–1652) *The Fortune Teller*. Oil
on canvas. J. 40 /8 in. W. 48 5/8 in. (101.9 × 123.5 cm.) Signed (upper
right): G. de La Tour Fecit Luneuilla Lothar: Metropolitan Museum of
Art, Rogers Fund, 1960 (60.30) Photograph © 1982 The Metropolitan
Museum of Art; **308** © Rijksmuseum Amsterdam; **311** © Rijksmuseum
Amsterdam; **Chapter 16: 319** Réunion des Musées Nationaux/Art

Resource, NY; **320** National Portrait Gallery Archive & Library; **327** The
Granger Collection, New York; **334** Scala/Art Resource, NY **Chapter 17:
339** Royal Cabinet of Paintings Mauritshuis The Hague; **341** By
Permission of The British Library (Maps C6C3. between 22-23); **352**
From the private collection of Peter V. Lape; **353** National Library **Chapter
18: 361** Reproduced by courtesy of the Trustees, © The National Gallery,
London (NG681); **367** Caravaque/Central Naval Museum, St. Petersburg;
372 Kunsthistorisches Museum; **376** The British Library/The Art Archive;
377 India Office Library/The Art Archive **Chapter 19: 383** Sameul H.
Kress Collection, © Board of Trustees, National Gallery of Art,
Washington, D.C. (1946.7.7[772]/PA); **384** Erich Lessing/Art Resource,
NY; **389** Reproduced by courtesy of the Trustees, © The National Gallery,
London (NG114); **393** Scala/Art Resource, NY **Chapter 20: 401** Spencer
Collection, The New York Public Library, Astor, Lenox and Tilden
Foundations; **403** Réunion Des Musées Nationaux/Art Resource, NY; **407**
Réunion des Musées Nationaux/Art Resource, NY; **416** Rouen, Musée des
Beaux-Arts. Don de J.M. Darcel, 1852. © Musée de la Ville de Rouen
Chapter 21: 421 Tate Gallery, London/Art Resource, NY; **427** akg—im-
ages; **428** The Granger Collection, New York; **430** Daumier, Honore
(1808–1879) *The Third Class Carriage*. Oil on canvas. H. 25 3/4 in. W. 35
1/2 in. (65.4 × 90.2 cm.) The Metropolitan Museum of Art, H. O.
Havemeyer Collection, Bequest of Mrs. H. O. Havemeyer, 1929.
(29.100.129) Photograph by Malcolm Varon. Photograph © 1984 The
Metropolitan Museum of Art **Chapter 22: 441** Gift of Quincy Adams
Shaw through Quincy A. Shaw, Jr. and Mrs. Marian Shaw Haughton.
Courtesy, Museum of Fine Arts, Boston (17.1505) Photograph © 2007
Museum of Fine Arts, Boston; **448** Bridgeman-Giraudon/Art Resource,
NY; **451** Mary Evans Picture Library **Chapter 23: 463** © bpk, Berlin; **469**
Bridgeman Art Library; **472** Bridgeman-Giraudon/Art Resource, NY; **473**
National Portrait Gallery Archive & Library **Chapter 24: 479** Bridgeman
Art Library; **486** Mary Evans Picture Library; **488** The Jewish
Museum/Art Resource, NY; **490** Museum of Modern Art, New York/Art
Resource, NY/© 2007 The Estate of Pablo Picasso/ Artists Rights Society
(ARS), New York; **491** (L) Staff finial, (mvuala), Kongo peoples,
Democratic Republic of the Congo, Congo, Angola, 16th–19th century,
Ivory, ceramic, camwood, resin. 6.5 × 5.1 × 6 cm (6 1/2 × 2 × 2 3/8 in.),
Museum purchase. National Museum of African Art, Smithsonian
Institution, Washington, D.C. (85-15-4); **491** (R) Face mask, Guro peo-
ples, Côte d'Ivoire, Mid-20th century, Wood, Paint. (21 1/4× 11 1/4 ×6
11/16 in.), Bequest of Eliot Elisofon. 73-7-167. Photograph by Franko
Khoury. National Museum of African Art, Smithsonian Institution
Chapter 25: 497 Mansell Collection/Time Life Pictures/Getty Images
Chapter 26: 518 (L) "Deutsche Frauen Arbeitet im Heimate-Heer!
Kriegsamtstelle Magdeburg" ("German Women Work in the Home-Army!
Magdeburg War Office" by George Kirchbach, Germany, 194-18. From
copy in the Bowman Gray Collection, Rare Book Collection, University of
North Carolina Library, Chapel Hill; **519** (R) "Take Up the Sword of
Justice" by Sir Bernard J. Partridge, England, 1915. From copy in Bowman
Gray Collection, Rare Book Collection, University of North Carolina
Library, Chapel Hill; **524** Imperial War Museum Photograph Archive; **528**
Imperial War Museum, London; **535** Brown Brothers **Chapter 27: 541**
Bildarchiv Preussischer Kulturbesitz/Art Resource, NY. © Estate of
George Grosz/Licensed by VAGA, New York, NY; **547** Michael Holford
Photographs; **549** (L) © Collection Roger-Viollet/Getty Images; **549** (C)
Liaison International/Getty Images; **549** (R) Liaison International/Getty
Images; **555** CORBIS **Chapter 28: 565** Osterreichische National
Bibliothek; **567** © Bettmann/Corbis; **569** Imperial War Museum, London;
572 Roger-Violet/Getty Images; **578** Bildarchiv Preussischer
Kulturbesitz/Art Resource, NY **Chapter 29: 587** © Bettmann/Corbis; **589**
Courtesy Consulate General of Germany; **591** Los Alamos National
Laboratory; **598** Courtesy of Sony Electronics, Inc.; **599** Rene
Burri/Magnum Photos, Inc.; **600** Popperfoto/ClassicStock; **604** David
Hurn/Magnum Photos, Inc. **Chapter 30: 611** AP/Wide World Photos; **613**
© Bettmann/CORBIS; **616** Vlastimir Shone/Saola-Agence de Presse; **624**
Steve McCurry/Magnum Photos, Inc.; **627** AFP/Getty Images

INDEX

Asia Minor, 130; Greek migration to, 33; Mycenaeans on, 28; Persians in, 41; Rome and, 79, 89

"Asocials": Nazis and, 557, 571

Asoka (Mauryan dynasty), 60

Assassinations: attempt on Hitler, 579; of Franz Ferdinand, 521–522; in Russia, 470, 486

Assemblies: in Athens, 49; in Corinth, 37; in Italian cities, 183; nobility in, 306; of Plebs, 75; in Rome, 74; in Sparta, 37

Assignats, in France, 409

Assimilation: foreign workers and, 624–625

Assizes (English count court sessions), 323

Assyria, 19; Hebrew kingdoms and, 19, 20; re-settlement of peoples by, 21

Assyrian Empire, 20–21

Astrolabe, 145, 244

Astrology, 210, 313–314, 342, 343

Astronomy, 340; Aristotelian, 340; Hellenistic, 64; Islamic, 145; mathematics in, 342; navigation and, 345; new science and, 340–341; Roman, 106

Astrophysics, 492

Ataulf (Visigoths), 123

Aten (god), 17

Athenian Empire, 47–48; Pericles and, 50; in Sicily, 51

Athens, 28, 32, 38–40, 106, 570; acropolis of, 35, 36; communities in, 49; democracy in, 39–40, 50, 51; lifestyle in, 48–49; ostracism in, 46; in Peloponnesian War, 51–52; Pericles in, 49–50; Persia and, 41, 46; reforms by Solon in, 39; sculpture on acropolis, 55; Sicilian expedition by, 52; Sparta and, 50; Syracuse and, 71; tyrants in, 33, 39. See also specific leaders

Athletic competitions: Greek, 34

Atilla (Huns), 123

Atom(s): nuclear structure theory of, 492; radioactivity and, 489

Atomic bomb(s), 489; France and, 590; Hiroshima and Nagasaki bombings, 581; Soviet Union and, 590; United States and, 588

Atrium, 81

Attalus III (Pergamum), 89

Attica, 29, 31, 50; Spartan invasion of, 50, 51

Auclert, Hubertine, 484

Augsburg, 198; executions in, 208–209; Peace of, 277, 293

Augustan Peace, 87

Augustine of Canterbury, 157

Augustine of Hippo, 120

Augustus (Octavian, Rome), 95–97; Altar of Augustan Peace, 86–87; divinity of, 96–97; Pax Romana and, 87, 95; poetry about, 97; successors to, 97–100

Aurelian (Rome), 115–118

Auschwitz: extermination camp at, 572, 573

Austen, Jane, 472

Australia, 577, 581; in World War I, 528

Australasia: kingdom of, 158

Austria, 198, 201, 258, 436, 594, 621, 624; alliance system and, 498; archduchy of, 248;

Cavour and, 465; decentralization of, 371; dual monarchy and, 467; France and, 409; German Confederation and, 444; in Grand Alliance, 351; as great power, 365; Habsburgs in, 365; Holy Alliance and, 446; "humiliation of Olmutz" and, 459; industrialization in, 434; Italy and, 444, 453, 458–459; Jews in, 486; liberalism in, 483–484; Napoleon and, 413, 414, 416; nationalist dissent in, 456; Nazi annexation of, 564–565; Netherlands and, 364, 365; Poland and, 444, 445; Prussia and, 466–467; Quadruple Alliance and, 446; railroads in, 437; religious toleration in, 388; revolutions of 1848 in, 458–459; rise of, 365; after Seven Years' War, 373; Spain combined with, 354; after World War I, 536, 543. See also Habsburg dynasty

Austria-Hungary, 294, 499; Bulgaria and, 500; Dual Alliance with Germany, 500; industrialization in, 437; liberalism in, 483–484; Slavic nationalism in, 521–522; in Three Emperors' League, 498; in Triple Alliance, 520; in World War I, 521

Austrian Empire, 370; disintegration of, 536; Italy and, 444

Austrian Netherlands: in Kingdom of the Netherlands, 444

Autarky: Germany and, 556

Authoritarianism: in Germany, 482–483

Authority: demise of royal, 471; in Islam, 143; monarchical principle of, 447

Autocracy: in Byzantine Empire, 133; Holy Alliance and, 446; in Russia, 470

Auxerre, 171

Avars, 155, 162

Averroës. See Ibn Rushd (Averroës)

Aviation, 492

Avicenna. See Ibn Sina (Avicenna)

Avignon, 443; popes in, 209

Axis Powers (World War II), 566, 568, 569; Japan as, 576; in North Africa, 578–579

Azerbaijan: nationalism in, 617

Aztec Empire, 243–244

B

Baal Hammon (god), 70

Baby and Child Care (Spock), 603

Baby boom: in United States, 602

Babylon, 21, 59

Babylonia: under Hammurabi, 12–13; mathematics in, 12–13; New Babylonian Empire and, 20, 21

Babylonian captivity: of Jews, 20

Babylonian language, 10

Bacaudae (resistance movements), 113

Bacchanalia, 82

Bacchiads (Corinth), 36

Bacchus: cult of, 82

Bacon, Francis, 320, 343

Bacteriology, 492

Bactria, 57

Baden, 467

Baghdad: as Islamic capital, 144; loss to Mongols, 149; as marketplace, 145

Baghdad Pact (1955), 590

Baghdad Railway, 499

Bahamas: Columbus in, 242

Baillis (administrative officials), 191

Bakelite, 492

Bakunin, Mikhail, 488

Balance of power: Bismarck and, 475; Congress of Vienna, alliance system and, 446; in 18th century, 360–379; 1870–1914, 498–505; Grand Alliance and, 351; in War of the Austrian Succession, 372; World War I and, 520–521, 545

Balboa, Basco Núñez de, 242

Baldwin, Stanley, 559

Balfour, Arthur, 530

Balfour Declaration, 530, 536

Balkan region, 248, 363; crises in, 499, 500; ethnic warfare in, 618–620; genocide in, 618; investment in, 513; in late 1800s, 499; Ottomans in, 149; rivalries in, 464; Russia and, 499; Turkey and, 500; before World War I, 521–522; World War II in, 569–570

Ballistics, 230

Balthild (wife of Clovis II), 160

Baltic region, 287; Dutch trade and, 348; eastern European borders and, 248; after Great Northern War, 366; Hanseatic League and, 207; Lutheranism in, 267; Muscovy cession to Sweden, 290; Peter the Great and, 332; Poland and, 287, 366; Soviet nationalities problem and, 617; Soviet Union and, 567, 589; Sweden and, 289, 293; trade in, 345; after World War I, 537, 543, 544

Ba Maw (Burma leader), 579

Banda Islands: nutmeg trade and, 352–353

Bandits: in Rome, 113

Banking. See Banks and banking

Bank notes: in England, 345

Bank of England, 426

Bankruptcies: in 18th century, 430; in Spain, 293

Banks and banking: in Amsterdam, 244, 345; in England, 345; in European Union, 621–622; in Florence, 233–234; in Great Depression, 547; industrial investment and, 426; Italian houses, 207; in London, 513; medieval merchant houses in, 182; new forms of, 345; regulation of markets and, 480; after World War I, 546

Banquet campaign, 456

Baptism, 101, 272; of Clovis, 158; of Constantine, 117

Bar, duchy of, 364

Baratieri, Oreste, 507–508

Barbados, 346

Barbarians: kingdoms of, 123–125, 154–158; migrations and invasions by, 124; Rome and, 91, 113–115, 122–125. See also Germanic peoples; specific groups

Barbary coast, 349

Barbed wire: in World War I, 524

Barcelona, 249, 326, 468

Bardi (banking house), 207

Bari, 147

Barlaam (monk), 61

Crimean Tatars, 251, 287

Crimean War, 464, 468, 470

Crimes and Punishments (Beccaria), 387

Criminal Code: of Napoleonic Code, 415

Crispi, Franceso, 508

Croatia, 619; Serbs in, 620; after World War I, 536

Croatian government: in Zagreb, 570

Croats, 569–570, 619–620

Crompton, Samuel, 428

Cromwell, Oliver, 329

Cromwell, Richard, 329

Cromwell, Thomas, 238, 253, 271

Crops: in early modern Europe, 300–301; enclosure and, 309; fodder, 395, 424; Renaissance trade in, 222; technology and, 480; trade in, 513; two-crop rotation and, 301; yields of, 424

Crossbow, 202

Crucifixion: of Jesus, 101; of Roman rebels, 89

Crusades, 180–181; First, 148; idea of, 181; sacks of Constantinople by, 148, 149; Seventh, 191

Crystal Palace Exhibition (London), 429, 433, 503

Cuba: communism in, 593

Cuban missile crisis, 593

Cubism, 490

Cult of the Supreme Being: in France, 411

Cults: of Akhenaten, 17; of Dionysus, 82; Egyptian cult of the dead, 15–16; Germanic, 114–115; in Greece, 34; of icons, 135; of one God, 117; Roman, 82, 97, 100; of Unconquered Sun, 117

Culture(s), 6; of Antonine Rome, 106–107; Athenian, 52–55; of Benedictines, 179; in Bohemia, 200; bourgeois, 391; Buddha and, 60–61; Byzantine, 147; crisis of, 478–479; in Egypt, 14–15; in 18th century, 382–388; Etruscan, 72; European peasant, 159; folk, in Russia, 368; in France, 253–254, 334, 483; Greek, 29; Hellenistic, 59–65; impact of Roman on Germanic peoples, 115; intelligence and, 493; Islamic, 145; of Japanese workplace, 599; monastic, 179; nationalism and, 449; Nazi Germany and, 556–557; of New World, 245–246; non-Western, 490; painting as record of, 6–7; popular, 397; race and, 513; Roman, 100, 102–106; Scandinavian, 166. *See also* Intellectual thought

Cumae, 33; battle at, 72

Cuneiform script: in Anatolia, 13; in Neolithic society, 10

Curia (Rome), 68, 74

Curie, Marie and Pierre, 489

Currency: Byzantine, 147; euro as, 621, 622–623; after World War I, 546

Curriculum: liberal arts as, 229

Cursus honorum (Rome), 75

Customs. *See* Lifestyle; specific cultures

Customs duties: economic integration and, 596

Customs union: Zollverein as, 436–437

Cybele: cult of, 100

Cycladic culture, 26

Cylinder seals, 10

Cylon (Athens), 38

Cynics, 64

Cyprus, 499; in EU, 623

Cypselus (Bacchiad), 36

Cyrene, 33, 71

Cyril (missionary), 146, 168

Cyrillic alphabet, 146

Cyrus II (Persia), 21, 41

Cyrus the Younger (Persia), 52

Czech language, 200

Czechoslovakia, 554, 564, 590; Hitler and, 566–567; industry in, 600; Prague Spring in, 601; reforms in, 600–601; revolution and democracy in, 614, 618; Soviet Union and, 582, 589, 597, 612; after World War I, 536, 543, 545

Czech people: after World War I, 543

Czech Republic, 614; in EU, 623

D

Dacia, 99

Da Gama, Vasco, 240, 246

Daguerre, Louis, 473

Daladier, Edouard, 566

Dalmatia, 80, 527, 536

Dalmatian coast, 444

Damascus, 128, 144

Dance of Death, 205

Danelaw, 166

Danes: in England, 166

Dante Alighieri, 213

Danton, Georges-Jacques, 410, 411

Danubian principalities, 464

Danzig: as "free city," 537

Darby, Abraham, 426

Dardanelles, 570; battle in, 527

Darius I (Persia), 41, 44, 46

Darius III (Persia), 44; Alexander's defeat of, 57; silk and, 136

Dark Age: in Greece, 28–30

Darwin, Charles, 473–474, 492

Dating system: in Islam, 140; Western, 6

Daughters: in Renaissance, 223

Daumier, Honoré, 430

Dauphin. *See* Charles VII (France)

David (Israel), 19–20

David (Michelangelo), 227

Dawes, Charles G., 546

Dawes Plan, 546, 547

Dayton Peace Accords, 620

D-Day, 568, 579

Deacons: in Calvinism, 271

Dead people: monastic cults of, 179

Death: in Renaissance, 224

Death rates. *See* Mortality

De Boisdenier, painting by, 416

De Bry, Theodore, 352

Debt: in England, 378; in Florence, 234; in France, 402

Decentralization: of Austria, 371; of Holy Roman Empire, 200–201

Declaration of Independence (U.S.), 387

Declaration of Rights (England), 330

Declaration of the Rights of Man and Citizen (France), 408

Declaration of the Rights of Woman and Citizen (Olympe de Gouges), 411

Declaratory Act (1766), 379

Decolonization: in Africa, 593; in Asia, 592–593; Cold War and, 591–592; in Latin America, 593; in Middle East, 593

Decurions (Rome), 117

Defense of Liberty Against Tyrants, A (Duplessis-Mornay), 326

Defense spending: national income and (1937), 556; by Soviet Union, 600

Deficits: Keynesian economics and, 595

Deflation, 480

Degas, Edgar, 490

De Gaulle, Charles, 569, 590, 593

Deification: of Roman emperors, 97

Deists, 386

Deities. *See* Gods and goddesses

Delacroix, Eugène, 448, 449

Delian League, 47–48

Delphi, 34

Demagogues: in Athens, 49

Demesne, 176

Demilitarization: of Japan, 597; after World War I, 535, 536

Demilitarized zone: in Rhineland, 544, 545

Deming, W. Edwards, 598–599

Democracies (democratic countries): Cold War ideology and, 588; before World War II, 557–560

Democracy: in Athens, 39–40, 50, 51; in Great Britain, 468–469; in Greece, 32; revolutions of 1848–1850 and, 455–456; social groups and, 479

Democratic Republic of the Congo, 593

Demography: birth control and, 602; in early modern Europe, 303; in 18th century, 394; in later Middle Ages, 204

Demos (the people), 37, 39

Denmark, 207, 248, 294, 445, 590, 594; in Common Market, 621; Germany and, 567; invasion of Sweden by, 289; Jews in, 574; Lutheranism in, 268; Scandinavian confederation and, 289; Schleswig and, 466; Sweden and, 290; Thirty Years' War and, 292; Vikings from, 167, 168

Départements (France), 408

De Pisan, Christine, 214

Depressions: definition of, 547; in19th century, 432. *See also* Great Depression

Descartes, René, 343, 386

Descent of Man, The (Darwin), 492

Desert War (World War II), 579

"Deserving poor," 308

Despotism: in Milan, 232; Montesquieu on, 386

De Staël, Germaine, 415, 448

De-Stalinization, 597–600

Détente, 613

Deterrence, 591

Developing nations, 2–3

Dhuoda (noblewoman), 164

Dialogue Between the Two Great Systems of the World, A (Galileo), 341, 344

Diamond mines, 508

in Soviet Union, 551; Uruk as, 9–10. *See also* Cities and towns
Urbino, 232
Ursuline order, 273
Uruk, Mesopotamia, 8–10, 12
'Uthman: as caliph, 143
Utica, 70
Utilitarianism, 447
Ut-napishtim (Mesopotamia), 11
Utopia (More), 238, 246
Utopianism, 449–450
Utrecht, Treaty of (1713–1714), 354–355, 362, 364, 365

V

Vaccination Act (Britain, 1853), 432
Vagrancy laws, 308
Valencia, 249
Valens (Rome), 122
Valerian (Rome), 112–113
Valla, Lorenzo, 228, 229
Valois (region), 191
Valois dynasty (France), 201, 253, 256, 283
Values: bourgeois, 390–391; in 19th century, 471–475; in Renaissance, 224–225; Roman, 83–84; urban, 229
Vandals, 123, 131, 154
Van Dyck, Anthony, 320
Van Gogh, Vincent, 493
Varro, Gaius Terentius (Rome), 78
Vasa family (Sweden), 289
Vasari, Giorgio, 227
Vase painting: in Greece, 35, 36, 54–55
Vasili (Russia), 251
Vassals, 162, 178
Vatican, 466
Veii, 75
Velázquez, Diego, 320
Velvet revolutions: in eastern Europe, 614, 618
Venaissin, 443
Venereal disease, 302, 450
Venetia, 444, 465
Venice, 232, 365; banking in, 182; *Book of Gold* in, 307; Byzantine Empire and, 147; commerce and, 147, 182; duchy of, 249; Fourth Crusade and, 182; glass industry in, 222; mercantile empire of, 232–233; Ottomans and, 235; religious procession in, 218–219; Republic of, 444; survival of, 236; trade by, 207; uprising in, 458; vagrant in, 308
Venus (goddess), 82, 110
Venus de Milo, 64
Vera Cruz, 243
Verdun, battle at, 526–527
Vermandois, 191
Vermeer, Jan, 311
Vernacular languages: of Anglo-Saxons, 166; literature in, 213–215; nationalism and, 449; in Russia, 368
Versailles, 318–319, 322, 333–334; Estates-General at, 403, 404; German Empire proclaimed in, 462; women's march to, 407–408
Versailles, Treaty of, 536; Hitler's renunciation of, 556; United States and, 545; after World War I, 545

Vesalius, Andreas, 342
Vespasian (Rome), 99
Vespucci, Amerigo, 235, 244
Vesta (spirit of hearth fire), 82
Vichy France, 569, 570, 574
Victor Amadeus II (Savoy), 365
Victor Emmanuel II (Sardinia, Italy), 464, 465–466
Victor Emmanuel III (Italy), 553
Victoria (England): as empress of India, 510
Victorian society: homemaking in, 472; reform and compromise in, 468–470
Vienna, 395; Congress of, 442–445; 1848 revolution in, 458; Ottomans and, 365; Prussia and, 371
Vietnam, 510
Vietnam War, 593, 603, 605
Viking (raiding): use of term, 167
Vikings, 167–168, 170; in Britain, 157, 166; in Scandinavia, 166
Villages: in Byzantine Empire, 133; in early modern Europe, 298–299, 312–314; Germanic, 114; in Mesopotamia, 8; peasant, 176, 177; Roman, 68, 74
Villanovans, 70
Villein, 307
Villon, François, 214–215
Violence: in French Revolution, 407; institutionalized, in Fascist Italy, 553; in mass society, 489; against Muslims and Arabs, 627; in Roman politics, 91. *See also* Terrorism
Virchow, Rudolf, 492
Virgil, 63, 97, 106
Virginia: slaves in, 347
Virtue: Aristotle on, 56; crisis of Roman, 83–84; in Roman philosophy, 94
Visconti family, 232
Visigoths, 111, 131, 154; in Gaul and Spain, 111; Jews and, 156; Rome and, 122; in Spain, 122, 123, 154, 156
Vladivostok, 498
Volk: in Nazi Germany, 557
Volscians, 75, 76
Voltaire (François-Marie Arouet), 385, 387, 391
Von Cocceji, Samuel, 387
Voting: in Austria, 484; Chartist movement and, 454; in England, 453–454, 469, 481; in France, 408, 410; in French Estates-General, 404; in Germany, 482; liberal attitudes toward, 447; movements for, 455–456; revolution of 1830 and, 453; in Rome, 74, 90; for Soviet women, 552; by women, 484–485
Vulgate Bible, 121, 260, 263

W

Wadis (fertile riverbeds), 14
Wages: in 18th century, 396; in France, 403; gender differences in, 600; for industrial workers, 432; men's vs. women's, 602; Ricardo on, 447; in rural manufacturing, 422; of working women, 454, 455
Waiblingen castle, 182
Wales, 250; English conquest of, 174, 175
Walesa, Lech, 613
al-Walid (Syria), 128–129
al-Walid, Khalid ibn (caliph), 141

Wallachia, 464
Walled cities: Etruscan, 72
Wallenberg, Raoul, 574
Wallenstein, Albrecht von, 292, 293
Walpole, Robert, 375
Wannsee conference: on Final Solution, 571
War debts: after World War I, 546
War Guilt Clause: after World War I, 536–537
War of 1812: trade depression after, 432
War of American Independence. *See* American Revolution
War of the Austrian Succession, 372
War of the Spanish Succession, 354–355, 360, 364, 371
War of the Three Henrys (France), 284
War posters: in World War I, 518–519
Warriors: Germanic, 115; nobility as, 306; in Sparta, 37; as vassals, 162. *See also* Knights
Wars and warfare: Anglo-Dutch, 350–351; *blitzkrieg* (lightning war), 569; changes in, 250–251; colonial, 355–356; over commerce, 350–356; democratization of, 32; over dynastic struggles, 256–258; in Europe (1598–1650), 330; in Florence, 234; by Germanic peoples, 114; in Greece, 28, 32; of Louis XIV, 351, 354–355; Marcomannian, 115; Napoleonic, 413–414; Persian, 41; population decline and, 325; Poussin's *Massacre of the Innocents* and, 280–281; renunciation of, 545; Roman, 74, 76, 91; selling to public, 518–519; Spain-Netherlands, 285–286; taxation for, 323–324; terrorism as, 625–628; trench warfare in World War I, 522–523, 524; by Venice, 233. *See also* specific battles and wars
Warsaw, 581; grand duchy of, 444, 445; Jews in, 572; revolution in, 452–453; after World War II, 586–587
Warsaw Confederation, 287, 288
Warsaw ghetto: Jewish resistance movement in, 574
Warsaw Pact, 590, 597, 600, 601, 613
Wars of Italy (1494–1529), 235, 256–258
Wars of Liberation (Germany), 447
Wars of religion: in France, 282–285
Wars of the Roses (England), 204, 252
Wastes: as fertilizer, 395
Water: in coal mines, 426
Water frame, 428
Waterloo, battle of, 360, 416
Waterways, 396; industrialization and, 425; for textile production, 184
Watt, James: steam engine of, 427
Way of Perfection, The (Teresa of Ávila), 273
Wealth: of bourgeoisie, 390; of Cistercians, 180; in Egypt, 16; English, 192; of European nobility, 389; expansion in Industrial Revolution, 432; in Germanic society, 115; new rich and, 307; physiocrats on, 388; in Rome, 74, 75, 112; in Russia, 368; social hierarchy and, 305; in western Europe, 602
Wealth gap, 629
Wealthy: in early modern Europe, 307–308; vs. poor, 221–222. *See also* Wealth
Weapons, 250, 256; in Africa, 507; Assyrian, 20; bronze, 10; in Ethiopia, 507; European

CONTEMPORARY EUROPE

Land Elevation

Feet		Meters
13,123		4,000
6,562		2,000
3,281		1,000
1,640		500
656		200
0		0
Below sea level		Below sea level

0   250   500 mi.

0   250   500 km

ICELAND

Norwegian Sea

FAROE IS.

KJØLEN MOUNTAINS

SCANDINAVIAN PENIN.

NORWAY   SWEDEN

L. Vänern

L. Vättern

SHETLAND IS.

HEBRIDES IS.

ORKNEY IS.

Scotland

Northern Ireland

UNITED KINGDOM

BRITISH ISLES

IRELAND

Wales

England

Celtic Sea

Thames R.

North Sea

JUTLAND PENINSULA

DENMARK

NETHERLANDS

RUHR VALLEY

Elbe R.

NORTH E

Oder R.

POL

GERMANY

ATLANTIC OCEAN

English Channel

BRITTANY PENINSULA

BELGIUM

Rhine R.

Seine R.

LUXEMBOURG

CZECH REPUBLIC

SLO

Loire R.

FRANCE

LIECHTENSTEIN

Danube R.

SWITZERLAND

L. Geneva

AUSTRIA

HU

HU

Bay of Biscay

CENTRAL MASSIF

A L P S

SLOVENIA

Drava R.

Garonne R.

Rhône R.

Po R.

CROATIA

Sava R.

ITALY

SAN MARINO

BOSNIA

PYRENEES

MONACO

A P E N N I N E S

DINARIC

Ebro R.

ANDORRA

Adriatic Sea

Duero R.

IBERIAN PENINSULA

CORSICA

PORTUGAL

Tagus R.

SPAIN

Guadiana R.

BALEARIC ISLANDS

SARDINIA

Tyrrhenian Sea

A

Guadalquiver R.

SIERRA NEVADA

Strait of Gibraltar

Ioni Se

M e d i t e r r a n e a n   S e a

SICILY

A F R I C A

MALTA

Arctic Circle

Balt

N

W   E

S

60°N

30°W

20°W

10°W

0°

70°N

10°E

20°

50°N

40°N

KOLA
PENINSULA

Barents Sea

30°E   40°E   50°E   60°E   70°E

Pechora R.

Ob R.

*White
Sea*

N. Dvina R.

FINLAND

L. Onega

*L.
Ladoga*

URAL MOUNTAINS

R U S S I A

Volga R.

Ural R.

Gulf of Finland

ESTONIA

*L.
Peipus*

LATVIA

PEAN PLAIN

CENTRAL RUSSIAN UPLAND

Oka R.

VOLGA UPLAND

THUANIA

BELARUS

Volga R.

Dnieper R.

Dniester R.

UKRAINE

Don R.

CASPIAN
DEPRESSION

*Caspian
Sea*

Prut R.

Siret R.

MOLDOVA

*Sea of
Azov*

PATHIAN MTS.

ROMANIA

CRIMEA

C A U C A S U S

RANSYLVANIAN ALPS

Danube R.

GEORGIA

BALKAN MTS.

Black Sea

ARMENIA

BULGARIA

ONIA

Bosporus

AZERBAIJAN

AN PENINSULA

TURKEY

GREECE

Dardanelles

A S I A

*Aegene
Sea*

S MTS.

CRETE

20°E 40°E 60°E 80°E 100°E 120°E 140°E 160°E

Barents Sea

ARCTIC OCEAN

Laptev Sea

SCANDINAVIA

NORTH EUROPEAN PLAIN

Volga R.

URAL MTS.

Ob R.

SIBERIA

Yenisei R.

Lena R.

Sea of Okhotsk

EUROPE

ALPS

Danube R.

CAUCASUS MTS.

Black Sea

Aral Sea

Caspian Sea

ASIA

L. Baikal

Amur R.

Sea of Japan

JAPAN

Mediterranean Sea

Tigris R.

ZAGROS MTS.

GOBI (DESERT)

Euphrates R.

Indus R.

HIMALAYA MTS.

TIBETAN PLATEAU

Huang He R.

Chiang Jiang R.

East China Sea

Tropic of Cancer

HARA SERT)

Nile R.

Red Sea

ARABIAN DESERT

Persian Gulf

THAR DESERT

Ganges R.

DECCAN PLATEAU

Mekong R.

South China Sea

PHILIPPINES

PACIFIC OCEAN

SUDAN

AFRICA

ETHIOPIAN HIGHLANDS

Arabian Sea

Bay of Bengal

Congo (Zaire) R.

CONGO BASIN

Victoria

SUMATRA

BORNEO

INDONESIA

NEW GUINEA

Zambezi R.

MADAGASCAR

INDIAN OCEAN

JAVA

KALAHARI DESERT

Cape of Good Hope

GREAT SANDY DESERT

Tropic of Capricorn

AUSTRALIA

GREAT VICTORIA DESERT

Darling R.

NEW ZEALAND

CONTEMPORARY WORLD

Land Elevation

Feet	Meters
13,123	4,000
6,562	2,000
3,281	1,000
1,640	500
0	0
Below sea level	Below sea level

Ice-covered

0   1,000   2,000 mi.

0   1,000   2,000 km

Robinson Projection

ANTARCTICA